EGYPT
THE ROUGH GUIDE

THE ROUGH GUIDES

OTHER AVAILABLE ROUGH GUIDES
SPAIN • PORTUGAL • PYRENEES • FRANCE • PARIS
PROVENCE • BRITTANY & NORMANDY • GREECE • CRETE
ITALY • VENICE • SICILY • TUSCANY & UMBRIA • IRELAND
SCANDINAVIA • BERLIN • WEST GERMANY • AMSTERDAM
HOLLAND, BELGIUM & LUXEMBOURG • YUGOSLAVIA
HUNGARY • EASTERN EUROPE • CZECHOSLOVAKIA
POLAND • TURKEY • ISRAEL • NEPAL • HONG KONG
MOROCCO • WEST AFRICA • ZIMBABWE & BOTSWANA
KENYA • TUNISIA • MEXICO • PERU • GUATEMALA & BELIZE
BRAZIL • CALIFORNIA & WEST COAST USA • FLORIDA
NEW YORK • SAN FRANCISCO • MEDITERRANEAN WILDLIFE
WOMEN TRAVEL • NOTHING VENTURED

FORTHCOMING
USA • CANADA • EUROPE • BARCELONA • BULGARIA
ROMANIA • THAILAND • WORLD MUSIC

EGYPT: THE ROUGH GUIDE CREDITS

Text Editor: Mark Ellingham
Proofreading: Kate Berens
Production: Susanne Hillen, Kate Berens, Andy Hilliard
Typesetting: Andy Hilliard and Gail Jammy

Rough Guide Series Editor: Mark Ellingham

The authors would like to **thank** the following individuals for their hospitality and help **in Egypt**: Hani Milad and his wonderful family in Luxor; Salah Mohammed Abdel Hafiez for many conversations and rides to Saqqara; Mustafa, Samir and Mohammed for fun evenings at the *Windsor*; Shoukry Sa'ad of Aswan's tourist office; Natasha Stacey and Didier Rouer (for saving Karen in Sinai); Martin and Monique (for Sudan information); Saartje Drijver (likewise for the Red Sea Monasteries); Mikael Kalos and Nathalie Garau (at Tell el-Amarna); Liane Colwell (for diverse scandal); Ali and Gamal of the *Plaza Hotel*; Emad and Jane (in Suez); and Jerome Hamers (for all things Shi'ite). For desert inspiration, we would also like to pay our dues to the late, great R.A. Bagnold, author of *Libyan Sands*.

Also thanks to those **in England**: Mark Ellingham (steadfast, brilliant editing); Andy Hilliard and Gail Jammy (ace graphics and typesetting); Kate Berens and Susanne Hillen (Horus-eyed proofing and production); Ali and Jane Nossarem (inspiring Arabic lessons and hospitality); David Jacobs; and Dorothy Stannard.

This **first edition** published **Autumn 1991** by
Harrap Columbus Ltd, 26 Market Square, Bromley, Kent BR1 1NA.

Illustrations in Part One and Part Three by Ed Briant
Basics and Contexts page illustrations by Henry Iles

Typeset in Linotron Univers and Century Old Style to an original design by Andrew Oliver.
Printed in the United Kingdom by Cox & Wyman Ltd (Reading).

640p. Includes index.

British Library Cataloguing in Publication Data

Richardson, Dan
Egypt: the rough guide. – (The Rough Guides).
1. Egypt – visitors' guides
I. Title II. Series
916.20455

ISBN 0–7471–0257–0

EGYPT

THE ROUGH GUIDE

Written and researched by

DAN RICHARDSON and KAREN O'BRIEN

With additional accounts by

Shirley Eber and David Lodge

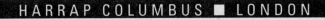

HARRAP COLUMBUS ■ LONDON

To Gagou with love

CONTENTS

Introduction viii

| PART ONE | BASICS | 1 |

Getting There from Europe (3); from the USA and Canada (8); from Australasia (11) / Visas and Red Tape (11) / Costs and Money (14) / Health and Insurance (18) / Information and Maps (21) / *Baksheesh* and Local Guides (23) / Attitudes and Behaviour (24) / Security, Police and Consulates (24) / From a Woman's Perspective (25) / Getting Around (26) / Accommodation (31) / Eating and Drinking (33) / Communications: Post, phones and media (38) / Moulids and public holidays (40) / Monuments, Mosques and Monasteries (43) / Disabled Access (43) / Working or Studying in Egypt (44) / Directory (45); Useful Things to Bring (46) / Metric Weights and Measures (46).

| PART TWO | GUIDE | 47 |

■ 1	CAIRO AND THE PYRAMIDS	49
■ 2	THE NILE VALLEY	236
■ 3	THE WESTERN DESERT OASES	390
■ 4	ALEXANDRIA AND THE MEDITERRANEAN COAST	449
■ 5	THE DELTA	488
■ 6	THE CANAL ZONE	500
■ 7	SINAI	517
■ 8	THE RED SEA COAST AND EASTERN DESERT	557

| PART THREE | CONTEXTS | 577 |

Historical Framework 579
Islam 593
Monumental Chronology 596
Music 600
Books 603
Language 609
Glossary 612

Index 613

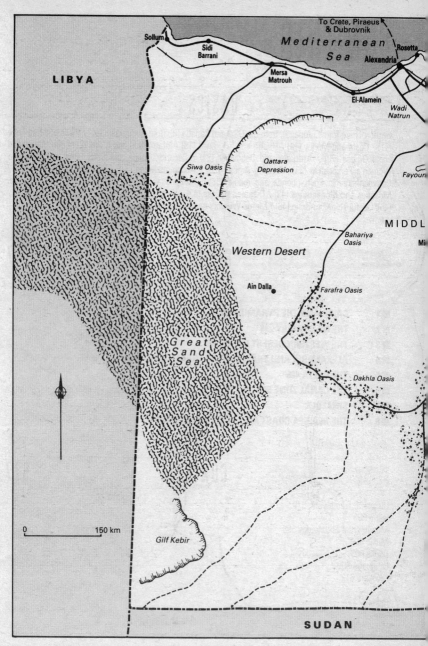

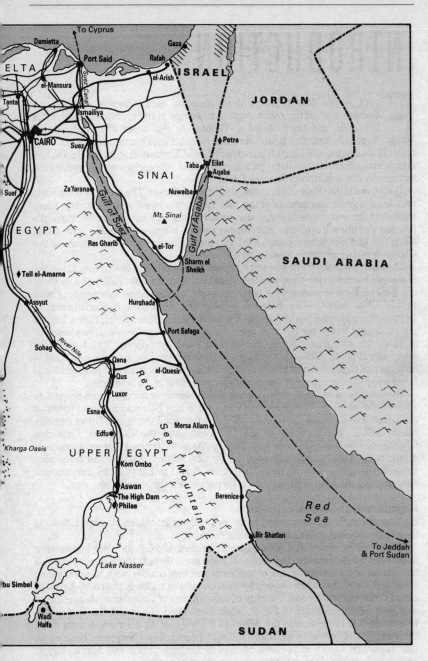

INTRODUCTION

E gypt is the oldest tourist destination on earth. Ancient Greeks and Romans started the trend, coming to goggle at the cyclopean scale of the Pyramids and the Colossi of Thebes. At the onset of colonial times, Napoleon and the British in turn looted Egypt's treasures to fill their national museums, sparking off a trickle of Grand Tourists that, by the 1860s, had grown into a flood of travellers, packaged for their Nile cruises and Egyptological lectures by the industrious Thomas Cook.

Today, the attractions of the country are little different. The focus of most visits remains the great monuments of the Nile Valley, combined with a few days spent exploring the *souks*, mosques and *madrassas* of Islamic Cairo. However, possibilities for Egyptian travel also encompass remote oases; snorkelling and diving along the Red Sea coasts; camel trips into the mountains of Sinai; or visits to the Coptic monasteries of the Eastern Desert.

The land itself is a freak of nature, whose lifeblood is the River Nile. From the Sudanese border to the shores of the Mediterranean, the Nile Valley and its Delta are flanked by arid wastes, the latter as empty as the former are teeming with people. This stark duality between fertility and desolation is fundamental to Egypt's character and has shaped its development since prehistoric times, imparting continuity to diverse cultures and peoples over five millennia. It is a sense of permanence and timelessness that is buttressed by religion, which pervades every aspect of life. Although the pagan cults of ancient Egypt are as moribund as its legacy of mummies and temples, their ancient fertility rites and processions of boats still hold their place in the celebrations of Islam and Christianity.

The result is a multi-layered culture, which seems to accord equal respect to ancient and modern. The peasants (*fellaheen*) of the Nile and Bedouin tribes of the desert live much as their ancestors did, a thousand years ago. Other communities include the Nubians of the far south, and the Coptic or Orthodox Christians, who trace their ancestry back to pharaonic times. What unites them is a love of their homeland, extended family ties, dignity, warmth and hospitality towards strangers. Though most visitors are drawn to Egypt by its monuments, the enduring memory is likely to be of its people and their way of life.

Regions and highlights

Each of the regions is discussed in its own chapter introduction; what follows is merely the briefest outline of the main attractions.

Most visitors arrive at **Cairo**. A seething megalopolis, its chief sightseeing appeal lies in its **bazaars** and medieval **mosques**, though there is scarcely less fascination in its juxtapositions of medieval and modern life, with fortified gates, villas and skyscrapers interwoven by flyovers whose traffic is halted by herds of camels. The immensity and diversity of this "Mother of Cities" is as staggering as anything you'll encounter in Egypt, while just outside Cairo are the first of the **pyramids** that range across the desert to the edge of the Fayoum, among them the unsurpassable trio at **Giza** and the vast necropolis of **Saqqara**. Besides all this, there are superb **museums** devoted to Ancient, Coptic and Islamic Egypt, and enough **entertainments** to occupy weeks of your time.

However, the main tourist lure remains, as ever, the **Nile Valley**, with its **ancient monuments** and timeless river vistas – *felucca* sailboat **cruises** being a great way to combine the two. The town of **Luxor** is synonymous with the magnificent temples of **Karnak** and the **Theban necropolis**, which includes the **Valley of the Kings** where Tutankhamun and other pharaohs were buried. **Aswan**, Egypt's southernmost city, has the loveliest setting on the Nile and a languorous ambience. From here, you can visit the island-temple of **Philae** and the rock-hewn colossi at **Abu Simbel**. Other sites not to be missed are **Abydos** and **Dendara** (north of Luxor), **Edfu** and **Kom Ombo** (between Luxor and Aswan). Those with more time and a particular interest in ancient Egypt should add **Beni Hassan** and **Tell el-Amarna** to the list.

Only recently accessible to tourists, the **Western Desert Oases** are scattered across a vast, awesomely desolate region. **Siwa**, out towards the Libyan border, has a unique culture and history, limpid pools and bags of charm. Another option is to follow the "Great Desert Circuit" (starting from Cairo or Assyut) through the four "inner" oases. Though **Bahariya** and **Farafra** hold the most appeal, with the lovely **White Desert** between them, the larger oases of **Dakhla** and **Kharga** also have their rewards once you escape their modernised "capitals". And for those equipped to make serious desert expeditions, there's the challenge of entering the **Great Sand Sea** or tracing part of the infamous **Forty Days Road**. By way of contrast to these deep-desert locations are the quasi-oases of **the Fayoum** and **Wadi Natrun**, with their diverse ancient ruins and **Coptic monasteries**.

Moving down to the **Mediterranean**, Egypt's second city, **Alexandria**, boasts a string of beaches where Cairenes flock over summer, and excellent seafood restaurants. Despite being founded by Alexander the Great and lost to the Romans by Cleopatra, the city hasn't much to show for its ancient glory or its famous decadence during colonial times, but romantics can still indulge in a nostalgic exploration of the "Capital of Memory". Further along the Mediterranean coast, beyond the World War II battlefield of **El-Alamein**, the low-key beach resort of **Mersa Matrouh** is the jumping-off point for Siwa Oasis.

The Nile **Delta**, east of Alexandria, musters few archaeological monuments given its major role in ancient Egyptian history, and is largely overlooked by tourists. However, for those interested in Egyptian culture, the Delta hosts colourful religious **festivals** at **Tanta**, **Zagazig** and other towns. Further east lies the **Canal Zone**, dominated by the Suez Canal and its three cities. **Port Said** and **Ismailiya** are pleasant, albeit sleepy places, where you can get a feel of "real Egypt" without tripping over other tourists. **Suez** is grim, but a vital transport nexus between Cairo, Sinai and the Red Sea coast.

Edged by coral reefs teeming with tropical fish, the **Sinai Peninsula** offers superb **snorkelling** and **diving**, and palmy **beaches** where women can swim without hassle. Resorts along the Gulf of Aqaba are varied enough to suit anyone, whether you're into upmarket hotels at **Na'ama Bay** or **Taba**, or cheap, simple living at **Dahab** and **Nuweiba**. From there it's easy to visit **Saint Catherine's Monastery** and **Mount Sinai** (where Moses received the Ten Commandments)

The **Arab Republic of Egypt** (*el-Gumhorriya Masr al-Arabiya*) covers an area of 1,002,000 square kilometres – roughly twice the size of France, or about equal to Texas – of which 96.4 percent is desert. Its population of 60 million is twice that of the next most populous Arab country (Morocco) and amounts to a quarter of the total population of the Arab world. Sixty-five percent of Egyptians work on the land.

in the mountainous interior. With more time, cash and stamina, you can also embark on **jeep safaris** or **camel treks** to remote oases and spectacular *wadis*.

Egypt's **Red Sea coast** has more reefs farther offshore, with snorkelling and diving centred around **Hurghada** and (to a lesser extent) **Port Safaga**. Inland, the mountainous **Eastern Desert** harbours the Coptic **Monasteries of Saint Paul** and **Saint Anthony**, Roman quarries and other antiquities, and dramatic rockscapes seen by few apart from the nomadic Bedouin.

When to go

Deciding on the best time for a visit involves striking a balance between climatic and tourist factors. Egypt's traditional season runs from **late November to late February**, when the Nile Valley is balmy, although Cairo can be overcast and chilly. However, at these times, particularly during the peak months of December and January, the major Nile resorts of Luxor and Aswan get unpleasantly crowded. This winter season is also the busiest period for the Sinai resorts.

With this in mind, **March or April** are good compromise options, offering decent climate and fewer visitors. However, there is a potential problem in the unpredictable *khamseen*, a dust-laden wind from the Sahara, which can blow for up to fifty days any time between March and early June. In **May and June** the heat is still tolerable but, after that, Egyptians rich enough to do so migrate to Alex and the coastal resorts. From **July to September** the south and desert are ferociously hot and sightseeing best limited to early morning or evening – though August still sees droves of backpackers. **October** into early November is perhaps the best time of all, with easily manageable climate and crowds.

Weather and tourism apart, the **Islamic religious calendar** and its related festivals can have a seasonal effect on your travel. The most important factor is **Ramadan**, the month of daytime fasting, which can be problematic for eating and transport, though the festive evenings do much to compensate. See "Festivals" in the *Basics* section following for details of its timing.

MINIMUM/MAXIMUM TEMPERATURES C (F)					
	Jan	**March**	**May**	**July**	**Sept**	**Nov**
Alexandria *Mediterranean*	11/18 (51/65)	13/21 (55/70)	18/26 (64/79)	23/29 (73/85)	23/30 (73/86)	17/25 (62/77)
Aswan *Southern Nile Valley*	10/23 (50/74)	14/31 (58/87)	23/39 (74/103)	26/41 (79/106)	24/39 (75/103)	17/31 (62/87)
Cairo *Northern Nile Valley*	8/18 (47/65)	11/24 (52/75)	17/33 (63/91)	21/36 (70/96)	20/32 (68/90)	14/26 (58/78)
Dakhla *Western Desert*	5/21 (41/70)	8/28 (47/82)	20/37 (68/99)	23/40 (74/104)	21/36 (70/96)	12/28 (53/82)
Hurghada *Red Sea Coast*	10/21 (50/70)	12/23 (61/74)	21/30 (70/86)	25/32 (77/90)	23/30 (74/86)	15/25 (59/77)

Note that these are *average* daily maximum/minimum temperatures. Summer peaks in Aswan, Hurghada or Sinai, for example, can hit the 120°s F (low 50°s C) in hot years. The dryness of the air and absence of cloud cover makes for drastic fluctuations, though they do also make the heat tolerably un-sticky outside Cairo and the Delta.

PART ONE

THE

BASICS

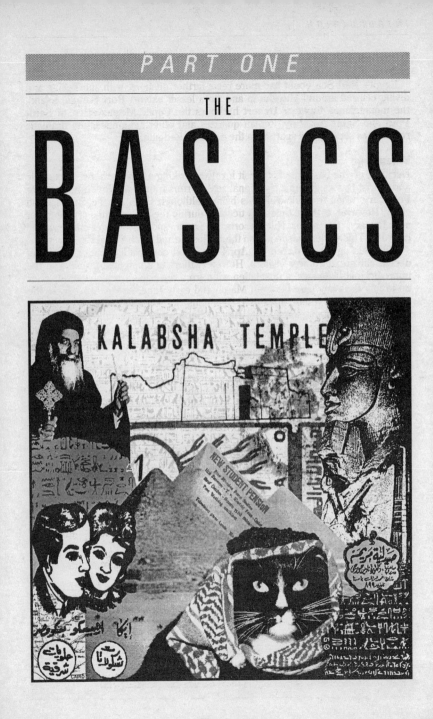

KALABSHA TEMPLE

GETTING THERE FROM EUROPE

The simplest way of getting to Egypt from northern Europe is to fly. From London, there are regular departures direct to Cairo and Luxor, and with a European connection to Egypt's three other international airports: Alexandria, Hurghada (Red Sea) and Sharm el-Sheikh (Sinai). At the time of writing, there are no direct flights to Egypt from any regional British airports, nor from Ireland: you either need connecting transport to London, or to fly on a European airline like *KLM* or *Lufthansa*, via their "home" airport.

Alternatively, for anyone wanting to take in Egypt as part of wider travels in the Mediterranean, other possible flight destinations include Athens, Crete, Cyprus, Israel or Jordan, from where you can make your own way on to Egypt by ferry or overland. At present, a charter flight to Israel is probably the cheapest way of reaching Egypt. As tourism picks up, however, following its Gulf War collapse, charters from London are likely to be resumed to Egyptian airports.

If you are pushed for time, or want things made a bit easier, buying a package holiday can make a lot of sense. As well as the standard Cairo-plus-Luxor tours, pioneered in the last century by Thomas Cook, many operators feature *felucca* trips on the Nile, while a number of independent companies specialise in activity or adventure holidays – diving on the Red Sea, for example, or camel trekking in Sinai.

DIRECT FLIGHTS FROM LONDON

Flying direct to **Egypt from London**, you have a straightforward choice of **scheduled flights** on *EgyptAir* or *British Airways*.

Both airlines operate out of **Heathrow**, *EgyptAir* from Terminal 3, *British Airways* from Terminal 4. *EgyptAir* flights are daily, leaving London either at 2pm or 5.25pm. *British Airways* flights are daily except Monday and Friday, leaving London at 4pm.

Agents quote **fares** of around £250–330 return, according to season (Nov–Feb is high season), on either airline. For addresses of the **airlines** and **agents**, see box overpage.

CHARTER FLIGHTS

Post Gulf War, **charter flights** from London to Egypt were heavily cut, leaving just *Monarch* running direct charters from London (Gatwick) to **Luxor**; flight-only deals are advertised by *Kuoni* (☎0306/740500) from £240. *Goldenjoy Holidays* (☎071/486 8403) are due to restart direct charters from London (Gatwick) to Hurghada; for other agents see overpage.

FLIGHTS VIA EUROPE

Most other major European airlines can sell you flights to Egypt (almost always Cairo), travelling via their own "home" airport. The majority work out more expensive than *EgyptAir* or *British Airways*, though agents in the know may direct you to special deals at various times of year.

Among the possibilities are:

KLM to Cairo, via Amsterdam. This is usually very expensive, at £400–450 return. However, *KLM* offer the advantage of flights for the first stage to Amsterdam from several regional British airports.

Lufthansa/Condor to Cairo, Alexandria and Luxor, via Munich or Frankfurt. *Condor* is *Lufthansa*'s charter wing. Add-on flights to a regular Britain–Germany flight can at times be decent value.

Olympic Airways to Alexandria or Cairo, via Athens. Another regular but quite pricey route; fares around £400–450 return.

TAROM to Cairo, via Bucharest. A bit unpredictable, but often cheap; return from £220.

Balkan-Bulgarian to Cairo, via Sofia. Can be good value, too; £250–350 return.

DISCOUNT AGENTS IN BRITAIN

In addition to the **recommended agents** listed below, useful **sources for finding a flight** are classified advertisements in the travel sections of newspapers like *The Independent* and *The Guardian* (Saturday editions), *The Sunday Times* or – in London – *Time Out* and *The Evening Standard*. High street travel agents are also worth a look for reductions on package holidays and charter flights.

Africa Travel Centre, 4 Medway Court, Leigh St, London WC1H 9QX (☎071/387 1211, Fax 071/383 7512). Helpful and resourceful.

Campus Travel, 52 Grosvenor Gardens, London SW1W 0AG (☎071/730 8111). Student/youth specialists.
Other branches at: 39 Queen's Rd, Bristol BS8 1QE (☎0272/292494); 5 Emmanuel St, Cambridge CB1 1NE (☎0223/324283); 5 Nicholson Sq, Edinburgh EH8 9BH (☎031/668 3303); 13 High St, Oxford OX1 4DB (☎0865/242067).

Nouvelles Frontières, 1 Hanover St, London W1 (☎071/629 7772). UK branch of the biggest French discount travel agency.

Soliman Travel, 233 Earl's Court Rd, London SW5 (☎071/370 6446). Regular *EgyptAir* flight consolidators.

South Coast Student Travel, 61 Ditchling Rd, Brighton BN1 4SD (☎0273/570226). A good agent with plenty to offer non-students as well.

STA Travel, 74 Old Brompton Rd, London W7 (☎071/937 9962, autoqueue). Large range of fares and airlines, from 20 offices in the UK and 120 worldwide. Special youth/student fares as well as a specialist Africa Desk at 117 Euston Rd, London (☎071/465 0486, Fax 071/388 0944).
Other branches at: 25 Queen's Rd, Bristol BS8 1QE; 38 Sidney St, Cambridge CB2 3HX; 75 Deansgate, Manchester M3 21BW; 19 and 48 High St, Oxford, OX1 4AH.

Trailfinders, 42–48 Earl's Court Rd, London W8 6EJ (☎071/938 3366). Respected discount flights agency that offers a convenient range of other services.

Wexas, 45 Brompton Rd, London SW3 1DE (☎071/589 3315). If you're unable to visit others, this membership-only organisation handles everything competently by post. Detailed brochures.

DISCOUNT AGENTS IN IRELAND

USIT. Student and youth specialist.
O'Connell Bridge, 19/21 Aston Quay, Dublin 2 (☎01/778117).
10–11 Market Parade, Cork (☎021/270 900).
31a Queen St, Belfast (☎0232/242562).

Joe Walsh Tours, 8–11 Baggot St, Dublin (☎01/789555). General budget fares agent.

Funtrek, 32 Batchelors Walk, O'Connell Bridge, Dublin 1 (☎01/733244). Agents for many of the adventure companies detailed on p.6.

AIRLINES

Balkan-Bulgarian Airways (LZ), 322 Regent St, London W1 (☎071/637 7637).

British Airways (BA), 75 Regent St, London W1 (☎081/897 4000).

Egyptair (MS), 29–31 Piccadilly, London W1 (☎071/734 2395 or ☎437 6426).

El Al (LY), 185 Regent St, London W1 (☎071/437 9255).

KLM Royal Dutch Airlines (KL), 8 Hanover St, off Regent St, London W1 (☎081/750 9000).

Lufthansa (LH), 23–26 Piccadilly, London W1 (☎071/355 4994).

Olympic Airways (OA), Trafalgar House, Chalkhill Rd, London W6 (☎081/846 9080).

TAROM (RO), 17 Nottingham St, London W1 (☎071/224 3693).

BY CARGO BOAT FROM BRITAIN

Travelling as a **paying passenger on a cargo boat** is not the most obvious way of getting to Egypt – nor, at £500 one-way from Tilbury or Felixstowe to Alexandria or Port Said, is it the cheapest. However, for enthusiasts, it's perfectly feasible, with several freight lines offering space for anything from two to a dozen paying passengers, in private cabins.

For details (and a brochure), contact: *Weider Travel/Strand Cruise Centre*, Charing Cross Shopping Concourse, The Strand, London WC2N 4HZ (☎071/836 6363).

BY TRAIN FROM BRITAIN

If you want to travel overland to Egypt, the easiest course is to take a **train to Piraeus**, the port of Athens, then catch one of the ferries to Alexandria outlined below.

The cheapest way to do this is to get an **InterRail** pass, which for its period of validity covers train travel throughout Europe (excluding the country of purchase) and offers discounts on various ferries. The passes are now available to **all ages**. Under-26s or over-65s pay £175 for a month, £145 for fifteen days. Everyone else pays £235 a month, or £175 for fifteen days. Passes are available through British Rail or most travel agents. Regular-fare return tickets from London to Athens work out more expensive than any of these passes.

Officially, you need to have been resident in Europe for at least six months to buy an *InterRail* pass (in practice, agents aren't always fussy about this). Vacationing **North Americans or Australasians** are supposed to buy, instead, a **Eurail pass** – not nearly such good value at $425 a month, $560 for two months, for under-26s. Over-26s have to buy an exorbitant first-class pass – scarcely worth consideration.

DRIVING TO EGYPT

Driving to Egypt is an expensive and pretty epic undertaking: it's close on 2000 miles from London to Athens, to pick up one of the ferries from Piraeus (see below). Arriving at **customs and immigration** at Alexandria or Port Said, or travelling into Egypt overland from Israel, you should expect tribulations worthy of Hercules.

Very few tourists bring their own cars and bureaucracy is very creaky. Officially, you can bring a car into Egypt via any border crossing providing you have an international *triptyque* or **carnet de passage en douane**, issued by an automobile club in the country where the vehicle is registered. The car is allowed to remain in Egypt for three months; an additional three-month extension can be arranged by the **Automobile and Touring Club of Egypt** (Cairo head office: 10 Sharia Qasr el-Nil; Sat–Thurs 9am–1pm; ☎743-355), or its representatives at the harbours of Alexandria, Port Said, Suez or Nuweiba.

Note that Egyptian regulations ban the importation of any **diesel-powered car** into the country.

TRAVELLING VIA GREECE OR CYPRUS

Combining Egypt with Greece or Cyprus is a distinctly attractive proposition if time is no great object. Flights to **Athens**, **Crete** or **Larnaka** (Cyprus) can be picked up quite cheaply (£130–200, according to season), and Greece is also included in the *InterRail* train pass (see above).

Moving on to Egypt **from Crete or Cyprus**, only ferries make sense. From **Athens**, however, you have a choice of a **ferry** or any number of cheap **flights** touted by discount travel agencies in Filellínon or Níkis streets (these include a branch of *USIT* at Filellínon 1; ☎324-1884). Keep in mind that flights may actually cost less than ferries for the trip from Athens, given the cost of food and drink aboard, and depending on the time of year you travel. The **high season** for ferries is from mid-July to mid-October.

GREECE/CYPRUS–EGYPT FERRIES

There are three companies currently operating ferries between **Greece/Cyprus and Egypt**:

Louis Cruise Lines The *C/F Princesa Marissa* laves from Limassol (Cyprus) for Port Said, every Monday at 3pm, arriving Tuesday at 6.30am. One-way fare starts at £50 in a basic cabin. You can also use the same company for a boat from Piraeus (the port of Athens) to Limassol.

Details: Louis Cruise Lines, c/o Viamare Travel, 33 Mapesbury Rd, London NW2 4HT (☎081/452 8231).

Adriatica Lines The *C/F Expresso Egitto* (joined out of season by its newer sister ship, the *C/F Sansovino*) runs from Piraeus to Alexandria, via Iraklion (Crete). The boats actually start out at Venice, on a first "cruise" leg to Piraeus. Fares from Piraeus to Alex start at around £85 one way but there are discounts for students, *InterRail* holders and anyone under 26.

Details: Adriatica, c/o Sealink Travel, PO Box 29, Victoria Station, London SW1V 1JX (☎071/828 1948).

Black Sea Shipping Company Three grungy Russian boats, *C/F Adjaria, C/F Armenia* and *C/F Bashkira* run from Istanbul to Piraeus and Alexandria, twice monthly. Some departures are more of a cruise, calling in at Larnaca (Cyprus) and Lattakia (Syria) between Piraeus and Alex. Piraeus to Alex fares from around £65 one way.

Details: Black Sea Shipping, c/o CNC Lines, 1–3 Lower Regent St, London SW1Y 4NN.

ADVENTURE HOLIDAYS AND PACKAGE TOURS

Tour operators to Egypt come in any number of shapes and sizes. The first group detailed below are small, independent, **"adventure holiday" companies**, who pride themselves on modest-sized groups, adventurous itineraries or special interest activities – for all of which Egypt offers a lot of scope. These are followed by a group of **diving holiday specialists**, which arrange trips to the Red Sea centres around Hurghada, usually inclusive of hire equipment and dives. And finally, we detail some of the better value **mainstream operators** who offer traditional tours and cruises, as well as flight-plus-hotel packages in Luxor, Aswan and elsewhere.

All **prices quoted** are inclusive of flights, unless otherwise stated.

ADVENTURE HOLIDAY COMPANIES

Exodus Expeditions, 9 Weir Rd, London SW12 0LT (☎081/675 5550). From an extensive programme, two trips stand out: a 23-day "Egypt and Sinai Safari", mixing desert drives with *felucca* cruises, camping and hotels (from £490 plus flights); and the "Middle East Expedition", a six-week London to Cairo overland trip by customised truck (from £760).

Explore Worldwide, 1 Frederick St, Aldershot, Hampshire, GU11 1LQ (☎0252/319448). Highly respected small groups operator with five Egyptian programmes, including a 15-day Nile tour with six days on a felucca (from £275 plus flights) and a 15-day Sinai camel trek (from £500 plus flights).

Guerba Expeditions, 101 Eden Vale Rd, Westbury, Wiltshire BA13 3QX (☎0373/827046). Long-established Africa-overland experts, *Guerba* runs a variety of Egyptian programmes, travelling by truck and felucca. A 22-day "Nile and Beyond" tour costs from £770. If you fancy an adventurous overland trip to Cairo, Guerba truck it from Istanbul in 29 days for £980.

High Places, The Globe Works, Penistone Rd, Sheffield S6 3AE (☎0742/822333). Extended camel treks and hiking in Sinai, from £985,

Top Deck, 131–135 Earl's Court Rd, London SW5 9RH (☎071/244 8641). "Tours for the 18–35s", long favoured by Australasian travellers, include the 15-day *felucca*, Nile Valley and desert "Egyptian Adventure" from £795.

Tracks Africa, 12 Abingdon Rd, London W8 6AF (☎071/937 3028-30). Fifteen-day *felucca* trips from £275; also quality hotel-based "Nile Valley Explorer" tours, from £575. *Flights extra.*

DIVING HOLIDAYS

Oonasdivers, 23 Enys Road, Eastbourne BN21 2DG (☎0323/648924).

Red Sea Aquarians, Newman House, 270 London Road, Wallington, Surrey SM6 7DJ (☎081/669 0068). Experienced divers only; no training offered.

Regal Diving Tours, Station Road, Sutton, Ely, Cambs CB6 2RL (☎0353/778096).

MAINSTREAM OPERATORS

Bales Tours, Bales House, Barrington Rd, Dorking, RH4 3EJ (☎0306/885923). An interesting range of tours includes a 12-day journey through the Western Desert Oases from £850.

Thomas Cook, PO Box 36, Thorpe Wood, Peterborough PE3 6SB (☎0733/332255). Thomas Cook more or less created tourism in Egypt, offering his first escorted tour in 1869, and the country remains one of Cook's specialities. They offer 9- to 16-day escorted tours, with Egyptologist guides, from £700 to £1200, as well as cheaper stays in Cairo, Luxor and Aswan.

Goldenjoy Holidays, 51 Dorset St, London W1H 3FA (☎071/486 8403). Features good value packages to Hurghada, using direct charter flights from London.

Hayes and Jarvis, Hayes House, 152 King St, London W6 0QU (☎081/748 5050). Charter flights to Luxor provide the basis of a variety of holidays: 7 nights in Luxor from £300, 7 nights in Hurghada from £450; cruises from £550.

Imaginative Traveller, 64 Kenway Rd, London SW5 0RD (☎071/244 7556). Good range of small-group tours (from £850 for 14 days) and cruises. Their "Nile in Style" trip features a cruise on a 1930s paddle steamer (14 days from £950).

Kuoni (☎0306/742000 or 0306/740500). Highly experienced operator, with a flexible and very good-value choice of trips, again based on charter flights to Luxor: eg, 7 nights in Luxor from £345, 7 nights in Hurghada (Red Sea diving) from £450, Nile Cruises from £480.

Speedbird, 152 King St, London W6 0QU (☎071/741 8041). *British Airways* holiday offshoot, with good-value, upmarket trips: eg Cairo and Luxor (7 nights from £500), Cairo and Red Sea (8 nights from £520), Nile Cruise (7 nights from £950).

GREECE/CYPRUS–ISRAEL FERRIES

A rather greater number of lines run ferries between **Piraeus and/or Limassol and Haifa (Israel)**, sometimes calling at **Iraklion** and **Rhodes** en route. Fares tend to be slightly lower than on boats direct to Egypt, and it's easy enough to travel on overland (see overpage).

Operators include *Louis Cruise Lines* and *Adriatica*, plus *Arkadia Lines*, *Marlines* and *Stability Lines* (all of which are represented by *Viamare Travel*). See p.5 for addresses.

TRAVELLING VIA ISRAEL

Scheduled and charter flights from **London to Tel Aviv** can be obtained for around £140–220. Once there, you can **fly to Cairo** on *El Al* or *Air Sinai* for around US$100. *El Al* offer half-price tickets if you book this as an add-on fare to one of their own international flights to Tel Aviv. Alternatively, it is easy and inexpensive to cross into Egypt's **Sinai peninsula**, or head on to Cairo, **overland**.

There are two border crossings: near the Mediterranean coast at the divided town of **Rafah**; and on the Gulf of Aqaba at **Taba**, near the Israeli resort of Eilat. The latter makes a fine jumping-off point for the Sinai coast resorts, Saint Catherine's Monastery or Cairo. Rafah and nearby el-Arish, by contrast, have little to offer and no direct communications with the rest of Sinai – just *service* taxi connections with Cairo.

Entering at either checkpoint, you're liable to **Israeli departure tax** (currently NIS15.60) and an **Egyptian entry fee** of US$6 (£E13) payable in any currency except shekels.

CROSSING AT RAFAH

It's possible to get a coach direct from **Tel Aviv or Jerusalem** into **Sinai** (or to **Cairo**); tickets are sold by most Israeli travel agents. Alternatively, you can make your own way by local buses and shared taxis. Doing it this way take a *sherut* (an Israeli shared taxi) to the Egyptian border at Rafah. You can then take local transport on into Sinai or beyond (see p.555 for details – and some background on the route).

Crossing the border (winter 9am–5pm; summer 10am–6pm), the Egyptian guards will examine your passport and visa (which cannot be issued here), and charge entry tax. The exchange office may specify US$, but should eventually accept traveller's cheques.

CROSSING AT TABA

Again, Israeli travel agents sell tickets on through coaches **from Eilat** into Sinai or on to Cairo. However, local transport is fairly simple if you are heading for a destination in Sinai. From Eilat, a taxi (NIS10) or #15 will get you to the Israeli checkpoint at **Taba** (daily 7am–9pm) for an exit stamp; you then board a bus for a short ride across no-man's-land to the Egyptian side where proceedings are similar to those at Rafah, except that **Sinai-only visas** can be obtained on the spot.

Buses from Taba (see p.542) down the Aqaba coast to Sharm el-Sheikh (4hr; £E14) don't always run as scheduled (7am, 9am, 1pm & 3pm), but they do stop at Nuweiba, Dahab and Na'ama Bay en route. Buses to Cairo (9hr; £E28) and Saint Catherine's (4hr; £E13) via Nuweiba leave more reliably at 10am and 1pm, and there's also the possibility of splitting the cost of a taxi to Nuweiba (£E35) or Saint Catherine's (£E105).

TRAVELLING VIA JORDAN

Coming from Jordan, you can **fly** from Amman to Cairo, or travel overland by **bus and ferry** into the Sinai and thence on to Cairo.

OVERLAND: THE FERRY TO NUWEIBA

Starting out at Amman, it's best to buy combined bus and ferry tickets to Nuweiba from a travel agent. These cost around US$45, which is little more than the cost of the ferry.

The **ferries** run between **Aqaba** in Jordan and **Nuweiba** in Sinai; they should be trouble-free. If you haven't bought a through ticket from Amman, they can be purchased from any agent in Aqaba; a second-class single currently costs JD8.40. Arrive an hour beforehand to go through customs and pay departure tax (JD6; JD40 for cars, not including driver). Boats are supposed to sail at 11am and 4pm, and take three hours, but rarely do. Everything you'll need to know on arrival is detailed under Nuweiba (p.538), as is travelling in the opposite direction, towards Aqaba.

See the "Red Tape and Visas" section on p.11 for details of **Egyptian and Sinai-only visas** and for addresses of **Egyptian consulates in Israel and Jordan**.

GETTING THERE FROM THE USA AND CANADA

The volume of North American travellers to Egypt is not great – and this is reflected in a relative dearth of flights. Other than on *EgyptAir*, which flies direct to Cairo from New York and Los Angeles, you'll have to transit via Europe or Israel. North American travel agents can arrange flights with no problem, or if you're heading to London anyway, you can arrange connections yourself, following the previous "Getting there from Europe" section.

On these and the following pages you'll find listings of offices of some of the best budget travel agencies in North America, plus a few Egypt specialists, and direct lines for the major airlines serving Egypt. Before booking a flight, it's a good idea to phone around several of the agencies to get an idea of the range of fares available. The airlines themselves are worth a call, too, as they sometimes have their own special fares and offers.

DIRECT FLIGHTS TO CAIRO

EgyptAir flights to Cairo from **New York** and **Los Angeles** don't come especially cheap. APEX round trip fares for the New York (JFK) flights range from around $1100 in low season to $1400 in high season; from LA, you need to count on an additional $150–200. *EgyptAir* flights from **Toronto** to Cairo (round trip fares from $CD1085) go via New York.

Departures are four times a week from New York (JFK airport), twice weekly from LA.

FLIGHTS VIA EUROPE OR ISRAEL

Travelling to Cairo via Europe or Israel, there's a considerably wider range of fares – and one that fluctuates greatly, depending on time of year and which agents you call. From New York, for example, you could hope to pick up a round trip ticket to Cairo for around $750–900 low season, $850–1400 in high season.

Good value airline routings include:
● *TWA*. New York to Cairo via Paris.
● *Sabena*. New York, Boston, Chicago or Montreal to Brussels, linking with *EgyptAir*.
● *British Airways*. All standard *BA* routings from North America into London, then on to Cairo.
● *United Airlines*. Flights from most US cities into Paris or Frankfurt, linking with other airlines for the Cairo leg.
● *El Al*. New York to Cairo via Tel Aviv. *El Al* flights from Miami, LA and Chicago route through New York; Boston routes through Montreal.
● *Lufthansa*. Flights to Cairo from several North American cities via Munich or Frankfurt.
● *KLM*. Again, flights to Cairo from several North American cities – via Amsterdam.
● *Air Canada*. Flights link with Lufthansa.

TOLL-FREE AIRLINE NUMBERS

American Airlines ☎1-800/433-7300

Air Canada ☎1-800/776-3000

British Airways ☎1-800/247-9297

EgyptAir ☎1-800/334-6787

El Al ☎1-800/223 6700

KLM ☎1-800/777-5553

Lufthansa ☎1-800/645-3880

Sabena ☎1-800/955-2000

TWA ☎1-800/221-2000

United Airlines ☎1-800/241-6522

COUNCIL TRAVEL IN THE US

Head Office: 205 E. 42nd St., New York, NY 10017; ☎212/661-1450

CALIFORNIA
2486 Channing Way, Berkeley, CA 94704; ☎415/848-8604
UCSD Price Center, Q-076, La Jolla, CA 92093; ☎619/452-0630
1818 Palo Verde Ave., Suite E, Long Beach, CA 90815; ☎213/598-3338
1093 Broxton Ave., Suite 220, Los Angeles, CA 90024; ☎213/208-3551
4429 Cass St., San Diego, CA 92109; ☎619/270-6401
312 Sutter St., Suite 407, San Francisco, CA 94108; ☎415/421-3473
919 Irving St., Suite 102, San Francisco, CA 94122; ☎415/566-6222
14515 Ventura Blvd., Suite 250, Sherman Oaks, CA 91403; ☎818/905-5777

COLORADO
1138 13th St., Boulder, CO 80302; ☎818/905-5777

CONNECTICUT
Yale Co-op East, 77 Broadway, New Haven, CT 06520; ☎203/562-5335

DISTRICT OF COLUMBIA
1210 Potomac St., NW Washington, DC 20007; ☎202/337-6464

GEORGIA
12 Park Place South, Atlanta, GA 30303; ☎404/577-1678

ILLINOIS
1153 N. Dearborn St., Chicago, IL 60610; ☎312/951-0585
831 Foster St., Evanston, IL 60201; ☎708/475-5070

LOUISIANA
8141 Maple St., New Orleans, LA 70118; ☎504/866-1767

MASSACHUSETTS
79 South Pleasant St., 2nd Floor, Amherst, MA 01002; ☎413/256-1261
729 Boylston St., Suite 201, Boston, MA 02116; ☎617/266-1926
1384 Massachusetts Ave., Suite 206, Cambridge, MA 02138; ☎617/497-1497
Stratton Student Center MIT, W20-024, 84 Massachusetts Ave., Cambridge, MA 02139; ☎617/497-1497

MINNESOTA
1501 University Ave. SE, Room 300, Minneapolis, MN 55414; ☎612/379-2323

NEW YORK
35 W. 8th St., New York, NY 10011; ☎212/254-2525
Student Center, 356 West 34th St., New York, NY 10001; ☎212/643-1365

NORTH CAROLINA
703 Ninth St., Suite B-2, Durham, NC 27705; ☎919/286-4664

OREGON
715SW Morrison, Suite 600, Portland, OR 97205; ☎503/228-1900

RHODE ISLAND
171 Angell St., Suite 212, Providence, RI 02906; ☎401/331-5810

TEXAS
2000 Guadalupe St., Suite 6, Austin, TX 78705; ☎512/472-4931
Exec. Tower Office Center, 3300 W. Mockingbird, Suite 101, Dallas,TX 75235; ☎214/350-6166

WASHINGTON
1314 Northeast 43rd St., Suite 210, Seattle, WA 98105; ☎206/632-2448

WISCONSIN
2615 North Hackett Avenue, Milwaukee, WI; ☎414/332-4740

STA IN THE US

BOSTON
273 Newbury St., Boston, MA 02116; ☎617/266-6014

HONOLULU
1831 S. King St., Suite 202, Honolulu, HI 96826; ☎808/942-7755

LOS ANGELES
920 Westwood Blvd., Los Angeles, CA 90024; ☎213/824-1574
7204 Melrose Ave., Los Angeles, CA 90046; ☎213/934-8722

2500 Wilshire Blvd., Los Angeles, CA 90057; ☎213/380-2184

NEW YORK
17 E. 45th St., Suite 805, New York, NY 10017; ☎212/986-9470;☎ 800/777-0112

SAN DIEGO
6447 El Cajon Blvd., San Diego, CA 92115; ☎619/286-1322

SAN FRANCISCO
166 Geary St., Suite 702, San Francisco, CA 94108; ☎415/391-8407

TRAVEL CUTS IN CANADA

Head Office: 187 College St., Toronto, Ontario M5T 1P7; ☎416/979-2406

ALBERTA

MacEwan Hall Student Centre, Univ. of Calgary, Calgary T2N 1N4; ☎403/282-7687. 10424A 118th Ave., Edmonton T6G 0P7; ☎403/471-8054

BRITISH COLUMBIA

Room 326, T.C., Student Rotunda, Simon Fraser University, Burnaby, British Columbia V5A 1S6; ☎604/291-1204. 1516 Duranleau St., Granville Island, Vancouver V6H 3S4; ☎604/687-6033. Student Union Building, University of British Columbia, Vancouver V6T 1W5; ☎604/228-6890 Student Union Building, University of Victoria, Victoria V8W 2Y2; ☎604/721-8352

MANITOBA

University Centre, University of Manitoba, Winnipeg R3T 2N2; ☎204/269-9530

NOVA SCOTIA

Student Union Building, Dalhousie University, Halifax B3H 4J2; ☎902/424-2054. 6139 South St., Halifax B3H 4J2; ☎902/494-7027

ONTARIO

University Centre, University of Guelph, Guelph N1G 2W1; ☎519/763-1660. Fourth Level Unicentre, Carleton University, Ottawa, K1S5B6; ☎613/238-5493. 60 Laurier Ave. E, Ottawa K1N 6N4; ☎613/238-8222. Student Street, Room G27, Laurentian University, Sudbury P3E 2C6; ☎705/673-1401. 96 Gerrard St. E, Toronto M5B 1G7; ☎ (416) 977-0441. University Shops Plaza, 170 University Ave. W, Waterloo N2L 3E9; ☎519/886-0400.

QUÉBEC (Known as *Voyages CUTS*)

Université McGill, 3480 rue McTavish, Montréal H3A 1X9; ☎514/398-0647. 1613 rue St. Denis, Montréal H2X 3K3; ☎514/843-8511. Université Concordia, Edifice Hall, Suite 643, S.G.W. Campus, 1455 bd de Maisonneuve Ouest, Montréal H3G 1M8; ☎514/288-1130. 19 rue Ste. Ursule, Québec G1R 4E1; ☎418/692-3971

SASKATCHEWAN

Place Riel Campus Centre, University of Saskatchewan, Saskatoon S7N 0W0; ☎306/975-3722

NOUVELLES FRONTIÈRES

In the United States

NEW YORK 12 East 33rd St, New York, NY 10016 ☎212/779-0600

LOS ANGELES 6363 Wilshire Blvd., Suite 200, Los Angeles, CA 90048; ☎213/658-8955

SAN FRANCISCO 209 Post St., Suite 1121, San Francisco, CA 94108; ☎415/781-4480

In Canada

MONTREAL 800 East Blvd. de Maison Neuve, Montréal, Quebec (☎514/288-9942)

QUEBEC 176 Grande Allée Ouest, Québec, P.Q. G1R 2G9; ☎418/525-5255

EGYPT SPECIALISTS

Galilee Tours
757 Main St, PO Box 96, Yarmouthport, MA 0267 (☎508/362-4022; ☎1-800/362-4022).

Homeric Tours
595 Fifth Avenue, New York, NY 10017 (☎212/753-1100; ☎1-800/223-5570).

Isis Travel
29 Birch Brook Rd, Bronxville, NY 10708 (☎914/793-7310).

Isram Wholesale Tours
630 Third Avenue, New York, NY 10017 (☎212/661-1193; ☎1-800/223-7460).

King Tut Tours and Travel
5 Willow St, Beth Pase, NY 11714 (☎516/433-3242).

Maupintour
408 East 50th St, New York, NY 10022 (☎212/688-4106; ☎1-800/255-4266).

Misr Travel
630 Fifth Avenue, #555, New York, NY 10011 (☎212/582-9210; ☎1-800/22-EGYPT).

Tursem
420 Madison Avenue, #1003, New York, NY 10017 (☎212/935-9210; ☎1-800/223-9169).

Wings Tours
6118 Franconia Rd, #204, Alexandraville, VA 22310 (☎703/719-0050).

ADVENTURE TOUR AGENTS

The following companies act as agents for the various **"adventure holiday" companies** detailed in the box on p.6. All of them can book complete packages to Egypt, including flights from North America.

USA

Campus Holidays, 242 Bellevue Ave, Upper Montclair, NJ 07043 (☎201/744-8724; ☎800/526-2915). **Top Deck** tours.

Safaricenter, 3201 North Sepulveda Blvd, Manhattan Beach, CA 90266 (☎213/546-4411; ☎800/223-6046). **Tracks** tours.

Adventure Center, 1311 63rd St, Suite 200, Emeryville, Oakland CA 94608 (☎415/654-1879; ☎800/227-8747). **Guerba** and **Explore Worldwide** tours.

CANADA

Travel Cuts (see box opposite for their numerous regional offices). **Exodus** and **Top Deck** tours.

Trek Holidays, Head office, 8412–109 Street, Edmonton, Alta T6G 1E2 (☎403/439-9118; ☎1-800/661-7265); also regional offices in major Canadian cities. Handles **Guerba** and **Explore Worldwide** tours.

GETTING THERE FROM AUSTRALASIA

Most Australians and New Zealanders visit Egypt as an extension of a European trip – and a flight to London, plus add-on fare to Cairo, almost always provides the cheapest access. However, you might want to consider taking in Egypt as a stopover on a Round-the-World (RTW) ticket, or take advantage of some reasonable budget fares to Cairo from the Far East.

Among routings to Cairo worth asking agents about are the **EgyptAir** flights from Bangkok (daily) and the **Singapore Airways** flights from Singapore. These can be linked with a range of flights from Australasian cities. Return fares to Cairo start from around AUS$1900. **RTW tickets** are around AUS$2700 for a route taking in Thailand/Singapore and Zimbabwe or Kenya, prior to Egypt.

The reliable **STA Travel** have branches throughout Australasia. Their head offices are: 1a Lee St, Sydney 2000 (☎02/519-9866); 64 High St, Auckland (☎9/309-0458).

VISAS AND RED TAPE

Bureaucracy has flourished in Egypt for 5000 years, pervading most aspects of life. In recent history, Nasser's promise of a civil service job for every graduate has led to a vastly overstaffed, inefficient administration, which you'll come up against when obtaining travel permits or visa extensions, and which may well defeat you if you try and do anything more complicated. However, it's hard to be categorical: rules change from place to place and individual bureaucrats may interpret them differently, or introduce new regulations, or simply be obstructive through caprice. Remain patient and good-humoured no matter what.

PASSPORTS AND VISAS

All visitors to Egypt must hold **passports** which are valid for at least **six months** beyond the proposed date of entry to the country. Almost all Europeans, plus all North Americans and Australasians, must also obtain **tourist visas** (see below).

PASSPORT PRECAUTIONS

Once **in Egypt**, you should always carry your passport with you: you'll need it to register at hotels, change money, collect mail, and for identification at police checkpoints. If you're travelling for any length of time, you may find it useful to **register with your embassy** on arrival in Cairo, which will help greatly if you lose your passport.

At the least, it's a wise precaution to **photocopy** the initial pages and keep them separately. If you are travelling to areas of the country that require permits, spare sets of photocopies are useful for producing with your application.

TOURIST VISAS

Regular **tourist visas** are available from Egyptian consulates abroad (see box below), or on the spot at Cairo International Airport and the docks at Alexandria and Port Said. You *cannot* get them at overland border crossings, Aswan,

Suez or Nuweiba (but see "Sinai-only visas", below). Both the **single-visit** and **multiple-entry** types of visa entitle you to stay in Egypt for one month, though the latter allows you to go in and out of Egypt three times within this period. Don't be misled by statements on the visa that it is "valid for three [or six] months"; this simply means that it can be used within that period (dating from the day of issue).

Visa applications can be made in person or by post. Applying in person, you can normally get a visa the same day in Athens, Tel Aviv, Eilat, Amman or Aqaba; within 48 hours in Britain, North America or Australia; and three or four days at consulates in other countries. Always turn up early in the day and expect to pay in cash. Postal applications take between ten days and six weeks to process. When returning the form, you need to include a registered or recorded stamped, addressed envelope, your passport, one photo, and a postal or money order (not a personal cheque).

The **cost** varies according to your nationality, and from place to place. A standard visa is currently US$13 for Americans and £15 for Brits on their home turf. In Israel, Americans are charged NIS25, most other nationalities NIS35. In Jordan, visa charges are higher in Aqaba than in Amman. Some consulates may demand that you

---

EGYPTIAN CONSULATES ABROAD

For visa applications, consulates listed below are usually open Mon–Fri 10am–noon; at most consulates, you will have to return on the following day to pick up the visa.

Britain
2 Lowndes St, London SW1X 9ET (☎071/235 9777).

Australia
125 Monaco Crescent, Red Hill, Canberra ACT 2603 (☎062/950-394).

US
2300 Decatur Place NW, Washington, DC 20008 (☎202/232-5400).
1110 Second Ave., New York, NY 10022 (☎212/759-7120).
3001 Pacific Ave., San Franciso, CA 94115 (☎415/346-9700).
300 S. Michigan 7th floor, Chicago, IL 60603 (☎312/443-1190).

2000 West Loop South #1950, Houston, TX 77027 (☎703/961-4915).

Canada
454 Laurier Ave., E. Ottawa, Ontario K1N 6R3 (☎613/234-4931).
3754 Cote des Neiges, Montreal, Québec H3H 1V6 (☎514/936-7781).

Greece
Zalakosta 1, Athens (☎612-954).

Israel
54 Basel St, Tel Aviv (☎03/546-4151).
68 Ha'Efroni St, Eilat (☎059/768-82 or 761-115).
Both open Sun–Thurs 9–11am.

Jordan
Jebel Amman, Amman (☎629-526).
Sharia al-Istiqlal, Aqaba (☎316-171).
Both open Sat–Thurs 9am–noon.

pay in US$ instead of local currency, or supply extra photos (and maybe glue to stick them down!). It's wise to allow for these eventualities.

SINAI-ONLY VISAS

If you don't mind being limited to a week in Sinai, you can obtain special, **Sinai-only visas at Taba** on the Israeli–Egyptian border, for around US$6. Valid for seven days only, this visa restricts you to the Aqaba coast down to Sharm el-Sheikh, and the vicinity of Saint Catherine's Monastery. It can't be extended, and there's no period of grace for overstaying.

Note: visas are not available at Rafah, the other crossing between Israel and Egypt.

OVERSTAYING AND EXTENSIONS

Tourists who **overstay** their (regular) visa are allowed a fifteen-day period of grace in which to renew it. After this, they're fined £E60 unless they can present a letter of apology from their embassy (which may in itself cost £E25).

One-month **visa extensions** are obtainable from the Mugamma in Cairo (see p.222) or offices in Alexandria, Luxor, Aswan, Suez, Sharm el-Sheikh, Mersa Matrouh and Ismailiya (addresses are detailed under their respective entries). You'll have to show bank receipts proving that you've cashed at least US$180 – or its equivalent in other foreign currency – during the last month (or week, at some offices); supply one (or two) photos; and pay about £E7. Procedures vary slightly from office to office, but shouldn't take longer than an hour. The bureaucrats will keep your receipts.

Visitors anticipating an extended stay may apply for a **tourist residence visa**. This is likewise issued against the exchange of US$180 per month, but for periods of up to six months at a time. Applications are made to the same offices as for ordinary extensions.

CUSTOMS & CURRENCY DECLARATIONS

Egyptian **customs** allow you to bring in 200 cigarettes (or 250g of tobacco) and one litre of **alcohol**. It's worth bearing in mind that Cairo International Airport has **duty-free shops** for arriving passengers *before and after* customs. The duty-free shop in the arrivals hall will ask to see your ticket, but doesn't enquire whether you've already stocked up. (For more about buying duty-free liquor, see p.220.)

ISRAELI PASSPORT STAMPS

Most Arab countries (excepting Egypt) will deny entry to anyone whose **passport shows evidence of a visit to Israel**. Although the Israeli customs are happy to give you an entry stamp on a separate piece of paper, an Egyptian entry stamp at Taba or Rafah in the Sinai will give you away – and the Egyptians insist on stamping your passport.

In practice, people with a Taba stamp can sometimes **get into Jordan**, but with a Rafah stamp you might as well forget it. If you want to combine travel to Egypt, Jordan, and Israel, visit Jordan ahead of Israel.

Though personal effects and cameras are exempt from duty, items such as **electronic equipment and video cameras** should be declared and listed on a "Form D". If you lose them during your visit, they will be assumed "sold" when you come to leave and (unless you have police documentation of theft) you will have to pay 100 percent duty. On items with a high resale value (eg laptop computers or video cameras) you may be required to pay a deposit against possible duty charges, which is refundable on departure. If customs insists on impounding goods, get a receipt and contact your consulate.

CURRENCY DECLARATION

Although the visa forms state that it's obligatory, visitors are seldom required to make a **currency declaration** unless they're bringing in over US$7000, so airlines no longer automatically issue the requisite form. Assuming you're not bringing in anything liable for duty or carrying the bulk of your money in cash, neglecting to fill in a declaration Form D probably won't matter. If an official asks for it when you leave Egypt, explain that you never received one and weren't told about it. However, it has been known for travellers carrying lots of undeclared cash to have it confiscated for suspected currency smuggling. Furthermore, you can't buy traveller's cheques with Egyptian money without producing a Form D, and the document may also be required for other transactions.

If you're staying for anything more than a couple of weeks, it's perhaps best to play safe and fill one of the forms in – that is, if you can persuade an official to dig one out for you.

REGISTRATION

Once inside Egypt, foreigners are required to register with the authorities within seven days, and obtain a triangular **registration** stamp in their passport (re-entry visa-holders must do this each time they return to Egypt). Fortunately, though, most hotels can arrange this for a modest sum, and upmarket places often do so automatically. Places to register are listed in the guide, but it's better to avoid doing so personally if you can. Failure to register incurs a £E40 fine.

TRAVEL PERMITS

You can travel without restriction through most areas of Egypt. However, special **travel permits** are required for the following regions and categories:

- All secondary roads in the Delta.
- The coastal road west of Mersa Matrouh towards the Libyan border.
- The Red Sea coast between (but not including) Suez and Hurghada, and beyond Mersa Allam.
- The interior of the Sinai peninsula, excluding Saint Catherine's monastery and environs.
- Along the Suez Canal between Ismailiya and Suez (but not including the towns themselves).
- Siwa Oasis.
- Off piste driving anywhere in the desert.

With the exception of the Siwa permits, which are granted on the spot (and often within an hour or so) in **Mersa Matrouh**, it's best to apply for permits in **Cairo** or **Alexandria** (see p.223 for details). The bureacracy usually takes about a week.

COSTS AND MONEY

Once you've arrived, Egypt is an inexpensive and excellent value destination. Costs for food, accommodation and transport are all low by European standards – sometimes ridiculously so. Much depends on the current rate of exchange, which is strongly in your favour at time of writing, with six Egyptian pounds to one pound sterling, and over three Egyptian pounds to one US dollar. However, to be on the safe side, we've assumed a less advantageous rate when reckoning the following costs.

If you stay in the cheaper hotels, eat local food, and share expenses and rooms with another person, £40 to £50 (US$65–85) a week would be enough to survive on. On £80 to £100 (US$130–170) you could live pretty well, and with £250 to £350 (US$400–575) a week between two people you would be approaching luxury.

SOME BASIC COSTS

Accommodation ranges from about £1.50–6 (US$2.50–10) a night for a double room in a basic, unclassified hotel to £80–150 (US$130–250) in Egypt's most luxurious establishments. On a limited budget, you can expect to get a decent double room in a one- or two-star hotel for around £5–8 (US$8–14). The occasional splurge in a four-star hotel, with a pool, will cost around £25–45 (US$40–75) for a double room off season, £50–80 (US$80–150) at peak periods.

The price of a **meal** reflects a similar span, but the basic Egyptian staple of *fuul* and *taamiya* (beans and felafel) or *kushari* (noodles and lentils with hot sauce) can be had in a local eatery for about 15p (25¢). Egyptian pizzas, chicken or kebabs cost about £1–2 (US$1.60–3), and European-style meals in restaurants from around £4 (US$6.50). Locally manufactured **drinks** are also cheap – a bottle of *Stella* beer costing less than £1 ($1.65), native spirits or wines under £3 (US$5) – but imported booze is dearer than back home, especially in hotels and restaurants, which are generally the only outlets serving alcohol.

Unless you take domestic flights or rely heavily on private taxis, **transport** is likewise cheap. You can rent a car for £15–20 (US$25–33) a day, including petrol (which costs less per litre than mineral water!). The cost of buses, trains and collective taxis is generally absurdly low. For instance, the 885km train ride from Cairo to Aswan costs £5 (US$8) for first class, under £1 (US$1.65) in third class.

REGIONAL VARIATIONS

To some extent, all these costs are affected by **where you are and when**. Though low-budget options exist, the cost of mid-range and upmarket hotels is higher in Cairo (all year), Alexandria, Hurghada and Sinai (during summer), Luxor and Aswan (over winter). Everyday items tend to be dearer in Sinai and the desert oases, where goods have to be trucked in from distant centres.

With many prices negotiable depending on the circumstances and a **knowledge of local rates**, tourists are often overcharged until they get the hang of things (and even then, sometimes). Try to strike a balance between defending your own wallet and interests and acquiescing gracefully when appropriate. It's crazy to spoil your mood and offend people over trifling sums.

HIDDEN COSTS

Hidden costs in Egypt are threefold. Visiting the Pyramids and the monuments of the Nile Valley entails spending a fair bit on **site tickets** (ranging from 75p to £2.50 – US$1.25–4), though card-carrying students get fifty percent reductions. The custodians of tombs and temples and the medieval mosques of Islamic Cairo also expect to be tipped. Aside from the hidden costs of sightseeing, most tourists end up buying some Egyptian **crafts**, usually in Cairo's Khan el-Khalili or the smaller bazaars in Luxor and Aswan.

A harder aspect to come to terms with is that you'll be confronted with real local **poverty**. As a tourist, you're not going to solve any problems, but with an average Egyptian's wage at around £E60 a month (roughly £15/US$25), even a small tip can make a difference to individual family life. For Egyptians, giving money and goods to the needy is a natural act – and a requirement of

Islam. For tourists, rich by definition, local poverty demands at least some response (see "Baksheesh", p.23).

PRICES AND INFLATION

Most of the **prices** in this book are given in local currency (see overpage). The main exceptions to this rule – airline fares, top-flight accommodation and special packages – are reckoned in US$, although most are actually payable only in Egyptian pounds backed by an exchange receipt.

Both of these price indications will certainly change, so costs in this guide can't be taken as read. However, the cost for tourists in *real terms* shouldn't rise much (if at all) compared to local prices, and might even decrease if your own currency is riding high.

Although Egyptian **inflation** is currently running at around thirty percent, it's unevenly distributed. Prices for luxury goods and services (ie most things in the private sector) rise faster than the cost of public transport, petrol and basic foodstuffs, which is held down by subsidies that the government dare not abolish.

Unlike Egyptians, you may also benefit from the post-Gulf War slump in tourism, which has depressed hotel rates and heightened competition. At the time of writing (autumn 1991), trade is only slowly beginning to pick up.

CURRENCY

Egypt's basic unit of **currency** is the **Egyptian pound** (called a *ginay* in Arabic, and written as £E or LE). Since being floated on the international money markets in 1987, its value has fluctuated (but generally declined) against hard currencies such as the US$.

It's easy to distinguish between **£E notes** since they bear Arabic numerals on one side, Western numerals on the other, and are colour coded: £E20 (green); £E10 (red); £E5 (blue); £E1 (brown). The new £E50 note has been suspect since forgeries came to light, and is almost impossible to change outside of banks.

The Egyptian pound is divided into 100 **piastres**, called *irsh* in Arabic and written as ﻗﺮﺵ (abbreviated by Westerners to pt). There are 50pt, 25pt, 10pt and 5pt notes; and 5pt and 10pt coins. Formerly, each piastre was divided into ten **milliemes**, making 1000 milliemes to the pound. Though no longer in circulation, this denomination is still often expressed in prices (which follow the continental European custom of using a comma instead of a decimal point: eg £1,30). It's usually obvious whether people are using the piastre or millieme: a bill for 30,750 means £E30 and 75pt rather than a small fortune.

Many of the notes in circulation are so ragged that merchants refuse them. Trying to palm off (and avoid receiving) decrepit notes can add spice to minor transactions, or be a real nuisance. Conversely, many vendors won't accept high denomination notes (£E5 upwards in most cases) due to a shortage of **change**. Whilst some offer sweets in lieu of coins, others round prices up. Try to hoard denominations under £E1 for tips, fares and small purchases.

CURRENCY REGULATIONS

Various **regulations** affect the exchange and use of currency by tourists in Egypt. It's illegal to import more than £E100 and export any at all – not that you're likely to, as banks abroad won't sell larger amounts, and Egyptian money is useless outside Egypt. Tourists are seldom required to complete a **currency declaration** form, but it's wise to do so (see p.13). Visitors are no longer obliged to change a set sum into Egyptian pounds on arrival. To buy an airline ticket or pay for upmarket accommodation with Egyptian money, you must produce a receipt proving that it was legally exchanged.

CARRYING YOUR MONEY

Arriving in Egypt, it is useful to have at least three days' survival money in **cash**. English pounds, US dollars, French francs or German Deutschmarks are easy to exchange. Aside from ordinary spending, hard cash (usually US$) may be required for visas, border taxes and suchlike. **Do not bring** Canadian and New Zealand dollars, Scottish pounds or Irish punts, which are not accepted in Egypt, even by banks.

The rest of your money should, ideally, be spread around different forms and currencies for the sake of security. Carry the bulk of it in a well known brand of **traveller's cheque**, with **credit cards** and/or **Eurocheques** for back-up. By taking cash in one currency and cheques in another, you can exchange whichever offers the better rate. Beware of tying up your capital in cheques or plastic with limited utility.

American Express, Barclays, Citibank and *Bank of America* **traveller's cheques** are accepted by all banks and exchange offices. *Thomas Cook* cheques are usually good, though may present problems in untouristed places. Any other brand will prove more trouble than it's worth. **Eurocheques** backed by a Eurocard can be cashed in some banks and hotels, but Eurotraveller's cheques are not recommended. Cashing **International Girocheques** at major post offices entails an incredible rigmarole.

Credit cards are accepted at major hotels, top-flight restaurants, some shops and airline offices, but virtually nowhere else. *American Express, Visa* and *Access/Mastercard* are safer bets than *Diner's Club* or *Carte Blanche*, but even the "big three" aren't infallible when it comes to buying airline tickets, and *Visa* gets a thumbs down from many outlets that display its logo. However, cash advances on *Visa* and *Access* can be obtained at most banks, and *American Express* cardholders can cash personal cheques at the main Amex branches (see following).

BANKS AND EXCHANGE

There doesn't seem much to choose between **Egyptian banks** for the purposes of exchange. The *Bank of Alexandria, Bank Misr, Banque du Caire* and *National Bank of Egypt* offer identical rates. What does vary (from branch to branch rather than between banks) is the speed of the transaction. If you're lucky, the whole business can be handled at a single desk, without queueing; if not, the process could stretch to half an hour, with forms being passed between a bevy of clerks and counters.

This extended transaction is a little less likely at **foreign banks** (found only in Cairo) or branches **in hotels** (which may levy a commission), but there are plenty of exceptions in practice. If you're carrying **American Express** or **Thomas Cook** traveller's cheques – or cash – it's often quicker to do business at their local branches (see below). In Suez, Ismailiya and Luxor there are also licensed **private exchanges**, which should offer similar rates.

HOURS, COMMISSION AND RECEIPTS

Hours for Egyptian banks are generally Monday to Thursday 8.30am–1pm; some also open similar hours on Saturday, and from 10am to noon on Sunday (details are given as relevant in the text). Most foreign banks are open from 8.30am to 1pm, Sunday (or Monday) to Thursday. For arriving visitors, the bank at Cairo Airport is open 24 hours daily, and the banks at ports open whenever a ship docks.

Commission is not generally charged on straight exchanges, but there is a 30pt stamp duty, which you can either pay on the spot or have them deduct from what you're owed (in which case you may lose a few piastres). The main thing is to ensure that you get a **postage stamp**, without which the **exchange receipt** is technically invalid for transactions such as extending your visa, buying an airline ticket, or whatever. Even if you're not planning to use them, it's wise to **keep all receipts** until you leave Egypt.

Rather than going through the hassle of **re-exchanging Egyptian pounds for hard currency**, it's better to spend it all before leaving (you *can't* use it at Cairo Airport's duty-free shop). Exchanging back entails a "deduction" of £E30 per day from the sum total of your exchange receipts; what remains is eligible for conversion into US$.

THE BLACK MARKET
Since the Egyptian pound was floated and a crackdown on money-changers was instituted, the **black market** for hard currency has withered. The fractional difference between the black market and official exchange rates offers zero incentive to deal with (possible) rip-off artists or *agents provocateurs*.

That said, you might find it expedient to change some cash unofficially in the Sinai or the desert oases, where banks are thin on the ground and the risk factor is lower.

AMERICAN EXPRESS AND *THOMAS COOK*

American Express has several offices in Cairo, branches in Luxor and Aswan, and a rep in Alexandria. All of them can hold client mail and cash Amex traveller's cheques, paying out in Egyptian pounds (you can only get US$ at the *Nile Hilton* branch in Cairo). Money may be wired to all except the Luxor office. Amex cardholders can buy traveller's cheques at every branch, and cash personal cheques at most of them. Green card-holders may draw up to US$1000 every 21

days (US$200 in cash, the rest in traveller's cheques); for gold card-holders the limit is US$5000 (the first US$500 in cash).

Amex addresses are:

CAIRO (main office): 15 Sharia Qasr el-Nil (☎750-881 or 750-892; telex: 92715 AMEXT UN; fax: 202 628975).

ALEXANDRIA: c/o *Eyeress Travel*, 26 Sharia al-Horriya (☎483-0084).

LUXOR: c/o *Old Winter Palace Hotel* (☎382-862).

ASWAN: c/o *Old Cataract Hotel* (☎323-222).

THOMAS COOK
Amex's old-established, but today rather more low-key, rival, **Thomas Cook**, will cash most brands of traveller's cheque, and sell their own cheques (in whatever hard currency you buy them with) to anyone who can show a currency declaration form. Like Amex, they can also receive money wired from abroad. Addresses are:

CAIRO (main office): 12 Midan el-Sheikh Youssef, Garden City (☎356-4650).

ALEXANDRIA: 15 Midan Sa'ad Zaghloul (☎482-7830).

LUXOR: c/o *Old Winter Palace Hotel* (☎382-402).

ASWAN: 59 Abtal el-Tahrir, Corniche el-Nil (☎324- 011).

PORT SAID: 43 Sharia el-Gumhorriya (☎236-111).

See the text for opening hours for both agencies.

EMERGENCY CASH

Despite traveller's tales, very few people lose (or are conned out of) all their money in Egypt – but it does happen. Access to an **emergency source** of money – whether it be a credit card or an arrangement with your bank or family to wire you money after a phone call (or telex) – is reassuring and may prove invaluable. Amex cardholders can cash personal cheques, as described on the previous page. *Visa* and *Mastercard* holders can get cash advances in Egyptian pounds at big city banks.

Transferring money from abroad is best done in Cairo (see p.221) and may be impossible in the provinces.

HEALTH AND INSURANCE

Despite the potential health hazards of travel in Egypt, the majority of visitors experience nothing worse than a bout or two of diarrhoea. For minor health complaints, a visit to a pharmacy is likely to be sufficient. Egyptian pharmacists are well trained and dispense a wide range of drugs, including many normally on prescription in Europe. If they feel you need a full diagnosis, they can usually recommend a doctor – sometimes working on the premises. Most doctors speak English or French.

Although the change of diet and climate accounts for most health problems, **individual responses** vary. Whilst some people adapt quickly to the heat and consume local food with impunity, others get sick and stay poorly (children and old people are likely to suffer the worst effects). If you're here for a week or two only, it makes sense to be cautious. But longer-staying visitors might prefer to get ill early, acclimatise, and worry less thereafter – a lot depends on your constitution. Bearing this in mind, take whatever precautions seem appropriate.

PREVENTATIVE MEDICINE

Although visitors to Egypt are not required to have **inoculations**, unless coming from an infected area, you should always be up to date with **polio** and **tetanus**. It's also worth being vaccinated against **typhoid** and **cholera**, which occasionally flare up in parts of Egypt – although some doctors doubt the efficacy of the cholera shot. If you're hoping to visit the Sudan or sub-Saharan Africa, a vaccination against **meningitis** is essential. Opinion is divided on the value of gamma-globulin shots as a protection against **hepatitis**. Though all these vaccinations can be obtained in Cairo (see p.226), it is vital to ensure that any injections are done with sterile needles. Disposable syringes are sold at pharmacies.

Other precautions are fairly obvious, though whether all of them are justified is debatable. Guard against **heatstroke** (see below) and **food poisoning**. Rare meat and raw shellfish top the danger list, which descends via creamy sauces down to salads, juice, raw fruit and vegetables – and if slavishly followed would prevent you from eating most of what's on offer. Visitors who insist on washing everything (and only cleaning their teeth) in mineral water are over-reacting. Just use common sense, and accustom your stomach gradually to Egyptian cooking. However, take prompt care of **cuts and skin irritations**, since flies can quickly spread infections. **Anthisan cream** (available abroad) is a good for bites, swellings and rashes.

PHARMACIES, DOCTORS AND HOSPITALS

Pharmacies, found in every town, form the advance guard of Egypt's health service. Private **doctors** are equally common, but charge for consultations; expect to pay about £E30 (roughly £7, US$15) a session, excluding the price of any drugs you are prescribed.

If you get seriously ill, private **hospitals** are generally preferable to public sector ones. Those attached to universities are usually well-equipped and competent, but small-town hospitals are often abysmal. Many hospitals (*mustashfa*) require a **deposit** of around £E150. Normally, you must pay this on admission; a delayed payment by your insurance company is not acceptable. Despite several good hospitals in Cairo and Alexandria, Egypt is basically no country in which to fall seriously ill.

HEAT AND DUST

Many visitors experience problems with Egypt's intense **heat**, particularly in the south. Because sweat evaporates immediately in the dry atmosphere, you can easily become dehydrated without realising it. **Dehydration** is exacerbated by both alcohol and caffeine. Drink plenty of other fluids (at least three litres per day; twice as much if you're exerting yourself) and take a bit of extra salt with your food. Wear a hat and loose-fitting clothes (not synthetic fabrics). Try to avoid going out in the middle of the day, especially in summer.

Heat exhaustion – signified by headaches, dizziness and nausea – is treated by resting in a cool place and drinking plenty of water or juice with a pinch of salt. An intense headache, heightened body temperature, flushed skin and the cessation of sweating are symptoms of **heatstroke**, which can be fatal if not treated *immediately*. The whole body must be cooled by immersion in tepid water, or the application of wet towels. Seek medical assistance.

Less seriously, visitors from cooler climes may suffer from **prickly heat**, an itchy rash caused by excessive perspiration trapped beneath the skin. Wearing loose clothing, keeping cool and bathing often will help relieve the symptoms until your body acclimatises.

In non air-conditioned environments, you might employ the traditional Egyptian method of pouring water on the ground to cool the surrounding area by evaporation – it also levels the dust.

DUST

Desert dust – or grit and smog in Cairo – may cause your **eyes** to itch and water. **Contact lens-users** should wear glasses instead, at least part of the time. If Murine eye drops don't help, try antihistamine, decongestant eye drops such as Vernacel, Vascon-A or Optihist. Persistent irritation may indicate **trachoma**, a contagious infection which is easily cured by antibiotics at an early stage, but eventually causes blindness if left untreated. Its traditional prevalence in Egypt explains the number of older folk with cloudy eyes, and the ophthalmologists in every town.

Spending time in the desert, you might find that your **sinuses** get painfully irritated by windborne dust. Covering your nose and mouth with a scarf helps prevent this, while olbas oil or a nasal decongestant spray (available at pharmacies) can relieve the symptoms.

SUNBURN

Wear a hat and a high-factor sunscreen to protect yourself from **sunburn**, especially during summer. The sun burns you even quicker in the water, so it's wise to wear a T-shirt when snorkelling.

WATER AND HEALTH HAZARDS

The **tap water** in Egyptian towns and cities is heavily chlorinated and safe to drink, but unpalatable and rough on tender stomachs. In rural areas, desert resthouses and oases, there's a fair risk of contaminated water.

Consequently, most tourists stick to **bottled mineral water**, which is widely available, tastes better, and won't upset sensitive tums. However, excessive fear of tap water is unjustified, and hard to sustain in practice if you're here for long. Once your guts have adjusted, it's usually okay to drink it without further purification (with Halazone tablets, iodine crystals, or by boiling).

What you should avoid is any contact with stagnant water that might harbour **bilharzia** (schistosomiasis) flukes. Irrigation **canals** and the slower stretches of the **River Nile** are notoriously infested with these minute worms, which breed in the blood vessels of the abdomen and liver (the main symptom is blood in the urine). Don't drink or swim there, walk barefoot in the mud, or even on grass that's wet with Nile water. But it's okay to bathe in the saline pools of the desert oases.

DIARRHOEA AND WORSE . . .

Almost every visitor to Egypt gets **diarrhoea** at some stage. Unless you're stricken by cramps, the best initial treatment is to simply adapt your diet. Fresh orange juice or lemon or lime juice makes a good stomach settler, as does live yogurt (if you can find it). Avoid other fruit and dairy produce, and keep your bodily fluids topped up by drinking plenty of bottled water (perhaps mixed with a rehydration sachet). If things don't improve after 24 hours – or if you have an "enteric" type attack with cramps or vomiting – resort to Imodium or Lomotil, being sure not to exceed the recommended dose. Avoid Enterovioform, which is still available in Egypt despite being suspected of damaging the optic nerve. Follow medical advice on giving any of these quite powerful drugs to children.

If symptoms persist longer than a few days, or if you develop a fever or pass blood in your faeces, get medical help immediately, since diarrhoea can also be a symptom of serious infection. Accompanied by vomiting and fever, it may indicate **typhoid**, which responds well to antibiotics. Rarer is **cholera**, which requires urgent treatment with antibiotics and rehydration fluids; it is marked by a sudden onset of acute diarrhoea and cramps. Except for the "rice-water shits" typical of cholera, similar symptoms occur with bacilliary **dysentery**, which is treated with antibiotics. Amoebic dysentery is harder to shift and can cause permanent damage if untreated. The normal remedy is Metronidazole (Flagyl), which should only be taken under medical supervision.

RABIES

Rabies is endemic in Egypt, where many wild animals and bats (sometimes found in temples and tombs) carry the disease. Avoid touching any strange animal, wild or domestic. Treatment must be given between exposure to the disease and the onset of symptoms; once these appear, rabies is invariably fatal. If you think you've been exposed, contact the *Hospital of the Rabies Institute* in Cairo (Maahad al-Kilab, Imbaba: ☎346-2042/2043).

MALARIA

Currently resurgent throughout Africa, **malaria**, spread by the Anopheles mosquito, could soon become a problem in Egypt. Consult your doctor, who may recommend a prophylactic course of Chloroquine, starting *before* you leave home. The first signs of infection are muscular soreness and a low fever; four to eight days later, the characteristic bouts of chills and fever appear.

MOSQUITOES AND BUGS

Beside the risk of malaria, **mosquitoes** can make your life a misery. Horribly ubiquitous over the summer, these blood-sucking pests are never entirely absent – even in Cairo, despite locals' assertions to the contrary. The only solution is total war, using fans, mosquito coils, rub-on repellent, and perhaps a plug-in *Ezalo* device, sold at pharmacies. However, the best guarantee of a bite-less night's sleep is to bring a mosquito net with long tapes, to pin above your bed. Outdoors, you'll have to depend on repellent, which soon sweats off. Mosquitoes favour shady, damp areas, and anywhere around dusk.

Equally loathsome – and widespread – are **flies**, which transmit various diseases. Only insecticide spray or air conditioning offers any protection. Some cheap hotels harbour fleas, scabies mites, giant roaches and **other bugs**. Consult a pharmacist if you find yourself with a persistent skin irritation.

SCORPIONS AND SNAKES

The **danger** from scorpions and snakes is minimal, as most species are nocturnal, hide during the heat of the day, and generally avoid people. However, you shouldn't go barefoot, turn over rocks or stick your hands into dark crevices anywhere off the beaten track. Whereas the sting of larger, darker **scorpions** is no worse than a bad wasp-sting, the venom of the pale, slender-clawed *Buthridae* is highly toxic. If stung, cold-pack the affected area and get a doctor.

Egypt has two main types of poisonous snakes. **Vipers** vary in colour from sandy to reddish (or sometimes grey) and leave two fang punctures. The carpet viper, Egypt's deadliest snake, has a light X on its head. **Cobras** are recognisable by their distinctive hood and bite mark (a single row of teeth plus fang holes). The smaller Egyptian cobra (coloured sandy olive) is found throughout the country; the longer black-necked cobra (which can spit its venom up to three metres) only in the south. All snake-bites should be washed immediately; if on an arm or a leg, tie a band between the wound and the body (but not so tight that it cuts off circulation). Get medical help.

AIDS

There is very little awareness of **AIDS** in Egypt – it's assumed to be a Western problem. The few cases reported are almost certainly the tip of an iceberg. With prostitution, extra-marital affairs and gay life so clandestine – and ignorance about AIDS so widespread – Egypt cannot be assumed to be "safe". As throughout the world, the need for extreme caution, and safe sex, cannot be overstressed. Likewise, be absolutely sure that any injections, tattooing or acupuncture is done with sterile instruments.

WOMEN'S HEALTH CONCERNS

Travelling in the heat and taking antibiotics for an upset stomach, you are liable to **vaginal infections** even if you wash regularly with mild soap, wear cotton underwear and loose clothing. Yeast infections are treatable with Nystatin pessaries (available at pharmacies); "one-shot" Canestan pessaries (bring some from home if you're prone to thrush); or douches of a weak solution of vinegar or lemon juice. Sea bathing can also help. Trichomonas is usually treated with Flagyl, under medical supervision.

Sanitary protection is available from pharmacies in cities and tourist resorts, but seldom anywhere else, so it's wise to carry a supply for your trip. **Tampons** are easier to dispose of (and take up less space) than sanitary towels.

Bring your own **contraceptives**, since the only forms widely available in Egypt are old-fashioned, high-dosage pills, and not too trusty condoms. Cap-users should pack a spare, and enough spermicide and pessaries. If you're on the pill, beware that persistent diarrhoea can render it ineffective. You cannot get abortions in Egypt.

TRAVEL INSURANCE

Travel insurance can buy you peace of mind as well as save you money. Before you purchase any insurance, however, check what you have already. North Americans, in particular, may find themselves covered for medical expenses and loss of or damage to valuables while abroad, as part of a family or student policy. Some credit cards, too, now offer insurance benefits if you use them to pay for tickets.

If you are travelling for any real length of time, however, additional or **specific travel insurance** is reassuring. Most policies on offer –

which can be bought through virtually any bank or travel agent – are quite comprehensive, anticipating everything from charter companies going bankrupt to delayed (as well as lost) baggage, by way of sundry illnesses and accidents.

Premiums are what vary. At the budget end there are good policies for under £20 (US$32) a month; at the other, there are those so expensive that the cost of two or three months of coverage will approach the cost of the worst possible combination of disasters. It pays to shop around. *ISIS*, formerly a "student" policy but now open to everyone, is reliable and fairly good value; it is available through most British travel agents.

REIMBURSEMENT

All insurance policies work by **reimbursing you** once you return home, so be sure to keep all your receipts from doctors and pharmacists. Any thefts should be reported immediately to the nearest police station and a police report obtained; no report, no refund.

If you have had to undergo serious medical treatment, with major hospital bills, contact your consulate. They can normally arrange for an insurance company, or possibly relatives, to cover the fees, pending a claim.

INFORMATION AND MAPS

Besides this book, readily available sources of information include the Egyptian Tourist Authority (which has offices abroad and throughout Egypt); travel agencies, hotels,

and local, often self-appointed, guides (see the section following).

TOURIST OFFICES

The **Egyptian Tourist Authority** (sometimes abbreviated as *EGAPT*) maintains general information offices in several countries (see box overpage), where you can pick up a range of pamphlets. However, most are simply intended to whet your appetite, and few hard facts can be gained from offices **abroad**.

In Egypt itself, you'll get a variable response from **local offices** (addresses are given throughout the guide). The most knowlegeable and helpful ones are in Luxor and Aswan. Staff in Alexandria and Cairo are also well informed, but may need prodding. Whilst Port Said's is desperate to please and Mersa Matrouh's couldn't care less, most provincial offices are good for a dated brochure, if nothing else.

TRAVEL AGENCIES AND HOTELS

Found in towns and cities, **travel agencies** can advise on (and book) transport, accommodation and excursions. Just remember that they are in business for themselves, so their advice may not be exactly unbiased.

The most ubiquitous agency is **Misr Travel**, the state-run tourist company, which operates hotels, coaches and limos, and can make bookings for most things. Their main office is in Cairo (1 Sharia Talaat Harb; ☎393-0010). *Misr Travel* is also represented in London (Langham House, Regent Street, W1; ☎071/255 1087), New York, Los Angeles, Sydney, Paris, Frankfurt, Rome and Stockholm. **American Express** and **Thomas Cook** (see p.17) offer various services besides currency exchange.

Receptionists at **hotels** can also be a source of information, and maybe practical assistance. In Luxor, Hurghada and some of the Western Desert oases, most pensions double as information exchanges and all-round "fixers".

TOURIST PUBLICATIONS

A series of **regional tourist booklets** under the generic heading *"By Night & Day"* are sporadically available free of charge at tourist offices and hotels. Currently there are four, covering Cairo, Alexandria, Upper Egypt (from Minya to Abu Simbel) and the Canal Zone. Each contains a dubious map, notes on local sites and listings of hotels, restaurants, agencies and banks – usually years out of date.

The best **guide to what's on** is the monthly magazine *Cairo Today*, which lists activities, entertainments and exhibitions in Cairo and Alexandria, and events in Luxor and Aswan. Its feature articles cover diverse aspects of Egyptian culture, and travel in Egypt. The magazine is sold in Cairo (£E4 per issue; overseas subscriptions US$40). Selected events are also listed in the daily *Egyptian Gazette* (see p.40).

MAPS

The best **general map of Egypt**, published by *Kümmerly & Frey* (1:950,000), is available in Cairo, Luxor and Aswan, and good map shops abroad. The more common *Bartholomew* map (1:1,000,000) is less detailed and way out of date. If the former is unavailable, *Freytag & Berndt's* 1:1,000,000 map makes a decent substitute.

Michelin map #154 covers Egypt and the Sudan – the latter is excellent, but the Egypt section is nothing special. Mobil's *Motoring Guide to Egypt* (sold at Mobil stations around the country) contains **road maps** and a number of town plans, but is really only worthwhile if you're planning to drive a lot.

Taken together, several local **city plans** cover Cairo in comprehensive detail (see p.54). Elsewhere, however, coverage is poor or non-existent. Aside from fairly crude maps of Alexandria, Luxor, Aswan and Port Said, and photocopied handouts in Minya, Mersa Matrouh and Siwa Oasis, there are no town plans to be had. Those in this book are as good as any.

Full-blown desert expeditions require **special maps**. The best Egyptian ones are published by the *Geological Survey and Mining Authority* in Cairo (3 Sharia Salah Salem, Abbassiya; ☎829-662; Sun–Thurs 8am–3pm). Alternatively, buy some *Tactical Pilotage Charts* (available from specialist map shops – see below) before leaving home. These include:

TPC H-5A Sinai.

TPC H-4B Siwa, the Qattara Depression and Bahariya Oasis.

TPC H-4C Farafra and Dakhla.

TPC H-5D Kharga.

TPC J-5A Approaches to Jebel 'Uweinat.

MAP SHOPS
Specialist map shops include:

Britain
Stanfords, 12–14 Long Acre, London WC2E 9LP (☎071 836 1321).

USA
Complete Traveller, 199 Madison Ave, New York, NY10016 (☎212/685-9007).

Rand McNally Mapstore, 150 East 52nd St, New York, NY10022 (☎212/758-7488).

BAKSHEESH AND LOCAL GUIDES

The word bakshîsh, which resounds perpetually in the traveller's ears during his sojourn in the East and haunts him long afterwards, simply means "a gift"; and, as everything is to be had in return for gifts, the word has many different applications.

Baedeker's Guide to Egypt, 1868 edition.

BAKSHEESH

As a presumed-rich *khawaga* (the Egyptian term for a foreigner), you will be expected to be liberal with **baksheesh** – as are wealthy Egyptians. The payments can be divided into three main varieties.

The most common is **tipping**: a small reward for a small service, which can encompass anyone from a waiter or lift operator to someone who unlocks a tomb or museum room at one of the ancient sites. The sums involved should be paltry – between 10 and 25pt – and you needn't feel railroaded into giving more.

A second common type is more expensive, rewarding the **bending of rules** – many of which seem to have been designed for just that purpose. Examples might include letting you into an archaeological site after hours (or into a vaguely restricted area), finding you a sleeper on a train when the carriages are "full", and so on. This should not be confused with bribery, which is a more serious business with its own etiquette and risks – best not entered into.

The last kind of *baksheesh* is simply **alms giving**. The crippled are traditional recipients of such gifts, and it seems right to join locals in giving out small change. Kids, however, are a different case, pressing their demands only on tourists. If someone offers some genuine help and asks for an *alum* (pen), it seems fair enough, but to yield to any request perhaps encourages a dependency Egypt could do without.

GUIDES

Official guides can be engaged through branches of *Misr Travel*, *American Express* and *Thomas Cook*, local tourist offices and large hotels. You can also hire them on the spot at the Antiquities Museum in Cairo and the Pyramids of Giza. They are normally paid at a fixed hourly rate (approximately £E5), which can be shared between a group of people, though obviously the latter would be expected to make some additional tip.

Such professional guides can be useful at **major sites**, like the Valley of the Kings, where they will be able to ease your way through queues at the tombs. If you feel intimidated by the culture, too, you might welcome an intermediary for the first couple of days' sightseeing. In general, however, there's no special need to employ anyone: they tend to have enough work already with tour groups.

Far more common are **local, self-appointed guides**, who fall into two main categories. On ancient sites, there are always plenty of loungers-around, who will offer to show you "secret tombs" or "special reliefs", or just present themselves in tombs or temples, with palms outstretched. They don't have a lot to offer you, and encouragement makes life more difficult for everyone following.

The other kind – most often encountered in a small town or village – are people who genuinely want to help out foreigners, and perhaps to practise their English at the same time. They are often teenagers. Services offered to you will be an escort from one taxi depot to another, or showing you the route to the souks or to a local site. The majority of people you meet this way don't expect money – kids included – and you could risk offence by offering. If people want money from you for such activities, they won't be reticent about asking.

An official version of this kind of guiding is offered by members of the **Tourist's Friend Association**, who often approach lost-looking foreigners at bus and train stations, and will swiftly produce their identity cards. They are generally students – very friendly and very helpful, and not on the make. Be courteous even if you don't want their help.

ATTITUDES AND BEHAVIOUR

If you want to get the most from a trip to Egypt, it is vital not to assume anyone who approaches you expects to profit from the encounter. Too many tourists do, and end up making little contact with an extraordinarily hospitable people.

Behaviour and attitude on your part are important. If some Egyptians treat tourists with contempt, it has much to do with the way the latter behave. It helps everyone if you can avoid **rudeness** or aggressive behaviour in response to insistent offers or demands. And be aware, too, of the importance of **dress**: shorts are acceptable only on beach resorts (and for women only in private resorts or along the Aquaba coast); shirts (for both sexes) should cover your shoulders.

Photography needs to be undertaken with care. If you are obviously taking a photograph of someone, ask their permission – especially in the more remote, rural regions where you can cause genuine offence. You may also find people stop you from taking photos that show Egypt in a "poor" or "backward" light. On a more positive front, taking a photograph of (and later sending it to) someone you've struck up a friendship with, or exchanging photographs, is often – in the towns at least – greatly appreciated. As ever, be wary of photographing anything militarily sensitive (bridges, railway stations, dams, etc).

When **invited to a home**, you normally take your shoes off before entering the reception rooms. It is customary to take a gift: sweet pastries (or tea and sugar in rural areas) are always acceptable. At a meal, never use the left hand when in the company of Egyptians.

SECURITY, POLICE AND CONSULATES

Egypt is a very safe country for visitors. Although it's wise to guard against pickpockets and casual theft, muggings are unheard of and cities feel unintimidating at night. Egyptians will generally respond to anyone in distress, and in rare instances of public crime the whole community may dish out rough justice to the offender before the cops arrive.

PETTY CRIME

Whilst relatively few in number, **pickpockets** are skilled and concentrate on tourists. Most operate in Cairo, notably in queues and on the crowded buses to the pyramids. To play safe, keep your valuables in a **money belt** or a pouch under your shirt (leather or cotton materials are preferable to nylon, which can irritate in the heat). Overall, though, **casual theft** is more of a problem. Campsites, hostels and cheap hotels often have poor security, making it unwise to leave valuables there. At most places, you can deposit them at the reception (always get a receipt for cash).

If you are **driving**, it almost goes without saying you should not leave anything you cannot afford to lose visible or accessible in your car.

THE POLICE

The **police** have a high profile (especially in Cairo, which has more cops per thousand citizens than any capital in the world) but seldom impinge on tourists. As a visitor, you will usually be treated with kid gloves and given the benefit of the doubt unless drugs or espionage are suspected.

The **Municipal Police** handle all crimes, and have a monopoly on law and order in smaller towns. Their uniform (black and white in winter, white in summer) resembles that of the **Traffic Police**, who wear striped cuffs. Both get involved in accidents and can render assistance in emergencies. However, relatively few officers speak anything but Arabic.

If you've got a problem or need to report a crime, it's better to approach the **Tourist Police**, who wear the regular police uniform with a *Tourist Police* armband. Found at tourist sites, museums, airports, stations and ports, they are supposedly trained to help tourists in distress, and speak a foreign language (usually English). In practice, the odds of getting such an officer are fifty-fifty – but it's worth trying them first.

Lastly, there are the **Central Security** police (dressed all in black and armed with Kalashnikovs) who guard embassies, banks and other public buildings. Though normally genial enough, this largely conscript force escalates rapidly from tear gas to live rounds when ordered to crush demonstrations or civil unrest. If you find yourself getting caught up in such actions, clear out quick. Ordinarily, though, they are nothing to worry about.

Addresses and phone numbers of local police stations appear in the text.

FOREIGN CONSULATES IN EGYPT

If you do find yourself in trouble – or simply need a visa – there are **consulates** for most nationalities in **Cairo** (see p.224). The US, UK and several other European countries also maintain consulates in **Alexandria** (p.474) and **Port Said** (p.515). Consulates can advise on legal matters and replace missing passports, but are unsympathetic towards drug offenders and will not make loans to penniless travellers (though they will repatriate you as a last resort).

FROM A WOMAN'S PERSPECTIVE

The biggest problem women travellers face in Egypt is the Hollywood perceptions of Egyptian men. Western women are seen as loose, willing to have sex at the most casual opportunity, and – in Egyptian social terms – virtually on a par with prostitutes.

The problem is compounded by the behaviour of travellers, who do a range of things no Egyptian woman would consider: dressing immodestly, showing shoulders and cleavage; sharing rooms with men to whom they are not married; drinking alcohol in public bars or restaurants; even travelling alone on public transport, without a family member as escort.

Without compromising your freedom too greatly, there are a few steps you can take to **improve your Egyptian image**. Most important and obvious is dress: loose clothes that cover all "immodest areas" (thighs, upper arms, chest) are a big help, and essential if you are travelling alone or in rural areas. On public transport (buses, trains, *service* taxis, etc), try to sit with other women – who may often invite you to do so. If you're travelling with a man, wearing a wedding ring confers respectability.

As anywhere, looking confident and knowing where you're going is a major help in avoiding hassle. Problems – most commonly hissing or touching up – tend to come in **downtown Cairo** and in the public **beach resorts** (with the exception of Sinai's Aqaba Coast, which is more or less the only place you'll feel happy about sunbathing). In the **oases**, where attractions include open-air springs and hot pools, it's okay to bathe – but do so in at least a T-shirt and shorts: oasis people are among the most conservative in the country.

Your **reaction to harassment** is down to you. Verbal hassle is probably best ignored but if you get touched up it's best to react: *imshee* ("get lost") or *sibnee le wadi* ("don't touch me") are suitable responses; if you shout the latter in a crowded area, you're likely to find people on your side, and your assailant shamed. Touching up an Egyptian woman would be judged totally unacceptable behaviour, so there's no reason why you should put up with it, either. Some women find that it occasionally helps to clout hasslers, if only to make yourself feel better.

On the positive side, **spending time with Egyptian women** can be a delight, if someone decides to take you under their wing. The difficulty in getting to know women is that fewer women than men speak English, and that you won't run into women in cafés or tourist facilities. However, public transport can be good meeting ground, as can shops and, best of all, local schools (Egypt has a high proportion of women teachers). It's generally a lot better to meet women off your own bat rather than through a male intermediary taking you home to meet the family.

GETTING AROUND

Egyptian public transport is, on the whole, pretty good. There is an efficient rail network linking the Nile Valley, Delta and Canal Zone, and elsewhere you can travel easily enough by bus or collective (*service*) taxi. On the Nile you can indulge in *feluccas* or cruise boats, and in the desert there's the chance to check out your camel-riding prowess. For the hurried, *EgyptAir*, *ZAS* and *Air Sinai* also offer a network of flights.

TRAINS

Covering a limited network of routes, **trains** are best used for long hauls between the major cities, when air-conditioned services offer a comfier alternative to buses and taxis. For shorter journeys, however, trains are slower and less reliable. There's a crucial distinction between relatively fast **air-conditioned (A/C) trains** (including **wagon lits** services) and the snail-like **non-A/C local-stop services**.

Students with ISIC cards get thirty to fifty percent reductions on all fares except sleepers and *wagon lits*.

A/C TRAINS

Air-conditioned trains nearly always have two classes of carriage. The most comfortable option is **first class** (*daraga oola*), which has A/C, waiter service, reclining armchairs and no standing in the aisles. Air-conditioned **second class superior** (*daraga tania mumtaaza*) is less plush and more crowded – but at half the price of first class it's a real bargain. Occasionally A/C trains will be first or second class only.

On certain services, along the Nile Valley for example, **sleepers** (again divided into first and second class) are available. A first-class sleeper costs about eighty percent on top of the normal fare; second class are cheaper but highly elusive for foreigners. Sleeping compartments are for four people; railway staff tend not to mix Egyptians and foreigners, and may not allow unmarried couples to share a compartment. Solo women travellers may be paired up with others, or alternatively asked to book a whole compartment.

Seats are **reservable** up to seven days in advance. There is occasional double booking but a little *baksheesh* to the conductor usually sorts out any problem. One common difficulty is that **round-trip bookings** can't be arranged at the point of origin, so if you're travelling back to Cairo from Aswan/Luxor (or vice versa), it's best to book a seat the day you arrive. Most **travel agencies** sell first-class tickets for a small commission, saving you from having to queue.

NON A/C TRAINS

Non-air-conditioned trains divide into **ordinary second class** (*daraga tania aadia*), which has padded bench seating, and **third class** (*daraga talata*), which is just wooden benches and open doors and windows for ventilation. Both classes are invariably crowded, the rolling stock is ancient and often filthy, and schedules fanciful.

There is no advance booking for seats on these services and you needn't queue for a ticket at the station. You simply walk on and buy a ticket from the conductor, paying a small penalty fee (about £E1).

WAGON LITS

A distinct notch above regular sleeper trains are **wagon lits** – often comprising a whole train, though sometimes just a few carriages tacked on to a normal A/C service. They are again divided into first and second class, costing around three times the equivalent normal sleeper services – still cheaper than a flight. For the extra money you get a comfortable two-bed cabin, with a sink; breakfast in bed; a dining car, bar and sometimes a disco.

Booking of *wagon lits* is best done through branches of *Thomas Cook* or *American Express*, or in Cairo through *Shepheard's Hotel*.

BUSES

Inter-city buses are an inexpensive way to travel, and often preferable to trains. Besides being quicker for short trips along the Nile Valley, buses serve areas beyond the railway network, such as Sinai, the oases, Abu Simbel and Hurghada. Travelling in Egypt for any length of time, you are likely to make considerable use of the various networks.

Where you can take a *service* taxi rather than a bus, however, do so. The difference in **fare** is small, and all except the A/C buses are much slower than *service* taxis, which for all their tight fit are still an improvement on old buses. Over long distances, though, A/C buses are more comfortable than *service* taxis, particularly during summer, when **night buses** are the coolest way of reaching Sinai or Hurghada from Cairo.

BUS SERVICES

Egypt's bus network is divided between three main operators, based in Cairo. The *Upper Egypt Bus Company* serves all points along the Nile Valley; the Fayoum and the inner oases; and the Red Sea coast as far down as el-Quesir. Company buses are dark green, or tan on the desert routes. Sinai and the Canal Zone are covered by the *East Delta Bus Company*, whose livery is green and yellow. The *West Delta Bus Company*'s blue vehicles serve Alexandria, Mersa Matrouh and the Delta.

On most routes there's a choice between **air-conditioned** (A/C) buses – which are usually new and fast – and **non-A/C** ones, generally old rattletraps. The former are invariably dearer, but their A/C doesn't always work.

On certain routes (from Cairo to Alexandria, Luxor, Aswan and Hurghada), there are also brand new *Superjets*, with toilets, A/C, in-flight videos and pricey snacks, operated by the *Arab Union Transport Company*, whose red, gold and black livery explains their nickname – "Golden Rockets".

TERMINALS AND BOOKING

Though most towns have a single bus depot for all destinations, cities such as Cairo, Alexandria, Port Said and Ismailiya have several **terminals** (detailed in the guide). English or French-speaking staff are fairly common at the larger ones, but rare in the provinces. **Schedules** – usually posted in Arabic only – change frequently, so timings in this guide should be verified in person. Hotels in Sinai and the oases, and the tourist offices in Luxor and Aswan can also supply information.

At city terminals, **tickets** are normally sold from kiosks, up to 24 hours in advance for A/C or long-haul services. In the provinces, tickets may only be available an hour or so before departure, or on the bus itself in the case of through-services, which are often standing-room only when they arrive. Passengers on A/C services are usually assigned a seat (the number is written in Arabic on your ticket), but seats on "local" buses are taken willy-nilly.

CITY TRANSPORT

Most Egyptian towns are small enough to cover on foot, especially if you stay in a hotel near the centre. In larger cities, however, local transport is definitely useful. Learn to recognise Arabic numerals and you can take full advantage of the cheap **buses**, **trams** and **minibuses** that cover most of Alexandria and Cairo (which also has river-taxis and an excellent new metro). Bus and tram routes are detailed under individual entries in the guide.

Equally ubiquitous are four-seater **taxis** (black and white in Cairo, black and orange in Alex), which often pick up extra passengers heading in the same direction. As meters are rarely used (or work), the trick is to know the fare and pay on arrival, rather than ask or haggle at the beginning. Above all, don't confuse these cabs with "special" taxis (usually Peugeot 504s or Mercedes), which

are three times dearer and prey on tourists. If you do hire a "special", establish the price – and bargain it down – before you get in.

You will also come across *caleches* – horse-drawn buggies, also known as *hantours*. These are primarily tourist transport, and you'll be accosted by drivers in all the major resorts: Alexandria, a few parts of Cairo, and most of all Luxor and Aswan. Fares are high by local taxi standards and, despite supposed tarifs set by the local councils, are in practice entirely negotiable. Some of the horses and buggies are in pristine condition; others painful to behold.

In a few small towns, mostly in Middle Egypt, *caleches* remain part of local city transport. Ask locals the price of fares before climbing on board, or simply pay what you see fit at the end.

SERVICE TAXIS

Collective **service taxis** are one of the best features of Egyptian transport. They operate on a wide variety of routes, and are generally quicker than buses and trains, and fares are very reasonable.

The taxis are usually big Peugeot saloons carrying seven passengers (four in the back, three in the front, plus the driver). Most business is along specific routes, with more or less non-stop departures throughout the day along the main ones, while cross-desert traffic is restricted to early morning and late afternoon. You just show up at the terminal (locations are detailed, city by city, in the guide) and ask for a *service* to your destination. As soon as seven people (or less, if you're willing to pay extra) are assembled, the taxi sets off.

On established routes *service* taxis keep to fixed **fares** for each passenger (detailed in the guide, but sure to rise). You can ascertain current rates by asking at your hotel (or the tourist office), or observing what Egyptians pay.

Alternatively, you can **charter a whole taxi** for yourself or a group – useful for day excursions or on odd routes. You will have to bargain hard to get a fair price (see entries in the guide).

TRUCKS AND HITCHING

In the countryside and the desert, where buses may be sporadic or non-existent, it is standard practice for **vans** and **lorries** (*camions*) and **pick-up trucks** (*bijous*) to carry and charge passengers. You may be asked to pay a little more than the locals, or have to bargain over a price, but it's straightforward enough. Getting rides from **tractors** is another possibility in rural areas. At Tell el-Amarna, locals drive a hard bargain for rides around the sprawling, sunbaked site; whereas farmers in the Fayoum and Dakhla Oasis often refuse money.

Also noteworthy are **pilgrim convoys**, bound for remote sites to celebrate a festival such as the *moulid* of Saint Damyanah (p.498) or Sheikh al-Shazli (p.575).

HITCHING

Hitching is largely confined to areas with minimal public transport (where anything that moves is considered fair game) or trunk routes (where hopefuls wait by the roadside for passing *service* taxis or scheduled buses). Since you'll probably end up **paying** anyway, there's no point in hitch-ing unless you have to. Indeed, foreigners who hitch where proper transport is available may inspire contempt rather than sympathy. As few tourists have their own car in Egypt, you can't expect much help from that quarter, either. **Women** should not attempt to hitch without a male companion.

CAR RENTAL

Renting a car pays obvious dividends if you are pushed for time or plan to visit remote sites, but whether you'd want to drive yourself is another matter. Roads in cities are hellish, congested trunk roads hardly less alarming, and it's not much more expensive to charter a car and driver.

Any branch of *Misr Travel*, and numerous local tour agencies, can fix you up with a **car and driver**. *Misr* tend to have big, air-conditioned Mercedes, which at around £E13 (£3/US$5) an hour is a brilliant deal for a group of people. An alternative is simply to negotiate with local taxi drivers (see above).

For a **self-drive car**, visitors can **make arrangements abroad** through *Hertz*, *Avis* or *Budget*, or directly with local **car hire companies in Egypt** (addresses given where relevant in the guide). It's worth shopping around for the best deal, since rates and terms vary considerably. At the cheaper end of the market, you can get a car with unlimited mileage for about US$25 (£16) a day. To hire a vehicle you must have an International Driving Licence and be at least 25 years old. Most companies require a hefty deposit (£E500), but not all accept credit cards.

Before making a booking, be sure to find out if you can pick up the car in one city and return it in another. Generally, this is only possible with cars from *Hertz*, *Avis* or *Budget*, found in the main cities and tourist centres. And before setting out, make sure the car comes with spare tyre, tool kit and full documentation – including insurance cover, which is compulsory issue with all rentals.

MOTORBIKES AND BIKES

Motorcycling could be a good way to travel around Egypt, but the red tape involved in bringing your own bike is diabolical (ask your AA and the Egyptian consulate for details). It's difficult to hire a machine except in Luxor, where the weedy bikes on offer are only fit for touring the Theban necropolis. Bikers should be especially wary of potholes, sand and rocks, besides other traffic on the roads.

Useful for getting around small towns and reaching sites or beaches in the vicinity, **bicycles** can be hired in Luxor, Aswan, Hurghada and other places for a modest sum. Cycling in big cities or over long distances is not advisable. Traffic is murderous, the heat brutal, and foreign cyclists are sometimes stoned by kids (particularly in the Delta). If you're determined to cycle the **Nile Valley**, the new east bank freeway that runs down as far as Minya is the safer route.

DRIVING IN EGYPT

Driving in Egypt is not for the faint-hearted or inexperienced motorist. Cities, highways, backroads and *pistes* each pose a challenge to drivers' skills and nerve. Pedestrians and carts seem blithely indifferent to heavy traffic. Though accidents are less frequent than you'd think, the crumpled wrecks alongside highways are a constant reminder of the hazards of motoring.

RULES OF THE ROAD

Although driving on the right is pretty much universal, other **rules** of the road vary. Traffic **in cities** is relentless and anarchic, with vehicles weaving to and fro between lanes, signalling by horn. Two beeps means "I'm alongside and about to overtake". A single long blast warns "I can't (won't) stop and I'm coming through!". Extending your hand, fingers raised and tips together, is the signal for "Watch out, don't pass now"; spreading your fingers and flipping them forwards indicates "Go ahead". Although the car in front usually has right of way, buses and trams always take precedence.

On country roads – including the two-lane west bank "highway" along the Nile Valley – trucks and cars routinely overtake in the face of incoming traffic. The passing car usually flashes its lights as a warning, but not always. Most roads are bumpy, with deep potholes and all manner of traffic, including donkey carts and camels. Beware, especially, of children darting into the road. If you injure someone, relatives may take revenge on the spot. Avoid driving **after dark**, when Egyptians drive without lights, only flashing them on to high beam when they see another car approaching. Wandering pedestrians and animals, obstructions and sand drifts present extra hazards. During spring, flash floods can wash away roads in Sinai.

The official **speed limit** outside towns is 90km per hour (100km on the Cairo–Alexandria Desert Road), but on certain stretches it can be as low as 30km per hour. Road signs are similar to those in Europe.

PISTE DRIVING

On **pistes** (rough, unpaved tracks in the desert or mountains) there are special problems. You need a good deal of driving and mechanical confidence – and shouldn't attempt such routes if you don't feel your car's up to scratch. **Desert driving** is covered in detail on p.392.

PETROL AND BREAKDOWNS

Petrol (*benzene*) stations are plentiful in larger towns but few and far between in rural and desert areas. Always fill your tank to the limit. A litre of *super* (81 octane) or *regular* costs under 50pt. Clean your oil filter regularly, lest impurities in the petrol, and Egypt's ubiquitous dust, clog up the engine.

Egyptian **mechanics** are usually excellent at coping with breakdowns, and all medium-sized towns have garages (most with a range of spare parts for French, German and Japanese cars). But be aware that if you break down miles from anywhere you'll probably end up paying a lot to get a lorry to tow you back.

If you are driving your own vehicle, there is also the problem of having to re-export any car that you bring into the country (even a wreck). You can't just write off a car; you'll have to take it out of Egypt with you.

VEHICLE INSURANCE

All car-hire agreements must be sold along with third-party liability insurance, by law. Though accident and damage insurance should be included in the package, always make sure. In the case of an accident, get a written report from the police and from the doctor who first treats any injuries, without which your insurance may not cover the costs. Reports are written in Arabic.

Driving your own vehicle, you will need to take out **Egyptian Insurance**. Policies are sold by the *al-Shark*, *Misr* and *National* insurance companies; offices are found in most towns and at border crossings. Premiums vary according to the size, horsepower and value of the vehicle.

AGE LIMITS

Important note: the **minimum age** for driving in Egypt is 25 years; the **maximum age** limit is 70 years.

BIKE REPAIRS

Most towns reveal a wealth of **general repair shops**, well used to servicing local bikes and mopeds. Though unlikely to have the correct spare parts for your make of bike, they can usually sort out some kind of temporary solution.

FLIGHTS

Egyptian domestic air fares are average by international standards, but probably too expensive for most low-budget travellers. In general, it's only worth flying if your time is very limited, or for the view – the Nile Valley and Sinai look amazing from the air.

There are three operators, all charging exactly the same rates. *EgyptAir*, the country's national airline, is the big one, operating a network more or less throughout the country. *Air Sinai* was specially created to serve the Sinai and Israel, after the 1979 treaty, in order to protect *EgyptAir* from the withdrawal of landing rights in other Arab countries. *ZAS*, originally a cargo carrier, is now a small passenger airline which competes with *EgyptAir* and *Air Sinai* on domestic routes. Details of each company's flights, and addresses of their local offices, are given in the main part of the text.

Fares are calculated in US$ (according to the price of aviation fuel) but payable in Egyptian currency, backed by an exchange receipt. As a rough guide to prices, Cairo to Luxor is currently around US$90 (no student discounts) but prices tend to get hiked up every couple of months. In the winter season, you would be very lucky to get any kind of flight between Cairo and Luxor, Aswan, Abu Simbel or Saint Catherine's Monastery. Always reconfirm 72 hours prior to the journey, as overbooking is all too common.

NILE CRUISES

Nile cruises are the classic tourist transport along the river, familiar from a score of films and novels. The luxurious boats with swimming pools, or the reconditioned old paddle steamers, can be wonderful, but you need to pick with care. Cheaper cruises, retailed by local agents, can be tacky and unhygienic, with hot, cramped cabins and unappetising food.

On the whole, you get pretty much what you pay for. Prices start from $150 (£90) for a three-day trip, and escalate dramatically with the luxury quotient. The most reliable cruises are generally those sold in association with package holidays (see p.6 for operators).

LOCAL FERRIES

Local ferries cross the Nile and the Suez canal at various points (specified as relevant in the guide). They are generally cheap, battered and crowded.

The only real long-distance ferry is between Hurghada and Sharm el-Sheikh across the Red Sea. This is a useful, direct route, so long as your boat doesn't break down and get towed back to port – a not infrequent occurrence.

FELUCCAS

Feluccas, the lateen-sailed boats used on the Nile since antiquity, still serve as transport along many stretches of the river. Favoured by tourists for sunset cruises, they allow you to experience the changing moods and scenery of the Nile whilst lolling in blissful indolence.

Many visitors opt for longer *felucca* **cruises**, stopping at the temples between Luxor and Aswan – downstream from Aswan is the most popular route. While it's easy to arrange a *felucca* cruise yourself (see p.372), several tour operators also offer packages (listed under "Getting There", p.6).

HORSES, DONKEYS AND CAMELS

Around the Pyramids and the major Nile sites, donkeys, horses and camels are all available for hire. **Horses** are fun if you want to ride across stretches of sand between the Pyramids. **Donkeys**, unless you're keen on the beasts, are not recommended – uncomfortable to ride and with notoriously avaricious boy-minders.

Camels (or, technically, dromedaries) make for pretty rigorous but exhilarating riding, and you'll probably want to try them at least once. They are good for short rides around Aswan, to the monastery of Saint Simeon, for example, but where they really come into their own is in the Sinai. Here, you can go camel-trekking up rocky wadis or across dunes that horses could never cope with. Trips – lasting anything from a half-day to a week – are easily enough arranged with local Bedouin operators, or arranged as part of "adventure holiday" packages before you set off (see p.6).

Camel riding is a real art, which gets a little easier on the body with experience. The mounting is done for you but be sure to hold onto the pommel of the saddle as the camel raises itself in a triple-jerk manoeuvre. Once on, you have a choice of riding it like a horse or cocking a leg around the pommel, as the bedouin do. Be sure to use a lot of padding around the pommel: what begins as a minor irritation can end up leaving your skin rubbed raw.

Beware also of being palmed off with a male (bull) camel that's in heat – they can get very vicious. Bad signs are an inflated mouth-sac, aggressive behaviour towards its mates, and a lot of noise and slobbering. When enraged, camels can launch a fierce attack – they've been known to grip someone's neck and shake them like a rag doll, or crush every bone in a leg.

ACCOMMODATION

The main tourist centres offer a broad spectrum of accommodation, with everything from luxury palaces – familiar from *Death on the Nile* movies – to homely pensions and flea-bitten dives. Even in high season, in Cairo, Sinai or the Nile Valley, you should be able to find something in your preferred range. Elsewhere, the choice is generally more limited, with only basic lodgings available in Middle Egypt and the desert oases.

HOTELS

Egyptian hotels are loosely categorised into **star ratings**, ranging from five-star deluxe class down to one-star pensions. Below this range, there are also unclassified hotels, mostly used by Egyptians in the towns, though travellers' haunts in places like the western oases.

Standards vary within any given category or price band – and from room to room in many places. The categorisations, also, tend to have more meaning in the higher bands. Once you're

down to one or two stars, the differences are often hard to detect.

Deluxe hotels are almost exclusively modern and chain-owned (*Hyatt*, *Hilton*, etc), with swimming pools, bars, restaurants, air conditioning and all the usual international facilities. **Four-star** places can be more characterful, including some famous (and reconditioned) names from the old tradition of Egyptian tourism: places like the *Old Cataract* in Aswan and the *Old Winter Palace* in Luxor. Again, all hotels in this class are air-conditioned, with a pool, café and restaurant, etc. They merge into **three-star** hotels, which again have the odd gem, though most are 1970s tower-block style, and often becoming a little shabby. Items like plumbing and air conditioning get a lot less reliable, too.

Down on the **two- and one-star** level, you rarely get air conditioning, though better places will supply fans, and old-style buildings with balconies, high ceilings and louvred windows are well designed to cope with the heat. Conversely, these places can be distinctly chilly in winter, as they scarcely ever have any form of heating.

Some of the cheaper hotels are classified as **pensions**, which makes little difference in terms of facilities, but tends to signify family ownership and a friendlier ambience. Cairo, in particular, has some wonderful pensions.

At the cheap end of the scale, in the most popular tourist towns, like Luxor and Hurghada, you also get a few **"student hotels"**, specifically aimed at backpackers. They are often quite well-run and equipped, if a bit cramped.

BOOKING AND CHARGES

Bookings for the **four- and five-star hotels** are best made through the central reservations office of the chain owning the hotel, or by telex.

Simply turning up at a ritzy hotel, or even phoning ahead, you may find a reluctance to book you in, with staff perhaps claiming the hotel is full. Many rely on tour groups for their business and are not very interested in individual travellers. You may alternatively prefer to book as part of a package through one of the British companies detailed on p.6.

At **mid-range hotels**, it is worth trying to book ahead if you want to stay in a particular place in **Cairo**, **Alex**, **Aswan or Luxor**. Elsewhere – and at all the **cheaper hotels** – most people just turn up. Phoning may itself prove unrewarding (see p.38).

Most hotels levy **service charge** (12 percent) plus **local tax** (2–9 percent) on top of their quoted rates. **Breakfast** is generally obligatory and may or may not be included in the room rate. It's not often anything to get excited about. **Extra charges** most commonly turn up at mid-range hotels, which may add on a few pounds for a fan or air conditioning, or TV that doesn't work.

HOTEL TOUTS

Hotel touts are found wherever tourists arrive: at Cairo Airport, railway stations in Luxor and Aswan, and oasis bus depots, to name but a few favoured locations. Though some actually work in the hotel they're touting, most are simply hustling for commissions and quite prepared to use trickery to deliver clients to "their" establishment – swearing that other places are full, or closed, or whatever. In some cases, the hotel being touted may be agreeable, or even the best deal going; all too often, however, it's the overpriced or grotty places that depend on touts.

By studying the hotel listings and town plans in this book, you should be able to detect most scams. Advice for travellers flying into Cairo appears on p.64.

YOUTH HOSTELS

Egypt's **youth hostels** are very cheap but their drawbacks are considerable. A daytime lock-out and night-time curfew are universal practice; so, too, is segregating the sexes and (usually) foreigners and Egyptians (which you might appreciate when riotous groups are in residence).

The most salubrious hostels are in Cairo, Sharm el-Sheikh and Ismailiya. These, however, are far from where the action is, as are grungier places in Alexandria, Mersa Matrouh, Luxor,

Assyut and Sohag. Though Aswan's hostel is smack in the centre, it's the foulest of the lot. Only the new hostel in Suez is both central and enticing – but the city is not.

It seems to be up to individual hostels whether you need an **International Youth Hostel Federation (IYHF) card**, and their rulings change constantly. If admitted, non-IYHF members are charged £E1–3 extra per night, and may be granted automatic membership after six days. For more information, contact the *Egyptian Youth Hostel Association* in Cairo (7 Sharia Abdul Hamid-Said; ☎758-099), near the *Odeon Cinema*.

Also worth noting are a couple of **YMCA hostels**, which admit anyone. The one in Port Said is nothing special, but the YMCA in Assyut is positively luxurious and excellent value.

Addresses for all hostels appear in the text.

RESTHOUSES

Chiefly found in the Western Desert oases, government **resthouses** offer basic triple-bed rooms (or dorms) and cold showers for £E2–3 per person. Aside from tourists making the "Great Desert Circuit", they're mostly used by truckers.

Resthouses are the only lodgings in Farafra Oasis. One of the resthouses in Dakhla Oasis offers hot springs and a pool. You can't rely on the outlying resthouses in Kharga Oasis, which are virtually derelict. The resthouses in Farafra and Dakhla double as tourist offices.

CAMPSITES

Egypt is not established camping territory. Such campsites as there are in the country tend to be **on the coast**, often shadeless and with few facilities, catering for holidaying Egyptian families. You'd have to be desperate to stay at these places.

Rather better are the occasional **campsites attached to hotels**, which may offer ready-pitched tents with camp-beds, plus use of the hotel shower and toilet facilities. And there are just a handful of really attractive, more upmarket sites – the standout being the campsite right beside **Dendara Temple**.

As for **camping wild**, you should always check with the authorities about any coastal site – some beaches are mined, others patrolled by the military. In the desert, it's less of a problem, though any land near water will belong to someone: so again ask permission.

EATING AND DRINKING

Egyptian food combines elements of Lebanese, Turkish, Syrian, Greek and French cuisine, modified to suit local conditions and tastes. Dishes tend to be simple and wholesome, made only with fresh ingredients, and therefore vary with the seasons. Nubian cooking, found in southern Egypt, is spicier than food in the north; in Alexandria, Mediterranean influences prevail. Cairo offers every kind of cuisine in the world.

Eating out falls into two camps. At a local level, there are cafés and diners, and loads of street stalls, which sell one or two simple dishes. More formally and expensively, restaurants cater to middle-class Egyptians and tourists. The latter have menus (most cafés don't) offering a broader range of dishes, and sometimes specialising in Greek or international food.

CAFÉS AND STREET FOOD

The staples of the Egyptian diet are bread ('*aish*, which also means "life"), *fuul* and *taamiya*. **Bread** is ubiquitous with all meals and snacks and comes either as pitta-type '*aish shami* (sun-raised bread made from white flour) or '*aish baladi* (made from coarse wholewheat flour).

Native beans or *fuul* (pronounced "fool") can be prepared in several ways. Boiled and mashed with tomatoes, onions and spices, they constitute *fuul madammes*, which are often served with a chopped boiled egg for breakfast. A similar mixture stuffed into '*aish baladi* constitutes the pitta-bread sandwiches sold on the street.

Deep-fried patties of *fuul* beans mixed with spices are known as **taamiya** or **felafel**, which again are served in pitta bread, often with a snatch of salad, *tahina* and pickles.

A frequent appetiser is **torshi**, a mixture of pickled radishes, turnips, gherkins and carrots; luridly coloured, it is something of an acquired taste.

Anther cheap café perennial is **makarona** – a clump of macaroni baked into a cake with mince-meat and tomato sauce inside. It's rather bland but very filling. Similarly common is **kushari**, which is a mixture of noodles, macaroni, lentils and onions, with a spicy tomato sauce. These are sold in tiled stand-up diners.

More elaborate, but a bit dearer, are **fatirs**, which can either be sweet or savoury. These are a cross between pizza and pancake, consisting of flaky filo pastry stuffed with either white cheese, peppers, mince, egg, onion and olives, or with raisins, jams, curds or just a dusting of icing sugar. They are served at café-like establishments known as *fatatri*.

Most **sandwiches** are small rolls with a minute portion of *basturma* (pastrami) or cheese. Other favourites include: grilled liver (*kibda*) with spicy green peppers and onions; tiny shrimps; and *mokh* (crumbed sheep's brains).

Lastly, and needing little explanation, are **shawarma** – essentially sliced doner kebabs, stuffed into pitta bread and maybe garnished with salad and *hummus* or *tahini*.

On the **hygiene** front, while cafés and tiled eateries with running water are generally safe, street grub is highly suspect unless it's peelable or hot.

RESTAURANT MEALS

The classic Egyptian restaurant or café meal is either a lamb **kebab** or **kofta** (spiced mince patties), accompanied or preceded by a couple of dips. The dips usually comprise **hummus** (made from chickpeas), **tahina** (from sesame seeds) and **babaghanoush** (tahina with aubergine).

In a basic place, this is likely to be all that's on offer, save for a bit of salad (usually lettuce/tomato based), *fuul* and bread. However, you may also find other **grilled meats**. Chicken (*firakh*) is a standard, both in cafés and as takeaway food

GLOSSARY OF EGYPTIAN FOOD

BASICS

'aish	Bread	*firakh*	Chicken	*shurba*	Soup
zibda	Butter	*zeit*	Oil	*izzaza*	Bottle
beyd	Eggs	*zeitun*	Olives	*kubbaya*	Glass
samak	Fish	*filfil*	Pepper	*showka*	Fork
gibna	Cheese	*melh*	Salt	*sikkeena*	Knife
gibna rumi	Yellow cheese	*sukkar*	Sugar	*mala'a*	Spoon
gibna beyda	White cheese	*skhudaar*	Vegetables	*tarabeyza*	Table
murabba	Jam	*salata*	Salad	*garson*	Waiter
'asal	Honey	*fawakih*	Fruit	*lista/menoo*	Menu
lahma	Meat	*zabadi*	Yoghurt	*il-hisab*	The bill

DRINKS

shai	Tea	*saada*	no sugar	*'asir*	Fruit juice
shai bi-na'ana	Tea with mint	*ahwa fransawi*	Nescafe or	*'asirburtu'an*	orange
shai bi-laban	Tea with milk		filter coffee	*'asir limoon*	lemon
laban	Milk	*mayya*	Water	*'asir manga*	mango
ahwa	Turkish coffee	*mayya*	Mineral	*karkaday*	hibiscus
ziyaada	very sweet	*ma'adaniyya*	water	*tamar hindi*	tamarind
mazboot	medium	*beera*	Beer	*'asab*	sugar cane
ariha	little sugar	*nibeet*	Wine		

SOUPS, SALADS AND VEGETABLES

Shurba	Soup	*Fasuliyya*	Beans
Shurbit firakh	Chicken soup	*Gazar*	Carrots
Shurbit 'adas	Lentil soup	*Bamya*	Okra (ladies fingers)
Shurbit khudaar	Vegetable soup	*Bisilla*	Peas
Salata	Salad	*Batatis*	Potatoes
Salatit khiyaar	Cucumber salad	*Ruz*	Rice
Salatit tamatim	Tomato salad	*Torshi*	Pickled vegetables
Salatit khadra	Mixed green salad	*Baytingan*	Aubergines
Basal	Onion		

MAIN DISHES

Kofta	Mincemeat flavoured with spices and onions, grilled on a skewer.	*Hamam mashwi*	Grilled pigeon
		Lahm dani	Lamb
		Kibda	Liver
Kebab	Chunks of meat, usually lamb, grilled with onions and tomatoes.	*Kalewi*	Kidney
		Mukh	(Sheep) brains
		Dik rumi	Turkey
Molukhiyya	Spinach-tasting dish made by stewing the leafy vegetable with meat or chicken broth and garlic.	*Samak mashwi*	Grilled fish served wih salad, bread and dips
		Gambari	Prawns
		Calamari	Squid
Firakh	Chicken grilled or stewed and served with vegetables.		

APPETISERS AND FAST FOOD

Fuul	Fava beans served with oil and lemon, sometimes also with onions, meat, eggs or tomato sauce.	*Kushari*	Mixture of noodles, lentils and rice, topped with fried onions and a spicy tomato sauce.
Taamiya	Balls of deep-fried mashed chickpeas and spices.	*Shakshouka*	Chopped meat and tomato sauce, cooked with an egg on top.
Shawarma	Slivers of pressed, spit-roasted lamb, served in pitta bread.	*Makarona*	Macaroni "cake" baked in a white sauce or mincemeat gravy.
Tahina	Sesame seed paste mixed with spices, garlic and lemon, eaten with pitta bread.	*Mahshi*	Literally, "stuffed", variety of vegetables (peppers, tomatoes, aubergines, courgettes) filled with mincemeat and/or rice, herbs and pine nuts.
Hummus	Chickpea paste mixed with tahina, garlic and lemon, sometimes served with pine nuts and/or meat.	*Wara einab*	Vine leaves filled as above and flavoured with lemon juice.
Babaghanoush	Paste of mashed aubergines and tahina.	*Fatir*	Sort of pancake/pizza made of layers of flaky filo pastry with sweet or savoury fillings.

DESSERTS, SWEETS, FRUITS AND NUTS

Mahallabiyya	Sweet rice or corn flour pudding, topped with pistachios.	*'Ishta*	Cream
		Tuffah	Apples
		Mishmish	Apricots
Balila	Milk dish with nuts, raisins and wheat.	*Mohz*	Bananas
		Balah	Dates
Baklava	Flaky filo pastry, honey and nuts.	*Tin*	Figs
		Tin shawqi	Cactus fruit
Basbousa	Pastry of semolina, honey and nuts.	*Shammam*	Melon
		Battikh	Watermelon
Umm (or Om) Ali	Corn cake soaked in milk, sugar, raisins, coconut and cinnamon, served hot.	*Farawla*	Strawberries
		Fuul sudani	Peanuts
		Libb battikh	Watermelon seeds
Gelati, ays kriml	Ice cream	*Loz*	Almonds

SOME PHRASES

ayyzeen il-menu min fadlak	We'd like the menu please	*bidoon sukkar*	Without sugar
ihna ayyzeen . . .	We'd like to have . . .	*ma talabtish di*	I didn't order this
ey da?	What is this?	*da mish . . .*	This is not . . .
ihna mush ayyzeen da	We don't want this	*. . . taza*	. . . fresh
ana makulsh . . .	I can't/don't eat . . .	*. . . mistiwi kwaiyis*	. . . cooked enough
. . . lahm	. . . meat	*da laziz aawi*	This is very tasty
. . . beyd	. . . eggs	*il-hisab, min fadlak (m) /fadlik (f)*	The bill, please
iddini/iddina . . .	Give me/us . . .		
. . . taba'	. . . a plate	*shokran*	Thank you
. . . futa	. . . a napkin		

from spit-roast stands. **Pigeon** (*hamam*), is common, too, most often served with *freek* (spicy wheat) stuffing. There's not much meat on a pigeon, so it's best to order a couple each. In slightly fancier places, you may also encounter pigeon in a ***tajine*** or *ta'gell*, stewed with onions, tomatoes and rice in an earthenware pot.

More expensive restaurants feature these same dishes, plus a few that are more elaborate. Some may precede main courses with a larger selection of dips, plus olives, stuffed vine leaves and so on – a selection known, as in Greek, as ***mezzes***. Soups, too, are occasionally featured, most famously ***molukhiyya***, which is made from stewing Jew's mallow in chicken stock – a lot tastier than its offputting, slimy appearance suggests.

Two common main dishes are ***mahshi*** – stuffed vegetables (tomatoes, aubergines, etc) – and ***torly***, a mixed vegetable casserole with chunks of lamb, or occasionally beef (which in reality may be donkey, water buffalo or camel meat).

Fish (***samak***) is featured on restaurant menus in Alexandria, Aswan, the Red Sea Coast and Sinai. It is invariably grilled, served with salad and chips, and usually very tasty. There are all sorts of types, ranging from snapper to Nile perch; you're usually invited to pick your own fish from the ice box and it'll then be priced by weight. In Greek restaurants you will also find squid (*calamari*) and shrimps (*gambari*).

One confusion that you'll frequently run up against is the idea that **macaroni**, **rice**, **chips** and even **crisps** are interchangeable. Order rice and you'll get chips, and your querying of the matter will be regarded as inexplicable.

VEGETARIAN EATING

Most Egyptians eat vegetables most of the time – meat and fish are seen as luxuries. However, the concept of **vegetarianism** is totally incomprehensible to most people, and you'll be hard pushed to exclude meat stock from your diet. If you do get across the idea that you "don't eat meat", you're as likely as not to be offered chicken or fish as a substitute.

CHESSE, NUTS, CAKES AND FRUITS

You can supplement regular cooked meals with a variety of fare available at corner shops, delicatessens, patisseries and street stalls.

CHEESE

There are two main types of Egyptian cheese: *gibna beyda* (white cheese), which tastes like Greek feta, and *gibna rumi* (Roman cheese), a hard, sharp yellow cheese.

For breakfast you will often be given imported processed cheeses such as *La Vache qui Rit* ("The Laughing Cow" – as Mubarak was nicknamed in the Seventies).

NUTS AND CAKES

Nut shops (*ma'la*) are a high-street perennial, offering all kinds of peanuts (*fuul sudani*) and edible seeds. *Lib abyad* and *lib asmar* are varieties of pumpkin seeds; *lib battikh* come from watermelon. Chickpeas (*hummus*) are roasted and sugar-coated or dried and salted – all of them are sold by weight. Most nut shops also stock candies and mineral water.

Cakes are available at patisseries (some of which are attached to quite flash cafés) or from street stalls. The classics will be familiar to anyone who has travelled in Greece or Turkey: *baklava* (filo pastry soaked in honey and nuts), *katif* (similar but with shredded wheat) and a variety of milk- or cornflour-based puddings, like *mahallabiyya* (sweet rice or cornflour, topped with pistachio nuts) and most famously *Umm Ali* (corn cake soaked in milk, sugar, coconut and cinnamon – served hot).

FRUITS

Fruits in Egypt are seasonal and wonderful. In winter, you get oranges, bananas and dozens of varieties of dates. In summer, you get melons, peaches, plums and grapes, plus a brief season (Aug–Sept) of cactus fruit (aka prickly pear). All are readily available at street stalls, or can be drunk at juice bars (see below).

DRINKS

As a predominantly Muslim country, Egypt gives alcohol a low profile. Drinks consist primarily of teas, coffees, fruit juices and familiar brands of soft drinks.

COFFEE AND TEA

Traditional Egyptian **coffeehouses** or **tearooms** – *ahwas* – are more or less exclusive male territory. Foreign women won't be turned away but may feel uneasy, especially unaccompanied by a man. For a more relaxed tea or coffee, frequent one of the middle-class places (in larger towns), which are often attached to patisseries, and where Egyptian women may be found.

All cafés serve **black "Turkish" coffee** (*ahwa*), pre-sugared to taste. Customers specify whether they want it *saada* (unsugared), *'ariha* (slightly sweetened), *mazboot* (medium sweet) or *ziyaada* (syrupy). **European-style coffee** is generally only found in middle-class or tourist establishments, where it can be ordered with milk (*bi-laban*) and may be *Nescafé* rather than the real thing. Even worse is *Misrcafé*, an inferior Egyptian brand.

Similarly, *ahwas* boil **tea** (*shai*) with leaves and serve it black, whereas posher cafés use tea-bags and supply milk. In hot weather, a glass of mint tea (*shai bia na'ana*) is refreshing; on cold evenings, try *sahleb*, a thick, creamy drink made from arrowroot, with cinnamon and nuts sprinkled on top.

JUICES AND SOFT DRINKS

Every main street has a couple of stand-up **juice bars**, recognisable by their displays of fruit. Normally, you order and pay at the cash desk before exchanging a plastic token for your drink at the counter (where customers leave 10–15pt tip).

Juices made from seasonal fruit include *burtu'an* (orange); *mohz* (banana; with milk *mohz bi-laban*); *manga* (mango); *farawla* (strawberry); *gazar* (carrot); *nus w nus* (carrot and orange, literally "half and half"); and *'asab* (the sickly-sweet, creamy juice of crushed sugar cane).

Street vendors also ladle out iced *asiir limoon* (strong, sweet lemonade), bitter-sweet liquorice-water, and deliciously refreshing *tamar hindi* (tamarind).

Western-style **soft drinks**, including *Coca-Cola* and *7-Up*, are available everywhere. Normally drunk on the spot, you'll have to pay a deposit on the bottle to take one away.

ALCOHOL

Alcohol in Egypt is rarely hard to obtain, but the range of outlets is limited and it can only be consumed indoors – even in restaurants or hotels if they overlook the street. In some regions – notably Middle Egypt – its sale is severely restricted or entirely prohibited. As a rule of thumb, hotels or Greek restaurants are the places to try; if you can't see anyone drinking it, there's none to be had. When you do manage to locate a drink, keep in mind that the hot, dry climate makes for dehydration, and agonising hangovers can easily result from over indulgence.

Beer, whose consumption goes back to pharaonic times, is the most widely available form of alcohol. Native *Stella* beer is a light lager served in large (roughly pint-sized) bottles, which are okay if they haven't sat in the sun for too long (some claim that the brown glass bottles are better than the green ones) and retail in most places for £E2.50–3. *Stella Export* with a blue rather than yellow label is dearer (£E3–4) and comes in smaller bottles. *Marzen*, a dark bock beer, appears briefly in the spring; *Aswali* is a dark beer produced in Aswan. Imported beer, the most expensive, only appears in bars, flash hotels and restaurants. There is also *Birrel*, a non-alcoholic beer.

Around Alexandria, a half-dozen or so **Egyptian wines** are produced. None is especially good, though they're drinkable with a meal. The most commonly found are *Omar Khayyam* (a dry red), *Cru des Ptolémées* (a dry white) and *Rubis d'Egypte* (a rosé). There are also a few **brandies** (a bit like Spanish brandy), a local **gin** (which is foul) and **zibib** – or *arak* – similar to Greek ouzo.

Note: Sale of alcohol is prohibited during the month of **Ramadan** and over the **Moulid al-Nabi** (see p.41) and, locally, during certain other festivals.

COMMUNICATIONS – POST, PHONES AND MEDIA

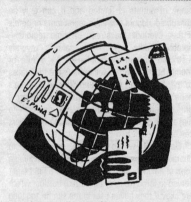

MAIL AND POSTE RESTANTE

Airmail **letters** between Western Europe and Egypt generally take around a week to ten days, two to three weeks to North America or Australasia. As a rule, around fifteen percent of one's correspondence (in either direction) never arrives; letters containing photos or other items are especially prone to go astray.

It's best to send letters from a major city or hotel; blue **mailboxes** are for overseas airmail, red ones for domestic post. Airmail (*bariid gawwi*) **stamps** can be purchased at post offices, hotel shops and postcard stands, which may charge 5pt above the normal rate (45/50pt for a postcard/letter to countries outside the Arab world). **Registered mail**, costing 15–30pt extra, can be sent from any post office. Selected post offices in the main cities also offer an **Express Mail Service** (36hr to Europe, 48hr to the US) costing £E26 for letters under 100 grammes.

To send a parcel, take the goods unopened to a major post office for customs inspection, weighing and wrapping. The procedure – explained in detail in the Cairo section (p.227) – is much the same throughout Egypt.

Post office hours are generally Sat–Thurs 8.30am–3pm (9am–3pm during Ramadan), though central offices may stay open until 7pm. Almost invariably, offices are closed on Fridays.

POSTE RESTANTE

Receiving letters **poste restante** is a bit of a lottery, since post office workers don't always file letters under the name you might expect. Ask for all your initials to be checked (including *M* for Mr or Ms, etc), and, if you're half expecting anything, suggest other letters as well. To have mail sent to you, it should be addressed (preferably with your surname underlined) to *Poste Restante* at the Central Post Office. To pick up mail, you'll need your passport.

A better option is to have mail sent to a major **hotel** (anything with three or more stars should be reliable) or **c/o American Express** (branches in Cairo, Alexandria, Luxor and Aswan; see p.17 for addresses). The latter service is officially only for Amex traveller's cheque or card-holders, but no one ever seems bothered. Note that **parcels** sent *c/o American Express* will be held at the post office (in the case of Cairo, at the branch on Sharia Mohammed Farid). The US Embassy will no longer accept mail for travelling Americans.

PHONES

Egypt's telephone system is erratic and frustrating, particularly for domestic calls (international connections are better).

All towns and cities have at least one **Telephone and Telegraph Office** (usually open 24hr) for calling long distance and abroad. Here, you give the number to a clerk and pay for the call in advance, either for a set amount of time or £E20–30 for an open line, settling the bill afterwards. Expect to queue and hang around a while. It's also possible to book (and pre-pay) for a call which is routed through to your hotel or some other number.

Alternatively, you can **make calls through a hotel** with a trunk or direct international line (most places with three or more stars have them), which entails paying 15–25 percent above the normal rate.

Phone boxes really only serve for local calls, which cost 10pt (though some kiosks only accept the old 5pt coins). You can also make local calls on semi-public phones owned by shopkeepers, who charge 25pt. Only in Cairo will you find payphones for direct dialling abroad (see below).

DIALLING

Overloaded exchanges and antiquated equipment make **local calls** a hit-and-miss business, especially during peak hours. Even dialling slowly, you'll often get a wrong number. To make matters worse, numbers vary from four or five digits to seven, the shorter ones gradually acquiring extra digits as the telephone system is overhauled. The **ringing tone** is similar to that used in Britain; the **engaged tone** consists of two-second bursts of tone separated by one second's silence. A persistent whine or silence indicates that the number is unobtainable, or the local exchange is overloaded.

Long-distance calls within Egypt are prefixed by a two- or three-digit area code (listed under the appropriate chapters in this book), followed by the individual number. However, to call Kharga Oasis or Sinai, you must dial the area code and get the exchange to connect you.

International calls are generally made through a telephone exchange or hotel switchboard (see above). Callers are charged in blocks of three minutes; calls over six minutes during **peak hours** (8am–8pm local time) cost triple the normal rate. The minimum charge at off-peak/peak **rates** is: Australia (£E19/£E25); Britain (£E12/£E16); Canada (£E14/£E19); France (£E14/£E19); Germany (£E12/£E16); Israel (£E13/£E17); USA (£E13/£E17). Remember that hotels add a hefty surcharge.

Facilities for **direct dialling** are limited to a few deluxe hotels, mostly in Cairo. Ask reception for the number connecting you to an international line, then dial the country code: Australia (161), Canada/USA (1), Britain (44), Netherlands (31), and finally the individual number, leaving out the initial 0 of its local code.

A trouble-free way to **dial the US from Cairo** is to make use of the *USDirect* phones at *American Express* on Qasr el-Nil Street, and in the *Marriott*, *Ramses Hilton* and *SemiRamis* hotels; these allow **credit-card and collect calls**. Alternatively, Americans with an *AT&T* **credit card** can use this to call abroad (in theory from anywhere in Egypt – though it's likely to prove difficult outside of the major cities): dial 146 and give the operator your international card number. The call will be billed to your (US) home address and charged as if it was made from the US.

CALLING EGYPT FROM ABROAD

Phoning Egypt from abroad, dial the international code (**010** in Britain; **011** in the US); then **20** (for Egypt) followed by the **area code** (see boxes in each chapter, but omit the initial 0) and finally the **subscriber's number**.

TELEGRAMS, TELEXES AND FAXES

Telegrams can be sent from any telephone office for so much per word (including the address) – 60pt a word to the US, for example.

Telex is probably the best way to reserve a hotel room from outside Egypt. Individual telex listings appear in the text. Where several hotels share the same telex number, messages should be addressed "Attention Ramses Hotel" (or whatever name is appropriate).

You can send **faxes** from the Telegraph and Telex Office on Cairo's Midan Ataba (which charges about £E12 for a one-page fax to the US) or the business service centres in major hotels (charging twice as much). Faxes **from abroad** can be sent to *American Express* on Qasr el-Nil Street (fax: 202 628975), who'll hold them like client mail, but won't notify the recipient.

THE MEDIA

As for other means of staying in touch, various British, US, French and German **newspapers** are available in Cairo, Alexandria, Luxor and Aswan, as are *Newsweek* and *Time* magazines. Elsewhere, however, you'll be lucky to find even the *Egyptian Gazette* (see below). In Cairo, one can also read **press agency reports** off teletype machines in the *Nile Hilton* and *Sheraton* hotels.

If you take a short-wave radio, you can pick up the **BBC World Service**, which is broadcast on 639KHz from 8.45am to noon, 3–5pm and 7–9pm; and on 1325KHz from 9pm to 3am (all local time). Reception is best in the north. The **Voice of America** broadcasts 24 hours on numerous frequencies on the AM (medium wave) or short wave. For full programme listings, write to VOA (PO Box 122, Dokki, ☎704-986). Both services carry news on the hour.

EGYPTIAN TV

Egypt has three **television** channels, all state-controlled.

Channel 1, running from 3.30pm to midnight, and found on 1 and 5 (or 6) on the dial, broadcasts mostly in Arabic, though subtitled Western movies are also shown, notably on Saturday nights at 10.30pm.

Channel 2, on the air from 3pm to midnight daily, and also from 10am to noon on Fridays and

Sundays, shows many foreign programmes, with Western movies presented on Thursday (10pm) and Friday (10am & 10pm), and news in English at 8pm daily.

Channel 3, limited to Cairo, broadcasts in Arabic from 5 to 9pm daily.

The *Egyptian Gazette* carries daily television schedules; its Monday edition lists all the movies that week.

THE EGYPTIAN PRESS

The **Egyptian press** encompasses a range of daily papers and weekly magazines, chiefly published in English, French or Arabic.

The **English-language** *Egyptian Gazette* (on Saturday, the *Egyptian Mail*) carries agency reports, articles on Middle Eastern affairs, and tourist features. Its **French-language** counterparts are *Le Journal d'Egypte* and *Le Progres Egyptien*. The weekly *Middle East Times* is good for regional affairs; the *Middle East Observer* concentrates on financial matters. All of them are bland and heavily censored.

There's more diversity of opinion **in Arabic**. Egypt's oldest newspaper, *al-Ahram* (The Pyramids), reflects official thinking, but less slavishly than *Mayo*, the organ of the ruling National Democratic Party. Other dailies with a party affiliation include *al-Wafd* (conservative); *al-Ahli* (socialist); *al-Shaab* (left of centre); and *al-Ahrar* (liberal). *Al-Da'wa* is the journal of the fundamentalist Muslim Brotherhood.

MOULIDS AND PUBLIC HOLIDAYS

Egypt abounds in holidays and festivals of all kinds, both Muslim and Christian, national and local. Coming across a local *moulid* can be the most interesting and enjoyable experience of any travel in the country – with the chance to witness music and dance, as well as great *souks*.

Perhaps surprisingly, there are rewards, too, in coinciding with one of the major Islamic celebrations – above all, Ramadan, when all Muslims (which means ninety percent of Egyptians) observe a total fast from sunrise to sunset for a month. This can pose some problems for travelling but the celebratory evenings are again good times to hear music and to share in hospitality.

ISLAMIC HOLIDAYS

Most Islamic holidays and festivals follow the Islamic calendar. This is lunar-based, so dates vary each year in relation to the western calendar. You may find it useful to get hold of an annual prayer calendar from a local Islamic cultural centre in your own country.

The twelve **months** are:

Moharrem (30 days)
Safar (29 days)
Rabi al-Awwal (30 days)
Rabi el-Tani (29 days)
Gumad al-Awwal (30 days)
Gumad el-Tani (29 days)
Ragab (30 days)
Sha'ban (29 days)
Ramadan (30 days)
Shawwal (29 days)
Zoul Qiddah (30 days)
Zoul Hagga (29 days – or 30 days in leap years).

See box below for estimated **starting dates** of *Moharrem* (which begins on Ras el-Sana el-Hegira) for the next three years. Note that a day in the Islamic calendar begins at sundown, as a consequence of which Islamic festivals start on the evening before you'd expect.

RAMADAN

Ramadan, in a sense, parallels the Christian Lent. The ninth month of the Islamic calendar, it commemorates the time in which the Koran was

RAMADAN AND ISLAMIC HOLIDAYS

Islamic religious holidays are calculated on the **lunar calendar**, so their dates rotate throughout the seasons (as does Ramadan's). Exact dates in the lunar calendar are impossible to predict – local Islamic centres can supply the year's calendar only – but approximate dates for the next three years are:

	1992	1993	1994
Ramadan	March 8	Feb 25	Feb 14
Eid al-Fitr	April 7	March 27	March 16
Eid al-Adha	June 12	June 1	May 20
Ras el-Sana el-Hegira	July 3	June 23	June 12
Moulid al-Nabi	Sept 10	Aug 31	Aug 20

revealed to Mohammed. In contrast to the Christian West, though, the Muslim world observes the fast rigorously.

What the fast involves is abstention from food, drink and smoking during daylight hours, and abstinence from sex throughout the month. Strict Muslims will even refrain from swallowing, lest they "drink" their own saliva.

With most local cafés and restaurants closing during the day, and people getting on edge towards the end of the month, Ramadan is in some respects a disastrous time to travel. It is certainly no time to try camel trekking in the Sinai – no guide would undertake the work – and it is probably safer to travel by bus during the mornings only, as drivers will be fasting, too. (Airline pilots are forbidden from observing the fast.)

But there is a compensation in witnessing and becoming absorbed into the pattern of the fast. At sunset, signalled by the sounding of a siren and the lighting of lamps on the minarets, an amazing calm and sense of well-being fall on the streets, as everyone eats *fuul* and *taamiya* and, in the cities at least, gets down to a night of celebration and entertainment. Through the evening, urban cafés – and main squares – provide venues for live music and singing, while in small towns and poorer quarters of big cities, you will often come across ritualised *zikrs* – trance-like chanting and swaying.

If you are a **non-Muslim** outsider you are not expected to observe Ramadan, but it is good to be sensitive about not breaking the fast (particularly smoking) in public. In fact, the best way to experience Ramadan – and to benefit from its naturally purifying rhythms – is to enter into it. You may not be able to last without an occasional glass of water, and you'll probably breakfast later than sunrise, but it is worth an attempt.

OTHER ISLAMIC HOLIDAYS

At the end of Ramadan comes the feast of **Eid al-Fitr**, a climax to the festivities in Cairo, though observed more privately in the villages. Equally important in the Muslim calendar is **Eid al-Adha** (aka *Corban Bairam* – the Great Feast), which celebrates the willingness of Ibrahim (Abraham) to obey God and sacrifice his son. The Eid al-Adha is followed, about three weeks later, by **Ras el-Sana el-Hegira**, the first day of the month of Moharrem, which marks the Muslim new year.

Both *eids* are traditional family gatherings. At the Eid al-Adha every household that can afford it will slaughter a sheep. You see them tethered everywhere, even on rooftops, for weeks prior to the event.

The fourth main religious holiday is the **Moulid al-Nabi**, the Prophet Mohammed's birthday. This is widely observed, with processions in many towns and cities.

MOULIDS

Moulids are the equivalent of medieval European saint's fairs: popular events combining piety, fun and commerce. Their ostensible aim is to obtain blessing (*baraka*) from the saint, but the social and cultural dimensions are equally important. *Moulids* are an opportunity for people to escape the monotony of their hard-working lives in several days of festivities, and for friends and families from different villages to meet. Harvest and farming problems are discussed, as well as family matters – and marriage – as people sing, dance, eat and pray together.

The largest events draw crowds of over a million, with companies of *mawladiya* (literally, "*moulid* people") running stalls and rides, and music blaring into the small hours. Smaller, rural *moulids* tend to be heavier on the practical devotion, with people bringing their children or livestock for blessing, or the sick to be cured.

DATES...

With the exception of the Moulid al-Nabi (the Prophet's Birthday – see previous page), which is celebrated throughout Egypt, most *moulids* are localised affairs, usually centred around the mosque or tomb (*qubba*) of a holy man. Most are scheduled according to the Islamic calendar, so dates vary from year to year when reckoned by the western calendar.

To complicate matters further, certain *moulids* start (or finish) on a particular day (eg a Tuesday in a given month), rather than on any specific date. However, a minority of festivals occur at the same time every year, generally following the local harvest. If you're planning to attend a *moulid*, it's wise to verify the (approximate) dates given in this guide by asking local people or the tourist office.

... AND SPECTACLES

At the heart of every *moulid* is at least one *zikr* – a gathering of worshippers who chant and sway for hours, striving to attain a trance-like state of oneness with God.

Frequently, the *zikr* participants belong to one of the **Sufi brotherhoods**, which are differentiated by coloured banners, sashes or turbans, and named after their founding sheikh. The current incumbent of this office may lead them in a *zaffa* (parade) through town, and in olden times would ride a horse over his followers – a custom known as "the Treading", nowadays only practised in the Luxor region.

Luxor's own festival features a parade of boats; elsewhere, the procession may be led by camels or floats. Accompanying all this are **traditional entertainments** – mock stick-fights, conjurers, acrobats and snake charmers; horses trained to dance to music; and, sometimes, bellydancers. Music and singing are a feature of every

moulid and locals often bring tape recorders to provide sounds for the rest of the year. If you are lucky enough to catch one of the major events, you'll get the chance to witness Egyptian popular culture at its richest.

The largest *moulids* are in Cairo, Tanta and Luxor. **Cairo** hosts three lengthy festivals in honour of el-Hussein, Saiyida Zeinab and the Imam al-Shafi'i (held during the months of Rabi el-Tani, Ragab and Sha'ban, respectively), plus numerous smaller festivals (see p.206). Following the cotton harvest in October, the Moulid of el-Bedawi in **Tanta** starts a cycle of lesser **Nile Delta festivals** which runs well into November (see p.489). Equally spectacular, albeit somewhat smaller, is the Moulid of Abu el-Haggag in **Luxor**, held during the month of Sha'ban (p.296).

COPTIC FESTIVALS

Egypt's Christian Coptic minority often attend Islamic *moulids* – and vice versa. **Coptic moulids** share some of the social and market functions of their Islamic counterparts, and, similarly, at their core is the celebration of a saint's nameday. As you'd expect, the major Christian events of the year are also celebrated.

Christmas (Dec 25), **Epiphany** (Jan 19) and the **Annunciation** (March 21) follow the western calendar. **Easter**, however, and its related feast days, is reckoned according to the Coptic calendar, which is solar, and can be up to a month apart from western dates.

Major **saints' day events** include the Moulid of Saint Damyanah (May 15–20), the Feast of the Apostles Peter and Paul (July 12), and various *moulids* of the Virgin and Saint George during August. Many of these are held at monasteries in Middle Egypt, the Delta and the Red Sea Hills.

Lastly, a Coptic festival (of pharaonic origin) celebrated by all Egyptians is the **Sham el-Nessim**, a coming-of-spring festival which provides the excuse for mass picnics.

PUBLIC HOLIDAYS

These secular public holidays are no longer celebrated in great style (having been more associated with military parades of the Nasser and Sadat years), though you'll find offices and the like closed.

January 1	New Year's Day	**October 6**	Forces Day
April 25	Liberation Day	**October 23**	Suez Day
May 1	Labour Day	**December 23**	Victory Day
July 23	Revolution Day Armed		

MONUMENTS, MOSQUES AND MONASTERIES

ANCIENT MONUMENTS

Egypt's **ancient sites and monuments** are maintained by the **Egyptian Antiquities Organisation (EAO)**. Most are kept open on a daily basis, with *ghaffirs* (caretakers) on hand to open tombs and point you towards the salient features. Local opening hours and so on are detailed in individual entries; for a few hints on *baksheesh*, see p.23.

If you're a committed Egyptologist and want to visit sites that are under excavation, closed for repairs or due to their dangerous state, you may want to contact the local branch of the EAO for a **special permit**. This is usually quite routine and you'll just be given a scrawled note in Arabic to show to the guards on site. If you have a particularly demanding or sensitive request – eg to venture into an area under military control – it may be best to go straight to the top, and make enquiries at the Ministry of Antiquities in Cairo (Sharia Fakhry Abdel Noor; ☎839-637 or ☎283-1117).

MOSQUES

Most of the **mosques** and their attached **madrassas** (Islamic colleges) that you'll want to visit in Egypt are in Cairo, and, with the exception of the el-Hussein and Saiyida Zeinab, are classified as "historic monuments". They are open routinely to non-Muslim visitors, although anyone not worshipping should avoid prayer times, especially the main service at noon on Friday. Elsewhere in the country, mosques are not used to seeing tourists and locals may object to your presence. Tread with care and if at all possible ask someone to take you in.

At all mosques, **dress** is important. Shorts (plus short skirts) and exposed shoulders are out, and in some places women may be asked to cover their hair (a scarf might be provided). Above all, remember to remove your **shoes** upon entering the precinct. They will either be held by a shoe custodian (small *baksheesh* expected) or you can just leave them outside the door, or carry them in by hand (if you do this, place the soles together, as they are considered unclean).

MONASTERIES

Egyptian monasteries (which are Coptic, save for Greek Orthodox Saint Catherine's) admit visitors at all times except during the Lenten or other fasts (local fasts are detailed where appropriate). Similar rules of dress etiquette as for mosques apply, though unless you go into the church itself you don't need to remove shoes.

DISABLED ACCESS

Egypt can be a very challenging place to visit if you have a **mobility** problem. There is virtually no provision for wheelchair (or blind) access, and little understanding of disabled visitors' needs; the hole-in-the-ground toilets, especially, are a nightmare. On the plus side, however, disability carries no stigma in Egypt, it is simply God's will, to be accepted and made light of – as Egyptians say, *Allah karim* (God is generous).

The **monuments** are a mix of the accessible and the impossible. Most of the major **temples** are built on relatively level sites, with a few steps here and there – manoeuvrable in a wheelchair or with sticks if you have an able-bodied helper. Your frustrations are likely to be with the **tombs**, which are almost always a struggle to reach – often sited halfway up cliffs, or down steep flights of stairs. In the Valley of the Kings, for example, the only really straightforward tomb is that of Ramses VI. The Pyramids of Giza are accessible to viewing but not entry; Saqqara would be difficult, being so sandy.

Cairo itself is bad news, especially Islamic Cairo, with its narrow, uneven alleys and heavy traffic, but with a car and helper, you could still see the Citadel and other major monuments. In the Egyptian Antiquities Museum, there's a lift.

On a strictly practical front, you would be well advised to make your **requirements** known in advance. The state tourist agency, *Misr Travrel*, can be helpful with arranging transport and accommodation. Better still, contact Dr Sami Bishara of *ETAMS Tours* in Cairo (13 Sharia Qasr el-Nil; ☎754-721 or 752-462), who specialises in custom-made tours for disabled individuals and groups.

WORKING OR STUDYING IN EGYPT

Cairo offers work possibilities for teaching English as a foreign language and – to a small extent – in journalism, modelling and tourism. The city's American University is a rewarding if relatively expensive place to study Arabic, Middle Eastern affairs or Egyptology.

TEACHING

Teaching in Egypt largely means working in Cairo, where there are various language schools, generally catering for adults. There's quite a big market for people wanting to learn both conversational and business English.

All of the following institutions are worth contacting:

British Council, 192 Corniche el-Nil, Aguza, Cairo (☎345-3281). TEFL or RSA certificates are required for jobs at the British Council, who recruit most of their staff in Britain (head office: 10 Spring Gardens, London SW1; ☎071/930 8466). Vacancies do occur locally from time to time, however, both here and at their branch in Alexandria. Upwards of £E1500 a month for a 24-hour week.

International Language Institute (ILI), off Sharia Merghani, Heliopolis, Cairo (☎666-704). Affiliated to International House abroad, ILI require an RSA certificate and a university degree. High turnover of staff, so good chance of work. Rates slightly lower than for the British Council.

International Language Learning Institute (ILLI), c/o Mr Nadr Yechya, 9 Orman Villas, Dokki, Cairo. A clearing house for a range of locally owned language schools. Certificates help but good English and determination may be requirement enough for some jobs. Rates are a lot lower: £E550–600 for unqualified staff; maybe £E700 for those with certificates. Long-term teachers may be offered deals including a flat. Do not hand over your passport to ILLI or to any college to which you are assigned.

Japanese Institute, in the *Marriott Hotel*, Zamalek, Cairo. Part-time teaching work at top rates (£E20–25 an hour) for the highly qualified only.

JOURNALISM

Cairo has been the launchpad for several journalistic careers, for it is easy to place work with the local English-language media. *Cairo Today* takes travel articles and photos. *The Egyptian Gazette* takes feature stories and may need subediting work from time to time.

International press agencies (listed in *Cairo: A Practical Guide* – widely available in the city) may also take stuff and possibly employ stringers.

MODELLING

Advertising agencies often require westerners to model for television or magazine commercials. You certainly aren't expected to be a professional model, nor are you paid like one: this is simply a day-to-day job for any western face that fits.

A number of agencies are again listed in *Cairo: A Practical Guide*. Women should keep their wits about them – and preferably a male escort.

TOUR GUIDING

Though most jobs in the tourism field are restricted to Egyptian nationals, and locally based companies will insist on a work permit, you can sometimes fix up a season's work with a foreign tour operator abroad as a rep or tour guide. See the lists on p.6 for companies to approach.

STUDYING

The **American University in Cairo** (113 Sharia Qasr al-Aini, just off Midan Tahrir; ☎354-2964) offers year-abroad and non-degree programmes, a summer school and intensive Arabic courses. A full year's tuition costs roughly US$7000. US citizens may apply for Guaranteed Student Loans. Contact the Office of Admissions, 866 UN Plaza #517, New York, NY 10017-1899 (☎212/421-6320).

Foreign students may also attend one- or two-term programmes at four **Egyptian universities**: Cairo, Ain Shams, al-Azhar and Alexandria. These are valid for transferable credits at most American and some British universities. In the US, contact the Egyptian Cultural and Educational Bureau, 2200 Kalorama Road NW, Washington DC (☎202/265-6400).

STAYING ON AND DIRECTORY/45

DIRECTORY

ABU AND UMM Literally "father" and "mother", Abu and Umm are used both as honorific titles and also figuratively as a nickname, picking out someone's salient characteristic: Flaubert, for example, was known as "Abu of the Moustaches".

ADDRESSES The words for street (*sharia*), avenue (*tariq*) and square (*midan*) always precede the name. Whole blocks often share a single street number, which may be in Arabic numerals.

CHILDREN evoke a warm response which makes travelling with them easier than one might expect. Most hotels can supply an extra bed and breakfast (which should be supplemented for variety), whilst baby food and disposable nappies are available at pharmacies and stores in all large towns. Children of any age should enjoy camel and felucca rides, snorkelling and (a few of) the great monuments. All the main resorts have discos and sports facilities. From an adult minder's standpoint, most hazards can be minimised or avoided by taking due precautions. Kids (especially young ones) are more susceptible than adults to heatstroke, dehydration and tummy upsets. Traffic is obviously dangerous, but stray animals (possible disease carriers), fenced-off beaches (probably mined – see below) and poisonous fish and coral in the Red Sea (see *Sinai*) are potentially enticing.

DRUGS In recent years, rising heroin addiction has prompted the state to clamp down on *all* drugs, ending the once-cosy relationship between

local cops and hashish dealers. In 1989, the first courier was executed under a law which makes **hanging or life imprisonment** mandatory for convicted smugglers and dealers (which could be interpreted to mean somebody caught with a few sachets of stuff). Mere possession or use merits a severe prison sentence and a heavy fine (plus legal costs, upwards of $1000). Given the risk of *agent provocateurs*, it's surprising how many tourists respond to approaches by dealers in Dahab, Luxor and Cairo (they're unlikely to be made anywhere else).

FOOTBALL is Egypt's national sport. The two Cairo-based rivals, *Ahly* and *Zamalek*, are the major teams and contributed most of the country's 1990 World Cup squad. Clashes between the two teams can be intense – and occasionally have led to rioting – but games are in general relaxed.

MINEFIELDS still exist from World War II along the Mediterranean coast, and from Israeli conflicts in the interior of Sinai and along the Red Sea Coast. Do not take any risks in venturing into fenced-off territory.

SPELLINGS Arabic is notoriously hard to transliterate into Roman script. The existence of several systems, and the popular familiarity of certain spellings, makes consistency a nightmare. Egyptians themselves employ English spelling loosely; basically, you get accustomed to different variations on the same Arabic name.

TIME is two hours ahead of GMT, and a more elastic concept than Westerners are used to. In practice, "five minutes" often means an hour or more; *bahdeen* ("later") the next day; and *bukkra* ("tomorrow") an indefinite wait for something that may never happen. Besides hinting that it won't, *inshallah* ("God willing") can be a polite way of backing away from unwanted commitments – a game which foreigners can also play. Remember, too, that Western abruptness strikes Egyptians as rude; never begrudge the time it takes to say *Salaam aleikum*, or return a greeting.

TOILETS Public ones are almost always filthy, and there's never any toilet paper (though someone may sell it outside). They're usually known as *Toileta*, and marked with WC, Men and Women signs. Expect squat toilets in bus stations, resthouses and fleapit hotels, and *always* carry toilet paper (75pt a roll in pharmacies).

USEFUL THINGS TO BRING

● **Alarm clock**. Vital for early-morning buses.

● **Clothes**. Keep both practicality and sensitivity in mind. As emphasised in the piece "From a Woman's Perspective", Egypt is a deeply conservative nation; the more modest your dress the less hassle you will attract.

On the practicalities front, bear in mind that northern Egypt can be cool and damp in the winter, while the desert gets distinctly chilly at night, even in the spring and autumn. A warm sweater is invaluable. So, too, are a solid pair of shoes: burst pipes are commonplace, and wandering around muddy streets in sodden sandals is a miserable experience..

● **Cool bottle**. Keeps juice and water at a refreshing temperature on those long desert journeys.

● **Film**. Kodak and Fuji film is available in most towns and major resorts, but it may well be pretty old stock. It's best to bring adequate supplies. For photography in dark alleyways, tombs and hidden corners, fast film (400–800 ASA) is useful. If you're looking for good landscape photographs, slow film (and/or early rising) is a must. See notes on behaviour.

● **Plug**. If you like your water to fill a basin, it is worth packing an omnisize plug: few hotels (even relatively upmarket ones) supply such equipment.

● **Sleeping bag**. A decent bag is invaluable if you're planning to sleep out in the desert in spring or autumn, or any low budget hotel over winter. In the summer, a sheet sleeping bag is handy if you're staying at cheaper hotels.

● **Snaps** of your family, home town, football team (or whatever) help bridge the language barrier. Locals will proudly show you their own.

● **Spare** contact lenses, hearing-aid batteries etc, if required.

● **Torch**. For exploring dark tombs, and use during power cuts.

METRIC WEIGHTS AND MEASURES

1 ounce = 28.3 grammes
1 pound = 454 grammes
2.2 pounds = 1 kilogramme (kg)
1 pint = 0.47 litres
1 quart = 0.94 litres
1 gallon = 3.87 litres

1 inch = 2.54 centimetres (cm)
1 foot = 0.3 metres (m)
1 yard = 0.91m
1.09 yards = 1m
1 mile = 1.61 kilometres (km)
0.62 miles = 1km

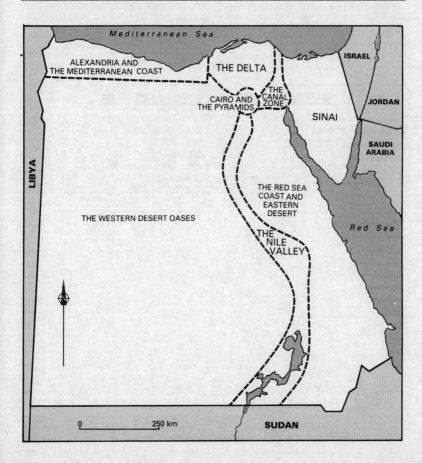

CHAPTER ONE

CAIRO AND THE PYRAMIDS

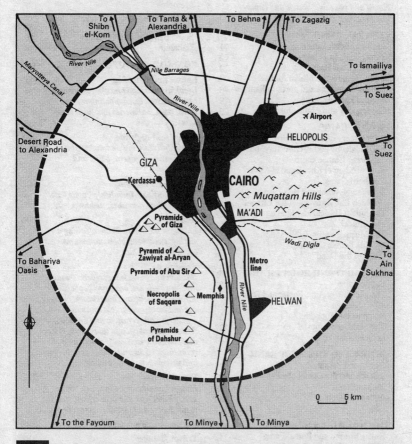

The twin streams of Egypt's history converge just below the Delta at **Cairo**, where the greatest city in the Islamic world sprawls across the Nile towards the **Pyramids**, those supreme monuments of antiquity. Every visitor to Egypt comes here, to reel at the Pyramids' baleful mass

FINDING YOUR WAY AROUND THIS CHAPTER

A brief historical outline 52

Orientation 53
Orientation and information; points of arrival

Getting around 58
Metro; taxis; buses; minibuses; walking; trams and rivertaxis; driving and car rental

Accommodation 64
Hotels and pensions; hostels and camping; long stays and flat-hunting

CENTRAL CAIRO 70
Around Midan Tahrir 71
Talaat Harb and Qasr el-Nil 72
East of Talaat Harb 73
Opera Square and Midan Ataba 77
Ezbekiya gardens and north to Ramses 78
Around Ramses Station 79
Garden City and Abdin Quarter 79

ISLAMIC CAIRO 82
Brief history of Islamic Cairo 83
A–Z of Islamic and Architectural terms 84
Exploring Islamic Cairo 87
Around Khan el-Khalili and al-Azhar 88
Northern Gates 92
Between al-Azhar and Bab Zwayla 99
Between Bab Zwayla and the Citadel 102
The Sultan Hassan and Rifai mosques 107
The Citadel 108
The Mosque of Ibn Tulun and the Saiyida Zeinab Quarter 111
Cities of the Dead 115

OLD CAIRO AND RODA ISLAND 121
Coptic Cairo 121
The Mosque of Amr, Fustat and Deir Abu'l-Safayan 129
North to the Aqueduct 131
The Southern Suburbs 132
Roda Island 133

GEZIRA AND THE WEST BANK 135
Gezira and Zamalek 135
Imbaba and the Camel Market 137
Mohandiseen 138
Aguza and Dokki 140
Giza 141

THE NORTHERN SUBURBS 142
Bulaq, Shubra and Rod el-Farag 142
Abbassiya, Hada'iq al-Qubba and Medinet Nasr 144
Heliopolis 146
Matariyya 147

THE MUSEUMS 150
Egyptian Antiquities Museum 150
Coptic Museum 160
Islamic Art Museum 163
Other museums 166

THE PYRAMIDS 168
The Pyramids in history 168
Giza 169
Kerdassa and Harraniyya 177
Zawiyat al-Ayran 177
Memphis 177
North Saqqara 178
Abu Sir 188
South Saqqara 190
Dahshur 190

CONSUMERS CAIRO 192

Eating and drinking 192
Breakfast and buffet meals; restaurants, cafés and street food; floating restaurants; cafés, patisseries and juice bars; bars

Music and nightlife 201
Music; bellydancing and nightclubs; discos; cinemas; opera, ballet and theatre

Traditional festivals 205
Muslim festivals (moulids); Coptic festivals; whirling dervishes; weddings

Activities 208
Riding in the desert; Felucca sailing and gliding; swimming pools; hammams; sport; chiefly for kids

Shopping 211
Bazaars and bargaining; markets; souvenirs and antiques; brass and copperware; carpets, appliqué and basketwork; clothing and leatherwork; gold and silver jewellery; glass, ceramics and precious stones; mashrabiya and inlay work; spices and perfumes; musical instruments and recordings; books and newspapers; books and newspapers; booze and cigs

Practicalities 220
Money, bureaucracy, visas, healthcare, post, phones, car and bike repair, etcCultural centres and language courses

Excursions from Cairo 229

Travel Details 231
Trains; buses; intercity service taxis; international coaches; domestic flights; international flights; boats – Nile cruises and international lines

and the seething immensity of Cairo, with its bazaars, mosques and Citadel and extraordinary Antiquities Museum. It's equally impossible not to find yourself carried away by the streetlife, where medieval trades and customs co-exist with a modern, cosmopolitan mix of Arab, African and European influences.

With so much to see (and overlook, initially), you can spend weeks in the city and merely scratch the surface. But as visitors soon realise, there are lots of reasons why people don't. Cairo's density, climate and pollution conspire against it, the culture shock is equally wearing. Tourists unfamiliar with Arab ways can take little for granted, regular visitors expect to be baffled, and not even Cairenes comprehend the whole metropolis. The downside weighs especially on newcomers, since it's the main tourist sites that generate most friction. A day at the Pyramids or Khan el-Khalili bazaar can feel like a course in sales-resistance and *baksheesh* evasion.

Generally, however, Cairenes are the warmest, best-natured city-dwellers going. They have to be to live in such a pressure cooker without exploding. Their sly wit and prying render pretension and secrecy impotent; their spirited ingenuity transcends horrendous conditions. Potential riots are defused by tolerance and custom; a web of ties resists alienation. Once you have something of the measure of this, Cairo feels an altogether different and more enjoyable place.

CAIRO (MASR, AL-QAHIRA)

CAIRO has been the largest city in Africa and the Middle East ever since the Mongols wasted Imperial Baghdad in 1258. Acknowledged as *Umm Dunya* or **"Mother of the World"** by medieval Arabs, and as Great Cairo by nineteenth-century Europeans, it remains, in Jan Morris's words, "one of the half-dozen supercapitals – capitals that are bigger than themselves or their countries . . . the focus of a whole culture, an ideology or a historical moment". As Egypt has been a prize for conquerors from Alexander the Great to Rommel, so Cairo has been a fulcrum of power in the Arab world from the Crusades unto the present day. The *ulema* of its 1000-year-old al-Azhar Mosque (for centuries the foremost centre of Islamic intellectual life) remains the ultimate religious authority for millions of Sunni Muslims, from Jakarta to Birmingham. Wherever Arabic is spoken, Cairo's cultural magnetism is felt. Every strand of Egyptian society knits and unravels in this febrile megalopolis.

Egyptians have two names for the city, one ancient and popular, the other Islamic and official. The foremost is **Masr**, meaning both the capital and the land of Egypt – an Ur-city that endlessly renews itself and dominates the nation: an idea rooted in pharaonic civilisation. (For Egyptians abroad, "Masr" refers to their homeland; within its borders it means the capital.) Whereas *Masr* is timeless, the city's other name, **al-Qahira** (The Conqueror) is linked to an event – the Fatimid conquest that made this the capital of an Islamic Empire stretching from the Atlantic to the Hindu Kush. The name is rarely used in everyday speech.

Both archetypes still resonate and in monumental terms are symbolised by two dramatic **landmarks**: the **Pyramids of Giza** at the edge of the Western Desert and the great **Mosque of Mohammed Ali** – the moderniser of Islamic Egypt – which broods atop the Citadel. Between these two monuments sprawls a vast city, the colour of sand and ashes, of diverse worlds and time zones, and gross inequities. All is subsumed into an organism that somehow thrives in the terminal ward: medieval slums and Art Deco suburbs, garbage-pickers and marbled malls, donkey carts and limos, sincere piety and "the oaths of men exaggerating in the name of God" – Cairo lives by its own contradictions.

This is a city, as Morris put it, "almost overwhelmed by its own fertility". Its **population** is today estimated at between twelve and fourteen million and is swollen by a further million commuters from the Delta and a thousand new migrants every day. One third of Cairene households lack running water; a quarter of them have no sewers, either. Up to 500,000 people reside in squatted cemeteries – the famous **Cities of the Dead**. The amount of green space per citizen has been calculated at thirteen square centimetres, not enough to cover a child's palm. Whereas earlier travellers noted that Cairo's air smelt "like hot bricks", visitors now find throat-rasping air **pollution**, chiefly caused by traffic. Breathing the atmosphere downtown is reputedly akin to smoking thirty cigarettes a day.

Cairo's genius is to humanise these inescapable realities with **social rituals**. The rarity of public violence owes less to the armed police on every corner than to the *dowshah*. When conflicts arise crowds gather, restrain both parties, encourage them to rant, sympathise with their grievances and then finally urge: *"Maalesh, maalesh"* (Let it be forgiven). Everyday life is sweetened by flowery gestures and salutations; misfortunes evoke thanks for Allah's dispensation (after all, things could be worse!). Even the poorest can be respected for piety; in the mosque, millionaire and beggar kneel side by side.

Extended-family values and neighbourly intervention prevail throughout the *baladi* quarters or **urban villages** where millions of first- and second-generation rural migrants live, whilst arcane structures underpin life in Islamic Cairo. On a city-wide basis, the colonial distinction between "native quarters" and *ifrangi* (foreign) districts has given way to a dynamic stasis between rich and poor, westernisation and traditionalism, complacency and desperation. Every year the polarities intensify, safety margins narrow, statistics make gloomier reading. The

---

A BRIEF HISTORICAL OUTLINE

Cairo reveals its history in a succession of sights and quarters and it's in the descriptions of these areas that we've provided the relevant background. What follows is the briefest of outlines, with page references for the main accounts.

Cairo is an agglomeration of half a dozen cities, the earliest of which came into existence 2500 years *after* ancient **Memphis**, the first capital of pharaonic Egypt, was founded (c.3100 BC) across the river and to the south. During the heyday of the Old Kingdom, vast necropoli developed along the desert's edge as the pharaohs erected ever greater funerary monuments, from the first Step Pyramid at **Saqqara** to the unsurpassable **Pyramids of Giza** (for more on this part of the history, see p.168–191). Meanwhile, across the Nile, flourished a sister-city of priests and solar cults known to posterity as **ancient Heliopolis** (see p.149).

It took centuries of Persian, Greek and Roman rule to efface both cities, by which time a new fortified town had developed on the opposite bank. **Babylon-in-Egypt** was the beginning of the tale of cities that culminates in modern Cairo, the first chapter of which is described under "Old Cairo" (p.121–134). Oppressed by foreign overlords, Babylon's citizens almost welcomed the army of Islam which conquered Egypt in 641. For strategic and spiritual reasons, their general, Amr, chose to found a new settlement beyond the walls of Babylon – **Fustat**, the "City of the Tent", which evolved into a sophisticated metropolis whilst Europe was in the Dark Ages.

abyss beckons in prognoses of **future trends**, yet Cairo confounds doomsayers by dancing on the edge.

Orientation and information

Greater Cairo consists of two metropolitan governorates: **Cairo**, on the east bank of the Nile, and **Giza**, across the river. The **River Nile** (*Bahr el-Nil*, or simply *el-Nil*) is the prerequisite of their existence and fundamental to basic orientation. Bear in mind that it flows northwards through the city, so that "down-river" means north, and "upriver" south, a reversal of the usual associations. The city's waterfront is dominated by the **islands** of Gezira and Roda and the **bridges** that connect them to the **Corniche** (embankment) on either side of the Nile.

There are four major divisions of the city:

● **Central Cairo** spreads inland to the east of the islands. Its **downtown** area – between Ezbekiya Gardens and the transportation hub of **Midan Tahrir** – bears the stamp of Western planning, as does **Garden City**, the embassy quarter farther south. At the northern end of central Cairo (beyond the downtown area) lies **Ramses Station**, the city's main railway terminus. Most of the banks, airlines, cheap hotels and tourist restaurants lie within this swathe of the city.

● Farther east sprawls **Islamic Cairo**, encompassing **Khan el-Khalili** bazaar, the Gamaliya quarter within the **Northern Walls** and the labyrinthine Darb al-Ahmar district between the **Bab Zwayla** and the **Citadel**, beyond which spread the eerie **Cities of the Dead** – the Northern and Southern Cemeteries.

● The Southern Cemetery and the populous **Saiyida Zeinab** quarter merge into the rubbish tips and wasteland bordering the **ruins of Fustat** and the **Coptic quarter** of **Old Cairo**, farther to the south. From there, a ribbon of development follows the Metro out to **Ma'adi**, Cairo's plushest residential suburb, and

Under successive dynasties of *khalifs* who ruled the Islamic Empire from Iraq, three more cities were founded, each to the northeast of the previous one, which itself was either spurned or devastated. When the schismatic Fatimids won the khalifate in 969, they created an entirely new walled city – **al-Qahira** – beyond this teeming, half-derelict conurbation. **Fatimid Cairo** formed the nucleus of the later, vastly expanded and consolidated capital that Salah al-Din (Saladin) left to the Ayyubid dynasty in 1193. But their reliance on imported slave-warriors caused power to ebb to these Mamlukes, ushering in a new era.

Mamluke Cairo encompassed all the previous cities, Salah al-Din's Citadel (where the sultans dwelt), the northern port of Bulaq and vast cemeteries and rubbish tips beyond the city walls. Mamluke sultans like Beybars, Qalaoun, Barquq and Qaitbey erected mosques, mausoleums and caravanserais that still enoble what is now called "Islamic Cairo". The like-named section of this chapter relates their stories, the Turkish takeover, the decline of **Ottoman Cairo** and the rise of Mohammed Ali, who began the modernisation of the city. Under Ismail, the most profligate of his successors, a new, increasingly **European Cairo** arose beside the Nile (see "Central Cairo"). During this century, Cairo's residential suburbs have expanded relentlesssly, swallowing up farmland and desert. The emergence of this **Greater Cairo** is charted under "Gezira and the West Bank" and "The Northern Suburbs".

Helwan, the city's heaviest industrial centre. Except for stylish **Heliopolis**, the **northern suburbs** likewise hold little appeal for visitors.

● Across the river on the west bank, the residential neighbourhoods of **Aguza** and **Dokki** aren't as smart as **Mohandiseen** or the high-rise northern end of **Gezira** island, known as **Zamalek**. The **Imbaba** district is only notable for its weekly **Camel Market**, but the dusty expanse of **Giza** (which lends its name to the west bank urban zone) is enlivened by **Cairo Zoo** and the nightclub-infested **Pyramids Road** leading to the **Pyramids of Giza**.

Maps and addresses

Cairo's more interesting areas are mapped in detail alongside their descriptions in this chapter. These **maps** – and the general plan overpage – should suffice for most sightseeing needs, although for an overview of the city they can't match that provided by *Lehnert & Landrock* city-plans, sold at most tourist bookshops (£E7). The free "souvenir" map issued by American Express conveys the city's layout even better, but can't be relied upon for navigation. The annually updated *Cairo: A Practical Guide* (£E20) also contains a useful set of maps, while most detailed of all is the weighty *Cairo A–Z* (£E25), whose five-year compilation was an epic task: the editor's phone was bugged and his researchers were tailed by Security agents, despite being authorised by the Ministry of the Interior.

It helps to memorise a few **geographical terms**. *Sharia* means "street" and always precedes the name (eg Sharia Talaat Harb). *Midan* denotes a square or open space. Narrower thoroughfares may be termed *Darb*, *Haret* or *Sikket*, instead of Sharia. *Bab* signifies a medieval gate, after which certain quarters are named (eg Bab el-Khalq); *Kubri* a bridge, and *Souk* a market. **Street names** are posted in English (or French) and Arabic in central Cairo and Zamalek; almost everywhere else in Arabic only, or not at all. The same goes for **numbers**, rendered in Western and Arabic numerals, or just the latter; a single number may denote a whole block with several entrance passageways – something to remember when you're following up addresses.

Don't expect **Cairenes** themselves to relate to maps; they comprehend their city differently. That said, however, people are remarkably helpful to visitors, going out of their way to steer them in the right direction; offer profuse thanks, but never *baksheesh* (which will offend in this situation).

Tourist offices and police

Cairo's downtown tourist office (☎391-3454) at 5 Sharia Adly (daily 8am–7pm) can supply a copy of *Cairo By Night* (see "Entertainments") and a useless free map, but little in the way of hard facts. After some sweet-talking, however, they will make enquiries over the phone, or write down questions or requests in Arabic to show other people who can help you out. There are also tourist offices at Cairo International Airport (☎667-475) and the Giza Pyramids (☎850-259).

Should the need arise, an alleyway to the left of the Sharia Adly office gives access to the headquarters of the **tourist police** (☎926-028), open 24 hours. Whether they're helpful or a waste of time largely depends on who you encounter; for serious matters, try to deal with Captain Tewfik. Other tourist police stations can be found at Ramses Station (☎764-214), Cairo Airport (☎692-584), the Giza Pyramids (☎850-259), Khan el-Khalili (☎904-827) and the Egyptian Antiquities Museum (☎754-319).

Points of arrival

Arriving in a big city can be a daunting experience, but you needn't worry about Cairo. Being overcharged by a taxi driver and spending your first night in a second-rate hotel is the worst that can happen to newcomers. Hustlers might try to lure you into overpriced perfume shops, but elaborate swindles are rare and robbery with violence is unheard of. If you're flying in from abroad, be sure to fill out the **customs declaration** on arrival (see "Red Tape" in *Basics*) and **register** with the authorities within seven days (see "Bureaucracy", p.222).

By air

Cairo International Airport has two main terminals, roughly 3km apart. **Terminal 1** (known as the old airport) is used by Egyptian carriers, *El Al* and most Arab, African and Eastern European airlines. Western European and US airlines use **Terminal 2** (aka the new airport).

Emerging from customs, you'll be waylaid by taxi drivers who'll swear that they're the only way of **getting into town**. Usually, this isn't so, but you might prefer going **by taxi** anyway. Though the fare is officially £E19, you'll have to bargain for it; most drivers start by quoting £E25–30.

On one side of Terminal 1's forecourt is the stop for #400 buses and #27 mini-buses to Midan Tahrir (45min–1hr). The **bus** (15pt) leaves roughly every half-hour by day, hourly late at night or early in the morning. The **minibus** (50pt) also operates 24 hours, but infrequently at night. The #422 bus from Terminal 2 to Midan Tahrir is unreliable after dark, but a free, CAA **shuttle bus** runs all through the night to Terminal 1.

Besides the above options, there's a **limousine taxi service** (£E14 per head; maximum four persons) next to Terminal 1's *Masr Travel* stand, which also runs an **airport service bus** (minimum five persons) that drops passengers at any hotel in central Cairo (£E13 per head) or Giza (£E4 extra).

By bus

Buses from Israel, Jordan and the Sinai usually wind up at the **Sinai Bus Terminal** (aka Abbassiya Station), 4km from the centre. Taxis outside often overcharge newcomers and try to inveigle them into hotels: resist them – Cairenes would feel generous if they paid £E3 for a black-and-white cab, or £E1 per person for a full seven-seater "special" taxi into the centre from here. Alternatively, turn left outside the station and walk on past the flyover to the hospital on Sharia Ramses, where you can catch a #32 minibus to Midan Tahrir (35pt).

Coming in from Bahariya or other oases on the great desert circuit, you'll end up at the **al-Azhar Bus Terminal**, midway between central and Islamic Cairo. If you turn left outside, it's a 400-metre walk beneath the flyover to Midan Ataba; turn right and head the other way to reach the al-Azhar Mosque in the heart of Islamic Cairo. Buses or *service* taxis from the Canal Zone or the Red Sea Coast drop passengers at the **Koulali Terminal** off Midan Ramses or the **Ahmed Helmi Terminal** behind Ramses Station.

By train

All trains into Cairo stop at **Ramses Station** (see map on p.80). There are hotels nearby, but the neighbourhood is so grotty that most visitors prefer to head downtown by metro, taxi (£E1.50) or bus #95 (along Sharia Ramses).

GREATER CAIRO

To Tanta

To Po

SHUBRA
EL-KHEIMA

River Nile

To Sadat City

Shubra
Palace

SHARIA BUR SAID

SHUBRA
AL-BALAD

HADA'IQ
AL-QUBBA

CORNICHE

SHARIA SHUBRA

ROD
EL-
FARAG

SHARIA RAMSES

Ain
Sham
Univers

IMBABA

ZAMALEK

BULAQ

Ramses
Station
2

4

8

Camel
Market

26TH JULY

MOHANDISEEN

GEZIRA

1

al-Azhar
Bus Station

3

SHARIA SALAH SALEM

AGUZA

Midan Tahrir

5

SHARIA AL-SUDAN

6

DOKKI

SAIYIDA
ZEINAB

Citadel

7

BULAQ
AL-DAKHROUR

Zoo

RODA

GIZA

OLD CAIRO

9

(MASR
AL-QADIMA)

EL
KHALIFA

0   2 km

Giza Station

Site of
Fustat

River Nile

10

To the
Pyramids

To the
Nile Valley

To Ma'adi, Helwan
& Minya

To
Sadat
City

To
Matariyya

To Ismailiya

EL-ZEITUN

Buses for
Cairo

Ter

Cairo International
Airport

Terminal 2

**HELIOPOLIS
(MASR EL-JEDIDA)**

Quba
Palace

SHARIA AL-HIGAZ

SHARIA AL-AHRAM

Midan Roxi

SHARIA AL-URUBAH

SHARIA MERGHANI

NOUZHA

Baron
Empain's
Palace

ILI

Nasser's
Tomb

ABBASSIYA

Cairo Stadium

To Suez

Sinai Bus
Terminal

Sadat's
Tomb

**MEDINET
NASR**

SHARIA SIKKIT AL-BAYDAH

Key to Map Enlargements
1. Central Cairo
2. Around Ramses Station
3. Around Khan el-Khalili & al-Azhar
4. To the Northern Gates
5. Between al-Azhar & the Bab Zwayla
6. Between Bab Zwayla & the Citadel
7. The Citadel
8. The Northern Cemetery
9. Around Ibn Tulun & the Southern Cemetery
10. Old Cairo & Roda Island

Muqattam Hills

Petrified
Forest

o al-Basatin

Getting around

Despite Cairo's complexity, **getting around** is relatively straightforward. The metro is simple to use, and taxis inexpensive once you understand their system. Familiarise yourself with Arabic numerals (see "Language" in *Contexts*) and you can also use buses and minibuses, which reach most parts of the city.

Since everyone drives like participants in the Paris–Dakar Rally, you might as well resign yourself to this. Accidents are surprisingly rare, all things considered. Unless you enjoy sweltering in traffic jams, it's best to avoid travelling during **rush hours** (9–11am & 3–7pm), when the streets are choked.

The metro

Cairo's **metro** (the first in the Arab world) works like nothing else in the city: pristine and efficient, with a well-enforced ban on littering and smoking. Trains run every few minutes from 6am to 1am; outside of peak hours (7–9am, 4–7pm) they are rarely crowded – indeed, only a minority of Cairenes can afford the fares.

Stations are signposted with a large "M"; signs and route maps appear in Arabic and English. **Tickets** (25–50pt) are purchased in the station; twin sets of booths cater for passengers heading in opposite directions, with separate queues for either sex. Hang onto your ticket to get through the automatic barriers at the other end. Travelling without a ticket will result in a fine (£E5).

The existing (red) metro line connects the northeastern suburb of El Marg with the southern industrial district of Helwan. From a tourist's standpoint, there are only six **crucial stations** (listed here from north to south):

Mubarak, beneath Midan Ramses, is for reaching or leaving Ramses Station.

Nasser, two stops on, leads onto 26th July Street near the top end of Talaat Harb (take the High Court exit).

Sadat, the most used (and useful) station, is set beneath Midan Tahrir, and doubles as a pedestrian underpass.

Saiyida Zeinab, two stops beyond, lies midway between that quarter and the northern end of Roda Island.

El-Malek el-Saleh, the next stop, can serve for exploring parts of Old Cairo.

Mari Girgis is the most useful stop for Coptic Cairo and Amr's Mosque.

Two more lines are planned for the future: **Shubra el-Kheima to Bulaq al-Dakhrour** (via Ramses, Ataba and Tahrir) and **Dirasa to Imbaba** (via al-Azhar, Ataba and Zamalek). If ever they materialise, Cairo will be rapidly traversable for the first time in modern history.

Taxis

The city has three kinds of taxi: **black-and-white cabs**, **service taxis** and **"specials"**. Though each requires different handling, some general rules apply. Firstly, choose the right sort of taxi. Secondly, try to discover the fare in advance; never start by asking how much. Third, don't expect drivers to speak English or know the location of every street. Identify a major landmark or thoroughfare in the vicinity and state that instead. If your destination is obscure or hard to pronounce, get it written down in Arabic. The best kind to use are four-seater **black-and-white taxis** (Fiats or Ladas), which often carry passengers collectively. Pick a major thoroughfare with traffic heading in the right direction, stand on the kerb, wave and holler out your destination (eg "Mohandiseen") as one approaches; if the driver's interested he'll stop and wait for you to run over. State your destination

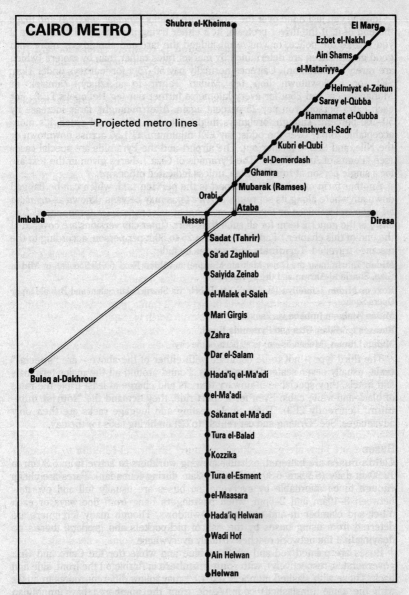

CAIRO METRO

Shubra el-Kheima

El Marg
Ezbet el-Nakhl
Ain Shams
el-Matariyya
Helmiyat el-Zeitun
Saray el-Qubba
Hammamat el-Qubba
Menshyet el-Sadr
Kubri el-Qubi
el-Demerdash
Ghamra
Mubarak (Ramses)

Orabi

Ataba

Imbaba

Nasser

Dirasa

Projected metro lines

Sadat (Tahrir)
Sa'ad Zaghloul
Saiyida Zeinab
el-Malek el-Saleh
Mari Girgis
Zahra
Dar el-Salam
Hada'iq el-Ma'adi
el-Ma'adi
Sakanat el-Ma'adi
Tura el-Balad
Kozzika
Tura el-Esment
el-Maasara
Hada'iq Helwan
Wadi Hof
Ain Helwan
Helwan

Bulaq al-Dakhrour

again, in more detail. If the driver starts talking money, say "forget it" (*maaleysh*) and look for another cab; otherwise jump in. Don't be alarmed by the circuitous routes taken to avoid bottlenecks, nor by other people getting in along the way. Near the end, direct him to stop where you want (bearing in mind one-way systems and other obstacles) with " *hina/hinak kwayees*" (here/there's okay).

Ideally, you just hand over the money with thanks (*itfuddel*, *shukran*) and that's the end of it. If the driver protests, he's either trying it on and will back down if you invoke the police, or you've misjudged the fare and should pay more with good grace. **Fares** are determined by market rates rather than by meters (which are rarely switched on). Cairenes normally pay 50–75pt for journeys under 1km; £E1 for a downtown hop (eg Midan Tahrir to al-Azhar), Zamalek or Mohandiseen; and 25pt for every kilometre further out (eg Heliopolis £E3). For each extra person, you pay 25 percent again. After midnight, fares increase by 50–100 percent. Though foreigners might get away with **local rates**, it's more acceptable to pay over the odds: say £E1 minimum, £E1.50 across downtown or the Nile, and £E3–6 further out. The airport and the Pyramids are special cases (see "Points of Arrival" and "The Pyramids of Giza"). Fares given in the text are for a single person at **tourist rates**, unless indicated otherwise.

Another form of collective transport is the **service taxi**, which can be flagged down anywhere along its set route. *Service* taxis may be vans (known as *arrabeya bil nafar*, microbuses or taxi-vans) or Peugeot saloons; *service* (pronounced "*serviis*") is the generic term for all such transport. (Inter-city versions are covered at the end of this chapter.) Fares range from 25 to 50pt per person, according to the distance travelled. **Terminals and routes** include:

Midan Tahrir (near the Omar Makram Mosque) to **Midan Roxi** (in Heliopolis), or **Midan Giza**, **Sharia al-Ahram** and **the Pyramids**.

Roxi or **Midan Ismailiya** (Heliopolis) to **Tahrir** via Sharia Salah Salem and Bab al-Luq or Opera Square.

Midan Ataba to **Imbaba** via Zamalek.

Ramses to **Midan Giza** and **Pyramids Road**.

Midan Libnan (Mohandiseen) to all parts of the city.

The third type – not to be confused with either of the above – are **"special" taxis**, usually seven-seater Peugeot 504s. Found around all the major terminals and hotels, they specialise in unwary tourists and charge at least triple the rates of black-and-white cabs. Even for a short ride, they demand the **"tourist minimum"** (currently £E3). Their ample seating and luggage racks are their only advantages. See "Driving and car rental" (p.62) on hiring taxis for the day.

Buses

Cairo's **buses** are battered, exhaust-spewing workhorses, active from 5.30am to 12.30am daily (6.30am–6.30pm, 7.30pm–2am during Ramadan). Fares are cheap enough to be affordable by everyone, so buses are usually full and overflow between 8–10am and 2–6pm, when passengers hang from doorways or each other and clamber in and out through windows. Though many foreigners are deterred from using buses by the risk of pickpockets and gropers, there's no denying that the network reaches virtually everywhere.

Buses are painted red and white or blue and white (for the Cairo and Giza governorates, respectively), with **route numbers** in Arabic on the front, side and back. Those with slashed numbers (eg *13/*) may follow different routes to buses with the same (unslashed) code. Aside from the numbered bays on Midan Tahrir, few **stops** are clearly signposted (look for metal shelters, plaques on lampposts or crowds waiting), and buses generally slow down instead of halting, compelling passengers to board and disembark on the run. Except at terminals, you must enter through the rear door (which is often removed to facilitate access); at official stops, you're supposed to exit from the front. Conductors sell **tickets** (10–15pt) from behind a crush-bar by the rear door. The front of the bus is usually less crowded, so it's worth squeezing your way forwards; start edging towards the exit well before your destination.

Most buses start from (or pass through) one of the smog-bound **terminals on Midan Tahrir**. Write the number(s) in Arabic to show to enquiry booths or bystanders, who'll point you towards the right lane. If possible, ask the conductor *"Raiya li . . .?"* (are you going to . . .?) to make sure.

FROM THE NILE HILTON TERMINAL
Services to Islamic Cairo are usually packed. To reach Ramses Station, catch any bus from the easternmost bay (nearest to Tahrir Square).

#50 Midan Ramses, Abbassiya
#60 Aguza
#63 and #66 al-Azhar, Khan el-Khalili
#72 Saiyida Zeinab, Ibn Tulun, the Citadel
#73 Imbaba (camel market)
#75 Museum of Islamic Arts, Bab Zwayla
#99 Midan Libnan (Mohandiseen)
#128 and #350 Ain Shams
#173 and #403 the Citadel
#302 Shubra al-Balad
#400 Heliopolis, Cairo Airport (Terminal 1)
#422 Heliopolis, Cairo Airport (Terminal 2)
#500 Midan Barquq and Heliopolis *or* the Giza Sheraton
#510 Heliopolis

FROM THE MUGAMMA TERMINAL
Between 7am and 7pm, all services to Manial and Giza or Islamic Cairo are very crowded.

#6 and #803 Midan Giza
#8 and #900 Qasr al-Aini, Manial, Pyramids (Mena House)
#16 Midan Dokki, Aguza
#160 Saiyida Zeinab, al-Basatin (Jewish Cemetery)
#166 Bulaq al-Dakhrour
#174 Saiyida Zeinab, Ibn Tulun, the Citadel
#182 Saiyida Zeinab, Imam al-Shafi'i Mausoleum
#913 directly to the Sphinx

FROM THE ARAB LEAGUE TERMINAL (50m BEFORE THE TAHRIR BRIDGE)
#13 Zamalek
#110, #182 and #203 Dokki

Minibuses
During the early 1980s, the Cairo governorate introduced orange-and-white **mini-buses** along many of the existing bus routes. Besides making better headway through traffic and actually halting at stops, they are far more comfortable and never crowded, as standing is not permitted. Tickets (25–50pt – prohibitively expensive for most Cairenes) are bought from the driver. Minibuses should not be confused with the older, multicoloured taxi-vans (see *service* taxis, above).

Midan Tahrir has two minibus terminals; others are found in Mohandiseen, Giza and Heliopolis (detailed as relevant in the text). It's possible that minibuses assigned to one Tahrir depot in the following rundown will leave from the other in the future. Ask on the spot.

FROM THE MUGAMMA TERMINAL
#2 Shubra al-Balad
#24 Ramses, Abbassiya, Heliopolis (Midan Roxi)
#27 Heliopolis (Midan Ismailiya), Airport (Terminal 1)
#32 Abbassiya, near the Sinai Terminal
#35 Abbassiya, Midan Ismailiya
#52 and **#56** Old Cairo, Ma'adi
#54 Saiyida Zeinab, Citadel, Sharia Imam al-Shafi'i
#59 Ramses Station *or* Old Cairo
#82 Qasr al-Aini, Giza, Sharia Faisal, Pyramids
#83 Dokki, Giza, Pyramids Road

FROM THE ARAB LEAGUE TERMINAL
The following services run in both directions from Tahrir. To reach the first destination listed, look for minibuses on the Egyptian Museum side; services to the latter destination leave from the Mugamma side.
#26 Midan Roxi *or* Dokki and Giza
#76 Midan Ataba and Zamalek *or* Bulaq al-Dakhrour
#77 Khan el-Khalili *or* Bulaq al-Dakhrour
#84 Midan Ataba *or* Dokki and Giza

Trams and river-taxis
As the metro and minibus systems expand, Cairo's original **tram network** (built in colonial times) is being phased out. Although the Heliopolis tram system will doubtless survive and remain useful (see "The Northern Suburbs" for details), we've paid less attention to other lines. Where trams *are* mentioned in the text, it's wise to check that services are still running. Like buses, they are cheap and battered with standing-room only; their Arabic route numbers are posted above the driver's cab.

The most relaxing way to reach Old Cairo is by river-taxi. **River-taxis** (aka waterbuses) leave from the Maspero Dock outside the Television Building, 600m north of the Antiquities Museum. Boats run every thirty to forty minutes to Old Cairo (via Giza and Roda), or over to Imbaba and thence to the Nile Barrages (see "Excursions from Cairo"). Buy tickets (25–50pt) at the dock.

Driving and car rental
The only thing scarier than **driving in Cairo** is cycling, which is tantamount to suicide. Dashes, crawls and finely judged evasions are the order of the day; donkey carts and jaywalkers trust in motorists' swift reactions. Any collision draws a crowd instantly. Minor dents are often settled by on-the-spot payoffs; should injury occur, it's wise to involve a cop right away, lest passions get uncontrollable. Multistorey car parks such as the one on Midan Ataba are ignored as motorists park bumper-to-bumper along every kerb, leaving their handbrakes off so vehicles can be shifted by the local *minairdy* (whom they tip 25pt–£E1). Given all this, it's no surprise that few foreigners drive in Cairo.

To rent a car you must be at least 25 years old and have an International Driving Licence. At last count, the cheapest of the "big three" agencies was *Hertz* (offices at the *Ramses Hilton, President Hotel* and Cairo Airport), which rents out Fiat 128s for the equivalent of $10 per day ($72 per week), plus 11 cents per kilometre, 12 percent tax and $5 daily collision waiver (insurance included). *Avis* or *Budget* (also found in big hotels) may do better deals in the future, while other companies worth checking include:

Europcar (24-hour service), 8 Sharia Qasr el-Nil (☎774-330).

Bita, 15 Sharia Mahmoud Bassiouni (☎774-330).

Cairo Car, 6b Sharia al-Salouli, Dokki (☎988-146).

Sunshine Tours, 106 Sharia Mohammed Farid (☎760-559).

Many of these agencies offer the preferable and reasonably priced option of **hired cars with drivers**. Average rates for a driver are around £E20 for a ten-hour day, plus £E5 for each extra hour of driving time. For overnight trips, you'll also be expected to pay about £E25 per night for his expenses and trouble. For shorter jaunts, consider hiring a chauffeur-driven Mercedes from *Misr Limousine* (☎259-9813; desks at major hotels), which charges £E13 an hour for local, one-day trips; or *Europcar* (☎340-8888). These rates can be used as a benchmark should you prefer to negotiate directly with "special" taxi drivers or anyone else.

Walking

The one advantage of Cairo's density is that many places of interest are within **walking** distance of Midan Tahrir or other transport ganglions. You can walk across downtown Cairo from Tahrir to Midan Ataba in fifteen to thirty minutes; the same again brings one to Khan el-Khalili in the heart of Islamic Cairo. Starting from here or the Citadel, you can make fascinating hikes through the medieval quarter, which doesn't suit other methods of exploration.

Arguably, walking is the only way to experience the city's pulsating streetlife. Though pavements are congested with vendors and pedestrians, they weave gracefully around each other, without the bullish jostlings of Western capitals. The commonest irritants are rubbish, noxious fumes and puddles, uneven pavements and gaping drains; in poorer quarters, the last two may not even exist. Women travellers must also reckon with gropers, who chiefly strike along Talaat Harb and around the Khan. Close proximity to a male escort confers some immunity, but the best solution is to develop an instant response (see "From a Woman's Perspective" in *Basics*).

COPING WITH TRAFFIC

To make faster headway you can walk along the edge of the road – obviously, always *facing* oncoming traffic. **Traffic** is heavy from 8am to midnight, and ceases for a few hours before dawn. Its daytime flow only diminishes during Ramadan, major football matches, and the midday prayer on Fridays, when many side streets are carpeted over and used as mosques.

At all times, crossing the road takes boldness. Drivers will slow down to give people time to dart across, but dithering or freezing midway confuses them and increases the risk of an accident. A prolonged horn-burst indicates that the driver can't or won't stop. Remember that motorists obey police signals rather than traffic lights, which were only installed in the 1980s and have yet to acquire any real local credibility.

Accommodation

Cairo is packed with **accommodation** to suit every tourist's taste and budget. Before the Gulf War decimated tourism, most hotels were busy or full through December and January, whilst the cheapest ones were also flooded with backpackers over the summer. Given time, this pattern will doubtless reassert itself, but meanwhile it's a buyer's market. Many hotels have held last year's **prices** or cut their rates to win back custom; even the ritziest may be into haggling if business remains slack – but price hikes are inevitable once trade recovers.

In the meantime, **hotel touts** compete more fiercely than ever. At Cairo Airport they masquerade as blazered "tourist officials" keen to book you into the dearest hotel that'll wash (say, £E40 a night for backpackers); downtown, they're more likely touting budget hotels. Taxi drivers are also on the game and may claim a split from both parties.

Yet **finding a room** needn't be traumatic if you take control of the situation. Officials can telephone about vacancies on your behalf from the airport, or you can simply hail a taxi and begin visiting downtown hotels (keyed to our map of central Cairo). Although the front doors of many blocks are locked at midnight, the doorman (*bowab*) can always be rousted.

Hotels and pensions

Cairo's hotels reflect the city's diversity: deluxe chains overlooking the Nile; functional high-rises; colonial piles and homely pensions with the same raddled facades as bug-infested flophouses. **Standards** vary within any given price range or star rating – and from room to room in many places. Try to inspect the facilities (A/C is air conditioning) before checking in. Also establish the price and any service tax or extra charges (which should be posted in reception) at the outset.

Hotels with three or more stars require payment in $US, or Egyptian currency backed by an exchange receipt. Offically, rates are the same all year, with an annual rise in early October. Bear in mind that **prices** specified below will inevitably become outdated, but comparative rates shouldn't change much.

DELUXE AND FOUR-STAR HOTELS – CITY WIDE

All the international chains are represented in Cairo, which has over thirty hotels with four- or five-star (deluxe) rating. At the time of writing most stand half-empty and will probably give discounts with a bit of arm-twisting, but as trade revives their prices will doubtless revert to the level indicated below (and then rise). Moderately flush visitors should take advantage while they can. Our **city wide selection** boasts fine locations, superlative facilities or splendid decor. The first four (sited on or near Midan Tahrir) are marked on our map of central Cairo (see p.74); the others can hardly be missed once you're in the vicinity.

Nile Hilton (☎740-777; telex 92222 HILTLS UN). Sited between Midan Tahrir and the Nile, this recently refurbished Fifties block is one of the first landmarks you'll get to recognise in

Cairo. In addition to the hotel, it contains a range of cafés and restaurants: the *Taverne du Champs de Mars*, *Ibis Café*, *Hilton Pizzeria* and *El Nile Rotisserie*. River-facing doubles cost $173 ($138 at the singles rate); rooms overlooking Tahrir are slightly cheaper. Winter night-club on the roof; during summer, action revolves around the pool.

Ramses Hilton (☎758-000/☎744-400; telex 94262 HIRAM UN). Cairo's tallest hotel, with three-storey atrium and glass elevator; pool, bars, restaurants and nightclub. Rooms are luxurious to a fault. Doubles $148–160; rented as singles for $115–130 plus $16 surcharge.

Semiramis Intercontinental (☎355-7171; telex 94257 IHC SM). Elegant rooms with every facility; gym, pool, *Al Rashid* nightclub. Singles $139–157; doubles $174–197; the dearer rooms have Nile views.

Shepheard's Hotel (☎355-3800; telex 21379 SHEPT UN). A 1950s, Nile-side version of the famous nineteenth-century establishment that stood on Opera Square. Currently being upgraded to five-star standards. Singles $80; doubles $97; rooms on the quieter side facing the Muqattam Hills are fractionally cheaper.

Hotel Meridien-Le Caire (☎845-444; telex HOMER UN). French-managed pile at the northern tip of Roda Island, commanding a superb river view and incorporating a French restaurant, nightclub, bars and 24-hour coffee shop. Singles $116; doubles $144; ten poolside cabanas costing $23 per day.

Manial Palace Club Mediterranee (☎846-014; telex 92353 MANIAL UN). Occupying half the grounds of the Manial palace on Roda Island, the *Manial*'s 2–6 person A/C bungalows are normally full of Club Med holidaymakers, but in off-season might be available for $90 for a double, roughly $70 for single occupancy, mandatory half-board included.

Cairo Marriott Hotel (☎340-8888; telex 93465 MAR UN). Modern guest rooms built around the lavish palace constructed to house Empress Eugenie in 1869. Singles $160; doubles $180. Restaurants, nightclub and pool; guests may use facilities at the *Gezira Club*, across the road. Non-residents can drink or dine in the khedival salons and billiard room.

El Gezirah Sheraton (☎341-1555; telex 22812 GEZEL UN). Overlooking the Nile from the southern end of Gezira Island, with a shuttle service to the Antiquities Museum across the river. Regular rooms $155; deluxe singles ($178) and doubles ($198) in the tower. *El Samar* restaurant-nightclub and *Regine's* disco.

Mena House Oberoi (☎857-999; telex 93096 OBHTL UN). Set in lush grounds near the Giza Pyramids, this one-time khedival hunting lodge witnessed Roosevelt and Churchill initiate the D-Day plan, and the formal signing of the peace treaty between Israel and Egypt. Its renovated arabesque halls and nineteenth-century rooms (singles $115; doubles $144) are delightful; the modern Mena Gardens annexe isn't. *Moghul* restaurant; pool, golf course and tennis courts; shuttle bus into town.

MID-RANGE PLACES, CHEAP HOTELS AND PENSIONS

The mid-range of the budgetry spectrum chiefly consists of **three-star hotels** whose rooms have private bathrooms and A/C, perhaps also fridges, phones and TV. If facilities fall short of what's advertised (and charged for), you're entitled to raise a stink. However, a couple of places in the centre are (more or less) refurbished colonial edifices whose old-world charm makes up for any trifling lack of modern gadgetry.

Budget travellers usually go for the **cheap hotels and pensions** on the upper floors of downtown office blocks. Designed to exlude sunlight and circulate air during summer, the unheated ones can be damp and draughty in winter. During the summer, bedbugs and mosquitoes may infest seedier places where hot water (or any water at all) is often lacking. By way of compensation some feature Art Deco rooms with sweeping balconies, and all can provide bottled water, tea and soft drinks. Most are reached from street level via an alleyway and/or lobby serving the entire building. Riding the elevators can feel like playing Russian roulette, but we've never heard of serious accidents.

The following rundown is by no means exhaustive, focusing as it does on places that are cheap, agreeable, or conveniently located (a few combine all these assets) – or bad enough to merit a warning. Rather than categorise them by fickle prices, we've listed hotels according to location, the areas corresponding to descriptive sections (and maps) in this chapter.

Garden City and the Abdin Quarter

Though deluxe hotels such as *Shepheard's* (see above) predominate, Garden City features one affordable option, and a somewhat less than desirable fallback on the edge of the Abdin quarter. Both are indicated on the map of central Cairo (see p.74).

Garden City House (keyed **A**), behind the *Semiramis Intercontinental* (☎354-4969). The Nile views from some rooms give this Thirties-style pension an edge on the otherwise superior *Anglo-Swiss* and *Pensione Roma* (see below). Singles £E25 (£E30 with shower); doubles £E42 (£E48); £E16 for an extra bed. Breakfast and one other meal included. Reservations essential.

Hotel Sphinx (Z) (☎355-7439). A tacky tower block east of the National Assembly, favoured by airport taxi touts. Singles, doubles and triples with private bathrooms for anywhere between £E20 and £E65; the singles are noisy holes; the doubles mangy suites with balconies facing the Citadel.

Downtown – between Tahrir and Ezbekiya

Talaat Harb, Mahmoud Bassiouni and Qasr el-Nil streets offer the widest range of budget hotels. A few are excellent, or really squalid; the majority fall somewhere in between. Richer tourists can choose between comfortable modern hotels or a number of vintage establishments redolent of prewar high society. All are keyed on the map of central Cairo (see p.74).

Cleopatra Hotel (B), corner of Sharia Bustan and Midan Tahrir (☎708-751). A three-star block with kitsch Seventies decor, Italian and Korean restaurants, A/C rooms with baths and phones. Singles £E75; doubles £E100; triples £E120. Breakfast included.

Anglo-Swiss Hotel (C), 14 Sharia Champollion (☎751-479). Charming Thirties-style pension with a piano, library, nifty spiral staircase and dining room. Singles £E17; doubles £E30; triples £E35; breakfast included. Hot water in spotless shared bathrooms. Reservations advisable.

Hotel Viennoise (D), 11 Sharia Bassiouni (☎743-153; telex 94285 UNDOS UN). Atmospherically decrepit warren of huge rooms and *fin-de-siècle* lounges, used for filming a Ramadan soap opera. Check the water-heater in singles (£E18) or doubles (£E23) with showers before accepting. Overpriced, but might appeal to some.

Hotel Suisse (E), 26 Sharia Bassiouni (☎746-639). Grubby but friendly, with hot water in the shared (if not the private) bathrooms. Singles £E10; doubles £E15; triples £E21; breakfast included.

Tulip Hotel (F), 3 Midan Talaat Harb (☎758-433). Decent old-style place facing *Groppi's*. Singles £E11 (£E13–15 with shower or bath); doubles £E16 (£E18–E20); triples £E21 (£E23–25). Hot water. Breakfast included.

Lotus Hotel (G), 12 Sharia Talaat Harb (☎750-627; telex 93839 DOSS UN, attention Lotus Hotel). Reception on the seventh floor, reached via an arcade signposted *Malév*. Clean, with friendly staff. Singles £E20 (£E24 with bath and A/C); doubles (£E26) with showers (£E32) may be small and damp; hot water 6–9am and evenings. Breakfast included.

Golden Hotel (H), 13 Sharia Talaat Harb (☎742-659). Battered third-floor flophouse open to considering discounts. Singles (£E5), doubles (£E8) and triples (£E12) all have cold water bathrooms.

Amin Hotel (I), 38 Midan Falaki (☎779-813). Gloomy rooms with fans. Singles £E14–15, doubles £E17–19; it's worth paying for a room with private bathroom and constant hot water – the shared facilities aren't so clean. Near the footbridge leading to Bab al-Luq market.

Cosmopolitan Hotel (J), off Qasr el-Nil (☎755-715; telex 7451 COSMO UN). Refurbished, monumental Art Nouveau building with a Grecian restaurant, Olde-English bar, bank and international calls facility. All singles ($35) and doubles ($45) have A/C and private baths. Amex, Visa and Diners Club accepted.

Odeon Palace Hotel (K), west of Talaat Harb (☎776-637). Modern three-star block with restaurant, bar and roof garden. Singles £E80; doubles £E100; extra bed £E10. Breakfast included.

Hotel Beau-Site (L), 27 Talaat Harb (☎747-877). Shabby, amiable backpackers' haunt (sells beer) with occasionally hot showers. Singles £E10; doubles £E12; dormitory bed £E5. Lift to the fifth floor usually kaput. Over winter they screen a film every night.

Pensione de Famille (M), just west off Talaat Harb – look for the faded sign. Downtown Cairo's cheapest flophouse (£E3 per head) would be grotty even without its owner's devotion to cats.

Oxford Pension (N), 32 Talaat Harb (☎758-173). Legendary scuzzpit favoured by hardcore travellers and junkies. Since the owner's spell in prison, it is only "cleaner" in the figurative sense, with access to the (one) hot shower limited to favourites, who may also use the kitchen, customise their rooms, and get reduced rates. Newcomers charged about £E4.50 per person, £E2–3 to sleep in the corridor. Beware of thefts and bedbugs.

Hotel des Roses (O), 33 Talaat Harb (☎758-022). Only refurbished rooms in this Art Deco hostelry are worth considering. Singles £E10 (£E13 with shower); doubles £E13 (£E17); triples £E17 (£E21). Fans for £E3, hot water after 5pm. A juddering lift ride to the third floor.

Hotel Minerva (P), between Talaat Harb and Sharia Sherif. Dimly lit doubles (£E7) with dusty Empire-style antiques; atmospheric if you don't mind gloom and roaches, but lone women might feel uneasy.

Hotel Claridge (Q), noisy location over 26th July and Talaat Harb. Some rooms large and freshly painted, others cramped and grimy; sporadic hot water in shared bathrooms. Surly staff. Singles £E10; doubles £E20; triples £E27; breakfast included.

Grand Hotel (R), 17 26th July St (☎757-700). Aptly-named Art Deco edifice with original lifts and furniture, a fountain, restaurant and bar. Pre-Gulf War rates for singles (£E20/£E30 with shower), doubles (£E40/£E43 with A/C and TV) and triple suites (£E65) are currently discounted by £E5–15 – enjoy it while you can.

Hotel Select (S), beside the synagogue on Sharia Adly. Simple, mostly triple rooms (£E6 per bed) and hot water bathrooms, eight floors up.

Hotel Kasr el-Nil (T), 33 Qasr el-Nil (☎754-523). Nice terrace, but shares the ninth floor with a disco and reeks of cats. Singles (£E11), doubles (£E15) and suites (£E25) with showers; breakfast included.

Plaza Hotel (U), 37 Qasr el-Nil (☎392-1939). This eighth-floor backpackers' haven charges £E5 per head for large doubles and triples, breakfast included. Congenial atmosphere compensates for lukewarm water, sporadic bedbugs and general tattiness.

Pensione Roma (V), 169 Sharia Mohammed Farid – entrance round the side of the *Gattegno* department store (☎391-1088). The stylish Forties ambience, immaculately maintained by Madame Cressaty, comes highly recommended and reservations are essential (call at 9am or the night before). Constant hot water; shared and private bathrooms; laundry service. Singles £E13; doubles £E23; triples £E30. The local muezzin wails like Hendrix.

Windsor Hotel (W), 19 Sharia Alfi Bey (☎915-810; telex 93839 DOSS UN). Agreeably faded vintage colonial grandeur, bags of character and the nicest bar in Cairo – worth a splurge. Singles £E44 (£E67 with bath); doubles £E57 (£E86); A/C £E2 extra; breakfast included. Run by the Doss family; Madame Doss's father was Ramses Wissa Wassef, founder of the weaving school at Harraniyya (see p.177).

Crown Hotel (X), 9 Sharia Emad el-Din (☎918-374). Salubrious and roomy, with hot water in shared bathrooms, on the fifth floor. Singles £E10; doubles £E15; triples £E18; quads £E25.

Downtown – nearer Ramses Station

Arriving late or leaving early from one of the terminals around Midan Ramses, three places commend themselves despite their grim surroundings. Like some quieter hotels a bit nearer the centre, they're marked on the map on p.80. Avoid three total pits which aren't: the *Nobel, Ramses* and *Africa House*.

Fontana Hotel, Sharia Ramses (☎922-145). Comfortable, with mod cons and a swimming pool which makes the cost of singles (£E50), doubles (£E70) and triples (£E90) tolerable. Bar, restaurant, patisserie – and discos or bellydancing some nights (see p.203).

Everest Hotel, Midan Ramses (☎742-707). Laid-back, tatty joint (on the fifteenth floor of the block advertising India Tea) used by most backpackers staying in the Ramses area. Singles £E8–10, doubles £E11–15, triples £E16 (breakfast included). Hot water and grand views of the surrounding sprawl; rooms 601–612 are best for sunsets. Overpriced café.

Cairo Palace Hotel, off Midan Ramses and el-Gumhorriya (☎906-327). Simple but clean, with helpful German-speaking manager and a nice bar/restaurant building on the roof. Singles £E12 (£E15 with shower); doubles £E16 (£E18); triples £E22.

New Cecil Hotel, 29 Sharia Emad el-Din (☎913-859). Cleanish, with fans and shared hot water bathrooms. Singles £E7; doubles £E16; triples £E18. On the fourth floor.

Big Ben Hotel, 33 Emad el-Din (☎908-881). Singles (£E10–14), doubles (£E19–23) and triples (£E28) with fans, soft beds and maybe a private bath. Take the left-hand elevator in the foyer to the eighth floor.

Victoria Hotel, 66 Sharia el-Gumhorriya (☎918-766; telex 92914 VICTOR UN). Revamped Thirties hotel once frequented by George Bernard Shaw; the widow of Ghana's first president still lives here. Large A/C rooms (many with mahogany furniture) and a tastefully appointed bar and restaurant. Singles $30, doubles $45, triples $60. Bank and hairdressers on the premises; international calls. Takes Amex and Visa.

Islamic Cairo

Islamic Cairo rubs shoulders with its medieval past; noises, smells and insects penetrate one's room, while the quarter's values and customs demand recognition outside. Excluding numerous bug-ridden dives around Saiyida Zeinab and Khan el-Khalili, three hotels are worth considering. The first is keyed to the downtown plan on p.74; the other two appear on the "Khan el-Khalili and al-Azhar" map on p.90.

New Rich Hotel (Y), 47 Sharia Abdel Aziz, off Midan Ataba (☎900-145). Located roughly midway between downtown and Islamic Cairo, with a female proprietor who looks after women guests. A/C singles (£E26/£E29 with bath) and doubles (£E36/£E47) may be discounted if you bargain. Breakfast included.

El Hussein Hotel (☎918-089). Entered via a passage into *Fishawi's*, the *Hussein's* balcony rooms overlooking Midan El-Hussein are harangued by Cairo's loudest muezzins, while the upper floors shake from wedding parties in its rooftop restaurant (great views, awful food). Sleep is impossible during religious festivals, when the square bops all night. Pleasant singles (£E14/£E21 with bath) and doubles (£E21/£E28), but it's worth paying for a private bathroom. Fine for women travelling alone. Reservations advisable.

Radwan Hotel (☎901-311). Just across the Muski, so equally noisy, but with smaller rooms and less character. Singles £E12 (£E18 with shower); doubles £E13 (£E25); triples £E23 (£E30). Sporadic hot water. Not advisable for women alone.

Zamalek

The northern half of Gezira Island is quieter and fresher than central Cairo, except along 26th July Street, where buses and *service* taxis shuttle between downtown and the west bank. Besides its *Cairo Marriott* and *Gezirah Sheraton* (see above), the island has modern **three-star hotels** like the *President* (22 Sharia Taha Hussein; ☎413-195) and *New Horus House* (21 Sharia Ismail Muhammed; ☎705-682), plus three **cheaper options**:

Mayfair Hotel, 9 Sharia Aziz Osman (☎340-7315). Quiet location and nice garden near the Polish embassy. Tidy pastel-painted singles (£E10/£E20 with shower) and doubles (£E15/£E30) with a view.

El-Nil Zamalek Hotel, 21 Sharia Maahad al-Swissry (☎340-1846; ☎340-02-20 from abroad). Spacious modern rooms with bath, phone, TV and A/C, and maybe a balcony overlooking the Nile. Singles £E32; doubles £E40.

Balmoral Hotel, 157 26th July St, behind the *Marriott* (☎340-6761). Noisy location and drab rooms – not the three-star place it pretends to be, but author Charlie Pye-Smith liked it. Rates for singles (£E26) and doubles (£E37) with baths are currently discounted by £E6–7. Breakfast included.

Hostels and camping

Hostelling and camping offer meagre rewards by comparison with downtown hotels, and any gains in clean air or seclusion tend to be negated by the extra travel involved in sightseeing from an outlying base.

That said, the **IYHF youth hostel** near the El-Gama'a Bridge on Roda Island (see map, p.122) is readily accessible by #83 minibus from Tahrir. Buses #803 and #904 also run nearby, or you can catch a river-taxi to the Giza University stop and walk back across the bridge. IYHF members pay £E4 for a bunk bed in spartan, noisy dorms. Non-members may be obliged to join on the spot (£E18; photo required) or allowed to stay for £E3 a night extra, with automatic membership after six days. Rules vary according to demand, so call ahead (☎840-729) to avoid disappointment. The hostel shuts its doors between 10am and 2pm (also 6–8pm during Ramadan), with an 11pm curfew, but functions all year.

Unless you've got private transport or an overwhelming urge to rusticate outside Giza, forget about **Salma Camping** (☎869-152). The manager prefers guests to pay in dollars for cabins ($5–10) with mosquito netting or the right to pitch a tent ($1) and use the hot showers (50pt). Despite its bar-buffet and delightful garden, the site's distance from everywhere but the Wissa Wassef School (next door) is bound to cause difficulties. It's reached by turning off Pyramids Road towards Saqqara, and then taking a signposted turn-off at Harraniyya village.

Long stays and flat-hunting

Should you decide to stay awhile, it's worth remembering that many hotels reduce their rates by ten percent after fifteen days' occupation. Depending on demand for rooms and your rapport with the management, it may be possible to negotiate further discounts for **long stays at pensions**. Unfortunately, the smart *Anglo-Swiss* and *Roma* are less open to persuasion than dives like the *Oxford*, which allows long-term residents to customise their rooms and cook on the premises.

In the longer term it's better **to rent a flat;** a base with a phone makes working or socialising in Cairo a lot easier. Given the range of localities and amenities, expect to look at half a dozen places before settling on one. Check the small ads in *Cairo Today, Maadi Messenger, British Community News* and *Egyptian Gazette;* and noticeboards at English-language institutes and cultural centres (see p.223), where asking around can also pay dividends. Foreigners working or studying in Cairo often seek flatmates or want to sublet during temporary absences. With luck, you can move into a fully furnished flat with little ado.

Another way involves using a *simsar* (flat agent), who can be found in any neighbourhood by making enquiries at local shops and cafés. Unless you spend a long, fruitless day together, he's only paid when you settle on a place; ten percent of your first month's rent is the normal charge. Flat agencies in Ma'adi levy the same commission on both tenant and landlord. Additional "key money" is illegal, but often demanded.

Before agreeing to **sign a lease**, **check** plumbing, water pressure, sockets, lighting, phone, stove and water-heater (*buta* gas cylinders need changing), and ask if power or water cuts are regular occurrences. Also determine whether utilities (phone, gas, electricity) and services (the *bowab*, garbage collection) are included in the rent, and paid-up to date when you move in (ask to see receipts if necessary). All the flat's contents should be accurately noted on an inventory, the responsibility for repairs and the size of the deposit established. A flat without a phone isn't likely to acquire one, whatever the landlord promises.

Cairo's **residential neighbourhoods** range from smart Western enclaves to countryfied *baladi* quarters. Quietly spacious **Ma'adi**, thirty minutes by metro from the centre, is home to most of Egypt's American community, and mega-wealthy natives. **Zamalek**, favoured by embassies and European expats, is likewise costly, but always has vacancies. Another focus for the foreign community is **Heliopolis**, a self-contained suburb where palatial Art Deco flats jostle with air-conditioned high-rises. Rents here are lower than in downtown Cairo, where few flats are available at any price unless you move into **Bulaq** or plumb the Qasr al-Aini side of **Garden City**. Across the Nile, middle-class **Dokki** merges into *baladi* market quarters whilst **Mohandiseen** parades blocks of flats and shopping centres along its shiny boulevards. Single males with a grasp of Arabic and Egyptian ways might enjoy living in **baladi quarters** (Islamic Cairo, Bulaq, Imbaba), which are cheap and cheerful, unhygienic and noisy. Foreigners are expected to contribute to the incessant drama of local life and do (verbal) battle when necessary – personal privacy doesn't exist in these urban villages.

CENTRAL CAIRO

Most people prefer to get accustomed to **central Cairo** before tackling the older, Islamic quarters, for even in this Westernised downtown area known as *wust al-Balad*, the culture shock can be profound. Beyond the sanctuary of the luxury hotels beside the Nile, crowds and traffic jostle for space in the fume-laden air; whistling cops direct weaving taxis and limousines, donkey-carts and buses; office workers rub shoulders with *baladi* folk, Nubians and soldiers. The pavements and shadowy lobbies of cavernous Art Deco or Empire-style apartment blocks are a lifetime's world for many vendors and doormen – both major contributors to Cairo's grapevine. Above the crumbling pediments and hoardings, pigeon-lofts and extra rooms spread across the rooftops – a spacious alternative to the streets below.

The area is essentially a lopsided triangle, bounded by **Ramses Station**, **Midan Ataba** and **Garden City**, and for the most part it's compact enough to explore on foot. Only the Ramses quarter and the further reaches of Garden City are sufficiently distant to justify using transport (see "Getting around"). Practical details of institutions and events mentioned in the following walkabout appear under "Accommodation", "Practicalities" and other sections, as indicated.

Around Midan Tahrir

The heart of modern Cairo is a concrete assertion of national pride which threatens to burst as it pumps traffic around the city. Created on the site of Britain's Qasr el-Nil Barracks after the 1952 revolution, **Midan Tahrir** (Liberation Square) embodies the drawbacks of subsequent political trends. During the Sixties, two bureaucratic monoliths and several transport depots responsible for much of Egypt and all of Greater Cairo were concentrated here, as Nasser adopted Soviet-style centralisation. A decade later, Sadat rejected his mentor's "Arab Socialism" in favour of an *Infitah* (Open Door) to Western capitalism, causing private car ownership to soar almost as fast as Cairo's population. Impending gridlock was only averted by digging a metro; in spite of which, buses and roads are still grossly overcrowded.

The entrances to **Sadat metro station** serve as pedestrian underpasses linking these depots and buildings with the main roads leading off Tahrir. Despite being clearly labelled in English, it's easy to go astray in the maze of subways and surface at the wrong location. Many Cairenes prefer to take their chances crossing by road – a nerve-wracking experience for newcomers. Though some **landmarks** are obvious, rooftop billboards and neon signs flanking the end of streets like Talaat Harb (between *Isis* and *7UP*) or Qasr el-Nil (beside the *Cleopatra Hotel*) also help with orientation. To watch the square over tea, try the Arab café beneath the *Saudia* sign or the tourist-oriented place on the corner of Sharia Tahrir.

Tahrir landmarks

Towards the Nile, where the Tahrir Bridge runs between guardian lions towards Gezira Island, the blue and white **Nile Hilton** was the first modern "international" hotel built along the Corniche. The **bus station** out front is used by municipal and inter-city services, ranging from battered workhorses to air-conditioned coaches (detailed under "Getting around" and "On from Cairo"). Its northern edge abuts the grounds of the domed **Museum of Egyptian Antiquities**, housing the finest collection of its kind in the world (see p.150). Behind here is the terminal for trams to Heliopolis; next door lurks the headquarters of the now defunct **Arab Socialist Union**, which Nasser founded to replace the political parties banned in the Sixties, and Sadat dissolved when it tried to supplant him.

Another vestige of the time when Egypt was acknowledged leader of the "progressive" Arab cause is the tan-coloured edifice just south of the *Nile Hilton*, which used to serve as the secretariat of the Arab League. After Sadat's treaty with Israel, the headquarters of the **Arab League** moved to Tunis and most of its members severed relations with Egypt. At the time of writing, deciding whether to return the League to Cairo seems almost as divisive an issue as was Iraq's invasion of Kuwait, so with diplomatic finesse, ad hoc sessions are being held at the **Semiramis Intercontinental** rather than the old building. Further down the Corniche, roughly opposite the new **Shepheard's Hotel**, was the site of the *Thomas Cook* landing stage, where generations of tourists embarked on Nile cruises and General Gordon's ill-fated expedition set off for Khartoum in 1883.

Across the Tahrir Bridge ramp from the Arab League building, Egypt's Ministry of Foreign Affairs is less conspicuous than the **Omar Makram Mosque**, where funeral receptions for deceased VIPs are held in brightly coloured marquees. But dominating the southern end of Midan Tahrir is a concave office block that inspires shuddering memories – **the Mugamma**. A "fraternal gift" from the Soviet Union, this Kafkaesque warren of gloomy corridors, dejected queues and idle bureaucrats houses the public departments of the Interior, Health and Education ministries, and the Cairo Governorate. How many of the 50,000 people visiting *El-Mugamma* each day suffer nervous breakdowns from sheer frustration is anyone's guess; an African supposedly flung himself through a window several years ago. (For advice on handling the Mugamma, see p.222.) Outside is Tahrir's principal **minibus station**.

On the corner of Sharia Qasr al-Aini, opposite the Mugamma, a handsome pseudo-Islamic facade masks the old campus of the **American University in Cairo**. (Entered via Sheikh Rihan Street, the Library is one block northeast.) Responsible for publishing some of the best research on Egypt in the English language, the AUC is also a Western-style haven for wealthy Egyptian youths and US students doing a year abroad, its shady gardens and preppy ambience seeming utterly remote from everyday life in Cairo. Visitors might experience a premonitory shiver that Iran's gilded youth probably looked pretty similar before the Islamic Revolution. Egyptian Marxists and Islamic Fundamentalists regard the AUC as a tool of US and Zionist imperialism.

Bab al-Luq

Worthy of a brief mention before moving on to the downtown area is the market quarter of **Bab al-Luq**, five minutes' walk from Tahrir Square. Following Sharia Tahrir to **Midan Falaki**, you'll find a pedestrian bridge of the kind which circumvented Midan Tahrir before its subways were dug. Off to the right, a broad street awash with fruit and veg stalls runs alongside **Bab al-Luq market**. Not a place for the sqeamish, and overpriced compared to other markets, it's still an interesting spot to watch haggling and gossiping over trussed poultry or tea and *sheeshas*. See "Eating and drinking" for details of cheap eateries around here.

The area beyond here and south of Tahrir is covered under "Garden City and the Abdin quarter", following the Ramses Station section.

Talaat Harb and Qasr el-Nil

Cutting an X-shaped swathe through downtown Cairo, the thoroughfares of **Talaat Harb** and **Qasr el-Nil** contain most of the city's budget hotels, airlines and travel agencies. Almost every visitor gravitates here at least once, while many spend a lot of time checking out the restaurants, shops and bars. Inevitably, hustling tourists is a major industry; the guys touting for perfume shops are especially adept at distinguishing gullible newcomers from *khawaga*s who've been around a while. But don't brush off every approach as a sales ploy – passers-by may bid you "Welcome to Egypt" with no motive other than courtesy.

Talaat Harb

Forty years ago, Suleyman Pasha Street was lined with trees and sidewalk cafés, a gracious ornament to the Europeanised city centre built in the late nineteenth century. Since being renamed **Sharia Talaat Harb** its trees have succumbed to traffic and its once elegant facades have been effaced by grime and neglect, tacky billboards and glitzy facings – yet its vitality and diversity have never been greater. Overflowing the pavements, thousands of Cairenes window-shop, pop into juice bars and surge out of cinemas with lurid hoardings. Imelda Marcos would drool over the profusion of shoe shops, some devoted to butterfly creations fit only for a boudoir. In the shadows of Western-style affluence, beggars lie with palms outstretched and barefoot urchins hump garbage pails onto donkey-carts – an accepted part of Cairo's street life.

Almost every tourist seeks a break from the crowds and culture shock at one of three places along the initial stretch of Talaat Harb. For a meal with beer and English-speaking waiters, there are the **Café Riche** and **Felfela's**, one just before the other, around the corner of Sharia Hoda Shaarawi. Folklore has it that the Free Officers plotted their overthrow of Egypt's monarchy in the *Café Riche*; another version maintains that they communicated over the telephone in **Groppi's**, a famous but nowadays dreary coffee house on **Midan Talaat Harb**, the intersection with Qasr el-Nil. Here stands a statue of Talaat Harb (1876–1941), nationalist lawyer and founder of the National Bank.

Up to this point traffic runs both ways, but thereafter northbound vehicles are restricted to Qasr el-Nil; because the streets cross over, it's easy to take the wrong one by mistake if you're on foot. Between Midan Talaat Harb and 26th July Street, Talaat Harb abounds in takeaways, **cinemas** and cheap **hotels** (see "Entertainments" and "Accommodation").

Qasr el-Nil

Although the racecourse that once ran beside **Sharia Qasr el-Nil** disappeared last century, northbound traffic tries to rival bygone derbys, and the shops, though functional enough, play second fiddle to Talaat Harb's. Heading up from Tahrir you'll pass *American Express* and the *Orientalist Bookshop* before coming upon a stall devoted to foreign newspapers and magazines, outside *Groppi's*.

Two blocks beyond Midan Talaat Harb, a side street on the right allows a glimpse of the carmine and gold Art Nouveau **Metropolitan Hotel**, an elegant leftover from colonial times. Kalashnikov-toting police and Central Security troops are ubiquitous in downtown Cairo, but never threatening. An amiable pair lounge outside the **National Bank** on the corner of Sharia Sherif, diagonally opposite a weirdly insectile shopfront.

Harbouring bookshops, bars and health clubs, some of the **backstreets** here also serve as **outdoor mosques**. For midday prayers on Fridays, the one running into Abdel Khaliq Sarwat is carpeted with green mats where the faithful perform a succession of *rekas*, swaying their heads, raising their hands and prostrating themselves whilst reciting parts of the Koran.

East of Talaat Harb

Although overshadowed by Talaat Harb and Qasr el-Nil, four streets running east–west off these avenues are equally integral to downtown Cairo: **Sharia Abdel Khaliq Sarwat, Sharia Adly, 26th July Street** and **Sharia Alfi Bey**.

Sharia Abdel Khaliq Sarwat and Sharia Adly

After the Khan el-Khalili bazaar, **Sharia Abdel Khaliq Sarwat** – the first major street you reach after the Midan Talaat intersection – has the city's highest concentration of **jewellers**, particularly around the Opera Square end, where a street of goldsmiths called Sikket al-Manakh leads off to the south. Because their marked prices are higher, canny shoppers can use them as benchmarks when haggling for lower rates in the Khan (see p.216).

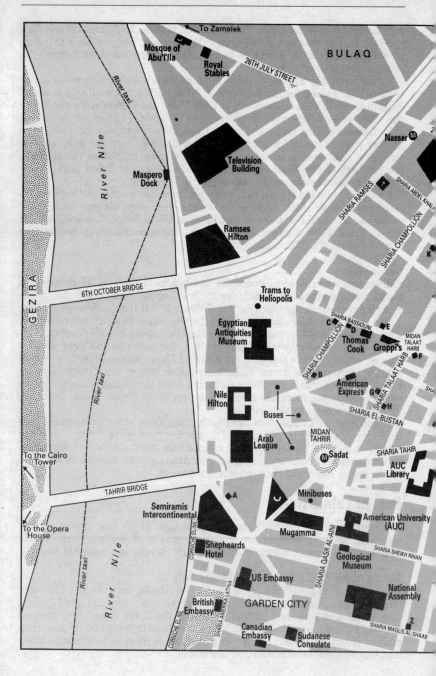

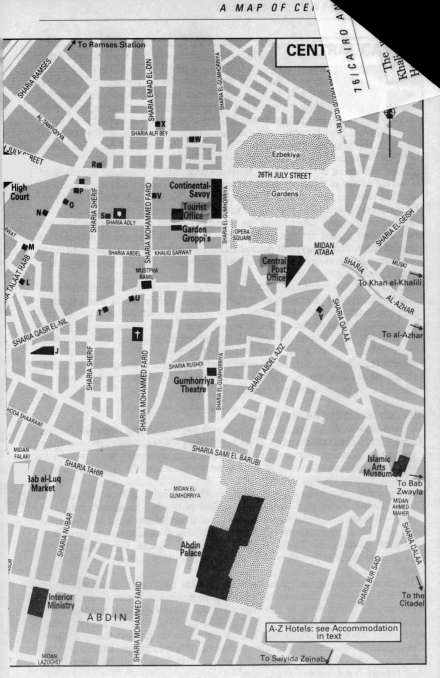

To Ramses Station

SHARIA RAMSES

SHARIA EMAD EL-DIN

SHARIA EL-GUMHORRIYA

SHARIA KHALUD (CLOT BEY)

AL-TAWFIQIYA

X

SHARIA ALFI BEY

W

JULY STREET

R

Ezbekiya

26TH JULY STREET

Gardens

High Court

P

O

SHARIA SHERIF

N

SHARIA ADLY

S

Continental-Savoy

Tourist Office

Garden Groppi's

V

SHARIA MOHAMMED FARID

SHARIA EL-GUMHORRIYA

OPERA SQUARE

MIDAN ATABA

SHARIA EL-GEISH

MUSKI

M

SHARIA ABDEL

KHALIQ SARWAT

Central Post Office

SHARIA

To Khan el-Khalili

ARWAT

L

SHARIA TALAAT HARB

MUSTPHA KAMIL

AL-AZHAR

U

SHARIA QALAA

V

To al-Azhar

SHARIA QASR EL-NIL

SHARIA SHERIF

T

J

SHARIA MOHAMMED FARID

SHARIA RUSHDI

Gumhorriya Theatre

SHARIA EL-GUMHORRIYA

SHARIA ABDEL AZIZ

HODA SHAARAWI

MIDAN FALAKI

SHARIA SAMI EL BARUBI

Islamic Arts Museum

SHARIA TAHIR

Bab al-Luq Market

MIDAN EL-GUMHORRIYA

To Bab Zwayla

MIDAN AHMED MAHER

SHARIA NUBAR

SHARIA QALAA

Abdin Palace

SHARIA MOHAMMED FARID

SHARIA BUR SAID

To the Citadel

Interior Ministry

ABDIN

A-Z Hotels: see Accommodation in text

MIDAN LAZOGHLI

To Saiyida Zeinab

ast Edwardian neo-Gothic apartment block at the junction of Abdel
Sarwat and Mohammed Farid frowns its northern face upon **Sharia Adly**.
eading east along this street you'll find a buff, temple-like edifice with Central
Security guards posing on a Cecil B. de Mille-like stairway. The arborial reliefs on
its columns represent the Tree of Manna whence Heaven's bounty fell upon the
Israelites, for the building is Cairo's last working **Synagogue**. Discreetly open on
Saturday mornings, its opulent marbled interior receives few worshippers these
days, the city's Jewish community having dwindled to around eighty, all aged.
For Rosh Hashana and Passover a rabbi is flown in from Tel Aviv; otherwise,
there's only the melancholy custodian and his Christian friend.

One block along is Cairo's main **tourist office**, with the **tourist police** sited
above; for details of both, see p.54. Across the road, **Garden Groppi's** spacious
patio and panelled salon are much nicer than the *Groppi's* on Midan Talaat Harb.
During World War II, this was one of the few posh establishments open to ordinary British troops – "other ranks" as they were called – whom the military top
brass decided should not mix socially with officers. Its high prices nonetheless
ensured that officers, Egyptian pashas and their fur-draped Levantine mistresses
predominated. Nowadays it's frequented by courting couples, journalists and
bourgeois matrons.

Another colonial institution that bit the dust still survives in moribund form
north of Sharia Adly's termination at Opera Square. Before World War I, tourists
could buy "anything from a boa constrictor to a fully grown leopard" outside the
grandiose **Continental-Savoy Hotel**, where a scandalised missionary insisted on
providing trousers to cover the genitals of a performing baboon. Orde Wingate,
the eccentric military genius who liberated Abyssinia from Italian rule for
Emperor Haile Selassie, attempted suicide in his room here. It's worth wandering
into the *fin-de-siècle* bar even if it's not functioning; whether the hotel will be
reopened or pulled down seems uncertain.

26th July Street and Sharia Alfi Bey

The busiest, widest thoroughfare of downtown Cairo is **Sharia setta w'ashreen
Yulyu** – more easily rendered as **26th July Street** – which runs all the way from
Ezbekiya to Zamalek. Formerly called Fouad I, after Ismail's son, its current
name commemorates the date of King Farouk's abdication in 1952, following a
bloodless coup by the Free Officers.

From a visitor's standpoint, everything worth mentioning lies east of the **High
Court** (Nasser metro station). Besides a slew of hotels – most noticeably the
Grand – this stretch of the street features two sleazy **nightclubs**; an off-licence
and cages full of pigeons awaiting buyers; plus almost as many shoe shops and
pavement hawkers as Talaat Harb. Behind the *Cicurel* department store,
expropriated from its Jewish owner in 1957, is a vintage Cairene restaurant, *El
Hatty*.

Better still for eating and drinking is **Sharia Alfi Bey**, two blocks north. Here
you'll find the Greek *Taverna* and *Alfi Bey* **restaurants**; a dirt cheap 24-hour
taamiya joint (next door to the *Nile Christian Bookshop*) and a wonderfully
relaxed bar inside the *Windsor Hotel*. Opposite the hotel entrance are two funky
Arab cafés. Though perfectly safe late at night, the backstreets that link these
thoroughfares retain an aura of illicit goings-on. When Lawrence Durrell and his
wife were evacuated from Greece to Cairo in 1941, they soon discovered that
their refugee hotel doubled as a brothel.

Opera Square and Midan Ataba

The layout of all these streets goes back to the 1860s, when Khedive Ismail had the centre rebuilt in the style of Haussmann's new Paris boulevards to impress dignitaries attending the inauguration of the Suez Canal. An Opera House was also constructed for staging an opus with an imperial Egyptian theme, though since Verdi couldn't finish *Aida* in time, *Rigoletto* was performed instead; symbolically, the building faced west, overlooking **Opera Square** and the modern city rather than Islamic Cairo. An equestrian statue of Ibrahim Pasha, by Cordier, honours Ismail's father. Though still the sprucest bit of greenery in central Cairo, the square lost its namesake when the Opera House burned down in 1971; a multistorey car park now occupies the site. To the north, a row of kiosks selling electrical goods marks the advent of Ezbekiya Gardens (see below).

Almost a century after Ismail mortgaged Egypt to foreign creditors, anti-colonial resentments exploded here on **"Black Saturday"** (January 26, 1952). The morning after British troops had killed native policemen in Ismailiya, demonstrators were enraged to find an Egyptian police officer drinking on the terrace of *Madame Badia's Opera Casino* (where the Opera Cinema stands today). A scuffle began and the nightclub was wrecked; rioting spread quickly, encouraged by the indifference of Cairo's police force. As ordinary folk looted, activists sped around in Jeeps torching foreign premises. Similarly, during the bread riots of 1977, nightclubs and boutiques were specifically targeted by the radical Islamic group *Al-Taqfir w'al-Higrah* (Repentance and Holy Flight).

Midan Ataba . . . and approaches to Islamic Cairo

Behind Opera Square car park, a bus and tram depot and split-level thoroughfares render **Midan Ataba** just as Yusuf Idris described it in *The Dregs of the City*: "a madhouse of pedestrians and automobiles, screeching wheels, howling claxons, the whistles of bus conductors and roaring motors." Originally called the Square of Green Steps, Ataba should rightly be renamed the Square of Flyovers. Local **transport** includes minibuses to Heliopolis (#20, #25), Medinet Nasr (#34) and Zamalek (#76); and trams to the Citadel (#13), al-Azhar (#19), Abbassiya (#3) and Shubra al-Balad (#8).

Using the **central post office** and Ataba fire station to get oriented, you'll be able to identify from here four **approaches to Islamic Cairo**:

● **Sharia Qalaa** (formerly Boulevard Mohammed Ali), across from the fire station. Like the #13 trams, this street runs directly to the Citadel. When Ismail's Minister of Public Works ordered the thoroughfare ploughed through the old quarter, he asked rhetorically: "Do we need so many monuments? Isn't it enough to preserve a sample?" The stretch down to Midan Ahmed Maher (where the Islamic Arts Museum is located) features musical instrument shops, all-night stalls and cafés. In pre-revolutionary times, Arab brothels and hashish dens infested the stepped lanes that rise between its tenements.

● **Sharia al-Azhar**. Overshadowed by a flyover running from Midan Ataba to the heart of Islamic Cairo, Sharia al-Azhar buzzes with traffic and cottage industries. The #19 trams rattle past the **al-Azhar bus terminal** (for the Western Desert Oases) near the Bur Said overpass, 400m along.

● **The Muski** is the classic approach to Khan el-Khalili: a narrow bazaar running parallel to Sharia al-Azhar, identifiable by the crowds passing between the *El Mousky* hotel and a clump of luggage stalls. For more details, see "Around Khan el-Khalili and al-Azhar".

● **Sharia el-Geish**. Also topped by a flyover, "Army Street" runs out towards Abbassiya and Heliopolis. Don't bother venturing beyond the Paper Market except to visit the derelict Mosque of Beybars the Crossbowman on Midan Zahir.

Ezbekiya Gardens and north to Ramses

The **Ezbekiya Gardens** were laid out by the former chief gardener of Paris in the 1870s, forming a twenty-acre park. Subsequent extensions to 26th July Street have reduced them to trampled islands amidst a sea of commerce and traffic, but they remain an important city focus, flanked by **booksellers** specialising in Islamic texts, images of the Grand Mosque and framed Koranic verses. Egyptians hawk clothes and gewgaws, shouting above the music and oratory that blares from **cassette kiosks** (see p.219), while taciturn Sudanese squat behind their incense cones and medicinal herbs. Beyond the clothes stalls on the right stands the **Cairo Puppet Theatre** (see p.211).

In medieval times a lake fed by the Nasiri Canal and surrounded by orchards existed here, but in 1470 the Mamluke general Ezbek built a palace, inspiring other Beys and wealthy merchants to follow suit. During the French occupation Napoleon commandeered the sumptuous palace of Alfi Bey, and his successor Kléber promoted Western innovations such as windmills, printing presses, and a balloon launch which embarrassingly failed. Another novelty was *Le Tivoli* club, where "ladies and gentlemen met at a certain hour to amuse themselves"; unheard of in a society where men and women socialised separately.

During Mohammed Ali's time, visitors could still witness Cairenes celebrating the Prophet's Birthday (12 Rabi al-Awwal) here with unrestrained fervour. Sufi dervishes entranced by *zikr*s lay prostrate to be trampled by their mounted sheikh in the famous *Doseh* (Treading) ceremony. However, snake-swallowing had already been ruled "disgusting and contrary to their religion" by the sheikh of the Sa'adiya, and under British rule popular festivals were discouraged and dispersed around the city. Nowadays, El-Hussein and other squares are more active during the *Moulid al-Nabi*.

Though nothing remains of them today, two bastions of colonialism once overlooked Ezbekiya from a site bounded by Alfi Bey and el-Gumhorriya, where Scottish pipers once played. Here, *Shepheard's Hotel* (founded in 1841) flourished alongside the *Thomas Cook Agency*, which pioneered tourist "expeditions" in the 1870s. Rebuilt more grandly in 1891, *Shepheard's* famous terrace, Moorish Hall, Long Bar and Ballroom (featuring "Eighteenth Dynasty Edwardian" pillars modelled on Karnak) were destroyed by Black Saturday rioters in 1952.

Between Ezbekiya and Ramses

When Mohammed Ali created a military high road to link the Citadel with Cairo's new railway station and named it after the French physician Antoine Clot – whom he enobled for introducing Western ideas of public health to Egypt – nobody foresaw that **Sharia Clot Bey** and the fashionable area north of Ezbekiya would degenerate into a vice-ridden "Open Land". By World War I, however, the quarter was full of honky-tonk bars, backstreet porn shows and brothels; shacks and plush establishments alike paying tribute to Ibrahim el-Gharby, the fearsome transvestite "King of the *Wasa'a*". During World War II, activities centred around Wagh el-Birket, known to troops as **"the Berka"**: a long street with curtained alleys leading off beneath balconies where the prostitutes sat fanning themselves. Only after the killing of two Australian soldiers (who were notorious for throwing women and pianos out of windows) was the Berka closed down in 1942.

Nowadays shabbily respectable, with cheap shops and cafés, this past has been further effaced by renaming Clot Bey **Sharia Khulud**. Any tram or bus heading up it from the gardens towards Ramses will take you past the hulking nineteenth-century **Cathedral of Saint Mark**, now superseded by the new Coptic Cathedral in Abbassiya. The derelict Moorish pile at the Ramses end of **Sharia el-Gumhorriya** (which runs up from the west side of the gardens) was the original premises of *Al-Ahram* (The Pyramids), the first – if not still the foremost – newspaper in the Arab world.

Around Ramses Station

The Ramses Station area is the northern ganglion of Cairo's transport system. Splayed flyovers and arterial roads haemorrhage traffic onto darting pedestrians, keeping **Midan Ramses** busy round the clock. Its main focus is **Ramses Station**, a quasi-Moorish shoebox to which **Kubri Lamun Station** was attached in 1910 to serve the burgeoning northeastern suburbs. Also contained within the complex is the **Egyptian Railways Museum** (see "Museums").

In ancient times, when the Nile ran farther east, Ramses was the site of *Tendunyas*, the port of Heliopolis. Renamed *al-Maks* (the Customs Point) by the Arabs, it was incorporated within Cairo's fortifications by Salah al-Din, whose Iron Gate was left high and dry as the Nile receded westwards, and was pulled down in 1847 to make way for the station. A thirty-foot-high red granite **Colossus of Ramses II**, moved here from Memphis by way of monumental compensation in 1955, now stands diminished by the Heliopolis flyover and an overhead walkway. A modern replica of this colossus stands beside the airport road.

Ramses Station: transport details
Mubarak metro station, beneath the square, offers rapid escape from an area with few incentives to linger. Indeed, you'll probably only come here to catch a train or use one of the **bus and service taxi depots** that cluster roundabout. Minibuses to Alexandria and the Delta cities leave from all over – just listen out for shouted destinations.

Koulali Terminal, off the road beneath the 6th October flyover, serves the Delta and Canal Zone, Alex and Northern Sinai, while separate bus and taxi parks at the chaotic **Ahmed Helmi Terminal** cover Middle and Upper Egypt, the Red Sea Coast and the Fayoum (see "On from Cairo" for transport details).

To reach Ahmed Helmi, cross the humpbacked iron bridge which overlooks Cairo's **army surplus market**, a warren of stalls where women may feel uneasy. Two **hotels** south of Midan Ramses deserve a mention for their facilities: the *Fontana* lets non-residents use its rooftop swimming pool, while the terrace of the *Everest* offers a panoramic view of Cairo's lights by night.

Midan Tahrir can be reached by metro, or overground transport heading southwest along Sharia Ramses. Travelling in the opposite direction, minibuses #24, #26 and #27 run through Abbassiya and Heliopolis (see "The Northern Suburbs").

Garden City and the Abdin quarter

Spreading south from Midan Tahrir towards Old Cairo and the Islamic districts are two very different, yet historically interlinked, quarters. Deluxe hotels follow the Corniche towards Roda Island, separating the old diplomatic quarter from the Nile just as Sharia Qasr al-Aini divides the leafy winding streets of **Garden City** from the grid of blocks where Egypt's ministries and parliament are located. Like

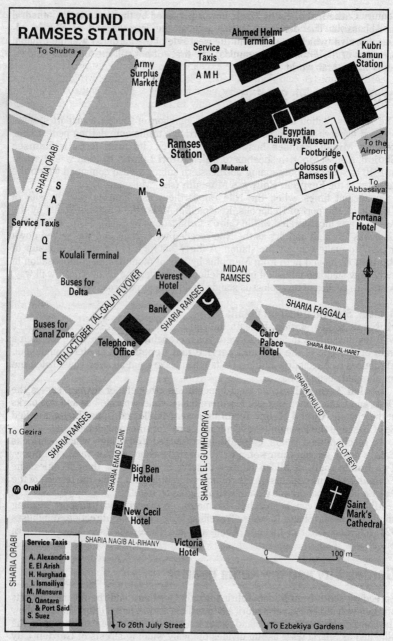

AROUND RAMSES STATION

To Shubra

Army Surplus Market

Service Taxis

A M H

Ahmed Helmi Terminal

Kubri Lamun Station

SHARIA ORABI

Ramses Station

M Mubarak

Egyptian Railways Museum

Footbridge

Colossus of Ramses II

To the Airport

To Abbassiya

S A I Q E

S M A

Service Taxis

Koulali Terminal

Buses for Delta

6TH OCTOBER [AL'GALA] FLYOVER

Everest Hotel

Bank

SHARIA RAMSES

MIDAN RAMSES

SHARIA FAGGALA

Fontana Hotel

Buses for Canal Zone

Telephone Office

Cairo Palace Hotel

SHARIA BAYN AL-HARET

SHARIA RAMSES

To Gezira

SHARIA EMAD EL-DIN

Big Ben Hotel

SHARIA EL-GUMHORRIYA

SHARIA KHULUD

(CLOT BEY)

M Orabi

New Cecil Hotel

Victoria Hotel

Saint Mark's Cathedral

SHARIA NAGIB AL-RIHANY

0   100 m

SHARIA ORABI

Service Taxis
A. Alexandria
E. El Arish
H. Hurghada
I. Ismailiya
M. Mansura
Q. Qantara
   & Port Said
S. Suez

To 26th July Street

To Ezbekiya Gardens

a spider in its web, the ex-royal, now presidential Abdin Palace lends its name to the convoluted **Abdin quarter** that merges into Saiyida Zeinab.

Since Garden City and Abdin meet around Midan Tahrir, both can claim to host Egypt's **National Assembly** (*Maglis al-Shaab*). During the late 1980s, Cairenes were agog over abusive exchanges and fisticuffs in parliament, as the hardline Minister Zaki Badr replied to allegations of torture, wrongful arrest and bugging by the **Interior Ministry**, sited a couple of blocks to the west in Abdin. Tourists need to visit the Ministry only to obtain travel permits for restricted areas (for details, see p.223), and few bother with the **Ethnological and Geological Museums** sited between the National Assembly and the AUC.

Garden City

When Ibrahim Pasha's al-Dubbarah Palace was demolished in 1906, British planners developed the site for diplomatic and residential use, laying down crescents and cul-de-sacs to create the illusion of lanes meandering through a **Garden City**. Until the Corniche road was ploughed through, embassies and villas boasted gardens running down to the Nile; nowadays, fishermen's shacks and vegetable plots line the river's edge.

Aside from the traffic, it's a pleasant walk along the Corniche towards Roda Island, past a cluster of **feluccas** available for Nile cruises (see p.209). Further inland, Art Deco residences mingle with heavily guarded **embassies** (addresses under "Practicalities"). Despite being outnumbered by the US – whose embassy is the largest in the world – the British enjoy grander buildings with more spacious grounds, a legacy of their pre-eminence in the days of Lord Cromer and Sir Miles Lampson. The main artery, running south from Tahrir towards Old Cairo, is **Sharia Qasr al-Aini**, which goes from riches to rags, banks and villas yielding to cheap backstreet eateries near the Sayala Bridge. A bygone "Palace of the Spring" lends its name to the mixed neighbourhood between Garden City and the slaughterhouse district, and to Cairo's largest public **hospital**, erected in the 1960s, where Yusuf Idris practised as a doctor before devoting himself to writing (see "Books" in *Contexts*). **Roda Island** and the mainland **further south** are described under "Old Cairo", see p.121.

WAR STORIES

During World War II, much of Garden City was comandeered by military organisations. At GHQ – which rapidly outgrew "Grey Pillars" to fill an entire neighbourhood – **R.A. Bagnold** proposed the formation of the Long Range Desert Group whose daring raids (with David Stirling's SAS) behind enemy lines were the genesis of a martial legend.

On Sharia Rustrum, the Middle Eastern headquarters of the **SOE** (Special Operations Executive) plotted operations from Yugoslavia to Libya, involving Fitzroy McLean, Evelyn Waugh, Patrick Leigh Fermor and others. At no. 13 Sharia Ibrahim Pasha Naguib, novelist **Olivia Manning** and her husband Reggie (the model for Guy Pringle in *Fortunes of War*) lived beneath Stirling's brother, Peter, who hosted wild parties in a flat crammed with captured ammunition.

British sang-froid only cracked once, when the Afrika Korps seemed poised to seize Alexandria and advance on Cairo. On "Ash Wednesday" (July 1, 1942) GHQ and the Embassy burned their files, blanketing Garden City with smoke. Half-charred classified documents were wafted aloft to fall on the streets, where peanut vendors twisted them into little cones.

The Abdin Quarter

With hindsight, several rulers must have regretted that Ismail moved the seat of State from the Citadel to what is now the **Abdin quarter**, where tenements surrounded the Palace enclave long ago. When Ismail began building the European-style **Abdin Palace**, in the 1860s, a worldwide scarcity of cotton had raised the value of Egypt's export crop to £25,000,000 a year, and his own civil list was double that of Queen Victoria. After prices slumped and creditors gathered, the palace was bequeathed to his successors together with vast debts that reduced them – and Egypt – to near vassal status.

The nadir of humiliation came in February 1942, when British armoured cars burst through the palace gates and Ambassador Lampson demanded that King Farouk sack the prime minister or abdicate himself. It was this that resolved Nasser to assemble the Free Officers, seize power and redeem Egypt. Ten years later, as Farouk displayed his long-awaited son at a magnificent reception, rioters burned downtown Cairo within earshot of the palace; six months afterwards, the Free Officers deposed him and declared a Republic.

Another mass protest – against Sadat's abolition of subsidies on bread and other essentials in January 1977 – actually happened outside the palace on **Midan el-Gumhorriya** (Square of the Republic). Chanting "Thieves of the *Infitah*, the People are Famished", crowds overwhelmed Central Security and rampaged against symbols of wealth and authority until the subsidies were restored. Still the state headquarters of Egypt's president, the Abdin Palace is flanked to the north by the Cairo Governorate building. During Ramadan a large tent is pitched in the middle of the square, where virtuoso performers recite the Koran.

Behind the palace grounds are blocks of crumbling *rabs* where families lower baskets from the upper windows to passing street vendors. The neighbourhood is chiefly residential, with many Nubians and Sudanese, several street **markets** (around Midan Lazoghli) and a reputation for *ghorzas* (see p.92). **Sharia Bur Said** (Port Said), which divides it from the Saiyida Zeinab quarter, marks the course of the Khalig al-Masri canal that was filled in early this century after the Aswan Dam reduced Cairo's dependency on Nile floodwater. Various stretches of Bur Said carry buses and minibuses to diverse locations around the city, but you need to know the routes well to take advantage of them. Slower **trams** are easier to suss: #5 and #22 run northeast past the Islamic Arts Museum, crossing the Muski; and southwards to el-Salakhana, near the Mamluke Aqueduct.

ISLAMIC CAIRO

The core of the city itself was circumscribed by the river and hills of refuse, the castle, the aqueduct and the abandoned slums. Most of the bazaars lay in the densely packed quarters of the North-East, nestling in amongst and parasitic upon the rubble of the old Fatimid palaces, and behind the commercial streets one found small courtyards and large tenements, into which were crowded communities of closely knit creeds and tribes . . . The city was like a disordered mind, an expression of archaic wishes and half submerged memories of vanished dynasties.

Robert Irwin, *The Arabian Nightmare*

Islamic Cairo sustains fantasy and confounds certainty. Few foreigners enter its maw without feeling excitement and trepidation. Streets are narrow and congested, slimy underfoot with donkey shit and burst water mains, overhung with latticed balconies. Mosques, bazaars and medieval lanes abound; the smell of *sheeshas* and frying offal wafts through alleys where muezzins wail "Allahu Akbar!" (God is Greatest) and beggars entreat "Ya Mohannin, ya Rabb" (O Awakener of Pity, O Master), as integral to street life as the artisans and hawkers. The sights, sounds, aromas and surprises draw you back time after time, and getting lost and dispensing *baksheesh* are a small price to pay for the experience.

You can have a fascinating time exploring this quarter of the city without knowing anything about its history or architecture, but to describe Islamic Cairo one has to refer to both. Islamic architecture has its own conventions, terminology and stylistic eras, which we've attempted to summarise in the box overpage. The potted history section provides a general context, with many of the personalities and events mentioned in more detail under the appropriate monument. Most of these are named after their various founders; modern-day Islamic fundamentalists shun them as *mesjid el-derar*: mosques built for self-glorification.

A brief history of Islamic Cairo

Islamic Cairo is the sum total of half a dozen cities whose varied names, ages and locations make for an unusually complex urban history. One helpful constant is that new cities have invariably been constructed to the north of the old, for quite simple reasons: an east–west spread was constrained by the Muqattam Hills and the Nile (which ran further east than nowadays), whilst the prevaling northerly wind blew the smoke and smell of earlier settlements away from newer areas.

Thus when the Muslim troops of Amr conquered Egypt for Islam in 641 AD, they sited their city **al-Fustat**, just north of Coptic Babylon (see "Old Cairo"). Here it grew into a powerhouse of religious conversion, surpassing Alexandria as Egypt's leading city, though remaining a mere provincial capital in the vast Islamic empire ruled from Iraq by the khalifs, whose only direct contact occurred when the last of the **Umayyads** (661–750) fled to al-Fustat, and then burned it. Their successors, the **Abbasids** (750–935), ordered the city to be rebuilt further north, and so *Medinet al-Askar* (City of Cantonments) came into being. More important in the long term was the Abbasid reliance on Turkish-speaking warriors, who were granted fiefdoms throughout the empire, including Egypt.

In 870, encouraged by popular discontent, the Abbasids' viceroy in Egypt asserted his independence, and went on to wrest Syria from their control. Like his predecessors, Ahmed **Ibn Tulun** founded a new city, reaching from Medinet al-Askar towards a spur of the Muqattam. Inspired by the imperial capital of Samarra, it consisted of a gigantic congregational mosque, palace and hippodrome, surrounded by "the Wards" (*al-Qitai*) or military quarters after which the city was named. However, when the Abbasids invaded Egypt in 905, al-Qitai was razed and ploughed under, sparing only the great Mosque of Ibn Tulun, which stands to this day.

The city regained a shadow of its former importance under the **Ikhshidids** (935–969), who seceded from the later Abbasid khalifs. But the impetus for its revival, and that of the Islamic empire, came from Tunisia, where adherents of Shia Islam had created their own theocracy, ruled by a descendant of Ali and Fatima – the dynasty of **Fatimids**. Aiming to seize the khalifate, they hit upon Egypt as an ill-defended yet significant power base, and captured it with an army of 100,000 in 969. The Fatimid general, Gohar (Jewel), a converted Greek, immediately began a new city where the dynasty henceforth reigned (969–1171).

AN A–Z OF ISLAMIC/ARCHITECTURAL TERMINOLOGY

ABLAQ Striped. An effect achieved by painting, or laying courses of different coloured masonry (the costlier method); usually white with red or buff. A Bahri Mamluke innovation, possibly derived from the Roman technique of *opus mixtum* – an alternation of stone and brickwork.

BAB Gate or door, as in the medieval city walls.

BEIT House. Segregated public and private quarters, the *malqaf, maq'ad* and *mashrabiya* are typical features of old Cairene mansions.

DARB Path or way; can apply to alleyways or thoroughfares.

FINIAL Ornamental crown of a dome or minaret, often topped by an Islamic crescent.

HAMMAM Bathhouse.

HARAMLIK Literally the "forbidden" area; ie women's or private apartments in a house or palace.

KHALIF Successor to the Prophet Mohammed and spiritual and political leader of the Muslim empire. A struggle over this office caused the Sunni–Shia schism of 656 AD. Most khalifs ruled from Baghdad or Damascus and delegated control of imperial provinces like Egypt.

KHAN Place where goods were made, stored and sold, which also provided accommodation for travellers and merchants, like a *wikala*. It's from khan that we get the word caravanserai.

KHANQAH Sufi hostel, analagous to a monastery.

KUFIC The earliest style of Arabic script; Foliate kufic was a more elaborate form, superseded by naskhi script.

KUTTAB Koranic school, usually for boys or orphans.

LIWAN Arcade or vaulted space off a courtyard, commonly found in mosques and madrassas. Originally, the term meant a sitting room opening onto a covered court.

MADRASSA Literally a "place of study" but generally used to designate theological schools. Each madrassa propagates a particular rite of Islamic jurisprudence.

MALQAF Wind scoop for directing cool breezes into houses; in Egypt, they always face north.

MAQ'AD Arch-fronted "sitting place" on the second floor of old Cairene houses, overlooking the courtyard.

MARISTAN Public hospital.

MASHRABIYA An alcove in lattice windows where jars of water can be cooled by the wind; and by extension, the projecting balcony and screened window itself, which enabled women to watch street life or the salamlik without being observed. Although flat latticework partitions are strictly termed *mashrafiya*, mashrabiya loosely covers both types of work.

MASTABA Stone or mudbrick benches at the entrance to buildings. Mohammed Ali had them removed to reduce idling and speed up the traffic.

MIDAN Open space or square; originally, most were polo grounds.

MERLONS Indentations and raised portions along a parapet. Fatimid merlons were angular; Mamluke ones crested, trilobed (like a fleur-de-lys) or in fancier leaf patterns.

MIDA'A Fountain for the ritual ablutions that precede prayer, located in a mosque's vestibule or courtyard.

MIHRAB Niche indicating the direction of Mecca, towards which all Muslims pray; in Egypt, facing southeast.

MINARET Tower from which the call to prayer is given; derived from *minara*, the Arabic word for "beacon" or "lighthouse".

MINBAR Pulpit from which an address to the Friday congregation is given. Often superbly inlaid or carved in variegated marble or wood.

MOULID Popular festival marking an event in the Koran or the birthday of a Muslim saint. The term also applies to the name-days of Coptic saints.

MOSQUE A simple enclosure facing Mecca in its original form, the mosque acquired minarets, riwaqs, madrassas and mausoleums as it was developed by successive dynasties. Large congregational mosques are called *Jami*, smaller, local "places of prostration" are known as *mesjid* – a very old distinction.

MUEZZIN A prayer-crier (who's nowadays more likely to broadcast by loud-speaker than climb up and shout from the minaret).

MURQANAS Stalactites, pendents or honeycomb ornamentation of portals, domes or squinches.

NASKHI Form of Arabic script with joined-up letters, introduced by the Ayyubids.

QASR Palace or castle.

QIBLA The direction in which Muslims pray, ie the wall where the mihrab is located.

QUBBA Dome, or domed tomb chamber.

RIWAQ Arcaded aisle around a mosque's sahn, originally used as residential quarters for theological students; ordinary folk may also take naps here.

SANCTUARY The liwan incorporating the qibla wall.

SABIL Public fountain or water cistern. During the nineteenth century it was often combined with a Koran school to make a SABIL-KUTTAB.

SAHN Central courtyard of a mosque, frequently surrounded by *riwaqs* or *liwans*.

SALAMLIK The "greeting" area of a house; ie the public and men's apartments.

SOFFITS Undersides of arches, often decorated with stripes (*ablaq*) or formalised plant designs (an Ottoman motif).

SQUINCH An arch spanning the right angle formed by two walls, so as to support a dome.

SUFIS Islamic mystics who seek to attain union with Allah through trance-inducing *zikrs* and dances. Whirling Dervishes belong to one of the Sufi sects.

TABUT A cenotaph or grave marker, sometimes embellished with a "hat" indicating the deceased's rank.

THULUTH Script whose vertical strokes are three times larger than its horizontal ones; Thuluth literally means "'third".

WAQF The endowment of some religious, educational or charitable institution in perpetuity. In Egypt, thousands of such bequests are overseen by the Ministry of Awaqf.

WIKALA Bonded warehouse with rooms for merchants upstairs. Here they bought trading licences from the *Muhtasib*, and haggled over sales in the courtyard. *Okel* is another term for a wikala.

ZIYADA Outer courtyard separating early mosques from their surroundings; literally "an addition".

ZAWIYA A *khanqah* centred around a particular sheikh or Sufi order (*tariqa*).

By this time distinctions between the earlier cities had blurred, as people lived wherever was feasible amidst the decaying urban entity known as **Masr** (which also means "Egypt"). The Fatimids distanced themselves from Masr by building their city of **al-Qahira** (The Conqueror) further north than ever, where certain key features remain. It was at the al-Azhar Mosque that al-Muizz, Egypt's first Fatimid ruler, delivered a sermon before vanishing into his palaces (which, alas, survive only in name); whilst the Mosque of al-Hakim commemorates the khalif who ordered Masr's destruction after residents objected to proclamations of his divinity. You can also see the great Northern Walls and the Bab Zwayla gate, dating from al-Gyushi's enlargement of al-Qahira's defences. But as the Fatimid city expanded, Fustat began disappearing as people scavenged building material from its abandoned dwellings; a process that spread to Masr, creating great swathes of *kharab*, or derelict quarters.

The disparate areas only assumed a kind of unity after **Salah al-Din** (Saladin to the Crusaders) built **the Citadel** on a rocky spur between al-Qahira and Masr, and walls which linked up with the aqueduct between the Nile and the Citadel, so as to surround the whole. Salah al-Din promoted Sunni, not Shia, Islam and built *madrassas* to propagate orthodoxy; he ruled not as khalif, but as a secular *sultan* ("power"). His successors, the **Ayyubids**, erected pepperpot-shaped minarets (only one remains) and the magnificent tombs of the Abbasid Khalifs and Imam al-Shafi'i (which still exist) in the Southern Cemetery, but they made the same error as the Abbasids: depending on foreign troops and bodyguards. When the sultan died heirless and his widow needed help to stay in power, these troops, the Mamlukes, were poised to take control.

The **Mamlukes** were a self-perpetuating caste of slave-warriors, originally from Central Asia but later drawn from all over the Near East and the Balkans. Their price in the slave markets reflected the "value" of ethnic stock – 130–140 ducats for a Tartar, 110–120 for a Circassian, 50–80 for a Slav or Albanian – plus individual traits: sturdy, handsome youths were favoured. Often born of concubines and raised in barracks, Mamlukes advanced through the ranks under *amirs* who sodomised and lavished gifts upon their favourites. With the support of the right amirs, the most ruthless Mamluke could aspire to being sultan. Frequent changes of ruler were actually preferred, since contenders had to spread around bribes, not least to arrange assassinations. The Mamluke era is divided into periods named after the garrisons of troops whence the sultans intrigued their way to power: the Qipchak or Tartar **Bahri Mamlukes** (1250–1382), originally stationed by the river (*bahr* in Arabic); and their Circassian successors the **Burgi Mamlukes** (1382–1517), quartered in a tower (*burg*) of the Citadel.

Paradoxically, the Mamlukes were also renowed as aesthetes, commissioning mosques, mansions and *sabil-kuttabs* that are still the glory of today's Islamic Cairo. They built throughout the city, from the Northern to the Southern Cemetery, and the Citadel to the Nile, and although urban life was interrupted by their bloody conflicts, the city nevertheless maintained civilised institutions: public hospitals, libraries and schools bequeathed by wealthy Mamlukes and merchants. The caravanserais overflowed with exotica from Africa and the spices of the East, and with Baghdad laid waste by the Mongols, Cairo had no peer in the Islamic world, its wonders inspiring the *Thousand and One Nights*.

But in 1517 the **Ottoman Turks** reduced Egypt from an independent state to a vassal province in their empire, and the Mamlukes from masters to mere overseers. When the French and British extended the Napoleonic War to Egypt they found a city living on bygone glories: introspective and archaic; its population dwindling as civil disorder increased. Eighteenth-century travellers like R.R. Madden were struck by "the squalid wretchedness of the Arabs, and the external splendour of the Turks", and the lack of "one tolerable street" in a city of some 350,000 inhabitants.

The city's renaissance – and an ultimate shift from Islamic to modern Cairo – is owed to **Mohammed Ali** (1805–48) and his less ruthless descendants. An Ottoman servant who turned against his masters, Mohammed Ali effortlessly decapitated the vestiges of Mamluke power, and raised a huge mosque and palaces upon the Citadel. Foreigners were hired to advise on urban development and Sharia Qalaa (Blvd. Mohammed Ali) was ploughed through the old city. As Bulaq, Ezbekiya and other hitherto swampy tracts were developed into a modern, quasi-Western city, Islamic Cairo ceased to be the cockpit of power and the magnet for aspirations. But as visitors soon discover, its contrasts, monuments and vitality remain as compelling as ever.

Exploring Islamic Cairo: practicalities

Most of Islamic Cairo's **monuments** are self evident and are often identified by little green plaques with Arabic numbers; these correspond to the numbers on Lehnert & Landrock's map of Cairo and the listings in the exhaustive *Islamic Monuments in Cairo: a Practical Guide*, published by the AUC. Although the area **maps** printed in this book should suffice, the AUC book and two fold-out maps published by *SPARE* (Society for the Preservation of the Architectural Resources of Egypt) have the advantage of greater detail.

Likewise, we can't hope to match the wealth of detail or evocations of time and place in certain **books**. Edward Lane's *The Manners and Customs of the Modern Egyptians* illuminates life during Mohammed Ali's time. The changes wrought this century underlie Naguib Mahfouz's *Midaq Alley* and *Cairo Trilogy*. Mameluke Cairo is the setting for Robert Irwin's surreal *The Arabian Nightmare*, whilst its fevered demise haunts *Zayni Barakat* by Gamal al-Ghitani. Life in the Cities of the Dead is captured in *Down to the Sea*, by Gamil Attiyah Ibrahim. For straight – but never dull – history try James Aldridge's *Cairo* or Desmond Stewart's *Great Cairo, Mother of the World*. All of these works are reviewed under "Books" in *Contexts* and a selection is available at tourist bookshops on Talaat Harb and Qasr el-Nil.

The best (if not the only) way **to explore Islamic Cairo** is by walking. Basically, you decide on a starting point that's readily accessible from downtown Cairo, and then follow an itinerary on foot from there. The most obvious **starting points** are Khan el-Khalili, the Bab Zwayla and the Citadel; see the beginning of each of these sections for details on getting there. Many of the **itineraries** can be linked up or truncated; the main limitations on how much you can see are the time factor, and your own stamina. It makes sense to read up on an area before striking out on foot.

Mosques are open all day, but tourists are unwelcome during **prayer times**, particularly the main Friday noon assembly, which lasts over an hour. A couple of mosques are permanently closed to non-Muslims (as indicated in the text). The regularly visited ones level **admission charges** of £E1 or so (students pay half), and guardians generally expect **baksheesh**: the footwear custodian merits 25pt, while someone who takes you into a tomb or up a minaret rates £E1. Excessive demands should be politely resisted, and asking for change is awkward and rude, so bring lots of small bills. Old **mansions**, charging along similar lines, theoretically have set **opening hours**, but in practice often close after 3pm, and all day Friday, whatever the official schedule.

How you **dress** is important. Anyone wearing shorts automatically diminishes their prestige in Egyptian eyes, and women wearing halter-necks, skimpy T-shirts, miniskirts etc will attract gropers and the disapproval of both sexes. Mosques baulk at admitting the "immodestly" dressed, and for Muslims and unbelievers alike it's obligatory to remove shoes (or don overshoes) to avoid sullying the sacred precincts. Comfortable, easy to slip off footwear is recommended; sandals offer scant protection against manure and leaking drains. Women may feel more comfortable sticking close to a male companion and covering their hair and shoulders with a shawl or veil.

It shouldn't need saying that intimate **behaviour** in public is a definite no-no. By remaining courteous and alert, you minimise the risk of hassles on the crowded streets. An effective yet graceful way of brushing off hustlers is to intone *la shokran* whilst smiling, touching your heart (a gesture of sincerity) and hurrying on. But never begrudge the effort of politeness, nor mistake every approach for a sales ploy. Ordinary Egyptians enjoy welcoming *khawagas* with the right attitude as much as they like watching arrogant tourists get misdirected and cheated.

Around Khan el-Khalili and Al-Azhar

Khan el-Khalili bazaar and the Mosque of al-Azhar form the commercial and religious heart of Islamic Cairo, and the starting point for several walking tours. **To get there from downtown Cairo** you can take a taxi, bus, or walk. Taxis (which usually go via the al-Azhar flyover) shouldn't cost more than £E1, although drivers normally try to overcharge tourists bound for Midan El-Hussein – the main square adjoining Khan el-Khalili that's best given as your destination. Buses #63 and #66 from the Nile Hilton depot on Tahrir Square provide cheaper (10pt) transport to al-Azhar, but they're grossly overcrowded.

APPROACHING ON FOOT: THE MUSKI
Walking **from Midan Ataba** there are two basic routes: along Sharia al-Azhar (beneath the flyover), which takes ten to fifteen minutes; or via the Muski, a more interesting half-hour approach.

The Muski is a narrow, incredibly congested street running eastwards from Midan Ataba; look for the faded *El Mousky Hotel* on the corner. Worming your way through the crowds – past windows full of wedding gear, tape decks and fabrics, and vendors peddling everything from salted fish to socks – beware of mopeds and other traffic thrusting up behind. Barrow-men still yell traditional warnings – "Riglak!" (Your foot!), "Dahrik!" (Your back!), "Shemalak!" (Your left side!). Itinerant drinks-vendors are much in evidence. Although the *saqi* (water-sellers) have been made redundant by modern plumbing, *susi* dispensing liquorice-water, and *sherbutli* with their silver-spouted lemonade bottles, remain an essential part of street life.

Halfway along the Muski you'll cross Sharia Bur Said and a series of tramlines where vendors stay put until the last minute; beyond here the Muski turns touristy, with hustlers emerging as it nears Khan el-Khalili.

El-Hussein Square

Midan El-Hussein (El-Hussein Square), framed by an eclectic mix of architecture, is a central point of reference.

To the north stands the tan-coloured **Mosque of Saiyidna Hussein**, where the Egyptian president and other dignitaries pray on special occasions, a sacred place, off-limits to non-Muslims. Its cool marble, green and silver interior guards the relic of a momentous event in Islamic history – the **head of Hussein**. The grandson of the Prophet Mohammed, Hussein was killed in Iraq in 680 by the Umayyads, who had earlier been recognised as Mohammed's successors against the claims of his son-in-law, Ali, Hussein's father, whom they had murdered. This generational power struggle over the khalifate caused an enduring schism within Islam. The Muslim world's *Sunni* ("followers of the way") majority not only recognised the khalifate, but forbade the office to anyone of Ali's line. Conversely, the *Shia* ("partisans of Ali") minority refused to accept any khalif but a descendant of Ali, and revered Hussein as a martyr. In predominantly Sunni Muslim Egypt, he's nevertheless regarded as a popular saint, ranked beside Saiyida Zeinab, the Prophet's granddaughter.

Hussein's annual *moulid* is one of Cairo's greatest **festivals** – a fortnight of religious devotion and popular revelry climaxing on the *leyla kebira* or "big night", the last Wednesday in the Muslim month of Rabi al-Tani. Here the Sufi brotherhoods parade with their banners and drums, and music blares all night, with vast crowds of Cairenes and *fellaheen* from the Delta (each of whose villages has its own café and dosshouse in the neighbourhood). El-Hussein is also a focal point during the festivals of *Moulid al-Nabi*, *Eid al-Adha*, *Ramadan* and *Eid al-Fitr*, all well worth seeing. A balcony room at the *El-Hussein Hotel* provides a perfect vantage point, but don't expect to get any sleep. Ablaze with neon lights (including green "Allahs"), the minarets boom sleepers into wakefulness with their amplified muezzins around dawn – and that's on ordinary nights of the year.

The Khan el-Khalili bazaars

Above all, the **Khan el-Khalili** quarter pulses with business, as it has since the Middle Ages. Except on Sundays, when most shops are shut, everything from spices to silk is sold in its bazaars. What follows is primarily a guide to the sights: for hard facts about merchandise, dealers and bargaining, see "Shopping", later in this chapter. The Khan itself is quite compact, bounded by Hussein's Mosque, Sharia al-Muizz and the Muski, with two medieval lanes (*sikkets*) penetrating its maze-like interior.

Generically speaking, all the bazaars around here are subsumed under the name Khan el-Khalili – after Khalil, a Master of Horse who founded a caravanserai here in 1382. Most of the shop fronts conceal workshops or warehouses and the system of selling certain goods in particular areas still applies, if not as rigidly as in the past. **Goldsmiths**, jewellers and souvenir-antique shops mostly congregate along Sikket al-Badetsan and Sikket Khan el-Khalili, which retain a few arches and walls from Mamluke times. When you've tired of wandering around, duck into **Fishawi's** via one of the passages off the Muski or the square. Showing its age with tobacco-stained plaster and cracked gilded mirrors, this famous café has been open day and night every day of the year for over two centuries, an evocative place to sip mint tea, eavesdrop, and risk a *sheesha*. Nobel prizewinning author Naguib Mahfouz sometimes takes coffee here.

South of the Muski you'll find the *Souk al-Attarin* or **Spice Bazaar**, selling dried crushed fruit and flowers besides more familiar spices. On the corner of the same street, screened by T-shirt and *galabiyya* stalls, stands the **Madrassa of al-Ashraf Barsbey**, who made the spice trade a state monopoly, thus financing his capture of Cyprus in 1426.

Any of the passages opposite will take you into the **Perfume Bazaar**, a dark, aromatic warren sometimes called the *Souk es-Sudan* because much of the incense is from there; in the last century, Baedeker's *Guide for Travellers* also noted "gum, dum-plant nuts" and "ill-tanned tiger-skins" amongst the merchandise. Mamluke sultans appointed a *Muhtasib* to oversee prices, weights and quality. Empowered to inflict summary fines and corporal punishments, he was also responsible for public morals, "enjoining what is right and forbidding what is wrong".

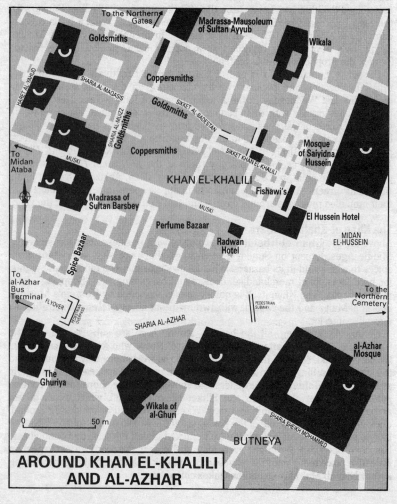

AROUND KHAN EL-KHALILI AND AL-AZHAR

Al-Azhar Mosque

To the southwest of El-Hussein Square, a pedestrian underpass leads towards the **Mosque of al-Azhar** (pronounced "al-*Azhar*"), whose name can be translated as "the radiant", "blooming" or "resplendent". Founded in 970, as soon as the enclosure walls of Fatimid al-Qahira were completed, al-Azhar claims to be the world's oldest university (a title disputed by the Kairaouine Mosque in Fes, Morocco). For more than a millennium, though, al-Azhar has provided students from all over the Muslim world with free board and with an education that, despite Nasserite reforms, remains largely as it was during the classical Islamic era. *Muqawrin* study every facet of the Koran and Islamic jurisprudence (*fiqh*); logic, grammar and rhetoric; and how to calculate the phases of the lunar Muslim calendar. Much of this involves listening in a circle (*halqa*) at the feet of a sheikh, and rote-memorisation; but with greater knowledge, students may engage in Socratic dialogue with their teachers, or instruct their juniors.

Given this, and the Sheikh al-Azhar's status as the ultimate theological authority for Egyptian Muslims, it's unsurprising that the mosque has always been politically significant. Salah al-Din changed it from a Shi'ite hotbed into a bastion of Sunni orthodoxy, while Napoleon's troops savagely desecrated it to make their power evident. (Omitting any mention of this, Baedeker cautioned visitors to this "fountain-head of Mohammedan fanaticism . . . not to indulge in any gestures of amusement or contempt".) A nationalist stronghold from the nineteenth century onwards, al-Azhar was chosen by Nasser for his speech of defiance during the Suez invasion of 1956. When Saudi King Fahd prayed here with Mubarak in 1989 it symbolised Egypt's return to the conservative Arab fold; yet, paradoxically, many of al-Azhar's 90,000 students revere the blind fundamentalist sheikh Omar Abd al-Rahman, officially regarded as an enemy of the state.

THE MOSQUE

The mosque itself is an accretion of centuries and styles, harmonious if confusing. Admission (Sun–Thurs & Sat 9am–3pm, Fri 9–11am & 1–3pm) costs £E1, with a small tip for the footwear custodian – and bigger *baksheesh* expected for anyone who shows you around; women are provided with shawls to cover hair and shoulders, whilst bare legs rules out entry for either sex.

You come in through the fifteenth-century **Barber's Gate**, where students traditionally had their heads shaved, onto a great **sahn** (courtyard) that's five hundred years older, overlooked by three minarets. The sahn facade, with its rosettes and keel-arched panels, is mostly Fatimid, but the latticework-screened *riwaqs* (residential quarters) of the **madrassas** (theological schools) on your right-hand side date from the Mamluke period. Unfortunately, these are rarely opened for visitors, but you can walk into the carpeted, alabaster-pillared **qibla liwan** where the *mihrab*, or prayer niche facing Mecca, is located.

You'll probably also be invited up to the **roof**, or onto a minaret, offering great views of Islamic Cairo's timeless vista of crumbling, dust-coloured buildings that could have been erected decades or centuries ago, the skyline bristling with dozens of minarets.

Butneya – and leaving al-Azhar

The warren of lanes and tenements behind al-Azhar – in the area known as **Butneya** – could be described as Cairo's "Thieves' Quarter", except that racketeering and drugs are more important. Until 1988, the main business was hashish: sold from "windows" and "green doors", it could be smoked with impunity in *ghorzas* (literally "stitches", small and hidden places) throughout the quarter. Local drugs barons like Kut Kut and Wilad Nasare entered Cairene folklore for their ostentatious wealth and devotion to their neighbourhood; Mustafa Marzuaa built a fifteen-room villa with VCRs in every room, smack in the middle. After the great crackdown in December 1988, when scores of corrupt officials were arrested, the drugs "mafiosi" decamped to the suburbs, leaving Butneya to local racketeers. Some gangs cream the profits from organised garbage collection and begging; others extort money from shops or restaurants, and one gang even specialises in weddings – families pay them to stay away rather than risk distur-bances: to hire bouncers would be a shameful admission of family weakness.

None of this should affect foreigners who stay outside the quarter (though you might be offered hashish, or even regaled with stories of the "good old days" when slabs were carved up on tables outdoors). In any case, the well-defined tour-ist trail leads elsewhere. **Leaving al-Azhar** by the Barber's Gate, you can turn left down an alley to reach the Wikala of al-Ghuri and other monuments described in the next-but-one walking tour; or return to Midan El-Hussein and check out the following itinerary.

To the Northern Gates and back again

As described below, this itinerary covers an array of monuments from different eras, occupying the one-time heart of Fatimid Cairo. Although one can walk the route – from El-Hussein Square to the Northern Gates and back again – within an hour, checking out the interiors of all the monuments could take half a day or more, so you might wish to be selective. If your time is limited, it's probably best to concentrate on the three big attractions: the Qalaoun–al-Nasir–Barquq complex, al-Hakim's Mosque and the Beit al-Sihaymi.

Midan El-Hussein to Bayn al-Qasrayn

Starting from Midan El-Hussein, walk 200m west along the Muski to a crossroads with two mosques, and then turn right onto the northern extension of **Sharia al-Muizz**. Here, jewellers' shops overflowing from the Goldsmiths Bazaar soon give way to vendors of pots, basins, and crescent-topped finials, after whom this bit of street is popularly called *al-Nahasen*, the **Coppersmiths' Bazaar**.

In Fatimid times this bazaar was a broad avenue culminating in a great parade ground between khalifal palaces – hence its name, **Bayn al-Qasrayn** (Between the Two Palaces), which is still used today although the palaces vanished long ago. Robert Irwin writes evocatively of the place as it was during the Mamluke era, when it was customary "for the men and even a few of the women to prome-nade in the cool twilight. Later, when respectable people had gone back to their homes, the streets were left to the lamplighters, carousing mamlukes, prostitutes and the sleepers."

To the right of the bazaar, a minaret poking above a row of stalls gives away the unobtrusive **Madrassa and Mausoleum of al-Silah Ayyub**, more interest-ing for its historical associations than anything else. Its founder, the last Ayyubid sultan, was responsible for introducing Mamlukes, or foreign slave troops (origi-nally Qipchaks from the lower Volga region), an act pregnant with consequences for Egypt. As related under "Cities of the Dead" (see p.116), the sultan's widow's daring bid for power made the Mamlukes aware that they were kingmakers – whence it was a short step to ruling Egypt themselves, as they did from 1250

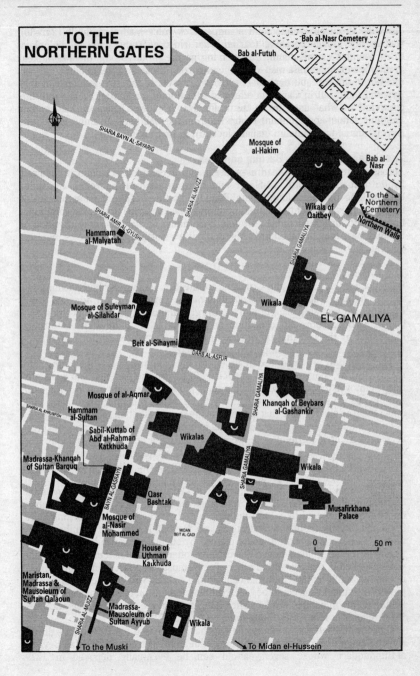

TO THE
NORTHERN GATES

Bab al-Nasr Cemetery

Bab al-Futuh

SHARIA BAYN AL-SAYARIG

Mosque of
al-Hakim

Bab al-
Nasr

To the
Northern
Cemetery

Northern Walls

Wikala of
Qaitbey

SHARIA AMIR AL-GYUSHI

SHARIA AL-MUIZZ

SHARIA GAMALIYA

Hammam
al-Malyatah

Wikala

EL-GAMALIYA

Mosque of Suleyman
al-Silahdar

Beit al-Sihaymi

DARB AL-ASFUR

Mosque of al-Aqmar

SHARIA GAMALIYA

Khanqah of Beybars
al-Gashankir

SHARIA AL-KHRUNFISH

Hammam
al-Sultan

Sabil-Kuttab of
Abd al-Rahman
Katkhuda

Wikalas

Madrassa-Khanqah
of Sultan Barquq

Wikala

BAYN AL-QASRAYN

Qasr
Bashtak

SHARIA GAMALIYA

Mosque of
al-Nasir
Mohammed

MIDAN
BEIT AL-QADI

Musafirkhana
Palace

House of
Uthman
Katkhuda

0   50 m

Maristan,
Madrassa &
Mausoleum of
Sultan Qalaoun

Madrassa-
Mausoleum of
Sultan Ayyub

Wikala

SHARIA AL-MUIZZ

To the Muski

To Midan el-Hussein

onwards. From an architectural standpoint, Ayyub's madrassa (built 1242–50) was the first to incorporate all four *mahhabs* (rites) of Sunni Islam, and be linked to its founder's mausoleum, thus serving as the prototype for the Mamlukes' great mosque-madrassa-mausoleum complexes. Beneath the minaret, whose *mabkhara* (incense burner) or "pepperpot" crown is the sole example of this Ayyubid motif left in Cairo, an alleyway with a gate (on the left) leads into the courtyard of what used to be the madrassa. A sixteenth-century sabil-kuttab (Koranic school and fountain) protrudes from the wall between the minaret and Ayyub's domed mausoleum (usually locked), further up the street.

The Qalaoun–al-Nasir–Barquq complex

Across the road from the madrassa, the medieval complex of buildings endowed by the sultans **Qalaoun**, **al-Nasir** and **Barquq** form an unbroken and quite breathtaking 185-metre-long facade. Founded by three of the most significant of the Mamlukes, each of these building groups was designed to serve several functions, yet to form a harmonious whole. Depending on restoration work, parts of the buildings may be off-limits to visitors, but it's worth trying to see as much as you can, *baksheesh*-ing as necessary.

THE QALAOUN COMPLEX

Influenced by the Syrian and Crusader architecture its founder had encountered whilst fighting abroad, **Sultan Qalaoun's Maristan, Madrassa and Mausoleum** arguably inaugurated the Burgi Mamluke style, which is typified by lavish ornamentation and execution on a grand scale. If modern visitors are impressed by the fact that these structures were completed in thirteen months (1284–85), Qalaoun's contemporaries were amazed.

The **Maristan** provided free treatment for every known illness (including cataract removals), storytellers and musicians to amuse the patients, and money to tide them over following their discharge. A modern eye clinic now occupies the site of Qalaoun's hospital, of which only three liwans remain; to see them, walk down the tree-shaded lane that starts opposite the sabil-kuttab mentioned above.

Further up the street, a main door clad in bronze with geometric patterns gives access to a corridor running between the madrassa and the mausoleum. The damaged **Madrassa** (entered to the left off this corridor) has a sanctuary liwan recalling the three-aisled churches of northern Syria, with Syrian-style glass mosaics around its prayer niche.

But the real highlight of the ensemble is Qalaoun's **Mausoleum**, across the corridor (daily 9am–5pm; £E1). First comes an atrium court with a mashrabiya doorway, surmounted by a beautiful stucco arch worked with interlocking stars, floral and Koranic motifs, as intricate as lace. Beyond is the tomb chamber, thirty metres high, with its soaring dome pierced by stained-glass windows in viridian, ultramarine and golden hues. Elaborately coffered, painted ceilings overhang walls panelled in marble, with mother-of-pearl mosaics spelling out "Mohammed" in abstract calligraphy. Until this century the mihrab was credited with healing powers, so supplicants could be "seen rubbing lemons on one of its pillasters, and licking up the moisture", whilst a stick hanging from the tomb's railings was used "to cure fools or idiots by striking them on the head".

Qalaoun himself was a handsome Qipchak, purchased for 1000 dinars during Ayyub's reign. He rose through the ranks due to the patronage of Sultan Beybars al-Bunduqdari, whose seven-year-old son he eventually deposed in 1279.

Qalaoun's sonorous titles *al-Mansour* and *al-Alfi* ("the Thousand", after his high price) were mocked by his name, which sounds comical in Arabic; it's supposedly derived from the Mongolian word for "duck", or an obscure Turkish noun meaning "great ransom" or "rich present". A tireless foe of the Crusaders – he died en route to Acre fortress in 1290, aged 79 – Qalaoun imported Circassians to offset Qipchak predominance amongst the Mamlukes, and founded a dynasty that ruled for almost a century, barring hiccups.

THE AL-NASIR COMPLEX

Qalaoun's second son, responsible for the **Mosque of al-Nasir Mohammed** next door, had a rough succession. Only nine years old when elected, he was deposed by his regent, then restored but kept in miserable conditions for a decade by Beybars al-Gashankir. He finally had Beybars executed and subsequently enjoyed a lengthy reign (1293–1340, counting interregnums), which marked the zenith of Mamluke civilisation.

The erection of thirty mosques, the great aqueduct and a canal north of Cairo attests to al-Nasir's enthusiasm for public works (matched apparently by his devotion to horses and sheep). If the **madrassa** is still undergoing restoration, you'll have to be content with the minaret – a superb ensemble of stuccoed Kufic and Naskhi inscriptions, ornate medallions and stalactites, probably made by North African craftsmen. Al-Nasir is actually buried in Qalaoun's mausoleum, and his own son occupies the **mausoleum** intended for him. Its official opening hours are 9am–4pm (£E1).

THE BARQUQ MADRASSA AND KHANQAH

The adjacent **Madrassa and Khanqah of Sultan Barquq** appears in the much reproduced nineteenth-century drawing by Owen Carter, which also depicts the Sabil-Kuttab of Ismail Pasha, opposite al-Nasir's mosque. Its broad facade, divided into shallow recesses, echoes Qalaoun's madrassa, although Barquq's complex (1384–86) has the taller dome, and also boasts a minaret.

Barquq was the first Circassian Sultan (1382–98), a Burgi Mamluke who seized power by intrigue and assassination. His name, meaning "plum" in Arabic, appears on the raised boss in the centre of the bronze-plated doors, behind which a vaulted passageway leads to an open court. The **madrassa**'s sanctuary liwan (on the right as you enter) has a beautiful ceiling supported by porphyry columns of pharaonic origin; upstairs are the cells of the Sufi monks who once inhabited the **khanqah** (monastery). To one side of the qibla liwan, a splendid domed mausoleum upheld by gilded pendives contains the tomb of Barquq's daughter.

Mansions and Sabil-Kuttabs

The domestic architecture of the Mamlukes was no less sophisticated: perfectly adapted to Cairene conditions, it offered greater comfort than contemporary European homes – for the well-to-do, at least. An example close at hand is the **House of Uthman Katkhuda**, so called after an eighteenth-century resident, although the mansion itself dates from 1350. You'll find it on the left-hand side of Sharia Beit al-Qadi, which runs eastwards opposite Qalaoun's mausoleum; look for the little green plaque halfway along. Knock, and someone should usher you into the *qa'a*, a narrow, sixteen-metre-high reception hall with a handsome fountain and wainscotting; cooled by a north-facing *malqaf*, or air-scoop, on the roof. The curator expects *baksheesh* for showing you around.

Back on Sharia al-Muizz, walk past Barquq's complex and cross the road, turning into a muddy alleyway on the right, where the second door on the left opens onto the fourteenth-century **Qasr Bashtak**. Here the qa'a is upstairs, with mashrabiya-screened galleries that permitted ladies to witness the amir's parties, and similar devices overlooking the street. Amir Bashtak was married to al-Nasir's daughter, so he could afford a five-storey palace with running water on every floor; alas, only a section has survived. If the Qasr Bashtak is locked when you arrive, its custodian can usually be found at the sabil-kuttab diagonally opposite.

Situated on a fork in the road, the **Sabil-Kuttab of Abd al-Rahman Katkhuda** rises in tiers of airy wooden fretwork above solid masonry and grilles at street level. Founded by an eighteenth-century amir who wished to make amends for roistering, this is an Ottoman-influenced example of a type of building once widespread throughout Cairo, intended to provide the "blessings" of water and education, mentioned in the Holy Koran. Thus, local people could draw water from the *sabil* on the ground floor (where the Ka'ba at Mecca is depicted in Syrian tilework), whilst their sons learned Koranic precepts in the *kuttab* upstairs. (Girls were deemed unworthy of schooling.) An old proverb suggests that teaching methods were simple: "A boy's ear is on his back – he listens when he is beaten."

By taking the left-hand fork at the sabil-kuttab and walking 70m north you reach the **Mosque of al-Aqmar** (on the right). Until the roofless interior is restored its interest lies in the dusty facade, whose ribbed shell hood, keel arches and stalactite panels were the first instance of a decorated mosque facade in Cairo. Built (1121–25) by the Fatimid khalif's grand vizier, the mosque gets its name – "the moonlit" – from the glitter of its masonry under lunar light. Notice the intricate medallion above the door; the way that the street level has risen well above the mosque's entrance; and the "cutaway" corner up the road, designed to facilitate the maneouvring of loaded camels.

One block further north, turn right into Darb al-Asfur, where the broad wooden door of no. 19 (on the left, halfway along) admits visitors to the finest mansion yet (9am–4pm; £E1). The **Beit al-Sihaymi** surrounds a lovely courtyard filled with bird noises and shrubbery, overlooked by a *maq'ad* or loggia, where males enjoyed the cool northerly breezes; the ground-floor reception hall with its marble fountain was used during winter, or for formal occasions. The *haramlik* section, reserved for women, is equally luxurious, adorned with faience, stained glass, painted ceilings and delicate latticework. The guided tour should include a visit to the bathhouse (lit by star-shaped apertures) and a small room with whalebones on the floor, over which women are invited to jump to ensure marriage and pregnancy.

Returning to the main street and continuing north brings you to the **Mosque of Suleyman al-Silahdar**, recognisable by its "pencil" minaret, a typically Ottoman feature. Built in 1839, the mosque reflects the Baroque and Rococo influences which reached Cairo via Istanbul during Mohammed Ali's reign – notably the fronds and garlands that also characterise sabil-kuttabs from that period. Shortly afterwards the street widens into a triangular square, beyond which it's busy with the colourfully painted carts of garlic and onion sellers who roll in through the mighty gate ahead.

Al-Hakim's Mosque

The **Mosque of al-Hakim**, abutting the Northern Walls, commemorates one of Egypt's most notorious rulers. Al-Hakim bi-Amr Allah (Ruler by God's

Command) was only eleven years old when he became the sixth Fatimid khalif, and fifteen when he had his tutor murdered. His reign (996–1021) was capricious and despotic by any standards, characterised by the persecution of Christians, Jews and merchants and by a rabid misogyny: al-Hakim forbade women to leave their homes (banning the manufacture of ladies' footwear to reinforce this) and once had a public bath full of noisy females broiled alive. His puritanical instincts were also levelled at wine, chess and dancing girls – all of which were prohibited – and all the city's dogs were exterminated as their barking annoyed him. Merchants found guilty of cheating during al-Hakim's inspections were summarily sodomised by his Nubian slave, Masoud, whilst the khalif stood upon their heads – comparatively restrained behaviour from a man who once dissected a butcher with his own cleaver.

In 1020, followers proclaimed al-Hakim's divinity in the Mosque of Amr, provoking riots which he answered by ordering Fustat's destruction, watching it burn from the Muqattam Hills, where he often rode alone at night. However, legend ascribes the conflagration to al-Hakim's revenge on the quarter where his beloved sister, Sitt al-Mulk (Lady of Power), took her lovers. Only after half of Fustat–Masr was in ruins was she examined by midwives and pronounced a virgin, whereupon he surveyed the devastation and asked, "Who ordered this?" Allegedly, it was his desire for an incestuous marriage that impelled her to arrange al-Hakim's "disappearance" during one of his nocturnal jaunts.

By governing as regent for the child-khalif Zahir and dying peacefully in her bed, Sitt al-Mulk forfeited the eternal fame that later accrued to Shagar al-Durr, renowned as the only female ruler of Egypt since Cleopatra (see "Cities of the Dead"). Meanwhile, al-Hakim's disciple, al-Durzi, persuaded many foreign Muslims that he would be reincarnated as the Messiah – the origin of the tightly knit Druze communities that still exist in Syria, Lebanon and Israel, and whose doctrines are secret. Conversely, the Copts maintain that al-Hakim experienced a vision of Jesus, repented, and became a monk.

At all events, though, his huge **mosque** was shunned or used thereafter for profane purposes until 1980, when it was restored by an Isma'ili sect based in India, which venerates al-Hakim. The sect's addition of brass lamps, glass chandeliers and a new mihrab outraged purists, but the original wooden tie-beams and stucco frieze beneath the ceilings remain. From the roof, you can gaze over Bab al-Nasr Cemetery (see below) and admire the mosque's minarets, which resemble bastions. Admission to the mosque (9am–4pm) costs £E1.

The Northern Gates

In times past, the annual pilgrim caravan returning from Mecca would enter Cairo via the **Bab al-Futuh** (Gate of Conquests), drawing huge crowds to witness the arrival of the *Mahmal*. This decorative camel-litter once carried Ayyub's widow on her pilgrimage, but thereafter it symbolised rather than signified the sultan's participation. Islamic pageantry is still manifest during the **Moulid of Sidi Ali al-Bayoumi**, in early October, when the Rifai brotherhood parades behind its mounted sheikh with scarlet banners flying. The procession starts from El-Hussein, passes through the Bab al-Futuh and north along Sharia Husseiniya, where locals bombard the sheikh and his red-turbanned followers with huge sweets called *arwah*.

Hang around the gate awhile and a custodian should appear to guide you across the moat of fetid black water, into the dark interior of the **Northern**

Walls. He'll point out archers' slits and bombardiers' apertures, shafts for pouring boiling oil, and bits of pharaonic masonry (featuring Ramses II's cartouche and a hippo) filched from Memphis, striking matches if you haven't brought a torch (£E1.50 admission, plus *baksheesh*). Erected in 1087 to replace the original mudbrick ramparts of Fatimid al-Qahira, the walls were intended to rebuff the Seljuk Turks, but never put to the test, although they later provided a barracks for Napoleonic, and then British, grenadiers.

A 200-metre tunnel connects the Bab al-Futuh with the **Bab al-Nasr** (Gate of Victory), whose inscription "No deity but Allah; Mohammed is the Prophet of God" includes a defiant Shi'ite addition, "And Ali is the Deputy of God". It was after entering this gate in 1517 that the victorious Ottoman sultan Selim the Grim had eight hundred Mamlukes decapitated, and their heads strung on ropes on Gezira Island.

Directly opposite the gate lies **Bab al-Nasr Cemetery**, a shantytown of squatted mausolea where kids use tombstones as goalposts. Before the construction of Sharia Salah Salem and a barracks, Bab al-Nasr merged with the Northern Cemetery, although it lacked the princely tombs of that vaster necropolis. The Swiss explorer Johann Burckhardt (1784–1817), who visited the holy cities of Arabia disguised as a Muslim sheikh, is buried here, though exactly where no one knows.

From Bab al-Nasr you could catch a taxi or walk 1.5km east, following the Walls and then Sharia Galal to reach Barquq's complex in the Northern Cemetery (see p.118).

Heading back along Sharia Gamaliya

Re-entering Islamic Cairo through the Bab al-Nasr you pass into *El Gamaliya*, whose name derives from the old camel road, Sharia Gamaliya, off which the quarter's alleys run; in one of them, Nobel prizewinning author Naguib Mahfouz was born in 1911. Immediately to your right stands the sturdy fifteenth-century caravanserai or **Wikala of Qaitbey**, now occupied by tinsmiths and their families. Such caravanserais naturally clustered near the city gates, and the facades of three more *wikalas* (the last reduced to a mere portal) are visible beyond a small domed mausoleum on the other side of Sharia Gamaliya.

Beyond these *wikalas* stands the **Khanqah of Beybars al-Gashankir**, with its unmistakably bulbous dome and stumpy minaret. Founded in 1310, and thus the oldest Sufi monastery in Cairo, the khanqah is entered via a "baffled" corridor which excludes street noises from the inner courtyard. Without tiles or mosaics, the courtyard escapes severity by the variety of its windows: ribbed, S-curved or keel-arched in styles derived from the Fatimid era. Al-Gashankir's tomb (off the corridor) is spectacular by comparison, with sunbeams falling through stained glass onto marbled walls inset with radiating polygons, and his cenotaph within its ebony mashrabiya cage. Sultan for one year only, Beybars was dubbed *al-Gashankir* (the Taster) to distinguish him from Beybars al-Bunduqdari (the Crossbowman), a mightier predecessor.

If you haven't already seen the Beit al-Sihaymi, this can be reached by heading west along the Darb al-Asfur, which starts opposite the khanqah. Otherwise, continue south along Sharia Gamaliya for 100m, past a ruined *wikala*, a fifteenth-century mosque built above shops (whose rent finance its maintenance), and then another mosque. Immediately after this, turn left into Qasr el Shook, an alleyway that bends left around a high stone wall to reach the **Musafirkhana Palace** (9am–4pm; closed Fri; £E1). Though semi-derelict and undergoing slow restoration, this eighteenth-century mansion (where Khedive Ismail was born) retains beautiful mashrabiyas, decorative ceilings, a fountain in the reception hall, and a peaceful atmosphere rarely disturbed by visitors.

Returning to the main street, you'll find that it narrows and forks as it runs south. Precise directions are difficult, but by turning right at one fork and passing through a medieval-looking gate, you should emerge onto a square with shops selling scrap metal and weighing machines, behind the El-Hussein Mosque.

Between Al-Azhar and the Bab Zwayla

Some of the most arresting sights in Islamic Cairo cluster between **al-Azhar Mosque** and the medieval gate known as the **Bab Zwayla** – a fairly brief itinerary (20–60min) which can be followed in either direction. We've described the sequence of places starting from al-Azhar and finishing at the gate, but you could equally well start at the Bab Zwayla (take bus #75 from the Nile Hilton depot on Tahrir, which runs via the Islamic Art Museum) and work north from there.

Bab Zwayla is also the starting point for **longer walking tours** of the Qasaba and Darb al-Ahmar, winding up beneath the Citadel and described in the section following; so you could also take this itinerary in reverse from there.

The Wikala, Mosque-Madrassa and Mausoleum of al-Ghuri

The **Wikala of al-Ghuri** is Cairo's best-preserved merchants' hostel (twenty such squatted or derelict structures remain, out of the 200 active in 1835). Its upstairs rooms have been converted into artists' studios, with a small exhibition on the culture of the Oases on the ground floor, and you can wander in and look around any day but Friday, between 9am and 5pm (9–11am & 2–4pm during Ramadan). With its stables and lock-ups beneath tiers of spartan rooms, the *wikala* is uncompromisingly functional, yet the rhythm of *ablaq* (striped) arches muted by the sharp verticals of shutters, and the severe masonry lightened by mashrabiyas and a graceful fountain, achieves elegance.

Although it was built (in 1505) just as the new Cape route to the East Indies was diminishing Cairo's role as a spice *entrepôt*, the *wikala* doubtless witnessed the kind of scenes described in *The Arabian Nightmare*:

> *The Muhtasib stood immovable, flanked by two huge Turks who carried lanterns on great staves. Black slaves staggered under trunks of merchandise that were being fought over. A party of men were unsuccessfully trying to persuade a camel to leave by the same gate that it had come in by. A sheep was being roasted in the centre of the compound.*

Located on a side street off Sharia al-Azhar, the *wikala* can be reached by turning left upon leaving the mosque of al-Azhar, then following the alley round past a market; or you can visit it after seeing the **Ghuriya** – the mausoleum and mosque-madrassa of al-Ghuri. Boldly striped in buff and white, this pair of buildings makes a set piece at the junction of Sharia al-Muizz and the al-Azhar high road, plainly visible from the footbridge. To the right (west) of the bridge stands the **Mosque-Madrassa**, offering glimpses of the Spice Bazaar from its rear windows, and a grand view of the neighbourhood from its rooftop (£E1 *baksheesh* if someone takes you up). Across the way, al-Ghuri's domed **Mausoleum** now serves as an adult educational centre, with temporary exhibitions on North African cultures, and a theatre with a splendid ceiling where performances by **Whirling Dervishes** are sometimes held (see p.207).

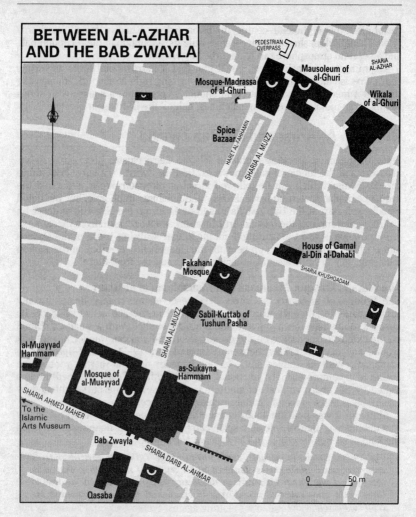

BETWEEN AL-AZHAR AND THE BAB ZWAYLA

Sixty years old when he became the penultimate Mamluke sultan in 1500, **Qansuh al-Ghuri** remained vigorous into his seventies, playing polo, writing poetry and discoursing with Sufis – not forgetting traditional pursuits like building, intrigue and arbitrary justice. Though not averse to filching marble for his mosque-madrassa, al-Ghuri wished to be remembered for his strict enforcement of Koranic precepts: sentencing a dervish accused of "atheism, sorcery, and the use of milk for his ablutions and intimate toilet" to be paraded naked on a camel, and then hanged; and berating his *kadis* (judges) for laxity. Al-Ghuri was killed in 1516 fighting the Turks outside Aleppo; his body was never found and his intended tomb was occupied by his luckless successor, Tumanbey (see below). Gamal al-Ghitani's *Zayni Barakat* is a fictionalised account of this Mamluke twilight.

Towards the Bab Zwayla

In olden times the **Sharia al-Muizz**, the street between the Ghuriya buildings, was roofed over, forming the Silk Bazaar where carpets were sold, the subject of a famous drawing by David Roberts. Nowadays, shops along here sell mostly household goods, making fewer concessions to tourism than Khan el-Khalili, though 75m past al-Ghuri's mosque there's a place making fezes* on brass moulds. The street is named after the conquering Fatimid khalif and it was the chief thoroughfare of Islamic Cairo, running from the Northern Gates down towards the Citadel, and meeting another main road – the Darb al-Ahmar – at the Bab Zwayla. Traditionally, each stretch of al-Muizz had its own name, usually derived from the merchandise sold there.

Roughly 200m down the street you'll find the "Fruit Seller" or **Fakahani Mosque**, whose arabesque-panelled doors are all that remain of the twelfth-century original after its reconstruction in 1735. From here, consider making a detour to the **House of Gamal al-Din al-Dahabi**, seventeenth-century Cairo's foremost gold merchant, whose domed and dadoed reception hall is only surpassed by the haramlik upstairs, with its coffered ceiling, beautiful stained glass and *mashrabiyas*. Athough the EAO's Islamic section Documentation Centre is based here, sightseers are admitted (9am–2pm; closed Fri). To reach the building, turn right at the mosque's northwestern corner, and then right again into Sharia Khushqadam: the mansion is on the left, at no. 6, roughly 100m along.

South of the Fakahani Mosque, Sharia al-Muizz curves around a row of shops that almost conceals the **Sabil-Kuttab of Tusun Pasha**, adorned with wrought-iron sunbursts, garlands and fronds. Shortly afterwards the street passes between two buildings structurally adjacent to the Bab Zwayla, whose formidable outline dominates the view ahead. To your right the wall of a *mashrabiya*-fronted *wikala* is preceded by an unobtrusive door (next to a jewellers' shop) that leads into the eighteenth-century **as-Sukanya Hammam**. The fires that heat the water for this atmospheric men's bathhouse are also used to cook *fuul mudammas* (broad beans) for the neighbourhood's breakfast. The traditional extra allure of such baths was described by Flaubert in 1839: "You reserve the bath for yourself (five francs including masseurs, pipe, coffee, sheet and towel) and you skewer your lad in one of the rooms". Nowadays, such practices are more furtive, so that most bathhouses are prudishly straight, with none of Flaubert's "naked *kellaas* . . . turning you over like embalmers preparing you for the tomb".

Across the way, the **Mosque of al-Muayyad** – also known as the "Red Mosque" from the colour of its exterior – occupies the site of a prison where its founder was once incarcerated for plotting against Sultan Barquq. Plagued by lice and fleas, he vowed to transform it into a "saintly place for the education of scholars" once he came to power. When he did, 40,000 dinars were dutifully lavished on the mosque's construction (1415–22).

The building is entered via a nine-tiered stalactite portal with a red and turquoise geometric frame around its bronze door. Off the vestibule lies a mausoleum where al-Muayyad and his son are buried in befittingly sized cenotaphs.

---

*The **fez**, called a *tarboush* in Egypt, was originally a mark of Ottoman allegiance, which came to represent the secular, westernised *effendi*, as opposed to the turbaned traditionalist. Still later, the *tarboush* was stigmatised as a badge of the *ancien regime* that the Nasserite revolution aimed to dispossess. Waiters and entertainers are the main wearers nowadays.

The kufic inscription on al-Muayyad's reads: "But the god-fearing shall be amidst gardens and fountains: Enter you them, in peace and security" – which seems appropriate for the mosque's courtyard, half filled with palms and open to the sky. Beneath the roofed section a thickly carpeted sanctuary precedes the qibla wall, niched and patterned with polychrome marble and mosaic. But best of all is the **view** from one of the minarets, sited atop the Bab Zwayla (*baksheesh* expected).

The Bab Zwayla

The al-Muayyad's minarets make **Bab Zwayla** look far mightier than the Northern Gates. All of the Fatimid city's defences (which included sixty gates) were in fact reinforced during the 1090s, using Anatolian or Mesopotamian Christian architects and Egyptian labour. Originally the main south gate, Bab Zwayla later became a central point in the Mamluke city, which had outgrown the Fatimid walls and pushed up against Salah al-Din's extensions. Nevertheless, the practice of barring the gates each night continued well into the nineteenth century, maintaining a city within a city. There's a strikingly medieval passage just on the north side of the gate, but the full awesomeness of the Bab itself is best seen from the south side. Note the barbells high up on the western gate-tower: a relic of medieval keep-fit enthusiasts.

The gate was named after Fatimid mercenaries of the Berber al-Zwayla tribe, quartered nearby, whom the Mamlukes displaced. Through the centuries it was the point of departure for caravans to Mecca and for drum-rolls greeting the arrival of senior "Amirs of One Hundred". Dancers and snake-charmers also performed here, and from the fifteenth century onwards punishments provided another spectacle. Dishonest merchants might be hung from hooks or ropes; garrotting, beheading or impalement were favoured for common criminals; while losers in the Mamluke power struggles were often nailed to the doors. It was here that Tumanbey, the last Mamluke sultan, was hanged in 1517, after a vast crowd had recited the *Fatah* and the rope had broken twice before his neck did. However, Bab Zwayla's reputation was subsequently redeemed by its association with Mitwalli al-Qutb, a miracle-working local saint said to manifest himself to the faithful as a gleam of light within the gatehouse.

A whole slew of places to the south of the Bab are covered by the next itinerary, but it's worth mentioning an alternative: namely, heading westwards along Sharia Ahmed Maher **towards the Islamic Art Museum**. En route you'll pass stalls selling waterpipes and braziers, piles of logs destined for the **al-Muayyad Hammam** (another bathhouse, see p.209), a nineteenth-century sabil-kuttab and a fifteenth-century mosque. It's a twenty-minute walk or a five-minute bus ride (#75) to the museum. See "The Museum of Islamic Art" (p.163) for details. The neighbourhood between Bab Zwayla and the Abdin district is known as the **Bab el-Khalq quarter**, after a long-vanished medieval gate.

Between the Bab Zwayla and the Citadel

There are two basic **routes between Bab Zwayla and the Citadel**: via the Qasaba, Sharia al-Muizz and Sharia Qalaa; or following the old **Darb al-Ahmar** (after which this quarter of Islamic Cairo is named). It's possible to get the best of both worlds by combining the Darb al-Ahmar with a detour into the **Qasaba** and **Saddlemakers' Bazaar**, located on the other route: a total distance of about

1.5km. Assuming you're **starting from the Bab Zwayla** like the itinerary below, it's logical to visit the Qasaba before embarking on the Darb al-Ahmar; whereas the reverse holds true if you're **coming from the Citadel**. Starting with the "Blue Mosque" of Aqsunqur on Sharia Bab al-Wazir (the Citadel end of Darb al-Ahmar), you can backtrack through the text from there.

From Bab Zwayla into the Qasaba

Emerging from Bab Zwayla, you'll see a cluster of Islamic monuments across the street, which is often flooded by burst water mains. On the right-hand corner stands a Sufi establishment, the **Zawiya of Farag ibn Barquq**, whose inlaid marble lintels and *ablaq* panels may be hidden by stalls. Opposite the zawiya, the **Mosque of Salih Tala'i** withdraws behind an elegant portico with five keel arches – a unique architectural feature. The shops around its base (whose rents again contribute to the mosque's upkeep) were once at street level, but this has risen well over a metre since the mosque was built in 1408. The last of Cairo's Fatimid mosques, the building shows an assured use of the motifs that were first employed on the Mosque of al-Aqmar: ribbed and cusped arches and panels, carved tie-beams and rosettes. Notice the capitals, plundered from pre-Islamic buildings, and the "floriated kufic" script around the arches.

Straight ahead lies the **Qasaba**, where colourful fabrics, appliqué and leather-work are piled in dens ranked either side of a gloomy, lofty passageway. Erected by Ridwan Bey in 1650, this is one of the best-preserved examples of a covered market left in Cairo. It is popularly known as the *Khiyamiyya*, or **Tentmakers' Bazaar**, as colourful printed fabrics are used here to make tents for moulids and weddings, and to screen unsightly building work – a big improvement on tarpaulins. Printed fabric is sold by the metre, quite cheaply; labour-intensive appliqué work is dearer (see "Shopping").

Beyond the Qasaba

Emerging from the southern end of the Qasaba, **Sharia al-Muizz** extends its path between two mosques and the facade of Ridwan Bey's former palace, beyond which the monuments thin out as vegetable stalls and butchers congest the narrow street. By Mamluke times most of the older quarters here were semi-derelict, merging into the "Tartar Ruins" near the Citadel. The Tartars, recruited by Sultan Kitbugha (1296–96), were despised by other Mamlukes as horse-eaters, and billeted in a quarter that's long since disappeared. About 150m on you'll pass the **Mosque of Gani Bak**, a protégé of Sultan Barsbey, who was poisoned by rivals at the age of twenty-five. Beyond, a few stalls selling donkey and camel wear constitute what remains of the *Souk es-Surugiyyah*, or **Saddlemakers' Bazaar**.

Assuming you don't turn back here to pursue the Darb al-Ahmar, it's a fairly mundane 350-metre walk to al-Muizz's junction with **Sharia Qalaa**. The Sultan Hassan and Rifai mosques below the Citadel are plainly visible at the boulevard's southern end, 300m away. You could do the last leg by bus or tram, or use services in the opposite direction to reach the Islamic Arts Museum, 1km up Sharia Qalaa. Some of the buses continue on to Midan Ataba; others to Abdin or al-Azhar.

Adventurous women might consider visiting the **Hammam Bashtak** bath-house, deep in the Darb al-Ahmar quarter. To get there, follow the backstreet

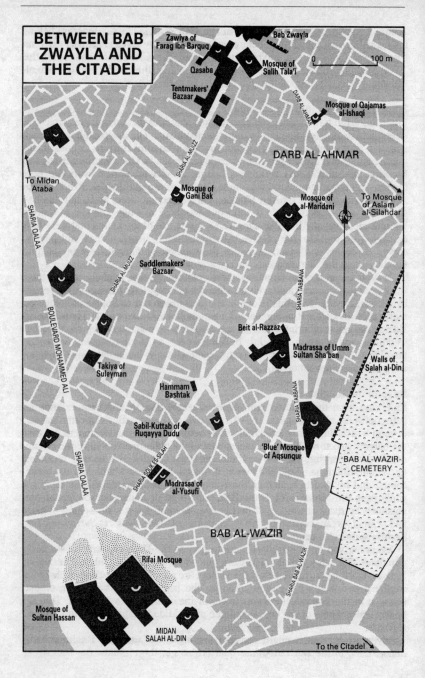

BETWEEN BAB ZWAYLA AND THE CITADEL

Zawiya of Farag Ibn Barquq

Bab Zwayla

Qasaba

Mosque of Salih Tala'I

0   100 m

Tentmakers' Bazaar

Mosque of Qajamas al-Ishaqi

DARB AL-AHMAR

DARB AL-AHMAR

To Midan Ataba

Mosque of Gani Bak

Mosque of al-Maridani

To Mosque of Aslam al-Silahdar

N

SHARIA QALAA

SHARIA AL-MUIZ

Saddlemakers' Bazaar

SHARIA TABBANA

SHARIA AL-MUIZ

BOULEVARD MOHAMMED ALI

Beit al-Razzaz

Madrassa of Umm Sultan Sha'ban

Walls of Salah al-Din

Takiya of Suleyman

SHARIA TABBANA

Hammam Bashtak

Sabil-Kuttab of Ruqayya Dudu

'Blue' Mosque of Aqsunqur

BAB AL-WAZIR CEMETERY

SHARIA QALAA

SHARIA SOUK ES SILAH

Madrassa of al-Yusufi

BAB AL-WAZIR

Rifai Mosque

SHARIA BAB AL-WAZIR

Mosque of Sultan Hassan

MIDAN SALAH AL-DIN

To the Citadel

running eastwards behind the Takiya of Suleyman, a block before al-Muizz's junction with Sharia Qalaa. After 250m it reaches a square, where you'll recognise the baths on the western side by their elaborate portal, whose ribbed keel arch bears the napkin symbol of a *jamdar*. In Mamluke society, this position – Master of Robes – ranked below the "Men of the Sword" (cabinet ministers, chosen from the Amirs of One Hundred), on a par with the sultan's Taster, Cup-Bearer, Slipper-Holder and Polo-Stick Keeper. Several Mamlukes who became sultans included their former rank (or slave-price) amongst their titles. Nowadays the bath serves women and children from the neighbourhood, whose own tenements (*rab*) lack washing facilities.

To reach the Citadel from the hammam, walk 300m down **Sharia Souk es-Silah** (formerly the Weapons Bazaar, now a second-hand ballbearings market), past the neglected gingerbread facade of the **Sabil-Kuttab of Ruqayya Dudu** and then the **Madrassa of al-Yusufi**, whose founder was a Cup-Bearer.

Along the Darb al-Ahmar

An alternative, more picturesque route towards the Citadel follows the "Red Road", or **Darb al-Ahmar**. Originally a cemetery beyond the southern walls of the Fatimid city, this quarter became a fashionable residential area in the fourteenth century, as al-Nasir developed the Citadel. The thoroughfare acquired its present name in 1805, when Mohammed Ali tricked the Mamlukes into staging a coup before slaughtering them "Between the Two Palaces". Stuffed with straw, their heads were sent to Constantinople as a sign of his power; six years later the surviving Mamlukes fell for another ruse, and were massacred on the Citadel.

Start by walking 150m east from Salih Tila'i's Mosque near the Bab Zwayla. On the corner where the Darb turns south, the **Mosque of Qajamas al-Ishaqi** looms over workshops sunk beneath street level. Its founder's blazon – a napkin, penbox, cup and horn of plenty – appears on the knots of the window-grilles, indicating the various positions that Qajamas held under Sultan Qaitbey. A marble panel with swirling leaf forms in red, black and white surmounts the entrance to a vestibule with a gilded ceiling; left off this is the mosque itself. Notice the sinuous decorations on the mihrab (incised grooves filled with red paste or bitumen) and the fine panelling on the floor near the qibla wall (ask the custodian to lift a mat). Best of all are the stained-glass windows in the tomb chamber occupied by one Abu Hurayba. A raised passage connects the mosque with a sabil-kuttab across the street; both were built in the 1480s.

A SHORT DETOUR: AL SILAHDAR'S MOSQUE

If you're not pushed for time, consider detouring off the Darb to visit the **Mosque of Aslam al-Silahdar**. From Qajamas's Mosque, walk through the tunnel around the side and on past a shrine where the street forks (either one will do); al-Silahdar's Mosque lies 250m ahead. The marble panel outside is typical of exterior decoration during the Bahri Mamluke period; inside, the layout is that of a cruciform **madrassa**. Students used to live in rooms above the north and south liwans, behind an ornate facade of stucco mouldings and screened windows. The mosque's founder was a Qipchak Mamluke who lost his position as Swordbearer after Sultan al-Nasir believed rumours spread by his enemies, and imprisoned him, only to reinstate Aslam as *silahdar* six years later.

To return to the Darb, either retrace your steps or take the street running southwest off the square, which joins the Darb further south, beyond al-Maridani's Mosque.

SOUTH ALONG THE DARB AL-AHMAR

South from the Qajamas Mosque, the Darb al-Ahmar passes the **Mosque of al-Maridani**, built in 1340 and still a peaceful retreat from street life. The mosque is usually entered via its northern portal, offset by a stalactite frieze with complex patterns of joggled voussoirs and *ablaq* panels. Inside, a splendid *mashrabiya* screen separates the open courtyard from the qibla riwaq, whose stained-glass windows and variegated columns (Mamluke, pre-Islamic and pharaonic) can be glimpsed through the lattice. Because it was economical with wood, and minimised the effect of warping in a hot, dry climate, *mashrabiya*-work was an ideal technique for Egyptian craftsmen. Architecturally speaking, the minaret marks the replacement of the Ayyubid "pepperpot" finial by a small dome on pillars, which became the hallmark of Mamluke minarets. Below the dome and above the minbar, arboreal forms in stucco may allude to the Koranic verse "A good word is as a good tree – its roots firm, its branches in heaven".

Leaving via the southern entrance, you'll need to turn left to rejoin the Darb – or **Sharia Tabbana** as it's called at this point. Roughly 200m on, past a small Turkish mosque, stands the hulking **Madrassa of Umm Sultan Sha'ban**. *Umm* (Mother of) Sha'ban was the concubine of a son of al-Nasir, whose own son erected the madrassa (1368–69) as a gesture of gratitude after he became sultan at the age of ten; murdered in 1376, he preceded her to the grave and was buried here since his own madrassa was unfinished. A wealth of *murqanas* and *ablaq* rims the entrance, which is flanked by a *sabil* and a drinking trough. Watering animals was meritorious in the eyes of Islam; the Prophet himself had seen a prostitute give water to a thirsty dog, and promised her, "For this action you shall enter paradise". Behind the mosque lurks the **Beit al-Razzaz**, a rambling, derelict palace which the American Research Centre hopes to restore.

Further along the street, now called **Sharia Bab al-Wazir** after the Gate of the Vizier that once stood here, lies the **"Blue Mosque"** or **Mosque of Aqsunqur**. Blue-grey marble outside and a qibla wall covered in indigo and turquoise tiling – with cypresses, tulips and other floral motifs either side of the magnificently inlaid mihrab – explain the mosque's name and popularity with tourists. Originally the mosque was plainer, its *ablaq* arches framing a sahn, now battered and dusty, with a palm tree and chirping birds. The Iznik-style tiles (imported from Turkey or Syria) were added in the 1650s by Ibrahim Agha, who usurped and redecorated the fourteenth-century mosque. However, the minbar inlaid with salmon, plum, green and grey stone is from the original building.

The mosque's founder, Shams al-Din Aqsunqur, intrigued against the successors of Sultan al-Nasir, his father-in-law, whose son al-Ashraf Kuchuk (Little One) was enthroned at the age of six, "reigned" five months, and was strangled by his brother three years later. The reign of al-Kamil Sha'ban (not to be confused with Sha'ban II, who erected the madrassa) lasted a year, ending in a palace coup and the crowning of his brother-in-law, Muzaffar Hadji. Recalling how Aqsunqur had manipulated Kuchuk (who's buried just inside the mosque's entrance) and deftly organised the coup against Sha'ban, Muzaffar promptly had him garotted.

From this mosque, Bab al-Wazir gradually slopes up to meet the approach road **to the Citadel**. If that's your destination, turn left and keep climbing.

Below the Citadel: the Sultan Hassan and Rifai mosques

The Citadel (covered in the following section) is the natural focus of a visit to Islamic Cairo, and as a prelude to a visit, the area just below it, around Midan Salah al-Din square, features two of the city's greatest monuments – the **Sultan Hassan** and **Rifai mosques**. To do justice to these, and to the Citadel itself, deserves a good half a day.

To reach the Citadel area, catch a taxi from downtown (£E1.50), a #72 bus or a less jampacked #54 minibus from Tahrir Square (both of which run past Saiyida Zeinab and Ibn Tulun's Mosque); or ride a tram from Ataba Square 2km along Sharia Qalaa – also an interesting walk if you've got the energy. Any of these approaches will leave you beneath the Citadel, either on Midan Salah al-Din or lower down behind the Sultan Hassan and Rifai mosques. Besides being the start (or finish) of the Darb al-Ahmar itinerary covered previously, Midan Salah al-Din and the Citadel are within walking distance of the superb Mosque of Ibn Tulun, and are a useful jumping-off point for exploring the Cities of the Dead.

Midan Salah al-Din

Prosaic traffic islands and monumental grandeur meet beneath the Citadel on **Midan Salah al-Din**, where makeshift swings and colourful *sewans* are pitched for local moulids. With an audience of lesser mosques on the sidelines, the scene is set for a confrontation of behemoths, given voice when the **muezzins** call. Both the Rifai and Sultan Hassan mosques have powerfully voiced muezzins whose duet echoes off the surrounding tenements. This amazing aural experience is best enjoyed seated in the **outdoor café** beside Sultan Hassan's Mosque; never mind that its tea is vastly overpriced.

From this café vantage point you can survey the **Rifai and Sultan Hassan mosques**, built so close as to create a knife-sharp, almost perpetually shadowed canyon between them. The dramatic angles and chiaroscuro, coupled with the great stalactite portal on this side of the Rifai, make this facade truly spectacular, although the view from Midan Salah al-Din and the Citadel takes some beating. A few centuries ago, all this area would have been swarming with mounted Mamlukes, escorting the sultan to polo matches or prayers.

The Mosque of Sultan Hassan

Raised at the command of a son of al-Nasir, the scale of the **Mosque of Sultan Hassan** was unprecedentedly huge when it was begun in 1356, and some design flaws soon became apparent. The plan to have a minaret at each corner was abandoned after the one directly above the entrance collapsed, killing 300 people; then Hassan himself was assassinated in 1391, two years before the mosque's completion. After another minaret toppled in 1659, the weakened dome collapsed; and if this wasn't enough, the roof was also used as an artillery platform during coups against sultans Barquq (1391) and Tumanbey (1517). But the mosque is big enough to withstand a lot of battering: 150m long, covering an area of 7906 square metres, its walls rise to 36m and its tallest minaret to 68m.

The mosque is best seen when the morning sun illuminates its deep courtyard and cavernous mausoleum, revealing subtle colours and textures disguised by shadows later in the day. The building is open from 8am to 6pm and charges £E1 admission. Entering beneath a towering stalactite hood, you're drawn by instinct through a gloomy domed vestibule with liwans, out into the central **sahn** – a stupendous balancing of mass and void. Vaulted **liwans** soar on four sides, their height emphasised by hanging lamp-chains, their maws by red and black rims; set off by a bulbous-domed ablutions fountain (probably an Ottoman addition). Each liwan was devoted to teaching a rite of Sunni Islam, providing theological justification for the cruciform plan the Mamlukes strove to achieve regardless of the site. At Sultan Hassan, four **madrassas** have been skilfully fitted into an irregular area behind the liwans to maintain the internal cruciform.

Soft-hued marble inlay and a band of monumental kufic script distinguish the sanctuary liwan from its roughly plastered neighbours. Left of the mihrab is a bronze door, exquisitely worked with radiating stars and satellites in gold and silver; on the other side is **Hassan's mausoleum**. Cleverly sited to derive *baraka* from prayers to Mecca, whilst overlooking his old stamping grounds, the mauso- leum is sombre beneath its restored dome, upheld by stalactite pendentives. Around the chamber runs a carved and painted Thuluth inscription, from the Throne verse of the Koran. Note also the ivory-inlaid *kursi*, or Koranic lectern.

The Rifai and Amir Akhur Mosques

The **Rifai Mosque** is pseudo-Mamluke, built between 1869 and 1912 for Princess Khushyar, the mother of Khedive Ismail. With the royal entrance now closed, you enter on the side facing Sultan Hassan. Straight ahead in a sandalwood enclo- sure lies the **tomb of Sheikh Ali al-Rifai**, founder of the Rifai *tariqa* of dervishes, whose moulid occurs during the sixth month of the Muslim calendar, Gumad el-Tani. Off to your left are the *mashrabiya*-screened **tombs of King Fouad** (who reigned 1917–36), his mother, and the last **Shah of Iran**, in whose cortège Sadat walked. The monumental sanctuary (left) is impressive, but after Ismail's chief eunuch had overseen its forty-four columns, nineteen sorts of marble, eighteen window grilles costing £E1000 apiece, and £E25,000 dispersed on gold leaf, dowdiness was scarcely possible – what it lacks is the power of simplicity embodied by the mosques of Ibn Tulun and Sultan Hassan.

Finally, facing the Citadel, you can't miss the **Mosque of Amir Akhur** (left), with its bold red and white *ablaq*, breast-like dome and double minaret finial, incorporating a sabil-kuttab at the lower end of its sloping site.

The Citadel

The Citadel is open daily 8.30am to 4pm; closed on Friday between 11.30am and 1pm. The museums start turning visitors away half an hour before closing. General tickets, cost- ing £E2.50 (students £E1.25), are sold inside the gate-tunnel. The Military and Carriage museums require separate tickets, sold on the spot.

The **Citadel** (*al-Qalaa*) presents the most dramatic feature of Cairo's skyline: a centuries-old bastion crowned by the needle-like minarets of the great Mosque of Mohammed Ali. Steeped in bloodshed and despotism, this fortified complex was begun by **Salah al-Din**, the founder of the Ayyubid dynasty – known throughout Christendom as Saladin, the Crusader's chivalrous foe. Salah al-Din's reign (1171–93) saw much fortification of the city, though it was his nephew, al-Kamil, who developed the citadel as a royal residence, later to be replaced by the palaces of Sultan al-Nasir.

The main features of the Citadel as it is today, however, are associated with **Mohammed Ali**, a worthy successor to the Mamlukes and Turks. In 1811 he feasted 470 leading Mamlukes in the Citadel palace, bade them farewell with honours, then had them ambushed in the sloping lane behind the **Bab al-Azab**, the locked gate opposite the Akhur Mosque. An oil painting in the Manial Palace on Roda Island depicts the apocryphal tale of a Mamluke who escaped by leaping the walls on his horse; in reality he survived by not attending the feast.

Nowadays the **main entrance** to the Citadel is at a higher level, closer to the centre of the complex; the road there curves up from Midan Salah al-Din in a clockwise direction past the start of Sharia Bab al-Wazir. Alternatively you can head straight up the stairs to the west of the Bab al-Azab. Having passed through the tunnel-gate and the inner Bab al-Wustani, you emerge into a courtyard with the **Police National Museum** on one side. This quirky exhibition includes sanitised "cells throughout the ages"; rooms devoted to Egypt's most sensational murders and assassinations (Sadat's is conspicuously absent); and a risible US "how to recognise drugs" kit. Apropos of Sadat and drugs, his brother Esmat is rumoured to have received a percentage on every kilo of hash sold in Cairo.

Mohammed Ali's Monuments

The **Mohammed Ali Mosque**, which so enables Cairo's skyline, disappoints at close quarters: its domes are sheathed in tin, its alabaster surfaces grubby. Nonetheless, it exudes *folie de grandeur*, starting with the ornate clock given by Louis Philippe (in exchange for the obelisk in the Place de la Concorde, Paris), which has never worked; and the Turkish Baroque ablutions fountain, resembling a giant easter egg. Inside the mosque, whose lofty dome and semi-domes are decorated like a Fabergé egg, the use of space is classically Ottoman, reminis-

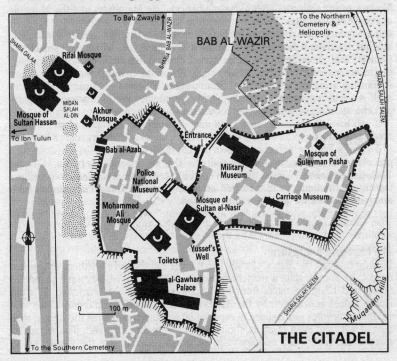

THE CITADEL

cent of the great mosques of Istanbul. A constellation of chandeliers and globe-lamps illuminates Thuluth inscriptions, a gold-scalloped mihrab and two minbars: one faced in alabaster, the other strangely Art Nouveau. Mohammed Ali is buried beneath a white marble cenotaph, behind a bronze grille on the right of the entrance. The mosque itself was erected between 1824 and 1848, but the domes had to be demolished and rebuilt in the 1930s.

Due south of here stands what remains of Mohammed Ali's **al-Gawhara Palace**, where he waited while the Mamlukes were butchered. Also known as the *Bijou* (Jewelled) Palace, its French-style salons exhibit portraits of the khedives and kings of Egypt and their wives; life-size models of monarchs and courtiers in nineteenth-century dress; royal furniture and tableware; and a collection of awful Impressionist works; the *tromp l'oeil* in the main salon is none too successful either. It was around here that al-Nasir's Striped Palace once stood, and that Saint Francis of Assisi preached to the Ayyubid ruler al-Kamil. For many of the hapless boy-sultans chosen by the Mamlukes, the palace amounted to a luxury prison, and finally an execution cell. Nevertheless, the Citadel remained the residence of Egypt's rulers for nearly 700 years, and Mohammed Ali prophesied that his descendants would rule supreme as long as they resided here. Ismail's move to the Abdin Palace did indeed foreshadow an inexorable decline in their power.

Medieval remains

For an idea of the Citadel's appearance before Mohammed Ali's grandiose recon-struction programme, visit the **Mosque of Sultan al-Nasir** (also called the Mosque of Ibn Qalaoun, after al-Nasir's father). The Mamlukes and the Mongols of Persia enjoyed good relations when the mosque was constructed (1318–35), and a Tabriz master mason probably designed the corkscrew minarets with their bulbous finials and faience decorations, if not the dome, which also smacks of Central Asia. Since Selim the Grim carted its marble panelling back to Turkey, the mosque's courtyard has looked ruggedly austere, with rough-hewn pillars supporting *ablaq* arches linked by Fatimid-style tie-beams – although the mihrab itself is a feast of gold and marble. Notice the stepped merlons around the para-pet, and the blue, white and silver decorations beneath the sanctuary liwan.

If you leave the mosque, turn right and walk clockwise around it, you'll find a wasteland with barbicans at the far end. There, a locked gate prevents admission to **Yussef's Well**, which spirals down 97m to the level of the Nile, whence water percolates through fissures in the bedrock. Dug by prisoners between 1176 and 1182, this so-called "Well of the Snail" had its steps strewn with soil to provide a footing for the donkeys that carried up water jars. The Citadel's infamous Jubb dungeon, "a noisome pit where foul and deadly exhalations, unclean vermin and bats rendered the pitchy darkness more horrible", was blocked up by al-Nasir in 1329, but reactivated under the latterday Mamluke Sultans.

The Northern Enclosure

Passing through the Bab al-Qullah, you'll enter the Citadel's northern enclosure, open to visitors despite a military presence. Straight ahead, beyond a parade of Soviet and US-made tanks from four Arab–Israeli Wars, Mohammed Ali's old Harim Palace is occupied by the **Military Museum** (£E1 admission). This vast exhibition devotes more space to ceremonial accoutrements than the savage real-ities of war, and even pacifists should enjoy the main salon, with its spectacular *tromp l'oeil*. Whilst in a military vein, it's worth recalling that the Citadel fell to

Mohammed Ali after he stationed cannons on the Muqattam heights. The military electronics that festoon them now are a reminder that strategic ground seldom loses its utility.

By turning right at the barracks near the enclosure entrance and following the lane around, you'll come out into a compound with a formal garden. At the northern end stands the **Carriage Museum**, with its row of horse-heads. Inside are six royal carriages and two picnic buggies, one of them an infant prince's; the largest state carriage – heavy with gold – was presented as a gift to Khedive Ismail by Emperor Napoleon and Empress Eugénie. Beware of the avaricious curator.

Behind here are two of the many bastions along the Citadel's ramparts, each with evocative names. Although the derivation of **Burg Kirkyilan** (Tower of the Forty Serpents) is unknown, the **Burg al-Matar** (Tower of the Flight Platform) probably housed the royal carrier pigeons. Neither can be entered, but it's worth visiting a neglected treasure at the other end of the compound. A cluster of verdigris domes and a pencil-sharp minaret identifies the **Mosque of Suleyman Pasha** as an early sixteenth-century Ottoman creation; borne out by the lavish arabesques and rosettes adorning the interior of the cupola and semi-domes. Inside, cross the courtyard to find a **mausoleum** where the tombs of amirs and their families have *tabuts* indicating their rank: turbans or hats for the men, floral-patterned lingums for the women. Adjacent to the courtyard is a **madrassa** where students took examinations beneath a riwaq upheld by painted beams.

On from the Citadel
Of the various itineraries emanating from the Citadel, the shortest takes you to the awesome Mosque of Ibn Tulun, whilst the longest ones (requiring transport) involve the Cities of the Dead; both are covered in sections following. The section *before* this one details the route along the Darb al-Ahmar/Sharia Bab al-Wazir from the Bab Zwayla; you could pick up the trail at the Blue Mosque and follow the directions in the text in reverse.

The Mosque of Ibn Tulun and the Saiyida Zeinab quarter

Two aspects of Islam are strikingly apparent in the great **Mosque of Ibn Tulun** and the quarter of the city named after Egypt's beloved saint, **Saiyida Zeinab**. The mosque evokes the simplicity of Islam's central tenet, submission to Allah, whereas the surrounding neighbourhoods are urban stews seething with popular cults. **Zeinab's moulid** is the wildest festival in Cairo, sucking 500,000 people into a pulsing vortex around her mosque, 1km west of Ibn Tulun's. Its high-octane blend of intense devotion and sheer enjoyment is also characteristic of **other moulids** honouring Saiyida Nafisa, Ruqayya and Aisha, whose shrines lie between Ibn Tulun and El-Khalifa (the Southern Cemetery).

The following section covers only Ibn Tulun, Saiyida Zeinab and sites along Sharia Saliba, which are shown in relation to the Citadel and Southern Cemetery on the **map** overpage. Conceivably, you could visit all of them in a single day – though a more leisurely approach seems advisable.

APPROACHES TO THE QUARTER
Bus #72 or minibus #54 provide the easiest access to Saiyida Zeinab **from Midan Tahrir**, running through the quarter past its namesake shrine and within sight of Ibn Tulun's Mosque, towards the Citadel.

Alternatively, the fifteen-minute walk **from the Mosque of Sultan Hassan** to Ibn Tulun takes you along **Sharia Saliba**, past a prison that serves as a barometer of law and order: whenever there's a crackdown you can see several arms thrust from each cell window. Next comes the lofty **Sabil-Kuttab of Qaitbey**, with its bold red, white and black facade. Farther along, beyond the **Khanqah of Shaykhu**, Sharia al-Khalifa turns off **towards the Southern Cemetery**, as described under the following section, "Cities of the Dead". By ignoring this and carrying on past the nineteenth-century *sabil* **of Umm Abbas** with its blue and red panels and gilt calligraphy, you'll see the huge walls of Ibn Tulun's Mosque on the left. Its entrance is that way, too, and not via the nearest portal, which belongs to the **Madrassa of Sarghatmish**, closed to non-Muslims.

The Mosque of Ibn Tulun

Open daily 9am–4pm; £E1 admission, students 50pt

Ibn Tulun's Mosque is a rare survivor of the classical Islamic period of the ninth and tenth centuries, when the Abbasid khalifs ruled the Muslim world from Iraq. Their purpose-built capital, Samarra, centred upon a congregational mosque where the entire population assembled for Friday prayer, and this most likely provided the inspiration for the Ibn Tulun. You enter the mosque via a **ziyada**, or enclosure, designed to distance the mosque from its surroundings; to the left stands the Gayer-Anderson House (see below). It's only within the inner walls that the vastness of the mosque becomes apparent: the sahn (courtyard) is 92 metres square; whilst the complex, measuring 140m by 122m, covers six and a half acres.

Besides sheer size, the **mosque** impresses by its simplicity. Strewn with pebbles and open to the sky, its vast court has the grandeur of a desert where all of Allah's worshippers are equally prostrated beneath the sun. Ibn Tulun's architects understood the power of repetition – see how the merlons echo the rhythm of the arcades – but also restraint: small floral capitals and stucco rosettes seem the only decorative motifs, although that isn't so. Beneath the arcades you'll find a sycamore-wood frieze over two kilometres long, relating roughly one fifth of the Koran in kufic script. The severely geometric *mida'a*, an inspired focal point, was added in the thirteenth century, when the mihrab was also jazzed up with marble and glass mosaics – the only unsuccessful note in the complex.

The **minaret** (reached by walking anticlockwise around the *ziyada*) is unique for its exterior spiral staircase, giving the structure a helical shape. Supposedly, Ibn Tulun twisted a scrap of paper into a spiral, and then justified his absent-minded deed by presenting it as the design for a minaret. But the great minaret at Samarra (itself influenced by ancient Babylonian ziggurats) seems a likelier source of inspiration.

The Gayer-Anderson House

Open 9am–4pm, Fri 9–11am & 1.30–3.30pm. Admission £E1; ticket also valid for same-day admission to the Islamic Arts Museum.

From the *ziyada* of the Ibn Tulun mosque a sign directs you to the **Gayer-Anderson House**, otherwise known as the *Beit al-Kritiliya* (House of the Cretan Woman), which abuts the southeast corner of the mosque.

Gayer-Anderson was a retired English major who during the 1930–40s refurbished two mansions dating from the sixteenth and eighteenth centuries, filling them with his Orientalist bric-a-brac. Amongst the many paintings is a self-

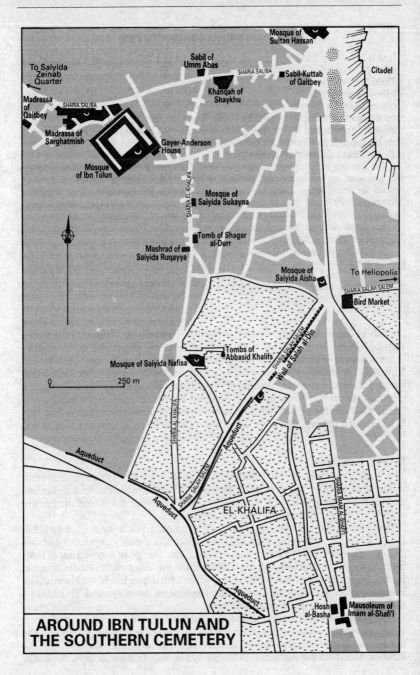

To Saiyida
Zeinab
Quarter

Madrassa
of Qaitbey

SHARIA SALIBA

Madrassa of
Sarghatmish

Mosque
of Ibn Tulun

Sabil of
Umm Abas

SHARIA SALIBA

Khanqah of
Shaykhu

Gayer-Anderson
House

Mosque of
Sultan Hassan

Sabil-Kuttab
of Qaitbey

Citadel

SHARIA EL-KHALIFA

Mosque of
Saiyida Sukayna

Mashrad of
Saiyida Ruqayya

Tomb of Shagar
al-Durr

Mosque of
Saiyida Aisha

To Heliopolis

SHARIA SALAH SALEM

Bird Market

0   250 m

Mosque of Saiyida Nafisa

Tombs of
Abbasid Khalifs

Wall of Salah al-Din

SHARIA SALAH SALEM

SHARIA EL KHALIFA

Aqueduct

Aqueduct

SHARIA SALAH SALEM

EL-KHALIFA

SHARIA IMAM AL-SHAFI'I

Aqueduct

Aqueduct

Hosh
al-Basha

Mausoleum of
Imam al-Shafi'i

AROUND IBN TULUN AND
THE SOUTHERN CEMETERY

IBN TULUN AND AL-QITAI

It was from Iraq that the Abbasids made Ahmed Ibn Tulun governor of Fustat in 868, and smarted as he declared his independence. Ibn Tulun (the "Son of Tulun", a Turkish slave) founded the Tulunid dynasty which ruled Egypt until 905, and established a new city to the northeast of Fustat. According to legends, Noah's Ark had come to rest on this site when the Flood receded; Moses confronted the pharaoh's magicians here; and Abraham had been ready to sacrifice his son on a nearby hillock. Unperturbed by this, nor by the existence of Christian and Jewish cemeteries on the site, he dictated the construction of **al-Qitai**, called "the Wards" after its division into military cantonments.

Ibn Tulun's performance on the polo field filled his doctors with foreboding, for in sickness he "refused to follow their orders, flouted their prescribed diet, and when he found himself still sinking, he had their heads chopped off, or flogged them till they died". But under his soft-living successor the al-Qitai *midan* was converted into a garden with a quicksilver lake, where the insomniac Khomaruya lolled on an air-bed guarded by a blue-eyed lion. The Tulinids could afford such luxury, for their annual revenue amounted to 4,300,000 dinars.

When the Abbasids subsequently reconquered Egypt in 905 they destroyed everything here but the mosque, which became derelict. Exploited as a makeshift caravanserai, and a hideout for bodysnatchers during the terrible famine of 1200, it was belatedly restored in 1296 by Sultan Laghin, who had hidden there as an amir suspected of murdering the sultan.

portrait of Gayer-Anderson wearing a pharaonic headdress. **Tours** of the house (the buildings are linked by a passage on the third floor) are conducted by charming women curators who refuse *baksheesh*. There are Persian, Chinese and Queen Anne rooms, and an amazing guest bedroom named after Damascus, whence its opulent wooden panelling originated. Women can sneak through a camouflaged *dulap* (wall cupboard) into the screened gallery overlooking the samalik, as in olden days. With its polychrome fountain, decorated ceiling and kilim-covered pillows, this is the finest reception hall left in Islamic Cairo. It was the set for a tryst and murder in the James Bond film, *The Spy Who Loved Me*.

Saiyida Zeinab

The backstreets west of Ibn Tulun harbour another gem of Islamic architecture in the **Madrassa of Qaitbey** (daily 9am–4pm; 50pt). Ignore the dust and grime and tip the curator to unlock the building, whose mosaic floors and minbar are superb examples of fifteenth-century craftsmanship.

Real aficionados can also track down other monuments in the area, detailed in the AUC guide. Otherwise, ride westwards into the densely populated **Saiyida Zeinab quarter**, where Islamic and modern Cairo merge in a confusion of tenement blocks and **markets**. Midan Lazoghli, on the edge of the Abdin quarter, hosts a daily car spares and repairs *souk*, while a **bird market** is held beneath an overpass in the direction of Qasr al-Aini Hospital on Mondays and Thursdays – hence its name, the *Souk Itnayn w Khamis*.

Like Saiyida Zeinab metro station, the market is on the quarter's periphery, where it merges with Garden City and Old Cairo (see map on p.122). To the northeast of the slaughterhouse district and the al-Abdin Mosque lies the **Brooke Hospital for Animals**. Founded by Dorothy Brooke in 1934, the hospital treats infirm donkeys and other beasts of burden free of charge, purchases the incurables and puts them out to grass. Egyptians find the whole idea bizarre, but appreciate the service; a stream of patients wends up Sikket el-Masbah, off Sharia Bayram el-Tonsi. Phone if you want to visit (☎849-312).

The quarter's highlight is the annual **Moulid of Saiyida Zeinab**, which features parades of Sufi orders by day, and nocturnal festivities that attract 500,000 people. Ecstatic devotion and pleasure rub shoulders (and other parts of the anatomy, should you be a woman) in this seething, mostly male crowd, transfixed by the music and spectacles. To see the *zikrs*, snake-charmers, conjurers, nail-swallowers and dancing horses performing, you'll have to force your way through a scrum of people and *sewans* – don't bring any valuables. The fifteen-day event takes place during Ragab, the seventh month of the Muslim calendar.

The focal point for these celebrations is the **Mosque of Saiyida Zeinab** (closed to non-Muslims), off Sharia Bur Said. Born in 628 AD, Zeinab, the Prophet's granddaughter, emigrated to Fustat after the Ummayads slew her brother, Hussein, and died there shortly afterwards. For Egyptian Muslims – especially women – Zeinab is a protectress whose *baraka* (blessing) is sought in matters of fortune and health; in other words, a popular saint. Although the Koran forbids the deification of mortals, the human urge to anthropomorphise religious faith seems irresistible. Every Muslim nation has its own "saints" (chosen by popular acclaim rather than a supreme authority), and respects bloodlines descended from the Prophet or his immediate kin. For the Shia, the martyrdom of Ali and Hussein is a parable of their own oppression, whilst Zeinab (whose *moulid* attracts foreign Shia) is honoured as their closest kinswoman.

To return to downtown Cairo from here, catch a Tahrir-bound #72 bus or #54 minibus from outside Zeinab's mosque, or ask for directions to the nearest metro entrance (ten minutes' walk). From Saiyida Zeinab station you can ride two stops north to Tahrir, or two stops south to reach Old Cairo (Mari Girgis station).

Cities of the Dead

Several hundred thousand Cairenes live amid the **Cities of the Dead**: two vast cemeteries which stretch away from the Citadel to merge with newer shantytowns below the Muqattam. The Southern Cemetery, sprawling to the southeast of Ibn Tulun's mosque, is only visible from the Muqattam, or at close quarters. The Northern Cemetery, by contrast, is an unforgettably eerie sight, with dozens of mausolea rising from a sea of dwellings along the road from Cairo Airport.

Although tourists generally – and understandably – feel uneasy about viewing the cemeteries' splendid **funerary architecture** with squatters living all around the tombs, few natives regard the Cities of the Dead as forbidding places. Egyptians have a long tradition of building "houses" near their ancestral graves and picnicking or even staying there overnight; other families have simply occupied them. By Cairene standards these are poor but decent neighbourhoods, with shops, schools and electricity, maybe even piped water and sewers. The saints buried here provide a moral touchstone and *baraka* for their communities, who honour them with **moulids**.

Though not a dangerous quarter, it's best to exercise some caution when **visiting**. Don't flaunt money or costly possessions, and be sure to dress modestly; women should have a male escort, and will seem more respectable if wearing a headscarf. By responding to local kids (who may request *baksheesh*) with the right blend of authority and affection, you can win the sympathy of their elders and seem less of an intruder; react wrongly, and you might be stoned out of the neighbourhood. You'll be marginally less conspicuous on Fridays, when many Cairenes visit their family plots; but remember that mosques can't be entered during midday prayers. At all events, leave the cemeteries well before dark, if only to avoid getting lost in their labyrinthine alleys – and don't stray to the east into the inchoate (and far riskier) slums built around the foothills of the Muqattam.

The Southern Cemetery

The older and larger **Southern Cemetery** is broadly synonymous with the residential quarter of **El-Khalifa**, named after the Abbasid Khalifs buried amidst its mudbrick *rabs*. Although the Abbasid tombs aren't half as imposing as those of the Mamlukes in the Northern Cemetery, one of the approach routes passes several shrines noted for their moulids, while another moulid is held at the beautiful **Mausoleum of Imam al-Shafi'i**, best reached by bus as a separate excursion. For this reason, we've described two different routes into what Egyptians call "the Great Cemetery" (*al-Qarafah al-Kubra*).

SHARIA SALIBA TO THE TOMB OF THE ABBASID KHALIFS

This walking route passes through one of the oldest poor neighbourhoods in Cairo, where it's thought that people started settling around their saints' graves as early as the tenth century. None of the tombs are remarkable visually, but the stories and moulids attached to them are interesting. The trail begins where **Sharia al-Khalifa** turns south off Sharia Saliba, just after the Khanqah of Shayku (see the previous section).

Heading south along this narrow street, full of commerce and capering children, you'll be "hey mistered" past a succession of tombs. The second on the left, within a green and white mosque, is that of **Saiyida Sukayna**, a daughter of Hussein, whose moulid (held during Rabi el-Tani) is attended by several thousand locals and features traditional entertainments like dancing horses and sticktwisters.

Such saintly graves invariably acquired an oratory (*mashrad*) or mosque, unlike the **Tomb of Shagar al-Durr**, 100m further on: a derelict edifice sunk below street level. Shagar al-Durr ("Tree of Pearls") was the widow of Sultan Ayyub, who ruled as *sultana* of Egypt for eighty days (1249–50) until the Abbasid Khalif pronounced "Woe unto nations ruled by a woman", compelling her to marry Aybak, the first Mamluke sultan, and govern "from behind the *mashrabiya*". In 1257 she ordered Aybak's murder after learning that he sought another wife, but then tried to save him; the assassins cried, "If we stop halfway through, he will kill both you and us!" Rejecting her offer to marry Qutuz, their new leader, the Mamlukes handed Shagar al-Durr over to Aybak's former wife, whose servants beat her to death with bath-clogs and threw her body to the jackals. Now totally gutted, her locked tomb once contained a *tabut* inscribed: "Oh you who stand beside my grave, show not surprise at my condition. Yesterday I was as you, tomorrow, you will be like me".

Slightly further down and across the street, three shrines are grouped within a compound entered via a green and white doorway. The **Mashrad of Saiyida Ruqayya**, on the left, commemorates the step-sister of Saiyida Zeinab, with whom she came to Egypt, the name of her father, Ali, adorns its rare Fatimid mihrab, and the devotion she inspires is particularly evident during Ruqayya's Moulid.

Ruqayya's devotion doesn't, however, compare with that accorded to the **Mosque of Saiyida Nafisa**, 100m to the south, past the market square. This, Egypt's third-holiest shrine, is closed to non-Muslims, though visitors can still appreciate the good-natured crowd that hangs around after Friday noon prayers, or Nafisa's *moulid*, held usually in the middle of the month of Gamad al-Tani (see p.206). Honoured during her lifetime as a descendant of the Prophet, a *hafizat al-Qur'an* (one who knows the Koran by heart) and a friend of Imam al-Shafi'i, Nafisa was famed for working miracles and conferring *baraka*. Her shrine has been repeatedly enlarged since Fatimid times – the Southern Cemetery possibly begun with devotees settling or being buried near her grave – and the present mosque was built in 1897.

If you walk through the passage to its left, turn right at the end and then right again, you should find yourself outside the compound enclosing the **Tombs of the Abbasid Khalifs**. Having been driven from Baghdad by the Mongols, the khalifs' surviving relatives gratefully accepted Beybars's offer to re-establish them in Egypt, only to discover that they were "No longer Commander of the Faithful, but Commander of the Wind". Beybars appropriated the domed mausoleum (usually kept locked) for his own sons; the khalifs were buried outdoors in less than grandiose tombs. Notice the beautiful foliate Kufic inscription on the cenotaph of Khadiga, under the wooden shed. In 1517 the last Abbasid Khalif was formally divested of his office, which the Ottomans assumed in 1538, and Ataturk abolished in the 1920s.

An alternative route back towards the Citadel passes the **Mosque of Saiyida Aisha**, whose moulid occurs during Sha'ban. To get there, retrace your steps to the market square south of Ruqayya's shrine and take the road leading off to the right. It's roughly 500 metres' walk to Aisha's Mosque on Sharia Salah Salem, which runs southwest alongside the medieval **Wall of Salah al-Din**. From here you can simply follow the tramlines **towards the Citadel** (1km). If you happen to be here on Friday, consider making a detour to the **bird market** (*Souk al-Asafeer* or *Souk al-Gom'a*), held on a side street to the south of the Salah Salem overpass.

THE MAUSOLEUM OF IMAM AL-SHAFI'I

Imam al-Shafi'i, revered as the founder of one of the four rites of Sunni Islam, occupies a great mausoleum 2km from the Citadel. Access is straightforward: #182 buses from the Midan Tahrir stop 20m up the road from the mausoleum, while comfier #54 minibuses turn off Sharia Imam al-Shafi'i 100m beforehand. If you miss the turn-off, ride on to the terminal, have a glass of tea with the minibus driver, and get dropped at the corner on the way back. Alternatively, a taxi from the Citadel costs about £E1.

Recognisable by its graceful dome, crowned by a metal boat like a weather vane, the **Mausoleum of Imam al-Shafi'i** lurks beside a mosque at the end of the street. The largest Islamic mortuary complex in Egypt, it was raised in 1211 by al-Kamil, Salah al-Din's nephew, a propagator of Sunni orthodoxy like the Imam himself, who died in 820. Al-Shafi'i's teak cenotaph – into which the faithful slip petitions – lies beneath a magnificent dome perched on stalactite squinches, painted red and blue, with gilt designs. The walls are clad in variegated marble, dating from Qaitbey's restoration of the building in the 1480s. In times past, the boat on the roof was filled with birdseed and water; boats are vehicles of spiritual enlightenment in Islamic symbolism, while birds are associated with souls.

Al-Shafi'i's **Moulid** attracts many sick or infirm people, seeking his *baraka*. The festival occurs in Sha'ban, the eighth month of the Muslim calendar, but the starting date varies. Normally it's the first Wednesday of the month; however, if this falls on the first or second day of Sha'ban, the moulid is delayed until the following Wednesday. Either way, it ends on Wednesday evening the following week. More prosaically, the street leading northwards to the mausoleum from the al-Basatin quarter is used for scrap, clothing and livestock **markets** every Friday morning.

By walking clockwise around the block in which the Imam's mausoleum is located, you'll find a five-domed complex directly behind it. Inside the courtyard are clumps of cenotaphs decorated with garlands and fronds, topped by a turban, fez or other headdress, indicating the deceased's rank. These constitute the **Hosh al-Basha**, where Mohammed Ali's sons, their wives, children and retainers are buried. The conspicuously plain cenotaph belongs to a princess with radical sympathies, who abhorred ostentation. Folklore has it that King Farouk was secretly buried here amongst his ancestors, following his death in exile.

The Northern Cemetery

The finest of Cairo's funerary monuments – erected by the Burgi Mamlukes from the fourteenth to sixteenth centuries – are spread around the **Northern Cemetery**. Most tourists who venture in from Sharia Salah Salem are content to see three main sites, plus whatever crops up in between, over an hour or so.

Aside from catching a taxi (ask for the *Qarafat al-Sharqiyyah* – "Eastern Cemetery" in Arabic), the surest way of **getting there** is to walk **from al-Azhar**. This takes ten to fifteen minutes, following the dual carriageway Bab al-Ghuriyab past university buildings and uphill to its roundabout junction with Salah Salem. Although the tombs of Anuk and Tulbey are amongst the nearby mausolea, you might prefer to head 250m north along the highway to *Dirasa* (also accessible by bus #500 **from Midan Tahrir or Midan Ataba**), and then cut east into the cemetery. That way you start with Qaitbey's Mausoleum – a known point on the circuit – whose ornate dome and minaret are clearly visible. Dirasa can also be reached by tram from Midan Triomphe in Heliopolis, and has been designated as the terminus of the cross-town metro line.

SULTAN QAITBEY'S MAUSOLEUM

Sultan Qaitbey was the last strong Mamluke ruler, and a prolific builder of monuments from Mecca to Syria; his funerary complex (depicted on £E1 notes) is amongst the grandest in the Northern Cemetery. His name meant "the restored" or "returned", indicating that he nearly died at birth; as a scrawny lad, he fetched only fifty dinars in the slave market. The rapid turnover in rulers after 1437 accelerated his ascent, and in 1468 he was acclaimed as sultan by the bodyguard of the previous incumbent, an old comrade-in-arms who parted from Qaitbey with tears and embraces. His twenty-eight-year reign was only exceeded by al-Nasir's, and Qaitbey remained "tall, handsome and upright as a reed" well into his eighties, still attentive to citizens' complaints at twice-weekly *diwaniyyas*.

An irregularly shaped complex built in 1474, the **Mausoleum of Sultan Qaitbey** is dynamically unified by the bold stripes along its facade, which is best viewed from the north. The trilobed portal carries one's eye to the graceful **minaret**, soaring through fluted niches, stalactite brackets and balconies to a teardrop finial. Inside, the **madrassa** liwans, floors and walls are a feast of marble and geometric patterns, topped by elaborately carved and gilded ceilings, with a lovely octagonal roof lantern. Qaitbey's **tomb chamber** off the qibla liwan is simi-

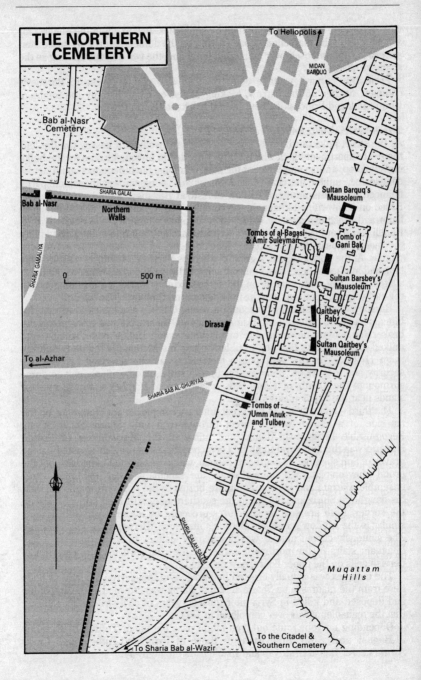

THE NORTHERN CEMETERY

To Heliopolis

MIDAN
BARQUQ

Bab al-Nasr
Cemetery

SHARIA GALAL

Bab al-Nasr

Northern Walls

SHARIA GAMALIYA

0   500 m

Sultan Barquq's
Mausoleum

Tombs of al-Bagasi
& Amir Suleyman

Tomb of
Gani Bak

Sultan Barsbey's
Mausoleum

Qaitbey's
Rab

Dirasa

Sultan Qaitbey's
Mausoleum

To al-Azhar

SHARIA BAB AL-GHURIYAB

Tombs of
Umm Anuk
and Tulbey

Muqattam
Hills

SHARIA SALAH SALEM

To Sharia Bab al-Wazir

To the Citadel &
Southern Cemetery

larly decorated, its lofty dome upheld by squinches. Ask to climb the minaret for a close view of the marvellous stone carving on the dome's exterior. A raised star-pattern is superimposed over an incised floral one, the two designs shifting as the shadows change.

From this minaret vantage point you can also plot a course to Barsbey's complex, further up the narrow, kinking street, or try to identify the tombs of Umm Anuk and Princess Tulbey, several blocks to the southwest.

THE BARSBEY AND BARQUQ COMPLEXES

As the street jinks northwards from Qaitbey's mausoleum it passes (on the left) the *rab* or apartment block which Qaitbey deeded to provide income for the building's upkeep, and as employment for poor relations. Such bequests could not be confiscated, unlike merchants' and Mamlukes' personal wealth, which partly financed the **Mausoleum of Sultan al-Ashraf Barsbey**, 200m beyond the *rab*. Based on a now-ruined khanqah, the complex was expanded to include a mausoleum and mosque-madrassa (1432) after Barsbey's funerary pile near Khan el-Khalili was found lacking. If there's a curator around, ask him to lift a mat hiding the marble mosaic floor inside the long mosque, which also features a superb minbar. At the northern end, a great dome caps Barsbey's tomb, its marble cenotaph and mother-of-pearl-inlaid mihrab softly lit by stained-glass windows, added at a later date. The stone carving on the dome's exterior marks a transition between the early chevron patterns and the fluid designs on Qaitbey's Mausoleum.

Barsbey was the sultan who acquired young Qaitbey at a knockdown rate. He himself had been purchased in Damascus for 800 dinars, but was "returned to the broker for a filmy defect in one of his blue eyes". Unlike other sultans who milked the economy, Barsbey troubled to pay his Mamlukes regularly and the reign (1422–38) of this well-spoken teetotaller was characterised by "extreme security and low prices". Fifty metres up the street, another finely carved dome surmounts the **Tomb of Gani Bak**, a favourite of Barsbey's, whose mosque stands near the Saddlemakers' Bazaar.

The third – and oldest – of the great funerary complexes lies 50m away, on the far side of a square with a direct through-road onto Sharia Salah Salem. Recognisable by its twin domes and minarets, the **Mausoleum of Sultan Barquq** was the first royal tomb in a cemetery that was previously noted for the graves of Sufi sheikhs. Its courtyard is plain, with sere, stunted tamarisks, but the proud chevron-patterned domes above the sanctuary liwan uplift the whole ensemble. Barquq and his son Farag are buried in the northern tomb chamber; his daughters Shiriz and Shakra in the southern one, with their faithful nurse in the corner. Both are soaring structures preceded by *mashrabiyas* with designs similar to the window-screens in Barquq's madrassa "Between the Two Palaces". The sinuously carved minbar was donated by Qaitbey to what was then a Sufi khanqah; stairs in the northwest corner of the courtyard lead to a warren of dervish cells on the upper floors, now deserted.

The complex was actually erected by Farag, who transferred his father's body here from the madrassa on Sharia al-Muizz. Farag was crowned at the age of ten and deposed and killed in Syria after thirteen years of civil strife – it's amazing that the mausoleum was ever completed in 1411.

Depending on your route out, you might pass the minor **Tombs of Barsbey al-Bagasi and Amir Suleyman**, or those of **Princess Tulbey and Umm Anuk**, nearer Bab al-Ghuriyab and visible from the highway.

OLD CAIRO AND RODA ISLAND

The southern sector of the city is divisible into three main areas, the most interesting of which is **Old Cairo** (*Masr al-Qadima*), the historic link between Egypt's pharaonic and Islamic civilisations. Here, the fortress-town of **Babylon**, where the Holy Family is thought to have taken refuge, developed into a powerhouse of native Christianity which today remains the heart of Cairo's **Coptic community**. Featuring several medieval churches, the superb **Coptic Museum** and an atmospheric synagogue, it totally eclipses the site of **Fustat** – Egypt's first Islamic settlement, of which little remains but the much-altered **Mosque of Amr** – or the largely uninteresting **southern suburbs** of Ma'adi and Helwan.

Connected by bridge to Old Cairo – and so covered in this section, too – is **Roda Island**, which boasts a venerable Nilometer and the wonderfully kitsch Manial Palace. The palace is, in fact, more easily accessible from Central Cairo.

APPROACHING OLD CAIRO: TRANSPORT LINKS

Depending on whether it's broadly or narrowly defined, **Old Cairo** covers everything beyond Garden City and Saiyida Zeinab – from the slaughterhouse district beside the Mamluke Aqueduct out to the ancient Jewish cemetery of al-Basatin – or a relatively small area near the Mari Girgis metro station, known to foreigners as **"Coptic Cairo"**. Cairenes themselves distinguish between the general area of *Masr al-Qadima* and specific localities such as *Fumm al-Khalig* ("Mouth of the Aqueduct") or *Qasr el-Sham'ah* (the erstwhile fortress of Babylon). Most tourists concentrate on Coptic Cairo, followed by a brief look at the Mosque of Amr.

The Coptic quarter is rapidly accessible by taking the **metro** from downtown Cairo to the **Mari Girgis** station (four stops from Midan Tahrir in the Helwan direction; 35pt). A lot slower but more fun are **river-taxis** from the Maspero Dock, which zigzag southwards upriver to make their fifth landfall on the embankment to the east: to reach the Coptic quarter from there, head inland, turn left and then cross the tracks at the end of the road. **Taxis** from downtown Cairo are reluctant to accept less than £E3, whilst **buses** (#92, #94, #134 & #140) from Tahrir to Amr's Mosque are usually packed on the outward journey but fine for getting back. To reach other points, see directions below.

Coptic Cairo

Coptic Cairo recalls the millennial interlude between pharaonic and Islamic civilisation, and the enduring faith of Egypt's Copts (see box overpage). Though not a ghetto, the quarter's huddle of dark churches suggests a mistrust of outsiders – an attitude of mind that has its roots in the Persian conquest and centuries of Greek or Roman rule.

Perhaps as early as the sixth century BC, a town grew up in this area, built around a fortress intended to guard the canal linking the Nile and the Red Sea. Some ascribe the name of this settlement – **Babylon-in-Egypt** – to Chaldean workmen pining after their home town beside the Euphrates; another likely derivation is *Bab il-On*, the "Gate of Heliopolis". Either way, it was Egyptian or Jewish in spirit long before Emperor Trajan raised the existing fortress in 130 AD. Resentful of Greek domination and Hellenistic Alexandria, many of Babylon's inhabitants later embraced Christianity, despite bitter persecution by the pagan

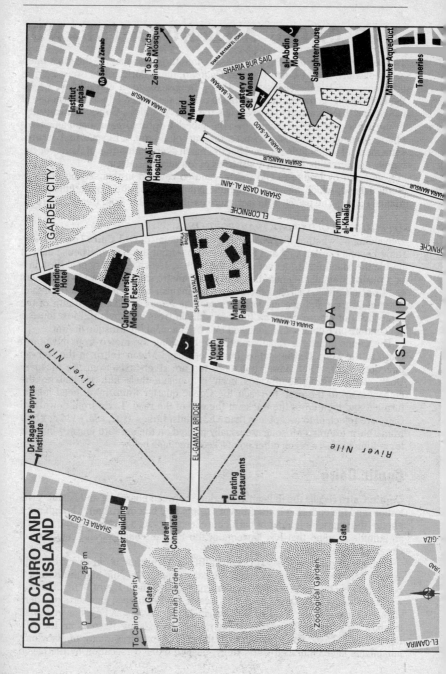

OLD CAIRO AND
RODA ISLAND

0   250 m

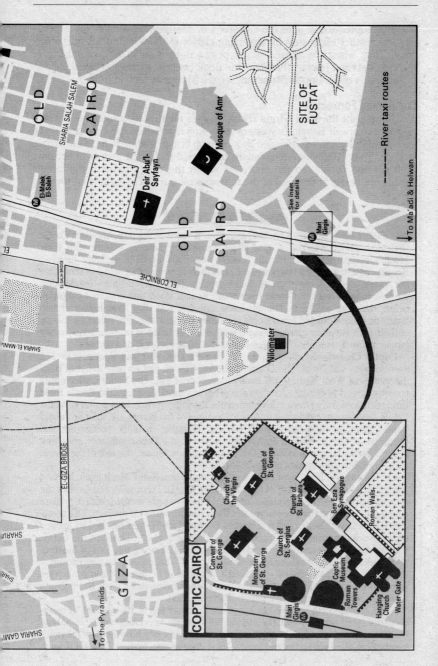

OLD CAIRO

SHARIA SALAH SALEM

El-Malek
El-Saleh

Deir Abu'l-
Sayfayn

Mosque of Amr

OLD   CAIRO

See inset
for details

Mari
Girgis

SITE OF
FUSTAT

River taxi routes

To Ma'adi & Helwan

EL SALIH BRIDGE

EL CORNICHE

SHARIA EL-MANIA

Nilometer

EL-GIZA BRIDGE

GIZA

SHARIA

SHARIA GAMI

To the Pyramids

COPTIC CAIRO

Convent of
St. George

Monastery
of St. George

Mari
Girgis

Church of
the Virgin

Church of
St. George

Church of
St. Sergius

Church of
St. Barbara

Ben Ezra
Synagogue

Roman Walls

Roman
Towers

Coptic
Museum

Hanging
Church

Water Gate

Romans. Subsequently, after the emperor Constantine's conversion, the community was further oppressed by Byzantine clerics in the name of Melkite orthodoxy. Thus when the Muslim army besieged Babylon in 641, promising to respect Copts and Jews as "People of the Book", only its garrison resisted.

For details of the **Coptic Museum**, see the Museums section (p.160).

The Roman Fortress

Almost opposite the **Mari Girgis** (Saint George) metro station you'll see the twin circular **towers** of Babylon's western gate. In Trajan's day, the Nile lapped the base of this gate and was spanned by a pontoon bridge leading to the southern tip of Roda. Today, Babylon's foundations are buried under ten metres of accumulated silt and rubble, so the churches within the compound and the streets outside are nearly at the level of the fortress's ramparts. The right-hand tower is

---

THE COPTS

While most Egyptians are Muslims, about ten percent of the population are Coptic Orthodox Christians. **The Copts** share a common national culture with their Muslim compatriots, but remain acutely conscious of their separate identity. Because inter-communal marriages are extremely rare, it's often said that the Copts are "purer" descendants of the ancient Egyptians than the Muslims – overlooking the infusions of Nubian, Greek, Jewish and Roman blood that occurred centuries before the Arab conquest. Though some maintain that they have higher cheekbones or almond-shaped eyes, Copts are rarely recognisable other than by tokens of their faith (wearing a cross around their neck, or tattooed on their wrist) or by forenames such as Maria, Antunius (Antony), Girgis (George) and Ramses.

Coptic Christianity differs from the Eastern Orthodox and Roman churches over doctrine and ritual. The Coptic Orthodox Church and its pope (chosen from the monks of Wadi Natrun) are totally independent from the Vatican, which only recently agreed to disagree for the sake of eccumenical harmony. The Coptic Bible (first translated from Greek c.300) antedates the Latin version by a century. Whilst Coptic services are conducted in Arabic, portions of the liturgy are sung in the old Coptic language descended from ancient Egyptian, audibly prefiguring the Gregorian chants of Eastern Orthodoxy. However, the Coptic influence goes well beyond music, for it was in Egypt that the monastic tradition, the cult of the Virgin and – arguably – the symbol of the cross originated.

Christianity reached Egypt early; tradition holds that **Saint Mark** made his first convert (a Jewish shoemaker of Alexandria) in 45 AD. From Jews and Greeks the religion spread to the Egyptians of the Delta – which teemed with Christian communities by the third century – and thence southwards up the Nile. The persecution of believers began under Emperor Decius (249–51) and reached its apogee under Diocletian, whom the Copts accuse of killing 144,000 Christians; the Coptic Church dates its chronology from his accession (284). During this **Era of Martyrs** many believers sought refuge in the desert. Paul of Thebes, Antony and Pacome – the sainted **"Desert Fathers"** – inspired a multitude of hermits and camp-followers whose rude communities became the first **monasteries** (see "Wadi Natrun" and "The Red Sea Monasteries" in chapters Three and Six).

The Christian faith appealed to Egyptians on many levels. Its message of resurrection offered ordinary folk the eternal life that was previously available only to those who could afford elaborate funerary rituals. And much of the new religion's **symbolism** fitted old myths and images. God created man from clay, as did Khnum

ruined, exposing a central shaft buttressed by masonry rings and radial ribs, which enabled it to withstand catapults and battering rams. Atop the other tower stands the Orthodox Church of Saint George (see below). Both towers are encased in alternating courses of dressed stone (much of it taken from pharaonic temples) and brick, a Roman technique known as *opus mixtum* or "mixed work".

By purchasing a ticket for the Coptic Museum, you can walk through the fortress's inner courtyard and down into the old **Water Gate** beneath the Hanging Church. The gate is now partly flooded and, though its arches and walls are visible from precarious walkways, the interior is only accessible by a stairway behind the three stone piers supporting the back of the church (bring a torch). It was through this gate that the last Byzantine viceroy, Melkite bishop Cyrus, escaped by boat under cover of darkness before Babylon surrendered to the Muslims.

on his potters wheel, and weighed the penitent's heart, like Anubis; Confession echoed the Declaration of Innocence; the conflict of two brothers and the struggle against Satan the myth of Osiris, Seth and Horus. Scholars have traced the **cult of the Virgin** back to that of the Great Mother, Isis, who suckled Horus. The resemblance between early **Coptic crosses** and pharaonic *ankhs* has also led some to argue that Christianity's principal symbol owes more to Egypt than Golgotha.

Although Emperor Constantine converted to Christianity and legalised his adopted faith throughout the empire (313–30), Byzantine converts known as **Melkites** continued to oppress the Copts. Political tensions were expressed in bitter theological disputes between **Arius** and **Athanasius** of Alexandria, which the Nicene Council (325) failed to resolve. When the Copts rejected the compromise verdict of the Council of Chaldeon (451) that Christ's human and divine natures were both unmixed and inseparable, and insisted that his divinity was paramount, they were expelled from the fold for this **Monophysite heresy** (meaning "Single Nature", a misrepresentation of their stance on Christ's divinity).

The association between Coptic Christianity and proto-nationalism was plain to Egypt's foreign rulers. "Copt" derives from the Greek word for Egypt, *Aigyptos*, truncated to *gibt* in Egyptian Arabic. Most Egyptians remained Christian long after the Arab conquest (640–41) and were treated justly by the early Islamic dynasties. Mass **conversions to Islam** followed harsher taxation, abortive revolts, punitive massacres and indignities engendered by the Crusades, until the Muslims attained a nationwide majority (probably during the thirteenth century, though earlier in Cairo). Thereafter Copts still participated in Egyptian life at every level, but the community retreated inwards and its monasteries and clergy stagnated until the nineteenth century, when Coptic reformists collaborated with Islamic and secular nationalists bent on overhauling Egypt's institutions.

In recent decades the Coptic community has undergone a **revival** under the dynamic leadership of its current pope, **Shenouda III**. The monasteries have been revitalised by a new generation of highly educated monks; community work and church attendances flourish as never before. Undoubtedly, this Coptic solidarity also reflects alarm at rising Islamic fundamentalism. Sporadic attacks on churches and Coptic students have bred tension in Middle Egypt (see "Beni Suef" and "Assyut", in Chapter Two, *The Nile Valley*). However, the fact that relatively few Muslims support bigoted radicalism remains a source of comfort for Egypt's six million Copts and 200,000 **Christians of other denominations** (Greek Orthodox, Maronite, Armenian, Catholic, Anglican and Baptist).

Whilst exploring the Coptic quarter, you'll also notice various sections of Babylon's Roman **walls**, rebuilt during the fourth and fifth centuries.

The Hanging Church

Built directly above the water gate, the **Hanging Church** (*al-Mu'allaqah*, "The Suspended" in Arabic) can be reached by a small gateway beyond the museum café, or via an ornate portal on Mari Girgis street. Ascending a steep stairway, you enter a nineteenth-century vestibule displaying cassettes and videos of Coptic liturgies and papal sermons. Above this are the monks' quarters; beneath it lies a secret repository for valuables, only discovered this century.

The main **nave** – whose ceiling is ribbed like an upturned boat or Ark – is separated from its side aisles by sixteen pillars, formerly painted with images of saints. Behind the marble pulpit, beautifully carved screens hide three **haikals** (altar areas) from the congregation. Accentuated by inlaid bone and ivory, their star patterns are similar to those found in mosques. Both pulpit and screens date from the thirteenth century, but the church was founded at least 600 years earlier and may even have originated in the fourth century as a chapel for the soldiers of the bastion. Amongst its relics, the church once claimed to own an olive stone chewed by the Virgin Mary, to whom *al-Mu'allaqah* is dedicated.

Coptic Masses are held on Fridays (8–11am) and Sundays (7–10am).

The Monastery of Saint George and into the Old Quarter

Returning to the Coptic Museum and heading north, go through the first gateway beyond the Coptic Museum entrance (ignoring demands for cash from "doormen") to reach the precincts of the **Monastery of Saint George**, now the seat of the Greek Orthodox Patriarchate of Alexandria. The monastery itself rarely admits tourists, but it's worth looking into the neighbouring **Church of Saint George**. The only round church in Egypt, its dark interior is perfumed with incense and pierced by sunbeams filtered through stained glass. A (barred) flight of steps descends into the bowels of the Roman tower, once believed to be "peopled by devils". The present church was built in 1904 after a fire destroyed the original structure, which dated back to the tenth century. Notwithstanding the church's Orthodox allegiance, its **Moulid of Mari Girgis** (April 23) is one of the largest Coptic festivals in Cairo.

Further up the main road, a **subterranean gateway** leads into the oldest part of Old Cairo, whose cobbled lanes flanked by high-walled houses wend between **medieval churches and cemeteries**. In 1929, Evelyn Waugh wrote disparagingly of a "constricted slum" whose Coptic residents hardly differed from their Muslim neighbours: "the only marked sign of their emancipation from heathen superstition was that the swarm of male and juvenile beggars were here reinforced by their womenfolk, who in the Mohammedan quarters maintain a modest seclusion." However, a decade ago the quarter was sanitised for tourists, so that "bearded patriarchs no longer rubbed shoulders with ascetics and paupers amid the stench and jostle" (Charlie Pye-Smith).

As renovation still continues, certain churches might be under wraps during your visit. Most of those that are open close around 4pm; there's no admission charge, but a modest donation is in order and curators may request *baksheesh*. As with mosques, visitors must be modestly dressed and remove their footwear before entering "working" churches.

The most interesting of the churches is reached through the first gate on the left, after you pass through the subterranean gateway. This is the Coptic **Convent of Saint George** (*Deir Mari Girgis*), whose main building, still a nunnery, is closed to visitors. However, you can walk down into a lofty hall that once belonged to a Fatimid mansion and into the chapel beyond, with its tall, narrow wooden doors, which boasts a cedarwood casket containing relics of Saint George; to the left of this building is a small room used for the **"chain-wrapping ritual"**, symbolising the saint's persecution by the Romans. Several of the nuns speak English and welcome questions about their faith; they might even wrap you in chains for a souvenir photo.

Upon leaving the convent, walk on to the end of the lane, where it meets another thoroughfare. At this intersection, turn right around the corner to stumble upon the Church of Saint Sergius, or head left to explore the quarter's northern reaches.

North to the churches of Saint George and the Virgin

The north part of the Coptic quarter contains nothing special, but its solitude is refreshing and you might enjoy wandering around the overgrown **cemeteries** – so far unsquatted Cities of the Dead.

Fifty metres up the road from the intersection, an alley to the right leads to yet another **Church of Saint George**, founded in 681 by Athanasius the Scribe. From the original foundation only the Hall of Nuptials survived a conflagration in the mid-nineteenth century, after which the current structure was erected.

Beyond it, at the end of the road, stands the smaller **Church of the Virgin**, also known as *Qasriyyat al-Rihan* (Pot of Basil) after the favourite herb of the Orthodox Church. Because al-Hakim's mother was of that faith, the church was given to the Greek community for the duration of his reign, but later returned to the Copts. Largely rebuilt in the eighteenth century, it's chiefly notable for several icons painted by John the Armenian in 1778.

The churches of Saint Sergius and Saint Barbara

Heading right from the intersection you pass a tourist bazaar before reaching the **Church of Saint Sergius**, whose site below street level attests to its great age. Probably founded in the fifth century and continuously rebuilt since medieval times, *Abu Serga* retains the basilical form typical of early Coptic churches. Major repairs have recently been under way, totally obscuring its low ceiling and the antique columns topped with Corinthian capitals that support the women's gallery, but by now you should be able to inspect its thirteenth-century *haikal* screen and bits of frescoes and mosaics in the central apse. Steps to the right of the altar descend into a (currently flooded) **crypt** where the Holy Family are believed to have stayed. A Coptic **festival** (June 1) commemorates their sojourn.

From Saint Sergius, you can wander along to the end of the lane where another thoroughfare leads to the Church of Saint Barbara (to the left) and Ben Ezra Synagogue (right).

The eleventh-century **Church of Saint Barbara** replaced an earlier Church of SS. Cyrus and John, which was razed during al-Hakim's assault on Fustat. Unlike others in the quarter, its wooden-vaulted roof is lofty, with skylights and windows which illuminate a nave flanked by Arabic arches with Fatimid tie-beams. Nor would its minbar-esque pulpit and inlaid *haikal* screen look amiss in a mosque. As if to refute such comparisons, the right-hand wall relates the life of Jesus in colourful tableaux, whilst the western sanctuary contains the relics of *Sitt Barbara*. Tradition holds that she was the daughter of a pagan merchant who was murdered for preaching Christianity in the third century, but sceptics might note that her belated recognition followed another questionable case (see "Saint Catherine's Monastery" in Chapter Seven, *Sinai*).

The Ben Ezra Synagogue

Down the road, through a gate blazoned with the Star of David, the **Ben Ezra Synagogue** is a sad relic of Cairo's ancient Jewish community. Renovation may yet save the building from collapse, but nothing can restore its former host of worshippers (see box below). Were it not for the efforts of one "Rabbi" Cohen, who shamelessly overcharged for souvenir postcards to fund renovation, the synagogue would have died in the Sixties; the Egyptian government and foreign donors have only recently stepped in to save it.

In form, the synagogue resembles a basilical church of the kind that existed here between the fourth and ninth centuries. Sold to the Jews in order to pay taxes raised from the Copts to finance Ibn Tulun's Mosque, this church was either demolished or incorporated within the synagogue which Abraham Ben Ezra, the Rabbi of Jerusalem, restored in the twelfth century. The inlaid marble and gilded stalactite niche date from around then, but most of the graceful mouldings and floral swirls are the result of nineteenth-century repairs which unearthed a cache of medieval manuscripts, including a sixth-century torah written on gazelle hide (now dispersed around Western libraries).

However, Jewish and Coptic traditions invest the site with ancient significance. Here, the pharaoh's daughter found Moses in the bulrushes; Jeremiah gathered survivors after Nebuchadnezzar destroyed Jerusalem; and the temple named

---

THE JEWS OF EGYPT

Egypt's Jewish community is dying out: fewer than 200 *Yahud* remain in Alexandria, Old Cairo and the Jewish Old People's Home in Heliopolis. The three synagogues that still exist will become empty memorials within a decade or so – a melancholy end to a story which begins **in the Old Testament**. *Genesis* relates how the descendants of Abraham escaped famine in Canaan (Palestine) by migrating to Egypt at the behest of Joseph, the pharaoh's favourite. Settling in the "Land of Goshen", they "multiplied and waxed mighty" until a new pharaoh enslaved them to build "the treasure-cities, Pithom and Raamses". Their flight from Egypt to the Promised Land is described in *Exodus*.

Squaring this with ancient Egyptian **history** presents difficulties. Whereas numerous sites are suggestive of Pithom and Raamses, there's no mention of the Exodus in pharaonic records. Assuming the Old Testament is based on genuine history, the Jews probably arrived sometime in the Ramessid era (c.1320–1237 BC), whilst the Exodus is generally ascribed to the reign of Merneptah (1236–23 BC). There's some evidence for the Prophet Jeremiah's foundation of a new community at Babylon-in-Egypt after the destruction of Jerusalem (585 BC), but there is no firm historical ground until the second century BC, when it is known that the Ptolemies encouraged an influx of Jews into Alexandria.

In contrast to the Alexandrian fusion of Greek and Jewish culture, the Jews of Babylon were more akin to native Egyptians. Mutual sympathies were strength-after him provided a haven for the Holy Family, who lived amongst the Jews of Babylon for three months. Moreover, the Copts believe that Peter and Mark pursued their apostolic mission in Egypt, whence Peter issued the First Epistle General. The rest of Christendom disagrees, however, arguing that the Biblical reference to Bablylon (*I Peter* 5:13) is only a metaphor for Rome.

The Mosque of Amr, Fustat and Deir Abu'l-Sayfayn

To get a feel for what happened after Babylon and Egypt surrendered to Islam, return to Mari Girgis street and follow it northwards, past the turning for Fustat and a small bus depot, to the **Mosque of Amr**. Though continuously altered, not to mention doubled in size in 827, this boasts direct descent from Egypt's first ever mosque, built in 641. A simple mudbrick, thatch-roofed enclosure without a *mihrab*, courtyard or minaret, it was large enough to contain the Muslim army at prayer. At its inauguration, **Amr Ibn al-As** told his 3500 Arab warriors:

> *The Nile floods have risen. The grazing will be good. There is milk for the lambs and kids. Go out with God's blessing and enjoy the land, its milk, its flocks and its herds, and take good care of your neighbours, the Copts, for the Prophet of God himself gave orders for us to do so.*

Until the fratricidal struggle between Sunni and Shia, this injunction was honoured: aside from paying a poll tax, non-Muslims enjoyed equal rights. It was Ibn Tulun and al-Hakim who introduced the discrimination (or worse) which later rulers either foreswore on principle or practised for motives of bigotry, fear or greed. But on an everday level, citizens of each faith amicably co-existed within the city of Fustat-Masr, as they do in modern Cairo.

ened by the **Jewish revolt** against Roman rule (115–17 AD) and the Coptic belief in the **Egyptian exile of the Holy Family**. Babylon's Jewish community would have been a natural haven for Mary, Joseph and the baby Jesus when Herod's wrath made Palestine too dangerous (it's harder to see why they should have hidden out near Assyut, as is also said).

As "People of the Book", Egypt's Jews were treated about as well (or badly) as the Copts **during the Islamic period**, acting as small traders, gold and silver-smiths, moneychangers or moneylenders. In Mohammed Ali's day, Lane estimated that they numbered about 5000. The British, however, introduced a new element: Jews who came as Europeans and shared their colonial disdain for the natives. Most of these new arrivals were merchants or professionals and settled in Alexandria or Cairo. A few families of *haute Juiverie* – the Menasces, Rolos, Hararis and Cattauis – were financiers who moved in royal circles. These **foreign Jews** lamented post-revolutionary restrictions on business and left en masse before and after the Suez Crisis (1956).

Meanwhile, native Jews were torn between Egypt and **Israel** as each war eroded their security. By the time of the 1967 war their numbers had declined from 75,000 to 2600 (mostly living in Cairo), though the capital still had 26 working synagogues, until mobs attacked them for the first time during the conflict. Thereafter, all but a few hundred Jews emigrated, leaving the poor, now aged community that remains today.

The site of the mosque was indicated by Allah, who sent a dove to nest in Amr's tent whilst he was away at war; on returning he declared it sacrosanct, waited until the dove's brood was raised, then built a mosque. The existing building follows the classic congregational pattern, arched *liwans* surrounding a pebbled *sahn* centred on an ablutions well. Believers pray or snooze on fine carpets in the sanctuary *liwan*, whose original *mihrab* is misaligned towards Mecca. When Amr introduced a pulpit, he was rebuked by Khalif Omar for raising himself above his Muslim brethren. The *mashrabiya*-ed **mausoleum** of his son, Abdullah, marks the site of Amr's house in Fustat. A nearby column bears a gash caused by people licking it until their tongues bled, to obtain miraculous cures. None of the mosque's two hundred **columns** is identical, incidentally; the pair on the left as you come in are said to part to allow the truly righteous to squeeze through, and another was whipped from Mecca by Omar. From the mosque's **well**, it is said, a pilgrim retrieved a goblet dropped into the Well of Zemzem in the Holy City.

Non-Muslims are charged £E1 **admission** to the mosque (or more if they don't know any better), and all the usual conventions apply.

The remains of Fustat, and Cairo's zebaleen

En route to Amr's Mosque you'll pass a rutted turn-off with a spray-painted "Fustat" sign, and piles of earthenware pots, jars and water pipes. Behind them, smouldering rubbish tips and hovels sprawl beneath a pall of smoke, seemingly as far as the Citadel.

Should you care to explore, a twenty-minute walk through this shantytown of potters and rubbish-gatherers will bring you to the **remains of Fustat** (admission £E1; students 50pt). Bring water, a few stones to deter wild dogs, and above all tread carefully – much of the site consists of centuries-old rubbish tips and kilns, prone to caving in. The foundation walls and water system (still being excavated by the American University) hardly do justice to Fustat's past, though the pottery shards which blanket the site are evocative; some fine early medieval and imported Chinese ware can be seen in the Islamic Arts Museum.

FUSTAT IN HISTORY

Originally a cluster of tribal encampments around Amr's Mosque, Fustat – the "City of the Tent" – evolved into a mudbrick beehive of multistoreyed dwellings with rooftop gardens, fountains, and a piped water and sewage system unequalled in Europe until the eighteenth century. As the Abbasids, Tulunids and Ikhshidids also built their own cities ever further to the northeast, a great conurbation known as **Fustat-Masr** was formed. Its decline began in Fatimid times, as the noxious potteries encouraged migration towards al-Qahira, thieves moved in and dereliction spread like cancer. In 1020, the mad khalif al-Hakim ordered his troops to sack Fustat-Masr for reasons worthy of Caligula (see p.97). Yet even in 1168, what remained was so vast that Vizier Shawar decided to evacuate and burn it rather than let the Crusaders occupy the old city beyond al-Qahira's walls. Set ablaze with 10,000 torches and 20,000 barrels of naphtha, Fustat smouldered for fifty-five days.

POTTERS AND ZEBALEEN

Settled in the ruins are two communities whose filthy work keeps Cairo tolerably clean. Whole families of **potters** slave over beehive kilns, churning out domestic ware for *baladi* households and piping for sewers and water mains. Even more important are the *zebaleen* or **rubbish-gatherers**. These families collect and sift Cairo's rubbish for anything edible or recyclable. All the glass, cardboard, metal, rags and leather are purchased in bulk by "Garbage Kings", who sell raw materials to workshops and markets. Though their daily forays into the city shame the authorities, no one has produced an alternative solution to Cairo's rubbish problem, or another livelihood for the *zebaleen*.

Deir Abu'l-Sayfayn

If the Coptic quarter hasn't satisfied your curiosity about medieval churches, pay a visit to **Deir Abul'-Sayfayn**, northwest of Amr's Mosque. This high-walled enclosure (open daily 8am–1pm) is entered via a humble wooden door facing the metro tracks; the original iron-bound door is now in the Coptic Museum. Within the compound are several churches of indeterminate age. First mentioned in the tenth century (when it served as a sugar-cane warehouse) and totally rebuilt after the burning of Fustat, the **Church of Saint Mercurius** claims older antecedents. Beneath its northern aisle lies a tiny crypt where Saint Barsum the Naked lived with a snake until his death in 317; a special Mass is held here on his name-day (September 10).

A doorway beside the crypt stairway leads through into the rest of the complex. The Upper Church, reached by steps, contains five disused chapels. Of more interest are the Small Church with its *haikal* dedicated to Saint James the Sawn-asunder, and the early seventh-century **Church of Saint Shenute**, featuring beautiful cedar-wood and ebony iconostases. From the same period comes the diminutive, icon-packed **Church of the Holy Virgin**, beyond which stands the **Convent of Saint Mercurius**, still inhabited by nuns. Adjacent to Deir Abul'-Sayfayn are extensive Protestant and Maronite **cemeteries**.

To return to central Cairo, walk to El-Malek el-Saleh metro station, or head back to the Amr's Mosque and catch a bus (#92, #94, #134 or #140).

North to the Aqueduct

Travelling between Coptic and Central Cairo by bus or taxi, you'll catch sight of the great **Aqueduct** that carried water to the Citadel. Originally a mere conduit supported by wooden pillars, it was solidly rebuilt in stone by Sultan al-Nasir in 1311 and subsequently extended in 1505 by al-Ghuri to accommodate the Nile's westward shift, to a total length of 3405m. River water was lifted by the **Burg al-Saqiyya**, a massive hexagonal waterwheel tower near the Corniche. On its western wall can be seen al-Ghuri's heraldic emblem and slots for engaging the six oxen-powered waterwheels, which remained in use until 1872.

The site of this tower is known as **Fumm al-Khalig** (Mouth of the Canal), after the waterway that once ran inland to meet the walls of Fatimid al-Qahira. This *Khalig Masri* (Egyptian Canal) supplied most of Cairo's water during Mamluke and Ottoman times, and was also linked to the ancient Nile Delta–Red Sea waterway, re-dug by Amr and al-Nasir. In an annual ceremony to mark the *Wafa el-Nil*, or Nile flood, the dike that separated it from the river was breached, sending fresh water coursing through the city. Pleasure boats were launched onto the lakes near Bab al-Luq and Ezbekiya, whilst fireworks heralded nocturnal revelries. But the taming of the Nile spelt the end of this practice, and after piped water was introduced early this century the canal was filled in to create Bur Said and Ramses streets.

Further inland

From the Fumm al-Khalig roundabout, Sharia al-Sadd al-Barrani runs up to Saiyida Zeinab (2km) past a swathe of **Christian cemeteries**. Within the northernmost cemetery, high walls enclose the **Monastery of Saint Menas** (*Deir Abu Mina*), whose sunken basilical church has been endlessly rebuilt since 724. Having returned the holy remnants of Saint Menas to his desert monastery (see p.478), its church now gives pride of place to the relics of Saints Behnam and Sarah, who were martyred by their own father. The monastery receives very few visitors and has no set opening hours.

Further south, the Aqueduct bestrides a medieval slum centred around a huge **slaughterhouse** and reeking **tanneries**. To outsiders, stark poverty seems all-pervasive; yet to those who live here, social distinctions are keenly felt. A slaughterhouse worker and his boss will both wear bloodstained *galabiyyas* during working hours, and possibly live on the same street – but the former can only speculate what riches the latter keeps indoors. Conversely, people will salvage designer-label bags and boxes to flaunt on the streets as if they were returning with a purchase.

Unlike the tanneries of Morocco, this is hardly on the tourist trail. Gustav Flaubert spent an afternoon here in 1850, shooting birds of prey and "wolf-like dogs", but the only recent case I've come across was that of two young Russian women who somehow wandered into the area, and were treated like princesses. However, the odd tourist has been known to attend Saturday evening *zikrs* outside the **Mosque of Sidi Ali Zein al-Abdin**, on the periphery of the quarter of Saiyida Zeinab (see p.114).

The southern suburbs

South of Old Cairo, a ribbon of development follows the east bank of the Nile down to Helwan. Though easily reached by metro, these **southern suburbs** hold little attraction for tourists, notwithstanding Ma'adi's popularity as a resident expatriate area. However, even the least-favoured quarters cast some light on various facets of Egyptian life.

Al-Basatin: the Jewish cemetery

A case in point is the **Jewish cemetery of al-Basatin**, 3km beyond El-Khalifa (bus #160 from Midan Tahrir or Saiyida Zeinab, or #505 from the Citadel). Tens of thousands of graves, up to nine hundred years old, have been stripped of their marble slabs, whilst squatters have occupied any mausoleums going (al-Basatin has few of these compared to the Muslim and Coptic cemeteries). Several years ago, the elders of Cairo's depleted Jewish community agreed to accept $80,000 in return for allowing a highway to be ploughed through al-Basatin. Then foreign rabbis intervened and the whole affair acquired diplomatic overtones; at the time of writing, legal wrangling still continues.

Ma'adi and the quarries of Tura

With its Corniche boutiques and takeaways, and acres of villas set amidst luxuriant grounds, **Ma'adi** is unmistakably wealthy. Besides native millionaires and Gulf Arabs, most of Egypt's American community lives here. US citizens can enjoy a free **Fourth of July Party** at the American School, courtesy of taxpayers back home (bring your passport). Trendy **restaurants** include the Sino-Korean *Four Seasons* (12 Sharia Mustapha Kamel; daily noon–midnight) and the *Seahorse* on Ma'adi's Corniche, near the **As-Salam International Hospital**.

The **Military Hospital**, further north, is the largest of its kind in the Middle East. It was here that the ex-Shah of Iran died of cancer, and President Sadat was rushed by helicopter from the blood-soaked reviewing stand in Medinet Nasr. As a young officer during World War II, Sadat was actually stationed in Ma'adi when he became embroiled in a Nazi spy ring (see p.140). Ma'adi is directly accessible from Midan Tahrir by minibus (#52 & #56) or metro (25min).

Farther south amidst the Muqattam foothills, the **quarries of Tura** have yielded fine limestone since pharaonic times (it was here that pyramid casing blocks were quarried), and now also produce cement. Less obtrusive is the **Sijn al-Salaam** or "Prison of Peace", a triumph of US penal technology used to hold politicians and religious leaders during Sadat's crackdown in September 1981, shortly before his assassination.

Helwan

The once-fashionable spa of **Helwan** is now grossly polluted by a gigantic **iron and steelworks** which exploits power from the Aswan Dam and iron ore from the Western Desert. The steelworks wreak eco-death on a nineteenth-century **Japanese Garden** – complete with Buddhas and a pagoda – located five blocks from Helwan metro station (turn left as you exit). Nearer Ain Helwan, one stop back, a tacky **Waxworks Museum** (daily 9am–5pm; 50pt plus *baksheesh*) portrays the gorier moments in Egyptian history.

Roda Island

The narrow channel between **Roda** and the mainland is bridged in such a way that the island engages with Garden City whilst distancing itself from Old Cairo – a reversal of historic ties. As its much rebuilt **Nilometer** suggests, it was the southern end of Roda that was visited by ferries en route between Memphis and Heliopolis, and Roman ships bound for Babylon-in-Egypt. However, nothing remains of the Byzantine fortress which defied the Muslim invasion, nor the vaster Ayyubid *qasr* where the Bahri Mamlukes were garrisoned, since Roda reverted to agricultural use as Cairo's focus shifted northeastwards. The island's main sight, the **Manial Palace**, re-established a fashion for palatial residences early this century, though it wasn't until the 1950s that Roda experienced a building explosion similar to Zamalek's.

APPROACHES

With Roda's tourist attractions sited 3km apart, choice of **transport** is a major consideration. Whereas the Manial Palace is easily accessible from central Cairo, the Nilometer may only be reached from Manial or Old Cairo by awkward detours on foot, or by taxi (see below). Should you decide to settle for only one site, make it the palace. Aside from a taxi (£E2), a #8 or #900 bus is the fastest way of getting there from Midan Tahrir; alight on Sharia Sayala, near the palace gates. Walking takes twenty-five to forty minutes, and on hot days can leave you totally bushed. Should you decide to anyway, don't cross the first bridge except to visit the **Meridien Hotel**, which commands superb river views and offers a reasonable pool-and-buffet deal, but is isolated from other parts of Roda.

The second bridge down leads to **Cairo University Medical Faculty**, a source of student cards (see p.228). By walking 150m south from here you can reach the palace gates without crossing the Sayala Bridge, used by traffic heading for Giza. Cairo's **youth hostel** overlooks the El-Gama'a Bridge, 500m further west.

The Manial Palace

The **Manial Palace** is a Cairo must. Built in 1903, its fabulously eclectic architecture reflects the taste of King Farouk's uncle, Prince Mohammed Ali, author of *The Breeding of Arabian Horses* and the owner of a flawless emerald which magically alleviated his ill-health (so legend has it). Each of the main buildings manifests a different style – Persian, Syrian, Moorish, Ottoman and Rococo – or mixes them together with gay abandon.

Having bought your ticket (£E1, students 50pt; admission from 9am to around 2–4pm), make a beeline for the **Reception Palace** just inside the gateway. Its magnificent *salamlik*, adorned with stained glass, polychrome tiles and ornate woodcarving, prepares you for the opulent guest rooms upstairs, of which the finest is the Syrian Room, which was quite literally transplanted from Damascus. On the stairs you'll notice a scale model of Qaitbey's Mausoleum, made entirely of mother-of-pearl.

Leaving the Reception Palace and turning right, you come upon a pseudo-Moroccan tower harbouring the prince's **mosque**, whose lavish decor is reminiscent of the great mosque of his namesake in the Citadel. Further along, the grotesque **Trophies Museum** features scores of mounted ibex heads and ineptly stuffed fowl, a hermaphrodite goat, a table made from elephants' ears and a vulture's claw candlestick.

The **Prince's Residence**, deeper into the banyan-shaded garden, is richly decorated in a mixture of Turkish and Occidental styles. The drab-looking building out back contains a long **Throne Hall** whose red carpet passes life-size royal portraits hung beneath a sunburst ceiling. Around the outside of this hall are the skeletons of the prince's horse and camel, and a stairway to the upper level (often closed). If accessible, visitors can admire its Obsidian Salon and the private apartments of the prince's mother, enriched by a silver four-poster bed from the Abdin Palace. Lastly, follow the signs to the **Private Museum**, a family hoard of manuscripts, carpets, glassware and silver plate – notice the huge banqueting trays.

Across a fence are the bungalows of a **Club Med** which occupies half of the Manial's grounds; the closely guarded complex is reached by a separate entrance west of – and around the corner from – the palace gates.

The Nilometer

From ancient times into the present century, Egyptian agriculture depended on the annual flooding of the Nile. Crop yields were predicted and taxes were set according to the river's level in August, as measured by Nilometers. A reading of 16 *ells* (8.6m) foretold the valley's complete irrigation; significantly more or less meant widespread flooding or drought. Public rejoicing followed the announcement of the *Wafa el-Nil* (Abundance of the Nile), whilst any other verdict caused gloom and foreboding.

Although the southern tip of Roda has probably featured a **Nilometer** since pharaonic times, the existing one dates from 861 and its Turkish kiosk is actually a modern replica. Descending well below the level of the Nile, its stone-lined shaft was connected to the river by three tunnels (now sealed) at different heights – the uppermost is still accessible. Around the shaft's interior are Koranic verses in kufic script, extolling rain as God's blessing; its central column is graduated into 16 *ells* of roughly 54cm each. The Nilometer is often locked, but its caretaker will turn out for rare visitors. With ten children to support – so he claims – the admission fee (officially 25pt) has to be negotiated, especially after the official 4pm closing time. West of here, the **Centre for Art and Life** within the former Manastirli Palace exhibits local arts and crafts (closed Fridays).

Unless you take a taxi (£E2–3), **getting to the Nilometer** entails a fifteen-minute walk from the river-taxi stage opposite Giza, or traipsing from the El-Malek el-Saleh metro station (25min). The latter is one stop north of Old Cairo's Mari Girgis station and within walking distance of Amr's Mosque and Deir Abu'l-Sayfayn (see p.129), making it feasible to combine them with the Nilometer in a day-long itinerary.

GEZIRA AND THE WEST BANK

Flowing northwards through Cairo, the Nile divides into channels around the two major islands of Roda and Gezira. **Gezira**, the larger island, is farther from the centre than Roda and notably more spacious and verdant than the rest of Cairo.

Across the island, elevated highways bear cross-town traffic to diverse **districts on the west bank** of the Nile, collectively known as **Giza** and administered as a separate Governorate from Cairo. Moving south through its neighbourhoods, **Imbaba** is the site of Cairo's main camel market – and a world apart from the adjoining **Aguza**, with its Corniche nightlife, and even more from the Dallas-style pretensions of **Mohandiseen**. Further south and inland is **Dokki**, whose wealthy enclaves give way to *baladi* market quarters, the green lungs of Cairo's zoo and scattered university faculties, before the dusty expanse of Giza city extends to the Pyramids. Giza's **transport** and utilities are functionally integrated with Cairo's. For an **orientation map** of the area, see the main city plan on p.56.

Gezira and Zamalek

Gezira (literally "island") dominates the waterfront from Garden City to Bulaq, its three sets of bridges spanning the Nile. Nearly 4km long and 1km wide, the island is big enough to encompass two distinct zones. The southern half, featuring the new Opera House complex, parks, a viewing tower and famous sporting clubs, is Gezira proper. **Zamalek** (pronounced "Zah-*mah*-lek"), further north, is pure real estate – apartments, villas, offices and embassies – with a westernised ambience and nightlife. Both seem so integral to Cairo that it's hard to envisage their absence, yet the island itself only coalesced early last century and remained unstable until the first Aswan Dam regulated the Nile's flood in the 1900s.

Almost a third of the island belongs to the **Gezira Sporting Club**, laid out by the British Army on land given by Khedive Tewfiq. The club's main pursuits were horse racing and polo, imbued with an extraordinary mystique. "It is on the Gezira polo grounds that the officers of the Cavalry Brigade are tested for military efficiency and fitness for command", wrote C.S. Jarvis in the 1920s. Diplomats and selected upper crust Egyptians also belonged to the club, and after Nasser decided against expropriation following the revolution it soon acquired members from the new elite. The hefty membership fees still restrict access to its golf course, tennis courts, stables (see p.209), gardens and pet cemetery.

APPROACHES TO GEZIRA: THE BRIDGES

The **6th October Bridge** high overhead the Sporting Club is more of a direct link between Aguza and central Cairo than a viable approach to Gezira (though there are stairs down to both banks of the island). However, it does overlook the **Ahly (National) Club**, home to one of Egypt's top football teams.

It's the southern bit of Gezira, however, that's accessible and worth seeing. Despite heavy traffic, it's enjoyable to walk across the **Tahrir Bridge** (10–15min from Midan Tahrir), catching the breeze and watching barges and *feluccas* on the river. Gaining the island, you can strike 200m northwards past the *El Borg Hotel* and turn left down an avenue to reach the Cairo Tower (10min), or follow the traffic heading for Dokki, which brings you to the Cairo Opera House and several museums (5–10min). Taxis or *caleches* are happy to oblige if you'd rather ride, but they expect the "tourist minimum".

Cairo Tower

Rising 187m above Gezira, the **Burg al-Qahira** or **Cairo Tower** offers a stupendous view of the seething immensity of Cairo (open daily 9am–midnight; £E3). Built between 1957 and 1962 with Soviet help, the tower combines pharaonic and socialist realist motifs within a latticework shaft of poured concrete which blossoms into a lotus finial.

On the fourteenth storey is an overpriced restaurant which occasionally revolves; above it is a Novosibirsk-style cafeteria serving tolerable tea. The attraction, though, is the view, provided by the café, restaurant and a **viewing platform** at the top, which provides a **panoramic vista of Cairo**. East across the river, the blue and white *Nile Hilton* and the antenna-festooned Television Building delinate an arc of central Cairo. Beyond it lies the medieval quarter, bristling with minarets below the Citadel and the sere Muqattam Hills. Roda Island and deluxe hotels dominate the view south (upriver); to the north are Zamalek, Shubra and the Nile Delta. Westwards, the city extends to meet the desert, with the Pyramids visible on the horizon on clear days. Come a while before sunset to witness Cairo transformed by nightfall, as a thousand muezzins call across the water.

The Opera House complex

Fans of post-Modernist architecture should check out the new **Cairo Opera House** near Tahrir Bridge. Outwardly Islamic in style, its interior melds pharaonic motifs with elements of the baroque opera houses of the nineteenth century: an audacious blend of Oriental and Occidental by Japanese architect Koichiro Shikida. A $30 million gift from Japan, it was built in 1988, belatedly replacing the old building on Opera Square which burned down in 1971. Director Magda Saleh, a Bolshoi-trained former prima ballerina, aims to put Cairo on the world opera circuit (see "Entertainments"). Off to the right as you walk towards the Opera House is the newly relocated **Modern Art Museum** (see "Museums").

Following Sharia Tahrir towards the west bank you'll pass the old Gezira Exhibition Grounds with its dilapidated pavilions housing the **Gezira Museum**, the **Museum of Egyptian Civilisation** (closed for renovation when last heard) and a still-functioning **Planetarium** (see "Activities"). Across the road from the entrance to the Ahly Club, just before the Galaa Bridge, the **Mukhtar Museum** honours the sculptor whose Renaissance of Egypt monument welcomes drivers into Dokki. (Again, see under "Museums".)

The 27-storey **El Gezirah Sheraton** at the southern tip of the island can be reached by slip roads from the Tahrir and Galaa bridgeheads. On public holidays, a **fountain** in the middle of the Nile between Gezira and Roda shoots an immense jet of water into the sky.

Zamalek

Originally a very British neighbourhood, despite its Continental grid of tree-lined boulevards, **Zamalek** still has bags of social cachet – renting a flat here is the Cairene equivalent of moving into Manhattan. Unlike most parts of Cairo, the quarter feels very private: residents withdraw into air-conditioned high-rises or Thirties apartment blocks, and with so many foreign companies and **embassies** in the area (see p.224), most streets are lifeless after dark.

That said, Zamalek also features some of the trendiest **nightspots** in Cairo. Near the Aguza side of the Gezira Sporting Club on Sharia Hassan Sabry, the *Four Corners* complex contains a deluxe French restaurant, *Justine*; pasta-oriented *La Piazza*; an American-style video-snackbar; and *Max's* disco. Other places congregate north of the 26th July flyover. Gay men and British expats favour *Pub 28* at the junction of Shagar al-Durr and Hassan Assim streets. The *Longchamp* disco is just around the corner on Sharia Ismail Mohammed. By heading 200m up Sharia Taha Hussein, you'll find *B's Corner* video-bar and *Il Capo* for live music, next to the *President Hotel*. For Arab music and belly-dancing, try the *Casino Abu el-Feda* opposite Imbaba, or the *Bateau Omar Khayyam*, an old houseboat moored alongside Saray el-Gezira, near the Sporting Club.

Zamalek by day has less to offer, though kids may enjoy the **aquarium grotto** in **Galabaya Park**, two blocks north of the Four Corners. For more cultural pursuits, head for the other end of Sharia el-Gezira as it curves around the northern edge of the Sporting Club. Here, a graceful nineteenth-century villa houses the **Mahmoud Khalil Museum**'s collection of Impressionist and Orientalist paintings (again, see "Museums"). The modern annexes of the adjacent **Cairo Marriott Hotel** screen what was originally a "madly sumptuous palace" built for Empress Eugénie, later sold to wealthy Copts in lieu of Ismail's debts and turned into a hotel. Non-residents can wander in and loll amidst khedival splendour for the price of a drink.

To save yourself a long walk from central Cairo, it's best to grab a taxi (which shouldn't cost over £E2) to any of these places. Buses from Tahrir to Zamalek (#95 & #170) are routed via Ramses, and whilst there's no lack of minibuses heading west along 26th July, it may prove hard to descend from the elevated highway. Having traversed the island, the highway crosses the **Zamalek Bridge** onto the west bank, where Midan Sphinx funnels traffic into Mohandiseen (see overpage).

Imbaba and the Camel Market

From Midan Kit-Kat, 300m north of Zamalek Bridge, Sharia al-Sudan arcs through the **Imbaba** district, whose overspill covers the site of the "**Battle of the Pyramids**" where Napoleon's army routed the Mamlukes on July 21, 1798, prior to taking Cairo. Unfortunately for Napoleon – who dreamed of "founding a religion, marching into Asia riding an elephant", bearing "the new Koran that I would have composed to suit my needs" – his strategic ambition to disrupt British power in India was literally scuppered when Nelson sank his fleet at Abu Qir Bay. Within eighty years, the Suez Canal had cemented the link between naval power, control of Egypt and Britain's empire "East of Suez"; a bond later reinforced by aviation. Although flying boats on the famous Cape-to-Cairo run used the Nile, most *Imperial Airways* flights used **Imbaba Airport**, now a flying school (see p.209).

The Camel Market

Across the railway tracks from the airport, a potholed road leads to Cairo's **Camel Market**, a weekly feast of drama and cruelty. Beaten into defecating ranks, the hobbled camels are assessed by traders who disregard their emaciation – caused by a month-long trek from northwestern Sudan to Aswan, followed by an overnight truck ride to Cairo – and concentrate on other features.

Strength and speed are discernible in the legs, chest, eyes, ears and position of the hump; teeth reflect age, whilst the clearly knackered are evaluated for their meat and hide. During rutting season, signs of irritation (an inflated mouth-sac, ferocious slobbering and gurgling) often herald a kick or bite from an enraged bull camel. Docile females are generally preferred as mounts: a prime *hageen* fetches over £E2000, a smaller camel roughly half that (although drought in the Sudan threatens to decimate future trade). They're also exchanged for goats and other livestock in an adjacent compound where Bishari herdsmen and Egyptian merchants gossip over tea, unperturbed by throat-slittings and disembowelments near the piles of saddlery and tack.

VISITING THE MARKET

Lasting from dawn till mid-morning every Friday, the *Souk el-Gamal* (pronounced "Gah*mell*") is busiest between 6 and 8.30am. There's no official entrance fee, but smart operators sometimes charge unwary tourists £E1 at the gate. It's far easier **to get there** by taxi (£E5 from downtown; a bit more for several passengers) than by public transport, although this is okay for the journey back. Should you opt for a #99 bus from the Nile Hilton, it's a ten-minute walk to the market from Sharia al-Sudan. Alternatively, minibuses from Tahrir and Giza Square run to Midan Kit-Kat (35pt), whence other minibuses shuttle to the market. Nile **river-taxis** also stop near Midan Kit-Kat (alias Midan Khalid Ibn al-Walid), offering a breezy trip. Walking back to central Cairo takes from an hour to ninety minutes, providing you don't go astray in Mohandiseen.

Mohandiseen

Laid out during the 1960s to house Egypt's new technocrats, "Engineers' City" (as the suburb was initially called) responded to an influx of business and media folk during the Sadat era by shortening its name to **Mohandiseen** and emulating America. Nowhere else in Cairo can you cruise down a boulevard glittering with boutiques and junk food outlets, squint and imagine that you're in LA. Even the palm trees seem to hail from Hollywood, rather than the Nile. But around midday on Fridays, the illusion is ruptured as herds of camels are driven through Mohandiseen en route to the slaughterhouse, bringing traffic to a standstill.

To **reach the quarter** from central Cairo, catch a #99 bus from the Arab League Building on Midan Tahrir (it follows a circuitous route to Mohandiseen's Midan Libnan before returning to downtown Midan Ataba via Sharia al-Sudan); or a #167 bus or shared taxi (£E2) heading west along 26th July Street. Either of the latter should speed you across Zamalek and down onto Midan Sphinx, beyond which Mohandiseen fans out along three boulevards.

Mohandiseen life

Sharia Orabi runs northwest for 1.5km, but except for the **International Language Institute** (ILI), two blocks from the al-Sudan ring road, it has no more to offer than the continuation of 26th July Street. Most of the action occurs along Mohandiseen's main axis, **Arab League Street** (*Sharia Gameat al-Dowal al-Arabiya*), also known as "The Mall", which is bisected by palms and shrubbery for its three-kilometre length, with the **Atlas Zamalek Hotel** towering 500m past Midan Sphinx. Starting with *King Grill* directly opposite the *Atlas*, fast food proliferates along the way to Midan al-Nasr, the centre of a radial grid of streets harbouring a dozen **embassies** (amongst them Kenya, Zambia, Ivory Coast and the CAR). Proper **restaurants** include the Moghul-esque *Tandoori* (11 Sharia Shehab), the Cairo Inn's *Taberna Espanola* (26 Sharia Suriya), and *Tia Maria* on Sharia Jeddah, at the bottom end of Arab League Street.

From Midan al-Nasr, another boulevard runs up to **Midan Libnan**, Mohandiseen's **transport** hub for #99 buses to Midan Ataba, #72 minibuses to Zamalek and Ramses Station, and *service* taxis to most parts of Cairo.

Beyond the ring road

Beyond the al-Sudan ring road lies **Bulaq al-Dakhrour**, an unplanned sprawl of ramshackle dwellings built by migrant *fellaheen* from Upper Egypt and the Delta. Devoid of any proper sewage network (like parts of Imbaba and Giza), the neighbourhood is a sanitary inspector's nightmare. Whilst some houses have cesspits, many households empty their waste into the drainage canals whose water is used by others for washing or drinking. Installing sewers here is merely one of the challenges facing the Cairo Wastewater Organisation (see box below).

Bulaq al-Dakhrour ends at the **Maryotteya Canal**, beyond which the village of **Kerdassa** (see "The Pyramids") precedes another canal before the strip of luxury hotels (*Mövenpick Jollie-Ville, Ramada Renaissance, Oasis*) along the Desert Road to Alexandria.

THE CAIRO WASTEWATER PROJECT

Designed by British engineers in 1910 to serve a population of one million, **Cairo's sewage system** reached breaking point in the late Seventies. Fractured pipes regularly flooded at 120 locations (in one incident, exposed power cables electrocuted a donkey-cart driving through a puddle). Worse still, a quarter of Cairo's by now twelve-million population lived in areas beyond the sewage network. Cases of what was termed "summer sickness" (in fact, cholera) occurred annually. Besides the risk of epidemics, the practice of flushing raw sewage into the Nile also threatened the ecology of Lake Manzala, the richest fishing grounds in the Delta. Action was urgently needed.

With US and British backing, the **Cairo Wastewater Project** aims to remedy these problems by the end of the century. On the west bank, where many areas have no sewers at all, an entirely new system is being created. The densely populated east bank poses a greater challenge, requiring extensive "blind" tunnelling. Plans of the old system were lost long ago; urban myth has it that a group of sewer repairmen have passed down their secret underground geography from father to son. Existing sewers are being fed into a huge new tunnel running from Fustat to Cairo's northern outskirts, where a gigantic pumping station is under construction; eventually, the sewage will also be treated at another plant. Given additional investments, the wastewater and nutrient-rich sludge could be used to irrigate and fertilise barren land.

Aguza and Dokki

A 100-metre-wide channel separates Zamalek and Gezira from the west bank districts of **Aguza and Dokki**. Being mainly residential and devoid of major "sights", they're only worth considering as a quieter place to stay than central Cairo, or for their nightlife; although you might just have business with certain local institutions. Yet it's typical of Cairo that these prim-looking neighbourhoods have generated as much scandal as the Clot Bey and Abdin quarters once did.

Aguza

Wedged between Mohandiseen and the Nile, **Aguza** ("Old Woman") stretches its legs **along the Corniche**. At the northern end of Sharia el-Nil, near the Zamalek Bridge, are the **Balloon Theatre** – a regular venue for the National and Reda dance troupes – and Egypt's **National Circus** (see "Entertainments"). Further south at no. 192 is the **British Council**, a fulcrum of expat life and a sought-after place of employment (see p.44 and p.223). Beyond the *Scherezade Hotel* and Aguza Hospital, couples seek privacy in nooks along the embankment, oblivious to cruising cars. A popular stopover for taxi drivers and nightclubbers is the 24-hour *Cafeteria Neima*, opposite the Police Hospital near the 6th October Bridge.

From here down to Dokki the riverside is colonised by **casinos**. These are family-oriented places for eating and listening to music (gambling isn't involved) which really come alive on Thursday nights. Some are taken over by wedding parties with traditional musicians and a belly dancer. Should you be invited to join a bash, accept without hesitation – they're always fun (see p.208). Street urchins and passers-by peer through the gates, shouting blessings or ribald comments. The downside to casinos is that some have poor food, and all of them are swarming with mosquitoes.

Fifty years ago the Corniche was also a mooring place for houseboats – then a fashionable alternative to rented flats. It was here the Nazi spy Eppler used a famous belly dancer, Hekmet Fathy, to inveigle secrets from Allied staff officers aboard her *dahabiya*. Also involved was a young Egyptian officer, Anwar Sadat, who attempted to convey messages to Rommel and was subsequently jailed by the British for treason. Post-revolutionary Egypt was austere by comparison, but hardly innocent. In 1988 the government tried to suppress the memoirs of Eitimad Khorshid, a *femme fatale* who cut a swathe through the Nasserite establishment of the Fifties, and promised to reveal all in what became an underground bestseller.

To reach any of the above locations, catch a taxi via 26th July or the 6th October Bridge. An elevated extension of the latter pushes 500m inland towards the **Agricultural Museum**, north of the Ministry of Agriculture. Set in beautiful grounds, its various pavilions include a **Cotton Museum** (see "Museums"). The Ministry of Agriculture marks the point where Aguza merges into Dokki.

To return to central Cairo from Aguza, catch bus #16 or #60

Dokki

The social geography of **Dokki** is more complex than Aguza's. Broadly speaking, the rich occupy the land nearest the river and the Dokki Sporting Club, a phalanx of private hospitals, VD clinics and covert bordellos separating their villas and flats from the market quarter to the southwest, where poorer folk live. Dokki is well served by buses (#19, #110, #166, #182, #203) from the Arab League Building on Midan Tahrir, but you'll have to check which route suits your objective.

Coming over the Galaa Bridge from Gezira Island you'll see Mahmoud Muktar's **Renaissance of Egypt statue** and the twin towers of the **Cairo Sheraton**. The hotel forecourt is the departure terminal for **buses to Tel Aviv and Jerusalem** (see "On from Cairo" at the end of this chapter). If anything remains in the former premises of Cairo's **Modern Art Museum** (now moved to Gezira), you can find it by heading 300m up Sharia al-Sad al-Ali, and then onto Ismail Abu al-Futuh beyond the square. Sharia al-Sad al-Ali itself continues on to meet Suleyman Gohar, Dokki's vibrant **market quarter**. For **cinemas** and **restaurants**, look along Sharia Tahrir and Midan al-Misaha, radiating west and southwest from the Galaa Bridge.

Two main roads head south from the Sheraton. Running one block inland, **Sharia el-Giza** passes the **Soviet Embassy** and the former residence of President Sadat, where his widow, Jihan, still lives in guarded seclusion (photography is prohibited in this area). Another once-famous resident of Dokki was Field Marshal Amr, a long-time friend and ally of Nasser's who committed suicide after being accused of plotting a coup against him, and was posthumously scapegoated for Egypt's defeat in the 1967 war.

Running parallel to Sharia el-Giza is the Corniche, **Sharia el-Nil**. Beyond **Dr Ragab's Papyrus Institute**, 100m south of the Galaa Bridge, are Cairo's **Rowing Club** and **Yacht Club**, both citadels of privilege. A few blocks nearer Giza, the Nasr Building contains two excellent **restaurants** owned by *SwissAir*: *Le Chalet* and *Le Château*.

Giza

In pharaonic times **Giza** lay en route between Heliopolis and Memphis and probably also housed the skilled corps of pyramid-builders. As Memphis declined during the Christian era, so Giza flourished, thanks to its proximity to the Fortress of Babylon, across the river; Amr's reopening of the ancient Delta/Red Sea canal subsequently boosted its prosperity under Muslim rule. Giza's apogee coincided with the reign of Salah al-Din – the Moorish traveller Ibn Jubayr described it as a "large and important burgh with fine buildings" – when its Sunday market attracted vast crowds. But the area's vulnerability to floods caused stagnation, and it wasn't until Ismail laid the Pyramids Road, drained swamps and built a palace in the 1860s that Giza became fashionable again. By Nasser's time, however, sheer expansion was paramount. As Giza's population topped a million, a tide of high-rise hovels, tacky nightclubs and roaring flyovers devoured crumbling villas, erstwhile farmland and desert, up to the Giza Plateau beneath the Pyramids.

Transport from Midan Tahrir approaches Giza via Gezira and Dokki (bus #6 or #803), or crosses over from Roda Island (bus #8 or #900). Either serves to reach the Zoo or Midan Giza.

Around Cairo Zoo and University

The extensive grounds which Deschamps laid out for Ismail's palace are now divided into Cairo's **Zoological Garden** – which is packed on Fridays and public holidays, but fun to visit at other times (see p.211) – and the smaller **El Urman Garden**. Like the **Israeli Consulate** and two **floating restaurants** near the **El-Gama'a Bridge**, they're marked on the "Old Cairo and Roda Island" map (see p.122).

The bridge is named after **Cairo University**, which was founded in 1908 as a counterweight to traditionalist al-Azhar but has never been any the less political. Access to its scattered faculties is vetted by Central Security, so foreigners may need a letter of introduction (or, at least, their passport) to pass beyond the gates. Aside from making student friends, morbid curiosity might inspire a visit to the Agricultural Faculty, near the bottom of Sharia Gameat al-Qahira. Occupying a former palace of Mohammed Ali, its swimming pool once delighted his harem and its basement features remnants of his torture chamber.

Midan Giza and Pyramids Road

West of the **El-Giza Bridge** and south of the university belt, Cairo's second largest **bus and taxi terminal** agitates **Midan Giza**. Even more chaotic than Tahrir, its seething ranks include buses (#3) to the Pyramids; minibuses (#26) to Tahrir, Ramses and Heliopolis; and *service* taxis to Fayoum city, Beni Suef and the Red Sea Coast.

Another batch of flyovers funnels traffic onto the **Pyramids Road** (Sharia al-Ahram), which runs the gauntlet of **nightclubs** and tourist bazaars for 8km. Just over halfway to the Pyramids of Giza, Sharia al-Ahram crosses two canals in quick succession – the second one marks the turning (left) for Saqqara. See "The Pyramids" for full details of both sites.

THE NORTHERN SUBURBS

During this century, Cairo's **northern suburbs** have swallowed up villages and farmland and expanded far into the desert to form a great arc of residential neighbourhoods stretching from the Nile to the Muqattam. **Heliopolis**, with its handsome boulevards and Art Deco villas, is still favoured above the satellite-suburbs that have mushroomed in recent decades and retains a sizeable foreign community. Otherwise, tourists usually only venture into **Abbassiya**, where the Sinai Terminal and the Coptic Patriarchate are located, and you have to be fanatically keen to bother hunting down the Virgin's Tree in **Matariyya**, Sadat's tomb in **Medinet Nasr**, or Mamluke edifices in **Bulaq**.

Bulaq, Shubra and Rod el-Farag

Bulaq and its neighbours **Shubra** and **Rod el-Farag** are run-down and overcrowded, averaging 166,000 residents per square kilometre – ten times the density of Garden City – and have a predominantly *baladi* ambience. But though more or less bereft of "sights", these quarters might appeal to visitors fascinated by ordinary Cairene life.

Getting there, buses (#302) and minibuses (#2) connect Tahrir with Shubra, and several trams wend their way from Saiyida Zeinab and Midan Ataba into Rod el-Farag. However, it's probably easiest to reach these districts using shared taxis. Look for vehicles heading in the right direction on Midan Tahrir, 26th July, or off Midan Ramses.

Bulaq

Immediately north of the 6th October flyover lies the oldest of the northern suburbs, **Bulaq**, whose name derives from the Coptic word for "marsh". During medieval times, the westwards shift of the Nile turned a sandbank into an island, which merged with the east bank as the intervening channel silted up. As the Fatimid port of al-Maks was left high and dry, Bulaq became the new anchorage in the 1350s; rapidly developing into an entrepôt after Sultan Barsbey re-routed the spice trade and encouraged manufacturing. When Mohammed Ali set about establishing a foundry, textiles factory and modern shipyards here in the 1820s, Bulaq was the obvious site. Unfortunately, the Ottomans permitted free trade, enabling British manufacturers to undersell local industries and force Egypt back into dependency on cotton exports to the Lancashire mills.

Since then, small workshops and apartment buildings have taken over Bulaq, while world affairs are handled in two towering landmarks along the Corniche: the **Television Building** and the **Cairo Plaza**. Inland of the latter (which harbours the Australian Embassy) is a one-time hostel for members of the Rifai order, next to the **Mosque of Sinan Pasha**, a sixteenth-century hybrid of Mamluke and Ottoman styles, attached to a still-working **hammam**. More revered by locals for its namesake's *baraka* is the fifteenth-century **Mosque of Abu'l'Ila**, three blocks before 26th July Street meets the Corniche. Nearby stand the abandoned **royal stables** of Mohammed Ali, recognisable by the model horse-heads protruding from its wings. Both are marked on the map of Central Cairo (see p.74).

Shubra

Two million Cairenes live in the sprawling beehive known as **Shubra**, the older part of which is called *Shubra al-Balad* to distinguish it from the newer outgrowth beyond the Ismailiya Canal, dubbed *Shubra el-Kheima*. Originally an island (its name, "Elephant", supposedly comes from a ship that ran aground), Shubra became attached to the mainland about the same time as Bulaq, but was given over to orchards and villages until the nineteenth century. In 1808, Mohammed Ali built a summer palace which caused Europeans to snigger ("The taste, alas! of an English upholsterer"), where he later died insane. Other palaces were erected by Ismail, who laid a carriage road to the original residence, planted with syca-more-fig and acacia trees, where Cairenes promenaded.

The 1891 edition of *Murray's Handbook* deemed **Sharia Shubra** "the most republican promenade in the world. No description of vehicle, nor manner of animal, biped or quadruped, is excluded, and the Khedive and his outriders are jostled and crossed in a most unseemly fashion by files of bare-boned and sore-covered mules and donkeys, whipped in by ragged urchins". Nowadays the avenue seems thoroughly proletarian, for Shubra has long since evolved from a garden suburb into densely packed quarters where educated Copts and Muslims rub shoulders with poor rural migrants.

Though self-help projects have improved some of the bleak low-rise estates in Shubra el-Kheima, dire poverty inclines a minority towards radical Islam, and re-inforces the traditional superstitions that most Cairenes at least half-believe. *Baladi* folk turn instinctively to **magic**, whereas educated people will exhaust rational solutions before resorting to a *sheikh* or *sheikha*. What psychologists might regard as mental illnesses are treated as cases of demonic possession, possibly caused by deliberate cursing. (One method of hexing is to recite the 33rd *sura* of the Koran backwards.) While certain moulids feature public **exorcisms**, most are private, especially those with pagan elements. Joseph McPherson, Cairo's secret police chief in the Twenties, witnessed a *zaar* where celebrants whirled to ancient and Muslim incantations; cymbals clashed; a ram, ganders, doves and rabbits were sacrificed, their blood being daubed on the particpants, whose frenzy increased:

> Sometimes they bent their bodies back, till they formed a writhing and vibrating bow, resting on the ground by the heels and back of the head, whilst the muscles of their bodies carried on the dance with unbelievable contortions.

When all concerned believe in the ritual's spiritual validity, the desired result is frequently achieved.

Rod el-Farag

During the 1950s, a slice of Shubra al-Balad was developed as a separate residential and commercial district, named "Farag's Orchard" after its previous role. The name remains appropriate, since **Rod el-Farag** hosts Cairo's largest **fruit and vegetable market**, *Abu el-Farag*. Like the others, it's the exclusive preserve of one of two cabals of wholesalers. In Rod el-Farag's case, they all hail from the villages around the capital, whereas elsewhere *Saiyidis* from Upper Egypt may control trade. The modern **Port of Cairo** is another local source of wealth with a shady underside.

Trams #6, #7, #8, #13 and #16 all return to central Cairo from Shurbra al-Balad or Rod el-Farag.

Abbassiya, Hada'iq al-Qubba and Medinet Nasr

In practice, the demarcation lines between these districts (which subdivide into other quarters) and Heliopolis are blurred by sheer density and overcrowding, and interlocking transport networks.

Abbassiya

The sprawling **Abbassiya** district gets its name from a palace built by Mohammed Ali's grandson, Pasha Abbas I, who dreaded assassination during his brief reign (1848–54) and kept camels saddled there for rapid flight into the desert – to no avail, for he was murdered by his servants. Nearer Cairo, the British established the Abbassiya Barracks (where the nationalist leader Orabi surrendered after his defeat at Tell el-Kebir), which vastly expanded during wartime. Like the Army GHQ (still located in Abbassiya), it was later seized by the Free Officers in a bloodless coup against Egypt's monarchy on the night of 22 July, 1952. Cairenes awoke next day to learn of a "revolution" led by General Naguib – a nominal figurehead, since it was Nasser who had engineered it and secretly controlled affairs until his public emergence as leader.

Abbassiya's Janus profile juxtaposes spacious institutions and crowded slums, marshalling yards and hospitals. Its main thoroughfare, Sharia Ramses, divides the oil-depot zone of al-Sharabiyya from Gamra and el-Sakakini, two residential market quarters. On Sharia Sakakini, near the end of the tramlines (#5, #7), the **Museum of Hygiene and Medicine** occupies an ornate rococo palace (see "Museums"). A more conspicuous edifice is the curvaceous new **Coptic Cathedral of Saint Mark**, the seat of the Coptic Patriarchate since it was raised in the 1970s. Visitors interested in joining pilgrim excursions to the Red Sea Monasteries should contact officials in the adjacent Church of Saint Peter and Paul (*al-Batrussiya*), at 222 Sharia Ramses (☎821-274).

Other landmarks include the **Misr Travel Tower**, housing the Ministry of Tourism, 500m from the **Sinai Bus Terminal** near the junction of Salah Salem and al-'Urubah, and a similar distance from the Engineering Faculty of **Ain Shams University**. Roundabout are sited numerous clubs (*nady*) and training schools belonging to professional unions, police and military. In December 1989, Egypt's hated Interior Minister, Zaki Badr, narrowly escaped a car-bomb outside one such club, following repressive action in Assyut (see Chapter Two, *The Nile Valley*).

Buses (#50, #400, #420 & #500) and minibuses (#24, #27, #32, #33, #34 & #35) run between Tahrir and Abbassiya. To reach the Sinai Terminal in particular, catch minibus #32, or a #69 bus from Midan Ataba.

Hada'iq al-Qubba: Nasser's Tomb

Northeast of Abbassiya along 23rd July Street (a continuation of Sharia el-Geish), a modern mosque stands beside a dusty shrine containing the **Tomb of Gamal Abdel Nasser**. When Nasser died in September 1969, a million Egyptians followed his bier through the streets of Cairo and the whole Arab world mourned. His cult was subsequently downplayed by Sadat (who feared comparisons) and in recent years most of the visitors to Nasser's shrine have been foreign admirers or gloating Israelis. Whatever Egyptians may think about Nasser's son, Khalid – who was recently acquitted of involvement in *Thawraat Masri* (Egypt's Revolution), a Libyan-backed group that attacked US and Israeli targets in the 1980s – his father's legend remains a potent one. Saddam Hussein's claim to be Nasser's "spiritual heir" was only the latest attempt by an Arab leader to metaphorically wrest the sword from the stone.

The tomb lies on the edge of **Hada'iq al-Qubba**, a district named after Ismail's **Qubba Palace**. Its 400 rooms were inherited by Khedive Tewfik and later contained King Farouk's vast collection of rare stamps, coins and other treasures, ranging from medieval Korans to a Fabergé thermometer. Now a presidential residence used for state conferences, it was here that the Shah of Iran spent the last days of his wandering exile, mortally stricken by cancer. The palace's walled grounds can be glimpsed along the #420 bus route; bus #300 also runs through Hada'iq al-Qubba en route between Tahrir and the Ain Shams quarter (see below).

Medinet Nasr – and Sadat's Tomb

During the 1960s and 70s a whole new satellite-suburb was created on the site of the Abbassiya Rifle Ranges and many government departments were relocated in this "Victory City". Despite some areas looking half-finished, **Medinet Nasr** is already connected to Midan Roxi in Heliopolis by bus #67 (starting from Tahrir) and local trams (see below), and accessible from Midan Ataba or Abbassiya by #34 minibus. But unless you've got business with the Inland Revenue or Transport Ministry, there's little here worth noting. Travellers coming in from Suez will pass the Olympic-sized **Cairo Stadium** at one end of Sharia al-Nasr, where the country's football cup finals are held (see "Entertainments").

Alongside the boulevard is a "desert Red Square" centred upon a pyramid-shaped **Victory Memorial** to the 1973 War. In 1981, Islamic radicals infiltrated the October 6 anniversary parade and blasted the reviewing stand with machine-guns and grenades, fatally wounding President Sadat (Mubarak, who stood beside him, was unharmed). Unlike the foreign leaders who paid homage at **Sadat's Tomb** beneath the Victory Memorial, most Egyptians seemed unmoved by their president's assassination. Two mass trials of alleged radicals have since been staged in the nearby **Cairo International Exhibition** grounds.

Heliopolis (Masr el-Jedida)

By the end of the nineteenth century, the doubling of Cairo's population and the exponential growth of its foreign community had created a huge demand for new accommodation, which fired the imagination of a Belgian entrepreneur. Baron Empain proposed creating a garden city in the desert, linked to the downtown area by an overground metro; a commercial venture attractive to investors, since Empain's company would collect both rents and fares from commuting residents of **Heliopolis**. Laid out by Sir Reginald Oakes in radial grid patterns, the suburb's wide avenues were lined with apartment blocks enobled by pale yellow Moorish facades and bisected by shrubbery. Named after the ancient City of the Sun near Matariyya (see overpage), Heliopolis soon acquired every facility from schools and churches to a racecourse and branch of *Groppi's*.

Wealthy Egyptians settled here from the beginning; merely prosperous ones moved in as foreigners left in droves throughout the 1950s. Meanwhile, poorer quarters started growing up around Heliopolis, ending its privileged isolation from Greater Cairo. During the 1970s, air-conditioned tower blocks began to replace spacious villas, the racecourse was turned into a fun park and burger joints proliferated. Today, visitors come for the restaurants and nightlife, or to admire the stylish architecture along its central boulevards; many foreigners also rent flats or work in Heliopolis, which is nowadays called "New Cairo" (*Masr el-Jedida*).

TRANSPORT

Depending on your starting point, choice of transport, and whether it's rush hour, Heliopolis is between fifteen and thirty minutes' ride from downtown Cairo. The fastest way is to hail **service taxis** heading there from Bab al-Luq, Opera Square and Midan Tahrir, via Salah Salem, which charge fixed rates. To reach Midan Roxi in Heliopolis, it's almost as quick to use **minibuses** from Tahrir (#24, #26) or Ataba (#20, #25); for Midan Ismailiya, catch a #27 or #35 from Tahrir.

During rush hour, **buses** from Tahrir and Ramses (#400, #420, #510) are slower than the suburb's original tram system, known as the **Heliopolis Metro**. From their downtown terminal behind the Egyptian Antiquities Museum, these three tram lines follow the same track through Abbassiya, diverging shortly before Midan Roxi. Each has colour-coded direction boards:

● The **Abd al-Aziz Fahmi line** (green) runs past Merryland and Heliopolis Hospital on Sharia al-Higaz before heading off towards the Shams Club.

● More centrally, the **Nouzha line** (red) veers off Sharia Merghani near the Heliopolis Sporting Club, and follows al-Ahram and Osman Ibn Affan up to Midan Triomphe.

● Initially running alongside the red line, the **Merghani line** (yellow) then follows the street of that name past the International Language Institute (ILI) to Midan Triomphe, and out towards the Armed Forces Hospital.

Meshing with this system are three **other tram routes**, only distinguished by Arabic signboards. Two connect Dirasa (near Islamic Cairo's Northern Cemetery) with the outlying quarters of Matariyya (see below) and Alf Maksan; the third runs between Roxi and Medinet Nasr. All three stop near the Girls' College (*Kulliyet Banat*) on the Merghani line, while the Matariyya tram also follows the Nouzha line through the centre, and the Alf Maksan service bridges a gap between Midan Triomphe and Midan Heliopolis.

Sights and activities

Nouzha-line, red-coded trams run through the heart of Heliopolis, whose finest **architecture** lines the boulevards between Sharia Merghani and Abu Bakr al-Saddiq. Stay on board to review Sharia al-Ahram's parade of handsome arcades topped with Andalusian balconies and pantiles, or alight near the **Heliopolis Sporting Club** and walk around the corner of the **Urubah Palace** onto Sharia Ibrahim.

Other side streets have more of a Twenties feel, with crisply graceful Art Deco apartments. But the most famous landmark lies off Sharia al-'Urubah, further southeast. Resembling a Hindu temple, **Baron Empain's Palace** originally boasted a revolving tower which enabled its owner to follow the sun throughout the day. The now derelict structure (dubbed "Le Baron" by locals) can be glimpsed from some of the airport-bound buses.

Not far away – and directly accessible by Merghani tram – the **International Language Institute** (ILI) employs many foreigners as teachers (see "Work" in *Basics*). Along the Merghani tram route, too, are the *Heliopolis* and *Heliolido* **sporting clubs**, with tennis and squash courts, swimming pools and gymnasiums. The *Heliopolis Sporting Club* only admits foreigners in the summer and seems snootier than the *Heliolido*. Northeast of the latter, **Merryland** contains a boating lake and funfair, a small zoo and an overpriced café – nothing to get excited about, but it's nice to be surrounded by greenery – and it's a safe place for children to play. Green-coded trams continue on past Merryland, up al-Higaz towards Midan Heliopolis.

Restaurants and facilities

Should hunger strike, Heliopolis abounds with **places to eat**. Around the centre you can lounge on the terrace of *Groppi's* or *Amphitrion*, overlooking Sharia al-Ahram; scoff a *Wimpy* or *Kentucky Fried Chicken* on al-Khalifa al-Ma'mun, which curves around towards Midan Roxi; or zap your taste buds on Sharia Abdel Wahid (one block north of al-Ahram), where there's a Korean restaurant and a *Chicken Tikka* takeaway. Opposite Merryland, the *Andalusia* resembles a set from *El Cid* propped up by a pizza joint. Near the hospital on Midan Heliopolis are another *Wimpy* and an excellent French restaurant, *La Terrine*. Equally good is the *Swiss-Air* run *La Chantilly* on Sharia Brazil. Hotels offer an even wider range of dining possibilities, plus **nightlife**. Until the *Sheraton Heliopolis* recovers from its fire, the main contenders are the *Hyatt Al Salam* on Sharia Abdel Hamid Badawi, *Le Baron Hotel* on Maahad al-Sahara, and the *Mövenpick* between the airport terminals – for details, see "Eating and Drinking" and "Entertainments".

Local **facilities** include *American Express* (Meridien Hotel), a 24-hour pharmacy (3 Osman Ibn Affan), hospitals (see "Listings"), cinemas and travel agencies. On Midan Ismailiya (not marked on maps, but accessible by minibus #27 or #35) is an **international coach station** from which services left for Baghdad and Amman before the Gulf War (and may yet resume). The square is also a depot for **service taxis** running back into town, via Bab al-Luq or Opera Square.

Matariyya and beyond

Northwest of Heliopolis, several former villages have evolved into ramshackle *baladi* suburbs. **El-Zeitun** (the Olives) merits a footnote in history as the site of

Sultan Selim's defeat of the Mamlukes in 1517 and of conspiratorial gatherings of Free Officers during the early 1950s. The adjacent **Helmiya** quarter gets its name from yet another khedival palace built last century. But for actual sights you have to venture even further out, into Matariyya.

The modern suburb of **Matariyya** traces its antecedents way back to the Old Kingdom and claims later acquaintance with the infant Christ. As evidence of the former, the neighbourhood's Midan al-Misallah displays a 22-metre-high, pink granite **Obelisk of Senusert I**. One of a pair raised to celebrate the pharaoh's Jubilee Festival (c.1900 BC), it originally stood outside the Temple of Re, erected by Amenemhat I, Senusert's father, who founded the XII Dynasty. Another pair, belonging to the XVIII Dynasty ruler Tuthmosis III, were moved by the Romans to Alexandria, whence they ended up in New York's Central Park and on London's Embankment. However, the significance of this site and its cult of the sun-god are far older, dating back to the earliest dynasties.

Cairo's new metro makes this sector of the northern suburbs readily accessible from the centre. Matariyya metro station is eleven stops from Tahrir, in the direction of El Marg; the neighbourhood can also be reached by tram from Heliopolis, or bus #43 from Midan Tahrir.

The Spring of the Sun, Virgin's Tree and Ain Shams

Nowadays, the **Spring of the Sun** waters a famous Christian relic, the **Virgin's Tree**. Located 500m south of the obelisk, this gnarled sycamore-fig is supposedly descended from a tree whose branches shaded the Holy Family during their Egyptian exile. Tradition has it that they rested here between Bilbeis and Babylon-in-Egypt (see p.129), and Mary washed the clothes of the baby Jesus in the stone trough which still lies beside the tree. Early this century, "Christian souvenir hunting was so bad that the owner of the sycamore tied a knife to the tree and put up a notice begging people not to hack at it any more with axes, and to leave some of it for others" (Aldridge). Now enclosed within a compound, it grows near the **Church of the Virgin**, a modern building occupying the site of far older churches.

The spring's Arabic name has attached itself to the **Ain Shams** quarter, one metro stop beyond Matariyya. Densely populated and solidly working-class, the neighbourhood is regarded by the police as a hotbed of Islamic fundamentalism. In August 1985, house-to-house searches provoked two days of rioting; veiled women hurled stones and chanted slogans from balconies, while the police fired gas and live rounds indiscriminately. After a plain-clothes cop was found with his throat cut later that year, several people were shot dead whilst "trying to escape" the police in Ain Shams.

The Lake of the Pilgrims

Still further out, beyond El Marg, caravans once prayed beside the **Lake of the Pilgrims** (*Birket el-Hagg*) before embarking on their journey to Mecca. Today, alas, the "covered litters of the female pilgrims and the picturesque corps of mounted *Bashi-Bazouks*" no longer "moves slowly forward on its desert route". Instead, the barren wastes outside Cairo have for several decades harboured rocket ranges, chemical weapons factories and other **military installations**, rendering vast tracts off-limits. Ironically, much of this research was undertaken in collaboration with Iraq, Egypt's main Arab ally before the Gulf War.

ANCIENT HELIOPOLIS, THE ENNEAD AND THE CULT OF RE

Although Anthony Trollope scoffed "Humbug!" when he saw what little remained in 1858, the site of **ancient Heliopolis**, near modern Matariyya, originally covered perhaps five square kilometres. The City of the Sun (called *On* by its founders, but better known by its Greek appellation) evolved in tandem with Memphis, the first capital of Dynastic Egypt (see "The Pyramids"). As Memphis embodied the political unification of Upper and Lower Egypt, so Heliopolis incarnated its theological aspect; syncretising diverse local cults into a hierarchical cosmogony which proved more influential than other creation myths of the Old Kingdom.

Cosmogony

In the **Heliopolitan cosmogony**, the world began as watery chaos (*Nun*) from which *Atum* the sun-god emerged onto a primal mound, spitting forth the twin deities *Shu*

Shu, Nut and Geb

(air) and *Tefnut* (moisture). They engendered *Geb* (earth) and *Nut* (sky), whose own union produced *Isis*, *Osiris*, *Seth* and *Nephthys*. Later texts often regarded this divine **Ennead** (Nine) as a single entity, while the universe was conventionally represented by the figures of Shu, Nut and Geb. Meanwhile (for reasons unknown), the primal deity Atum was subsumed by *Re* or *Ra*, a yet mightier aspect of the sun-god.

Re manifested himself in multiple forms: as hawk-headed Re-herakhte (Horus of the Horizon); the beetle Khepri (the rising sun); the disc Aten (the midday sun); and as Atum (the setting sun). The Egyptians believed that Re rose each morning in the east, traversed the sky in his solar barque and sank into the western land of the dead every evening, to voyage through the Duat (nether world) during the night, emerging at sunrise. This journey inevitably linked Re to the Osirian myth, and from the V Dynasty onwards it became *de rigueur* for pharaohs to claim descent from Re by identifying themselves with Horus and Osiris. The **cult of Re** was exclusive, for only the pharaoh and priesthood had access to Re's sanctuary, whose daily rituals were adopted by other divine cults and soon became inextricably entangled with Osiris-worship (see "Karnak" and "Abydos", *The Nile Valley*).

Ordinary folk – whose participation was limited to public festivals – worshipped lesser, more approachable deities.

Re

Remains

Having been eclipsed by Karnak and Amun-worship during the New Kingdom, Heliopolis was devastated by the Persians in 525 BC. Once rebuilt, however, its intellectual reputation attracted visitors such as Plato, Eudoxus (who probably invented the sundial after studying Egyptian astronomy) and Herodotus. But as Alexandria became the new focus for science and religion, Heliopolis inexorably declined; Strabo found it nearly desolate and the Romans totally ignored it. Today, the only tangible reminders of its existence are **Senusert's obelisk** and the **Spring of the Sun**, where Atum supposedly washed himself at the dawn of creation.

THE MUSEUMS

Although Cairo has over a dozen museums, most visitors limit themselves to the big three, devoted respectively to **Egyptian Antiquities**, **Coptic** and **Islamic Art**. Of these, the Antiquities Museum is the most popular and by far the largest, necessitating at least two visits to do it any kind of justice. The Coptic and Islamic Art museums can each comfortably be seen in a couple of hours and make fitting adjuncts to exploration of their quarters of the city.

On a practical note, unless you're planning to buy a photo permit, it's best to leave your **camera** at the hotel. Otherwise you'll have to check it in at the entrance to all three main museums, a process which occasionally leads to the wrong camera being returned to the wrong owner.

The Museum of Egyptian Antiquities

Open Sat–Thurs 9am–4pm, Fri 9–11.15am & 1.30–4pm. Admission £E4, students £E2. On Fridays a separate ticket is required for the morning and afternoon sessions. Cameras only admitted with a permit (£E10); no flashes or tripods.

The **Museum of Egyptian Antiquities** feels almost as archaic as the civilisation it records. Founded in 1858 by Auguste Mariette, who excavated the Serapeum at Saqqara and several major temples in Upper Egypt (and was later buried in the museum grounds), it has long since outgrown its present building on Midan Tahrir, which now scarcely provides warehouse space for the pharaonic artefacts. Allowing one minute for each, it would take about nine months to view its 100,000 exhibits. Thousands more items lie crated in the basement, where many have sunk into the soft ground, necessitating excavations beneath the building itself. Yet for all the chaos, poor lighting and captioning, the richness of the collection makes this one of the great museums of the world.

Although most guided **tours** last two hours, the museum deserves at least six. To avoid museum fatigue and the coach parties which pack in every morning, it's best to look around on successive afternoons. A single visit of three to four hours suffices to cover the Tutankhamun exhibition, the newly reopened Mummy Room and a couple of other **highlights**. The Amarna gallery and the selection of masterpieces hit the spot on each floor, but everyone has their own favourites. A reasonable shortlist might include the cream of statuary from the Old, Middle and New Kingdoms (**Rooms 42, 32, 22 and 12**) and the Nubian funerary cache (**Room 44**) downstairs; the Fayoum Portraits (**Room 14**) and model figures (**Rooms 37, 32 and 27**) on the upper floor.

A Guide to the Egyptian Museum (£E5), sold at the kiosk, lists exhibits by **catalogue** number but doesn't identify their location, so unless you're keen to look things up (labels on most exhibits are perfunctory) it's of little practical use. Should you want running commentary, it's easy to tag along behind a tour group. To break up morning and afternoon visits, there's a first-floor **café-restaurant**, entered via the souvenir shop from outside the museum.

Ground Floor

Exhibits are arranged more or less chronologically, so that by starting at the entrance and walking in a clockwise direction around the outer galleries you'll pass through the Old, Middle and New Kingdoms before ending up with the Late and Greco-Roman periods in the east wing. This approach is historically and artistically coherent but rather plodding. A snappier alternative is to proceed instead through the Atrium – which samples the whole era of pharaonic civilisation – to the superb Amarna gallery in the northern wing; then backtrack to cover sections that sound interesting, or instead head upstairs to see Tutankhamun.

To suit either option, we've covered the ground floor in six sections: the Atrium, Old, Middle and New Kingdom galleries, the Amarna gallery, and the East Wing. Whichever approach you decide on, it's worth starting with the Atrium foyer (**Room 43**), where the dynastic saga begins.

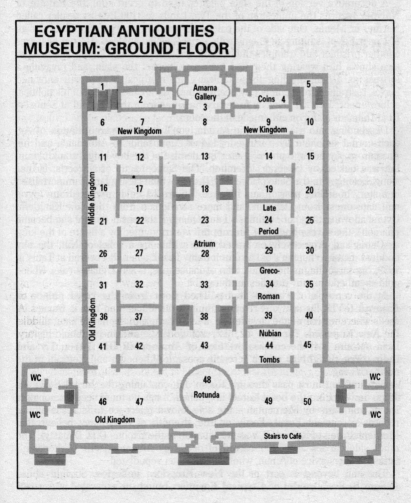

EGYPTIAN ANTIQUITIES
MUSEUM: GROUND FLOOR

ATRIUM

The **Rotunda**, inside the museum entrance, kicks off with **monumental sculptures** from various eras, notably a giant head of Pharaoh Userkaf (V Dynasty), three colossi of Ramses II (XIX Dynasty) and a statue of Amenhotep, son of the XVIII Dynasty royal architect Hapu. On the threshold of the Atrium foyer sits the limestone **statue of King Zoser** installed within its *serdab* beside his Step Pyramid at Saqqara in the twenty-seventh century BC, and removed by archaeologists 4600 years later. Those who regard Zoser's reign as the start of the Old Kingdom categorise the preceding era as the Early Dynastic or **Archaic Period**. The actual forging of dynastic rule is commemorated by a famous exhibit just beyond Zoser's statue.

A decorative version of the slate palettes used to grind kohl, the **Palette of Narmer** records the unification of the Two Lands (c.3100 BC) by a ruler called Narmer or Menes. One side of the palette depicts him wearing the White Crown of Upper Egypt, smiting an enemy with a mace, whilst a falcon (Horus) ensnares another prisoner and tramples the heraldic papyrus of Lower Egypt. The reverse face shows him wearing their Red Crown to inspect the slain, and ravaging a fortress as a bull; dividing these tableaux are mythical beasts with entwined necks, restrained from conflict by bearded men, an arcane symbol of his political achievement. Two XII Dynasty **funerary barques** from the pyramid of Senusert III at Dahshur stand on either side of the room.

Descending into the well of the Atrium, you'll pass the **sarcophagus of Ay**, each corner enfolded by a winged goddess. Counsellor to Akhenaten and his successors, Ay became pharaoh after the demise of the boy-king Tutankhamun, but was ousted by General Horemheb. The Sarcophagus of Nitrocris, farther along, belonged to the Saite princess of Thebes whom Henry James immortalised in a story of sibling passion and revenge. **Room 33** holds **pyramidions** (pyramid capstones) from Dahshur, and more sarcophagi from the New Kingdom. Overshadowing those of Tuthmosis I and Queen Hatshepsut (before she became pharaoh), the **sarcophagus of Merneptah** is surmounted by a figure of the king as Osiris and protectively embraced from within by a relief of Nut, the sky goddess. But Merneptah's bid for immortality failed: when discovered at Tanis in 1939, his sarcophagus held the coffin of Psusennes, a XXI Dynasty ruler whose gold-sheathed mummy now lies upstairs.

At the centre of the atrium is a **painted floor from the royal palace at Amarna** (XVIII Dynasty). A river brimming with ducks and fish is framed by reeds where waterfowl and cows amble, a fine example of the lyrical naturalism of the Amarna period. For more of this revolutionary epoch in pharaonic history, head upstairs past the **colossal statues of Amenophis III, Queen Tiy and their three daughters**, which serenely presage Akhenaten and Nefertiti in the northern wing.

But first you must pass through **Room 13**, containing the **Israel Stele**. Its name derives from the boast "Israel is crushed, it has no more seed", amongst a list of conquests by Merneptah – the sole known reference to Israel in all the records of ancient Egypt. Partly on the strength of this, many believe that Merneptah, son of Ramses II, was the Pharaoh of the Exodus (XIX Dynasty). The other side carries an earlier record of deeds by Amenophis III (Akhenaten's father) in the service of Amun, whom his son later repudiated.

The hall beyond is part of the **New Kingdom galleries**. Straight ahead **(Room 8)** lies a **model of a typical Egyptian house**, as excavated at Amarna, the shortlived capital of Akhenaten and Nefertiti – who are honoured with their own gallery across the hall.

OLD KINGDOM GALLERIES

The southwest corner of the ground floor is devoted to the **Old Kingdom** (c.2700–2181 BC), when the III–VI dynasties ruled Egypt from Memphis and built the pyramids. Lining the central aisle of **Rooms 46–47** are funerary statues of deceased VIPs and servants (the custom of burying live retainers ended with the II Dynasty). Notice the **statuettes** of the dwarf Khnum-hotep, Overseer of the Wardrobe; a man with a deformed head and a hunchback afflicted by Pott's disease (Case B); also menial *shabti* (worker) figures, depicted preparing food (Case D).

To the north are three **slate triads of Menkaure flanked by Hathor** and the goddess of the Aphroditopolis nome, from the Mycenius valley temple at Giza. The **panel from Userkaf's temple**, against the back wall, is the first known example of natural scenes being used as decoration within a royal funerary edifice. A pied kingfisher, purple gallinule and sacred ibis are clearly recognisable; likewise the **beard of the Sphinx**, at the end of the hall.

Beside the entrance to **Room 41**, **reliefs** from a V Dynasty tomb at Maidum depict a desert hunt and other rural activities. The women wear long chemises, the men loincloths or sometimes nothing (revealing them to be circumcised, according to Egyptian custom). A pair of **lion tables**, probably used for sacrifices or libations towards the end of the II Dynasty, flanks the doorway into **Room 42**, which boasts a superb **statue of Chepren**, his head embraced by Horus. Carved from black diorite, whose white marbling emphasises the sinews of his knee and clenched fist, the statue comes from Chepren's valley temple at Giza. Equally arresting is the wooden **statue of Ka-aper**, a plump figure with an introspective gaze which Arab diggers at Saqqara called "Sheikh al-Balad" because it resembled their own village headman. The **statue of a scribe**, poised for notation with an open scroll across his knees, is also memorable.

On the left-hand wall of **Room 31**, six **wooden panels** from the tomb of Hesy-Re portray this senior scribe of the III Dynasty, who was also a dentist – the earliest known to history. Another wall bears sandstone reliefs from Wadi Maraghah, near the ancient turquoise mines of Sinai. Twin limestone **statues of Ra-Nufer** signify his dual role as Memphite high priest of Ptah and Sokar; aside from their wigs and kilts, they look virtually identical. Both were created in the royal workshops, possibly by the same artist.

Room 32 is dominated by life-size seated **statues of Prince Rahotep and Princess Nefert**, from their *mastaba* at Maidum (IV Dynasty). His skin is painted brick red, hers a creamy yellow – a distinction common in Egyptian art. Nefert wears a wig and diadem and swathes herself in a diaphanous wrap; the prince is simply clad in a waist cloth. Look out for the **tableaux of the dwarf Seneb and his family**. Embraced by his wife, this Overseer of the Wardrobe seems contented; his naked children hold their fingers to their lips. Nearby hangs a perfectly observed, vividly stylised mural, known as the **Maidum Geese** (III/IV Dynasty). Although the heyday of the Old Kingdom is poorly represented by a **statue of Ti**, its twilight era boasts the first known metal sculptures (c.2300 BC): two **statues of Pepi I and his son**, made by hammering sheets of copper over wooden armatures.

MIDDLE KINGDOM GALLERIES

With **Room 26** you enter the **Middle Kingdom**, when centralised authority was restored and pyramid-building resumed under the XII Dynasty (c.1991–1786 BC). A relic of the previous era of civil wars (termed the First Intermediate Period) sits in the corner, glum-faced. Endowed with hulking feet to suggest power, and black skin, crossed arms and a curly beard to link it to Osiris, the **statue of Mentuhotep Nebhepetre** was buried near his funerary shrine at Deir el-Bahri and discovered by Howard Carter – whose horse fell through the roof. If the Mummy of Dagi were still around, it could use the pair of "eyes" carved inside its sarcophagus to espy a statue of Queen Nofret wearing a sheath dress and a Hathor wig, across the corridor.

Room 22 contains expressive likenesses of Amemenhat III, Senusert I and the daughters of Djehutyhotep, but your attention is grabbed by the **burial chamber of Harhotpe** from Deir el-Bahri, covered inside with pictorical objects, charms and texts. Surrounding the chamber are ten limestone **statues of Senusert** from his pyramid complex at Lisht, stiffly formal in contrast to his cedarwood figure. The sides of these statues' thrones bear variations of the *sematawy* symbol of unification: Hapy the Nile-god, or Horus and Seth, entwining the heraldic plants of the Two Lands.

This basic imperative of statecraft might explain the unique **double statue of Amenemhat III** in *Room 16*. Personified as the Nile-god bringing his people fish on trays, the dual figures may represent Upper and Lower Egypt, or the living king and his deified *ka*. Five **lion-headed sphinxes with human faces** watch your exit from the Middle Kingdom; the anarchic Second Intermediate Period and the Hyksos invasion go uncommemorated.

NEW KINGDOM GALLERIES

With **Room 11** you pass into the **New Kingdom**, an era of renewed pharaonic power and imperial expansion under the XVIII and XIX dynasties (c.1567–1200 BC). A grey schist **statue of Tuthmosis III** honours the founder of Egypt's African and Asian empire, whose ambitions were thwarted whilst his stepmother Hatshepsut ruled as pharaoh. From one of the Osiride pillars of her great temple at Deir el-Bahri comes a commanding crowned **head of Hatshepsut**.

Room 12 is crammed with masterpieces of XVIII Dynasty art. The **Hathor Shrine** from Tuthmosis III's ruined temple at Deir el-Bahri contains a statue of the goddess in her bovine form, emerging reborn from a papyrus swamp. Tuthmosis stands beneath her cow's head, and is suckled as an infant in the fresco behind Hathor's statue, overshadowed by a star-spangled ceiling. To the right of the shrine is a block statue of Hatshepsut's vizier, Senenmut, and her daughter Neferure: the trio's relationship has inspired much speculation. From the same period comes a section of the Deir el-Bahri "**Punt reliefs**", showing the obese Queen of Punt and her donkey, observed by Hatshepsut during her expedition to that fabled land.

Two **statues of Amenhotep** portray him as a young scribe of humble birth, and as an octogenarian priest, honoured for his direction of massive works like the Colossi of Memnon. Between Amenhotep's figures stands a pink granite **statue of Tutankhamun as Khonsu** (with the side-lock of youth), removed from the temple of the moon-god at Karnak. Another striking figure is that of Sennefer, builder of the tomb with the grape-arbour ceiling at Thebes.

Turning the corner into the northern wing, you encounter two **lion-headed statues of Sekhmet**, found at Karnak. **Sphinxes** with the heads of Hatshepsut and her family dominate the central aisle of **Rooms 6–7**. Some of the reliefs along the southern wall come from the Tomb of Maya at Saqqara, which was uncovered last century but subsequently lost until its rediscovery in 1986. From **Room 8**, most visitors check out the Amarna gallery before walking through the cast of statues and sarcophagi in **Room 9**. Here, note the relief on a block from Ramses II's temple at Memphis, which shows him subjugating Egypt's foes. In a motif repeated on dozens of temple pylons, the king grabs the hair of a Libyan, Nubian and Syrian, and wields an axe. Ramessid pharaohs who never fought a battle were especially keen on such **reliefs**.

Many of the ancient **coins** in **Room 4** bear the head of Alexander the Great; some on the left side of the first case on the right carry the profile of Cleopatra. From **Room 10** you can follow the New Kingdom into the east wing (covered shortly), or climb the stairs to the Tutankhamun galleries on the upper floor.

THE AMARNA GALLERY
Room 3 focuses on the **Amarna period**: a break with centuries of tradition which barely outlasted the reign of Pharaoh Akhenaten (c.1379–1362 BC) and Queen Nefertiti. Rejecting Amun and the other deities of Thebes, they decreed the supremacy of a single god, the Aten; built a new capital at Amarna in Middle Egypt to escape the old bureaucracy; and left enigmatic works of art that provoke a reaction.

Staring down from the walls are four **colossi of Akhenaten**, whose attenuated skull and face, flaring lips and nostrils, rounded thighs and belly are suggestive of a hermaphrodite or a primaeval earth goddess. Because this is carried over to the figures of his wife and daughters on certain stele (Cases F and H) and tomb-reliefs, it has been argued that the Amarna style pandered to some physical abnormality in Akhenaten (or the royal family) – the captions hint at perversions. Others retort that the exquisite **head of Nefertiti** proves that it was just a stylistic device, eschewed when inappropriate. Another feature of Amarna art was its note of intimacy: a **stele of the royal family** (Case F) portrays Akhenaten dandling their eldest daughter, Meritaten, whilst Nefertiti cradles her sisters. For the first time in Egyptian art, breakfast was depicted. The Amarna focus on this world rather than the afterlife infused traditional subjects with new vitality – witness the freer brush-strokes on the fragments of a **marsh scene**.

The carnelian, gold and glass-inlaid **coffin** is usually ascribed to Smenkhkare, who ruled alongside Akhenaten in his final years and is variously identified as the pharaoh's son-in-law, brother, lover – or as Nefertiti herself (see p.253). The **Amarna Letters** (Case A) note pleas for troops to aid the pharaoh's vassals in Palestine, the impact of his death, and Nefertiti's search for allies against those who pressed Tutankhamun to reverse the Amarna revolution. Originally baked into earthen "envelopes" for delivery, these cuniform tablets were stored in the Foreign Office archives at Amarna.

THE EAST WING
As an inducement to follow the New Kingdom into the east wing, **Room 15** has a sexy statue of the wife of Nakht Min (Case 196). Inside **Room 14**, a statue of Ramses VI dragging a grovelling Libyan by the hair (XX Dynasty), and a painted sunk-relief of Ramses II doing likewise to three prisoners, already seem tedious. More interesting is the huge **statue of Seti I**, whose sensitive facial modelling recalls Nefertiti's head. Originally, it would have worn a *nemset* headdress like the one on Tutankhamun's funerary mask.

Waning with the XX Dynasty and expiring with the XXI, the New Kingdom was followed by the so-called **Late Period** of mostly foreign rulers. **Room 25** contains a granite **head of Taharqa**, the XXV Dynasty Nubian king who conquered Thebes and is mentioned in the Bible (*II Kings* 19:9). From the same period comes an alabaster **statue of Amenirdis the Elder**, whom the pharaoh made divine votaress of Amun to watch over the Theban priesthood (**Room 30**). Dressed as a New Kingdom queen, Amenirdis wears a falcon headdress crowned with *uraei*, originally topped by a Hathor crown bearing a solar disc and horns. Of the diverse **statues of deities** in **Room 25**, it's Taweret (or Tweri), the pregnant-hippopotamus goddess of childbirth, that most visitors remember.

Rooms 34–35 cover the **Greco-Roman Period** (332 BC onwards), when classical art engaged with ancient Egyptian symbolism. The meld of styles is typified by the two stele near the back wall, and bizarre **statues and sarcophagi** in **Room 49**. That of Petosiris, high priest of Thoth at Hermopolis (c.300 BC), features nubile Nuts carved on the bottom of the sarcophagus and inside its lid, to comfort him through eternity. **Room 50** contains a comical **bust of Serapis**, the made-to-order Ptolemaic god with the taurine necropolis at Saqqara.

Even if you decide to skip the rest of the wing, it's worth visiting **Room 44**, devoted to **artefacts from royal Nubian tombs** south of Abu Simbel. The burial of Blemmye royalty involved the strangulation of servants and the butchery of horses. An equine skeleton, saddlery, crowns and weaponry were unearthed in graves at Qustul and Ballana, where the Blemmye still worshipped Isis and Horus long after Egypt had become Christian.

First Floor

The upper floor is dominated by the Tutankhamun galleries, which occupy the best part of two wings. Once you've seen Tut's treasures, everything but the Mummy Room and the display of masterpieces seems lacklustre – even though the other galleries feature artefacts just as fine as those downstairs. Come back another day and check them out.

TUTANKHAMUN GALLERIES

The funerary impedimenta of the boy-king **Tutankhamun** numbers 1700 items and fills a dozen rooms. Given the brevity of his reign (1361–1352 BC) and the paucity of his tomb in the Valley of the Kings, one's mind boggles at the treasure that must have been stashed with great pharaohs like Ramses or Seti. Tutankhamun merely fronted the Theban counter-revolution that effaced Amarna and restored the cult of Amun and its priesthood to their former primacy. However, the influence of Amarna is apparent in some of the **exhibits**, which are laid out roughly as they were packed into his tomb: chests and statues (**Room 45**) preceding furniture (**Rooms 40, 35, 30, 25, 20 and 10**), shrines (**Rooms 9–7**) and gold appurtenances (**Room 4**). Adjacent to this are jewellery (**Room 3**; closes half an hour early) and other treasures from diverse tombs (**Rooms 2 and 13**). Most visitors make a beeline for the last four, ignoring the sequence just outlined. If that includes you, skip ahead through the following rundown.

When Carter's team penetrated the sealed corridor in 1922 they found an antechamber stuffed with caskets and detritus ransacked by robbers, and two life-size **ka statues of Tutankhamun**, whose black skin symbolised his rebirth. Pass between these into **Room 45** to see a **shrine of Anubis**, carried in his cortege: the protector of the dead as a vigilant jackal with gilded ears and silver claws. To ensure quality-of-afterlife, Tut also packed an ebony and ivory **gaming set** for play-

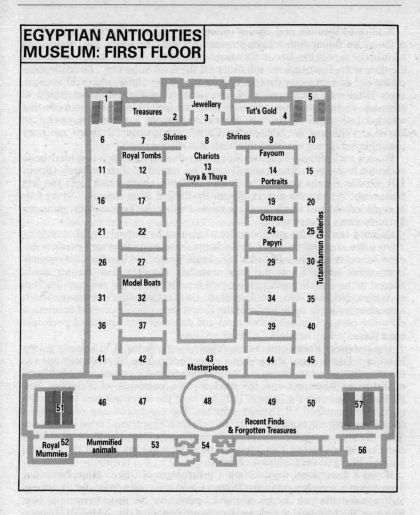

EGYPTIAN ANTIQUITIES
MUSEUM: FIRST FLOOR

1

Treasures 2

Jewellery 3

Tut's Gold 4

5

6 7

Shrines 8

Shrines 9

10

Royal Tombs
11 12

Chariots
13
Yuya & Thuya

Fayoum
14
Portraits

15

16 17

19 20

Ostraca
24

Tutankhamun Galleries

21 22

25

Papyri

26 27

29 30

Model Boats
31 32

34 35

36 37

39 40

41 42

43
Masterpieces

44 45

51

46 47

48

49 50

57

Royal 52
Mummies

Mummified
animals

53

54

Recent Finds
& Forgotten Treasures

56

ing *senet*, and a host of **shabti figures** to fulfil any tasks the gods might set him. A **golden shrine** covered in repoussé scenes of conjugal harmony once held statues of Tut and his wife Ankhesenamun that were stolen in antiquity (**Room 40**).

The king's clothes and unguents were stored in two magnificent **chests** (**Room 35**). On the lid and sides of the "Painted Chest", he is depicted hunting ostriches and antelopes and devastating ranks of Syrians in his war-chariot, larger than life; the end panels show him trampling other foes in the guise of the sphinx. By contrast, the lid of the "Inlaid Chest" bears a gentle, Amarna-style vignette of Ankhesenamun (daughter of Nefertiti and Akhenaten) offering lotus, papyrus and mandrake to her husband, framed by poppies, pomegranates and cornflowers. Note the **Amarna toilet-seat** outside **Room 34** and the **statue of Tutankhamun hunting with a harpoon** between **Rooms 35 and 30**.

Next come **thrones and chairs (Rooms 30, 25 and 20)**. On the backrest of the gilded throne with winged-serpent arms and clawed feet, the royal couple relax in the rays of the Aten, their names given in the Amarna form – dating it to the time when Tutankhamun still observed the Amarna heresy. The "ecclesiastical throne" (the prototype for episcopal thrones of the Christian church) is exquisitely inlaid with ebony and gold, but looks uncomfortable. More typical of pharaonic design are the wooden *Heb* chair and footstools, and a commode that wouldn't look amiss at Harrods. **Room 20** features a **gilded trumpet** (last played in 1939) and the **"Prisoners' Cane"**, whose ebony (Nubian) and ivory (Asian) inlaid figures symbolise the unity of north and south.

From ivory headrests in **Room 15**, it's a natural progression to **gilded beds** dedicated to the gods whose animal-forms are carved on their bedposts (**Room 10**). Similar figures protect the golden **canopic chest** which held the jars containing the pharaoh's viscera (**Room 9**). Ranged along **Rooms 7–8** are four boxy **gilded shrines** which fitted one inside another like Russian dolls, enclosing Tutankhamun's sarcophagus.

Room 4 contains the **gold**, some of which may be on tour abroad. Assuming it's in Cairo, the centrepiece is Tutankhamun's haunting **funerary mask**, wearing a *nemset* headdress inlaid with lapis lazuli, quartz and obsidian. His mummiform **coffin**, adorned with the same materials, comes a close second; hands clasped in the Osiride position, the figure is protected by the cloisonné feathers of Wadjet, Nekhbet, Isis and Nephthys. On Tutankhamun's mummy (which remains in his tomb at the Valley of the Kings) were placed scores of **amulets**, a cloisonné **corselet** spangled with glass and carnelian, gem-encrusted **pectorals** and a pair of golden **sandals** – all displayed here.

The **Jewellery Room** next door is equally overpowering. A VI Dynasty golden **head of a falcon** (once attached to a copper body) from Hieraconpolis rates as the star attraction, but there's stiff competition from the **crown and necklaces of Princess Khnumyt** and the **diadem and pectorals of Princess Set-Hathor**. Buried near the latter at Dahshur were the **amethyst belt and anklet of Mereret**, another XII Dynasty princess. The ceremonial **axe of Ahmosis**, commemorating his expulsion of the Hyksos from Egypt, was buried in the tomb of his mother, Queen Ahhotep. From the same cache (found by Mariette in 1859) came a rigid bracelet of lapis lazuli and the bizarre **golden flies** of the Order of Valour – bug-eyed decorations for bravery.

Room 2 displays two royal caches. The **furniture of Queen Hetepheres** has been expertly reconstructed from heaps of gold and rotten wood. As the wife of Snofru and mother of Cheops, she was buried near her son's pyramid at Giza with a sedan chair, gold vessels and a canopied bed. From the XXI–XXII Dynasty, when northern Egypt was ruled from the Delta, comes the **Treasure of Tanis**. Of the three royal caches unearthed by Montet in 1939, the richest was that of Psusennes I, whose electrum coffin was found inside the sarcophagus of Merneptah (see downstairs). His gold necklace is made from rows of discs, in the New Kingdom style.

Between **Room 8** and the Atrium stand two wooden **chariots**, found in the antechamber of Tutankhamun's tomb. Intended for state occasions, their gilded stucco reliefs show Asiatics and Nubians in bondage; pharaonic war-chariots were lighter and stronger. The finest **objects from the tomb of Yuya and Thuya (Room 13)** are Thuya's gem-inlaid gilded mask, their mummiform coffins and statues of the couple. As parents of Queen Tiy (wife of Amenophis III), they were buried in the Valley of the Kings; their tomb was found intact late last century.

Having finished with Tut, you can either head down the western wing to the Mummy Room, or tackle the other galleries (see below).

MUMMIES
The museum's southwest corner harbours two rooms full of mummies. **Room 53** exhibits **mummified animals and birds** from necropoli across Egypt, evincing the strength of animal cults towards the end of the pagan era, when devotees embalmed everything from bulls to mice.

Modern Egyptians regard these relics of ancestoral superstition with equanimity, but the exhibition of human remains offended many – hence Sadat's closure of the famous Mummy Room in 1981. At the time of writing, however, **Room 52** has just been reopened to display fifteen of the museum's twenty-five **royal mummies**. From the XVIII Dynasty come Ahmosis I, Queen Nefertari, Tuthmosis I, II and III, Amenophis III and (maybe) Smenkhkare; from the XIX Dynasty, Seti I and II, Ramses II and III, and Merneptah.

THE OTHER GALLERIES
To view the other galleries in approximate chronological order you should start at **Room 43** (overlooking the atrium) and proceed in a clockwise direction, as on the ground floor. However, since most visitors wander in from Tut's galleries, we've described the western and eastern wings from that standpoint.

Starting with the **western wing**, notice the "**Heart Scarabs**" that were placed upon the throats of mummies, bearing a spell that implored the deceased's heart not to bear witness against him or her during the Judgement of Osiris (**Room 6**). **Room 12**'s hoard of **objects from XVIII Dynasty royal tombs** includes the mummies of a child and a gazelle (Case I); priestly wigs and wig-boxes (Case L); two leopards from the funerary cache of Amenophis II; and the chariot of Tuthmosis IV. **Room 17** holds the **contents of private tombs**, notably that of Sennedjem, from the Workmen's village near the Valley of the Kings. With skills honed on royal tombs, Sennedjem carved himself a stylish vault; its door depicts him playing *senet*. The sarcophagus of his son Khonsu carries a design showing the lions of Today and Yesterday supporting the rising sun, while Anubis embalms his mummy under the protection of Isis and Nephthys.

Whilst the corridor displays **canopic chests and coffins**, the inner rooms feature **Middle Kingdom models**. From Meketre's tomb at Thebes come marvellous domestic figures and tableaux: a woman carrying wine-jars on her head; peasants netting fish from reed boats; cattle being driven past an estate-owner (**Room 27**). Compare the fully crewed model boats in Case F of **Room 32** with the unmanned solar barques for voyaging through eternity, in Case E. In the corridor outside stands a unusual *ka* statue of Pharaoh Hor, mounted on a sliding base to signify his posthumous wanderings. Model-soldier buffs will delight in the phalanxes of Nubian archers and Egyptian pikemen from the tomb of Prince Mesehti at Assyut, in **Room 37**.

The museum's **southern wing** is best seen at a trot. The eastern part contains a **model of a funerary complex** showing how the pyramids and their temples related to the Nile (**Room 49**), and the square **leather funerary tent** of an XXI Dynasty queen (by the southeast stairway). More striking are two exhibitions in the central section. **Recent finds and forgotten treasures** are showcased outside **Room 54**; a **selection of masterpieces** nearer the atrium. The latter includes a panel of blue faience tiles from Zoser's burial hall at Saqqara; a stone head of Queen Tiy which prefigures the Amarna style; and "dancing dwarves" modelled on equatorial pygmies.

If approached from the north, the **eastern wing** begins with **Room 14**, containing the superbly lifelike **"Fayoum Portraits"** found by Petrie at Hawara. Painted in encaustic (pigments mixed into molten wax) whilst their sitters were alive, the portraits were glued onto Greco-Roman mummies (100–250 AD). The staggering diversity of Egypt's pantheon by the late pagan era is suggested by the **statues of deities** in **Room 19**. Next door and the room after are devoted to **ostraca and papyri**. Ostraca were limestone flakes or potshards, on which were scratched sketches or ephemeral writing; papyrus was used for finished artwork and lasting **manuscripts**. Besides the *Book of the Dead* (**Room 24**) and the *Book of AmDuat* (depicting the Weighing of the Heart ceremony), note the *Satirical Papyrus*, showing mice being served by cats in a parody of offerings to the gods. **Room 29** also displays a scribe's writing kit and an artist's paints and brushes. Although the **miscellaneous and everyday objects** in **Rooms 39 and 34** are hardly thrilling, it's worth popping into **Room 44** to see the **faience panels** from the palaces of Ramses II and III.

The Coptic Museum

Open Sat–Thurs 9am–4pm, Fri 9–11am & 1–4pm (the old wing closes 30min earlier). Admission £E2, students £E1; photography permit £E5.

Nestled between the Hanging Church and the Roman towers of Babylon, the **Coptic Museum** is one of the highlights of Old Cairo. Its peerless collection of Coptic artefacts is enhanced by the beautiful carved ceilings, beams and stained-glass domes inside its *mashrabiya*-ed wings, which enclose peaceful gardens. Founded in 1908 under the patronage of Patriarch Cyril V and Sultan Kamil, the museum was intended to save Christian antiques from the ravages of neglect and foreign collectors, but soon widened its mandate to embrace secular material. With artefacts from Old Cairo, Upper Egypt and the desert monasteries, the museum traces the evolution of Coptic art from Greco-Roman times into the Islamic era (300–1000 AD). Notwithstanding debts to pharaonic and Greco-Roman culture, its spirit was refreshingly unmonumental: "realistic, at times humorous", Coptic art reflected "plebian or agricultural concerns" (Stewart) and often seems homespun compared to pharaonic and Islamic craftsmanship; appropriately enough, its finest expression was in textiles.

Though spread over three floors, the collection isn't so large that visitors become jaded. You can do it justice within a couple of hours, or cover it at a trot in half that time. A **café** in the grounds sells tea and biscuits; the gateway beyond gives access to the courtyard of the Hanging Church.

New Wing

Entering the museum grounds from Mari Girgis street, you'll find the **New Wing**, built in 1937, straight ahead. The **ground floor** is arranged in chronological order in an anticlockwise direction, starting with **Room 1**. The other exit from this room leads into a garden containing tombstones and funerary stelae, with stairs down to the Water Gate beneath the Hanging Church (see p.125) and up into the old wing (see below).

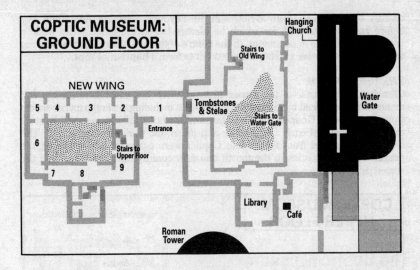

Centred upon a fountain from one of the old houses of the quarter, **Room 1** displays **pagan reliefs and statues** of figures from classical mythology. Their squat proportions and oversized heads make Aphrodite, Daphnae, Pan, Leda and the Swan look more African than Greco-Roman. The tendency to superimpose two flat layers, and the motif of a broken pediment with a shell, were both characteristic of proto-Coptic art. Artefacts in **Room 2** evince a **shift towards Christian symbolism** from the third century onwards. Pharaonic *ankhs* are transmuted into looped crosses, whilst true crosses appear on the shell-pediments and coexist with Horus hawks on a basket-weave capital.

Coptic artistry reached its zenith between the sixth and ninth centuries, as exemplified by the **stone-carvings and frescoes from Bawit Monastery**, near Assyut. Along the north wall of **Room 3** is a splendid apse niche depicting Christ enthroned between the creatures of the Apocalypse and the moon and sun; below, the Virgin and Child consort with Apostles whose homely faces can still be seen in any Egyptian city today. In **Room 4**, notice the eagle, an early Christian symbol of resurrection (as was the peacock). **Room 5** is also filled with miscellaneous objects, notably a painted capital carved with sinuous acanthus leaves, a motif borrowed from the Greeks and Romans but apparently devoid of symbolic meaning for the Copts.

Capitals with acanthus leaves and grapevines mingle with pharaonic palm fronds and lotus motifs in **Room 6**. Among other **objects from the Monastery of Saint Jeremiah** at Saqqara is the earliest known example of a stone pulpit, possibly influenced by the *heb-sed* thrones of Zoser's funerary complex. The fresco beside it, like the Bawit apse, subtly identifies the Virgin Mary with Isis. Other instances of recycled iconography can be seen around the corner in **Room 7**: a fresco of the grape harvest (a theme favoured by pharaonic nobles) and a small sphinx (between Greek columns).

Room 8 moves on to **Biblical scenes** (Abraham and Isaac, Christ with angels) and **friezes** of animals offset in plant rondels – a motif that was later adopted by Fatimid woodcarvers. Entering **Room 9** you'll encounter a tenth-century diptych from Umm al-Birgat in the Fayoum, depicting Adam and Eve before and after the Fall, for which he blames her in the latter scene while a serpent relishes the denouement. In the centre of the hall is an elaborate papyrus and lotus basket-weave capital, hollowed out to form a **baptismal font**.

THE UPPER FLOOR

Climbing the staircase to the **upper floor**, one reaches casefuls of *ostraca* and manuscripts produced by monastic scriptoriums, including several papyrus sheets from the **Gnostic Gospels of Nag Hammadi**, whose 1200 pages shed light on the development of early Christianity and its mystic tradition (see p.278). The Gospels (translated from Greek into Coptic) were probably buried during the purges against Gnostics in the fourth and fifth century; farmers unearthed the sealed jar in 1945.

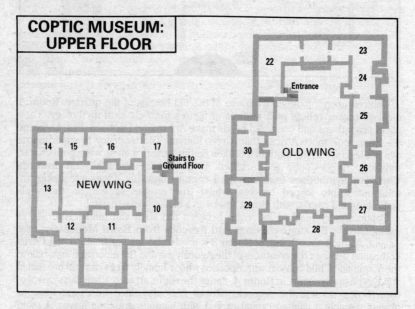

COPTIC MUSEUM: UPPER FLOOR

Proceeding clockwise through **Room 10**, a 1600-year-old towel presages a host of **textiles**. From the third or fourth century onwards, Coptic weavers (chiefly women) developed various techniques to a pitch of sophistication. Tapestry and pile weave designs blended human and bird forms with plant motifs; tunics were appliqued with bands and rondels. In **Room 12** there's a magnificent silk robe embroidered with pictures of the Apostles, dating from the eighteenth century.

Room 13 displays Alexandrian-style **ivory-work** and cruder efforts from Upper Egypt alongside a selection of **icons** from Old Cairo, Aswan and Kharga Oasis. Some believe that the change from murals to icons resulted from the need to hide sacred treasures from hostile interlopers. The next three rooms showcase **metalwork**, ranging from crosses and censers to musical instruments and tools. In **Room 15** are patriarchal crowns, a lamp emblazoned with both a Christian cross and an Islamic crescent, and an eagle from the Fortress of Babylon.

The upper floor concludes with an exhibition of **Nubian paintings** salvaged during the 1950s and 60s from villages about to be drowned by Lake Nasser. Like Isis-worship in ancient times, Christianity persisted as the dominant religion in Nubia for several centuries after it had waned in Egypt. The figures are darker, with larger eyes and rounder heads than the Copts.

Old Wing

Entered via stairs from the sculpture garden, the **Old Wing** has even finer ceilings and *mashrabiyas*, now emerging from a bout of renovation. The exhibits are laid out on the **upper floor** in a clockwise direction.

On the left as you enter **Room 22** are the original **fourth-century altar** and a Fatimid-era dome from the Church of Saint Sergius. In the other direction lie two halls full of Nubian wall paintings, plus a pair of lunettes (semicircular paintings) from Bawit Monastery (**Room 23**). Rounding the corner, an original screen from the Church of Saint Barbara inaugurates the **woodwork** section. Fragments in the following alcove show a similar mixture of Hellenistic mythology, pharaonic symbolism and Coptic naturalism to the stone-carving in the other wing, whilst later pieces feature human activities. A **panel depicting Christ's entry into Jerusalem**, taken from the Hanging Church, is the highpoint of **Room 25**.

Sharing **Room 26** with Coptic toys and domestic utensils are several **mummy portrait panels**, latterday versions of the Roman "Fayoum Portraits" displayed in the Egyptian Antiquities Museum. In the far right-hand corner is a remarkable **Early Coptic crucifix** (one of the few in existence) which combines a beardless Christ with a Horus hawk and sun-disc. Byzantine and Sassanid (Persian) influences underlie the **friezes** of hunting scenes and fabulous creatures – motifs which continued into Islamic times until the Sunni restoration. The episcopal chairs in the annexe to **Room 27** are similar to the reception-thrones used by wealthy Amirs.

The last quarter of the wing displays **pottery**, arranged by type or form rather than antiquity. Ancient motifs such as fish, ducks and plants are widely employed. At the end of **Room 29** are **Pilgrim's flasks** showing Saint Menas between two camels (see p.478). Amongst the later work in **Room 30** are lustreware pieces like those made by Muslim potters at Fustat, but here emblazoned with a Coptic fish or cross. The annexe beyond contains a small collection of **glassware**.

The Museum of Islamic Art

Open Sat–Thurs 9am–4pm, Fri 9–11am & 1.30–4pm. Admission £E2, students £E1; ticket also valid for the Gayer-Anderson House (see p.112) on the same day. Photography permit £E5.

Try to visit the **Museum of Islamic Art** midway through exploring Islamic Cairo, since the historic architecture lends meaning to the museum's artefacts, which, in turn, enhance your appreciation of the old city. It was the ruinous state of many of its mosques and mansions that impelled Khedive Tewfiq and the historians Herz and Cresswell to establish an Islamic collection in 1880. Pieces were stored in al-Hakim's Mosque until 1902, when a museum was created on the ground floor of the imposing neo-Mamluke *Dar al-Kutub* (National Library) at the junction of Bur Said and Qalaa streets, 600m west of the Bab Zwayla.

The museum is currently entered from Sharia Bur Said via its garden door, which messes up the already confusing arrangement of **exhibits** by period and medium. To view them in order, walk straight through Rooms 7, 10, 4B and 2 (which contain some of the finest work) and begin with Room 1. However, the cool, deserted halls tempt one to wander through the collection, which can be seen in around ninety minutes.

Because Sunni Muslims extended the Koranic strictures against idolatry to any images of humans or animals, these are largely absent. Instead of paintings and statues there are exquisite designs based on geometry, Islamic symbolism, plant motifs and Arabic calligraphy – a totally different aesthetic. You'll also note that dates are given as *AH* – After the Hegira (Mohammed's flight from Mecca) – the starting point of Islamic chronology (622 AD by Western reckoning).

Touring the museum

Assuming you proceed through the central halls without getting sidetracked by the marvellous woodwork and fountains, the exhibition starts with a display of **recent acquisitions** in **Room 1**. If time is short, take the opportunity to visit the **masterpieces** in **Room 13**, next door, which include mosque lamps, carpets, glassware, ceramics, and a lavish door from the Mosque of Saiyida Zeinab.

During the **Umayyad period** (661–750), art was representational and influenced by Hellenistic and Sassanian traditions. Amongst an assembly of objects in **Room 2** are a bronze ewer with a spout in the form of a crowing cockerel, which probably belonged to the last Umayyad khalif (who was slain near Abu Sir), and an **early Muslim tombstone**, dated AH 31.

In **Abbasid and Tulunid times** (750–905) **stucco** was developed into a high art form, principally in Iraq. From being deeply cut and crisply textured with relatively naturalistic vines and acanthus scrolls, stucco panels became increasingly abstract and flowing, no longer carved but moulded. The three different styles from Samarra were also imitated by the Tulunids in wood; compare the stucco panels with the woodwork from al-Qitai in **Room 3**.

Passing through a huge door from Sultan Qalaoun's Maristan into **Room 4** you enter the **Fatimid era** (969–1171). As Shi'ites, the Fatimids had no doctrinal objection to depicting animals and birds (a theme popular amongst their co-religionists in Persia), as attested by **panels from the Western Palace**. Also exhibited are inlaid ivory and jewellery, rock crystal, and early **lustreware from Fustat**. **Room 4B** (part of the main hall) is a lovely composite of Mamluke columns, an Ottoman fountain and floor and intricate *mashrabiya* work.

Walking from Room 4 into Room 5 you pass through the original doors of the Mosque of Beybars, surmounted by stained-glass "moon windows" set in open plasterwork, from Ottoman times. **Room 5** covers the **Mamluke period** (1250–1517) and centres upon a lovely sunken mosaic fountain, which the curator sometimes turns on. Roundabout are displayed **mosque lamps** and stucco mihrabs; enamelled glass, woven and printed textiles; inlaid metalwork, polychrome pottery, and a wooden **cenotaph from the El-Hussein Mosque**. At the far end of the room is a wooden door from the Mosque of Sultan Ayyub, bearing square kufic and cursive naskhi inscriptions.

A pair of doors from the al-Azhar Mosque lead into **Room 6**, the first of three devoted to **woodwork**, whose evolution paralleled that of stucco. The deeply incised, naturalistic forms of Umayyad woodcarving gave way to interlocking arches and concentric circles under the Abbasids, followed by bevelled, stylised birds and animals in Tulunid times. Gradually confined to small areas during the

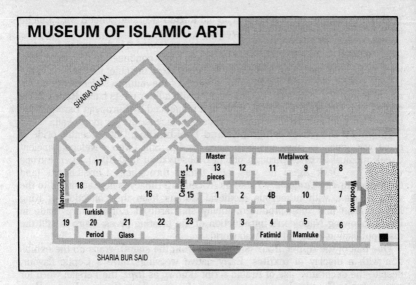

MUSEUM OF ISLAMIC ART

SHARIA QALAA

Manuscripts

17

18

Turkish
Period
19   20

Glass
21

22

Ceramics
14
15
16
23

Master
13
pieces
1

12
2
3

Fatimid

11
4B
4

Metalwork
9
10
5
Mamluke

8
7
6

Woodwork

SHARIA BUR SAID

Fatimid era, figures were then progressively simplified into arabesques by Ayyubid craftsmen. However, representational art could still be found under the early Mamlukes, as evinced by a **frieze from Qalaoun's Maristan**, showing hunting, music and dancing. Also featured in **Room 6** are carved panels from the Western Palace, the original mihrab from Saiyida Ruqayya's Mashrad, and a portable prayer niche for use on military campaigns. **Room 7** contains a series of *mashrabiyas*, minbars and **panelled ceilings**, including one with *murqanas*. In **Room 8**, note the wooden frieze in Hebrew script.

Wooden caskets overspill into **Room 9**, where bronze mirrors and brass lamps inaugurate the metalwork section. The adjacent main hall reflects Ottoman tastes in **interior design**. Beneath an exquisitely coffered ceiling, guests could socialise around a graceful fountain, secretly overlooked by the women of the household. The furnishings in **Room 10** date from the seventeenth and eighteenth centuries.

From Mosul in Iraq came the techniques of inlaying copper or silver into bronze, which characterised Egyptian **metalwork**. A brass-plated door from the Mosque of Salih Tala'i stands at the entrance to **Room 11**. Inside you'll find candlesticks and vases; incense burners inlaid with gold and silver (some with Christian symbols); a "Cup of Terror" given to shock-victims; and a case of astrolabes, used by Muslim navigators. **Room 12** contains a fraction of the Mamluke **Armoury** (most of which was taken to Istanbul by Selim the Grim). Case 7 holds the swords of Mehmet II and Suleyman the Magnificent (the respective conquerors of Constantinople and the Balkans); in Case 11 is the sword of Mamluke general Murad Bey, captured by the French at the Battle of the Pyramids, and subsequently by Wellington at Waterloo.

Rooms 14–16 shift the focus to **ceramics**, ranging from native bowls and ewers to tiles from Tunisia and Turkey; potshards from Italy, Holland and Spain show the extent of Fustat's commercial reach. Notice the *ahlaq* (chokes) that were inserted in the necks of Fatimid water jars to regulate their flow, fretted with bird, boat and tree motifs. In **Room 16** are various stucco mihrabs, a tiled

Turkish fireplace, and a section of an old **kuttab** (Koranic school) with a niche for the teacher to sit beneath its *murqana*-ed ceiling.

With Rooms 17 and 18 closed, one proceeds to **Room 21**, devoted to Egyptian **glass**. Various techniques perfected in ancient times continued to be used; lustre-ware (a Fatimid speciality) and enamelled glass were the chief innovations in the Islamic period. Amongst the **Persian objects** of the ninth to seventeenth centuries in **Room 22**, notice the ceramic camel with a litter on its back. **Room 20** is stuffed with **Ottoman material**, some of it influenced by European Baroque; the bejewelled, gold-encrusted perfume-sprayer and incense burner most of all.

Room 19 showcases **calligraphy and bookbinding**. Until recently, pride of place was given to manuscripts penned by Ibn Sina, who developed ancient Greek medical theories through practical observation (980–1037) when Europe was in the Dark Ages; he was later famed throughout Christendom (and mentioned in *The Canterbury Tales*) as Avicenna. Primacy is now accorded to the word of God, with numerous medieval Korans from the collection of King Farouk. The first mass-produced, totally standardised Korans were made in Egypt following Napoleon's introduction of the printing press; Cairo is still the main publishing centre of the Arab world.

One hall of the **upper floor** (signposted from the stairs) wraps up the exhibition with a display of **textiles**. Early native weavings have a Coptic flavour, despite the decorative use of Arabic script (known as *tiraz*, the Persian word for embroidery). There's also a superb range of carpets from Turkey, Yemen, Iran and Central Asia.

Other Museums

Aside from places on the Citadel and Roda Island (covered under those sections), Cairo has a dozen **other museums** which deserve a mention, if not necessarily a visit. However, given temporary closures and erratic opening hours, it's worth telephoning the distant ones before setting out.

Mahmoud Khalil Museum

In a fine old mansion next to the Cairo Marriott Hotel on Zamalek. Sat–Thurs 9.30am–2.30pm; £E1, students 50pt; bring your passport. ☎341-8672.
Impressionist works by Monet, Pissaro, Sisley, Gaughin, van Gogh, Toulouse Lautrec, Corot etc. Upstairs are Fauvist and Orientalist paintings. Definitely worth visiting.

Modern Art Museum

Now in the Opera House complex on Gezira, though it may have left a residue at its former home in Dokki (18 Sharia Ismail Abu Fetouh). Daily 9am–1.30pm, Fri closes 1pm).
Paintings, sculptures and graphics by Egyptian artists since 1908; there is always something new on show.

Gezira Museum and Museum of Egyptian Civilisation

The Gezira Museum consists of thousands of *objets d'art* collected by the royal family, stored in the Agricultural Pavilion of the Gezira Exhibition Grounds (☎806-982). Adjacent is a Museum of Egyptian Civilisation, iillustrating national history from pharaonic to modern times. Both are scheduled to reopen soon.

Mukhtar Museum

Near the Galaa Bridge, Gezira. Tues–Sun 9am–1.30pm; £E1. ☎340-2519.

Bronze and marble sculptures by Mahmoud Mukhtar (1891–1934), creator of several patriotic monuments, who is buried in the basement. Ramses Wissa Wassef designed the building.

Egyptian Railways Museum

At the east end of Ramses Station. Tues–Sun 8.30am–1pm, Fri closes noon); £E1. ☎763-793.

Ismail's private train heads a cast of antique steam engines and railway coaches. Egypt's current rolling stock comes from Romania.

Museum of Hygiene and Medicine

Sharia Sakakini, Abbassiya (tram #5 or #7). Sat–Thurs 9am–2pm.

Even if displays of anatomy and pathology don't appeal, the rococo Sakakini Palace (built in 1898) certainly merits a look.

Agricultural Museum

In the grounds of the Ministry of Agriculture, Dokki; follow Sharia Abdel Aziz Radwan, beyond the 6th October exit-ramp. Tues–Sun 9am–3pm; 10pt. ☎702-366.

Exhibits on farming, with stuffed animals and models of village life, plus quirky items such as an Egyptian flag made from insects. The nearby **Cotton Museum** (same hours) gives the rundown on Egypt's main cash crop.

Ethnological Museum

109 Sharia Qasr al-Aini, just south of the American University. ☎354-5350.

Village crafts, costumes and equipment – worth seeing when it reopens. Previously Sat–Thurs 9am–1pm; admission free.

Geological Museum

Due to return to its old home on Sharia Sheikh Rihan (near the National Assembly) from temporary premises on the Corniche between Old Cairo and Ma'adi. Sat–Thurs 9am–2pm. ☎982-608.

Fossils of sea-cows, giant snakes and rock hyraxes from the Eocene beds of the Fayoum, amongst other curiosities.

Post Office Museum

On the second floor of the Central Post Office, Midan Ataba. Sat–Thurs 9am–1pm; admission free. ☎390-9686.

Egypt's postal service (?!) through the ages plus stamps galore, including the rare Suez Canal commemorative issue.

Dr Ragab's Papyrus Institute

Daily 9am–7pm; admission free. ☎348-8676.

The ancient craft of papyrus making (which died out in the tenth century AD and was revived in modern times by Dr Ragab) demonstrated aboard three boats moored between the Giza Sheraton and the University Bridge, with papyrus growing alongside and papyri for sale.

THE PYRAMIDS

All things dread Time, but Time dreads the Pyramids
— Anonymous Egyptian proverb

For millions of people the pyramids epitomise ancient Egypt: no other monument is so instantly recognised the world over. Yet comparatively few foreigners realise that over eighty pyramids are spread across seventy kilometres of desert, from the outskirts of Cairo to the edge of the Fayoum.

Most visitors are content to see the great **Pyramids of Giza** and part of the sprawling necropolis of **Saqqara**, both easily accessible from Cairo. Only a minority ride across the sands to **Abu Sir**, whilst the **Dahshur** pyramid field is effectively out of bounds. Still farther south, the dramatic "Collapsed Pyramid" of **Maidum** and the lesser Middle Kingdom pyramids of **Hawara**, **Lisht** and **Lahun** are easier to reach from the Fayoum, so for the sake of convenience we've covered them in *The Western Desert Oases* chapter.

The Pyramids in history

The derivation of the word "pyramid" is obscure. *Per-em-us*, an ancient Egyptian term meaning "straight up", seems likelier than the Greek *pyramis* – "wheaten cake", a facetious descriptive term for these novel monuments. Then again, "obelisk" comes from *obeliskos*, the ancient Greek for "skewer" or "little spit".

Whatever, the pyramids' sheer **antiquity** is staggering. When the Greek chronicler Herodotus visited them in 450 BC, as many centuries separated his lifetime from their creation as divide our own time from that of Herodotus, who regarded them as ancient even then. For the Pyramid Age was only an episode in three millennia of pharaonic civilisation, reaching its zenith within 200 years and followed by an inexorable decline, so that later dynasties regarded the works of their ancestors with awe. Fourteen centuries after the royal tombs of the Old Kingdom were first violated by robbers, the Saite (XXVI) Dynasty collected what remained, replaced missing bodies with surrogates, and reburied their forebears with archaic rituals they no longer comprehended.

The Pyramid Age began at Saqqara in the twenty-seventh century BC, when the III Dynasty royal architect Imhotep enlarged a *mastaba* tomb to create the first **step pyramid**. As techniques evolved, an attempt was made to convert another step pyramid at Maidum into a true pyramid by encasing its sides in a smooth shell, but the design was faulty and the pyramid collapsed under its own weight, necessitating hasty alterations to its counterpart at Dahshur. Not until the IV Dynasty were all the problems solved and a sheer-sided **true pyramid** arose at Giza. After two more perfect pyramids, less resources and care were devoted to the pyramid fields of Abu Sir and south Saqqara, and the latterday pyramids near Fayoum Oasis never matched the standards of the Old Kingdom.

Their enigma has puzzled people ever since. Whereas the ancient Greeks vaguely understood their function, the Romans were less certain; medieval Arabs believed them to be treasure houses with magical guardians, and early European observers reckoned them the Biblical granaries of Joseph. The nineteenth century was a golden era of discoveries by Belzoni, Vyse, Petrie, Mariette, Maspero and Lepsius, which all suggested that the pyramids were essentially containers for royal tombs and nothing else. It was also the heyday of Pyramidologists like Piazzi Smyth and David Davidson, who averred that their dimensions in "pyramid inches" proved the supremacy of Christianity and the Jewish origin of the pyramid-builders.

Archaeologists now agree that the pyramids' **function** was to preserve the pharaoh's *ka*, or double: a vital force which emanated from the sun-god to his son, the king, who distributed it amongst his subjects and the land of Egypt itself. Mummification, funerary rituals, false doors for his *ba* (soul) to escape, model servants (*shabti* figures) and anniversary offerings – all were designed to ensure that his *ka* enjoyed an afterlife similar to its former existence. Thus was the social order perpetuated throughout eternity and the forces of primaeval chaos held at bay, a theme emphasised in tomb reliefs at Saqqara. On another level of **symbolism**, the pyramid form evoked the primal mound at the dawn of creation, a recurrent theme in ancient Egyptian cosmogony, echoed in megalithic *benben* and obelisks whose pyramidion tips were sheathed in glittering electrum.

Although the limestone scarp at the edge of the Western Desert provided an inexhaustible source of building material, finer stone for casing the pyramids was quarried at Tura across the river or came from Aswan in Upper Egypt. Blocks were quarried using wooden wedges (which swelled when soaked, enlarging fissures) and copper chisels, then transported on rafts to the pyramid site, where the final shaping and polishing occurred. Shipments coincided with the inundation of the Nile (July–November), when its waters lapped the feet of the plateau and Egypt's workforce was released from agricultural tasks.

Herodotus relates that 100,000 slaves took a decade to build the causeway and earthen ramps, and a further twenty years to raise the Great Pyramid of Cheops. Archaeologists now believe that, far from being slaves, most of the workforce were actually peasants who were paid in food for their three-month stint (papyri enumerate the quantities of lentils, onions and leeks), while a few thousand skilled craftsmen were employed full time on its **construction**. One theory holds that a single ramp wound around the pyramid core, and was raised as it grew; when the capstone was in place, the casing was added from the top down and the ramp was reduced. Apparently, pulleys were only used to lift the plug blocks that sealed the corridors and entrance; all the other stones were moved with levers and rollers. It is estimated that during the most productive century of pyramid building some twenty-five million tons of material were quarried. To put this in perspective, this is equivalent to one month's quarrying in 1990s Britain – or the material for 125 miles of motorway.

Whether or not the ancient Egyptians deemed this work a religious obligation, the massive levies certainly demanded an effective bureaucracy. Pyramid-building therefore helped consolidate the state. Its decline paralleled the Old Kingdom's, its cessation and resumption two anarchic eras (the First and Second Intermediate Periods) and the short-lived Middle Kingdom (XII Dynasty). By the time of the New Kingdom, other monumental symbols seemed appropriate. Remembering the plundered pyramids, the rulers of the New Kingdom opted for hidden tombs in the Valley of the Kings.

The Pyramids of Giza

Of the Seven Wonders of the ancient world, only the **Pyramids of Giza** have withstood the ravages of time. "From the summit of these monuments, forty centuries look upon you", cried Napoleon; "A practical joke played on History", retorted another visitor. The Great Pyramid of Cheops has inspired more learned and crackpot speculation than any monument on earth. For millions of people, the Giza Pyramids embody antiquity and mystery. Burdened with expectations, you may find the reality disappointing. Resembling small triangles from afar and corrugated mountains as you approach, their gigantic mass can seem oddly two-dimensional when viewed from below. Far from being isolated in the desert as carefully angled photos suggest, they rise just beyond the outskirts of Giza City. During daytime, hordes of touts and tourists dispel any lingering mystique, as do sound and light shows after dark. Only at sunset, dawn and late at night does a brooding majesty return.

Visiting the pyramids

The site is directly accessible from Cairo by the 11-km-long Sharia al-Ahram (Pyramids Road) built by Khedive Ismail for the Empress Eugénie. Though heavy traffic can prolong the journey, **getting there** is straightforward. Taxi drivers often quote upwards of £E20, but the proper fare is about £E7 for a one-way trip. A cheaper option is to catch a bus (25pt) or minibus (35pt) from Midan Tahrir. Bus #913 runs directly to the village of Nazlat al-Samman, near the Sphinx, and two other services from the depot outside the Antiquities Museum go via Qasr al-Aini, Manial Island and Giza: the #8 terminates near the site entrance, whilst the #900 turns off just before the Mena House hotel. Minibuses from outside the Mugamma building (whose drivers shout, "Al-Ahram, al-Ahram!") can drop you at the Saqqara road turn-off, whence it's a fifteen-minute walk to the site.

Opposite the Mena House is a **tourist office** (Sat–Thurs 8am–5pm, Fri 9am–4pm) which can supply the official rates for horse and camel rides around the Giza plateau – not that these mean much in practice. Until a couple of years ago access to the site was free, but nowadays you must buy a ticket to visit during **opening hours** (8am–4.30pm; the pyramids shut a bit earlier); after that, no one bothers. Sold near the Sphinx and the Pyramid of Cheops, **tickets** (£E10, students £E5) are valid for entry to whichever pyramids are open, plus Chephren's valley temple, but *not* the solar boat museum. Con men may try to extort "special fees" or act as guides, offering commentary along the lines of "Cheops Pyramid very old" – ignore them, or threaten to call the tourist police if necessary.

Plan on spending half a day at the pyramids, which are best entered early in the morning before the heat and crowds become unbearable, or in the late afternoon – by 5pm most tour groups have departed and people have yet to arrive for the nightly **Sound and Light Show**. These consist of two one-hour shows in different languages; schedules (posted in tourist offices and hotels) vary according to season. As the melodramatic commentary is rather naff, you might prefer one of the performances in Arabic. Hundreds of Egyptians enjoy a free show from vantage points around the site, eschewing seats (£E10) on the terrace facing the Sphinx. Bring a sweater, since nights are cold even in summer.

Behind the grandstand is a row of stables **hiring horses and camels** which are generally in better shape than the animals touted around the site by Nagama Bedouin. To have your pick of mounts, come early in the morning or after 4pm; by comparing them and engaging their owners in competitive bargaining, you should be able to get the price down to £E6 with a guide, £E4 without. As the site

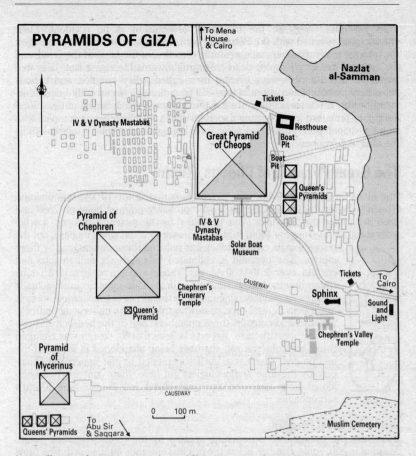

PYRAMIDS OF GIZA

To Mena House & Cairo

Nazlat al-Samman

Tickets

IV & V Dynasty Mastabas

Resthouse

Great Pyramid of Cheops

Boat Pit

Boat Pit

Queen's Pyramids

Pyramid of Chephren

IV & V Dynasty Mastabas

Solar Boat Museum

Tickets

To Cairo

CAUSEWAY

Chephren's Funerary Temple

Queen's Pyramid

Sphinx

Sound and Light

Chephren's Valley Temple

Pyramid of Mycerinus

CAUSEWAY

0   100 m

Queens' Pyramids

To Abu Sir & Saqqara

Muslim Cemetery

is small enough to cover on foot, riding is more of an experience than a time-saver. Consider a short ride into the desert even if you're not interested in a longer jaunt to Saqqara (3hr one-way; £E20–25). Be warned, however, that some guides set horses galloping across the sands and only curb their flight in return for *baksheesh*.

In Baedeker's day, it was *de rigueur* for visitors to climb the Great Pyramid: whilst two Bedouin seized an arm apiece and hauled from above, a third would push from below. **Climbing the pyramids** is now forbidden, but attempts are still made. If you're determined to risk it, the northeast corner of the Great Pyramid offers the least dangerous ascent (15–20min) to the platform at the top. The last person to sleep there rolled off the edge and smashed his skull open. Should guards apprehend you coming down (which is riskier than the ascent), you'll need to bribe them. Though **going inside** is quite safe, anyone suffering from claustrophobia or asthma should forget it; I once tried it during a bout of flu and nearly fainted. Clambering through all three shafts in the Great Pyramid will make your leg muscles ache the following day.

As site plans suggest, the pyramids' **orientation** is no accident. Their entrances are aligned with the Polar Star (or rather, its position 4500 years ago); the internal tomb chambers face west, the direction of the Land of the Dead; and the external funerary temples point eastwards towards the rising sun. Less well preserved are the causeways leading to so-called valley temples, and various subsidiary pyramids and *mastaba* tombs. The entire site is currently being renovated by the EAO, particularly around the Sphinx. During Sadat's time, a local developer proposed incorporating the site within a $4 billion resort complex with an *ankh*-shaped golf course, "a kind of Palm Springs by the Nile" – but thankfully the idea was dropped.

The Great Pyramid of Cheops (Khufu)

The oldest and largest of the Giza pyramids is that of the IV Dynasty pharaoh **Khufu** – better known as **Cheops** – who probably reigned between 2589 and 2566 BC. Called the "Glorious Place of Khufu" by the ancient Egyptians, it originally stood 140m (roughly 480ft) high and measured 230m along its base, but the

Cheops

removal of its casing stones has reduced these dimensions by three metres. The pyramid is estimated to weigh six million tons and contain over 2,300,000 blocks whose average weight is 2.5 tons (though some weigh almost 15 tons). This gigantic mass actually ensures its stability, since most of the stress is transmitted inwards towards its central core, or downwards into the underlying bedrock. The pyramid contains three chambers: one in the bedrock and two in the superstructure. Experts believe that its design was changed twice, the subterranean chamber being abandoned in favour of the middle one, which was itself superseded by the uppermost chamber. By the time archaeologists got here, their contents had been looted long ago, and the only object left *in situ* was Khufu's sarcophagus.

Inside the Great Pyramid

You enter the pyramid via an opening created by the treasure-hunting Khalif Ma'mun in 820, some distance below the original entrance on the north face (now blocked). After following this downwards at a crouch, you'll reach the junction of the ascending and descending corridors. The latter – leading to an unfinished chamber below the pyramid – is best ignored or left until last, and everyone heads up the 1.6-metre-tall **ascending corridor**. According to medieval Arab chroniclers, intruders soon encountered an "idol of speckled granite" wreathed by a serpent which "seized upon and strangled whoever approached", but latter-day visitors are merely impeded by the 1:2 gradient of the passage, which runs for 36m until another junction.

To the right of this is a **shaft** that ancient writers believed to be a well connected to the Nile; it's now recognised as leading into the subterranean chamber and thought to have been an escape passage for the workmen. Straight ahead is a horizontal passage 35m long and 1.75m high, leading to a semi-finished limestone chamber with a pointed roof, which Arabs dubbed the "**Queen's Chamber**". Petrie reckoned this was the *serdab*, or repository for the pharaoh's statue, whilst the eccentric Davidson saw it as symbolising the ultimate futility of

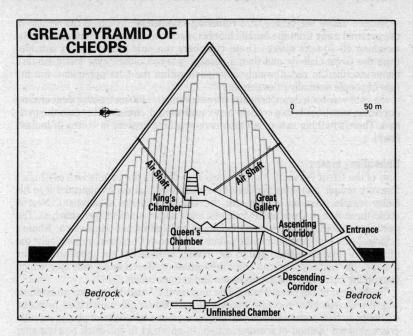

GREAT PYRAMID OF CHEOPS

0   50 m

Air Shaft

Air Shaft

King's Chamber

Great Gallery

Queen's Chamber

Ascending Corridor

Entrance

Descending Corridor

Bedrock

Bedrock

Unfinished Chamber

Judaism. Either way, there's no evidence that a queen was ever buried here. In the northern and southern walls are two holes made in 1872 for the purpose of discovering the chamber's ventilation shafts.

However, most people step up into the **Great Gallery**, the finest section of the pyramid. Built of Muqattam limestone, so perfectly cut that a knife blade can't be inserted between its joints, the 47-metre-long shaft narrows to a corbelled roof 8.5m high. (Davidson believed that its length in "pyramid inches" corresponded to the number of years between the Crucifixion and the outbreak of World War I.) The incisions in its walls probably held beams that were used to raise the sarcophagus or granite plug blocks up the steep incline (nowadays overlaid with wooden steps). Though no longer infested by giant bats, as nineteenth-century travellers reported, the Great Gallery is sufficiently hot and airless to constitute something of an ordeal, and you'll be glad to reach the horizontal antechamber at the top, which is slotted for the insertion of plug blocks designed to thwart entry to the burial chamber.

The **King's Chamber** lies 95m beneath the apex of the pyramid and half that distance from its outer walls. Built of red granite blocks, the rectangular chamber is large enough to accommodate a double-decker bus. Its dimensions (5.2 by 10.8 by 5.8 metres) have inspired many abstruse calculations and whacky prophecies; Hitler ordered a replica built beneath the Nuremberg Stadium, where he communed with himself before Nazi rallies. To one side of the chamber lies a huge, lidless **sarcophagus** of Aswan granite, bearing the marks of diamond-tipped saws and drills. On the northern and southern walls, at knee height, you'll notice two air shafts, leading to the outer world.

Unseen above the ceiling, five **relieving chambers** distribute the weight of the pyramid away from the burial chamber; each consists of 43 granite monoliths weighing 40–70 tons apiece. These chambers can only be reached by a ladder from the Great Gallery, and then a passage where Colonel Vyse found Khufu's name inscribed in red (the only inscription within the Giza pyramids), but the flow of people normally rules this out.

On your way back down, consider investigating the 100-metre-long **descending corridor**, which leads to a crudely hewn **unfinished chamber** beneath the pyramid. There's nothing to see, but the nerve-wracking descent is worthy of Indiana Jones.

Subsidiary tombs

East of the Great Pyramid, it's just possible to discern the foundations of Khufu's funerary temple and a few blocks of the causeway that once connected it to his valley temple (now buried beneath the village of Nazlat al-Samman). Nearby stand three ruined **Queens' Pyramids**, each with a small chapel attached. The northern and southern pyramids belonged to Merites and Hensutsen, Khufu's principal wife (and sister), and the putative mother of Chephren, respectively; the middle one may have belonged to the mother of Redjedef, the third ruler of the dynasty. Farther east, you can enter the **tombs of Meres-ankh and Qar**, which contain life-size statues of the deceased and various reliefs.

To the west of the Great Pyramid lie dozens of **IV and V Dynasty mastabas**, where archaeologists recently uncovered a 4600-year-old mummified princess, whose body had been hollowed out and encased in a thin layer of plaster – a hitherto unknown method of mummification. In an effort to win back tourists after the Gulf War, the Egyptian Antiquities Office has also opened fifteen **tombs** that had been closed to the public since their discovery last century, including that of Ra-Kha-Ef-Ankh, director of the royal hairdressers. Their custodian usually hangs out in a hut to the east of the pyramid.

The Solar Boat Museum

Perched across the road from another cluster of *mastabas* is a humidity-controlled pavilion (9am–4pm; £E5, students £E2.50) containing a reconstructed **boat** from one of the five boat pits sunk around Khufu's pyramid. (Another boat has been located by X-rays and video cameras, but for the present is left unexcavated.)

When the pit's limestone roofing blocks were removed in 1954, a faint odour of cedarwood arose. Restorer Hagg Ahmed Yussef spent fourteen years rebuilding a graceful craft from 1200 pieces of wood, originally held together by sycamore pegs and halfa-grass ropes. Archaeologists term these vessels "solar boats" (or barques), but their purpose remains uncertain – carrying the pharaoh through the underworld (as shown in XVII–IX Dynasty tombs at Thebes) or accompanying the sun-god on his daily journey across the heavens are two of the many hypotheses.

The Pyramid of Chephren (Khafre)

Sited on higher ground, with an intact summit and steeper sides, the middle or **Second Pyramid** seems taller than Khufu's. Built by his son **Khafre** (known to posterity as Chephren), its base originally covered 214.8 square metres and its weight is estimated at 4,883,000 tons. As with Khufu's Pyramid, the original rock-hewn burial chamber was never finished and an upper chamber was subsequently constructed. Classical writers such as Pliny believed that the pyramid had no entrance, but when Belzoni located and dynamited open the sealed portal on its north face in 1818, he found that Arab tomb-robbers had somehow gained access nearly 1000 years earlier, undeterred by legends of an idol "with fierce and sparkling eyes", bent on slaying intruders.

If the pyramid is open, you can follow one of the two entry corridors downwards, and then upwards, into a long horizontal passage leading to his **burial chamber**, where Belzoni celebrated its discovery by writing his name in black letters. This ebullient circus strongman-turned-explorer went on to find Seti I's tomb in the Valley of the Kings, and died searching for the source of the River Niger. Set into the chamber's granite floor is the sarcophagus of Khafre, who reigned c.2558–2533 BC. The square cavity near the southern wall may have marked the position of a canopic chest containing the pharaoh's viscera.

Chephren

Chephren's Funerary Complex and the Sphinx

The funerary complex of Chephren's Pyramid is the best-preserved example of this typically Old Kingdom arrangement. When a pharaoh died, his body was ferried across the Nile to a riverside valley temple where it was embalmed by priests. After the process was complete, mourners gathered here to purify themselves before escorting his mummy up the causeway to a funerary (or mortuary) temple, where further rites preceded its interment within the pyramid. Thereafter, the priests ensured his *ka*'s afterlife by making offerings of food and incense in the funerary temple on specific anniversaries.

Chephren's **funerary temple** consists of a pillared hall, central court, niched storerooms and a sanctuary, but most of the outer granite casing has been plundered over centuries and the interior may not be accessible. Amongst the remaining blocks is a 13.4-metre-long monster weighing 163,000 kilos. Flanking the temple are what appear to be boat pits, although excavations have yielded nothing but pottery fragments. From here you can trace the foundations of a **causeway** which runs 400m downhill to his valley temple, near the Sphinx.

The **valley temple** lay buried under sand until its discovery by Mariette in 1852, which accounts for its reasonable state of preservation. Open from 9am to 4pm, it should be accessible with a site ticket, though touts may try to extract an extra £E1. Built of limestone and faced with polished Aswan granite, the temple faces east and used to open onto a quay. Beyond a narrow antechamber you'll find a T-shaped hall whose gigantic architraves are supported by square pillars, in front of which stood diorite statues of Chephren. Contrary to the widely accepted theory, a few scholars believe that mummification occurred at Memphis or Chephren's mortuary temple, this edifice being reserved for the "Opening of Mouth" ceremony, whereby the *ka* entered the deceased's body.

The Sphinx

This legendary monument is carved from an outcrop of soft limestone that was left standing after the harder surrounding stone was quarried for the Great Pyramid. Chephren is credited with the idea of shaping it into a figure with a lion's body and a human head, which is often identified as his own (complete with royal beard and *uraeus*), though it may represent a guardian deity. Some thousand years later, the future Tuthmosis IV dreamt that if he cleared the sand that engulfed the Sphinx it would make him ruler; a prophecy fulfilled, as recorded on a stele that he placed between its paws. The name "Sphinx" was actually bestowed by the ancient Greeks, after the legendary creature that put riddles to passers-by and slew those who answered wrongly; the Arabs called it *Abu 'l-Hol*, the awesome or terrible one.

Used for target practice by Mamluke and Napoleonic troops, the Sphinx lost its beard to the British Museum and was sandbagged for protection during World War II. Early modern repairs have done more harm than good, since its porous limestone "breathes", unlike the cement used to fill its cracks, but the latest renovation hopes to solve the problem of rising damp from Cairo's water table. During Sound and Light shows, the Sphinx is given the role of narrator. In 1979 and 1989 it formed the backdrop for concerts by, respectively, Frank Sinatra and the famous Lebanese singer Farouz.

The Pyramid of Mycerinus (Menkaure)

Sited on a gradual slope into undulating desert, the last and smallest of the Giza Pyramids bespeaks of waning power and commitment. Though started by Chephren's successor, **Menkaure** (called Mycernius by the Greeks), it was finished with unseemly haste by his son Shepseskaf, who seemingly enjoyed less power than his predecessors and depended on the priesthood. Herodotus records the legend that an oracle gave Mycernius only six years to live, so to cheat fate he made merry round the clock, doubling his annual quantum of experience. Another story has it that the pyramid was actually built by Rhodophis, a Thracian courtesan who charged each client the price of a building block (the structure is estimated to contain 200,000 blocks). In any event, no subsequent pyramid ever matched the standards of the Giza trio.

Because its lower half was sheathed in Aswan granite, this is sometimes called the **Red Pyramid**. Its relative lack of casing stones owes to a twelfth-century

Mycernius

sultan whose courtiers persuaded him to attempt the pyramid's demolition, a project he wisely gave up after eight months. Medieval Arab chroniclers frequently ascribed the Giza Pyramids to a single ruler, who supposedly boasted: "I, Surid the king, have built these pyramids in sixty-one years. Let him who comes after me attempt to destroy them in six hundred. To destroy is easier than to build. I have clothed them in silk; let him try to cover them in mats." Recently reopened, the **interior** is unusual for having its unfinished chamber in the superstructure and the final burial chamber underground. Here Vyse discovered a basalt sarcophagus later lost at sea en route to Britain, plus human remains which he assumed were Menkaure's but are now reckoned to be a XXVI Dynasty replacement and rest in the British Museum.

The complex also features three subsidiary pyramids, a relatively intact funerary temple, and a causeway to the now-buried valley temple. Northwest of the latter lies the sarcophagus-shaped **Tomb of Queen Khentkawes**, an intriguing figure who appears to have bridged the transition between the IV and V dynasties. Apparently married to Shepseskaf, the last IV Dynasty ruler, she may have wed a priest of the sun-god after his demise and gone on to bear several kings who were buried at Saqqara or Abu Sir (where she also built a pyramid).

KERDASSA AND HARRANIYYA

These two villages have no connection with the pyramids, but tour groups often pay one or both of them a visit. **KERDASSA**, roughly due east of Imbaba (but accessible by minibus from Midan Giza), is where most of the scarves, *galabiyyas* and shirts in Cairo are made, plus carpets which are sold by the metre. Although no longer a place for bargains, it's still frequented by collectors of ethnic textiles, particularly Bedouin robes and veils (the best quality ones retail for hundreds of dollars). In times past, Kerdassa was also the starting point of the camel trail across the Western Desert to Libya.

Folks on Salah's tours (see "Saqqara") are inevitably taken to **HARRANIYYA**, the site of the famous **Wissa Wassef Art School** (daily 8am–5pm; ☎850-403). Founded fifty years ago by Ramses Wissa Wassef, an architect who wanted to preserve village crafts and alleviate rural unemployment, the school teaches children to design and weave carpets, and has now branched out into batik work and pottery. Superintended by his widow and the original generation of students, pupils produce beautiful tapestries which now sell for thousands of dollars and are imitated throughout Egypt. You can see them at work between 8am and 3pm (except at lunchtime and on Fridays), and admire a superb collection in the museum designed by Hassan Fathy, a masterpiece of mudbrick architecture. To reach the Art School under your own steam, catch a taxi or minibus 2.5km south along the Saqqara road and follow the signs to *Salma* (or *Salome*) campsite, next door.

The Pyramids of Zawiyat al-Aryan

The **Zawiyat al-Aryan pyramid field** lies roughly midway between Giza and north Saqqara, and can be seen if you ride across the desert. Both its pyramids are sanded over and scacely worth a detour, but Egyptologists still ponder their place in the evolution of pyramid-building.

The northerly **Unfinished Pyramid** makes extensive use of granite, suggesting that it might hail from the IV Dynasty, but never got beyond its foundations and enclosure wall – unfinished blocks and stone chippings are scattered all around. To the southeast lies a **Layer Pyramid** built of small stone blocks, which seems to have been intended as a step pyramid and thus presumably belongs to the III Dynasty. From here it's about 3.5km to the Sun Temples of Abu Ghurab, described under "Abu Sir" (see p.189).

Memphis

Most tour excursions to Saqqara include a flying visit to the scant **remains of Memphis** in the village of MIT RAHINA. Sadly, these hardly stir one's imagination to resurrect the ancient city effaced over centuries by Nilotic silt, which now lies metres below rustling palm groves and oxen-ploughed fields. Although something of its glory is evident in the great necropoli ranged across the desert, and countless objects in Cairo's Antiquities Museum, to appreciate the significance of Memphis you have to recall its history.

The city's foundation is attributed to Menes, the quasi-mythical ruler (known also as Narmer – and possibly a conflation of several rulers) who was said to have unified Upper and Lower Egypt and launched the I Dynasty around 3100 BC. At that time, Memphis was sited at the apex of the Delta and thus controlled over-

Ptah

land and river communications. If not the earliest city on earth, it was certainly the first imperial one. Memphis was Egypt's capital throughout the Old Kingdom, regained its role after the anarchic Intermediate Period, and was never overshadowed by the parvenu seat of the XII Dynasty. Even after Thebes became capital of the New Kingdom, it still held sway over Lower Egypt and remained the nation's second city until well into the Ptolemaic era, only being deserted in early Muslim times after 4000 years of continuous occupation.

Alas for posterity, most of this garden city was built of mudbrick, which returned to the Nile silt whence it came, and everyone from the Romans onwards plundered its stone temples for fine masonry.

Nowadays, leftover statues and stelae share a garden (daily 9am–4pm; free) with souvenir kiosks. The star attraction, found in 1820, is a limestone **Colossus of Ramses II**, similar to the one on Midan Ramses, but laid supine within a concrete shelter. A giant **alabaster sphinx** weighing eighty tons is also mightily impressive. Both these figures probably stood outside the vast Temple of Ptah, the city's patron deity.

By leaving the garden and walking back along the road, you'll notice (on the right) several alabaster **embalming slabs**, where the holy Apis bulls were mummified before burial in the Serapeum at Saqqara. In a pit across the road are excavated chambers from Ptah's temple complex; climb the ridge beyond them and you can gaze across the cultivated valley floor to the Step Pyramid of Saqqara.

North Saqqara

Whilst Memphis was the capital of the Old Kingdom, Egypt's royalty and nobility were buried at **Saqqara**, the limestone scarp that flanks the Nile Valley to the west – the traditional direction of the Land of the Dead. Although superseded by the Theban necropolis during the New Kingdom, Saqqara remained in use for burying sacred animals and birds, especially in Ptolemaic times, when these cults enjoyed a revival. Over 3000 years, it grew to cover seven kilometres of desert – not including the associated necropoli of Abu Sir and Dahshur, or the Giza

Pyramids. As such, it is today the largest archaeological site in Egypt. Its name – pronounced "sah-*kah*-rah" – probably derives from Sokar, the Memphite god of the dead, though Egyptians may tell you that it comes from *saq*, the Arabic word for a hawk or falcon, the sacred bird of Horus.

Besides the pyramids and *mastabas* seen by visitors, Saqqara has an incalculable wealth of monuments and artefacts still hidden beneath windblown sands. As recently as 1986, the **tomb of Maya**, Tutankhamun's treasurer, was discovered, stuffed with precious objects (it won't be open to the public for some time). Yet aside from Zoser's Pyramid, the site was virtually ignored by archaeologists until Auguste Mariette found the Serapeum in 1851.

The necropolis divides into two main sections: **North** and **South Saqqara**. The following pages cover North Saqqara, the more interesting area; South Saqqara is described after Abu Sir (see p.190), since both entail lengthy detours. North Saqqara alone boasts a score of sights, so anyone with limited time should be selective. The **highlights** are Zoser's funerary complex, the Serapeum, and two outstanding *mastabas*; if time allows, add other tombs to your itinerary. To encompass the whole site would take several days.

Getting there and other practicalities

North Saqqara lies 21km south of the Giza Pyramids as camels cross the desert, or 32km from Cairo by road, being roughly opposite Helwan on the east bank of the Nile. Getting there **by public transport** is awkward and time-consuming. One way is to take the metro to Helwan station (50pt), catch a minibus (10pt) or taxi to the riverside, then a ferry to the village of El-Badrashein on the west bank, and finally a taxi to Saqqara (£E5). El-Badrashein is also accessible by third-class train from Ramses Station, but this takes two hours! Another approach entails reaching Abu Sir (see p.188), and then walking the further three kilometres to Saqqara.

To save time and energy for the site, it's best to avail yourself of **tours** run by the affable Salah Mohammed Abdel Hafiez. You can sign up in budget hotels like the *Plaza* and *Beau Site*, or contact him (☎768-537) between 1 and 3pm the day before. Leaving around 8am, you'll be driven to Memphis, North Saqqara, the Wissa Wassef tapestry school at Harraniyya and the Pyramids of Giza, before returning to Cairo at about 5pm. Salah promises *Rough Guide* users £E2 off the normal rate (£E10 per head), which doesn't include admission tickets. *Thomas Cook*, *Misr Travel* and *American Express* also run tours to Saqqara for upwards of £E30 per person. Another option is to hire a **private taxi** for the day (£E50–60), splitting the cost between however many people you can assemble to fill a seven-seater Peugeot 504. Be sure to specify which sites are included when you negotiate with the driver.

Lastly, you could plump for riding across the desert from the Pyramids of Giza **by horse or camel** (3hr). Although touts swear that the route takes you through the desert, past Zawiyet al-Aryan, the sun temples of Abu Ghurab and the Pyramids of Abu Sir, they often guide you along a more direct village track on the edge of the cultivated area, supposedly due to military restrictions. Either way, the journey will leave you stiff for days afterwards (see "Getting Around" in *Basics* for the rudiments of camel-handling.) Most people opt for a one-way ride (£E30 for a horse, £E35 for a camel, which can carry two riders); return trips cost twice that, plus a negotiable sum for waiting time. Be warned that some guides threaten to strand travellers in the middle of nowhere unless they receive hefty *baksheesh*; it's usually safe to call their bluff.

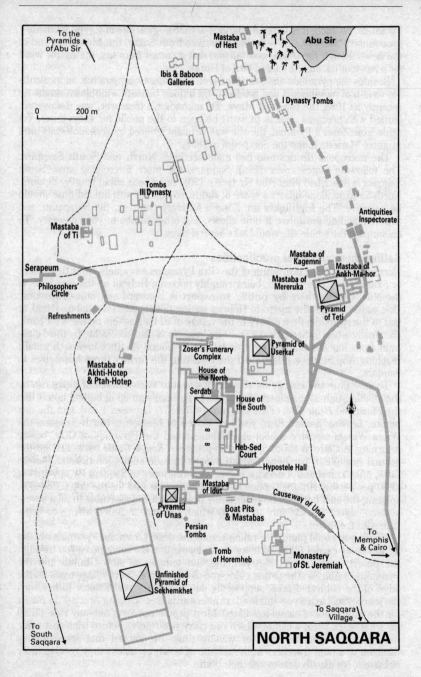

To the Pyramids of Abu Sir

Abu Sir

Mastaba of Hest

Ibis & Baboon Galleries

I Dynasty Tombs

0   200 m

Tombs III Dynasty

Mastaba of Ti

Antiquities Inspectorate

Serapeum

Philosophers' Circle

Refreshments

Mastaba of Kagemni

Mastaba of Ankh-Ma-hor

Mastaba of Mereruka

Pyramid of Teti

Zoser's Funerary Complex

House of the North

Pyramid of Userkaf

Serdab

Mastaba of Akhti-Hotep & Ptah-Hotep

House of the South

Heb-Sed Court

Hypostele Hall

Mastaba of Idut

Causeway of Unas

Pyramid of Unas

Boat Pits & Mastabas

Persian Tombs

To Memphis & Cairo

Tomb of Horemheb

Monastery of St. Jeremiah

Unfinished Pyramid of Sekhemkhet

To South Saqqara

To Saqqara Village

NORTH SAQQARA

Even if you don't emulate Lawrence of Arabia, bear in mind **conditions** at Saqqara. Over winter, the site can be swept by chill winds and clouds of grit; during the hottest months, walking around is exhausting. Beware of deep pits, which aren't always fenced off. Bring at least one litre of water apiece, as vendors at Memphis and the refreshments tent at north Saqqara are grossly overpriced, like every restaurant along the Saqqara road; a packed lunch is also a good idea.

OPENING HOURS
Though **opening hours** are 9am–4pm daily, guards start locking up the tombs half an hour early. A kiosk at the foot of the plateau sells **tickets** (£E10, students £E5) valid for all parts of Saqqara; a permit to photograph without a flash inside pyramids or tombs costs £E5. Some guards encourage unauthorised snapping in the expectation of *baksheesh*, but aside from this you're not obliged to give anything unless they help with lighting or provide a guided tour. If you don't want a running commentary, make this clear at the outset.

To reduce footslogging around the site, consider **hiring a camel, horse or donkey** (roughly £E2 per hour after bargaining) from outside the refreshments tent near the Serapeum.

Zoser's Funerary Complex

The funerary complex of King Zoser (or Djoser) is the largest in Saqqara, and its **Step Pyramid** heralded the start of the pyramid age. When Imhotep, Zoser's chief architect, raised the pyramid in the twenty-seventh century BC, it was the largest structure ever built in stone – the "beginning of architecture", according to one historian. Imhotep's achievement was to break from the tradition of earth-bound *mastabas*, raising level upon level of stones to create a four-step, and then a six-step pyramid, which was clad in dazzling white limestone. None of the blocks was very large, for Zoser's builders still thought in terms of mudbrick rather than megaliths, but the concept, techniques and logistics all pointed towards the true pyramid, finally attained at Giza.

Before it was stripped of its casing stones and rounded off by the elements, Zoser's pyramid stood 62 metres high and measured 140 by 118 metres along its base. The original entrance on the northern side is blocked, but with permission and keys from the site's Antiquities Inspectorate you can enter via a gallery on the opposite side, dug in the XXVI Dynasty. Dark passageways and vertical ladders descend 28m into the bedrock, where a granite plug failed to prevent robbers from plundering the burial chamber of this III Dynasty monarch (c.2667–2648).

Surrounding the pyramid is an extensive **funerary complex**, originally enclosed by a finely cut limestone wall, 544m long and 277m wide, now largely ruined or buried by sand. False doors occur at intervals for the convenience of the pharaoh's *ka*, but visitors can only enter at the southeastern corner, which has largely been rebuilt. Beyond a vestibule with simulated double doors (detailed down to their hinge pins and sockets) lies a narrow colonnaded corridor whose forty "bundle" columns are ribbed in imitation of palm stems, which culminates in a broader **Hypostele Hall**.

From here you emerge onto the **Great South Court**, where a rebuilt section of wall (marked * on our site plan) bears a **frieze of cobras**. Worshipped in the Delta as a fire-spitting goddess of destruction called Wadjet or Edjo, the cobra was adopted as the emblem of royalty and always appeared on pharaonic headdresses – a figure known as the *uraeus*. Nearby, a deep shaft plummets into Zoser's

Southern Tomb, decorated with blue faience tiles and a relief of the king running the *Heb-Sed* race. During the Jubilee festival marking the thirtieth year of a pharaoh's reign, he had to sprint between two altars representing Upper and Lower Egypt and re-enact his coronation, seated first on one throne, then upon another, symbolically reuniting the Two Lands. Besides demonstrating his vitality, the five-day festival confirmed the renewal of his *ka* and the obedience of provincial dignitaries.

Although the festival was held at Memphis, a pair of altars, thrones and shrines were incorporated in Zoser's funerary complex to perpetuate its efficacy on a cosmic timescale. The B-shaped structures near the centre of the Great Court are the bases of these altars; the twin thrones probably stood on the platform at the southern end of the adjacent **Heb-Sed Court**. Both shrines were essentially facades, since the actual buildings were filled with rubble. This phoney quality is apparent if you view them from the east: the curvaceous roof-line and delicate false columns wouldn't look amiss on a yuppie waterfront development. Notice the four **stone feet** beneath a shelter near the northern end of the court.

Beyond this lies the partially ruined **House of the South**, whose chapel is fronted by proto-Doric columns with lotus capitals, and a spearhead motif above the lintel. Inside you'll find several examples of XVIII–IXX Dynasty tourist graffiti, expressing admiration for Zoser or the equivalent of "Ramses was here" – banalities which one scornful ancient graffitist likens to "the work of a woman who has no mind". Continuing northwards, you'll pass a relatively intact row of casing stones along the eastern side of Zoser's pyramid. The **House of the North** has fluted columns with papyrus capitals; the lotus and papyrus were the heraldic emblems of Upper and Lower Egypt.

On the northern side of the pyramid, a tilted masonry box or **Serdab** ("cellar" in Arabic) contains a life-size statue of Zoser gazing blindly towards the North and circumpolar stars, which the ancients associated with immortality – seated thus, his *ka* was assured of eternal life. Zoser's statue is a replica, however, the original having been removed to Cairo's Antiquities Museum. The ruined mortuary temple to the right of the *Serdab* is unusual for being sited to the north rather than the east of its pyramid, and for the underground tunnel which originally led to Zoser's burial chamber.

Around the Pyramid of Unas

South of Zoser's funerary complex are several tombs and other ruins, dating from various dynasties. During the Old Kingdom, nobles were buried in subterranean tombs covered by large mudbrick superstructures; the name *mastaba* (Arabic for "bench") was bestowed upon them by native workmen during excavations last century. Three such edifices stand outside the southern wall of Zoser's complex, although two of them are currently closed. The open one, the **Mastaba of Idut**, has interesting reliefs in five of its ten rooms. Among the fishing and farming scenes, notice the crocodile eyeing a newborn hippo, and a calf being dragged through the water so that cows will ford a river. The chapel contains a false door painted in imitation of granite, scenes of bulls and buffaloes being sacrificed, and Idut herself.

Idut was the daughter of Pharaoh Unas, whose pyramid stands just beyond the **Mastaba of Nebet**, his queen. If accessible, its reliefs are also worth seeing: in one scene, Nebet smells a lotus blossom.

The Pyramid of Unas

Although its frontal aspect resembles a mound of rubble, the **Pyramid of Unas** retains many casing stones around the back, some carved with hieroglyphs. A low passageway on the northern side leads into its **burial chamber**, whose alabaster walls are covered with inscriptions listing the rituals and prayers for liberating the pharaoh's *ba*, and articles for his *ka* to use in the afterlife. These **Pyramid Texts** are the earliest known example of decorative writing within a pharaonic tomb chamber, and formed the basis of the New Kingdom *Book of the Dead*. Painted stars adorn the ceiling, whilst the sarcophagus area is surrounded by striped, checked and zigzag patterns. Thomas Cook & Sons sponsored the excavation of the tomb by Gaston Maspero in 1881.

Unas was the last pharaoh of the V Dynasty, so his pyramid follows those of Abu Sir, which evince a marked decline from the great pyramids of Giza. Given the duration of pharaonic civilisation, it's sobering to realise that only 350 years separated the creation of the Step Pyramid from this sad reminder of past glories. Originally, it was approached by a 1000-metre-long **causeway** enclosed by a roof and walls. Reliefs inside the short reconstructed section depict the transport of granite from Aswan, archers, prisoners of war, and a famine caused by the Nile failing to rise. The ruins of a valley temple face the ticket office below the plateau.

To the south of the causeway are two gaping, brick-lined **boat pits** which may have contained solar barques like the one at Giza, or merely symbolised them, since nothing was found when the pits were excavated.

Other tombs and ruins

A stone hut to the south of the pyramid gives access to a spiral staircase which descends 25m underground, where three low corridors lead into the vaulted **Persian Tombs**. Chief physician Psamtik, Admiral Djenhebu and Psamtik's son Pediese were all officials of the XXVII Dynasty of Persian kings founded in 525 BC, yet the hieroglyphs in their tombs invoke the same spells as those written 2000 years earlier. The dizzying descent and claustrophobic atmosphere make this an exciting tomb to explore. Though often locked, it's not "forbidden" as guards sometimes pretend, hoping to wangle excessive *baksheesh*.

Unas

Further to the southeast lies the recently rediscovered **Tomb of Horemheb**. Built when he was a general, it became redundant after Horemheb seized power from Pharaoh Ay in 1348 BC and ordered a new tomb to be dug in the Valley of the Kings, the royal necropolis of the New Kingdom. Many of the finely carved blocks from his original tomb are now in museums around the world. Another set of paving stones and truncated columns marks the nearby **Tomb of Tia**, sister of Ramses II. The **Tomb of Maya**, Tutankhamun's treasurer, was found nearby in 1986 and is still under excavation. Due east lie the sanded-over mudbrick ruins of the **Monastery of Saint Jeremiah**, which the Arabs destroyed in 960, four hundred years after its foundation. Practically all of the monastery's carvings and paintings have been removed to the Coptic Museum in Old Cairo.

It's indicative of how much might still be hidden beneath the sands at Saqqara that the **unfinished Pyramid of Sekhemkhet** was only discovered in 1950. Beyond his monuments, nothing is known of Sekhemkhet, whose step pyramid and funerary complex were presumably intended to mimic those of his predecessor, Zoser, and may also have been built by Imhotep. The alabaster sarcophagus inside the pyramid (which is unsafe to enter) was apparently never used, but the body of a child was found inside an auxiliary tomb.

From Sekhemkhet's pyramid and the monastery it's roughly 700m to the nearest part of South Saqqara (see p.190).

Around the Pyramids of Userkaf and Teti

Whilst neither of these pyramids amount to much, the *mastabas* near Teti's edifice contain some fantastic reliefs. If you're starting from Zoser's complex, it's only a short walk to the pulverised **Pyramid of Userkaf**, the founder of the V Dynasty, whose successors were buried at Abu Sir (see p.189).

From here, a track runs northwards to the **Pyramid of Teti**, which overlooks the valley from the edge of the plateau. Excavated by Mariette in the 1850s, it has since been engulfed by sand and may be closed; in one of the funeral chambers (accessible by a sloping shaft and low passageway), the star-patterned blocks of its vaulted roof have slipped inwards.

Although most of the VI Dynasty kings who followed Teti chose to be buried at South Saqqara, several of their courtiers were interred in a **"street of tombs"** beside his pyramid, which was linked to the Serapeum by an Avenue of Sphinxes (now sanded over). To do justice to their superbly detailed reliefs takes well over an hour, but it's rare to find all of them open.

Teti

The Mastaba of Mereruka

The largest tomb in the street belongs to **Mereruka**, Teti's vizier and son-in-law, whose 32-room complex includes separate funerary suites for his wife, Watet-khet-hor, priestess of Hathor, and their son Meri-Teti. In the entry passage, Mereruka is shown playing a board game and painting at an easel; the chamber beyond depicts him hunting in the marshes with Watet-khet-hor (the frogs, birds, hippos and grasshoppers are beautifully rendered), along with the usual farming scenes. Goldsmiths, jewellers and other artisans are inspected by the couple in a room beyond the rear door, which leads into another chamber showing taxation and the punishment of defaulters. A pillared hall to the right portrays them watching sinuous dancers; a room to the left depicts offerings, sacrifices and birds being fed, with a *serdab* at the far end.

Beyond the transverse hall with its tomb shaft, false door and reliefs of grape-treading and harvesting lies the main offering hall, dominated by a statue of Mereruka emerging from a false door. The opposite wall shows his funeral procession; around the corner are boats under full sail, with monkeys playing in their rigging. To the left of the statue, Mereruka is supported by his sons and litter bearers, accompanied by dwarves and dogs; on the other side, children frolic whilst dancers sway above the doorway into Meri-Teti's undecorated funerary suite.

To reach **Watet-khet-hor's suite**, return to the first room in the *mastaba* and take the other door. After similar scenes to those in her husband's tomb, Watet-khet-hor is carried to her false door in a lion chair.

The Mastabas of Kagemni and Ankh-ma-hor

East of Mereruka's tomb and left around the corner, the smaller **Mastaba of Kagemni** features delicate reliefs in worse shape. The pillared hall beyond the entrance corridor shows dancers and acrobats, the judgement of prisoners, a hippo hunt and agricultural work, all rich in naturalistic detail. Notice the boys feeding a puppy and trussed cows being milked. The door in this wall leads to another chamber where Kagemni inspects his fowl pens whilst servants trap marsh birds with clap-nets; on the pylon beyond this he relaxes on a palanquin as they tend to his pet dogs and monkeys. As usual in the offerings hall, scenes of butchery appear opposite the false door. On the roof of the *mastaba* (reached by stairs from the entrance corridor) are two boat pits. As vizier, Kagemni was responsible for overseeing prophets and the estate of Teti's pyramid complex.

The **Mastaba of Ankh-ma-hor** is also known as the "Doctor's Tomb" after its reliefs showing circumcision, toe surgery and suchlike, as practiced during the VI Dynasty. If the tomb is open it's definitely worth a look, unlike the sand-choked **I Dynasty tombs** which straggle along the edge of the scarp beyond the **Antiquities Inspectorate**.

Two outstanding mastabas

If your time is limited, these are the tombs to visit. The **Double Mastaba of Akhti- and Ptah-Hotep** lies 200m off the road to the refreshments tent, whilst the **Mastaba of Ti** lies 500m in the other direction and is best visited after the Serapeum. Outside the **refreshments tent** (£E2 minimum charge) you'll be importuned to hire a horse or camel.

The Mastaba of Akhti-Hotep and Ptah-Hotep

This *mastaba* belonged to **Ptah-Hotep**, a priest of Maat during the reign of Unas's predecssor, Djedkare, and his son **Akhti-Hotep**, who served as vizier, judge and overseer of the granaries and treasury. Though smaller than Ti's *mastaba*, its reliefs are interesting for being at various stages of completion, showing how a finished product was achieved. After the preliminary drawings had been corrected in red by a master artist, the background was chiselled away to leave a silhouette, before details were marked in and cut. The agricultural scenes in the entrance corridor show this process clearly, although with the exception of Ptah-Hotep's chapel, none of these reliefs was ever painted.

Off the pillared hall of Akhti-Hotep is a T-shaped chapel whose inside wall shows workers making papyrus boats and jousting with poles. More impressive is the chapel of his father, covered with exquisitely detailed reliefs. Between the two door-shaped stelae representing the entrance to the tomb, Ptah-Hotep enjoys a banquet of offerings, garbed in the panther-skin of a high priest. Similar scenes occur on the facing wall, whose upper registers show animals being slaughtered and women bringing offerings from his estates. The left-hand wall swarms with activity, as boys wrestle and play *Khaki la wizza* (a leapfrog game still popular in Nubia); wild animals mate or flee from hunting dogs, whilst others are caged. A faded mural above the entrance shows the priest being manicured and pedicured at a time when Europe was in the Stone Age.

The Mastaba of Ti

Discovered by Mariette in 1865, this V Dynasty tomb has been a rich source of information about life in the Old Kingdom. A royal hairdresser who made an advantageous marriage, **Ti** acquired stewardship over several mortuary temples and pyramids, and his children bore the title "royal descendant".

Ti makes his first appearances on either side of the doorway, receiving offerings and asking visitors to respect his tomb **[a]**. The reliefs in the courtyard have been damaged by exposure, but it's possible to discern men butchering an ox **[b]**, Ti on his palanquin accompanied by dogs and dwarves **[c]**, servants feeding cranes and geese **[d]**, and Ti examining accounts and cargo **[e]**. His unadorned tomb (reached by a shaft from the courtyard) contrasts with the richly decorated interior of the *mastaba*.

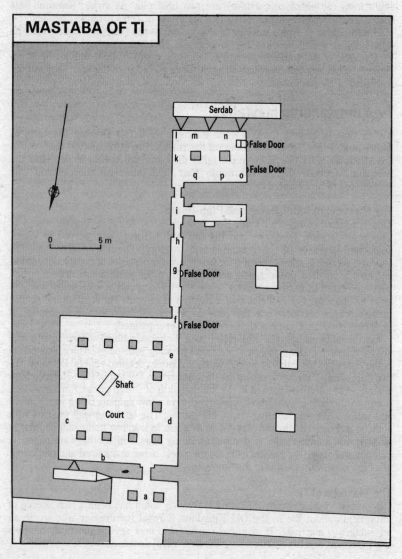

MASTABA OF TI

Serdab

False Door

False Door

False Door

False Door

0   5 m

Shaft

Court

Near his son's false door, variously garbed figures of Ti **[f]** appear above the portal of a corridor where bearers bring food and animals for the sustenance of his *ka* **[g]**. Beyond a doorway **[h]** over which Ti enjoys the marshes with his wife, funerary statues are dragged on sledges above scenes of butchery, and his Delta fleets are arrayed **[i]**. Potters, bakers, brewers and scribes occupy the rear wall of a storage room **[j]**, while dancers shimmy above the doorway to Ti's chapel.

Feeding cranes

In the harvesting scene, notice the man twisting a donkey's ear to make it behave **[k]**. Further along, Ti inspects shipwrights shaping tree trunks, sawing and hammering boards **[l]**. Goldsmiths, sculptors, carpenters, tanners and market life are minutely detailed **[m]**, like the musicians who entertain Ti at his offerings table **[n]**. Peer through one of the apertures and you'll see a cast of his statue inside its *serdab*.

Reliefs on the northern wall depict fishing and trapping in the Delta **[o]**; Ti sailing through the marshes whilst his servants spear hippopotami **[p]**; harvesting papyrus for boatbuilding, and ploughing and seeding fields **[q]**. The scene of hunting in the marshes is also allegorical, pitting Ti against the forces of chaos (represented by fish and birds) and evil (hippos were hated and feared).

The Serapeum

Saqqara's weirdest monument lies underground near a derelict building downhill from the refreshments tent. Discovered by Mariette in 1851, the rock-cut galleries of the **Serapeum** held the mummified corpses of the Apis bulls, which the Memphites regarded as manifestations of Ptah's "blessed soul" and identified with Osiris after death. Having been embalmed on alabaster slabs at Memphis, they were interred in sarcophagi weighing up to seventy tons apiece. Meanwhile, the priests began searching for Ptah's reincarnation amongst the sacred herd.

The **cult of the Apis bulls** was assailed by Egypt's Persian conqueror, Cambyses, who stabbed one to disprove its divinity, whilst Artaxerxes I avenged his nickname "the donkey" by ordering that a namesake beast be buried here with full honours. But the Ptolemies encouraged native cults and even synthesised their own. "Serapeum" derives from the fusion of the Egyptian Osarapis (Osiris in his Apis form) and the Greeks' Dionysos into the cult of *Serapis*, whose temple stood in Alexandria.

Exploring the Serapeum

Now that the lighting has been improved, the galleries are much less spooky than when Mariette broke in. Although tomb robbers had plundered them centuries before, he found a single tomb miraculously undisturbed for 4000 years. The finger mark and footprints of the ancient workman who sealed the tomb were still visible, and Mariette also found a mummified bull and the coffin of Khamenwaset, son of Ramses II and high priest of Ptah.

The oldest of the galleries dates from that era, and is now inaccessible, the second from the Saite period, and the main one from Ptolemaic times. Enormous granite or basalt sarcophagi are ranged either side of the Ptolemaic gallery, at the end of which is a narrow shaft whereby robbers penetrated the Serapeum. The finest sarcophagus squats on the right, whilst another one lies abandoned near the entrance to the Ramessid gallery.

Other curiosities

En route to the Serapeum you'll notice a concrete slab sheltering broken statues of Plato, Heraclitus, Thales, Protagoras, Homer, Hesiod, Demetrius of Phalerum and Pindar – a **Philosopher's Circle**. The statues formerly stood near a temple that overlaid the Serapeum, proof that the Ptolemies juxtaposed Hellenistic philosophy and ancient Egyptian religion with no sense of incongruity.

A cluster of **III Dynasty tombs** to the east of Ti's *mastaba* is now reckoned a likely site for the tomb of Imhotep, as yet undiscovered. The architect of Zoser's Step Pyramid was revered throughout pharaonic history and eventually became a demigod, credited with powers of healing; the Ptolemies associated him with Asclepius, the Greek god of medicine.

Farther northeast lie the **Ibis and Baboon Galleries** sacred to Thoth, which Flaubert visited in the 1840s: "we go down into a hole and then crawl along a passageway almost on our stomachs, inching over fine sand and fragments of pottery; at the far end the jars containing ibises are stacked like blocks of sugar at a grocer's, head to foot".

The Pyramids of Abu Sir

Northwest of Saqqara, a necropolis of V Dynasty (c.2494–2345 BC) pharaohs covers an arc of desert beyond the village of **ABU SIR**. The mortuary complexes here are smaller than the Giza Pyramids of the previous dynasty, suggesting a decline in royal power; their ruinous state and the effort required to reach them also means that few tourists come here. Those who do often feel that Abu Sir's splendid isolation compensates for its monumental shortcomings; its helpful custodians and friendly villagers are certainly different from those at Saqqara.

Getting there

The Pyramids of Abu Sir can only be reached by riding or walking across the desert. The boldest option is to visit them **en route between Giza and Saqqara**, spending three hours in the saddle. Making a round trip **from north Saqqara** is less demanding, but still requires commitment. With the pyramids clearly visible 6km away, you can either walk (90–120min) or conserve energy by hiring a horse or camel from near the refreshments tent (£E10 one-way).

Getting to Abu Sir **from Cairo** is more uncertain and time-consuming. In theory you can catch a minibus from Midan Giza to Abu Sir village (35pt) and then walk 2.5km: cross a small canal, turn right, then left, follow a garden wall to the desert's edge and you'll finally reach the causeway of Sahure's Pyramid. In practice, however, taxi drivers take advantage of stranded travellers, and it's easy to mistake one turning for another. A Beau Geste approach from Saqqara makes better sense.

The pyramid complexes

The four pyramid complexes are ranged in an arc which ignores chronological order. At the southern end of the pyramid field a low mound marks the core of the unfinished **Pyramid of Neferefre**, whose brief reign preceded Nyuserre's. As the core is composed of locally quarried limestone and was never encased in finer Tura masonry, no causeway was ever built. However, the desert may yet disgorge other structures: during the 1980s, Czechoslovak archaeologists uncovered another pyramid complex, thought to belong to Queen Khentkawes, the mother of Sahure.

Dominating the view north is the much larger **Pyramid of Neferirkare**, the third ruler of the V Dynasty, who strove to outdo his predecessor, Sahure. If finished, it would have been 70m high – taller than the third pyramid at Giza – but Neferirkare's premature demise forced his successor to hastily complete a modified version using perishable mudbrick. More humiliatingly, its valley temple and grand causeway were later usurped to serve the **Pyramid of Nyuserre**, further north. A battered mortuary temple with papyriform columns mocks the original name of this dilapidated pyramid, "The Places of Nyuserre are Enduring"; the pharaohs who followed him preferred burial at Saqqara.

A cluster of *mastabas* to the northwest includes the **Tomb of Ptahshepses**. Currently entered via a rickety ladder, the tomb's most curious feature is the double room off the courtyard, which may have held solar boats. If so, the only other known example of this in a private tomb is that of Kagemni in north Saqqara. Ptahshepses was chief of works to Sahure, the first of the V Dynasty kings to be buried at Abu Sir.

The **Pyramid of Sahure** is badly damaged, but its associated temples have fared better than the others. A 235-metre-long causeway links the ruined valley temple to Sahure's mortuary temple on the eastern side of the pyramid. Though most of its reliefs (which were the first to show the king smiting his enemies, later a standard motif) have gone to various museums, enough remains to make the temple worth exploring. It's also possible to crawl through a dusty, cobwebbed passage to reach the burial chamber within the pyramid (whose original name was "The Soul of Sahure Gleams"). From its summit, ten or more pyramids are visible on clear days.

The sun temples of Abu Ghurab

If you're riding between Giza and Saqqara, ask your guide to stop at the site known as **Abu Ghurab**, northwest of Abu Sir. Its twin temples were designed for worship of Re, the sun-god of Heliopolis, but their Jubilee reliefs and proximity to a pyramid field suggests that they fulfilled a similar function to Zoser's Heb-Sed court at Saqqara.

Unlike the ruinous **Sun Temple of Userkaf**, 400m from Sahure's Pyramid, the more distant **Sun Temple of Nyuserre** repays a visit. Approached from its valley temple by a causeway, the great courtyard is centred upon an alabaster altar where cattle were sacrificed. At its western end stood a *benben* or megalith symbolising the primordial mound, of which only the base remains. From the courtyard's vestibule, corridors run north to storerooms and south to the king's chapel. The "Chamber of Seasons" beyond the chapel once contained beautiful reliefs; to the south you can find the remnants of a brick model of a solar boat.

South Saqqara

Like their predecessors at Abu Sir, the pharaohs of the VI Dynasty (c.2345–2181 BC) established another necropolis – nowadays called **South Saqqara** – which started 700m beyond Sekhemkhet's unfinished pyramid and extended for over three kilometres. Unfortunately for sightseers, the most interesting monuments are those farthest away across the site; hiring a donkey, horse or camel (about £E10 for the round trip) will minimise slogging over soft sand.

Two tracks run either side of several pyramids before meeting at the Mastabat al-Faraun. The western one is more direct than the (soon to be upgraded) route which goes via SAQQARA VILLAGE, set amidst lush palm groves 2km from North Saqqara's ticket office.

The site

Heading south along either track, you'll pass a low mound of rubble identified as the **Pyramid of Pepi I**. The name "Memphis", which classical authors bestowed upon Egypt's ancient capital and its environs, was actually derived from one of this pyramid's titles. To the southwest, another insignificant heap indicates the **Pyramid of Merenre**, who succeeded Pepi. French archaeologists are excavating the latter's pyramid, but neither site is really worth a detour.

Due west of Saqqara village, sand drifts over the outlying temples of the **Pyramid of Djedkare-Isesi**. Known in Arabic as the "Pyramid of the Sentinel" (*Ahram es-Shawaf*), it stands 25m high and can be entered via a tunnel on the north side. Although a shattered basalt sarcophagus and mummified remains

---

DAHSHUR AND THE RIDDLE OF THE PYRAMIDS

The **Dahshur pyramid field lies** within a **military zone** that's off-limits to civilians. Specialists might be able to wrangle a permit from Corps HQ in Heliopolis or the Ministry of the Interior, but tourists should disregard camel or donkey owners who promise "Dahshur pyramids, no problem", knowing full well that visitors are turned back long before the site. However, even if you don't intend to visit, Dahshur's archaeological significance merits some explanation.

The pyramid field consists of two groups. To the east are three **Middle Kingdom complexes**, dating from the revival of pyramid-building (c.1991–1790 BC) that culminated near the Fayoum. Though the pyramids proved unrewarding to nineteenth-century excavators, their subsidiary tombs yielded some magnificent jewellery (now in the Antiquities Museum). More intriguing are the two **Old Kingdom pyramids** farther into the desert, which have long tantalised archaeologists with a riddle.

Both of these pyramids are credited to **Snofru** (c.2613–2588 BC), father of Cheops and founder of the IV Dynasty, whose monuments constitute an evolutionary link between the stepped creations of the previous dynasty at North Saqqara and the true pyramids of Giza. Despite its lower angle (43.5°) and height (101m), Snofru's northern **Red Pyramid** clearly prefigures his son's edifice. But his southern one is uniquely different, rising more steeply (54.3°) than the Great Pyramid for three-quarters of its height, before abruptly tapering at a gentler slope – hence its sobriquet, the **Bent Pyramid**. The explanation for its shape, and why Snofru should have built two pyramids only 3km apart, is a longstanding conundrum of Egyptology.

were found here last century, it wasn't until 1946 that Abdel Hussein identified them as those of Djedkare, the penultimate king of the V Dynasty. Far from being the first ruler to be entombed in South Saqqara, Djedkare was merely emulating the last pharaoh of the previous dynasty, whose own mortuary complex is uniquely different, and the oldest in this necropolis.

Built of limestone blocks, Shepseskaf's mortuary complex resembles a gigantic sarcophagus with a rounded lid; another simile gave rise to its local name, **Mastabat al-Faraun** – the Pharaoh's Bench. If you can find a guard, it's possible to venture through descending and horizontal corridors to reach the burial chamber and various storerooms. The monument was almost certainly commissioned by Shepseskaf, who evidently felt the need to distance himself from the pyramid of his father, Mycerinus. However, the archaeologist Jequier doubted that the complex was ever used for any actual burial and Shepseskaf's final resting place remains uncertain.

Northwest of here lies the most complete example of a VI Dynasty mortuary complex, albeit missing casing stones and other masonry, plundered in medieval times. The usual valley temple and causeway culminate in a mortuary temple whose vestibule and sanctuary retain fragments of their original reliefs. Beyond this rises the **Pyramid of Pepi II**, whose reign supposedly lasted 94 years, after which the VI Dynasty expired. A descending passage leads to his rock-cut burial chamber, whose ceiling and walls are inscribed with stars and Pyramid Texts. These also appear within the subsidiary pyramids of Pepi's queens, Apuit and Neith, which imitate his mortuary complex on a smaller scale. Various nobles and officials are buried roundabouts.

Mindful of the truism that a pharaoh required but one sanctuary for his *ka*, many reasoned that the Bent Pyramid resulted from a change of plan prompted by fears for its stability, and when these persisted, a second, safer pyramid was built to guarantee Snofru's afterlife. But for this theory to hold water, it's necessary to dismiss Snofru's claim to have built a *third* pyramid at Maidum as mere usurpation of an earlier structure; and the possibility that its sudden collapse might have caused the modification of the Bent Pyramid must likewise be rejected on the grounds that he needed only one secure monument.

In 1977, a professor of physics at Oxford University reopened the whole debate. Arguing that Snofru did, indeed, build the "Collapsed Pyramid" at Maidum, whose fall resulted in changes to the Bent one at Dahshur, Kurt Mendelsson overcame the "one pharaoh–one *ka*–one pyramid" objection by postulating a pyramid production line. As one pyramid neared completion, surplus resources were deployed to start another, despite the satisfaction of the reigning king's requirements. The reason for continuous production was that the task of building a single pyramid required gigantic efforts over ten to thirty years; inevitably, some pharaohs lacked the time and resources. A stockpile of half-constructed, perhaps even finished pyramids was an insurance policy on the afterlife.

Snofru

Egyptologists greeted Mendelssohn's theory with delight or derision, and partisans are still going hard at it in the *Journal of Egyptian Archaeology*. Unlike the Great Pyramids or the lives of Hatshepsut, Nefertiti and Akhenaten, however, the enigma of Snofru's pyramids hasn't excited great public interest.

CONSUMERS' CAIRO

As befits its size, Cairo has the most varied culinary scene, shopping and nightlife in North Africa. Much of it is new, having developed in the Sadat era after the decades of Nasserite austerity, and for those that can afford it conspicuous consumption is very much the order of the day. As a visitor, you're well catered for, whether you're into sailing on the Nile, watching a belly dancer, or absorbing a whole world of popular culture at Cairo's religious festivals. All of this is fun to discover but more mundane practicalities can involve hassles and bureaucracy, mysteries and intricacies which we've tried to unravel in the final "Practicalities" section.

Eating and drinking

The culinary scene in Cairo has diversified enormously since the 1970s, making it possible to eat anything from *sukiyaki* to Kentucky Fried Chicken. Don't fall into the trap of eating only in tourist restaurants or thinking that Egyptian food doesn't rise beyond *koftas* and kebabs. You can satisfy most tastes if you know where to look. The options range from Arab cafés offering a few simple dishes to extravagant "food weeks" at deluxe hotels (advertised in *Cairo Today*). Though few natives would agree with them, foreigners are generally pleasantly surprised by the cost of eating out in Cairo. Drinking, whilst more limited, is also quite affordable. Places where dancing or live acts are paramount are covered in the following "Entertainments" section.

Breakfast and buffet meals

There are two solutions to the monotony of hotel breakfasts (rolls and jam and/ or cheese spread). Either you buy savouries, juice etc, to store in the hotel fridge and consume in the morning, or you go elsewhere for **breakfast**, picking up a glass of freshly squeezed juice from one of the many tiled street outlets to get the appetite going. Downtown Cairo provides the most substantial breakfast options, including dozens of cafés (see following section) and a range of deluxe hotels whose **buffets** are open to non-residents.

Downtown

Lappas, 17 Qasr el-Nil. Once a *Groppi's*-style coffeehouse, now a shiny stand-up delicatessen eatery with a supermarket out back. A cheaper option than any of the following.

Ibis Café, on the ground floor of the Nile Hilton. Ideal for a slap-up continental breakfast (£E7) between 6 and 10am. From 11am to 2pm and 6 to 10pm, you can have free run of a fantastic salad bar (£E7) or hot and cold buffet (£E14). Open 24 hours.

Taverne du Champ de Mars. A splendidly ornate *fin-de-siècle* Brussels tavern reconstructed next to the *Hotel Ibis*, which offers a single entrée with soup or salad bar and dessert for £E18. Drinkers also receive nibblets. Smart casual dress required. Expensive, but worth it for the ambience (see also "Bars", below).

Islamic Cairo

Cafeteria Khan el-Khalili, 5 Sikket al-Badestan. Filling if expensive breakfast fare in a rather antiseptic environment.

Nameless eatery beneath the *El-Hussein Hotel*. This, uniquely, features baguettes with clotted cream and honey (mingled with the stench of frying offal).

Roda Island

Le Café, in the *Meridien Hotel* on Roda Island. Breakfast buffet (£E15) with chocolate croissants from 7 to 10am. Later on, a huge buffet lunch is laid out on the terrace overlooking the Nile; £E18 gets you unlimited food, use of their swimming pool and foreign newspapers. A nice place to spend a hot afternoon.

Manial Palace Club Med, on Roda Island. For £E28, non-residents can enjoy a superb buffet lunch and use a pool set amidst the former grounds of Mohammed Ali's palace on Roda Island.

Pyramids of Giza

Khan el-Khalili Coffeeshop. Luxurious A/C cafeteria in the *Mena House Hotel*, near the Pyramids of Giza. Skip the paltry continental breakfast (£E7.50) and have a £E14 "special". The "Oberoi" version includes fruit juice, pancakes and croissants; the "Egyptian" one yoghurt with honey and *fuul* with eggs.

Restaurants, cafés and street food

Restaurants, cafés and street food comprise a culinary spectrum rather than distinctly separate categories. **Restaurants** run the gamut from *nouvelle cuisine* salons to backstreet kebab houses, while **cafés** range from air-conditioned bourgeois havens to open-fronted tiled diners. The ones devoted to *kushari* (50pt a bowl) or *fuul* and *taamiya* (£E1 with salad and pickles) provide the cheapest nutritious meals going. A third type of outlet purveys *fatir* or Egyptian pizzas, which are tastier and cheaper (£E2–5 depending on size and ingredients) than most Western-style pizzas in Cairo.

Despite the blurred line between hole-in-the-wall eateries and outright **street food**, running water remains a crucial factor – anywhere without it is risky. Markets and terminals offer the best outlets: a number of places off Ramses, Orabi, Ataba, Falaki, Lazoghli and Giza squares, and midway down Sharia Qalaa function **all night**.

At the other end of the gastro-cultural spectrum, every hotel rated three stars or above has at least one restaurant and coffeeshop (maybe 24-hour) that's accessible to non-residents. If familiar food and no hassle are top priority, **hotel dining** is usually a safe bet.

Note that telephone numbers have been included for all restaurants where reservations are a good idea. At others, there's no need to bother – if, indeed, you could get through and make yourself understood.

PRACTICALITIES: MENUS AND TIPPING

Between these extremes there's a huge variation in **standards** of cleanliness and presentation, and whether somewhere seems okay or grotty depends partly on your own values. We've tried to present a cross-section of what's available in various parts of the city. The majority of places listed have **menus** in English or French and staff who understand both, but others only deal in Arabic; fortunately, many of them display what's on offer, so you only have to point.

Though restaurant bills include tax and service (8–12 percent), you are also expected to tip – conventions for which are byzantine. Basically, you tip in inverse proportion to the size of the bill, dropping below ten percent in expensive places and above it where the sums involved are trifling. In juice bars and diners, customers simply put 10–25pt on a plate by the exit.

Downtown Cairo

Virtually every type of food except Indian cuisine can be had in downtown Cairo. The following places are listed not in order of price but according to location, progressing (roughly) **northwards from Midan Tahrir**.

Fatatri el-Tahrir, look for the marble facade on the right-hand side, two blocks east along Sharia Tahrir. Small *fatirs* (with meat and egg) or larger, crustier versions topped with hot sauce, cheese and olives make a delicious meal for around £E8. Also pancake-*fatirs* filled with apple jam and icing sugar. Open 24 hours.

El Tahrir, further along Sharia Tahrir. A good *kushari* diner.

El-Guesh, 2 Midan Falaki, on the corner of Tahrir and Falaki streets. A family place serving spicy kebab (£E6). Open daily noon–midnight.

Kowloon Restaurant, next to the *Hotel Cleopatra* on the corner of Midan Tahrir and Sharia el-Bustan. Reasonably priced Korean and Japanese food; open for dinner 7.30–11.30pm. *Valentino's*, in the same building, offers pizzas (£E6–8) and pasta dishes (£E5–8).

Arabesque, 6 Sharia Qasr el-Nil (☎759-896). French and Levantine cuisine, strong on soups and meat dishes (£E14–18), but chiefly remarkable for its Oriental decor and contemporary art gallery. Wine and beer. Daily noon–3.30pm & 7.30pm–midnight.

Caroll, 12 Qasr el-Nil – in the passage (☎746-434). Posh service and decent Franco-Levantine food (main dishes £E10–20); wine and beer; A/C. Usually full of package tourists. Daily 1–4pm & 7.30pm–midnight.

Estoril, 12 Talaat Harb – in the passage (☎743-102). Similar menus to the *Caroll*, at cheaper prices and in quieter surroundings. Its vintage bar deserves a Bogart. Daily noon–3.30pm & 7–10pm; closed Aug.

Café Riche, 17 Talaat Harb. Indifferent food and service, but perennially popular. Shady patio for outdoor dining; to drink alcohol you have to sit indoors (amid portraits of famous artists who once frequented the café). Serves the coldest beer in Cairo. Daily 10am–10pm.

Felfela, 15 Sharia Hoda Shaarawi. Another Mecca for tourists, offering diverse veggy and meaty Egyptian dishes (£E1–12) in a funkily decorated hall that goes back forever. Sells beer. Open daily 7am–1pm. *Felfela's* **takeaway**, around the corner on Talaat Harb, does cheap *shwarmas* and *taamiya* sandwiches.

American Fried Chicken, 8 Hoda Shaarawi. Inexpensive chicken, burgers and milkshakes from the best Western chain outlet in central Cairo. Usually open to midnight.

The Greek Club, above *Groppi's* on Talaat Harb square – entrance on Sharia Bassiouni. Cheap, excellent Greek cooking; indoors in winter, pleasant outdoor terrace in summer. Run by Greeks with Greek-only advertising.

Fu-Shing, 28 Talaat Harb – in the passage. Founded by ethnic Muslim refugees from China. Filling quasi-Chinese meals in a relaxed ambience. The spring rolls make a great snack. Sells beer. Inexpensive. Open 12.30pm–10pm, except Mon.

Coin de Kebab, aka *Kebab Corner*, one block west off Talaat Harb, towards the Odeon Palace Hotel. Generous portions of kebab and tahina for about £E13.

Rex, 14 Sharia Abdel Khaliq Sarwat – west of Talaat Harb. Cheese omelette, macaroni with meat sauce, chicken and beef dishes for £E2–7. Sat–Thurs 1–4.30pm & 6–10pm.

La Chesa, 21 Sharia Adly (☎393-9360). Salubrious, *Swiss Air*-managed establishment serving decent Western food and scrumptious pastries at affordably upmarket rates. Open 10.30am–11pm.

Valley of the Kings, on the first floor of the *Grand Hotel*. Complete with elegant fountain and stained-glass windows overlooking 26th July Street. Reasonably priced Franco-Levantine cuisine; the three-course set meals are good value. Beer and wine. Seldom crowded. Open 12.30–2pm & 7–9.30pm daily.

El-Kamaal, halfway up al-Tawfiqiyya, a narrow market street starting diagonally opposite the Grand; Arabic sign only. Okra, rice and noodles, or a beef or chicken salad, costs about £E5.

Al Haty, Midan Halim, behind the Cicurel department store on 26th July. Vintage decor, with mirrors and fans; the fare is traditional: kebab, fish, stuffed vine leaves, *mezzas*, roast lamb; main dishes around £E7–8. No alcohol. Open daily 11am–10pm.

Alfi Bey, 3 Sharia Alfi. Another vintage restaurant run by strict Muslims. Some of the staff claim to have been here since the 1940s; the panelling and chandeliers certainly have. Best for lamb dishes, chicken, macaroni, or pigeon stuffed with liver; reckon on around £E10 a head. Open daily noon–midnight.

Taverna, signposted in Greek a few doors west of Alfi Bey. This no-frills seafood place serves great *calamari*, shrimp, salad and tahina; beer and *ouzo*. May ignore set hours (noon–4pm & 7pm–midnight) and close down over summer. Inexpensive to moderate.

Paprika, 1129 Corniche el-Nil, just south of the TV Building (☎749-447). Tasty European dishes (£E10 upwards) and *mezzas*. Frequented by media folk. Noon–midnight daily.

REALLY CHEAP DOWNTOWN OPTIONS

Several downtown areas are good for **really cheap meals**. On and off **26th July Street** are numerous *kushari* diners; *Lux*, near the corner with Sharia Sherif, is probably the best. Two blocks farther north, there's a 24-hour *fuul* and *taamiya* joint next to the Nile Christian Bookshop on Sharia Alfi Bey, plus all kinds of eateries in the backstreets north of the High Court and along that end of Sharia Champollion.

Another area is **Midan Falaki**, several blocks east of Midan Tahrir. Near the northern end of its pedestrian overpass are *Doumyati* (11am–11pm; closed Fri), another homely *fuul* place, and the *Souk al-Hamadea*, offering macaroni and diverse sandwiches for under £E1. Across the bridge, sausage stalls and a hole-in-the-wall *fatir* place coexist with fruit stalls along **Sharia Mansur**, outside Bab al-Luq market.

Garden City

Besides its hotels, a floating restaurant (see section following) and *fuul*, *fatir* and *kushari* joints (east off Qasr al-Aini before the hospital), Garden City can also offer:

Sit-In Restaurant, 1 Sharia Amerika Latina. Look for the Donald Duck sign, near the British Embassy. Cheap sandwiches, hamburgers, grilled chicken and other dishes. 8am–midnight.

Abu Shakra, 69 Sharia Qasr al-Aini, opposite the hospital (☎848-711). Decorated in marble and alabaster, this famous, strictly Muslim establishment specialises in *kofta* and kebab sold by weight (£E21 per kilo – enough for 2–3 persons), accompanied by salads and dips. Open 1–5pm & 7–11pm. Closed Fri, and daytime during Ramadan.

Islamic Cairo

Although every main street and square features poky eateries serving cheap grub, most tourists stick to the four places in Khan el-Khalili detailed below. But for those inured to flies and roaches, there are discoveries to be made, like the hole-in-the-wall near the market on Sharia Qalaa, which does freshly grilled shrimp sandwiches.

Cafeteria Khan el-Khalili, 5 Sikket al-Badestan. Pricey, A/C "Oriental" restaurant managed by the Oberoi, near the old gate 40m west of El-Hussein's Mosque. Western and Egyptian snacks and light meals (£E2–14) in the dining room; coffee, mint tea or fresh orange juice in the **Naguib Mahfouz Coffeeshop**, facing the street.

Egyptian Pancake House, Between Midan el-Hussein and al-Azhar. Made to order *fatirs* filled with egg, cheese, coconut, rasins, jam or honey (or any combination thereof). Inexpensive. Only tapwater to drink. Open noon–midnight.

El-Hussein, on the roof of the *El-Hussein Hotel*. Fantastic views but grotty food – consume as little as possible. Used for wedding parties at least two nights a week. *Loud* music. 8am–midnight. Inexpensive.

El Dahan/Chicken Home, several doors apart on the Muski, near Midan el-Hussein. One does *kofta* and kebabs, the other grilled chicken. Both have seating upstairs and operate from noon to midnight. No alcohol. Inexpensive.

Zamalek

As befits a high-rent, cosmopolitan neighbourhood, Zamalek boasts several upmarket restaurants devoted to foreign cuisine, plus **trendy nightspots** like *B's Corner*, *Longchamp* and *Pub 28* (see "Bars" below, and the "Entertainments" section). The following places are listed according to location, starting near the Gezira Sporting Club and working northwards. Most of them are within ten minutes' walk of 26th July Street.

Justine, 4 Hassan Sabry, in the Four Corners complex two blocks south of Galabaya Park (☎341-2961). Probably the finest and most expensive restaurant in Cairo. *Nouvelle cuisine*, soft lighting and music; formal dress required.

La Piazza (☎340-7510). A stylish Italian restaurant (pasta dishes £E8–10) in the same building, which also contains **Matchpoint**, an American-style video snackbar frequented by Cairene preppies (1pm–1am daily; £E6–8 minimum charge), and *Max's* disco (see "Entertainments").

Zamalek Restaurant, 118 26th July Street, near the intersection with Sharia al-Aziz Osman. Cheap sit-down joint for *taamiya*, *fuul* and tahina. Soft drinks only.

Balmoral Hotel Chinese Restaurant, corner of 26th July and Sharia Maahad al-Swissry. Tasty Cantonese dishes (£E9–15) in quiet surroundings. Daily 11am–11pm.

Tokyo, 4 Maahad al-Swissry, one block north of the 26th July Bridge (☎340-0502). Excellent Japanese food served by kimono-clad waiters. Main dishes £E12–18; imported *sake*. A place to splurge. Daily noon–2.30pm & 6–10.30pm.

Hana Korean Restaurant, 21 Maahad al-Swissry; next to the *El-Nil Zamalek Hotel* (☎340-1846). Small, friendly place offering various Asian dishes. A huge portion of *sukiyaki* (do-it-yourself stir-fry soup) costs £E13. Daily noon–11pm.

Angus Brasserie, 34 Sharia Yehia Ibrahim, inside the *New Star Hotel*. Charcoal-grilled steaks and other Argentine specialities. Noon–midnight.

Five Bells, 9 Sharia Adil Abu Bakr, north of the Zamalek Bridge (☎340-4102). It's worth dressing up for this swish Italianate joint, complete with a grand piano, garden and fountain. Entrées £E10–15; a few *mezzas* (£E2–8) make a meal. Open daily noon–1am.

Don Quichotte, 9a Sharia Ahmed Heshmat (☎340-6415). Tiny, elegant restaurant sampling great cuisines of the world. Expensive. Reservations advisable. 12.30–4pm & 7.30–midnight.

Il Capo, 22 Sharia Taha Hussein (☎341-3870). Tasty *antipasti*, pizzas and spaghetti (£E8) in slick, A/C surroundings. Often has live music. When popular groups play, there's a minimum charge of £E10 per head. In the same building as *B's Corner* (see "Bars"), next to the *President Hotel*. Daily 10am–1.30am.

Mohandiseen

The 1980s saw a proliferation of fast-food outlets and chic restaurants, mostly situated along or just off Arab League Street (*Sharia Gameat al-Dowal al-Arabiya*, also nicknamed "The Mall"), which can be reached by #167 bus from the Nile Hilton terminal and 26th July Street in downtown Cairo, or, easier still, by taxi.

Abu Shakra, 17 Arab League St. Another branch of the famous kebab and *kofta* restaurant in Garden City, keeping similar hours (see above).

King Grill, opposite the *Atlas Zamalek Hotel*, Arab League St. Chiefly a takeout, their speciality is grilled chicken with fifteen different spices (£E6).

Al-Omdah, 6 Sharia al-Gaza'ir, around the corner from the Atlas. Upmarket, A/C *kushari* outlet; a bowl costs £E2.50. Open daily 11am–2am.

Tandoori, 11 Sharia Shehab, two blocks west of Arab League St (☎348-6301). Cool marble decor, fine service and Indian cuisine. Try the tandoori chicken, curried lamb (*kema*) or prawns (*jhinga*). Expect to pay about £E15 for a full meal; takeouts cost less. No alcohol. Open noon–4pm & 7.30–11pm.

Tikka, 47 Sharia Batal Ahmed Aziz (☎346-0393). A cheaper place for Indian and Egyptian food. Does takeouts and deliveries. Open 10am–midnight.

Maria, 32 Sharia Jeddah, at the bottom end of Arab League St (☎713-0661). Tasty home-made pasta and other Italian dishes; relaxed ambience; average prices. Daily 11am–11pm.

Taberna Espanola, 26 Sharia Suriya, in the *Cairo Inn* (☎346-0661). Excellent Spanish food, with cocktails (£E4) and guitar music in the evenings. Open 24 hours.

Le Tirol, 38 Sharia Gazirit al-Arab (☎344-9725). Swiss-chalet decor and tasty Central European cuisine (main dishes £E12–22). No alcohol. Daily noon–1am.

Prestige Pizza, 43, Gazirit al-Arab, just east of Sharia Wadi el-Nil (☎347-0383). Smart ambience with chairs outside. Pizzas (£E5–8) and other Italian food. Daily noon–2am.

Bon Appetit, 21 Sharia Wadi el-Nil (☎346-4937). Elegant decor and *haute cuisine* variations on native fare such as fish kebab and shrimp *kofta* (£E14), or stewed quail stuffed with onions (£E10). Also salad bar, appetisers, children's menu (£E5 each) and superb pastries. Their takeaway does huge club sandwiches.

Aguza, Dokki and Giza

The rest of the west bank is less tempting than Mohandiseen, but hardly bereft of options. Cheap eateries abound in market quarters like Suleyman Gohar (Dokki) and Midan Giza, whilst overpriced kebab restaurants and hotel dining loom large along the Pyramids Road. Visitors with kids should enjoy the **outdoor family restaurants** beside the Maryotteya Canal, farther north (bring mosquito repellent), or the floating restaurants near the El-Gama'a Bridge (see overpage).

AGUZA

Okamoto, 7 Sharia Ahmed Orabi – off Midan Sphinx, towards Mohandiseen (☎349-5774). Excellent Japanese food, well worth the expense; also does takeouts. Tues–Sun noon–4pm.

Cafeteria Niema, 182 Corniche el-Nil, Aguza, opposite the Police Hospital near the 6th October Bridge. The best takeaway *fuul* and *taamiya* sandwiches in Cairo – so taxi drivers swear; open 24 hours.

Flying Fish, 166 Corniche el-Nil (☎349-3234). Seafood specialities. Daily noon–midnight.

GIZA

El Mashrabia, 4 Sharia Ahmed Nessim, opposite the El Urman Garden, Giza (☎725-059). Elegant Moorish decor and excellent Middle Eastern food. Salads (£E2), lamb, *kofta* and turkey dishes (£E15). No alcohol. Daily 11am–1am. The *Swiss Chalet Bar B Q*, across the road, does inexpensive grilled chicken (noon–2am).

Le Chalet, in the Nasr Building, Giza – see map on p.122 (☎729-488). Run by *Swiss Air*, clean and pleasant, with fine views of the Nile. Quiches, salads and fondues (£E7–13); hot meat or fish platters (£E12–18); delectable pastries and ice creams. Children's menu £E5. Daily 10.30am–11.30pm. The plush **Le Chateau** restaurant, upstairs, offers rich main courses (£E20–30) and scrumptious desserts. Open for lunch (1–3.30pm) and dinner (8–11pm). Reservations advisable (☎729-487).

MARYOTTEYA CANAL

The Farm, 23 Maryotteya Canal (☎861-901). Playground and coffeehouse, with outdoor dining and daily folkloric shows (2–7pm). Moderately priced.

La Rose, 58 Maryotteya Canal (☎855-712). Air-conditioned, fly-free dining amidst arabesque hangings. A full meal of appetisers, main course (chicken, kebab or pigeon), salad and fruit costs about £E17. Open daily 11am–1am.

Andrea's Chicken Restaurant, 60 Maryotteya Canal – signposted on Pyramids Road (☎851-133). Indoor and outdoor feasting on similar fare.

Felfela Village, Maryotteya Canal (☎854-209). From *Andrea's*, cross the bridge, turn right and double back along the canal for a block or so. This rambling outdoor complex features a zoo and playground, camel rides, acrobats, puppet shows, music and belly dancers – even dancing horses. The show (noon–6pm) is presented daily over summer, and on Tues, Fri, Sat and Sun in winter; the restaurant is open 10am–7pm daily.

Felfela Cafe, 27 Alexandria Desert Road (☎850-234). *Felfela's* latest offshoot, whackily adorned with fake birds and trees, presents daily folkloric shows (10am–1pm) and the usual menu, plus a salad bar and appetisers. Open daily 8.30am–1.30am.

Heliopolis

Deluxe hotels in Heliopolis offer a variety of restaurants, coffeeshops, nightclubs and snack bars.

Tikka, Sharia Abdel Wahid, one block north of the central drag Sharia al-Ahram. Spicy takeouts.

Amphitrion, Sharia al-Ahram. Middle Eastern and Western dishes, snacks and takeouts; tea and coffee. Pleasant terrace. Inexpensive. Daily 7.30am–1pm.

Andalusia – look out for the fake castle opposite Merryland on Sharia al-Higaz (☎258-1292). Western and Egyptian food outdoors, sometimes with music. Open 1pm–midnight.

Granada City Pizzeria, next door to the Andalusia. Moderately priced.

La Terrine, 105 Sharia al-Hiugaz, near Heliopolis Hospital (☎257-8634). Excellent French cuisine and stylish service. Almost as good – and significantly less exorbitant – than *Justine* in Zamalek. Reservations advisable.

Floating restaurants

Before the Gulf War decimated Egypt's tourist industry, floating restaurants seemed the wave of the future; since then, however, some cruises have been cut until business picks up, so you'll have to verify schedules. Under normal circumstances, it's advisable to book for cruises anyway.

Scarabee (☎355-4481). Docked along the Corniche near *Shepheard's Hotel* and affiliated with the *Wagon-Lits* company. Sails three times daily (11am–1pm; 7–9pm; 10pm–midnight) complete with an "Oriental" floorshow and a dance band on the evening cruises (£E40 excluding drinks).

Bateau Omar Khayyam (☎340-8553). An old houseboat permanently moored alongside Saray el-Gezira, near the Sporting Club, this offers traditional Egyptian fare and entertainment, and is mostly patronised by Cairenes. Open noon–4pm & 8pm–1am.

Nile Pharaoh (☎738-914). A mock-pharaonic barge with lotus-flower stern and prow, Eyes of Horus, scarab friezes, and picture windows. Aside from Ramadan (when schedules vary) there are three ninety-minute cruises daily. The lunch cruise starts at 2.30pm and costs £E30 per person. Dinner cruises with music and belly dancing (£E45) leave at 8 and 10.45pm in the summer, 7.30 and 10pm during winter. The boat cruises upriver to Ma'adi and then drifts with the current towards Gezira before returning to dock. There's also a stationary "docked" lunch (£E16).

Golden Pharaoh. The Nile Pharoah's new sister-ship may now be operating from the same dock, offering longer cruises, a folklore show, belly dancers, and separate decks for buffet and a la carte meals. Contact the Nile Pharaoh (above) or the *Mena House Hotel* (☎855-4444) for information.

Cafés, patisseries and juice bars

Cairene males have socialised in **coffeehouses** (*ahwa*) ever since the beverage was introduced from Yemen in the early Middle Ages. Although professional *qasas* (storytellers) have largely been supplanted by broadcast or taped music, other traditional diversions such as backgammon and dominoes are still popular, and smokers remain loyal to their waterpipes. Most *ahwas* are shabby and high-ceilinged, with chairs overlooking the street. Certain places are the haunt of hobbyists – stamp collectors at *Mukhtallat* (14 Abdel Khaliq Sarwat), literati at *Ali Baba* (Midan Tahrir) – or rural migrants – oasis folk frequent *al-Wahia* (Sharia Qadry, off Bur Said) – but most have an eclectic clientele. Those around Bab al-Luq, Midan Ramses Sharia Qalaa and other market areas stay open **all night**, as do the coffeeshops in the *Intercontinental*, *Meridien* and other deluxe hotels.

Upmarket coffeehouses and tearooms also serve pastries, rice pudding, creme caramel and suchlike. To take away or consume on the spot, it's cheaper to buy at **patisseries** like *El Abd* or *Haroun al-Rashid* on Talaat Harb.

Every main street also has a couple of stand-up **juice bars**, recognisable by their displays of fruit. The ones near the *Café Riche* and *Felfela* charge more than most, but they're never expensive. Normally, you order and pay at the cash desk before exchanging a plastic token for your drink at the counter (where customers leave a 5–15pt tip). **Nut shops** (*ma'la*) are another high street perennial, offering all kinds of peanuts (*fuul sudani*) and edible seeds. Most nut shops also stock candies and mineral water.

See Basics *for a rundown on coffee-drinking and preparation, and details of the various types of juices and nuts.*

Coffeehouses/tearooms

A brief selection of the more famous and some personal favourites . . .

GROPPI'S

The classic **Groppi** chain is now at four locations. The once-palatial branch on Midan Talaat Harb (7am–10pm daily) has lost its charm since "renovation" and the service is awful, but it's still fun to hang out at *Garden Groppi's* on Sharia Adly (7.30am–9pm), whose panelled interior hasn't changed since World War II. *Groppi's* in Heliopolis has a pleasant terrace overlooking Sharia al-Ahram. Each levies a minimum charge of £E1 per person and doubles as a delicatessen – the main function of yet another downtown outlet on the corner of 26th July and Mohammed Farid streets.

DOWNTOWN

Indian Tea Centre, 23 Talaat Harb – in the passage. Cheap snacks, imported teas and Indian-style pastries.

Brazilian Coffee Shop, 38 Talaat Harb. Delicious café au lait, espresso and cappuccino; greasy burgers and grills; no seats. Open daily 7am–midnight.

Café à l'Americaine, corner of Talaat Harb and 26th July. Good ice cream and creme caramel; awful meals. A/C and £E1.50 minimum charge; a lawyers' hang-out. Daily 7am–11pm.

GARDEN CITY

La Poire, Sharia Rustrum, near the British Embassy in Garden City. Home-made *baklava* and éclairs for under £E1. Open daily 8am–midnight.

ISLAMIC CAIRO

Fishawi's, behind the *El-Hussein Hotel* in Khan el-Khalili. Cairo's oldest teahouse has been managed by the same family – and remained perpetually open – since 1773. Cracked mirrors, battered furniture, haughty staff and wandering vendors imbibe the atmosphere with a pot of mint tea (50pt) and a *sheesha* (£E1). Never closes.

Sukariya, on the corner of Sikket al-Badestan near Fishawi's. This *ahwa* still hosts storytellers and conjurers.

ZAMALEK

Simmonds Coffee Shop, 112 26th July St – near the intersection with Hassan Sabry. Excellent cappuccino, espresso, hot chocolate, lemonade, fresh croissants and *ramequins* (cheese in a mould). Open daily 8am–9pm.

Rigoletto, 3 Sharia Taha Hussein (in the Yamaha Centre). Great ice cream and cheesecake (£E2–3) acompanied by piped Springsteen. A place to forget Egypt. Open 9am–midnight.

HELIOPOLIS

Al-Sokkareya, 61 Sharia Abdul Hamid Bedawi, near the al-Salam Hyatt (bus #50, #128 or #330 from downtown Cairo). An upmarket garden café featuring singers, musicians and sideshows during Ramadan (8pm–3am); the £E10 admission charge includes all (soft) drinks and a *sheesha*. Call the Hyatt (☎245-5155) to confirm shows.

Bars

As throughout Egypt, the sale of alcohol is banned during Ramadan and other major Muslim festivals, and drinking is limited to indoor locations at all times. Besides restaurants and hotels, there are various **bars**, some of which are chiefly meeting places for men and prostitutes (the only Egyptian women found there).

Inevitably, there's also some overlap between bars and discos or nightclubs (covered under "Entertainments").

DOWNTOWN

Taverne du Champs de Mars, in the *Nile Hilton*. Come evening, this plush Belle Epoque enclave becomes a predominantly gay pick-up joint, with piano music from 8am–midnight (Thurs–Tues). Expensive drinks; £E5 cover charge; smart dress required. Daily 11am–1am.

Stella Bar, corner of Talaat Harb and Hoda Shaarawi, next to *Felfela's* takeaway. A cheap dive open till midnight or later. Men and beer only; strictly for drinking and arguing.

Barrel Lounge, on the first floor of the *Windsor Hotel*, Sharia Alfi Bey. Faded Anglo-Egyptian decor and charming ambience; popular with Cairene intellectuals and utterly safe for women. Native brandy with Coke is the cheapest bevvy, followed by Stella beer and *zibib*. Open daily until midnight or later.

Kings Restaurant, in a passage to the east of Qasr el-Nil, 20m up from Midan Talaat Harb. A misnamed hostess-bar serving beer and whisky.

Stereo Restaurant, 33 Qasr el-Nil – follow the "Dar al-Kitab" sign to the first floor and bear right. A similar place which sometimes features Arab music and dancing after 10pm. You can hear from the street if anything's cooking.

Honolulu. A luridly obvious joint opposite the *Pension Roma* on Sharia Mohammed Farid.

Garden Bar, inside the *Atlas Hotel* on Sharia el-Gumhorriya, south of Opera Square. Chiefly active on Thursday and Friday nights, when rock music attracts a mostly gay crowd (11pm–1am). Drinks are expensive but there's no cover charge.

Oxford Pension, 32 Talaat Harb (sixth floor). The hotel lobby is Cairo's only **all-night** bar – a sleazy spot where droppers-in can quaff Stella beer; a couple of other fleabag hotels also keep bottles in the fridge.

ZAMALEK

Matchpoint in the Four Corners complex, 4 Sharia Hassan Sabry. A pseudo-American bar/snack bar with sports and pop videos, frequented by rich young Cairenes attending the AUC. It's easy to exceed the minimum charge (£E6 till 9pm; £E8 afterwards). Daily 1pm–1am.

Pub 28, 28 Shagar al-Durr. The bar section – modelled on a British pub – stocks diverse foreign beers. Popular with expatriates and gay men but noted for its peremptory evictions. There's also a restaurant serving *mezzes*. Open daily noon–1pm.

El Patio, west off Shagar al-Durr, one block north of 26th July. A Cairene homage to Hollywood, complete with salon swing-doors, old movie posters and a piano. Serves imported beers (£E8) and cheesecake (£E2.50). Open daily 6pm–midnight.

B's Corner, 22 Sharia Taha Hussein. A kind of lounge-cum-dance club with a dartboard, popular with expats and AUC students. No cover charge. Daily 3pm–1am. Next door to *Il Capo* (see "Restaurants" above, and "Entertainments" overpage).

Music, nightlife, theatre and film

For current information about **what's on** at cinemas, concert halls and nightclubs, get hold of the daily *Egyptian Gazette* (on Saturday, the *Egyptian Mail*); the monthly *Cairos* (£E1) or *Cairo Today* (£E3.50); the Thursday (English weekly edition) of *al-Ahram* newspaper; or the free weekly *Cairo By Night*.

Music

Aside from discos and the Opera House, you're unlikely to hear much Western music outside of tourist restaurants – Egyptians prefer music from the Arab world. For contemporary music, by far the liveliest time is after the school and university exams, from late June to November; you'll need an Arabic-speaking friend to tell you what's happening as none of it is advertsied in the foreign press.

Contemporary music: shaabi and al-Jeel

Contemporary Egyptian music can be categorised as *Shaabi* – the urban folk music of *baladi* Cairo, blending traditional *mawals* (laments) with raunchy, satirical lyrics – or *al-Jeel* – a fusion of Nubian, Libyan and Bedouin rhythms with disco-beat, reflecting the tastes of upwardly mobile Cairene youth.

Though both sounds are played everywhere, live acts are more elusive. *Shaabi* stars like **Ahmed Adaweer**, **Hamdy Batchan** and **Magdy Talaat** now perform at nightclubs along Pyramids Road, rich weddings and private parties. Hotel nightclubs, open air concerts at the Gezira and Heliopolis clubs or Cairo University (usually during summer vacation) are likelier venues for *al-Jeel* stars such as **Mohammed Moneer**, **Amr Dieb**, **Ehab** and **Hanan**. Up and coming performers might appear at downtown nightclubs or *Il Capo* in Zamalek.

Dance music

Cairo's nightclubs harbour **oriental dance music**, whose golden age was the 1940s and 50s. Purists distinguish between classical *raqs sharqi* and music influenced by Umm Kalthoum or Western jazz – the torrid sounds associated with belly dancing and pre-revolutionary Cairo. Meanwhile, those who can afford it lap it up regardless at weddings (see p.208) and nightclubs (see overpage).

Folk music and dance

During the Nasser era, numerous troupes were established to preserve Egyptian folk music and dance in the face of urbanisation. Traditional rural numbers like *The Gypsy Dance* or *The Mamluke* are performed at the **Balloon Theatre** (☎347-7457) on Aguza's Corniche by the **National Troupe** and the **Reda Troupe**, whilst the **Folklore Orchestra of Egypt** (aka the Nile Music Orchestra) plays reproduction ancient instruments at various venues (☎735-153/728-004 for information). However, none of this music commands a wide following today.

Classical Arab music

Another tradition on the wane is **classical Arab music**, with its oriental scales and passionate rhetoric, bravura soloists, massed orchestras and male choirs. On alternate Thursday evenings, the **Arab Music Troupe** performs at the **Gumhorriya Theatre** (☎742-864) in central Cairo. Real enthusiasts should attend the **Saiyid Darwish Concert Hall** in Giza, where the **Umm Kalthoum Classical Arabic Music Troupe** fronts a choral ensemble backed by violinists and cellists on alternate Thursday evenings from September to May (☎852-473). The concert hall (named after the blind musician who revived and adapted this form of music early this century) is on Sharia Gamal al-Din al-Afghani, behind the City of Art south of Pyramids Road (£E5 by taxi from downtown Cairo).

Religious music

All the *moulids* listed under "Festivals" feature **religious music** (the reading or chanting of the Koran), whilst few everyday sounds are more evocative than the call to prayer. Outstanding *muezzins* inspire local pride and professional jealousy. (In a celebrated court case it was ruled that no copyright existed on any expression of the Koran, since Allah created it.) The duet between the Rifai and Sultan Hassan mosques, and the *muezzin* near the *Pension Roma*, are superb.

Belly dancing and nightclubs

A Marxist critique of **belly dancing** would point the finger at imperialism, and with good reason. The European appetite for exotica did much to create the art form as it is known today: a sequinned fusion of classical *raqs sharqi* (oriental dance), stylised harem eroticism and the frank sexuality of the *ghawazee* (public dancers, many of whom moonlighted as prostitutes during the nineteenth century). The association with prostitution has stuck ever since, notwithstanding the fact that most dancers today are dedicated professionals, and the top stars wealthy businesswomen. Dancers tread a line between sensuality and eroticism and Egypt's Moral Majority, thanks to whom they must now wear bodystockings over their midriffs.

Performers

Each star has their own style. **Fifi Abdou** exemplifies the *bint balad*, or streetwise village girl in the big city. Her act includes circus tricks, vulgar posturing and rapping; with awesome vitality, she does three shows a night. **Nagwa Fouad** relies heavily on tight choreography and backup dancers; a regal figure who dances little, but wonderfully during *taqasim* (solo instrumental interludes).

Another of the "older generation" is **Soheir Zaki**, who draws upon the *baladi* style of dance found on Mohammed Ali Boulevard around the turn of the century. In contrast to this artless innocence, **Sahar Hamdi** specialises in obscenity, acting the brothel Madame and sometimes getting busted by the police. **Lucy** (Saad Mohammed Abdel Wahhab) is an all-round show woman who loves singing and includes pop songs, Saudi and Ottoman dances in her repertoire. Young Egyptian men are also enamoured of **Dina**, who dances well but affects simpering coquetry.

Venues

These dancers only do shows at **deluxe hotel nightclubs** (advertised in hotel lobbies and tourist magazines), which provide a delicious four-course meal to tide you through the warm-up acts until the star comes on sometime between midnight and 3am. There's either a minimum rate or flat charge (£E40–60) for the whole deal. Reservations and smart dress are required. The twice nightly show (7.30pm & 10.30pm) at *Felfela's Restaurant* in the Ramses Hilton (☎758-000) centres around the Hassan folkloric troupe and costs £E40.

A step down from this are the somewhat sleazy, rip-off nightclubs **along Pyramids Road**, where the entertainments are varied and sometimes good, but food is usually poor. Two places that are halfway recommendable are *El Leil* and the *Auberge des Pyramids* (both known to taxi drivers), where the music and dancing start around 11pm. Dinner is served as early as 9.30pm.

Cheaper places lurk **downtown**. *Scheherzade*, at the western end of Sharia Alfi Bey, presents an enjoyable mixture of variety acts. Another venue that's reasonably decent is the *Fontana* in the hotel of the same name on Midan Ramses (Sun & Thurs; £E8 minimum charge). Other nightclubs are definitely seedy (prostitution is rife) but can be good fun for mixed groups or self-confident males. The *Arizona* (a little way east of the *Scheherzade*) and the *Miami* (in a passage opposite the *Chemla* store on 26th July Street) charge about £E4 admission and the same for beer – unless you sit right up front, in which case drinks are dearer. The *Stereo Restaurant*, 35 Sharia Qasr el-Nil, sometimes has a belly-dancer after 10pm, but is otherwise just a hostess bar.

Discos

Cairo has a fair number of **discos** but nowhere to rave about. The music is usually last year's hits back home or current Egyptian stuff; lightshows are unsophisticated. But dance floor manners are good, boozy boors are at a minimum and casual/smart dress is acceptable at all but the ritziest places. More problematical is the trend towards a **mixed couples only policy**. Though you might imagine this is to prevent women from being swamped, locals say that it's to stop discos from becoming **gay haunts** (see *Taverne du Champs de Mars*, *Pub 28* and the *Garden Bar* under "Eating and drinking"). In practice, women can usually get in without escorts, but men without women have little chance. Call first to avoid disappointment.

Unless otherwise specified, all of the venues below are open nightly.

Hotel venues

Most of the hotel discos cater to rich foreigners and Westernised Egyptians. *Jackie's* in the Nile Hilton and *Regine's* (of Paris, London and New York) in the

Gezirah Sheraton (both 10am–3pm) admit hotels guests and members only. Other places maintain their cachet by high prices and standards of dress: the *36 Club* on the 36th floor of the Ramses Hilton (5pm–5am; minimum charge £E12 per person); *Sultana* in the Semiramis Intercontinental (10am–5pm); *The Saddle* in the Mena House (10am–3pm); and *Le Baron* in the Heliopolis Sheraton (10pm–4am; £E15 minimum charge for men, £E20 for both sexes on Thurs). More aggravatingly, the *Tamango* atop the Atlas Zamalek Hotel in Mohandiseen (10.30pm–3am; £E11 minimum charge) and the *Club Med* disco on Roda Island (similar hours and rates) restrict admission to mixed couples. Another couples-only venue is *Max's* in the Four Corners complex on Zamalek (10pm–2am).

Cheaper and seedier ...

Less fastidious, **cheaper venues** include *Longchamp* at 21 Sharia Ismail Mohammed, Zamalek (open till 1am; minimum charge £E8), and the *Fontana Hotel* disco (closed Thurs & Sun; same rates). *After Eight*, in the passage at 6 Sharia Qasr el-Nil, is more of a brasserie and does good food (closed July & Aug).

The seediest spot in town is *Audio 9* on the 9th floor of 35 Qasr el-Nil, whose low tables and black drapes reek of the Sixties, sweat and hashish. Active most nights and packed out on reggae night (usually a Thursday), it charges around £E6 admission or the equivalent minimum for drinks. Together with *Longchamp* and *Il Capo*, it may serve as a venue for **transitory events** such as *Africana*, an African disco advertised by word of mouth and posters in cheap hotels, where the music is excellent (£E6 admission charge).

Pub 36 in Ma'adi (take a taxi and ask the driver to get directions from locals) is good for **jazz and African music**.

Cinemas

Most **cinemas** in downtown Cairo are Art Deco relics of the 1930s and 40s, purpose-built for foreigners and trashed by rioters on "Black Saturday" in 1952. Never properly refurbished and now distinctly seedy, they still attract huge, virtually all-male audiences, who cat-call at anything remotely risqué. Lurid hoardings portray grotesquer versions of Hollywood mega-heroes, or the stock characters beloved of *baladi* films (indomitable matriarch, broken patriarch, starcrossed lovers, the hussy and the villain).

Though **foreign movies** are shown throughout the year, there's most choice during winter and Ramadan; see listings in the *Egyptian Gazette*. Because they're subtitled in Arabic, audiences chatter and vendors hawk snacks, drowning out the soundtrack – you have to sit near the front to hear anything. However, the spanking new *Al-Tahrir Cinema* on Sharia Tahrir, past the *Concorde Hotel* in Dokki, has ultra-plush seats (£E2.50–5.50), stereo sound, A/C, and prohibits chattering and smoking. Elsewhere, it's usually okay to buy tickets (£E1) an hour or so beforehand, except during Ramadan when extra evening showings draw full houses and the *Metro Cinema* on Talaat Harb screens a different movie every night (no reserved seats).

To a greater or lesser extent, all films suffer from **censorship**, which sometimes leaves the plot in shreds. The only chance to view uncensored foreign movies comes during the **Cairo International Film Festival**, usually held in the autumn or December. Check the *Egyptian Gazette* or the tourist office for details.

Opera, ballet and theatre

The new **Cairo Opera House** on Gezira (☎342-0603/601-589) is now the chief centre for performing arts. Its main hall hosts performances by prestigious foreign acts (anything from Kabuki theatre to Broadway musicals) and the **Cairo Ballet Company** (from January onwards); the Cairo Opera season begins in March. The smaller hall is used by the **Cairo Symphony Orchestra**, which gives concerts on Friday nights from September to mid-June. Programme listings appear in *Cairo Today* and the *Egyptian Gazette*. Tickets (£E5–30) should be booked several days beforehand (daily 10am–3pm & 4–8pm). A jacket and tie are compulsory for men.

Another venue for Western-style performing arts is the AUC's **Wallace Theatre** (☎354-2964), which produces two English-language **plays** or **musicals** and sponsors diverse concerts from October to May, advertised on campus and in local newspapers. You might also hear about productions by two theatre groups run by Cairo's expat community, the **Cairo Players** (☎712-862) and the **Ma'adi Players** (☎350-3193) – both open to anyone who's interested – while for those who understand Arabic, the range encompasses everything from **avant garde drama** at the **Thalia Theatre** (☎937-948) on Midan Ataba to **politcal satire** at the **Miami Theatre** on Talaat Harb (closed Mon).

Religious festivals and weddings

Though few foreign visitors frequent them, Cairo's **religious festivals** are quite accessible to outsiders – and a lot of fun. Many begin with a *zaffa* (parade) of Sufis carrying banners, drums and tambourines, who later perform marathon *zikrs*, chanting and swaying themselves into the trance-like state known as *jazb*. Meanwhile, the crowd is entertained by acrobats, stick dancers, dancing horses, fortune-tellers and other sideshows – Cairenes see nothing incongruous in combining piety with revelry.

Whilst most festivals are specifically Muslim or Christian, people of both faiths attend the birthday or name-day celebrations of holy persons with *baraka* (the power of blessing) – known as **moulids**. Aside from the crowds (don't bring valuables, or come unescorted if you're a woman), the only problem is ascertaining festival **dates**. Different events are related to the Islamic, Coptic or secular calendar, and sometimes to a particular day rather than a certain date, so details below should be double-checked with Egyptian friends or the tourist office. As a rule, all the longer *moulids* climax in a *leyla kebira* (literally "big night") on the last evening or the eve of the last day – the most spectacular and crowded phase.

Muslim festivals

Most **Muslim festivals** follow the Islamic calendar, whose New Year begins on *Ras el-Sana el-Hegira*, the first day of Moharram.

MOHARRAM
The initial ten days of this first month are blessed, especially the eve of the tenth day (*Leylat Ashura*), which commemorates the martyrdom of Hussein at Karbala. Until this century, it witnessed passionate displays by Cairo's Shia minority, whose menfolk lashed themselves with chains. Nowadays, Sunni Muslims

observe the following day (*Yom Ashura*) with prayers and charity; wealthy folk often undertake to feed poor families, serving them personally to demonstrate humility. But aside from *zikrs* outside Hussein's Mosque, there's little to see.

THE HADJ AND PROPHET'S BIRTHDAY

In olden days the **return of the pilgrims** from Mecca (*Nezlet el-Hagg*) occasioned great festivities at the Bab al-Futuh towards the end of Safar, the second month. Nowadays, celebrations are localised, as pilgrims are feasted on the evening of their return, their homes festooned with red and white bunting and painted with *Hadj* scenes. However, it's still customary to congregate below the Citadel a week later and render thanksgiving *zikrs* in the evening.

Previously, these gatherings blended into the celebrations of the **Prophet's birthday** (*Moulid al-Nabi*) during the next month, Rabi al-Awwal, which run from the third day to the night of the twelfth, the last being its great day. The eve of the twelfth – known as the Blessed Night (*Leylat Mubarak*) – witnesses spectacular processions and fireworks, with *munshids* (singers of poetry) invoking spiritual aid whilst crowds chant "*Allahu Hei! Ya Daim!*" (God is Living! O Everlasting!). Midan el-Hussein, the Rifai Mosque and Ezbekiya Gardens are the best sites to observe the festivities.

RABI EL-TANI

During the following month, Rabi el-Tani, the **Moulid of El-Hussein** gathers pace over a fortnight, its big day invariably falling on a Tuesday, its *leyla kebira* on Wednesday night. Hussein's Mosque in Khan el-Khalili is surrounded by crowds chanting "*Allah Mowlana!*" (God is our Lord!), dozens of *zikrs* and amplified *munshids*, plus all the usual sideshows.

Sometime during the same month, the smaller **Moulid of Saiyida Sukayna** takes place at her mosque on Sharia el-Khalifa (see map on p.113).

GUMAD EL-TANI

On a Thursday or Friday in the middle of the sixth month, Gumad el-Tani, Sufis of the Rifai order attend the **Moulid of al-Rifai** at his mosque below the Citadel. Those carrying black flags belong to the mainstream Rifaiyah; subsects include the Awlad Ilwan (once famous for thrusting nails into their eyes and swallowing hot coals) and the Sa'adiya (snake charmers, who used to allow their sheikh to ride over them on horeseback).

Dervishes are less evident at the **Moulid of Saiyida Nafisa** (on a Wednesday or Thursday mid-month, or a Tuesday towards the end of the month), but the event is equally colourful.

RAGAB

Ragab, the seventh month, is dominated by the great **Moulid of Saiyida Zeinab**, Cairo's "patron saint", which lasts for fifteen days and attracts up to one million people on its big day and *leyla kebira*, falling on a Tuesday and Wednesday in the middle of the month.

A much smaller, "local" event is the **Moulid of Sheikh al-Dashuti** on the 26th Ragab, at his mosque near the junction of Faggala and Bur Said streets, 1km northwest of the Bab al-Futuh.

The eve of the 27th is observed by all Muslims as the *Leylat el-Mirag* or **Night of Ascension**, occasioning *zikrs* outside the Abdin Palace and principal mosques.

WHIRLING DERVISHES

The *Mowlawiyya* are Egyptian adherents of a Sufi sect founded in Konya, Turkey, during the mid-thirteenth century, and known to Westerners as the **Whirling Dervishes**. Their Turkish name, *Mevlevi*, refers to their original Master, who extolled music and dancing as a way of shedding earthly ties and abandoning oneself to God's love. The Sufi ideal of attaining union with God has often been regarded by orthodox Muslims as blasphemous, and only during Mamluke and Ottoman times did the Whirling Dervishes flourish without persecution.

In modern Egypt, the sect is minuscule compared to other Sufi orders and rarely appears at *moulids*, but a tourist version of the famous whirling ceremony is staged at the Ghuriya cultural centre in al-Ghuri's Mausoleum (see map on p.100). If the *Mowlawiyya* are in Cairo, **performances** are held on Wednesdays and Saturdays around 8–9pm; drop in during the day and ask if one is scheduled.

Each element of the **whirling ceremony** (*samaa*) has symbolic significance. The music symbolises that of the spheres, and the turning of the dervishes that of the heavenly bodies. The gesture of extending the right arm towards heaven and the left towards the floor denotes that grace is being received from God and distributed to humanity without anything being retained by the dervishes. Their camelhair hats represent tombstones; their black cloaks the tomb itself; their white skirts shrouds. During the *samaa* the cloaks are discarded, denoting that the dervishes have escaped from their tombs and all other earthly ties.

SHA'BAN

During the eighth month, Sha'ban, the week-long **Moulid of Imam al-Shafi'i** enlivens his mausoleum in the Southern Cemetery (see p.117) from one Wednesday to another. The eve of the 15th is believed to be the time when Allah determines the fate of every human over the ensuing year, so the faithful hope to gain *baraka*.

RAMADAN AND THE EID AL-FITR

The sighting of the new moon on the *Leylat er-Ruyeh* (Night of Observation) marks the onset of **Ramadan** – a month of fasting from sunrise to sunset, with festivities every night (see p.40). *Zikrs* and Koranic recitations draw crowds to el-Gumhorriya and el-Hussein squares, whilst secular delights are concentrated around Ezbekiya and other areas. For £E10, you can enjoy unlimited soft drinks, musicians, singers and fortune-tellers within the garden of *Al-Sokkareya* (8pm–3am) near the *al-Salam Hyatt* in Heliopolis (bus #50, #128 or #330). The *Leylat el-Qadr* (Night of Power) on the eve of the 27th was traditionally marked by Whirling and Howling dervishes at Mohammed Ali's Mosque on the Citadel.

The end of Ramadan heralds the three-day **Eid al-Fitr** or "Little Feast", when people buy new clothes, visit friends, mosques, shrines and family graves. In bygone days, this was followed by the procession of the *kisweh* (the brocaded cloth which covers the sacred Ka'ba at Mecca), a prelude to the departure of the pilgrims around the 23rd day of Shawwal. Given modern transport, however, most pilgrims now depart the following month, Zoul Qiddah, with local send-offs that counterpoint the *Nezlet al-Hagg*.

ZOUL HAGGA

The twelfth month, Zoul Hagga, is notable for the "Feast of Sacrifice" or **Eid al-Adha** (the "Great Feast", **Corban Bairam**), which involves the mass slaughter of sheep and other livestock on the 10th, commemorating Ibrahim's willingness to sacrifice Ismail to Allah (the Muslim version of the story of Abraham and Isaac).

MOULID OF SIDI ALI AL-BAYOUMI
Last but not least, there's another colourful parade of dervishes at the **Moulid of Sidi Ali al-Bayoumi**, the Rifai sects proceeding from El-Hussein's Mosque to the Bab al-Futuh and thence into the Husseiniya quarter. Unlike most Muslim festivals, this is unrelated to the Islamic calendar, happening early in **October**.

Coptic festivals

It should be emphasised that **Coptic festivals** are primarily religious, with fewer diversions than Muslim ones. Unless you're into church services, the "moveable" feasts centred around Easter (which follow the Coptic calendar rather than the Western one), Christmas (January 7), Epiphany (January 19) and the Feast of Annunciation (March 21) have little to offer.

However, there's more to enjoy at two festivals in Old Cairo: the **Moulid of Mari Girgis** at the round Church of Saint George (April 23) and the **Moulid of the Holy Family** at the Church of Saint Sergius (June 1). Moreover, all Egyptians observe the ancient pharaonic-Coptic spring festival known as **Sham el-Nessim** (literally "Sniffing the Breeze"), when families picnic on salted fish, onions and coloured eggs in gardens and cemeteries.

Weddings

There's nothing bashful about Cairo **weddings** or the curiosity of spectators. On Thursday nights the city resounds with convoys of honking cars conveying guests to Nile-side hotels and casinos; ululations, drums and tambourines welcoming the newlyweds (often preceded by a belly dancer), whom relatives shower with rose petals. In poorer quarters all the bridal furniture and wedding guests are first displayed to admiring neighbours.

At the reception itself, the couple sit receiving congratulations ("*Alf mabrouk*" is the formal salutation) whilst relatives and friends perform impromptu dances. Guests may be segregated, allowing both sexes to let their hair down: women can dance and smoke, men indulge in spirits (or hashish, in private homes). Although it's not uncommon for foreign onlookers to be invited into middle-class or *baladi* wedding parties, rich ones are predictably exclusive, but good for a brief show.

Activities and kids' stuff

The two classic tourist activities are riding in the desert near the Pyramids and sailing on the Nile in a *felucca*. Other more or less adventurous trips are covered at the end of this chapter under "Excursions from Cairo".

Riding in the desert

Despite the pitfalls mentioned under "The Pyramids of Giza", **riding in the desert** is a fantastic experience. Unless you relish haggling, authorised stables are a safer bet than footloose Bedouin operators. Stables behind the Sound and

Light grandstand near the Sphinx include *AA* (☎850-531), which is good for kids, *Eurostables* (☎855-849) and *MG Stables* (☎853-832/851-241). To avail yourself of *Omar Stables* (☎850-301), ask for Mohammed or Adel Omar in the Pyramids Bazaar opposite the Mena House. You can also use the *Ferrosea Riding Club* on the south edge of the Gezira Club, Zamalek, and take lessons at Heliopolis Racing Club (☎245-4090).

Felucca sailing and gliding

Something as restful as **sailing on the Nile in a felucca** can hardly be termed an activity. Since the boatman does all the work, the only effort involved is negotiating rates of hire (£E8–10 an hour by day, £E12–17 in the evening). Most of the *feluccas* moored along the riverbank between *Shepheard's Hotel* and the northern tip of Roda can seat eight people. Bring a picnic dinner and lots of mosquito repellent. For a cheaper no-frills ride on the Nile, catch a river-taxi (25pt) from the Maspero Dock to Giza.

An off-the-wall alternative which might appeal is **gliding** at Imbaba airport over the weekend. Besides giving lessons, the Egyptian Gliding Institute offers hour-long **sightseeing flights over Cairo or the Pyramids of Giza** for about £E35 per person. Ask the tourist office to phone and fix things up.

Swimming pools

Swimming pools take on an extra allure in Cairo, whose only "public" pool is the *Heliolido* (☎258-0070) off Midan Roxi (open April–Oct; £E3.50 admission). The nearby *Heliopolis Sporting Club* (☎671-414) on Sharia Merghani has a larger pool and admits foreigners over the summer (bring your passport), but the entrance fee (£E5) doesn't cover use of the facilities. The *Gezira Sporting Club* (☎342-0800) limits access to members ($30/$50 per week; $55/$100 per month for single/married tourist membership) or their guests (£E3 daily).

Hotel pools are more accessible, the best being the *Gezirah Sheraton* (£E15), *Cairo Marriott* (£E25) and *Atlas Zamelek* (April–Oct only; £E8 minimum charge), and the **poolside buffets** at the *Manial Palace Club Med* (☎344-083) and *Meridien* hotels on Roda Island (£E36 and £E18, respectively). The rooftop pool of the *Fontana Hotel*, off Ramses, is cheaper for dipping (£E7) but hardly big enough to swim. For those who'd rather sweat it out, £E15 buys a **sauna** at the *Gezirah Sheraton*, a sauna and Turkish bath at the *Nile Hilton*, or both plus **jacuzi** at the *Ramses Hilton*.

Hammams

A totally different experience is available at traditional **hammams** (bathhouses), whose nondescript facades conceal gloomy warrens of sweatrooms and tubs. The only real difference from Ottoman times is that male bathers are prudish rather than promiscuous. With no mixed bathing, women can ignore taboos and talk frankly; foreigners may be adopted into their circle, which usually includes kids being scrubbed.

Some baths serve men in the morning and women in the afternoon; others assign them separate days, or only admit one sex. Ask **around Islamic Cairo** – most of the baths are located on maps in that section. The oldest, dating from

1261, is the *Hammam al-Sultan*, beside Barquq's complex on Sharia al-Muizz. Nearer to the Northern Walls are the eighteenth-century *Hammam al-Malatyah* (on Sharia Amir al-Gyushi) and the harder-to-find *Hammam al-Tanbali* (near the el-Geish end of Bayn al-Haret, 1km east of Ramses). Around the Bab Zwayla are the Mamluke *as-Sukayna* and *al-Muayyad* baths, and the Ottoman *Hammam al-Sukkariyya*. A medieval facade halfway down Sharia es-Silah screens the modernised *Hammam Bashtak*, for **women only**.

Sports

Keeping fit in Cairo is difficult but not impossible. The expatriate *Hash House Harriers* (contact Philip Wanless ☎291-7687 or Terry Evans ☎351-6911) are one of several clubs organising **street running**, best done on Gezira, Roda or the west bank Corniche before 8am or after 10pm to avoid heavy traffic and air pollution. By paying £E1 to enter the Youth Club under the Giza side of the 6th October Bridge, you can "stray" into the Gezira Sporting Club – just keep away from the built-up area near the running track, where guards check for tickets.

Although the Gezira Sporting Club's extensive facilities are only available to members and guests (see above), anyone can use **gymnasiums** in the *Marriott* (£E25 a visit), *Nile Hilton* (£E5 per hour) and *Atlas Zamalek* (£E10 per day) hotels. Sweaty local clubs include the *Gamaet al-Subayn el Muslimeen* (12 Sharia Ramses), *Nady Mahad el-Continental* (26th July Street) and *Nady Shababeen Musrayeen* (Sharia Nubar, near Midan Lazoghli) – contact the *Egyptian Weightlifting Federation* (13 Sharia Qasr el-Nil; ☎753-296) for details.

Non-residents can play **golf** at the *Mena House Hotel* for about £E25 a day. Contact Seif (☎392-2907/341-5121) about *Cairo Diver's Club* courses in **scuba diving** and trips to the Red Sea reefs.

Spectator sport: football, horse racing and rowing

During the **football** season (Sept–May), premier league teams *Ahly* and *Zamalek* take on challengers like *Mahalla* and *Naseig Helwan* at the Cairo Stadium in Heliopolis (Fri, Sat & Sun). Tickets cost 50pt–£E10; kick-off is at 3pm. Riot policemen with machine-guns are regularly in attendance at matches since football riots, though infrequent, are extremely bloody.

The Saturday *Egyptian Mail* also gives details of **horse racing** at the Heliopolis Hippodrome Course and the Gezira race track, from mid-October to mid-May. Races start at 1.30pm every other Saturday and Sunday. From November to April, Cairo's bridges provide a fine view of **rowing** races every Friday.

Chiefly for kids

Besides the following places, children (and adults) should enjoy *felucca* and camel rides, the Sound and Light show and theme-restaurants at Giza (see "The Pyramids" and "Eating and drinking"). Because of Cairo's density, most of the parks and pleasure grounds are on the islands or the west bank.

The Aquarium and Zoo

The **Aquarium Grotto** in Galabaya Park on Zamalek (daily 8.30am–3.30pm; 20pt) displays 195 kinds of tropical fish amidst a labyrinth of passageways and stairs that kids will love to explore.

For a larger park and more to see, check out **Cairo Zoo** – regarded as the finest in the world when it was founded in 1890 (daily 6am–5pm; 20pt) – and the **El Urman Gardens** (Sat–Wed 8am–8pm, Thurs 8am–noon; 10pt) across the road, a stately remnant of the Khedival Gardens laid out by the French. Both can be reached from Midan Tahrir by buses (#8 or #900) which run past the Manial Palace (see p.134) – another place that kids should enjoy. Try to avoid Fridays, weekends or public holidays, when the zoo is packed with picnicking families.

Dr Ragab's Pharaonic Village

Reached by half-hourly boats from the Corniche 2km south of the Giza Bridge, **Dr Ragab's Pharaonic Village** (☎729-053/729-189) is a kitsch simulation of ancient Egypt on Jacob Island, upriver from Roda. During the two-hour tour, visitors survey the Canal of Mythology (flanked by statues of gods) and scores of costumed Egyptians performing tasks from their floating "time machines", before being shown around a replica temple and nobleman's villa; a pyramid is under way. It is open daily 9.30am–3.30pm in winter, 9am–8pm in summer; tickets £E20 per head, free for children under six.

The Circus, puppets and Planetarium

Those who enjoy animals performing tricks, acrobats, clowns and trapeze artists should visit the **National Circus** (☎346-4870) in Aguza, next to the Balloon Theatre near the Zamalek Bridge. The box office opens at 2.30pm (tickets £E2–5); performances run from 9.30 to 11.30pm. Another traditional diversion is the **Cairo Puppet Theatre** (☎910-954) in Ezbekiya Gardens, which stages *Sinbad the Sailor*, *Ali Baba* and other favourites (Thurs–Sun at 6.30pm; also at 11pm on Fri & Sun), or campy musicals during season (Oct–May).

Shows in the **Gezira Planetarium** (Sat–Thurs 7pm) are likewise in Arabic, but groups can arrange English-language performances through Dr M. Ahmed Sulayman (☎341-2453).

Rides and games

Fun rides and games are on offer at the **Cookie Amusement Park** near the Giza Pyramids (from 3pm till late; opens at noon on Fri) and the larger **Sinbad Amusement Park** near Cairo airport, which has bumper cars, a small roller coaster and lots of rides for tots (winter Sat–Thurs 2–11pm, Fri 10am–11pm; summer daily 5pm–2am). **Merryland** on Sharia al-Higaz, off Midan Roxi in Heliopolis, is a safe environment to play, with a merry-go-round, pedallo lake and small zoo (daily 9.30am–midnight; 20pt).

Shopping: bazaars and markets

Shopping in Cairo is a time-consuming process, which suits most locals fine. Cairenes regard it as a social event involving salutations and dickering, affirmations of status and servility; smoothly impersonal transactions are not an ideal. Excluding Government Stores, there are basically three types of retail outlet:

● **Department stores** (generally open 9am–1pm & 5–8pm; closed Sun) have fixed prices and the tedious system where you select the goods and get a chit, pay the cashier and then claim your purchases from a third counter.

● **Smaller shops**, usually run by the owner, stay open till 9 or 10pm and tend to specialise in certain wares. Although most of them have fixed prices, tourists who don't understand Arabic price tags or Egyptian currency are liable to overcharging (around the Khan and Talaat Harb, especially). If you know the correct price, attempts can be thwarted by handing over the exact sum (or as near as possible).

● In **markets** and **bazaars** haggling prevails, so it's worth window-shopping around fixed-price stores before **bargaining** for lower rates in bazaar stalls. When asked for a quote, merchants often riposte: "What do you think?" Suggest an absurdly low sum to make them respond and don't be fazed by mockery – it's all part of the game. Buyers' tactics include stressing any flaws that might reduce the object's value; talking of lower quotes received elsewhere; feigning indifference or having a friend urge you to leave. Avoid being tricked into raising your bid twice in a row, or admitting your estimation of the object's worth (just reply that you've made an offer).

Providing you don't make an offer they're willing to accept, it's okay to terminate a lengthy session without buying anything.

MARKETS

Although the bazaars deal in more exotic goods, Cairo's **markets** provide an arresting spectacle, free of the touristy slickness that prevails around the Khan. Watch how people bargain over the humblest items (often recycled from other products), a paradigm of free enterprise in the gutter. What isn't apparent are the customs, guilds and rackets that govern business, as exemplified by the vast wholesale market at Rod el-Farag (see p.144), whence **fruit and vegetables** are distributed throughout the city. Street markets in central Cairo can be found at Bab al-Luq, half-way up Sharia Orabi, at the eastern end of Sheikh al-Rihan, and along Sharia Qalaa – all of which do business through the night, accompanied by local coffeehouses. With the kilo price displayed on stalls in Arabic numerals, you shouldn't have to bargain unless they try to overcharge.

Elsewhere haggling is *de rigueur*. Promising locations are listed below.

• The daily **Army Surplus Market** near Ramses Station (see map on p.80) sells everything from boots and tents to jerrycans and insignia; be sure to wash anything purchased here.

• Secondhand clothing can also be found in the *canto* section of the **Imam al-Shafi'i Market**, which straggles for 1km along the road leading from al-Basatin to the Imam's mausoleum in the El-Khalifa district. Other parts of this Friday morning market sell scrap, grain, poultry, sheep and cattle.

• The famous **Imbaba Camel Market** is described on p.138.

• Cairo's **Bird Markets** are named after the days on which they're held (10am–2.30pm): *Souk al-Hadd* (Sun; Giza Station), *Souk al-Gom'a* (Fri; by the Salah Salem overpass, south of the Citadel), and *Souk Itnayn w Khamis* (Mon & Thurs; in the Abu Rish area of Saiyida Zeinab). The locations of the last two are shown on p.113 and p.122.

• On Sharia el-Geish near Midan Ataba there's a daily **Paper Market**, with all types of paper, dyed leather and art materials.

• For **fabrics** (from handloomed silk to cheap offcuts), **tools** and much else, you can't beat the daily **Wikalat al-Bulah**, on Sharia Abu'l'Ila in the Bulaq district.

• For **car spares**, visit the daily **Souk Lazoghli** on Midan Lazoghli (between Abdin and Saiyida Zeinab), where repairs can also be arranged.

• **Cars** are bought and sold at the Friday market (10am–3pm) on Midan al-Ittihad in Ma'adi, along **Road 105**.

RAMADAN HOURS

During Ramadan (see p.40), shopping hours go haywire, as some places close all day and operate through the night, whilst others open later and close earlier. Given that people splurge after sundown, Cairo's boutiques and bazaars are busy then as Western stores before Christmas.

Souvenirs and antiques

Scores of shops in the Khan and central Cairo purvey **souvenirs**, mostly kitsch reproductions of pharaonic art – scarabs, statuettes of deities, busts of Nefertiti, eyes of Horus – which are cheaper to buy at source in Luxor or Aswan.

Sheets of **papyrus** painted with scenes from temples or tombs are equally ubiquitous, though much is actually made from banana leaves – genuine papyrus should be able to withstand crumpling without cracking (though paint won't!). But the important thing is whether you like the painting. Prices range from around £E4 to £E80 depending on size, intricacy, the quantity of gold paint used and where you're buying: places around the Pyramids, in big hotels and the Khan tend to be overpriced; if you've got the stomach to bargain them down, itinerant street-vendors give better deals. You can see papyrus-making demonstrated at Dr Ragab's Papyrus Institute (p.167).

Copies of **prints** by David Roberts and other nineteenth-century illustrators also make nice souvenirs. For cheap poster-sized or postcard editions, check out *Reader's Corner* and *Lehnert and Landrock*; costlier original engravings are sold at *L'Orientalist* (addresses under "Books and Newspapers", following).

Antiques

Selling fake *antikas* (with spurious certificates) is an old tradition. Genuine pharaonic, Coptic or Islamic **antiques** cannot be exported without a licence from the Department of Antiquities. Old reproductions and foreign-made antiques are a safer bet. Dealers in the Khan include *Lotus Palace* (7 Sharia Khan el-Khalili), and *Oriental Souvenirs* and *Ahmed Dahba* (both at 5 Sikket al-Badestan).

Brass and copperware

Egyptian craftsmen have been turning out **brass and copperware** for over a thousand years, and aside from the tourist trade there's still a big domestic market for everything from banqueting trays to minaret finials. Amongst the items favoured as souvenirs are candlesticks, waterpipes, gongs, coffee sets, embossed plates and inlaid or repoussé trays (the larger ones are often mounted on stands to serve as tables). All of these are manufactured and sold within the Khan, particularly along the stretch of Sharia al-Muizz just before Qalaoun's complex, known as the **Coppersmiths' Bazaar** (*Souk al-Nahhasin*).

Although the Khan offers the best range of decorative pieces (small plates from about £E6), it's cheaper to buy Turkish coffeepots and hubble-bubbles between the Ghuriya and the Bab Zwayla, along Ahmed Maher, or from workshops on Sharia Khulud and other streets around Ramses, where a set of five **coffeepots** costs £E12–14. Be sure that anything you intend to drink out of is lined with tin or silver, since brass and copper react with certain substances to form toxic compounds. Test **waterpipes** for leaky joints (the glass-bottomed ones are usually better) and remember to call them *sheeshas* or *narghiles* rather than *hookahs* (which signifies hashish-smoking). *Mohammed Hassan* and *Mahmoud Eid*, facing the Barquq complex, both specialise in waterpipes, backgammon boards and other coffeehouse sundries.

Carpets, appliqué and basketwork

Pure wool kilims and knotted carpets are an expensive (and bulky) purchase in any country, so serious buyers are advised to read *Egyptian Carpets* (see "Books" under *Contexts*) before spending hundreds of pounds on one. As most Egyptian **kilims** (pile-less rugs) and **knotted carpets** have half as many knots (16 per centimetre) as their Turkish counterparts, they should be significantly cheaper – especially the ones made from native wool rather than the high-grade imported stuff used in finer kilims. Prices posted in downtown stores like *Kazarouni* (22 Qasr el-Nil), *Ismail Ali* (Midan Opera), *Abdou Moustafa* and *Ashraf Exhibition* (both on Sharia Sherif) can give you an idea of what to aim for in the bazaar.

Tapestries and rugs
More affordable – and ubiquitous – are the **tapestries and rugs** woven from coarse wool and/or camel hair. These come in two basic styles. Bedouin rugs carry geometric patterns in shades of brown and beige and are usually loosely woven (often purely from camel hair). The other style, deriving from the famous Wissa Wassef School at Harraniyya (p.177), features colourful images of birds, trees and village life. Beware of stitched-together seams and gaps in the weave (hold pieces up against the light), and unfast colours – if any colour wipes off on a damp cloth, the dyes will run when the rug is washed. Depending on size and complexity of design, rugs cost anywhere between £E10 and £E200 in Cairo; prices in Aswan are generally a bit lower.

Whilst the suburban village of Kerdassa (p.177) replicates every style imaginable, the only authorised outlet for genuine Harraniyya tapestries and batiks is *Senouhi*, on the fifth floor of 54 Sharia Abdel Khaliq Sarwat (☎910-955; Mon–Fri 10am–5pm, Sat 10am–1pm). Crammed with carpets, jewellery, Bedouin embroidery and modern paintings, this small store is a fascinating place to browse. The best site in the bazaar is Haret al-Fahhamin (see "Spices and Perfume", below), where you can compare *Rashidi* and *Shahatta Talba Manna* (both at no. 11) with *Hamid Ibrahim Abdel Aal* (no. 5). *Marc Antoine Fouad Hajj* (5 Sikket Khan el-Khalili) specialises in rugs woven by families in Assyut and the Fayoum.

Tent-making and appliqué
The traditional Cairene crafts of tent-making and appliqué work are still practised in half a dozen tiny workshops inside the Qasaba, near the Bab Zwayla – hence its sobriquet, the **Tentmakers' Bazaar** (*Souk al-Khiyamiyya*). Colourful **appliqué work** comes in various forms. Some designs are pictorial, based on pharaonic motifs or romantic Arab imagery; others are abstract, delicate arabesques (which tend to be dearer). Prices vary according to size and intricacy. A zippered pillowslip or cushion cover costs £E10–50; larger pieces, to be used as hangings, go for upwards of £E100, whilst bedspread-sized ones start at roughly £E300. A much cheaper alternative is the riotously patterned **printed tent fabric**

used for marquees at *moulids* or to screen unsightly building work. This costs about £E4 per metre length, cut from a bolt of cloth roughly 1.5m wide; offcuts are cheaper still.

Another cheap souvenir is palm-frond **basketwork**, mostly from the Fayoum and Upper Egypt. Fayoumi baskets (for sewing, shopping or laundry) are more practical, but it's hard to resist the woven platters from Luxor and Aswan, as vibrantly colourful as parrots. You may also find baskets from Siwa Oasis, trimmed with tassels. Most baskets cost between £E2 and £E10.

Clothing and leatherwork

As a cotton-growing country with a major textiles industry, Egypt is big on retail **clothing**. Smartly dressed Cairenes are forever window-shopping along Talaat Harb and 26th July (downtown), Sharia al-Ahram (Heliopolis) and Arab League Street (Mohandiseen), to name only the main clusters of **boutiques** (open till 9–10pm). For those who want familiar labels, there's a branch of *Benetton* at 114 Sharia Mohammed Farid. Staider threads can be had in **department stores** like *Chemla* and *Cicurel* on 26th July Street, or *Omar Effendi* on Talaat Harb and Sharia Adly (9am–1pm & 5–8pm). The cheapest outlet for clothes are **street vendors** in Ezbekiya Gardens and the Muski (see also "Markets", below).

Egyptian clothes

Although few tourists can wear them outdoors without looking silly, many take home a caftan or *galabiyya* for lounging attire. Women's **caftans** are made of cotton, silk or wool, generally A-line, with long, wide sleeves and a round or mandarin collar (often braided). Men's **galabiyyas** come in three basic styles. *Ifrangi* (foreign) resembles a floor-length tailored shirt with collar and cuffs; the *Saudi* style is more form-fitting, with a high-buttoned neck and no collar; whilst *baladi* galabiyyas have very wide sleeves and a low, rounded neckline.

The fixed prices in downtown shops should be beatable by hard bargaining **in the Khan**, which also features two fixed-price stores. *Ouf* (pronounced "oaf"), at the end of an alley leading west off the Spice Bazaar, stocks a wide assortment of ready-mades at reasonable prices, including black dresses with Bedouin-style embroidery (£E15). *Atlas*, on Sikket al-Badestan, does made-to-order garments in handwoven fabrics with intricate braidwork (allow several weeks; keep all receipts). Their cheapest caftans (£E60) and *galabiyyas* (£E25) are dearer than most garments in other shops.

Another fetching item are the heavy, woven, fringed or tassled black **shawls** worn by *baladi* women, which are sold along the Muski for upwards of £E8, depending on their size and composition (nylon or silk); check for any snags or tears in the weave. If you want to go the whole hog, invest in a *melaya*, the flowing black ankle-length wraps which *baladi* women wear over their house dresses when they go outdoors.

Shoes

The biggest retail item has to be **shoes**, which fill dozens of shops along Talaat Harb and 26th July, where assistants have to dust every pair before closing (around 9–10pm). *Bedros* and *Bellina* (20 Talaat Harb) have a big selection; funky canvas shoes and coloured boots can be bought at *Lofti* (Midan Talaat Harb); for cheap trainers, try around Ezbekiya and the Muski.

Leatherwork

Egyptian **leatherwork** is nice and colourful, if not up to the standards of its Turkish rival. You can get an idea of the range of products from several shops along Sikket Khan el-Khalili. Leather jackets cost £E120–200. Cheaper wallets, handbags and pouffes (tuffets) are sold throughout the Khan and central Cairo, whilst camel-saddles in a variety of colours and sizes (£E20–50) are still produced in the **Saddlemakers' Bazaar** (*Souk es-Surugiyyah*), south of the Qasaba.

Gold and silver jewellery

Most Egyptians still regard **jewellery** as safer than money in the bank; for women in particular, it constitutes a safety net in case of divorce or bereavement. Pharaonic, Coptic and Islamic motifs, Bedouin, Nubian and oasis designs, work from Syria, Jordan, Yemen and Arabia – Cairo's jewellers stock them all, and can also make pieces to order.

Gold and silver are sold by the gramme, with a percentage added on for workmanship. Bullion prices fluctuate but Egyptian wages remain low. The current ounce price of gold is printed in the daily *Egyptian Gazette*; one ounce equals about 28 grammes. Barring antiques, all **gold** work is stamped with Arabic numerals indicating its purity: usually 21 carat for Bedouin, Nubian or *fellaheen* jewellery; 18 carat for Middle Eastern and European-style charms and chains. Sterling **silver** (80 or 92.5 percent) is likewise stamped, whilst a gold camel in the shop window indicates that the items are **gold-plated brass**.

The Goldsmiths' Bazaar

Downtown jewellers are concentrated along Sharia Abdel Khaliq Sarawt and Sikket al-Manakh, near Opera Square. In Islamic Cairo, the **Goldsmiths' Bazaar** (*Souk es-Sagha*) covers Sharia al-Muizz between the Muski and Sultan Qalaoun's complex, and infiltrates the heart of the Khan via Sikkets al-Badestan and Khan el-Khalili, two medieval lanes whose gateways now denote addresses (eg Bab al-Awwal, "First Gate"). For gold-plated *fellaheen* designs, check out *Sigal* and *Al Gamal Jewellery* on Sharia al-Muizz. Oasian gold can be found at *Adel Rizk*, off to the right near Bab al-Awwal, and at *Gundi Shenouda*, Bab al-Talat; the latter also sells original *faraoni* necklaces from Upper Egypt. *Adly Fam* (72 Muski) specialises in 21-carat *fellaheen* jewellery; *Youssef Moustapha Sudani* (16 Sharia al-Maqasis) in Nubian goldwork. There are several good **silversmiths** in the Wikala al-Gawarhergia (ask for directions).

The most popular souvenirs are gold or silver **cartouches** with given names in hieroglyphics. The price depends on the quantity of metal used, and whether the characters are engraved or glued on. Thin gold cartouches with glued letters cost about £E60; thicker ones with soldered letters £E90–170; silver cartouches are much cheaper (£E10 upwards).

Glass, ceramics and precious stones

A number of primitive factories on Haret al-Birkedar in the Gamaliya quarter still produce **Muski glass**, an inferior form of hand-blown glassware popular in medieval times, which is nowadays made from recycled bottles. Recognisable by its air bubbles and extreme fragility, Muski glass comes in five main colours (navy blue, turquoise, aquamarine, green and purple) and is fashioned into inexpensive glasses, plates, vases, candle-holders and ashtrays – sometimes painted with arabesque designs in imitation of enamelled Mamluke glassware. Aside from the factories, the main stockist is *Saiyid Abd al-Raouf* (8 Sikket Khan el-Khalili).

Pottery and alabaster

Robust **household pottery** is sold outdoors near the Mosque of Amr in Old Cairo, along Sharia al-Ahram in Giza and the Corniche between Cairo and Ma'adi. For more refined **ceramics**, check out *Senouhi* (see above), *Sornaga* (on Sharia Labanas, between Qasr el-Nil and Mohammed Sabri street) and Ma'adi galleries such as *Al Patio* (6, Road 77c) and *Haddouta* (Sharia Amira, New Ma'adi).

Vases and sculptures made from **alabaster** are ubiquitous in Cairo's tourist marts, but you can get better deals at source, in Luxor.

Precious stones

Although nothing can substitute for experience, it's worth relating a few tips about **precious stones**, which Egypt imports from all over, having exhausted its own by centuries of mining. Most emeralds in Egypt are of poor quality (good ones are clear, dark green); very large or transparent rubies (from India and Burma) are almost certainly fake, and real sapphires should also be opaque. True amber will float when put in salt water. Pearls (from the Gulf Emirates and Japan) should feel like glass if tapped against your teeth, whilst German onyx should be opaque and make a sharp sound if dropped onto glass, and genuine turquoise (from Sinai, Iran or the USA) should contain streaks and impurities. To test the authenticity of Brazilian topaz, amethyst or aquamarine, place them on a sheet of white paper – genuine ones should have only two shades within the stone.

Dealers on Sikket Khan el-Khalili include *Ali Ahmed al-Kolaly* (no. 5), *Farouk Abd al-Khalek* (no. 6), *Ali Koborrassany* (no. 12) and *Emil Sif Falamon* (☎906-168).

Mashrabiya and inlay work

With little demand for the huge latticed screens that once covered nearly every window in Cairo, modern **mashrabiya-work** is usually confined to decorative screens and table stands (see "Brass and copperware", above). Generally made of imported red birch or oak, they consist of scores or hundreds of turned wooden beads, joined by dowels and glue, without nails. The technique is also applied to Koran stands (which make splendid magazine racks), the fancier ones being embellished with mother-of-pearl, bone and other inlays.

Inlay work: boxes, backgammon and chess boards

Inlaid **boxes** come in all sizes, from cigar holders to multi-drawer jewellery caskets. Small boxes cost upwards of £E7; prices increase with size and quality of workmanship. **Backgammon boards** (*thowla* – pronounced "dow-la") broadly come in two varieties: very simple, with minimal (often poor quality or plastic) inlay, for around £E35; and larger sets made of hard woods, intricately inlaid with mother-of-pearl, bone or ivory, costing upwards of £E150.

Many backgammon sets have chess boards on the back; **chess pieces** in every style and material are widely available, but good backgammon counters are hard to find. Now that Egypt has stopped legal imports, fresh supplies of **ivory** (whose sale is not illegal) are smuggled in from Sudan and Kenya, where poachers are decimating elephant herds. If that's not sufficient reason to boycott ivory products, numerous countries (including Australia, Britain, Germany and the USA) prohibit their importation. Inlaid or carved **bone** makes an acceptable, cheaper substitute.

Dealers

Shops in the Khan that specialise in *mashrabiya* and inlay work include *Mother of Pearl Products* (6 Khan el-Khalili); *Hassan and Ali Abdel Aal* (☎903-361); *Ibrahim Zayed* (Chevikan building); *Salah Badr Ali Sherif* and the *Mashrabiya Factory* (both at 5 Rabeh al-Salihdar).

The two coffeehouse **shops** near the Barquq complex are also worth investigating for **backgammon** sets, whilst real woodwork buffs might visit the *House of Mashrabiya* on the outskirts of Giza (17 Maryotteya Canal, just before the *Farm Restaurant*; Sat–Thurs 9am–5pm).

Spices and perfume

As the world's main spice entrepôt from Fatimid times until the eighteenth century, Cairo remains the largest market for perfumes and spices in the Arab world, with some of its business still conducted in bazaars.

Spices and herbs

The Muski end of the **Spice Bazaar** is generally disappointing, with tourist tat impinging on old shops like *Donia al-Henaur* (incense, spices, candles) and *Khedar al-Attar* (herbal cures) between the Madrassa of Barsbey and Sharia al-Azhar. However, at the other end of the *Souk al-Attarin*, a narrow lane behind the Mosque-Madrassa of al-Ghuri, the **Haret al-Fahhamin**, is a welter of vivid colours and aromas, mingling with the dirt and stench of ages. Here, piled high and named in Arabic, *'irfa* (cinnamon) and *simsim* (sesame) are still evocative of distant lands. The best buy is saffron (*za'faraan*), which costs about £E2 for 100 grammes – a hundred times less than you'd pay back home.

Some shop owners are also **herbalists** (*etara*), whose traditional remedies for every ailment from impotence to constipation are widely used. There are several *etara* on al-Fahhamin and outside Barsbey's madrassa, but the most famous establishment is *Abdul Latif Mahmoud Harraz* (39 Sharia Ahmed Maher), in the Bab el-Khalq quarter, which has been run by the same family since 1885. Notice the jar of dessicated crocodiles, to be boiled into a potion for the oversexed.

Incense and perfume

Just as herbal medicine blends into folk magic (many stalls purvey amulets), both make use of **incense**. The Spice and Perfume bazaars offer the widest range of musks and resins, but you can also find Sudanese vendors squatting beside aromatic cones and medicinal roots in the Ezbekiya Gardens.

Alongside the northern half of the *Souk al-Attarin* lies a warren of covered alleys that forms the **Perfume Bazaar**. Egypt produces many of the **essences** used by French perfumiers, which are sold by the ounce to be diluted 1:9 in alcohol for perfume, 1:20 for eau de toilette and 1:30 for eau de cologne. Local shops will duplicate famous perfumes for you, or you can buy brand-imitations (sometimes unwittingly – always scrutinise labels).

Reputable shops like the one on the southeast corner of the intersection of Sharia al-Muizz and the Muski charge £E6–15 an ounce, depending on the type of essence, and will only dilute to order, but many places overcharge and cheat –

around Talaat Harb especially. Whilst boasting that their "pure" essence is undiluted by alcohol, crooked salesmen omit to mention that oil has been used instead, which is why they rub it into your wrist to remove the sheen. A half-pint of scented oil costs about £E4.

Musical instruments and recordings

Cairo is a good place to buy **traditional musical instruments** such as the *kanoon* (dulcimer), *oud* (lute), *nai* (flute), *rabab* (viol), *mismare baladi* (oboe), *tabla* (drum), *riq* and *duf* (both tambourines; the latter is played by Sufis). All of them are made and sold by half-a-dozen shops on the right-hand side of **Sharia Qalaa** (walking from Midan Ataba towards the Islamic Art Museum), which also deal in Western instruments and cheaper imitations from China.

Traditional instruments are also sold by itinerant vendors, especially during *moulids*, when people buy a hand-held dummy that claps its cymbals together when squeezed (called a *Shoukoukou* after the famous comic monologist).

Recordings

As the centre of the Arab music world and a melting-pot for every tradition (see "Music" in *Contexts*), Cairo is a superb place to buy **recordings**. Authorised cassettes (nobody uses LPs or CDs) and pirated versions are sold from kiosks where it's quite acceptable (indeed, advisable) to listen before buying. Given that non-Arabic labelling is minimal, it helps to recognise labels like *Sout el-Beiruit* (a green cedar-pine logo; Gulf and Levantine music), *SLAM!* (mostly *al-Jeel* music) or the *shaabi* imprint *Fel Fel Phone* (which has a retail outlet on Sharia Khulud, near Midan Ramses).

The kiosk beside the *Café Riche* is good for all kinds of music, whereas those on Ezbekiya chiefly stock religious and folk (often cheap, inferior copies). For quality recordings (£E5) of Umm Kalthoum, Abdel Wahaab and orchestral music, visit *Sono Cairo* on Sikket Ali Labib Gabr, between Qasr el-Nil and Talaat Harb (opposite the Radio Cinema). Cairo's main distributor, *Abdullah*, has a shop in the alley behind the Café a l'Americaine, with vast stocks and an even bigger mail-order catalogue of new wave Arab music.

Sheet music is available from *Papasian* (9 Sharia Adly) and several of the musical instrument shops on Sharia Qalaa.

Books and newspapers

Egypt is the world's largest publisher of Arabic books and newspapers, so those who know the language can find almost any type of **Arab literature** in Cairo. Aside from magazine and paperback stalls along the downtown thoroughfares, good sources include *Dar al-Kitab al-Masri wal-Libnani* (on the first floor of 33 Sharia Qasr el-Nil) and *Dar al-Maaref* (27 Sharia Abdel Khaliq Sarwat); for Islamic heritage books, try *Dar al-Oras* (22 Sharia Gumhorriya) and around Ezbekiya Gardens.

Unlike most other places in Egypt, Cairo also has plenty of **books in foreign languages** (chiefly English, French and German). For a huge range of material on all things Egyptian, plus novels, travel guides and dictionaries, visit the *American University in Cairo Bookshop* (closed Aug) at the back of the main campus. Also good for fiction, Egyptology and local literature are *Al Shourouk* and *Madbouli* (on Midan Talaat Harb); *Lehnert and Landrock* (44 Sharia Sherif); and *Reader's Corner* (33 Abdel Khaliq Sarwat). *Shady* (29 Abdel Khaliq Sarwat) has a decent collection of African fiction; the *Anglo-Egyptian Bookshop* (169 Sharia Mohammed Farid) specialises in Arab politics, history and culture; *L'Orientalist* (15 Qasr el-Nil) in rare and antique editions.

Most of these **downtown bookshops** are closed on Sunday. For **secondhand books**, try the stalls around Ezbekiya, especially in the northwestern corner.

Newspapers and magazines

The best source of **foreign newspapers and magazines** is the stall on Qasr el-Nil, outside *Groppi's*. Craftily, the owner keeps the most recent editions (1–2 days old) under the counter and displays older copies on the racks. Purchasers of weekend editions of British papers should note that colour supplements are sold separately. Total news junkies can read **press agency releases** off telex machines in the lobbies of the *Nile Hilton* and *Cairo Sheraton*.

Booze and cigs

For those who enjoy tippling in their room or want a cache for consumption in "dry" parts of Egypt, there are several places which sell alcohol.

Downtown **off-licences**, run by Greek or Maronite Christians, maintain a low profile; furtive Muslim customers are served at once, with hardly a word exchanged. You'll find *Orphanides* next to the Rivoli Cinema on 26th July; *Cava Kasr el-Nil* at 24 Sharia Bassiouni; and another place below the *Hotel Claridge* on Talaat Harb. All three stock Egyptian beer, wine, *zibib*, *raki*, brandy, rum and gin; open from mid-afternoon till 8pm, Monday to Friday; and close down entirely during Ramadan and other major Muslim festivals.

New liquor regulations entitle foreigners to buy up to four litres of **imported alcohol at duty-free prices** within one month of entering Egypt. To take advantage of this offer, bring your passport along to the well-stocked Diplomatic Section of the *Egypt Free Store*, beyond the *Atlas-Zamalek Hotel* on Arab League Street in Mohandiseen.

Cigarettes

With **cigarettes** available on every corner, only smokers addicted to certain foreign brands need hunt down specialist outlets. Try the stall outside the Metropole Theatre (near the *Windsor Hotel*) on Sharia Alfi, or *Carvellis Freres* (beside the *Zeina* restaurant on Talaat Harb), which also sells pipe tobacco and cigarette papers, and never overcharges.

Practicalities

The following sections cover most of the remaining **practicalities**. Bear in mind that vital details such as opening hours, costs and regulations governing currency exchanges or visas may change, so be sure to phone to confirm anything important.

For a comprehensive rundown of services, regulations and much else, if you need to supplement our listings, check the current edition of *Cairo: A Practical Guide*, published by the AUC and available from most bookshops (£E20).

American Express and Thomas Cook

Aside from its overpriced tours and travel services, **American Express** (*Amex* for short) can be very useful to travellers. Their main office at 15 Sharia Qasr el-Nil (☎750-881/750-892; telex: 92715 AMEXT UN; daily 8.30am–6pm, 9am–4pm during Ramadan) is the best place to send money or letters. Although their client mail service (closed Fri) is only available to holders of Amex traveller's cheques or cards, nobody seems to check if you are or not. As a rule, it's quicker to change foreign currency or Amex cheques here than in commercial banks. There's also a US direct telephone service (see "Phones", p.38).

Other **Amex branches** can be found in the hotels *Nile Hilton* (☎743-383), *Ramses Hilton* (☎773-690), *Giza Sheraton* (348-8937), *Marriott* (☎341-0136) and *Meridien* (☎844-017), and at Cairo International Airport (☎670-895). The *Nile Hilton* branch is the only place in Cairo that pays out $US for Amex traveller's cheques, which are sold only to Amex card holders.

If you're exchanging money to buy an airline ticket, make sure that Amex doesn't invalidate your exchange receipt with an Arabic stamp that translates as "not for airline tickets" (for more on this, see p.234). Note, too, that parcels addressed to Amex must be collected at the post office on Sharia Mohammed Farid. Transferring money from abroad via Amex is explained below.

Thomas Cook

The modern-day descendant of the world's first tourist company, **Thomas Cook**, also comes in handy. Besides changing foreign currency or any brand of travel-ler's cheque into Egyptian money, their central branch (17 Sharia Bassiouni; ☎743-955) also *sells* traveller's cheques in return for dollars or sterling, with no nonsense about card holders.

There are **other branches** of Thomas Cook in Heliopolis (7 Sharia Baghdad; ☎670-622) and Dokki (Shops 9 & 10, 26th July Street; ☎346-2429).

Banks and currency transactions

As rates of exchange are the same everywhere, **banks** are chiefly distinguished by their opening hours and relative (in)efficiency. Egyptian banks are open 8.30am–1pm and close on Fridays, Sundays and public holidays; foreign banks keep the same hours but also take Saturdays off.

Exchanging money

Aside from Thomas Cook or Amex, it's usually quickest to **exchange money** or traveller's cheques in the *Nile Hilton*'s **24-hour** *Bank Misr*, or branches in other major hotels and off Midan Ramses, open daily till 8pm. **VISA** or **Mastercard** holders can obtain cash advances in £E from the *Bank of America* at 106 Sharia Qasr al-Aini (☎354-7788; telex 92425 BOFA UN), a couple of blocks south of Midan Tahrir; it takes about an hour to get confirmation by telex. Except for Amex in the *Nile Hilton* (which gives $US for Amex traveller's cheques on request), all **pay outs** are in Egyptian currency only.

Transfers

There are several ways of **transferring money from abroad**. Foreign banks can send money orders through the central Amex office in their own country to the

Qasr el-Nil branch, which deducts one percent commission before paying out in hard currency or traveller's cheques the following day. (Thomas Cook offers a similar service).

The cost and speed of bank-to-bank transactions vary considerably. *Cairo Barclays International Bank* (☎354-2195; telex 92343 CABAR UN), opposite the AUC on Sharia Qasr al-Aini, will deal with any bank abroad. Charges are made at the sender's end, telex transfers are dearer than by phone, but almost immediate; the cost is the same whatever the amount.

Other banks include:

Bank of America (see above).

Citibank, 4 Sharia Ahmed Pasha, Garden City (☎355-1873; telex 92832 CITAR UN).

Deutsche Bank, 23 Qasr el-Nil (☎762-341; telex 92306 DEUCAI).

Lloyds Bank International, 44 Sharia Mohammed Mazhar, Zamalek (☎341-8366; telex 92344 LLOYD UN).

Manufacturer's Hanover, 3 Sharia Ahmed Nesim, Giza (☎726-703; telex 92660 MHTCO UN).

Midland Bank, same address (☎726-934; telex 92439 MIDBK UN).

Royal Bank of Canada, Abu el-Feda Tower, Zamalek (☎340-8115; telex 92725 ROCAR UN).

If you wish to use money received at banks to **buy traveller's cheques** at Thomas Cook or Amex, you must produce a Certificate of Transaction (which you have to request at the issuing bank) rather than an ordinary exchange receipt proving that your Egyptian currency was legally acquired.

Bureaucracy

All foreigners are required to register with the authorities within seven days of entering Egypt and obtain a triangular **registration stamp** in their passport (re-entry visa-holders must do this each time they return to Egypt). However, since most hotels can arrange this for £E1–2 (ritzier places may do so without being asked), there's no need to do it yourself.

Registering at the Mugamma

Registering in person or extending your visa entails visiting the **Mugamma**, that bureaucratic behemoth on Midan Tahrir (open Sat–Wed 8am–4pm, Thurs 8am–1.30pm, Fri 10am–1pm and every evening 7–9pm; variable hours during Ramadan). Display patience and good humour when dealing with the Mugamma; only stage a tantrum or nervous breakdown as a last resort. To avoid the crush, arrive first thing in the morning or during the evening shift. Unless you're certain which numbered "window" is currently appropriate (details below may become outmoded), check with the **information** desk on the second floor (through the left-hand door, then left).

For **registration**, simply bring your passport to window #50 on the same floor. To get a **visa extension** you need to show bank receipts proving that you've exhanged $190 (or its equivalent) into Egyptian currency during the past month, and provide one passport photo. Pay the fee (roughly £E7) and collect a form at the cashiers; then take the completed form to windows #23–27 (marked "Non Arab: Europe, North and South America, Australia"), where your new visa will be issued. The same windows also issue **tourist residence visas; re-entry visas** are handled by windows #12–13. In case of lost or stolen passports (see below), replacement entry-stamps are obtainable from room #90.

Travel permits: the Ministry of the Interior

Other matters are dealt with by the **Ministry of the Interior** in the Abdin quarter (Sat–Thurs 9am–2pm; ☎355-6301/354-8661), whose Travel Permits Department can grant **permission to travel in restricted areas** (Siwa Oasis; minor Delta and Sinai roads; between Mersa Matrouh and Libya, or Mersa Allam and the Sudanese border).

Applications require two photos and photocopies of the first three pages of your passport and Egyptian entry visa; plus a justification for your journey. Processing takes anywhere between 24 hours and seven days.

If you're only interested in **Siwa**, it's much easier to obtain permission in Mersa Matrouh (see Chapter Four).

Passport photos, photocopying and translations

The smudgy black and white copies (£E2) of passport photos produced by guys with antique box cameras outside the Mugamma building are *not* acceptable to bureaucrats. Though colour isn't obligatory, they require high definition **passport photos**, which can be obtained from the studio in room #99 on the ground floor of the Mugamma (£E8), or a photo-booth in the *Nile Hilton*.

Several shops along 26th July Street and Sharia Mahmoud (near the AUC Library) advertise **photocopying** services. For cheap **translations**, contact Fouad Nemab (27 Sharia Qasr el-Nil; ☎392-8306).

Cultural centres, clubs and language courses

Cultural centres are good for catching up on home news and making contacts; longer-staying visitors can join their libraries and sign up for **language courses**.

Institutes

American Cultural Centre, 4 Sharia Ahmed Ragab (☎355-0532). Anyone who's going to be in Egypt at least three months can join (bring two photos and your passport); members can borrow books and cassettes. World news round-up (Sun noon & Mon 3pm) plus occasional free films and lectures. Summer Sun–Fri 10am–4pm; winter Mon & Wed 10am–8pm, Tues, Thurs & Fri 10am–4pm.

British Council, 192 Corniche el-Nil, Aguza; near the Circus (☎345-3281). Large library (annual membership £E14), including videos and cassettes. Also sponsors visting cultural acts. Mon–Sat 9am–2pm & 3–8pm.

Egyptian Centre for International Cultural Cooperation, 11 Sharia Shagar al-Durr, Zamalek (☎341-5419). Organises Arabic classes, tours to the Red Sea Monasteries, exhibitions and recitals. Sat–Thurs 9.30am–5pm.

Goethe Institute, 2 Sharia el-Bustan (just off Midan Tahrir), second floor (☎759-877). Public reading room; library membership and borrowing rights with ID. Mon, Wed & Thurs 11am–7pm, Tues & Fri 9am–2pm.

Institut Francais, 1 Madraset al-Huquq al-Fransia, near Saiyida Zeinab metro station; see map of Old Cairo (☎355-3725). Regular films, lectures and exhibitions.

Japanese Cultural Centre, 106 Sharia Qasr al-Aini, third floor (☎355-3962). Screens films Wed 6pm; open Sun–Thurs 9am–2pm.

Netherlands Institute, 1 Sharia Mahmoud Azmi, Zamalek (☎340-0076). English lectures about Egypt on Thursdays at 5pm (Sept–June).

Spanish Cultural Centre, 20 Sharia Adly – in the passage (☎756-476). Exhibitions and lectures; Spanish language courses October–May. Mon–Fri 11am–4pm.

Associations

Archaeology Club, 2 Midan Qasr al-Dubbarah, Garden City (☎354-8239/355-3052).

Baladi Association, 47 Sharia Ramses, third floor (☎743-813). Concerned with environmental issues.

SPARE (Society for the Preservation of Architectural Resources of Egypt). Conservation society which occasionally organises lectures and historic walks; contact Elizabeth or John Rodenbeck (☎351-8863).

Language courses

Arabic Language Centre, Sharia Mahmoud Azmi, Mohandiseen (☎346-3087). Forty-hour courses in modern, standard and colloquial Arabic for about £E300.

Egyptian Centre for Cultural Cooperation (see above). Three-day intensive courses in classical Arabic for $120.

Berlitz School, 165 Sharia Mohammed Farid (☎391-5096). Specialises in classical Arabic.

AUC Public Service Division, 28 Sharia Falaki (☎354-2964).

International Language Institute, off Sharia Merghani, Heliopolis (☎666-704).

Private tutors (£E15–20 per hour) advertise in all these places.

Embassies, foreign visas and missing passports

Most **embassies and consulates** are in Garden City, Zamalek, Dokki or Mohandiseen. All of them are listed in *Cairo: A Practical Guide* and located in the *Cairo A–Z*. Since everyday business is handled by consulates rather than embassies, we've listed the former only if there are two separate addresses. The following partial rundown includes notes on **applying for foreign visas**.

Australia, 5th floor of the south Cairo Plaza Tower, 1097 Corniche el-Nil, Bulaq; 1km north of the Maspero Dock (☎777-900). Sun–Thurs 8am–3.30pm; enquiries 9am–12.30pm.

Britain, 7 Sharia Ahmed Ragheb, Garden City – see map of central Cairo (☎354-0850). Letters of recommendation cost £E23. Sun–Thurs 8am–1pm. Also handles affairs for **New Zealand** nationals.

Canada, 6 Sharia Mohammed Fahmi el-Sayed, Garden City; west of the above (☎354-3110/354-3119). Sun–Thurs 7.30am–3pm.

Germany, 8a Sharia Hassan Sabry, Zamalek (☎340-6017/340-3687).

India, 5 Sharia Aziz Abaza, Zamalek (☎340-6053/341-0052). Bring one photo and $15 or equivalent sum. Must show an onward return ticket. No visas issued on arrival.

Ireland, Abu el-Feda Tower, north of the Zamalek Bridge, Zamalek (☎340-8264).

Israel, 6 Sharia Ibn Malek, Giza; near the El-Gama'a Bridge – see map of Old Cairo and Roda (☎361-0528/361-0380). Look for the security guards at the entrance or the Israeli flag flying aloft. Most foreigners can, in fact, obtain tourist visas at the border. Daily 9am–noon.

Jordan, 6 Sharia Gohaini, Dokki, two blocks west of the *Sheraton* (☎348-5566/348-6169). Visas require one photo and a letter of introduction, and are free for US, Canadian and Australian citizens; New Zealand and British nationals must pay £E25 and £E74, respectively. (It's cheaper to buy visas on arrival in Aqaba, if possible; see Sinai, p.541). Sat–Thurs 9am–12.30pm.

Kenya, 20 Sharia Boulos Hanna, south of Midan al-Sad al-Ali in Dokki (☎704-546/704-546). With luck, you might get a 30-day visa within 24 hours.

Netherlands, 18 Sharia Hassan Sabry, Zamalek (☎340-8744/340-6872).

Sudan, 1 Sharia Mohammed Fahmi el-Sayed, Garden City – see central Cairo map (☎354-5043). Supposedly open Sun–Thurs 9am–noon. Five application forms and photos, plus a letter of recommendation from your embassy, are required for visas. As Sudan's plight has worsened, delays have extended to months; at the time of going to press no visas are being issued.

Syria has yet to reopen its embassy in Cairo, so the nearest place to obtain a visa is their embassy in Amman. British citizens should check if they're still banned from entering Syria.

Turkey, 25 Sharia Falaki, Bab al-Luq (☎354-8364). Most Western nationals don't require visas; British and Irish citizens can obtain them routinely on arrival.

Uganda, 9, Midan al-Misaha, Dokki (☎981-945/980-329).

United States, 5 Sharia Amerika Latina, Garden City – see map of central Cairo (☎355-7371). Lost or stolen passports replaced overnight for £E100; limited passports issued for travel to Israel on request. Sun–Thurs 8.30am–4pm.

Yemen, 28 Sharia Amin al-Rafi'i, Dokki (☎348-6754). Letter of recommendation required. A temporary visa is normally issued within 48 hours; you must travel to Yemen within fourteen days of issue, or it becomes invalid. On arrival at Sanaa airport you must cash $150 (or equivalent) and should receive a one-month visa.

Lost or stolen passports

Lost or stolen passports should be reported to the police as soon as possible. You'll receive a slip of paper indicating the police file number; take this and two photos plus any personal ID to your consulate to apply for a new passport. Then bring this and the police report to the Mugamma for verification of entry (see above). You'll also need to obtain a new Egyptian visa.

Health care

For minor complaints, simply consult the nearest **pharmacy**; pharmacists can prescribe a wide range of drugs, including antibiotics.

24-hour pharmacies

Ataba, 17 Midan Ataba (☎910-831).

Isaaf, 3 26th July St (☎743-369).

Al Ezabi, 1 Sharia Ahmed Taysir, Heliopolis (☎663-409).

Zamalek, 3 Sharia Shagar al-Durr, Zamalek (☎340-2406).

As-Salam International Hospital, Ma'adi (see below).

Opticians

Mounir Nassif, 30 Sharia Talaat Harb.

Ibrahim Abd al Hamid, 5 Sharia Sherif (☎392-0058).

Sphinx Opticals, 160 26th July Street.

Baraka Optical Co, 10 Sharia Baghdad, Heliopolis (☎678-165).

Doctors and dentists

There are English- or French-speaking **private doctors** all over Cairo. A consultation normally costs about £E30, excluding drugs. Some practices used to foreign patients include:

General practice: Dr Naguib Badir at the Anglo-American Hospital, Zamalek (☎340-6162).

Internal medicine: Dr Victor Fanous, *Nile Hilton Hotel* clinic (☎740-777/754-623).

Tropical medicine: Dr Zoheir Farid, 16 Abdel Khaliq Sarwat (☎745-023/745-478).

Gynaecologist: Dr Sherif Gohar, 2 Midan Talaat Harb).

Dentists: Dr Aida A. Bastawi (☎354-7554) or Maher Barsum (☎915-069).

Herbal medicine and spiritual healing

Those who prefer **herbal medicine and spiritual healing** might consult:

Khedr al-Attar, in front of Sultan Barsbey's Mosque (☎900-865).

Ahmed Sadek Zalat, 10 Sheikh Mohammed Abdu, alongside the al-Azhar Mosque (☎903-773).

Hospitals

Hospitals require a cash deposit of about £E150 to cover the cost of treatment; medical insurance is *not* accepted (though you can reclaim expenses later). The following are well equipped and used to foreigners:

Anglo-American Hospital, next to the Cairo Tower on Gezira Island (☎341-8630).

As-Salam International Hospital, on the Corniche to Ma'adi (☎363-8050/363-4196/363-8424).

Cairo Medical Centre, on Midan Roxi in Heliopolis (☎258-0237/258-0636).

For any of these hospitals, take a taxi if you can; otherwise use the private **As-Salam ambulance service** (same phone numbers as the hospital). **Public ambulances** offer free transport to the *nearest* hospital: ☎770-227 or 770-123 in Cairo; ☎720-123 in Giza.

Vaccinations

Two places provide **vaccinations** against meningitis, cholera, yellow fever and other diseases.

Public Health Vaccination Centre, at the rear of the lobby of the *Hotel Continental-Savoy* on Midan Opera (8.30am–1pm). Highly efficient, with no red tape or fuss. A cholera shot costs £E6.50 (£E1.15 with your own syringe).

Vaccination and Serum Centre, 51 Sharia Wazart el-Zaraa – near the Aguza end of the 6th October Bridge (8am–2pm daily; 9.30am–1.30pm during Ramadan). If you're staying on the west bank, it's easier to use this centre, where injections cost £E3–5.

Post and phones

The **central post office** on Midan Ataba (open Sat–Thurs 9am–7pm, Fri 8am–noon; 9am–4pm daily during Ramadan) and other main branches (Sat–Thurs 8.30am–3pm; 9am–3pm during Ramadan) are often extremely crowded. Rather than using the **poste restante** (Sat–Thurs 8am–6pm) on Sharia Bidek (west around the corner from Ataba post office), it's better to have mail sent to American Express (see above).

Mail services

Although letters posted in the lobby of the *Nile Hilton* are said to arrive faster than those dropped in ordinary mailboxes (painted blue for overseas mail), **airmail letters** can still take two weeks to reach Europe, three weeks for the USA (80pt). However, Ataba's **express mail service** (daily 8.30am–7pm) promises delivery to Europe in two days, the USA in three; the European/US rate for items weighing under 100 grammes is £E26. Any post office can send **registered letters**.

It's quicker to buy **stamps** from hotel shops or cigarette kiosks, which charge about 5pt above normal rates (45/50pt for a postcard/letter to countries outside the Arab world).

PACKAGES

Until recently, packages weighing under two kilos could be sent from any post office and/or Cairo International Airport, whilst anything heavier (up to 20kg, or 1.5m total dimensions) had to be dispatched from the Ataba or Ramses post offices. Reports now suggest that **sending parcels** is restricted to Ramses only, but it's unclear whether you obtain customs clearance there, or at Ataba's Parcel and Customs section (opposite poste restante on Sharia Bidek), as before.

Whichever holds, you'll have to bring the unsealed parcel for inspection, weighing and sealing. The overseas rate is about £E4 a kilo. Items worth more than £E100 require an **export licence** from the Ministry of Foreign Trade (8 Sharia Adly; ☎919-661). Many of the larger tourist shops can arrange this, and shipping, for a charge (keep all receipts). Anyone **receiving parcels** in Egypt should beware of **import duty** (eg £E40 on a pair of contact lenses).

Phones

Cairo's telephone system has been undergoing major restructuring since 1986, with new exchange numbers and/or extra digits being introduced in some areas – but not consistently. Older places tend to have 4–6 digit numbers; newer establishments numbers with 5–7 digits (often resulting from a 3, 5 or 7 being added at the beginning).

Although **local calls** now cost 10pt, many public phones only accept the old 5pt coins, and generally fail to work anyway. It's better to use the semi-public phones provided by many shops and kiosks (25pt a call), or the bank of payphones in the lobby of the *Nile Hilton* (50pt tokens sold) – but expect to be frustrated even so.

The same goes for **long-distance calls** to other parts of Egypt, best arranged through your hotel or a telephone office.

INTERNATIONAL CALLS

Facilities for international calls are more reliable. Central Cairo has four main **Telephone and Telegraph Offices** (open 24hr) and various branch offices (7am–10pm daily). The main offices downtown (8 Sharia Adly and alongside the *Windsor Hotel* on Sharia Alfi Bey) are less chaotic than those on Sharia Ramses and Midan Tahrir. Calls are booked and paid for in advance, and can either be taken in a booth at the office or directed to an outside number such as a hotel.

Many **hotels** can also place calls for a 15–25 percent surcharge. **Collect and credit-card calls to the USA** can be made from *USDirect* phones in the *Marriott*, *Ramses Hilton* and *SemiRamis* hotels (all 24hr) and Amex on Qasr el-Nil. You cannot make collect calls anywhere else in Egypt.

The cheapest time to call is betwen 8pm and 7.59am. For details of rates, see p.39.

TELEGRAMS, TELEXES AND FAXES

Telephone offices can also send **telegrams** for so much per word (including the address) – 60pt a word to the USA, for example. Like the 24-hour **Telegraph and Telex Office** on Midan Ataba (opposite the post office), they also handle **telexes**.

You can send **faxes** from the Ataba office or business service centres in deluxe hotels; the former charges about £E12 for a one-page fax to the USA, hotels roughly double that. Faxes **from abroad** can be sent to Amex on Qasr el-Nil (fax: 202-628975), who'll hold them like client mail, but won't notify the recipient.

Other services

Car repairs

Authorised **dealers and garages**, who should use imported or factory-made parts when repairing, include:

Audi/VW: *Egyptian Automotive & Electric Co.*, Sharia Murad, by Giza Zoo (☎751-964).

Buick/GM: *Magar*, 19 Sharia Talaat Harb (☎744-063).

Citroen/Ford: *Anglo-Egyptian Motors Co.*, 27 Sharia Adly (☎754-411).

Chevrolet: Arab League Street, Mohandiseen (☎460-087).

Chrysler/Mitsubishi: *Electessadia*, 2 Sharia Mohammed Farid Wagdi, Manial (☎842-215).

Datsun: *Saudi*, Midan al-Misaha, Dokki.

Fiat: 1097 Corniche el-Nil, Garden City (☎354-9660/355-7596).

Mercedes: *Engineering Car Co.*, 14 Route 9, Ma'adi (☎351-3128/350-0931).

Peugeot: 4 Sharia Wadi el-Nil, Mohandiseen (☎463-069/650-394).

Renault: 37 Sharia Lutfi Hassouna, Dokki.

Toyota: *Alpha Trade Centre*, Sharia Zaafaran, Giza (☎851-946).

Volvo: 26th July Street, opposite the Rivoli Cinema.

If these can't help you, *baladi* **repair shops**, skilled at improvising parts (cheaper than imported ones), probably can. Ask around Sharia Champollion Sharia Orabi or Ramses Square in downtown Cairo, or the *Souk Lazoghli* on Midan Lazoghli, which is a daily **spare parts market**.

Film and processing

Outside of big hotels, you can buy **film** cheaply. *Actina* (4 Sharia Talaat Harb; Mon–Sat 10am–4pm; ☎767-236) and *Photo Greenwich* (16 Sharia Adly; ☎906-990) both sell Kodachrome and Agfa films for £E7–8.

If you care about quality, leave **photo-processing and printing** until you get home; Egyptian work is second-rate at best. *Kodak Egypt* (20 Sharia Adly; Mon–Sat 9am–8pm; ☎749-037) is slightly cheaper and less abysmal than the Kodak kiosk on 26th July. Both offer 24-hour or 1-hour printing; expect to pay 35pt per exposure, plus extra charges unmentioned in the sales spiel.

Laundry

Guests at deluxe hotels or the *Pension Roma* can avail themselves of **laundry** services (50pt per item). Elsewhere, hotel receptionists or block janitors can probably put you in touch with the local *makwagi*, who does washing and ironing at piece rates. Washing powder is sold in most pharmacies and corner shops.

For **dry-cleaning**, enquire at *Hollywood*, opposite the Stella Bar on Hoda Shaarawi. Delicate silks and woollens are better entrusted to the *Top-Matic Laundry* next to the *Safir Hotel* on Midan al-Misaha in Dokki.

Student cards

The big student discounts on rail and airline tickets have encouraged fraudulent applications for **ISIC Student Cards**, which were easily obtainable until recently. Now, however, firm proof of student status is demanded at the issuing office in Cairo Medical University on Roda Island (Sat–Thurs 10am–1.30pm), which can be reached by taking bus #803 or #904 from Midan Tahrir, passing through the main gates to the second block on the left, and then turning right around the corner.

EXCURSIONS FROM CAIRO

The Nile Valley – most people's target after Cairo – is too distant for **day excursions** from the city. Elsewhere, however, you can choose between a jaunt to the seaside or remoter pyramids, a river trip or desert monasteries – and still be back in Cairo the same night. The notes below are an outline of possibilities and are intended (with the exception of the entries on the Nile Barrages and Muqattam Hills) to be used in conjunction with full accounts in other chapters.

THE NILE BARRAGES AT QANATIR

Roughly 20km downriver from Cairo, the Nile divides into two great branches which define the Delta, whose flow is controlled by the **Nile Barrages** at **Qanatir**. Decoratively arched and turreted, this splendid piece of Victorian civil engineering is surrounded by shady parks and lush islets – an ideal spot for a picnic.

Originally conceived by Mohammed Ali's French hydro-engineer, Mougel Bey, the Barrages were later realised as part of the nationwide hydrological system designed by Sir Colin Scott-Moncrief. At the eastern end of the 438-metre-long Rosetta Barrage lies the *Istarahah al-Qanatir* or **Presidential Villa** that Islamic Jihad once considered attacking with an anti-aircraft cannon in the garden of one of their member's homes, across the river. Egypt's **State Yacht** (originally King Farouk's, on which he sailed into exile) is often moored at the quay.

Providing you don't come on Friday, when the area is ridiculously crowded, the Barrages make a pleasant excursion. Qanatir is accessible by bus #210 from the *Nile Hilton* terminal on Midan Tahrir, or by ferry from the Maspero Dock in front of the Television Building. Ferries (£E1) leave hourly (6am–6pm) and take two hours; the bus journey is less appealing. Travelling by *felucca* is very slow, since the mast must be lowered at every bridge.

THE MUQATTAM HILLS AND WADI DIGLA

The **Muqattam Hills**, rising beyond Cairo, are seldom visited by tourists but readily accessible by #401 buses from Midan Tahrir and Ataba. Zigzagging up the hillside past caves and quarries, ruined shrines and guarded outposts, they terminate at **Medinet Muqattam**, an upmarket suburb whose avenues are flanked by villas and casinos. The Muqattam Corniche, circling the edge of the plateau, offers spectacular views across the Citadel and most of Cairo – an unforgettable vista at sunset.

People planning desert expeditions might consider a few training runs below the Muqattam. Victorian travellers used to engage a dragoman to lead them to the **Petrified Forests** – two expanses littered with broken, fossilised trunks, thought to date from the Miocene Period. The larger one (marked on our map of Greater Cairo) is really only accessible with a guide, but would-be explorers can easily find the "Little Forest" on the Jebel el-Khasab plateau, north of the Digla–Ain Sukhna road.

The **Digla–Ain Sukhna road** turns east off the new Nile Valley expressway near a *zebaleen* village beyond Ma'adi. Roughly 25km from the turn-off, you'll pass the Jebel el-Khasab on the left; if you keep heading on, you'll notice various tracks leading off to the right, which eventually converge on a main desert track running east–west. By following it west, back towards Digla, you'll pass through several meandering wadis before the way is blocked by **Wadi Digla**. This miniature canyon is good for **rock-climbing** and **birdwatching**; bring water, food and shade.

THE FAYOUM

Fayoum Oasis, 100km southwest of Cairo, is another place to escape. Though Fayoum City holds little appeal, you can walk from its centre into lush countryside within half an hour. Irrigated by waterwheels and canals, the Fayoum was a major centre during the Middle Kingdom, Ptolemaic and Roman times, as evinced by various ruins around its periphery. Whilst some involve bumpy rides into the desert, others are reasonably accessible from Fayoum city by local bus or *service* taxi, with a pleasant walk to the site itself. The **ruins of Karanis** lie just off the Fayoum–Cairo road; the dramatic **"Collapsed Pyramid" of Maidum** a short ride from El Wasta. Both sites are usually deserted, in blissful contrast to Giza and Saqqara. Either makes a good day excursion, but you should bring food and drink and be under way by mid-morning. *Service* taxis from Midan Giza are the fastest way of reaching Fayoum City (2hr). See *The Western Desert Oases* chapter for details.

ALEXANDRIA AND THE MONASTERIES OF WADI NATRUN

A three-hour journey from Cairo, Egypt's second city and summer capital embraces the Mediterranean with its sweeping Corniche. **Alexandria** has little to show for its ancient glory (personified by Cleopatra) or former decadence (celebrated by Lawrence Durrell), but its fresh seafood and cool breezes are delightful. A few hours suffice to visit its Graeco-Roman ruins or to make a literary pilgrimage around the haunts of Durrell, E.M. Forster and the poet Constantine Cavafy. Alex can be reached by bus, train or *service* taxi; the latter (leaving from Midan Ramses) is the easiest method. For details, see the *Alexandria and the Mediterranean Coast* chapter.

The Desert Road to Alex passes the turn-off for the fortified **Monasteries of Wadi Natrun**, which have long provided the Coptic Church's spiritual leadership. When not undergoing periodic fasts, the monks welcome pilgrims and other visitors. The most accessible of the monasteries are **Deir Anba Bishoi** and **Deir al-Suryani**, 10km from the rest stop on the highway. To visit all four, it's best to hire a taxi or car for the day, either in Cairo or at the rest stop, which is roughly midway between Alex and Cairo. Wadi Natrun is described in *The Western Desert Oases* chapter.

Unless you start very early or have a car, it's not really feasible to visit both Alexandria and the monasteries in one day.

ISMAILIYA, AIN SUKHNA AND THE RED SEA MONASTERIES

The canal city of **Ismailiya** is verdantly peaceful, with handsome promenades and colonial-era villas – a nice place to stroll or bicycle, also favoured by Egyptians as a honeymoon destination. Its museum and Garden of Stelae attest to ancient canals that once linked the Delta with the Red Sea; the House of Ferdinand de Lesseps commemorates the founder of the Suez Canal, one of the world's crucial waterways. Outside town you can watch boats slip between the desert on either side. Along the eastern embankment runs the Bar-Lev Line, a fortified Israeli barrier that was stormed on the first day of the 1973 War. Ismailiya itself can be reached by bus or *service* taxi from Cairo's Koulali Terminal (2–3hr), or by train. For details, see *The Canal Zone* chapter (p.506).

Cairenes with transport visit **Ain Sukhna** on the Gulf of Suez for its **beaches** and offshore coral reefs. If you fancy swimming and **snorkelling**, it's worth hiring a car for the day rather than switching buses at Suez and having to hitch back. Bring food and drink (plus snorkel if required), since they're not obtainable there. Don't wander into areas ringed by barbed wire, which are still mined. Ain Sukhna is approachable via Suez (3hr) or by the Digla–Ain Sukhna desert road (see above). Farther south and high inland are the **Red Sea Monasteries** of Saint Paul and Saint Anthony. With a car, you could combine a visit to Saint Anthony's with a swim at Ain Sukhna, but unless you leave at the crack of dawn it's impossible to make both monasteries and return that night. All three places are described in *The Red Sea Coast and Eastern Desert* chapter.

travel details

Cairo is the linchpin of Egypt's transport network and its main link to the outside world. Many parts of the country are accessible from the capital by several forms of transport, whilst numerous airlines compete over flights to Europe, Africa and Asia.

Trains

Virtually all trains depart from **Ramses Station** (*Mahatat Ramses*), a cavernous beehive seemingly designed to bemuse. Almost all trains halt at **Giza Station** 15min after leaving Ramses.

RAMSES STATION LAYOUT

Entering **Ramses Station** from Ramses Square, you'll find the tourist police, *wagons lits* and sleeper bookings offices on the left; through to your right are platforms serving Alexandria, the Delta and Canal Zone. Tickets for these destinations are sold at the rear, left-hand side of the main hall, where window #1 can supply **information** and advise on muddles, rescheduling and other problems (English spoken). Card-carrying members of the Student Friends Association may also approach you, offering to help; they're quite sincere and don't expect *baksheesh*.

Through the back of the hall are platforms 8–11, for southbound trains to Upper Egypt; linked by an underpass leading to the ticket offices beyond platform 11.

TICKETS

Buying tickets is rarely easy. Both sets of ticket offices have separate windows for 1st class/2nd class superior seating (which is reservable and has A/C) and ordinary 2nd class/3rd class (which isn't and doesn't); the placement of these windows varies from day to day. You have to find the right queue and get your requirements (it helps to have them written down in Arabic) across to clerks who may not give a damn. Tickets can be booked up to a week in advance; 1st and 2nd class superior seats sell out first. The peak seasons for travel are winter (for Upper Egypt) and summer (for Alexandria).

Card-carrying students are eligible for 30–50 percent **reductions** on all trains except **sleepers and wagon lits**, which must be booked at their own counters in the main hall. Prices given below are ordinary rates.

REGULAR SERVICES

All **services** are individually numbered on timetables.

The fastest ones **to Alexandria** are the #905 (leaving 8am), #917 (2pm) and #927 (7pm); during summer there's also another high-speed train, #577 (3.40pm).

For the long haul down **to Luxor and Aswan**, the quickest services (11–12hr and 14–17hr respectively) are #82 (6.40pm), #84 (7pm) and #86 (7.20pm), all of which are sleeper trains. For ordinary seats (not sleeping berths), current fares to Luxor are: 1st class £E25; A/C 2nd class £E15; non-A/C 2nd class £E9; for Aswan, the costs are £E30, £E16 and £E10, respectively.

You may also prefer trains **to Mersa Matrouh** (7am daily; 1st class £E18; A/C 2nd class £E10; non-A/C 2nd class £E5) to going by bus.

WAGONS LITS SERVICES

In addition to regular services, there are two daily **wagon lits** services to **Upper Egypt**, which include a bar and disco on the train. The cost per person for a double cabin is about £E150 to Luxor or Aswan. Solo travellers can reserve the entire cabin for £E200, or consent to share it with a stranger of the same sex and pay the normal fare. During summer, there are also thrice-weekly *wagon lits* to **Mersa Matrouh** (£E22 per head).

The Ramses *wagon lits* **bookings office** is notoriously bloody-minded: they'll happily announce that everything's booked solid for the next fortnight, whilst denying that one can reserve more than seven days ahead. You can, in fact, do this at their branch in *Shepheard's Hotel*, or at their main offices: 9 Sharia Menes, Heliopolis (☎290-8802/290-8804) and 48 Sharia el-Giza, Giza (☎348-7354/349-2536). Bring the passports of everyone travelling with you.

Buses

Inter-city buses reach most parts of Egypt, making equal or better time than trains. Vehicles range from sleek A/C *Superjets* serving overpriced snacks to battered rattletraps missing panes of glass; the majority being nominally A/C but actually ventilated by ill-fitting rear doors. Services depart from several terminals, none of which will take **bookings** over the phone; tickets must be purchased in person. You can usually only get information on the spot. Unless stated otherwise, all services below run daily; however, **schedules** change, so you shouldn't rely on our timings.

Two companies operate from the **Nile Hilton Terminal** outside the hotel arcade. The *West Delta Bus Co* has a row of ticket kiosks facing the arcade; the red booths nearest the Mugamma belong to the *Arab Union Travel Co* (☎772-663) – better known as the *Golden Rocket* or *Superjet* company from the livery of its A/C buses.

Blue *West Delta* buses **to Alexandria** (every 15min from 5.30 to 10am, then hourly till 10pm) cost £E4.50–10 according to their ventilation. Be sure not to take one of the decrepit vehicles routed via the Delta rather than the Desert Road. *Golden Rockets* leave every 60–90min between 5.30am and 8.30pm; a ticket to Alex costs £E10. A couple of each line's early-morning services carry on **to Mersa Matrouh** (8hr from Cairo); *West Delta* charge £E7.50–12, *Golden Rockets* £E20. Seats should be booked the day before, or earlier during summer, when demand is heavy.

Note: All Superjets and some West Delta buses originate at Cairo Airport (Terminal 1); passengers who board there pay £E2 extra.

SINAI BUS TERMINAL

Whilst the **Sinai Bus Terminal** will doubtless continue serving **all parts of the Sinai Peninsula**, schedules and prices change so rapidly that it's impossible to predict either with any accuracy. However, you can be sure of 3–4 services daily to Sharm el-Sheikh, Na'ama Bay, Dahab and Nuweiba; a similar number to Saint Catherine's Monastery (via Wadi Feiran); and several buses daily to El Arish in northern Sinai. Nuweiba is also served directly via a newly reopened route across the peninsula's interior; when last heard, this was an overnight service (5–6hr).

All seats should be booked the day before. You can reach the terminal (aka the *Abbassiya Station*, or *Mahatat Seena* in Arabic) via minibus (#32, #33 or #34) from Tahrir or Ataba square – look for the yellow billboard 500m beyond the Masr Travel Tower in Cairo's Abbassiya district.

AHMED HELMI TERMINAL: HURGHADA AND UPPER EGYPT

The **Ahmed Helmi Terminal** behind Ramses Station is more noticeable for its *service* taxis

than the muddy yard screened by fruit-stalls, used by the *Upper Egypt Bus Co* (☎746-658). The ticket-hutches for Middle and Upper Egypt are to the right and back as you come in; those for the Red Sea coast are along to your left. Most tourists come here for buses **to Hurghada** (6–8hr; 4 non-A/C between 7.30 and 9pm, £E12; two overnight *Superjets*, £E20) or services **to Upper Egypt** (3 to Luxor: 10hr; non A/C £E15, A/C *Superjet* £E28; two to Aswan: 15hr; £E18–34). Like buses to el-Quesir on the Red Sea (7am & 10pm; £E25 with A/C), they should be booked the day before. Non-A/C services **to Middle Egypt** can generally be booked an hour or two in advance. Destinations include Beni Suef (hourly 6am–7pm); Minya (every 1–2hr, 6.30am–6.30pm); Sohag (6 daily) and Assyut (8 daily). Cronky old vehicles run **to Fayoum City** every 15–30min between 6.15am and 6.45pm.

KOULALI TERMINAL: CANAL ZONE AND THE DELTA

From the nearby **Koulali Terminal** (also notable for its *service* taxis), the *East Delta Bus Co* covers the Canal Cities and much of the Delta.

Their green-and-yellow buses **to the Canal Zone** come with or without A/C, departing every half-hour for Suez (6am–8.30pm; £E3.50), Ismailiya (6.30am–6.30pm; £E3.50) and Port Said (6–9am; then hourly till 7pm; £E6–8). The Port Said run (3hr) is also covered by A/C *Superjets* (£E7).

Buses **to the Delta** are less salubrious but equally frequent, running every 15min to el-Mansura (6am–6pm) and Zagazig (5.30am–5pm, then hourly till 9pm); half-hourly to Behna (6am–9pm) and Faqus (8.30am–6pm); and hourly to Damietta (6am–5pm). During summer, there are services to the beach resorts of Gamasa (hourly; 8am–3pm) and Ras el-Bahr (7.15am, 9.15am, 1.15pm, 3pm & 5pm).

AL-AZHAR TERMINAL: WESTERN DESERT OASES

Another hole-in-the-wall base is the **al-Azhar Bus Terminal**, sited 400m east of Midan Ataba, just before Sharia al-Azhar meets the Bur Said flyover. From here, dusty vehicles embark on lengthy journeys **to the Western Desert Oases** (excluding Siwa, which is reached from Mersa Matrouh).

Unless schedules change radically, buses for **Bahariya Oasis** (6–7hr; £E8/£E12 with A/C) should leave twice daily around 7am and noon (no midday service on Wed). On Monday, Thursday and Saturday, the morning service continues on through **Farafra** to **Dakhla Oasis** (4–5hr for each leg). Dakhla is also the terminus for one of the three daily buses from Cairo to Kharga Oasis, routed via Assyut. You can get the latest details from helpful, English- and French-speaking Mahmoud Mustapha, who runs the ticket office (☎390-8635) every morning except Friday. To play safe, book tickets two days beforehand (one is pushing it). Be sure to bring food and drink for the journey.

Inter-city service taxis

If you don't mind a slightly cramped and definitely hair-raising journey, **service taxis** are usually the fastest way to reach a host of destinations. Their biggest advantage is that they leave as soon as they're full; just turn up, and you'll probably be away in 15min (mornings and late afternoon are prime time).

Drivers drum up custom by shouting out their destinations; anybody can point you towards the right taxi(s) for your destination. Prices are posted in Arabic on the windscreen; **fares** to specific destinations are detailed in subsequent chapters, but generally work out 20–30 percent above the bus fare. Watch what Egyptians pay and you can hardly go wrong. If you're alighting halfway (eg at Wadi Natrun, along the Desert Road to Alex), it's normal to pay the full fare.

The keyed map on p.80 gives an idea of *service* depots around the **Koulali and Ahmed Helmi terminals**, which serve the Delta and Canal Zone, Alexandria and the Mediterranean coast (including El Arish), the Red Sea coast down to Hurghada and the Nile Valley as far south as Minya or Assyut. If in doubt, try the Ahmed Helmi depot first. A third terminal on **Midan Giza** serves the Fayoum and Suez (and maybe farther down the Red Sea coast).

International coaches

International coaches are highly vulnerable to political upheavals, so none of the schedules and fares mentioned below can be taken for granted – double-check everything, including the availability of foreign visas (see "Practicalities").

Of most interest to tourists are the services **to Tel Aviv and Jerusalem** – an 8–10hr journey via El Arish and Rafah. *Travco* (13 Sharia Mahmoud Azmi, near the *Marriott Hotel*, Zamalek; ☎342-0488; open daily 9am–4pm) runs a service to both cities, departing from the *Giza Sheraton* (5am) and the *Sheraton-Heliopolis*

(5.30am) every day except Saturday. The one-way fare is about £E60; returns cost roughly £E100. A similar service, operated by the *East Delta Transportation Co* (☎824-773), departs from the Sinai Bus Terminal (Sun, Mon, Wed & Thurs) at 7.30am, and costs slightly more. For a modest surcharge, you can also buy tickets from *Misr Travel* or *Abydos Travel* (both on Talaat Harb).

Less well known are *Arab Union Bus Co* services **to Amman**, which formerly departed three times daily from Midan Ismailiya in Heliopolis (#35 minibus from Tahrir). Previously, the ticket ($50 single, payable in $US only) included the price of a Red Sea ferry to Aqaba, and the journey to Amman took about 24hr. Before the Gulf Crisis blew up, buses also ran to **Damascus**, **Baghdad** and **Kuwait**, though no one seems to know if these services will ever resume. In any case, most tourists prefer to reach Jordan via Nuweiba and Aqaba under their own steam (see *Sinai*).

Domestic flights

Egypt has three domestic carriers which charge identical rates.

EgyptAir flies 3–5 times a day to Aswan, Luxor, Abu Simbel and Alexandria; daily to Hurghada; and regularly to Mersa Matrouh (Thurs, Fri & Sun) and Kharga Oasis (Wed & Sun). Its Cairo offices (mostly open Sat–Thurs 8am–5pm) include: 6 Sharia Adly (☎390-2444); 9 Sharia Talaat Harb (☎392-2835/393-2836); *Nile Hilton* (☎759-806/759-703); *Giza Sheraton* (☎348-8600); and 22 Sharia Ibrahim al-Lakani, Heliopolis (☎664-305).

Air Sinai, based in the *Nile Hilton* (☎760-948), flies regularly to Sharm el-Sheikh (Tues, Thurs, Fri & Sat), Saint Catherine's Monastery (Mon & Sat), Hurghada (Mon & Fri) and El Arish (Thurs & Sat).

ZAS flies daily except Thursday to Luxor, Aswan, Hurghada and Saint Catherine's; its main office (☎291-8030) is in the *Novotel* near Cairo Airport.

TICKETS AND TERMINALS

During winter, flights to the Nile Valley or Hurghada are often fully booked by groups – reserve as far in advance as possible. Although **tickets** must be purchased in Egyptian currency backed by an exchange receipt, fares are generally reckoned in $US. With prices set to rise as this book goes to press, the following one-way

fares are only estimates: Luxor $85; Aswan $90; Abu Simbel $120; Saint Catherine's $60; Sharm el-Sheikh $70; Hurghada $65; El Arish $60; Alexandria $35; Kharga Oasis (New Valley Airport) $70; Mersa Matrouh $45. Return fares cost double. There are no reductions on domestic flights.

All these flights leave **from Terminal 1**, the "old airport", which can be reached by #400 bus from the *Nile Hilton* or #27 minibus from the Mugamma (both hourly), or by taxi (drivers usually demand £E15). During rush hour the journey takes over an hour. Always allow plenty of time.

International flights

Many airlines make Cairo a stopover between the Near and Far East, or Europe and sub-Saharan Africa, ensuring a competitive market in fares, student and youth discounts – but also heavy demand for flights. Don't leave **buying tickets** until the last moment. Especially during August, you should book weeks in advance on Eastern European airlines (which have the cheapest flights to Turkey, Greece and Western Europe) or popular long-haul destinations like Nairobi, Bangkok and Dehli.

All **reservations** should be **reconfirmed** 72 hours before departure. Also check which terminal you are flying from – most Western airlines use **Terminal 2**, the "new airport" (*al-mattar jedid*). Rather than rely on #422 buses from the *Nile Hilton*, it's safer to take a taxi.

AGENTS AND TICKETS

Agents such as *Wonder Travel* (9 Midan Tahrir; ☎759-774) or *Bon Voyage Egypt* (16 Sharia Adly; ☎390-7032) can often find seats when the airline itself swears that none exist. Expect queueing and shoving in agencies and offices.

Although some agents and airlines may accept credit card payments for **tickets**, most don't – it's certainly not something to count on. Generally, tickets must be purchased with Egyptian currency backed by an exchange receipt. To do this, ascertain the fare (including tax, which mysteriously varies from 1 to 10 percent), then exchange an equivalent sum in foreign currency or TCs at a bank, making sure that they don't invalidate the exchange receipt with an Arabic stamp meaning "not for airline tickets" (as *Amex* does). Then return to the airline with the cash and receipt to buy your ticket. (They'll keep your receipt, so it can't be used for visa extensions.)

STUDENT DISCOUNTS AND COURIER FLIGHTS

To qualify for student discounts (20–50 percent) you must have a valid ISIC card and be under an age limit (24–26 years, depending on the airline or agency). The same age limit determines eligibility for youth discounts, which don't require an ISIC card. There are rarely any **student/youth discounts** on flights to black Africa, India and the Far East, nor on *Royal Jordanian Airlines*.

Persistent under-26s might also get discounted or free **courier flights** by ringing around express mail services such as *Skypac International Express* (☎348-8204), *Federal Express*, 1079 Corniche el-Nil, Garden City (☎355-0427), and *East Courier Service*, 1 Sharia Mahmoud Hafez, Heliopolis (☎245-9281).

AIRLINE OFFICES

Most of the **airline offices** are in central Cairo:
Air France, 2 Midan Talaat Harb (☎743-300) .
Air India, 1 Sharia Talaat Harb (☎754-864).
Air Malta, 2 Talaat Harb (☎760-307).
Alitalia, *Nile Hilton* arcade (☎743-488).
British Airways, Midan Tahrir (☎759-977/772-981).
Bulgarian/Balkan Airlines Sharia el-Bustan, east off Talaat Harb.
CSA, 9 Talaat Harb (☎750-395).
El Al, 5 Sharia el-Makrizi, Zamalek (☎341-1620).
Iberia, 15 Midan Tahrir (☎749-955).
JAT, 9a Sharia al-Sharifein (☎743-166).
Kenyan Airways, *Nile Hilton* arcade (☎762-494).
KLM, 11 Sharia Qasr el-Nil (☎740-999).
LOT, 1 Qasr el-Nil (☎747-312).
Lufthansa, 9 Talaat Harb (☎750-343/750-425).
Malev, 12 Talaat Harb (☎753-111).
Olympic Airways, 23 Qasr el-Nil (☎751-381).
Pan Am, 2 Talaat Harb (☎747-399).
Sudan Airways, 1 Sharia el-Bustan (☎747-251).
Turkish Airways, 26 Sharia Bassiouni (☎758-939).
TWA, 1 Qasr el-Nil (☎960-300/749-900).

Boats – Nile cruises and international lines

The colonial tradition of **Nile cruises** has spawned an industry deploying 200 steamers, which virtually collapsed during the Gulf Crisis and is only now recovering. Previously, most cruise boats were booked months in advance by tour companies and it was difficult for individuals to make **bookings** in Egypt – but right now, it's easier.

Although luxury cruises operated by the *Hilton*, *Sheraton* and *Oberoi* remain prohibitively expensive, budget travellers may consider less ritzy boats run by *Eastmar Tours* (13 Sharia Qasr el-Nil; ☎753-216), which charges about $150 for a three-day cruise between Luxor and Aswan. However, sailing on a *felucca* is a funkier experience and much cheaper (see *The Nile Valley*, p.372).

INTERNATIONAL LINES

If you're planning to leave Egypt by sea, several agencies can supply info and tickets for **international lines**.

Gaby Travel (1 Midan Talaat Harb; ☎393-8567) is the booking agent for *Adriatica* ferries from **Alexandria to Irakilon, Piraeus and Venice**.

Assuming you manage to get a visa, the **Sudan** can be reached by weekly ferries from **Suez to Port Sudan** (enquire at *Misr Travel*, 1 Sharia Talaat Harb), or more frequent boats from **Aswan to Wadi Halfa**, operated by the *Nile Navigation Co* (Ramses Station; ☎753-555) and the *Nile Maritime Agency* (8 Sharia Qasr el-Nil; ☎740-883). For more about these routes, see "Alexandria", "Suez" and "Aswan".

CHAPTER TWO

THE NILE VALLEY

E gypt has been called the gift of the Nile, for without the river it could not exist as a fertile, populous country, let alone have sustained a great civilisation 5000 years ago. Its character and history have been shaped by the stark contrast between the fecund **Nile Valley** and its Delta (covered in Chapter Five), and the arid wastes that surround them. To the ancient Egyptians, this was the homeland or *Kemet* – the Black Land of dark alluvium, where life and civilisation flourished as the benign gods intended – as opposed to the desert that represented death and chaos, ruled by Seth, the bringer of storms and catastrophes.

Kemet's existence depended on an annual miracle of rebirth from aridity, as the Nile rose to spread its life-giving waters and fertilising silt over the exhausted land during the season of inundation. Once the flood had subsided, the *fellaheen* (peasants) simply planted crops in the mud, waited for an abundant harvest, and then relaxed over summer. Whilst empires rose and fell, this way of life persisted essentially unchanged for over 240 generations, until the Aswan Dam put an end to the inundation in 1967 – a breathtaking period of continuity considering that Jesus lived only eighty generations ago.

This continuity and ancient history is literally underfoot. Almost every Nile town and village is built upon layers of previous **settlements** – pharaonic, Ptolemaic, Roman and Coptic – whose ancient names, modified and Arabised, have sometimes survived. When treasure-hunting "archaeologists" first turned their attention to the ancient temples and tombs in the 1830s they had to sift through metres of sand and debris before reaching their goal. Yet the centuries of burial preserved a panoply of ancient reliefs and carvings which would otherwise have been defaced by Coptic or Muslim iconoclasts, who hacked away at the pagan gods on the accessible friezes, pillars and ceilings, and plundered masonry for their own churches and mosques.

After a century and a half of excavation by just about every Western nation – and by the Egyptians since independence – the Nile's **monuments** constitute the greatest open-air museum in the world. Revealed along its banks are several thousand tombs (Thebes alone has over 900) and scores of temples: so many, in fact, that most visitors feel satiated by just a fraction of this legacy.

To enjoy the Valley, it's best to be selective and mix sightseeing with *felucca* rides on the river, roaming around bazaars or camel markets, or attending the odd *moulid* (religious festival). Most visitors succeed in this by heading straight for Upper Egypt, travelling by train or air to **Luxor** or **Aswan**, then making day trips to the sights within easy range of either base, in addition to exploring the New Kingdom temples and tombs of **Karnak** and the **Theban Necropolis** from Luxor. If you choose to move against the river's current, taking time to travel south from Cairo through **Middle Egypt**, the monuments begin less impressively, with a ragbag of Middle and New Kingdom and Coptic sites.

The river, its gods and pharaohs...

The Nile originates in the highland lakes of Uganda and Ethiopia, which give rise to the White and Blue Niles. These join into a single river at Khartoum in the Sudan, then flow northward over a series of cataracts through the Nubian desert, before forming the Egyptian Nile Valley. The river's northward flow, coupled with a prevailing wind towards the south, made it a natural highway.

As the source of life, the Nile determined much of ancient Egyptian **society and mythology**. Creation myths of a primal mound emerging from the waters of chaos reflect how villages huddled on mounds till the flood subsided and they could plant their crops. Even more crucially, the need for large-scale irrigation works in the Valley and the consequent mobilisation of labour may have engendered the region's system of centralised authority – in effect the state.

Both the Valley and its Delta were divided into **nomes** or provinces, each with a nomarch or governor, and one or more **local deities**. As political power ebbed and flowed between regions and dynasties, certain of the deities assumed national significance and absorbed the attributes of lesser gods in a perpetual process of religious mergers and takeovers. Thus, for example, Re, the chief god of the Old Kingdom, ended up being assimilated with Amun, the prime divinity of Thebes during the New Kingdom. Yet for all its complexity, ancient Egyptian religion was essentially practical and intended to get results. Its pre-eminent concerns were to perpetuate the beneficent sun and river, maintain the righteous order personified by the goddess Maat, and achieve resurrection in the afterlife.

Abundant crops could normally be taken for granted, as prayers to Hapy the Nile god were followed by a green wave of humus-rich water around June. However, if the Nile failed to rise for a succession of years there ensued the "years of the hyena when men went hungry". Archaeologists reckon that it was the **famine** – caused by overworking of the land, as well as lack of the floodwaters – that caused the collapse of the Old and Middle Kingdoms, and subsequent political anarchy. But each time some new **dynasty** arose to reunite the land and re-establish the old order. This remarkable conservatism persisted even under foreign rule: the Nubians, Persians, Ptolemies and Romans all continued building temples dedicated to the old gods, and styled themselves as pharaohs.

... and its people

Although the Nile Valley and its Delta represents a mere four percent of Egypt's surface area, it is home to ninety-five percent of the country's population. Whilst Cairo and Alexandria account for about a quarter of this, the bulk of the people still live in small towns and villages and, as in pharaonic times, the **fellaheen** or peasant farmers remain the bedrock of Egyptian society.

Most **villages** consist of flat-roofed mudbrick houses, with chickens, goats, cows and water buffaloes roaming the unpaved streets, and elaborate multi-storeyed pigeon coops (the birds are eaten and their droppings used as fertiliser). The plastered outside walls of the houses are often painted light blue (a colour believed to ward off the Evil Eye) and if the householder has made the pilgrimage to Mecca, it will be decorated with characteristic *Hadj* scenes (recalling the journey with images of ships and charter jets, lions and the sacred Ka'ba). Children begin work at an early age: girls feed the animals, fetch water and make the dung-patties which are used for fuel (though primus stoves are increasingly popular), while boys, by the age of nine or ten, are learning how to farm the land which will one day be theirs.

Rural life might appear the same throughout the Nile Valley, but its character changes as you go further south. The northern part of the Valley is wider and greener, unconstrained by the desert hills; its people have a reputation for being quiet-spoken and phlegmatic, notwithstanding a recent turn towards Islamic radicalism. By contrast, Egyptians characterise the **Saiyidis** of Upper Egypt as mercurial in character, alternating between hot-blooded passion and a state known as *kismet* – a kind of fatalistic stasis. To non-Saiyidis, they are also the butt of jokes mocking their stubbornness and stupidity. A further ethnic contingent of the southern reaches of the valley are the black-skinned **Nubians**, whose traditional homeland extended into the Sudan but has now been submerged beneath the waters of Lake Nasser.

Nile wildlife

The Nile wildlife depicted on ancient tomb reliefs – hippos, crocodiles, elephants and gazelles – is largely a thing of the past, though you might just see a croc on the Sudanese shores of Lake Nasser. However, the Valley has a rich diversity of **birds**. Amid the groves of palms (dates all along the valley and dom-palms south of Assyut), fruit and flame trees, sycamores and ecalyptus, and fields of *besoom* (Egyptian clover) and sugar cane, you can spot hoopoes, turtle- and laughing-doves, bulbuls, blue throats, redstarts, wheatears and dark-backed stonechat; purple gallinules, egrets and all kinds of waders are to be seen in the river; while common birds of prey include a range of kestrels, hawks and falcons.

THE TWO LANDS, PHARAONIC SYMBOLS AND CARTOUCHES

Much of the symbolism of ancient Egypt referred to the union of the **Two Lands**, the **Nile Valley** (Upper Egypt) and its **Delta** (Lower Egypt), whose establishment marked the onset of the Old Kingdom (c.3100 BC).

Each Land had its own deity – the Delta had **Buto**, the cobra-goddess, while the Valley had **Nekhbet**, the vulture-goddess. With union, however, their images were combined with the

winged sun disc

sun disc of the god Re to form the **winged sun disc**, which often appeared on the lintels of temple doors. Another common image was that of the Nile god, **Hapy**, binding together the **heraldic plants** of the Two Lands, the papyrus of the Delta and the lotus of the Valley.

Hapy binding the Two Lands

Much the same process can be observed in the evolution of **pharaonic crowns**. At state rituals, the pharaoh customarily wore first the **White Crown** of Upper Egypt and then the **Red Crown** of Lower Egypt, although by the time of the New Kingdom (c.1570 BC) these were often subsumed into the **Combined Crown**. Pharaonic crowns also featured the **uraeus** or fire-spitting cobra, an incarnation of Buto believed to be a guardian of the kings.

Another image that referred to the act of union (an act which had to be repeated at the onset of the Middle and New Kingdoms) was the **Djed column**,

Approaches to the Nile Valley

Setting out **from Cairo**, you are faced with a variety of approaches to the Nile. In ascending order of price, these include:

● **Trains** Regular services from Ramses station run down as far as Aswan. The fastest ones (the #82, #84 and #86 sleeper services) reach Luxor in 11–12hr, Aswan 3–5hr later. Most of the trains stop en route at Minya (3–4hr) and Assyut (7hr) in Middle Egypt but it's always wise to check on this.

● **Buses** Departures from the Ahmed Helmi Terminal include: Minya (non A/C services every 1–2hr; 5hr); Luxor (3 daily; 10hr; non-A/C £E15; *Superjet* £E28); and Aswan (2 daily; 15hr; £E18–34).

● **Service taxis** There are standard runs, again leaving from Ahmed Helmi, to Minya (5hr) and Assyut (6hr), where you can pick up connections south.

● **Wagon lits** These luxury coaches are fitted to certain sleeper trains to Luxor or Aswan. Prices are steep (£E140 to either destination).

● **Flights** Trips to Luxor (US$85), Aswan (US$90) or Abu Simbel (US$120) allow spectacular views from 35,000 feet over the Nile's green belt of cultivated land and glittering water.

● **Nile cruises** These are all comparatively expensive – certainly if you want to set out from Cairo, which would mean a minimum five-day cruise to Luxor, eight days to Aswan. The cheaper tours on offer usually start off in Luxor, sailing down to Aswan, with stops at Esna, Edfu and Kom Ombo; these take three days and charge from US$150 per person. If you're interested, take some time to shop around in Cairo (or Luxor) and don't necessarily take the cheapest – some boats leave a lot to be desired in terms of hygiene and living conditions. If at all possible, always try to look around the boat first. The most reliable and luxurious boats are those run by big hotel chains like the *Hilton* and *Sheraton*.

a symbol of steadfastness. Additional symbols of royal authority included the **crook** (or staff) and the **flail** (or scourge), which are often shown crossed over the chest – in the so-called Osiride position – on pharaonic statues. A ubiquitous motif was the **ankh**, symbolising breath or life, which pharaohs are often depicted receiving from gods in tombs or funerary texts.

However, the archetypal symbol of kingship was the **cartouche**, an oval formed by a loop of rope, enclosing the hieroglyphs of the pharaoh's **nomen** and **prenomen**. Traditionally a pharaoh's title consisted of five names: four adopted on accession to the throne (Horus name, Nebty name, Golden Horus name and prenomen) and a birthname (nomen), roughly corresponding to a family name. The prenomen was introduced by a group of hieroglyphs meaning "He who belongs to the sedge and the bee" and was nearly always compounded with the name of Re, the sun god. The nomen – the name by which pharaohs are known to posterity – was likewise introduced by an epithet, "Son of Re".

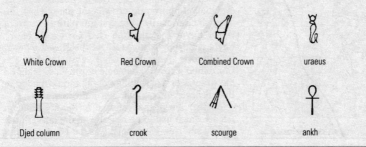

| White Crown | Red Crown | Combined Crown | uraeus |

| Djed column | crook | scourge | ankh |

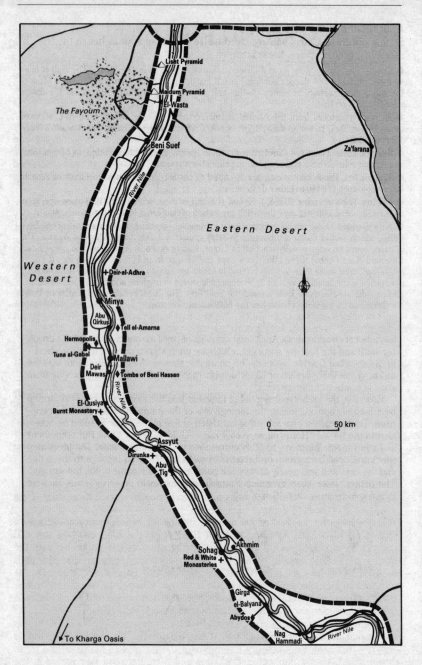

MIDDLE EGYPT

It was nineteenth-century archaeologists who coined the term **Middle Egypt** for the stretch of river between Cairo and the Qena Bend; in native useage and current administration there's no such area, unlike Upper and Lower Egypt, which are ancient divisions. Nevertheless, it's a handy label for a region that's subtly distinct from Upper Egypt, farther south. Owing little to tourism, the towns are solidly provincial with social conservatism providing common ground for those wanting to preserve peaceful relations between the Muslim majority and Middle Egypt's Coptic community (about twenty percent of the local population, roughly double the national average). The strength of the Muslim Brotherhood in the area, however, is apparent in the guards posted outside churches in the towns – and in a dearth of publicly available alcohol.

Most tourists rate Middle Egypt a low priority, which is good news in some respects. Compared to Luxor, towns like **Minya** and **Sohag** are refreshingly normal and hustler-free, and if local antiquities aren't so grand as Upper Egypt's, they're also less overrun by visitors. The rock tombs of **Beni Hassan** and the necropolis of **Tuna al-Gabel** are well-preserved relics of Middle Kingdom artistry and Ptolemaic cult-worship, while the desolate remains at **Tell el-Amarna** stand as an evocative a reminder of the "heretic" Pharaoh Akhenaten as any great temple exalting Ramses II. Half a dozen Coptic **monasteries** and **moulids** are also accessible from Minya, Sohag or Assyut thanks to good transport connections along the Valley. Buses and *service* taxis also link Middle Egypt with Kharga Oasis and the Fayoum.

Beni Suef

The only reason for outsiders to visit the ramshackle provincial capital of **BENI SUEF**, 130km up the Nile from Cairo, is to switch transport – an operation easily enough completed (see overpage). If by some misfortune you need to stay, the town does have one decent **hotel**, the *Semiramis*, opposite the post office. Their dearer singles (£E8–10) and doubles (£E13–20) have private bathrooms, and when last heard, the hotel had the only **bar** in town.

Forgotten cities: Heracleopolis and Oxyrhynchus

Two ancient cities – **Heracleopolis** and **Oxyrhynchus** – once flourished along this stretch of the Nile Valley.

Heracleopolis is marked by a huge mound of rubble near the village of IHNASYA EL-MEDINA, 15km west of Beni Suef. Founded early in the Old Kingdom and long the capital of the twentieth nome, its rise coincided with the decline of the VIII Dynasty, which barely controlled the region around Memphis by 2160 BC. Whilst anarchy reigned throughout the Two Lands, Achthoes, the nomarch of Heracleopolis, forged a new dynasty. Although his successors never achieved control of southern Egypt, their reassertion of centralised authority in the north paved the way for the XII Dynasty and the Middle Kingdom.

Of similarly academic interest, **Oxyrhynchus**, 9km west of BENI MAZAR, was the capital of the nineteenth nome. It's noted for the discovery of numerous papyri – including third-century fragments of the gospels of Matthew and John, portions of plays by Sophocles, Euripides and Meander, and summaries of the lost books of Livy. More frivolously, it deserves to be remembered for revering the Elephant-snout fish – perhaps the weirdest totemic creature on record.

Moving on from Beni Suef

From Beni Suef's **bus station**, which is sited just east of the railway terminal, you can catch half-hourly services to Cairo (£E3.50) or Fayoum city (£E1); less frequent buses to Tanta and other Delta towns; and twice-daily (8am & 2pm) A/C coaches to Alexandria. For quicker, if hair-raising, transportation to the Fayoum and other destinations, ask around the **service taxi** depots west of the bus and train stations. Mornings are the best time to look for taxis to Za'farana on the Red Sea coast, whose route passes the turn-off for Saint Anthony's Monastery (see p.561); it was across the river from Beni Suef that Anthony first lived as a hermit.

Minya and Mallawi

The best archaeological sites in Middle Egypt fall within a 50km radius of the towns of **Minya**, 109km south of Beni Suef, and **Mallawi**, a further 47km south. Most trains between Cairo and Luxor stop at both towns. From Cairo, the journey to Minya takes about four hours by **train** (1st class £E9; A/C 2nd class £E6), although the 7.30am service (#980) does it in just over three.

More frequent **buses** from Cairo's Ahmed Helmi Terminal (every 1–2hr; £E5) take about five hours to Minya, as do **service taxis** from the adjacent depot and Midan Giza (£E5.50). If you're **driving**, use the new expressway that runs down the east bank of the Nile almost as far as Minya; despite rough patches, sparse traffic enables you to make better time than on the congested west bank "highway". Coming up **from Luxor** by bus or *service* taxi usually entails a change of vehicles at Assyut.

> All telephone numbers in the Minya/Mallawi area are prefixed ☎086.

Minya

Whilst **MINYA** is farther from most of the sites, it's infinitely preferable to Mallawi as a base for excursions: the provincial capital, it derives considerable charm from the old villas built by Italian architects for Greek and Egyptian cotton magnates – now picturesquely decaying amidst their overgrown gardens – and from its people, known in Egypt for their warmth and honesty. Beneath the palm trees that shadow its squares, couples canoodle and vendors hawk sweet potatoes, and during Ramadan half the population seems to sleep outdoors.

Emerging from the train station you'll find a square redolent of some ex-colonial *ville* in North Africa. Follow **Sharia Gumhorriya** past a row of cafés to reach **Midan Tahrir** (aka Midan Qasr), the hub of small-town life. Come evening, locals promenade between Midan Tahrir and **Midan Sa'a** (Clock Square), past shops and eateries replicated farther up Gumhorriya, which terminates at the **Corniche** (aka Sharia Ramadan or Sharia el-Nil).

Across the river rise the striated hills of the Eastern Desert. Thus constrained, Minya spreads alongside the riverbank and westwards across the **Ibrahimiya Canal**, encroaching on the agricultural plain beyond.

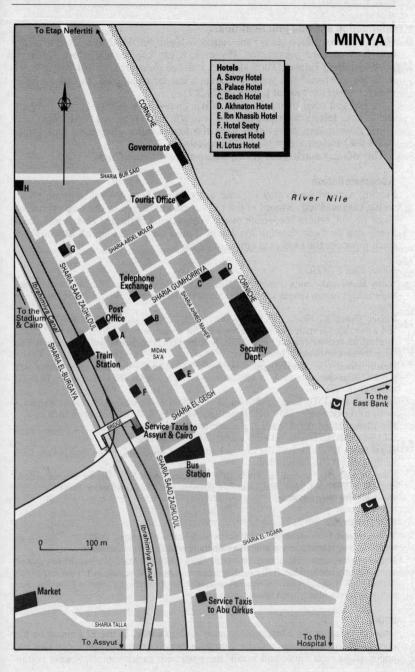

MINYA

To Etap Nefertiti

CORNICHE

Governorate

Hotels
A. Savoy Hotel
B. Palace Hotel
C. Beach Hotel
D. Akhnaton Hotel
E. Ibn Khassib Hotel
F. Hotel Seety
G. Everest Hotel
H. Lotus Hotel

River Nile

SHARIA BUR SAID

H

Tourist Office

SHARIA ABDEL MOLEM

G

SHARIA SAAD ZAGHLOUL

Telephone
Exchange

SHARIA GUMHORRIYA

D

C

CORNICHE

Ibrahimiya Canal

To the
Stadium
& Cairo

Post
Office

B

SHARIA AHMED MAHER

A

Security
Dept.

SHARIA EL-BURGAYA

MIDAN
SA'A

Train
Station

E

F

To the
East Bank

BRIDGE

Service Taxis to
Assyut & Cairo

SHARIA EL-GEISH

0   100 m

SHARIA SAAD ZAGHLOUL

Bus
Station

Ibrahimiya Canal

SHARIA EL-TIGARA

Market

Service Taxis
to Abu Qirkus

SHARIA TALLA

To Assyut

To the
Hospital

Information and and practicalities

Minya's **tourist office** (daily 8am–2pm & 5–10pm; ☎320-150) is anxious to please but short on hard information. However, it can confirm the latest admission prices for Beni Hassan, Tuna al-Gabel and Tell el-Amarna, or put you in touch with drivers should you want to engage a car for excursions. In case of emergency, contact the **tourist police** (☎324-527).

Should you need them, the **post office** (Sun–Thurs 8.30am–2pm & 5–10pm) and 24-hour **telephone exchange** are smack in the centre, and two **banks** (Sun–Thurs 8.30am–2pm & 5–10pm) flank the tourist office. There are both public (☎324-098) and private (☎323-077) **hospitals**.

The Monday **market** has been a fixture since Ottoman times.

Accommodation

Finding somewhere to stay is never a problem. There are half a dozen places within easy walking distance of the railway station (keyed to the map overpage), some decent, others borderline cases. Reservations at the *Ibn Khasib* and *Beach* hotels can be made through *Ibn Khasib Travel Co* (☎758-409), off Sharia Talaat Harb (opposite the *Lufthansa* office) in Cairo.

NEAR THE STATION

Savoy Hotel (A), Sharia Gumhorriya. Noisy, high-ceilinged single (£E8), double (£E8) and triple (£E10) rooms. Guests are charged for rarely hot showers. There's a funky *ahwa* next door.

Palace Hotel (B), Sharia Gumhorriya (☎327-071). Tattily nostalgic, with a dayglo Nefertiti and a fine colonial staircase to prepare you for the rooms, some of which have hot baths or overlook an outdoor cinema. Singles £E5, doubles £E8. Breakfast of *fuul* and omelette £E2. Once the smartest hotel in Minya.

Beach Hotel (C), Sharia Gumhorriya (☎322-307). Clean, carpeted rooms, mostly with private bathrooms, fans or A/C, a balcony and fridge. Singles £E13–16, doubles £E15–20, triples £E26. **(C)**

Akhnaton Hotel (D), beside the Corniche (☎325-918). Salubrious, simple rooms with wind-swept balconies. Singles £E10, doubles with shower £E14, A/C £E4. Give breakfast a miss.

Ibn Khasib Hotel (E), 5 Sharia Ragab (☎324-535). Nice garden and restored vintage rooms (£E18–21 with half board), but sniffy management. Fans available.

Hotel Seety (F), 71 Sharia Sa'ad Zaghloul. Antiquated, dusty and noisy – don't bother. Ditto for the **Everest (G)**, farther north.

Lotus Hotel (H), far end of Sharia Sa'ad Zaghloul (☎324-541). Decent singles (£E19), doubles (£E26) and triples (£E32) with hot showers; fans £E1. Top-floor restaurant with fine views, serving beer and wine.

FURTHER OUT

Youth Hostel, by the stadium, 1.5km north along Sharia el-Burgaya (☎322-029). Dorm beds for £E1 in a semi-official environment; a swimming pool almost compensates.

Etap-Nefertiti, 1km north of town (☎326-281; telex 23608 ETPMN UN). Doesn't rate its five-stars, but very comfortable. A/C rooms or bungalows with TV, private bathroom and phone. Singles $30–34, doubles $37–40, depending on whether they have a garden or Nile view. Pool and restaurants. Mostly used by tour groups.

Food

Unless staying at the *Etap*, most tourists end up **eating** in the *El Fairouz* on the corner of Sharia Salatin and the Corniche, which serves burgers, chicken and juices, plays rock music and assails the eyes with garish murals. Staider restaurants in the *Lotus* and *Akhnaton* hotels do tasty three-course meals for around £E10; the former has the only **bar** in town.

For cheap *shwarma* sandwiches and gooey pastries, visit the *Cafeteria Aly Baba*, just north of the Governorate, which is also good for morning coffee. Both squares feature Arab **cafés**, *kushari* and grilled-chicken takeaways.

Transport and excursions from Minya

Though *hantours* (buggies) are happy to drive you around, Minya itself is compact enough for walking, with transport depots relatively close together.

Service taxis are the fastest way to reach most places between Cairo and Assyut (the point to change for destinations further south); the fare to Mallawi is 60pt; to Assyut £E1.30. The "local" and inter-city *service* taxi depots between the station and the bus terminal cover all destinations except for Abu Qirkus (the jumping-off point for Beni Hassan), which is served by a depot 300m farther south. Many routes are also covered by **bijous** (minivans or covered pick-ups), which charge similar rates to *service* taxis.

Trains are of little use for exploring the sites around Minya, and slower than other transport to most points in the Nile Valley. **Buses** for Assyut leave every hour on the hour; services to Cairo (£E5; 5hr) every two hours on the half-hour.

Mallawi

MALLAWI has gone to the dogs ever since Minya supplanted it as the regional capital. Its streets are littered and stink of open drains; hovels are more prevalent than villas. As Stanley Stewart wrote, it seems like the kind of place where people grow embittered; Sadat's assassin, Khalid al-Islambouli, was born into a well-respected local family. The only relics of Mallawi's former status are a derelict, Hindu-Gothic-style **feudal palace** and a small **museum** (Thurs–Tues 9am–1pm) of archaeological finds, notably painted coffins from the Middle Kingdom – neither of which justify visiting town.

Rooms, meals and other practicalities

Along Sharia Essim you'll notice the green-painted, roach-ridden *Samir Amis* hotel (☎652-955), which charges £E5 a head for basic rooms and cold showers. Only consider staying here in order to cut the journey time to each site, allowing you to visit several in a single day.

Below the hotel is a **restaurant** serving meat and rice with salad and bread, soft drinks and tea. On Bank al-Misr Street, just across the bridge from the railway station, the *El-Horriya Restaurant* does hearty *kofta* meals. To finish off with a sticky pastry, track down the *Deaael Deen* by following the street to the right of the hotel until its end, turning left and then right, and looking on the left one block along.

Mallawi's *Bank Misr* (Sun–Thurs 8am–2pm & 6–9pm) can **exchange** foreign currency and TCs. To reach the **post office** (Sat–Thurs 8.30am–3pm), follow the dirt road to the left of the bank and turn left after 100m.

Transport

Unfortunately for those who come into Mallawi for **transport** on to Beni Hassan, Tuna al-Gabel and Tell el-Amarna, the various terminals are dispersed either side of the Ibrahimiya Canal.

On the **east bank**, *service* taxis for points south of town leave from south of the railway station. Northbound taxis leave from a depot 200m north of the small bridge spanning the canal. On the other side of this is **Sharia Essim**, the main drag, along which buses and *service* taxis shuttle between Minya and Assyut.

Sites around Minya and Mallawi

Each of the sites around Minya and Mallawi is relatively isolated, so it's difficult to visit more than one or two in a single day unless you've got private transport – read up on them first and be selective. The number one target must be the rock tombs of **Beni Hassan**, roughly midway between the towns, which contain the finest surviving murals from the Middle Kingdom. Nearer to Mallawi are the ruins of **Hermopolis** and its partially subterranean necropolis, **Tuna al-Gabel**, while the Coptic **Monastery of the Virgin** lies across the river north of Minya.

Note: The major site of Tell el-Amarna, 12km south of Mallawi on the east bank, is covered separately in the section following.

Across the river from Minya: the East Bank

Before moving onto the more well-trodden pharaonic sites south of Minya, it's worth mentioning a few alternatives across the river and north of town: Minya's **City of the Dead**, and the **Monastery of the Virgin** and the temple of **Tehna al-Gabel**. Thanks to the new Minya Bridge and *service* taxis from the "local" depot, all are now reasonably easy to reach, and by aiming for the Monastery of the Virgin first, you could conceivably visit all three sites in a circuitous excursion (bring food and water).

Minya's City of the Dead and the Church of Aba Hur

Beyond the east bank village of **AL-SAWADAH**, 4km south of Minya, stretches an immense cemetery resembling Cairo's City of the Dead. Dubbed **Zawiyet el-Mayyiteen**, the "Corner of the Dead", it consists of thousands of mausoleums – confessional enclaves interspersed by the homes of the living. A rash of mudbrick domes marks the Muslim quarters; a forest of crosses, Coptic burial grounds. Somewhere amongst them lies the **Mausoleum of Hoda Shaarawi**, an early feminist who campaigned for women's liberation.

Traditionally, locals visit their ancestral tombs during the Muslim months of Shawwal, Ragab and Zoul-Hagga, at the time of the full moon. On July 6, the cemetery is also a campground for pilgrims attending the **Moulid of Aba Hur** at the subterranean rock church of **Deir Aba Hur**, 1km from al-Sawadah. The church – entered via a narrow, stepped tunnel – contains finely inlaid *haikal* screens and a nineteenth-century icon of Aba Hur, a blacksmith's son whose faith under torture converted the Roman governor of Pelusium to Christianity.

Deir al-Adhra: the Monastery of the Virgin

About 20km downriver from Minya, the east bank extrudes a cliff-like hill known as **Gabel el-Teir** (Bird Mountain) after the flocks said to haunt it on the birthday of a local saint – a name that's also applied to the Coptic monastery on its summit. The **Monastery of the Virgin**, properly called **Deir al-Adhra**, was inhabited until late last century, when Baedeker dismissed it as a "group of miserable huts, occupied not only by the monks but by laymen with their wives and children", whose reaction to passing tourist-steamers had previously amused Flaubert: "You see these fellows, totally naked, rushing down their perpendicular cliffs and swimming towards you as fast as they can, shouting '*Baksheesh, baksheesh*'."

Nowadays a place of pilgrimage, the monastery's rude outbuildings screen a **rock-hewn church**, reputedly founded in 328 by Empress Helena, inside a cave where the Holy Family sheltered. One of its six columns has been hollowed out and serves for baptisms; the tales attached to it are only surpassed by the miraculous cures attributed to a picture of the Virgin that weeps holy oil. On August 22, thousands of pilgrims come here for the **Feast of the Assumption**; at other times the church is locked, but a caretaker can admit visitors (£E1 *baksheesh*).

To **get to the monastery from Minya**, catch a *service* taxi 30km north to SAMALUT (40pt); get off at the canal bridge and take a *bijou* to the Nile, where you can cross by canoe-ferry (25pt) to the east bank. Here, walk through a field to the rock-hewn stairway that ascends 130m up the cliffside to the hamlet beside the monastery, or hope for a pick-up truck heading up the bumpy track.

Tehna al-Gabel

To continue from Deir al-Adhra to **TEHNA AL-GABEL**, descend the steps to the dirt track below and wait for another pick-up, heading south (10km; 40pt). Alternatively, you can reach Tehna direct from Minya by *service* taxi (50pt).

Tehna **village** huddles below a limestone cliff riddled with ancient tombs. By walking 100m towards the hills and then turning right, you'll come upon a **ruined temple** dedicated by Nero to Amun and Sobek. Beware of bats when exploring its interior. An anti-clockwise circuit around the ruins will take you past the remnants of several Hathor-columns; farther along is a room whose barred window permits glimpses of mummified crocodiles. Climb the twelve-metre ledge to a higher level, where an ornate doorway leads into a sanctuary containing reliefs of Roman and native officials, in fairly good condition. A Greek inscription to the right of the doorway asserts, "This is our home".

The Rock Tombs of Beni Hassan

Roughly midway between Minya and Mallawi, barren cliffs east of the Nile shelter the **rock tombs of Beni Hassan** (daily 8am–4pm), named after an Arab tribe that once settled roundabouts. The vivid murals in this necropolis shed light on the Middle Kingdom (2050–1800 BC), a period when provincial dignitaries celebrated their greater independence by having grand burials locally, rather than at Saqqara. To stretch a visit to the tombs into a longer excursion, you could walk from Beni Hassan to the isolated temple of **Speos Artemidos**. Neither site has food or water.

Getting there

To reach Beni Hassan, catch a *bijou* or *service* taxi (30–40min; 60–70pt) from Minya or Mallawi to the large village of ABU QIRKUS. Once there, cross the main canal bridge and grab another *bijou* at the end of the street for the 3km ride (25pt) to the riverbank, where an office sells tickets (£E3.75; six or more £E1.25 each) valid for the ferry crossings and minibus rides to and from the tombs, 500m inland. There you buy an admission ticket (£E8, students £E4).

The tombs

Although most of Beni Hassan's thirty-nine tombs are unfinished, the four shown to visitors evince their **stylistic evolution** during the XI–XII Dynasties. Their variously shaped chambers represent a transitional stage between the lateral *mastaba*-tombs of the Old Kingdom and the deep shafts in the Valley of the Kings, gradually acquiring porched vestibules and sunken corridors to heighten the impact of the funerary effigies at the back. The actual mummies were secreted at the bottom of shafts, accompanied by funerary texts derived from the royal burials of the Old Kingdom.

Pharaonic iconography and contemporary reportage are blended in the **murals**, whose innovative wrestling scenes presaged the battle vistas of the New Kingdom. Though battered or effaced in parts, their details reward careful study; the following descriptions (keyed to tomb plans) should help.

TOMB OF BAQET III (#15)

Taking the chambers in chronological order, you should start with the **Tomb of Baqet III**. Like other tombs, its images are arranged in registers whose height above floor level reflects their spatial relationship. Thus, Nile scenes go below those involving the Valley, above which come desert vistas, the highest ones most distant.

Mural **[a]** shows papyrus-gathering in the marshes; **[b]** a desert hunt (notice the copulating gazelles) above pictures of ball-players, women spinning and fullers beating cloth. The rear wall depicts nearly 200 wrestling positions **[c]**, while the south wall **[d]** is covered with episodes from the life of this XI Dynasty nomarch; in one scene, his underlings count cattle and punish tax defaulters.

TOMB OF KHETI (#17)

Baqet bequeathed the governorship of the Oryx nome to his son, buried in the nearby **Tomb of Kheti**, which retains two of its structually inessential papyrus-bud columns. In the murals, hippopotami ignore the papyrus harvest **[a]** as desert creatures are hunted **[b]** above registers of weavers, dancers, artists and *senet*-players; metalsmiths labour, musicians entertain Kheti and his wife **[c]** and minions bring offerings of gazelles and birds **[d]**.

On the rear wall, warriors storm a fortress below a compendium of wrestling positions **[e]**. Grape harvesting and wine-making **[f]**, herding cattle **[h]** and ploughing **[i]** are only some of the tasks overseen by Kheti, who appears beneath a sunshade attended by his dwarf and fan-bearers **[g]**, and elsewhere receives offerings. Notice Kheti's boats, and bulls locking horns, near the entrance **[j]**.

TOMB OF AMENEMHET (#2)

Columned porticos and a niche for statues (which replaced the Old Kingdom *serdab*) are hallmarks of the XII Dynasty tombs, 150m north. Proto-Doric columns uphold a vaulted ceiling painted with chequered reed-mat patterns in the **Tomb of Amenemhet**. This nomarch's campaign honours are listed beside the door near a text relating the death of Senusert I. Leather-workers, armourers, masons and weavers **[a]** precede the customary hunting scene **[b]**, beneath which Amenemhet collects tribute from his estates – a scene with scribes brow-beating defaulters at the bottom.

Below the wrestling and siege tableaux, boats escort him towards Abydos **[c]**, while a niche **[d]** holds broken effigies of Amenemhet, his mother and his wife

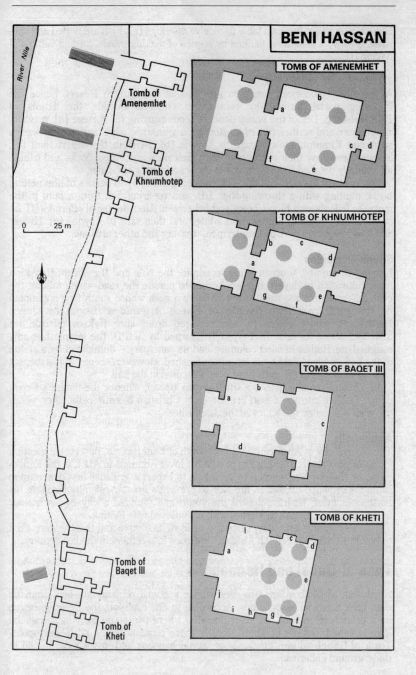

BENI HASSAN

River Nile

Tomb of Amenemhet

Tomb of Khnumhotep

0   25 m

Tomb of Baqet III

Tomb of Kheti

TOMB OF AMENEMHET

a   b   c   d   e   f

TOMB OF KHNUMHOTEP

a   b   c   d   e   f   g

TOMB OF BAQET III

a   b   c   d

TOMB OF KHETI

a   b   c   d   e   f   g   h   i   j   l

Heptet, who sits at her own table to receive offerings [e]. Fish are netted and spit-roasted above a false door flanked by scenes of making music, fording cattle and baking [f].

TOMB OF AMENEMHET (#3)

Amenemhet's successor was also governor of the Eastern Desert, hence the imposing portal framed by proto-Doric columns outside the **Tomb of Khnumhotep**. Left of the *muwu* dancers accompanying his cortege [a], servants weigh grain and scribes record its storage in granaries; while agricultural scenes surmount Khnumhotep's voyage to Abydos [b]. Beneath the desert hunt [c], Semitic Amus pay their respects to him; their alien costumes, flocks and tribute all minutely detailed – the governor is shown accepting eye-paint.

Remnants of his statue in the niche are eclipsed by vivid scenes of him netting birds, hunting with a throwing-stick [d], and spearing fish from a punt in the marshes [e], above a hippo, crocs and fishermen. After the usual offerings [f], he inspects boat-building timber from a litter and then sails to Abydos [g]. Higher and lower registers portray laundrymen, weavers and other artisans.

Speos Artemidos

Leaving the tombs, tourists linger to admire the Nile and the abrupt transition from cultivation to desert, but few bother to pursue the road which follows the cliffs 2.5km south, and then heads 500m up a wadi whose south face is pimpled by the small rock-hewn **temple of Speos Artemidos**. Begun by Queen Hatshepsut, whose claims to have restored order after Hyksos misrule are inscribed above its door (but typically usurped by Seti I), the temple has only roughed-out Hathor-headed columns, and its sanctuary – dominated by a statue of the lion-goddess Pakht – is largely unfinished. However, scenes of Hatshepsut making offerings to the gods have been executed in the hall.

Just before the site there's a small **grotto** (*speos*), whence the temple's Greek name. Farther into the desert are the early Christian **hermit cells**, after whom the wadi was called the Valley of the Anchorites.

Antinopolis

The ancient city of **Antinopolis**, 10km south of Beni Hassan, deserves a mention for its origins alone. Touring Egypt with his lover Antinous in AD 130, the Roman emperor Hadrian was warned by an oracle to expect a grievous loss, whereupon Antinous drowned himself in the Nile to prevent a greater calamity befalling his master. In grief, Hadrian deified the youth and founded a city in his honour before continuing south to Thebes with his unloved wife Plotina.

There's nothing left today, since the ruins of its temple and theatre were used to build the village of Sheikh Abadah, or turned into cement in the last century.

Tuna al-Gabel and Hermopolis

Northwest of Mallawi are two sites whose vestigial remains are less dramatic than their mythical associations. According to one tradition, the Creation began on a primordial mound near **Hermopolis**, where two stone baboons recall the long-vanished Temple of Thoth. Rather more remains of the city's necropolis, **Tuna al-Gabel**, where thousands of sacred baboons and ibises were buried in underground galleries.

By hiring a **taxi** or pick-up from Mallawi, you can visit both sites in a half-day excursion (group rate £E20), or Tuna al-Gabel alone (£E10) within a couple of hours. Getting there by erratic public transport connections seems more trouble than the sites are worth. Bring plenty of water, as the necropolis is isolated amidst scorching desert.

Tuna al-Gabel

The **necropolis** (daily 9am–5pm; £E8, students £E4; photo permits an outrageous £E5 per house) gets its name from the small town of TUNA AL-GABEL, 6km from the site. Halfway along the road from town, keep your eyes fixed on the distant rockface, where a boundary stele marks the edge of the agricultural land claimed by Tell el-Amarna, across the river (see section following). On arrival at the necropolis you must buy an admission ticket and pay a 25pt toll to enter the desert. The site is awash with sand, wind-rippled drifts casting its angular mausolea into high relief, but obscuring other features.

A path to the right of the entrance leads to the **catacombs** (*al-Saradeb*), which some believe stretch as far as Hermopolis. The section open to visitors consists of several main corridors with blocked-off side passages, where the mummified baboons and ibises were stacked (a few bandages remain). A shrine near the ladder contains a baboon fetish and a pathetic-looking mummy; baboons were sacred to Thoth (see box below). Beneath the main gallery lies the tomb of a temple priest. Sadly, the agreeably spooky atmosphere vanishes once the lights go on and coach parties arrive.

THOTH AND THE HERMOPOLITAN OGDOAD

In Egyptian mythology, **Thoth** was the divine scribe and reckoner of time, the inventor of writing and the patron god of scribes. His cult probably originated in the Delta, but achieved the greatest following in Middle Egypt; later, by association with Khonsu, he acquired the attributes of the moon-god and mastery over science and knowledge. Though usually depicted with a man's body and the head of an ibis (his sacred bird), Thoth also assumed the form of a great white baboon, invariably endowed with an outsize penis. Baboons habitually shriek just before dawn, and the Egyptians believed that a pair of them uttered the first greetings to the sun from the sand dunes at the edge of the world.

Thoth's role is rather more complex in relation to the Hermopolitan cosmogony, which ordained that the chaos preceding the world's creation had four characteristics, each identified with a pair of gods and goddesses: primordial water (*Nun/Nanuet*), infinite space (*Heh/Hehet*), darkness (*Kek/Keket*) and invisibility (*Amun/Amunet*). From this chaos arose the primaeval mound and the cosmic egg whence the sun-god was hatched and proceeded to organise the world. Whilst stressing the role of this **Hermopolitan Ogdoad** (company of eight), Thoth's devotees credited him with laying the cosmic egg in the guise of the "Great Cackler", so it's difficult to know who got star billing in this Creation myth. By the New Kingdom it had generally succumbed to the version espoused at Heliopolis (see p.149), but Thoth's cult continued into Ptolemaic times.

Thoth

Farther along the main track is a miniature **City of the Dead** with "streets" of mausolea which mostly reflect Hellenistic influences. The finest structure is the **Tomb of Petosiris**, High Priest of Thoth (whose coffin is in the Cairo Museum), dating from around 300 BC. Its vestibule walls depict traditional activities such as brick-making, sewing and reaping (left), milking, husbandry and wine-making (right) – with all the figures wearing Greek costume. Inside the tomb are colourful scenes from the *Book of Gates* and the *Book of the Dead*. The most vivid shows nine baboons, twelve women and a dozen cobras, each set representing a temporal cycle. Notice the Nubians at the bottom of the opposite wall.

Behind this is another "house" whose upper room displays the **Mummy of Isadora**, a young woman from Antinopolis who drowned in the Nile around 120 BC. Victims of the life-giving river acquired posthumous sanctity, but the leathery state of Isadora's corpse owes to 2000 years of desert air rather than embalming techniques, which had by then degenerated. From here, walk past the columns 100m beyond to find the brick superstructure of *al-Saqiyya*, a great **well** that once supplied the necropolis and its sacred aviary with fresh water, drawn up from 70m below the desert by a huge **water wheel**. For *baksheesh*, the guard will unlock the well and let you climb down – though beware bats and scorpions.

The ruins of Hermopolis

The pulverised ruins of Hermopolis spread beyond the village of ASHMUNEIN, off the secondary road linking Mallawi with Tuna al-Gabel. If possible, take the access road curving off to the west of Ashmunein, which brings you to a pair of **giant sandstone baboons** that once sported erect phalluses (hacked off by early Christians) and upheld the ceiling of the Temple of Thoth. Built by Ramses II using masonry from Tell el-Amarna, the temple stood within an enclosure covering 640 square metres, the spiritual heart of the city of the moon-god.

Hermopolis was a cult centre from early Dynastic times, venerated as the site of the primeval mound where the sun-god emerged from a cosmic egg. Like Heliopolis (which made similar claims) its priesthood evolved an elaborate cosmogony, known as the Hermopolitan Ogdoad (see box on previous page). Though ancient Egyptians called the city *Khmunu*, history remembers it as **Hermopolis Magna**; its Ptolemaic title reflecting the Greek association of Thoth with their own god Hermes. However, none of the mounds of earth and rubble that remain seem credible as the site of Creation, and there's little to see except 24 slender rose granite **columns**, farther south. Re-erected by archaeologists who mistook the ruins for a Greek *Agora*, they previously supported a Coptic basilica, but originally belonged to a Ptolemaic temple.

Tell el-Amarna

TELL EL-AMARNA is the familiar name for the site where **Pharaoh Akhenaten** and **Queen Nefertiti** founded a city dedicated to a revolutionary idea of God, which later rulers assailed as heretical. During their brief reign, Egyptian art cast off its preoccupation with death and the afterlife to revel in human concerns; bellicose imperialism gave way to pacifistic retrenchment, and the old gods were toppled from their pedestals. The interplay between personalities, beliefs and art anticipates the Renaissance – and their story beats Shakespeare for drama.

The interest of the **site** – located between Mallawi and Assyut (see p.256 for access details) – is chiefly romantic, for what remains is hardly comparable to the great temples farther up the Nile. Only the faintest outline of the city is discernible, whilst the reliefs in its rock-cut tombs have been badly mutilated (initially by reactionaries, who defaced the images of Akhenaten and his deity). Nonetheless, it strikes some visitors as intensely evocative: a place of mystery whose enchantment grows the more one knows about it.

The story of Akhenaten and Nefertiti

Few figures from ancient history have inspired as much conjecture as Akhenaten and Nefertiti, as scholars dispute even fundamental aspects of their story – let alone the interpretation of the events.

The tale begins with Pharaoh **Amenophis III**, who flouted convention by making Tiy, his Nubian concubine, Great Wife, despite her lack of royal blood. **Queen Tiy** remained formidable long after Amenophis entered his dotage and their eldest son ascended the throne as **Amenophis IV**. Some believe this event followed his father's death, others that mother and son ruled jointly for twelve years. To square the former theory with the period of his reign (c.1379–1362 BC) and his demise around the age of thirty means accepting that Amenophis Jr embarked on his religious reformation between the age of nine and thirteen. It seems an unusually early age, though a marriage at thirteen is quite possible.

The origins of Amenophis's wife, **Nefertiti**, are obscure. Her name – meaning "A Beautiful Woman Has Come" – suits the romantic legend that she was a Mesopotamian princess originally betrothed to Amenophis III. However, others identify her as Amenophis III's child by a secondary wife, or as the daughter of his vizier **Ay**, whose wife, **Tey**, was almost certainly Nefertiti's wet-nurse. The pharaonic custom of sister-brother and father-daughter marriages allows plenty of scope for speculation, but the fair-skinned bust of Nefertiti in the Berlin Museum suggests that she wasn't Tiy's child, at any rate.

Early in his reign, Amenophis IV began to espouse the **worship of the Aten** (see box overpage), whose ascendancy threatened the priesthoods of other cults. The bureaucracy was equally alarmed by his decree that the spoken language should be used in official documents, contrary to all tradition. To escape their influence and realise his vision of a city dedicated to the Aten, the pharaoh founded a **new capital** upon an empty plain beside the Nile, halfway between Memphis and Thebes, which he named **Akhetaten**, the "Horizon of the Aten".

It was here that the royal couple settled in the fifth year of their reign and took Aten's name in honour of their faith. He discarded Amenophis IV for **Akhenaten** (Servant of the Aten) and vowed never to leave the city, whilst she took a forename meaning "Beautiful are the Beauties of the Aten", styling herself **Nefernefruaten-Nefertiti**. Her status surpassed that of any previous Great Wife, approaching that of Akhenaten himself. Bas-reliefs and stelae show her participating in state festivals and her own cartouche was coupled with Aten's – an unprecedented association. Tableaux from this period depict an idyllic royal family life, with the couple embracing their daughters and banqueting with Queen Tiy.

There's no sign that their happiness was marred by his decision to take a second wife, **Kiya**, for dynastic ends; nor of the degenerative condition that supposedly afflicted Akhenaten in later life. However, the great ceremony held at Akhetaten in their twelfth regnal year marked a turning point. Whether or not this was Akhenaten's true coronation (following his father's death), he subse-

ATEN-WORSHIP AND AMARNA ART

Many scholars herald **Aten-worship** as a breakthrough in human spirituality and cultural evolution: the world's first monotheistic religion, and thus representing "a peak of clarity which rose above the lowlands of superstition".

Aten was originally just an aspect of the sun-god (the "Globe" or "Disk" of the midday sun), ranking low in the Theban pantheon until Amenophis III privately adopted him as a personal deity. Then Akhenaten publicly exalted Aten above other gods, subsuming all their attributes into this newly omnipotent being. Invocations to Ma'at (truth) were retained, but otherwise the whole cast of underworld and celestial deities was jettisoned. Morbid Osirian rites were also replaced by paeans to life in the joyous warmth of Aten's rays (which are usually shown ending in a hand clasping an *ankh*), as in this extract from the *Hymn to Aten*:

When you rise from the horizon the earth grows bright; you shine as the Aten in the sky and drive away the darkness; when your rays gleam forth, the whole of Egypt is festive. People wake and stand on their feet, for you have lifted them up . . . Then the whole of the land does its work; all the cattle enjoy their pastures, trees and plants grow green, birds fly up from their nests and raise their wings in praise of your spirit. Goats frisk on their feet and all the fluttering and flying things come alive.

Similarities between the *Hymn* and *The Song of Solomon* (supposedly written 500 years later) have encouraged speculation about the influence of Atenism on early Jewish monotheism. In *Moses and Monotheism*, Freud argued that Moses was an Egyptian nobleman and the Biblical Exodus a "pious fiction which a remote tradition has reworked in the service of its own biases". Conversely, a recent book by Ahmed Osman advances the theory that Akhenaten's deity derived from tales of the Jewish God related to him by his maternal grandfather Yuya, the Joseph of the Old Testament (see p.328).

quently launched a **purge against the old cults**. From Kom Ombo to Bubastis, the old temples were closed and their statues disfigured, causing widespread internal unrest. Although this was quelled by Akhenaten's chief of police, **Mahu**, his foreign minister apparently ignored pleas from foreign vassals menaced by the Hittites and Haibru (Hebrew) tribes, and the army was less than zealous in defending Egypt's frontiers. Akhenaten was consequently blamed for squandering the territorial gains of his forefathers.

What happened in the last years of Akhenaten and Nefertiti's reign is subject to various interpretations. The consensus is that Neferiti and Akhenaten became estranged, and he took as co-regent **Smenkhkare**, a mysterious youth married to their eldest daughter, **Meritaten**. Whilst Nefertiti withdrew to her Northern Palace, Akhenaten and his regent lived together at the other end of the city; the poses struck by them in mural scenes of the period have prompted suggestions of a homosexual relationship. Whatever the truth of this, it's known that Smenkhkare ruled alone for some time after the **death of Akhenaten** (c.1362 BC), before dying himself. Nefertiti's fate is less certain, but it's generally believed that she also died around the same time. To date, none of their mummies have been found (or, rather, definitely identified).

In the late 1970s, a novel solution to the puzzle of Smenkhkare's identity and the **fate of Nefertiti** was advanced by Julia Samson of the Petrie Museum. Samson argued that Smenkhkare *was* Nefertiti, who, far from being spurned by Akhenaten, finally achieved pharaonic status, adopting Smenkhkare as her

Equally intriguing is the artwork of the Amarna period and the questions it raises about Akhenaten. **Amarna art** focussed on nature and human life rather than the netherworld and resurrection. Royal portraiture, previously impersonally formalised, was suffused by naturalism (a process which began late in the reign of Amenophis III, as evinced by the stele depicting the obese king listlessly slumped beside Tiy). Whilst marshes and wildlife remained a popular subject, they no longer implicitly associated birds and fish with the forces of chaos. The roofless Aten-temples made new demands on sculptors and painters, who mixed sunk- and bas-relief carving to highlight features with shifting shadows and illumination.

Most striking is the rendering of **human figures**, especially Akhenaten's, whose attenuated cranium, curvaceous spine and belly, matronly pelvis and buttocks (evident on the colossi in the Cairo Museum) have prompted speculation that the pharaoh had a hydrocephalus condition, or was a hermaphrodite. Some argue that the Amarna style was essentially an acquiesence to Akhenaten's physiognomy, others that such distortions were simply a device that could be eschewed, as in the exquisite bust of Nefertiti. Advocates of the "Akhenaten was sick" theory point out that this was the only time when vomiting was ever represented in Egyptian art; however, Amarna art also uniquely depicted royalty eating, yet nobody asserts that other pharaohs never ate.

Nefertiti and Akhenaten

"throne name". Since the faces on the stelae depicting Akhenaten and his co-regent have been obliterated, only their cartouches identify them; and previous hypotheses have never satisfactorily explained why Smenkhkare's should be coupled with "Nefernefruaten", Nefertiti's Aten-name. Conversely, the youth shown with a princess isn't identified as her husband, nor by name, but he does wear the royal *uraeus*.

Unfortunately, this figure looks too old to be the famous boy-king who succeeded Smenkhkare at the age of nine – known to posterity as **Tutankhamun**. Tut's own genealogy is obscure (some hold that his parents were Amenophis III and his half-sister Sitamun; others favour Ay and Tey, or Akhenaten and Kiya), but it's certain that he was originally raised to worship Aten, and named Tutankh*aten*. By renouncing this name for one honouring Amun, he heralded a return to Thebes and the old gods, fronting a **Theban counter-revolution** executed by Vizier Ay and General Horemheb.

Some think this was relatively benign whilst Tut and his successor Ay ruled Egypt, blaming **Horemheb** and Seti I for a later and ruthless extirpation of Atenism. Certainly, in time-honoured tradition, Seti plundered the abandoned city of Akhetaten for masonry to build new temples, ordered its site cursed by priests to deter reoccupation, and excised the cartouches of every ruler tainted with the "Amarna heresy" from their monuments and the List of Kings. So thorough was this cover-up that Akhenaten and Nefertiti remained unknown to history until the nineteenth century.

The site of Akhetaten

The remains of Akhenaten's city are spread across a desert plain girdled by an arc of cliffs. Except for a few palm groves beside the Nile, the site is utterly desolate, a tawny expanse of low mounds and narrow trenches littered with potshards. These fragments of pale terracotta, cream and duck egg blue-glazed pottery seem more tangible links to the city's past than its vestigial remains. Because the city was created from scratch and deserted soon after Tut moved the court back to Thebes, its era of glory lasted only twelve years, and much was never completed, so don't expect to find imposing ruins or statues, as everything of value has been removed to museums. However, a century of archaeological research has identified the city's salient features, assisted by pictures found in contemporary tombs.

Visiting Tell el-Amarna: el-Till

Tell el-Amarna lies on the east bank of the Nile, 12km south of Mallawi and roughly halfway between Minya and Assyut. Starting from either of the latter, an excursion will take the best part of a day, as the widely dispersed attractions are time-consuming and tiring, unless you have a car.

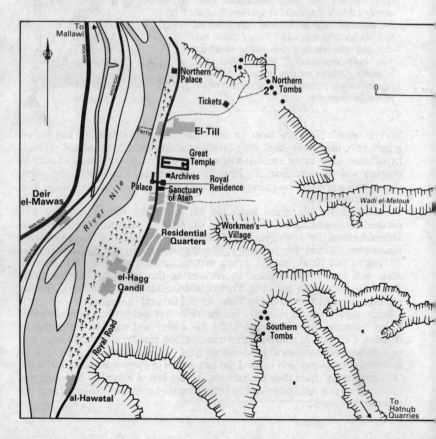

Wherever you start out from, you're best off making a connection at **Mallawi**. From here, drivers should turn east at KAFR KHUZAM, the second village south of town, to reach the ferry crossing. By public transport, any southbound bus or local pick-up truck (*bijou*) from the depot south of Mallawi's railway station can take you out to the ferry crossing on the west bank of the river for 25pt; private taxis charge £E3–5. From here, you can either cross by *felucca* (£E3), car ferry (£E50pt per head, vehicles £E2; last ferry at 6pm) or canopied motorboat (£E5 group rate) to the village of el-Till. There are also smaller ferries from DEIR EL-MAWAS to the southern village of EL-HAGG QANDIL, but this isn't such a good approach.

Landing at **EL-TILL,** you'll be greeted by hordes of children touting colourful basketwork. Left of the landing-stage is a small office selling **tickets** (£E2.50) which cover the ruins of the city, though not the Northern Tombs. These are reached by a spine-jolting **tractor-driven trailer** or occasional minibus (£E1.50); the former returns to El-Till via the palace district of the ruined city. To see more than that, you'll have to find a car-owner willing to risk his suspension **driving around** the site. After hard bargaining, reckon on paying £E40–60 for a full day's hire or £E15 for the round-trip to the Southern Tombs.

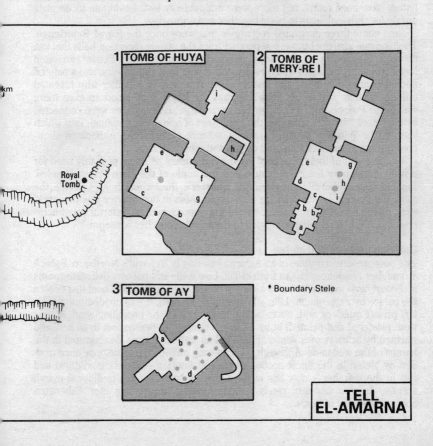

Royal Tomb

1 TOMB OF HUYA

2 TOMB OF MERY-RE I

3 TOMB OF AY

* Boundary Stele

TELL EL-AMARNA

Though most people head directly for the Northern Tombs, we've described the city first; an idea of how it was and who lived there adds to an appreciation of the tombs.

The City

The dirt track running south from el-Till follows the old **Royal Road** that formed Ancient Akhenaten's main axis, and is known locally as the *Sikket es-Sultan*, the Road of the Sultan. A twenty-minute walk brings you to a Muslim cemetery which overlies part of a vast rectangle stretching eastwards towards the ridge.

This was once the **Great Temple of Aten**, whose northern wall incorporated the Hall of Foreign Tribute where emissaries proffered treasure (as depicted in tombs). Unlike traditional temples, which got darker as one approached the sanctuary, Aten's was roofless, admitting the rays of its namesake. It's thought that Horemheb ordered the temple's destruction after Akhenaten's death, and Ramses II quarried its foundations for his temples at Hermopolis, across the Nile.

Farther south (and hard to distinguish beneath shifting sands) are the remnants of the Foreign Office **Archives**, where the *Amarna Letters* were discovered. Written in the Akkadian script used for diplomatic correspondence with Asiatic states, these clay tablets have revealed much about the period. Over 360 letters have been found, but more were undoubtedly lost, leaving an incomplete puzzle for archaeologists to piece together and argue over.

Next come three excavated rectangles that were once the **Royal Residence**. Their private apartments were separated from the stately reception halls that ran through the centre of the huge palace compound. When Petrie excavated Nefertiti's suite, he found wall-tiles decorated with fruit and flowers, and a painted floor depicting fish, birds and insects (later smashed by a farmer who resented tourists walking across his fields). Across the Royal Road stood an even more vast **State Palace**, with a dock for the royal barge. Both palaces were connected by a covered "flyover" spanning the road (part of one pylon remains), into which was set the **Window of Appearances**, whence Nefertiti and Akhenaten showered favoured courtiers with gold collars and other rewards.

To the south of their residence lay the **Sanctuary of Aten**, probably used for private worship by the royal family, and the home of the High Priest, Panehsi. Beyond spread the city's **residential quarters**; the richest homes beside the road, the poorest hovels backing onto desert. Also in this quarter was the workshop of the sculptor Tuthmosis, where the famous bust of Nefertiti was uncovered in 1912, before being smuggled to Berlin's Ägyptisches Museum.

Outlying palaces and stelae

The best-preserved outline of an Amarna building is Nefertiti's **Northern Palace** or summer residence, 1500m from el-Till. Low walls and hollows delineate rooms and courtyards grouped around a garden which once contained a pool that cooled the palace by evaporation. Like all Amarna residences, it was divided into public and private quarters, with north-facing doors to catch the prevailing wind. Rooms were plastered and painted, lit by oil lamps hung from pegs or set in niches, and warmed by braziers over winter. Fitted toilets and bathrooms also featured in the homes of the well-to-do. Although you can walk on bits of mosaic floor once trodden by Nefertiti, the finest section of painted flooring – depicting wildfowl and fish in the marshes – now lies in the Cairo Museum. Unlike traditional marsh scenes, Amarna tableaux rarely feature hunting, suggesting that Akhenaten abjured the sport of kings.

In summer, Akhenaten and Nefertiti would ride in their electrum-plated chariot to the other end of the Royal Road, where another palace called *Maru-Aten* stood near the modern-day hamlet of al-Hawatah. Alongside this **Southern Palace** lay a pleasure-lake surrounded by trees and shrubs, which fed smaller pools within the palace. The walls of its columned hall were painted with flowers and inlaid with figures and Aten-symbols. It was here that Petrie found hundreds of glazed pieces and flakes of paint adhering to blocks which bore Meritaten's cartouche superimposed over another assumed to be that of Nefertiti – the rather shaky basis upon which archaeologists devised the theory of Nefertiti's rejection in favour of Smenkhkare. In 1974, however, Professor John Harris re-examined the fragments and concluded that the hidden cartouches really belonged to Kiya, whose existence was unknown to earlier scholars. From this point, Samson developed her theory that Nefertiti and Smenkhkare were one and the same.

Akhetaten's periphery was defined by **boundary stelae** carved high up on the cliffs (marked * on our map); erected over successive years, their inscriptions and family portraits have enabled archaeologists to deduce many events during Akhenaten's reign. Fine alabaster for the temples and public buildings was dragged from the **Hatnub Quarries**, 10km southeast of the city (only accessible by donkey or four-wheel drive). On the way up the wadi are remains of workmen's huts and pottery from diverse periods.

The Northern Tombs

Most visitors are content to see the **Northern Tombs** (open daily 7am–5pm), 4km from el-Till village. The office near the landing stage can arrange lifts on the tractor-pulled trailer (usually scheduled to coincide with coach parties), whilst motorists should follow a poorly signposted track towards the cliffs. Admission **tickets** (£E1.50, students #75pt) are either sold at the yellow building halfway along the track, or at the **café** (toilets; overpriced drinks) below the cliffs; ask which applies before leaving el-Till.

Although guards manipulate foil-covered boards to reflect sunlight into tombs without electric lighting, it's advisable to bring a torch to study the reliefs and paintings (now less clear than the exquisite copies made by Norman de Garis Davies, a century ago), and spotlight uneven floors or deep shafts with flimsy railings. Note that, unless you insist, you won't be shown the most distant of the six **tombs** (#1 and #2).

TOMB OF HUYA (#1)

As Steward to Queen Tiy and Superintendent of the Royal Harem, **Huya** is shown praying at the entrance beside a hymn to the Aten **[a]**. In the following banqueting scene **[b]**, involving Tiy, the royal couple and two princesses, it may be significant that the dowager queen is merely drinking (which was acceptable by Theban standards of decorum), whereas the Amarna brood tuck in with gusto (an act of royalty never hitherto portrayed). Across the way they imbibe wine, *sans* princesses **[c]**, followed by a royal procession to the Hall of Tribute, where emissaries from Kush and Syria await Akhenaten and Nefertiti **[d]**.

On the rear wall, Akhenaten decorates Huya from the Window of Appearances (notice the sculptor's studio, lower down **[e]**), who displays his awards **[f]** on the other side of the portal, the lintel of which portrays three generations of the royal family, including Amenophis III. Along the east wall, Akhenaten leads Tiy to the temple built for his parents **[g]**. Huya's mummy was stashed in a burial shaft **[h]** below the transverse hall, beyond which is a shrine painted with offerings, containing an unfinished statue of Huya **[i]**.

TOMB OF MERY-RE II (#2)

The last resting place of **Mery-Re II**, Overseer of the Two Treasuries, is similar in shape to Huya's tomb, but was constructed late in Akhenaten's reign, since his cartouches have been replaced by Smenkhkare's, and Nefertiti's by Meritaten's. Beyond the entrance (whose adoration scene and *Hymn to Aten* are largely destroyed), the inner walls portray Nefertiti straining a drink for the king, who is seated beneath a sunshade (to your left); and Mery-Re receiving a golden crown, followed by a warm welcome from his household (right). The rear wall bears an unfinished scene of Mery-Re being rewarded by Smenkhkare and Meritaten, drawn in black ink.

TOMB OF AHMOSE (#3)

This battered tomb is one of the four that visitors usually see. The entrance walls show **Ahmose**, Akhenaten's fan-bearer, praying to the Aten, with a now-illegible inscription enjoining the deity to ensure "that there is sand on the shore, that fishes in the stream have scales, and cattle have hair. Let him sojourn here until the swan turns black and the raven white". Inside, you can just discern Ahmose carrying an axe and a fan, his official regalia. On the left-hand wall are reliefs of archers, shield-bearers and pikemen, crouched and moving, followed by an outsized horse and chariot outlined in red pigment (presumably intended to represent Akhenaten leading his army into battle, which never happened).

TOMB OF MERY-RE I (#4)

High Priest **Mery-Re I** (father of Mery-Re II) rated a superior tomb with a coloured cornice around its entrance **[a]** and columns of painted flowers at the rear of the vestibule **[b]**. Reliefs of Mery-Re and his wife, Tenro, at prayer flank the portal **[c]** into the main chamber, which retains two of its original papyrus-bud columns. Proceeding clockwise around the room, you'll see Mery-Re's investiture with a golden collar **[d]** and the royal family leaving the palace **[e]**, Akhenaten in a chariot (his face and the Aten symbol have been chiselled out, as usual). Scenes of offerings **[f]** and Aten-worship **[g]** flank the doorway into the unfinished rear chamber, which lacks any decoration. More interesting is the eastern wall **[h]**, depicting Akhenaten and the Great Temple (which has helped archaeologists visualise the city's appearance). Notice the sensitive relief of blind beggars awaiting alms, low down in the corner **[i]**.

TOMBS OF PENTU (#5) AND PANEHSI (#6)

The third tomb in this cluster belongs to **Pentu**, the royal physician, whose statue in the endmost chamber has been disfigured. Its reliefs are in even worse shape, so there's no point wasting time here when you could be checking out the isolated tomb of High Priest **Panehsi**, 500m south along the cliff path. Unlike most of the others, its decorative facade has remained intact, but the interior has been modified by Copts who used it as a chapel. On the left of the entrance the royal family pray above their servants. The painted, apse-like recess in the main chamber is probably a Coptic addition. In one corner, steps spiral down into an underground sarcophagus chamber containing broken urns. Lower down the cliff are strata of rubble and potshards – vestiges of a medieval Coptic village.

The Royal Tomb

Secreted in a wild valley 5.5km from the plain, the **Royal Tomb** is kept locked to prevent further damage, but the office in el-Till might arrange for it to be opened. Assuming you can persuade a taxi to make the journey (which involves muscling the vehicle through patches of soft sand), the round-trip takes three to four hours. You're bound to have to wait until the watchman turns up and then join him for tea.

The tomb is the first from the XVIII Dynasty to run directly from a corridor to a burial chamber. The burial scene and text were virtually obliterated by Amun's priests, and no mummies were ever found here. However, one of the side chambers off the main corridor contained fragments of a granite sarcophagus bearing Tiy's cartouche, suggesting this might have been a family vault. Almost certainly, it served for the burial of Meketaten, the royal couple's second-eldest daughter, for the walls bear scenes of her funeral and their grief. Although visitors still leave offerings in their memory, no one knows whether Akhenaten and Nefertiti were interred here (and perhaps dragged out to rot a few years later) or elsewhere. Some believe that the mysterious mummy found in Tomb #55 in the Valley of the Kings is Akhenaten's (see "The Theban Necropolis").

Akhenaten

The Southern Tombs

Visiting the **Southern Tombs** entails a separate 14km excursion (£E15 from el-Till if you can find a driver who'll oblige) and tracking down the *gaffir* with the keys. The tombs are scattered over seven low hills in two clusters: #7–#15 and #16–#25. Amarna notables buried here include Tutu, the foreign minister, and Ramose, Steward of Amenophis III, but the ones to look out for are Mahu and Ay.

TOMB OF MAHU (#9)

Set amongst the northernmost group is the **Tomb of Mahu**, Akhenaten's chief of police and frontier security. The structure has a long, rough-cut corridor without decoration. On the right-hand entrance wall of the first chamber, Mahu appears before the Vizier with two intruders whom he accuses of being "agitated by some foreign power". Farther back are two more chambers at different levels, linked by a winding stairway and decorated with scenes of Mahu mixing with royalty.

TOMB OF AY (#25)

Ay's Tomb, the finest at Tell el-Amarna, lies some distance beyond the southern group and was never finished, since Ay built himself a new vault at Thebes after the court returned there under Tutankhamun. However, such paintings as were executed show the Amarna style at its apogee.

Both sides of the tomb's vestibule **[a]** are decorated. On the left, the king and queen, three princesses, Nefertiti's sister Mutnedjmet and her dwarves lead the court in the worship of Aten. Across the way is a superb relief of Ay and his wife Tey rendering homage and the most complete text of the famous *Hymn to Aten*. The really intriguing scenes, however, are in the main chamber. On the left side of the entrance wall, Ay and Tey are showered with decorations from the *Window of Appearances*, acclaimed by fan-bearers, scribes and guards **[b]**. Palace life is intimately observed: a concubine has her hair done, girls play the harp and dance, cook and sweep; farther along, Ay is congratulated by his friends, as servants carry the gifts away **[c]**. The top register shows doormen and peasants gossiping, whores and soldiers, and other street life. Along the rear wall are a ruined door-shaped stele **[d]** and a stairway leading to an unfinished burial shaft.

Ay and Tey are mysterious figures, honoured as "Divine Father and Mother", but never directly identified as being royal. Some reckon Ay was a son of Yuya and Thuya, Akhenaten's maternal grandparents; others that Tey bore Nefertiti, or that both conceived Tutankhamun. Certainly, Ay was Vizier to Amenophis III, Akhenaten and Tutankhamun, and reigned briefly himself (1352–1348 BC).

Assyut and around

Every country has at least one city which is universally loathed by all but those who live there. In Egypt, Assyut holds this honour.

Douglas Kennedy

Power cuts, sectarian tensions and sporadic violence have given **Assyut**, largest city of the Nile Valley, a forbidding reputation and most tourists only come here for connections to Tell el-Amarna or Kharga and Dakhla oases. That said, some find the place briefly compelling, exuding indolence and battered charm. More conventionally appealing are a pair of **monasteries** and various **moulids** in the vicinity. And for those arriving from – or about to visit – the spartan Western Desert oases, Assyut's hotels and restaurants will seem like the height of luxury.

All telephone numbers in the Assyut area are prefixed ☎088.

Assyut

Seething terminals and traffic await visitors to downtown **ASSYUT**, whose street names (mostly in Arabic or outdated) are even less help than usual. However, hotel billboards facilitate orientation. Don't bother searching for the now-defunct tourist office in the Governorate – ask at the ritzier hotels if you need information.

Accommodation

If nothing else, Assyut offers a good range of accommodation, with decent options at all budgets, most within a few minutes' walk of the train station.

HOSTELS AND CAMPING
YMCA (☎323-218). With pleasant, carpeted A/C double (£E9) and deluxe rooms (£E15), and a swimming pool due soon, this is unbeatable value and well worth the taxi ride (£E1) – it's otherwise hard to find, in the north of the city.
Youth Hostel, Lux Houses, Building #503 (☎324-846). Again in the suburbs, accessible by *service* taxi, though the fusty dorm beds (£E2; £E3 for non-IYHF members) are uninviting.
Camping is permitted at the **Officers' Club** (☎322-134) and **Sporting Club** (☎233-139), both near the Assyut Barrage. You can also camp on Banana Island, *sans* facilities.

CHEAP HOTELS
Hotel El-Haramein (C), Sharia el-Hellaly. Fanless but OK rooms; singles £E5, doubles £E8.
Zam Zam Hotel (D), Sharia el-Hellaly. Similar accommodation at £E3.50 per head.
Omar Khaiam Hotel (G), near the souks. Functional rooms for £E12 a double.

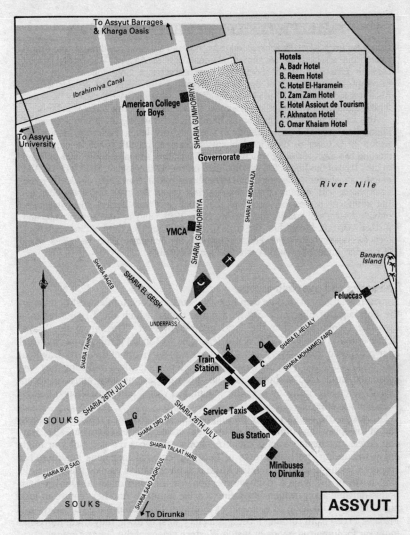

Hotels
A. Badr Hotel
B. Reem Hotel
C. Hotel El-Haramein
D. Zam Zam Hotel
E. Hotel Assiout de Tourism
F. Akhnaton Hotel
G. Omar Khaiam Hotel

ASSYUT

Hotel Assiout de Tourism (E), Sharia el-Geish. Renovated singles (£E8) and doubles (£E12) behind a grotty facade. Very noisy.

The *El Ryad*, *Savoy*, *Windsor*, *Semiramis*, *Venus* and *Lotus* hotels are not recommended.

MORE UPMARKET HOTELS

Hotel Akhnaton (F), Sharia 26th July (☎327-723). Comfy, reasonably priced A/C rooms with private baths and TV; singles £E15–25, doubles £E25–35.

Hotel Reem (B), Sharia el-Hellaly. Similar to the above; doubles £E40.

Badr Hotel (A), Sharia el-Geish (☎329-811). Aspiringly palatial, the *Badr* cocoons tour groups and VIPs within its padded, mirrored chambers (£E60–110 plus 12 percent tax).

TORM WARNINGS: TROUBLE IN ASSYU

Heavy Security, sexually segregated cafeterias and a ban on co-ed music and drama reflect the strength of Muslim fundamentalism at **Assyut University**, where *Gamaat Islamiya* (Islamic Societies) have attracted a large following by their uncompromising pursuit of the *Sharia*, alarming Christians and secular leftists. Muslims, too, have run afoul of club-wielding militants on day trips where male and female students travel together, or similar violations of fundamentalist standards.

Attacks are usually blamed on **al-Jihad** (Holy Struggle), the group accused of killing President Sadat as a prelude to attempted revolution. Following his assassination on October 6, 1981, local Jihadists stormed Assyut's police headquarters, starting two days of rioting which caused 55 fatalities. Amongst those later indicted at the "Trial of the Jihad 302" was the blind university theologian, Sheikh Omar Abd el-Rahman, allegedly their "spiritual leader" (see p.403). Nowadays, *al-Jihad* is more amorphous, with dozens of autonomous cells which the state ruthlessly pursues. Indiscriminate repression – such as the shooting of worshippers and bystanders outside Assyut's Sharia Mosque in December 1989 – only creates new recruits and further reprisals. Meanwhile, the city's Christians (roughly a third of the population) feel increasingly beleaguered: stigmatised by fundamentalists as allies of a "Crusader" imperialism which exploits Egypt's Muslims.

The souks and riverside quarter

Assyut has largely erased its own history. Scores of rock tombs west of town are the only sign of pharaonic *Sawty*, a nome capital which the Greeks renamed *Lycopolis* (Wolftown) after the local god, Wepwawet, "Opener of the Ways". Represented as a wolf or jackal of the desert, he was an apt symbol for a city which later prospered from slavery, for it was here that survivors of the Forty Day Road (see p.432) emerged from the desert to be traded wholesale. Trafficking may have continued until 1883, although Amelia Edwards saw nothing amiss a decade earlier, when she enthused over the "quaint red vases" and "bird-shaped bottles" in Assyut's **souks**.

Nowadays the souks purvey nothing worse than flyblown meat at the seedy end of the sprawling commercial district that opens with jewellers on Talaat Harb and peters out beside a fetid canal. A shoppers' mecca it's not, but you might enjoy wandering the backstreets of decaying colonial mansions smothered in creepers, trying to locate a derelict **khan** that once stabled camels (on your right, 50m north of the souk's main intersection) or the **Hammam al-Qadim** bathhouse, farther along, which has a fine marble fountain. Another feature of local nightlife is the invasion of a couple of thousand **Romanians** on Thursdays and Fridays. Freed from running a cement factory west of town, they trade Romanian footwear for imported goods or watch Western videos at the *Omar Khaiam*.

The leafy **riverside quarter** is also worth a ramble, with cool breezes along the Corniche. Sharia el-Hellaly leads directly to the Nile, where you can catch a *felucca* (50pt) to lush **Banana Island** (*Gezira el-Mohz*), a nice picnic spot.

Two kilometres downriver, the British-built (1898–1903) **Assyut Barrage** links the *Officers'* and *Sporting* clubs on opposite banks. Staff at the **Lillian Thrasher Orphanage** on the eastern side are happy to explain their work and goals to visitors. Nineteenth-century missionaries also founded the **American College for Boys** at the canal end of Sharia Gumhorriya, which includes a small **museum** of Coptic and pharaonic artefacts.

Eating and drinking

All three of the upmarket hotels incorporate **restaurants**. Spicy *ads*, salad and roast chicken at the *Reem* costs about £E6; an à la carte meal at the *Akhnaton* roughly twice that, or a bit more at the *Badr*. Both the latter serve alcohol; at the *Badr* bar you may run into Sabur, the Levi-capped, self-styled "King of Assyut" who offers various tourist services – we'd advise against any dealings. Other middle-class establishments include the *Officers'*, *Engineers'* and *Sporting* **clubs** (see above), former consulates which generally admit *pukka*-looking tourists.

Assyut's commercial district, west of the station, features **cheaper eating options**. The *Express Restaurant*, 100m along 26th July, sells hamburgers and *shwarma* or kebab sandwiches, while you can buy a whole grilled chicken at the *Mattam al-Azhar*, 100m down Sa'ad Zaghloul (on the left, with a fancy screen above the door), whose second floor overlooks the quarter. Along 26th July and Talaat Harb you'll find juice bars, patisseries and *kushari* joints; coffeehouses and *taamiya* stands cluster opposite the station.

Other facilities and transport

Assyut's 24-hour **telephone exchange**, beside the railway station, is near the **post office** on the street to the right of the *Hotel Assiout de Tourism*. In the commercial district around Talaat Harb, the *Alexandria* **bank** (Sat–Thurs 8.30am–2pm & 6–9pm, Fri 9am–12.30pm & 6–9pm) will change traveller's cheques. For medical treatment, contact the *El-Mabara* **hospital** (☎323-600) on Sharia el-Mohafaza; you dial ☎123 for an ambulance.

Over a dozen **trains** per day make the 375km run to Cairo (7hr; 2nd class A/C £E9.50), stopping at Mallawi (2hr; £E2) and Minya (3hr; £E3) along the way. Half a dozen A/C services also forge southwards, calling at Sohag (2hr; £E4.50), Qena (4–5hr; £E6.50) and Luxor (6–7hr; £E7.50) en route to Aswan (12hr; £E10). Alternatively, there are seven daily **buses** to Cairo (7hr; £E5) and four to Qena (4hr), plus half-hourly services to Sohag or Minya (2hr) between 6am and 6pm. You'll have to check exactly when the five daily buses to Kharga Oasis (5hr; £E5) leave, and which one continues on to Dakhla (8–9hr; £E9). Seats on oasis buses should be booked the day before.

In the morning, it's easier to reach Kharga by shared **service taxi** (5hrs; £E6) from the depot south of the station. *Service* taxis also run to every town along the Valley between Minya and Qena, and a few points farther afield.

Excursions from Assyut

Close to Assyut are a couple of monasteries – the **Convent of the Virgin** and the **Burnt Monastery** – which testify to the roots Christianity put down in this region in the fourth century. If you start early enough it's also feasible to make long day excursions to **Tell el-Amarna** (see p.252) or **Abydos Temple** (p.271). Mallawi, jumping-off point for Tell el-Amarna, can be reached by *service* taxi (90min; £E2), bus or train (both slower); for Abydos, catch a taxi (2hr) or stopping train to el-Balyana, the nearest town. The **monasteries outside Sohag** (see following section) lie in the same direction and are equally accessible.

BENI MARR, south of Assyut, also deserves a mention, if nothing else, as the village where Nasser spent much of his childhood. Although born and educated in Alexandria, his family's roots were in the village, which still contains a small **Nasser Museum**.

Dirunka: the Convent of the Virgin

The Copts believe that when the Holy Family fled from Herod into Egypt, they sought refuge in caves at **DIRUNKA**, 12km outside Assyut – as did later Christians. From such troglodyte origins, however, the present **Convent of the Virgin** (aka *Deir el-Adhra,* or Santa Maria) on the site has grown into what looks like a fortified shopping mall – not at all the dinky place depicted on brochures.

The expansion is justified by the monastery having to accommodate 50,000 pilgrims for the **Moulid of the Virgin** (Aug 7–22). This occasions the parading of icons around the spacious cave-church where they stand for most of the year. Coptic altars face east because it's from there that Jesus will return, but also because He is "the sun" of their religion. Pilgrims are photographed against a huge portrait of the Virgin, or the verdant plain overlooked by the convent's terrace, below which is a Coptic village where nuns operate a dispensary.

Getting to the monastery by private taxi (£E6 round-trip) will save you the fifteen-minute uphill slog from the roadside, where minibuses from Assyut (25pt) drop visitors. If you can't beg a lift back at the convent, returning minibuses can be flagged down on the main road. The ridge between Dirunka and Assyut is honeycombed with long vandalised rock tombs from pharaonic times.

The Burnt Monastery

By taking a *service* taxi 42km north to **EL-QUSIYA** (1hr; £E1) and then letting kids guide you to this small town's other terminal, you can catch a covered pickup (25pt) 5km out to the **Burnt Monastery** (*Deir el-Muharaaq*), near the desert's edge. Its tinderbox surroundings explain the name and protective walls; the crenellated inner rampart is still blackened from a conflagration during the **Moulid of the Virgin** (June 21–28) a few years ago.

Except on fast days, visitors are shown around the thriving, modernised establishment. Many of the 100 students at its Theological College will become monks when they turn twenty-five. Within the inner compound are grouped the Abbot's residence, a fourth-century keep and two churches. Believers maintain that the **cave-sanctuary** of the small Church of the Annointed once hid the Holy Family for a month, and what is now the altar-stone was used to block its entrance. When an abbot ordered its replacement, the mason's hand was paralysed and a vision of Jesus appeared, intoning "Leave it alone". The *Virgin and Child* icon is said to be painted by Saint Luke; those in the Church of Saint George come from Ethiopia.

Foreigners with passports can stay at the monastery's **guesthouse**, where simple meals are provided. Even for brief visits, a donation seems appropriate.

Sohag

Set on a rich agricultural plain bounded by the hills of the Eastern and Western deserts, **SOHAG** (pronounced "Sohage") is an industrious town of 75,000 with a large Christian community and a small university. A little ramshackle and quite untouristy, its friendly atmosphere makes an agreeable stopover. The **Red and White Monasteries** and **Akhmim** (see overpage) are the nearest sights, but the town also makes a good base for excursions to Abydos Temple (see p.271).

All telephone numbers in the Sohag area are prefixed ☎093.

Rooms and food

The *Andalos Hotel* (☎324-328) has the best **accommodation**, offering clean singles (£E5) and doubles (£E8–£E10) with fans, plus a *fuul* breakfast. Unfortunately, hot water depends on bottled gas deliveries, like boilers at the *El-Salaam* (☎323-317), which has similar singles (£E4) and doubles (£E7).

In the unlikely event that both hotels are full, there's a spartan youth hostel (☎324-395) on Sharia Bur Said, which charges IYHF members £E2, non-members £E6 (lock-out 10am–2pm; 11pm curfew). The *Ramses* (☎323-313) and *Sohag*, without fans or hot water, are last resorts.

To **eat** in town, either sit down for chicken and tahina (£E3.50) at *El Eman*, north of the *Andalos*, or buy food from street vendors.

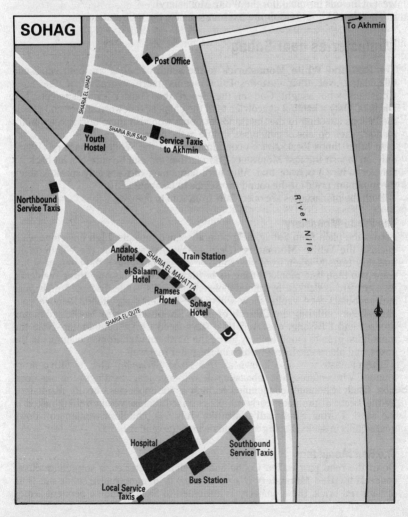

SOHAG

To Akhmin

Post Office

SHARIA EL JIHAD

SHARIA BUR SAID

Youth Hostel

Service Taxis to Akhmin

Northbound Service Taxis

River Nile

Andalos Hotel

SHARIA EL MAHATTA

Train Station

el-Salaam Hotel

Ramses Hotel

Sohag Hotel

SHARIA EL QUTE

Hospital

Southbound Service Taxis

Bus Station

Local Service Taxis

Transport

Don't bother with **trains** except to reach Luxor (4hr; 2nd class A/C £E5.30) or Cairo – buses and *service* taxis provide faster, easier access to Valley towns.

There are five **buses** daily to Minya and Cairo (6.30–10.30am), and a similar number to Luxor (last one at 3pm). Half-hourly services to el-Balyana (1hr; 85pt), Qena (3hr; £E2.75) and Assyut (2hr; £E1.75) run until early evening.

Assyut (1hr 30min; £E2.50) is the farthest destination for northbound **service taxis**, while Qena (1hr; £E3.50) is the normal limit for southbound vehicles, which also call at the bus station. To el-Balyana – the jumping-off point for Abydos – takes between thirty minutes and an hour (£E1.25). Local *service* taxis depart from two separate depots: north of the railway station (for Akhmim) and west of the bus terminal (for the White Monastery).

There's a 24-hour **telephone exchange** inside the train station.

Monasteries near Sohag

The **Red and White Monasteries** to the south of Sohag are both small and dilapidated, yet their near-desolation seems more evocative of the early Christians who sought God in the desert than busier establishments like Dirunka. Only a handful of acolytes tend the chapels; timeworn stones and plastic medallions attesting to the thousands of Copts who visit them during Shenoudi's *moulid*, when dozens of minibuses shuttle in the pilgrims.

At other times local *service* taxis (25pt) run to the White Monastery (10km) only, so to visit the Red Monastery (4km farther on) and be sure of a lift back it's simpler to hire a **private taxi**. After hard bargaining (drivers only speak Arabic), the minimum price for the round trip seems to be about £E10.

Both the monasteries are open daily from 9am to 5pm.

The White Monastery

Across the plain from Sohag, near an arabesqued mosque, high limestone walls enclose the **White Monastery** (*Deir al-Abyad*). Named for the colour of its masonry (mostly taken from pharaonic or Roman buildings), the monastery had some two thousand monks during its heyday. Today, it has only three residents, its courtyard is flanked by ruined cloisters and cells, while discarded millstones and soot-blackened vaults show where the kitchen once stood. Remove your shoes before entering the **Church of Saint Shenoudi**, a lofty basilica admitting breezes and birdsong, observed by a stern-faced Christ Pantokrator. Note the monolithic granite pulpit halfway along the northern wall, Roman columns in the apses, and pharaonic hieroglyphics on the outer rear wall.

The monastery is also known as *Deir Anba Shenouda* after its fifth-century founder, who enforced the monastic rule with legendary beatings – on one occasion, fatally. Shenoudi condemned bathing as an upper-class luxury maintained by the sweat of the poor; early monks cleansed themselves by rolling naked in the sand. During **Shenoudi's Moulid** (July 14), childless women roll down nearby hills in sacks, hoping to obtain divine intervention.

The Red Monastery

Down the road past walled Coptic and Muslim cemeteries, a straggling village conceals the **Red Monastery** (*Deir al-Ahmar*) in an unobtrusive cul-de-sac. Built of dark red brick, the monastery is attributed to Saint Bishoi, a penitent armed robber who became Shenoudi's disciple (retaining his club as a reminder); hence its other sobriquet, *Deir Anba Bishoi*.

The monastery's principal **church** is darker than Shenoudi's, its blackened tenth-century murals less remarkable than the finely carved tiers of niches. Whereas purloined Roman columns and the White Monastery's pharaonic-style corvetto cornice betray artistic debts, the intricate floral capitals inside the outer gate evince that Coptic architecture soon transcended mere imitation. In the courtyard's far corner squats the smaller **Red Church**, whose inner sanctum is barred to women.

Akhmim

Only a century ago, guidebooks ranked Sohag as less important than **AKHMIM**, across the Nile – a place reckoned "the oldest city of all Egypt" by the sixteenth-century Moorish geographer-historian Leo Africanus. Known to the Greeks as *Panopolis*, Akhmim was originally dedicated to the god Min, whose ruined temple lies near the cemeteries west of town, where a princess's tomb was recently discovered. The town these days is noted for its traditionally manufactured silk-fringed shawls and its blue cloth for workday *galabiyyas*. Come for the **Wednesday market** and you might avoid the attention of excited kids, who at other times are likely to dog your every move.

Another reason for making the trip is that many of the **service taxis** that shuttle between Sohag's Sharia Bur Said and Akhmim (25pt) are lovely **vintage cars** from the Thirties and Forties. From Akhmim's depot there are also minibuses back to Sohag (15min).

UPPER EGYPT

In antiquity, **Upper Egypt** started at Memphis and ran as far south as Aswan on the border with Nubia. Nowadays, with the designation of Middle Egypt, borders are a little more hazy, though the **Qena Bend** is generally taken as the region's beginning and **Aswan** is still effectively the end of the line.

Within this stretch of the Nile is the world's most intensive concentration of ancient monuments – temples, tombs and palaces constructed from the onset of the Middle Kingdom (c.1990 BC) up until Roman and Byzantine times. The greatest of the buildings are the **cult temples** of **Abydos**, **Dendara**, **Karnak**, **Esna**, **Edfu**, **Kom Ombo**, **Philae** and **Abu Simbel**, each conceived as "homes" for their respective deities and an accretion of centuries of building. Scarcely less impressive are the multitude of tombs in the **Theban Necropolis**, most famously in the **Valley of the Kings**, across the river from **Luxor**, where Tutankhamun's resting place is merely a hole in the ground by comparison with such great pharaohs as Seti I and Ramses II.

Monuments aside, Upper Egypt marks a subtle shift of character, with the desert closing in on the river, and dom-palms growing alongside barrel-roofed houses, designed to reflect the intense heat. One of the greatest pleasures to be had here – indeed one of the highlights of any Egyptian trip – is to absorb the riverscape slowly from the vantage point of a **felucca**. This is easily arranged on the spot at Luxor or Aswan – the latter being the preferred starting point so that you can sail downriver with no fear of being becalmed.

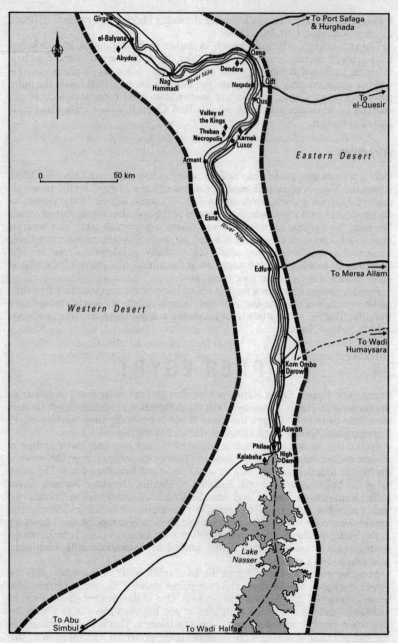

Abydos

As Muslims endeavour to visit Mecca once in their lifetimes and Hindus aspire to die at Benares, the ancient Egyptians devoutly wished to make a pilgrimage to **ABYDOS**, cult-centre of the god Osiris. Those who failed to make it hoped to do so posthumously; relatives brought bodies for burial, or embellished distant tombs with scenes of the journey to Abydos (represented by a boat under sail, travelling upriver). Egyptians averred that the dead "went west", for the entrance to the underworld was believed to lie amidst the desert hills beyond Abydos. By bringing other deities into the Osirian fold, Abydos acquired a near monopoly on death-cults, which persisted into Ptolemaic times. Nowadays, people come to admire the **Temple of Seti I** rather than to achieve resurrection.

Access: transport from Luxor and el-Balyana

Abydos lies 10km from the small town of EL-BALYANA, midway between Sohag and Qena, and an easy half-day excursion from either. Most tourists, however, visit Abydos on a long **day trip from Luxor**, hiring a private taxi and taking in Dendara Temple along the way (£E40–75). Attempting this by public **transport**, it's wise to visit Abydos – the more time-consuming and distant site – first, using *service* taxis for each leg of the journey. From Luxor to Qena (1hr; £E2) and thence to el-Balyana (40min; £E3.75) entails changing vehicles in Qena, whereas taxis from Sohag run directly to el-Balyana (40min; £E1.25).

Despite being a halt for five of the ten daily Cairo–Luxor trains (11hr from Cairo; A/C 2nd class £E4.50), **EL-BALYANA** is as ramshackle as they come, and there's no reason to suffer its fleabag *Wadi Melouk* (☎801-658) and *Eman* **hotels** when superior lodgings can be had in Luxor or Nag Hammadi (see p.278). The map below is printed simply to help you get out as quickly as possible.

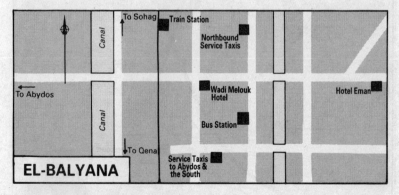

From el-Balyana, the **site of Abydos** is reached by a canal-side road clogged with carts and camels bearing loads of sugar cane from the surrounding fields. Rather than haggle with private cabbies (£E4 each way) or wait for an infrequent, crowded bus (15pt), it's best to catch a local *service* taxi (50pt) to the village of AL-ARABA EL-MADFUNA, beside the ruins. Here, a restaurant and soft-drink stalls precede the kiosk selling **tickets** (admission daily 7am–6pm; £E5, students £E2.50). One ticket covers the entire site.

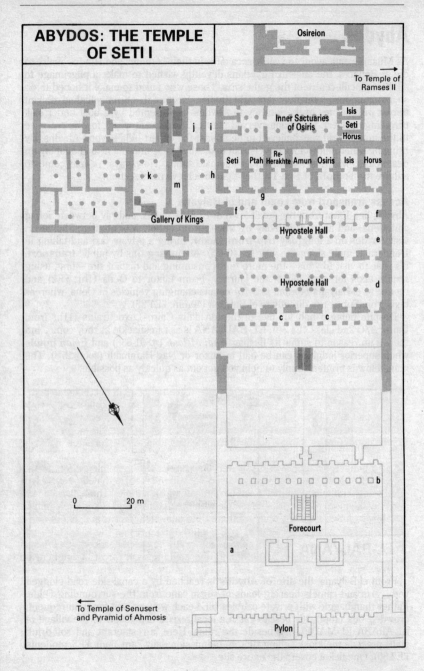

ABYDOS: THE TEMPLE OF SETI I

Osireion

To Temple of Ramses II

Inner Sactuaries of Osiris

Isis
Seti
Horus

Seti   Ptah   Re-Herakhte   Amun   Osiris   Isis   Horus

j   i

k   m   h

g

l

f   f

Gallery of Kings

Hypostele Hall   e

d

Hypostele Hall

c   c

0   20 m

b

Forecourt

a

To Temple of Senusert
and Pyramid of Ahmosis

Pylon

The Temple of Seti I

Whilst Karnak and Deir el-Bahri are breathtaking conceptions executed on a colossal scale, it is the exquisite quality of its bas-reliefs that distinguishes the **Temple of Seti I** at Abydos. The reliefs are amongst the finest works of the New Kingdom, harking back to Old Kingdom forms in an artistic revival that mirrored Seti's political efforts to consolidate the XIX Dynasty and recover territories lost under Akhenaten. The official designation of Seti's reign (1318–1304 BC) was "the era of repeating births" – literally a renaissance.

Seti I

It was in fact Seti's son, Ramses II (1304–1237 BC), who completed the reconquest of former colonies and the construction of his father's temple at Abydos. Strictly speaking, the building was neither a cult nor a funerary temple in the ordinary sense (see box overpage), for its chapels contained shrines to a variety of deities concerned with death, resurrection and the netherworld, and one dedicated to Seti himself. Its purpose was essentially political: to identify the king with these cults and with his putative "ancestors", the previous rulers of Egypt, thus conferring legitimacy on the Ramessid dynasty.

The forecourt and Hypostele Halls

The temple's original **pylon** and **forecourt** have almost been levelled but you can still discern the lower portion of a scene depicting Ramses II's dubious victory at Qadesh **[a]**, women with finely plaited tresses **[b]**, and Seti making offerings to Osiris (behind a pillar, nearby). From the damaged statues currently stored in the upper, second court, your eyes are drawn to the square-columned **facade**, where tiny birds inhabit fissures in the wall behind pillars covered with scenes of Ramses greeting Osiris, Isis and Horus **[c]**. Originally, the temple was entered by seven doors (corresponding to the shrines within), but Ramses ordered all except the middle one blocked up.

The ponderous reliefs in the **outer Hypostele Hall**, completed by Ramses after Seti's death, suggest that he used second-rate artists, having redeployed Seti's top craftsmen on his own (now destroyed) temple. The entrance wall portrays Ramses measuring the temple with the goddess Selket and presenting it to Horus on Seti's behalf, while on the wall to your right Horus and Thoth douse him with holy water (represented by the interlinked signs for life and purity) **[d]**. To the left of this tableau, Horus and Wepwawet (the jackal-headed god of Assyut and Abydos) lead Ramses to the temple and hold the *ankh* (breath) sign beneath his nostrils. To the right, he stands beyond Hathor and proffers a falcon-headed box of papyrus to Isis, Horus and Osiris.

The deeper, darker **inner Hypostele Hall** was the last part of the temple decorated before Seti's death, and some sections were never finished. On the right-hand wall Seti stands before Osiris and Horus – who pour holy water from garlanded vases – and makes offerings before the shrine of Osiris, attended by Maat and Ronpet (the goddess of the year) in front, Isis, Amentet (goddess of the west) and Nephthys behind **[e]**. Seti's profile is a stylised but close likeness to his mummy (now once again on display in the Cairo Museum). The east and west walls are of sandstone, the north and south of limestone. Two projecting piers **[f]** near the back of the hall depict Seti worshipping the *djed* column whilst wearing the crown of Upper or Lower Egypt.

The sanctuaries
The finest **bas-reliefs** at Abydos are in the sanctuaries dedicated to Seti and six deities. Though retaining much of their original colouring (showing how most temple reliefs once looked), their graceful lines and subtle moulding are best appreciated on the unpainted reliefs. Seti's classical revival eschewed both

---

ANCIENT EGYPTIAN TEMPLE ARCHITECTURE

From earliest times, two distinct types of temple evolved in Egypt: **cult-temples**, dedicated to the principal god of the region, and **mortuary temples**, devoted to the worship of the dead king. Cult-temples were regarded as the *pr-ntr* or "house of the god", whose effigy was cosseted with daily rituals and periodically taken to visit its divine spouse in another temple. Such centres were immediately elaborate, unlike mortuary temples, which began as two-roomed structures attached to the king's pyramid and joined to a valley temple by a causeway, only being divorced from their tombs and burgeoning into massive complexes during the New Kingdom.

Most of the great temples of the Nile Valley embody centuries of work by successive kings and dynasties, some of whom added major sections whilst others merely decorated a wall or carved their name on another pharaoh's statue. Built from stone, to last forever, their general form and layout hardly changed over millennia, being imitated still during Ptolemaic and Roman times.

Temple layout
Because each temple was envisaged as a progression from this world into the realm of divine mysteries, halls got darker and lower and doors narrowed as they approached the sanctuary. In accordance with this convention, additional halls or pylons had to increase in size as they grew more distant from the sanctuary. As a corollary of this, the architecture is generally older the farther in you venture.

Temples were seldom accessible to commoners, being set within enclosures surrounded by lofty mudbrick walls. These **precincts** often contained priestly residences, workshops and storehouses, along with a **Sacred Lake** for ritual ablutions. In Ptolemaic and Roman times, they also usually featured a **Birth House** or *Mamissi* which emphasised the king's divine antecedents. Entering the temple proper meant passing through a series of gated **Pylons** whose towers bore giant reliefs of the pharaoh offering to the gods and smiting Egypt's enemies. A few also boasted graceful **obelisks** whose tips were sheathed in gold or electrum (an alloy of gold and silver). Between the pylons were open **courts**, often flanked with **colonnades** of Osiride pillars and guarded by **colossi** of a pharaoh or deity.

Another pylon (or a screen wall surmounted by open columns) divided the court from a **Hypostele Hall**, whose forest of columns was intended to resemble a papyrus thicket, dimly illuminated by shafts of sunlight penetrating apertures in the roof. Beyond lay a series of **vestibules** or antechambers (often preceded by a smaller hypostele hall), climaxing in the **Sanctuary** where the deity's effigy and sacred boat reposed. Smaller rooms and **chapels** for storing valuables or worshipping subsidiary deities were grouped off the halls and behind the sanctuary. Some temples also had a **rooftop shrine** or kiosk for celebrating the resurrection of Osiris and revitalising the divine effigy at New Year.

Amarna expressionism and the bombastic XVIII Dynasty imperial style, which his son embraced and raised to new heights of megalomania. The seven sanctuaries are roofed with false vaults carved from rectangular slabs, and culminate in false doors (except for Osiris's chamber, which leads into his inner sanctuaries).

To ancient Egyptians, these chambers constituted the abode of the gods, whom the king (or his priests) propitiated with **daily rituals**, shown on the walls. Having opened the shrine, the pharaoh offers the god sacrifices and washes and dresses its statue, which is then purified and presented with gifts. After further offerings before the god's barque, he scatters sand on the floor, sweeps away his footprints and withdraws, leaving the deity alone till next morning.

Decoration

Virtually every temple wall is covered in **reliefs**, either carved proud (ie bas-reliefs, the most delicate and time-consuming method), recessed into the surface (sunk reliefs) or simply incised (the quickest form to execute). Lintels are always adorned with a winged sun-disc, symbolising the Two Lands whose heraldic plants are a common motif. Some Ptolemaic temples also feature astronomical ceilings depicting heavenly bodies and creatures of the zodiac. Since reliefs were generally painted in bright colours, temples must once have looked far gaudier than their present state suggests.

Also striking are the variegated **columns**, which evolved from two basic types. Square-sectioned pillars were sometimes faced with a statue of the pharaoh as a god (usually Osiris – hence the term Osiride pillars) or crowned with the head of the goddess Hathor (perhaps surmounted by a sistrum, her sacred instrument). A wider variety derived from plant forms, with different permutations of shafts and capitals. The palm column had a plain shaft and leafy capital; the papyrus column chevron markings and a flowering or closed bud capital; whilst a cluster of rounded stems gave the lotus column its distinctive "bundle" appearance. By Ptolemaic times, capitals resembled baroque bouquets and the established forms were mixed to create composite columns.

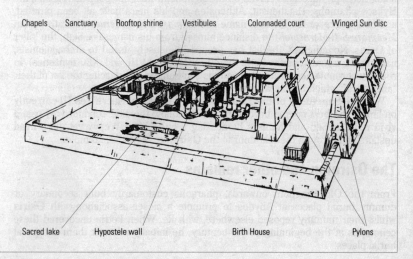

| Chapels | Sanctuary | Rooftop shrine | Vestibules | Colonnaded court | Winged Sun disc |

| Sacred lake | Hypostele wall | Birth House | Pylons |

An exception to this rule is the **Sanctuary of Seti**, which emphasises his recognition by the gods, who lead him into the temple and ceremonially unite the Two Lands along the northern wall. Below the barque on the southern wall, Seti receives a list of offerings from Thoth and the High Priest Iunmutef, wearing the leopardskin and braided side-lock of his office. Finally, Seti leaves the temple, his palanquin borne by the souls of jackal-headed deities from the Upper Egyptian town of Nekhen and hawk-headed gods from the Delta capital of Pi-Ramses.

With the Sanctuary of Ptah under restoration, it's more rewarding to study the **pier** that separates it from Re-Herakhte's sanctuary. Shine a torch upwards to catch Seti kneeling before Osiris and Horus, with the sacred persea tree in the background **[g]**. The fine unpainted reliefs of Seti and seated deities in **Re-Herakhte's chamber** make interesting comparison with similar painted scenes in the sanctuaries of Amun-Re, Osiris and Isis. On the side wall just outside the Sanctuary of Horus, the pharaoh presents Maat to Osiris, Isis and Horus, a XIX Dynasty motif symbolising righteous order, the restoration of royal legitimacy.

The **inner sanctuaries of Osiris** boast three side chapels whose colours are still fresh and shiny – as near perfect as you could hope for.

The southern wing

From the inner Hypostele Hall you can enter the southern wing of Seti's temple. The portal nearest his sanctuary leads into the columned **Hall of Sokar and Nefertum**, two deities of the north representing the life-giving forces of the earth and the cycle of death and rebirth, who were integrated into the Osirian cult by Seti's time. The niches along the far wall once contained Osiride statues. Reliefs across the way **[h]** depict Seti receiving a hawk-headed Sokar, and Nefertum in both his human and leonine forms (crowned with a lotus blossom). In the **Chapel of Sokar [i]**, Osiris appears in his bier and returns to life grasping his penis, whilst Isis hovers over him in the form of a hawk on the opposite wall. There are also delicate reliefs in the **Chapel of Nefertum**, next door **[j]**.

The other portal leads through into the **Gallery of Kings**, so called after the list of Seti's predecessors carved on the right-hand wall. For political reasons, the Hyksos pharaohs, Hatshepsut, Akhenaten and his heirs have all been omitted, and Seti has recorded his own name as *Menmare Osiris-Merneptah* (rather than *Menmare Seti-Merneptah*) to distance himself from his namesake Seth, the killer of Osiris. Nonetheless, the list has proved immensely useful to archaeologists, naming 34 kings (chiefly from the VI, VII, XII, XVIII and XIX dynasties) in roughly chronological order. Seti and his son Ramses stand facing the list of their "ancestors", which begins with Menes (Zoser).

With the **Sanctuary of the Boats [k]** and the **Hall of Sacrifices [l]** currently off-limits, the best course beyond here is to follow the side corridor **[m]** past a vivid relief of Seti and Ramses harnessing a bull before Wepwawet, then head upstairs and through the rear door to the **Osireion**, behind the temple.

The Osireion and other remains

From the Old Kingdom onwards, pharaohs customarily built secondary or dummy burial places at Abydos to promote a closer association with **Osiris** whilst their mummy reposed elsewhere, with Re. When Petrie uncovered these cenotaphs at the beginning of the century, he initially mistook them for actual burial places.

THE CULT OF OSIRIS

Originally the corn-god of Busiris in the Delta, **Osiris** attained national significance early in the Old Kingdom, when he was co-opted into the Heliopolitan Ennead. According to legend, Re (or Geb) divided the world between Osiris and his brother Seth, who resented being given all the deserts and murdered Osiris to usurp his domain. Although the god's body was recovered by **Isis**, the sister-wife of Osiris, Seth recaptured and dismembered it, burying the pieces (and feeding the penis to a crocodile, in one version). Aided by her sister Nephthys, Isis collected the bits and bandaged them together to create the first mummy, which they briefly resurrected with the help of Thoth and Anubis. By transforming herself into a hawk, Isis managed to conceive a child with Osiris before he returned to the netherworld to rule as lord and judge of the dead. Secretly raised to manhood in the Delta, their child **Horus** later avenged his father and cast Seth back into the wilderness (see p.350).

As the reputed burial place of the torso (or head) of Osiris, **Abydos** was the setting for two annual **festivals**. The "Great Going Forth" celebrated the search for and discovery of his remains, whilst the Osiris Festival re-enacted his myth in a series of Mystery Plays. In one scene, the god's barque was "attacked" by minions of Seth and "protected" by **Wepwawet**, the jackal-headed god of Assyut. This marked the final stage in a process of religious mergers, for it was Wepwawet who supplanted **Khentamenty**, the original death-god of Abydos, as the "Foremost of the Westerners", before his own assimilation into the cult of Osiris. The total identification of Abydos with **death-cults** was completed by its association with **Anubis**, the jackal-headed god of embalming.

Osiris

The Osireion and Temple of Ramses II

The only Osirian burial place visible nowadays is the Cenotaph of Seti I – more commonly known as the **Osireion** – and even this is half-buried and rendered inaccessible by flooding. Built of massive blocks, it once enclosed a room containing a mound surrounded by a moat (symbolising the first land arising from the waters of Chaos at the dawn of Creation), where a pseudo-sarcophagus awaited resurrection.

Abydos once covered a huge area, with various temple complexes, necropoli and sacred lakes, and a town centred upon the great Temple of Osiris. Nowadays, almost everything has been demolished or sanded-over, and not many visitors bother with what remains. If you feel like stretching your legs, however, the **Temple of Ramses II** is 300m from the Osireion. Though now much ruined and reduced in height, the temple was surely once magnificent, incorporating fine limestone, red and black granite and alabaster masonry. Fragments of the Battle of Qadesh and offering scenes can be discerned on the remnants of its enclosure walls and pillared courtyard.

Further afield

Only the most devoted archaeology buff will venture further afield. Another 300m or so beyond Ramses II's temple lies an Old Kingdom burial ground that stretches to the cliffs of the Western Desert, where several I and II Dynasty kings were actually interred. Its Arabic sobriquet, **Umm al Qa'ab** (Mother of Pots), refers to the shards of votive pots left by ancient pilgrims, which litter the desert's edge. On the far side of this cemetery is another necropolis, dating from the Middle Kingdom. Nearby stands a double-walled, mudbrick enclosure which locals call **Shumet el-Zibib** (Storeroom of Dates) and scholars identify as one of several funerary complexes dating back to Pre-Dynastic times.

The city of Abydos lay northeast of here, towards the modern village of AL-KHIRBAH, whose inhabitants coined the name **Kom al-Sultan** (Mound of the Sultan) for the indistinct heap marking the site of the Temple of Osiris, supposedly built upon the spot where Seth buried the god's head. Even less worthwhile are the ruins 2–3km southeast of Seti's temple, where the XII Dynasty king Senusert III erected his own mortuary temple and Pharaoh Ahmosis raised a pyramid in the XVIII Dynasty.

Nag Hammadi

At **NAG HAMMADI**, 40km from Abydos and 560km from Cairo, the Nile sweeps eastwards into the "Qena Bend" and the main road and railway transfer from the west bank to the eastern side of the river. Nag Hammadi itself is an important agricultural centre whose Nile barrage irrigates over 622,000 *feddans*, though there's nothing here to attract tourists save for the *Aluminium Hotel* (☎757-947), 7km south of town. This is probably the most comfortable **accommodation** between Assyut and Luxor (singles £E30, doubles £E40) and might come in handy if more distant options prove impractical.

THE GNOSTIC GOSPELS

The **Nag Hammadi Codices** – better known as the **Gnostic Gospels** – were found near town, below the caves of Jebel el-Tur, in 1945. The gospels are fourth-century Coptic translations of second-century Greek originals, although the Gospel of Thomas might date from 50–10 AD, and therefore be as early as – or even older than – the gospels of Matthew, Mark, Luke and John.

The Gnostics (from *Gnosis*, Greek for "knowledge") were early mystics who believed that God could only be known through self-understanding and the recognition that the world was illusory. Regarding self and the divine as one, they saw Jesus as a spiritual guide rather than the crucified son of God, pointing to his words in the Gospel of Thomas: *"If you bring forth what is within you, what you bring forth will save you. If you do not bring forth what is within you, what is within you will destroy you"*. But the official church thought otherwise and condemned Gnosticism as a heresy; hence the burial of these codices (some of which can be seen today in Cairo's Coptic Museum).

Qena and Dendara

Tourists pass through **Qena** for two reasons: its **connections** between the Nile Valley and the Red Sea, and local transport to the fantastic **temples** of **Dendara** (9km west of town) and **Abydos** (see preceding section). Both temples make a grand day excursion from Luxor, only an hour's ride from Qena; for groups it's almost as cheap to hire a private taxi for the whole jaunt (£E40–75) as to get about by public transport. Just try to avoid having to stay overnight in Qena – a dubious prospect at the best of times.

All telephone numbers in the Qena area are prefixed ☎096.

Qena

Wandering the bazaars of **QENA** "inhaling the odour of sandalwood" in 1850, Gustav Flaubert's sexual tourism was tinged with "sweet sadness" by what he called the *almehs* (Wise Women), in reality professional singers or *ghawazi* whom Mohammed Ali exiled from Cairo to Qena, Aswan and Esna for their "indecent" dances and prostitution. You'll find no *ghawazi* in modern Qena, however, which is today the Nile Valley's staidest provincial capital. Were it not for the proximity to the Dendara temples, it would only merit a footnote in history for its military air base, used as a staging post during the abortive mission to rescue the US hostages from Iran.

Accommodation

Since it's possible to spend the night near Dendara (see overpage), the only reason to stay in Qena is to catch an early morning transport connection. The most comfortable **hotel** in town is the *New Palace* (☎322-509) behind the Mobil garage, whose singles (£E10 with bath) and doubles (£E10/£E15 with bath) have mosquito netting, and sometimes fans. Another fairly decent place is the *Al-Salaam* (singles £E3, doubles £E5; fans £E2.50). Avoid the *El Fath*, *Cleopatra* and *Mecca* hotels – all very basic and scuzzy.

Diversions and food

Despite vestiges of nineteenth-century prettiness, Qena exudes boredom and frustration, as locals themselves complain. Should you have to stay here for any

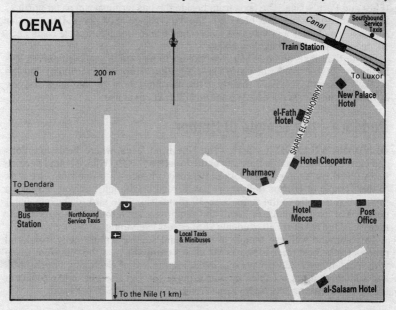

length of time, walk down to the Nile (1km from the centre) and enjoy the sunset over a glass of *shai*. Outside of the **Moulid of Abdel Rahim al-Qenawi** (held on the 14th day of Sha'ban) and the Thursday **market**, *Qenawis* settle for Nile-side cafés or window-shopping along the nameless main street as the only diversions going. Homes and shops are deprived of electricity until 6pm, but the call to prayer booms from grandiose mosques throughout the day.

Foodwise, things are slightly better. *El Prince*, on the main intersection, does standard Egyptian **meals**. On the main street 100m towards the bus station, you can get filling plates of chicken, okra, salad and dessert at the *Hamdi Restaurant*. Between them lies *Maradona 86*, a sports fans' hangout offering *kofta* and *tahina* with salad. None of these places should set you back more than £E4–6.

Other practicalities

EgyptAir, halfway towards the bus station, keeps similar hours to the **post office** (Sat–Thurs 8am–2pm & 6–8pm) at the other end of the main drag, near a moribund **State Information Office**. For enquiries it's better to go to Qena's English-speaking **pharmacist** or the 24-hour **police** (☎325-724) in the railway station.

Transport

To avoid the twenty-minute walk between Qena's transport terminals you can take a horse-drawn *caleche*, which seats three (£E1–1.50 with bargaining).

Air-conditioned **trains** (6 daily) are the surest way to Cairo (11–12hr; 2nd class A/C £E12) or Aswan (6hr 30min; £E7), but less convenient for reaching Luxor (2hr; £E2) than **service taxis** (1hr; £E2). Taxis to Luxor and other points south leave from the square with the mosque, across the canal from the railway station; to reach Esna, change at Luxor; for Edfu or Kom Ombo you'll have to pay the full fare to Aswan (£E5). Past the mosque is another depot for taxis to Hurghada (£E8) and Port Safaga. The taxis from beside the bus terminal run as far north as Sohag, charging 25pt per head for Dendara village, £E4 for el-Balyana (for Abydos). To charter a private taxi for a round-trip to Dendara temple costs £E5–10, depending on your haggling ability.

Slower than taxis and needing reservations to be sure of seats, **buses** are less handy for Assyut, Sohag or Cairo (11–12hr; £E6). However, you might find the six daily buses to Hurghada (hourly in the morning; some go onto Suez; last one at 7pm) or the 6am service to Alexandria (13hr; £E25) of use.

Dendara – the Temple of Hathor

DENDARA VILLAGE lies across the Nile from Qena, where fields of onions and clover recede towards the cliffs of the Western Desert. Village-bound **service taxis** (25pt) can drop you at a fork in the road, whence it's a one-kilometre walk to the Temple of Hathor (follow the paved road on the left); or you can take a private taxi directly to the ruins (£E5–10 round-trip). The **site** (daily 7am–6pm) deserves at least a couple of hours and requires a torch to illuminate its darker recesses. One ticket (£E10, students £E5) covers everything.

To commune with the temple at sunset and sunrise – a distinctly wonderful prospect – the best place to stay is Mr Imalt's **campsite** near the ruins. For those with tents, it costs £E3 per person, including the use of electricity, hot showers and a kitchen. If not occupied by tour groups, you can also get simple rooms in the **Hotel Dendara** (aka *Happy Land Hotel*; ☎322-330) for £E6 per head.

The Temple of Hathor

Although there have been shrines to Hathor, the goddess of joy, at Dendara since Pre-Dynastic times, the existing **Temple of Hathor** is a Graeco-Roman creation, built between 125 BC and 60 AD. Since the object of the exercise was to confer legitimacy on Egypt's foreign rulers, it emulates the pharaonic pattern of hypostele halls and vestibules preceding a darkened sanctuary, "a progression from the light of the Egyptian sun to the mystery of the holy of holies" (T.H.G. James).

THE FACADE

The temple **facade** is shaped like a pylon, with six Hathor-headed columns rising from a screen. Here and inside, Hathor appears in human form rather than her bovine aspect (see box). Because this section was built during the reign of Tiberius, its reliefs depict Roman emperors making offerings to the gods, namely Tiberius and Claudius before Horus, Hathor and their son Ihy **[a]**, and Tiberius as a sphinx before Hathor and Horus **[b]**. Nineteenth-century engravings show the temple buried in sand almost to the lintel of its portal, which explains why its upper sections bore the brunt of Coptic iconoclasm.

THE HYPOSTELE HALL

Entering the **Hypostele Hall** with its eighteen Hathor-headed columns, let your eyes grow accustomed to the gloom before examining its famous **astronomical ceiling**, which retains much of its original colouring. This is not a sky chart in the

---

THE CULT OF HATHOR

Worshipped from the earliest times as a cow-goddess, **Hathor** acquired manifold attributes – body of the sky, living soul of trees, goddess of gold and turquoise, music and revelry – but remained essentially nurturing. Her greatest role was that of wet-nurse and bed-mate for **Horus**, and giver of milk to the living pharaoh. In her human aspect (with bovine ears and horns), the goddess paid an annual visit to Horus at his temple in Edfu. Escorted by priests and cheered by commoners, her barque proceeded upriver, where Horus sailed out to meet her on his own boat. After much pomp and ritual, the idols were left alone to re-consummate their union whilst the populace enjoyed a **Festival of Drunkenness** which led the Greeks to identify Hathor with their own goddess of love and joy, Aphrodite. However, drunkenness at other times drew condemnation, as in this timeless rebuke to a lager lout: "You trail from street to street smelling of beer, you have been found performing acrobatics on a wall, people run from your blows. Look at you beating on your stomach, reeling and rolling about on the ground covered in your own filth!".

Some believe that Hathor's cult expressed a yearning for the bygone pastoral, nomadic lifestyle of Pre-Dynastic Egypt. Several Nilotic peoples still base their culture on **cattle**. In ancient Egypt, gods such as Amun and Min were identified with great bulls, as were the kings, who hunted herds of aurochs. Milch cows were especially venerated by the *fellaheen*. One tomb relief shows a herd fording a canal where a lurking crocodile snarls, "Hey! You scum! Give the beasts a shove"; but the herdsmen assures his cows, "I am watching your baby, mother".

Hathor

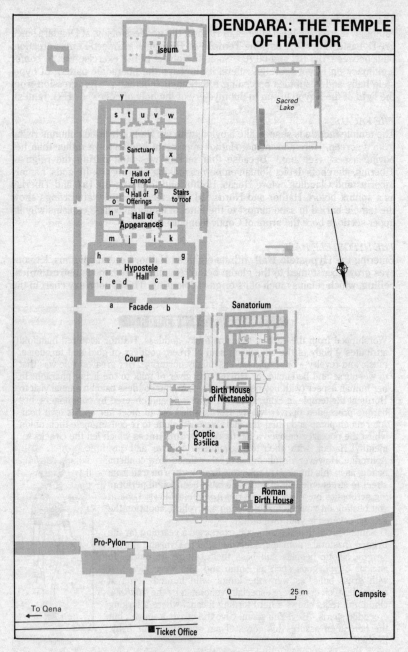

DENDARA: THE TEMPLE OF HATHOR

Iseum

Sacred Lake

y

s t u v w

Sanctuary

x

r Hall of Ennead

q Hall of Offerings p

Stairs to roof

o

n

Hall of Appearances

m j i k

l

h g

Hypostele Hall

f e d c e f

a Facade b

Sanatorium

Court

Birth House of Nectanebo

Coptic Basilica

Roman Birth House

Pro-Pylon

0 25 m

Campsite

To Qena

■ Ticket Office

modern sense, but a symbolic representation of the heavenly bodies, the hours of the day and night, and the realms of the sun and moon. Although the Qena Bend dictates a north–south orientation rather than the customary east–west axis (since temples always faced the Nile), the ceiling maintains the traditional dichotomy between the northern and southern halves of the sky.

Above the central aisle, a row of flying vultures and winged discs separates the left-hand bays representing the southern heavens from those to the right, dedicated to the northern sky. Here, the first row **[c]** begins with the full moon, followed by the Eye of Re in its barque, above which appear the fourteen days of the waning moon. Next come the fourteen stages of the waxing moon (each with its own deity), culminating in the full disc worshipped by Thoth, and lastly the moon as Osiris, protected by Isis and Nephthys. Souls in the form of jackals and birds adore Re's barque as it journeys across the sun's register **[d]**.

Following these are two bands **[e]** showing the planets, the stars of the twelve hours of the night, and the signs of the zodiac. The end rows **[f]** are dominated by Nut, who gives birth to the sun at dawn and swallows it at dusk. On one side, the rising sun Khepri (the scarab beetle) is born **[g]**; on the other, the sun shines down on Hathor **[h]**.

THE HALL OF APPEARANCES
The Ptolemaic section of the temple begins with the columned **Hall of Appearances**, where Hathor consorted with fellow deities before her voyage to Edfu (see box on previous page). Reliefs on the entrance wall depict offerings **[i]**, the foundation of the temple and its presentation to the gods **[j]**. Holy objects of precious metal were kept in the Treasury **[k]**, to your right. Next door is the so-called Nile Room **[l]**, which provided access to the well outside, and is decorated with various river scenes.

Corresponding chambers across the hall include the laboratory **[m]**, where perfumes, incense and unguents were mixed and stored (notice the reliefs showing recipes, and bearers bringing exotic materials from afar); and another room for storing valuables, whose doorway carries a liturgical calendar listing festivals celebrated at the temple **[n]**.

THE HALL OF OFFERINGS AND HALL OF ENNEAD
Beyond lies the **Hall of Offerings**, the entrance to the temple proper, with a **stairway** to the roof (see overpage) and a corridor through which sacrificial animals were led **[o]**. A list of offerings appears on the rear wall **[p]**, across the way from a relief showing the king offering Hathor her favourite tipple **[q]**.

Next comes the **Hall of the Ennead**, where statues of the gods and kings involved in ceremonies dedicated to Hathor once stood. Her wardrobe was stored in a room to your left, where reliefs show the priests carrying the chests that held the sacred garments. Just outside the sanctuary you can see the text of the hymns of Awakening. The **Sanctuary** housed Hathor's statue and ceremonial barque, which priests carried to the riverside and placed upon a boat that worshippers towed upriver to Edfu for a conjugal reunion with Horus. Reliefs depict the daily rituals (described in the Abydos account – see p.275), and the king presenting Maat to Hathor, Horus and Harsomtus (rear wall).

SIDE CHAPELS
Two corridors with side chapels run alongside (and meet behind) the sanctuary. Above the low doorway into the Corridor of Mysteries, Hathor appears as a cow

within a wooden kiosk mounted on a barque [r]. Past the chapels of Isis, Sokar and the Sacred Serpent, you'll find the "Castle of the Sistrum" (Hathor's musical instrument), where niches depict her standing on the sky, and the coronation of Ihy as god of music [s]. This is entered via the *Per-Nu* chapel [t], whence Hathor embarked on her conjugal voyage to Edfu.

The New Year procession began from the *Per-Ur* chapel [u], where a hole in the floor leads into the **crypts** (you'll have to plug in the light, or use a torch to explore them). The *Per-Neser* chapel [v] shows Hathor in her terrible aspect as a lioness, for by Ptolemaic times she had assimilated the leonine goddess Sekhmet and the feline goddess Bastet. The temple's most valuable treasures were stored in a crypt beneath the Chapel of Re [w].

If you haven't already stumbled upon it, return to the Hall of the Ennead and bear left, then right, to find the "Pure Place" [x], better known as the **New Year Chapel**, whose ceiling bears an exquisite relief of Nut giving birth to the sun, which shines on Hathor's head. It was here that rituals were performed prior to Hathor's communion with the sun on the temple's roof. Check out the rooftop shrines before leaving the building to see Cleopatra and her son Caesarion, larger than life along the rear wall of the temple [y]. The chubby face below the Hathor-crown is so unlike the beautiful queen of legend that most people prefer to regard this as a stylised image rather than a lifelike **portrait of Cleopatra**.

ROOFTOP SANCTUARIES

From the Hall of Offerings a stairway ascends to the roof of the temple; the scenes on its walls depict the New Year procession, when Hathor's statue was carried up to an open pavilion at the southern end of the roof to await the dawn. Touched by the rays of the sun, her father Hathor's *ba* was revitalised for the coming year. Although such **rooftop sanctuaries** were a feature of most temples, those at Dendara are uniquely intact. Also here are two suites of rooms dedicated to the death and resurrection of Osiris. Reliefs in the western suite show him being mourned by Isis and Nephthys, passing through the gates of the netherworld (guarded by knife-carrying gods) and finally bringing himself to erection to impregnate Isis, who appears as a hovering kite.

The eastern suite contains a plaster cast of the famous **Dendara Zodiac** ceiling filched by Lelorrain in 1820 and now in the Louvre. Upheld by four goddesses, the circular carving features a zodiac which only differs from our own by the substitution of a scarab for the scorpion, and the inclusion of the hippo-goddess Tweri. The zodiac was introduced to Egypt (and other lands) by the Romans.

Outlying buildings

Surrounding the temple are various other structures, now largely ruined. Ptolemaic temples were distinguished by the addition of *mamissi* or Birth Houses, which associated the pharaoh with Horus, the deified king. When the Romans surrounded the temple with an enclosure wall, it split in two the **Birth House of Nectanebo** (XXX Dynasty), compelling them to build a replacement. The **Roman Birth House** has some fine carvings on its south wall, and tiny figures of Bes and Tweri on the column capitals and architraves. Between the two *mamissi* lies a ruined, fifth-century **Coptic Basilica**, built with masonry from the adjacent structures; notice the incised Coptic crosses.

As a compassionate goddess, Hathor had a reputation for healing and her temple attracted pilgrimages from the sick. In the **Sanatorium** here patients were prescribed cures during dreams, probably induced by narcotics. Water for ritual ablutions was drawn from a **Sacred Lake** now drained of liquid and full of reeds and wildlife.

Nearby stands a ruined **Iseum** erected by Augustus and used for the worship of Isis and Osiris, whose cults were ubiquitous by then.

Other excursions from Qena

Other sites around Qena are inevitably eclipsed by the Temple of Dendara, but for those into "undiscovered" locations, a cluster of places to the south of town are worth considering.

All those detailed below should be accessible by *service* taxis from Qena's southbound depot (25pt–£E1). By day, you can also catch ferries across the Nile between el-Ballas and Qift, and Naqada and Qus.

Along the west bank

There are two places worth mentioning – and one that's just quirky enough to merit a visit – on the west bank.

EL-BALLAS, 23km from Qena, has manufactured white earthenware jars since antiquity; they are sold at Qena's **pottery** market alongside the town's own traditional wares – the porous water-jars that women carry on their heads from childhood. South of here lay ancient *Ombos*, whose crocodile-worshipping residents never forgave the people of Dendara for eating one: a grudge reaffirmed at every Festival of Drunkenness (see p.281).

Further south, half an hour's taxi ride from Qena, the predominantly Coptic village of **NAQADA** lends its name to two **Pre-Dynastic cultures** that existed between around 4000 and 3000 BC: Naqada I (early) and Naqada II (late). However, the reason to come here is to see the **Pigeon Palace**, built by a monk at the turn of the century. Located in a field 200m west of the main road through Naqada, the mudbrick, pyloned *Qasr el-Hamam* enables 10,000 birds to recuperate from overflying the Western Desert; food is provided – and in turn the keepers eat their resident charges.

Along the east bank

Crowded with traffic for Luxor, the east bank, south of Qena, marks the start of hairpin desert roads to Quesir and Safaga on the coast. The Valley comes closest to the Red Sea near **QIFT**, ancient *Kebt* or *Koptos*: a mining depot which became a commercial entrepôt once a route to the coast was found. Nowadays well-paved but lacking petrol stations, the 216-kilometre-long **road to Quesir** is covered in *The Red Sea Coast and Eastern Desert* chapter.

South towards Luxor, a new factory for converting *bagasse* (the waste product of sugar refining) into paper is underway outside **QUS**, a large town second only to Cairo during Fatimid and Mamluke times, when it served as a place of exile for deposed sultans. A relic of its former status is the eleventh-century **al-Amri Mosque**, containing a fine arabesque mihrab and teak minbar.

Farther south, near Khuzam, a sideroad leads to the Coptic community of **GARAGOS**, which produces arty **ceramics** but is hard to reach without private transport. Further still, nearing Luxor, you pass by **EL-MADAMUD**, harbouring a **ruined Temple of Montu** whose Ptolemaic-Roman avenue of sphinxes and monumental gateway belie its Old Kingdom origins.

Luxor

The dusty town of **LUXOR** has been a tourist mecca ever since Nile cruisers began calling in the nineteenth century to view the remains of Thebes, ancient Egypt's New Kingdom capital, and its associated sites. The concentration of relics in this area is overwhelming. The town itself boasts **Luxor Temple**, a graceful ornament to its waterfront and "downtown" quarter, while just to the north is **Karnak Temple**, a stupendous complex built over 1300 years. Across the river are the amazing tombs and mortuary temples of the **Theban necropolis**, and if this wasn't enough, Luxor also serves as a base for trips to Esna, Edfu, Dendara and Abydos temples, up and down the Nile Valley.

Luxor's dependency on **tourism** also has its downside. The genuine warmth found in other parts of Egypt has little place in a town whose non-stop hustle too often brings out the worst in people. Locals need tourists' money but feel contempt for their naivety and package-holiday vision of Egypt; hassled and over-charged at every turn, tourists reciprocate with scorn. It's hard to break free from these stereotypes. On top of this, there's a Hobson's choice of whether to come in winter – when sites and hotels are overrun – or in summer, when clouds of flies and the stench of dung adds to the misery of the heat. Balancing crowds and **climate**, the optimum times for a visit are either early November or March.

A little history

The name Luxor derives from the Arabic *el-Uqsur* – meaning "the Palaces" or "the castles" – a name which may have referred to a Roman *castrum* or the town's appearance in medieval times, when it squatted admidst the ruins of **Thebes**. This, in turn, was the Greek name for the city known to the ancient Egyptians as *Weset*, originally an obscure provincial town during the Old Kingdom, when Egypt was ruled from Memphis. After power ebbed to regional overlords in the First Intermediate Period, Weset/Thebes gained ascendancy in Upper Egypt under Mentuhotep II (c.2100 BC), who reunited Egypt under the Middle Kingdom. Though this dissolved into anarchy, the town survived as a power base for local princes who eventually liberated Egypt from the Hyksos invaders, reunited the Two Lands and founded the XVIII Dynasty (c.1567 BC).

As the capital of the **New Kingdom**, whose empire stretched from Nubia to Palestine, Thebes' ascendancy was paralleled by that of **Amun**, whose cult-temple at Karnak became the greatest in Egypt. At its zenith under the XVIII and XIX dynasties, Thebes may have had a population of around a million; Homer's *Iliad* describes it as a "city with a hundred gates". Excluding the brief **Amarna Period** (c.1379–62 BC) when the "heretic" Akhenaten moved the capital north-wards and forbade the worship of Amun, the dynasty's – and city's – supremacy lasted some 500 years. Even after the end of the Ramessid line, when the capital returned to Memphis and thence moved to the Delta, Thebes remained the fore-most city of Upper Egypt, enjoying a final fling as a royal seat under the **Nubian** rulers of the XXV Dynasty (c.747–645 BC).

Though Thebes persisted through **Ptolemaic** into **Roman** times, it retained but a shadow of its former glory, and might have been abandoned like Memphis were it not for Christian settlements. During Muslim times its only claim to fame was the tomb of Abu el-Haggag, a twelfth-century sheikh. However, Napoleon's expedition to Egypt awakened foreign interest in its **antiquities**, which were grad-ually cleared during the nineteenth century, and have drawn visitors ever since.

> All telephone numbers in the Luxor area are prefixed ☎095.

Orientation and getting around

Luxor spreads along the east bank of the Nile, its outskirts encroaching on villages and fields. For a general layout of the city, together with Karnak and Thebes, see the map on p.312; a map of central Luxor is to be found overpage.

Orientation in central Luxor is simplified by a relatively compact tourist zone defined by three main roads. **Sharia al-Mahatta** runs 500m from the railway station towards Luxor Temple, where it meets **Sharia el-Karnak**, the main drag heading north to Karnak Temple (2.5km). Karnak is also accessible via the riverside **Corniche**, though tourists generally stick to the 1.5km stretch between Luxor Museum and the *Old Winter Palace Hotel*. The "circuit" is completed by a fourth street, **Sharia el-Birka** – also known as Sharia al-Souk after its bazaar.

Two of the other main roads have aliases, too: Sharia el-Nil (or el-Bahr) for the Corniche, and Sharia el-Lokanda and Sharia el-Markaz for the downtown sections of Sharia el-Karnak.

Getting around

You can easily explore central Luxor on foot since almost everywhere is within fifteen to twenty minutes' walk of the railway station. However, **horse-drawn carriages** (*caleches*) are fun to ride and useful if you're burdened with luggage. Fares are set by the authorities but drivers charge whatever they can get. Expect an argument if you pay the official rate (£E1.50 for a ride within Luxor) during winter; rides to Karnak are a special case (see p.299). **Taxis** serve for trips to outlying hotels or the airport (£E5).

Many people rent **bicycles** from places such as the *New Karnak Hotel*, *Boulos Bicycles* (52 Sharia al-Mahatta) or the *Bike Shop* opposite the *Hotel Philippe*. Prices vary from £E5–6 a day in the winter to £E2–4 over summer; a passport or other ID is generally required as security. Though most bikes are one-speed only, the *Etap* and *Windsor* hotels rent superior models (£E10 per day). You can also rent 150cc **motorbikes** from *Sinbad*, opposite the *Ramoza Hotel* on Sharia al-Mahatta, for about £E30 a day. The owner doesn't care whether you've got a licence or not, but the police will. Bikes can be carried on local ferries to the west bank, for getting around the Theban necropolis.

One you've found somewhere to stay, it's a good idea to visit the **tourist office** (☎382-215; open daily 8am–8pm) south of Luxor Temple to discover the current official rates for taxis, *caleches*, *feluccas* or any other service you might be interested in. There's also a branch at the airport (☎382-306), open 24 hours. The **tourist police** (☎386-620) can be found in the same building as the main tourist office, and maintain a branch in the railway station; both are open 24 hours. The regular **police** (☎382-006) are based off Sharia el-Karnak, north of Luxor Temple.

Accommodation

The cost and availability of **accommodation** varies with the time of year. Officially, there are simply "high" (Nov–May) and "low" (June–Oct) **seasons**, the former being dearer than the latter. In practice, however, many hotels hike their prices still further during the period of peak demand (Dec & Jan), receptionists

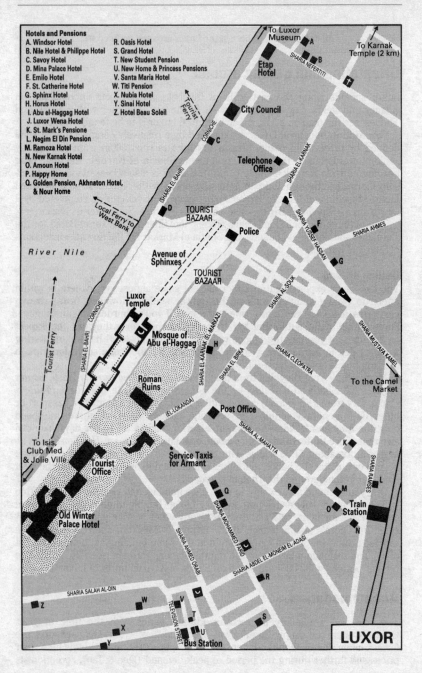

Hotels and Pensions

A. Windsor Hotel
B. Nile Hotel & Philippe Hotel
C. Savoy Hotel
D. Mina Palace Hotel
E. Emilo Hotel
F. St. Catherine Hotel
G. Sphinx Hotel
H. Horus Hotel
I. Abu el-Haggag Hotel
J. Luxor Wena Hotel
K. St. Mark's Pensione
L. Negim El Din Pension
M. Ramoza Hotel
N. New Karnak Hotel
O. Amoun Hotel
P. Happy Home
Q. Golden Pension, Akhnaton Hotel,
   & Nour Home
R. Oasis Hotel
S. Grand Hotel
T. New Student Pension
U. New Home & Princess Pensions
V. Santa Maria Hotel
W. Titi Pension
X. Nubia Hotel
Y. Sinai Hotel
Z. Hotel Beau Soleil

To Luxor Museum
To Karnak Temple (2 km)
SHARIA NEFERTITI
Etap Hotel
City Council
Tourist Ferry
CORNICHE
Telephone Office
SHARIA EL KARNAK
SHARIA EL BAHRI
SHARIA YUSSEF HASSAN
SHARIA AHMES
Local Ferry to West Bank
TOURIST BAZAAR
Police
SHARIA AL-SOUK
River Nile
Avenue of Sphinxes
TOURIST BAZAAR
Luxor Temple
SHARIA MUSTAFA KAMEL
CORNICHE
Mosque of Abu el-Haggag
SHARIA KARNAK (EL-MARKAZI)
SHARIA EL BIRKA
SHARIA CLEOPATRA
Tourist Ferry
Roman Ruins
To the Camel Market
(EL-LOKANDA)
Post Office
SHARIA AL-MAHATTA
To Isis, Club Med & Jolie Ville
Tourist Office
Service Taxis for Armant
SHARIA RAMSES
Train Station
Old Winter Palace Hotel
SHARIA MOHAMED FARID
SHARIA AHMED ORABI
SHARIA ABDEL EL-MONEIM EL-ADASI
SHARIA SALAH AL-DIN
Z
W
V
X
Y
TELEVISION STREET
T
U
Bus Station
R
S

LUXOR

pocketing the difference between the actual and official price. If you're fussy about lodgings, make reservations over this period, when all the low-budget and mid-range places in the centre are likely to be booked up (though you might be allowed to stay one night pending the arrival of a group), and the only cheap vacancies are around Television Street, in the southern part of town. The obverse of this is that places compete with each other as demand dwindles towards zero during the hottest months, when hotels slash their rates by up to fifty percent, knock off taxes, or both. Because of the slump in tourism caused by the Gulf War, you might get a better deal than the (high season) rates below. But as trade recovers, prices should rise.

If you want to stay in the centre when all the hotels are full, you might try renting **private accommodation** on Sharia Yussef Hassan. Rather than going through receptionists at local hotels (who take a cut), it's best to negotiate directly with Hani Milad, who can usually be found at his print shop opposite the *St Catherine's Hotel* (see "Mid-range" listings, overpage). The longer your stay, the lower the price of a double room at Hani's (£E10–20 a night).

Most hotels listed below are keyed to the map of Luxor opposite. There are also a youth hostel and campsite in the northern part of town, plus half a dozen hotels on the west bank of the river; all of them are keyed on the map on p.312.

Cheap hotels and pensions

Budget hotels and pensions range from cosy home-from-homes to utter fleapits, all varieties being represented on and off Yussef Hassan, al-Mahatta and Television streets. The biggest selection lies around mosquito-ridden Television Street, in the southern part of town – the places to *avoid* here are the *Thebes, Mubarak, Salam* and *Salah al-Din* hotels. All places listed below are to some degree recommend ed.

Sphinx Hotel (G), Sharia Yussef Hassan (☎382-830). Simple rooms with fans and shared hot-water bathrooms, cleaned daily. Singles £E8, doubles £E10, triples £E13; private bath £E2 extra. Thirty percent reductions over summer. Rooftop restaurant.

St Mark's Pensione (K), 19 Sharia Michael Bolus, off Sharia al-Mahatta. A tiny pension with several doubles (£E10) with a shared bathroom and kitchen, regularly cleaned.

Negim El Din Pension (L), next to the railway tracks, so noisy all night (☎382-852). Desperate for custom, they charge only £E3 per person (less over summer). Poky but clean rooms; shared hot showers; kitchen and washing machine. Shady tropical garden and verandah.

Ramoza Hotel (M), Sharia al-Mahatta, 100m from the railway station (☎382-270; telex 23647 PBLXR). May be fully occupied by low-budget tour groups during January. Spotlessly clean A/C rooms with hot showers. Rates for singles (£E19), doubles (£E22) and triples (£E25) include breakfast.

New Karnak Hotel (N), opposite the station and usually full (☎382-427). Basic, noisy rooms with fans and shared bathrooms (sporadic hot water); singles £E6, doubles £E8 (£E10 with bath), triples £E11. Book exchange; restaurant next door.

Amoun Hotel (O), a few doors along. Similar rooms and rates, but hot water on the first floor only. Vacancies more likely.

Happy Home (P), off Sharia al-Mahatta (☎385-811). Longtime cheapie haven: cramped, fairly clean rooms with shared hot showers. Singles £E4, doubles £E6, triples £E9.

Golden Pension (Q), Sharia Mohammed Farid, two blocks south of al-Mahatta (☎382-234). A cosy pension with four rooms (£E8–10) which fill rapidly. Clean and friendly; kitchen and washing machine available.

Nour Home, Sharia Mohammed Farid – beside the *Golden* (☎380-416). Four rooms sharing a bathroom (£E3 per person) and one double with a private shower (£E10), all with fans. Hot water most of the day. Helpful management.

Akhnaton Hotel, Sharia Mohammed Farid – next door to the *Nour* (☎383-979). Cramped but clean rooms with fans (singles £E10, doubles £E15; private bath £E2). Hot water.

Oasis Hotel (R), Sharia Mohammed Farid (☎383-279). A new place further down the street. Decent rooms (£E6 per person, plus £E3 apiece for A/C), shared bathrooms, kitchen and free laundry service. Breakfast included.

Grand Hotel (S), on a side street between Mohammed Farid and Ahmed Orabi (☎384-186). Singles (£E4–5), doubles (£E8–10) and triples (£E12) are tiny but clean. Hot water and a small roof garden. A budget travellers' haunt for the last fifteen years.

New Student Pension (T), off Television Street. Quiet rooms, most with fans and small balconies, for £E5 per person. Hot baths, washing machine and roof garden. Breakfast included in the singles' price. Hires bikes.

New Home Pension (U), across the road (☎383-059). Similar facilities to the above – and likewise popular with backpackers. £E6 per person.

Princess Pension (☎383-997). Quieter rooms with fans, mosquito screens and balconies, two doors along from the *New Home*. Somewhat creepy staff.

Titi Pension (W), west off Television Street (☎383-803). Clean and cosy, with friendly management. Rates (including breakfast) are negotiable, starting at £E7. Hot showers.

Nubia Hotel (X), Sharia Gesr al-Awamia. Another good deal, one block south of the *Titi*. Singles (£E6), doubles (£E10) and quadruples (£E12) up to fifty percent cheaper over summer. Hot showers, kitchen, washing machine and TV, even the occasional free meal.

Sinai Hotel (Y), Sharia Gesr al-Awamia – farther along (☎384-752). Clean and simple, with a pushy manager. Big rooms with fans for £E10–25 (the dearer ones have A/C and/or private shower). Hot water; washing machine; rooftop restaurant.

Mid-range hotels

Mostly modern or modernised, the following mid-range hotels feature private bathrooms, A/C and TV unless otherwise stated. Being geared to tour groups, some of them treat independent travellers shabbily, and may overcharge when vacancies in town are scarce (reservations are advisable). Conversely, sizeable reductions may be negotiated in the summer.

Windsor Hotel (A), off Sharia Nefertiti (☎382-847; telex 23647 PUBLUX UN). Salubrious carpeted rooms with lounges – for tour groups, anyway: others may get dingy holes. Singles £E45, doubles £E70, suites £E90. No credit cards accepted. Garden and pool underway.

Nile Hotel (B), Sharia Nefertiti, near the landmark *Hotel Etap* (☎382-859). Refurbished rooms, some with balconies; a few without A/C or private bathrooms – prices vary. Front-facing singles (£E28) and doubles (£E35) are best. Bar and disco underway.

Philippe Hotel, Sharia Nefertiti (☎382-284; telex PBLXR). A smarter joint almost next door. Carpeted rooms with double beds, video, fridge and bath. Singles £E42, doubles £E60; breakfast included. Roof garden, bar, dining room. Deservedly popular.

Mina Palace Hotel (D), on the Corniche north of Luxor Temple (☎382-074; telex 23674 PUBLUX). The balcony of most rooms overlooks the Nile – "06" rooms also possess an extra balcony facing Luxor Temple. The dearer singles (£E26–35) and doubles (£E30–35) have phones and mini-fridges.

Emilio Hotel (E), Sharia Yussef Hassan, just off the main drag (☎383-570; telex PUBLUX UN). Comfy rooms with phone and video channel; some have balconies overlooking Luxor Temple. Rates for singles (starting at £E50) and doubles (£E65 upwards) include breakfast, but not 21 percent tax. Shady rooftop terrace. Reservations essential.

St Catherine Hotel (F), Sharia Yussef Hassan (☎382-684). A homier place up the road, popular with German tour groups. Singles £E23, doubles £E29; plus 21 percent tax. Across the road is the similarly priced **El Aref Hotel**.

Horus Hotel (H), opposite Luxor Temple, backing onto the souk (☎382-165; telex 23647 PUBLUX). Revamped vintage hotel. Take your pick of views (top-floor front rooms overlook the Nile), but bear in mind the *muezzin* across the road. Singles £E25, doubles £E35, triples £E45, quadruples £E55. Laundry service, currency exchange, restaurant/bar and café.

Abu el-Haggag Hotel (I). Bang opposite Luxor Temple, with great views from the upper floor, this former cheapie hotel is heading upmarket, and rates for A/C singles (£E18), doubles (£E23) and triples (£E28) with private bathrooms may well rise soon.

Santa Maria Hotel (V), Television Street (☎382-603). Three-star facilities spoilt by a grotty location. Singles £E22, doubles £E27, triples £E37, quadruples £E43.

Hotel Beau Soleil (Z), Sharia Salah al-Din, near the impending *Novotel* (☎382-671). Cheerful rooms (soon to get TV and phones) and a pleasant garden. Prices include half-board: singles £E30, doubles £E50, triples £E60.

Upmarket hotels

The post-Gulf War slump in tourism hit **upmarket hotels** especially hard, since tour groups are their mainstay. Following a season of desperate price-cutting, they are now hoping for a better year and rising prices; figures below are only estimates – don't be shy about angling for reductions if business looks slack.

Etap Hotel, on the Corniche between Luxor Temple and the Museum (☎328-011; telex 92080 ETAPLX UN). A modern complex featuring three restaurants, a nightclub/disco, pool and other facilities. Luxurious singles (US$80) and doubles (US$100).

Savoy Hotel (C), nearer the temple and ferry dock (☎382-200; telex 24126 LUXTL UN). Now somewhat run-down and under Saudi management (no alcohol served). A/C bungalows in the garden (singles £E85, doubles £E115); rooms in the main building cost half as much.

Luxor Wena Hotel (J), near Luxor Temple (☎382-011). Recently upgraded to four stars, this renovated Twenties pile retains a splendid Moorish-style verandah and some Art Deco features. Set amidst a lush garden with a pool. Double rooms from US$49.

Old Winter Palace Hotel (☎382-000; telex WINTER UN). The doyen of Luxor's hotels, founded in 1887, has played host to heads of state, Noël Coward and Agatha Christie (parts of *Death on the Nile* were written and filmed here). Combines old-fashioned elegance with modern facilities. Its spacious singles (US$70) and doubles (US$90) overlook the Nile or hotel garden. Next door stands the charmless but similarly equipped *New Winter Palace*.

Isis Hotel (☎382-750; telex 92078). Just south of town along the Corniche, with a wonderful view of the Nile. A/C singles (US$85) and doubles (US$95) with all mod cons; balconies overlook the garden or the river. Buffet and restaurant; tennis and squash courts, water sports and bike rental.

Akhenaton Club Med (☎377-7575; telex 93156 MEDLX UN) Stylish, self-contained resort hotel, next door. Simple, modern A/C singles (US$62) and doubles (US$78). Pool, night-club/disco.

Movenpick Jolie Ville, on leafy Crocodile Island, 5km south of town (☎384-855; telex 23825 MPL UN). Lavish singles (US$100) and doubles (US$130) set amidst gardens. Buffet terrace, restaurants, "folkloric" nightclub, bank, pool, tennis courts, children's playground and zoo. Linked to town by an hourly shuttle (7am–11pm) from the *Old Winter Palace*.

Hostels and camping

IYHF Youth Hostel, halfway between Luxor and Karnak temples, a fair distance from the centre (☎382-139). Though relatively clean, with dorm beds (£E3), double rooms (£E12) and free lockers, this offers less value for money than places around Television Street, with the added drawback of a 10am–2pm lockout and 11pm curfew. Furthermore, non-members must purchase a guest card (£E1 per night) or IYHF membership (£E18).

YMCA campsite, across the road (☎382-425). Tent-space and hot showers, chiefly used by Egyptian families and tour groups, who party till midnight or later; the site is guarded 24 hours. £E3 a head, plus a charge for motorbikes (£E1), cars (£E3) or caravans (£E5).

Luxor Temple

Luxor Temple stands aloof in the heart of town, ennobling the view from the waterfront and tourist bazaar with its grand colonnades and pylons, which are spotlit at night. Though best explored by day – when its details can be thoroughly examined in a couple of hours – you should come back after dark to imbibe its atmosphere and drama with fewer people around. It was in this temple, in 1987, that Verdi's opera *Aida* was staged with a cast of thousands, including Placido Domingo, Maria Chiara, a squadron of cavalry and a caged lion.

The site is open daily (winter 6am–9pm; summer 6am–10pm; 6am–6.30pm & 8–11pm during Ramadan), the lights going on at 7.30pm year-round. Admission costs £E5 (students £E2.50); the entrance is on the Corniche.

The temple's dedication and construction

Dedicated to the Theban Triad of Amun-Min, Mut and Khonsu (see box on p.301), Luxor Temple was the "Harem of the South" where Amun's consort Mut and their son Khonsu resided. Every spring a flotilla of barques escorted Amun's effigy from Karnak Temple to this site for a conjugal reunion with Mut in an *Optet* or fertility festival noted for its public debauchery.

Whereas Karnak is the work of many dynasties, most of Luxor Temple was built by two rulers during a period when New Kingdom art reached its apogee. The temple's founder was **Amenophis III** (1417–1379 BC) of the XVIII Dynasty, whose other monuments include the Third Pylon at Karnak and the Colossi of Memnon across the river. Work halted under his son Akhenaten (who erased his father's cartouches and built a sanctuary to Aten alongside the temple), but resumed under Tutankhamun and Horemheb, who decorated its court and colonnade with their own reliefs. To this, **Ramses II** (1304–1237 BC) of the XIX Dynasty added a double colonnaded court and a great pylon flanked by obelisks and colossi. Despite additions by later pharaohs and the rebuilding of its sanctuary under Alexander the Great, the temple has a coherence that reproaches Karnak's inchoate giganticism.

The clarity of its **reliefs** owes to the temple having been half-buried by sand and silt, and overlaid by Luxor itself. Nineteenth-century visitors found a "labyrinthine maze of mud structures" nesting within its court; colonnades turned into granaries where dishonest merchants were hung by their ears. "So stirs a mini-life amid the debris of a life that was far grander," wrote Flaubert. When the French desired to remove an obelisk, and archaeologists to excavate the temple, they had to pay compensation for the demolition of scores of homes.

Approaching the temple

The gradual slope inside the temple entrance obscures the fact that the site lies some six metres below street level – a measure of the debris that accumulated here over centuries. To your left stands a mudbrick **Roman chapel** which still contains a battered statue of Isis. Beyond this, the courtyard opens into an **Avenue of Sphinxes** with human faces that once led to Karnak – a XXX Dynasty addition by Nectanebo I.

The gateway proper is flanked by massive pylons and enthroned colossi, with a single **Obelisk** soaring 25m high. Carved with reliefs and originally tipped with electrum, this was one of a pair until its mate was removed in 1835, taken to France and re-erected on the Place de la Concorde. The four dog-faced baboons at the base of each obelisk also sported erect phalluses until prudish Frenchmen hacked them off. Behind loom three of the six **colossi of Ramses II** that originally fronted the pylon (four seated, two standing). The enthroned pair have Schwarzenegger physiques and double crowns; reliefs of the Nile-god binding the Two Lands adorn their thrones.

Notched for flagpoles and carved with scenes of Ramses' victory at Qadesh (the battle uppermost, the Egyptian camp below), the **Pylon** was later embellished by Nubian and Ethiopian kings, as evinced by the relief of Pharaoh Shabaka running the *heb* race before Amun-Min, on the left as you walk through.

Courts and colonnades

Beyond the pylon lies the **Court of Ramses II**, surrounded by a double row of papyrus-bud columns, once roofed over to form arcades. The courtyard is set askew to the temple's main axis, doubtless to incorporate the earlier **barque shrine** of Tuthmosis III, whose triple chapels were dedicated to Khonsu (to the right as you enter), Amun (centre) and Mut (nearest the river).

Incongruously perched atop the opposite colonnade (which is still buried up to its capitals), the **Mosque of Abu el-Haggag** is a much rebuilt edifice, bearing the name of Luxor's patron saint, whose demolition the townsfolk refused to countenance when the temple was excavated. To the right of the portal at the back of the court, carvings depict Amun's procession approaching the temple during the Optet festival, when the god was presented with lettuces, symbolising his fertility. Here, Ramses offers to Mut and Mont (the Theban war-god), observed by his queen and seventeen of the hundred or so sons that he sired over ninety years.

The portal itself is flanked by black granite statues of Ramses, their bases decorated with bound prisoners from Nubia and Asia. Beyond lies the older section of the temple, inaugurated by the lofty **Colonnade of Amenophis III**, with its processional avenue of papyrus columns whose calyx capitals still support massive architraves. On the walls are more scenes from the Optet festival, intended to be "read" in an anticlockwise direction. After sacrifices to the boats at Karnak (northwest corner), Amun's procession (west wall) arrives at Luxor Temple (southeast corner), returning to Karnak 24 days later (east wall). The pharaoh shown here is Tutankhamun, who had the colonnade decorated, but the cartouches honour his successor, Horemheb.

The colonnaded **Court of Amenophis III** is the chief glory of the temple, surrounded on three sides by double rows of papyrus-bundle columns with bud capitals – the most elegant form devised by the ancient Egyptians. Its decorations include artwork from the time of Alexander and Philip of Macedon, with traces of colour visible on the eastern and western colonnades. The southern one merges into a **Hypostele Hall** with 32 papyrus columns, serving as a vestibule to the temple proper. Between the last two columns on the left of its central aisle is a Roman altar dedicated to Constantine (before his conversion to Christianity). On either side of the hall's rear wall, Amenophis makes offerings to the gods.

The inner sanctums

Beyond the hall lies a columned **portico** or antechamber, whose central aisle was flanked by the barque shrines of Mut and Khonsu. Roman legionaries later plastered over the pharaonic reliefs and turned it into a chapel where local Christians were offered a choice between martyrdom or obeisance to the imperial cults.

Paintings of Roman emperors are visible near the top of the walls; elsewhere the stucco has fallen away to reveal Amenophis offering sacrifice to Amun. In the smaller, four-columned **Hall of Offerings**, beyond, reliefs show the pharaoh leading sacrificial cows and presenting incense and sceptres.

By erecting a granite chapel within the next columned hall, Alexander the Great converted it into the **Sanctuary of Amun's Barque**, adorned with "doors of acacia inlaid with gold". The remaining chambers to the south constituted the private apartments of the gods, reached by a **transverse hall** whose end walls show the barques of Day and Night. However, this section of the temple is badly damaged and really only notable for the name *Rimbaud*, carved high up on the wall near the river. Rimbaud spent the last sixteen years of his life roaming the Near and Far East; whilst living in Ethiopia he was feared dead, so Verlaine published his poems (all written by the age of twenty-one), which took Paris by storm and inspired the Decadent movement.

More interesting pharaonic reliefs survive in two rooms situated alongside the Sanctuary and Hall of Offerings. The first, opening eastwards (left) off the Sanctuary, contains hacked about scenes of Amenophis III being crowned, and hunting in the marshes. From here, you can walk north into the **Birth Room**, whose left-hand wall emphasises his divine paternity. The much defaced lower register shows Amun, Hathor and Queen Mutemuia embracing; Thoth leading Amun (disguised as Tuthmosis IV) into the queen's bedchamber. Examined from left to right, the middle register depicts Thoth foretelling Amenophis' birth; Mutemuia's pregnancy and confinement; Isis presenting the child to Amun; and the god cradling his son. Along the top register, Amenophis and his *ka* are nurtured by deities and presented to Amun; in the far right corner, Amenophis becomes pharaoh.

It was near this room in 1989 that workers uncovered a cache of twenty-two New Kingdom statues buried at the start of the Roman conquest (c.30 BC), including effigies of Amenophis III, Tutankhamun, Ramses II, Queen Nefertari, Hathor and Horus.

Luxor Museum

Intended to be seen after a hard day's touring, **Luxor Museum** has a small but choice collection of antiquities (winter daily 4pm–9pm; summer 5pm–10pm; admission £E3, students £E1.50; photo permit £E5, no flashes or tripods).

The exhibits have recently been rearranged to include a number of statues from the Luxor Temple cache; everything is clearly labelled, but some names may be rendered differently from those in this book (eg Amenhotep for Amenophis; Sestosiris for Senusert). An illustrated guidebook can be purchased at the information desk.

Works in stone include a large pink granite head of Amenophis III; a fine statue of Tuthmosis III in green-black schist; a jug-eared Senusert III (XII Dynasty); a human-bodied, crocodile-headed Sobek in alabaster; and two haunting busts of Amenophis IV (Akhenaten) from his temple at Karnak. Figures on a lovely mural from this temple also evince the strange physiognomy associated with Akhenaten's reign.

From **Tutankhamun's tomb** in the Valley of the Kings come a funerary bed, two model boats and a stunning gold-inlaid cow's head representing Merit Weri (an aspect of Hathor); the rest of the Tut finds are housed in Cairo.

Other highlights include a dazzling mummy casing from the tomb of Lady Shepenkhonsu; canopic jars with animal- or human-headed lids; and a scowling statue of Amenhotep, Steward of Amenophis III, the probable architect of Luxor Temple.

The collection is rounded off with some **Greek, Roman, Coptic and Mamluke artefacts**, and **prints** of Luxor, Karnak and the Theban necropolis as they looked in the nineteenth century.

Bazaars and markets

The streets around Luxor Temple are infested with **tourist bazaars** whose importunate salesmen make the "official" bazaar centre beside the *New Winter Palace* seem a haven of peace. Luxor's merchants have been gulling tourists with phoney *antikas* for generations, and are masters of the hard sell. Despite fierce competition, you must bargain hard for a good price, since merchants can rely upon fresh-off-the-plane tourists to pay way over the odds. They and the rash of curio and carpet shops have long been driving hardware, spices, vegetables and clothing stalls northwards up Sharia el-Birka, the traditional *souk*. The main **fruit and veg market** is now held on Television Street on Tuesday.

Luxor's weekly **Camel Market** is smaller than the *Souk el-Gamal* at Darow (near Aswan) or Imbaba, but just as rough on the nerves of animal lovers. The name of its location – Sharia el-Salakhana, "Slaughterhouse Street" – says it all. The market is usually held every Tuesday (7–11am), but it's worth checking ahead at the tourist office before setting out. To reach the site, follow Sharia Mustafa Kamel across the railway tracks, turn right down el-Salakhana and keep going – it's about a kilometre's walk in all.

Activities

Sailing on the river in a *felucca* is a relaxing way to spend an afternoon, whilst a sunset cruise is the perfect way to end the day. Find out the current rates before conducting negotiations with boatmen along the Corniche. Bargaining is easier during summer, when trade is slack. Expect to pay about £E15–20 an hour for a boat carrying two people, £E20–25 for a craft seating up to six or seven. The favoured destination for a longer trip is **Banana Island** (*Gezira el-Mohz*), a lush peninsula 4km upriver, where visitors can stuff themselves with finger bananas for £E1 or so. It's not quite an idyll, however: there are also souvenir and drinks stalls, and lads who hijack the clothes of tourists who strip to swim and hold them to ransom. The round-trip takes between two and three hours depending on the wind. A group of four should reckon on paying about £E8 each, plus *baksheesh*.

A pricier experience is offered by the *Airship and Balloon Company*, whose **hot-air balloon flights** over Luxor, Karnak and the Theban necropolis lift off daily at 7am. For about ninety minutes you drift above the town and temples, across the glittering river and parched Theban Hills, enjoying the godlike view attributed to Re and Horus. Travel agents along the Corniche can make bookings.

Non-residents may use the **swimming pools** at the *Old Winter Palace* (7am–sunset; £E10), *Etap* (£E8) and *Luxor Wena* (£E5) hotels. Should you feel like **horse-riding**, mounts are available just south of the village where the local ferry docks on the west bank. Details can be obtained from *American Express* in the arcade below the *Old Winter Palace*.

Nightlife

Aside from the **Sound and Light show at Karnak Temple** – which is the best in Egypt (see p.300) – Luxor's nightlife is a paler version of Cairo's. The *Isis*, *Etap*, *Winter Palace* and *Sheraton* hotels feature **music** and **belly-dancing** most nights, with a mandatory buffet or minimum drinks charge; whilst the *Jolie Ville* offers an all-inclusive "folklore" evening that starts with a sunset cruise to *Fellah's Village* – ask at reception for details. A mixed-couples-only policy restricts access to the **discos** in the *Etap* and *Isis* (nightly in winter from 9.30pm; £E8).

For locals who can't afford such pleasures, the main diversions are playing backgammon (*thowla*) or dominoes in **cafés** like the *Amoun* and *Oum Kalsoum*, near the Abu el-Haggag mosque. Though café life is exclusively masculine, foreign women can feel comfortable in the *Amoun*, even alone. Most places stay open as long as there are customers; Sharia Ramses has several all-nighters.

Festivals

Should you happen to be around during the Muslim month of Sha'ban, there's no wilder spectacle than the **Moulid of Abu el-Haggag**, the town's patron sheikh, whose mosque overlooks the Luxor Temple. His *moulid* on the 14th is the largest festival in Upper Egypt. The parading of a large boat (or even three boats) through town is often compared to the solar barque processions of pharaonic times, though in Islamic symbolism boats represent the quest for spiritual enlightenment. Huge crowds attend the *zikrs* outside his mosque, and revel in traditional entertainments. There are mock fights (*tahtib*) with sticks to the music of drums and *mizmars*, and horse races (*mirmah*) where the riders gallop hell-for-leather, halting in a flurry of dust just before they plough into the crowd.

Yussef Abu el-Haggag (Father of the Pilgrimage) was born in Damascus (c.1150), moved to Mecca in his forties and finally settled in Egypt, where he founded a *zawiyah* in Luxor and met with other Sufi sheikhs such as al-Mursi and al-Shazli. Many of his descendants still live in the area, and the tradition of venerating local sheikhs persists in Old Qurna, across the river, where another *moulid* honours Abu Qusman (see p.316). To compensate for the daytime rigours of **Ramadan**, townsfolk also gather to hear *zikrs* and dance outside Abu el-Haggag's mosque in the evenings. At all these festivals *fellaheen* indulge in booze and hash.

In previous years the municipality has staged an **Amun Festival** that re-enacts the procession of Amun from Luxor Temple to Karnak, with participants dressed in "pharaonic" costumes. If held in the future (most likely in January or February), details will be available at the tourist office.

Eating and drinking

Compared to Cairo or Alexandria, the culinary scene is lacklustre. The best Middle Eastern and European food is served in upmarket **hotel restaurants** such as the Jolie Ville's *Movenpick* (noon–4.30pm & 6.30pm–midnight) and *La Terraza* at the *Isis Hotel*. If you're into splurging, it's also worth considering the latter's evening **buffets** (from 6.30pm onwards; all you can eat for £E40), or the salad bar (£E10) at the *Etap*'s *Champollion Coffeeshop* (open 24hr).

Though all the usual **street food** can be found along el-Karnak, Ramses and Yussef Hassan streets, it's hard for foreigners to escape being grossly overcharged, even if they know the proper price. The same is also true for tea, coffee and *sheeshas* at cafés; cigarettes, pastries and other items.

Budget restaurants
Most of the following **restaurants** are inexpensive by Western standards, and largely cater to low-budget tourists. All are open from mid-morning (or earlier) till 9–10pm, but the range of meals shrinks as the evening wears on. Unless specified otherwise, they don't sell alcohol.

Salt and Bread. A hang out for hotel touts in front of the railway station, serving chicken, kebab and pigeon.

New Karnak Restaurant, next to the like-named hotel. Similar fare, plus okra, salads and spaghetti with a smidgin of sauce.

Limpy's, just across the way, does lunch and poor breakfasts, and likewise offers a ringside view of Sharia al-Mahatta.

Mensa Restaurant. Similar food at slightly higher prices, with surlier staff and semi-A/C.

Cafeteria El Hussein, Sharia el-Karnak, behind Luxor Temple. Tasty fare, served indoors or on the terrace.

Amoun Restaurant, north of Abu el-Haggag's mosque. Set meals of chicken, fish or *kofta* with soup, salad and rice pudding. There's a café for playing backgammon next door.

Restaurant Abu El Hassan El Shazly, farther up the street, does similar food.

Maharba (☎382-633). Above the tourist office, with a rooftop terrace overlooking the Theban hills and a darkened indoor restaurant. Serves the usual food at upmarket rates, plus beer.

Drinking
Aside from bars in the top hotels, or quaffing beer at the *Hotel Ramoza*'s restaurant, there's not much **drinking**. Since the *Old Winter Palace* came under strictly Muslim management, one can no longer sink a Stella on its garden terrace.

Listings

American Express outside the *Old Winter Palace* can hold mail, change money and travellers' cheques, but will only sell them to Amex cardholders. Open daily 8am–8pm (☎382-862).

Banks *National Bank of Egypt*, 50m south of the Old Winter Palace (Sat–Thurs 8.30am–2pm & 5–8pm, Fri 8.30–11am & 5–8pm); *Banque Misr* on Sharia Nefertiti (Sun–Thurs 8.30am–9pm); *Bank of Alexandria*, just north of the Nefertiti/el-Karnak street intersection (Sun 6–9pm, Wed 5–8pm). Currency also exchanged at the *Bazaar Radwan* at the junction of el-Karnak and Mohammed Farid streets (daily 10am–11pm).

Bookshops *Abdoui* in the tourist bazaar, near the tourist office, and *Hachette*, in the arcade of the *Hotel Etap*, stock novels and books on Egyptology in foreign languages. A kiosk on the Corniche near the Winter Palace sells foreign **newspapers**.

Hospital *Al-Amiri* (☎382-025), on the Corniche near the youth hostel, is open 24 hours; English is spoken but the place is pretty grim – if you can, seek treatment in Cairo. The town's **emergency** number (☎123) doesn't always work.

Passport office on the second floor of the City Council (☎382-318). Open daily 9am–3pm and 6–9pm, but only registers passports and extends visas in the mornings.

Pharmacies *Ashraf* (☎382-834), near the *Horus Hotel*, is open 24 hours.

Post office with *poste restante* on Sharia al-Mahatta (Sun–Thurs 8am–2pm). However, it's probably better to have letters sent to you c/o Amex.

Telephone calls The 24-hour Central Telephone Office on Sharia al-Karnak, behind the *Etap*, can make domestic and international calls, though for the latter you'd do better to pay more and call from one of the luxury hotels.

Excursions from Luxor – and moving on

With Karnak Temple and the Theban necropolis (see following sections) in the immediate vicinity, it'll be a while before you start considering **excursions** to other sites up and down the Nile Valley. However, the **temples of Dendara and Abydos** lie downriver, beyond Qena, and in the other direction the **temples of Esna, Edfu and Kom Ombo** are spaced along the way to Aswan. Any of these sites makes a feasible day excursion from Luxor, *service* taxis being the most efficient form of public transport (see below).

To cover two or more sites, you really need to hire a private taxi for the day. A round-trip **to Dendara and Abydos** costs £E40–75, depending on the size of the cab and your bargaining skills. For a day-long trip **to Esna, Edfu and Kom Ombo**, concluding in Aswan, expect to pay £E65–75 for a four- or five-seater taxi, £E95–100 for a seven-person vehicle. The **journey to Aswan** can also be made **by felucca**, with stops at the temples en route, but since boats are dependent on the wind to travel upstream, most visitors prefer to sail downriver from Aswan. The ins and outs of *felucca* trips are covered on p.372.

Moving on to these and other points in Egypt may be affected by seasonal factors. Flights and trains are heavily booked over winter, as are direct buses to Hurghada on the Red Sea (which are also popular in summer). *Service* taxis are generally the easiest way to reach most points in Upper Egypt.

Buses

Although the terminal is on Television Street, most buses load up on either side of **Sharia el-Karnak** near the *Horus Hotel* and the inconspicuous green kiosk of the *Upper Egypt Bus Co*, where you can get information and sometimes buy tickets the day before (if not, then on the bus).

There are three express buses to **Cairo** (10hr; A/C £E26, non-A/C £E15) every day, plus the chance of seats on the A/C through-service from Aswan. Seedier southbound buses run every hour or so to **Aswan** (£E4), the morning services making longer stops at **Esna** (£E1.25), **Edfu** (£E2.50) and **Kom Ombo** (£E3.25). Direct services to **Hurghada** (4hr; £E6) leave around 6am, noon and 4pm; otherwise, travel to **Qena** and switch buses (last one at 7pm). Seats on the left side of the bus get less sun-baked crossing the **Eastern Desert**.

Trains

If you're planning to return to **Cairo** by train it's best reserve a seat on the day you arrive in Luxor. Schedules are posted in the station, but trains often run late. There are six daily A/C trains to Cairo (12–14hr; 1st class £E25, 2nd class £E15), plus two *wagon lits* sleepers. Trains to **Aswan** are equally full and unreliable (4–6 per day; 5hr; 1st class £E9, A/C 2nd class £E5). The queues for tickets are enough to make you travel by bus or taxi.

Service taxis

The **service taxi depot** in the north of town (just off Sharia el-Karnak before the YMCA) has signs in English for each destination. Per person fares can be obtained from the tourist office, so you needn't worry about being overcharged. Just turn up at the depot and you should be off within fifteen minutes. Current times and prices include: **Qena** (1hr; £E1.50); **Esna** (45min; £E1.50); **Kom Ombo** (2–3hr; £E3); Aswan (3–4hr; £E4). Most taxis have luggage racks.

Flights

Flight schedules vary seasonally and prices change regularly, so it's best to get the latest details from **EgyptAir** (☎580-581) and **ZAS** (☎385-928), outside the *Old Winter Palace* (both open daily 8am–8pm), which charge identical rates for flights to **Cairo**, **Aswan**, **Abu Simbel** and **Hurghada**. The first three destinations are served by between four and seven flights a day in summer, and up to twenty a day in winter; there are two to three flights to Hurghada a week. Book as far in advance as you can, or try for last-minute cancellations.

Luxor Airport (☎384-655) is 6km east of town (£E5–8 by taxi).

Karnak

The temple-complex of **Karnak** beats every other pharaonic monument but the Pyramids of Giza. Built on a leviathan scale to house the gods, it comprises three separate temple enclosures, the grandest being the **Precinct of Amun**, dedicated to the supreme god of the New Kingdom and a structure large enough to accommodate ten top-league cathedrals.

Karnak's magnitude and complexity owes to 1300 years of aggrandisement. From its XII Dynasty core, Amun's temple expanded along two axes – towards the river and the **Temple of Mut** – while its enclosure wall approached the **Precinct of Mont**. Though Pharaoh Akhenaten abjured Amun, defaced his images and erected an Aten Temple at Karnak, the status quo was soon restored. At the zenith of Amun's supremacy, Karnak drew tribute from 65 towns and cities, owned vast estates, scores of ships, 81,000 slaves and 240,000 head of cattle. T.G.H. James likens it to an industrial giant "which generated a mass of business subsidiary to the practice of the cults and a huge army of officials and working people". Yet ordinary folk were barred from its precincts and none but the pharaoh or his representative could enter Amun's sanctuary. The whole area was known to the ancient Egyptians as *Iput-Isut*, "the most esteemed of Places".

Visiting Karnak

The **site** of Karnak covers over 100 acres, 2.5km north of central Luxor. The only part that's readily accessible is the Precinct of Amun, which is open daily (winter 6am–5.30pm; summer 6am–6.30pm; £E7, students £E3.50) and also hosts nightly Sound and Light shows. This alone covers almost 62 acres, requiring at least two hours for a lookover, three or four hours for a closer examination. With little shade, it's best to start fairly early in the morning; wear a hat and bring water. A café by the Sacred Lake sells tea and soft drinks, whilst toilets can be found near the grandstand and the open-air museum.

There are two **approaches** from town: via the Corniche, which turns inland and passes the ticket kiosk en route to the temple entrance; or along Sharia el-Karnak, roughly following the **Avenue of Sphinxes** that once connected Luxor and Karnak temples, past the towering **Gateway of Euergetes II** and the precinct's **enclosure wall**. You could cycle or walk, but it's best to conserve your energy for the site. The cheapest way to get there (and back) is by covered pick-up trucks or *bijous*, which shuttle between Luxor railway station and a depot across the road from Karnak's ticket office (25pt per person). Luxor tourist office can supply the official rates for private taxis and horse-drawn *caleches*, which provide a benchmark for haggling with drivers.

Expect to pay more for rides to the **Sound and Light Show** (twice nightly; schedules widely posted; £E10 tickets sold on the spot). The first half consists of a four-stop tour through the temple, ineffably grander when gloomy and spotlit. Although the second half – when you view the ruins from a grandstand beyond the lake – drags on too long, the whole experience is unforgettable, not least for the crowd, which is so dense that people faint. *Caleches* cram in extra passengers for the homeward journey, and race back for a second load.

The Temple of Amun

The great **Temple of Amun** seemingly recedes towards infinity in an over-whelming succession of pylons, courts and columned halls, obelisks and colossi. Compared by T.G.H. James to "an archaeological department store containing something for everyone", it bears the stamp of dozens of rulers, spanning some thirteen centuries of ancient history. Half-buried in silt for as long again, the ruins were subsequently squatted by *fellaheen*, before being cleared by archaeologists in the mid-nineteenth century. The Karnak thus exposed was far more ruinous than today, with columns and colossi lying amidst piles of rubble and frogs croak-ing from the swampy enclosure. Since major repairs early this century, the temple has been undergoing slow but systematic restoration.

Making sense of its convoluted layout is not easy, with the ruins themselves getting denser and more jumbled the farther in you go. To simplify **orientation**, we've assumed that the temple's alignment towards the Nile corresponds with the cardinal points, so that its main axis runs east–west, and the subsidiary axis north–south (as on the map overpage).

It's worth following the main axis all the way back to the **Festival Hall**, and at least seeing the **Cachette Court** of the other wing. A break for refreshments by the lake is advisable if your itinerary includes the **open-air museum** or the **Temple of Khonsu**, off the main circuit.

Entering the temple

Walking towards the Precinct of Amun from the ticket office, and crossing over a dry moat, you'll pass the remains of an **ancient dock**, whence Amun sailed for Luxor Temple during the Optet festival. Before boarding a full-sized boat, his sacred barque rested in the small **chapel** to the right, which was erected (and graffitied by mercenaries) during the brief XXIX Dynasty. Beyond lies a short **Processional Way** flanked by ram-headed sphinxes (after Amun's sacred animal) enfolding statues of Ramses II, which once joined the main avenue link-ing the two temples.

Ahead of this rises the gigantic **First Pylon**, whose yawning gateway exposes a vista of receding portals, dwarfing all who walk between them. Composed of regular courses of sandstone masonry, the 43-metre-high towers are often attrib-uted to the Nubian and Ethiopian kings of the XXV Dynasty, but may have been erected as late as the XXX Dynasty (when Nectanebo I added the enclosure wall). Although the northern tower is unfinished and neither is decorated, their 130-metre width makes this the largest pylon in Egypt.

Inside the gateway to your right, Napoleonic surveyors have inscribed Karnak's vital statistics and the distances to other temples in Upper Egypt. For *baksheesh*, you might be allowed to climb a stairway to the top of the north tower, which offers a superb **view** of the temple and its environs.

AMUN AND THE THEBAN TRIAD

Originally merely one of the deities in the Hermopolitan Ogdoad (see p.251), **Amun** gained ascendancy at Thebes shortly before the Middle Kingdom, presumably because his cult was adopted by powerful local rulers during the First Intermediate Period. After the expulsion of the Hyksos (c.1567 BC), the rulers of the XVIII Dynasty elevated Amun to a victorious national god, and set about making Karnak his principal cult-centre in Egypt.

As the "Unseen One" (whose name in hieroglyphic script was accompanied by a blank space instead of the usual explicatory sign), Amun assimilated other deities into such incarnations as **Amun-Re** (the supreme creator), **Amun-Min** (the "bull which serves the cows" with a perpetual erection). or ram-headed **Auf-Re** ("Re made Flesh"), who sailed through the underworld revitalising the souls of the dead, emerging reborn as Khepri. However, Amun most commonly appears as a human wearing ram's horns and the twin-feathered *atef* crown.

His consort, **Mut**, was a local goddess in Pre-Dynastic times, who became linked with Nekhbet, the vulture protectress of Upper Egypt. Early in the XVIII Dynasty she was "married" to Amun, assimilated his previous consort Amunet and became Mistress of Heaven. She is customarily depicted wearing a vulture headdress and *uraeus* and the Combined Crown of the Two Lands.

Amun and Mut's son **Khonsu**, "the Traveller", crossed the night sky as the moon-god, issued prophecies and assisted Thoth, the divine scribe. He was either portrayed with a hawk's head, or as a young boy with the side-lock of youth.

Karnak was the largest of several temples consecrated to this **Theban Triad** of deities.

| Amun | Mut | Khonsu |

The **Forecourt** is another late addition, enclosing three earlier structures. In the centre stands a single papyriform pillar from the **Kiosk of Taharqa** (an Ethiopian king of the XXV Dynasty), thought to have been a roofless pavilion where Amun's effigy was placed for its revivifying union with the sun at New Year. Off to the left stands the so-called **Shrine of Seti II**, actually a way station for the sacred barques of Amun, Mut and Khonsu, built of gray sandstone and rose granite.

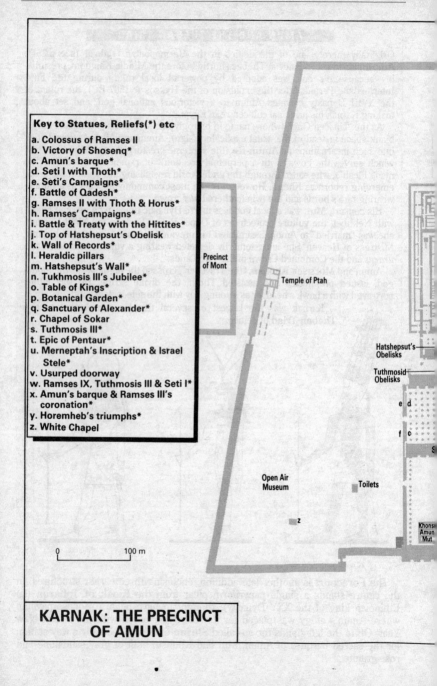

Key to Statues, Reliefs(*) etc

a. Colossus of Ramses II
b. Victory of Shosenq*
c. Amun's barque*
d. Seti I with Thoth*
e. Seti's Campaigns*
f. Battle of Qadesh*
g. Ramses II with Thoth & Horus*
h. Ramses' Campaigns*
i. Battle & Treaty with the Hittites*
j. Top of Hatshepsut's Obelisk
k. Wall of Records*
l. Heraldic pillars
m. Hatshepsut's Wall*
n. Tukhmosis III's Jubilee*
o. Table of Kings*
p. Botanical Garden*
q. Sanctuary of Alexander*
r. Chapel of Sokar
s. Tuthmosis III*
t. Epic of Pentaur*
u. Merneptah's Inscription & Israel Stele*
v. Usurped doorway
w. Ramses IX, Tuthmosis III & Seti I*
x. Amun's barque & Ramses III's coronation*
y. Horemheb's triumphs*
z. White Chapel

Precinct of Mont

Temple of Ptah

Hatshepsut's Obelisks

Tuthmosid Obelisks

e d

f o

Open Air Museum

Toilets

z

Khonsu Amun Mut

0   100 m

KARNAK: THE PRECINCT OF AMUN

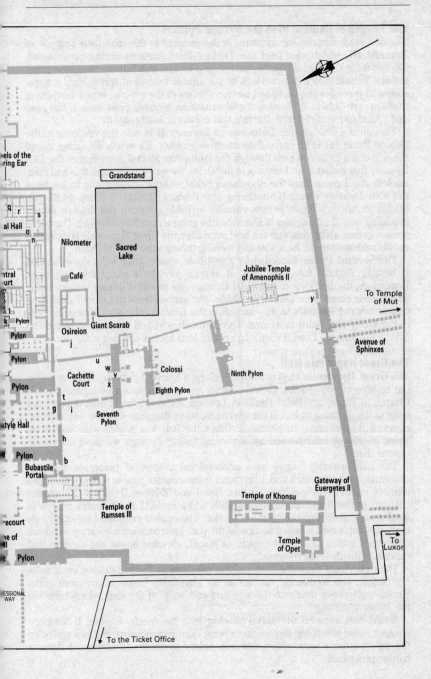

Grandstand

Sacred
Lake

Nilometer

Café

Jubilee Temple
of Amenophis II

Osireion

Giant Scarab

j

Cachette
Court

u
w
v
x

Colossi

Ninth Pylon

Eighth Pylon

Seventh
Pylon

t
i
g
h

b

Bubastile
Portal

Temple of
Ramses III

Temple of Khonsu

Gateway of
Euergetes II

Temple
of Opet

els of the
ring Ear

q r   s
o
n

al Hall

ntral
urt

l
k

Pylon

Pylon

Pylon

Pylon

style Hall

Pylon

ecourt

e of
l

Pylon

ESSIONAL
WAY

To Temple
of Mut

y

Avenue of
Sphinxes

To
Luxor

To the Ticket Office

The Temple of Ramses III to the Second Pylon

The first really impressive structure in the precinct is the columned **Temple of Ramses III**, which also held the Theban Triad barques during processions. Beyond its pylon, flanked by two colossi, is a festival hall with mummiform pillar-statues, behind which are carvings of the annual festival of Amun-Min. A hypo-stele hall precedes the darkened barque-shrines of the temple, whose dedication reads in part: "*I built it, sheathed it with sandstone, bringing great doors of fine gold; and I filled its treasuries with offerings that my hands had brought*".

Though the pink granite **Colossus of Ramses II** beside the vestibule to the Second Pylon **[a]** is an immediate attention-grabber, it's worth detouring round the side of his temple to pass through the **Bubastite Portal**, named after the XXII Dynasty that hailed from Bubastis in the Delta. By walking through this and turn-ing left, you'll come upon the **Shoshenq relief**, commemorating the triumphs of the XXII Dynasty Pharaoh Shoshenq (the Biblical Shishak; I Kings 14:25–26). Whilst Shoshenq's figure is now virtually invisible, you can still discern Amun, presiding over the slaughter of Rheoboamite prisoners in Palestine **[b]**. The battle scenes farther along this wall are best seen after the Great Hypostele Hall, which entails returning to the forecourt and walking through the Second Pylon.

The **Second Pylon**, preceded by a vestibule whose inner walls show Ramses II besting Amun's foes, was one of several jerry-built structures begun by Horemheb, the last king of the XVIII Dynasty. As revealed during repairs in the 1920s, their cores were filled with blocks and statues from the demolished Aten temple beyond Karnak's walls – including the famous colossi of Akhenaten now in the Luxor and Cairo museums. The cartouches of Seti I (who completed the pylon) and Ramses I and II (Seti's father and son) appear just inside the doorway.

The Great Hypostele Hall

The **Great Hypostele Hall** is Karnak's glory, a forest of gigantic columns cover-ing an area of 6000 square metres – large enough to contain both Saint Peter's Church in Rome and Saint Paul's in London. Its grandeur is best appreciated early in the morning or late in the afternoon, when diagonal shadows enhance the effect of the columns. In pharaonic times the hall was roofed with sandstone slabs, its gloom interspersed by sunbeams falling through windows above the central aisle.

The hall probably began as a processional avenue of twelve or fourteen **columns**, each 23m high and 15m round (requiring six people with outstretched arms to encircle their girth). To this, Seti I and Ramses II added 122 smaller columns in two flanking wings, plus walls and a roof. All the columns consist of semi-drums, fitted together without mortar. The central ones have calyx capitals that once supported a raised section of the roof incorporating clerestory windows (the stone grilles of several remain in place), elevated above the papyrus-bud capitals of the flanking columns.

Their **carvings** show the king making offerings to Theban deities, most nota-bly Amun, who frequently appears in an ithyphallic (sexually aroused) state. Similar cult-scenes decorate the side and end walls of the hall, which manifest two styles of carving.

Whilst Seti adorned the northern wing with bas-reliefs, Ramses II favoured cheaper sunk reliefs for the southern wing. You can compare the two styles on the far (western) wall, which features nearly symmetrical scenes of Amun's barque procession.

In Seti's **northern wing**, the procession begins on the northern wall with a depiction of Amun's barque, initially veiled, then revealed **[c]**. Thoth inscribes the duration of Seti's reign on the leaves of a sacred persea tree **[d]** just beyond the doorway. By walking out through this door you'll come upon Seti's battle reliefs, whose weathered details are best observed in the early morning or late afternoon. The first section relates his campaigns to restore Egypt's empire in Palestine and Syria **[e]**, including battles with Bedouin and Canaanites, and an upper register depicting Lebanese felling cedars to provide masts and flagstaffs. The second portrays Seti capturing the Hittite fortress of Qadesh, and repulsing Libyans **[f]**.

Returning to the hypostele hall, you can find similar reliefs commissioned by Ramses II in the **southern wing**. Beyond the barque scenes on the inner wall, Ramses is presented to Amun and enthroned between Wadjet and Nekhbet, whilst Thoth and Horus adjust his crowns **[g]**. The extramural battle scene **[h]** is more rigidly stylised than Seti's, and devoted to the second Battle of Qadesh (c.1300 BC). Though historians reckon it was probably a draw, Ramses claimed total victory over the Hittites. The text of their peace treaty (the earliest such document known) continues along the outer wall of the Cachette Court **[i]**.

Pylons and obelisks

Beyond the XIX Dynasty Hypostele Hall lies an extensive section of the precinct dating from the XVIII Dynasty. The **Third Pylon** that forms its back wall was originally intended by Amenophis III to be a monumental gateway to the temple. Like Horemheb forty years later, he demolished earlier structures to serve as core-filler for his pylon. Removed by archaeologists, these blocks are now displayed – partly reassembled – in the open-air museum.

The narrow court between the Third and Fourth pylons once boasted four **Tuthmosid Obelisks**. The stone bases near the Third Pylon held a pair erected by Tuthmosis III, chunks of which lie scattered around. Of the pink granite pair erected by Tuthmosis II, one still stands 23m high, with an estimated weight of 143 tons. Once tipped with glittering electrum, the finely carved obelisk was later appropriated by Ramses IV and VI, who added their own cartouches.

At this stage it's best to carry on through the **Fourth Pylon** rather than get sidetracked into the Cachette Court on the temple's secondary axis (see p.307). Beyond the pylon are numerous columns which probably formed another hypostele hall, dominated by the rose granite **Obelisk of Hatshepsut**, the only woman to rule as pharaoh. To mark her sixteenth regnal year, Hatshepsut had two obelisks quarried in Aswan and erected at Karnak, a task completed in seven months. The standing obelisk is over 27m high and weighs 320 tons, with a dedicatory inscription running its full height. Its fallen mate has broken into sections, now dispersed around the temple. After Hatshepsut's death, the long-frustrated Tuthmosis III took revenge, defacing her cartouches wherever they occurred and hiding the lower part of her obelisks behind walls – which inadvertently protected them from further vandalism during the Amarna Period.

The carved tip of Hatshepsut's fallen obelisk **[j]** can be examined near the Osireion and Sacred Lake. On the way there, you'll pass a granite bas-relief of Amenophis II target-shooting from a moving chariot, protruding from the **Fifth Pylon**. Built of limestone, this pylon is attributed to Hatshepsut's father, Tuthmosis I. Beyond it lies a colonnaded courtyard with Osiride statues, built by one of the Tuthmosid pharaohs and possibly part of a large inner court surrounding the original Middle Kingdom temple of Amun.

Though the **Sixth Pylon** has largely disappeared, a portion either side of the granite doorway remains. Its outer face is known as the *Wall of Records* **[k]** after its list of peoples conquered by Tuthmosis III: Nubians to the right, Asiatics to the left. Beyond the latter is a text extolling the king's victory at Megiddo (Armageddon) in 1479 BC. By organising tribute from his vanquished foes rather than simply destroying them, Tuthmosis was arguably the world's first imperialist.

Around the Sanctuary

The section beyond the Sixth Pylon gets increasingly confusing, but a few features are unmistakable. First come a pair of square-sectioned **heraldic pillars**, their fronts carved with the lotus and papyrus of the Two Lands, their sides showing Amun embracing Tuthmosis III **[l]**. North of here are two **Colossi of Amun and Amunet**, dedicated by Tutankhamun (whose likeness appears with them) when orthodoxy was re-established after the Amarna Period. Against the west wall is a seated **statue of Amenophis II**.

Next comes a granite **Sanctuary** built by Philip Arrhidaeus, the cretinous half-brother of Alexander the Great, on the site of a Tuthmosid-era shrine which similarly held Amun's barque (whose pedestal is still in situ). The interior bas-reliefs show Philip offering to Amun in his various aspects, topped by a star-spangled ceiling. On the outside walls are sunk reliefs depicting his coronation, Thoth's declaration of welcome, and Amunet suckling the young pharaoh.

Around to the left of the sanctuary and farther back is a wall inscribed with Tuthmosis III's victories, which he built to hide reliefs by Hatshepsut, now removed to another room **[m]**. The left-hand section of **Hatshepsut's Wall** retains much of its original colouring, but the figures of the queen have been chiselled away. On the facing portion, Tuthmosis has replaced them by offerings tables or bouquets, and substituted his father's and grandfather's names for her cartouches.

Beyond here lies an open space or **Central Court**, thought to mark the site of the original temple of Amun built in the XII Dynasty, whose alabaster foundations poke from the pebbly ground.

The Jubilee Temple of Tuthmosis III

At the rear of this court rises the **Jubilee Temple of Tuthmosis III**, a personal cult-shrine in Amun's back yard. As at Memphis during the Old Kingdom, the Theban kings periodically renewed their temporal and spiritual authority with jubilee festivals. The original entrance **[n]** is flanked by reliefs and statues of Tuthmosis in *hed-seb* regalia. A left turn brings you into the **Festival Hall**, with its unusual tentpole-style columns, their capitals adorned with blue and white chevrons. The lintels – carved with falcons, owls, *ankhs* and other symbols – are likewise brightly coloured. During Christian times the hall was used as a church, hence the haloed saints on some of the pillars.

A chamber off the southwest corner **[o]** contains a replica of the *Table of Kings* (the original is in the Louvre), depicting Tuthmosis making offerings to previous rulers – Hatshepsut is naturally omitted from the roll-call. Behind the hall are further chambers, mostly ruinous. The best preserved is the so-called **Botanical Garden**, containing four papyrus-bundle columns and carvings of plants and animals which Tuthmosis encountered on his campaigns in Syria **[p]**. Across the way is a chamber decorated by Alexander the Great, who appears before Amun and other deities [q]. The **Chapel of Sokar** constitutes a miniature temple to the Memphite god of darkness [r], juxtaposed against a (now inaccessible) shrine to the sun. A further suite of rooms is dedicated to Tuthmosis III [s].

Chapels of the Hearing Ear

Excluded from Amun's Precinct and lacking a direct line to the Theban Triad, the inhabitants of Thebes used intermediary deities to transmit their petitions. These lesser deities rated their own shrines, known as **Chapels of the Hearing Ear** (sometimes actually decorated with carved ears), which straddled the temple's enclosure wall, presenting one face to the outside world. At Karnak, however, they became steadily less approachable and were finally surrounded by the present enclosure wall.

Directly behind the Jubilee Temple is a series of chapels built by Tuthmosis III, centred upon a large alabaster statue of the king and Amun. On either side are the bases of another pair of obelisks erected by Hatshepsut, of which nothing else remains. Still farther east lie the ruined halls and colonnades of a Temple of the Hearing Ear built by Ramses II. Behind this stands the pedestal of the tallest obelisk (31m) known, which Constantine had shipped to Rome and erected in the Circus Maximus; it was later moved to Lateran Square, hence its name, the **Lateran Obelisk**. As the ancient Egyptians rarely erected single obelisks, it was probably intended to be accompanied by the Unfinished Obelisk which lies in a quarry outside Aswan, abandoned after the discovery of flaws in the rock.

The other axis

The temple's **north–south axis** is sparser and less variegated than the main section, so if time is limited there's little reason to go beyond the Eighth Pylon. The Gate of Ramses IX, at the southern end of the court between the Third and Fourth Pylons, gives access to this wing of the temple, which starts with the Cachette Court.

The **Cachette Court** gets its sobriquet from the discovery of a buried hoard of statues early this century. Nearly 17,000 bronze statues and votive tablets, and 800 figures in stone seem to have been cached in a "clearance" of sacred knick-knacks during Ptolemaic times. The finest statues (dating from the Old Kingdom to the Late Period) are now in the Cairo Museum. The court's northwest corner incorporates the tail end of Ramses II's battle reliefs on the outside of the hypostele hall – known as the *Epic of Pentaur* [t]. Diagonally across the court are an eighty-line inscription by Merneptah and a copy of the *Israel Stele* [u] that's now in Cairo, which contains the only known reference to Israel in pharaonic history.

Built by Tuthmosis III, but decorated during the XIX Dynasty, the **Seventh Pylon** features usurped cartouches on its door jambs [v]; reliefs of Ramses IX, Tuthmosis III and Seti I [w]; Amun's barque and Ramses III's coronation [x]. In front are seven statues of Middle Kingdom pharaohs, salvaged from pylon cores. On the far side are the lower portions of two **Colossi of Tuthmosis III**.

Although repair work has closed the **Eighth Pylon**, you can walk around the edge for a distant view of its four seated colossi, or pay some *baksheesh* to be sneaked in for a closer look. The most complete figure is that of Amenophis I. Beyond a featureless court rises the **Ninth Pylon**, one of three erected by Horemheb and stuffed with masonry from the demolished Aten Temple, which archaeologists have removed and hope to reassemble. Flanking the east wall of the final court is the ruinous **Jubilee Temple of Amenophis II**, which fulfilled a similar function to Tuthmosis III's temple in the main wing. Its central chapel is decorated with fine low reliefs, still brightly coloured in places. In the far corner near the **Tenth Pylon** are pro forma scenes of Horemheb leading captives from Punt before the Theban Triad **[y]**. The Avenue of Sphinxes beyond this pylon formed a processional way to the Temple of Mut (see overpage).

Around the Sacred Lake

A short walk from the Cachete Court or Hatshepsut's Obelisk brings you to Karnak's **Sacred Lake**, which looks about as holy as a municipal boating pond, with the grandstand for the Sound and Light Show at the far end. The EAO is currently laying pipes to convey fresh Nile water into the lake, which has stagnated since the inundation ceased.

Meantime, the main attraction is a shady **café** where you can take a break from touring the complex and imagine the scene in ancient times. At sunrise, Amun's priests took a sacred goose from the fowl-yards which now lie beneath the mound to the south of the lake, and set it free on the waters. As at Hermopolis, the goose or Great Cackler was credited with laying a cosmic egg at the dawn of Creation; but at Karnak the Great Cackler was identified with Amun rather than Thoth. During the Late Period, Pharaoh Taharqa added a subterranean **Osireion**, linking the resurrection of Osiris with that of the sun. The **giant scarab beetle** nearby represents Khepri, the reborn sun at dawn.

The Temples of Khonsu and Opet

Located in the southwest corner of Amun's Precinct are two smaller temples related to his cult. The **Temple of Khonsu** is dedicated to the son of Amun and Mut. Mostly built by Ramses III and IV, with additions by later kings, it is well preserved but crudely carved and dark inside. Many of the reliefs depict Herihor, first of Thebes' priest-kings, who ruled Upper Egypt after the Ramessid pharaohs moved their capital to the Delta. This shift in power is also evident on the pylons, which show Pinundjem, another high priest, worshipping the gods as a king.

Alongside stands a smaller **Temple of Optet**, the hippopotamus-goddess traditionally believed to be the mother of Osiris. Its reliefs – dating from Ptolemaic and Roman times – are finer than Khonsu's, but it may not be possible to enter. The towering **Gateway of Euergetes I**, with its winged sun-disc cornice, was raised in Ptolemaic times and is now barred shut.

The open-air museum and northern sector

Aside from mounds of spoil from excavations, the northern sector of Amun's Precinct contains an interesting museum and a small temple. To reach the **open-air museum** (£E1, students 75pt), follow the signs outside the forecourt of Amun's temple. Its prime attractions are two early barque shrines, re-assembled from blocks found inside the Third Pylon. From the XII Dynasty comes a lovely **White Chapel**, carved all over with bas-reliefs **[z]**. Whilst most depict *djed* columns, *ankhs* and other symbols, it's the scenes of Senusert I embracing a priapic Amun-Min that one remembers. The plainer **Alabaster Chapel** of Amenophis I contains more innocuous scenes of the pharaoh offering to Amun and his barque. Along the way you'll pass rows of blocks from Hatshepsut's **Red Chapel**, which archaeologists have been unable to reconstruct since each block features a self-contained design rather than a segment of a large relief; and granite **statues of Sekhmet.**

SEKHMET

Sekhmet – "the Powerful" – was the violent counterpart of the Delta goddess Bastet (see p.495). As the daughter of Re, she personified the sun's destructive force, making her a worthy consort for Ptah, the Memphite creator-god. In one myth, Re feared that humanity was plotting against him and unleashed his avenging Eye in the form of Sekhmet, who would have massacred all life had not Re relented and slaked her thirst with red beer, which the drunken goddess mistook for blood.

With the rise of Thebes and Amun's association with Ptah, a corresponding relationship was made between their consorts, Mut and Sekhmet. The New Kingdom pharaohs adopted Sekhmet as a symbol of their indomitable prowess in battle; the statues of the goddess at Karnak bear inscriptions such as "smiter of the Nubians". As "Lady of the Messengers of Death", Sekhmet could also send – or prevent – plagues, so her priests served as doctors and veterinarians.

Sekhmet

The statues come from the **Temple of Ptah** alongside Karnak's enclosure wall, whose ruins aren't much reward for a 300-metre trek across broken ground. Dedicated to the patron god of Memphis and his consort, the temple was built by Tuthmosis III and enlarged by the Ethiopian king Shabaka and several Ptolemies. You approach its sanctuary via five miniature pylons and a four-columned vestibule with flowery capitals. In the central chapel stands a headless statue of Ptah, lit through a tiny hole in the roof. By scrambling up the embankment or peering through the gate in the enclosure wall, you can see the jumbled ruins of the Precinct of Mont.

Other temples at Karnak

Beyond the Precinct of Amun is a host of other ruins, intermingled with canals and villages. None of them are readily accessible or officially open to tourists, and sites under excavation are off-limits without prior permission from the Antiquities Office in Luxor (sited near the *Etap Hotel*); but anyone willing to hike from the main road or Amun's Precinct can probably get in.

The Precinct of Mont

Dedicated to the falcon-headed Theban war-god of the Old Kingdom, who continued to be venerated after Amun gained primacy, the overgrown and ruinous **Precinct of Mont** is unusual for being orientated northwards rather than towards the river. Its main **Temple of Mont** (or Montu) dates from the XVIII–XIX Dynasty, whilst the **Temple of Amun** was added in the XXX Dynasty. Both are currently being excavated by the French Institute of Archaeology in Cairo.

Also worth noting are the **chapels** of Amenirdis, daughter of the Nubian king Kashta (honoured by another chapel at Medinet Habu in the Theban necropolis), and Nitocris, daughter of Psammetichus I, who is said to have avenged her brother's murder by constructing a sunken festival hall near the Nile, inviting the suspects to party, opening hidden sluices and drowning them all.

The Aten Temple

Likewise undergoing excavation, the **Aten Temple** 100m east of Amun's Precinct was demolished by Horemheb during the Theban counter-revolution that followed the brief Amarna Period. The temple was constructed early in Akhenaten's reign, before he quit Thebes for Tell el-Amarna, and, like the Aten shrine at Luxor Temple, constituted his opening move towards a revolutionary monotheism. A team from Toronto University hopes to match and reconstruct blocks and statues recovered from the pylons with what remains in situ.

The Precinct of Mut

As Amun's consort, the goddess Mut rated her own temple complex, linked to her husband's by an Avenue of Sphinxes. The **Precinct of Mut** covers roughly twice the area of Mont's enclosure, and centres around a kidney-shaped **lake**. Locals informed Flaubert that Karnak's priests submerged all the gold and silver ornaments here when the Persian emperor Cambyses sacked Thebes, but so far the site has merely yielded masonry. Near the enclosure entrance lies a headless granite colossus, recently matched with a serene head and mighty forearm held by the British Museum (attributed to Amenophis III, Tuthmosis II or Ramses II). It was Amenophis III who commissioned the scores of grey diorite **statues of Sekhmet** that rise from the long grass.

The Theban Necropolis

Across the Nile from Luxor, the **Theban Necropolis** testifies to the same obsession with death and resurrection that produced the pyramids. Mindful of how these had failed to protect the mummies of the Old Kingdom pharaohs, later rulers – along with their families and chief priests – opted for concealment, sinking their tombs in the arid Theban Hills whilst perpetuating their memory with gigantic mortuary temples on the plain below. The necropolis straddled the border between the lands of the living and the dead: verdant floodplain giving way to boundless desert, echoing the path of the dead "going west" to meet Osiris as the sun set over the mountains and descended into the underworld.

Though stripped of its treasures over millennia, the necropolis retains a peerless array of funerary monuments. The grandest of its tombs are in the **Valley of the Kings** and the **Valley of the Queens**, but there's also a wealth of vivid detail in the smaller area known as the **Tombs of the Nobles**. Equally amazing are the mortuary temples which enshrined the deceased pharaoh's cult: among these, **Deir el-Bahri** is timelessly magnificent and **Medinet Habu** rivals Karnak for grandeur, while the shattered **Ramesseum** and **Colossi of Memnon** mock the pretensions of their founders. On a humbler level, but still executed with great artistry, are the funerary monuments of the craftsmen who built the royal tombs and the ruins of their homes at **Deir el-Medina**.

Visiting the necropolis

Spread across wadis and hills beyond the edge of the cultivated plain, the Theban Necropolis is too diffuse and complex to encompass in a single visit. Even limiting yourself to the Valley of the Kings, Deir el-Bahri and one or other of the major sites, you're likely to feel all-tombed-out by the end of the day. Most people favour a series of visits, taking into account the climate and crowds – both major factors to the enjoyment of a visit. In **winter**, mornings are pleasantly hot, afternoons baking but bearable, and most coach tours are scheduled accordingly, making the Valley of the Kings extremely crowded between 9am and 2pm (other sites are less overrun). As lots of people come early "to beat the crowds", the royal tombs are actually emptiest in the late afternoon. In **summer**, it's simply too hot throughout the afternoon, and you should get here as early as possible.

Official **opening hours** for all the sites are 6am–4pm daily in winter, 6am–5pm in summer, though lesser tombs may close two to three hours earlier in summertime. It's worth mulling over an itinerary and making preparations before you set out. Useful **things to bring** include a torch, plenty of water and small change. If you're planning to cycle or donkey it, a hat and double rations of water are vital.

Crossing the Nile

Crossing over from **Luxor** to the west bank is simple. **Tourist ferries** sail frequently (6am–5pm daily) from the docks near the *Savoy* and *Winter Palace* hotels to the site **ticket office** on the west bank (£E1 round-trip; no bicycles). Alternatively, there are two antiquated **local ferries** (6am–midnight; 25pt), departing from near Luxor Temple and the *Etap Hotel*, which dock 700m further south along the west bank, where taxis and donkey-boys await tourists. Bicycles (10pt) are allowed on both these ferries; the one from the *Etap* dock also carries cars if the water level permits. Tourists should dress modestly in deference to the *fellaheen* who use these boats.

Getting around

How you choose to get around will largely be determined by the time of year and what you plan to see.

The easiest way of getting around the necropolis is **by taxi**, an economical method for groups. Taxis are usually engaged for a half-day tour (4hr): a four-seater cab can be hired for £E15, a seven-seater for £E20. You can also hire slightly cheaper, non-private, taxis which scoot off for other business while you're exploring, and catch up with you when needed later on. Luxor's tourist office can supply current official rates, but in practice all fares must be negotiated. Taxis wait by both landing stages on the west bank; some drivers even tout for business on the boat. Pay at the end and reward good service with *baksheesh*.

If you'd prefer to have everything organised, **guided tours** in A/C coaches with English-speaking guides can be arranged through *Misr Travel*, *Isis Travel* and other agencies for £E40–80 per person, including admission tickets. Some outfits will tag you onto existing tour groups; others may tailor a trip to your specifications. Most tours feature the tombs of the Kings and Queens, Deir el-Bahri and the Colossi of Memnon. Tour groups get priority access to the royal tombs and a higher standard of commentary than offered by unofficial guides, but lack atmosphere and spontaneity.

To experience the west bank at close quarters, reasonably fit winter visitors could try **cycling**. In the dry air, you'll feel cool when riding but start sweating profusely once you stop. Guard against heatstroke and keep swigging water. A day's touring might involve cycling 30km: for example, 3km from the riverbank to the student ticket kiosk, 8km from there to the Valley of the Kings (beware of traffic), and 3km from Deir el-Bahri to Medinet Habu. The main drawback is that you can't walk over the hills from the Valley of the Kings to Deir el-Bahri. Cycling

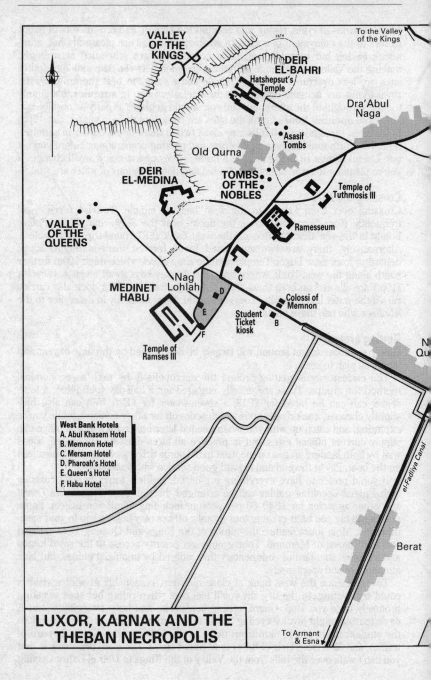

To the Valley
of the Kings

VALLEY OF THE KINGS

PATH

PATH

DEIR EL-BAHRI

Hatshepsut's Temple

Dra'Abul Naga

PATH

Asasif Tombs

Old Qurna

DEIR EL-MEDINA

TOMBS OF THE NOBLES

Temple of Tuthmosis III

PATH

Ramesseum

VALLEY OF THE QUEENS

PATH

C

Nag Lohlah

D

MEDINET HABU

E

Colossi of Memnon

Student Ticket kiosk

B

F

Temple of Ramses III

el-Fadliya Canal

N
Qu

West Bank Hotels
A. Abul Khasem Hotel
B. Memnon Hotel
C. Mersam Hotel
D. Pharoah's Hotel
E. Queen's Hotel
F. Habu Hotel

Berat

LUXOR, KARNAK AND THE THEBAN NECROPOLIS

To Armant
& Esna

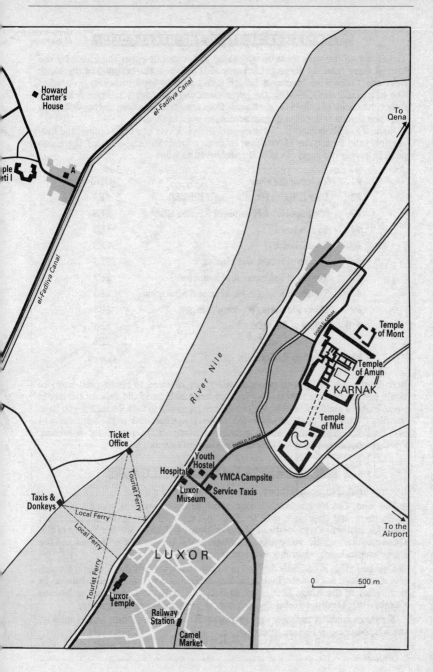

Howard Carter's House

el-Fadliya Canal

To Qena

ple eti I

A

el-Fadliya Canal

River Nile

SHARIA EL KARNAK

Temple of Mont

Temple of Amun

KARNAK

Temple of Mut

SHARIA EL KARNAK

Ticket Office

Youth Hostel

Hospital

YMCA Campsite

Tourist Ferry

Luxor Museum

Service Taxis

Taxis & Donkeys

Local Ferry

Local Ferry

To the Airport

Tourist Ferry

LUXOR

Luxor Temple

Railway Station

Camel Market

0   500 m

TICKETS FOR VISITING THE NECROPOLIS

Tickets for all the sites must be purchased in advance at either the **kiosk by the tourist ferry landing stage** (which only sells tickets at the full rate) or the **kiosk near the Colossi of Memnon** (which sells half-price student tickets on production of an ISIC card). Usually, the latter kiosk can also supply full rate tickets (or rather, two student tickets for each site). Both are open from 6am to 4pm daily. You can't buy tickets at the sites or gain admission without them.

Since it's unlikely that you'll use more than five tickets in a day's outing, and they are only valid for the day of purchase (with no refunds for unused ones), there's no point in buying too many. Tickets are numbered as follows:

#1	Valley of the Kings	£E10
#2	Deir el-Bahri (Hatshepsut's Temple)	£E5
#3	Medinet Habu (Temple of Ramses III)	£E5
#4	Ramesseum	£E3
#5	Asasif Tombs	£E3
#6	Tombs of Nakht and Menna	£E3
#7	Tombs of Rekhmire and Sennofer	£E3
#8	Tombs of Ramose, Userhat and Khaemhat	£E3
#9	Deir el-Medina (Workers' village)	£E3
#10	Valley of the Queens	£E3
#11	Temple of Seti I	£E3
#12	Tomb of Pabhasa	closed

Both kiosks also sell **photo permits**, which are required to photograph interiors (£E10 per tomb). Like tickets, they are non-refundable and valid only for the day of issue. Flashes are forbidden as they cause the pigments to fade, so unless you have fast film it's useless to shoot inside the tombs. Don't succumb to the temptation to use flashes, even though some guards encourage it in return for *baksheesh*. Photography is not permitted inside Tutankhamun's tomb.

SOME SUGGESTED ITINERARIES

If you're limited to a couple of days, two **itineraries** make sense.

● **Day one.** Catch a taxi to the **Valley of the Kings** before 9am, spend a couple of hours there and then walk over the hills to **Deir el-Bahri**, arranging to be met there for another ride to **Medinet Habu** or **Deir el-Medina** and the **Valley of the Queens**. Alternatively, you could spend time at the **Tombs of the Nobles** and the Ramesseum before returning to the landing stage.

● **Day two.** This is basically devoted to whatever you missed the first time around. If you're forced to cram the highlights into half a day, a minimalist schedule might run: **Valley of the Kings** (2hr); **Deir el-Bahri** (30min); the **Tombs of the Nobles** (30min–1hr); **Medinet Habu** (30min) and/or the **Ramesseum** (15min).

For those who like to linger over every mural or relief, the tombs and temples on the west bank easily require three days.

during summer is a lot more demanding, so it's imperative to take the long uphill stretch to the Valley of the Kings early in the morning, allowing you to coast back downhill in the afternoon heat. Most bikes are one-speed only; roads vary from smooth macadam to stony *pistes*. It's cheaper to hire bikes in Luxor than at the landing stages.

Unless you're nostalgic for the era when it was only possible to tour the necropolis **by donkey**, there's nothing to recommend them except over short distances which you could walk anyway. Donkeys are slow and uncomfortable, and their minders may turn nasty when your position is most precarious. That said, many of the pensions around Television Street organise morning excursions by ass for around £E20 a head, including a carriage from the hotel to the ferry and the services of a guide. The standard six-hour tour features the Valley of the Kings, Deir el-Bahri, the Ramesseum and the Colossi of Memnon, but itineraries, like prices, are negotiable.

The really gung-ho could explore parts of the necropolis **on foot** (outside of summer, anyway). Catch a local taxi (25–50pt) from the landing stage to the student kiosk and you'll be within twenty or thirty minutes' walk of Medinet Habu or the Ramesseum. Walking from the latter to Deir el-Bahri takes about fifteen minutes, but you'd be foolish not to visit the Tombs of the Nobles and the Asasif Tombs, en route. Even if you plan to rely on taxis, it's definitely worth hiking over the hills from the Valley of the Kings to Deir el-Bahri or vice versa.

Staying on the west bank

To avoid the hassles of Luxor and to get closer to the sights, consider staying on the west bank, which musters half a dozen **hotels**, all but one of them (*Pharaoh's Hotel*) fairly basic, though they do all feature fridges. Before crossing the Nile with your luggage it's advisable to phone ahead. Where we list three-digit numbers below, dial 25 or 10 in Luxor and request "west bank number . . . ".

The high season rates given below are slashed by half over summer. A taxi from the landing stage to any of the following should cost £E1–2.

Abdul Kasem Hotel (A), east of the Temple of Seti I, so distant from other sites (☎438, or ☎382-502 in Luxor). Singles (£E16), doubles (£E27) and triples (£E33) with fans; the best are on the top floor. Terrific views from the rooftop. Bikes for rent (£E2 per day).

Memnon Hotel (B), opposite the Colossi of Memnon (☎705). Spartan rooms with hard beds and shared hot water facilities; £E10 gets you bed and breakfast. There are also three "suites" with private bathrooms (negotiable), space and shade for camping (£E3 per head).

Mersam Hotel (C), near the Antiquities Office (☎382-403). Mudbrick doubles (£E20) and triples (£E30) in a rustic setting, popular with archaeologists. Breakfast included; serves dinner (£E6) and rents bikes (£E2 per day). Run by a son of the late Sheikh Ali Abdul Rasul, who helped excavate the Tomb of Seti I.

Pharaoh's Hotel (D). New, two-star hotel, a short walk from the student kiosk along an unpaved road (☎384-797). Comfortable singles (£E28) and doubles (£E45) with A/C or fans; shared bathrooms. Breakfast included. Large reductions in summer.

Queen's Hotel (E), near Medinet Habu (☎616 or ☎384-797; ☎382-502 in Luxor). Simple, garishly decorated rooms, some with sinks (£E6; £E7 with breakfast). The genial *patron*, Hagg Ali Hassan Khalifa, boasts testimonials from archaeologists.

Habu Hotel (F), facing the Temple of Ramses III (☎382-477; ☎382-677 in Luxor). Temperate in all weathers thanks to its Nubian-style architecture. Simple, cheery doubles (£E15) and triples (£E20) with fans and shared baths. You can also sleep on the terrace or camp in the back yard (winter only) for about £E3. Breakfast (£E3), lunch and dinner (£E6) available.

Qurna and other west bank villages

The **west bank villages** are incidental to most tourists visiting the Theban necropolis, but integral to the landscape and atmosphere. Their fields stretch from the riverbanks to the temples on the desert's edge; their goats root amidst the Tombs of the Nobles. Though many villagers make a living from tourism, it hasn't touched their *souks* or festivals. For every *antika* salesman or curio grinder, a dozen villagers work on the land much as their ancestors have done for centuries, if not millennia. Richard Critchfield's *Shahhat* (sold in most Luxor bookshops) gives a fascinating glimpse into their lives.

En route to the necropolis you'll pass **NEW QURNA** (*Qurnat el-Jedid*), whose spacious mudbrick homes were designed by the late Hassan Fathy, a lifelong advocate of architecture suited to local conditions. Alas, this model village has not lured many people away from insalubrious **OLD QURNA** (*Sheikh Abd el-Qurna*), which hugs the barren slopes of the Theban Hills. Besides a sentimental attachment to their ancestral homes (many of which are painted with *Hadj* scenes), the villagers are loath to lose a traditional source of income – **tomb-robbing**. Over 900 tombs are dug into the hills, and rumours of undisclosed finds persist. The villagers are also adept at **faking antiquities** (a favoured technique is passing scarabs through the intestines of turkeys to give them an aged finish). More authentically, at the **alabaster workshops** you can see craftsmen shaping vases and bowls with primitive hand-grinders.

Qurna's **Moulid of Abu Qusman** (March 29) still features the practice of *doseh* (treading), where the sheikh walks over his followers. Many tales are told about Abu Qusman, who died in 1984. On one occasion he supposedly crossed the Nile on his handkerchief after the ferry refused to take him because he lambasted the tourists on board for immorality.

The Colossi of Memnon

A kilometre or so beyond New Qurna the road passes the **Colossi of Memnon**, rearing nearly sixty feet above the fields. This gigantic pair of enthroned statues originally fronted the mortuary temple of Amenophis III, which later pharaohs plundered for masonry until nothing remained but the king's colossi. Both have lost their faces and crowns, and the northern one was cleaved to the waist by an earthquake in 27 BC. Subsequently, this colossus was heard to "sing" at dawn – a sound probably caused by particles breaking off as the stone expanded, or wind reverberating through the cracks. The phenomenon attracted many visitors in antiquity, including the Roman emperors Hadrian (130 AD) and Septimus Severus, who gave orders for the statue to be repaired (199 AD), after which it never sang again.

Previously, the sound had been attributed to the legendary Memnon, whom Achilles killed outside the walls of Troy, greeting his mother, Eos, the Dawn, with a sigh. The Greeks identified the colossi with Memnon in the belief that his father, Tithonus, had been an Egyptian king. Before this, the colossi had been identified with Amenhotep, Steward of Amenophis III, whom posterity honoured as a demigod long after his master was forgotten. This association had some grounds in truth, since it was Amenhotep who supervised the quarrying of the monoliths at Silsilah, and their erection on the west bank. He was also probably responsible for Amenophis III's section of Luxor Temple.

At close quarters you can appreciate what **details** remain, mostly on the thrones and legs of the sandstone colossi. On the sides of the nearest one, the Nile-gods of Upper and Lower Egypt bind the heraldic plants of the Two Lands together. The legs of each colossus are flanked by smaller statues of Queen Tiy (right) and the king's mother, Mutemuia (left). As high as one can reach, both are covered in graffiti, including Roman epigrams.

The Valley of the Kings

Secluded amidst the bone-dry Theban Hills, removed from other parts of the necropolis, the **Valley of the Kings** was intended as the ultimate insurance policy on life eternal. These secretive tombs of New Kingdom pharaohs were planned to preserve their mummies and funerary impedimentia for eternity. While most failed the test, their dramatic shafts and phantasma-
gorical murals are truly amazing. The descent into the under-
world and the fear of robbers who braved their traps is still
imaginable in the less crowded, darker tombs.

Royal burials in the "Place of Truth" date from the early XVIII to the late XX Dynasty. The first to do so was probably Tuthmosis I (1525–1512 BC). Until the time of Ramses I, queens and royal children were also buried here. **The tombs** were hewn and decorated by skilled craftsmen (known as "Servants at the Place of Truth") who dwelt at nearby Deir el-Medina. Work began early in a pharaoh's reign and never exceeded six years, duration; even so, some tombs were hastily pressed into service, or usurped by later kings. Broadly speaking, there are two types: the convoluted, split-level ones of early XVIII rulers such as Tuthmosis I and Amenophis II; and the straighter, longer tombs of the XIX–XX Dynasty.

Seal of the Valley
of the Kings

The weaker rulers of the XX Dynasty were unable to prevent **tomb-robbing** on a massive scale. Both the vizier and police chief of Thebes were implicated in the disposal of treasure, while many of the robbers were the workmen who had built the tombs, embittered over arrears in pay. In desperation, the priests reburied many sarcophagi and objects in two **secret caches** which were only discovered in the nineteenth century.

The exploration of the Valley began in earnest with a series of **excavations** sponsored by Theodore Davis in 1902–14, when over thirty tombs and pits were cleared. In 1922, the discovery of Tutankhamun's tomb made headlines around the world, while as recently as 1987 archaeologists used remote sensing devices to locate a new tomb. The principal worry today for the Egyptian Antiquities Office is the impact of mass **tourism**. To prevent further damage to the reliefs and pigments caused by friction, moisture and carbon dioxide, they are currently building **replica tombs**, the first of which is scheduled to be opened to visitors in 1993.

Visiting the tombs

The main **approach** to the valley (known as *Biban el-Melouk*, "Gates of the Kings" in Arabic) is via a serpentine road that follows the route of ancient funeral processions. Before the road, when donkeys were the only means of travel, its silence and emptiness were striking ("White earth; sun; one's rump sweats in the saddle", noted Flaubert). Nowadays, though, you'll only get this feeling on the trail across the hills from Deir el-Bahri, which visitors generally follow in the other direction (see p.329).

The valley is surrounded by limestone crags, the loftiest of which was the abode of Meretseger, snake-goddess of the necropolis. This natural suntrap is baking hot even in winter, the heat permeating even the deepest tombs, whose air is musty and humid (drink plenty of water). The site can feel like a missile

---

MUMMIFICATION AND THE UNDERWORLD

The **funerary beliefs** manifest in the Valley of the Kings derive from two myths, concerning Re and Osiris. In that of **Re**, the sun-god descended into the underworld and voyaged through the hours of night, emerging at dawn to sail his barque across the heavens until sunset, when the cycle began anew. **Osiris**, king of the underworld, offered hope of survival in the afterlife through his death and resurrection.

Mummification and burial

To attain the afterlife, it was necessary that the deceased's name (*ren*) and body continued to exist, sustaining the **ka** or cosmic double that was born with every person and inhabited their mummy after death. **Mummification** techniques evolved over millennia, reaching their zenith by the New Kingdom, when embalmers offered three categories of mummification. The deluxe version entailed removing the brain (which was discarded) and the viscera (which were preserved in canopic jars); dehydrating the cadaver in natron salts for about forty days; packing it to reproduce lifelike contours, inserting artificial eyes and painting the face or entire body red (for men) or yellow (for women); then wrapping it in gum-coated linen bandages, and finally cocooning it in mummiform coffins. On the chest of the mummy and its coffin were placed heart scarabs, designed to prevent the deceased's heart from bearing witness against him during the judgement of Osiris.

Royal burials were elaborate affairs. Escorted by priests, mourners and musicians, the coffin was dragged on a sledge to the Valley of the Kings, where the sarcophagus was already occupied by a *sem* (death) priest, who performed the **Opening of the Mouth** ceremony, touching the lips of the mummy with an adze and reciting spells. As the mummy was lowered into its sarcophagus, priests slashed the forelegs of sacrificial animals, whose limbs were burned as the tomb was sealed. The tomb's contents (intended to satisfy the needs of the pharaoh's *ka* in the afterlife) included food, drink, clothing, furniture, weapons, and dozens of *shabti* figures to perform any task that the gods might require. Then the doors were walled up, plastered over and stamped with the royal seal and that of the necropolis. To thwart robbers, royal tombs featured deadfalls and false burial chambers; however none of these devices seem to have succeeded in protecting them.

The Journey of Re
From right to left: Sunset; Year; Eternity; Everlastingness; Maat (justice); Re; Heka; Sunrise.

base in Nevada on open day, sightseers wandering from one bunker-like entrance to another. Tour groups take precedence, so you may have to wait till they emerge. Rather than queue outside popular tombs like Tut's or Ramses VI's, check out less frequented ones (eg Ramses IX and IV). Most people find three to five tombs enough for one visit; of the 64 tombs (numbered in order of discovery, not chronologically), less than a score merit attention. Toilets, drinks and snacks are available at the resthouse (daily summer 6am–5pm; winter 8am–3.45pm).

The journey through the underworld and Judgement of Osiris

Funerary artwork dwelt on the **journey through the underworld**, whose pictorial representation inverted the normal order, so that each register was topped by sand instead of sky. The **descent** (*Duat*) echoed that of a sarcophagus into its tomb, involving ramps, ropes and gateways. Each of the twelve **gates** was personified as a goddess and guarded by ferocious deities (for example, the "Lady of Duration" and the "Flame-eyed" serpent at the fifth gate). In the darkness between them lay twelve **caverns** inhabited by such as the jackal-headed gods who fed on rottenness at the first cavern, or the wailing goddesses with bloody axes who waited at the tenth. Voyaging through the twelve **hours** of the night in his solar barque, Re had to overcome the serpent Apophis and other lesser denizens of **primaeval chaos**, which threatened to overwhelm the **righteous order** personified by the goddess Maat.

It was Maat's feather of Truth that was weighed against the deceased's heart (believed to be the seat of intelligence) during the **Judgement of Osiris**. With Anubis on the scales and Thoth waiting to record the verdict, the deceased had to recite the **negative confession** before a tribunal of forty-two **assessor gods**, each attuned to a sin. While the hearts of the guilty were devoured by crocodile-headed Ammut, the righteous were pronounced "true of voice" and led into the presence of Osiris to begin their **resurrection**, which paralleled Re's passage through the underworld. Helped by Anubis, Isis and Nephthys (often shown as serpents), Aker the earth-god (whose back bore Re's barque) and Khepri the scarab beetle, Re achieves rebirth in the fifth hour, and is fully restored to life by the tenth. Here the two myths part company, for whereas Re emerges from the body of the sky-goddess Nut to travel the heavens again, the Osirian journey concludes in an after-life that is sometimes identified as the **Fields of Yaru**.

Since many of the scenes were duplicated or supplemented by papyri buried with the mummy, funerary **artwork** is categorised in literary terms. The *Book of the Dead* is the name now given to the compendium of Old and Middle Kingdom *Pyramid Texts* and spells, known in the New Kingdom as the *Book of Coming Forth*. Other **texts** associated with the New Kingdom include the *Book of Gates*, *Book of Hours*, *Book of Day and Night* and *Book of Amduat* (That which is in the Underworld).

The Judgement of Osiris
From left to right: Anubis escorts the deceased and weighs his heart before Ammut and Thoth; then Horus leads him to Osiris, Isis and Nephthys.

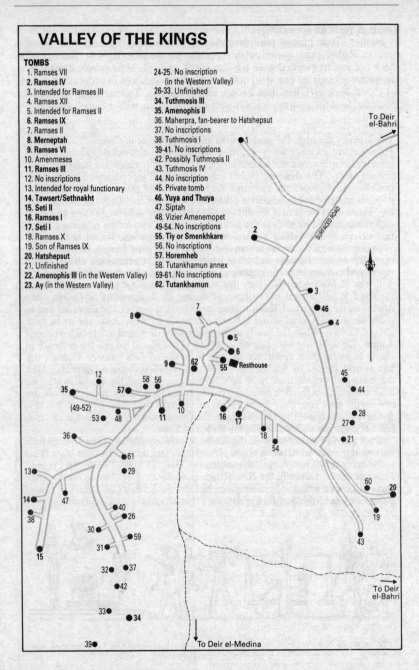

VALLEY OF THE KINGS

TOMBS

1. Ramses VII
2. **Ramses IV**
3. Intended for Ramses III
4. Ramses XII
5. Intended for Ramses II
6. **Ramses IX**
7. Ramses II
8. **Merneptah**
9. **Ramses VI**
10. Amenmeses
11. **Ramses III**
12. No inscriptions
13. Intended for royal functionary
14. **Tawsert/Sethnakht**
15. **Seti II**
16. **Ramses I**
17. **Seti I**
18. Ramses X
19. Son of Ramses IX
20. **Hatshepsut**
21. Unfinished
22. **Amenophis III** (in the Western Valley)
23. **Ay** (in the Western Valley)

24-25. No inscription
(in the Western Valley)
26-33. Unfinished
34. **Tuthmosis III**
35. **Amenophis II**
36. Maherpra, fan-bearer to Hatshepsut
37. No inscriptions
38. Tuthmosis I
39-41. No inscriptions
42. Possibly Tuthmosis II
43. Tuthmosis IV
44. No inscription
45. Private tomb
46. **Yuya and Thuya**
47. Siptah
48. Vizier Amenemopet
49-54. No inscriptions
55. **Tiy or Smenkhkare**
56. No inscriptions
57. **Horemheb**
58. Tutankhamun annex
59-61. No inscriptions
62. **Tutankhamun**

Tomb of Tutankhamun (#62)

The world's most famous tomb is neither large nor imposing by the standards of the Valley of the Kings, reflecting Tutankhamun's short reign (c.1361–1352; see p.255) as a XVIII Dynasty boy-pharaoh. Its renown stems from its belated discovery and its amazing hoard of treasures (now mostly in the Cairo Museum). Having spent £50,000 sterling on five seasons of digging, **Lord Carnarvon** was about to give up when the tomb was found on November 4, 1922. Fears that it had been plundered were dispelled when they broke through the second sealed door – officially on November 26, though in fact Carnarvon and his chief archaeologist, Howard Carter, secretly looked in the previous night, stole 35 items and resealed the door. Otherwise, the tomb was cleared meticulously. Each of its 1700 objects was documented, drawn and photographed in situ before being removed to an improvised laboratory in the tomb of Seti II, for stabilising and cleaning by Arthur Mace. Unpacking everything took nearly ten years, the whole process being recorded in over 1800 superb photographs by Harry Burton, who converted an empty tomb into a darkroom.

Lord Carnarvon's death in Cairo from an infected mosquito bite in April 1923 focused world attention on a warning by the novelist Marie Corelli, that "dire punishment follows any intruder into the tomb". (At the moment of Carnarvon's death, all the lights in Cairo went out.) The **Curse of Tutankhamun** gained popular credence with this and each successive "mysterious" death. The US magnate Jay Gould died of pneumonia resulting from a cold contracted at the tomb; a famous Bey was shot by his wife in London after viewing the discovery; a French Egyptologist suffered a fatal fall; Carter's secretary died in unusual circumstances at the Bath Club, and his right-hand man Arthur Mace sickened and died before the tomb had been fully cleared. However, of the twenty-two who

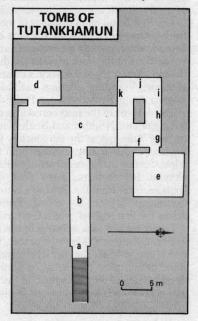

had witnessed the opening of Tut's sarcophagus, only two were dead ten years later. Howard Carter died in 1939 at the age of 64, whilst others closely involved lived into their eighties (not least Dr Derry, who performed the autopsy which suggested that Tut died from a blow to the head, aged about 19).

Visitors usually spend longer waiting to gain entry than inside the tomb, being hustled out after five minutes. Carter found the door at the bottom of the stairway **[a]** walled up and sealed with Tut's cartouche and the seal of the necropolis, but signs of repairs, the detritus in the corridor **[b]** and another resealed door at the end indicated that robbers had penetrated the antechamber **[c]** during the XX Dynasty.

Most of the funerary objects now in the Cairo Museum were crammed into the undecorated chambers **[c]**, **[d]** (now walled up) and **[e]**. Another wall (now replaced by a barrier) enclosed the burial chamber, which was almost filled by four golden shrines packed one inside another, containing Tut's stone sarcophagus and triple-layer mummiform coffin, of which the innermost, solid gold coffin still remains.

The colourful murals run in an antclockwise direction, starting with the funeral procession where nine friends and three officials drag Tut's coffin on a sledge [f]. Next, his successor Ay performs the Opening of the Mouth ceremony [g] and sacrifices to the sky-goddess Nut [h]. The deceased king embraces Osiris, followed by his *ka* (in the black wig) [i]. His solar boat and sun-worshipping baboons appear on the left wall [j]. On the hard-to-see entrance wall, Anubis and Isis escort Tutankhamun to receive life from Hathor [k].

Tomb of Ramses VI (#9)

One reason why Tut's tomb stayed hidden for so long was that it lay beneath mounds of rubble from the tomb of Ramses VI (1156–1148 BC), which has been a tourist attraction since antiquity, when the Greeks called it the *Tomb of Memnon*. The first two corridors have suffered from centuries of graffiti, but the varied imagery and brilliant colours farther in still make this a favourite with visitors.

The tomb was begun by Ramses V but usurped and enlarged by his successor, whose offering of a lamp to Horus of the Horizon opens the *Book of Gates* [a], which faces other sunk reliefs from the *Book of Caverns* [b]. Like the astronomical ceiling, this continues through a series of corridors (note the winged sun-disc over the lintel and Ramses' cartouches on the door jambs [c]). Where the *Book of Gates* reaches the Hall of Osiris [d], a flame-breathing snake and catfish-headed gods infest the *Book of Caverns* [e]. As Re's barque approaches the Seventh Gate, beyond which twelve gods hold a rope festooned with whips and heads [f], the *Book of Caverns* depicts a procession of *ka* figures [g]. From here on, the astronomical ceiling features an attenuated sky-goddess and the *Book of Day and Night*.

The eighth and ninth divisions of the *Book of Gates* [h] and fifth division of the *Book of Caverns* [i] decorate the next chamber, originally a vestibule to the hall beyond, which marked the limits of Ramses V's tomb. This contains the concluding sections of the *Book of Gates* [j], the seventh division of the *Book of Caverns* [k] and a summary of the world's creation [l]. The rear wall also features a scene of Ramses VI making offerings and libations to Osiris. On the pillars, he offers to Khonsu, Amun-Re, Meretseger, Ptah-Sokar, Ptah and Re-Herakhte [m].

The descent to the next corridor is guarded by winged serpents representing the goddesses Nekhbet and Neith (left), Meretseger and Selket (right). On the corridor walls appear the introductory [n] and middle sections [o] of the *Book of Amduat*; on the ceiling, extracts from the *Books of Re* and the *Book of Day and Night*. Scenes in the next corridor relate the fourth and fifth [p] and eighth to eleventh [q] chapters of the *Book of Amduat*. The small vestibule beyond contains texts from the *Book of Coming Forth by Day*, including the "Negative Confession" [r]. On the ceiling, Ramses sails the barques of Day and Night across the first register, whilst Osiris rises from his bier in the second.

Lovely back-to-back versions of the *Book of Day* and *Book of Night* adorn the ceiling of Ramses VI's burial chamber, where his image makes offerings at either end of one wall [s]. The rear [t] and right-hand walls carry portions of the *Book of Aker*, named after the earth-god of the underworld who fettered the coils of Apopis, safeguarding Re's passage. Incarnated as a ram-headed beetle, the sun-god is drawn across the heavens in his divine barque [u]. Lower down, you can

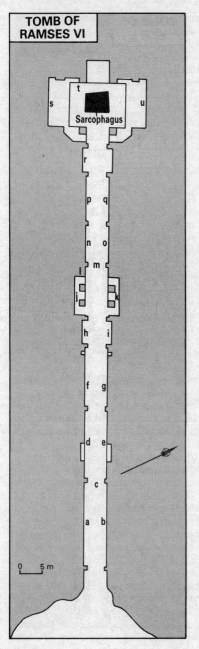

TOMB OF RAMSES VI

see a mummy on a mound. The king's black granite sarcophagus was smashed open by treasure hunters in antiquity.

Tomb of Merneptah (#8)

Merneptah (1236–1223 BC), grandson of Seti I, may have been the Pharaoh of the Exodus. Like other XIX Dynasty tombs, his descends through stepped corridors whose ceilings are painted with flying vultures or nocturnal skies, their walls with extracts from the *Litany of Re*, *Book of Gates* and *Book of Amduat*.

Similar scenes adorn the gigantic lid of Merneptah's outer sarcophagus, discarded by looters in an antechamber. Down another flight of stairs is the pillared burial chamber, containing the lid of his inner sarcophagus, carved in high relief with Merneptah as Osiris. The best preserved murals are those in the false burial chamber, halfway into the tomb; a device to fool robbers which seldom worked.

Tomb of Ramses IX (#6)

Sited nearer the resthouse but less crowded than the tombs of Tut or Ramses VI, this monument belonged to one of the last rulers (1140–1123 BC) of the XX Dynasty. Its stepped corridors are bisected by inclined ramps (to facilitate moving the sarcophagus); the walls depict Ramses before the gods and symbolic extracts from the *Book of Caverns*. For example, the mast of Re's boat is formed by the penis of Babi, an Old Kingdom baboon-god whose phallus was the bolt on the door of heaven. The burial chamber is memorable for its *Book of Night* in yellow upon a dark blue background. Two sky-goddesses stretch back-to-back across the ceiling, encompassing voids swirling with creatures, stars and heavenly barques. Whilst the king's sarcophagus pit gapes empty, his resurrection is still heralded on the walls by Khepri, the scarab-incarnation of the reborn sun at dawn.

Tomb of Seti I (#17)

It was Seti I (1318–1304 BC) who consolidated the XIX Dynasty, regained the colonies lost under Akhenaten, and paved the way for Ramses II to reach new heights of imperialism. Found in 1817, Seti's tomb is the longest (100m) and finest in the valley, boasting carvings and gilded paintings comparable to those in his temple at Abydos. Unfortunately, these have suffered from the humid exhalations of tourists, necessitating the tomb's closure several years ago. Whether it'll reopen once they've finished restoration work and solved the ventilation problem is uncertain.

The tomb descends through several corridors, their ceilings painted with flying vultures. In the first, Seti appears before falcon-headed Re-Herakhte **[a]**, Aten, Khepri and other solar incarnations, in a *Litany of Re* that continues along the facing wall **[b]** and both sides of the stairway beyond, flanked by Isis and Nephthys. On the upper part of the left-hand recess **[c]** are depicted the 37 forms of the sun-god, whose journey through the underworld features in the next corridor **[d]**. In the fifth hour of the night (left), Re overcomes the Serpent of Chaos. His own ram-headed form is that of Re-made-Flesh, whose mortal avatar – the king – consorts with deities **[e]**. Beyond a pit lies a pillared hall depicting the fifth division of the *Book of Gates* **[f]**; Horus presenting Seti to Osiris **[g]** near the stairs into a Hall of Offerings **[h]** with extracts from the *Book of Amduat*.

The descent continues via steps across another pit, into a corridor showing the Opening of the Mouth **[i]**, a winged disc surmounting the portal to another passage, where Seti sits before an offerings table **[j]**, with a *Litany of the Eye of Horus* to the left of the door at the end. In the next chamber **[k]** he is embraced and given life by the gods. The pillared hall **[l]** forms an ante-room to the burial chamber, which features an astronomical

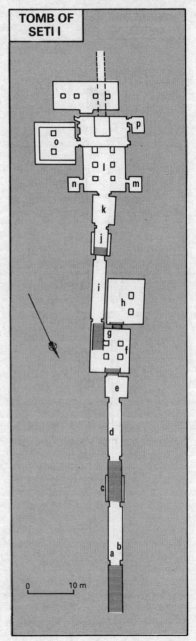

TOMB OF SETI I

0   10 m

ceiling, scenes from the *Book of Amduat*, and a depression where Seti's sarcophagus (now in the Sir John Soane Museum, London) once rested. One of the side-chambers depicts the sky-goddess Nut in the form of a cow **[m]**; the others carry extracts from the *Book of Gates* and the *Book of Amduat* (**[n]**, **[o]** and **[p]**).

Tomb of Ramses I (#16)

Buried next door to Seti is his predecessor Ramses I, founder of the XIX Dynasty, whose brief reign (1320–1318 BC) only allowed a modest tomb. Its steep, featureless corridor leads to a small but finely painted burial chamber, the colours still bright against a blue-grey background. On the left wall are nine black sarcophagi in caverns, above twelve goddesses representing the hours of the night, from the *Book of Gates*. Elsewhere, Ramses appears with Maat, Anubis, Ptah, Osiris and other deities.

Tomb of Ramses III (#11)

If Seti's tomb is closed, Ramses III's makes a fair consolation prize, being almost as grand. His reign (1198–1166 BC) marked the heyday of the XX Dynasty, whose power declined under the later Ramessids. Like his temple at Medinet Habu, the tomb harks back to the earlier glories of the New Kingdom. Uniquely for royal tombs, its colourful sunk-reliefs include scenes of everyday life. From another vignette derives its popular name, the *Tomb of the Harpers*.

Off the entrance corridors lie ten side-chambers, originally used to store funerary objects. Within the first pair are scenes of butchery, cooking and baking **[a]**, and ships setting sail, those with furled sails bound downriver **[b]**. Next, Hapy blesses grain-gods and propitiates snake-headed Napret, with her escort of aproned *uraei* **[c]**. The bull of Meri (right) and the cow of Hesi (left) coexist with armoury scenes **[d]**, while hermaphrodite deities bring offerings **[e]** to a

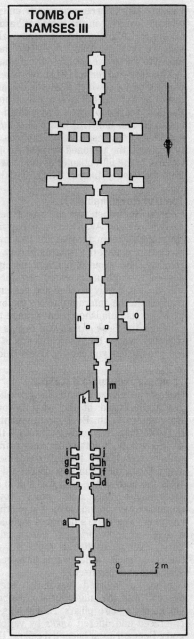

TOMB OF
RAMSES III

treasury **[f]**. Ramses owns cattle and minerals **[g]**, and from his boat inspects peasants working in the Fields of Yaru **[h]**. In a famous scene, two harpists sing to Shu and Atum, whilst Harsomtus and Anhor greet the king; the lyrics of the song cover the entrance wall **[i]**. The twelve forms of Osiris **[j]** are possibly linked to the twelve *decans* of the night.

The dead-end tunnel **[k]** shows where diggers accidentally broke into a neighbouring tomb, at which point the original builder, Pharaoh Sethnakht, abandoned it and appropriated Tawsert's (see below). When construction resumed under Ramses, the tomb's axis was shifted west. The corridor has scenes from the fourth **[l]** and fifth **[m]** hours of the *Book of Amduat*. Part of the *Book of Gates* specified four races of men: Egyptians, Asiatics, Negroes and Libyans **[n]**. On the facing wall, the pinioned serpent Apopis is forced to disgorge the heads of his victims, in the fifth chapter of the *Book of Gates*. In the small room **[o]** are scenes from the *Book of Amduat*. The rest of the tomb is barred to visitors.

Tomb of Horemheb (#57)

General Horemheb was the power behind the throne of Tutankhamun and his aged successor Ay. Despite being married to Nefertiti's sister Mutnedjmet, Horemheb's reign (1348–1320 BC) marked the height of the Theban counter-revolution against the Amarna heresy (see p.255), and the last gasp of the XVIII Dynasty. The layout of his tomb prefigures Seti's (see above), with a long, steep descent through undecorated corridors to a well room which depicts Horemheb with deities, highly detailed and coloured. Hathor, Isis, Osiris, Horus and Anubis reappear in the anteroom before the burial chamber, whose entrance is guarded by Maat. Its unfinished scenes range from stick-figure drawings to fully worked carvings; the *Book of the Dead* begins to your left and runs clockwise round the chamber, whose huge sarcophagus is carved with a relief of Nut. In the second room to the left, you can see Osiris before a *djed* pillar.

Tomb of Amenophis II (#35)

One of the deepest tombs in the valley lies at the head of the wadi beyond Horemheb's tomb. Built for Amenophis II (1450–1425 BC) midway through the XVIII Dynasty, it gets hotter and stuffier with each sublevel, having over ninety steps. When the tomb was discovered in 1898, the body of the king was still in its sarcophagus and nine other royal mummies were found stashed in another chamber. The tomb's defences included a deep pit (now bridged) and a false burial chamber to distract robbers from the lower levels (which would have been sealed up and disguised).

From a pillared vestibule, steps descend into the huge burial chamber. On its six square pillars, Amenophis is embraced and offered *ankhs* by various gods. Beneath a star-spangled ceiling, the

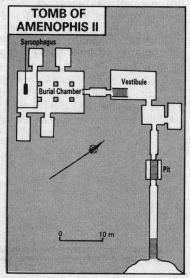

TOMB OF
AMENOPHIS II

Sarcophagus

Burial Chamber

Vestibule

Pit

0   10 m

walls are painted yellow and inscribed with entire *Book of Amduat*, like a continuous scroll of papyrus. When found in his quartzite sarcophagus (still in situ), the king's mummy had a floral garland about its neck. The second chamber on the right served as a cache for the mummies of Tuthmosis IV, Merneptah, Seti II, Ramses III and IV and Queen Tiy, after their original tombs were proved insecure.

Tomb of Tawsert/Sethnakht (#14)
Located en route to Seti II's tomb, this originally held the mummy of his wife, Queen Tawsert, but was usurped by Pharaoh Sethnakht (c.1200–1085 BC) after his own tomb (now Ramses III's) ran into difficulties. A series of corridors leads into an eight-chambered hall, decorated throughout with well-preserved extracts from the *Book of the Dead*, *Book of Gates* and the Opening of the Mouth ceremony. A further passage bears scenes from the *Book of Caverns*. Sethnakht offers to gods on the pillars in his tomb chamber, where fragments of his granite sarcophagus remain.

Tomb of Seti II (#15)
At the end of the wadi lies the seldom-visited tomb of Seti II (1216–1210 BC), which Arthur Mace used as a storage and restoration area during the excavation of Tutankhamun's tomb. Its long, straight corridors are typical of the XIX Dynasty, but although the low-reliefs on the walls are in decent condition, their style is unsophisticated. Seti's demise brought an abrupt end to the tomb's construction, and his mummy was later hidden in Tomb #35 (see above); the example in situ belongs to an anonymous dignitary.

Tomb of Tuthmosis III (#34)
Likewise secreted in a separate wadi, high up in a cleft, the tomb of Tuthmosis III (1504–1450 BC) is one of the oldest in the valley. Its concealment and (futile) defences make this tomb especially interesting, though some are disappointed by its artwork. Having ascended a wooden stairway to the cleft, you descend through several levels, crossing a pit by footbridge to reach a vestibule. Its walls depict 741 deities as stick-figures in imitation of the format used on papyrus texts from the Middle Kingdom onwards, which was favoured for murals early in the New Kingdom. Reduced to their essentials, the ramps and shafts that led into the underworld, and Khepri's role in pulling Re's barque, are clearly visible.

The unusual rounded burial chamber is similarly decorated with matchstick figures and symbols. Although the yellow background simulates the look of aged papyrus, the texts were only

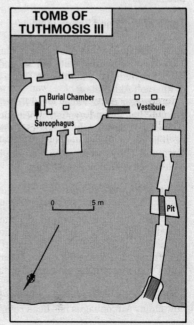

TOMB OF TUTHMOSIS III

Burial Chamber

Sarcophagus

Vestibule

0   5 m

Pit

painted after Tuthmosis had been laid to rest; on the "instruction" fresco there's a crossed-out mistake.

Elsewhere you'll notice double images, used to suggest motion (as at Abu Simbel). On one of the pillars, Tuthmosis's mother stands behind him in a barque; the register below shows three wives and a daughter, to the right of which, a tree-goddess suckles the young king. By shining a torch inside the quartzite sarcophagus, you can admire a lovely carving of Nut, whose arms would have embraced his mummy before priests removed it to a safer hiding place near Deir el-Bahri (see below).

Tomb of Queen Tiy/Smenkhkare (#55)

This undecorated tomb near the resthouse has been an archaeological conundrum ever since its discoverer, Theodore Davis, failed to record its contents before removing the mummy in 1907, thus destroying crucial evidence. The decrepit mummy was initially attributed to Queen Tiy due to its pelvic shape and feminine position (left arm bound across the chest, right arm alongside the body), and a gilded panel which depicted her with Akhenaten. Later, however, the bones were identified as those of a man under 26 with signs of hydrocephalus, which seemed to fit Akhenaten instead. Yet another examination in 1933 found no signs of hydrocephalus, but diagnosed a platycephalic skull similar to Tutankhamun's – suggesting that this was the mummy of his mysterious predecessor, Smenkhkare.

Although new evidence has since been advanced for this being the mummy of Akhenaten, the Egyptian Museum remains unconvinced, and still attributes it to Smenkhkare.

Tomb of Yuya and Thuya (#46)

Another tomb with nothing to see (its contents are in the Cairo Museum) but a story attatched is that of Yuya and Thuya. Though seemingly not of noble birth, Yuya was the highest state official under Tuthmosis IV and Amenophis III. The latter married Tiy, daughter of Thuya and Yuya, making them the grandparents of Pharaoh Akhenaten.

In *Stranger in the Valley of the Kings*, Ahmed Osman argues that Yuya – whose mummy has a non-Egyptian appearance – was the Joseph of the Old Testament (Genesis 41:39-40), whose talk of Yahweh subsequently inspired the monotheistic religion of Akhenaten (see "Tell el-Amarna"). However, others believe that Yuya and Thuya were of Nubian origin, as evinced by the famous bust of Tiy, whose face is indubitably African.

Tomb of Ramses IV (#2)

Situated beyond the site entrance, a hundred metres back along the road, this tomb has much of the appeal of Ramses VI's (which it resembles), but is less crowded with visitors. Its cheerful colours make amends for the inferior carving and abundant Greek and Coptic graffiti (notice the haloed saints on the right near the entrance). The ceiling of the burial chamber is adorned with twin figures of Nut. On the enormous pink granite sarcophagus are magical texts and carvings of Isis and Nephthys, to protect the mummy from harm. When these seemed insufficient, the priests stashed Ramses in the tomb of Amenophis II, whence the now empty sarcophagus has been returned.

HIKING ACROSS THE HILLS TO DEIR EL-BAHRI

This wonderfully scenic hike is easiest over winter, but feasible at other times so long as you guard against heatstroke. Though **the hike** can be done in thirty minutes, it's worth taking it slowly once you've shaken off the donkey boys who wait above the start of the trail (near Tomb #16). Crossing the hills **by donkey** is not advisable, as passengers who fail to comply with exorbitant demands for cash may be knocked off their mounts. (Some of the lads also hassle women, making it safer to hike in groups.)

When the path forks, take the left-hand track running flat along the top of a rock "loaf", before crossing the ridge to behold the Nile Valley. Directly beneath the sheer cliff lies Hatshepsut's temple; to see it, walk right for a bit before peering *carefully* over the edge. To descend, follow the path alongside the wire fence till you reach a crag where the trail divides. Ignore anyone who tries to lure you down the steeper trail, to render "help" for *baksheesh* – the left-hand path is the one to take. On the hillside lower down, younger boys wait to sell fake *antikas* which their friends have "just found" nearby.

Should you fancy a longer walk (45–60min), another trail runs over the hills to Deir el-Medina, starting at the first fork in the path described above. Don't attempt this trail without carrying plenty of water to drink.

Deir el-Bahri

Of all the sites on the west bank, none can match the breathtaking panache of **Deir el-Bahri**. Set amidst a vast natural amphitheatre in the Theban Hills, the temple rises in imposing terraces, the shadowed verticals of its colonnades drawing power from the massive crags overhead. Its great ramps and courts look modern in their stark simplicity, but in ancient times would have been softened and perfumed by gardens of fragrant trees. Although its uppermost level may still be off-limits, the lower colonnades and chapels attest to a woman's will and a man's spite.

Deir el-Bahri (Northern Monastery) is the Arabic name for the **Mortuary Temple of Hatshepsut**, the only woman ever to reign over Egypt as pharaoh (1503–1482 BC). A daughter of Tuthmosis I, married to his successor Tuthmosis II, Hatshepsut was widowed before she could bear a son. Rather than accept relegation in favour of a secondary wife who had produced an heir, Hatshepsut made herself co-regent to the young Tuthmosis III and soon assumed absolute power.

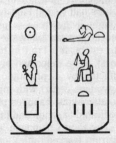

To legitimise her position, she was depicted in masculine form, wearing a pharaoh's kilt and beard; yet her authority ultimately depended on personal willpower and the devotion of her favourite courtier, Senenmut, who rose from humble birth to the stewardship of Amun's estates before falling from grace for reasons unknown. When Tuthmosis came into his inheritance after her death, he defaced Hatshepsut's

Hatshepsut

cartouches and images, consigning her memory to oblivion until her deeds were rediscovered by archaeologists.

Hatshepsut's temple

Hatshepsut called her temple *Djeser Djeseru*, the "Splendour of Splendours". In ancient times an avenue of sphinxes probably ran from the Nile to its **Lower Terrace**, which was planted with myrrh trees and cooled by fountains (the stumps of a few trees remain). At the top and bottom of the ramp to the next level stood pairs of stone lions (one of each pair is still in situ). Before ascending the ramp, check out its flanking **colonnades**, whose reliefs were defaced by Tuthmosis III, and later by Akhenaten. Whilst Hatshepsut's image remains obliterated, those of Amun were restored after the Theban counter-revolution. Behind the northern colonnade (right of the ramp) are idealised scenes of rural life; reliefs in the southern (left) colonnade show the transport by river of two obelisks from Aswan – doubtless the pair that she erected at Karnak.

The **Middle Terrace** once also boasted myrrh trees which Hatshepsut personally acquired from the Land of Punt in a famous expedition that's depicted along one of the square-pillared colonnades flanking the ramp to the uppermost level. Together with the Birth reliefs behind the other colonnade, and scenes in the chapels at either end, these are the highlights of her temple.

THE BIRTH AND PUNT COLONNADES

To the right of the ramp is the so-called **Birth Colonnade**, whose reliefs assert Hatshepsut's divine parentage. Starting from the left, its rear walls show Amun (in the guise of Tuthmosis I) and her mother Queen Ahmosis (seated on a couch), their knees touching. Next, bizarre deities lead the Queen into the birth chamber, where the god Khnum fashions Hatshepsut and her *ka* (both represented as boys) on his potter's wheel. Her birth is attended by Bes and the frog-deity Heqet; goddesses nurse her, whilst Thoth records details of her reign. The sensitive expressions and delicate modelling convey a sincerity that transcends mere political expediency.

At the far end of the colonnade, steps lead back into a **Chapel of Anubis** with its fluted columns and colourful murals. Tuthmosis III and a falcon-headed sun-god appear over the niche to the right; Hathor on the facing wall; offerings by Hatshepsut and Tuthmosis to Anubis on the other walls. As elsewhere, the images of Hatshepsut were defaced after her death by order of Tuthmosis.

On the other side of the ramp is the famous **Punt Colonnade**, relating Hatshepsut's journey to that land (thought to be modern-day Somalia). Though others had visited Punt to obtain precious myrrh for temple incense, Hatshepsut sought living trees to plant outside her temple. Despite the faintness of the reliefs, you can follow the story as it unfolds (left–right). Commissioned by Amun "to establish a Punt in his house", the Egyptian flotilla sails from the Red Sea coast, to be welcomed by the king of Punt and his grotesquely fat wife (perhaps afflicted by elephantitis). In exchange for metal axes and other goods, the Egyptians depart with myrrh trees and resin, ebony, ivory, cinnamon wood and panther-skins; baboons playing in the ships' rigging. Back home, the spoils are dedicated to Amun and the precious myrrh trees bedded in the temple gardens.

The Punt Colonnade leads into a larger **Chapel of Hathor**, whose face and sistrum (sacred rattle) form the capitals of the square pillars. In the first pillared chamber, the goddess appears in her bovine and human forms, and suckles Hatshepsut (whose image has not been defaced here) on the right-hand wall. The next chamber features delicate reliefs of festival processions (still quite freshly coloured) in a similar location. Peering into the gated sanctuary, you'll see another intact Hatshepsut worshipping the divine cow (left) and an alcove (right) containing a *portrait of Senenmut*, which would have been hidden when the doors were open. Apocryphally, it was this claim on the pharaoh's temple that caused his downfall. After fifteen years of closeness to Hatshepsut and her daughter Neferure (evinced by a statue in the Cairo Museum, which some regard as proof of paternity), Senenmut abruptly vanished from the records late in her reign.

THE UPPER TERRACE AND SANCTUARIES

Reached by a ramp terminating in vulture's heads, the **Upper Terrace** is now emerging from decades of research and restoration work by Polish and Egyptian teams, and may be open to visitors in the near future. Beyond its Osiride portico lies a courtyard flanked by colonnades and sanctuaries. In the **Sanctuary of Hatshepsut** (left) are stylish reliefs of priests and offerings bearers. On the other side is the **Sanctuary of the Sun**, an open court with a central altar.

The central **Sanctuary of Amun** is dug into the cliff, aligned so that it points towards Hatshepsut's tomb in the Valley of the Kings on the other side of the mountain. In Ptolemaic times the sanctuary was extended and dedicated to Imhotep and Amenhotep, the quasi-divine counsellors of Zoser and Amenophis III. Beneath it lies another burial chamber for Hatshepsut, presumably favoured over her pro forma tomb in the Valley of the Kings, since it was dug later.

Other temples

From the heights of Hatshepsut's temple you can gaze southwards over the ruins of two similar edifices. The **Mortuary Temple of Tuthmosis III** was long ago destroyed by a landslide, but a painted relief excavated here can be seen in the Luxor Museum. More remains of the far older **Temple of Nebhetepre Mentuhotpe**, the first pharaoh to chose burial in Thebes (XI Dynasty). Unlike his XVIII Dynasty imitators, Nebhetepre was actually buried in his mortuary temple; his funerary statue is now exhibited in the Cairo Museum.

Secret tombs and lavatory humour

Whereas Nebhetepre's remains weren't discovered till modern times, many of the New Kingdom royal tombs were despoiled soon after the last burial in the Valley of the Kings. The priests subsequently hid the contents of several tombs in a **secret cache** above Nebhetepre's temple, which the villagers of Qurna found in 1875 and quietly sold off for years until rumbled by the authorities, who forced them to reveal its location. Amongst the mummies recovered were Tuthmosis III, Seti I and Ramses II and III. As the steamer bore them downriver to Cairo, villagers lined the banks, ululating in sorrow or firing rifles in homage.

Worth a look if you can persuade a guard at Deir el-Bahri to unlock it is the **Tomb of Senenmut**, just beyond the temple precincts. Its steep shaft descends past a bust of Senenmut into a chamber with a lovely astronomical ceiling; on its walls are extracts from the *Book of the Dead*. Why Senenmut should have built this tomb when he already had one at Qurna is uncertain; in any event, its unfinished burial chamber was never used.

Finally, there's a rare example of ancient Egyptian lavatory humour in a **cave** to the north of Hatshepsut's temple (on a line with its lower colonnade). Amongst the doodles and inscriptions is a drawing of a man buggering a figure wearing pharaonic headgear and women's underwear. Could this be Senenmut and Hatshepsut – or a fantasy of revenge by the juvenile Tuthmosis?

The Asasif Tombs

Midway between Deir el-Bahri and the Tombs of the Nobles lies a burial ground known as the **Asasif Tombs**, currently being studied by several archaeological teams. While some of its 35 tomb-chapels date from the XVIII Dynasty, the majority are from the Late Period (XXV–XXVI Dynasty), when Thebes was ruled by Nubian kings, and then from the Delta. Several of the tombs may be open to visitors (ask at the ticket office).

The finest scenes are in the **Tomb of Kheruef (#192)**, a Steward of Queen Tiy during the Amarna period, and depict a Jubilee Festival, Tiy and Amenophis III, musicians, dancers and playful animals – as lyrical as those in Ramose's tomb (see below). Roughly ten metres north of here lies the **Tomb of Kiki (#409)**, whose soul is weighed by Anubis and Thoth at the entrance. In the unfinished burial shrine are faceless figures outlined in red.

More noteworthy is the **Tomb of Pabasa (#279)**, twenty metres west of Kiki's. Pabasa was Steward to a Divine Votaress of Amun during the XXVI Dynasty and his tomb reflects the Saite obsession with the Old Kingdom. Its massive gateway leads into a pillared court with scenes of hunting, fishing and viticulture (note the bee-keeping scene on the central column). A funeral procession and the voyage to Abydos appear in the vestibule.

The Tombs of the Nobles

The **Tombs of the Nobles** are a study in contrasts to their royal counterparts. Whereas royalty favoured concealed tombs in secluded valleys, Theban nobles and high officials were ostentatiously interred in the limestone foothills overlooking the great funerary temples of their masters and the city across the river. Whilst royal tombs are filled with scenes of judgement and resurrection, the nobles' chosen artwork dwells on earthly life and its continuation in the hereafter. Given more freedom of expression, the artists excelled themselves with vivid paintings on stucco (the inferior limestone on this side of the hills militates against carved reliefs).

The **tombs' layout** marks a further evolution in funerary architecture since the Middle Kingdom tombs of Beni Hassan. Most are entered via a courtyard, with a transverse hall preceding the burial shrine with its niche containing an effigy of the deceased (or statues of his entire family). Strictly speaking, they are tomb-chapels rather than tombs, since the grave itself lies at the bottom of a shaft (usually inaccessible).

Excluding the Asasif Tombs nearer Deir el-Bahri (see above), all the tombs open to visitors cluster around the village of Old Qurna, where they're divided into three groups (each requiring a separate ticket), namely: **Rekhmire and Sennofer; Ramose, Userhat and Khaemhat;** and **Nakht and Menna**. The first two lie furthest west and back from the road; the next trio downhill towards the Ramesseum; and the last pair to the northeast, closer to Deir el-Bahri. Until signposting improves, you'll have to ask kids for directions or try to locate them by their modern brick enclosure walls.

As visiting all seven tombs takes a couple of hours, most people limit themselves to a single group or the highlights from each (marked * in the accounts following). The *gaffir* will use a mirror to reflect sunlight inside (which is how they were illuminated for artists to work), but it's worth bringing a torch.

Tomb of Rekhmire (#100)*

This richly decorated tomb casts light on statecraft and foreign policy under Tuthmosis III and Amenophis II, whom Rekhmire served as Vizier. Paintings in its transverse hall show him collecting taxes from Upper [a] and Lower [b] Egypt; inspecting temple workshops, charioteers and agricultural work [c]. Around the corner from his ancestors [d], grapes are trod in large tubs and the juice is strained and put in jars [e].

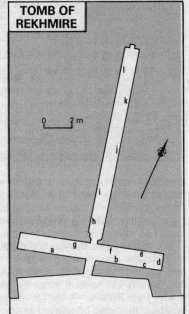

TOMB OF REKHMIRE

The rear portal is flanked by a desert hunt [f] and a famous scene of Rekhmire receiving tributes from foreign lands [g], including vases from Crete and the Aegean Islands (top); chariots and horses from Syria (middle); a giraffe, monkeys and elephant tusks from Punt and Nubia (bottom).

Growing taller as it recedes towards the false door at the back, the long corridor is decorated with scenes of work and daily life. Slaves store grain in silos [h], whence it was later disbursed as wages to armourers, carpenters, sculptors and other state-employed craftsmen [i]. An idealised banqueting scene [j] merges into an Afterworld with a lake and trees [k]. Also note Rekhmire's funeral procession and offerings to sustain him in the afterlife [l].

Tomb of Sennofer (#96)

From Rekhmire's tomb, you can slog fifty metres uphill (to the west) to find the deeply buried "Tomb of Vines", whose rounded antechamber simulates an arbour, its filigree texture casting the painted grapes and vines into relief. As Mayor of Thebes and Overseer of Amun's estates under Amenophis II, Sennofer's responsibilities included local viticulture. The walls of the burial shrine beyond depict his funeral procession (left), voyage to Abydos (back) and mummified sojourn with Anubis (right). Its pillars have Hathor-headed capitals whose eyes follow you around the room; a tree goddess appears on the inner side of the rear left-hand pillar.

Tomb of Ramose (#55)*

Down a dirt road to the southeast lies the tomb of Ramose, who was Vizier and Governor of Thebes immediately before and after the Amarna revolution. His spacious tomb captures the moment of transition from Amun to Aten-worship, featuring both classical and Amarna-style reliefs, the latter unfinished since Ramose followed Akhenaten to his new capital. Besides its superb reliefs, the tomb is notable for retaining its courtyard – originally a feature of all these tombs.

Along the entrance wall of its pillared hall are lovely carvings which reflect the mellowing of classicism during the reign of Amenophis III, Akhenaten's father.

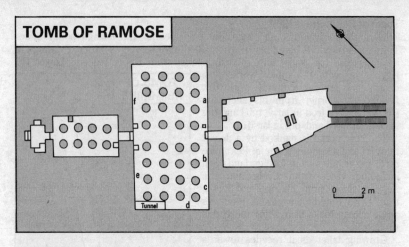

TOMB OF RAMOSE

0   2 m

Predictable scenes of Ramose and his wife **[a]**, Amenophis III and Queen Tiy **[b]** making offerings come alive thanks to the exquisite rendering of the major figures, carried over to their feasting friends and relatives **[c]**. The sinuous swaying of mourners likewise imparts lyricism to the conventional, painted funerary scene **[d]**, where Ramose, wife and priests worship Osiris.

The onset of Aten-worship and the Amarna style is evident in the reliefs at the back, despite their battered condition. Those on the left **[e]** were carved before Amenophis IV changed his name to Akhenaten and espoused Aten-worship, so the pharaoh sits beneath a canopy with Maat, the goddess of truth, receiving flowers from Ramose. (At the far end, note the red grid and black outlined figures by which the artist transferred his design to the wall before relief-cutting took place.) However, the corresponding scene **[f]** depicts the pharaoh as Akhenaten, standing with Nefertiti at their palace window, bathed in the Aten's rays. Ramose is sketched in below, accepting their gift of a golden chain; his physiognomy is distinctly Amarnan, but less exaggerated than the royal couple's (see p.255).

By a quirk of Egyptian security, a gate bars access to Ramose's inner shrine, but nothing prevents one from venturing into a dark tunnel leading off the hall, which suddenly plummets into his grave, fifteen metres below – beware.

Tomb of Userhat (#56)

Immediately south of Ramose's tomb lies that of Userhat, a royal scribe and tutor in the reign of Amenophis II. Although some of the figures were destroyed by early Christian hermits who occupied the shrine, what remains is freshly coloured, with unusual pink tones.

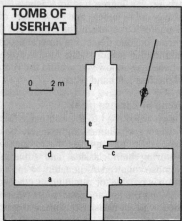

TOMB OF USERHAT

0   2 m

Along the entrance wall of the antechamber are scenes of wine-making, harvesting, herding and branding cattle, collecting grain for the royal storehouse [a], and the customary obeisances by Userhat before the pharaoh, whose face has been gouged out [b]. On the rear wall are reliefs of baking, assaying gold-dust, and – lower down – a barber trimming customers beneath a tree [c].

The funerary feast scene [d] was extensively damaged by hermits, particularly the female figures. The inner hall contains paintings of Userhat hunting gazelles, hares and jackals from a chariot in the desert [e]; fowling and fishing amidst the reeds [f]; and funerary scenes [g].

Tomb of Khaemhat (#57)

Next door is the tomb of Khaemhat, royal scribe and inspector of granaries under Amenophis III, which is reached via a forecourt off which two other tombs once led. Flanking its doorway are reliefs of Khaemhat worshipping Re, and the complete set of instruments for the Opening of the Mouth ceremony. In the transverse antechamber with its red and black patterned ceiling, the best reliefs are on the left as you enter. Although Renenet the snake-headed harvest goddess has almost vanished, a scene of grain boats docking at Thebes harbour is still visible nearer the niche containing statues of Khaemhat and Imhotep.

On the facing wall Khaemhat presents a report to the king, and breastfeeding is depicted beside the door into the inner chamber, where fowling, fishing and family scenes decorate the left-hand wall, near the triple-niched chapel containing seated statues of Khaemhat and his family.

Tomb of Nakht (#52)*

Northeast of Ramose's tomb lies the burial place of Nakht, royal astronomer and overseer of Amun's vineyards and granaries under Tuthmosis IV. The only decorated section is the transverse antechamber, whose ceiling is painted to resemble woven mats, with a *kherker* frieze running above the brilliantly coloured murals.

To one side, Nakht supervises the harvest in a scene replete with vivid details [a]. Whilst one farmer fells a tree, another swigs from a waterskin; of the two women gleaning, one is missing an arm. Beyond a stele relating Nakht's life [b] is the famous banqueting scene [c], where sinuous dancers and a blind harpist entertain friends of the deceased, who sits beside his wife with a cat scoffing a fish beneath his chair.

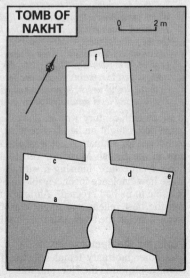

The defacement of Nakht's image and Amun's name is usually ascribed to Amarna iconoclasm, but the gouging out of his eyes and throwing sticks in the hunting scene [d] suggests a personal animus. Happily, this has not extended to the images in the corner [e], where peasants tread grapes in vats, and birds are caught in clap-nets and hung for curing (below). The plain inner chamber contains a replica of the funerary statue of Nakht lost at sea en route to America in 1917 [f]; a false door painted to resemble Aswan granite; and a deep shaft leading to the (inaccessible) burial chamber.

Tomb of Menna (#69)

If restoration work is complete, you can admire more scenes of rural life in the nearby tomb of Menna, an XVIII Dynasty inspector of estates. Accompanied by his wife and daughter, Menna worships the sun in the entrance passage. In the left wing of the first chamber, he supervises field labour (notice the two girls pulling each other's hair), banquets and makes offerings with his wife. Across the way they participate in ceremonies with Anubis, Osiris, Re and Hathor. Though chiefly decorated with mourning and burial scenes, the inner chamber also features a spot of hunting and fishing, vividly depicted on the right-hand wall.

The Ramesseum

The **Ramesseum** or mortuary temple of Ramses II was built to awe the pharaoh's subjects, perpetuate his existence in the afterlife and forever link him to Amun-United-with-Eternity. Had it remained intact, the Ramesseum would doubtless match his great sun temple of Abu Simbel for monumental grandeur and unabashed self-glorification. But by siting it beside an earlier temple on land that was annually inundated, Ramses unwittingly ensured the ruination of his monument, whose toppled colossi would later mock his presumption, inspiring Shelley's sonnet *Ozymandias*:

> *I met a traveller from an antique land*
> *Who said: Two vast and trunkless legs of stone*
> *Stand in the desert . . . Near them on the sand,*
> *Half sunk, a shattered visage lies, whose frown,*
> *And wrinkled lip, and sneer of cold command*
> *Tell that its sculptor well those passions read*
> *Which yet survive, stamped on these lifeless things,*
> *The hand which mocked them, and the heart that fed.*
> *On the pedestal these words appear:*
> *'My name is Ozymandias, King of Kings:*
> *Look upon my works ye Mighty, and despair!'*
> *Nothing beside remains. Round the decay*
> *Of that colossal wreck, boundless and bare*
> *The lone and level sands stretch far away.*

Nineteenth-century writers knew the ruins as the *Memnonium*. The present name only caught on late last century, by which time the Ramesseum had been plundered for statuary – not least the seven-ton head of one of its fallen colossi, now in the British Museum. Yet its devastation lends romance to the conventional architecture, infusing it with the pathos that moved Harriet Martineau to muse how "violence inconceivable to us has been used to destroy what art inconceivable to us had erected". Although an hour suffices to see the famous colossi and the best reliefs, you might consider breaking a hard day's touring with a picnic beneath the trees near the First Pylon.

Exploring the Ramesseum

Like other mortuary temples in the Theban necropolis, the Ramesseum faces southeast towards the Nile, and was originally entered via its **First Pylon**. Today,

Ramses II

this stands marooned beyond a rubble-strewn depression that used to be the **First Court**, now reduced to a colonnade of Osiride pillars. One side of this court abutted a palace where Ramses stayed during visits to his cult-temple, but centuries of flooding have almost effaced it (a similar arrangement survives at Medinet Habu).

Nowadays visitors enter the temple via the northern flank of its **Second Court**, to be confronted by the **fallen colossus of Ramses II**. This seated megalith once towered over the stairs from the first into the second court; over fifty-foot tall and weighing some nine hundred tons, it was only surpassed by the Colossi of Memnon thanks to their pedestals. When the colossus toppled some time after the first century AD, its upper half smashed through the Second Pylon into the court, where its monolithic head and torso lie today, measuring seven metres across the shoulders. In the lower court are other fragments, notably feet and hands; the forefinger alone is one metre long. As Dean Stanley wrote in 1852, "You sit on his breast and look at the Osiride statues which support the porticos of the temple, and they seem pygmies before him".

Behind the chunky Osirian pillars rises what's left of the **Second Pylon**, whose inner face mimics that of the First with scenes from the Battle of Qadesh, surmounted by a register depicting the festival of the harvest-god Min. At the far end of the second courtyard, where three ruined stairways rise to meet a colonnaded portico, lies a **smaller fallen colossus** of Ramses, more fragmented though its face has suffered merely nasal damage. Originally there were two colossi, but the other – dubbed the "Young Memnon" – was acquired for Britain in 1816 by Belzoni, who wrote his name next to that of Ramses on the remaining throne. Some 1700 years earlier, Diodorus had fancifully misread the king's inscription and distorted his praenomen *User-Maat-Re* into "Ozymandias".

Beyond here, the core of the Ramesseum is substantially intact. The first set of reliefs worth noting occurs on the rear wall of the **portico**, between the central and left-hand doorways. Above a bottom register depicting eleven of his sons, Ramses appears with Atum and Mont (who holds the hieroglyph for "life" to his nose), and kneels before the Theban Triad whilst Thoth inscribes his name on a palm frond (right). The top register shows him sacrificing to Ptah and making offerings to an ithyphallic Min.

The now roofless **Great Hypostele Hall** had 48 columns, of which 29 are still standing. The taller ones flanking the central aisle have papyrus shafts and lotus capitals which once supported a raised section of roof, admitting sunlight into the hall; the lower side columns have papyrus bud capitals. On the wall to the left as you come in, an upper register depicts Egyptian troops storming the Hittite city of Dapur, shields slung over their backs to protect them from arrows and stones. At the back of the hall, incised reliefs show lion-headed Sekhmet presenting Ramses to an enthroned Amun, who gives him an *ankh*; along the bottom are depicted some of the king's hundred sons.

Beyond this lie two **smaller hypostele halls**. The first retains its astronomical ceiling, featuring the oldest known twelve-month calendar (whether lunar or solar months is debatable). Notice also the barques of Amun, Mut and Khonsu on the entrance wall, and the scene of Ramses beneath the persea tree with Sheshat and Thoth, just before you enter the inner hall. The utterly ruined sanctuaries beyond were presumably dedicated to Amun, Ramses the god and his glorious ancestors, for the edifice stood alongside an earlier temple of Seti I, which itself contained shrines to Seti and his father, both of whom were linked to Amun. Its scant remains lie to the northeast of the portico and hypostele hall.

The whole complex is surrounded by mudbrick **magazines** that once covered about three times the area of the temple and included workshops, storerooms and servants' quarters, all originally enclosed by high walls.

Other mortuary temples

In ancient times, the Ramesseum was one of half a dozen mortuary temples ranged along the edge of the flood plain with no regard for chronological order. To the southwest were arrayed the mortuary temples of Tuthmosis IV, Merneptah and Amenophis III (of which only the latter's colossi remain), followed by those of Tuthmosis II, Ay and Horemheb. The furthest temple at Medinet Habu was closely modelled on the Ramesseum (see p.340).

Since all bar Medinet Habu are virtually non-existent, the only one worth consideration is the **Temple of Seti I**, beyond the village of Dra' Abul Naga. Rarely visited by tourists, it comprises a hypostele hall, chapels and sanctuary; the latter dedicated to Amun, the former to Seti and his father Ramses I. All are decorated with reliefs. To justify carving his own image on the columns of their hypostele hall, Ramses II added a (now ruinous) wing dedicated to Re-Herakhte.

Deir el-Medina: the Workmen's Village

Anyone who saw the television series *Ancient Lives* will recall **Deir el-Medina**, the **Workmen's Village** that housed the masons, painters and sculptors who created the royal tombs in the Valley of the Kings. Because many were literate and left records on papyrus or *ostracae*, we know such details as who feuded with whom, and about labour disputes. As state employees, they were supposed to receive fortnightly supplies of wheat, dried meat and fish, onions, pulses and beer, corresponding in value to the price of a bull. When these failed to arrive (as often happened during the ramshackle XX Dynasty), the workers downed tools, staged sit-ins at Medinet Habu, or demonstrated in Luxor.

Normally they worked an eight-hour day, sleeping in huts near the tombs during their ten-day shift before returning to their families at Deir el-Medina – a pattern followed over generations, as most occupations were hereditary. In their spare time craftsmen worked for private clients or collaborated on their own tombs, built beneath man-sized pyramids. Their own murals appropriated imagery from royal and noble tombs, which was parodied in the famous *Satirical Papyrus*, showing animals judging souls, collecting taxes and playing *senet*.

Whilst the now-ruined village is of little interest to non-specialists, the terraced necropolis is definitely worth visiting. The nearest mini-pyramid marks the **Tomb of Sennedjem** (or Sennutem), whose vaulted burial chamber is reached by a steep flight of steps. Its colourful murals feature ithyphallic baboons, Osiris and the Fields of Yaru, Anubis ministering to Sennedjem's mummy, and a cat killing a snake beneath the sacred persea tree. Other tombs cluster at the far end of the terraces. In the **Tomb of Peshedu** (#3), you can see the deceased praying beneath the tree of regeneration, below which flow the waters of the *Amuntit*, the "Hidden Region" where souls were judged. Unusually for Deir el-Medina, the **Tomb of Iphy** (#217) eschews ceremonial scenes and deities for tableaux from everyday life.

Just north of the village stands a **Ptolemaic temple** dedicated to Maat and Hathor, whose head adorns the pillars between the outer court and naos. Each of its three shrines is decorated with scenes from the *Book of the Dead*; in the left one, a monstrous reptilian "Devourer of Souls" awaits those who fail the Judgement of Osiris. Marauding Blemmye from Nubia have left a drawing of a camel on the outer wall. Early in the Christian era, the temple and village were occupied by monks – hence the site's Arabic name *Deir el-Medina* (Monastery of the Town).

Valley of the Queens

The **Valley of the Queens** is something of a misnomer, for it also contains the tombs of high officials (who were interred here long before the first queen was buried in this valley during the XIX Dynasty) and royal children. Polygamy and concubinage produced huge broods whose blood lines were further entangled by incestuous marriages between crown princes and their sisters, in emulation of Osiris and Isis. Princes were educated by priests and scribes, taught swimming, riding and shooting by officers, and finally apprenticed to military commands around the age of twelve. Less is known about the schooling of princesses, but several queens were evidently well versed in statecraft and architecture.

Originally named the "Place of Beauty", but now known in Arabic as *Biban el-Harem* (Gates of the Harem), the valley contains nearly eighty tombs, most of which are uninscribed and simple in plan. Although the finest murals rival those in the Valley of the Kings for artistry, many have been corroded by salt deposits, or badly vandalised. The exquisite **Tomb of Nefertari**, wife of Ramses II, is indefinitely closed for restoration work, whilst others may be temporarily shut. Ask at the ticket office before paying a visit, since only three tombs were accessible when last heard.

Tomb of Prince Khaemweset (#44)
Relatively few tourists visit this colourfully painted tomb, which lies uphill behind the souvenir stalls. Prince Khaemweset was one of several sons of Ramses III who died in a smallpox epidemic, and the murals in his tomb give precedence to images of Ramses, making offerings in the entrance corridor and worshipping funerary deities in the side chambers. In the second corridor, decorated with the *Book of Gates*, Ramses leads Khaemweset past the fearsome guardians of the Netherworld to the Fields of Yaru; bearing witness for him before Osiris and Horus in the burial chamber. Notice the four sons of Horus on the lotus blossom.

Tomb of Queen Titi (#52)
Sited along the well-trodden route to Amun-Hir-Khopshef's tomb, this cruciform structure was commissioned by Queen Titi, wife of one of the Ramessid pharaohs of the XX Dynasty. A winged Maat kneels in the corridor (where Titi appears before Thoth, Ptah and the sons of Horus) and guards the entrance to the burial chamber with Neith (left) and Selket (right).

This boasts jackal, lion and baboon guardians, plus three side chambers, the finest being the one to your right. Here, Hathor emerges from between the mountains of east and west in her bovine form, whilst the tree-goddess pours Nile water to rejuvenate Titi, who reposes on a cushion across the room. Unfortunately, most of these murals are faded or damaged.

Tomb of Amun-Hir-Khopshef (#55)

Further along lies the tomb of Khaeweset's brother, Amun-Hir-Khopshef, who was given a royal burial and portrayed as a boy with the braided side-lock of a prince even though he died in infancy. Descending the steps, you'll find a hall and corridor with lustrous murals of Ramses conducting him through funeral rituals, past the Keepers of the Gates, to an unfinished burial chamber containing a granite sarcophagus. A glass case displays a shrivelled foetus which his mother supposedly aborted through grief – a grisly curio which makes this the most visited tomb in the Valley of the Queens.

Medinet Habu

Medinet Habu is the Arabic name for the gigantic **Mortuary Temple of Ramses III**, a structure second only to Karnak in size and complexity. Modelled on the Ramesseum of his illustrious ancestor, Ramses II, this XX Dynasty extravaganza deserves more attention than it usually gets, being the last stop on most tourists' itinerary. The site itself was hallowed long before Ramses erected his "House of Millions of Years" and is still imbued with magical significance by the local *fellaheen*. Its massive brick enclosure walls sheltered the entire population of Thebes during the Libyan invasions of the late XX Dynasty and for centuries afterwards protected the Coptic town of *Djeme*, built within the great temple.

The temple precincts

The entire complex was originally surrounded by **enclosure walls**, sections of which rise at intervals from the plain. You enter the temple precincts through a lofty **Gatehouse** resembling an Assyrian fortress. The statue of Ptah beside the entrance served to transmit the prayers of pilgrims to Amun, who dwelt within the temple. If the crumbling stairs are still negotiable, it's worth investigating the upper storeys where Ramses relaxed with his harem (as depicted inside the top apartment) – but take care, since the timber floors disintegrated long ago.

North of here stands a **Small Temple**, reputedly sited where the primaeval mound arose from the waters of Chaos, preceding the creator-god Re-Atum of the Hermopolitan Ogdoad. The existing structure was built and partly decorated by Hatshepsut, whose cartouches and images were erased by Tuthmosis III. Akhenaten did likewise to those of Amun, but Horemheb and Seti replaced them. The most interesting reliefs [a] show Tuthmosis presiding over the foundation ceremonies, "stretching the cord" before the goddess Seshat, "scattering the gypsum" and then "hacking the earth" before a priapic Min.

Ramses III

Whilst the Small Temple antedates Ramses' work by three centuries, the **Chapels of the Votaresses** are Late Period additions. Several date from the XXV Dynasty of Nubian kings, who appointed these high priestesses of Amun and *de facto* governors of Thebes. The best reliefs are in the forecourt and shrine [b] of Amenirdis, sister of King Shabaka, whose alabaster funerary statue is now in the Cairo Museum. Ironically, these chapels remained objects of veneration long after Ramses' temple had been abandoned.

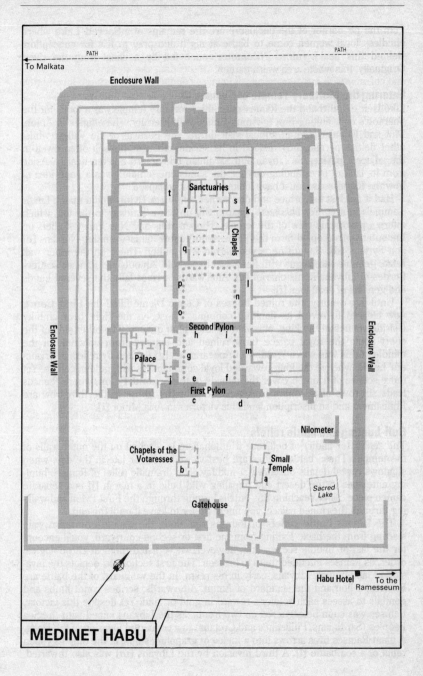

PATH

PATH

To Malkata

Enclosure Wall

Sanctuaries

t

s

r

k

Chapels

q

p

l

n

o

Second Pylon

h

i

Palace

g

m

j

e

f

First Pylon

c

d

Enclosure Wall

Enclosure Wall

Nilometer

Chapels of the
Votaresses

Small
Temple

b

a

Sacred
Lake

Gatehouse

Habu Hotel

To the
Ramesseum

MEDINET HABU

In the far corner of the enclosure are the remains of a **Sacred Lake** where childless local women come to bathe at night and pray to Isis for conception. Behind this lies a ruined **Nilometer**, once fed by a canal from the river. Originally, this whole area was a garden.

Entering the Mortuary Temple of Ramses III

Like Deir el-Bahri and the Ramesseum, this mortuary temple was a focus for the pharaoh's cult, linking him to Amun-United-with-Eternity. The effigies of Amun, Mut and Khonsu paid an annual visit during the Festival of the Valley, whilst other deities permanently resided in its shrines. Ramses himself often dwelt in the adjacent palace, his Libyan and Sardinian bodyguard billeted nearby. Aside from its lack of freestanding colossi, the sandstone temple gives a good idea of how the Ramesseum must have looked before it collapsed.

Had it not lost its cornice and one corner, the **First Pylon** would match Luxor Temple's in size. For *baksheesh*, guards will unlock a stairway to the top, which offers a panoramic view of the temple, Theban Hills and Nile Valley. Reliefs on the outer walls (copied from the Ramesseum) show Ramses smiting Nubians **[c]** and Syrians **[d]**, though he never warred with either. Those on the inner wall relate genuine campaigns with Ramessid hyperbole. An outsized Ramses scatters hordes of Libyans in his chariot **[e]**. Afterwards, scribes tally the severed hands and genitals of dead foes **[f]**.

Until last century, the ruined houses of Coptic Djeme filled the **First Court**, now cleared to reveal its flanking columns. Those on the right bear chunky Osiride statues of the king, attended by knee-high queens. The other side of the court abuts the royal palace (now ruined and entered from outside). In the middle of this wall was a Window of Appearances **[g]** flanked by reliefs of prisoners' heads, whence the king rewarded loyal commanders with golden collars. Yet more scenes of triumph cover the outside of the **Second Pylon**, where Ramses leads six rows of prisoners to Amun and Mut **[h]** (those in the third row are Philistines) and an inscription lauds his victories in Asia Minor **[i]**.

Bull-hunting and battle reliefs

The zenith (or nadir) of bellicose triumphalism is reached on the outer walls of the temple. These battle scenes are best viewed early or late in the day, when shadows reveal details obscured at midday. The dramatic relief of Ramses hunting antelopes in the desert and impaling wild bulls in a marsh **[j]** is a separate cameo piece. Since reaching this entails leaving through the First Pylon and walking through the ruined palace, you might prefer to leave it until the end.

The famous **battle reliefs** of Ramses run along the temple's northern wall, starting from the back. Exiting from the first or second courtyard, you'll encounter the last or middle scenes first; however, we've listed them in chronological order, as Ramses intended them to be seen. The first section **[k]** depicts the invasion of land-hungry Libyans, early in his reign. In the vanguard of the battle are Ramses, a lion and the standard of Amun. Afterwards, scribes count limbs and genitals to assess each soldier's reward in gold or land. Yet despite this victory, Ramses was soon beleaguered on two fronts, as the Libyans joined with the Sea Peoples (Sardinians, Philistines and Cretans) in a concerted invasion of the Delta. A giant Ramses fires arrows into a melee of grappling ships, in the only Egyptian relief of a sea battle **[l]**. A third invasion by the Libyans **[m]** was also thwarted, but their descendants would eventually triumph and rule Egypt as the XXIII and XXIV dynasties.

Halls and sanctuaries

During Coptic times most of the Osiride pillars were removed to make room for a church, and a thick layer of mud was plastered over the reliefs in the **Second Court**. Now uncovered, these depict the annual festivals of Min **[n]** and Sokar **[o]** (upper registers), and relate the events of Ramses's fifth regnal year **[p]** (lower register). As usual, Min is hung like a horse.

The now-roofless **Hypostele Hall**, beyond, once had a raised central aisle like the great hall at Karnak. To the right lie five **chapels** dedicated to Ramses, his XIX Dynasty namesake, Ptah, Osiris and Sokar. On the opposite side are several treasure chambers whose reliefs show the weighing of myrrh, gold, lapis lazuli and other valuables bestowed upon the temple **[q]**.

Beyond this lie two **smaller halls** with rooms leading off. To the left of the first hall is the funerary chamber of Ramses III **[r]**, where Thoth inscribes his name on the sacred tree of Heliopolis. The other side – open to the sky – featured an altar to Re. On the architraves **[s]**, Ramses and several baboons worship the sun. The central aisle of the next hall is flanked by statues of Ramses with Maat or Thoth. At the back are three **sanctuaries** dedicated to the Theban Triad of Mut (left), Amun (centre) and Khonsu (right). The false door behind the central one was for the use of Ramses' *ka*.

Though little remains of the mudbrick magazines and stone palace that abutted the temple, its outer wall still displays a recognisable calendar of religious festivals **[t]**.

Nag Lohlah, Malkata, Armant and Riziq

Having seen Medinet Habu temple, you'll probably feel like a cold drink at the *Habu Hotel*, across the road. Its aged owner appears in Richard Critchfield's superb book *Shahhat*, whose euphonymous hero was born in **NAG LOHLAH** village. Indeed, most of the characters described by Critchfield still live here, or in other villages such as Qurna or Berat.

Their fields have almost effaced the **remains of Malkata**, a pleasure palace erected by Amenophis III, where Akhenaten spent his youth. From the Theban Hills, however, you can still discern a huge depression where the king created a lake for Queen Tiy to sail upon in the royal barge, named *Aten Gleams*. But unless you fancy a walk through the countryside, there's no reason to make the kilometre's trek from Medinet Habu.

Between February and May, the villagers harvest their crops of sugar cane, which are transported by rail to the refinery at **ARMANT**. As the cane's value declines the longer it sits in the sun, farmers are anxious to load it quickly. But wagons are in short supply, leading to accusations of favouritism and bribery, and even fights. Armant itself was anciently known as *Pathyris* and used to have a temple built by Cleopatra and Ptolemy Caesarion (her son by Julius Caesar).

Farther south, the small town of **RIZIQ** (or *el-Rizeiqat*) deserves a mention for its annual **Moulid of Saint George**, sometime in November, which draws Copts and Muslims alike. Though worth attending, the festival is not for the squeamish, involving mass circumcisions and the slaughter of animals.

Esna

Smalltown life and ancient stone are boldly juxtaposed at **ESNA**, where a huge pit in the centre of town exposes part of the **Temple of Khnum**. Some visitors are disappointed by what they find: the only part to have been excavated is the hypostele hall, whose somewhat inferior reliefs detract from the forest of columns and lofty astronomical ceiling. That said, Esna is worth a stopover en route to the fabulous temple at Edfu, 50km upriver, and is often the last port of call for *feluccas* from Aswan. Unless you care to visit the early Saturday morning **camel market**, there's no reason to linger after seeing the temple, which takes under an hour.

Access and practicalities

Esna lies on the west bank of the Nile 54km south of Luxor and 155km north of Aswan. **Service taxis** are the fastest way of getting there from Luxor (1hr; £E2), Aswan (2–3hr; £E2.50) or Edfu (1hr; £E2), and drop you about ten minutes' walk from the temple. Though **buses** are frequent in the morning, anyone boarding at Esna could find all the seats taken, while only 2nd- and 3rd-class **trains** stop at the railway station, which is farthest from the temple (take a *caleche*; £E1–2).

There are two routes into town from the taxi depot. Either cross the canal and head 800m south past a **market** until you reach the temple, or aim for the river and walk south along the Corniche until you find the temple ticket kiosk; the temple itself is 50m inland through a covered tourist bazaar.

The first route passes the **police**; the second a **bank** (Sat–Thurs 8.30am–2pm & Sun 6–9pm & Wed 5–8pm; during Ramadan 10am–1.3pm) and some old *mash-rabiya*-ed houses along the riverside. There are no restaurants as such, but **cafés** and *taamiya* stands cluster around the central square and the **souk**. By walking a kilometre past the riverside ticket kiosk, then heading 100m inland beside a concrete building and turning left, masochists can find the fanless and grimy *El Haramin* (☎400-340), Esna's only **hotel**.

The Temple of Khnum

When Amelia Edwards visited Esna, the **Temple of Khnum** was "buried to the chin in the accumulated rubbish of a score of centuries" and built over with houses. To minimise their destruction, only a portion was excavated in the 1860s. Now ten metres below ground level, the temple resembles a pharaonic Fort Knox: its boxy mass fronted by six columns rising from a screen; the open space above them covered with wire mesh to discourage nesting birds. Visiting hours are 6am–6pm daily; tickets (£E5, students £E2.50) are sold at the riverside kiosk and by guards at the top of the stairs.

A Ptolemaic-Roman replacement for a much older structure dedicated to the ram-headed creator god of ancient myth, the temple faced eastwards and probably rivalled Edfu's for size. Since what you see is merely the Roman section (dating from the first century AD), the **facade** bears the cartouches of Claudius **[a]**, Titus **[b]** and Vespasian **[c]**, and the winged sun disc above the entrance is flanked by votive inscriptions to these emperors.

Entering the lofty **Hypostele Hall**, your eyes are drawn upwards by a forest of columns which bud and flower in variegated capitals. Their shafts are covered with festival texts (now defaced) or hiero-glyphs in the form of crocodiles **[d]** or rams **[e]**. The hall's **astronomical ceiling** rivals Dendara's for finesse and complexity, but gloom, soot and distemper render much indiscernible. However, the zodiac register **[f]** visibly crawls with two-headed snakes, winged dogs and other creatures. Note especially the pregnant hippo-goddess Tweri, whom the Greeks called Thoeris. Registers on the wall below show Septimus Severeus, Caracalla and Geta before the gods.

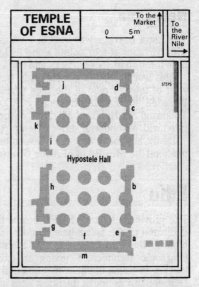

TEMPLE OF ESNA

To the Market

To the River Nile

0   5 m

STEPS

Hypostele Hall

The last Roman emperor mentioned is Decius **[g]**, whose persecution of Christians (249–51) anticipated the "Era of Martyrs" under Diocletian. Farther along **[h]** is the cartouche of Ptolemy VI Philometor (Mother Lover), whose father began the construction of Esna temple. To the right of the portal, Decius makes offerings to Khnum, including a potter's wheel **[i]**. The liveliest reliefs are near the foot of the northern wall **[j]**, where Khnum, Horus and Emperor Commodus net fish and malignant spirits. To the left of this tableau stands an ibis-headed Thoth; to the right, Seshat, goddess of writing. Around the outer walls of the temple are texts dedicated to Marcus Aurelius **[k]** and stiffly executed scenes of Titus, Domitian and Trajan smiting Egypt's foes before the gods (**[l]** and **[m]**). Several blocks from an early Christian church lie in front of the temple; notice the lion-headed font.

KHNUM AND HAPY

In Upper Egypt, **Khnum** was originally the ram-headed creator god who moulded man on a potter's wheel, and the guardian of the Nile's source (which myth assigned to the caves just beyond the First Cataract, although the ancient Egyptians must have known better).

Later, however, Khnum was demoted to an underling of Amun-Re and shared his role as river deity with **Hapy**, god of the Nile in flood, who was also believed to dwell in an island cavern near the First Cataract. Shown with a blue-green body and a female breast, wearing a crown of lotus or sedge (the heraldic plants of Upper and Lower Egypt), he should not be confused with Hapi, son of Horus, the ape-headed deity of canopic jars.

Khnum

Hapy

Near Esna

The **Esna barrage** was built in 1906 as part of a grand scheme to tame the Nile with barrages at four points along its length. Whilst cruise boats and barges can pass through its locks, trucks and carts trundle across the top of the barrage.

Also worth a passing mention is **Deir Manayus w al-Shuhada**, 6km southwest of town, a relic of the time when Esna was a centre of early Christianity. Founded in the fourth century AD, the high-walled "Monastery of Three Thousand Six Hundred Martyrs" now contains two churches, one of them decorated with a wonderful series of tenth-century murals.

Lastly, anyone in the area between the 13 and 15th days of Sha'ban might want to attend the **Moulid of al-Amir Ghanem** at ASFUN, 10km north of Esna.

Edfu

The provincial town of **EDFU** boasts the best preserved **cult-temple** in Egypt, dedicated to the falcon-headed god Horus (see box on p.350). Though actually built in the Ptolemaic era, this mammoth edifice respects all the canons of pharaonic architecture, giving an excellent idea of how most temples once looked. In terms of sheer monumental grandeur, it ranks alongside Karnak and Deir el-Bahri as one of the finest sites in the Nile Valley.

The town: practicalities

Situated on the west bank of the Nile, roughly equidistant from Luxor (115km) and Aswan (105km) and 65km north of Kom Ombo, Edfu is readily accessible by public transport. **Service taxis** from Aswan (90min; £E2), Kom Ombo (45min; £E2), Esna (1hr; £E2) or Luxor (90min; £E3.50) drop you near the bridge, about twenty minutes' walk from the temple. Cheaper, slower **buses** terminate nearer the temple. Arriving by 2nd- or 3rd-class **train** at the station across the river, you can catch a pick-up (25pt) or private taxi (£E2–3) to the site. *Caleches* shuttle furiously between the boat landing stage and the temple; the ride costs 75pt–£E2, depending on your bargaining skills.

The two simple **restaurants** in town close around 9pm. *Happy Land* offers a slightly wider menu than the *Zahrat el-Medina*, but neither is anything to rave about. There's a daily fruit and vegetable **market** along the upper stretch of Sharia Gumhorriya, and a **bank** (Sun–Thurs 8.30am–2pm) farther down the street. If forced to stay, the *Dar es-Salaam* (☎701-727) is the cleanest of Edfu's **hotels**, with sporadic hot showers (£E5 per person), but there's a friendlier ambience at the shabby *El-Medina* (☎701-326), where some rooms have balconies (singles £E6, doubles £E8, triples £E12; breakfast £E3, dinner £E5). Give the *Sami Ramis* and *El-Magdi* hotels a miss.

The Temple of Horus

From the tourist bazaar at the end of Sharia al-Maglis is an excavated compound (daily 7am–6pm; £E10 admission, students £E5) overlooked by mudbrick houses and catcalling children. Ahead stretch the sandstone enclosure walls and towering pylon of the **Temple of Horus**, which lay buried to its lintels until the 1860s,

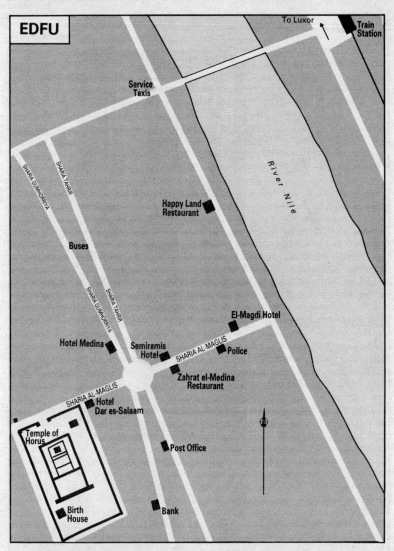

when Mariette cleared the main building; a splendid drawing by David Roberts shows the courtyard full of sand and peasant houses built atop the hypostele hall. Yet the mammoth task of excavation was nothing compared to the temple's construction, which outlasted six Ptolemies; the final touches being added by the twelfth ruler of that dynasty.

Traditionally, one entered through a huge **Pylon**, erected by Ptolemy IX before he was ousted from power by his brother Alexander in 107 BC. The pylon, too, was later usurped, for its exterior reliefs show Neos Dionysos smiting foes before

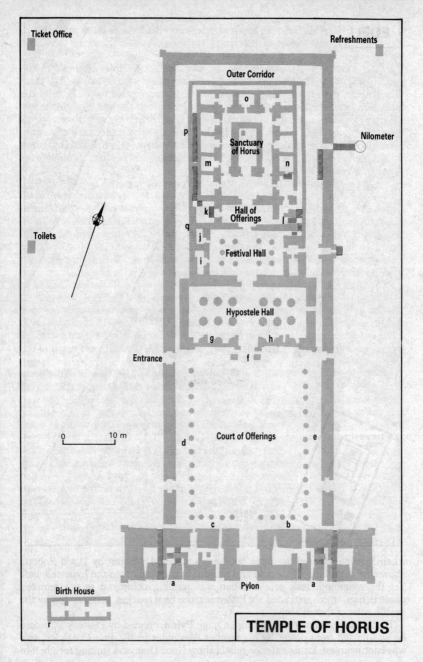

Ticket Office

Refreshments

Outer Corridor

o

p

Sanctuary
of Horus

Nilometer

m

n

k

Hall of
Offerings

l

q

j

Festival Hall

i

Toilets

Hypostele Hall

g

h

f

Entrance

0   10 m

d

Court of Offerings

e

c

b

a

a

Pylon

Birth House

r

TEMPLE OF HORUS

Horus the Elder **[a]**. But with repairs underway, visitors now enter at the north end of the immense **Court of Offerings**, entailing some backtracking to see the festival reliefs on the pylon's inner wall.

In the *Feast of the Beautiful Meeting*, Horus's barque tows Hathor's to the temple, where the deities retire to the sanctuary after suitable rituals **[b]**. Later they emerge from the temple, embark and drift downstream to the edge of the Edfu Nome, where Horus takes his leave **[c]**. Beneath the western colonnade, Ptolemy IX makes offerings to Horus, Hathor and Ihy **[d]**; his successor appears before the Edfu Triad across the way **[e]**. However, most visitors are content to photograph the pair of **Horus statues** outside the hypostele hall **[f]**. One hawk stands higher than a man, the other lies decapitated in the dust; in olden days they flanked the pylon gate.

The great **Hypostele Hall** dates from the reign of Ptolemy VII (145–116 BC), known to his contemporaries as "Fatty". Its entrance wall harbours two small rooms: the Chamber of Consecrations, where the king or his priestly stand-in dressed for rituals **[g]**; and a Library of sacred texts adorned with a relief of Seshat, the goddess of writing **[h]**. The foundation of the temple and the deification of Horus are depicted at the back of the hall. From here on you encounter the oldest section of the temple, begun by Ptolemy III in 237 BC and completed 25 years later by his son, who styled himself Philopator (Father Lover).

Try to imagine the shadowy halls during the annual festivals rhapsodised in temple texts, when the **Festival Hall** was decorated with faience, strewn with flowers and herbs and perfumed by myrrh. Incense and unguents were blended according to recipes inscribed on the walls of the Laboratory **[i]**. Non-perishable offerings were stored in the room next door **[j]**, whilst liquids, fruit and sacrificial animals were brought in through a passageway across the hall, connected to the outside world.

The sacred barques of Horus and Hathor are depicted either side of the doorway into the **Hall of Offerings**. During the New Year Festival, Horus was carried up the ascending stairway **[k]** to the rooftop; after being revitalised by the sun-disc, his statue was returned to the sanctuary via the descending stairway **[l]**. For a grand view of the temple and the Nile, bribe a guard to unlock one of the gates and let you up onto the roof. Otherwise, carry on to the **Sanctuary of Horus**, dimly illuminated by three apertures in the ceiling. Reliefs on the lower half of the right-hand wall show Philopator entering the sanctuary and worshipping Horus, Hathor and his deified parents.

Off the surrounding corridor are several chambers worth noting, but hard to see without a torch. The Linen Room **[m]** is flanked by chapels to Min and the Throne of the Gods, while the middle room of the Osiris Suite now contains a model of Horus's barque **[o]**. Finest of all is the **New Year Chapel**, with a lovely relief of the sky-goddess Nut stretched across its ceiling **[n]**.

From the Hall of Offerings, walk through into the outer corridor behind the enclosure wall and follow it round past a **Nilometer** to see two sets of reliefs along the western wall. In a scene lifted from Old Kingdom iconography, the king and Horus ensnare birds, animals and men representing evil spirits **[p]**. Farther along, you'll see tableaux from the Triumph of Horus over Seth, depicting Mystery Plays in which Seth was cast as a hippopotamus **[q]**. The annual Coronation Festival re-enacting the divine birth of Horus and the reigning pharaoh centred upon the **Birth House** outside the temple. Don't miss the reliefs of Isis suckling Horus, and an erect Amun, around the corner **[r]**.

THE CULT OF HORUS

Originally the sky-god of the Nile Valley, whose eyes were the sun and moon, the falcon deity **Horus** was soon assimilated into the Osirian myth as the child of Isis and Osiris (see p.377 and p.277). Raised in the swamps of the Delta by Isis and Hathor, Horus set out to avenge his father's murder by his uncle Seth. During their titanic struggle at Edfu, Horus lost an eye and Seth his testicles. Despite this, Seth almost prevailed until Isis intervened on her son's behalf and Osiris pronounced judgement upon them from the netherworld, exiling Seth back to the wilderness and awarding the throne to Horus. Thus good triumphed over evil and Osiris "lived" through his son.

All pharaohs claimed to be the incarnation of Horus the "living king" and reaffirmed their divine oneness in an annual **Festival of Coronation**. A live falcon was taken from the sacred aviary, crowned in the central court and then placed in an inner chamber where it "reigned" in the dark for a year as the symbol of the living king. Another event, sometimes called the **Festival of Triumph**, commemorated the Contendings of Seth and Horus in a series of Mystery Plays. At the equally lavish **Feast of the Beautiful Meeting**, his wet-nurse and wife Hathor sailed from Dendara aboard the *Lady of the Lake* to be met near Edfu by his own barque, *The First Horus*. Public ceremonies preceded their conjugal encounters in the privacy of

the temple's sanctuary. Besides these festivals, Horus also underwent a reunion with the sun-disc at New Year, similar to Hathor's at Dendara.

To complicate the cult of Horus still further, he was also associated with the Divine Ennead of Heliopolis and another variant of the Creation myth. Having distinguished the Osirian Horus from the Heliopolitan deity by terming the latter **Horus the Elder**, the Egyptians split him into archetypes such as **Herakhte** (often conjoined with Re), **Hariesis** (stressing his kinship to Isis) and **Haroeris** (see p.352). His priesthood asserted a place for Horus in the Creation myth by crediting him with building the first house amidst swamps at the dawn of the world, or even laying the Cosmic Egg whence the sun-god hatched. In rituals associated with the **Myth of the Great Cackler**, they launched a goose onto the sacred lake near Edfu temple, whose egg contained air and the potential for life – crucial elements in the world's creation.

Horus

South from Edfu: el-Kab and Silsilah

Fifteen kilometres downriver from Edfu, the east bank road between Luxor and Kom Ombo passes the site known as **EL-KAB**, once the ancient city of *Nekheb*, dedicated to the vulture-goddess of Upper Egypt. Only opened to tourists in the late 1980s, the scattered ruins are meagre compared to other sites and you have to be pretty keen to bother. The nearest village accessible by *service* taxi is EL-MAHAMID, 2.5km away. Tickets (£E2, students £E1) are sold from a kiosk by the road, which bisects the site (open daily 8am–6pm).

The site lies towards the Nile, where the vast mudbrick **walls** that once enclosed the city stand, along with the conjoined **temples** of Nekhbet and Thoth, now reduced to stumps of painted columns and a series of **crypts** (notable for a scene of baboons dancing to the rituals of Mut). Across the road and up the slope from the ticket office, other ruins are scattered eastwards across the desert. If you don't fancy hiking 3.5km to a small Chapel of Thoth and a Ptolemaic Temple of Nekhbet, there are four **tombs** dug into the nearest ridge of hills.

Silsilah

Travelling between Edfu and Kom Ombo by *felucca*, you'll pass a succession of ancient quarries, most notably at **Silsilah**, where the river is constricted by sheer sandstone cliffs and the bedrock changes from Egyptian limestone to Nubian sandstone. The site's ancient name, *Khenu* (Place of Rowing), suggests that rapids once existed here during the season of inundation. If your boatman is willing to stop, the most imposing **quarries** lie on the east bank, approached by a narrow defile down which cut stones were dragged to waiting barges. Workmen's graffiti covers the rocks, while two formal inscriptions record the cutting of stone for Aten's temple at Karnak, and the reopening of the quarry early this century to provide stone for the Esna Barrage.

The desert road – and a moulid

Lastly, real devotees of off-the-beaten-track experiences should bear in mind the desert road linking Edfu to the Red Sea Coast. Once a year, trucks decked with banners and loudspeakers convey thousands of Sufis along this route to Wadi Humaysara, high in the Red Sea Hills, for the **Moulid of Abul Hassan al-Shazli** (see p.575).

Kom Ombo

Thirty kilometres downriver from Aswan the arid hills of the Eastern Desert recede from the riverbanks and bumper crops of sugar cane are harvested on reclaimed land. Here, too, around the town of **KOM OMBO**, many of the **Nubians** displaced by Lake Nasser have settled. In ancient times this town stood at the crossroads of the caravan route from Nubia and trails from the gold mines of the Eastern Desert, becoming the capital of the Ombos Nome and a training depot for war elephants during the Ptolemaic era.

Whilst modern-day Kom Ombo is known to the *fellaheen* for its sugar refinery and annual *moulid*, tourists associate it with the Ptolemaic **Temple of Haroeris and Sobek**, 4km outside town. Unlike other temples in the valley, this still stands beside the Nile, making the approach by river one of the highlights of a *felucca* journey. (Another method is to join a day cruise from Aswan.) By way of compensation for land-based travellers, Kom Ombo is easily combined, using *service* taxis, with a visit to the Tuesday **camel market** at nearby **Darow**.

Practicalities

Kom Ombo lies along the east bank "highway" between Luxor (170km) and Aswan (45km), roughly 60km south of Edfu. Although buses and slow trains call at Kom Ombo, the best way of **getting there** is to grab a *service* taxi in Edfu (1hr; £E2) or Aswan (45min; £E1). Approaching from Aswan or Darow, you can ask to be dropped at the signposted "tembel" turn-off, 2km south of town, whence it's a 1.5-kilometre walk past cane fields to the temple site. Should you start from town instead, the cheapest method is to catch a pick-up to the ferry landing-stage 50m from the temple. Pick-ups leave from behind a white mosque with a minaret on Sharia Gumhorriya, one block off the highway, and charge 20pt per head, but don't always run all the way to the river. Alternatively, you can engage a private taxi for the trip (£E3–5 one-way).

Kom Ombo's **service taxi depot** is on 26th July Street, just south of the intersection with Sharia Gumhorriya (which crosses the highway to meet the railway station); continue south for another 350m to find the bus terminal.

Should you wish **to stay**, the *Cleopatra Hotel* (☎500-325), by the taxi depot, has clean rooms (singles £E3.50, doubles £E6; fans £E1.50) and balconies. The newly opened *Restaurant El-Noba*, 150m south of the white mosque on the highway, provides an alternative to **eating** at *fuul* and *taamiya* stands.

A small alley next to the mosque harbours a **bank** (Sun–Thurs 8.30am–2pm; 10am–1.30pm during Ramadan).

The Temple of Haroeris and Sobek

The **Temple of Haroeris and Sobek** stands on a low promontory near a bend in the river whose sandbanks were a basking place for crocodiles in ancient times. This proximity to the Nile has both preserved and damaged the site (daily 6am–6pm; £E5, students £E2.50), covering the temple with sand which protected it from Coptic iconoclasts, but also washing away its pylon and forecourt. What remains was aptly described by Amelia Edwards as a "magnificent torso"; truncated and roofless, it is still imposing, with traces of its original paint.

However, its main characteristic is its bisymmetry, with twin entrances and sanctuaries, and halls that are nominally divided down the middle. The left side is dedicated to the falcon-headed Haroeris the "Good Doctor" (a form of Horus the Elder) and his consort Ta-Sent-Nefer the "Good Sister" (an aspect of Hathor). The crocodile-god Sobek (here identified with the sun as Sobek-Re), his wife (another form of Hathor) and their son Khonsu-Hor are honoured on the right side of the temple.

THE FACADE AND HYPOSTELE HALLS

With the forecourt (added by Trajan in 14 AD) reduced to low walls and stumps of pillars, your eyes are drawn to the **facade** of the hypostele hall. Rising from a screen wall, its surviving columns burst in floral capitals beneath a chunk of cavetto cornice bearing a winged sun-disc and twin *uraei* above each portal. Bas-reliefs on the outer wall show Neos Dionysos being purified by Thoth and Horus **[a]**, and yet again in the presence of Sobek **[b]**. Around the lintels and jambs of the easternmost portal, the Nile gods bind the Two Lands together.

Wandering amidst the thicket of columns inside the **first Hypostele Hall**, notice the heraldic lily of Upper Egypt or the papyrus symbol of the Delta carved on their bases. On the inner wall of the facade are splendid paintings of Neos Dionysos' coronation before Haroeris, Sobek, Wadjet and Nekhbet (the goddesses of the north and south) **[c]**, and his appearance before Isis, Horus the Elder and a lion-headed deity **[d]**. Having propitiated four weird creatures by the easternmost door, he mingles with Nile gods and field goddesses along the side walls and appears with hymnal texts at the back of the hall, whose left side retains much of its roof, decorated with flying vultures.

Entering the older, **inner Hypostele Hall**, you'll find a relief of Sobek in his reptilian form between the two portals **[e]**. Ptolemy VII makes sacrifices to

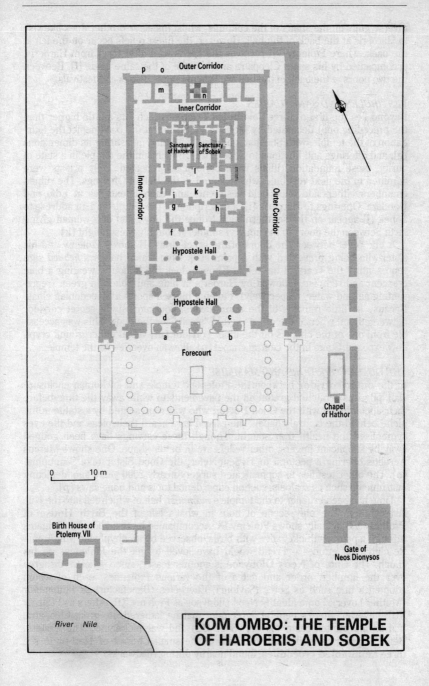

Outer Corridor

p o

m

n

Inner Corridor

Sanctuary of Haroeris Sanctuary of Sobek

Inner Corridor

Outer Corridor

l

i k j

g h

f

Hypostele Hall

e

Hypostele Hall

d c

a b

Forecourt

0 10 m

Chapel of Hathor

Birth House of Ptolemy VII

Gate of Neos Dionysos

River Nile

KOM OMBO: THE TEMPLE OF HAROERIS AND SOBEK

diverse gods on the shafts of the columns, whilst his elder brother does likewise to Haroeris at the back of the hall. However, the finest reliefs occur on the left at the back, where Ptolemy VII receives the *hps* (sword of victory) from Haroeris, accompanied by his sister Cleopatra and his wife of the same name **[f]**. Between the two doors at the back of the hall are lists of temple deities and festivals.

VESTIBULES AND SANCTUARIES

Beyond lies the first of three **vestibules** (each of which sits a little higher than the preceding one) decorated by Ptolemy VI. Scenes at the back depict the foundation of the temple, with Sheshat, goddess of writing, measuring its dimensions **[g]**; and offerings and libations to Sobek **[h]**. To maintain the temple in a state of purity, these foundation rituals were periodically repeated. Only priests were admitted to the next vestibule, which served as the Hall of Offerings. The ruined chambers either side once held vestments and sacred texts, as at Edfu and Dendara. Offerings to Haroeris **[i]**, a description of the temple and an address to Sobek **[j]** appear on the southern wall. Notice the tiny relief of a woman giving birth between the doors to the inner vestibule, at roughly waist height **[k]**.

A fine relief between the doors of the sanctuaries **[l]** shows Ptolemy and his sister-wife being presented with a palm stalk from which hangs a *heb-sed* sign representing the years of his reign. Khonsu does the honours, wearing a blue crescent and red disc, followed by Haroeris in blue and Sobek in green (representing air and water, respectively); Ptolemy himself sports a Macedonian cloak. Because so little remains of the **sanctuaries**, you can espy a secret corridor between them, whence the priests would "speak" for the gods. This was accessible from one of the chapels off the inner corridor **[m]** via an underground crypt, now exposed. Stairs in the central chapel **[n]** allow an overview of the temple.

THE OUTER CORRIDORS AND MAMMISI

In the **outer corridor** between the Ptolemaic temple and its Roman enclosure wall, pilgrims scratched graffiti on the pavements to while away the time before their appointment with the Good Doctor, who was represented by a statue in the niche behind the central chapel. The carved ears heard their pleas and the eyes symbolised the health they sought. Though these carvings have been gouged away by supplicant fingers, other reliefs are in better shape. One shows Marcus Aurelius offering a pectoral to Ta-Sent-Nefer, the Good Sister (aka Sennuphis) **[o]**. The other testifies to sophisticated surgery nearly 2000 years ago, depicting instruments such as scalpels, suction cups, dental tools and bone saws **[p]**.

Time has been crueller to the temple's *mammisi*, half of which fell into the Nile last century. The only scene of note in what's left of the **Birth House of Ptolemy VII** actually shows Ptolemy IX. Accompanied by two gods, he navigates through a papyrus thicket alive with birds, observed by an ithyphallic Min-Amun-Re clutching lettuces – Freud would have loved to get the Ptolemies on his couch. The **Gate of Neos Dionysos** is another teaser, since scholars disagree over the number, order and dates of the various Ptolemies, each of whom adopted a title such as Soter (Saviour), Euergetes (Benefactor) or Philometor (Mother Lover). Some identify Neos Dionysos as Ptolemy XII, others as Ptolemy XIII; however, there's general agreement that he fathered the great Cleopatra, had an interrupted reign (80–58, 55–51 BC) and was nicknamed The Bastard. Before leaving, peer through the bars of the small **Chapel of Hathor** to see three **mummified crocodiles**, found nearby during roadworks.

Darow Camel Market

Traditionally, **DAROW** (pronounced "De-*rau*") marks the point where Egypt begins to shade into Nubia: a distinction underlined by its camel market, which is attended by tribesmen and bactrians from the northern deserts of the Sudan. The village is a ramshackle sprawl of mudbrick compounds either side of the highway and railway line, where *service* taxis from Kom Ombo (5min; 50pt) or Aswan (40min; £E1) will drop you near a bridge that functions as a taxi depot, level crossing, bus stop and general meeting point. Private taxis in Darow might agree to take you to Kom Ombo Temple and back for about £E10.

The **Camel Market** (*Souk el-Gamal*) happens every **Tuesday** throughout the year, and maybe also on Sundays or Mondays over winter. Although hours (7am–2pm) remain constant, with activities winding down after 11am, the location of the market changes seasonally. Over winter, it's often held in two dusty compounds on the eastern outskirts of Darow (15-min walk from the main intersection; cross the bridge, walk on past the cane fields and turn right down a lane flanked by mudbrick walls). During summer, it may take place on the other side of town beyond the fruit, veg and poultry *souk* – just follow the crowds. The giveaway is truck-loads of camels bumping hither and thither along a dusty lane.

At the end you'll find several hundred camels with their forelegs hobbled in the traditional manner, and scores of drovers and buyers drinking tea and smoking *sheeshas* beneath awnings. As the principal camel market between Dongola and Cairo, Darow is a good place to do business. A prime *hageen* (riding camel) costs 25 to 50 percent less than at the Imbaba market. The buyers are Egyptian peasants who need a beast of burden, or merchants who plan to sell them for a profit in Cairo or abroad. More notable – but negligibly rewarded – are the herdsmen who drive the camels up the Forty Days Road (see box below).

The Tuesday *Souk el-Gamal* coincides with a **livestock market** where donkeys, sheep and cows jostle for space with people and trucks amidst trampled mud and dung. Over summer, the two markets are often held side by side. It's also worth catching Darow's annual **Moulid of Sidi Amr** should you happen to be around between the 13th and 15th of Sha'ban.

THE LAST FORTY DAYS ROAD

The camel trail from northern Sudan to Upper Egypt is one of the last great desert droving routes still active. The camels are reared in Sudan's Darfur and Kordofan provinces and herded 300–400km eastwards across the Libyan Desert to Dongola on the Nile, whence they follow the river into Egypt. Herdsmen call this month-long route the **Forty Days Road** (*Darb al-Arba'in*), perhaps from folk-memory of the old slave trail from Kobbe to Assyut (see p.432), which was even longer and harder.

Now, as then, the drovers are usually Bishariyyn or Rizayqat nomads, who sometimes appear at Egyptian markets in their traditional garb of flowing trousers, woollen cloak, dagger and sword (serious weapons like AK-47s are stashed before crossing the border). For what amounts to three months' work in atrocious conditions, each drover receives the equivalent of £50 sterling, the guide (*khebir*) about £150. The camel owners are town-dwelling Sudanese merchants who fly up to supervise the sale. But with drought and famine ravaging northwestern Sudan, herds dying and nomads fleeing to the towns, the last Forty Days Road may soon follow its predecessor into oblivion.

Aswan

Egypt's southernmost city and ancient frontier town has the loveliest setting on the Nile, and all the charm that Luxor lacks. At **ASWAN** the deserts close in on the river, confining its sparkling blue between smooth amber sand and rugged extrusions of granite bedrock. Lateen-sailed *feluccas* glide past the ancient ruins and gargantuan rocks of Elephantine Island; palms and tropical shrubs softening the islands and embankments till intensely blue skies fade into soft-focus dusks. The city's **ambience** is palpably African; its Nubian inhabitants are lither and darker than the *Saiyidis*, with different tastes and customs. Women dressed in flowing *tobes* can be seen drinking beer with men, for example: louche behaviour by the standards of provincial Egypt, but quite acceptable here.

Although its own monuments are insignificant compared to Luxor's, Aswan is the base for **excursions** to the **temples of Philae and Kabasha**, near the great dams beyond the First Cataract, and the Sun Temple of Ramses II at **Abu Simbel**, far to the south. It can also serve for day trips to Darow camel market, Kom Ombo, Edfu and Esna – the main temples between here and Luxor. But the classic approach is to travel downriver by *felucca*, experiencing the Nile's moods and scenery as travellers have for millennia. The delights and pitfalls of **felucca journeys** are described on p.372; the uncertainties of travelling **on to the Sudan** on p.388. However, Aswan itself is so laid-back that one could easily spend a week here simply hanging out, never mind going anywhere.

Climate

The time of year is a major influence on people's level of activity. Situated near the Tropic of Cancer, Aswan is hot and dry nearly all the time, with average daily **temperatures** ranging from a delicious 23–30°C in the winter to a searing 38–54°C over summer. Late autumn and spring are perfect times to visit, being less

---

THE NUBIANS

Nubians – the primary people of the Nile between Aswan and Khartoum – are seemingly unrelated to other Nilotic or desert tribes of the same region. They have lived along the Nile's middle reaches as long ago as anyone can establish. In ancient times, when the region was known as **Kush**, the pharaohs used the Nubians as mercenaries and traders – roles in which they are often depicted in tomb and temple art. Several of the XXV Dynasty ("Ethiopian" or "Kushite") pharaohs were probably of Nubian birth, and some claim that Cleopatra (or *Kilu baba tarati* – "Beautiful Woman") was a Nubian born near Wadi Halfa.

Traditional Nubian life centred around **villages** of extended families, each with its own compound of domed houses. The people made a livelihood farming the verges of the river, planting date palms, corn and *durra* melons, as well as fishing and transporting trade goods. Socially and spiritually, the Nile formed the basis of their existence. The whole village celebrated births, weddings and circumcision ceremonies with Nile rituals, and, despite converting first to Christianity and then to Islam, they retained a belief in water spirits, petitioning them for favours.

This way of life – which had existed pretty much unchanged for five millennia – was shattered by the **Aswan Dams**. The first dam, built in 1902 and successively raised, forced the Nubians to move onto higher, unfertile ground; unable to subsist

crowded than the peak winter period, yet not so enervating as summer, when long siestas, cold showers and air conditioning commend themselves, and the number of tourists dwindles to a minimum.

Aswan in history
Elephantine Island – opposite modern Aswan in the Nile – has been settled since time immemorial, and its fortress-town of *Yebu* (or *Abu*) became the border post between Egypt and Nubia early in the Old Kingdom. Local governors, known as the "Guardians of the Southern Gates", were responsible for border security and trade with Nubia, huge quarries for fine red granite, and mining in the desert hinterland of amethysts, quartzite, copper, tin and malachite. Military outposts further south could summon help from the Yebu garrison by signal fires and an Egyptian fleet patrolled the river between the First and Second Cataracts.

Besides this, Yebu was an important cult-centre, for the Egyptians believed that the Nile welled up from subterranean caverns at the First Cataract, just upriver (see p.371). Its local **deities** were Hapy and Satet, god of the Nile flood and goddess of its fertility, though the region's largest temple honoured Khnum, the provincial deity (see Esna section, preceding).

During settled periods, the vast trade in ivory, slaves, gold, silver, incense, exotic animal skins and feathers spawned a **market town** on the east bank (slightly south of modern Aswan, its linear descendant), but the island remained paramount throughout classical times, when it was known by its Greek appellation, *Seyene*. In the Ptolemaic era, the Alexandrian geographer **Eratosthenes** (276–196 BC) heard of a local well into which the sun's rays fell perpendicularly at midday on the summer solstice, leaving no shadow; from this he deduced that Seyene lay on the Tropic of Cancer, concluded that the world was round and calculated its diameter with nearly modern accuracy. (Since that time, the Tropic of Cancer has moved further south.)

on agriculture, many of the menfolk left for Cairo and the cities, sending back remittances to keep the villages going. With construction of the High Dam, the Nubians' traditional homeland was entirely submerged, displacing the entire 120,000-strong community. Around half of the villagers moved north, settling around Aswan and Kom Ombo, where the government provided homes and assistance with agriculture and irrigation. The rest were repatriated to the Sudan where many ended up at Khashm el-Quirba beside the Blue Nile, 1000 miles to the south, where they today find themselves embroiled in the Sudan's civil war.

In Egypt, the **post-dam Nubian community** has done reasonably well. Many have taken advantage of higher education and business opportunities, making their mark in government and commerce. Others from the first wave of emigration continue to provide the backbone of Cairo's janitors and servants; Nubians as a whole have always been noted for their honesty and reliability. Remarkably, the community has maintained its cultural identity, with the resettled villages (which took their old names) acting as guardians of the old traditions.

A few Nubian phrases
Erraigray minnabou?	How are you?	*Irr sharrifeso*	I am honoured
Anta mezhroul?	Are you busy?	*Afwan*	Thank you
Togis	Sit down	*Ena fiadr*	Goodbye

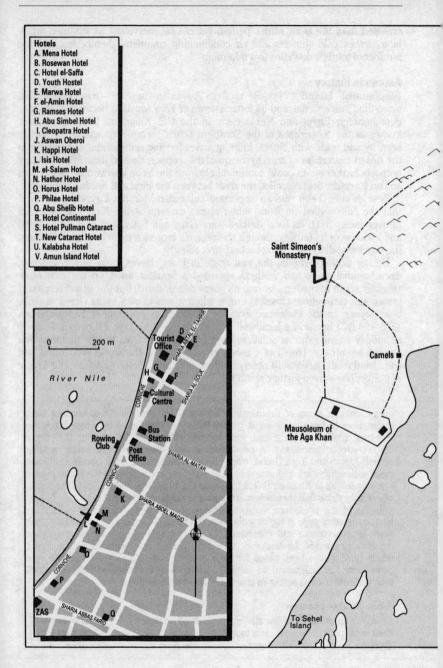

Hotels
A. Mena Hotel
B. Rosewan Hotel
C. Hotel el-Saffa
D. Youth Hostel
E. Marwa Hotel
F. el-Amin Hotel
G. Ramses Hotel
H. Abu Simbel Hotel
I. Cleopatra Hotel
J. Aswan Oberoi
K. Happi Hotel
L. Isis Hotel
M. el-Salam Hotel
N. Hathor Hotel
O. Horus Hotel
P. Philae Hotel
Q. Abu Shelib Hotel
R. Hotel Continental
S. Hotel Pullman Cataract
T. New Cataract Hotel
U. Kalabsha Hotel
V. Amun Island Hotel

Saint Simeon's
Monastery

Camels

Mausoleum of
the Aga Khan

0   200 m

River Nile

Tourist
Office

Cultural
Centre

Bus
Station

Rowing
Club

Post
Office

SHARIA SA'D EL-TAHRIR

SHARIA AL-SOUK

SHARIA AL-MATAR

SHARIA ABDEL MAGID

SHARIA ABBAS FARID

CORNICHE

CORNICHE

CORNICHE

ZAS

To Sehel
Island

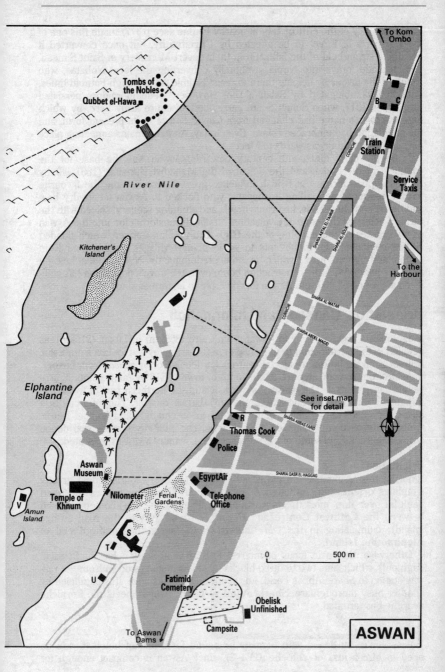

To Kom
Ombo

A

B C

Train
Station

Service
Taxis

River Nile

To the
Harbour

*Kitchener's
Island*

J

D

D

*Elphantine
Island*

See inset map
for detail

N

R

Thomas Cook

Police

EgyptAir

Aswan
Museum

Telephone
Office

Temple of
Khnum

Nilometer

Ferial
Gardens

V

*Amun
Island*

S

T

U

0   500 m

Fatimid
Cemetery

Obelisk
Unfinished

To Aswan
Dams

Campsite

ASWAN

SHARIA MATAR EL TAHRIR

SHARIA AL SOQA

CORNICHE

SHARIA AL MATAR

SHARIA ABDEL MAGID

CORNICHE

SHARIA ABBAS FARID

SHARIA QASR EL-HAGGAG

Qubbet el-Hawa

Tombs of
the Nobles

The potency of the **cult of Isis** at nearby **Philae** (see p.377) made this one of the last parts of Egypt to be affected by **Christianity**, but once converted it became a stronghold of the faith. From their desert Monastery of Saint Simeon, monks made forays into Nubia, eventually converting the local Nobatae, who returned the favour by helping them to resist Islamic rule through Fatimid times, until finally subjugated by Salah al-Din. However, Bedouin raiders persisted through to 1517, when Sultan Selim garrisoned an entire army here, by which time the town's name had changed from Coptic *Sawan* to its present form, and the population had embraced **Islam**. Even today, Aswan remains a meeting place for pilgrims trekking eastwards to Mecca.

From the early nineteenth century onwards, Aswan was the base for the conquest of the Sudan and the defeat of the Mahadist Uprising (1881–98) by Anglo-Egyptian forces. As British influence grew, it also became the favourite **winter resort** of rich, ailing Europeans, who flocked to Aswan for its dry heat and therapeutic hot sands, luxurious hotels and stunning scenery, spiced with the thrill of being "at the edge of civilisation". Its final transformation into the Aswan of today owes to the building of the **High Dam**, 15km upriver, which flooded Nubia, compelling its inhabitants to settle in new villages built around Kom Ombo and Aswan itself, which is now predominantly Nubian (see box on previous page). With the construction boom over, the town's population has stabilised at around 55,000, and Aswan has reverted to its former languor.

Orientation, transport and information

Most tourists travel directly to Aswan from Cairo (889km) or Luxor (215km), as detailed in the introduction to this chapter; a few arrive by *service* taxi from Esna, Edfu or Kom Ombo (see respective entries for details), or by *felucca* from Luxor.

Aside from **Aswan airport**, 23km south of town (£E10 by taxi), points of arrival are fairly central. The **railway station** lies in the northern part of town, five minutes' walk from the Corniche or Aswan's bazaar quarter. The inter-city **bus station** is smack in the middle of town, at the lower end of Sharia Abtal el-Tahrir, whilst **feluccas** tie up alongside the Corniche. The inter-city **service taxi** depot, across the tracks and south of the railway station, is more awkwardly located.

Orientation

Ignoring the residential and industrial suburbs (as every tourist does) greatly simplifies orientation. Although Aswan's sinuous **Corniche** follows the riverbank for over 4km, most things worth noting lie along the two-kilometre stretch between the **Cultural Centre** and **Ferial Gardens** (where the road swings inland), culminating in the *Old Cataract Hotel* facing the southern end of **Elephantine Island**.

Otherwise, the main focus of interest is **Sharia al-Souk** (aka Sharia Sa'ad Zaghloul), which runs two to three blocks inland as it snakes down from the railway station to Sharia Abbas Farid. For about half this distance, it is paralleled by another busy thoroughfare, **Sharia Abtal el-Tahrir**, which meets the Corniche near the bus terminal.

Getting around

Unless you're burdened with luggage or bound for a distant hotel, there's no need to hire a **taxi** or **caleche** (£E1–2), since Aswan is compact enough for getting around on foot. Alternatively, **bicycles** can be rented from shops on Abtal el-Tahrir (100m south of the *Ramses Hotel*) and Sharia al-Matar (opposite the King Aswan Lab) for roughly £E1 an hour, £E10 per day. However, bikes are virtually irrelevant until you want to visit Philae, Kalabsha or Abu Simbel; all the attractions close at hand are reached by river – mostly by **felucca**.

For better or for worse, **felucca** are inseparable from the Aswan experience. It's wonderfully relaxing to drift downstream whilst egrets swoop overhead, or tack between rocky islands, but, on the downside, it's all too easy to get irked by boatmen who fritter away time before demanding *baksheesh* for an unfulfilled itinerary, or wearied of the persistent touts along the Corniche. Despite **rates** being fixed by the authorities at £E10 for an hour's sailing, or £E26 for a three-hour tour of Elephantine and Kitchener islands and the west bank sites (regardless of the number of passengers), market rules and haggling prevail. If big-spenders abound, boatmen will sniff at official rates; if business is slack, they'll undercut each other. Unsurprisingly, prices are highest at the landing stage beneath the luxurious *Old Cataract Hotel*. (Longer felucca trips to Sehel Island, or downriver towards Luxor, are covered on p.372).

Information and assistance

The current rates of hire for *feluccas* and private taxis (to Philae, Abu Simbel etc) can be checked at the **tourist office** (daily 9am–2pm & 6–8pm; during Ramadan 9am–3pm; ☎323-297). Both the officers, Farag Gomaa and Shoukry Sa'ad, can advise on just about anything. Shoukry wishes visitors to know that the townsfolk are offended by immodest attire and brusque requests, and would rather talk about deeper matters than prices. Be polite and stay for a chat once he's answered your questions. Above the office is the main branch of the **tourist police** (☎324-393/323-163; open 24hr), which maintains another office on the south side of the railway station.

All telephone numbers in the Aswan area are prefixed ☎097.

Accommodation

As in Luxor, the **accommodation** situation varies greatly with time of year. Although high season officially runs from October 1 to April 30, the squeeze is really only felt from December to January (especially just after New Year), when many hotels are block-booked by Egyptian groups and it's advisable to make **reservations**. The nadir of the low season (May 1–Nov 30) comes in the summer, when most places are empty and desperate for business. Many offer **reductions** of fifteen to fifty percent or will waive service charges and taxes (sometimes amounting to twenty percent) after a bit of haggling. With temperatures in the 50s°C, A/C (or at least a fan) is almost essential in summer.

Prices quoted below are for current high season (winter) rates.

Cheap places

Mena Hotel (A), 250m walk from the railway station (☎324-388). Immaculate, well-furnished rooms, some with double beds, most with A/C, cleaned daily and all with baths. Table tennis and roof garden. Singles (£E7), doubles (£E12) and five-person suites (£E28); A/C £E2 extra. Small breakfast included.

Rosewan Hotel (B), near the railway station (☎324-497). Turn right as you leave the station, head past a petrol station and take the next left; the hotel is on the right. Tidy and welcoming. Large singles (£E9) and doubles (£E12) with fans; private bathrooms £E5 extra.

El Saffa Hotel (C), near the railway station (☎312-172). Darker, dingier rooms (£E3–5) with fans and sinks, worth considering only if the *Rosewan* is full.

Youth Hostel (D), Sharia Abtal el-Tahrir (☎322-313). A grungy fleapit with beds in crowded dorms (£E2–4); lock out 10am–2pm; 11pm curfew . . . forget it.

Marwa Hotel (E), Sharia Abtal el-Tahrir. Across the road from the hostel, near a mosque and cinema (noisy at dawn and late at night). Clean, simple rooms with fans, and a hot shower on every floor. Doubles £E10, triples £E12.

El-Amin Hotel (F), Sharia Abtal el-Tahrir (☎323-189). Just off the bazaar. Singles £E7, doubles £E13 (£E16 with shower), triples £E18 (£E21). Reductions negotiable.

Abu Shelib Hotel (Q), Sharia Abbas Farid (☎323-051). Clean, simple rooms with fans and bathrooms. Singles £E10–15, doubles £E15–21, triples £E23.

Hotel Continental (R), just off the Corniche (☎322-311). A wonderful location, but totally grungy: fleas and roaches, filthy loos and cold-water bathrooms; tables or planks sometimes substitute for beds (£E4 upwards). The café out front is a budget travellers' rendezvous.

Mid-range

Ramses Hotel (G), Sharia Abtal el-Tahrir (☎324-000; telex 23602 PBASW UN). Comfy A/C rooms with balcony, TV, phone and fridge. Most singles (£E40) and doubles (£E53) overlook the Nile; rear-facing rooms are slightly cheaper. Restaurant, bar and disco.

Abu Simbel Hotel (H), Corniche (☎322-888; telex 23602 PBSAW UN). A/C singles (£E25), doubles (£E30–35) and triples (£E40) with private bathrooms and great views of the Nile. Patisserie, nightclub, bank and shady gardens. Breakfast included.

Cleopatra Hotel (I), Corniche (☎324-001; telex 23602 PBSAW UN). Near the *souk*, this very salubrious establishment has A/C singles (£E70) and doubles (£E90) with phones and showers, plus a juice bar and restaurant.

Happi Hotel (K), off the Corniche (☎322-028; telex 23602 PBSAW UN). Cramped singles (£E22) and roomier doubles (£E30), all with phones and bathrooms. Most have A/C (for a few pounds extra) and a balcony with river views. Reasonable evening meals.

El Salaam Hotel (M), Corniche (☎322-651). Decent Nile-facing singles (£E19), doubles (£E30) and triples (£E35), but the back rooms are dark and dingy. All rooms have baths. Breakfast included.

Hathor Hotel (N), Corniche (☎322-590). A friendlier place with a sun roof. Simple, clean rooms with private bathroom, A/C or fans. Singles (£E17) and doubles (£E25) overlooking the river; rooms at the back are a few pounds cheaper.

Horus Hotel (O), off the Corniche (☎323-323). Pleasant rooms with A/C, bath, and balconies overlooking the Nile. Singles £E17, doubles £E25; breakfast included.

Hotel Philae (P), Corniche (☎322-117). Small, clean rooms with showers; fans or A/C for a modest surcharge. Singles £E18, doubles £E25, triples £E32.

Upmarket hotels

Aswan Oberoi (J), Elephantine Island (☎323-455; telex 92120 OBEROI UN). Resembling an airport control tower, this five-star blight is reached by a ferry got up like a pharaonic barge. Rooms with all mod cons (singles US$120, doubles US$140), or villas with private gardens. Restaurants, nightclub and disco.

Isis Hotel (L), beside the Oberoi landing stage (☎324-905; telex 23459 ISFMT UN). Single (US$75) and double (US$90) bungalows with A/C, TV and other facilities, in a garden.

Hotel Pullman Cataract (S), by the Ferial Gardens (☎323-222; telex 92720 ASCTE UN). Known to all as the "Old Cataract", this splendid Edwardian-Moorish relic has river-facing rooms with glorious views, and others overlooking a fine garden; the former are dearest. Singles US$65–80, doubles US$70–100.

New Cataract Hotel (T), by the Ferial Gardens (☎333-222; telex 92720 ASCTE UN). A modern, *PLM*-managed block that shares facilities with the *Old Cataract*. Nile-facing singles (US$70), doubles (US$120) and suites (US$150) are about ten percent dearer than rooms overlooking the garden. Restaurants, bar and 24-hour café. Olympic-sized pool.

Kalabsha Hotel (U), inland of the above (☎323-434; telex 92720 ASCTE UN). This *Pullman*-managed block has A/C singles (US$45) and doubles (US$60), a bank, bar and restaurant-nightclub. Ask at reception for a free pass to use the *New Cataract* pool.

Amun Island Hotel (V), on its own island, across from the *Old Cataract* (☎322-555; telex CMAMN UN). A Club Med resort set amid a lush garden and exotic bird life; pool, bars and restaurant. A/C singles (US$70) and doubles (US$90) with private bathrooms.

Camping

Aswan Campsite. Situated outside town near the Unfinished Obelisk, this site is hopelessly inconvenient unless you've got private transport, and chiefly serves trans-African Safari groups. It costs £E3 to pitch a tent in the spacious but shadeless compound, which has showers and toilets (vendors sell firewood); motorbikes (£E2), cars (£E5) and caravans (£E10).

Aswan's bazaar and Corniche

Aswan's **bazaar** is renowned as the best in Egypt outside Cairo, and until a few years ago was largely uncorrupted by tourism. Traditional wares such as spices, ebony, basketwork and rugs are still in evidence, but souvenir shops are gradually forcing humdrum vendors into the alleys off Sharia al-Souk. Nonetheless, it's a pleasure to wander around, with its smells and colours evoking the Sudan and camel caravans across the Sahara. Fresh produce is chiefly sold around the junction of Saiyida Nafisa Street (running inland from the *Isis Hotel*) and Sharia al-Souk, and at the station end of the latter. Shop in the morning, since quality drops as the temperature rises. Conversely, the spice, textiles and jewellery *souks* are barely active before 3pm, but thronged with shoppers after sundown.

The city's **Corniche** is the finest in the country, less for its architecture (which is mostly modern and undistinguished) than for the superb vista of Elephantine Island, *feluccas* gliding over the water like quill pens across a page, and the tawny wastes of the Western Desert on the far bank. Unfortunately, you can't walk along the esplanade without being pestered by boatmen or their juvenile sidekicks; stay on the other side of the street and they'll leave you alone. Sunset is best enjoyed from the rockbound **Ferial Gardens** or the grand terrace of the **Old Cataract Hotel** (featured in the movie *Death on the Nile*). After dusk, locals promenade the Corniche in spotless white *galabiyyas* or gorgeously patterned *tobes*, as coolly elegant as the tourists look dishevelled. For several hours every evening, hidden spotlights turn the Tombs of the Nobles into a visual approximation of Moon Base Alpha.

Elephantine Island

Elephantine Island takes its name from the huge black rocks clustered around its southern end, which resemble a herd of pachyderms bathing in the river. Its spectacular beauty is marred only by the towering *Aswan Oberoi Hotel*, reached by its own private ferry and cut off from the rest of the island by a lofty fence.

South of this, three **Nubian villages** nestle amidst lush palm groves, their houses painted sky blue, pink or yellow and often decorated with *Hadj* scenes. Alongside the houses run mudbrick alleys where chickens peck around the dust and tethered goats chew garbage. The villagers prefer foreigners to keep out unless invited in, as they don't want to become a tourist sideshow. However, this doesn't cause any problems since all the tourist attractions are at the southern end of the island, accessible by public **ferries** from the landing stage near *EgyptAir* (every 15min 6am–midnight; 25pt) or *feluccas* (negotiable rates), both of which dock just below the Aswan Museum.

The Aswan Museum

The small **Aswan Museum** (daily 8am–5pm; £E1.50 ticket also valid for the ruins farther south) casts light on the island's past, when its southern end was occupied by the town of *Yebu* (meaning both "elephant" and "ivory" in the ancient Egyptian language). Exhibits on the ground floor include a careworn-looking Governor Ameni sculpted in black granite; assorted jewellery and pots; and slate palettes in the form of birds, fish, buffalo and hippos. The basement displays a golden bust of Khnum, a mummified ram (his sacred animal) once interred in a gilded sarcophagus, and several human mummies. Hopes of expanding this into a Museum of Nubia, detailing the region's culture and the salvaging of its ancient monuments, are currently stymied by lack of cash.

Originally the villa of Sir William Willcocks, designer of the first Aswan Dam, the verandahed house overlooks fragrant, shady **gardens**. Come back and enjoy them once you've visited the Nilometer and the ruins of Yebu.

The Nilometer

In ancient times the **Nilometer** at Aswan was the first to measure the river's rise, enabling priests to calculate the height of the inundation, crop yields over the next year and the rate of taxation (which peasants paid in kind). Ninety enclosed rock-hewn steps lead down to a square shaft by the riverside; the stair walls are graduated in Arabic, Roman and (extremely faint) pharaonic numerals, reflecting its usage in ancient times and during the late nineteenth century.

Should you approach the Nilometer by river, notice the rock embankments to the south, which bear **inscriptions** from the reigns of Tuthmosis III, Amenophis III, and the XXVII Dynasty ruler Psammetichus II. To reach the Nilometer from the museum, follow the path southwards for 300m to find a sycamore tree (pharaonic symbol of the fruitful earth-goddess) which shades the structure. Its *gaffir* usually keeps the barbed-wire gate shut in the hope of exacting *baksheesh*.

The ruins of Yebu

The southern end of the island is littered with the **ruins** of the ancient town, which covered nearly two square kilometres by Ptolemaic times. To the southwest of the Nilometer, a massive platform and foundation blocks mark the site of the **Temple of Khnum**, god of the Aswan Nome, founded in the Old Kingdom (when it accounted for two-thirds of the town's area) but entirely rebuilt during the XXX Dynasty. On its north side are the remains of pillars painted by the Romans, and Greek inscriptions; to the west stands the imposing gateway added by Alexander II, shown here worshipping Khnum.

Depending on the state of excavations, parts of the area to the north may be off-limits. Immediately to the north lies a Greco-Roman **Necropolis of Sacred Rams**, unearthed in 1906. Further to the northwest stands the small **Temple of Hekayib**, a VI Dynasty Nomarch buried in the Tombs of the Nobles (see overpage) who was later deified; the stelae and inscriptions found here by Labib

Habachi in 1946 revealed much about Aswan during the Middle Kingdom. However, the most interesting site lies due east of here.

This is the **Temple of Satet** (currently closed to visitors). Built by Queen Hatshepsut around 1490 BC, it was the last of more than thirty such temples on this site, dating back four millennia, which were dedicated to the goddess who incarnated the fertile aspect of the innundation. Beneath the temples, German archaeologists have found a shaft leading nineteen metres into the granite bedrock, where a natural **whirl hole** is thought to have amplified the sounds of the rising water table (the first indication of the life-giving annual flood) and been revered as the "Voice of the Nile". Although the High Dam has since silenced its voice, a half-buried statue near the temple still draws new brides and barren women longing for the gift of fertility.

To the southwest of Khnum's Temple, the layered **remains of ancient houses** have yielded Aramaic papyri attesting to a sizeable **Jewish colony** on Elephantine in the sixth century BC. A military order by Darius II permitting the Yebu garrison to observe Passover in 419 BC suggests that they defended the southernmost border of the Persian empire. Although nothing remains of their temple to Yahweh, the German team have used leftover blocks from Kalabsha to reconstruct a **Ptolemaic sanctuary** with decorations added by the Nubian Pharaoh Arkamani in the third century BC, at the southern tip of the island.

The rocky passage between Elephantine and Amun Island looks its best from a *felucca*. If you're not already waterborne, the surrounding coves are frequented by lads who'll happily sail you across to Kitchener's Island or the west bank, but drive a hard bargain. **Amun Island** itself features a reclusive *Club Med*.

Kitchener's Island

Almost hidden from town by the bulk of Elephantine, the smaller, lusher "Island of Plants" (*Geziret al-Nabatat*) is still commonly referred to by tourists as **Kitchener's Island**. Presented with the island in gratitude for his military exploits in the Sudan, Consul-General Kitchener indulged his passion for exotic flora, importing shrubs and seeds from as far afield as India and Malaysia. This beautiful island-wide **botanical garden** (daily 8am–sunset; £E5) is an ideal place to spend the afternoon, having seen the other sites. Colourful **bird life** flits through the trees and hundreds of white ducks paddle in a closed-off cove at the southern end of the island, where a duck-breeding institute is ensconced.

The island is only accessible by *felucca* (£E2–5 from the west bank or Elephantine) or private motorboats (roughly £E28 an hour for 10–12 passengers; groups assemble on the Corniche). If you wait until 7pm, when the Egyptians who work here head home, you can catch a rowing boat back to Elephantine for 50pt.

The west bank: the Aga Khan Mausoleum, Saint Simeon's Monastery and the Tombs of the Nobles

The main attractions on the **west bank** of the river are the **Mausoleum of the Aga Khan** and the desert **Monastery of Saint Simeon**. Unless you're prepared to hike for over two kilometres across the hills, the more northerly **Tombs of the Nobles** are best visited as a separate excursion. When negotiating a price for a *felucca*, be sure to establish how long you plan to spend at both sites.

The Agha Khan's Mausoleum

Just uphill from the embankment is a walled estate comprising a private villa and riverside garden, and a stairway ascending the barren hillside to the **Mausoleum of the Aga Khan** (Tues–Sun 9am–4.45pm; free). Outwardly modelled on the Fatimid tombs of Cairo, its open court culminates in a Carrara marble *mihrab* and sarcophagus, enshrining the late Aga Khan III (1877–1957), the forty-eighth Imam of the Isma'ili sect of Shi'ite Muslims, who was weighed in jewels for his diamond jubilee in 1945.

The Agha Khan was initially drawn to Aswan by its climate and hot sands, which relieved his rheumatism; subsequently he fell in love with its beauty, built a villa and spent every winter here. His widow, the Begum, still does likewise, and ensures that a fresh red rose is placed on his sarcophagus every day; legend has it that when none were available in Egypt, a rose was flown in by private plane from Paris on six successive days. Since the mausoleum is a holy place for Shi'ite Muslims, you will not be admitted unless decorously dressed.

The Monastery of Saint Simeon

Unless you bunk over the wall that the Begum erected to prevent tourists from simply walking along the ridge (15min), the ruined **Monastery of Saint Simeon** (*Deir Anba Samaan*; daily 9am–4pm; £E1.50, students 75pt) must be approached from the valley below. You can either slog uphill through soft sand (25min) or hire a camel from the pack near the landing stage (£E10 round-trip with an hour's waiting; a camel seats two); the latter is more fun and less effort, but whichever way you approach, it's a good idea to bring water.

Founded in the seventh century and rebuilt in the tenth, the monastery crowns the head of a desert valley, which used to be cultivated down to the river's edge. Built like a fortress, it was originally dedicated to Anba Hadra, a local saint of the fourth century who encountered a funeral procession the day after his wedding and decided to renounce the world for a hermit's cave before the marriage was consummated. From here, monks made evangelical forays into Nubia, where they converted the Kingdom of the Nobatae to Christianity. After the Muslim conquest, the Nobatae used the monastery as a base during their own incursions into Egypt, until Salah al-Din had it destroyed in 1173.

One of the *gaffirs* will show you around the split-level complex, whose lower storeys are made of stone, the upper ones of mudbrick. The now-roofless **Basilica** bears traces of frescoes of the Apostles, their faces scratched out by Muslim iconoclasts. In a nearby chamber with a font you're shown the place where Saint Simeon (about whom little is known) used to stand sleeplessly reading the Bible, with his beard tied to the ceiling so as to deliver a painful tug if he nodded off. The central **Keep** has room for 300 monks sleeping five to a cell, a tunnel-like refectory, bathhouse, ovens and bakeries (notice the millstones). Beware of sheer drops when exploring. At sunset the surrounding desert turns madder-red and violet; hawks can sometimes be seen soaring on the thermals.

The Tombs of the Nobles

Relatively few tourists bother with the **Tombs of the Nobles** (daily 8am–4pm; £E1.50, students 75pt; photo permit £E10), hewn into the hillside further up the west bank. If you're curious, they are best reached via *baladi* **ferries** from the Corniche near *Seti Tours*; these run every half-hour from 6am to 6pm, then hourly till 9pm (50pt). In order to combine a visit with the monastery and mausoleum, start early with the tombs, then ascend to the Muslim **Qubbet el-Hawa** (Tomb of the Wind) and walk across the desert to Saint Simeon's (roughly 40min; bring plenty of water).

The tombs lie at different heights (**Old and Middle Kingdom** ones upper-most, **Roman** tombs nearest the waterline), and are numbered in ascending order from south to north. Taking the path up from the ticket kiosk you reach the high-numbered ones first.

TOMB OF SIRENPUT I

Turn right at the top of the steps and follow the path downhill around the cliffside to find the tomb of **Sirenput I**, overseer of the priests of Khnum and Satet and Guardian of the South during the XII Dynasty. The six pillars of its vestibule bear portraits and biographical texts. On the left-hand wall he watches bulls fighting, and spears fish from a papyrus raft accompanied by his sandal-bearer, sons and dog. On the opposite wall he's portrayed with his mutt and bow-carrier, and also sitting above them in a garden with his mother, wife and daughters, being enter-tained by singers; the lower register shows two men gambling. Amongst the badly damaged murals in the hall beyond, you can just discern fowlers with a net (on the lower right wall), a hieroglyphic biography (left), and a marsh-hunting scene (centre). Beyond lies a chapel with a false door set into the rear niche; the corridor to the left leads to the burial chamber.

TOMB OF PEPI NAKHT (#35) AND HARKHUF

To reach the other tombs from Sirenput I's, return to the top of the steps and follow the path southwards. Amongst a cluster of tombs to the left of the steps are two rooms ascribed to Hekayib (whose cult-temple stands on Elephantine), called here by his other name, **Pepi-Nakht**. As overseer of foreign troops during the long reign of Pepi II (VI Dynasty), he led colonial campaigns in Asia and Nubia, which are related on either side of the door of the left-hand room.

A bit further south lies the (unnumbered) tomb of **Harkhuf**, who held the same position under Pepi I, Merenre and Pepi II. A badly eroded hieroglyphic biography just inside the entrance mentions his gifts to the young Pepi II, which included incense, leopard skins and ebony, and a "dancing dwarf from the land of spririts" (thought to be a pygmy from Equatorial Africa).

TOMB OF SIRENPUT II (#31)

The largest and best-preserved tomb belongs to **Sirenput II**, who held the same offices as his father under Amenemhat II, during the apogee of the Middle Kingdom. Beyond its vestibule (with an offerings slab between the second and third pillars on the right) lies a corridor with six niches containing Osiride statues of Sirenput, still brightly coloured like his portraits on the four pillars of the chapel, where the artist's grid-lines are visible in places. Best of all is the recess at the back, where Sirenput appears with his wife and son (left), attends his seated mother in a garden (right), and receives flowers from his son (centre). Notice the elephant in the upper left corner of this tableau.

TOMB OF MEKHU (#25) AND SABNI (#26)

At the top of the double ramps ascending the hillside (up which sarcophagi were dragged) are the adjacent tombs of a father and son, which are chiefly interesting for their story. After his father **Mekhu** was killed in Nubia, **Sabni** mounted a punitive expedition which recovered the body. As a sign of respect, Pepi II sent his own embalmers to mummify the corpse; Sabni travelled to Memphis to personally express his thanks with gifts, as related by an inscription at the entrance to his tomb. Both tombs are crudely constructed and decorated, with small obelisks at their entrances, and twin vestibules which form a single rectangular room. Sabni's chapel has columns painted with fishing and fowling scenes.

Eating out

Eating out in Aswan is marginally better than in Luxor, chiefly due to abundant fresh fish and Nubian dishes such as okra in spicy tomato sauce or meaty *kab hala* stew. The following **restaurants** are listed according to location (north–south) rather than cost; most lie along the Corniche. Places marked with an asterisk sell beer and (maybe) wine.

Roseway, next to a cinema on Abtal el-Tahrir, north of the railway station. Handy for those staying at the *Mena Hotel*. Fish and chips (£E5) and seasonal specials.

El Gomhoreya, on the left in front of the station. Tables outside and fans indoors. Mostly does chicken and caters to tourists; no longer cheap.

Carre Ace Restaurant, next to the *Ramses Hotel*. Another tourist joint – full meals of *kofta* or kebab with dips, cooked vegetables and spaghetti, for about £E7.

El Medina, Sharia al-Souk, opposite the *Cleopatra Hotel*. Good Egyptian food, popular with locals and still cheap.

La Trattoria*, in the *Isis Hotel* on the Corniche. Outdoor tables facing Elephantine. Expensive pizzas and pasta dishes.

Saladin Restaurant, on the Corniche – directly on the waterfront. Does moderately priced fish or chicken with cooked vegetables.

Aswan Moon*, just along the Corniche, with a mock-castle gate. Cool by day, loud and lively at night; a place to meet locals and hear Nubian music. Fish, chicken, vegetable dishes and *kab hala* at reasonable prices.

Mona Lisa, on the Corniche, next door. A sweatbox over summer, but serves good baked fish, rice and salad for about £E5. Breakfast £E1.50. Blends a delicious cocktail of fruit juices.

El Shatte, on the Corniche opposite the *Hotel Continental* (☎324-117). Indoor and outdoor dining. Set meal of beef, chicken or fish with salad, bread and fruit (£E5). Also breakfast (£E2) and diverse juices.

El Nil, on the Corniche, a few doors down (☎326-020). A grilled pigeon, chicken and kebab eatery. Similar prices to the above.

Aswan Panorama, on the Corniche, across the road. Serves a wide range of entrées, so-called vegetarian and diabetic dishes, iced drinks and various kinds of herbal teas and coffees. A meal averages £E8–10.

Old Cataract Buffet, on the hotel terrace at sunset. Earl Grey tea, cakes and sandwiches (£E9), or the cheapskate alternative of tea alone (£E2).

Entertainments

Traditional *Aswani* diversions are promenading the Corniche and bazaar, meeting friends in riverside restaurants, and listening to Nubian music. For tourists, there are clubs, swimming, and the Philae sound and light show to consider.

Nubian music and folklore events

Although Nubian stars like Saiyid Hussein or Saiyid Jayr only visit town occasionally, taped music plays everywhere and impromptu sounds can be heard in cafés and backstreets, or sometimes at Ferial Gardens. Over winter, locals flock to see the **Nubian Folk Troupe** perform stories of village life, wedding and harvest numbers and the famous Nubian stick-dance, which pantomimes a sword fight. Performances at Aswan's **Cultural Centre** (☎323-344) usually happen every night (9.30–11pm) except Friday from October to February; tickets (roughly £E4) are sold on a first-come, first-served basis.

Nightclubs

When not attending the **Sound and Light Show at Philae** (see p.376), package tourists usually opt for **nightclubs** in the *Oberoi, New Cataract* and *Kalabsha* hotels, which offer a floor show of Nubian and Western music, accompanied by a meal and perhaps a belly dancer for upwards of £E40 a head (ask at reception for details). The *Philae Hotel* runs a nightly **disco** (10am–2pm) year-round, and may waive the cover charge (£E6) if business is slack.

Swimming

Sooner or later, you'll find the idea of **swimming** irresistible. Though Aswan's municipal baths won't admit foreigners any more, non-residents may use the pools at the *New Cataract* (£E10; 9am–9pm daily), *Isis* (£E10; 7am–6pm) and *Oberoi* (£E15; 7am–6pm) hotels. With crocodiles held at bay behind the High Dam and no bilharzia upstream of Esna, it should also be safe to **swim in the Nile**; pick a likely cove on Elephantine or jump off a *felucca*.

    Water sports equipment can sometimes be hired by the day at the *Rowing Club* on the Corniche.

Festivals and weddings

On **Aswan Dam Day** (January 15), the Corniche witnesses a good-natured parade of civic and military hardware; fire engines and ambulances following Jeep-loads of perspiring frogmen and rubber-suited decontamination troops. To appreciate the joke, catch the farcical orgy of drilling and polishing that transpires outside Police Headquarters and the Governorate Building the day before.

    Although Aswan itself isn't noted for religious festivals, there's a large **Moulid of Abu Yazid al-Bistami** at KUBANIYAH, 13km north of town (just beyond Kattarah), sometime between the 13th and 15th of Sha'ban.

    Foreigners may also be invited to **Nubian weddings** in the villages (guests from distant lands are held to be auspicious), but you shouldn't presume – tread with care.

Listings

Airlines *EgyptAir* (☎322-400) and *ZAS* (☎326-401) on the Corniche; daily 8am–8pm. Reserve flights as far in advance as possible. Aswan **airport** (☎480-320/322-987; police ☎480-509) is near the High Dam, 23km south of town (£E10 by taxi).

American Express (☎323-222; daily 8am–2pm & 5–8pm; during Ramadan 8am–2pm) in the lobby of the *Old Cataract* hotel can exchange currency and TCs, and hold client mail.

Banks Cash and TCs exchanged at *Bank Misr* (☎323-156; Sun–Thurs 8.30am–2pm), *Banque du Caire* (☎322-458; daily 8.30am–2pm & 5–8pm), *Bank of Alexandria* (☎322-765; Sun–Thurs 8am–2pm) and the *National Bank of Egypt* (☎322-013), all on the Corniche.

Foreign newspapers and books are sold next to the *ZAS* office on the Corniche, and sidewalk kiosks further north.

Medical emergencies The *German Evangelical Hospital* (☎322-176) south of *EgyptAir* will provide treatment now and accept insurance payments later. Open 24 hours. Public ambulance ☎123.

Passport office (☎322-238) Under a large yellow sign near the Hotel Continental; enter on the left side of the building (Sat–Thurs 8am–2pm & 6–8pm, Fri 8am–2pm). All day passport registration; visa extensions mornings only.

Pharmacies *El Nile* (☎322-674; 7am–midnight), opposite the *Isis Hotel*; *Atlas Pharmacy* (☎324-400; Mon–Sat 9am–2.30pm & 6–11pm). Both sell drugs and contraceptives over the counter.

Photo-developing *King Aswan Lab* (☎323-124; Sat–Thurs 8am–10pm) on Sharia al-Matar will do 36 colour prints in an hour (£E18) or overnight (for slightly less); if you're prepared to wait three days, it costs roughly half that at *Photo Sabry* on the Corniche (☎326-452; Sat–Thurs 8.30am–11pm, Fri 6.30–11pm). Both sell film.

Post office Main GPO (Sat–Thurs 8am–2pm) near the *Rowing Club*; poste restante (Sat–Wed 7–11am & 5–8pm, Thurs 7–11am, Fri 5–8pm) is one block inland behind the Bank of Alexandria. Outward-bound mail often arrives quicker if posted from a major hotel.

Telecommunications International calls from the 24-hour Telephone Office near *EgyptAir*, or the branch in the railway station (daily 8am–10pm). The *Oberoi* has a fax machine (off-peak rates 8pm–8am).

Thomas Cook on the Corniche and in the *Oberoi* hotel (☎323-455) can change money and arrange tours (see below).

Excursions from Aswan

Aswan is a base for **excursions** to numerous sites, some of which can only be reached from here, whilst others are also accessible from Luxor. With the exception of **Sehel Island** and the Sun Temple of **Abu Simbel** (see p.383) – which would leave you too exhausted to think about visiting anywhere else that day – it's possible to fit two or more sites into a half or **full day's itinerary**, albeit one which doesn't allow you to linger at each place for long. Much depends on whether you engage a private taxi for the whole jaunt or rely on public transport, which is more time-consuming.

Bearing this in mind, there are two basic circuits:

● The classic day excursion is to **Philae Island** (see p.376) with its lovely Temple of Isis, situated in the lake between the **Aswan Dams**. Typically, a group of tourists hires a private taxi to take them to the Philae launch dock, then the dams and back to Aswan, briefly visiting the **Unfinished Obelisk** and the **Fatimid Cemetery** on the outskirts of town (see below). The tourist office in Aswan can supply official prices, but you'll still have to bargain with a driver over the deal. For a four- to five-hour tour (which suffices for the above), four-seater taxis should accept about £E30; larger Peugeot 504s, seating seven or eight, roughly £E35.

For £E40, you can probably persuade them to extend the tour to include **Kalabsha Temple**, which otherwise entails a separate trip (see p.381). Whether you go through hotels (the *Marwa*, *Ramses* and *Mena* are among ones to contact), Corniche "fixers", or approach drivers directly, the main thing is to establish exactly what the package includes.

● The other main circuit takes in one or more of the **temples between Aswan and Luxor**. Relying on public transport, you could feasibly combine **Kom Ombo** with **Edfu**, but to see **Esna** as well really calls for a private taxi. Expect to pay £E65 for a four-seater taxi, or £E95 for a larger vehicle to take you to each site for an hour and then on to Luxor.

Half-day tours to Kom Ombo, Edfu and back, and full day tours to all three sites, concluding in Luxor, are also available from *Thomas Cook* (see addresses above).

By starting early, it's also possible to combine **Kom Ombo** and/or **Edfu** with the **Camel Market at Darow** (see under respective towns for details). Alternatively, you can visit these temples whilst sailing between Aswan and Luxor in a *felucca* (see box overpage).

The Unfinished Obelisk and the Fatimid Cemetery

Past the Aswan campsite, off the highway south, is one of the **granite quarries** that supplied fine red stone for temples and colossi in ancient times (daily 6am–6pm; £E1.50, students 75pt). In one section lies a gigantic **Unfinished Obelisk**, roughly dressed and nearly cut free from the bedrock, but abandoned after a flaw in the stone was discovered. Had it been finished, the obelisk would weigh 1168 tons and stand over 120-foot high. It's reckoned that this was the intended mate for the so-called Lateran Obelisk in Rome, which originally stood before the temple of Tuthmosis III at Karnak and is still credited as the largest obelisk in the world. From chisel marks and abandoned tools, archaeologists have been able to deduce pharaonic quarrying techniques, such as soaking wooden wedges to split fissures, and using quartz sand slurry as an abrasive.

Beside the turn-off and sprawling back towards town are hundreds of mudbrick tombs ranging from simple enclosures to complex domed cubes. This veritable lexicon of Islamic funerary architecture is known as the **Fatimid Cemetery**, though the majority of tombs actually date from Tulunid times. Alas, most of their marble inscriptions were removed to Cairo in 1887 without any record of their original locations, leaving the tombs starkly unadorned.

Though neither of these sites is worth the effort of **getting there** by yourself, which involves a two-kilometre walk or bike ride, **taxi tours to Philae** often stop here on the way back for a brief look.

Sehel Island and the First Cataract

Travellers enamoured of *felucca* journeys should consider visiting **Sehel Island**, four kilometres upriver. With a strong wind behind you, it can be reached in an hour or so; on calmer days, allow longer. The official rate for a three-hour *felucca* trip is about £E25. Bring water and a hat, and come well shod; although the river is cool, the sun, rocks and sand are scorchingly hot. Landing on the east side of the island, you may be lured into the **Nubian village** (to the west) by promises of tea, or mobbed by kids eager to lead you to the "ruins" (south); the expected *baksheesh* supplements family incomes.

Sehel is dominated by two hills of jumbled boulders bearing over 250 **inscriptions** from the Middle Kingdom until Ptolemaic times, "bruised" rather than carved into the weathered granite. The majority record Egyptian expeditions beyond the First Cataract or prayers of gratitude for their safe return, but atop the eastern hill you'll find a Ptolemaic **Famine Stele** (#81). Backdated to the reign of Zoser, it relates how he ended a seven-year famine during the III Dynasty by placating Khnum, god of the cataract, with a new temple on Sehel and the return of lands confiscated from his cult-centre at Esna, which had provoked Khnum to withhold the inundation.

The summit provides a superb view of the **First Cataract**, a cliff-bound stretch of river divided into channels by outcrops of granite. Before the Aswan Dams, the waters foamed and boiled, making the cataract a fearsome obstacle to upriver travel. Until this century, it was necessary to offload cargo and transport it overland whilst the lightened boats risked rowing against the rapids. Amelia Edwards described "the leap – the dead fall – the staggering rush forward", waves and spray flooding the boat and the oars audibly scraping the rocks on either side.

In ancient times the cataract was credited as the source of the Nile (which was believed to flow south into Nubia as well as north through Egypt) and the abode of the deity who controlled the inundation (either Hapy or Khnum, or perhaps both working in tandem). The foaming waters were thought to well up from a subterranean cavern where the Nile-god dwelt. Offerings continued to be made at Sehel even after its putative location shifted to Biga Island during the Late Period or Ptolemaic times (see "Philae").

Moving on from Aswan

Details of how to reach Philae, Kalabsha, the Aswan Dams and Abu Simbel appear in subsequent sections, and hints on travelling into the Sudan after that.

Service taxis
Service taxis are the fastest overland transport to everywhere as far north as Qena, and don't involve complicated schedules, queuing or fighting for seats – but you'll have to resign yourself to a death-defying ride.

The main depot beyond the railway tracks serves **Darow** and **Kom Ombo** (£E1), **Edfu** (£E2), **Esna** (£E2.50), **Luxor** (£E5.50) and other points north. **Aswan environs**, **Hazan/the Old Dam** (25pt) and **points south** are served by a smaller depot next to the *Happi Hotel*.

Buses
Slower buses feel safer than taxis, but have their own drawbacks. Depending on who's on duty at the terminal it may be hard to ascertain schedules, which change periodically. Roughly thirteen services daily (5.45am–3pm) stop at every town **between Aswan and Luxor** (5hr; £E5), of which half continue on to **Qena** (6hr; £E7). However, you'll make faster time on the "expresses" (9.30am, 11am,

---

FELUCCA JOURNEYS BETWEEN ASWAN AND LUXOR

The Nile's timeless scenery is best appreciated on longer *felucca* journeys between Aswan and Luxor. **Travelling downstream** (ie towards Luxor) is a safer bet, since boats sailing upriver depend on the wind to make progress and may reach their destination later than expected. Whether your *felucca* trip is blissful or boring, tragicomic or simply unpleasant, largely depends on factors such as your captain and fellow passengers, the weather and cooking – and your own expectations.

Typically, a large *felucca* has an English-speaking Nubian captain and carries up to eight passengers who either sleep ashore after the boat has tied up, or on wooden slats aboard. Nights are chilly (and maybe damp) for most of the year, so a sleeping bag or plenty of blankets are essential. **Bring** at least three litres of bottled water per person for each day, unless you're willing to drink Nile water as the boatmen do. Also strongly recommended are a hat and sunscreen lotion (the river feels cool but reflects sunlight with great intensity) and bug repellent (the shallows swarm with mosquitoes).

The first step is to assemble a group of six to eight people, which is easily done by asking around in Corniche restaurants or responding to messages posted in the tourist office. Since you'll be spending many hours in close proximity, the character and habits of your **fellow travellers** are a prime consideration (*viz* Sartre, "Hell is other people"). Having ascertained the official rate for the journey, the next step is to find a captain and negotiate the deal. Aswan **captains and boats** recommended by travellers include: Noury-Dawi Mohammed (the *Oregon*); Cptn. Sabri (*Lucky Boat, Washington*); Cptn. Abed (*Jamaica*); Cptn. Tariq (*Nile Star*); and Cptn. Fowzy (*Sheraton*). Avoid the scar-faced guy who skippers the *Zezo*.

2.30pm & 3.30pm), which only call at **Kom Ombo, Esna** and **Edfu** en route to Luxor. There are three daily buses to **Cairo** (5.30am, 3.30pm & 4.30pm): deluxe, with videos, A/C and toilet (£E34); A/C 1st class *sans* toilet (£E30); and no frills at all (£E18). Travellers bound for the Red Sea Coast or Sinai can use a new daily A/C bus (3.30pm; £E25) to **Hurghada**, which continues on to Cairo via Suez.

Trains

It's only worth using trains for long hauls. There are six daily services to **Luxor** (5hr; 1st class £E10, A/C 2nd class £E5), all of which continue on to **Cairo** (18hr; 1st class £E30, A/C 2nd class £E16). Heading for Luxor, it's probably safe to board without a ticket, since walk-on seats may be available for a £E1.50 surcharge; but the journey to Cairo is too long to risk standing, so you'll have to join the huge queues for tickets (or go through *Thomas Cook* or some other agency). **Express #85** (to Luxor, Cairo and Alexandria) has A/C sleepers and a restaurant; **#87** to Cairo (which also stops at Qena) has the same *sans* A/C; **#89** also musters a bar and buffet. Two daily *wagon lits* (leaving around 3.40pm & 6.30pm; £E150) are hitched onto the last two. A cheaper, non-sleeper option is train #981, which has A/C first and second class.

Flights

For those with the money, *EgyptAir* and *ZAS* offer identical services to **Luxor** (45min; $25 one-way) and **Cairo** (90min; $90). During the summer season, both do from two to four flights daily to Cairo, five a week to Luxor; over winter, the frequency doubles or triples. Even so, it's wise to book a week or more before-hand; alternatively, you might get lucky with last-minute cancellations.

Rates vary according to the length of the journey, but also (unofficially) with fluctuating demand (big reductions are negotiable over summer). The tourist office quotes £E50 per person for a group of six to eight to sail between Aswan and Luxor, stopping at Kom Ombo, Edfu and Esna over five days and four nights. Many travellers prefer to sail only as far as Edfu (three days and nights; roughly £E30 per person) or Esna (three nights and four days; £E40 each), or even just to Kom Ombo (one night; £E25); travelling on to Luxor or returning to Aswan by *service* taxi. Whether you can obtain these prices is another matter – as always, bargaining is what counts. Don't pay until you reach your destination, lest the boat "break down" and curtail the trip prematurely.

The **food arrangements** are another ticklish issue. Most captains argue that they can buy supplies more cheaply than you and press for an additional sum (say, £E4–7 each per day) up front to cover this. Unscrupulous captains then deliver less than promised and pocket the difference. Buying your own supplies is a safer bet, but requires some face-saving excuse like stringent dietary requirements. Don't leave shopping till the night before or you'll be vulnerable to railroading tactics. Most *feluccas* carry a stove on which the captain cooks and brews tea.

Travellers starting out from Aswan are required **to register** their passports and pay £E5 each (including for the boatman) at agencies like *Luxor Tours* (☎322-615) or *Seven Tours* (☎323-679) on the Corniche. Strangely, however, this is not required if one starts from Luxor (unless regulations have changed). By law, *feluccas* cannot sail on the river after 8pm. Between January 1 and February 5 every year, the **locks** between Luxor and Esna are closed for maintenance, so downriver trips at these times must end at Esna.

The Aswan Dams

Under a good administration the Nile gains on the desert; under a bad one the desert gains on the Nile.

Napoleon

The **Aswan Dams** attest that Egypt's fundamental dilemma is more intractable than suggested by John Gunther's pithy diagnosis: "Make more land. Make fewer people. Either solution would alleviate the problem, but neither is easy." Although each dam has brought large areas under cultivation, boosted agricultural productivity and provided hydroelectricity for industry, the gains have been eroded by a population explosion which again threatens to outstrip resources.

Ever conscious of the dams' significance, Egyptians are inclined to view them as a tourist attraction, whereas most foreigners simply regard the edifices as a route to the temples of Abu Simbel, Philae and Kalabsha, which were reassembled on higher ground following construction of the High Dam. Views from the top of the dams are spectacular, though, so don't begrudge tours' obligatory stopovers – nor forget that **photography** is strictly prohibited around both dams.

The Aswan Dam

Just upriver from the First Cataract stands the old **Aswan Dam**, built by the British (1898–1902) and subsequently twice raised to increase its capacity. Once the largest dam in the world, it stands 50m tall, 2000m long, 30m thick at the base and 11m at the top. Driving across, you'll notice the 180 sluice gates which used to be opened during the inundation and then gradually closed as the river level dropped, preserving a semi-natural flood cycle. Now that its storage and irrigation functions have been taken over by the High Dam, it chiefly serves to generate hydroelectricity for the nearby *Kima* factory, producing chemical fertilisers. Philae is visible amongst the islands to the south of the dam.

Near the eastern end of the dam lies a former Reservoir Colony, now called **HAZAN**, where colonial villas nestle amidst peaceful gardens. Though few tourists come here, it can easily be reached from Aswan by *service* taxi (25pt) or buses #20 and #59 from the city's corniche (14 daily 6am–9.30pm; 25pt).

The High Dam (al-Sadd al-Ali)

By 1952 it was apparent that the Aswan Dam could no longer satisfy Egypt's needs nor guarantee security from famine. Nasser pledged to build a new **High Dam**, six kilometres upstream, that would secure Egypt's future, power new industries and bring electricity to every village. When the World Bank reneged on its promised loan under pressure from the USA, Nasser nationalised the Suez Canal to generate revenue for the project and turned to the USSR for assistance. The dam's construction (1960–71) outlasted his lifetime, however, as well as the era of Soviet-Egyptian collaboration. When Egypt decided to install more powerful turbine generators in the late 1980s, they bought them from America.

Lake Nasser and environmental consequences

The most visible consequence of the High Dam is **Lake Nasser**, which backs up for nearly 500km, well into the Sudan. Over 180m deep in places, with a surface area of 6000 square kilometres, the lake is the world's largest reservoir. During the decade of drought that saw the Nile fall to its lowest level in 350 years, it saved Egypt from the famine that still wracks Ethiopia and the Sudan. When heavy rainfall caused the Nile to flood in August 1988, the High Dam prevented Aswan from being inundated like Khartoum. Since a dam burst would wash most of Egypt's population into the Mediterranean, its security is paramount. The surrounding hills bristle with radar installations and anti-aircraft missiles; threats to bomb the dam made by Israel during the 1967 and 1973 wars, and by Gadaffi in 1984, have not been forgotten.

Although its human, cultural and environmental costs are still being evaluated, the dam has delivered most of its promised **benefits**. Egypt has been able to convert 700,000 *feddans* of cultivated land from the ancient basin system of irrigation to perennial irrigation – doubling or tripling the number of harvests – and to reclaim over one million *feddans* of desert. The dam's turbines have powered a thirty percent expansion of industrial capacity, too; humming pylons carry megavolts to Aswan's chemical and cement factories, the Helwan Iron and Steel Mill, and the refineries of Suez. A fledgling fishing industry on Lake Nasser provides an additional source of protein and a livelihood for the locals, or *arraqa* (literally, "those who sweat"). Evaporation from the lake has caused haze, clouds and even rainfall over previously arid regions, and the water table beneath the Sahara has risen as far away as Algeria. The main losers have been the **Nubians**, whose homeland was submerged by Lake Nasser (see box on p.356).

Other **environmental consequences** are still being assessed. Because the dam traps the silt that once renewed Egypt's fields, farmers now rely on *Nitrokima* fertilisers, which have entered the food chain. The soil salinity caused by perennial irrigation can only be prevented by extensive drainage projects, which create breeding grounds for mosquitoes and biharzia-carrying snails. Ancient monuments have been affected by damp and salt-encrustation, blamed on the rising water table and greater humidity.

It's estimated that the lake itself will be filled by silt within 500 years. But whereas some reckon that the Nubian desert may have reverted to its prehistoric lushness by then, others fear international conflicts over water resources within the next century. Civil wars have hitherto prevented Ethiopia and the Sudan from harnessing the White Nile and the watery Sudd for their own needs, while Egypt has already expressed its objections, citing a vested interest in the Nile's headwaters.

Visiting the High Dam

The High Dam can be crossed anytime between 7am and 5pm; all vehicle passengers are charged £E1.50 **toll**, and may also have to show their passports. Along the western approach, a giant lotus-blossom **tower** built to commemorate Soviet-Egyptian Friendship now symbolises goodwill and the dam's benefits – depicted in heroic, Socialist Realist bas-reliefs; its observation deck, reached by elevator, is sometimes open. Off the road at the east end of the dam is a **visitor's pavilion** (daily 7am–5pm) which the curator will unlock for *baksheesh*. Exhibits include a fifteen-metre-high model of the dam, plans for its construction (in Russian and Arabic), and a photo-narrative of the relocation of Abu Simbel.

However, unless you ask to visit the tower (*burg*) or "model" (*mekat*), taxis will only **stop midway across the dam** for a brief look. From this vantage point the dam's height (111m) is masked by the cantilever, but its length (3830m) and width at the top (40m) and base (980m) are impressive. From the southern side of the dam you can gaze across Lake Nasser to Kalabsha temple. The **view** northwards includes the huge 2100-megawatt power station on the east bank and the channels through which water is routed into the Nile, rushing out amidst clouds of mist, sometimes crowned by a rainbow. Philae lies amongst the cluster of islands farther downriver.

Trains south from Aswan (9 daily 6am–10.30pm; 25pt) terminate at **Sadd al-Ali Station**, 5km south of the High Dam. Being so close to the dock for **ferries to Wadi Halfa**, the station is usually full of Sudanese, especially Bishari tribespeople, waiting for a boat home (see p.388 for more about this journey).

Philae

The island of **PHILAE** and its **Temple of Isis** have bewitched visitors since Ptolemaic times, when most of the complex was constructed. The devout and curious were drawn here by a cult that flourished throughout the Roman empire well into the Christian era. Although the first Europeans to "rediscover" Philae in the eighteenth century could only marvel from a distance after their attempts to land were "met with howls, threats and eventually the spears of the natives living in the ruins", subsequent visitors revelled in this mirage from antiquity. "If a procession of white-robed priests bearing aloft the veiled ark of the God were to come sweeping round between the palms," mused Amelia Edwards, "we would not think it strange."

After the building of the first Aswan Dam, rising waters lapped and surged about the temple, submerging it for half the year, when tourists admired its shadowy presence beneath the translucent water. Once it became apparent that the new High Dam would submerge Philae forever, however, UNESCO and the EAO organised a massive operation (1972–80) to **relocate its temples** on nearby **Aglika Island**, which was landscaped to match the original site. The new Philae is magnificently set amidst volcanic outcrops, like a jewel in the royal blue lake, but no longer faces Biga Island, sacred to Osiris, whence its holiness derived.

Getting there

Most people visit Philae on **taxi tours from Aswan** (see p.370), which is the best way of getting there and back. The alternative entails catching a #20 or #59 **bus** from Aswan's corniche to the checkpoint at the eastern end of the Old Dam, and then walking two kilometres to the Shallal motorboat dock, where taxis drop visitors and you buy site **tickets** (£E10, students £E5; daily 7am–5pm, during Ramadan 7am–4pm). Having agreed on a price for a motorboat to the island (officially £E10 per boat-load, round-trip), you shouldn't pay anything until you're back on shore, obliging the boatmen to wait while you explore; if you linger more than an hour, however, *baksheesh* is in order. There's nowhere to buy food or drink on the island, and the toilets are grisly.

Sound and Light shows

To attend Philae's **Sound and Light show** (one or two performances nightly except Thurs & Sun), check the posted schedules. As at Karnak, the show consists of a one-hour tour through the ruins, whose floodlit forms are more impressive than the melodramatic soundtrack. By maneouvring yourself into the front row, you can enjoy a panoramic view of the entire complex without having to swivel your head during the second stage of the tour. Unlike by day, motorboats charge each passanger a flat fare (currently £E1) for the return trip. Tickets (£E10) for the show are sold at the dockside.

The Temple of Isis

Philae's cult status dates back to the New Kingdom, when Biga Island was identified as one of the burial places of Osiris – and the first piece of land to emerge from the primordial waters of Chaos. Since Biga was forbidden to all but the priesthood, however, public festivities centred upon neighbouring **Philae**, which was known originally as the "Island from the Time of Re".

Excluding a few remains from the Late Period, the existing **Temple of Isis** was constructed over some eight hundred years by Ptolemaic and Roman rulers who sought to identify themselves with the Osirian myth and the cult of Isis (see below). An exquisite fusion of ancient Egyptian and Graeco-Roman architecture, the temple complex harmonises perfectly with its setting, sculpted pillars and pylons gleaming white or mellow gold against Mediterranean-blue water and black Nilotic rock.

Approaching the temple

Motorboats land near an ancient quay at the southern end of the island. In ancient times, on the original Philae, visitors ascended a double stairway to the **Vestibule of Nectanebo** at the entrance to the temple precincts. Erected by a XXX Dynasty pharaoh in honour of his "Mother Isis", this was the prototype for the graceful kiosks of the Ptolemaic and Roman era. Notice the double capitals on the remaining columns; traditional flower shapes topped with sistrum-Hathor

---

THE CULT OF ISIS

Of all the cults of ancient Egypt, none endured longer or spread farther than the worship of the goddess **Isis**. As the consort of Osiris, she civilised the world by instituting marriage and teaching women the domestic arts. As an enchantress, she collected the dismembered fragments of his body and briefly revived him to conceive a son, Horus, using her magic to help him defeat the evil Seth and restore the divine order. As pharaohs identified themselves with Horus, the living king, so Isis was their divine mother; a role which inevitably associated her with Hathor, the two goddesses being conflated in the Late Period. By this time Isis was the Great Mother of All Gods and Nature, Goddess of Ten Thousand Names, of women, purity and sexuality.

By a process of identification with other goddesses around the Mediterranean, **Isis-worship** eventually spread throughout the Roman empire (the westernmost *Iseum* or cult-temple extant is in Hungary). The nurturing, forgiving, loving Isis was Christianity's chief rival between the third and fifth centuries. Many scholars believe that the cult of the Virgin Mary was Christianity's attempt to wean converts away from Isis; early Coptic art identifies one with the other, Horus with Jesus, and the Christian cross with the pharaonic *ankh*.

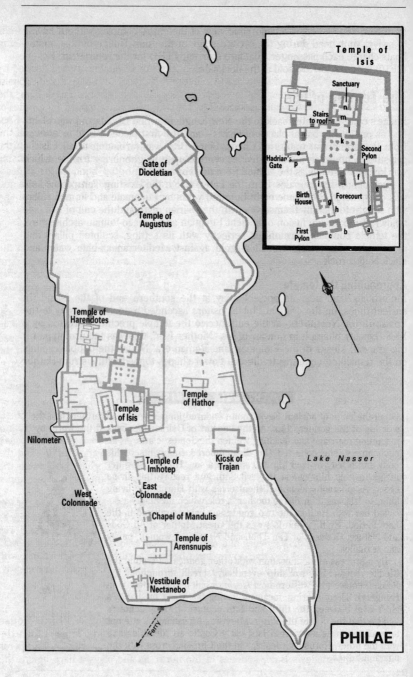

Temple of Isis

Sanctuary

Stairs to roof

Hadrian's Gate

Second Pylon

Birth House

Forecourt

First Pylon

Gate of Diocletian

Temple of Augustus

Temple of Harendotes

Temple of Isis

Temple of Hathor

Nilometer

Lake Nasser

Temple of Imhotep

Kiosk of Trajan

West Colonnade

East Colonnade

Chapel of Mandulis

Temple of Arensnupis

Vestibule of Nectanebo

Ferry

PHILAE

squares that supported the architrave. The screens which once formed the walls are crowned with cavetto cornices and rows of *uraeus* serpents, a motif dating back to Zoser's complex at Saqqara, nearly three thousand years earlier.

Beyond the vestibule stretches an elongated trapezoidal courtyard flanked by colonnades. The **West Colonnade** is better preserved, with fine carved capitals, each slightly different. The windows in the wall behind once faced Biga, the island of Osiris; the one opposite the first two columns is topped by a relief of Nero offering two eyes to Horus and Isis. The plainer, unfinished **East Colonnade** abuts a succession of ruined structures. Past the foundations of the **Temple of Arensnupis** (worshipped as the "Goodly Companion of Isis" in the Late Period) lies a ruined **Chapel of Mandulis**, the Nubian god of Kalabsha. Near the First Pylon, an unfinished **Temple of Imhotep** honours the philosopher-physician who designed Zoser's Step Pyramid and was later deified as a god of healing. Its forecourt walls show Khnum, Satis, Anukis, Isis and Osiris, and Ptolemy IV before Imhotep.

The Pylons and Forecourt

The lofty **First Pylon** was built by Neos Dionysos, who smites enemies in the approved fashion at either corner, watched by Isis, Horus and Hathor. Set at right angles to the pylon, the Gate of Ptolemy II **[a]** is probably a remnant of an earlier temple. The pylon's main portal **[b]** is still older (dating from the reign of Nectanebo II) and was formerly flanked by two granite obelisks; now, only two **stone lions** remain. Inside the portal are inscriptions by Napoleon's troops, commemorating their victory over the Mamlukes in 1799. The smaller door in the western section of the pylon leads through to the Birth House and was used for *mamissi* rituals; the entrance depicts the personified deities of Nubia and the usual Egyptian pantheon **[c]**. On the back of the pylon are scenes of priests carrying Isis' barque.

Emerging into the **Forecourt**, most visitors make a beeline for the Birth House (see below) or the Second Pylon, overlooking the colonnade to the east. Here, reliefs behind the stylish plant-columns show the king performing rituals such as dragging the barque of Sokar **[d]**. A series of doors lead into six rooms which probably had a service function; one of them, dubbed the Library **[e]**, features Thoth in his ibis and baboon forms, Maat, lion-headed Tefnut and the goddess of writing. At the northern end stands a ruined chapel **[f]** which the Romans erected in front of a granite outcrop that was smoothed into a stele under Ptolemy IV and related his gift of lands to the temple.

Set at an angle to its forerunner, the **Second Pylon** changes the axis of the temple. A large relief on the right tower shows Neos Dionysos placing sacrifices before Horus and Hathor; in a smaller scene above he presents a wreath to Horus and Nephthys, offers incense and anoints an altar before Osiris, Isis and Horus. Similar scenes on the other tower have been defaced by early Christians, who executed the paintings in the upper right-hand corner of the pylon passageway, leading into the temple proper.

The Birth House

The western side of the forecourt is dominated by the colonnaded **Birth House** of Ptolemy IV, which linked his ancestry to Horus and Osiris. Most of the exterior reliefs were added in Roman times, which explains why the Emperor Augustus shadows Buto, goddess of the north, as she plays a harp before the young, naked Horus and his mother at one end of the central register behind the Hathor-headed colonnade **[g]**. Farther south and higher up, the Roman reliefs overlay inscriptions in hieroglyphs and demotic characters which partly duplicate those on the Rosetta Stone **[h]**. Inside the *mamissi*, a columned forecourt and two vestibules precede the sanctuary, which contains the finest scenes **[i]**. Although iconoclasts have defaced the goddess suckling the child-pharaoh on the left-hand wall, you can see Isis giving birth to Horus in the marshes at the bottom of the rear wall. Around the back of the sanctuary behind the northern colonnade is a corresponding scene of Isis nursing Horus in the swamp **[j]**.

Inside the Temple of Isis

Immediately behind the Second Pylon lies a small open court that was originally separated from the **Hypostele Hall** by a screen-wall, now destroyed. A lovely drawing by David Roberts shows this "Grand Portico" in its rich original colours: the flowering capitals in shades of green with yellow flowers and blue buds; crimson and golden winged sun-discs flying down the central aisle of the ceiling, which elsewhere bear astronomical reliefs. The unpainted walls and column shafts show the hall's builder, Ptolemy VII Euergetes II, sacrificing to various deities. After the emperor Justinian forbade the celebration of Isis rituals at Philae in 550 AD, Copts used the hall for services and chiselled crosses into the walls. On the left-hand jamb of the portal **[k]** into the vestibule beyond, a piece of Roman graffiti asserts *B Mure stultus est* ("B Mure is stupid").

As at other temples, the **vestibules** get lower and darker as you approach the sanctuary. By a doorway **[l]** to the right of the first vestibule, a Greek inscription records the "cleansing" of this pagan structure under Bishop Theodorus, during the reign of Justinian. On the other side of the vestibule is a room giving access to the **stairs** to the roof (see below). The next vestibule has an interesting scene flanking the portal at the back **[m]**, where the king offers a sistrum (left) and wine (right) to Isis and Harpocrates. On the left-hand door jamb, he leaves offerings to Min, a basket to Sekhmet and wine to Osiris, with the sacred bull and seven cows in the background. In the partially ruined transverse vestibule, the king offers necklaces, wine and eye-paint to Osiris, Isis, Hathor and Nephthys outside the sanctuary **[n]**.

Dimly lit by two apertures in the roof, the **Sanctuary** contains a stone pedestal dedicated by Ptolemy III and his wife Berenice, which once supported the goddess's barque. On the left wall, the pharaoh faces Isis, whose wings protectively enfold Osiris. Across the room, an enthroned Isis suckles the infant Horus (above) and stands to suckle a young pharaoh (below, and now defaced). The other rooms, used for rites or storage, contain reliefs of goddesses with Nubian features.

The Osirian Shrine

Try to persuade a guard to unlock the stairway to the roof, where a series of sunken rooms dwells on the resurrection of Osiris. After scenes of lamentation in the vestibule of this **Osirian Shrine**, you can see Isis gathering up his limbs, and the slain god lying naked and tumescent upon a bier (as always, the phallus has been vandalised). Mourned by Isis and Nephthys, Osiris revives to impregnate his sister-wife, whilst Selket and Douait reconstruct his body for its solar rebirth. Cast as the hawk-headed Sokar, Osiris is borne away to a papyrus swamp by the four sons of Horus, to be anointed with holy water with Anubis in attendance.

Hadrian's Gate

By leaving the temple through the western door of the first vestibule you'll emerge near **Hadrian's Gate**, set into the girdle wall that once encircled the island. Flanking your approach are two walls from a bygone vestibule, decorated with notable reliefs. The right-hand wall [o] depicts the origin of the Nile, whose twin streams are poured forth by Hapy the Nile-god from his cave beneath Biga Island, atop which perches a falcon. To the right of this, Isis, Nephthys and others adore the young falcon as he rises from a marsh.

Above the door in the opposite wall [p], Isis and Nephthys present the dual crowns to Horus, whose name is inscribed on a palm stalk by Sheshat (right) and Thoth (left). Below, Isis watches a crocodile drag the corpse of Osiris to a rocky promontory (presumably Biga). Around the gate itself, Hadrian appears before the gods (above the lintel) and the door-jambs bear the fetishes of Abydos (left) and Osiris (right). At the top of the wall, Marcus Aurelius stands before Isis and Osiris; below he offers Isis grapes and flowers.

North of the gateway lie the foundations of the **Temple of Harendotes** (an aspect of Horus), built by the emperor Claudius.

The Temple of Hathor and Trajan's Kiosk

To complete the cast of deities involved in the Osirian myth, a small **Temple of Hathor** was erected to the east of the main complex. Aside from two Hathor-headed columns in situ and fragmented capitals out back, the ruined temple is only notable for a relief of musicians, amongst whom the god Bes plays a harp. More eye-catching and virtually the symbol of Philae is the graceful open-topped **Kiosk of Trajan**, nicknamed the "Pharaoh's Bedstead". Removed from its watery grave by a team of British navy divers, the reconstructed kiosk juxtaposes variegated floral columns with a severely classical superstructure; only two of the screen-wall panels bear reliefs.

Last in order of priority come the ruined **Temple of Augustus** and the **Gate of Diocletian**, which shared the northern end of old Philae with a mudbrick Roman village that was so eroded by repeated soakings that it was left to be submerged by the lake. The **toilets** lie in this direction.

Kalabsha Temple

The hulking **Temple of Kalabsha** broods beside Lake Nasser near the western end of the High Dam, strung out on a promontory or marooned on an island depending on the water level. Between the site and the dam lies a graveyard of boats and fishy remains, enhancing its mood of desolation. The main temple originally came from Talmis (later known as Kalabsha), 50km south of Aswan; in a German-financed operation, it was cut into 13,000 blocks and reassembled here in 1970, together with other monuments from Nubia. Although military restrictions were lifted in 1987, the site only became readily accessible to tourists a few years ago, and is still under-visited.

Getting there

Taxis are the best way of getting to Kalabsha and back. Official rates for a round-trip from Aswan are about £E10–15 for a four-seater taxi, £E15–20 for a seven-seater Peugeot 504. Better still, include Kalabsha in a half-day taxi tour taking in

Philae, the dams and the Unfinished Obelisk (see p.370). Either is preferable to the penny-pinching alternative of taking a **train** to Sadd al-Ali Station (see p.376), then walking or hitching up to the dam and across to the other side of the lake (almost 10km in all).

If Lake Nasser has risen so that it's necessary to reach **Kalabsha by boat**, an oarsman will materialise to row you across. Specify when you want to return, and pay for the boat (£E10) when you're back on the mainland. Most visitors find that an hour at **the site** (open daily 6am–6pm) is sufficient; **tickets** (£E5, students £E2.50) are sold at the temple itself.

The Temple of Mandulis

The **Temple of Mandulis** is a Ptolemaic-Roman version of an earlier XVIII Dynasty edifice dedicated to the Nubian fertility-god *Marul*, whom the Greeks called Mandulis.

By Ptolemaic times, Egypt's Nubian empire was a token one, dependent on the goodwill of the powerful Nabatan Empire ruled from Merowe near the Fourth Cataract. Having briefly restored old-style imperialism, the Romans abandoned most of Nubia during the reign of Diocletian, falling back on deals with local rulers to safeguard Egypt's southern border. As the linchpin of the last imperial town south of Aswan, the temple bears witness to this patronage and the kingdoms that succeeded the Nabatan Empire, which disintegrated under the onslaught of marauding Blemmyes – a group of nomadic tribes who were perhaps the ancestors of the modern Beja.

The causeway, court and facade

Approaching the sandstone temple from behind, you miss the dramatic effect of the great **causeway** from the water's edge, used by pilgrims in the days when Kalabsha was a healing temple, like those at Edfu and Dendara. For reasons unknown, its chunky **pylon** is skewed at a slight angle to the temple, a blemish rectified by having a trapezoidal **courtyard** whose pillars are set closer together along the shorter, southern side.

The first batch of reliefs worth a mention occur on the **facade** of the hypostele hall at the back of the court. While Horus and Thoth anoint the king with holy water in a conventional scene to the left of the portal, the right-hand wall bears a decree excluding swineherds and their pigs from the temple (issued in 249 AD); a large relief of a horseman in Roman dress receiving a wreath from the winged Victory; and a text in poor Greek lauding Siklo, the Christian king of the Nobatae, for repulsing the Blemmye (c.550).

The Hypostele Hall and Sanctuary

The now roofless **hypostele hall** is distinguished by columns with ornate flow-ered capitals, and some interesting reliefs along the rear wall. Left of the portal, a Ptolemaic king offers crowns to Horus and Mandulis, whilst Amenhotep II (founder of the XVIII Dynasty temple) presents a libation to Mandulis and Min. Across the way, a nameless king slays a foe before Horus, Shu and Tefnet.

Within the **vestibules** beyond, look for figures personifying the Egyptian Nomes, below a scene of the king offering wine to Osiris and a field to Isis and Mandulis (near the stairs off the pronaos); and a rare appearance by the deified Imhotep (low down on the left-hand wall of the naos or inner vestibule).

The **Sanctuary** is similar in size to the vestibules and, like them, once had two columns. Along its back wall you can identify (left–right) the emperor offering lotuses to Isis and the young Horus and milk to Mandulis and Wadjet; then incense to the former duo and lotuses to the latter. Although the god's cult statue has vanished, Mandulis still appears at either end of the scene covering the temple's **rear wall**: in his royal form, with a pharaonic crown, sceptre and *ankh* sign (right); and as a god whose ram's horn crown is surmounted by a solar disc, *uraeus* and ostrich plumes (left).

From the temple's pronaos, you may be able to ascend a stairway to the **roof**, which features an abbreviated version of the Osirian shrines found at other complexes.

The Kiosk of Qertassi and Beit al-Wali

Re-erected near the lakeside at the same time as Kalabsha temple, the **Kiosk of Qertassi** resembles a knocked-about copy of the "Pharaoh's Bedstead" at Philae, but actually came from another ancient settlement, 40km south of Aswan. Aside from its fine views of Lake Nasser, this Ptolemaic-Roman edifice is chiefly notable for two surviving Hathor-headed columns which make the goddess look more feline than bovine.

Beit al-Wali

The oldest monumental relic from Nile-inundated Nubia is a temple dug into the hillside behind Kalabsha temple. Originally hewn under Ramses II, who left his mark throughout Nubia, this cruciform rock-cut structure is known by its Arabic name, **Beit al-Wali** (House of the Governor). The weathered reliefs flanking its narrow court depict the pharaoh's victories over Nubians and Ethiopians (left), Libyans and Asiatics (right). By contrast, scenes in the transverse hall are well preserved and brightly coloured. Here, Ramses makes offerings before Isis, Horus and the Aswan Triad, and is suckled by goddesses inside the sanctuary, whose niche contains a mutilated cult-statue of three deities.

Abu Simbel

The great **sun temple** of **ABU SIMBEL** epitomises the monumentalism of the New Kingdom during its imperial heyday, when Ramses II (1304–1237 BC) waged colonial wars from the Beka'a Valley to the Fourth Cataract. To impress his power and majesty on the Nubians, Ramses had four gigantic statues of himself hewn from the mountainside, from whence his unblinking stare confronted travellers as they entered Egypt from Africa. The temple he built here was precisely orientated so that the sun's rays reached deep into the mountain to illuminate its sanctuary on his birthday and the anniversary of his coronation. The deified pharaoh physically overshadows the sun-god **Re-Herakhte**, to whom the temple is nominally dedicated, just as his queen, **Nefertari**, sidelines **Hathor** in a neighbouring edifice, also hewn into the mountain.

The first European to see Abu Simbel since antiquity was the Swiss explorer Burckhardt, who found the temples almost completely buried by sand-drifts in 1813. Although Belzoni later managed to clear an entrance, lack of treasure discouraged further efforts and the site was soon reburied in sand so fine "that every particle would go through an hour glass"; a process repeated throughout the nineteenth century. After Robert Hay took a cast of the face of the northern colossus, leaving it disfigured by lumps of plaster, Amelia Edwards ordered her sailors to remove them and tint the white stains with coffee, dismaying the vessel's cook, who had never "been called upon to provide for a guest whose mouth measured three feet and a half in width". Finally cleared, the temple became the scenic highlight of Thomas Cook's Nile cruises.

It was the prospect of losing Abu Simbel to Lake Nasser that impelled UNESCO to organise the salvage of Nubian monuments in the 1960s. Behind the temporary protection of a coffer dam, Abu Simbel's brittle sandstone was stablised by injections of synthetic resin and then hand-sawn into 1050 blocks weighing up to thirty tons apiece. Two years after the first block was cut, Abu Simbel was reassembled 210m behind (and 61m above) its original site, a false mountain being constructed to match the former setting. The whole operation (from 1964 to 68) cost US$40 million and is still being paid for; the cost of Egyptian tourist visas supposedly goes towards repayments.

Visiting Abu Simbel

Abu Simbel lies on the west bank of Lake Nasser, 280km south of Aswan and 40km north of the Sudanese border. Before the road from Aswan was completed in 1985, it could only be reached by water (which is no longer feasible) or by air. Though a road to the border is under construction, communications with Wadi Halfa (see p.389) are likely to remain non-existent for years to come.

Getting there

The quickest way of getting to Abu Simbel is to fly from Cairo (2hr), Luxor (1hr) or Aswan (30min). *EgyptAir* and *Zas* run three **flights** a day in summer, rising to a dozen services daily during wintertime peak season. Make reservations as far in advance as possible, whatever the time of year. Although overnight stopovers can be arranged, most tickets are sold on the assumption that you'll return the same day. Round-trip fares from Cairo (US$240), Luxor (US$120) and Aswan (US$174) will surely rise, but should include a free bus from Abu Simbel airport to the site and back again, two hours later. Planes usually circle above the temple before landing; seats on the left side give the best view.

Misr Travel's **luxury coach tours** are another upmarket option. The US$62-a-head package includes admission to the site, lunch at the nearby *Hotel Nefertari*, and a coach with A/C, toilet and videos. Departure schedules vary (usually 6am in the summer, 8am over winter), but you should get two to three hours at the site, plus time for lunch. These tours should not be confused with the A/C, daily **public bus** that leaves Aswan's terminal at 8am, reaches Abu Simbel at 11.30am, and starts its return journey from the *Hotel Nefertari* between 1.30pm and 2pm. Purchase your outbound ticket at the station at least one day before; tickets for the return journey are sold aboard the bus (£E18 round-trip). Both services are comfortable and efficient, but their simultaneous arrival (coinciding with the first flights) means that the temple is immediately crammed with people.

Others prefer to join **taxi tours** from Aswan, organised by hotels like the *Mena, el-Amin, Continental* and *Ramses*, which charge £E20 per person; by Corniche "fixers" who'll offer to do it for slightly less, but might not deliver; and

---

PHOTOGRAPHING ABU SIMBEL

Abu Simbel is an awkward subject for photography. The immense facade should be snapped in the morning before it's cast into shadow, and needs a wide-angle lens to do it justice; whereas details are best captured with a telephoto lens (it also helps to underexpose the shot by 1–1.5 stops). To photograph Abu Simbel from the air, sit on the left side of the plane and use a telephoto (at least 200mm) with a haze filter. Unless you get there very early or just before the temple closes, its interior is so crowded that photography is hopeless.

---

by groups of travellers who've negotiated their own deal with a driver. Make arrangements the day before, since taxis normally leave around 4–5am to reach Abu Simbel by 8.30am and be back in Aswan by 1–2pm. The ride is cramped and sticky, and may take over three and a half hours if the engine is knackered. Coachloads start arriving not long after you reach the temple, so it's best to visit it right away and leave the tea-stands till later.

The desert road

The reason for an early start becomes apparent once the sun gets up on the **desert road to Abu Simbel**. After clearing the High Dam you see nothing of Lake Nasser until Abu Simbel, and the monotony of dust flats, pink or grey outcrops and distant reddish hills is only relieved by silvery lakes and other **mirages**, caused by the intense heat from mid-morning onwards.

On the return journey, vehicles often stop at a teahouse in the middle of nowhere, said to mark the point where one crosses the **Tropic of Cancer**. By this time the heat is infernal, and tired drivers start nodding off at the wheel; keep the radio playing loudly and prod them when necessary to avert **crashes**.

Accommodation: Abu Simbel Town

Roughly two kilometres before the temple you'll pass the new **town** of ABU SIMBEL, a huddle of breeze-block dwellings in a dusty wilderness that belies its Arabic name, "Father of the Ear of Corn".

Should you decide **to stay** overnight to enjoy the temples at their deserted best, there are several options to consider. The state-owned *New Ramses Hotel*, near the tourist police, is spartan and moderately priced, like the half-built, utterly dismal *Pharaoh's Village*, with its *Ramses Supermarket* and *Tutankhamun Tourist Centre*. Halfway between the airport and the site, the three-star *Nefertari Hotel* has A/C rooms, a swimming pool, tennis courts and restaurant, and is usually booked up over winter (make reservations in Aswan ☎326-841 or Cairo ☎757-950) but often half-empty in summer. Rates for singles (US$36/$24), doubles (US$45/$34) and suites (US$90/US$60) vary accordingly. The hotel also has a **campground** where tents can be pitched for £E5; camping out at Abu Simbel is now forbidden.

The site

Open daily from 6am to 5pm (or later if planes land in the evening), **the site** lies downhill and around the corner from the ticket kiosk. Following the Gulf War, the **admission charge** (which includes an obligatory, non-existent guide) has been hiked to £E20, but might perhaps be reduced as trade recovers.

The Sun Temple of Ramses II

Rounding a shoulder of the hill, visitors are confronted by the great **Sun Temple**, seemingly hewn from the cliffs overlooking Lake Nasser. Having been depicted on everything from T-shirts to £E1 notes, its impact is perhaps a little diminished by familiarity: the technicolour contrast between red rockscape and aquamarine water is more startling than the cleanswept facade, which looks less dramatic than the sand-choked Abu Simbel of nineteenth-century engravings. For all the meticulous reconstruction and landscaping, too, it's hard not to sense its artificiality . . . then the temple's presence asserts itself and your mind boggles at its audacious conception, the logistics of hewing and moving it, and the unabashed megalomania of its founder.

Although Re-Herakhte, Amun-Re and Ptah are also billed as patron deities, they're clearly secondary to Ramses, the pharaoh-god whom courtiers lauded as "a powerful lion with claws extended and a terrible roar".

The colossi and facade

The temple facade is dominated by four enthroned **Colossi of Ramses II**, whose twenty-metre height surpasses the Colossi of Memnon at Thebes (though one lost its upper half following an earthquake in 27 BC). Their feet and legs are crudely executed but the torsos and heads are finely carved, and the face of the left-hand figure is quite beautiful. Between them stand figures of the royal family, dwarfed by Ramses' knees. To the left of the headless colossus is the pharaoh's mother, Muttuy; Queen Nefertari stands on the right of the colossus; Prince Amunherkhepshef between its legs. On the left leg of this same figure, an inscription records that Greek mercenaries participated in the Nubian campaign of the Saite king Psammetichus II (c.590 BC).

The **facade** is otherwise embellished with a niche-bound statue of **Re-Herakhte**, holding a *was* sceptre and a figure of Maat. This composition is a pictorial play of words on Ramses' prenomen, *User-Maat-Re*, so the flanking sunk-reliefs of the king presenting the god with images of Maat actually signify Ramses honouring his deified self. Crowning the facade is a corvetto cornice surmounted by baboons worshipping the rising sun. On the sides of the colossal thrones flanking the temple entrance, twin Nile-gods entwine the heraldic papyrus and sedge around the hieroglyph "to unite". The rows of captives depicted beneath them are divided between north and south, so that Asiatics feature on the northern (right-hand) throne, Nubians on its southern (left-hand) counterpart.

Cross-section of the Sun Temple

The Hypostele Hall and Sanctuary

This schematic division reappears in the lofty rock-cut **Hypostele Hall**, flanked on either side by four pillars fronted by ten-metre-high statues of Ramses in the Osiris position, carrying the crook and flail (the best is the end figure on the right). Beneath a ceiling adorned by flying vultures, the walls crawl with scenes from his campaigns, from Syria to Nubia. On the entrance walls, Ramses slaughters Hittite and Nubian captives before Amun-Re (left) and Re-Herakhte (right), accompanied by his eight sons or nine daughters, and his *ka*. But the most dramatic **reliefs** are found on the side walls (all directions as if you're facing the back of the temple).

The right-hand wall depicts the **Battle of Qadesh** on the River Orontes (1300 BC), starting from the back of the hall. Here you see Ramses' army marching on Qadesh, followed by their encampment, ringed by shields. Acting on disinformation tortured out of enemy spies, Ramses prepares to attack the city and summons his reserve divisions down from the heights. The waiting Hittites ford the river, charge one division and scatter another to surround the king, who single-handedly cuts his way out of the trap. The final scene claims an unqualified Egyptian triumph, even though Ramses failed to take the city. Notwithstanding this, the opposite wall portrays him storming a Syrian fortress in his chariot (note the double arm, which some regard as an attempt at animation), lancing a Libyan and returning with fettered Nubians. Along the rear wall, he presents them to Amun, Mut and himself (left), and the captured Hittites to Re-Herakhte, lion-headed Wert-Hekew and his own deified personage (right).

The eight **lateral chambers** off the back of the hall were probably used to store cult-objects and tribute from Nubia. Reliefs in the smaller **pillared hall** show Ramses and Nefertari offering incense before the shrine and barque of Amun (left) and Re-Herakhte (right). Walk through one of the doors at the back, cross the transverse vestibule and head for the central **Sanctuary**. Originally encased in gold, its four (now mutilated) cult-statues wait to be touched by the sun's rays at dawn on February 22 and October 22. February 21 was Ramses' birthday and October 21 his coronation date, but the relocation of Abu Simbel has changed the timing of these **solar events** by one day. Perhaps significantly, the figure of Ptah is situated so that it alone remains in darkness when the sun illuminates Amun-Re, Re-Herakhte and Ramses the god. Before them is a stone block where the sacred barque once rested.

The False Mountain

To see behind the scenes at Abu Simbel, look for a grey door in the mountainside beyond the northern colossus. Inside you'll find air conditioning, a guy selling soft drinks, and stairs which lead up into a vast dome ringed by a walkway. Here, displays show how the temple was removed from its original site and reassembled beneath the dome, which was covered with landfill to create a **false mountain**.

The Hathor Temple of Queen Nefertari

A little further north of the Sun Temple stands the smaller rock-hewn **Temple of Queen Nefertari**, identified here with the goddess Hathor, who was wife to the sun-god during his day's passage and mother to his rebirth at dawn. As with Ramses' temple, the rock-hewn facade imitates a receding pylon (whose corvetto cornice has fallen); its plane accentuated by a series of rising buttresses separating six **colossal statues of Ramses and Nefertari** (each over 30ft tall), which seem to emerge from the rock. Each is accompanied by two smaller figures of their children, who stand knee-high in the shadows. A frieze of cobras protects the door into the temple, which is simpler in plan than Ramses', having but one columned hall and vestibule, and only two lateral chambers.

The best **reliefs** are in the hall with square, Hathor-headed pillars whose sides show the royal couple mingling with deities. On the entrance wall Nefertari watches Ramses slay Egypt's enemies; on the side walls she participates in rituals as his equal, appearing before Anuket (left) and Hathor (right). In the transverse vestibule beyond, the portal of the sanctuary is flanked by scenes of the royal couple offering wine and flowers to Amun-Re and Horus (left), Re-Herakhte, Khnum, Satet and Anuket (right). The **Sanctuary** niche contains a ruined cow-statue of Hathor, above which vultures guard Nefertari's cartouches. On the side walls, she offers incense to Mut and Hathor (left), whilst Ramses worships his own image and that of Nefertari (right). The predominance of yellow in the paintings may allude to Hathor's title, "The Golden One".

Into the Sudan?

As things stand at present, **visiting the Sudan** is neither possible nor desirable. The military regime of Brigadier Omar Bashir (who mounted a coup in 1988) is xenophobic and repressive and even aid workers have been denied visas or forced to leave for criticising gross violations of human rights – especially in the war-torn south. Drought has stricken Darfur, Kordofan and the Red Sea Hills, driving thousands more into refugee camps around Khartoum and Kassala. The civil war has aborted plans to exploit untapped oil reserves and the Sudd (the swampwaters of the Blue Nile), which once offered Sudan the hope of breaking free from a vicious cycle of poverty and conflict.

These grim realities currently outweigh the positive side of what used to be the ultimate hard-core traveller's destination: Africa's largest country and arguably its most fascinating, with its 300 ethnic groups and diverse cultural traditions. Up until the mid-1980s, the country was also one of the most enjoyable (if not the most easy) travel destinations. The Sudanese had an unshakeable reputation for hospitality and until dire poverty cramped their generosity would commonly invite foreigners home to eat or settle their bills without saying a word.

Though it's hard to be optimistic, the following pointers might have some relevance should things improve and the Sudan becomes accessible again. Bear in mind that conditions change all the time, but bureaucracy (as for decades past) is invariably sluggish and frustrating.

Visas

Obtaining Sudanese **visas** was always a lengthy process, involving month-long delays, and a mass of forms and photographs. Officially, visas can still be obtained through Sudanese consulates abroad, but at the time of writing they simply aren't being issued – endless delays rather than outright refusal being the preferred tactic. If you want to make enquiries, the **Sudanese consulate in Cairo** is at 1 Sharia Mohammed Fahmi el-Sayed, Garden City (☎354-5043; Sun–Thurs 9am–noon).

Getting there by ferry: Wadi Halfa

Due to the numbers of Sudanese working in Egypt, **ferries** continue to operate between **Aswan and Wadi Halfa**. For details and tickets contact the *Nile Navigation Co*, beside Aswan's tourist office (☎323-348; Sat–Thurs 8am–2pm). Boats currently run on Mondays and Thursdays, sometimes on an extra day in the summer; getting the Thursday boat is not a good idea as you'll arrive in Wadi Halfa on the Friday to find everything (customs, immigration, etc) closed. The ferry theoretically takes twenty hours and connects with a train to Khartoum; both passengers and cars are carried.

Arriving at Wadi Halfa, you must fill in a **currency declaration** (valid for three weeks only; seemingly non-extendable) and obtain a **travel permit** listing all the places along the way to Khartoum that you might want to visit. These permits are required to travel around all parts of the country; Wadi Halfa is the easiest place to get one and could in the past give permission to visit most points to Khartoum and possibly Port Sudan and other places on the coast.

Getting there by air

Sudan Air no longer flies from Aswan to Khartoum, but still flies to the Sudanese capital from Cairo. Note that *EgyptAir* will no longer carry passengers out of the Sudan unless they have yellow fever and meningitis vaccination certificates (check the latest regulations). Also, beware that getting the travel permit (see above) in Khartoum is very time-consuming, involving an application to two separate offices – each of whom demands to keep your passport, compelling you to stay in the capital. All official business is like this in Khartoum.

Conditions

Outside of Khartoum, all **accommodation** is pretty basic: rooms around a hotel courtyard are used as lock-ups, while everyone drags their cots outdoors. Likewise, you'll rarely come across a restaurant as such: the population basically subsists on *fuul*, bread and lentils – if they're lucky. Bring as much food as possible with you, both for personal consumption and as gifts: things like tea, sugar, rice and lentils are always appreciated.

Most **transport** in the country is by lorry, across potholed tracks; it is extemely crowded and bumpy and journeys can last for days.

Keep in mind that **alcohol** is strictly prohibited and renders you liable for a whipping if caught. Beware, also, **black market** money-dealers in the Sudan – security agents are everywhere, making it extremely risky.

CHAPTER THREE

THE WESTERN DESERT OASES

For the ancient Egyptians civilisation began and ended with the Nile Valley and the Delta, known as the "Black Land" for the colour of its rich alluvial deposits. Beyond lay the "Red Land" or desert, whose significance was either practical or mystical. East of the Nile it held mineral wealth and routes to the Red Sea coast; west of the river lay the Kingdom of Osiris, Lord of the Dead, who "went west" to meet him. But once it was realised that human settlements existed out there, Egypt's rulers had to reckon with the **Western Desert Oases** as sources of exotic commodities and potential staging posts for invaders.

Strictly speaking, only five of the places covered in this chapter qualify as true oases. **Bahariya, Farafra, Dakhla** and **Kharga** – the four "inner" oases – have been influenced by the Valley since pharaonic times and are now linked by roads and buses in a 1000-kilometre desert circuit. Power plants and apartment buildings increasingly conceal the romantic stereotypes of palm groves and camels, but Bahariya and Farafra, at least, remain basically desert villages, living off their traditional crops of dates and olives. Dakhla and Kharga, both essentially modern towns, have stronger appeal in the journeying – across hundreds of miles of awesome barrenness, most of it gravel pans rather than pure "sand desert". The fifth oasis, **Siwa**, is located out by the Libyan border and came under Egyptian control only in the last century. Its culture remains quite distinct and the trip out again conjures up a startling sense of isolation.

Much nearer to Cairo (and suitable for day excursions) are two quasi-oases – the Fayoum and Wadi Natrun. **The Fayoum** partakes of the Nile literally and figuratively, with a dozen ancient ruins to prove its importance since the Middle Kingdom. **Wadi Natrun** is significant mainly for its Coptic monasteries.

The Desert

Much of the fascination of this region lies in the desert itself. It's no accident that Islam, Judaism and Christianity were forged in deserts whose vast scarps and depressions displayed the hand of God writ large, with life-giving springs and oases as manifestations of divine mercy in a pitiless landscape. Although much of this landscape was once savannah, it was reduced to its current state millennia ago by geological processes and overgrazing by Stone Age pastoralists.

The **Western Desert**, which covers 681,000 square kilometres (over two-thirds of Egypt's total area), is merely one part of the Sahara belt across northern Africa. Its anomalous name was bestowed by British cartographers who viewed it from the perspective of the Nile – and, to complicate matters further, designated

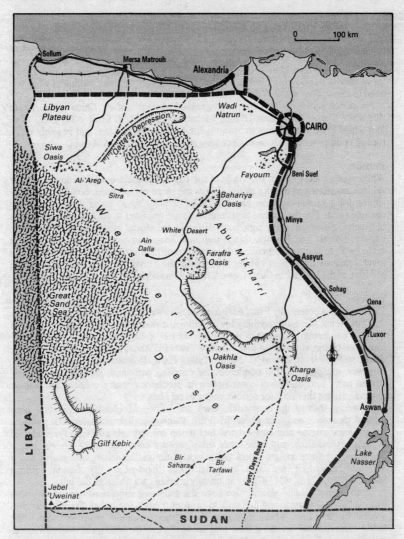

its southern reaches and parts of northwestern Sudan as the "Libyan Desert". Aside from the oases, its most striking features are the **Qattara Depression**, whence dunes extend 700km southwards, and the **Great Sand Sea** along the Libyan border. Both are discussed under Siwa Oasis, while the old slave trail from the Sudan is covered after Kharga Oasis, the penultimate stop on the **Forty Days Road**.

All the **practicalities** of visiting the oases (including the best times to go) are detailed under the respective oasis entries.

DESERT DRIVING: SOME PRACTICALITIES

Although most of the places in this chapter can be reached by public transport or locally arranged excursions, a few of them entail real **desert expeditions**. The following advice should be borne in mind even if you're going to stick to main roads; for motorists considering more ambitious trips, it's only the bare outline of what you need to know. (For detailed handbooks, see "Books" in *Contexts*.)

An easier option is to take an **organised desert safari**. Cairo-based *Acacia Adventure Travel* (27 Sharia Libnan, Mohandiseen; ☎347-4713 or ☎345-1022) does four-wheel drive expeditions to Siwa via the Qattara Depression, and possibly other routes; enquire well in advance, since they're often booked from abroad.

Permits

When visiting sites within the limits of the oases, the main considerations are your vehicle, supplies and driving skills. Things get more complicated, however, if you're aiming for a remote location like Ain Dalla, or planning to cross the desert by an unusual route. For their own safety, motorists are required to stick to the main roads between the oases, and any significant detours need official **permission**. In Bahariya, Farafra, Dakhla and Kharga, this is the local army garrison; for Siwa, authority is vested with military intelligence at Mersa Matrouh. For cross-desert routes spanning several military districts, it's better to approach the Travel Permits Department of the Ministry of the Interior in Cairo (see p.231) or Alexandria.

Vehicles

The desert is a potentially lethal environment, so it's crucial to get the right vehicle.

If you're not planning anything too ambitious, a **camper** (mobile home) might be worth considering. You can hire one for £E100 a day (plus steep mileage and insurance charges) from *Sea and Caravan Tours* (55 Abdel Monim Hafez, Heliopolis, Cairo; ☎660-978) or *Starco* (1 Midan Talaat Harb, Downtown Cairo; ☎392-1205). However, campers are too ponderous for crossing soft sand, salt flats or boulder-strewn pans, and their fuel consumption is prodigious (carry a full extra tank in reserve), ruling them out for serious ventures off *piste*.

Providing they're up to scratch, **cars** are better. Mechanical reliability, high ground clearance and four-wheel drive are absolutely vital; non-automatic gears, a water-cooled engine and an electrical fuel pump are strongly advised. Tyres should be in good condition and have inner tubes; always carry two spare wheels, a tyre pump and pressure gauge, levers and a jack. A fire extinguisher, vital spares and a full tool/repair kit are also essential. *Max Rent-a-Car* (27 Sharia Libnan, Mohandiseen, Cairo; ☎347-4712) can usually provide cars which fit the bill.

Ideally, your vehicle should also have the following **modifications**: steel plates welded below the sump and fuel tank to prevent them being holed; fireproof lagging around the fuel lines where they pass the exhaust manifold; crossover seat belts; fabric covered seats; an extra, false roof above the cab (painted gloss white for maximum cooling effect); and a "trip" odometer for navigational calculations.

Equipment

You can *never* carry too much **water** (in metal or heavy-duty polythene jerrycans, securely fixed to brackets) or **fuel**; travelling off *piste* can reduce a car's normal mileage by half. Even staying within the limits of an oasis depression, it's vital to be able to orientate yourself. A vehicle-mounted **compass** must be adjusted to the car's magnetic field, which will also distort readings on hand-held compasses if you stand too close (as do ferrous rocks in Bahariya Oasis).

Desert driving

For deep desert expeditions it's wise to follow the tradition of travelling in pairs. More fundamentally, never set off – or keep going – during **sandstorms**; should you get caught in one, turn the car's rear end towards the wind, lest it sand-blasts the front windscreen and headlights into opacity.

Driving at **night** is likewise taboo: potholes are vicious and it's easy to crash or get lost. The **best times for driving** are early morning or late afternoon, when there's less risk of overheating or misjudging the terrain. During the middle of the day, the details of the landscape are lost in the glare, making it harder to judge **distances and scale**. Both are distorted by the desert, where drivers often perceive near-vertical slopes as level ground, or discarded jerrycans as villages. These kind of optical illusions are commoner than **mirages** of shimmering "lakes".

If you are driving cross-country, stay alert for **changes in the desert's surface**, often indicated by a shift in colour or texture. Wheel ruts left by other vehicles can also yield clues: a sudden deeping and widening usually means softer sand (another sign of which is vegetation around the edges of dunes). Generally speaking, gravel plains provide a firm surface, whilst salt flats and dunes are the most unstable. Deflating one's **tyres** increases their traction on soft sand, but also their surface temperature and the car's fuel consumption, so keep a reasonable speed.

Dunes

There's no substitute for experience of **dunes**, but a few points need making. Never crest a dune at high speed in case the far side has collapsed, leaving a slipface. If you *do* go over, accelerate hard (which tends to lower the rear of the vehicle), charge down the slope and hope to butch it out. Braking or slewing sideways seems the natural reaction, but it's likely to somersault or roll the car over the edge.

When deflating tyres for better traction, do this just before you drive onto sand, and pump them up again before gaining firm ground. Shifting into a lower gear should likewise be done in advance. If stuck in soft sand, revving the engine will only dig you in deeper. Stop at once, change into low gear and try driving out slowly. If this fails, deflate the tyres as far as possible (or put traction mats, brushwood etc, beneath the rear wheels) and try again.

Emergencies

Getting stuck, breaking down or crashing in the desert can be fatal if you compound the misfortune by acting wrongly. Assuming you're driving solo, *never leave your own vehicle* unless you're within 5km of a plainly visible settlement or major highway. Otherwise, stay put, keep cool (literally) and try to attract attention. By day you can burn oil-soaked sand or bits of rubber to produce thick black smoke; at night, make a fire. A vehicle, smoke or fire are hard enough for search parties to locate; a person on their own is virtually impossible.

Other **emergencies** arise simply through drivers getting lost. The moment you suspect this, stop and try to get orientated using a compass, the sun, or the watch or stick method; take your time calculating how much water and fuel remain, and deciding on a course of action. The worst thing to do is simply drive on by instinct – it's a sure way of wandering even further in the wrong direction.

Although proper spares are obviously preferable, **improvised materials** can serve for vital **repairs** – nylon tights make a substitute fan belt and chewing gum can plug holes in fuel tanks or radiators.

Maps

For details of the best relevant maps for exploring the oases, see p.22.

WADI NATRUN

The quasi-oasis of **Wadi Natrun** lies just off the Desert Road between Cairo and Alexandria, a place that takes its name – and oasis stature – from deposits of natron salts, a vital ingredient in ancient mummifications. Wadi Natrun's most enduring legacy, however, is its **monasteries**, which date back to the dawn of Christian monasticism, and have provided spiritual leadership for Egypt's Copts for the last 1500 years. Their fortified exteriors, necessary in centuries past to repel Bedouin raiders, cloak what are today very forward-looking, purposeful monastic establishments. Coptic monasticism experienced a revival during the 1980s, twenty years after Cottrell dismissed the monasteries as "decaying" and "of little interest except to the specialist".

The area surrounding Wadi Natrun is known as **Liberation Province** (*Mudiriyat el-Tahrir*). In the 1950s, model villages, olive groves and vineyards were planted here to reclaim 25,000 hectares of land from the desert, a project initially financed by the sale of King Farouk's stamp collection and other valuables. The soil is potentially fertile, but lacks water; hitherto, the main springs and lakes in Wadi Natrun have been saline. Currently a whole new conurbation, SADAT CITY, is being laid out to the east of the Desert Road. A planner's vision mix of science park and dormitory suburb, it is about as far removed as it's possible to imagine from the existing village of BIR HOOKER (named after one Mr Hooker, an early manager of the Egyptian Salt and Soda Co), a teeming shantytown straggling the entrance to the Natrun valley.

The monasteries: practicalities and transport

Wadi Natrun makes a memorable **day excursion** from Alex or Cairo, but a few caveats are in order. Getting within striking distance of the oasis requires little effort, time or cash, but reaching the widely dispersed monasteries can be difficult without using hired vehicles – and consequently expensive for solo travellers who can't split the cost. In addition, **Deir al-Suryani** monastery doesn't allow women visitors, while **Deir Abu Maqar** is generally reluctant to admit anyone without a letter of introduction from the Patriarchate in Cairo (next to the new Cathedral of Saint Mark, 222 Sharia Ramses, Abbassiya) or Alexandria (Nabi Daniel Street).

The Patriarchate may also grant permission for men **to stay** overnight, in which case a donation of £E10 is in order. Guests are fed, and expected to attend morning or evening prayers. There's nowhere else to stay, and the only alternative places to eat are the **cafés** on the Desert Road (most of which sell drinks and basic snacks).

Visiting hours for the monasteries are normally from around 10am to 5pm. Note, however, that visitors are excluded from the monasteries during the five seasons of **fasting**: 43 days before the Nativity; 3 days in commemoration of Jonah in the Whale; 55 days preceding Lent; the fast of the Holy Apostles (from Pentecost to July 12); and 15 days marking the Assumption of the Virgin Mary (Aug 7–22).

GETTING THERE

Unless you hire a car from the outset, getting to Wadi Natrun is a two-stage process. First you must reach the **Wadi Natrun turn-off on the Desert Road**, roughly 95km from Cairo. Any *service* taxi going that way between Cairo (Ahmed

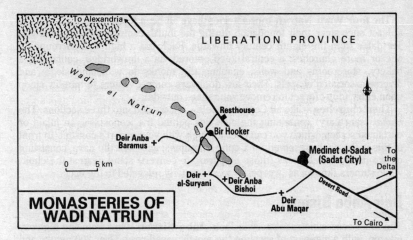

MONASTERIES OF WADI NATRUN

Helmi/Ramses Square) or Alex (Midan el-Gumhorriya) can drop you there within ninety minutes, though they'll charge the full inter-city fare (£E5.50). Slower *West Delta Bus Co* services (£E3.50) shuttling between the Arab League building on Tahrir Square in Cairo and Alexandria's Midan Orabi usually stop here as well, but check for sure.

Once you've arrived **at the turn-off**, have a drink at the pit-stop café and psych yourself up for negotiations with a taxi driver. For the trip to the two nearest monasteries, 10km away, taxis charge £E5 (for the car); any waiting time or trips to remoter sites means paying by the hour (£E10–15). Taking into account time spent driving there and chatting with the monks, reckon on spending at least an hour per monastery. If you don't retain a taxi, you'll have to walk or hitch rides, as young Copts do; there's most traffic on Fridays.

The Monasteries of Wadi Natrun

Christian monasticism was born in Egypt's Eastern Desert, where the first Christian hermits sought to emulate Saint Anthony, forming rude communities; however, it was at Wadi Natrun that their rules and power were forged. Peter Levi's study of monasticism, *The Frontiers of Paradise*, notes how this coincided with the persecution of Christians in urban areas, especially under Diocletian. Certainly, several thousand **monks** and hermits were living here by the middle of the fourth century, harbouring bitter grudges against paganism – scores which they settled after Christianity was made the state religion in 330 by sacking the temples and library and murdering scholars in Alexandria. E.M. Forster judged them "averse to culture and incapable of thought. Their heroes were Saint Ammon, who deserted his wife on their wedding eve, or Saint Anthony, who thought bathing was sinful and was consequently carried across the canals of the Delta by an angel". The Muslim conquest and Bedouin raids encouraged a siege-mentality amongst the monks, who often lapsed into idle dependence on monastic serfs. Nineteenth-century foreign visitors unanimously described them as slothful, dirty, bigoted and ignorant – the antithesis of the monks here today.

The **four Wadi Natrun monasteries** have all been totally ruined and rebuilt at least once since their foundation during the fourth century; most of what you see dates from the eighth century onwards. Each has a high wall surrounding one or more churches; a central keep entered via a drawbridge, containing a bakery, storerooms and wells, enabling the monks to withstand siege; and diverse associated chapels. Their low doorways compel visitors to humbly stoop upon entry (don't forget to remove your shoes outside).

Their **churches** – like all Coptic chapels – are divided into three sections. The *haikal* (sanctuary) containing the altar lies behind the iconostasis, an inlaid or curtained screen, which you can peer through with your escort's consent. In front of this is the choir, reserved for Coptic Christians; and then the nave, consisting of two parts. *Catechumens* (those preparing to convert) stand nearest the choir, while sinners (known as "weepers") were formerly relegated to the back.

Deir Anba Bishoi

The most accessible monastery is **Deir Anba Bishoi**, 10km from the highway pit-stop, with a signpost of sorts on the mostly paved road. Over 200 monks and novices live here, and the monastery of Saint Bishoi (or Pishoi) receives a steady stream of Coptic pilgrims.

The legend of **Bishoi** suggests he was one of the earliest monks at Wadi Natrun. An angel told the saint's mother that he was chosen to do God's work even before his birth in 320; two decades later he moved here to study under Saint Bemoi alongside John "the Short". Adopting a seemingly rather imaginative chronology, the legend also recalls that Bishoi met Christ as an old man, carried him to church, washed his feet and was allowed to drink the water as a reward. Whatever the truth, since Bishoi's death in 407 his body has reportedly stayed uncorrupted, and occasionally reaches out from beneath its red shroud to shake the hands of devout believers. Next to him lies Paul of Tammuh, who was revered for committing suicide seven times.

The complex

Saint Bishoi's is the oldest of the five **churches** in the monastery, and features three *haikals* dating from the ninth or tenth century. The **keep**, built three to four hundred years later, has chapels at ground level (around the back) and on the second storey, one floor above its drawbridge. There's also a fifth-century **well** where Berber tribesmen washed their swords after massacring the 49 Martyrs of the Monastery of Saint Makarius.

The multi-domed building farthest away from the entrance is the **residence of Pope Shenouda III**, the current Coptic pope. He uses it normally as an occasional retreat, though he was exiled here for some years by President Sadat. Most of the Coptic popes have been chosen from the monks of Wadi Natrun.

Deir al-Suryani

A sixth-century dispute over the theological importance of the Virgin led dissenting monks to found another monastery, 500m from Saint Bishoi's. After they returned to the fold it was purchased for a group of Syrian monks, hence its name, **Deir al-Suryani**. It was here that Robert Curzon came searching for ancient manuscripts (the ostensible reason for his tour of Balkan and Levantine

THE MONASTIC RULE AND WORKING DAY

All Egyptian monasteries are cenobitic, meaning that the monks share food and possessions and unconditional submission to the rule of their abbot (a word that derives from the Arabic *abu*, "father").

The **monastic day** begins at 3am with an hour of silent prayer in individual *laura* (cells), before two hours of collective worship in the chapel, followed by unrelenting labour until the main meal of the day at noon. Afterwards, the monks work until 5pm, assemble for prayers and then return to their tasks until sheer exhaustion forces them to bed.

Work and prayer are seen as equal holy obligations, and many of the younger monks and novices are qualified engineers or scientists. High-tech coexists with spiritualism, which is clearly apparent during liturgies. Black garments symbolise their death to the world of bodily desires; their hoods (possibly representing the "helmet of salvation" in *Ephesians* 6) are embroidered with twelve crosses, after Christ's disciples.

monasteries in the 1830s), and found them lying on the floor or serving as covers for jars, all "well begrimed with dirt". The keep's oil cellar held a "mass of loose vellum pages", whilst the consistory of Abyssinian monks contained a library of Aramaic texts, hanging from pegs in individual leather satchels. Nowadays, the monastery's antique volumes are lovingly maintained in a modern **library**.

al-Adra church

Deir al-Suryani's principal **Church of the Virgin** (*al-Adhra*), built around 980, contains a *haikal* with Tulunid-style stucco ornamentation, and a superb ebony "**Door of Prophecies**", inlaid with ivory panels depicting the disciples and the seven epochs of the Christian era. A dark passageway at the back of the church leads to the **cave** where Bishoi tied his hair to a chain hanging from the ceiling to prevent himself sleeping for four days, until a vision of Christ appeared. The marble basin (*lakan*) in the nave is used by the abbot to wash the feet of twelve monks on Maundy Thursday, emulating Christ's act during Passion week.

In the grounds is a tamarind tree said to have been planted by Pope (later Saint) Ephraim, who established cordial relations with the Fatimid khalif between 977–81; and a pair of embalmed armadillos.

Deir Anba Baramus

If you're keen on seeing one of the remoter monasteries, **Deir Anba Baramus** fits the bill. A newly built road running 4km north from the vicinity of Saint Bishoi's Monastery has reduced its isolation amidst barren sands, but it still feels far from the madding crowd. Visitors are greeted outside by a picture of Saint Moses "the Strong", a Nubian convert whose relics have joined Saint Isidore's within the Church of the Virgin's shrine. People drop petitions onto their bier, next to which hangs a photo of a T-shirt bearing their names and a bloody cross, resulting from an exorcism in the early 1980s. (For more about Egyptian exorcisms, see p.497.)

Tradition ascribes the monastery's foundation to Maximus and Domidus, two sons of the Roman Emperor Valentinus who died from excessive fasting; the younger one was only nineteen years old. Both are reputedly buried in a crypt beneath the altar, which is only used once a day – just as Mary's womb begot but one child. An adjacent altar, normally curtained off, serves the "Immaterial Fathers", the spirits of bygone saints and abbots who occasionally leave droplets of water sprinkled there. Restoration work since 1987 has revealed layers of medieval frescoes in the nave, the western end of which incorporates a fourth-century column with Syriac inscriptions. It was behind here that Saint Arsanious prayed with a pebble in his mouth, regretful only of the few words that he'd spoken (including a statement to that effect).

The ninth-century church (whose belfries of unequal height symbolise the respective ages of Maximus and Domidus) shares a vine-laden courtyard with a **keep** and four other churches. Deir Anba Baramus currently has eighty monks and novices, one of whom will doubtless show you around.

Kilia

The monks may also tell you about **Kilia**, a name given to the ruins of some 500 hermitages – covering a wide area 30km north of here – that French archaeologists have unearthed over the last decade. It's thought that the hermitages might have maintained links with the pilgrim city of Abu Mina (see p.478) until their freshwater springs dried up. There's also a chain of **saline lakes** rimmed by crusts of **natron**, a mixture of sodium carbonate and sodium bicarbonate which the ancients used for dehydrating bodies and making glass. Ducks, water-hens, jack snipes and sandpipers are typical of the **bird life** around these lakes.

Deir Abu Maqar

The oldest and furthest of the monasteries, **Deir Abu Maqar** lies 18km southwest of Saint Bishoi, and can also be reached by an eight-kilometre spur off the Desert Road, midway between the main turn-off and Sadat City.

Enclosed by a circular wall 10m high, the monastery requires visitors to pull a bellrope; in times past, two giant millstones stood ready to be rolled across to buttress the door against Bedouin raiders. Its founder, **Saint Makarius**, died in 390 "after sixty years of austerities in various deserts", the last twenty of which were spent in a hermit's cell at Wadi Natrun. He's said to have been so remorseful over killing a gnat that he withdrew for six months to the marshes, getting stung all over until "his body was so much disfigured that his brethren on his return only knew him from the sound of his voice". A rigorous faster, his only indulgence was a raw cabbage leaf for Sunday lunch.

The monastery

Despite repeated sackings, Abu Maqar has hung onto the bodies of the numerous Coptic popes that have been buried here, plus the 49 Martyrs whom the Berbers killed in 444. (In 1978, monks discovered what they believed to be the head of John the Baptist; however, this is also claimed to be held in Venice, Aleppo and Damascus.) Since its nadir in 1969, when only six monks lived here, the monastery has acquired 100 brethren, a modern printing press and a farm employing 600 workers. The monks have mastered pinpoint irrigation systems and bovine embryo transplant technology in an effort to meet their abbot's goal of feeding 1000 laypersons per monk, revitalising a landscape which "might be supposed to boast of nothing but the salt and natron for which it is indebted to its barrenness and its name" (*Murray's Handbook,* 1891).

THE FAYOUM

Likened in Egyptian tradition to a bud on the stem of the Nile and an "earthly paradise" in the desert, **the Fayoum** depends on river water – not springs or wells, like a true oasis. The water is distributed around the depression by a system of canals going back to ancient times, creating a lush rural enclave of palm trees dividing cotton and clover fields, orchards, and carefully tended crops of tomatoes and medicinal plants in the sandier outlying regions. Pigeons nest in mudbrick *burg al-hamam* shaped like Victorian trifles, blindfolded cattle turn threshing machines and water buffalo plod home for milking. Along one shore of Lake Qaroun are fishing communities, while on the periphery are encampments of semi-nomadic Bedouin.

Given easy access from Cairo, there have to be good reasons why foreign tourists are so thin on the ground. Number one is the Governorate capital, **Fayoum City**, which has all of Cairo's **drawbacks** and few of its advantages. Avaricious drivers bedevil day excursions to the distant **antiquities**, whilst *baksheesh*-hungry locals pester visitors to **Lake Qaroun**, where wealthy tourists are bussed in for shooting holidays. It is possible to get into the diverse **bird life**, local **moulids** or **desert expeditions**, but you have to be committed. If you're only lukewarm, a brief day trip will probably discourage further contact.

FAYOUM CLIMATE

The Fayoum's winters are warmer and drier than Cairo's; its summers milder than in Upper Egypt. Cold winds in spring precede the *khamseen*, which coats everything with dust. At other times, the clarity of the air causes the sun's rays to burn more strongly than you'd expect.

Getting there

The **road from Cairo** to the Fayoum starts near the Pyramids of Giza, whose silhouette sinks below the horizon as the road gains a barren plateau dotted with army bases, then (76km on) reaches the edge of the Fayoum depression. Once here, the Ptolemaic-Roman site of Kom Oshim is passed (on the left) before you sight Lake Qaroun and cruise down through Sinnuris into Fayoum City, driving past the Obelisk of Senusert I.

Buses (£E2) from Cairo's Ahmed Helmi and Giza stations (every 30min between 6.15am and 6.45pm) do the 100-kilometre journey in two hours; advance bookings are usually only necessary from midday Thursday till late on Saturday, or during Ramadan, Fayoumi *moulids* or public holidays. An alternative is to go to Midan Giza (bus #8 from Midan Tahrir) and grab a **service taxi**. These seven-seater Peugeots or pack'em-in minibuses run practically non-stop between early morning and late at night, charging £E2–3 for a stomach-churning high speed ride past the wrecks of previous crashes, reaching Fayoum City in just over an hour – *inshallah*. Both services use the depot just north of the Bahr Yussef canal in the centre of town.

Coming from the Nile Valley, catch one of the half-hourly buses (75pt) or *service* taxis (£E1) **from Beni Suef**, which reach Fayoum City in an hour. The road runs through a cultivated strip beside the Bahr Yussef, so there's little sense of entering an oasis; en route it passes the start of tracks to the Lahun and Hawara pyramids. Buses and *service* taxis coming from this direction terminate at the al-Hawatim depot in the southwest of town.

Fayoum City

A kind of pocket-sized version of Cairo, with the Bahr Yussef canal in the role of the Nile, **FAYOUM CITY*** makes a grab at the wallets of middle-class Egyptians who come to bask beside Lake Qaroun during summertime, and any foreigners that come to hand. Most of the latter are whisked through in coaches and remain immured in luxury hotels, so independent travellers bear the brunt of local hustlers – and obnoxious teenagers, if you're a woman. Another major drawback is that mosquitoes swarm from every nook and waterway, making evenings a misery. Add makeshift buildings, weaving traffic and malodorous canals and you've got half a dozen reasons not to linger.

On the plus side, the city has the cheapest accommodation in the area and serves as the jumping-off point for almost everywhere you might consider visiting in the oasis. It also musters a pleasant **souk**, a couple of venerable **mosques** and some colourful **moulids** – the biggest of which (see overpage) is that of Ali er-Rubi in the middle of the month of Sha'ban .

Orientation and getting around

Most things worth seeing in the city can be reached on foot, with the Bahr Yussef canal facilitating **orientation**. When locals can't be bothered to walk, they catch minibuses (15pt) or horse-drawn buggies called *hantours*. Minibus routes are hard to figure out without local advice, so *hantours* are better for getting around if you've got luggage or lack confidence about directions. Fares are negotiable before or after the ride; reckon on around £E1.50 for a trip across town (al-Hawatim terminal to the centre, for example).

Arriving from Cairo by bus or taxi, you'll be dropped about 50m east of the **tourist office** (☎225-86), a prefab box keeping irregular hours (closed Fri). If you're planning to explore the Fayoum, it's worth checking here that locations of the various *service* taxi depots are still current.

Accommodation

There shouldn't be any difficulty **finding a room** outside of er-Rubi's *moulid*. Fayoum has several moderately priced hotels, while other options exist at Ain es-Siliyin and Lake Qaroun (see sections following).

Montazah Hotel, Sharia Ismail al-Medany (☎324-633). Marked on our plan – north of the centre. Run by Copts, this has slightly tatty but otherwise agreeable singles (£E7; £E10 with private shower), doubles (£E11/£E13) and triples (£E17), with breakfast, fans, fridges and sporadic hot water included in the deal.

Palace Hotel, by the Bahr Yussef – see plan (☎323-641). Wide range of singles (£E9–12.50) and doubles (£E15–25); the grasping owners charge whatever they can get away with. Beware of the besuited spiv called Magdi, who claims to be the manager's cousin.

Queen Hotel, Sharia Menshat Luftallah (☎326-819). Ask the tourist office for directions to this newly-opened hotel with modern singles (£E10), doubles (£E17) and suites (£E25) with A/C, TV and phones.

The **Ramla Hotel**, across the canal, is a total fleapit, and you have to be pretty stingy to bother with the **youth hostel** (☎36-82; £E2 per night, opens 2pm; see plan).

---

*The city is officially **Medinet el-Fayoum**, but known as **el-Fayoum** or **Fayoum** in colloquial usage (not *el-Medina*, as some guidebooks say). The word "Fayoum" probably derives from *Phiom*, the Coptic word for "sea", although folklore attributes it to the pharaoh's praise of the Bahr Yussef: "This is the work of a thousand days" (*alf youm*).

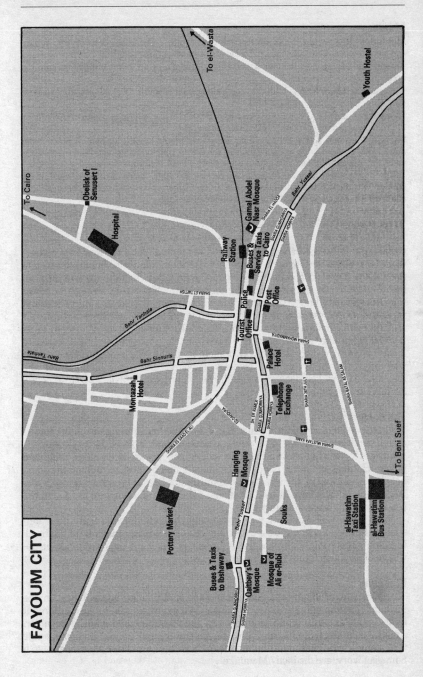

FAYOUM CITY

To el-Wasta

Youth Hostel

To Cairo

Obelisk of
Senusert I

Hospital

Gamal Abdel
Nasr Mosque

Bahr Yussef

Railway
Station

Buses &
Service Taxis
to Cairo

SHARIA EL-MAHDI

SHARIA GUMHORIYA

SHARIA HORRIYA

SHARIA ET TATSH

Police

Post
Office

Tourist
Office

SHARIA MOHAMMADIYA

Bahr Tanhala

Bahr Sinnuria

Bahr Tanhala

Palace
Hotel

SHARIA 26TH JULY

SHARIA BATAL AS SALAM

Montazah
Hotel

Telephone
Exchange

SHARIA GUMHORIYA

SHARIA MUSTAFA KAMIL

SH. EK ALM LA

SHARIA HORRIYA

SHARIA ES SAADE AL

Hanging
Mosque

To Beni Suef

Pottery Market

Bahr Yussef

Souks

al-Hawatim
Taxi Station

al-Hawatim
Bus Station

Buses & Taxis
to Ibshaway

Qaitbey's
Mosque

Mosque of
Ali er-Rubi

SHARIA GUMHORIYA

SHARIA HORRIYA

Meals

Mokhimar Restaurant, 100m west of the tourist office. The best cheap eatery, serving excellent chicken, *tahina*, kebabs and salad at reasonable prices; soft drinks only.

Cafeteria el-Medina, by the four waterwheels. A bit of a rip-off, but you might succumb to breakfast (£E3).

Governorate Club, Nadi al-Muhafza, north along Bahr Sinnuris (50pt admission). Western-style food, with a nice garden out back.

L'Auberge – at Lake Qaroun (see overpage). If you feel like splurging, make a trip here for the wild duck and other treats (£E20–30 for a meal).

Sherif's, Mustapha Kamil, between Bahr Yussef and Sharia Ramleh; **unnamed place** 100m north along the east bank of Bahr Sinnuris. Ice cream, milk puddings and *bilea* – hot wheat and milk, topped with nuts, raisins and sugar that's a local wintertime favourite.

Other places for sit-down Egyptian meals are **Kebabgi** (opposite *Sherif's*) and **Hagg Khaled** (Sharia Muhammadia). **Said's**, next to the Sinnuris taxi stand, serves cheap *kushari*, and fried fish is sold by weight near the main level-crossing.

The City

Groaning away in the background, behind the tourist office, are four large **water-wheels**, symbolic of Fayoumi agriculture. Because Nile water is introduced into the sloping depression at its highest point, gravity does half the work of distribution. Sluices at el-Lahun regulate the current, which is strong enough to power waterwheels for lifting irrigation water where needed – except during January, when the whole system is allowed to dry out for cleaning and maintenance.

Coptic and Muslim folklore ascribes the **Bahr Yussef** (River of Joseph) to its Biblical namesake, who's believed to have been the pharaoh's architect. In reality it was originally a natural waterway branching off the Nile near Beni Suef, which was regulated from the XII Dynasty onwards. Since the building of the Ibrahimiya Canal last century, it has drawn water from the Nile at Dairut, nearly 300km further south.

The souks

Walking west alongside the canal and crossing the fourth bridge from the tourist office, you'll notice a side street with a wooden roof. This is the city's **souk**: a compact labyrinth of alleys with stalls selling copperware and spices, grain and pulses, clothing and other goods – all without a hint of tourism. Behind the souk, keeping slightly aloof, the street of **goldsmiths** (*es-Sagha*) is crammed with jewellery shops, mostly owned by Christians. (There's a church nearby, and three larger ones on Sharia 26th July.)

More persistent hawkers flog ornamental baskets (*sabat*) near the water-wheels. For ceramics, there's a better choice at the **pottery market** off Sharia el-Mudaris (Tues only). Most of the red, pink or unglazed pots are made at the village of an-Nazla, south of Ibshaway.

Mosques

The **Mosque of Khawand Asal-Bey**, west of the souk, is the oldest in the Fayoum. Traditionally attributed to Sultan Qaitbey, who's said to have ordered it built for his favourite concubine in 1499, the mosque could actually be older. Ancient columns from Kiman Faris (see box overpage) uphold its dome, while the stone carving around the doorway, and the ebony *minbar* inlaid with Somalian ivory, are distinctly Mamluke.

The twin-arched bridge nearby, once also named after Khawand, is now called the "Bridge of Farewells" because it leads to a cemetery. By walking east and turning right before the next bridge, and then right again further up the street, you should come upon the Mosque and **Mausoleum of Ali er-Rubi**. The *darih* or carved box-frame around the tomb is often surrounded by Fayoumis muttering or shouting supplications to this revered sheikh. On the other bank opposite the souk, the **Hanging Mosque** – built above five arches – is undergoing restoration.

Moulids

It's worth visiting Fayoum purely for its moulids, as loads of *fellaheen* do. Hotels overflow during **Ali er-Rubi's moulid** in Sha'ban, when the alleys around his mosque are crammed with stalls purveying sugar dolls and horsemen, and all kinds of amusements, whilst the devout perform *zikrs* in the courtyard.

The other big occasion is the "viewing" (*er-Ruyeh*) of the new moon that heralds **Ramadan**. This calls for a huge procession from the Gamal Abd en-Nasir Mosque. Headed by the security forces, followed by imams and Sufi sheikhs, a parade of carnival floats "mimes" the work of different professions and bombards spectators with "lucky" prayer-leaflets.

During the month of Ramadan, there's a small *moulid* at the domed white tomb of **Sheikha Mariam** (between the sluice of the Bahr Sinnuris and the *Cafeteria el-Medina*). The **Great Feast** (starting on the tenth of Zoul Hagga) is a more private occasion, with most eateries closed, so avoid coming then.

Lastly, on the Monday after the moveable **Coptic Easter**, everyone "Smells the Breeze" along the Bahr and the shore of Lake Qaroun.

FUNDAMENTALIST POLITICS IN THE FAYOUM

On the off-chance that future festivities could turn nasty, it's best to know about the **troubles** since April 1989, when a protest march by Islamic fundamentalists exploded into a riot after the police moved in with clubs and tear-gas and grabbed Sheikh Omar Abd el-Rahman. Having lived here under house arrest since his acquittal in the "Trial of the Jihad 302" (see p.264), the blind sheikh is currently once again on trial for conspiracy against the state, accused of sending followers to be trained by the Afghan *mujahadin*. Another group, New Islamic Jihad, actually seized control of an outlying Fayoumi village in May 1990 and five other breakaway groups allegedly exist in the oasis.

As a visitor to the Fayoum, it pays to say nothing about past troubles yet keep alert for signs of aggro – for all that it's unlikely to happen.

The Seven Waterwheels and the Obelisk of Senusert I

For a pleasant half-hour's walk in the morning or evening, follow the Bahr Sinnuris northwards out of town to reach the **Seven Waterwheels**. First comes a single wheel near a farm; slightly further on, a quartet revolves against a backdrop of mango trees and palms; the final pair is a little way on, near a crude bridge. The Fayoum has about 200 such waterwheels (introduced by Ptolemaic engineers in the third century BC), which have a working life of ten years if properly tarred and maintained.

Entering or leaving town by the Cairo road you can't miss the 13-metre-high red granite **Obelisk of Senusert I**, which doesn't merit a closer look. Senusert was the second king of the XII Dynasty, which displayed a special fondness for the Fayoum and was the first to regard it as more than just a hunting ground, building the Lahun and Hawara pyramids, Medinet Ma'adi and Qasr es-Sagha. Following the XII Dynasty (1991–1786 BC), interest in the Fayoum declined, and didn't properly revive until the advent of the Ptolemies, fourteen centuries later.

SOBEK AND CROCODILOPOLIS

Kiman Faris (Horseman's Mounds) is the local name for a site on the northern outskirts of Fayoum City, rapidly disappearing beneath new colleges. Although

Sobek

nothing exists to justify a visit, it deserves a mention as the **site of Crocodilopolis** (later renamed *Arsinoë* after Ptolemy II's sister-wife), the Fayoum's ancient capital and centre of the crocodile cult. This supposedly began with Pharaoh Menes, the legendary unifier of Upper and Lower Egypt, whose life was saved by a croc whilst he was hunting in the Fayoum marshes. Crocodiles infested the lake beyond Kiman Faris (which was much larger in ancient times), so an urge to propitiate the creatures is understandable.

The crocodile-deity, **Sobek**, was particularly favoured by Middle Kingdom rulers but assumed national prominence after he became identified with Re (as Sobek-Re) and Horus. He was variously depicted as a hawk-headed crocodile or in reptilian form with Amun's crown of feathers and ram's horns. At the Sacred Lake of Crocodilopolis, reptiles were fed and worshipped, and even adorned with jewellery, by the priests of Sobek.

Around Fayoum oasis

The oasis's other populous centres – Sinnuris, Ibshaway, Itsa and Tamiya – hold little interest. However, there are enjoyable scenic spots easily accessible from Fayoum City in the form of the springs of **Ain es-Siliyin** and **Lake Qaroun**. Reaching the seldom-visited **ancient sites** on the periphery of the oasis is more tricky, entailing a bus or taxi ride out to a turn-off and then a fair bit of walking. Don't undertake a jaunt lightly, nor set off without adequate water and food for the day – you can't rely on finding them in the sticks. Short of hiring a private taxi, you'll have to **get around** in *service* taxis, *bijous* (covered pick-ups with fixed fares and routes), local buses or trains. *Bijou* and taxi drivers frequently overcharge, so it's wise to check fares beforehand and pay with the exact money. Having said that, rural truck drivers often carry hitchhikers for free, and it's worth trying to flag down anything that moves.

Aside from being alert for tractors, kids and livestock, **drivers** should take care in visiting the remoter sites (see the "Desert Driving" box at the beginning of this chapter). You'll need a car with high ground-clearance, if not four-wheel drive; adequate water (for people and radiators); and shovels and traction mats or boards (for digging cars out of soft sand). Always travel with at least one other car and heed local advice about the weather; never travel during the *khamseen*.

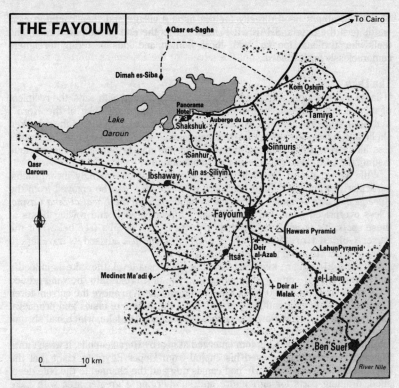

THE FAYOUM

To Cairo

Qasr es-Sagha

Dimah es-Siba

Kom Oshim

Panorama Hotel

Lake Qaroun

Shakshuk

Auberge du Lac

Tamiya

Qasr Qaroun

Sanhur

Sinnuris

Ibshaway

Ain as-Siliyin

Fayoum

Hawara Pyramid

Deir al-Azab

Lahun Pyramid

Itsa

Medinet Ma'adi

Deir al-Malak

el-Lahun

Beni Suef

River Nile

0   10 km

Ain es-Siliyin

Fayoumis rate **Ain es-Siliyin** as a major beauty spot – and perhaps it was in the days before two cafeterias, a football pitch, pool and chalets were built in the hollow where the Siliyin **springs** bubbled forth. Nowadays they spurt from pipes, and hordes of picnickers (Fridays are busiest) have trampled the surrounding vegetation. The pool itself is perennially packed with kids and, whatever Egyptians say, it's *not* a good idea to drink the spring water.

To reach the springs, which are sited 9km north of town just before the village of the same name, ask for directions to the taxi and *bijou* depot serving Sanhur, Shakshuk and other points north. This is currently located just off the railway tracks several blocks west of Bahr Sinnuris, but it moves from time to time. Public **transport** is cheap: to the springs or Sanhur by *bijou* costs about 25pt; don't be fooled into hiring a private taxi instead of a *service*. Should you want **to stay**, the *Ain as-Siliyin Hotel* has seedy, fanless rooms for £E16.

Lake Qaroun

To reach **Lake Qaroun**, ride on to SANHUR and catch a pick-up heading for "*el-Birka*" (The Pond), as it's familiarly known. Some *bijous* join the lakeside road 3km east of the *Auberge du Lac* hotel and then run west along the shore towards

Shakshuk; others head directly for the fishing village and then continue eastwards past the hotels. SHAKSHUK itself marks the end of the paved road, and feels like a village too far, with local women and kids pestering foreigners remorselessly for *baksheesh*.

The Lake

"Glassy and brooding, surrounded by beaches encrusted with salts, the recipient of all the drainage canals in the region", Lake Qaroun ("Lake of the Horn") makes an unlikely resort. Egyptians seem undeterred by the beach of broken shells and a lack of showers for removing saline gunk, but you may feel rather less like **swimming**. (The enthusiastic may be glad to note that, though foultasting, the lake's water is at least free of bilharzia.)

With barren desert on its far shore, the lake looks strikingly incongruous, particularly when the fishing boats are out. The view can be enjoyed from the *Auberge du Lac*'s verandah, lemonade in hand, or from the *Gabal al-Zina Casino*, a less overpriced joint 1km west. Besides hiring parasols and rowing **boats** at these spots, it's possible to negotiate trips to Dimeh es-Siba (see below) or the barren **Golden Horn Island** where *Murray's Handbook* advised its travellers to camp in order "to avoid the hyenas and Arabs".

Covering 214 square kilometres at 45m below sea level, the **lake** is indeed a mere *birka* (pond) compared to when the Nile first broke into the wind-eroded Fayoum depression 70,000 years ago, forming a lake 40m above the current level. Egyptian mythology identified this with *Nun*, the waters of chaos and primaeval life; from the Stone Age onwards people lived around the lake, which had shrunk considerably by Dynastic times.

Although the Middle Kingdom emerged at nearby Heracleopolis, it wasn't until Pharaoh Amenemhat I moved his capital from Upper Egypt to Lisht that the Fayoum became important. He had canals dug and the channel to the Nile deepened, draining parts for agriculture and submerging a greater area with Lake Moeris. It was this that the Ptolemies lowered to reclaim land for their settlements, whose decline by the end of the Roman period matched the lake's drop to 36m below sea level. Increasing salinity was a problem by medieval times, and after the lake came into equilibrium with the water-sheet 40m beneath the Libyan Desert in 1890, it became too salty for its freshwater fish; since when, new marine species have been introduced.

The Fayoum nonetheless abounds in **bird life**, from the ubiquitous cattle egrets and grey herons to hard-to-spot wagtails, skylarks, kestrels, kites and Senegal coucals. But it's the vast numbers of ducks, geese and quail wintering here which brings hunters from all over to the lakeside hotels, making reservations advisable at this time of year.

Hotels

King Farouk's former lodge, where heads of state met in 1945, has become the *Auberge du Lac* (☎324-924; in Cairo ☎725-848; telex 93095 AUB FA UN), with the swankiest singles (£E70) and doubles (£E85) around. Nearly as good is the *Panorama Shakshuk* (☎725-848 in Cairo), with singles (£E43), doubles (£E55) and suites (£E77). Midway between them lies the *Oasis Motel*, with A/C doubles (£E30) and rather erratic power and water. Ask about its planned caravan and campsite.

Kom Oshim: Ancient Karanis

The most accessible of the ancient sites in the Fayoum is **Kom Oshim**, 30km from Fayoum City, where the Cairo road descends into the depression.

Ask a bus or taxi driver to drop you off at *Mat'haf Kom Oshim*, the small **museum** (Tues–Sun 9am–4pm) by the road. Delicate pottery and glassware, terracotta figures used for modelling hairstyles and a lifelike "Fayoum portrait" (see below) convey the wealth and sophistication of the ancient frontier town whose ruins lie behind the museum.

The **ruins of Karanis** clearly show the layout of this Ptolemaic-Roman town, founded by Greek colonists during the third century BC, which had a population of 3000 or so until the fifth century AD. Although the mudbrick houses have been reduced to low walls, two stone temples are better preserved – no thanks to the nineteenth-century Antiquities Department, which allowed contractors to destroy Roman buildings for their bricks. During Petrie's excavations, "incessant feuds, alarms, and nightly plunderings went on".

Snack stands and a **campsite** of sorts operate in the vicinity; to return to Fayoum or Cairo, flag down any passing bus or *service* taxi. During opening hours the museum can usually provide a guide for excursions to Qasr es-Sagha and Dimeh es-Siba (see below).

Qasr es-Sagha and Dimeh es-Siba

Adventurous types might go for visiting the ancient sites of **Qasr es-Sagha** and **Dimeh es-Siba** in the desert north of Lake Qaroun. Because of looting, you need to obtain permission from the Karanis museum (see above), which strongly recommends that you take a guide. Even with the right sort of vehicles it's important to stick to the vaguely marked track (starting by the police station opposite the museum), for soft sand lurks off *piste*. The forty-kilometre journey to Qasr es-Sagha takes about ninety minutes; Dimeh, 9km further south, can also be reached by paying a boatman to row you across the lake (1–2hr) and return some hours later; either way, the excursion will take the best part of an afternoon.

The sites
Qasr es-Sagha (Palace of the Jewellers), a small Middle Kingdom temple, nestles inconspicuously halfway up a scarp. Although lacking any friezes or inscriptions, it's still remarkable for its masonry, which is unlike that of any other Egyptian temple. The blocks are irregularly shaped, with odd angles and corners fitting together like a jigsaw; the overall effect is of a transplanted Inca edifice. Lake Qaroun, which once lapped its feet, now lies 11km away, beyond the ruins of a Ptolemaic settlement which pegged out as the lake shrank.

Starkly visible against the desert, the ruins of **Dimeh es-Siba** (Dimeh of the Wolves) are ringed by a wall up to 10m high and 5m thick. In the centre is a rough-hewn, ruined temple that was dedicated to Soknopaios, a form of Sobek (see box on p.404); the hill on which it stands was originally an island in the crocodile-infested lake. Approaching from that direction – a 2.5-kilometre walk – you'll come first to a 400-metre-long road (flanked by stone lions as late as the nineteenth century) running past ruined houses into the temple enclosure. Dimeh used to be the last stop for caravans before they entered the desert, and its majestic desolation exceeds that of el-Bagawat in Kharga Oasis.

Qasr Qaroun

Qasr Qaroun, a better preserved and more accessible Ptolemaic temple, lies on the northwestern edge of the oasis, roughly 45km from Fayoum City. To get there, take a *service* taxi from the rank on the canal near Khawand's Mosque to IBSHAWAY, and then another one from there towards the village of QAROUN; the temple is close to the road just before its namesake.

Not a palace as its Arabic name suggests, Qasr Qaroun is an outwardly plain but inwardly labyrinthine temple. You'll need a torch to explore its warren of chambers, stairs and passageways at different levels; beware of scorpions, bats, snakes and lizards – the latter resemble miniature crocodiles, as befits a temple dedicated to Sobek. Roundabout are the **ruins of Dionysias**, a Ptolemaic-Roman town believed to have been abandoned in the fourth century AD when the lake shrank (it's now 45 minutes' walk away), leaving dessicated stalks of vegetation. Early European travellers undertook nine-hour horse rides to this site, believing that it was the famous Labyrinth described by Herodotus and Strabo.

Medinet Ma'adi

Medinet Ma'adi – "Ma'adi's Town" – is another temple site in the desert, roughly 35km southwest of Fayoum City. **Getting there** entails catching the el-Qasmiya bus from the al-Hawatim depot (7am & 11am) and riding on through Itsa, el-Minia and Abu Gandir. Ask to be dropped off at Menshat Sef, roughly one hour later. From this bridge it's about an hour's walk to the temple. Turn right, follow the canal to the next bridge, cross over and take a narrower canal path past a small village on your left, aiming for a stone hut on the rise ahead, beyond which lies the site.

Squatting in a sandy hollow where excavations are revealing an avenue of sphinxes and lions (one of them ruffed and bearded like a Renaissance grandee), the **Temple of Medinet Ma'adi** was built for the XII Dynasty pharaohs Amenemhat III and IV, and dedicated to twin deities. Sobek appears in relief on the outside of the rear wall, whilst Renenutet the serpent goddess (also associated with harvests) can be seen in the left-hand room of the limestone edifice. Ptolemaic additions include two female winged sphinxes, and the **ruined town** of mud- and fired-bricks to the southeast. Although legend attributes its destruction to a tribe of eleventh-century Nejd warriors enraged by King Ma'adi's refusal of hospitality, the real cause of its blight was probably the shrinking of the lake. What looks like an embankment north of the temple was actually the storm beach of the lake in ancient times, 68m above its present level.

To return to Fayoum City, catch the bus from Menshat Sef at 12am or 4pm (going in the same direction, because the route is circular).

Pyramids around the Fayoum

The Fayoum is associated with four separate **pyramid sites**, two of them beyond its limits, the other pair more conveniently sited off the Beni Suef road. The latter, at **Lahun** and **Hawara**, both date from the XII Dynasty, which governed Egypt – and ordered the waterworks that transformed the Fayoum – from its capital *Itj-tway* (Seizer of the Two Lands). This lay 30km to the northeast, near **Lisht**, where the dynasty's founder Amenemhat I built his own pyramid.

The fourth site, **Maidum**, is unconnected with the others (which it predates by seven centuries), but its dramatic-looking "Collapsed Pyramid" marks an evolutionary step between the pyramids at Saqqara and Giza.

Hawara Pyramid

Stripped of its limestone casing, the mudbrick **Pyramid of Amenemhat III** has degenerated into a humpy mound offering great views of the surrounding area. Unlike most pyramids, its entrance (now blocked) was on the south side: one of many ruses devised to foil tomb-robbers – to no avail. The body of the pharaoh (1842–1797 BC) had been looted and burned centuries before Petrie rediscovered his sarcophagus alongside that of his daughter, Nefru-Ptah, which was stored here while her own tomb was being constructed. (It was found intact with her treasures in 1956.) East of the pyramid (the direction from which visitors approach) lies a bone- and bandage-littered necropolis, with deep shafts to ensnare the unwary.

Amenemhat III

To the south, towards and beyond the canal, a few column stumps and masses of limestone chippings mark the **site of the Labyrinth**. All that's known about Amenemhat III's mortuary temple comes from Strabo and Herodotus (who was prone to exaggeration). Reportedly, it contained over 3000 chambers hewn from a single rock, half of them underground (where the kings and mummified crocs were buried): surpassing "all the walls and other great works of the Greeks ... put together".

In the Roman cemetery north of the pyramid, Petrie unearthed 146 brilliantly naturalistic **"Fayoum Portraits"**, dating from 100–250 AD. Executed in beeswax-based paint whilst their sitters were alive, they were cut to size and stuck on to the bandaged cadavers, whose mummification was perfunctory compared to the embalming of Dynastic times. One such portrait graces the Karanis museum (see previous page); others can be admired in Cairo's Egyptian Museum.

Getting to the pyramid involves a ten-kilometre *service* taxi ride from al-Hawatim depot to just beyond the village of HAWARA, whence you take the left-hand turning, cross the Bahr Yussef by a shaky bridge and walk on for about 3km until the pyramid appears. From its summit (easily reached by climbing the southwest corner) you should be able to see the Lahun Pyramid on the southeastern horizon.

Lahun Pyramid

Nine kilometres beyond Hawara, the incoming Nile waters pass through EL-LAHUN, where modern sluices stand just north of the **Qantara of Sultan Qaitbey**; the thirteenth-century equivalent of the regulators installed by Amenemhat III. (Photographing these installations is forbidden.) Lahun gets its name from the ancient Egyptian *Le-hone* (Mouth of the Lake), and gives it to the Pyramid of Senusert II sited 5km away. Most of the *service* taxis from al-Hawatim to el-Lahun stop where the track leaves the main road; it's well over an hour's walk to the pyramids from there.

Built seven or eight centuries after the pyramids at Giza, the **Pyramid of Senusert II** employed a new and different technique. The core consists of a rock

Senusert II

knoll on which limestone pillars were based, providing the framework for the mudbrick overlay, which was finally encased in stone. Mindful of flooding, the pharaoh's architect, Anupy, surrounded the base with a trench full of sand and rolled flints, to act as a "sponge".

Alas, the subsequent removal of its casing stones left the mudbrick pyramid exposed to the elements, which eroded it into its present mess. When Petrie entered the pyramid and found Senusert's sarcophagus it had been looted long ago; however, Brunton discovered the jewellery of Princess Sat-hathor, which is now divided between Cairo's museum and the Metropolitan Museum of Art in New York.

Senusert II (1897–78 BC) was Amenemhat III's grandfather, and ordered eight rock-cut mastabas for his family to the north of his pyramid; east of them is the shapeless, so-called Queen's Pyramid, apparently lacking any tomb.

Maidum Pyramid

Although technically outside the limits of the Fayoum, the **"Collapsed Pyramid" of Maidum** is best reached from there. Take an early morning train from Fayoum to EL-WASTA (1hr), and then a *service* taxi to the village of MAIDUM (10–15min). From the far end of the village it's a short walk across the fields and two canals into the desert; beware of potholes and skulls as you tread. The pyramid is visible from the Nile Valley road, and during the last stage of the train journey.

Standing isolated and truncated amidst the sands "with much of its outer layers collapsed into piles of rubble, it looks more like the keep of a medieval castle than a proper pyramid", as T.G.H. James observed. It rises, in fact, in sheer-walled tiers above mounds of debris: a vision almost as dramatic as the act of getting inside used to be, when "visitors had to hang by their hands from the ledge above and drop into the entry guided by a guard". Nowadays you climb a thirty-metre stairway on the north side, descend to the bedrock via a passageway, and then ascend to the airless, corbelled burial chamber (bring a torch). Roundabout the pyramid are subsidiary, unfinished buildings, reduced to "ruinous lumps", where the exquisite "Maidum Geese" frieze and the famous statue of Prince Ra-Hotpe and his wife Nofret were found (both can now be seen in Room 32 of the Cairo Egyptian Museum).

Archaeologists ascribe the pyramid to **Snofru** (see p.190), the first king of the IV Dynasty (c.2613–2494 BC), or to **Huni**, the last ruler of the preceding dynasty. Partisans of Huni argue that Snofru is recognised as having built the Red and Bent pyramids at Dahshur, and would therefore not have needed a third repository for his *ka*. Mendelssohn's *The Riddle of the Pyramids* advances the contrary theory that Maidum was started by Snofru as a step-pyramid (like Zoser's at Saqqara), and then later given an outer shell to make it a "true" pyramid. But the design was faulty, distributing stresses outwards rather than inwards, so its own mass blew the pyramid apart. Mendelssohn argues that Snofru had already embarked on another pyramid at Dahshur, whose angle was hastily reduced (hence the Bent Pyramid), and that the Red Pyramid was a final attempt to get things right. Crucial to his argument is the idea that pyramids were built in production-line fashion, whether there were pharaohs to be buried in them or not; thus, kings who died before the completion of their own pyramid could be allotted one from the "stockpile".

Lisht Pyramids

The **Pyramids of Lisht** are the most inaccessible and ruined of the Fayoum collection, with little claim to anyone's attention. The larger of them, the **Pyramid of Amenemhat I** (1991–1962 BC), commemorates the founder of the XII Dynasty, whose capital, *Itj-tway*, was somewhere in the vicinity. Slightly to the south and harder to reach is the **Pyramid of Senusert I**, Amenemhat's son.

Fayoumi monasteries

Tradition has it that Saint Anthony personally inspired the first hermits in the Fayoum during the fourth century, and within 200 years the depression held 35 monastic communities. As elsewhere in Egypt, Coptic monasticism gradually declined after the Muslim conquest, and has only started to revive during this century. But the habit of pilgrimage never faded, and still ensures visitors to monasteries which are virtually deserted except on holy days.

Deir al-Azab

Deir al-Azab, the nearest monastery to Fayoum City, is reached by heading 5km out along the Beni Suef road, and turning left at a fork; the monastery is on the right after just over a kilometre. Founded during the twelfth century and recently rebuilt *sans* style, the "Bachelor's Monastery" no longer houses monks, but draws many Coptic visitors on Fridays and Sundays, and the **Moulid of the Virgin** (Aug 15–22). It's the burial place of Saint Abram, the revered Bishop of Fayoum and Giza between 1882 and 1914, whose portrait is said to reach out and shake hands with blessed visitors.

Deir el-Malak

The remoter, more picturesque **Deir el-Malak** (Angel Monastery) squats on a desert hillside overlooking the cultivated lowlands, a single monk in attendance. Pilgrim buses may turn up for the **Moulid of Archangel Gabriel** (Dec 18), but otherwise it's very quiet. Wolves have been known to make their dens in the hillside caves; from the ridge you can see the Lahun gap, and sometimes the Lahun and Hawara pyramids. *Service* taxis for Qalamsha run past a yellow stone barn in the village of QALHANA, whence a dirt track leads to the monastery (1hr walk).

Deir Mari Girgis and Deir Anba Samwil

Two yet remoter sites which we didn't check out are the monasteries of Saint George and Saint Samuel.

Deir Mari Girgis was restarted early this century by two monks whose relics are in the refectory, and hosts the **Moulid of Saint George** a week before the Feast of Ascension. For the occasion, there should be a boat there from SIDMANT AL-GABAL, 10km southwest of el-Lahun.

Deir Anba Samwil is totally isolated in the desert, 30km south of the oasis rim, and can only be reached (with a guide) by donkey or four-wheel drive. Two neighbouring springs sustain it in the Valley of Salts (*Wadi al-Mawalih*); Saint Samuel and other early hermits lived in caves on Jebel al-Qalamun, 4–5km east of the present monastery, which has been rebuilt recently by monkish engineers.

THE GREAT DESERT CIRCUIT

Only feasible for tourists since the 1980s, the **Great Desert Circuit** is one of the finest journeys Egypt has to offer. Starting from Cairo or Assyut, it runs for over 1000km through a desert landscape pockmarked by sculpted dunes and lofty escarpments. En route, amid a group of wind-eroded depressions, four **oases** are sustained: **Bahariya**, **Farafra**, **Dakhla** and **Kharga**.

Although each of the oases has a focus in its scattered springs and palm groves, differences between them are as marked as similarities. **Bahariya** and **Farafra** both score highly on their hot springs and picturesque old quarters, but the former is laid-back and hedonistic while the latter is given to religious fervour. In **Dakhla** and **Kharga** the modern centres are less appealing than the ancient ruins and villages on their periphery, redolent of links with the Nile Valley or the old slave trail from the Sudan. Staying overnight in the haunting **White Desert** between Bahariya and Farafra is a must, while for those with transport and a lust for adventure there are remoter destinations like **Ain Dalla** and **Jebel 'Uweinat**.

Exploring the circuit

Local **conditions** are pretty tough for visitors. Accommodation (in government resthouses or private hotels) is generally basic; there's little choice of things to eat, rarely any alcohol, and no bright lights or air conditioning. Passengers might have to stand during five-hour bus journeys, while motorists must reckon on potholed roads and only three petrol pumps, hundreds of kilometres apart. Keep your passport handy to show at checkpoints and save the receipt once you've paid the governorate **tax** (£E4.10 per person) to avoid being charged again in other oases. Only Kharga and Dakhla have **banks** and **telephone** communications with the outside world.

Broadly speaking, the oases share the **climate** of Nile Valley towns on the same latitude – Bahariya is like Minya and Kharga like Luxor – but the air is fresher (although the dust sometimes causes swollen sinuses). Winter is mild by day and near freezing at night (bring a sleeping bag); during summertime temperatures can soar to 50°C at midday and hover in the 20°s after dark. Over **winter** each oasis can usually muster half a dozen visitors, making it easy to assemble a group for excursions to the White Desert or other sites – unlike during summer, when tourism evaporates.

Most people visit Bahariya or Kharga before deciding whether to complete the circuit, and it's quite feasible to limit yourself to one or two oases. If so, start with Bahariya rather than Kharga, whose main centre is a real letdown. The briefest **itinerary** should include the hot springs at Bahariya or Farafra, and a night in the White Desert. Going on to Dakhla, you could take in a day trip from the oasis capital to the Muzawaka Tombs and Al-Qasr. Completing the circuit (skipping Kharga if desired) and emerging from the desert, you'll find varied menus and comfy hotels in Assyut, which has connections up and down the Nile Valley. Travellers *starting* from there should be prepared for Kharga City, the antithesis of a romantic oasis town.

TRANSPORT FROM CAIRO

As extra services are introduced, getting to the oases becomes easier every year. Starting from Cairo, book seats a day or two beforehand at the al-Azhar bus terminal for the two buses daily to Bahariya (currently at 7am & noon, Wed 7am only);

some of these buses (Mon, Thurs & Sat only) carry on to Farafra and Dakhla. Dakhla is also the terminus for one of the three daily buses from Cairo to Kharga, routed via Assyut. As many oasians moved to Cairo in the 1940–50s, Bahariya is also accessible by **service taxi** from the *Ahwa al-Wahia* café on the corner of Sharia Qadry (a few blocks south of Sharia Bur Said) in the Saiyida Zeinab quarter, where the immigrants congregated. On Wednesday and Sunday there are **flights** from Cairo to Kharga Oasis (New Valley airport) for the equivalent of about US$70. Kharga (and, to a lesser extent, Dakhla) may also be reached by daily **buses and service taxis from Assyut**.

For details of the journeys to (and between) each oasis, see the main text.

"THE NEW VALLEY"

The four "Great Desert Circuit" oases are situated along a dead, prehistoric branch of the Nile, and depend on springs and wells tapping the great water sheet beneath the Libyan Desert. In 1958 the government unveiled plans to exploit this, irrigate the desert, and relocate landless peasants from the overcrowded Nile Valley and Delta to the "**New Valley**" (*al-Wadi al-Jedid*).

Work on the New Valley began in the 1970s, but the project has since been scaled down: investments proved costlier than expected, and doubts surfaced about the subterranean water table. Previously it was thought to be replenished by underground seepage from Lake Chad and Equatorial Africa, whereas nowadays it's believed to be a finite geological legacy, sufficient for 100–700 years. As a result, the oases have been caught in mid-stride, partly modernised but unsure of their long-term viability. Hopes of prosperity and fears of decline still turn on the caprices of hydrology and the wits of the oasis folk, as they have since ancient times.

Bahariya Oasis

The 360-kilometre **journey from Cairo** to Bahariya takes six to seven hours by bus (£E8; £E12 with A/C) or five to six hours by *service* taxi (£E10; runs evenings only). It can take an hour merely to reach Giza, where the Pyramids are visible (on the left) as you enter the Western Desert. Not long afterwards you'll pass 6TH OCTOBER CITY, one of the dismal satellite towns under construction outside Cairo. To relieve the tedium of traversing flat, featureless desert, vehicles stop at a halfway resthouse (*pita, fuul*, soft drinks, toilets). Running alongside is a railway for transporting iron ore to the steel mills at Helwan; supplied by a vast open cast mine (resthouse, petrol) which imparts a ferrous hue to the surrounding desert.

Entering **Bahariya Oasis**, soon afterwards the road passes a gravel track to the outlying settlement of el-Harra, and then forks towards the villages of Zabu and Mandisha. Don't get off if the bus calls at any of these places – wait for the end of the line at the oasis "capital", **Bawiti**.

As in most of the oases, people, springs and palm groves are scattered around a large depression. Although Bahariya's covers 2000 square kilometres, less than one percent is actually cultivated with date palms, olive and fruit trees, vegetables, rice and corn. Since a dramatic slump earlier this century, when 32 springs dried up, 63,900 palm trees died, and thousands emigrated to Cairo, the population has risen again. Depending on who you talk to, the oasis has between 10,000 and 30,000 inhabitants, two-thirds of them resident in Bawiti and al-Qasr.

Bawiti and al-Qasr

BAWITI harbours a picturesque nucleus of old houses on a ridge overlooking luxuriant palm groves, but that's not what you see on **arrival**. The lower ground beside the Cairo–Farafra road is littered with half-finished New Valley projects, well-intended but depressingly ugly. Buses trundle past the police station and a measly market to drop passengers near the *Lamey Hotel*.

Accommodation

The *Lamey Hotel*'s scuzzy communal rooms are the last place to seek a bed. Better, not far away, is the white-walled *Paradise Motel*, which has bright rooms with fans (beds E£2.50, breakfast included). However, most people prefer to stay at the *Alpenblick Hotel*, which charges £E3 a head and does good breakfasts (£E2), or the quieter *Oasis Hotel*, where all the rooms (£E3 per person) have fans. Their managers are deadly rivals who've entered travellers' folklore: *Let's Go* raves about the *Alpenblick's* Salah Sherif and his hound Crazy Max, whereas the German guidebook *Reise Know-How* accuses him of having left a group of tourists stranded in the desert. Salah's mannerisms are cruelly aped by Mohammed, who rather outshines his boss at the *Oasis*, Magdi Deyab. If you fancy neither place, you can stay at the new resthouse or grass huts **outside town** (see overpage).

Water is only on from 7am to noon and 4 to 7pm in all these hotels.

The Old Quarter

By following the unpaved road past the *Popular Restaurant* you'll find Bawiti's **old quarter**, a huddle of mudbrick homes and mausolea flanking a main street where Bahariyans sit and gossip on *mastabas*.

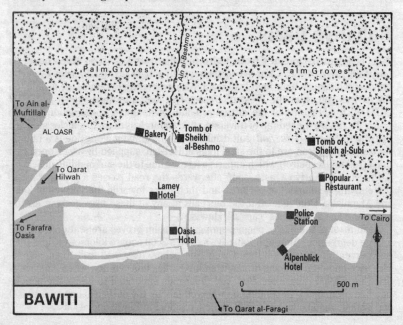

To appreciate Bawiti's commanding position, take the alley winding off behind an incinerator on the second square you come to, which leads to **Ain al-Beshmo**. A craggy fissure in the bedrock where a spring was hewn in Roman times, it gushes hot water (30°C) which irrigates the dense **palm groves** below. Mostly owned by the al-Dawawida family (like the spring itself), the gardens look especially lovely when they're spangled with apricot blossom during springtime. If the view and the crumbling edges of the gorge aren't dramatic enough, local kids will happily lead tourists into the **qubba** of Sheikh al-Beshmo; it's full of dead goats – they love to get a horrified reaction.

Al-Qasr and local antiquities

Although you can scramble down into the palm groves from Ain al-Beshmo, it's worth returning to the main street and walking on past a hole-in-the-wall bakery. At some point here Bawiti gives way to **AL-QASR**, its older sister village. Sited on top of Bahariya's ancient capital, al-Qasr's houses incorporate stones from a bygone XXVI Dynasty temple, and a Roman triumphal arch which survived until the mid-nineteenth century. The ancient town extended 3km northwest to **Ain al-Muftillah**, where four ruined chapels depict King Amasis and various deities, amongst them Bes, whose leering visage used to be a favoured tattoo on the thighs of dancing girls. A similar distance to the southwest lies the ridge of **Qarat Hilwah**, which is gouged with tombs; that of Amenhotep contains badly defaced scenes from the life of this XXVI Dynasty governor.

Due to looting and vandalism the best **antiquities** were closed for restoration during our visit, so you'll have to ask Salah or Mohammed at the hotels if they've reopened. **Qarat Qasr Salim**, on the eastern outskirts of Bawiti, contains two burial chambers with pillars and murals, excavated by Fakhry in 1938. Unfortunately, the paintings began to blacken after exposure to the air, particularly in the **Tomb of Bannentiu** where the journeys of the Sun and Moon are depicted just inside the entrance, with Horus and Thoth flanking the doorway to the burial chamber.

Ibises, falcons, armadillos and quails merited their own cemetery 500m south of Bawiti, known to locals as **Qarat al-Faragi** (Ridge of the Chicken Merchant), which can't be entered nowadays. En route lies the Muslim cemetery, where the burials of old people are accompanied by rituals to prevent younger kinsfolk from following them to the grave. Bahariyans are superstitious and pleasure-loving, like most *fellaheen*. Children are guarded against the Evil Eye, while any supplication at the tomb of Sheikh al-Subi (or Sheikh Badawi at Al-Qasr) is preceded by dancing and clapping to put the saint in a good mood. **Sheikh Badawi's moulid** on the night of a summer full moon is a special cause for singing and dancing.

Meals and other practicalities

Perhaps influenced by their sojourn in Cairo, local men indulge in beer and home-grown grass, unlike the puritanical Farfaronis. Otherwise, **entertainments** boil down to *sheeshas*, tea and backgammon at one of the cafés along the main drag. The *Popular Restaurant* is just that, perhaps because it's one of the few places serving **meals**. If it's not chicken, any meat on offer will most likely be camel. Biscuits, soft drinks and feta cheese are available from shops and the *Alpenblick* kiosk.

Bawiti has a **hospital** and a **petrol** pump; motorists should fill up as there's no more fuel until Dakhla Oasis, 500km away.

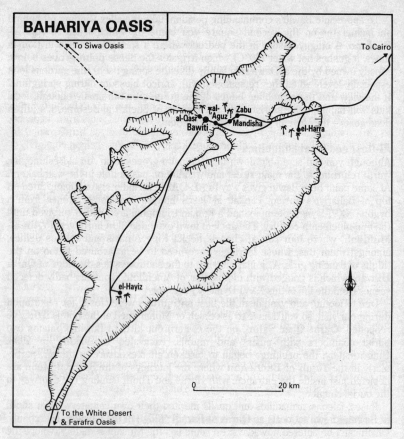

Around Bahariya oasis

Trips around Bahariya focus on bathing in **hot springs** around the oasis – and can be arranged most easily through one of the Bawiti hotels. Closer to town, you can walk out to the palms for a glimpse of the oasis ecology and **wildlife**; Bahariya abounds in insect and bird life – most noticeably wheatears, which semaphore to each other with their black and white tails, while birds of prey stay aloft, soaring on thermals.

Bir Mathar

The most popular Bahariya excursion is to the **hot springs** at **Bir Mathar**, 6km from Bawiti. Both the *Oasis* or *Alpenblick* hotels run van-trips but be warned that mixed couples need to juggle times: by day the springs can only be used by men, by night only by women (who bathe in modest clothes). The "spring" is actually a concrete tank into which faintly sulphurous water pours from a viaduct. Nearby lies a brand new government **resthouse** with bungalows (£E5 per head) and tents (£E2.50 per person), a swimming pool, restaurant and volleyball courts.

Bir al-Ghaba

For more privacy, sign up for a visit to **Bir al-Ghaba**, another spring, 15km from Bawiti (again, trips can be arranged through hotels). The track out there crosses a desert plain, skirting palm groves and fields where camels graze; all Bahariya's camels belong to the Naggi family, whose menfolk own up to sixty animals apiece (worth £E2000 each when fully grown).

Cruising down an avenue of acacias towards a natural pyramid on the horizon, you'll finally come to the **spring**, where both men and women can bathe (women should expect a small audience). The lichen-encrusted tank gains from its peaceful surroundings. Just nearby is a *kraal*-like enclosure of grass **huts**, owned by the *Alpenblick* (£E3 per head including breakfast), where you can get changed.

Further afield: Jebel al-Mi'ysrah and villages

Even a brief visit to the springs will give you an impression of Bahariya's wildlife and topography. The depression is ringed and pimpled by **hills** whose blackish colour results from their ferruginous quartzite and dolorite composition. Most of the settlements and cultivated areas are visible from the summit of the 50-metre-high **Jebel al-Mi'ysrah**, which bears a ruined house built for Captain Williams, who commanded Bahariya's resistance to the Senussi during World War I.

Jebel Mandisha separates Bawiti from three more **villages**, 8–12km away by road. First comes AL-AGUZ, a small oasis hamlet reputedly founded by adulterous women exiles from Siwa Oasis, which still has a relatively louche reputation. Beyond here a side road forks 3km north to MANDISHA, another ancient centre effaced by mudbrick and breeze blocks, themselves menaced by an advancing dune, the **Ghird Mandisha**.

Over 2km long and 300m wide, this, the largest of Bahariya's dunes, also threatens to engulf ZABU, 1500m further northeast. There's a scalding hot spring, **Ain Siwa**, not far away from Zabu, and a huge rock inscribed with medieval **Libyan graffiti** 2.7km further on, known to locals as *Qasr al-Zabu*. Ask Mohammed or Salah at the hotels for advice on **getting there**.

Between Bahariya and Farafra: the White Desert

Most visitors break the 180-kilometre journey between Bahariya and Farafra with a night out in the **White Desert**, experiencing some of its magic at sunset and sunrise. During winter it's easy to assemble a group of travellers and split the cost of an excursion offered by the *Paradise Motel* (E£120), or the *Oasis* and *Alpenblick* (£E140); prices are per van-load and include hot meals, scanty bedding and the military permission required for camping out.

Motorists travelling independently must arrange all this themselves, not forgetting water, petrol and firewood; a warm sleeping bag is also essential for winter nights. Allow three hours to reach the White Desert, preferably a while before sunset – it's risky to drive after dark.

The route

Much of the way the road crosses a gravelly **Black Desert** with charred outcrops and tabletop rocks. Some stretches are quite smooth, but others – like solidified lava flows – compel detours off *piste*.

Roughly 30km from Bawiti there's a white **tomb** atop a crag in the desert to the right: a monument to an elderly Swiss who fell asleep in his car and died of heatstroke (not because Salah abandoned him, as Mohammed claims). Another ten kilometres on, the road passes **EL-HAYIZ**, Bahariya's southernmost oasis, with two villages (pop. 4000) and some ruins from early Christian times, when the community was far larger. The Copts believe that one of Christ's apostles, Saint Bartholomew, visited Bahariya before his martyrdom, and perhaps even died there. Military permission is required to visit the **ruined Roman camp and church**, marked with Coptic graffiti. Fakhry reckons that el-Hayiz was the "fourth oasis" described by texts in the Temple of Edfu.

Huge drifts of golden sand wave up to the escarpment separating the Bahariya and Farafra depressions; a magnificent sight from the **al-Sillim Pass**. In the excitement of photographing it, don't point your lens anywhere near the microwave mast. Sixty kilometres or so into the pebbly Farafra depression, a checkpoint marks the turning for the **road to Ain Dalla** (see below). Farther along the Farafra road, the desert undergoes a startling transformation.

The **White Desert** itself is a surreal landscape of fungoid shapes which glint pale gold in the midday sun and turn pink and violet around dusk, resembling icebergs at dawn and snowdrifts by moonlight. (Moonless nights are better for stargazing.) The Arabic term for such wind-eroded rock formations is *yardang*. Herds of **gazelles** may be glimpsed at daybreak, when they forage for a couple of hours. Some miles from the usual camping site there's a "spring" (actually a water pipeline valve) where you can wash; some drivers suggest a visit. Unfortunately, the White Desert is short-lived, petering out into a dusty pan for the last 20km to Farafra.

Farafra Oasis

A single village in a windblown depression, **Farafra Oasis** seems the most isolated of the five main oases in the Western Desert. When camels were the only means of travel, the Farafonis had less contact with Bahariya (a journey of four days) than with Dakhla, which was tenuously connected to the Forty Day Road. Fakhry relates how the villagers once lost track of time and could only ascertain the right day for Friday prayers by sending a rider to Dakhla. Before the paved road was built in 1978 it took four-wheel drive and a winch truck a whole day to climb the Bahariya escarpment. Yet the oasis had dealings with the Nile Valley as early as the V Dynasty, when it was called *Ta-iht*, the "Land of the Cow".

Two extended families account for most of Farafra's 2300 inhabitants, whose piety is obvious during Ramadan, when the village mosque overflows with robed *imams* and sheikhs. The nineteenth-century explorer Rohlfs described them as "bigoted, fanatic and inhospitable" after his caravan had stupidly announced its arrival by firing shots into the air – causing the Farafonis to retreat into their mudbrick fort. This, the *qasr*, had 116 rooms where each family stored vital provisions; it finally collapsed in 1958.

Qasr al-Farafra: the village

The fort's memory is enshrined in the village's official name, **QASR AL-FARAFRA**, though the appellation is never used in everyday speech. As in Bawiti, the oldest part occupies the highest ground, backing onto the palm groves, while New Valley developments line the lower, main road.

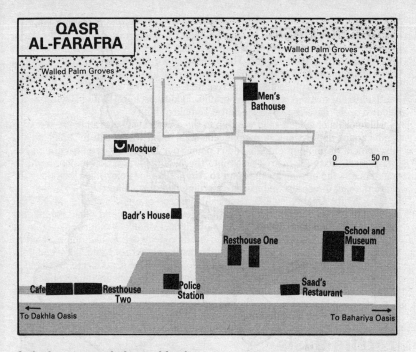

Arrival, accommodation and food

On arrival, you'll probably be dropped outside *Saad's Restaurant* near *Resthouse One*, which charges £E3.50 per head (£E2 to sleep in the tent in the yard), or by a café farther down the road, where the dingier *Resthouse Two* has beds for £E2.50. Both **resthouses** are utterly basic, with shared rooms and cold water (when it's running at all). The sporadically functioning *President Sadat* **hotel** seems to have closed down entirely.

Pending new additions, the only **places to eat** are *Saad's Restaurant* – favoured by tourists for its juices, omelettes and lentil soup – and the café where locals hang out over tea and *sheeshas*. The **shop** next door is Farafra's best source of cigarettes, sweets and tinned food.

Around the village

Many of Farafra's houses are decorated with geometric friezes, flying eagles or snarling lions painted by **Badr**, a young local artist, whose sculptures and colourful canvases have recently been transferred to a purpose-built **museum** (free admission, donations welcome). As an amateur taxidermist, he also enjoys demonstrating the snares with which Farafonis catch falcons (for export to Saudi Arabia) and gazelles (supposedly a protected species).

From the main square, uphill, you can follow paths into the **walled palm groves**, Farafra's nicest feature – just respect the privacy of the men's bathhouse and family gardens. Generators provide electricity from 7am to midnight, but the military own the only radio-telephone and petrol in Farafra, which they're unlikely to share with civilians.

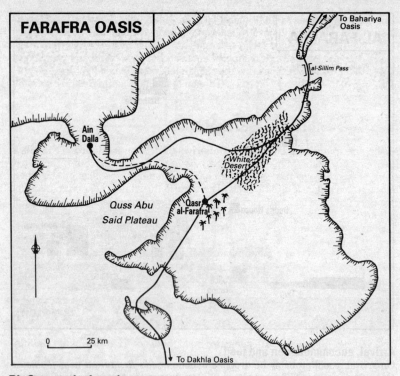

FARAFRA OASIS

To Bahariya Oasis

al-Sillim Pass

Ain Dalla

White Desert

Quss Abu Said Plateau

Qasr al-Farafra

0   25 km

To Dakhla Oasis

Bir Setta and other trips

Saad (of *Saad's Restaurant*) and his German buddy Achim organise trips to **Bir Setta** (Well Six), 4km west of town, for about £E15 per van-load. The tank of sulphurous hot water here is good for wallowing but stains clothes brown. The thorny bushes roundabouts provide little cover, but you should be able to change unobserved once a **tourist camp** of grass huts is completed.

Saad and Achim also run **excursions** to the nearby White Desert (day trips £E60; overnight £E80; see previous section); el-Mufid lake, which is warm enough for swimming during summer (£E15); or the small oasis of Ain el-Tanien (£E25). All these prices are per van-load.

Ain Dalla and the Lost Army of Cambyses

Motorised travellers with jerrycans of fuel and water and military permission from Bahariya or Farafra might consider visiting **Ain Dalla**, a remote spring 80km northwest of Farafra. A local guide is essential if one uses the track curving around the northern end of the Quss Abu Said plateau; for an easier approach, take the paved road turning off between Farafra and Bahariya (see above), which runs for 120km across the desert floor and through the scarp.

Attempting the 300-kilometre round trip without due precautions is potentially suicidal. As the last waterhole before the Great Sand Sea, Ain Dalla was a vital springboard for motorised explorers during the Twenties and Thirties, and is believed to have been the last known location of the **Lost Army of Cambyses**. Despatched by Egypt's Persian conqueror to destroy the famous Oracle of Amun, the 50,000-strong army disappeared en route to Siwa Oasis in 524 BC. Herodotus relates how the troops were resting when a sandstorm blew up and completely buried them; Fakhry reckons that they separated, panicked and got lost, eventually dying of thirst. Archaeologists still dream of finding Cambyses' army beneath the outlying dunes of the Great Sand Sea (see p.445).

Moving on: the road to Dakhla

Moving on from Farafra, **buses to Bahariya** (£E7; 3hr) and **Cairo** (£E18; 8hr) leave around 10am (Mon, Thurs & Sat) or 7am (Tues, Fri & Sun); the latter services start here so there's a better chance of getting a seat than on the other buses, which originate from Dakhla. There's also the chance of **service taxis** to Bahariya (£E5), or lifts from cars which have just deposited tourists after a night in the White Desert, and are heading back.

Buses to Dakhla (£E7; 4–5hr) normally depart from the café beside *Resthouse Two*; check their schedules at *Saad's*. Seats are easily obtained on the early morning bus which starts from Farafra four days a week; on other days it's necessary to stand on through-services from Cairo, which pull in here any time between 2 and 4pm. Alternatively, ask around if anyone's prepared to drive you to Dakhla **by car** (£E40–80) or truck. **Hitchhiking** from the military checkpoint outside town is feasible, but be sure your ride is going all the way.

Farafra to Dakhla
Few vehicles follow the 310-kilometre road **between Farafra and Dakhla Oasis**, where the only water and fuel en route are reserved for road gangs and military outposts.

Heading south, the first sight is the tiny AIN EL-TANIEN OASIS, partly cultivated by Farafran farmers, with a stretch of rotund white boulders farther on. Over the next hour the desert shifts from white stone to gravel and sand before the guarded pass of **Abu Minqar**, 250km from the Libyan border. Here the road veers southwest, and for the next 230km or so it skirts the edge of the vast escarpment that delineates **Dakhla Oasis**. Entering this from the northeast, you'll pass Garb Mawhub, al-Qasr and the *Roadside Resthouse* before reaching Mut, Dakhla's main centre.

Dakhla Oasis

Verdant cultivated areas and a great wall of rose-hued rock across the northern horizon make a feast for the eyes in **Dakhla Oasis**. Partitioned by dunes into more or less irrigated, fertile enclaves, the oasis supports 65,000 people living in fourteen settlements strung out along the Farafra and Kharga roads. Although it's the outlying sites that hold most attraction, the majority of travellers base themselves in **Mut** (pronounced "moot"), Dakhla's "capital", which has a virtual monopoly on accommodation. The buses and *bijous* that run between Mut and the villages enable you to see how the Dakhlans have reclaimed land, planted new crops, and generally made the best of New Valley developments.

Mut

Dakhla's capital, **MUT**, was branded a miserable-looking place by travellers earlier this century, but it has come on apace since the 1950s, as the Dakhlans have subverted or embraced planned "modernity" according to their needs and tastes. The architect of Mut's already crumbling low-rise flats is unlikely to have foreseen their balconies being converted into extra rooms or pigeon coops, and the four-lane highway that snakes through town rarely carries anything heavier than cyclists. Yet the locals have welcomed innovations like the hospital, cultural centre and school which flank Sharia Wadi Jedid between Midan Tahrir and New Mosque Square, and the old Mut of mudbrick and palms has been banished from sight behind an embankment.

In this dusty, friendly, slow-moving town, social life centres around the illuminated mosque and cafés (useful landmarks after dark) and everything is within walking distance. Buses from the outside world terminate on New Mosque Square after stopping near the police station, where foreigners are obliged **to register** on arrival. Come first thing next morning if you arrive after hours (daily 8am–2pm & 7–9pm); just wave your passport and act lost to be directed to the proper room on the first floor. Visitors must also pay £E4.15 **governorate tax** at the **tourist office** (8am–2pm and sometimes 9–11pm; ☎407), where English-speaking Ibrahim Mohammed Hassan can advise on local buses and possibly supply oasis maps. Keep your tax receipt to avoid being charged again in Kharga.

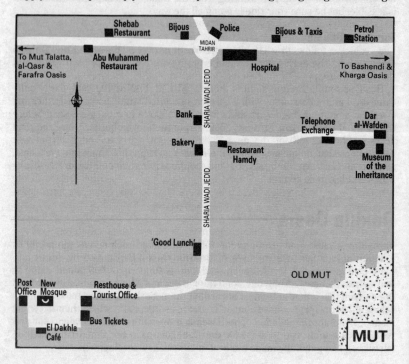

Accommodation and information

You'll find the **tourist office** in the **resthouse** on the corner of New Mosque Square, which is handily sited for late arrivals but provides poor accommodation. A bed in a shared room costs £E1.40, or £E3 if the room has a private shower and toilet – well worth having given the filthy shared facilities. The **Hotel Dar al-Wafden** (☎778), a ten- to fifteen-minute walk away, is a better deal, with doubles and triples (£E1.75 per head), clean facilities and a pleasant terrace. Awkwardly located at the end of the street with the telephone exchange and sports ground, and lacking any sign, it's next door to the Museum of the Inheritance. Between 10pm and 4am there's no **water** in either place.

Alternatively, catch a *bijou* (25pt) to the hot springs at **Mut Talatta**, 3km out of town. Its **Roadside Resthouse** or "Villa" has clean rooms with fans and screens and the use of a kitchen. Nearer the springs is the *Poolside Resthouse* or "Bungalows": six cramped doubles with private bathrooms but no fans. Its walled pool offers some privacy, but the water is so dirty that most guests prefer the boiling hot springs, despite lurking peepers. Both places charge £E3.60 per bed, and can supply meals by prior arrangement. You can also pitch tents here, even though the **campsite** isn't ready yet.

The Museum of the Inheritance

Mut's only "sight" is the **Museum of the Inheritance**, which sheds light on traditional Dakhlan culture. Arranged like a family dwelling with household objects on the walls and a complex wooden lock on the palm-log door, its seven rooms contain clay figures posed in scenes from village life. Notice the gazelle-hide receptacle for carrying fat on long camel journeys, and the spiked basket that Dakhlans hid beneath the sand to ensnare gazelles. Preparing the bride and celebrating the pilgrim's return from Mecca are two scenes that remain part of oasis life today.

Admission costs £E1; visits can be arranged through the tourist office or by contacting the museum curator, Ibrahim Kemal Abdallah, at the multistorey building north of the *Hamdy Restaurant* between 8am and 2pm or 6 and 9pm.

Food and practicalities

The best **places to eat** in Mut are the *Hamdy* and *Abu Muhammed* restaurants, run by two brothers. Both places serve soup, chicken, rice and salad, hot drinks and canned juices, accompanied by Western pop music – ensuring that all the foreigners in town hang out there. For a more Dakhlan ambience, try a generous kebab or a tea and *sheesha* at the place signposted *Good Lunch*, whose all-male clientele sits transfixed by female wrestling on the TV come evening. The *el-Dakhla café* is good for sandwiches but overpriced, and there's nothing to recommend the *Shebab Restaurant* except for the patisserie next door (great apple *fatirs*), past the minuscule fruit and veg **market** on Midan Tahrir.

Mut's *Misr Bank* (Sun–Thurs 8.30am–2pm) and the branch in Kharga are the only places to legally exchange **money** or travellers' cheques in the oases. The **post office** on New Mosque Square is open from Saturday to Thursday between 8am and 2pm, while the telephone exchange – where **international calls** can be made – functions 24 hours. To call Dakhla from other Egyptian cities, dial the New Valley **telephone code** (☎088) and then the exchange (☎901-101/901-102/901-103), which connects callers to local numbers.

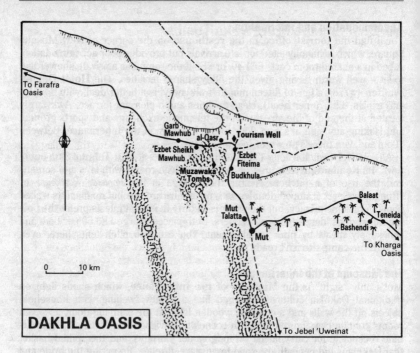

To Farafra Oasis

Garb Mawhub • al-Qasr • ✦ Tourism Well

'Ezbet Sheikh Mawhub •

'Ezbet Fiteima

Muzawaka Tombs • Budkhula

Mut Talatta •

Balaat

Teneida

Bashendi

• Mut

To Kharga Oasis

0   10 km

To Jebel 'Uweinat

DAKHLA OASIS

Mut's **hospital** (☎332/ambulance ☎333) is well equipped by the standards of the Western Desert, and most of the villages have a medical post. There's no other **petrol** station between here and Bahariya, 500km away.

Transport around the oasis

Transport around Dakhla is hit and miss, depending on your destination. **Taxis** are the dearest option, with hard bargaining required should you wish the driver to wait at sites and return to Mut (reckon on £E15–20 for al-Qasr and the Muzawaka tombs); ask around New Mosque Square. **Bijous**, shuttling past Mut Talatta to the western villages, cost only 25–40pt, and locals flag them down anywhere but particularly at Midan Tahrir. The *bijou* depot 200m past the hospital is mainly for services to the eastern villages or Kharga Oasis, which run less frequently. *Bijous* are quicker than local buses, and most active in the morning.

Local buses from New Mosque Square run to both ends of the oasis, stopping at villages along the way (50pt). Buses for Gharb Mawhub, calling at Qasr, leave around 10.30am, 1pm and 2pm; turning around and returning to Mut roughly half an hour after reaching their destination. Teneida-bound services, departing around 6.30am and 2pm, can drop you at the turning for Bashendi, but return unpredictably, if at all. You can also use long-distance buses to reach outlying villages. In both cases, simply buy tickets on board. Out of town it's worth **hitching**. Although payment at *bijou* rates is customary, one often gets a free lift.

The workshop on New Mosque Square hires **bicycles** (£E2–3 a day after bargaining); cycling is feasible in wintertime, at least.

Al-Qasr and the Muzawaka Tombs

If you're limited to a single day excursion at Dakhla, make it to **al-Qasr** and the **Muzawaka Tombs**, 30–40km along the western arm of the oasis. Using *bijous* or buses a certain amount of walking is unavoidable, but by visiting the tombs first and then Qasr this can be minimised. However, since the tombs lie further west, Qasr – the main attraction – is described first.

Al-Qasr

Heading out from Mut past rice paddies, reservoirs and the villages of BUDKHULA and 'EZBET FITEIMA, the road curves west as it nears the great cliff wall. A few kilometres before Qasr you'll see a palm-fringed, azure-coloured saline lake, 4km into the desert: the "Tourism Well", fit for camping if you bring food and water. Visitors to Qasr are usually dropped near a roadside café, with reedy pools and old Qasr scenically arrayed behind, although the bus might stop at the modern village, 300m away.

New Qasr – whose main street is called Sharia al-Kuwait after the source of the remittances that financed it – is pleasant enough, but it's the old village that's the reason for the strip. More of a warren than its Arabic name ("castle" or "palace") suggests, **AL-QASR** was a Roman settlement and Dakhla's medieval capital, acquiring a pepperpot minaret and other distinctively Ayyubid features along the way. Mud-walled alleys snake through dark passageways upheld by acacia-wood lintels, whose cursive or kufic inscriptions name the former builders or occupants (just three houses are still inhabited). You can follow the signs to a tenth-century **madrassa** (school and court) offering great views from its rooftop, or visit a **pottery** and **waterwheel** (*saqqiya*) accompanied by local kids, who may want to sell pots or rush sewing baskets (£E3–5), or simply practice their English. Qasr's schoolteachers also enjoy a chat, and the guys in the café will happily accept a challenge to ping-pong.

The Muzawaka tombs

Five kilometres west along the highway, a signpost "To Muzawaka Mon" points down the track to the **al-Muzawaka Tombs**. Hewn into the "Hill of Decoration" during the first century AD, they're reached by walking for twenty minutes through silent desert, past dessicated buttes gouged with empty tombs.

Their dozing custodian appreciates some banter before unlocking the **Tomb of Petosiris**, vividly painted with Roman-nosed blonds in pharaonic poses, curly-haired angels and a zodiac with a bearded Janus-figure on the ceiling. In the back, right-hand corner, notice the man standing on a turtle, holding a snake and fish aloft – a curious amalgam of Egyptian and Graeco-Roman symbolism. Better preserved, cruder murals in the **Tomb of Sadosiris** show Anubis (weighing the deceased's heart in one scene), Osiris judging on the rear wall, and another Janus – looking back on life and forward into the hereafter – just inside the entrance.

Roughly 2km west of al-Muzawaka, the desert also boasts a grey sandstone temple, known to locals as the "Stone Convent", **Deir al-Hagar**. Dedicated to the Theban triad, this temple with its hypostele hall, sanctuary, and pyloned brick enclosure wall was probably rebuilt under the Roman emperors Nero and Titus. Nearby there's a **hot sulphur spring**.

Heading back from the tombs, you can try hitching towards Qasr, or cut across the desert towards the village as the guard suggests. There's little risk of getting lost, since by climbing a table-plateau you can always get orientated – and the views are splendid. Notice the **dunes** swelling proudly on the far side of the highway, and how millennial exposure to extremes of heat and cold has made the tabletops friable, shedding rock "scales".

Dakhla's westernmost villages – old 'EZBET SHEIKH MAWHUB and new, built-in-one GARB MAWHUB – aren't particularly interesting.

East of Mut

Villages on the east side of the oasis are more or less accessible by Teneida-bound buses, though *bijous* rarely venture far beyond Balaat. Along the way, you'll see where rice and peanuts have been sown to prepare the land for frailer crops, defying dust clouds blowing off the barren areas.

Balaat
BALAAT, 35km from Mut, prospered through trade with Kush (ancient Nubia) as early as the VI Dynasty. Since 1977, when French archaeologists discovered the unplundered tomb of a governor from the time of Pepi II, scholars have been excavating an immense **funerary mastaba** nearby (closed to visitors). Architecturally speaking, it's the linear ancestor of the humble mudbrick bench outside Balaat's café (a good place to wait for lifts). Some of Balaat's older buildings still have palm-log doors opened with pegged wooden keys.

Bashendi
Five or six kilometres past Balaat, buses can drop you at the turn-off for **BASHENDI**, with its sign promising carpet-weaving, Roman tombs and other goodies. Having walked 4km across an African-looking landscape of acacia trees and red earth, you reach the village, whose sugary pink mosque with its three white domes resembles from afar a marquee.

A charming maze of curvaceous blue-washed houses decorated with floral friezes and *hadj* scenes, Bashendi backs onto the desert, where its tombs lie. Some empty sarcophagi separate the domed **qubba** of village holy man Bash Endi (where locals pray for the recovery of lost items) from the **Tomb of Kitnes**, of first-century BC, Roman origin. One of its four rooms depicts the owner meeting the desert gods Min, Seth and Shu, but if no one materialises to unlock the tomb you'll have to be satisfied with viewing its pharaonic lintels.

Locals can direct you to the **carpet-weaving** factory, where carpets bearing scenes of Dakhlan life are produced. However, with a derelict resthouse and no shops, you can't really stay. Since there's no bus out you must trudge back to the main road and hope for a lift. There's supposed to be a bus from Tineida around 4.30pm, but it's pretty unreliable. Rather than wait, start walking and hitching back towards Balaat, where it's easier to find a *bijou* for the one-hour ride to Mut.

Teneida
Five kilometres away, the easternmost settlement in the oasis is a large affair centred around a leafy square. The brick tombs in its Muslim cemetery are **TENEIDA**'s main claim to antiquarian interest, but an incident in its history deserves a mention. In 1931, three men staggered out of the desert, alerting the authorities to a tragedy that was already weeks old. Bombed from their homes at Kufra Oasis in Libya by the Italians, 500 Zwayah nomads had trekked 320km

south over waterless desert to Jebel 'Uweinat, where they found springs but no grazing. Faced with starvation, half the tribe struck out towards Dakhla without knowing the way, while the others remained to await their end. Thanks to the men's 21-day, 670-km march (a feat of endurance with few parallels), search parties managed to rescue almost 300 stragglers from the wilderness.

Leaving Dakhla, and the road to Kharga

If you're doing the desert circuit in reverse, there's a **bus to Farafra, Bahariya and Cairo** on Monday, Thursday and Saturday, leaving around 6am. Heading on clockwise, there are five buses (and possibly shared taxis) to **Kharga**, the staging post for services to Assyut (leaving Mut at 8.30am), and buses taking the Nile route to Cairo (6am & 4.30pm); all of these run daily. Try to buy tickets one hour in advance (or the day before for 6am departures); the office is four doors along, on the left-hand side of New Mosque Square. Before leaving Mut, motorists should fill up at the gas station 1km out along the Kharga road; there's no more **petrol** until Kharga or Bahariya.

The route: Dakhla to Kharga

For most of the 197km **between Dakhla and Kharga** the only sights are gravelly sand and dun-coloured tabletops; buses break the three-hour journey at a filthy **resthouse** near kilometre 105. Nearer Kharga, golden sand emerges as the tabletops recede towards cliffs on the horizon, and the final 20km stretch is menaced by advancing **dunes**, which have buried earlier roads and even telegraph poles. These outstretched fingers of the Abu Mikharri range are of the ridged type known as *seif* or "sword" dunes, better described by Ralph Bagnold as "whalebacked". Folk wisdom asserts that the less common *barchan* or crescent-shaped dunes are always separate from whalebacks; you'll see a cluster of baby ones in the desert to the left, nearer town.

Kharga Oasis

If your time or appetite for the desert is limited, **Kharga Oasis** is the one to consider missing. Of the 60,000 people in the oasis, three-fifths live in sprawling, charmless **Kharga City** – and with *service* taxis and buses from here to Assyut there's no compulsion to stay. Having said that, there are some fine Christian and pharaonic ruins near the town, others at remoter points in the oasis, and the prospect of dramatic scenery as you ascend the scarp wall en route to Assyut. And for those smitten by the desert, Kharga gains something from its association with the famous **Forty Days Road**, way to the south.

El-Kharga (Kharga City)

Of all the oases Kharga has been most affected by the New Valley programme, which has transformed **EL-KHARGA** into a city of burgeoning blocks and highways, swollen by migrants (including 1000 Nubians displaced by Lake Nasser), and aided by technical advisors from as far away as Korea. Only around its souk and along the palm-lined street between the bus station and the Fellaheen Monument will you find mudbrick houses redolent of the oasis of old.

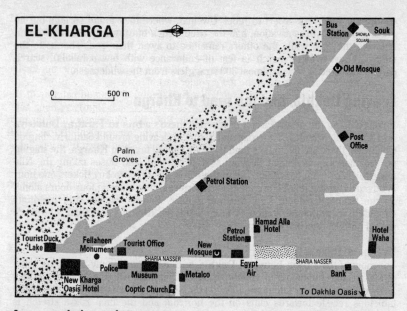

Accommodation and transport

Arriving in el-Kharga, ask to be dropped at one of the **hotels** along the way to Showla Square bus station. The *New Kharga Oasis* (☎901-450) has spacious rooms with hot showers (singles £E20, doubles £E25, extra bed £E5), a nice restaurant, bar and peaceful garden terrace; the only thing missing is A/C – bad news from April onwards, when the temperature climbs to 98°F. Alternatives are the unsanitary huts of the *Metalco*, or the overpriced *Hamad Alla* (singles £E18, double with bath £E24). The *Hotel Waha* (singles £E4–9, doubles £E7–12) is clean and simple, its cold showers no hardship in the Khargan climate.

The town is too visually monotonous and widely dispersed for pleasant walking, but *bijous* are perfect for **getting around**. These covered pick-ups shuttle almost non-stop between Showla Square and the Fellaheen Monument, stopping on request at metal shelters all along Nasser Street. The turning near the *Hotel Waha* marks the "fare stage", being a 5pt ride from each terminus; the full journey costs 10pt. To let the driver know when you want to get off, stamp on the floor or bang on the partition.

Almost everywhere you might need to visit can be reached like this, not least the **tourist office** (Sat–Thurs 8am–2pm and sometimes 8–10pm; during Ramadan Sun–Thurs 10am–2pm & 9pm–midnight; ☎901-205). Helpful, English-speaking Mr Tewfik can advise on transport to *outré* destinations, and maybe supply the map that was "expected any day" during our visit. The **tourist police** (8am–2pm; ☎901-502) are across the road.

Around town – food and services

Heading east along Sharia Nasser you'll pass a new red-brick, white-arched **Museum**, whose opening has been delayed after the looting of its storage facility in 1989. A couple of blocks along and 100m right down a side street, Kharga's

Coptic Church is a sky-blue breeze-block erection with a lethargic police guard. Beyond the *Metalco* hotel and the equally new but nicer-looking **Mosque** on Nasser Street, are the **EgyptAir** office (see below) and the *Misr* **bank** (Sun–Thurs 8.30am–2pm, Fri & Sat 9am–1pm), which will exchange foreign currency and travellers' cheques. The ornamental park is a bit of a focal point, but for life and colour you need to go to the lower, older part of town.

The first junction past the *Hotel Waha* has several shops and eateries of the *fuul*-and-offal variety, with a **post office** (Sat–Thurs 9am–2pm), 24-hour **telephone** exchange (calls abroad also possible from the *New Oasis Hotel* for a 25 percent mark-up) and juice bar before you reach the main downhill drag. A left turn brings you to unexpected **palm groves**, while a right down the slope takes you past Kharga's **Old Mosque**, a bastion of traditionalism.

At the bottom of the slope, running east of Showla Square, a small **souk** purveys food and hides, tools and poultry; goats and palm trees encroaching on the far end of alleys whose mudbrick houses are painted apricot or azure, and daubed with the lucky Hand of Fatima. If you turn right at the souk's intersection and then left, you should find yourself in **al-Darb al-Sendediya**, a sunken alley running beneath houses supported by huge wooden beams.

For decent **food** and an ambience where women can feel relaxed, there are really only two places. The joint beside the *Hotel Waha* does chicken, rice, soup and not much else; the slightly overpriced restaurant in the *New Oasis* runs to beer and fancier meals.

Moving on from Kharga

If you've got the money, *EgyptAir* **flights** from el-Kharga's New Valley airport can get you to Cairo in two hours, *inshallah*. Departures are on Wednesdays and Sundays at 7.50am (June–Sept at 8.50am); a one-way ticket costs the equivalent of US$90. The airport turn-off is 3km north along the Assyut road, then 2km southeast; minibuses or shared taxis do the run from Showla Square for 50pt–£E1.

Otherwise, there are **buses** to Cairo (6am, 6pm & 8pm), Dakhla (6am, 1pm & 4.30pm) and Assyut (6am, 7am, noon, 1pm & 2pm), all on a daily basis. If there's no bus imminent, cross the square and ask about **service taxis** (Peugeot cars or Toyota vans) to **Assyut**, whence you can reach most points along the Nile. The journey costs around £E5 a head and takes five to eight hours – it's worth travelling by day and getting seats on the left to see the magnificent rock escarpment, one of the most dramatic vistas Egypt has to offer.

Around el-Kharga

Worthwhile visits from el-Kharga include a couple of local sites – the Temple of Hibis and the Necropolis of Bagawat, both a short distance north of the city.

To the Temple of Hibis

For the Temple of Hibis, take a *bijou* to the Fellaheen Monument, then walk up past the *New Kharga Oasis Hotel*. Before reaching the temple, you'll pass the **Tourist Duck Lake**, whose shade and cool and relaxing quacking sounds are best appreciated when you're hot and tired, having seen the sights. One kilometre out along the Assyut road, you'll also catch sight of the ruined Ptolemaic **Temple of Nadura** atop a low hill in the desert to your right – though quite honestly, its sandstone wall and pronaos aren't worth the 1km trudge.

The **Temple of Hibis** stands just up the road amidst the palm groves, a short walk away by tarmac path (beyond the swamp). Besides reminding sightseers that most pharaonic sites originally looked verdant, the lush vegetation around it covers the site of Ancient Hibis, a XVIII Dynasty settlement that prospered under the Saïtes, Persians and Ptolemies.

One of the few Persian monuments left in Egypt, the sixth-century BC **temple** itself respects pharaonic conventions. Well preserved from the Third Pylon onwards, it features painted vultures (beneath the pylon), squat columns with variegated capitals, and (locked) hypostele halls. By peering through the gates you can see graffiti by Francis Catherwood, later famous for discovering Maya temples in Central America. Carrying a stone to deter wild dogs, walk around the outer walls, with their huge reliefs of Darius I greeting Egyptian gods, and noticeably Persian hairstyles. For *baksheesh*, the guard will unlock an unsafe subterranean tomb containing fine reliefs of dolphins.

The Necropolis of el-Bagawat

Roughly ten metres beyond the Hibis temple road, a dirt track leads off towards crumbling ruins in the desert. Follow this through a palm grove and then cut across to a **ruined Christian village**, where the sand chokes low walls with flowery friezes, and disgorges shards of Coptic pottery. From here you can see the **Necropolis of el-Bagawat** – 263 mudbrick chapels ascending a ridge.

Used for Christian burials between the third and seventh centuries, these **chapels** display diverse forms of mudbrick vaulting or Roman-influenced portals, but they are best known for their Coptic murals. A guard should appear to unlock the **Chapel of Peace**, whose dome is decorated with images of Adam and Eve, the Ark, Abraham and Isaac, sadly defaced by Greek inscriptions. Flowery motifs and doves of peace can be seen inside **Tomb no. 25**, one of three adjacent family vaults on the ridge, where the guard usually asks "Shouf bebe?" If you reply affirmatively he'll produce a hideous mummified child, expecting male tourists to react with sang-froid and women with dismay, not to mention *baksheesh* worthy of his efforts. Give him his due, but not until you've seen the frescoes in the **Chapel of the Exodus**. Crudely executed yet vivid, they depict Roman-looking pharaonic troops pursuing the Jews, led by Moses, out of Egypt, and other biblical scenes.

From behind the chapel you can gaze across the desert towards the scarp wall or the isolated Jebel Terif. Notice how the four mighty crescent **dunes** to the north have spawned two infants downwind, either side of the Assyut road, near a crowd of whalebacks. Though disproving the notion that *barchan* and *seif* dunes don't mix, its physical causes are still explicable in terms of formulae devised by the late desert explorer Ralph Bagnold, whose classic book *The Physics of Blown Sand and Desert Dunes* (1939) later helped NASA to interpret data from its Martian space probes. The book was written after five years' experimentation with a home-made wind-tunnel and builder's sand; after his desert journeys of the 1920s, Bagnold felt "it was really just exploring in another form".

Further afield north of el-Kharga

For those with four-wheel drive, a couple more ruins scattered around the northern part of the depression provide an excuse for driving off *piste*. **Qasr Ain Mustapha Kachif**, roughly a kilometre to the northeast of Bagawat, is an

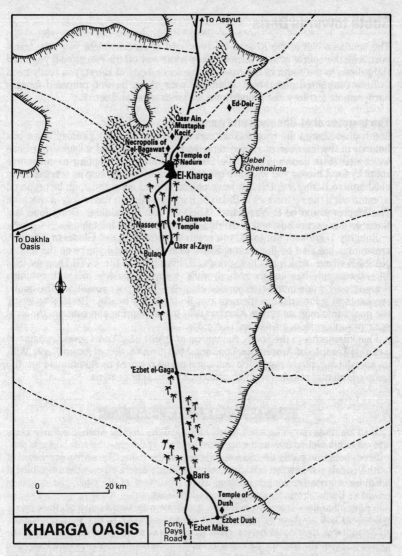

To Assyut

Qasr Ain
Mustapha
Kacif

Ed-Deir

Necropolis of
el-Begawat

Temple of
Nadura

Jebel
Ghenneima

El-Kharga

To Dakhla
Oasis

Nasser

el-Ghweeta
Temple

Qasr al-Zayn

Bulaq

'Ezbet el-Gaga

0   20 km

Baris

Temple of
Dush

KHARGA OASIS

Ezbet Dush

Forty
Days
Road

'Ezbet Maks

abandoned fortified convent with a tower, vaulted chambers, chapel and
refectory, near a spring. Before the road to Assyut was built, vehicles and heavy
freight could only reach the oasis by a railway from the Nile. Now likewise
abandoned, this runs to the north of **Ed-Deir**, a ruined Roman fort, with a temple
and a round tower, approximately 30km northeast of Kharga City. Intended to
guard the shortest camel route to the Nile, it provides a less magnificent view of
the oasis than the heights of **Jebel Ghenneima**, 3km to the south.

South towards Baris

The southern half of the Kharga Oasis is hard of access unless you have transport, with the couple of local **temple sites** some way off the road; and if you head right down to the south of the oasis, to the second city of **Baris**, you really need to be a committed desert-buff. Whatever your plans, be well prepared for this hard, remote territory and properly stocked with water and petrol.

The temples of el-Gheetwa and Amenebis

South of el-Kharga the road follows part of the old "Forty Days Road" (see box below), past a number of ruined temples in the desert, and villages that once welcomed slave caravans from the Sudan. If you are attempting to cover this route by local **buses** you will have to count on an overnight stop as services from el-Kharga to Baris (2hr; £E1.25) leave only at around noon and 2pm; be prepared to camp out if the resthouses at Bulaq or Baris are full. An easier way of reaching the temples would be to hire a **taxi** (£E60–70 with bargaining). Bring food and water on day excursions, and, if **driving**, be sure to have a full tank.

Roughly 17km south of town, you reach the first sight, **el-Ghweeta Temple**, crowning a hill 2km off the main road (or 5km to the east if you're on the fork to NASSER village, which has hot springs). Dating back to the XXVII Dynasty (522 BC), the temple has ten-metre-high walls, a small hypostele hall with columns missing, and crude murals in rounded chapels – all in poor condition. The adobe remnants of a Ptolemaic settlement can be made out nearby. Besides watering the ducks that migrate across Kharga Oasis in early spring and autumn, the local springs support palm groves and rice crops.

Five kilometres to the south, the village of QASR EL-ZAYAN gives its name to a ruined **Temple of Amenebis**, honouring the divine fusion of Amun-Neph. With its open-lotus capitals, mudbrick walls, and portal restored by Antoninus Pius, the temple is all that remains of another ancient town, Tchonemyris.

THE FORTY DAYS ROAD

Of all the trade routes between North Africa and the tropical south, the **Forty Days Road** (*Darb al-Arba'in*) was the one most involved in slavery – the only business profitable enough to justify the risks and rigours of the route. The slaves, purchased at the Dongola slave market or kidnapped by the fierce desert tribes, were assembled at **Kobbé**, a town (no longer existing) 60km northwest of el-Fasher, the capital of Sudan's Darfur Province, once an independent kingdom.

After a few days' march from Kobbé, the slaves were unchained from their yokes, for there was nowhere to run. With no permanent water source until Bir Natrun, 530km away, they could only survive on the ox-skins of water that burdened the camels. From **Bir Natrun**, caravans trekked 260km northeast across waterless, open sands, vulnerable to attack by bandits from the Arab Kababish and Bedayatt tribes, or the black Gor'an based at Nukheila Oasis. The next oasis, **Laqiya al-Arba'in**, had water but scant grazing for camels, and with reserves of fodder exhausted they could easily weaken and stumble along the rocky 280-kilometre journey to **Selima Oasis**. Whilst human losses were erased by the sands, the road gained definition from its bactrian casualties; a 1946 survey of northwestern Sudan noted "a track about one mile wide marked with white camel-bones".

BULAQ, 3km further south, has better developed **thermal springs** than Nasser, but an equally basic **resthouse** (beds £E3.50). It's the only settlement of any size until you reach Baris.

Baris and beyond

BARIS, 90km south of el-Kharga, is the oasis's second largest settlement, having mushroomed even faster than the capital under the New Valley programme. Half a dozen kiosks and a place dispensing *fuul* and *taamiya* (except on Fridays) ensure that you won't starve here, and there's an unsignposted **resthouse** on the northern edge of town at right angles to the highway. North of here stands a housing complex designed along traditional Nubian lines by the late Hassan Fathy; unfortunately, work stopped in 1967, and the villagers have since refused to occupy a building that reminds them of tombs.

A recently paved road runs 23km southeast of Baris to 'EZBET DUSH, not far from the **Temple of Dush**, currently under excavation. Built during Trajan's reign for the worship of Serapis and Isis, the temple originally served the town of Kysis, which archaeologists are still unearthing. The discovery of an elaborate system of clay pipes and a Christian church suggests that Kysis was abandoned when its wells dried up, some time after the fourth century AD. "Dush" is believed to derive from Kush, the name of the ancient Sudanese kingdom with whom the Egyptians traded along the Nile.

Desert routes developed later, with two factors providing the spur. Camels, introduced to North Africa sometime after the Persian invasion of 525 BC, enabled travellers to cover far greater distances between wells, making new routes feasible. But caravans lacked an incentive to make such a long and dangerous journey until well into the Mamluke era, when rising tolls and bribes for customs officials along the Nile made a desert route more profitable. Thus arose the famous *Darb el-Arba'in* or **Forty Days Road**, which entered Kharga Oasis at 'EZBET MAKS, 10km west of Dush (see below).

W.G. Browne, the only European to complete the Forty Days Road, estimated the slave caravan's value at £115,000 sterling – a huge sum for the time (1762). During the nineteenth century a customs post was established at Maks to tax caravans arriving in **Kharga Oasis**, the last stage before their ultimate destination, Assyut. As the caravans approached, small boys were hidden in empty waterskins to evade tax, but officials would beat them to thwart this ploy. The most valuable slaves were young Nubian women – prized as concubines because their skin remained cool whatever the heat. Having sold their chattels at **Assyut**, traders bought "fabrics, jewellery, weaponry and kohl" for the return journey.

The Forty Days Road effectively ended in 1884, after the rise of the Dervish empire closed the Egyptian–Sudanese border. When it reopened, slavery had been prohibited, rendering the road's premier commodity worthless; this thousand-mile journey was made no more. As the illiterate slave-drivers died off, memories of the *Darb al-Arba'in* faded, as Michael Asher discovered when he tried to retrace the route from Darfur in the 1980s. The borderlands, however, were – and still are – rendered perilous by Bedayatt and Gor'an raiders whose automatic weapons outgun local tribesmen and Sudanese police. Tribal alliances and blood feuds have become fatally entangled with international politics; rumours abound of Libyan-trained infiltrators, fundamentalist-backed guerrillas and bandit gangs – and Darfur Province is increasingly chaotic.

SIWA OASIS

Isolated by hundreds of kilometres of waterless desert, **Siwa Oasis** remained virtually independent of Egypt up until the last century, and has only become accessible to tourists in the last few years. Yet Siwa has fascinated outsiders ever since antiquity. The legendary Army of Cambyses was heading this way when it disappeared into a sandstorm; Alexander the Great journeyed here to consult the famous Oracle of Amun in 331 BC; and fantastic Arabic tales of *Santariyah* (as the oasis was known) were common currency into the last century.

Insular and archaic, Siwa's romantic aura lingers on. The oasis is set amidst thick palm groves clustered around freshwater springs and salt lakes, and though its crumbling fortified villages have been abandoned in favour of new houses, other aspects of traditional life seem little changed. Women still wear silver jewellery by the kilo, and shroud themselves from head to foot outdoors; Siwans still observe their own festivals and wedding customs; and among themselves they speak *Siwi*, a Berber tongue. Just how much longer these idiosyncrasies survive is questionable: after centuries of resisting invaders the Siwans have recently welcomed the ultimate cultural subversive – a thousand television sets were ordered the week after electricity was installed in the oasis.

SIWA PRACTICALITIES

All visitors to Siwa require **military permission**, which should be obtained at Mersa Matrouh on the Mediterranean coast, 290km west of Alexandria (*not* in Alex or Cairo, as some guidebooks suggest). Ask for more time than is necessary (say, seven days) as permits can't be extended in Siwa; permission to stay longer than a week might be denied, while trips to the eastern villages beside Lake Zeitun and the remoter Qara and Girba oases require special permission, which is rarely granted. Details of how to obtain the permit, and get from Matrouh to Siwa, are given under "Mersa Matrouh" (see p.486).

Getting there: the route

Unless you sign up with a desert safari, which might reach Siwa via the Qattara Depression or the half-finished road from Bahariya Oasis, the well-surfaced **road from Matrouh** is the only feasible approach. Travelling by **bus** (£E5; £E8 with A/C) or **service taxi** (£E6), be sure to give your permit to the driver and reclaim it at the end of the 300-kilometre journey.

The trip takes five hours, with a stop at a halfway resthouse (tea, soup, soft drinks; no petrol) whose toilets are the nearest one gets to the horrors of this route before the road was built. Until this century there was only a camel trail (eight days from Matrouh) across this flat desert and the few landmarks might be obscured by dust clouds or sandstorms. The sharp limestone ridges and hollows beneath the powdery surface of this *shabak* ("net") desert also made the route hazardous for early motorists, who followed the line of telegraph poles. Nowadays the monotonous vistas – interspersed with army camps – keep going until the last 40km, when rock outcrops presage the appearance of the oasis.

Climate

The **best time** to come is during spring (before the *khamseen*) or autumn, when the Siwans hold festivals and the days are pleasantly warm. During winter, windless days can also be nice, but nights – and gales – are chilling. From May onwards, rising

A little history

Beyond the fact that it supported hunter-gatherers in Palaeolithic times, little is known about Siwa Oasis before the XXVI Dynasty, when the reputation of its **Oracle** spread throughout the Mediterranean world.

Siwa's inhabitants – who probably migrated here from the Libyan oases – were always at risk from predatory desert tribes, so their first settlement was a fortified acropolis. Classical accounts of the Oracle reveal little about this beyond its name, **Aghurmi**, and its position as a major caravan stop between Cyrenaica and the Sudan. Its later history, however, is detailed in the *Siwan Manuscript*, a turn-of-the-century compilation of oral histories which relate how Siwa's rulers considered poisoning the springs with mummies in order to thwart the Muslim conquest (date uncertain), and how Bedouin and Berber raids reduced Aghurmi's population to a mere 200 by the twelfth century AD.

SHALI AND SIWAN SOCIETY

Roundabout 1203, seven families quit Aghurmi to found a new settlement further west, called **Shali** (the town). Their menfolk are still honoured as the "forty ancestors", and these pioneering families were probably the most vigorous of the surviving Siwans. Like Aghurmi, Shali was walled and built of *kharsif*: a salt-

---

temperatures keep people indoors between 11am and 7pm, and summer nights are sultry and mosquito-ridden. Even when the climate is mild you'll probably feel like taking a midday siesta or a swim.

Facilities – and attitudes

Aside from **lacking a bank** (bring enough cash for your stay), Siwa has all the basic **facilities**, including a special hospital for women. Before its inauguration in 1987, sick women were driven to Matrouh to be treated by strangers; local men refused to let their wives be examined by a fellow Siwan.

Bearing in mind such attitudes, visitors are advised to **dress** modestly. Women should cover their legs and shoulders in town, and their bathing costume with a baggy T-shirt at the pools. Tourists of both sexes can get away with wearing shorts in town, but the Siwans don't like it, as several notices proclaim. People are generally more reserved than the Egyptians, and invitations home are less common. Siwan households are segregated, with the women's quarters on the ground floor; foreign women who get invited upstairs have reason to be suspicious.

Photography

Besides the official ban on photographing military installations (including the airport, and sandbagged dug-outs in unexpected locations), visitors should respect Siwan feelings on the issue. As a rule, local women are taboo subjects, whereas Siwan males – particularly the younger ones – don't mind being snapped (but always ask them first). Discreet long-shots are easier than close-ups. For streetlife and visual clarity, take your pictures before 9am, or during the hour or so before sunset; people stay indoors when the sun is high, and its glare bleaches colours and textures from photographs.

A few words of Siwi

yes	*mashi*	donkey	*zitan*	camel	*dalghrumt*
no	*oola*	horse	*tegmirt*	dates	*ragawen*

impregnated mud which dries cement-hard, but melts during downpours – fortunately, it only rains heavily here every fifty years or so. Fearful of raiders, Shali's *agwad* (elders) forbade families to live outside the walls, so as the population increased the town could only expand upwards. Siwan households added an extra floor with each generation, whilst the *agwad* regulated the width of alleys to one-donkey's breadth in an effort to ensure some light and air within the labyrinth.

Siwan bachelors aged between twenty and forty were obliged to sleep in caves outside town, guarding the fields – hence their nickname, the "club-bearers". Noted for their love of palm liquor, song and dance, these *zaggalah* shocked outsiders with their open **homosexuality**. Homosexual marriages were forbidden by King Fouad in 1928, but continued in secret until the late 1940s; the dowry and matrimonial expenses were equivalent to a bride's.

Another feature of Shali was the tradition of the violent **feuds** between two neighbourhood gangs – the Westerners and Easterners – in which all able-bodied males were expected to participate. Originally ritualised, with parallel lines of combatants exchanging blows between sunrise and sunset whilst their women-folk threw stones at cowards and shouted encouragement, feuds became far deadlier with the advent of firearms. Fifty years after the Easterners' victory at the savage Battle of the Sands (1712), W.G. Browne found that "hostile families fire on each other in the streets, and from the houses . . . on the slightest grounds". Yet the Siwans immediately closed ranks against outsiders – Bedouin raiders, khedival taxmen or European explorers.

EGYPTIAN AND BRITISH CONTROL

Visitors of the eighteenth and nineteenth centuries regularly experienced Siwan **xenophobia**. "Whenever I quitted my apartment, it was to be assailed with stones and a torrent of abusive language," Browne wrote. Having poked around the antiquities in Muslim guise, Frederick Hornemann was pursued into the desert, where "the braying of 300 donkeys announced the arrival of the Siwan army", and only escaped thanks to his assistant's recitation of Koranic verses. Frederic Cailliaud was permitted to visit the gardens and ruins in 1819 but the town remained barred to strangers until 600 troops sent by Mohammed Ali compelled the oasis to recognise **Egyptian authority** in 1820.

Although the Siwans subsequently revolted against their governor (*Ma'mur*) and defaulted on taxes (payable in dates) half a dozen times over the next sixty years, the oasis began to change. With the desert tribes suppressed, and Shali rendered unsafe by heavy rains, the *agwad* permitted families to settle outside the walls. From the 1850s onwards the great reformist preacher Mohammed Ibn Ali al-Senussi cast a spell over the desert peoples from Jaghbub Oasis just over the border, and Siwa – the site of his first *zawiya* – supported **Senussi** resistance to the Italian conquest of Libya (1912–30) until it became clear that their "liberators" would not restore Siwan independence. Thus in 1917, British forces were "welcomed by the cheering Siwans, who declared their loyalty as they always did with every new victorious conqueror" (Fakhry).

Anglo-Egyptian control of Siwa was maintained by the Camel Corps and Light Car Patrols. Agricultural advisors, a school and an orthodox *imam* were introduced following King Fouad's visit to the oasis in 1928. When the British withdrew as the Italians advanced across North Africa in 1942, the Siwans accepted Axis **occupation** with equal resignation. Unlike Rommel, who made a favourable impression during his flying visit, King Farouk dismayed the Siwans by wearing shorts, and asking if they "still practised a certain vice" when he visited the oasis in 1945.

MORE RECENT DEVELOPMENTS

Paradoxical as it sounds, Siwa suffers from an excess of fresh water, which gushes from springs and drains into salt lakes, increasing their volume and salinity. As the desert explorer Ralph Bagnold put it: "the air, hot and breathless, has a characteristic oasis smell, slightly sweet, of rank grass faintly charred, decaying through increasing saltiness". Various **land reclamation** projects have tried to tackle the problem since 1907, but creating drainage catchment areas in an oasis lying 18m below sea level has always proved hugely expensive – if not futile, given the local labour shortage.

Health care, education and the new road (completed in 1984, at the Siwans' request) are the best examples of **recent developments**: the military bases only serve Egyptian interests, whilst tourism's contribution is debatable. Even the Swiss couple resident here for several years, who won international backing for the Woman and Child Hospital, are not universally accepted.

International affairs, meanwhile, remain relevant to the oasis, for if the rapprochement between Libya and Egypt lasts, Siwans may start crossing the border to work in oilfields around Jaghbub Oasis, as they did in the 1960s.

Siwa Town

Most visitors rate **SIWA TOWN** and the pools, rocks and ruins around as the oasis's main attractions, and not many bother to visit al-Maraqi on the western side of the oasis, as their permits allow.

Made of mudbrick and breeze block, Siwa Town radiates outwards from limestone crags encrusted with the jagged ruins of Shali. A triumphal arch and broad roads debouch onto a central market area, but the town slips away into a maze of alleyways, and loses itself amidst the encircling palms. Boys driving donkey carts transport fodder and decorously wrapped Siwan women, and the braying of donkeys resounds from every quarter of town. After dark, as the lights go out across town, a thousand stars emerge and military radio becomes Siwa's sole link to the world beyond the Great Sand Sea.

Accommodation

There's no problem finding **somewhere to stay**, but little choice either, and at all places the water supply usually conks out at midday. The options are:

Hotel Arous el-Waha (Bride of the Oasis), by the guardhouse as you enter town. Luxurious by Siwan standards, with fitted showers and toilets in airy, carpeted rooms, a pleasant patio and a roof for stargazing. Singles cost £E15, doubles £E20, triples £E25 and quadruple rooms £E28; you can get a better breakfast elsewhere for the £E2 that's charged.

Hotel el-Madina, off the market area. Charges £E2 a head for clean, very basic rooms; cold water and paraffin lamps are the order of the day.

Badawi Hotel, opposite the Intelligence Office. Small and clean but will only allow couples to share a room (£E3) if they have proof of marriage.

New Siwa Hotel, on the road towards the hospital and bus station. It's hard to think of any reason for staying at this small, cramped fleapit.

The *Alexandria Rest House* is defunct at present.

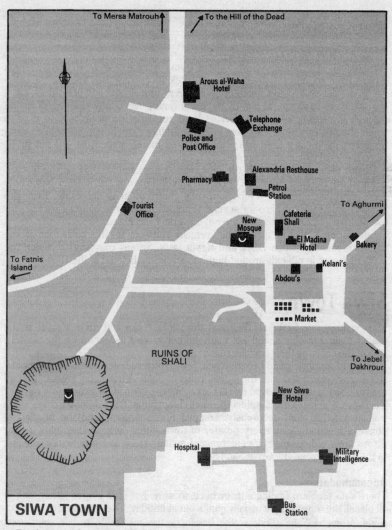

To Mersa Matrouh

To the Hill of the Dead

Arous al-Waha Hotel

Telephone Exchange

Police and Post Office

Alexandria Resthouse

Pharmacy

Petrol Station

Tourist Office

To Aghurmi

New Mosque

Cafeteria Shali

El Madina Hotel

Bakery

To Fatnis Island

Kelani's

Abdou's

Market

RUINS OF SHALI

To Jebel Dakhrour

New Siwa Hotel

Hospital

Military Intelligence

Bus Station

SIWA TOWN

Don't consider **camping** out unless the tourist office gives the okay. Depending on relations with Libya, the oasis may be swarming with soldiers "alert" for saboteurs and smugglers.

Information

Siwa's **tourist office** (Sat–Thurs 9am–1pm, Fri 6–8pm) is the place to find Mr Mahdi Mohammed Ali Hweiti, a native Siwan and English-speaking graduate of Alexandria University, who also runs a handicrafts emporium (see below). Mohammed the barber, who has travelled all over the Arab world and wants to practice his English, is another possible source of information.

City sights: Shali and the Hill of the Dead

The **ruins of Shali**, looming above New Mosque Square, are best entered near the generator, where a passage ascends into the crumbling labyrinth. You have to beware of sudden deadfalls where roofs have collapsed, exposing palm-log beams and decaying goat carcasses.

It's the **views of Siwa** that make it all worthwhile. You can see the whole town, its palm groves, the salt lakes and tabletop rocks beyond; and providing you don't peer too obviously into the courtyards below, it's possible to glimpse the Siwans at home. Downstairs, women busy themselves with cooking (cockerels and goats roam the alleys) and childcare; a few mats, and painted chests for storing the family valuables, constitute the only furniture.

The Hill of the Dead

By following the Matrouh road out of town and then bearing right, you'll soon reach the unmistakable *Jebel al-Mawta*, or **Hill of the Dead**, also known as the Ridge of the Mummified. Amongst scores of XXVI Dynasty and Ptolemaic tombs reused by the Romans, who cut *loculi* for their own burials, four locked ones still retain murals or inscriptions. For access, there is a custodian on the hill every day, between around 10am and 1pm.

In the **Tomb of Si-Amun**, murals depict this bearded, Greek-looking merchant and his family worshipping Egyptian deities with great artistry; unfortunately, they were vandalised by Allied soldiers after the tomb's discovery in 1940, when the Siwans dug into the necropolis to escape air raids and also found the **Tomb of Mesu-Isis**. Another third-century BC creation, this was used for two burials although the decorators never got far beyond the entrance.

Whereas Si-Amun's tomb bespeaks of Cyrenaician influence, the **Tomb of the Crocodile** reflects Siwa's longstanding ties to the Fayoum, where the Crocodile cult (see p.404) flourished – with a dash of Hellenistic style in the painting of gazelles nibbling at a tree.

Lastly, there's the battered XXVI Dynasty **Tomb of Niperpathot**, with a ruined court, side rooms, and a tiny burial chamber covered with red inscriptions, including praise of Niperpathot as "the straightforward one".

Jewellery and crafts

A glimpse of earrings or ankle-bracelets aside, you won't see much of **Siwan jewellery** on the streets, unless you check out the shops.

Unlike the gold-loving Egyptians, the Siwans prefer **silver jewellery**, which likewise serves as bullion assets for a people mistrustful of banks and paper money. Broad silver bracelets and oval rings wrought with geometric designs – the most popular items with visitors – are usually modern reproductions which might come from Khan el-Khalili, whence the locals have imported stuff for centuries: "Siwan jewellery" isn't necessarily synonymous with "made in the oasis". *Al-salhat*, with six pendants hung from silver and coral beads, is the easiest type of necklace to identify. You'll also recognise the *ti'laqayn*, a mass of chains tipped with bells, suspended from huge crescents; an ornament for the head, like the silver hoops and bells suspended from matching chunks of bullion, known to the Siwans as *qasas*. Finally, there's the *aghraw*, a silver collar from which girls hang a decorative disk or *adrim*, removed on their wedding day.

SIWAN FESTIVALS AND WEDDINGS

Siwan festivals are the most public side of a largely private culture, so it's worth making an effort to attend one.

Two of the Siwan festivals are celebrated by Muslims everywhere: the **Lesser Bairam**, at the end of Ramadan, occasioning festivities similar to those elsewhere in Egypt; and the **Corban Bairam** (Greater Feast), which starts earlier in Siwa. The gathering of fuel and salt by the *zaggalah* over the preceding nine days is reckoned as much a part of the event as the mass slaughter of sheep after festival prayers on the tenth day of Zoul Hagga. The sheep's hide is stewed together with its offal in an earthenware pot; its head and stomach are eaten the next day, when cuts of meat are distributed amongst relatives (new brides especially); and finally, any leftovers are preserved.

The **Moulid of Sidi Suleyman** is a less carnivorous affair, with banners, candles and *zikrs* outside the tomb of this local holy man, next to the New Mosque in Siwa Town. Siwans recall how its doors refused to open after their ancestors spurned some poor Bedouin pilgrims, and how Sidi Suleyman once conjured up a sandstorm to bury an army of Tibbu raiders from the Sudan. Held shortly after the corn harvest, his *moulid* subsumes two older, pagan festivals, where vast quantities of *labgi* were openly consumed. Public drinking of palm liquor is now forbidden, but the *zaggalah* still have a rowdy three-day bash near Shali.

Ashura, on the tenth of Moharram, was once Siwa's principal feast, and fervently Shi'ite; the Fatimid Shia reached Egypt via the North African oases. Nowadays it's chiefly an event for children, who decorate their homes with palm-stalks soaked in olive oil, and fire them at sunset, singing whilst the town is illuminated by torchlight. Afterwards children go from house to house exchanging presents.

Weddings

Although you might be invited to join the tea-drinking crowd outside the bridegroom's family house, foreigners rarely witness the intricate ritual of **Siwan weddings**. Preceded by reciprocal visits of kinsfolk, and a bath in a limpid pool where the removal of an item of jewellery symbolises her abandonment of maidenhood, the bride is "kidnapped" by her spouse's family, returned, and then delivered wrapped in a sheet. The wedding dress of embroidered shawls and skirts is as flamboyant as the outdoor garb of married women is drab.

Traditionally, a Siwan widow commanded the same *mahr* (dowry) as a virgin since both were "daughters of the forty ancestors", but could only remarry after one year of bereavement. Cruelly, the Siwans regarded newly bereaved widows as "devourers of the soul" (*ghulah*), and forced them to spend forty days in solitary confinement before they were "cleansed".

If that taboo has lapsed, Siwan attitudes remain profoundly patriarchal: women are virtually housebound, and expected to shroud themselves in blue-grey cloth if they venture outdoors.

Other local **handicrafts** include black robes with orange or red piping; intricately embroidered wedding clothes spangled with antique coins; and various types of woven baskets, notably the one called *margunah*. Buying recently made items helps maintain local handicraft traditions, as Siwa's mayor asserts, but the sale of antique pieces is questionable. Not only is Siwa's artistic heritage leaving the oasis, probably forever, but the silver anklets or pendants might be the financial assets of a woman who's powerless to stop her husband disposing of them.

Food, facilities and buses back to Matrouh

There are really only two **places to eat**, both on the main "shopping street" that runs back-to-back with Siwa's market. *Abdou's Restaurant* does great *karkaday* and spicy mixed vegetables, and the usual oasis staples like pasta, noodles and omelette; *Kelani's* offers the same, plus *fuul* and *taamiya* for homesick Egyptians – but *Abdou's* (run by the engaging Abd al-Ghani) produces tastier, safer meals.

Across the road are a couple of **shops** selling basic provisions, while if you're serious about self-catering, the **market** stocks seasonal vegetables, dates and olive oil galore. Fresh pita bread is available from dawn to dusk at the hole in the wall **bakery**. The *Cafeteria Shali*, run by a friendly English-speaking Egyptian, has *sheeshas* and also a copy of Fakhry's *Siwa Oasis* available for reading.

Other facilities

Among useful services and facilities, there's a **pharmacy** (some English spoken) and also a **hospital** – the latter a kilometre from the centre.

Modern blocks along the road between the triumphal arch and New Mosque Square contain Siwa's **police** station, **post office** and telephone exchange (daily 7am–10pm – they can place **international calls**). The **petrol** station on the corner is the only one in the oasis.

Returning to Mersa Matrouh

Though **buses** to Mersa Matrouh can be boarded outside the New Mosque or the Arous el-Waha, it's necessary to **book** the night before and board at the terminal before departure to be sure of a getting a seat; however, standing passengers are never turned away, and seats should become vacant as soldiers are dropped off along the way. Non A/C buses leave daily at 6am and 2pm (£E6), the afternoon service continuing to Alexandria; on Sunday, Monday and Tuesday there is also a 10am A/C service to Matrouh (£E7) and Alex (£E8).

Alternatively, enquire at *Abdou's* about **service taxis**, which leave mid-morning or late afternoon, depending on demand. Drivers charge £E6 per head for a full seven-seater car or fourteen-person minibus; more to run less than fully loaded.

Whatever your transport, give the driver your **permit** to show at checkpoints.

Around Siwa Oasis

Although the **Siwa Oasis** depression is some 82km long and up to 28km wide, cultivated areas amount to less than 2000 acres and the total population is just over 14,000; in some areas both population and cultivation have diminished since salination turned ancient gardens into barren *karshif*. Nearer town, dense **palm groves** and wiry olive trees are carefully tended in mud and palm-leaf walled gardens: dates and olives are the Siwans' chief crops. The tourist board proclaims Siwa "the oasis of a million palm trees", of which around 23,000 are male palms, only valued for the white heart at the top of the tree, a local delicacy.

Palms form a backdrop for most places that you're likely to go, especially the **pools** or **baths**, which for many visitors are the highlight of the oasis. The nearer sites can be reached by donkey *caretta* or by walking; just time your visit to avoid travelling at the hottest time of day. A place in the market rents bicycles (£E1 per hour; £E5 for the day), but the track to Fatnis is unbelieveably rough.

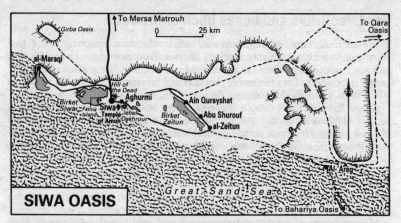

SIWA OASIS

Should you be invited to visit **private springs and gardens** it's wise to consider your would-be host's motives before accepting. Financial designs aren't necessarily a deterrent – it's quite acceptable to pay for a good experience – but lecherous intentions are something else: women without male escorts should definitely be wary.

The Oracle and Cleopatra's Bath

A *caretta* (£E2) or a twenty-minute walk through the palm groves will bring you to **AGHURMI**, just a kilometre east of town. The modern village lies just beyond the rock where ancient Siwans built their first **acropolis** (signposted "Alexander crowning hill"). Behind its *karshif* walls, palm-logs uphold the shells of buildings straggling up towards a bulky, battered **temple** on the summit, whose sanctuary once housed the **Siwan Oracle**.

The Oracle of Amun
Fakhry's *Siwa Oasis* dates the acropolis **temple** to the reign of Amasis the Drunkard (570–526 BC) but reckons it evolved from a seventh- or eighth-century BC site dedicated to Amun-Re. Though others have attributed the primal shrine to the ram-headed Libyan god Ammon, experts agree that the **Oracle of Amun** was renowned from the XXVI Dynasty onwards.

Its history is subsequently much documented: a Persian army sent to destroy it was obliterated by the desert; emissaries sent by Cimon of Athens were told of his death as it happened; assured of success by the Oracle, Eubotas of Cyrenaica took his own victory statue to the 93rd Olympiad; Lysander tried bribery to win the oracle's endorsement of his claim to the Spartan throne.

But the most famous petitioner was Alexander the Great. Having liberated Egypt from its hated Persian rulers and ordered the creation of a city on the Mediterranean, Alexander hurried to Siwa in the spring of 331 BC. It's thought that he sought confirmation that he was the son of Zeus (whom the Greeks identified with Amun), but the Oracle's reply – whispered by a priest through an aperture in the wall of the sanctuary – is unrecorded. Alexander kept it secret unto his death in Asia eight years later. Despite his personal wish to be buried near the Oracle, he was interred at Alexandria, the capital he never saw.

The site

From the minaret on the acropolis you can gaze across clusters of palms to a cream-coloured pillar – part of a **ruined Temple of Amun** viewed side-on. A bas-reliefed wall and blocks of rubble are all that remain of this once substantial XXX Dynasty creation after it was dynamited by a treasure-hunting *Ma'mur* in 1897. Locals call the ruin *Umm 'Ubaydah*, but its likely founder was King Nectanebo II (360–343 BC), who also rebuilt the Temple of Hibis at Kharga Oasis.

Follow the path on for ten to fifteen minutes to reach the enticing **Cleopatra Bath**, a deep pool of gently bubbling water near an adobe laundry (where women can get changed). Although you're fully visible to anyone passing along the donkey trail, most foreigners feel relaxed about bathing here, and even Siwan brides used to do so before ritual ablutions were transferred to the **Tamusi Bath**, secluded in a thicket 150m back along the path. The Tamusi is where brides-to-be pass on their *adrims* to their younger sisters and boys are circumcised; foreigners would be advised to keep a respectful distance.

Heading on from the Cleopatra Bath, pick your way through groves of palms and clover fields towards **Jebel Dakhrour**: a fifteen- to twenty-minute walk. This rocky hill is the site for a great **feast** in October. At other times you can easily scramble up to enjoy memorable views from its summit. In contrast to the verdant oasis, the southern horizon presents a desolate vista of crescent dunes and blackened mesas, shimmering with heat – the **Great Sand Sea** (see overpage).

To return to town, follow the first unpaved road you come to and hitch rides on donkey-carts; it takes thirty to forty minutes to reach the back alleys of Siwa.

Fatnis Island

One of the best spots in the oasis is **Fatnis – or "Fantasy" – Island**, on the salt lake of **Birket Siwa**, 6km west of town. The trail gets rougher and the scenery becomes wilder with each kilometre of this forty-minute donkey *caretta* journey (you could walk it instead, temperature permitting). If you hire a *caretta*, pay your donkey boy once back in town for the return journey plus time spent at the pool; between £E6–10 seems about right.

The route down to the island and its pools runs past the **Abu Alif Bath**, where farmhands wash in a concrete tank. The track then enters the palm groves, emerging onto a bone-shakingly rutted causeway across salt-encrusted pans onto **Fatnis Island**, where palms surround a large circular **pool**. The dark reflections and clumps of algae on its surface can make this look a bit off-putting, but once you take the plunge it's invigorating. Diving is quite safe and minimises contact with the slippery steps and sides. Fresh water constantly wells up from clefts in the rock 15m below, but you'll need to bring drinking water (plus food).

Before returning, take a look at **Birket Siwa** receding towards sculpted table-tops on the western horizon. You can see the process of crust-formation at the edges, where evaporation gradually renders fresh water saline, then crystalline, blackening the surrounding vegetation.

Al-Maraqi

As far as public transport and standard visitors' permits go, the only other place in the oasis that's accessible is the western village of **AL-MARAQI**. Buses (35pt) leaving Siwa town at 7am and 2pm (double-check) take around two hours to cover the 25km, twisting through a desertscape of fissured ochre buttes riddled with caves and Roman tombs. From the Roman era until the fifteenth century, this area was thickly populated and intensely cultivated, whereas nowadays the oasis (separated by desert from the rest of Siwa) is largely used for grazing by the Bedouin al-Shihaybat tribe, of whom a dozen families inhabit al-Maraqi village. Buses return after an hour's wait, so you have to catch the morning service to avoid being stranded in a place with no tourist facilities (pick-ups or donkeys are possible alternatives to walking back).

En route between al-Maraqi and town, where the road nears Birket Siwa, a spur heading northwest is the upgraded version of the old *Mashrab el-Ikhwan* camel trail to GIRBA OASIS, now inhabited only by soldiers.

Lake Zeitun and further afield

Areas **beyond the limits of standard visitors' permits** range the gamut of accessibility. If you can find a willing Siwan with a pick-up, sites along the eastern shore of **Lake Zeitun** (Birket Zeitun) are readily accessible, and the penalty for being caught out by officials shouldn't exceed a reprimand. But sites further out require a properly equipped desert expedition with military permission, vital if you're not to die from the environment or travel in fear of soldiers. Egyptian nationals running desert safari tours find permits hard enough to obtain; for independent foreign motorists it could prove impossible.

Birket Zeitun

Ringed by a good road, the largest salt lake in the oasis takes its name from the southernmost hamlet on its far shore, now practically deserted. **Birket Zeitun's** increasing salinity is both the cause and result of depopulation: as less irrigation-works are maintained, more of the freshwater from the **Ain Qurayshat** spring flows unused into the lake, crystallising mineral salts as it evaporates.

Near the spring are two ancient **ruins**, roughly 100m apart: a heap of rubble, which still constituted a temple during Steindorff's visit in 1900, and the remains of a brick building attributed to "the abode of king al-Ghashsham" by the *Siwan Manuscript*. Though Siwans still dig roundabouts in the hope of finding loot, Ain Qurayshat is better for bathing than antiquities.

The best of the lake's **bathing** is around 35km south of Siwa Town at the hamlet of ABU SHUROUF: a huddle of brick houses around a small stone **temple**. Abu Shurouf also contains a Bedouin encampment and all the female **donkeys** in the oasis, which are kept and mated here.

Further south along the lake, the village of AL-ZEITUN was once a model Senussi community tending the richest gardens in the oasis. Damaged by Italian bombs in 1940, it is nowadays abandoned, partially burying a ruined temple.

Northeast to Qara Oasis

Travelling 119km northeast of Siwa across the gravel plain, you'd be following the former *Mashrab al-Khalida* to QARA OASIS, a stuffy hollow surrounded by cliffs, where meagre palms struggle to survive in salt-encrusted ground. Qara is the poorest, remotest oasis in the Western Desert, hardly changed since Bagnold described it in 1929, perched atop "a solitary white mushroom of rock . . . a single mud-cap edged by a high smooth wall, impregnable to raiders, with one black tunnel for a street into which open windowless cells without ventilation".

Northeast of Qara the land plummets into the **Qattara Depression**, 120–134m below sea level, where "a long narrow salt marsh" winds "like a petrified river close beneath the cliffs". Ever since Dr Ball first proposed it in the 1920s, Egyptian planners have dreamed of piping water from the Mediterranean to the depression, utilising the fall in height to generate hydroelectricity, run desalination plants and irrigation systems. However, all attempts have foundered through lack of capital and the danger of World War II minefields, and nothing seems likely to happen in the foreseeable future.

Siwa to Bahariya

By contrast, the **road between Siwa and Bahariya** should be completed by the mid-1990s, and should open up the Western Desert considerably. Aside from direct communications between Siwa and the New Valley, travellers will be able to enjoy views of the great **dunes** running southeast from the Qattara Depression, whose sandy crests Bagnold likened to "unclipped horses' manes".

The route seems likely to pass through AL-'AREG, where ancient, often-plundered tombs attest to past inhabitation. A mummy from here found its way to the Alexandria Museum after the tomb-robber's maid found it in his apartment, thought it was a murder victim, and rang the police.

The Great Sand Sea and the "Lost Oasis"

The **Great Sand Sea** that laps Siwa and floods the Libyan–Egyptian border still has areas beyond the "limits of reliable relief information" on Tactical Pilotage Charts, but its overall configuration is known. From thick "whalebacks" and a mass of transverse dunes near Siwa, it washes south in parallel ridges (orientated north–south, with a slight northwest–southeast incline) as far as the eye can see.

Although its general existence was known in the time of Herodotus, the extent to which it stretched southwards wasn't realised until the Rohlfs' expedition of 1874 headed west from Dakhla into the unknown. With seventeen camels bearing water and supplies, they soon met the *erg*'s outermost ranges: "an ocean" of sand-waves over 100m high, ranked 2–4km apart. Rohlfs estimated that their camels could scale six dunes and advance 20km westwards on the first and second days, but their endurance would rapidly diminish thereafter, so with no prospect of water or an end to the dunes they were forced to turn north-northwest and follow the dune-lanes towards Siwa. The isolation, as they described it, was intense:

> *If one stayed behind a moment and let the caravan out of one's sight, a loneliness could be felt in the boundless expanse such as brought fear even in the stoutest heart . . . Nothing but sand and sky! At sea the surface of the water is moved, unless there is a dead calm. Here in the sand ocean there is nothing to remind one of the great common life of the earth but the stiffened ripples of the last simoon; all else is dead.*

By the eighteenth day the expedition could no longer water every camel and the animals began dying, yet it wasn't until the thirty-sixth day that the party reached Siwa. They had trekked 675km, 480 of them, across the waterless dunes.

The feat wasn't repeated until 1921–24, when Colonel de Lancy Forth entered the Sand Sea twice by camel from Dakhla and Siwa. Beneath a layer of sand he found campfires, charred ostrich eggs, flint knives and grinders from Neolithic times, when the desert was lush savannah.

Meanwhile, Ball and Moore had managed to round the Sand Sea's southeastern tip (near latitude 24) by car in 1917. However, it was an Egyptian, Hassanein Bey, who circumvented the Sand Sea's western edge (1923) as part of an extraordinary 3550-kilometre camel journey from Sollum on the Mediterranean to el-Fasher in Sudan's Darfur Province. He also confirmed the existence of the hitherto legendary massif, **Jebel 'Uweinat** (see below), whose water source encouraged motorised explorers of the 1920s to seek new routes to the southwest. For Prince Kemal al-Din in his fleet of caterpillar-tracked Citroens, and Ralph Bagnold and co – who found customised Model-T Fords more effective – the next obstacle was the **Gilf Kebir**: a vast limestone plateau south of the Sand Sea, which barred the way to remoter Libyan oases.

Jebel 'Uweinat

On a map of North Africa, the ruler-straight borders of Libya, Egypt and Sudan intersect at **Jebel 'Uweinat**, the highest point in the Libyan Desert. A flat-topped block of sandstone 16km wide, it rises from foothills through a "vertical battlement" to heights of 1800m, just enough to attract a little rainfall, which collects in pools at either end of the massif's southern face.

Although 'Uweinat's semi-permanent water and grazing supported small numbers of Gor'an pastoralists, the massif's location remained a mystery to the

---

SAND SEAS AND DUNES

The true life of the desert is not made up of the marches of tribes in search of pasture, but of the game that goes endlessly on. What a difference in substance between the sands of submission and the sands of unruliness! The dunes, the salines, change their nature . . . as the code changes by which they are governed.

Antoine de Saint-Exupéry *Wind, Sand and Stars*

Though gravel plains, limestone pans and scarp account for ninety percent of the Sahara, it's the **sand seas** or *ergs* that captivate the imagination. Covering hundreds of thousands of square kilometres of Algeria, Libya and Egypt, these sand sheets and dune fields are awesomely lifeless, yet shift and reproduce. Formed by wind and particles, vortices and accretion, their shapes, hues and textures are defined by light and shadow, a mutable reality. Venturers into this unearthly world must accept its whims and logic – this is elemental, not mortal terrain. Its sandstorms have buried armies and scoured paint from cars; soft spots and slipfaces can trap the unwary, break limbs or axles; getting lost and dying of heat and thirst are real possibilities here.

While prevailing winds are the dominant factor, local geology and whatever precipitation or vegetation exists also determine the shape of **dunes**. Where sand is relatively scarce and small obstructions are common, windblown particles tend to form crescent-shaped *barchan* dunes, which advance horns first. Fully-grown specimens (weighing up to 450 million kilos) are capable of spawning infants downwind, but their mass is nothing compared to ridged *seif* dunes, which can rise over 100m (500 feet) high and run unbroken for 50km – the longest straight lines in nature. Each has a hard-packed windward face, and a softer, gently sloping leeward side. The latter is prone to shallow quicksand spots and sudden slippages (stop and look before cresting dunes!), and even the firm windward surface can become unstable once its "piling" has been disturbed.

outside world until 1923, when it was reached by Hassanein Bey from Kufra Oasis in Libya. This spurred attempts by Dr Ball, Prince Kemal al-Din and other motorised explorers to find a route from Egypt, circumventing the Great Sand Sea and the plateau of the Gilf Kebir, described by explorer Ralph Bagnold as "unscalable":

> *For a hundred miles the great cliff went on. It seemed like the frontier of some "lost world" . . . unbroken except where the mouths of deep unlit gorges appeared as black slits, from the bottom of which an ancient debris of boulders spilled out fanwise for miles into the plain. It was tempting to go and explore one of those gorges. What might there not be far inland up the valleys which they drained? . . . But it was impossible to get close to the foot of the cliff without risking the cars.*

Nowadays, desert-smitten travellers can reach 'Uweinat by two rough desert roads, running 300–400km southwest from Kharga and Dakhla. A suitable car, loads of jerrycans of fuel (there's none available en route), ample food and water are essential; not to mention military permission, usually slow to get in either oasis. Armchair travellers can visit via the pages of Ralph Bagnold's *Libyan Sands*.

Zerzura: the "Lost Oasis"

With the "discovery" by motorised explorers of Selima, Merga and the Forty Day Road's waterholes, the number of unlocated oases diminished until only the

---

It's easy to imagine a sand ridge developing in the lee of soft, eroded rock, but **dune formation** in open desert requires some explanation. The ingredients include coarse sand and gravel whose weight immobilises them as lag deposit – and lighter particles (between 0.1 and 0.5 millimetres in size) which travel by a series of hopping movements, termed saltation. Transverse dunes (producing a "washboard" affect) are generally attributed to multi-directional winds – the prevailing one moderate, the stronger wind intermittent – but there's disagreement about the cause of parallel ridged dunes. Some think they evolve from transverse dunes buffeted by fierce crosswinds; others that they're whipped up by "longitudinal roll vortices" (horizontal whirlwinds). When the wind direction alters constantly, it can even form star-shaped (*rhourd*) or ring dunes.

Entering the Sand Sea

It's reasonably safe to enter the Sand Sea during the cooler months, but never during sandstorms, the *khamseen* period (see *Introduction*) or summertime. The outermost dunes are only a few kilometres beyond Siwa's cultivated edge, so a day trip or an overnight stay are quite feasible. The low-tech method is to hire a donkey and a boy minder, bring water, food and firewood, and simply trek into the Sand Sea. Don't venture beyond the first couple of dunes and keep orientated in relation to the oasis; a compass is essential unless you can take bearings from the sun or stars. (The red light on Siwa's radio mast might also be visible at night.)

Motorised transport increases one's range, but also the risk of getting lost, which is the worst situation to be in. You might find a Siwan with a pick-up truck who's willing to drive you into the dunes, but think long and hard before entrusting your life to him. The alternatives are to join a safari (some Cairo-based companies run them) or travel independently; though in the latter case, lots of caveats apply. Besides needing military permission (apply beforehand in Mersa Matrouh) and a properly equipped vehicle, some experience of driving and navigating amidst dunes is required. See "Desert Expeditions" at the beginning of this chapter for more information.

"Lost Oasis" of **Zerzura** remained. First mentioned in 1246 as an abandoned village in the desert southwest of the Fayoum, it reappeared as a fabulous city in the fifteenth-century treasure-hunters' *Book of Hidden Pearls*:

> This city is white like a pigeon, and on the door of it is carved a bird. Enter, and there you will find great riches, also the king and queen sleeping in their castle. Do not approach them, but take the treasure.

Citing native sources, the first European reference to Zerzura (1835) placed the oasis "five days west of the road from el-Hez [al-Hayiz] to Farafra", or "two or three days due west from Dakhleh". *Murray's Handbook* (1891) reported an "Oasis of the Blacks . . . also called Wady Zerzura" to the west of Farafra, and described it quite matter-of-factly. But Zerzura was still unlocated, and the stories placing it west of Dakhla gained credibility after Europeans "discovered" Kufra Oasis in Libya, which the same tales had mentioned. However, both the Rohlfs and Harding-King (1911) expeditions heard accounts of black men who periodically raided Dakhla from an oasis seven or eight days' journey to the southwest.

Weighing the evidence for various speculative locations in the last chapter of *Libyan Sands*, Bagnold demarcates three zones. The "northern" one – encompassing the whole Sand Sea, but rating the areas west of Dakhla and Farafra as likeliest – was propounded by de Lancey Forth, citing the story of a town with iron gates, seven days' camel journey to the south, in the *Siwan Manuscript*; plus tales of Bedouin chancing upon unknown oases whilst pursuing missing camels.

Unfortunately, similar yarns also pointed towards the far south – that vast wilderness between Dakhla, Selima and Merga oases. Dr Ball and Newbold favoured this area, largely free of dunes and often low enough to approach the subterranean water table; in addition, Newbold thought he glimpsed an oasis during a flight over the desert (one of several by the Hungarian aviator, Almassy).

The third, "central" zone extended southwest from Dakhla as far as 'Uweinat. Championed by Harding-King, it rested largely on native accounts of incursions by "strange cows", Tibbu raiders and a "black giantess". When Ball discovered a cache of Tibbu water-jars 200km southwest of Dakhla in 1917, it supported the stories but argued against an oasis; if a water-source existed, why bother to maintain a depot in the middle of nowhere?

Accepting Ball's theory of a consistent water level beneath the Libyan Desert, Bagnold argued that Zerzura could only exist in low-lying areas or deep, wind-eroded hollows. As the desert was surveyed, the possibility of such sites escaping notice diminished, and Bagnold doubted that an undiscovered oasis existed. Perhaps Zerzura might once have been a waterhole or an area favoured with periodic rainfall, but the fabled oasis of palms and ruins must be a figment of wishful thinking: a Bedouin Shangri-la that tantalised foreign explorers. Only Thesiger struck a dissenting note by claiming that Zerzura's discovery would have left him "unmoved" had it been accomplished by motor vehicle.

CHAPTER FOUR

ALEXANDRIA AND THE MEDITERRANEAN COAST

For ancient Egyptians, the **Mediterranean coast** marked the edge of the "Great Green" – the measureless sea that formed the limits of the known world. Life and civilisation meant the Nile Valley and the Delta, an outlook which still seems to linger in the country's subconscious. For, despite the white beaches, craggy headlands and turquoise sea that stretch for some 500km, the Egyptian Med is eerily vacant and underpopulated.

Anywhere on the European side of the sea, mass tourism would have taken hold years ago. Here, though, in part due to a lack of fresh water sources, towns are few and generally small, and far outnumbered by military bases. Such tourism as exists is largely domestic and overwhelmingly male; there is virtually no alcohol on sale and standards of dress verge on the puritanical. Foreign women, especially, could well find that the hassles far outweigh any pleasure to be gained here – in contrast to the much more relaxed beaches in the Sinai. If you explore nonetheless, the best resorts are **Mersa Matrouh** (a jumping-off point for the Siwa Oasis) and **Sidi Abd el-Rahman**, whilst historical interest focuses chiefly on the World War II battlefield of **El-Alamein**.

Alexandria, however, at the east end of the coast, is an entirely different animal. Egypt's second city feels as Mediterranean and cosmopolitan as Athens or Marseille, its nineteenth-century architecture redolent of the colonial days immortalised by E.M. Forster, the poet Cavafy and, most famously, Lawrence Durrell. But its sights look back to an earlier age of greatness, when it was the capital of Greco-Roman Egypt, and the seat of Cleopatra, the last of the Ptolemies.

ALEXANDRIA (EL-ISKANDARIYA)

Alexandria, princess and whore. The royal city and the anus mundi.
Lawrence Durrell *The Alexandria Quartet.*

ALEXANDRIA turns its back on the rest of Egypt and faces the Mediterranean, as if remembering its glorious past; a hybrid city characterised by Durrell as the "Capital of Memory". One of the great cities of antiquity, Alex slumbered for 1300 years until it was revived by Mohammed Ali and transformed by Europeans, who gave the city its present shape and made it synonymous with cosmopolitanism and decadence. This era ended in the 1950s with the mass flight of non-Egyptians and a dose of revolutionary puritanism, but Alexandria's beaches, restaurants and breezy climate still attract hordes of Cairenes during the summer, whilst its jaded historical and literary mystique remains appealing to foreigners. And when *el-Iskandariya* (Alex's Arabic name) palls, you can easily enough take a bus to Mersa Matrouh and continue on to Siwa Oasis.

Alex in history

When **Alexander the Great** wrested Egypt from the Persian empire in 332 BC at the age of twenty-five, he decided against Memphis, the ancient capital, in favour of building a new city linked by sea to his Macedonian homeland. Choosing a site near the fishing village of **Rhakotis**, where two limestone spurs formed a natural harbour, he gave orders to his architect, Deinocrates, then travelled on to Siwa and thence to Asia, where he died eight years later. His corpse was subsequently returned to Egypt, where the priests refused burial at Memphis, so it was laid to rest in a glass coffin at the crossroads of Alexandria, the city he had founded but never saw.

Thereafter Alexander's empire was divided amongst his Macedonian generals, one of whom took Egypt and adopted the title **Ptolemy I Soter**, founding a dynasty. Avid promoters of Hellenistic culture, the **Ptolemies** made Alexandria an intellectual powerhouse: among its scholars were Euclid, the "father of geometry", and Eratosthenes, who accurately determined the circumference and diameter of the earth. Alexandria's great lighthouse, the **Pharos**, was literally and metaphorically a beacon, rivalled in fame only by the city's **Mouseion**, which incorporated laboratories, observatories and a library of 500,000 volumes.

The later, mostly enfeebled Ptolemies, however, increasingly depended on Rome to maintain their position, and even the bold **Cleopatra** VII (51–30 BC) came unstuck after her lover, Julius Caesar, was murdered, and his successor in Rome (and in Cleo's bed), Mark Antony, was defeated by Octavian. The latter proved immune to her charms and in fact so detested Cleopatra's capital at Alexandria that he banned Roman citizens from entering Egypt on the pretext that its religious orgies were morally corrupting.

ROMAN RULE AND ARAB CONQUEST

Whereas Alexandria's Egyptians and Greeks had previously respected one another's deities and even syncretised them into a common cult – the worship of Serapis – religious conflicts developed under **Roman rule** (30 BC–313 AD). The empire regarded Christianity, which was supposedly introduced by Saint Mark in 45 AD, as subversive, and the persecution of Christians from 250 onwards reached a bloody apogee under Emperor Diocletian, when the Copts maintain that 144,000 believers were martyred. (The Coptic church dates its chronology from 284, the "Era of Martyrs", rather than Christ's birth.)

After the emperor Constantine made **Christianity** the state religion a new controversy arose over the nature of Christ, whose theological subtleties essentially cloaked a political rebellion by Egyptian **Copts** against Byzantine (ie Greek) authority. In Alexandria, the Coptic Patriarch became supreme and his monks waged war against paganism, sacking the Serapis Temple and Library in 391, and later murdering the female scholar Hypatia.

Local hatred of Byzantium disposed the Alexandrians to welcome the **Arab conquest** (641), whose commander, Amr, described the city as containing "4000 palaces, 4000 baths, 400 theatres, 1200 greengrocers and 40,000 Jews". But while the Arabs incorporated elements of Alexandrian learning into their own civilisation, they cared little for a city which "seemed to them idolatrous and foolish", preferring to found a new capital at Fustat (now part of Cairo). Owing to neglect and the silting-up of waterways which connected it to the Nile, Alexandria inexorably declined over the next millennium, so that Napoleon's expeditionary force found a mere fishing village of 4000 inhabitants when it landed in 1798.

MOHAMMED ALI AND COLONIAL RULE

Alexandria's **revival** sprang from the sultan Mohammed Ali's desire to make Egypt a commercial and maritime power, which necessitated a seaport. The Mahmudiya Canal, finished in 1820, once again linked Alexandria to the Nile, while a harbour, docks and arsenal were created with French assistance. European merchants erected mansions and warehouses, building outwards from the Place des Consuls (modern-day Midan Tahrir), and the city's population soared to 230,000.

Nationalist resentment of foreign influence fired the **Orabi revolt** of 1882, in retaliation for which British warships shelled the city, whose devastation was completed by arsonists and looters. Yet such was Alexandria's vitality and commercial importance that it quickly recovered.

Having survived bombing during World War II, Alexandria experienced new turmoil in the postwar era, when anti-British riots expressed rising **nationalism**. The **revolution** that forced King Farouk to sail into exile from Alexandria in 1952 didn't seriously affect the "foreign" community (many of whom had lived here for generations) until the Anglo-French-Israeli assault on Egypt during the Suez Crisis of 1956. The following year, however, Nasser expelled all French and British citizens and nationalised foreign businesses, causing 100,000 non-Egyptians to emigrate. Jewish residents also suffered after the discovery of an Israeli-controlled sabotage unit in the city, so that by the year's end only a few thousand Alexandrian Greeks and Jews remained. Foreign institutions, street names and suchlike were Egyptianised, and the custom of moving the seat of government to Alexandria during the hot summer months was ended (though it was later revived by Sadat).

CONTEMPORARY ALEX

Though "old" Alexandrians undoubtedly regret the **changes** since Suez, Durrell's complaint that they've produced "leaden uniformity" and rendered Alexandria "depressing beyond endurance" seems jaundiced and unjustified. Egypt's second city (pop. 4,000,000) has become more Egyptian and less patrician, but it doesn't lack contrasts and vitality (except by comparison with Cairo). The difference is that middle-class Egyptians set the tone, not Greeks, Levantines and European expats. If Cavafy, *arak* and child-brothels represented the old days, Michael Jackson, Coke and Wimpy symbolise a new and brasher kind of cosmopolitanism. Overcrowding, pollution and traffic have all worsened, but the Med still keeps Alex cool, unlike pressure-cooker Cairo.

With few monuments to show for its ancient lineage and much of its modern heritage rejected, one seeks Alexandria's past in institutions like *Pastroudis*; minutiae such as old nameplates; the reminiscences of aged Arabs, Greeks and Jews; and in the **literary dimension**. E.M. Forster's *Alexandria: A History and a Guide* (1922) remains the classic source book, but Forster reckoned that the best thing he did was to publicise the work of Alexandrian-born Constantine Cavafy. Nostalgia, excess, loss and futility – the leitmotivs of Cavafy's *Collected Poems* – also pervade Lawrence Durrell's *The Alexandria Quartet*; indeed, Durrell used Cavafy as the basis for his character Balthazar. However, bearing in mind the ancient quip that "a big book is a big nuisance", you might prefer Naguib Mahfouz's *Miramar*, a concise evocation of post-revolutionary Alex from an Egyptian standpoint. For more recent, foreign views of Alex, check out Charlie Pye-Smith's *The Other Nile* and Douglas Kennedy's *Beyond the Pyramids*.

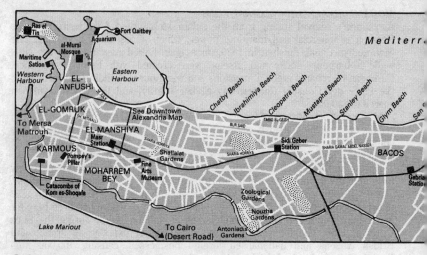

Orientation and arrival

Alexandria runs along the Mediterranean for 20km without ever venturing more than 3km inland – a true waterfront city. Its great **Corniche** sweeps around the **Eastern Harbour** and along the coast past a string of city **beaches** to **Montazah** and **Ma'amoura**, burning out before the final beach at **Abu Qir**. Away from the beach, visitors hang around the downtown quarter of **el-Manshiya**, where most of the restaurants, hotels and nightclubs are within a few blocks either side, or inland, of **Sa'ad Zaghloul Square**.

The modern city overlies the ancient one, hence a fine collection of Graeco-Roman **antiquities**, but few monuments remain *in situ*: a Roman theatre near el-Gumhorriya, Pompey's Pillar and the Catacombs in the **Karmous quarter**. The Islamic era is better represented by **Fort Qaitbey** and the old Turko-Arabic neighbourhoods of **el-Gomruk** and **el-Anfushi**, both of which are notable for their souks and streetlife.

Maps and street names

The Corniche (and breezes blowing inland) make basic orientation quite simple, but the finer points can still be awkward. Unlike Cairo, downtown Alex has yet to be properly mapped. The standard Lehnert & Landrock's *Alexandria Tourist Map* (£E3) omits whole streets and blocks, and our **maps** aren't faultless either.

Street names are also problematic, for signs don't always square with the latest official designation or popular usage (usually one change behind). Other street names have simply been Arabised: *Rue* or *Place* to *Sharia* or *Midan*; *Alexandre le Grand* to *Iskander el-Akbar*.

Getting to Alex

Alex is easily reached **from Cairo**, with a choice of train, bus, *service* taxi or flights. Buses and *service* taxis offer a choice of routes to Alex, travelling by the flat and dreary Desert Road past the turn-off for Wadi Natrun (whose monasteries are covered in *The Western Desert Oases*), or by the scenic, congested Delta Road,

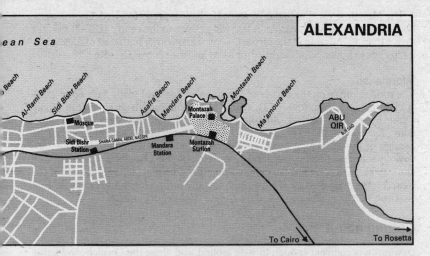

which is much slower though the distance is roughly similar (about 225km). Remember that transport can get booked up during "the season" (mid-June to late Sept), so reserve seats unless you're prepared to use *service* taxis.

The best buses from Cairo, which do the journey in three hours, are operated by *Golden Rocket* (aka *Superjet*). The fastest trains, the thrice-daily A/C *Turbini* services, take just over two hours. *Service* taxis do the run in about three hours, their advantage being that they leave all through the day, as soon as they're full; in Cairo both car- and minibus-taxis cluster outside Ramses Station, on Koulali Square and around the Ahmed Helmi bus terminal, their drivers bawling "*Iskandariya! Iskandariya!*". For details on bus, train and taxi schedules and terminals, see the "Travel Details" at the end of the Cairo chapter (p.231–233).

Getting to Alex **from other parts of Egypt**, buses and/or *service* taxis are your best bet. Transport from the Delta and the Canal zone is fairly regular; from the Nile Valley, daily buses run from Beni Suef, Qena and Luxor, and there's a chance of *service* taxis from Assyut. See the relevant chapters for details.

Alex can also be reached **from abroad** by plane or boat. Ferry routes (most usefully from Greece) and flights are detailed on p.3–5.

Points of arrival

Blue and *Golden Rocket* **buses** drop passengers on **Midan Sa'ad Zaghloul**, the social hub of downtown Alex, a stone's throw from the Corniche and the *Cecil Hotel*, with two cheap pensions just around the corner. However, *Delta* buses (and the really knackered blue ones) might terminate instead at **Midan el-Gumhorriya**. This vast square – portioned up into bus parks and taxi ranks – lies about 1km south of Midan Sa'ad Zaghloul, flanked on one side by **Masr Station**.

Arriving by **train** you should get off at Masr Station – don't make the error of getting off at Sidi Gaber station in the eastern suburbs. From Masr Station/Midan el-Gumhorriya, it's about twenty minutes' walk up Nabi Daniel Street to Sa'ad Zaghloul Square.

Service taxis might drop you at either square, or at **Midan Orabi**, 700m west of Sa'ad Zaghoul.

The **Maritime Station** in the Western Harbour is pretty frenzied, like the warehouse and slum district outside. A taxi will get you to the centre (£E2–3) quicker than a tram #6. Arriving at the **airport**, several kilometres southeast of Alex, catch a #203 bus to Midan Sa'ad Zaghloul, or a taxi into the centre (£E7–10).

Information

The **tourist office** on the corner of Midan Sa'ad Zaghloul (daily 8am–6pm; 9am–4pm during Ramadan; ☎80-76-11), staffed by helpful English-speakers, can supply a free information booklet, *Alexandria Night and Day*, and answer most questions; the port (☎492-59-86) and Masr Station branches (8am–8pm) should be capable of the former, at least. The university and foreign cultural centres are obvious sources of **contacts** (students and expats); Alex has its insiders-only side like every city. If you're considering staying for some time, try getting hold of the *Newcomers' Guide to Alexandria*, written by (and for) resident Americans, or Neil Hewison's forthcoming guide to the city (see "Books" in *Contexts*).

Getting about

Downtown is compact enough to walk around, and along the Corniche to Pharos makes a healthy constitutional. However, you really need transport to reach other outlying areas.

Trams, buses and microbuses

Ramleh (just east of Midan Sa'ad Zaghloul) and **Midan Orabi** are the main terminals for **trams**, which rattle almost incessantly from dawn until midnight or 1am, charging 5pt a ride. **Buses** (keeping similar schedules and likewise numbered in Arabic) are dirtier and faster, with passengers boarding on the run between Sa'ad Zaghloul, Orabi, Tahrir and el-Gumhorriya squares – the major terminals. Nippy **microbuses** also run along the Corniche to the beaches (25pt).

Useful routes include:

TRAMS

#1–4: eastwards from Ramleh to Sidi Bishr.

#15: from Ramleh through el-Gomruk and el-Anfushi to Fort Qait Bey.

#6: to the Maritime Station.

#5 and #16: from Midan Orabi, south to Karmous and Pompey's Pillar.

BUSES

#129: Midan Orabi to Montazah and Abu Qir.

#120, 220 and 300: Along the Corniche to Montazah.

#209: Ramleh to Pompey's Pillar.

#455 and #500: along the Corniche to Agami and Hannoville beach.

#41: Masr Station to the Zoological Gardens.

#203: Midan Sa'ad Zaghloul to the airport.

#307 and 310: Midan Orabi to the airport.

BUSES

#725: along the Corniche to Ma'amoura.

#729: along the Corniche to Abu Qir.

> All telephone numbers in the Alexandria area are prefixed ☎01.

Taxis and caleches

Regular black and orange **taxis** often go by the meter (add 25–50pt *baksheesh*; more late at night), though the practice of overcharging for the ride between Masr Station and Midan Sa'ad Zaghloul is widespread. A typical journey within the downtown area should cost £E1; a trip to Montazah about £E4–5. The larger, monochrome Peugeots are a lot dearer than regular taxis.

Leather-hooded, brass-trimmed **horse-drawn carriages** solicit passengers with cries of "*caleche, caleche*" outside Masr Station and along the Corniche. Providing you don't get stuck in traffic jams or feel self-consciously "colonial", they can be a good way of touring the quieter parts of Alex and enjoying the sea breezes. You'll have to negotiate a price – roughly £E3–5 an hour.

Accommodation

Alexandria's **hotels** run the gamut from evocative old pensions to glitzy citadels of nouveau riche and Sheraton-style internationalism, with something for every visitor's taste and budget. Whereas foreign visitors usually stay downtown, many Egyptian holidaymakers prefer hotels near the Corniche beaches. A sea view is definitely an asset, and hotels charge accordingly. Two drawbacks that only later become apparent are tram noise and giant orange cockroaches – the twin banes of hotels near the waterfront. Basically, you either learn to live with them or move further inland.

Bear in mind that the choice and availability of rooms declines during "the season" (officially starting June 1, when prices rise), making **reservations** advisable from mid-June onwards.

Downtown

All downtown hotels are marked on the map overpage.

CHEAP TO MODERATE

Youth Hostel, 32 Sharia Bur Said (☎597-5459). Opposite Saint Mark's College in the Chatby district, a tram ride east from Ramleh station – though why pay £E4.50 (non-members £E6) for a bed in noisy, flyblown segregated dormitories (open 7–10am & 2–11pm) when you can stay at a decent pension for a little more?

Hotel Acropole, 1 Sharia Gamal al-Din Yassin (☎805-980). Friendly Thirties-style pension favoured by budget travellers, on the side street behind the *Hotel Cecil*, just off Sa'ad Zaghloul Square. All rooms have sinks, with hot water in the clean, shared bathrooms in the early mornings and evenings. Singles £E6 (£E10 with view), doubles £E15 (£E18); breakfast included.

Hotel Triomphe, Sharia Gamal al-Din Yassin – across the street on the 5th floor (☎807-585). A tattier alternative to the *Acropole*. Singles £E5, doubles £E8, triples £E10. Hot water unlikely.

Hotel Normandie, Sharia Gamal al-Din Yassin – further up the street (☎806-830). Still furnished with the antiques of its original French owner but now in the care of her Egyptian manager. Atmospherically musty. Singles £E11, doubles £E13.

Hotel Ailema, 21 Sharia Amin Fikry, 7th floor (☎493-2916). Atmospherically faded, Greek-run place. Basic singles £E11 and doubles £E17, but it's worth paying £E1.50–2 extra for rooms with a sea view or bath. Breakfast included. Facilities for making international calls.

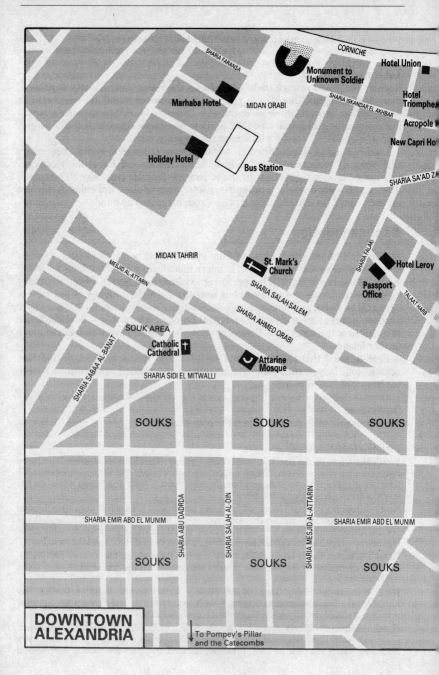

CORNICHE

Hotel Union

SHARIA FARANSA

Monument to
Unknown Soldier

Hotel
Triomphe

SHARIA ISKANDAR EL AKHBAR

Marhaba Hotel

MIDAN ORABI

Acropole

New Capri Ho

Holiday Hotel

Bus Station

SHARIA SA'AD Z

SHARIA FALAKI

MIDAN TAHRIR

St. Mark's
Church

Hotel Leroy

MESJID AL-ATTARIN

SHARIA SALAH SALEM

Passport
Office

TALAAT HARB

SHARIA AHMED ORABI

SOUK AREA

Catholic
Cathedral

Attarine
Mosque

SHARIA SABAA AL-BANAT

SHARIA SIDI EL MITWALLI

SOUKS

SOUKS

SOUKS

SHARIA ABU DADRDA

SHARIA SALAH AL-DIN

SHARIA MESJID AL-ATTARIN

SHARIA EMIR ABD EL MUNIM

SHARIA EMIR ABD EL MUNIM

SOUKS

SOUKS

SOUKS

**DOWNTOWN
ALEXANDRIA**

To Pompey's Pillar
and the Catacombs

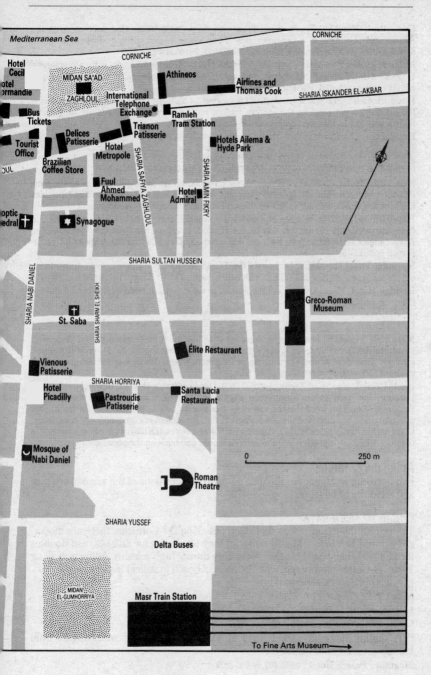

Hyde Park Hotel, 21 Sharia Amin Fikry, 8th floor (☎493-5666). One floor up from the *Ailema* and also nice in a run-down way. Four single rooms without showers at £E10; doubles £E15 (£E17 with bath), triples £E20 (£E22). Breakfast £E1.50.

Admiral Hotel, 24 Sharia Amin Fikry (☎483-1787). Clean and comfy, with a restaurant. Singles £E18 (£E21 with bathroom), doubles £E28 (£E30), triples £E35, suites £E35–40; all with breakfast included. Facilities for international calls.

Hotel Piccadilly, 11 Sharia Horriya, 6th floor (☎493-4802). Art Deco, bright and airy, this is the nearest decent place to the railway station; on the downside, its beds are lumpy and there's only one hot shower. Singles £E10, doubles £E16.

Hotel Leroy, 25 Sharia Talaat Harb, 8th floor (☎483-3439). Once splendid Art Deco pile across from the Passport Office, now run-down and seldom occupied, its location provides great views. Singles £E18 (£E22 with bath), doubles £E32 (£E35); breakfast and one meal included. Author Charlie Pye-Smith (*The Other Nile*) stayed here.

New Capri Hotel, 23 Sharia Portest, 8th floor (☎809-310). In the building housing the tourist police, with a broken lift. Most of the rooms with views lack baths (singles £E17, doubles £E24, triples £E31), although a few doubles (£E30) have them. Surly management.

Hotel Union, 164 26th July Street, reception on the 5th floor (☎807-312). Comfy beds and clean, carpeted, airy rooms, but stay on the 4th floor to escape the noisy 6th-floor *Belvedere Disco*. Singles £E15 (£E23 with bath and sea view), doubles £E21 (£E32), triples £E27, four-person suite £E45.

Marhaba Hotel, 10 Midan Orabi (☎800-957). All rooms have phones, some have baths, others sea views; singles £E23 (£E29 with bath), doubles £E43 (£E49). Breakfast included.

Holiday Hotel, Midan Orabi. Like the *Marhaba*, a comfortable middle-class establishment, charging similar rates.

UPMARKET

Metropole Hotel, 52 Sharia Sa'ad Zaghloul (☎482-1456). A modernised period piece with wonderful Art Deco/Nouveau decor, notably on the first floor (above the *Trianon Patisserie*), formerly the offices of the Third Circle of Irrigation, where Cavafy worked. Rooms start at around £E50, with 17 percent tax on all bills.

Hotel Cecil, Midan Sa'ad Zaghloul (☎807-055). Dead central, with great views of the Eastern Harbour, the *Cecil* is an Alexandrian institution. Durrell, Churchill, Noël Coward and Somerset Maugham head the roll call of former guests (ask to see the visitors' book), but modernisation has dispelled the old ambience, faintly redolent of corruption and conspiracy. Comfortable A/C singles (£E77), doubles (£E95) and suites (£E125), with two restaurants, a casino, tea lounge, nightclub, *Monty's Bar*, *Avis* desk and bank on the premises.

Along the Corniche

For Corniche locations see the map on p.457; descriptions of the various beaches and areas are to be found on p.468–470.

CHEAP TO MODERATE

Though it's the ritzier places that stand out along the Corniche, there are moderately priced hotels too. Mostly two-star, they let singles for £E20–30 and doubles for £E40–50 (half-board is often mandatory during high season). Addresses along **Tariq el-Geish** (numbered, with the nearest beach in italics) include:

Dubai, #41, *Camp Cizar* (☎596-1139).

Nobel, #152, *Cleopatra* (☎963-374).

Lolowa, opposite *Miami Casino* (☎969-362).

Corail, #802, *Mandara* (☎968-996).

A slightly more upmarket hotel at **Ma'amoura beach**, with singles from US$18, doubles from US$25 is :

Maamura Palace Hotel (☎865-401 or 865-383).

UPMARKET

Prices at these hotels run from around US$50 a head; all these places have mandatory half-board during high season.

Montazah Sheraton, Montazah (☎968-550). Luxurious isolation from the city, featuring a private beach and heated pool, all mod cons, a nightclub and several restaurants.

Ramada Renaissance, Sidi Bishr (☎866-111). The *Sheraton's* main rival – an equally ugly tower block.

Palestine Hotel, Montazah beach. Another haunt of international businessmen, visiting diplomats and mega-wealthy Egyptians.

Samalek Hotel, Samalek. Built in the style of an Alpine chalet to please the khedive's Austrian mistress. Currently closed for a major refit,

RENTALS AND CAMPING

If there's a group of you staying awhile, it's worth considering **renting a flat in Ma'amoura** from *Menatours* (between the beach and the entrance, and maybe also the city branch on Sa'ad Zaghloul Square).

The impecunious beachcomber's alternative is to hire a seven-person tent – or pitch their own – at Abu Qir's jam-packed **campsite** (☎560–1541), located on Sharia Bahr al-Mait, about 500m south of the *Xephyron*.

Exploring the city

> *I loved the shabbiness of the streets and cafes, the melancholy which hung over the city late of an evening, the slow decay (not destruction, mind you) of what the Europeans had left behind when they fled.*
>
> Charlie Pye-Smith *The Other Nile*

Alex encourages nostalgia trips and random exploration, if only because "the sights" are limited and chance incidents often more revealing. Don't be afraid of following your nose and deviating from the usual itineraries, which could be completed in a day if one did them at the trot.

For convenience, these accounts start with the downtown area and work outwards, interweaving the ancient, remembered and existing cities.

Midan Sa'ad Zaghloul to the Roman Theatre

Since E.M. Forster wrote his guide to Alexandria in 1922, the city's centre has shifted eastwards from the former Place Mohammed Ali to the seafront **Midan Sa'ad Zaghloul**, a square named after the nationalist leader (1860–1927) whose statue gazes towards the Mediterranean. His deportation by the British to Malta provoked nationwide rioting (1919) and guaranteed Zaghloul a hero's return, though the national independence he sought was denied for another generation. Zaghloul is referred to as "the Pasha" in Naghuib Mafouz's novel, *Miramar*.

With no trace of the Caesareum which stood here in ancient times, the square today looks post-colonial. Decrepit edifices that could have been lifted from Naples or Athens overshadow the new **bus terminal** and **tourist office**. The dominant building is the pseudo-Moorish **Hotel Cecil**, where British Intelligence hatched the el-Alamein deception plan. Although it is no longer the "moribund" establishment of *The Alexandria Quartet*, palms still "splinter and refract their motionless fronds" in its gilt-edged mirrors.

A similar mystique used to attend Alexandrian **patisseries**. Among these, *Délices*, beneath a tatty facade on the south side of the square, remains unpretentious, while the famous old *Trianon* has installed a doorman and air conditioning. For the sheer elegance of its *fin-de-siècle* mirrors and mouldings, you can't beat *Athineos* on Midan Ramleh, a block or so east, by Ramleh train station.

South down Sharia Nabi Daniel

Starting as an inconspicuous backstreet beside the tourist office, **Sharia Nabi Daniel** grows wider as it runs south along the route of the ancient Street of the Soma. Paved in marble and flanked by marble colonnades, this dazzled the Arabs in 641, even though its finest buildings had already vanished.

Before its destruction by feuding Christians in the fourth century, the north end of the street was crowned by the **Caesareum**, a temple begun by Cleopatra for Antony, which Octavian completed and dedicated to himself. Full of "choice paintings and statues", it was fronted by two obelisks which remained *in situ* until the 1870s, when they were relocated on London's Embankment and in New York's Central Park. Their popular title, **"Cleopatra's Needles"**, is a misnomer: erected in Heliopolis fourteen centuries earlier, the obelisks were moved to Alexandria fifteen years after her suicide.

A short way along the street, guarded wrought-iron gates front Alexandria's principal **Synagogue**, entered via an alley (Sun–Fri 10am–1pm, Sat 8–10am; bring your passport). An old woman speaking French, English and a little Hebrew will show you round its pastel-coloured, Italianate interior, turning on giant *menorahs*. Tracing its ancestry back to the city's foundation, Alexandria's Jewish community numbered 15,000 before 1957; nowadays only about 100 elderly Jews remain (religious services Fri evening).

Further down Nabi Daniel stands the **Coptic Orthodox Cathedral** of Saint Mark, whose body was smuggled out of Muslim-ruled Alexandria in a barrel of salt pork in 828. Outwardly unimpressive, its interior was recommended by Forster as "fatuously ugly". The street, and Rue de l'Eglise Copte around the corner, are classic Durrell territory; Darley and Pombal shared a flat here.

Bygone monuments

Ancient Alexandria's crossroads lay near the modern-day intersection of Nabi Daniel, Sidi el-Mitwalli and Horriya streets. The latter used to be the Canopic Way, flanked by marble colonnades extending from the Gate of the Sun, where visitors entered the city. Our word "museum" derives from the **Mouseion**, a colossal institution which once stood beside the crossroads. Medieval Europe mythologised its destruction as proof of Arab barbarism: an apocryphal tale had the ruler Amr pronouncing "If these writings of the Greeks agree with the Koran they are useless, and need not be preserved; if they disagree, they are pernicious, and ought to be destroyed", before consigning them to the boilers of Alexandria's bathhouses, which they fuelled for six months. In fact, it was Christian mobs that sacked the Library. (Foreign states recently pledged $64,000,000 to found a new *Bibliotheka Alexandria*, scheduled for completion in 1995.)

Where the Mouseion once stood you'll find a French Cultural Centre and a nameless mosque; the antique columns serving as the latter's gateposts possibly came from the Mouseion. In ancient times it faced the **Soma**, a temple where Alexander and several Ptolemies were entombed. Here the victorious Octavian paid his respects to Alexandria's founder but disdained his heirs: "I wished to see a king, I did not wish to see corpses". Part of the site is occupied by the nine-teenth-century **Mosque of Nabi Daniel**, whose inconspicuous entrance is set back between two buildings. The mosque's crypt is popularly believed to hold the remains of the Prophet Daniel (in reality, those of Mohammed Danyal al-Maridi, a Sufi sheikh, and one Lukman the Wise). More importantly, legend has it that Alexander the Great lies buried yet deeper underground; the EAO plans to exca-vate the crypt in the near future.

Beyond the next crossroads is **Midan el-Gumhorriya**, the Edwardian bulk of **Masr Station** rising behind car parks and traffic swathed in gritty fumes. You can beat a retreat westwards into the **souk**, or follow the track behind the station to reach Alexandria's Fine Arts Museum (see overpage), but the nearest refuge is the Roman Theatre off Sharia Yussef.

The Roman Theatre

Sat–Thurs 9am–4pm, Fri 9–11.30am & 1.30–4pm; Ramadan daily 9am–3pm. Admission £E3, students £E1.50. Camera permit £E10.

Since 1959 Polish archaeologists have removed the Turkish fort and slums upon *Kom el-Dik* (Mound of Rubble), revealing a substratum of Roman remains beneath a Muslim cemetery. In a hollow to the east lies an elegant **Roman Theatre** with marble seating for 700–800, *opus mixtum* galleries and a forecourt boasting two patches of mosaic flooring. During Ptolemaic times this was the Park of Pan, a hilly pleasure garden with a limestone summit carved into a pine-cone, onto which Roman villas and baths later encroached.

Further north they're excavating a **residential quarter** whose jumbled arches and walls resolve into streets, shops and houses at close quarters. Many of the buildings are constructed from alternating courses of brick and stone, a tech-nique called *opus mixtum* (mixed work). In Forster's day one could also see remnants of the Arab walls built to enclose the shrunken city in 811, between Kom el-Dik and Masr Station.

Fine Arts Museum

Sat–Thurs 8am–2pm; free. From Masr Station, walk east along Sharia Mahmoud Bey (parallel to, and south of the tracks) for 150m before turning right; the museum lies ahead at 18 Sharia Menasce. Alternatively, tram #14 from Ramleh stops nearby.

The ground floor of the museum gives pride of place to Mohammed Naghi's Fauvish canvases and the pen and wash drawings of Ragheb Ayad, both preoccu-pied with rural life; Mahmoud Bey Said's Cubist-influenced portraits of urban sophisticates were considered faintly suspect after the revolution. When "socialist realism" was abandoned in the Seventies, artists leapt at Surrealism and Abstract Expressionism, which is why much of the stuff upstairs seems derivative. Painting in the Fifties, Seif el-Wahly had already captured the essence of the jazz and flamenco era, Alexandria's previous engagement with Mediterranean culture.

Up Safiya Zaghloul to Ramleh

Turning the corner of the archaeological site and heading northwards up **Sharia Safiya Zaghloul**, you'll reach a cluster of cinemas and restaurants. The *Santa Lucia* is for splurging on seafood, the *Elite* for a slow beer and cheaper meals, whilst the *Cafeteria Asteria* further up the street has a nice conservatory. A right turn just after the *Metro Cinema* will bring you to a quiet square and the **Graeco-Roman Museum** (see overpage).

In the years when Safiya Zaghloul was called Rue Missala, **Constantine Cavafy** (1863–1933) picked up boys in its cafés and lived around the corner from the Greek Orthodox Church of Saint Saba. The flat where Cavafy reached the zenith of his poetic talent was located above a bordello at 10 Rue Lepsius. "Where could I live better?" he asked, "Below, the brothel caters for the flesh. And there is the church which forgives sin. And there is the hospital where we die." He died there indeed, and was buried in the Greek Cemetery at Chatby.

Since then his old home has become the sleazy *Pension Amir* (the address is now 4 Sharia Sharm el-Sheikh), but his apartment has been recreated as a **museum** on the top floor of the Greek Consulate (63 Sharia Iskandar el-Akbar; open consular hours).

Perhaps Cavafy's most poignant poem about Alex was *The City*:

You won't find a new country, won't find another shore.
This city will always pursue you.
You'll walk the same streets, grow old
in the same neighbourhoods, turn grey in the same houses.

You'll always end up in this city. Don't hope for things elsewhere:
there's no ship for you, there's no road.
Now that you've wasted your life here, in this small corner,
you've destroyed it everywhere in the world.

The pervasive mystique of loss and regret doesn't fit real life further up the street, where Safiya Zaghloul debouches onto **Ramleh**. Tavernas, takeaways and Ramleh **tram station** provide a backdrop for the **promenade** that waxes and wanes around midday and after sundown.

The Greco-Roman Museum

Daily 9am–4pm; closed 11.30am–1.30pm on Fridays; Ramadan daily 9am–3pm. Admission £E1.50, students 75pt. Camera permit £E5. Coming from Ramleh, walk four blocks down Safiya Zaghloul and turn left just before you reach the Metro Cinema; the museum's classical facade is visible at the far end of Sharia al-Mathaf.

Turning left off the entrance vestibule into Room 6, you encounter **relics of the Serapis cult** promoted by Ptolemy I. A fusion of Osiris and Dionysos, Serapis was represented as a bearded, avuncular-looking fellow, and by a giant granite bull carved during the reign of Hadrian (who's commemorated by a bust). Besides maintaining the old cults, the Romans added flourishes like the **death masks** they hung indoors as memento mori.

The Ptolemies also adopted the Fayoumi cult of Sobek (see p.404), hence the **mummified crocodile**, fragmentary chapel and funerary accoutrements in Room 9. The most remarkable of the human **mummies** bears a superbly lifelike portrait of the deceased, executed in the Fayoum c.100–250 AD, when naturalism was taking hold. Although a life-size Marcus Aurelius dominates the other **statues** in Room 12, it can't hide the resemblance between Ptolemy X (who mortgaged Egypt to Rome) and the actor Donald Pleasence.

Amongst the **busts of Roman emperors** in Room 14 are Julius Caesar, a cold-faced Augustus (Octavian) and a bearded Hadrian, and there's more evidence of sculptural talent in Rooms 16–17, beyond the chunk of wall decorated with a **Ptolemaic mural** of an oxen turning a *saqiyya*. The colossal headless red porphyry statue has been identified variously as Christ Pantokrator (Christ in Majesty) or the rabidly anti-Christian Diocletian.

Pharos-shaped lamps can be seen in Room 18, whose annexe showcases delicate **tanagra figures**, buried with young women and children. Notice the hideous effigy of Bes (Room 20) and the finely carved schist head of a young man (Room 23) that precede a huge collection of **antique coins**.

Finally, you can catch a breath of air with **rock-cut tombs** and a giant head of Mark Antony in the garden before going in search of the mummy with a cross on its neck, amongst the **Christian antiquities** (Rooms 1–5).

Around Midan Orabi and Midan Tahrir

The old heart of **"European" Alexandria** lies five blocks west of Midan Sa'ad Zaghloul, inland of the Neoclassical Monument to the Unknown Soldier. Where the **bus terminal** blights what greenery remains on **Midan Orabi**, expatriates once strolled amongst the acacia trees and shrubs of the French Gardens ("French Street", Arabised to Sharia Faransa, still exists nearby).

Midan Tahrir

South of the French Gardens lay **"Frank Square"**, the European city's social hub; "There is nothing in Alexandria but the Frank Square and the huts of the Alexandrians", wrote Florence Nightingale in 1849. Originally the Places des Consuls, it was renamed in honour of Mohammed Ali, whose equestrian statue forms its centrepiece. After the Orabi Revolt of 1882, rebels were tied to the acacias, shot and buried there by British forces. Not surprisingly, its name was changed to Liberation Square – **Midan Tahrir** – following the revolution.

Midan Tahrir also witnessed two crucial events of the Nasser era. In October 1954, a member of the Muslim Brotherhood fired on Nasser during a public speech; the botched assassination gave Nasser an excuse to ban the Brotherhood and supplant General Naguib (who was falsely implicated in the conspiracy) as Egypt's acknowledged leader. Two years later, on the fourth anniversary of King Farouk's abdication, he delivered a three-hour speech broadcast live from here on national radio, climaxing in the announcement that Egypt had taken possession of the Suez Canal; Nasser's repetition of the name "Lesseps" earlier in his peroration was actually the codeword for the operation to begin.

Antiques and jewellery

A few streets around Midan Tahrir deserve a mention. Leading off to the southeast, the erstwhile Bond Street of Alexandria, Rue Chérif Pacha, was Cavafy's birthplace; on the corner stood the Cotton Exchange that once echoed with the "howls and cries" of European merchants. Renamed **Sharia Salah Salem** after a colleague of Nasser's, the street is less chic but still the place to find **antiques and jewellery**.

The Cotton Exchange itself was demolished after being gutted in the food riots of 1977; C.S. Jarvis, stationed here in the 1920s, considered Alex "one of the finest towns for a riot in all the world". Past the Anglican Church of Saint Mark, near Salah Salem's junction with Sharia Sidi el-Mitwalli, you'll notice a copy of the Palazzo Farnese in Rome (once the *Banco di Roma*, now an Egyptian bank); Durrell worked around the corner in a propaganda bureau at 1 Rue Toussoum Pacha. A plaque at no. 2 marks the first trading company established by the Al Fayeds – two poor lads born in Alex's Sharbangi Alley, now multi-millionaire businessmen and controversial owners of *Harrods*.

Jewellers also crop up in the backstreets north of Salah Salem, and along two thoroughfares further south: Ahmed Orabi and Mesjid al-Attarin. The latter (formerly Rue de la Mosquée d'Atarine) gets its name from the **Attarine Mosque** which occupies the site of the legendary "Mosque of a Thousand Columns". It was from here that Napoleon's forces removed a seven-ton sarcophagus, thought to be Alexander's, and later surrendered it to the British Museum, which attributed it to Nectanebo I. The Mosque of a Thousand Columns was built over the Church of Saint Theonas, whose rector Athanasius argued the "dual nature" of Christ against his theological opponent, Arius the Monophysite.

Northwest of Tahrir, the former European district merges into the erstwhile Turko-Arab Anfushi quarter (see below). **Sharia Tatwig**, one of the main roads into this old "native quarter", was notorious for its child-bordellos in pre-revolutionary days. In *The Alexandria Quartet*, Justine sought her kidnapped daughter here; Mountolive was mauled by child prostitutes; and Sobie killed his neighbours with moonshine whisky. Real life was equally decadent: a former drinking-chum of King Farouk's recalls parties where the men snipped away the women's gowns with golden scissors.

Trams from Midan Orabi run south to Pompey's Pillar (#5, #16), or northwards through the Anfushi district towards Qaitbey's Fort (#15, #25). There's also a tram from Midan Tahrir/Sharia Mesjid al-Attarin to Nouzha Gardens.

Anfushi and the harbours

In ancient times, the site of Midan Orabi was underwater and a seven-league dike – the *Heptastadion* – connected Alexandria with Pharos, then an island. Allowed to silt up after the Arab conquest, the Heptastadion gradually turned into a peninsula which the newcomers built over, creating the **Anfushi quarter**. Its Ottoman mosques and some old *mashrabiya*-ed houses are the only "sights" as such, but the variety of streetlife makes this an interesting area to explore.

It's possible to reach the al-Mursi Mosque and Qaitbey's Fort by tram or bus; if you prefer to walk, the **Terbana Mosque**, 700m along Faransa or Tatwig Street, is worth a look en route. With its Delta-style facade of wood and brick heavily plastered over, the mosque is chiefly remarkable for its antique columns, taken from Allah knows where. A huge pair with Corinthian capitals supports the minaret; lesser columns are ranged eight to an arcade within and painted gloss white; there's also some fine tiling quietly going to pot – the mosque has been subject to slapdash "improvements" ever since it was built in 1685.

The city's foremost religious building, the **Mosque of Abu al-Abbas al-Mursi** is located the same distance again further north, accessible by tram #15 or #25, which run one block back from the Corniche. Fronted by a smaller mosque whose illuminations sparkle at night, the al-Mursi honours the patron saint of Alexandria's fishermen and sailors, a thirteenth-century Andalusian sheikh. Although the present building was erected as recently as 1943 – in gratitude for al-Mursi's supernatural defence of the quarter against Luftwaffe bombers, so legend has it – it looks as old as the sixteenth-century original. Bold keel-arched panels, elaborately carved domes and cornices make a visually satisfying pastiche. Women are only allowed into a room at the back of the mosque.

After a visit, have a drink in the arcade across the street and watch life go by; if you're feeling adventurous, investigate the maze of old houses behind the mosque; otherwise, press on to Qaitbey's Fort.

Fort Qaitbey and the Pharos

One tram-stop after al-Mursi's Mosque and a short walk past the fishing port and boatyard will bring you to the promontory bearing Sultan Qaitbey's Fort. The **Aquarium** and **Institute of Oceanography** en route are not worth the time of day: the first is cramped and miserable, the other musters a weird collection of lacquered sea creatures.

Fort Qaitbey (Sat–Thurs 9am–4pm, Fri 9am–noon & 2–4pm; Ramadan daily 10am–2.30pm; £E1.50, students 75pt; photo permit £E5) is an Alexandrian landmark, a doughty limestone sentinel buffeted by windborne spray, its flag forever rippling. Built during the 1480s and later beefed up by Mohammed Ali, it commands great views of the city and the spume-flecked Mediterranean. Within the keep there's a mosque whose minaret was blown away by the Royal Navy in 1882; upstairs, relics of Roman and Napoleonic sea battles comprise a small **Naval Museum**.

The fort occupies the site of the **Pharos**, Alexandria's great lighthouse, one of the seven wonders of the ancient world. Combining aesthetic beauty and scientific prowess, it transcended its practical role as a navigational aid and early-warning system, becoming synonymous with the city itself. Possibly conceived by Alexander himself, it was built during Ptolemy II's reign (c.279 BC) under the direction of an Asiatic Greek, Sostratus, and exceeded 125m – perhaps even 150m – in height, including the statue of Poseidon at its summit.

Its square base contained 300 rooms* and possibly hydraulic machinery for raising the fuel up the second, octagonal storey; otherwise, this would have been accomplished by an endless procession of pack-mules climbing a spiral ramp. The cylindrical third storey housed the lantern, whose light is supposed to have been visible 56km away. Some chroniclers also mention a "mirror" which enabled the lighthouse-keepers to observe ships far out to sea; a form of lens (whose secret was lost) has been postulated.

Around 700 AD the lantern collapsed, or was demolished by a treasure-hunting khalif; the base survived unscathed and Ibn Tulun restored the second level, but earthquakes and neglect reduced the whole structure to rubble by the fourteenth century. Fragments of the Pharos are embedded in the northwest section of the fort's enclosure walls and the facade of its keep.

The Anfushi Tombs, Ras el-Tin and the Western Harbour

A small park some 2km west of Qaitbey's Fort, near the end of the tram line and Sharia Ras el-Tin, features the seldom-visited **Anfushi Tombs**. Sharing a pair of atriums, these four limestone-cut tombs are painted to simulate costly alabaster or marble. The right-hand set has pictures of Egyptian gods, warships and *feluccas*, crudely executed around 250 BC; a Greek workman has also immortalised his mate's virtues in graffiti. Hang around and a keeper should appear to unlock the tombs (daily 9am–4pm, closed Fri 11.30am–1pm; £E1) for *baksheesh*.

Further west, formal gardens precede **Ras el-Tin Palace**, overlooking the Western Harbour. In the days when Pharos was an island, a Temple of Neptune stood here. Now strictly off-limits as Admiralty Headquarters, the "Cape of Figs"

---

*Legend has it these rooms once housed the seventy rabbis who translated the Hebrew scriptures into Greek for Ptolemy Philadelphus (c.200 BC), producing identical texts despite having worked alone. In fact, this *Septuagint* version of the Bible wasn't completed until 130 BC, and the rabbis lived in huts on the island.

palace was built for Mohammed Ali, its audience hall sited so that he could watch his new fleet at anchor whilst reclining on his divan. Rebuilt and turned into the summer seat of government under Fouad I, it witnessed **King Farouk's abdication** on July 26, 1952. "What you have done to me I was getting ready to do to you," the king informed General Naguib, "Your task will be difficult. It is not easy to govern Egypt." Wearing an admiral's uniform, Farouk departed on the royal yacht to a twenty-one gun salute; with him went the royal family, an English nursemaid, three Albanian bodyguards, a dog trainer and 244 trunks.

Egypt's main port and naval base since the mid-nineteenth century, the **Western Harbour** is not for sightseeing. Inland, blocks of warehouses with foreign names still faintly visible are given over to the **cotton industry**, "greasy fluff" and rags littering the streets as in Forster's day. Another major industry is smuggling, for which the **port** is notorious. Before the revolution, the traditional right of Alexandrian customs officials to levy duties at their own discretion made corruption inevitable, and opportunities blossomed again during Sadat's *Infitah*.

The Eastern Harbour

Although the **Eastern Harbour** is no longer the busy port of ancient times, its graceful curve is definitely appealing. At the Qaitbey end, fishermen cast rods and mend nets while the fresh catch is marketed and shipwrights show off their hulls to anyone visiting the boatyard. Nearer to al-Mursi's Mosque, the Corniche is flanked by stately palms and weathered colonial mansions, calling to mind a set from *Casablanca*, an effect somewhat spoiled by crass new buildings further east around the bay.

Walking **along the Corniche** from Sa'ad Zaghloul to al-Mursi takes roughly half an hour, and is highly recommended. If you peg out over longer distances, switch to minibuses or caleches – it's a good six-kilometre trek from Qaitbey's Fort to **Silsileh** ("the Chain"). This promontory has shrunk since the days when it enclosed the royal harbour, and nothing now remains of the palace where Cleopatra died* or the Arab beacon called *Pharillon* (the seond monument Forster took for his essay on the city – *Pharos and Pharillon*). A club on the seaward edge that used to offer guests trap-shooting seems to have been appropriated by the military, who sometimes declare the promontory off-limits. Naghuib Mahfouz located his fictional *Pension Miramar* near its juncture with the mainland.

Pompey's Pillar and the Catacombs of Kom es-Shoqafa

The poor **Karmous quarter** contains two of Alexandria's best-known ancient monuments. **Pompey's Pillar** can be reached by bus #209 from Ramleh, or tram #16 or #5 from Midan Orabi. Prepare to alight when the vehicle runs alongside a high-walled Muslim cemetery: the pillar's capital is visible closer to the stop. From Pompey's Pillar you can easily walk to the **Catacombs**. If you've just arrived in Egypt the intervening neighbourhood might seem shocking – this is how poor Egyptians live in towns and cities. Tread respectfully, treating kids with warmth and firmness, and the adults will afford you safe passage.

---

*Antony fell on his sword and was carried, dying, to Cleopatra, but her famous death by asp-bite could have been invented by Plutarch or Shakespeare. Forster ascribes Cleopatra's suicide to the chilly response that her "seductive negligence of grief" got from Octavian, and the realisation that she was now thirty-nine.

Pompey's Pillar

"An imposing but ungraceful object", **Pompey's Pillar** towers 25m above a lime-stone ridge and garden, surrounded by the fruits and pits of excavations. Despite its name, the red granite column was actually raised to honour Diocletian, who threatened to massacre the dissenting populace until their blood reached his horse's knees, but desisted when his mount slipped and bloodied itself prematurely. The column came from the ruined Temple of Serapis, which once rivalled the Soma and Caesareum in magnificence.

Three subterranean galleries where the sacred Apis bulls were interred (see Saqqara, p.187) are all that remain: you'll find them west of the ridge, which also features three sphinxes and some underground cisterns. Overall, however, the site (daily 9am–4pm; closes 3pm during Ramadan; £1.50, students 75pt) is pretty disappointing considering what used to exist here.

The Catacombs of Kom es-Shoqafa

The **Catacombs of Kom es-Shoqafa** combine spookiness and kitsch, never mind their prosaic Arabic name, "Mound of Shards". To reach them, turn right around the corner after leaving Pompey's site and follow the road uphill and straight on for about 500m; the entrance to the catacombs is on the left (daily 9am–4pm; closes 3pm during Ramadan; £E3, students £E1.50; camera permit £E5).

Visitors descend a spiral stairway, past the shaft down which bodies were lowered. From the vestibule with its well and scalloped niches, you can squeeze through a fissure (right) into a lofty **Caracalla** riddled with tombs, or walk into the **Triclinium** (left), where relatives toasted the dead from stone couches. But the main attraction is the **Central Tomb** downstairs, whose vestibule is guarded by reliefs of bearded serpents with Medusa-headed shields. Inside are comically musclebound statues of Sobek and Anubis wearing Roman armour, dating from the second century AD when "the old faiths began to merge and melt". Water has flooded the **Goddess Nemesis Hall** (still accessible) and submerged the lowest level, hastening the catacombs' decay.

Gardens and canals

A kilometre or so east of the Masr train station, along Sharia Horriya, the Waterfalls or **Shallalat Gardens** blaze with scarlet flame trees. Their French designer utilised remnants of the Arab walls and the Farkha Canal to create rock-eries and ornamental ponds; if any trace of it remained, the ancient Gate of the Sun would have doubtless been accorded pride of place. Further out along Horriya (formerly called Rue de Rosette, and still the Rosetta road) are the university's Faculty of Engineering and the posh **Alexandria Sporting Club**.

The Zoo and Nouzha Gardens

Another cluster of gardens lies 3km to the southwest, alongside the Mahmudiya Canal. You can get there by bus #41 from Masr Station, or by tram from Sharia Mesjid al-Attarin. The northern **Zoological Gardens**, opened in 1907, cover 26 acres; the macaws swear like troopers, tutored by long-departed British soldiers.

Next door, diverse trees planted by Khedive Ismail have grown to maturity in the **Nouzha Gardens**, where military bands formerly played. Here, E.M. Forster had his first date with Mohammed el-Adl, a tram conductor whom he met at Ramleh in the winter of 1916–17. Before Mohammed, Forster's sexual passions had never been reciprocated; "you have to take it or die spiritually", Forster said of their affair. The racial, class and sexual barriers it challenged underlie the finale of *A Passage to India*, which Forster was struggling with when he learned of Mohammed's death in Egypt.

Both the Zoo and Nouzha Gardens are open daily from 8am to 4pm, and charge 10–15pt admission. Just to the south of Nouzha are the tranquil **Antoniaidis Gardens** (open 8am–4pm; 25pt). Embellished with classical statuary, the gardens were once the private grounds of a wealthy Greek family.

The Mahmudiya Canal and beyond

In ancient times, the Nouzha area was a residential suburb inhabited by the likes of Callimachus (310–240 BC), head librarian, poet and author of the quip about big books. It was around here, too, that Amr's Muslim forces camped before entering the city in 641.

Following the digging of the **Mahmudiya Canal** which claimed 20,000 lives, rich merchants erected mansions along its banks, described by *Murray's Handbook* as the "fashionable afternoon promenade". Nowadays the canal is choked and filthy, the mansions derelict and squatted, merging into the industrial slums of **Moharrem Bey**. In August 1987, a warehouse explosion produced clouds of choking gas which killed seven people and hospitalised 400; officials described the gas as "nontoxic". It was an ominous sign of how polluted Egypt's towns and cities have become. Near the huge Iron and Steel Works, madder-rose lakes of industrial effluent are only separated from the reedy fishing grounds of **Lake Mariout** by low dikes.

The Corniche beaches

Alexandria's beaches are an overworked asset. Hardly a square metre of sand goes unclaimed during high season, when literally millions of Egyptians descend on the city. Before June the beaches furthest out are relatively uncrowded, with predominantly local users; however, Alexandrians alone can number hundreds on Fridays, Saturdays and public holidays – days to be avoided.

The popularity of the beaches doesn't imply Western-style beach culture. On most of the beaches you will rarely see any woman past the age of puberty wearing a swimsuit – though they may wander into the sea fully clad. For Western women who want to swim without the hindrance of a *galabiyya*, or a lot of attention, the only place where even a modest one-piece seems okay is the Westernised enclave of **Ma'amoura**. As far as facilities go, most beaches have parasols and chairs for hire, and sometimes public showers, while fish restaurants, soft-drink and snack vendors are ubiquitous. So, too, alas, are sewage outlets, which number some forty-seven between the centre of town and Montazah.

East to Ma'amoura and Abu Qir

Buses #120, #129, #220 or #300 will whisk you eastwards along the Tariq el-Geish section of the Corniche past a string of **city beaches**. Mostly quite small, with a single hotel and casino (for food, drink and light music, not gambling) in the vicinity, they're hard to differentiate. Unless you've got somewhere in mind, simply get off at the least crowded, cleanest-looking one. Travelling by tram (#1–

#4) three to five blocks inland, you'll only have the stops – mostly named after beaches – to go on.

Chatby to Glym

The beach at **Chatby** could have spawned *The Swamp Thing*, but it's worth noting in passing Saint Mark's College (now a faculty of the university) and the district's cemeteries: Jewish, English, Greek, Armenian and Catholic. **Camp Cizar** ("Caesar") was once the site of *Eleusis Maritimus*, a Roman settlement.

After **Ibrahimiya**, tram #2 turns further inland, visiting **Sidi Gaber Station** and passing through the **Bacos quarter** where Gamal Abdel-Nasser was born on January 15, 1918. He was eleven years old when he attended his first nationalist demonstration, got truncheoned and was jailed overnight.

Meanwhile, tram #1 runs closer to **Sporting Beach** and **Cleopatra**. There's no connection between Cleopatra Beach and the queen herself, but the nearby district of **Mustapha Pasha** was the site of *Nikopolis*, which Octavian (or Augustus Caesar, as he then styled himself) founded because he hated living in Alexandria. The British also built barracks there, and houses, in the districts they named Stanley, Glym and San Stefano.

Glym boasts a **Royal Jewellery Museum** (daily 9am–4pm; Fri closed 11.30am–1.30pm; £E2, students £E1; tram #2 or any Corniche bus to *Zezeniya*). Housed in an ornate mansion at 27 Sharia Ahmed Yehia, behind the governor's residence, this glittering collection was accumulated by Mohammed Ali and his descendants. Farouk had to leave them behind when he sailed into exile; so, too, his priceless stamp collection. Also worth a look at Glym is *Pastroudis Loveboat*, an old-established **patisserie-restaurant**, with a ballroom and outside dining.

San Stefano and Sidi Bishr

San Stefano – named after a famous resort hotel of the 1930s (now featuring a small private beach) – used to entertain promenaders with an orchestra. As in Forster's day, the tram lines converge nearer the coastal fort of **al-Raml** (the sands), terminating at Victoria (now Nasser) College.

Buses carry on to **Sidi Bishr**, 14km east of the centre, where Sidi Bishr's Mosque stands between two beaches with the same name. Below the Automobile Club, east of the mosque, are the "Spouting Rocks" of Bir Mas'ud, where the ancients placed water-powered horns and mills, delighting as ever in gadgetry. It was here, too, that Hero invented the world's first hurdy-gurdy and coin-operated vending machine (dispensing holy water) in the first century AD.

Beyond Sidi Bishr, the **Miami** Casino gives way to two more sandy inlets, **Asafra** and **Mandara**; at the latter, the *New China* restaurant (daily noon–4pm & 6–11pm; serves alcohol) in the *Hotel Corail* makes for a change.

Montazah

Eighteen kilometres east of downtown Alex you reach **Montazah**, the city's walled pleasure grounds. You can enter the grounds (daily 7am–sunset; £E1) by the gates opposite the *Sheraton*. The 350 acres are well laid out and tended, with brass lamps, diverse pines, palms and flowers, plus a *Wimpy* and *Kentucky Fried Chicken* that might have pleased the gluttonous King Farouk.

Farouk's ancestor Khedive Abbas II ordered the fabulous **Montazah Palace**, a Turko-Florentine hybrid whose central tower mimics the Palazzo Vecchio in Florence; it was from here that Farouk fled to Ras el-Tin before abdicating. Sadat spent £E7 million on restoring the building, which is now a state guesthouse, closed to the public. Nearby are a few luxury hotels, the *Salamlek* and *Palestine*.

Montazah's **beach** is separated from Ma'amoura by a promontory supporting a picturesque "Turkish" belvedere; gaps in the fence may enable one to reach Ma'amoura directly, rather than via the distant fee-paying entrance.

Ma'amoura and Canopus

East of the palace grounds, **Ma'amoura** has developed into an enclave of holiday flats and villas, charging visitors 85pt before they've even glimpsed the **beach**. The sands are actually cleaner than most, and women can get away with wearing one-piece costumes. The main beach entrance is off a roundabout on the Abu Qir road, about 1km east of the Montazah *Sheraton*. A #725 microbus will deliver you to the toll-gate; other buses stop at the roundabout; microbuses back to Alex leave from outside the *Maamura Palace Hotel*.

Past Ma'amoura Beach, the road runs inland of a swathe of military and naval bases, occupying the ancient site of **Canopus**. Not that anything significant remains of this once-great Delta city, which flourished when a branch of the Nile reached the sea by the nearby "Canopic Mouth", but declined as this dried up and Alexandria arose. Classical mythology has it that Canopus was founded by a Greek navigator returning from the Trojan war, whom the locals later worshipped in the form of a jar with a human head. Nineteenth-century archaeologists bestowed the title **Canopic jars** on similar receptacles used to preserve mummies' viscera. Each organ had its own protective deity (a minor son of Horus) whose visage adorned the stopper (human heads went out of fashion late in the XVIII Dynasty). Even after XXI Dynasty embalmers began replacing organs in the mummies, the practice of leaving Canopic jars in tombs continued.

Abu Qir

When a straggle of jerry-built houses appears beyond the bases, you know you're entering **Abu Qir**. This small fishing town can be reached by *service* taxi, bus #129 or microbus #729; if you're coming from Montazah (25pt), the microbus stop is under the bridge and left around the corner of the palace walls from the *Sheraton Hotel* – look for knots of people waiting near the butchers. Abu Qir is garbage-strewn and ugly, and the raw sewage flowing down its **beach** should deter anyone but Egyptians from bathing; the only things going for it are itinerant vendors peddling everything from dolls to candelabras, and its restaurants.

The *Xephiron* at Abu Qir is rated one of Alexandria's best seafood **restaurants**. It's the blue and white building (☎560-1319) with green awnings overlooking the beach, entered from an alley running off the bus terminal. Guests select their own crab, fish or king prawns, sold per kilo; with chips, tahina, salad and beer, expect to pay at least £E25 a head. Beware of the walk-in oyster-sellers, whose wares are dearer still. Cheaper options include the *Bella Vista* next door and makeshift beach cafés along the sands.

Formerly, Abu Qir was better known for two **historic battles**. Admiral Nelson's defeat of the French fleet at Abu Qir Bay (1798) effectively scuppered Napoleon's dream of an eastern empire, but Bonaparte had his revenge the following year, when he personally led 10,000 cavalry against 15,000 Turks landed by the Royal Navy, pushing them back into the sea. It was the naval battle (remembered as the "Battle of the Nile") that inspired Mrs Hemans to write, "The boy stood on the burning deck . . . ".

Food and nightlife

Alexandria can't match Cairo for culinary variety, but it beats the capital when it comes to **seafood and Greek restaurants** – and when these pall you can always fall back on Egyptian favourites like *shwarmas*, pizzas, *fuul* and *felafel*, or seek refuge in a few Oriental-ish places. **Coffeehouses**, too, are an Alex speciality, though **bars**, despite its European past, are not greatly evident.

Restaurants

The following **restaurants** more or less represent the culinary and budgetary spectrum downtown; almost all of them are in the triangle of streets delineated by Sharia Safiya Zaghloul and Sharia Nabi Daniel, south of Ramleh Station, and Sharia Horriya, north of the Roman Theatre. For Corniche recommendations, see the entries for Mandara and Abu Qir, in the preceding section.

Taverna Ramleh Station, opposite the tram terminal. A "Greek" chain restaurant favoured by tourists, with a *shwarma* and kebab takeaway downstairs. Does Egyptian and Western-style pizzas, seafood, soup and has a fabulous salad bar at reasonable rates. Even cheaper *shwarmas*, pies and juices are available from the **nameless takeaway** on the corner of Safiya Zaghloul, just past the inexpensive stand-up patisserie almost next door to the *Taverna*.

Denis, 1 Sharia Ibn Basaam (☎483.0457). Just off Ramleh and the Corniche, this Thirties-style Greek fish bar lets you select your *samak* or *calamari* from the freezer. A kilo of shrimps with chips, salad, *tahina* and beer should cost around £E25. Lugubrious service. Beer and wine available. Open 9am–1am.

La Pizzeria, 14 Sharia Horriya. Serves cheap pizzas, lasagne, spaghetti and other filling meals. Near the *Vienous* and *Pastroudis* patisseries, down towards the Roman Theatre.

Fuul Ahmed Mohammed. Simple family place serving excellent *fuul*, *arroz bi khalto* ("rice with everything") and other cheap Egyptian eats (just over £E1 per head). Soft drinks only. To find it, walk along the street with the *Zenah* shop and the Bank of Alexandria on the corner, running parallel to and between Safiya Zaghloul and Nabi Daniel streets (see our Downtown Alex map).

Al-Ekhlas, 49 Sharia Safiya Zaghloul. Join the haughty bourgeoisie supping tasty Egyptian dishes (£E6–12) in the restaurant upstairs, or go for pizzas (£E3–4) and a rather mingy salad bar (£E1.85) in the plastic *Papillon Coffee Shop* on the ground floor.

Elite, 43 Sharia Safiya Zaghloul. Behind the blue-painted bar facing the Metro Cinema, this restaurant is decorated with murals and prints, and serves *calamari*, fish and *kofta* dishes (£E7–11). Its Greek owner, Madame Christina, mourns the passing of old Alexandria, and enjoys reminiscing about the artists and writers she has known. Daily 9am–midnight (or later). Beer and *ouzo* served.

Cafeteria Asteria, Sharia Safiya Zaghloul – diagonally across the street from the *Elite*. Sandwiches, macaroni, pizzas, ice cream and hot drinks at reasonable prices. Walk through the dingy outer room to find a nice glass-roofed annexe, popular with lovebirds. Friendly, English-speaking Greek proprietor. Daily 9am–midnight.

Santa Lucia, 40 Sharia Safiya Zaghloul (☎482-0332). On the corner opposite the *Elite*, this is one of Alexandria's best and dearest seafood restaurants. Reckon on paying £E25–30 for a meal; a lot more if you're seriously drinking. A huge plate of *taramasalata* and bread makes an affordable snack (£E10). Open daily noon–4pm & 7pm–1am; Amex accepted. Nightclub and music. Beer and wines.

Tikka Grill, on a promontory near al-Mursi's Mosque, overlooking the Eastern Harbour. Plush surroundings and great service, though only the hot chicken *tikka* tastes remotely Indian. By ordering a main dish (around £E11) you're entitled to plunder the delicious salad bar. A meal for two works out around £E30. Serves alcohol. Daily 1–5pm & 7.30pm–2am.

Street food, provisions and booze

Taamiya, *fuul* and other **street food** can be found throughout the **souks**, where fresh produce is also sold on al-Attarin, Abu el-Daarda and al-Sabaa Banat streets.

If you're unaccustomed to such fare it's probably wiser to buy from **shops**. Several grocers selling cheese, *basturma*, etc, lie a few blocks west of Midan Zaghloul along Iskandar el-Akbar; for fresh bread you have to jostle with locals outside backstreet **bakeries**. There's a discreet **wine and beer shop** on the left, west along Iskandar el-Akbar.

Coffeehouses and patisseries

Coffeehouses and patisseries like *Athineos* and the *Trianon* have accumulated a heavy load of mystique, and even if you couldn't give a croissant about Cavafy or Durrell, their opulent interiors and cakes should not be missed.

The Trianon, corner of Sa'ad Zaghloul and Ramleh. Redecorated and air-conditioned, the dearest and swankiest of Alexandria's patisseries boasts gilt columns and a splendidly ornate restaurant; Cavafy used to work upstairs. The patisserie serves light meals, beer, creamy cakes and beverages (£E2 minimum charge).

Athineos, Midan Ramleh. Decorated with classical motifs and mirrors and frequented by eccentrics, *Athineos* is a good place to read Durrell over coffee or a beer and sandwich, and it is also cheaper than the *Trianon*. Check out the gilded friezes and columns in the restaurant upstairs – the entrance is around the corner.

Délices, between Midan and Sharia Sa'ad Zaghloul. Appealing in a shabby sort of way, with creaking fans and a magnificent teak bar reduced to selling lukewarm Stella. Inexpensive.

Vienous, corner of Nabi Daniel and Horriya, opposite the *Hotel Piccadilly*. Faintly chintzy with its cream and gilt, mirrored salon, but restful.

Pastroudis, 39 Sharia Horriya, 100m from *Vienous* (☎492-9609). Established in 1923, this dark-panelled bar (8.30am–midnight) and café feature in *The Alexandria Quartet*, and was another haunt of Cavafy.

Brazilian Coffee Store, just down the alley from the tourist office. This popular stand-up breakfast spot features antique coffee-mills, a glass map of Brazil and other period furnishings. Great coffee and pastries. Open daily 6.30am–3pm (closed Fri).

Arab cafés

Traditional **Arab cafés** (*ahwas*) are another world from the European patisseries, and a male preserve not recommended for single women. If you're into sipping tea or *karkaday* surrounded by guys slapping down backgammon counters or dominoes between lung-charring tokes on *sheeshas*, there are loads of places around el-Gumhorriya. You can almost locate them by the sound of coughing, audible above Koranic recitals or Umm Kalthoum sobbing from the radio.

24-hour coffee bars

For nocturnal types, there are **24-hour coffee bars** in the *Marhaba*, *Dubai*, *Sheraton*, *Ramada Renaissance*, *Landmark*, *Plaza* and *San Giovanni* hotels.

Bars, nightclubs and discos

Alex is the centre of Egypt's wine and spirits industry (the vineyards are near Lake Mariout), but it's not much of a drinking town. Plush hotels and restaurants are the main source of **bars**, which tends to inflate prices. If you're flush with money, it's worth checking out the *Metropole* or *Cecil*; if cash is tighter, go for no-frills drinking at the *Elite Restaurant*. Expatriates and native preppies favour the *Spitfire Bar* off Sharia Goufra el-Togariya, two blocks west of Midan Sa'ad Zaghloul – a place to hear rock music and grow maudlin (look for the Jumbo Jet sign). It's open Monday to Saturday till 2am.

Several **nightclubs** offer a programme of dinner, glitz and dancing for £E40–60 a head, with a belly dancer after 1am. These include *Layli* in the *Hotel Cecil* (10.30pm–4am), *el-Phanar* in the *Sheraton* (10.30pm–3am), and *Queen's Hall* in the *San Giovanni Hotel* at 205 Tariq el-Geish (10.30pm–3am). For live music and dancing, there's also the *Santa Lucia* restaurant and the *Crazy Horse* (inside *Athineos*), both going strong from 10pm to 2am during high season. There's no cover charge, but patrons are expected to consume £E6–10 worth of drinks apiece (which isn't difficult).

Young Egyptians prefer the kind of **discos** which exude sweat and Arabic pop from the upper floors of seedy buildings. There's one above the Ramleh takeaway and another on the sixth floor of the *Hotel Union*; neither gets going much before 10pm. Punters who aren't in mixed-sex couples might be refused admission to the dearer, Westernised discos in the top hotels. The *Ramada Renaissance* hotel's *Black Gold* gushes from 9pm to 1am (closed Mon); *Aquarius* in the *Montazah Sheraton* from 10.30pm to 2.30am (closed Wed).

Arts and festivals

The two main venues for **performing arts** are the *Saiyid Darwish Theatre* (☎482-5106) on Sharia Fouad, for plays, classical music and ballet; and the *Firquit Reda Theatre* (☎597-9960) in Chatby, home of the Reda Dance Company. Performances occur most nights during the high season; ask the tourist office for details.

The timing of **festivals** varies from year to year, so you'll have to get the latest word from the tourist office. Late summer normally witnesses an **International Film Festival** which gives Egyptians a rare opportunity to see foreign movies in an uncensored state; every cinema in town screens a few. Other cultural festivals take place from time to time. In 1989, 45 cities named Alex were invited to send cultural delegations to a *Festival of the Alexandrias of the World* – an event which that be repeated in future years.

The Egyptian, Islamic side of Alex revels in five **moulids** over five consecutive weeks, starting with *zikrs* outside the Mosque of al-Mursi. The day after its "big night", the action shifts to Sidi Gaber's Mosque, then Sidi Bishr's; followed by the *moulids* of Sidi Kamal and Sidi Mohammed al-Rahhal. They don't seem to be fixed according to the Muslim or the secular calendar, unlike most *moulids*.

Listings

American Express c/o *Eyeress Travel* (26 Sharia Horriya; ☎483-0084; Mon–Thurs 8.30am–1pm & 5.30–6pm, Fri & Sat 8.30am–1pm) can cash and sell Amex TCs, and hold clients' mail.

Arabic language courses can be arranged through the British Council (see overpage).

Banks/changing money *Bank of Alexandria* (downtown branches open Sun–Thurs 8.30am–2pm; 10.30am–1pm during Ramadan), *Chase Manhattan* (19 Sharia Dr Ibrahim el-Sayd), *Bank of America* (Sharia Lomomba; ☎493-1115), *Barclays* (10 Sharia Fawoteur; ☎482-1308), *Thomas Cook* (Midan Ramleh; ☎278-30; daily 8am–5pm) and bureaux in the hotels *Cecil*, *Metropole*, *San Stefano* and *Palestine* can all exchange currency and cash TCs.

Bookshops *El-Ma'aref* (between Midan and Sharia Sa'ad Zaghloul, next to *Délices*), the *Book Centre* (51 Sharia Sa'ad Zaghloul) and *al-Ahram* (10 Sharia Horriya) stock a limited selection of books in English, and the secondhand stall (opposite the Centre Française on Nabi Daniel) yields occasional finds, but there's little evidence of the old literary cosmopolitanism. You can buy three- to thirty-day-old foreign **newspapers and magazines** on the southwestern corner of Sa'ad Zaghloul Square.

Car rental *Avis* (☎80-75-32) in the *Hotel Cecil* rents Fiat 127s for around £E60 a day; you must be over 25. *Budget* (59 Tariq el-Geish, Chatby; ☎597-1273) does likewise, but you only have to be over 20.

Car repairs Try the *baladi* workshops around the far end of Sharia Amin Fikry.

Cultural centres *British Council* (9 Sharia Batalsa, Bab Sharki; ☎482-9890); *France* (30 Sharia Nabi Daniel; ☎492-0804; 9am–1pm & 4–8pm; closed Fri and Sat); *Goethe Institute* (10 Sharia Ptolemy, Azarita; ☎483-9870); *Italy* in the Italian Consulate on Midan Sa'ad Zaghloul; *Spain* (101 Sharia Horriya; ☎422-0214; open 5–8pm); *USA* (3 Sharia Pharana; ☎482-1009; Mon–Fri 9am–4pm; video viewing from 11am).

Consulates *Britain* (3 Sharia Mena, Roushdi; ☎847-166; Mon–Fri 8am–1pm); *Federal Republic of Germany* (5 Sharia Mena, Roushdi; ☎845-475); *France* (2 Midan Orabi; ☎483-5613); *Greece* (63 Sharia Iskandar el-Akbar; ☎492-2318); *Israel* (453 Sharia Horriya, Roushdi; ☎840-933); *USA* (110 Sharia Horriya, 2km east of downtown; ☎482-1911; Sun–Thurs 8am–4.30pm). Australia, New Zealand and Canada have no consular representation; other consulates are listed in *Alexandria Night and Day*.

Hospitals *al-Moassah* (☎421-2886 or 421-6662) on Sharia Horriya. For non-emergencies, ask your hotel or consulate to recommend a doctor. The *Medical Care Advisory Team* (*MCAT*) at Glym (97 Sharia Abel-Salem Aref; ☎586-2323) is used to dealing with foreigners.

International calls The circular exchange on Midan Ramleh functions 24 hours. State your number and pay (minimum period three minutes; £E5 to Europe at peak rate) at the far end of the counter, then wait – hopefully no longer than fifteen minutes – to collect your call. The process is smoother (but 50–70 percent dearer) at major hotels.

Passport office For registering your arrival in Egypt, or renewing your visa (two photos needed), go to the office at 28 Sharia Talaat Harb (☎482-4366; Sat–Thurs 8.30am–2pm, Fri 10am–1pm; and between 7–9pm, in theory). It's not as bad as Cairo's Mugamma.

Pharmacies *Khalid*, on Iskandar el-Akbar just west of Sa'ad Zaghloul Square (☎806-710), is open daily until 10pm. There are many others along Safiya Zaghloul and Nabi Daniel streets.

Photography/film developing Kodak film sold and developed opposite the Rialto Cinema on Safiya Zaghloul; other places can be found on Sharia Sa'ad Zaghloul.

Post offices Midan Ramleh, Sharia Iskandar el-Akbar, and Masr Station: all open daily 8am–8pm. The Iskandar el-Akbar branch has a **post restante** service (9am–3pm; postal code 21519), but you might prefer to have your mail sent care of American Express (see above). There's an Express Mail Service from the branch in Masr Station.

Swimming pools Non-residents are sometimes allowed to use the pools at the *Ramada Renaissance* (☎868-188), *Sheraton* (☎548-0550) and *Summer Moon* (☎430-0367) hotels. Phone to check before turning up.

Tourist police above the tourist office on Midan Sa'ad Zaghloul (☎807-611), and in Montazah Palace grounds (☎863-804). Both open Sat–Thurs 8am–8pm, Fri 8am–2pm.

On from Alexandria

Most of the places covered in the remainder of this chapter can be reached from Alexandria by some form of public transport. Using the quickest available method it's also feasible to make **day excursions** to Rosetta and Tanta in the Delta (see Chapter Five) or the Monasteries of Wadi Natrun (see Chapter Three). Moving on from the city, there are also direct services to the Canal Zone, and a range of **international connections**.

Buses

Alexandria's inter-city **bus terminals** are spread around downtown.

● **Sa'ad Zaghloul** Terminal for A/C express buses to **Cairo** (every 30min–1hr between 6am and 6.30pm), for which bookings should be made at the kiosk on the square itself. Another kiosk handles the yellow and green *East Delta Bus Co* services to **Ismailiya** (leaving 7am and 2pm; 5hr; £E7).

● **Iskandar el-Akbar** The ticket office just around the corner from Sa'ad Zaghloul on Iskandar el-Akbar (next door to *Khalid* pharmacy) is where you make reservations for the 9am express bus to **Mersa Matrouh**, plus the *West Delta Bus Co* services that leave from **Midan Orabi**. The most useful of these are the non-express services that call at **el-Alamein** and **Sidi Abd el-Rahman** en route to Mersa Matrouh; currently departing at 7am, 11am, 1pm, 3pm and 5pm.

● **Gumhorriya** Facing the entrance to the Roman Theatre, on Gumhorriya, there's a depot for buses to **Rashid** and **Damietta**, which seem to ignore schedules and leave at their drivers' whim. A kind of sub-depot nearer **Masr Station** has buses for Bahig, which continue on to the Monastery of Abu Mina on Fridays and Sundays.

Trains

Train services between Alex and Cairo are detailed on p.231; westbound services are covered under "El-Alamein" and "Mersa Matrouh". There is also a daily train to Luxor and Aswan (2nd class with and without A/C); book well in advance.

Unless you travel first-class A/C, trains are generally slower and less comfortable than buses and/or service taxis. Hope to get sympathetic treatment from the info desk and booking clerks in **Masr Station**. Services to Tanta and Cairo can also be boarded at Sidi Gaber Station.

Service taxis

Midan el-Gumhorriya seethes with Peugeots, Japanese minibuses and minivans going to almost everywhere that's worth mentioning within 200km of Alexandria. Listen for the drivers shouting out destinations, or simply ask for directions to the right clump of *service* taxis. If you don't mind a hair-raising trip with strangers, *service* taxis are the quickest way to get anywhere.

Flights

Alexandria's airport (bus #310 or #307 from Midan Orabi; taxis upwards of £E5) is a gateway to Cairo, Athens or Paris. Any travel agency can book *EgyptAir* flights to Cairo (2–3 times daily); *Olympic* on Midan Ramleh (Mon–Fri 8.30am–4pm, Sat 8.30am–12.30pm) flies to Athens on Thursdays and Fridays at 9.30am; *EgyptAir* flies to Athens on Wednesdays and Sundays. *Air France* (22 Sharia Salah Salem; ☎807-061) has a Sunday flight to Paris.

All tickets must be paid for in £E backed by an exchange receipt.

Ferries

Adriatica ferries to Iraklion, Piraeus and Venice sail every eight to twelve days over the summer (less frequently during low season). *De Castro & Co* (33 Sharia Salah Salem; ☎357-70) or *Menatours* (Midan Sa'ad Zaghloul; ☎806-909) can make bookings in Alex; *Gaby Travel* (1 Midan Talaat Harb; ☎393-8567) from Cairo.

Rates and reductions are identical to incoming ferries (see p.5), but you have to pay in £E backed by an exchange receipt. Book as early as possible, and ask about **customs** regulations; it may be necessary to check in at the Maritime Station, hours (sometimes even days) before departure.

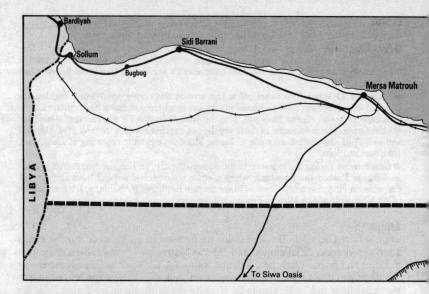

THE MEDITERRANEAN COAST

Egypt's 500-kilometre-long **Mediterranean coast** has beautiful beaches and sparkling sea all the way to Libya. However, lengthy stretches are still mined from World War II (see box below), others are off-limits due to military bases, or simply hard to reach; while many of the accessible sites are undergoing "development". The Ministry of Tourism dreams of attracting millions of European holidaymakers, like Greece or Spain, but its current clientele is overwhelmingly Egyptian. Both domestic **tourism** and beach culture are fairly recent phenomena and hardly square with Western notions of either.

Most travellers heading this way go directly to the new resort town of **Mersa Matrouh** and thence to Siwa Oasis (see *The Western Desert Oases*). Aside from the **beaches** near Matrouh, other coastal sites are awkward to reach (or leave) without private transport, though you may consider it worth making the effort to get to the famous World War II battlefield of **El-Alamein**, or the swanky resort at **Sidi Abd el-Rahman**. In general, though, even the sea seems reclusive here, hidden from sight of the H55 "coastal" highway by dunes and ridges, while the B-road and railway along which most of the region's villages are located runs still further inland.

MINEFIELDS: A WARNING

Sections of the Mediterranean coast and the desert inland are still littered with **unexploded shells and minefields**. Never stray into wired-off areas or anything that resembles an abandoned camp or airfield. The best indication of safe and dangerous areas is the behaviour of locals. By sticking to well-worn paths and regular beaches you'll be quite safe.

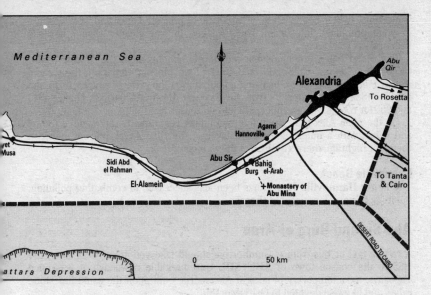

Between Alexandria and El-Alamein

The "sights" **between Alex and El-Alamein** are relatively neglected by tourists, in some cases deservedly so. Getting there can involve much to-ing and fro-ing around unsignposted crossroads miles from anywhere and, without a car, none of the places below are easy to reach as stops en route to Alamein or Matrouh. Using public transport, it's better to consider them as day excursions from Alex.

Agami and Hannoville

West of Alex are two **beaches** – **Agami** and **Hannoville** – whose white sands and relative privacy were first appreciated by rich, villa-building Egyptians. Nowadays, both attract plenty of ordinary day-trippers, but offer little in the way of cheap accommodation, encouraging the *hoi polloi* to leave by nightfall.

Getting to the beaches is easiest by microbus from el-Gumhorriya (25pt; services every 10–30min during daytime, calling at both resorts) or by *service* taxi (£E3–5). Buses #455 (from the embankment stop on Midan Sa'ad Zaghloul), #760 and #600 (from Masr Station and Midan Orabi) also run to both beaches but they are sardine-cans on Fridays and weekends. En route, you'll pass through the heavily industrialised suburb of **Mex** (or Max), whose only possible attraction is the *Sea Gull* restaurant (☎445-575) in the "castle" on the Corniche. An upmarket seafood joint, it promotes itself as a "paradise for children".

Agami Beach

A pale slip of sand beside cerulean water, **Agami Beach** beckons 20km west of Alex. On weekends and during high season it gets packed by lunchtime; at other times the beach is relatively uncrowded, though never quite deserted even in wintertime (when hotels close or slash their prices). Litter and pollution are growing problems, but Agami has managed to stay cleaner than other city beaches – at least so far.

The resort has a few modest-priced **hotels**, among them the *Minass* (☎431-0150), *New Admiral* (☎337-338) and *Queen Ann*. Moving upmarket, the tasteful *Agami Palace* (☎430-0386), boasting a pool, halves the price of singles ($78) and doubles ($83) over winter; its rival, the *Summer Moon* (☎430-0582), charges $43 and $55 for rooms over summer, $10 less off-season.

On the main Alex road you'll find two Italian **restaurants**, *Leonardo da Vinci* and *Ciino*, with a quiet, vine-shaded taverna, the *Blue Angel*, midway between them; for nightlife, there's a **disco** at the *Summer Moon*.

Hannoville Beach

The larger **Hannoville Beach** has been less successful in combating pollution, but its hotels aren't noticeably cheaper.

Abu Sir and Burg el-Arab

A *service* taxi or bus from el-Gumhorriya should take you 48km west along the H55 to the coastal town of **ABU SIR**. Unremarkable nowadays, it was once Taposiris, a contemporary of ancient Alexandria, built upon the same limestone ridge, and likewise devoted to Osiris-worship.

The enclosure walls of a long-vanished temple crown the ridge, with gate towers offering lovely views over the Mariout marshes and the azure sea. A few hundred metres to the east stands the solitary **Burg el-Arab** (Arab Tower), actually a Ptolemaic lighthouse replicating the Pharos, but one tenth of its size; it was part of a chain that once illuminated the coastline from Alexandria to Cyrenaica.

Burg el-Arab

Just west of Abu Sir, a minor road runs inland across reedy marshes, passing fragments of an ancient causeway (on the left) that connected Taposiris with the desert. There it meets **BURG EL-ARAB**, a "model" village resembling a walled, medieval Italian town, designed by W.E. Jennings-Bradley early this century. Commandeered as the RAF headquarters during the battle for Alamein, Burg el-Arab was subsequently graced with a presidential villa (near the carpet factory outside its walls).

The town is on the B-road from Alex to Matrouh, with a fair chance of *service* taxis to the nearest small town, BAHIG (also a railway halt).

The Monastery of Abu Mina

Seven kilometres along the road from Burg el-Arab to Bahig, a poorly marked track turns off and runs 15km south into the desert, to the Coptic **Monastery of Abu Mina**. The site is directly accessible by bus from Alex (leaving Masr Station at 7.30am, 8.30am, 12.30pm and 1pm) on Fridays and Sundays; on other days the service terminates at Bahig.

Deir Mari Mina (as it's known locally) honours **Saint Menas**, an Egyptian-born Roman legionary who was martyred in Asia Minor in 296 after refusing to renounce Christ. His ashes were buried here when the camel that was taking them home refused to go any further. Miraculous events on the spot persuaded others to exhume Menas in 350 and build a church over his grave, later enclosed within a huge basilica. A pilgrim city grew up as camel-trains spread his fame (Menas is depicted between two camels), and "holy" water from local springs was exported throughout Christendom. But when these dried up in the twelfth century the city and its vineyards were abandoned and soon buried by sand, only a small community of monks remaining.

With its belfry towers visible from way out on the roads west and east, the present **monastery** hides its concrete buildings within a stone enclosure. Erected in 1959, the building is outwardly graceless and luridly decorated within, like all modern Coptic architecture. Not that monks and believers would agree, or even think it relevant; what counts is the spirit of devotion, most evident on November 11 (15 Hathor by the ancient calendar), when pilgrims celebrate **Saint Menas' day**. (A Coptic papal encyclical of 1943 asserted that it was Menas the "wonderworker of Egypt" who ensured the Allies' victory at el-Alamein.)

In addition to Menas, the crypt houses the body of Pope Kyrillos VI (1959–71), whom Copts regard as a saint, writing petitions on his marble grave. Tombs aside, though, there are only paltry **antiquities** to see. Amidst some low mounds several hundred metres beyond the monastery are broken marble paving, granite and basalt columns – the foundations of the original church and the basilica raised around Menas's original tomb. Remnants of the pilgrims' town lie all around (artefacts found here can be seen in the Greco-Roman Museum); to the north is a ruined hospice once equipped with hot and cold baths.

El-Alamein

Before Alamein we never had a victory. After Alamein we never had a defeat.

Winston Churchill, *The Hinge of Fate*

EL-ALAMEIN ("Two Flags") is an apt name for a place that witnessed the turning point of the North African campaign, determining the fate of Egypt and Britain's empire. When the Afrika Korps came within sixty miles of Alexandria on July 1, 1942, the city and the capital experienced "The Flap": documents were burned, civilians mobbed railway stations, and Egyptian nationalists prepared to welcome their Nazi "liberators". Control of Egypt, Middle Eastern oil and the Canal route to India seemed about to be wrested from the Allied powers by Germany and Italy. Instead, at el-Alamein, the Allied Eighth Army held, and then drove the Axis forces back, to ultimate defeat in Tunisia. Around 11,000 soldiers were killed and 70,000 wounded at el-Alamein alone; total casualties for the North African campaign (September 1940–March 1943) exceeded 100,000.

Travellers who wish to pay their respects to the dead or have an interest in military history should find the **cemeteries** and the **war museum** worth the effort of getting there.

Getting there – and leaving
The village of EL-ALAMEIN squats on a dusty plain 106km west of Alexandria, 2km from its railway halt in the middle of the desert. Although spurs connect it to the highway and B-road, anyone driving past could blink and see nothing except construction debris; the new oil pipeline and port hardly justify tourist bumpf about "Alamein City".

If you can afford it, the easiest way of visiting Alamein is by **hired car**. *Thomas Cook* in Alex quotes US$50 a head for a full day excursion, inclusive of meals and admission fees; or, less exorbitantly, they can supply a car with driver for around £E120, split between however many people you can get together and cram in. Depending on your bargaining skills, it should also be possible to hire a **taxi** for the day in Alex (from Midan el-Gumhorriya) for £E60–80. A third option is to rent your own vehicle from *Budget* or *Avis* (see p.474). Though comparatively expensive, a car enables you to reach the far cemeteries and leave Alamein without difficulty – a major advantage over public transport.

Non-express **buses** usually call at *Alamein's Resthouse* (the *de facto* bus stop) between Alex and Matrouh. Leaving Midan Orabi around 7am, 11am, 1pm, 3pm and 5pm, they also stop at Sidi Abd el-Rahman, further west of Alamein. Booking a seat means paying the full fare to Matrouh (£E7); by just turning up and possibly standing throughout the two-hour journey, it costs £E3.50. Leaving Alamein can be tricky, as buses are packed when they arrive and you can't reserve seats from here. There's more chance of standing room on buses to Matrouh than on services to Alex.

Service taxis from Midan el-Gumhorriya could drop you off along their run to Matrouh, but will probably expect the full fare (£E7). If that's the deal, make sure you're dropped in the village proper, and not at some distant intersection. The *Resthouse* is the place to seek drivers leaving Alamein. **Trains** are even less convenient. Aside from having to trudge to the station (trains in both directions call at el-Alamein in the late morning and mid-afternoon), there's the discomfort of spending four hours in third-class.

The Battle and its legacy

Rather than the single relentless clash of armies that people usually imagine, the **Battle of el-Alamein** alternated between vicious fighting and relatively bloodless lulls over a period of four months. The **Afrika Korps'** initial advance on Alamein faltered through lack of fuel and munitions, and stiff Allied resistance organised by Auchinleck (July 17). But once resupplied, **Rommel** had the advantage of 88mm cannons that outranged the Allies' guns, and faster, better-armoured tanks.

After **Montgomery** took over the Allied **Eighth Army**, he negated this weakness by siting his tanks hull-down, protected until the panzers came within range. Having suffered heavy losses attacking Alam Halfa ridge (August 31 to September 6), the Afrika Korps withdrew behind a wall of minefields, while Monty amassed *materiél* and plotted a counter-offensive. A crucial element was the deception plan which led the Germans to expect the main assault on their southern flank. When the Allies punched through the central front (October 23) instead, Rommel was obliged to concentrate his mobile units further north (a flanking attack inland, followed by a thrust to the coast, were standard tactics in desert warfare), stranding four Italian divisions in the south. As the Eighth Army broke out (November 5) and surged west, the Afrika Korps fought rearguard actions back through Libya until its inevitable surrender six months later.

The War Museum and Cemeteries
Armoured vehicles, weaponry and kit, maps and other items are displayed in a **War Museum** near the *Resthouse* on the main square (daily 9am–6pm; 9am–3pm during Ramadan; £E1). As if to prove that Egypt is no martial slouch either, a

separate room recalls the storming of the Bar-Lev line along the Suez Canal during the October War of 1973 – a tactical victory that still inspires pride, even though Israel ultimately prevailed on the battlefield.

In a valley to the east of town, poignantly neat rows of headstones fill the **Allied War Cemetery**, where 815 of the 7367 dead are nameless, only "known unto God". Though over half were Britons, the dead included Australians, New Zealanders, Indians, Malays, Melanesians, Africans, Canadians, French, Greeks and Poles. The curator who keeps the cemetery immaculate appreciates some *baksheesh*, and may offer militaria for sale.

At the point where the Australian Division assaulted Tell el-Eisa ridge, 8km west of town, is the seldom-visited, high-walled Axis burial grounds. The **Italian War Cemetery** nearest the highway is a square enclosure with a central column; from here a track runs 4km to the **German War Cemetery**, whose giant obelisk holds the ashes of those named on bronze tablets in the memorial arcades. A separate grave, inscribed "Death knows no country", commemorates thirty-one fatalities whose nationality was never ascertained. About one hundred surviving members of the Afrika Korps return here every October for a memorial service.

Another legacy of the conflict, forgotten by the nations that pursued it, are the **minefields** they sewed across the Western Desert, which still kill or maim Bedouin to this day. Casualties were highest in the 1950s, when a foreign scrap-metal dealer taught them to make bombs from unexploded shells, and blow derelict tanks into portable chunks. Such memories disposed many Libyans to support Gaddafi's demands for war reparations in 1989, which the Western media dismissed as a propaganda stunt. For Egypt, the minefields are also a major obstacle to implementing the Qattara Depression project (see p.445).

Accommodation and Sidi Abd el-Rahman

Located too far from its beach for comfort, el-Alamein offers no incentive to stay at the *Hotel al-Amana* (singles £E6, doubles £E12), opposite the museum, although the *Resthouse* serves decent **meals** (£E3–5), including local treats like armadillo eggs. However, well-heeled and mobile travellers have a couple more **accommodation** options, starting with the all-mod-cons *Atic Hotel* (☎4921-340), 16km back towards Alex, which boasts a pool and private beach; it charges £E80 for double rooms or four-person bungalows.

Sidi Abd el-Rahman

A better upmarket option, perhaps, is the four-star *Alamein Hotel* (open May–Oct) at **SIDI ABD EL-RAHMAN**, 26km west of Alamein: an isolated resort with a lovely white beach. Rich Egyptians flock here over summer, when it's necessary to reserve rooms (£E50) or seven-person villas (£E150) up to a year in advance (☎586-3580; telex 92726 EGYPTL UN). Lunch and dinner cost £E20 a head at the hotel restaurant, the only place selling food. Torn tents are available for rent (£E20); pitching your own is strictly forbidden.

The resort is a world apart from the small village, 3km inland, where the government is trying to settle **Bedouin** of the Awlad Ali tribe. Originally from Libya, they moved onto the lands of the weaker Morabiteen tribe a couple of centuries ago. Many have abandoned their traditional goat's-hair tents for stone houses, but they maintain the flocks, which they graze on scrubland or pen behind their now-immobile homes.

Mersa Matrouh

Judging by **MERSA MATROUH**, Egypt's Mediterranean coast is unlikely to become the Costa del Sol of the 1990s. Donkey carts outnumber cars on its unpaved main street, and its cafés are full of youths gawping at demurely clad families. The **beaches**, however, are exceptional: Agiiba and Ubbayad, furthest from town, are truly magnificent, but by no stretch of the imagination does this staid middle-class resort fit the tourist board's promise of a hedonist's playground. The only people likely to think so are the Libyans who've started coming here since the border was reopened; Egyptians go the other way, seeking work in Libya; whereas Western visitors are usually more interested in reaching Siwa Oasis (see p.486) than lolling on Matrouh's beaches.

A grid of mould-poured low-rise blocks housing 20,000 people, the **town** spreads up from the coast towards a ridge festooned with radar dishes. As Matrouh has gone from being a quiet fishing port to the booming capital of the vast Mediterranean Governorate within ten years, immigrants have poured in from other parts of Egypt, inspiring mixed feelings amongst the locals. The Bedouin in particular often regard the newcomers as "*khlifty*" (untrustworthy, dishonourable) – though they're too varied a bunch to fit any such generalisation.

Getting there from Alex or Cairo

The 290km journey **from Alex** is best accomplished by either *Golden Rocket* **buses** (2–3 daily; £E15) or the A/C, non-stop blue bus (£E12), which currently leave Midan Sa'ad Zaghloul at 9am; both take four hours and seats should be booked the day before. Other blue buses – stopping at Alamein and Sidi Abd el-Rahman – take five hours (£E7) and usually leave from Midan Orabi. Quicker but scarier are the **service taxis** which depart from outside Masr Station until around 6pm (£E7; 3hr 30min). The daily **train services** (6–19hr!) aren't really worth bothering with, though you might want to make use of the overnight *wagon-lit* which runs between June 1 and October 31 (Sun, Tues & Thurs; £E12) and must be booked well in advance.

Both *Golden Rocket* (2–3 daily; £E20; 8hr) and blue **buses** (hourly 7–11am; £E9–12 depending on A/C) also run to Matrouh **from Cairo**, departing from outside the *Nile Hilton* on Midan Tahrir; book seats a day or two beforehand. Mornings are the best time to catch sporadic **service taxis** (£E13) from Ahmed Helmi and Koulali squares, near Ramses Station, which take about seven hours; an alternative is to ride to Alex and get another *service* taxi. The slowness of **trains** is again a real deterrent. Fastest of all are *EgyptAir* **flights** (Thurs, Fri & Sun; 90min) between June 1 and October 28; one-way costs around US$45.

Arrival and accommodation

On **arrival**, catch a taxi from the airport (£E5–7), or a donkey cart from the train or bus station, into the centre. Donkey *carettas* are the mainstay of **transport** around town (50pt–£E1) and useful for reaching the nearer beaches (£E1–3). As in Cairo, you pay what seems appropriate when you arrive. Matrouh's **tourist office** (daily 9am–2pm & 8–10pm, in theory) is utterly useless, so in the unlikely event of your needing information it's better to ask at one of the posher hotels.

Many of the pricier **hotels** close down (or slash their prices) over winter, to reopen once the tourist season has got going in July. To **phone Matrouh from anywhere outside the area**, use the prefix ☎094.

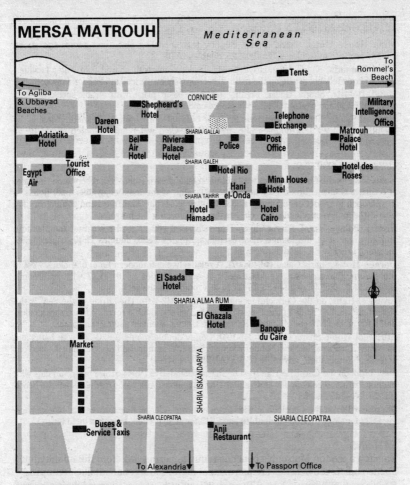

CHEAP LODGINGS

Women are advised to give the cheap hotels between the bus terminal and Sharia Iskandariya a miss; men should be safe there, though their belongings might not be. Most of the following places are accustomed to foreigners.

Youth Hostel, northwest of the *Adriatika Hotel* (☎94-23-31). Dinky shared rooms (unsuitable for women) and a kitchen. IYHF members £E2, non-members £E5.

Hotel el-Gazala, Sharia Alma Rum (☎943-519). Clean and simple, this is the budget traveller's favourite. Beds in double, triple or quadruple rooms (without locks) for £E5; free hot showers. Often group-booked in July & Aug. The "comments" book makes amusing reading.

Hotel Rio, Sharia Galeh (☎942-811). Clean, bare rooms, some with balconies. Singles £E8, doubles £E12, triples £E15. Could be quieter and less mosquito-ridden.

Hotel des Roses, Sharia Galeh (☎942-755). Cool and tidy, but the mosque next door blasts sleepers awake before dawn. Singles £E19, doubles £E36. Dinner and breakfast included. Open June–Sept.

Hotel Cairo, Sharia Tahrir (☎942-648). Small, luridly decorated rooms around a vine-shaded courtyard. Friendly English-speaking manager, Mr Adih. Double rooms £E5 (£E7 with bath).

Mina House Hotel, Sharia Tahrir. Slightly less appealing place just across the street, equally prone to mosquitoes. Singles £E5, doubles £E10.

Hotel Hamada, Sharia Iskandariya. Dusty, basic rooms with shared cold water facilities, above a crowded, noisy café on the main street. Grossly overpriced at £E18 for a double.

Hotel Bel-Air, Sharia Gallai. Freshly painted, basic place with Arabic-speaking staff. Doubles (£E9) and triples (£E14) with shared cold water facilities.

Hotel el-Saada, Sharia Iskandariya. Friendly but malodorous place, frequented mainly by Egyptians. Singles £E3, doubles £E6, triples £E9. Cold water only. Women would be ill-advised to stay here.

UPMARKET HOTELS

Beau Site, on the Corniche 2km west of Sharia Iskandariya (☎942-066; reservations in Cairo at 6 Sharia Osman Ahmed Osman, ☎259-9480). One of the most enjoyable small hotels in Egypt, open May–Oct only. Singles £E33, doubles £E41, plus £E22 per head compulsory full board (the food is excellent). Also chalets for rent, sleeping 3–8 persons.

Riviera Palace Hotel, Sharia Gallai. Three-star joint with a good restaurant (no alcohol), and an organist in the lounge most evenings. Singles £E25, doubles £E40, triples £E90, including breakfast. Closed during winter.

Dareen Hotel, Sharia Gallai (☎945-607). A relatively plush modern hotel one block west of the *Bel-Air*, guaranteeing breakfast and hot water. Singles £E10 (£E17 with bathroom), doubles £E20 (£E34), extra bed £E8 (£E14 in a room with shower).

Arous el-Bahr, on the Corniche facing the Med (☎942-420). The "Bride of the Sea" is the sister hotel to the "Bride of the Desert" in Siwa. Two-star double rooms – mostly with balconies – for £E18, £E13 out of season. Restaurant. Helpful about arranging transport.

Adriatika Hotel, Sharia Gallai (☎945-194). Comfy double rooms (£E20–30) with baths and balconies. Cafeteria, bar and 24-hour room service. TV, laundry and dry cleaning. Closed out of season. Reservations advisable (Telex: ADRIT UN 54591).

New Lido, on the Corniche 1km west of Sharia Iskandariya (☎944-515). Four-room flats with kitchen, bath and balcony for £E46 a night; or bungalows with baths further down the beach (£E25). Closed in winter.

Shepheard's, on the Corniche in the centre of town. A large, black, three-star block charging £E27 for singles, £E36 for doubles and £E13 for an extra bed; breakfast included.

CAMPING

To pitch a tent on Matrouh's beaches requires permission from the military intelligence office; the beaches are patrolled at night, so forget about illicit **camping**.

Badr Camp, on Ubayyad Beach. Two-person tents with cots can be rented during the tourist season; per-person rates range from £E18 to £E33, but the deal includes three meals and access to showers and toilets. Reservations can be made through *Badr Camp* in Cairo (8 Qasr el-Nil; ☎770-132), though they charge more than double what you'd pay on the spot.

Beaches

Beaches are Matrouh's saving grace, so it's a real shame that women can't enjoy them. As in Alex, Egyptian women sunbathe and swim fully clothed, accompanied by male relations; a foreigner acting differently is liable to persistent eyeballing and pestering, and maybe an encounter with an exhibitionist masturbator whom the authorities have tolerated for years. An exception to this rule is the *Beau Site*'s **private beach**, where non-guests are expected to rent a beach umbrella (£E3 per hour) or surf kayak (£E6 per hour).

The nearer beaches are accessible by *caretta* (£E2–3) or hired bicycle (£E7 for 24hr; hire shop open 6am–midnight); **transport** to the western beaches varies with the season. From June onwards you should be able to catch a shared taxi or microbus (£E2–3 to Agiiba), or the open-sided *tuf-tuf* bus (£E1.25) which shuttles back and forth between around 8am and 5pm from near the bus station. At other times, ask your hotel to arrange a private taxi; to Agiiba and back (with several hours there, and the option of a stopover at Cleopatra's Beach) costs about £E10. During summer, the *Beau Site* runs weekly car excursions (£E8 per head including refreshments) and occasional boats to Cleopatra's Beach (£E4).

Beaches close to town

The three beaches around Matrouh's crescent-shaped bay are separated by a litter-strewn swathe and a small port farther east. Beyond this, a spit of land curves around to face the town, rimmed on the landward side by **Rommel's Beach**. The Desert Fox supposedly bathed here in between plotting the Alam Halfa offensive from a nearby cave, now turned into a small **Rommel Museum** (9.30am–4pm; 50pt). His maps, desk and greatcoat are amongst the exhibits, which carry amusing captions like: "Rommel was the professor of contemporary military leaders to the extent that he was in every place at the same time". With a surf kayak you can paddle out towards a red buoy, twenty metres from which (in the direction of the mosque) lies a **sunken U-boat**, visible underwater with a mask. Soldiers discourage people from lingering on the rockier, deserted, seaward side of the peninsula.

Having ruined **Lido Beach**, curving west around the bay, litterbugs are doing the same to the **Beach of Lovers** on its western horn. Farther west (roughly 7km from town) lies the cleaner, windier **Cleopatra's Beach**, which drops away sharply a metre offshore. Across the dunes on its far right-hand side is **Cleopatra's Bath**, a hollow rock whirlpool bath where she and Mark Antony reputedly frolicked. Outside of the bath, heavy surf and sharp, slippery rocks make this a bad place to swim. The road to these beaches is a continuation of the Corniche, which turns south at the end of Lido Beach and then winds westwards.

Ubayyad Beach

Twenty kilometres out of town the sands have disgorged a tiny **ruined temple-fort** dedicated to Ramses II by his general Nebre. **Zawiyat Umm al-Rukham** (its local name) isn't signposted on the coastal road, and can really only be reached by private taxi or a long walk from **Ubayyad Beach**, farther west. Probably the finest expanse of beach in Egypt, Ubayyad hosts the *Badr Camp* (see opposite), a sterile conglomerate of A/C double rooms (no baths) and beachside tents favoured by middle-class Egyptians.

Agiiba Beach

From the next headland, 28km west of town, a path slopes down to **Agiiba Beach**. Agiiba ("miracle of nature") is an apt name for this stunningly beautiful cove, but "beach" is rather a misnomer. To swim in the calm, crystal-clear turquoise water you have to dive off rocky shelves protruding into the sea, for the beach itself is gunged up with algae.

From July onwards it's necessary to walk around the headlands and along the shore to find uncrowded sites. Bring food and drink as there's no guarantee of stalls operating on the clifftop, which overhangs some caves.

Food and other practicalities

Matrouh is not exactly a metropolis, but it has a fair spread of restaurants and most services that you might want to make use of.

Restaurants

Hani el-Onda, Sharia Tahrir. This dimly-lit café offers a real bargain – three meals for £E6. Breakfast consists of *fuul*, eggs, bread and jam; lunch is macaroni, chicken, salad and a desert; while supper features meat and beans, bread and cheese.

Alexandria Tourist Restaurant, nearer to the Corniche. Another cheapie, charging £E4–5 for meals or packed lunches.

Restaurant Panayotis, opposite. Excellent Greek salads and the cheapest beer in town,

Mansour Fish Restaurant, past the *Mina House Hotel*. Popular with trendy young Egyptians, who can watch videos over their fish and salad (£E5–6).

Anji Restaurant, Sharia Cleopatra. Decent food and an okay environment for solo women.

Hotel Riviera Palace, **Hotel Beau Site**. The two swanky options for a set dinner and smooth service, respectively £E13 and E£16. No alcohol at the former.

Discos

The *Beau Site* also hosts the better of Matrouh's two **discos**; the other, the *Disco 54* at the Radi Hotel, 700m west along the Corniche, doesn't get going until well into the tourist season, like the nightclubs in other three-star hotels.

Practicalities

You'll find the **post office** (daily 9am–3pm), **police** station and 24-hour **telephone exchange** on the street running off beside a small park. Should you need to register, use the **passport office** two blocks south of Sharia Cleopatra.

Matrouh's **hospital**, near the railway station at the top of Sharia Iskandariya, is relatively ill-equipped, so it's advisable to fly to Cairo for treatment if possible. For less serious ailments, visit the *M.M.* **pharmacy** south of the *Riviera Palace Hotel* (daily 9am–2pm & 5pm–midnight).

The *Banque du Caire* (daily 8.30am–2.30pm & 6–9pm) and other **banks** (daily 9am–2pm & 6–8pm) west of **EgyptAir** can all change traveller's cheques, as can some three-star hotels.

South to Siwa Oasis

Many travellers come to Matrouh simply **to visit Siwa Oasis**, deep in the Western Desert, which is famed for its strange customs, beautiful pools and legendary antiquities (see p.434). The once hazardous journey has become relatively easy since the mid-1980s, when a new road was completed, buses from Matrouh were introduced and the rule that all visitors had to have a military escort was abolished – although travellers still require permission to visit this strategically sensitive zone near the Libyan border.

Getting permission is quite straightforward, starting with the copying of your passport. In Matrouh, both the kiosk near the tourist office and the Kodak shop on the main street know which pages need photocopying. Next, take the photocopy and original to the barracks at the end of Sharia Gallai and knock on the steel gates. If Military Intelligence is working (officially 8am–2pm & 8–11pm), you should get shown into the guardhouse and receive your free permit within fifteen minutes; otherwise you'll be told to come back later. Permits are valid for a specified number of days (which can't be extended in Siwa), so it's worth asking for a week even if you're planning to leave the oasis sooner. You'll need to give your permit to the driver to show at checkpoints along the way.

There are one or two **buses** to Siwa daily. A non-A/C bus leaves Matrouh every morning at 7am (£E5). Three times a week (Sat, Mon & Wed) there is also an A/C service which originates in Alexandria, passing through Matrouh around 3pm (£E8), by which stage there may be standing room only. The journey takes around five hours, or slightly less if you catch one of the **service taxis** (£E6) which leave during the morning and afternoon (until 4–5pm) to avoid travelling in the midday heat. Besides doing likewise, **motorists** should fill up in Matrouh since there are no petrol pumps along the 300km route. The Siwa road is reached by following the Corniche west out of town, turning inland and passing the airport turn-off, and then heading south at the next junction.

Remember to **change money** before you set out, as Siwa has no bank.

West of Matrouh: the road to Libya

The **road to Libya** reflects relations between the Arab Republic of Egypt and the Libyan *Jamahiriyah* (State of the Masses). During the 1960s, when Gadaffi regarded Nasser's Egypt as the vanguard of revolutionary Arab nationalism, people and goods flowed both ways, encouraging the Libyan leader to propose that the two countries unite in 1973 – an ambition that came to nought as President Sadat cultivated the Western powers and finally signed a peace treaty with Israel. In response, Libya severed relations, closed the border and began agitating for the overthrow of the Egyptian government; a cold war ensued, with sporadic incursions by Libyan warplanes and saboteurs during the 1980s.

It wasn't until the end of the 1980s that relations were restored and the border was reopened. Despite an upturn in civilian traffic there's still an overwhelming military presence along the 150km to SIDI BARRANI – a small port (resthouse; petrol) bitterly contested during the Western Desert campaign – and the 70km to SOLLUM, whence it's 10km to the actual border crossing.

Although Egyptians and Libyans cross over regularly, tourists have yet to discover the attraction. Libya certainly presents little opportunity for an impulse visit, as advance **visas** must be obtained from a Libyan Consulate abroad (if the one in Cairo hasn't reopened). UK citizens are allowed into Libya even though the two countries have no diplomatic relations; US citizens are forbidden to travel there by their own government. A rare account of visiting Libya as a tourist appears in Eric Newby's *On the Shores of the Mediterranean*.

CHAPTER FIVE

THE DELTA

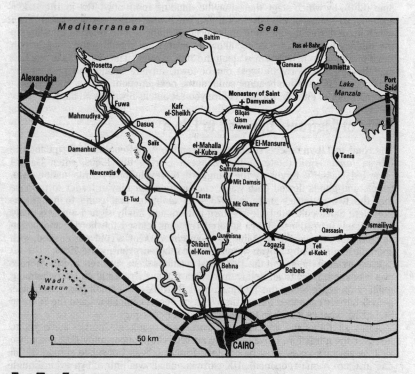

W hile the Nile Valley's place in ancient Egypt remains writ large in extraordinary monuments, the **Nile Delta**'s role has largely been effaced by time and other factors. Although several pharaonic dynasties arose and ruled from this region – Lower Egypt – little of their twenty provincial capitals remains beyond mounds of debris, known as *tell* or *kom*. The pharaohs themselves set the precedent of plundering older sites of their sculptures and masonry – hard stone had to be brought to the Delta from distant quarries, so it was easier to recycle existing stocks – and nature performed the rest. With a yearly rainfall of nearly 20cm (the highest in Egypt, most of it during winter) and an annual inundation by the Nile which coated the land in silt, mudbrick structures were soon eroded or swept away. More recently, *sebakheen* have furthered the cycle of destruction by digging the mounds for a nitrate-enriched soil called *sebakh*, used for fertiliser; several sites catalogued by nineteenth-century archaeologists have all but vanished since then.

Of the Delta's show of ancient monuments, the spooky **Cat Cemetery of Bubastis** near Zagazig makes the best pharaonic site, and if you had to pick a runner-up, it would be the ruins of **Tanis** in the eastern Delta. As for Islamic architecture, there's a sprinkling of "Delta Style" mansions and medieval mosques in the coastal towns of **Rosetta** and **Damietta**.

Practically everywhere else on the map is an industrialised beehive or a teeming village, only worth visiting for **moulids** or popular festivals, of which the region has, literally, dozens. Combining piety, fun and commerce, the largest events draw crowds of over 1,000,000, with companies of *mawladiya* running stalls and rides while the Sufi *tariqas* perform their *zikrs*. People camp outdoors and music blares into the small hours. Smaller, rural *moulids* tend to be heavier on the practical devotion, with people bringing their children or livestock for blessing, or the sick to be cured.

The great **Moulid of Saiyid el-Bedawi**, held at **Tanta** just after the cotton harvest in October, starts a cycle of **Muslim** festivals lasting well into November. At one- to two-week intervals, pilgrims and revellers congregate for week-long bashes at **Basyouni**, **Dasuq**, **Mahmudiya**, **Fuwa** and **Rosetta**. The Muslim month of Shawwal (following Ramadan) also occasions *moulids* at **Bilbeis** and **Zagazig**. During May, the remote **Monastery of Saint Damyanah** witnesses one of Egypt's largest **Christian moulids** and, come August, another event transpires at the village of **Mit Damsis**. In January a unique **Jewish moulid** takes place at **Damanhur**.

The Delta's other possible attraction is its flat, intensely green **landscape**, riven by waterways where *feluccas* glide past mudbrick villages and wallowing buffaloes. The northern **lakes** are a wintering ground for herons, storks, great crested grebes and other water birds, while doves and pigeons – reared for human consumption in cotes shaped like Khmer temples – join other **bird life** pecking around the cotton, rice and cornfields. In ancient times, wealthy Egyptians enjoyed going fowling in the reeds, using throwing sticks and hunting cats; their modern-day counterparts employ shotguns. The Delta is also still a habitat for wildcats and Pygmy white-toothed shrews, but boars have been driven out and the last hippopotamus was shot in 1815.

More sombrely for the ecology, the Delta is one of the world regions most vulnerable to the effects of **global warming**. Oceanographers predict that a two- to three-metre rise in the sea level would swamp Alexandria and submerge the Delta as far inland as Damanhur, destroying about one fifth of Egypt's cultivable land and rendering one in six of the population homeless. The freshwater Delta lagoons, which provide much of the nation's fish catch, would also be ruined.

Practicalities

As few visitors have the time for more than one *moulid* or site, we've dealt with the region in less detail than other parts of Egypt. Depending on where you're aiming for, it might be better to start from Alex, Cairo or the Canal Zone; in any case, a shortage of local **accommodation** makes day trips more feasible than overnight stays.

Trains are okay for reaching major towns, but *service* taxis and buses are the best way of **getting around**. Renting a car isn't necessarily a good idea: it's easy to have accidents on the Delta roads, and the minor ones are legally off-limits to foreign drivers – a hangover from Sixties spy-phobia. Should the police decide to make a fuss, you could conceivably spend a night in jail.

Rosetta, Damanhur and the Western Delta

The broader Rosetta branch of the Nile delineates one edge of the **Western Delta**, whose other flank fades into desert. Its cottonfields and mill towns are quite visible enough from the Delta Road or the Cairo–Alexandria railway, and few places merit closer inspection. **Rosetta** makes a nice day excursion from Alex and **Damanhur** hosts two remarkable *moulids*, but you have to be pretty keen on archaeology to bother with the *koms* off the Tanta road.

All telephone numbers in the Rosetta/Damanhur area are prefixed ☎045.

Rosetta (Rashid)

The coastal town of **ROSETTA** has waxed and waned in counterpoint to the fortunes of Alexandria, 65km away. When Alex was moribund, Rosetta burgeoned as a port, entering its heyday after the Ottoman conquest of Egypt in the sixteenth century, only to decline after Alexandria's revival. The modern-day town is still "surrounded by groves of orange and lemon trees", as Eliza Fay wrote home in 1817, but its "appearance of cleanliness . . . gratifying to the English eye" has dissipated and these days few tourists come to wander through its run-down, littered streets in search of once-elegant Ottoman mansions. It's certainly a far cry from the early nineteenth century, when E.D. Clarke saw "English ladies from the fleet and the army" wearing "long white dresses", riding "the asses of the country".

This earlier European fascination owed to the discovery of the **Rosetta Stone** by French soldiers in 1799. Their officer realised the significance of this second-century BC basalt slab inscribed with ancient hieroglyphs, demotic Egyptian and Greek script, which was forwarded to Napoleon's savants in Cairo. Although their archaeological booty had to be surrendered in 1801 – which is how the Stone, "Alexander's Sarcophagus" and many other objects wound up in the British Museum – it was a French professor, Jean-François Champollion (1790–1832), who finally deciphered the hieroglyphs by comparison with the Greek text, and unlocked the secret of the ancient Egyptian tongue.

Around the town

Rosetta's main appeal lies in its **"Delta Style" architecture**. The Delta hallmarks are pointed brickwork (usually emphasised by white or red paint), inset beams and carved lintels, and a profusion of *mashrabiya*-work. Some of the mansions also incorporate ancient columns. Here, the finest examples lie on, or just off, the main street running parallel to the river, with the railway station at its northern end. Starting from the bus and taxi depot, you can find this by walking past the nearest mosque and taking the second turning on your left. The first house worth investigating stands on the left, 200m ahead, bearing a blue sign in Arabic. It's now a workshop for producing and restoring *mashrabiyas*, but the craftsmen don't mind visitors.

For a better idea of how the Ottomans lived, visit the **Beit al-Amasyali**, 50m further on, straddling a corner. A superb wooden ceiling and mother-of-pearl-inlaid *mashrabiyas* ennoble the reception room upstairs. Downstairs you'll find the Abu Shahim Mill, with its huge wooden grinders and delicately pointed keyhole arches. Both were built around 1808 for the Turkish Agha, Ali al-Topgi, who bequeathed them to his servant al-Amasyali. The curator can point you towards the eighteenth-century **Beit Qili**, and the century-older **Beit Ali al-Fatairi**. By bringing food and taking a taxi-boat from the dock, you can enjoy a picnic at the tranquil **Mosque of Abu Mandar**, 5km upriver.

Roundabout mid-November, the chain of festivals which started in Tanta the previous month should reach Rosetta. Don't despair if you come a few weeks earlier, since similar **moulids** occur at Fuwa, Mahmudiya and Dasuq, further inland. Salted fish (*fisikh*) and *humous* are the traditional snacks at these events.

Transport

A **service taxi** (1hr; £E2) or bus (90min; 75pt) from Alexandria's Gumhorriya Square is the quickest way to reach Rosetta. **Trains** are slower, though you might find them useful for reaching Fuwa and Dasuq (on the Tanta line), or Mahmudiya (on the Damanhur branch), in order to attend their *moulids*. But *service* taxis provide the widest choice of destinations. Most Delta towns are within a couple of hours' ride; to Cairo takes an hour longer. To find a *service* taxi from Cairo to Rosetta, ask around Ahmed Helmi Square, behind Ramses Station.

There is no accommodation in Rosetta.

Damanhur

Most of the land between Alex and Tanta is given over to **cotton**, Egypt's major cash crop, whose intensive cultivation began under Mohammed Ali. His French hydro-engineer's scheme to regulate the flood waters by means of barrages across the Rosetta and Damietta branches of the Nile was ultimately realised by Sir Colin Scott-Moncrief in 1880–90. The shift from flood to perennial irrigation enabled three or four crops a year to be grown in the Delta, as is still the case.

Hardly surprising, then, that local towns are heavily into textiles; particularly the Beheira Governorate capital, **DAMANHUR**, once *Tmn-Hor*, the City of Horus. Although much of it is drably functional, this city of 170,000 people gains a dash of colour from green-shuttered houses and bougainvillea-laden archways, and blossoms during its festival.

Turbaned Sufis perform *zikrs* and *munshids* to enthusiastic crowds during Damanhur's **Moulid of Sheikh Abu Rish**. This occurs a week or so after the festival at Dasuq, across the river (and directly accessible from here by bus or *service* taxi). With venues so close together, the *mawladiya* (*moulid* people) can easily move on to the next event; barbers, circumcisers and all.

Egypt's only **Jewish moulid**, held over two days in January, is a very different scene. The shrine of **Abu Khatzeira** (Father of the Mat), a nineteenth-century mystic, is cordoned off by security police who rigorously exclude non-Jewish Egyptians, fearing a terrorist attack. Within the cordon a few thousand mostly French or Israeli visitors bring sick relatives or bottled water to be blessed, and "bid" for the key to Abu Khatzeira's shrine; the money raised supports its upkeep.

Between Damanhur and Tanta

A couple of **ancient sites** reduced to *kom* lie off the road **between Damanhur and Tanta** (64km). Roughly 23km out of Damanhur, a track leads 3km left off the main road to the village of EL-NIBEIRAH, near two low mounds marking the site of **NAUCRATIS**. During the XXVI Dynasty, when Egypt was ruled from the Delta, King Amasis (570–26 BC) granted it a monopoly of trade between Egypt and Greece. Excavating the site for the British Museum in the nineteenth century, Flinders Petrie found it littered with shards of Greek pottery, and imagined that he was "wandering in the smashings of the Museum's vase-room".

At ITAI EL-BAROUD, the last town before crossing the Rosetta branch of the Nile, another turn-off runs 14km south to EL-TUD, by the "Mound of the Fort", *Kom el-Hisn*. This used to be **IMAOU**, which became the capital of the Third Nome during the New Kingdom, and was turned into a necropolis by the Hyksos pharaohs. A temple enclosure and numerous tombs are still evident.

Tanta and the Central Delta

Tanta, Egypt's fifth largest city, hosts the country's greatest *moulid*, which is worth experiencing for at least a day. The city also serves as a jumping-off point for practically everywhere else in the **Central Delta**. Depending on your bent, there are several other *moulids* and a host of ancient sites scattered around the region. With regular trains and service taxis to Alex (a roughly 2hr-journey) and Cairo (1hr–90min) running from early morning till nigh on midnight, you don't have to stay in Tanta; indeed, you'd be lucky to find a vacant room while the *moulid*'s on. Elsewhere, tourist accommodation is virtually non-existent anyway. Because the northwestern corner of this part of the Delta is easier to reach from Damietta or Mansura, we've allocated sites there to the "Eastern Delta" section.

Numbers in the **Tanta** area are prefixed ☎040; those around **Kafr el-Sheikh** ☎047.

Tanta

A bustling city with strong rural ties, **TANTA** marks the end of the cotton harvest in October with Egypt's largest festival, the **Moulid of Saiyid Ahmed el-Bedawi**. Tanta's population jumps from 230,000 to well over two million as visitors pour in from the Delta villages, other parts of Egypt and the Arab world. Streets and squares fill with *sewans* and stalls; Sufis prepare for *zikrs* while musicians test their amps ("Allah, two, three"). Thousands camp out amidst heaps of blankets and cooking pots, though sleep seems impossible. Music and chanting, vendors and devotees, a circus with lions and tigers and a levitation act – Tanta becomes a seething cacophony.

The *moulid* honours the founder of one of Egypt's largest Sufi brotherhoods. Born in Fes in Morocco in 1199, **Saiyid Ahmed el-Bedawi** was sent to Tanta in 1234 by the Iraqi Rifaiyah order, and later established his own *tariqa* (brotherhood), the Ahmediya. His name is invoked to ward off calamity – *"Ya saiyid, ya Bedawi!"* – but his *moulid* is anything but angst-ridden. "Although a religious festival, pleasure is the chief object of the pilgrims, and a few *fatahs* at the tomb of the saint are sufficient to satisfy every pious requirement", noted *Murray's Handbook* in 1891. The climax to the eight-day festival occurs on a Friday, when the Ahmediya – whose banners and turbans are red – parade with drums behind their mounted sheikh. Events focus on the triple-domed, Ottoman-style **mosque** wherein Bedawi and a lesser sheikh, Abd el-Al, are buried.

Should you wish **to stay** during the *moulid* (or other festivals in the vicinity – see below), book a room in the three-star *Hotel Arafa* (☎26-952) outside the railway station as far in advance as possible. Tanta's **service taxi** depot is the place to ask about rides to wherever you hope to go.

Sites around Tanta

Some of the places below – **moulid venues** and **ancient sites** – are directly accessible from Tanta; to reach others you might have to change once or twice. For the committed, hiring a **taxi** privately gives the greatest scope for excursions.

Two moulids: Dasuq and Fuwa

A week or so after Tanta's festival, the agricultural town of **DASUQ** holds the **Moulid of Ibrahim al-Dasuqi**, drawing almost as many people. Al-Dasuqi (1246–88) was the only native-born Egyptian to found a major Sufi order, the Burhamiya (whose chosen colour is green): the other brotherhoods originated abroad, or were started here by foreigners.

Should you decide to attend the eight-day event, Dasuq is probably easiest to reach from Damanhur by bus or *service* taxi. Coming from Tanta or Rosetta you could either take a slow stopping train, or catch a *service* taxi, changing at KAFR EL-SHEIKH if necessary. Most trains also call at **FUWA**, 13km from Dasuq, where another **festival** occurs in late October or early November.

Buto and Xois

Only those with private transport and a consuming passion for **ancient sites** will bother trying to reach **Tell al-Faraoun** (Mound of the Pharaoh), on the edge of some marshes north of IBTU village, itself 5km north off the Dasuq–Kafr el Sheikh road. The site appears on maps as **Buto**, the Greek name for a dual city known to the ancient Egyptians as *Pr Wadjet*. **Wadjet**, the Cobra Goddess of Lower Egypt (whom the Greeks called Buto) was worshipped in the half known as Dep. The other city, known as **Pe**, was dedicated to the Djbut, the Heron God, who was later supplanted by Horus. Nothwithstanding all this, the 180-acre site had been obliterated down to its paving stones by the time Petrie excavated it.

Should you carry on to **KAFR EL-SHEIKH** (*Hotel Salam*) and follow the Tanta road south, you'll pass the village of SAKHA, occupying the site of **Xois**, ancient capital of the Sixth Nome.

Saïs

Nothing but a few pits filled with stagnant water remains of the once great city of Saïs, near the modern village of SA EL-HAGAR, beside the Rosetta branch of the Nile. Founded at the dawn of Egyptian history, it was always associated with the Goddess of War and Hunting, **Neith**, whose cult emblem appeared on Pre-Dynastic objects. In Egyptian cosmology, she was also the protectress of embalmed bodies; the Greeks identified her with Athena.

The city became Egypt's capital during the **Saïte Period**, when the XXVI Dynasty (664–525 BC) looked back to the Old Kingdom for inspiration, refurbishing the Pyramid tombs and reviving archaic funerary rituals. In 525 BC the Dynasty was overthrown by the Persian emperor Cambyses, who's said to have had the body of the penultimate Saïte king, Amasis "the Drunkard", removed from its tomb, whipped and burnt.

El-Mahalla el-Kubra and Sammanud

EL-MAHALLA EL-KUBRA, 24km northeast of Tanta, is Egypt's fourth largest city (**hotel** *Omar Khayyam* on 23rd July Square), and a taxi staging-post for journeys to the riverside town – almost a suburb, these days – of **SAMMANUD**.

Immediately west of the Sammanud taxi depot, near the hospital, a large mound and a scattering of red and black granite blocks marks the site of the **Temple of Onuris-Shu**, rebuilt by Nectanebo II to grace **Tjeboutjes**, the capital of the Twelfth Nome. Another city, **Busiris**, occupied a bluff overlooking the river further south, along the road out of Sammanud. Part of an XXVI Dynasty basalt statue and fragments of a monumental gateway, however, are all that remain of this reputed birthplace of Osiris.

The H8 road, which runs northeast from Sammanud to Talkha, takes one past the site of ancient **Pr-Hebeit**, 10km to the west, better known by its Roman name, **Iseum**. Here, the great **Temple of Isis** which Nectanebo began and Ptolemy II completed has been reduced to an enclosure wall, some carved granite blocks and Hathor-headed capitals. From Talkha, you can easily cross the river to Mansura (see overpage).

Sadat's birthplace

As a footnote to bygone rulers, it's worth mentioning (but not visiting) the village of MIT ABU EL-KOM, near the small town of Quweisna to the south of Tanta, as the **birthplace of Anwar el-Sadat**. Born in 1908, he escaped rural life by joining the army, became a nationalist and conspired with like-minded officers to overthrow King Farouk. As Nasser's heir, President Sadat waged war against, and then signed a peace treaty with Israel; opened Egypt to Western capitalism, generating a consumer boom and massive corruption; and was finally assassinated by Islamic fundamentalists in 1981.

The Eastern Delta

The **Eastern Delta** scores on several counts. **Bubastis** and **Tanis** are the best **pharaonic ruins** that Lower Egypt can offer; there are **moulids** aplenty, both Christian and Muslim; and if you include places on the Central Delta coast which are easier to reach from here, then the region can also boast three low-key **beach resorts** and some fine **bird-watching**.

For some of these destinations it might be simpler to approach the Eastern Delta from Port Said or Ismailiya in the Canal Zone than from Alex.

> Phone prefixes in the **Eastern Delta** area are:
> **Zagazig** ☎055; **Behna** ☎013; **Mansura** ☎050; **Damietta** ☎057.

Zagazig and the ruins of Bubastis

Aside from its delightful name, **ZAGAZIG** has the merit of being highly accessible. You can travel the 80km from **Cairo** by *service* taxi from Ahmed Helmi Square (1hr; £E1.50); regular buses from Koulali Square (£E1.25); or any Port Said-bound train (80min). *Service* taxis from the other major **Delta towns**

and Alexandria also run to Zagazig, and there are hourly bus links with **Ismaliya**.

Only founded in 1830, Zagazig was the birthplace of Colonel Ahmed Orabi (1839–1911), leader of the 1882 revolt against British rule, and has since become the capital of the Sharqiya Governorate. Its **Moulid of Abu Khalil**, on the square outside the central mosque (held sometime during the month of Shawwal), is one reason to pay a visit. But the main attraction is undoubtedly the ruins of Bubastis, to the southeast of town. Before heading out there, you might want to browse through the archaeological exhibits in the small **Orabi Museum** (9am–1pm; closed Tues).

Bubastis

Situated on an area of wasteland between Sharia Mustapha Kamal and the Bilbeis road (*service* taxis can drop you off), the ruins of **Bubastis** recall a site known to the ancient Egyptians as *Pr Bastet* (House of Bastet), a city dedicated to the Cat Goddess, in whose honour licentious festivals were held. Pilgrims sailed to Bubastis in high spirits, saluting riverside towns with music, abuse and exposed loins. In the fifth century BC, Herodotus noted that 700,000 revellers consumed more wine than "during the whole of the rest of the year", and described how the city lay on raised ground encircling a canal-girt temple, "the most pleasing to look at" in all of Egypt.

Begun by the VI Dynasty pyramid-builders, Bubastis was enlarged and embellished with items removed from other sites for over 1700 years, leaving a chronological puzzle for Naville to solve when he excavated Bubastis in 1887–89. Little remains of the city but a *kom* and scattered blocks, but 200m down the road you can explore the twisting passages of an underground **Cat Cemetery** which has yielded dozens of lovely bronze statues of Bastet.

BASTET THE CAT GODDESS

The feline goddess **Bastet** was originally depicted as a lioness, her head surmounted by a solar disc and *uraeus* serpent. As the daughter of Re, she was associated with the destructive force of the sun-god's eye. This aggressive side of Bastet can be seen in texts and reliefs describing the pharaoh in battle. Her epithet, "Lady of Asheru", also linked her to the goddess Mut at Karnak, where temple reliefs show the pharaoh running ritual races in front of Bastet.

After about 1000 BC, however, this side of Bastet became subsumed by Sekhmet (see p.309), and the goddess herself was portrayed more commonly as a cat, often with a brood of kittens, and carrying a sacred rattle. The Coffin Texts of the Middle Kingdom frequently invoke her protection as the first-born daughter of Atum (another aspect of the sun-god). In return, the Egyptians venerated cats and mummified them at several sites, including Bubastis and Memphis.

The Greeks later identified Bastet with Artemis, the Virgin huntress, who was believed to be able to transform herself into a cat.

Bilbeis and Behna

To the south and southwest of Zagazig a couple of rather minor towns are worth a passing mention – and perhaps a visit.

BILBEIS, 10km away by road or rail, hosts a couple of festivals during Shawwal: its **moulids** of Abu Isa and Abu Alwan predate Abu Khalil's in Zagazig.

Further west, beside the Damietta branch of the Nile, **BEHNA** (on the Cairo–Alex main line; half-hourly buses to Cairo between 6am and 9pm) is near another ancient site. To the northeast of town, 150m off the road, *Kom el-Atrib* is what remains of **Athribis**, once the capital of the Tenth Nome. This was the birthplace of Psammetichus I (664–610 BC), who restored pharaonic authority over Upper and Lower Egypt, replacing the so-called *Dodekarchy* with centralised government by the Saïte dynasty.

Tanis and the "Land of Goshen"

Early archaeologists were drawn to the eastern marches of the Delta in search of clues to the Israelites' Biblical sojourn, but what they found proved more important to knowledge of ancient Egypt. Fragmented statues and stelae, papyrus texts and layers of debris have shed light on dynastic chronologies and religious cults, the movement of Delta waterways and imperial borders, invasions and famines.

Tanis (San el-Hagar)

One of the oldest, most revealing sites was a huge *kom* near the village of SAN EL-HAGAR, 167km northeast of Zagazig. Barring a stint by Petrie, the excavation has mostly been in French hands since the 1860s. Although best known by its Greek name, **TANIS**, the city dated back to the Old Kingdom, when it stood beside the Tanite branch of the Nile, which has long since dried up.

Several dynasties are associated with Tanis. It was around here that Asiatic settlers carved out their own state and went on to create the XV Dynasty (1674–1567 BC) of **Hyksos kings**. (Hyksos derives from *hekatu-khasut*, meaning "princes of foreign lands".) Their capital, *Avaris*, was assumed to be Tanis renamed; but postwar archaeologists located it further south, at Tell el-Daba. Long after Ahmose expelled the Hyksos, Tanis was the birthplace of another formidable dynasty, the **Ramessids**. Ramses I was a local prince made good, while his successor, Ramses II (1304–1237 BC), the man responsible for some of the most monumental Nile Valley pyramids, also founded a new royal city, *Pi-Ramses*, filled with plundered statuary. (This, too, was later conflated with Tanis, but is now located 25km further south, near QANTIR: there's not a lot to see there).

The Tanis **site**, reached by turning off before San el-Hagar, is more extensive if not immediately illuminating. It looks as if the huge Ramessid **Temple of Amun** was shattered by a giant's hammer, scattering chunks of masonry and fragments of statues everywhere. Some predate the Hyksos, who carved their own cartouches upon them; others were brought here from distant sites by the XXI Dynasty kings – testing the wits of archaeologists, who are still investigating a royal necropolis (officially closed, but you might get a look by pleading).

Unfortunately, **getting to San el-Hagar** entails a four-hour taxi ride from Zagazig, with no certainty of a lift back unless you fix things with the driver. San el-Hagar has nowhere to eat or stay, even if one wanted to. Between 8.30am and 6pm, there are regular buses between FAQUS and Cairo.

The "Land of Goshen"

Travelling the 80km **between Zagazig and Ismailiya** (see *The Canal Zone*) via Wadi Tumaylat (hourly buses), you pass a couple more sites of historic significance.

It was at **Tell el-Kebir**, 7km east of Zagazig, that Orabi's forces were finally defeated by the British in September 1882. In the 1920s, the government sponsored a reforestation project in what was then virgin desert, and now supports timber plantations and orchards.

Another *kom*, visible south of the road 13km beyond Qassasin, is **Tell el-Maskhuta** – site of the capital of the Eighth Nome, known to posterity by its Biblical name, *Pithom*. Edouard Naville, who first excavated the mound in 1883, reckoned it was the other city of the Exodus, *Raamses*, which Montet later (wrongly) identified as Tanis. Both lay within the **"Land of Goshen"** where the Israelites toiled for the pharaoh before Moses led them out of Egypt. Petrie was amongst those who shrewdly plugged the Biblical connection to raise money for digs with other aims, particularly at Tanis. Some intact burial chambers were discovered at Tell el-Maskhuta as recently as 1978, but everything of interest has been removed from the site.

Mit Damsis and el-Mansura

Trains and inter-city buses take the shortest route **between Zagazig and el-Mansura**, and for most of the year that's a sensible option. In August, however, you might consider the alternative Mit Ghamr–Aga road in order to visit **Mit Damsis** village near the Damietta branch of the Nile, site of the Coptic **Moulid of Saint George**.

Mit Damsis: the Moulid

The **Moulid of Saint George** (Aug 2–28) is notable primarily for its **exorcisms**. Copts attribute demonic possession to improper baptism or deliberate curses, and specially trained priests bully and coax the *afrit* to leave through its victim's fingers or toes rather than via the eyes, which is believed to cause blindness.

Egyptian Muslims likewise believe in possession, but don't always regard it as malign; in some cases they try to harmonise the relationship between the spirit and its human host rather than terminate it. Egyptians of both faiths take precautions against the Evil Eye. Christians put store in pictures of Saint George and the Virgin, while Muslims display the Hand of Fatima – literally hand-printed on the walls of dwellings – and perhaps the legend, *B'ismallah, masha' Allah* ("In the name of God, whatever God wills").

Because the **moulid** is well attended there's a fair chance of lifts along the seven kilometre-long track that turns west off the main road, 15km south of Aga. MIT DAMSIS rarely appears on maps; don't confuse it with Damas, which does.

El-Mansura

EL-MANSURA was founded as the camp of Sultan al-Kamil's army during the 1218–21 siege of Damietta, though its name ("The Victorious") was a premature boast, since the Crusaders reoccupied Damietta in 1247. Weakened by cancer and tuberculosis, Sultan Ayyub was unable to dislodge them, and died here in 1249 – a fact concealed by his widow, Shagar al-Durr, who issued orders in Ayyub's name, buying time until his heir could return from Iraq. Encouraged by the Mamlukes' withdrawal, Louis IX led a sortie against the enemy camp, slaying their general in his bath. But with victory in sight, the Crusaders fell sick after eating corpse-fed fish, just before a devastating counterattack launched by Beybars the Crossbowman. Louis was captured and ransomed for Damietta's return, and later met a similar fate on his Tunisian crusade.

The medieval **Beit Luqman** where Louis was imprisoned still stands near the Mwafi Mosque, but most of today's el-Mansura is modern, with tree-lined avenues, a university, and a central mosque whose twin minarets are visible from far away. For outsiders, the town's most interesting feature is delicious buffalo-milk ice cream.

Buses run between Cairo and Mansura every quarter of an hour from 6am to 8pm (£E2), as do **service taxis** (£E3). These also link Mansura with Zagazig and Damietta, plus a number of sites in the Central Delta beyond the west bank suburb of TALKHA. Mansura proper has a few simple **hotels**; try asking for directions to the *Hotel Cleopatra* (☎67-89).

The Monastery and Moulid of Saint Damyanah

Normally hard to reach without private transport, the **Monastery of Saint Damyanah** becomes accessible during its namesake's **Moulid** (May 15–20), when *service* taxis and hired buses convey pilgrims across to BILQAS QISIM AWWAL, whence it's 3km by track to *Deir Sitt Damyanah*.

The monastery – whose four churches date from the nineteenth and twentieth centuries – is, in fact, rather less interesting than **Damyanah's story** and her **festival**, which is one of the largest Christian *moulids* in Egypt. The daughter of a Roman governor under Diocletian, she refused to marry and insisted that her father build a palace into which she and forty other virgins could retire. All refused to worship Roman gods, and their example eventually converted her father – enraging Diocletian, who had the lot of them executed.

As with the Church of Saint George at Mit Damsis, Copts ascribe the building of Damyanah's shrine to Saint Helena, the mother of the Roman emperor Constantine. Pilgrims bring sick relatives (or livestock) to be blessed, and believe that Damyanah manifests herself at night as a pigeon, which can be distinguished from other birds by the trajectory of its flight. Icons and special pottery (inscribed "Happy returns, Damyanah") are popular buys at the fair, where Muslim tattoo-ists do a brisk trade in Saint George, Christ Crucified, snakes, birds and other motifs, which punters select from display boards.

Damietta (Dumyat)

Sited near the mouth of the eastern branch of the Nile, the port city of **DAMIETTA** became prosperous in medieval times, through its trade in coffee, linen, dates and oil. However, it was always wide open to seaborne invasions and was seized by the Crusaders in 1167–68 and 1218–21, on the latter occasion accompanied by Saint Francis of Assisi – who ignorantly imagined that the Sultan al-Kamil knew nothing of Christianity, although he numbered Copts amongst his advisors. The main function of the Crusaders in Egypt, however, was pillage and Damietta suffered heavily during its occupations. When Louis "the Pious" returned with a further crew in 1247, the inhabitants fled or deliberately sold the Crusaders putrid fish – one cause of their defeat at el-Mansura (see above).

Unfortunately, Damietta suffered a far worse attack under the Mamlukes, who razed the town and rendered its river impassable as a punishment for suspected disloyalty and a precaution against future invasions.

It was the Ottomans who revived the town and built **Delta Style mansions** of the kind found in Rosetta; their last Pasha surrendered to the Beys here just before the rise of Mohammed Ali. With the opening of the Suez Canal, Damietta had to reorient its trade towards Port Said, 70km away. Nowadays it's a thriving port city of 120,000 inhabitants, with the status of a provincial capital.

Having said that, there's little call to come here unless you're mad on Delta architecture, or into bird-watching or beachcombing. If so, the Nile-side Corniche is where to find the modest *Al Shatt* (☎80-29), *Al Mogarbel* (☎23-51) and *New Cecil* (☎28-10) **hotels**. As for **transport**, Damietta is linked by rail to Tanta, Zagazig, Alex and Cairo; and by hourly buses (6am–5pm; £E3) or *service* taxis (£E4) to Cairo. Closer at hand are Port Said (30min drive along the causeway between Lake Manzala and the Med) and the beach resorts of the Central Delta.

Lake Manzala

East of Damietta lies **Lake Manzala**, a great place for **bird-watching** if you can find a boatman to take you through the reeds. Nineteenth-century European visitors tended to be more interested in shooting wildfowl than observing it. "Their compact mass formed living islands upon the water; and when the wind took me to these, a whole island rose up with a loud and thrilling din to become a feathered cloud in the air", wrote one hunter.

Winter is the best time to see herons (*balashon* to locals), spoonbills (*midwas*), pelicans (*begga*) and flamingoes (*basharus*). Along the Nile, these last are called "water camels" (*gamal el-bahr*).

Three Delta resorts

Ranged along the coast of the Central Delta are three beach resorts popular with middle-class Egyptians: **Ras el-Bahr**, **Gamasa** and **Baltim**. During summer, they can be reached by special A/C buses from Cairo's Koulali bus station, and probably by *service* taxi from Ramses or Ahmed Helmi squares. Buses and taxis from Damietta are another option, at least to Ras el-Bahr or Gamasa.

Ras el-Bahr and Gamasa

RAS EL-BAHR, where the eastern branch of the Nile flows into the Med north of Damietta, is a pleasant beach resort with several **hotels** and restaurants. Try *Abou Tabl* (4 Sharia 17), *Marine Fouad* (☎81-75), *Marine el-Nil* (☎80-06) or *Marine Ras el-Bar*. Buses leave Cairo at 7.15am, 9.15am, 1.15pm, 3pm and 5pm during the summer; the three-and-a-half-hour journey costs £E3.50.

Between 8am and 3pm, there are also regular bus services (£E3.50) to **GAMASA**, further down the coast, which has simple cabin-type hotels: the *Marine Fuad al-Nil* and *al-Malek*, *At Home* and *Al-Shatt*.

Baltim

The last resort, **BALTIM**, is actually halfway to Rosetta, but only accessible from there by a long detour inland. It has two or three **hotels**.

CHAPTER SIX

THE CANAL ZONE

N o longer fêted as a triumph of nineteenth-century engineering, nor regarded as the linchpin of Britain's empire, the **Suez Canal** seems as Joseph Conrad described it: "a dismal but profitable ditch" connecting the Red Sea and the Mediterranean. Except around the harbour mouths or where ships are glimpsed between sandbanks, it's a pretty dull waterway, too, relieved only by the Canal Cities of Port Said and Ismailiya.

With its evocative waterfront, prosaic beaches and duty-free shopping, **Port Said** feels like Alexandria less its cultural baggage – and a place that's somehow more authentic as a maritime city. By contrast, the canal scarcely impinges on the leafy, villa-lined streets of **Ismailiya**, once the residence of the Company's European staff and now a popular honeymoon destination. Foreigners generally overlook both cities, prejudging them on the basis of **Suez**, a real dump but a vital transport nexus between Cairo, Sinai and the Red Sea Coast, and with irregular passenger boats, also, to Port Sudan and Cyprus.

Heading to Sinai, bus passengers (or car drivers) cross the Suez Canal at either the **Ahmed Hamdi Tunnel** (12km north of Suez City) or the **car-ferry 7km north of Ismailiya**; at **Qantara**, between Ismailiya and Port Said, there's a passenger ferry across to East Qantara, where buses and *service* taxis run to el-Arish in Sinai. Drivers should be aware that stretches of the canal are **off-limits** and should stick to main routes to avoid questioning by the military.

The Canal's history

The **first attempts** to link the Red Sea and the Mediterranean by means of a canal are usually attributed to Necho II (610–595 BC) of the XXVI Dynasty. Herodotus claims that 120,000 workers died before the project was abandoned after an oracle predicted that only Egypt's foes would benefit from it. Sure enough, it was the Persian emperor **Darius**, around 500 BC, who completed the first canal in the region, linking the Red Sea and the Great Bitter Lake, whence an older waterway created by Ramses II connected with Bubastis on the Nile and thence to the Mediterranean.

Refined by the Ptolemies and Trajan (who added an extension to Babylon-in-Egypt), this system of waterways was restored by **Amr** following the Muslim conquest and was used for shipping corn to Arabia until the eighth century, when it was deliberately abandoned to starve out rebels in Medina. Although the Venetians, Crusaders and Ottomans all considered renewing the old system, the idea of a canal running direct between the Red Sea and the Mediterranean was first mooted – and then vetoed – by Napoleon's engineers, who miscalculated a difference of 10m between the two sea levels.

The discovery of their error, in the 1840s, encouraged a junior French consul, **Ferdinand de Lesseps**, to present his own plan to Said Pasha, who approved it despite British objections. ("It cannot be made, it shall not be made; but if it were made, there would be a war between England and France for the possession of Egypt," Palmerston asserted).

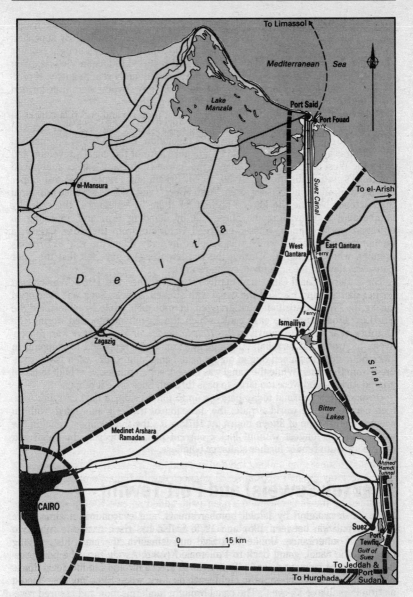

Work began at the Mediterranean end in 1859 and continued throughout the reign of Said's successor, Ismail (hence the names of Port Said and Ismailiya). Of the 20,000 Egyptians employed in the **construction of the Suez Canal**, thousands died from accidents or cholera, while Ismail himself went bankrupt financing his one-third share of the £19 million sterling investment.

In 1875 Ismail was forced to sell his shares to Britain for a mere £4 million sterling and the Suez Canal effectively became an imperial concession. By appealing to the Rothschilds for a loan over dinner, Prime Minister Disraeli bought Ismail's shares before France could make an offer, and reported to Queen Victoria: "You have it, Madam". The **Suez Canal Company** subsequently remitted its vast profits abroad and acted as a state within a state, while two world wars transformed the **Canal Zone** into the largest military base on earth.

Following the end of World War II, nationalist protests and guerrilla attacks in the Zone led to the British assault on Ismailiya's police barracks that sparked "Black Saturday" in Cairo. After the 1952 revolution, Egypt's leaders demanded the withdrawal of British forces and a greater share of the canal's revenue, and when the West refused loans to finance the Aswan High Dam, Nasser announced the canal's **nationalisation** (July 26, 1956). Britain and France tried to hamper this process, smearing Nasser as an "Arab Hitler", and Israel's advance into Sinai that October became the agreed pretext for them to "safeguard" the canal by bombarding and invading its cities. But by standing firm and appealing to outraged world opinion, Nasser emerged victorious from the **Suez Crisis** (a memorable quote about which was supplied by Lady Eden, the wife of Britain's premier, who complained "During the last few weeks I have felt that the Suez Canal was flowing through my drawing room").

The battered Canal Cities had hardly recovered when the **1967 War** caused further damage and blocked the canal with sunken vessels. Suez was evacuated during the "War of Attrition" that dragged on until 1969, while Israel fortified the **Bar-Lev Line** along the east bank, which the Egyptians stormed during the **October War** of 1973 (known as the *10th Ramadan* or *Yom Kippur* war, respectively, to Arabs and Israelis). Although the canal was reopened to shipping in 1975, both sides remained dug in on opposite banks until 1982, when Israel withdrew from the Sinai. While the canal was closed, supertankers were built to travel around Africa – and were too large to pass through Suez once it reopened.

Despite this, the canal today handles up to ninety ships a day, carrying fourteen percent of the world's trade; the direction of traffic is alternated, with an average transit time of fifteen hours. At 167km, it's the third longest canal in the world and the longest without locks; current plans to deepen the canal and double its width render further statistics pointless.

Suez (el-Suweis) and Port Tewfiq

Since its devastation by Israeli bombardments, and evacuation of almost the entire population between 1967 and 1973, SUEZ has risen from the rubble to reclaim its inheritance. Unlike Port Said and Ismailiya, the city's history long predates the canal, going back to Ptolemaic *Klysma*. As *Qulzum*, the port prospered from the spice trade and pilgrimages to Mecca throughout medieval times, remaining a walled city until the eighteenth century, when Eliza Fay described it as "the Paradise of Thieves". The canal brought modernisation and assured revenues, later augumented by the discovery of oil in the Gulf of Suez.

All this was lost during the wars with Israel, requiring a massive reconstruction programme financed by the Gulf states. While petrochemical refineries, cement and fertiliser plants and a new *Hadj* (the pilgrimage to Mecca) ferry terminal ring the outskirts, most of the city's 270,000 inhabitants have been rehoused in prefabricated estates or the patched-up remnants of older quarters. Despite the friendliness of local people, gritty, jerry-built *el-Suweis* holds no intrinsic appeal. In addition, solo women need to be aware that Suez is a thoroughly conservative town – it's best to dress and act with extreme decorum.

All numbers in the Suez City area are prefixed ☎062.

Arriving – and transport

Arriving by **bus or service taxi**, the chances are you'll arrive at Suez's **Arba'in Terminal**, the place for connections to more exciting destinations. During daytime, the *Tourists' Friends* kiosk can advise on bus times and *service* taxi rates. Be polite and have a chat; brusque interrogations make these student volunteers wonder, why bother? The **train station** is 50m north of the Arba'in Terminal.

Bus and taxi connections

● **Cairo** Like the other Canal Cities, Suez has most regular connections with Cairo by **bus** (every 30min 6am–8.30pm) or **service taxi** (even more frequently, from the Koulali Terminal near Ramses Station). Both cover the 134km in a little over two hours and charge about £E4. Direct **express** trains (four daily; 3hr; £E3.50) with A/C are also worth considering, but don't board one of the half dozen slow trains routed via Ismailiya (6–7hr).

● **Sinai** Except for the **Taba** service, it's usually possible to get a seat on daily **buses** to Sinai by booking an hour or so beforehand. Buses for Sharm el-Sheikh (£E9) currently leave at 10.30am and 2pm, the morning bus continuing on to Dahab (£E11). Buses depart for Saint Catherine's Monastery at 9.30am (£E9) and 1pm (£E11); for Nuweiba (6hr; £E13–15) at 9.30am and 2pm; the early Nuweiba bus runs on to Taba (£E15). A group of travellers can split the cost of a hired taxi to Sharm (£E90–100) or Saint Catherine's (£E80–90).

● **Hurghada/Nile Valley** *Service* taxis also fill gaps between the five daily buses to Hurghada, which leave around 6am, 6.30am, 7am, 5pm and 5.30pm; fares £E10–12.

● **Hurghada/Nile Valley** For **Luxor (via Qena)** you need to book in the morning (or two days before at the time of Abu Haggag's *moulid* in the month of Sha'ban) for seats on the 7pm bus. Ask about other daily buses to Assyut, Sohag or Beni Suef in the Nile Valley.

● **Ismailiya** Buses run every thirty minutes and service taxis at least as frequently to Ismailiya, many of them continuing to **Qantara** and **Port Said** (£E4).

● **Alexandria** Reserve an hour or so beforehand for seats on buses (9am & 11pm).

Ferries

Ferries to Port Sudan sail four times a month, calling en route at the Saudi port of Jeddah – except during the *Hadj* season (six weeks either side of the Muslim month of Zoul Haggah), when they shuttle between Suez and Jeddah. To Port Sudan takes two days and two nights; the one-way fare at deck class is about US$40. Make enquiries at any *Misr Travel* agent, or the *Canal Shipping Agencies Co* in Port Tewfiq – minibuses can drop you at *Bab Tissa'* (Gate 9) nearby.

Around the city – and accommodation

Should you decide to stay (or simply pass a few hours between buses), Suez City is readily accessible from the Arba'in depot – just follow the alley past some motor dealers to reach **Sharia el-Geish**, a two kilometre-long swathe where cruising minibuses drop and collect passengers along the way to Port Tewfiq (15pt).

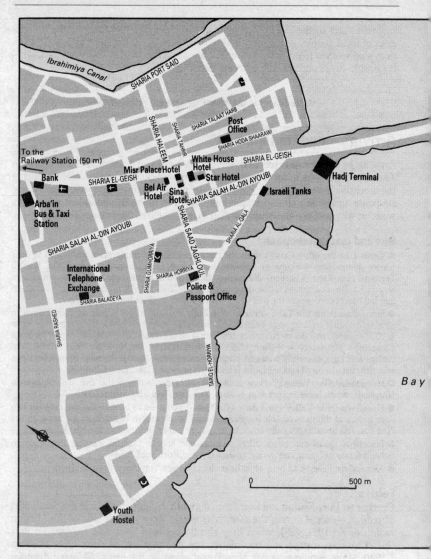

Ibrahimiya Canal

SHARIA PORT SAID

SHARIA HALEEM

SHARIA TAHRIR

SHARIA TALAAT HARB

Post
Office

SHARIA HODA SHAARAWI

To the
Railway Station (50 m)

SHARIA EL-GEISH

White House
Hotel

SHARIA EL-GEISH

Bank

Misr Palace Hotel

Star Hotel

Hadj Terminal

Bel Air
Hotel

Sina
Hotel

SHARIA SALAH AL-DIN AYOUBI

Arba'in
Bus & Taxi
Station

Israeli Tanks

SHARIA SALAH AL-DIN AYOUBI

SHARIA AL-QALA

SHARIA SAAD ZAGHLOUL

SHARIA GUMHORRIYA

International
Telephone
Exchange

SHARIA HORRIYA

SHARIA BALADEYA

Police &
Passport Office

SHARIA RASHED

TARIQ EL-HORRIYA

Bay

0   500 m

Youth
Hostel

Dusty palms and decrepit colonial-era buildings (including several churches) are followed by a strip of hotels, restaurants and legitimate moneychangers (but check bank rates first). South of here, the backstreets harbour cheap cafés, while **Sharia Sa'ad Zaghloul** runs past consulates and a fun park towards the Governorate. North of el-Geish, a tawdry souk overflows **Sharia Haleem**, presaging a quarter of workshops and chandlers, crumbling turn-of-the-century apartments with wooden balconies interspersed by modern low-rises. There's a better **bazaar** to the northwest of the bus station.

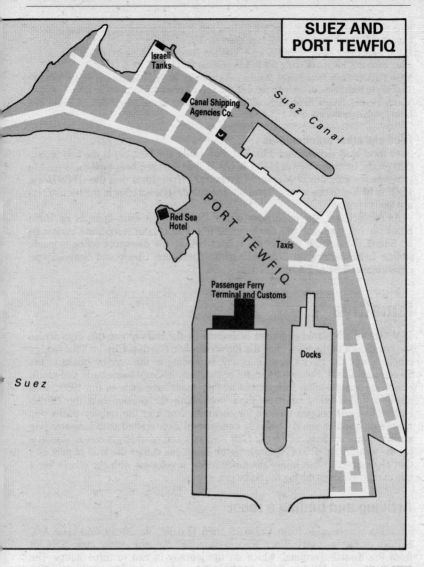

Along the Bay of Suez promenade and the main **corniche** around **PORT TEWFIQ**'s northeastern corner stand four US-made tanks captured from Israel in the 1973 War.

Accommodation

Outside of the *Hadj* season, **finding a room** should be easy. The options are:

White House, Sharia el-Geish. £E22 for a single, £E28 for an A/C double with TV and private bathroom.

Red Sea Hotel, Port Tewfiq (☎23-339). Best option if you're arriving or leaving by ferry. Singles (£E28) and doubles (£E36) have every facility.

Hotel Star, Bank Masr Street. A salubrious but poky establishment, lacking fans or any other comforts. Rooms sleeping one to four persons (£E11–27).

Misr Palace, Bank Masr Street. Similar but gloomier; singles, doubles and triples for £E7–16 (£E8–40 with bath), roughly on par with the **Saint James** across the main drag.

Youth Hostel, Sharia Sa'ad Zaghloul, four blocks south of the *Misr Palace*. A brand new hostel, with dormitory beds at £E3-4.

Food and other practicalities

Suez **food and drink** is a bit limited. For meals, the best bet is the fish restaurant on the northern side of el-Geish, but as it doesn't sell beer foreigners tend to gravitate towards the *El Magharbel Restaurant* (7am–1pm) past the *White House Hotel* (which also has a bar). Naturally, the *baladi*-style eateries in the backstreets are loads cheaper.

As for facilities, the main **post office** (Sat–Thurs 8.30am–2pm) is on Hoda Sharaawi. International calls can be made from the 24-hour **telephone exchange** on Sharia Baladeya. If you need a visa extension, the **passport office** is inside **police** headquarters on Sharia Horriya. There are Greek and Scandinavian **consulates** on Sa'ad Zaghloul Street.

Ismailiya

ISMAILIYA's schizoid character is defined by the railway line that cuts across the city. South of the tracks lies the European-style **Garden City** built for foreign employees of the Suez Canal Company, extending to the verdant banks of the Sweetwater Canal. Following careful restoration, its leafy boulevards and placid streets of colonial villas look almost as they must have done in the 1930s, with newly installed bilingual street-signs nourishing the illusion that the British empire has just popped indoors for cocktails. North of the railway tracks you move into another world of hastily constructed flats grafted onto long-standing **slums**, a quarter financed by the Gulf Emirates and providing a *cordon sanitaire* for the wealthy suburb of **Nemrah Setta**. From one comes the kind of militancy that challenged British imperialism before the revolution; with the others lies a tale of rags-to-riches during the Sadat era.

Arriving and finding a room

Ismailiya is accessible **from Cairo** by train (7 daily; 3hr 30min; 2nd class A/C £E2.50) or buses (every 30min 6.30am–7pm; £E3.50) and *service* taxis (£E4.50) from the Koulali Terminal, which do the journey in two to three hours. The 120km desert road runs through KHANKA, a byword for insanity (after its mental asylum), and on past MEDINET ASHARA RAMADAN, one of several satellite cities intended to reduce Cairo's overpopulation. Buses from Cairo (and Alex) use a small terminal on Midan Orabi, near the railway station and hotels in the salubrious part of town.

Approaching **from Zagazig** (see the *Delta* chapter) or from anywhere in the **Canal Zone**, you'll be dropped at the depot that straddles Sharia Gumhorriya on the wrong side of the tracks.

> All telephone numbers in the Ismailiya area are prefixed ☎064.

Accommodation

Accommodation in Ismailiya spans just about all budgets. In ascending order of cost, the choices are:

Youth Hostel. Perversely inconvenient, though by dint of asking directions to the "*Beit es-Shabbab*", you might be able to locate it in the Sheikh Zayid quarter, northwest of Sharia Hussein and the railway tracks.

Hotel Minerva, Sa'ad Zaghloul Street. A skulking, flea-ridden dosshouse that even at £E6 a night is a definite last resort.

Hotel des Voyageurs, Sharia Ahmed Orabi. Cheap, colonial-style hotel that's stronger on atmosphere than creature comforts.

Ramsis Hotel, just off Midan Orabi. The best budget choice: clean doubles with A/C, TV and a phone for about £E15.

Nefetary Hotel, Sultan Hussein (☎32-822). Excellent value, with baths and A/C in its singles (£E14) and doubles (£E18), a bar, coffeeshop and nightly disco on the smart premises, and breakfast included.

Crocodile Inn, Sa'ad Zaghloul Street (☎222-724). Similar amenities and slightly sniffier ambience for £E10–20 extra.

Hotel Isis (☎227-821), **El Bourg Hotel** (☎226-327), both on Midan Orabi. Egyptian honeymoon couples gravitate towards these outwardly impressive establishments. The former's dearer singles (£E10), doubles (£E17) and suites (£E30) have private showers; the latter charges £E10 more for A/C rooms in an amazingly pretentious nineteenth-century pile.

Etap Hotel, Forsan Island (☎765-322). Luxurious singles (£E80) and doubles (£E90) amidst the leafy seclusion of Forsan Island, a taxi ride northeast of town.

Sights and stories

Ismailiya's old town is a pleasure to walk or bike around, shaded by pollarded trees. Most of the sights can be reached on foot within ten minutes, although a couple of places outside town warrant renting a bicycle in the backstreets off Mohammed Ali Quay, or catching a *service* taxi from the turn-off near the Fountain Park.

The Lesseps House and the Battle of Ismailiya

First on the trail is the large, vaguely Swiss-looking **House of Ferdinand de Lesseps**, who lived here during the canal's construction. Though supposedly a museum (Wed–Mon 9am–4pm), it's often used as a state guest house; getting inside might require permission from the public relations department of the Suez Canal Authority. You could also try asking at the **tourist office** (Sat–Thurs 8am–2pm) on the Mohammed Ali Quay, which shares a new Governorate Building with the police (☎270-08).

The old police barracks, out towards Tell el-Kebir, was wrecked in the "**Battle of Ismailiya**" (January 25, 1952) after its Egyptian garrison refused to surrender their weapons to British forces, whose hold on the canal was threatened by guerrilla attacks and an economic boycott. Only when fifty policemen were dead and their ammunition was exhausted did the survivors give in. Next day – "Black Saturday" – outraged mobs attacked European hang-outs in Cairo, where the police simply watched as looters, Muslim Brotherhood and Communist arsonists set to work.

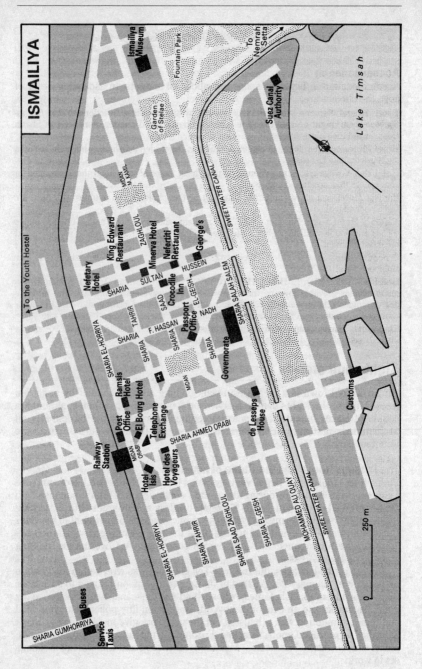

ISMAILIYA

Ismailiya Museum

Fountain Park

Garden of Stelae

To Nemrah Setta

Lake Timsah

Suez Canal Authority

SWEETWATER CANAL

MIDAN M. KAMIL

King Edward Restaurant

Nefertari Hotel

SHARIA

ZAGHLOUL

Minerva Hotel

SULTAN

Nefertiti Restaurant

SAAD

Crocodile Inn

HUSSEIN

George's

Passport Office

EL-GEISH

NADH

SHARIA TAHRIR

F. HASSAN

SHARIA

SHARIA

SHARIA

SHARIA SALAH SALEM

Governorate

To the Youth Hostel

SHARIA EL-HORRIYA

Ramsis Hotel

Post Office

El Bourg Hotel

MIDAN

Telephone Exchange

de Lesseps House

Railway Station

MIDAN ORABI

Hotel Isis

Hotel des Voyageurs

SHARIA AHMED ORABI

Customs

SHARIA EL-HORRIYA

SHARIA TAHRIR

SHARIA SAAD ZAGHLOUL

SHARIA EL-GEISH

MOHAMMED ALI QUAY

SWEETWATER CANAL

250 m

0

Buses

SHARIA GUMHORRIYA

Service Taxis

The Muslim Brotherhood and Osman Ahmed Osman

Ismailiya – the most Europeanised of Egyptian towns – was actually the birth-place of **Muslim Brotherhood** and its founder, **Hassan el-Banna**. As a child, Hassan nailed up leaflets calling upon Muslims to renounce gold and silks, and awoke his neighbours before dawn prayers. When older he campaigned against female emancipation, delivering fiery sermons in rented cafés. He founded the *Ikhwan el-Muslimeen* in 1928 and within fifteen years the Brotherhood had spread throughout Egypt and spawned offshoots across the Middle East, articulating an Islamic response to modernisation on Western terms.

From campaigning for moral renewal it went on to organise paramilitary train-ing and terrorist cells, and was outlawed by Farouk (whose agents purportedly assassinated el-Banna) in 1949. Legalised after the revolution but then suppressed for trying to kill Nasser, the Brotherhood fared similarly under Sadat, and is currently undergoing a quasi-legitimate phase with Mubarak.

Another native son who left his mark is **Osman Ahmed Osman**, a self-made millionaire contractor whom Sadat appointed as Minister of Housing and Reconstruction in 1975. As Gulf investments poured into the Canal Zone, bill-board-sized pictures of Osman began to outnumber those of his patron, who finally agreed to opposition demands for an audit. By the time it was discovered that millions had been stashed in Swiss banks, Osman had fled the country. However, subsequent investigations into his political connections proved incon-clusive and he is now back in business.

Ismailiya's Museum and Garden of Stelae

Eschewing local scandal, the **Ismailiya Museum** (Sat–Thurs 9am–4pm, Fri 9–11am & 2–4pm; Ramadan daily 9am–2pm; £E1) leans towards ancient history, devoting a section to the waterways of Ramses and Darius. The highlights of its collection of 4000 Graeco-Roman and pharaonic artefacts are some lovely mosaics dating from the fourth century AD.

With permission from the museum, one can also visit a dull bunch of sphinxes, plaques and obelisks from Ramses II's time, in the **Garden of Stelae**, backing onto the pleasant **Fountain Park**.

The shady **Sweetwater Canal** edging the park, and fed by lake Timsah, was originally dug to provide fresh water for labourers building the Suez Canal. Previously, supplies had to be brought across the desert by camels, or shipped across Lake Manzala to Port Said.

The Bar-Lev Line and Nemrah Setta

Service taxis turning off near Fountain Park are usually bound for the "Ferri Setta" (50pt), outside town, where locals use a primitive **ferry crossing** to the east bank of the canal.

Here, a vast sand rampart breached by deep cuts marks the former **Bar-Lev Line**, named after its Israeli creator. Intended to stall any attack on Sinai for 48 hours, this 25-metre-high embankment was defended by forty mined strong-points. In the event, they were totally surprised by Egypt's assault on October 6, 1973. As hidden artillery opened up at 2pm, 8000 commandos dragged launches to the water's edge, roared across the 180-metre-wide canal and scaled the ramparts with ladders. Within hours, high-pressure hoses ordered from Bavaria "for the Cairo Fire Department" were blasting gaps for the Egyptian armour massing behind pontoon bridge-layers.

However, although "The Crossing" was an Egyptian triumph (still remembered with pride), the war subsequently turned against them. An Israeli force under Ariel Sharon counterattacked across the canal between Lake Timsah and the Great Bitter Lake, wheeled inland to cut the Cairo–Suez road, and had virtually encircled the Egyptian army in Sinai by the time the superpowers imposed a ceasefire. Disengagement on the ground began with UN-sponsored talks at Kilometre 101 – the nearest Israeli tanks came to Cairo.

Not far from the ferry, a fine view of the Suez Canal can be had from **Nemrah Setta**, an exclusive suburb of French colonial-style villas on a hilltop outside town (accessible by private taxi).

Lake Timsah

Notwithstanding its name, "Crocodile Lake", there are several nice **beaches** around **Lake Timsah**. Owned by resort-clubs which often include a buffet for the price of admission (£E5–10), they're popular with students and professionals at weekends. During warm weather, wealthier citizens patronise the *Hotel Etap*'s **water-skiing**, **windsurfing** and **tennis** facilities; its lunchtime buffet (Fri & Sat; £E15) and nightly barbecue are supervised by a French chef.

Food and practicalities

The smartest **restaurants** in town are *George's* and *Nefertiti* on Sultan Hussein, and the *King Edward* at 171 Sharia Tahrir. All of them have bars, A/C and varied menus (dishes for £E6–13). A cheaper, more *baladi*-style establishment is the *El Gandool Restaurant* on the same backstreet as the *Hotel Minerva*. For dirt cheap grub, try the kebab stalls and smokey *ahwas* near the bus and taxi terminal.

Facilities are straightforward. You can't miss the **post office** (Sat–Thurs 9am–3pm) and 24-hour **telephone exchange** on Midan Orabi, nor the **passport office** on the corner of Gumhorriya Square.

Moving on, the gritty **bus and taxi depots** either side of Sharia Gumhorriya serve to reach anywhere in the Delta or the Zone. Buses to Cairo (£E3.50) also fill up there after leaving from the smaller terminal on Midan Orabi: the point of departure for several daily services to El Arish (£E4) and Alexandria (£E7). For these you need to book an hour or so beforehand.

Between Ismailiya and Port Said

Seven kilometres north of Ismailiya, a **car-ferry** crosses the canal more or less non-stop during daylight hours. Together with the Ahmed Hamdi Tunnel outside Suez, it carries almost all the traffic between mainland Egypt and Sinai, with a first stop at el-Arish. By dint of being the most direct route from Cairo to Israel, the car-ferry also takes **international coaches and tour buses**. In February 1990, one of these buses was ambushed along the Ismailiya road; nine Israeli passengers were killed by gunshots and grenades. Whether the attack was carried out by Palestinian or Egyptian radicals remains unclear. On the premise that lightning *can* strike twice, you might wish to avoid international coaches and stick to domestic services.

Besides direct buses from Cairo and Ismailiya, el-Arish is easily accessible from Qantara, 44km north of Ismailiya, where a bridge crosses the canal.

Qantara

Even before the canal was dug, pilgrims and armies usually crossed the Isthmus of Suez via **QANTARA** ("bridge" in Arabic).

Most of the town clusters on the **west bank**, whose unpaved main drag has a busy souk and lines of **service taxis** going to Cairo (£E3) and the Canal Cities (£E1.25–2); nearby stands an old mosque where pilgrims pray for a safe journey. The battered, poorly rebuilt houses are a reminder that armies clashed here as recently as 1973, while the oldest residents might even remember the Sinai Campaign of World War I, when Qantara became an "enormous camp". Nowadays the pontoon bridges have gone but a crowded *baladi* **ferry** transports locals, bikes and donkeys for free during daytime to East Qantara – whence you can make connections to Sinai.

East Qantara – and the Exodus

East Qantara (*Qantara Sharq*) is poised to hit Egypt's archaeological map following excavations in the late 1980s (still continuing) which suggest that this might have been the site of Ramses II's Delta capital, Pi-Ramses – the town from which **Moses led the Israelites out of Egypt**. Initial excavations have revealed the existence of a temple and palace and a dozen huge granaries.

More immediately, on this side of the river, there's a cafeteria and numerous **service taxis for El Arish** (2hr 30min; roughly £E5).

Port Said (Bur Said)

Founded at the start of the canal excavations, **PORT SAID** was long synonymous with smuggling and vice, boasting an "even larger stock of improper photos than Brussels or Buenos Aires". De Monfreid was amused by the Arab cafés where "native policemen as well as coolies" smoked hashish in back rooms, supplied by primly respectable Greeks. "If anyone had even had the bad taste to pronounce the forbidden word, I believe that they would have all turned into pillars of salt. All the same, every single one of them got his living from trafficking in hashish, either as a retail seller, or as a small-scale smuggler who haunted the liners."

Nowadays, this bustling city of 250,000 people earns its living as a free port and beach resort, yet a faintly raffish atmosphere lingers around its old streets of timber-porched houses, vaguely resembling the French Quarter of New Orleans. *Bur Said* is currently luring native tourists away from Alexandria by promising better shops and less crowded beaches, cheap hotels and good restaurants; only failing to deliver much in the way of nightlife. Aside from day-trippers off cruise liners, Western tourists seldom visit the city and hustlers are rare, making it an agreeable place to relax for a day or two if you don't mind the lack of "sights" and diversions.

Arriving and finding a room

Trains **from Cairo** (5 daily; 2nd class A/C £E5.50, students £E2) take at least four and a half hours to reach Port Said via Ismailiya, and are grimy to boot, making it quicker and more salubrious to do the 220km journey by bus (every 30–60min from 6am to 7pm; *Superjet* £E7–8; regular A/C buses £E6.50–8) or *service* taxi (£E6) from Koulali Terminal (roughly 3hr). In the absence of direct trains, seats on the once-daily *Golden Rocket* (5hr; £E10) and A/C blue buses (6hr; £E6) **from Alexandria** should be reserved the day before. *Service* taxis provide the fastest transportation **from Suez and Ismailiya** and augument buses **from the Delta**, where Damietta and Mansura have the best connections. Coming **from el-Arish** in northern Sinai, catch a taxi from West Qantara (40min; £E1.75).

Because Port Said is a **duty-free port**, visitors are supposed to pass through **customs** upon entering and leaving the city. Coming in, declare any cameras or other gadgets which they might think you bought at a discount here, or you may be subject to a twelve percent levy as you go out (ship's passengers are exempt). If you somehow enter town without making a declaration, it's advisable to get a letter of explanation from the tourist police to show to customs when leaving.

Arriving at the **railway station** near the Arsenal Basin, or the **Cairo/Alex bus depot** alongside Ferial Gardens, you're within ten minutes' walk of Gumhorriya and Filastin streets, where most of the cheap hotels and restaurants are concentrated. Otherwise you'll be dropped at the **Delta bus terminal** at the bottom end of Sharia al-Amin, or the **service taxi depot** near the intersection of Mustapha Kamel and Shohada streets; a municipal taxi from either of these to the downtown area costs £E1–1.50.

Down on the waterfront where **Sharia Filastin** (Palestine Street) runs past ships' chandlers, the **tourist office** (Sat–Thurs 8am–8pm; ☎223-868) is keen to answer questions and supply a nicely drawn but useless map of town.

All telephone numbers in the Port Said area are prefixed ☎066.

Accommodation

Sharia el-Gumhorriya offers the widest range of **hotels**, from modern blocks to old-style pensions. If one's full up or seems uncongenial, there's always another within easy walking distance. Be aware, however, that accommodation can be hard to find on Thursday and Friday nights, when many Egyptians come here to do weekend duty-free shopping.

ALONG SHARIA EL-GUMHORRIYA

Hotel Vendome (☎220-802). Clean singles (£E4.50), triples (£E10) and quadruples (£E11) without baths; doubles (£E11) and suites (£E21) with private showers. Breakfast included.

Hotel Akri (☎221-013). Run-down, atmospheric Greek pension near the harbour. Basic, clean rooms without fans or breakfast: singles (£E8), doubles (£E12–13) and triples (£E15–16). Sporadic hot water.

Regent Hotel (☎223-802). Old-fashioned rooms with hardwood floors and armoires going to seed, for £E10–15. Around the corner is the modern **New Regent Hotel** with singles (£E41), A/C doubles (£E51) and triples (£E61) equipped with fridges, TV and hot showers – a lot more comfortable but shorter on character.

Hotel de la Poste (☎229-994). Rambling Forties-style place with high-ceilinged double rooms with fans and bathrooms for £E20 (single occupancy £E13), not including breakfast. Good value bar, restaurant and patisserie. The manager is a hero of the 1956 invasion and a former governor of Girga Province.

Abu Simbel Hotel (☎221-150). Clean, comfy rooms with fans, fridges, TV and hot showers, marred only by gloomy decor. Singles (£E17), doubles (£E26) and triples (£E32), some with A/C. On the third floor, next to the *Gianola* restaurant and patisserie.

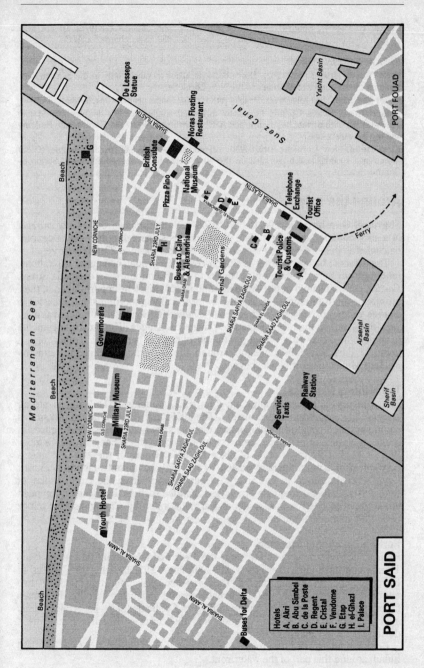

PORT SAID

Mediterranean Sea

Beach

Suez Canal

Yacht Basin

PORT FOUAD

Arsenal Basin

Sherif Basin

Ferry

De Lesseps Statue

Noras Floating Restaurant

British Consulate

Pizza Pino

National Museum

Telephone Exchange

Tourist Office

F

D

E

B

C

A

Tourist Police & Customs

Buses to Cairo & Alexandria

H

Feria Gardens

Governorate

Military Museum

Youth Hostel

Service Taxis

Railway Station

Buses for Delta

I

G

NEW CORNICHE

OLD CORNICHE

SHARIA 23RD JULY

SHARIA DIAB

SHARIA PILASTIN

SHARIA PILASTIN

SHARIA SAFYA ZAGHLOUL

SHARIA SAAD ZAGHLOUL

SHARIA EL NUZZA

SHARIA SAFYA ZAGHLOUL

SHARIA SAAD ZAGHLOUL

SHARIA DIAB

SHARIA 23RD JULY

SHARIA AL-AMIN

SHARIA AL-AMIN

Hotels
A. Akri
B. Abu Simbel
C. de la Poste
D. Regent
E. Cristal
F. Vendome
G. Etap
H. el-Ghazl
I. Palace

Cristal (☎221-961). Singles (£E15/£E24 with view) and doubles (£E19/£E30) are dear enough even before fourteen percent tax is added, plus £E1.65 surcharge for A/C.

ELSEWHERE IN TOWN
IYHF Youth Hostel (☎223-202). Dorm beds (£E5) for members only in the Sea Rangers' Building on the corner of al-Amin and the New Corniche.
Hotel El Ghazl, 23rd July Street. Simple, rather noisy rooms near the beach for £E15–30.
Palace Hotel, Sharia Ghandi. Pleasantly furnished singles (£E30), doubles (£E45) and suites (£E66) with private bathrooms and A/C, near the beach, by the Governorate Building and the New Corniche.
Etap Hotel, New Corniche (☎220-892). All-mod-cons single (£E75) and double (£E85) rooms in a swanky beach complex on the New Corniche, at the north end of Sharia el-Gumhorriya.

Around the city

Sharia el-Gumhorriya reflects Port Said's metamorphosis from a salty *entrepôt* to a slick commercial centre, plate glass facades superseding turn-of-the-century balconies as the street progresses from the Arsenal Basin to 23rd July Street.

The adjacent **bazaar** quarter is a microcosm of Egyptian consumer aspirations, ranging from humble stalls on el-Togary to smart boutiques on el-Nahda Street. *Baedeker's* complained of the "intrusive and almost insolent importunities of their proprietors" but foreigners nowadays are practically ignored, making it easier to change money or traveller's cheques at *Thomas Cook* (43 el-Gumhorriya; daily 9am–6pm) rather than the ubiquitous private exchanges. The only inducements to venture up **23rd July Street** are the novel sight of teenage girl traffic cops (a uniquely Port Saidi phenomenon) around the Governorate Building, and the Military Museum a few blocks beyond.

The Military Museum
The **Military Museum** (daily 8am–3pm; £E2, students £E1) leaves a strong sense of the canal's embattled history. The 1956 Anglo-French-Israeli invasion is commemorated by lurid paintings and dioramas (notice the headless figures in scene of Nasser at al-Azhar), whilst another room is dedicated to the October War of 1973. This gives pride of place to the storming of the Bar-Lev Line, a heroic feat of arms ultimately wasted by the high command's failure to exploit Egypt's breakthrough in the Sinai. Curiously absent from the large display of weaponry are the Soviet-made *Strella* and *Molutka* rockets that enabled Egyptian infantrymen to destroy Israeli jets and armour, rated by strategists as a minor revolution in modern warfare.

Port Said National Museum
Housed in a gleaming new building, the **Port Said National Museum** (Sat–Thurs 9am–4pm, Fri noon–2pm; £E3, students £E1.50) runs the gamut of Egyptian history. Highlights of the well-displayed collection include two mummies, an exquisitely worked faience shroud and painted coffin; Ptolemaic funerary masks; Islamic tiles and *mashrabiyas*; Coptic textiles – especially a tunic adorned with images of the Apostles; and the coach of Khedive Ismail, used during the canal's inauguration ceremonies.

Cool and uncrowded, the museum makes a pleasant retreat from the heat and hubub around this part of the waterfront.

The Waterfront and beach

Come evening, townsfolk **promenade** near the National Museum, watching dozens of vessels at anchor, their bulky hulls dwindling to lights bobbing far offshore. A **statue of de Lesseps** accepts their homage at the end of the quay.

Port Said's uninspiring **beach** provides views of ships underway, but a better sense of the canal's workings can be gained by taking a cruise (see below) or catching the free **ferry** across to Port Fouad (every 15min).

Port Fouad

Founded as a suburb for canal bureaucrats in 1927, **PORT FOUAD** is quieter than its sister city. Residents boast of commuting between Asia and Africa – an enjoyable ride in a battered ferry reeking of everything but intercontinental status. Travellers hoping to work their passage to the Med or the Indian Ocean occasionally strike lucky at Port Fouad's **yacht basin**. East of town there's a new branch of the canal, cut to speed up maritime traffic.

Food and practicalities

There are several **patisseries and coffeeshops** on el-Gumhorriya, **cinemas** on Safiya Zaghloul, and a fair host of **eateries** scattered around town, concentrated mainly on el-Gumhorriya and the New Corniche.

Restaurants

Noras floating restaurant, Sharia Filastin. One-hour **cruises** (6.30pm; £E5) with a drink, plus lengthier jaunts over lunch (3pm; £E17) or dinner (9.30pm; £E25).

Hotel de la Poste, Sharia el-Gumhorriya. Reasonably priced pizzas, grills and sandwiches on the terrace.

Popeye's Café, Sharia el-Gumhorriya – opposite the *Hotel de la Poste*. More of a burger bar with trimmings and piped music.

Reana House, Sharia el-Gumhorriya – diagonally across from the *Hotel Akri*. Generous helpings of Korean food (£E9–20) above a bar frequented by old Greeks – both open late.

Pizza Pino, corner of Gumhorriya and 23rd July. The town's trendiest joint, with a slick decor and seductive range of Italian dishes and ice cream.

The Seahorse, New Corniche. Good seafood restaurant; another, nameless seafood place is on the same street, near the *Hotel Etap*.

Other practicalities

Consulates British (☎226-963), French (☎221-532) and Belgian (☎223-314) citizens can seek help from their representatives in the modern Commercial Centre just beyond the museum. The US consulate (11 Sharia el-Gumhorriya; ☎223-868) confines itself to shipping matters. Along the waterfront, a block north of the tourist office, at Sharia Sultan Hussain 30 (fourth floor), Denmark, Sweden and Norway maintain consuls c/o the Norwegian Seaman's Service (☎227-514).

Hospitals Of the three hospitals, *el-Mabbarrah* (☎220-560 or 561) at the western end of 23rd July and *Deliverande* (☎225-965) on el-Shaheed el-Gayar Street are most accustomed to foreigners.

Pharmacy All-night pharmacy on Safiya Zaghloul Street near Sharia Shohada (☎227-919).

Post office The main branch is on the corner of Ferial Gardens (daily 7am–5pm). There's a 24-hour **telephone exchange** (international calls) on the waterfront.

Tourist police Two branches: a 24-hour branch in the railway station, another in the Customs building (☎223-868).

Moving on

Buses to Cairo leave from the northern side of Ferial Gardens; *Superjets* should be booked a day ahead, but seats on ordinary buses (leaving from a nearby side street) can safely be purchased an hour or so before. To board either, you must first go through customs, so come a little early.

The same goes for **buses to the Delta**, leaving from the other depot, though passengers in **service taxis** often seem to avoid customs entirely.

A possible international alternative is to ask shipping agencies along el-Gumhorriya (starting at no. 31) about **ferries to Cyprus or beyond**. The most regular sailing is the *Princessa Marissa* service to Limassol (Cyprus), every week (usually Tues) for most of the year. The same company that operate the Marissa have a sister ship, the *Princessa Cypria* which cruises between Limassol and Piraeus, the port of Athens, via the island of Rhodes; joint tickets may be on offer. Single cabins to Limassol go for as little as £E165; there is a twenty percent discount for under-28s.

CHAPTER SEVEN

SINAI

The **Sinai** peninsula has been the gateway between Africa and Asia since time immemorial and a battleground for millennia. Prized for its strategic position and mineral wealth, Sinai is also revered by disparate cultures as the site of God's revelation to Moses, the wanderings of Exodus and the flight of the Holy Family. As Burton Bernstein wrote, "it has been touched, in one way or another by most of Western and Near Eastern history, both actual and mythic", being the supposed route (there's no archaeological proof) by which the Israelites reached the Promised Land and Islam entered North Africa, then a theatre for Crusader-Muslim and Arab-Israeli conflicts, and finally transformed into an internationally monitored demilitarised zone.

Though mostly wilderness, Sinai looks far too dramatic – and too beautiful – to be dismissed as "24,000 square miles of nothing". The **south** of the peninsula is an arid moonscape of jagged ranges harbouring **Mount Sinai** and **Saint Catherine's Monastery**, where pilgrims climb the Steps of Repentance from the site of the Burning Bush to the summit where God delivered the Ten Commandments. Farther north, the vast **Wilderness of the Wanderings** resembles a Jackson Pollock canvas streaked with colour and imprinted with tank-tracks. Remote springs and lush oases can be reached by **camel-trekking** or **jeep safaris**, providing some insights into **Bedouin culture**.

Above all, however, the south has the lure of exquisite coral reefs and tropical fish in the **Gulf of Aqaba**, one of the finest **diving** and **snorkelling** grounds in the world. The beach resorts at **Sharm el-Sheikh**, **Na'ama Bay**, **Dahab** and **Nuweiba** cater to every taste and budget. From Sharm or Na'ama you can also make expeditions to Egypt's deepest reefs and most diverse aquatic life at **Ras Mohammed**, a mini-peninsula at the southern tip of Sinai.

Northern Sinai is, by contrast, visited by almost no Western tourists. A barren coastline, which you scarcely glimpse from the road, it has a single town and focus in **el-Arish**, a laid-back if conservative place with a palm-fringed beach and a Bedouin market. The few foreign visitors who do come here are mostly crossing the border into Israel and the Occupied Territories.

Visiting Sinai

The differences between Sinai and mainland Egypt can induce culture shock in travellers who arrive from Israel or Jordan, spend some days on a Sinai beach and then go on to Cairo. For those accustomed to Egyptian towns and beaches, Sinai will seem amazingly uncrowded, laid-back and hassle free – especially so for women. Pressing on into mainland Egypt, of course, you experience the reverse. Native Bedouins and recent settlers from the mainland both assert Sinai's distinctive character and disparage Egyptian government, often comparing it unfavourably with the period of Israeli rule, when tourists arrived in droves. Even the customary salutation is different: "*Marhabba kaif halak*" (Greetings and Good Health) instead of "*Salaam aleikum*".

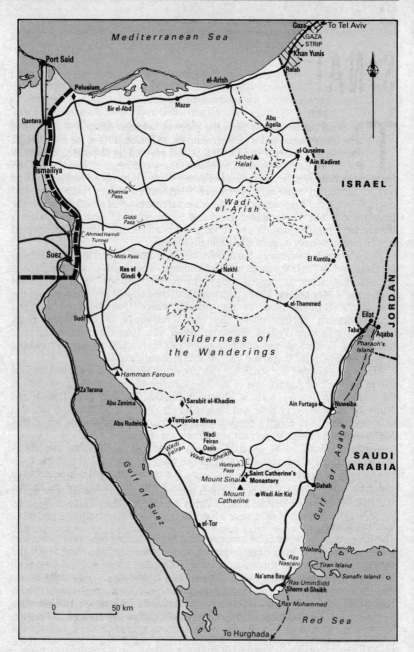

Note: For information on **entering Sinai from Israel or Jordan**, see p.7.

SINAI ZONES
Broadly speaking, Sinai divides into three zones, only two of which are in direct communication. The **coastal strip** along the Aqaba and Suez gulfs connects with the interior at certain points, whereas **northern Sinai** is effectively sundered from both. This chapter is structured accordingly, with transport from mainland Egypt described at the start of each section, while the **approaches** from Israel and Jordan are covered in *Basics*. Check with the Egyptian Ministry of the Interior regarding current restrictions on taking rented or four-wheel drive vehicles into Sinai; private cars brought across the border require a *carnet de passage en douane*. Moving around, you will come across **MFO** (Multinational Force of Observers) personnel and bases, rather than the Egyptian military.

GETTING AROUND AND TOURS
All the main tourist spots are accessible by well-paved roads and some form of public transport. Most travellers find getting around fairly easy, despite the unpunctuality of *East Delta Company* **buses** (whose schedules tend to vary slightly every year) and the infrequency of **service taxis**, which hike their prices in the absence of other transport (be ready to bargain). **Motorists** are generally restricted to main roads, where a 60km-per-hour speed limit is enforced.

Given the baking heat, scarcity of traffic and huge distances, **hitchhiking** is a dubious proposition unless your destination is nearby or you're certain of a ride all the way (or at least to somewhere with shade and buses). Women should never hitch alone. MFO personnel are forbidden to give lifts.

Although **tourism** is a year-round business in Sinai, winter is traditionally the busiest period for the Aqaba coast resorts and the only season when it's feasible to run **jeep safaris** or lengthy **camel treks**. You can join these by contacting local operators (see Na'ama Bay, Dahab and Nuweiba listings) or any of three agencies in Cairo: *Acacia Adventure Travel* (27 Sharia Libnan, Mohandiseen; ☎347-4713), *South Sinai Travel* (79 Sharia Merghani, 11th floor, Heliopolis) and *Sinai Safari* (c/o *American Express* ☎750-444 or *Isis Travel* ☎847-060).

CLIMATE
Sinai's **climate** is extreme. On the coast, daytime temperatures can reach 50°C (120°F) during summer, while nights are sultry or temperate depending on the prevailing wind. In the mountains, which receive occasional snowfall over winter and the odd rainstorm during spring, nights are cooler – if not chilly or freezing. Outside of winter, you should wear a hat, use high-screen suntan lotion and drink four to six litres of water a day (more if you're trekking) to avoid sunburn and heatstroke.

COSTS
The **cost** of everyday items, meals and transport is generally higher in Sinai than elsewhere in Egypt, but still cheaper than in Israel. All the main resorts have banks, while US dollars can be furtively exchanged in many shops. Bottled water and toilet paper are stocked by supermarkets, but tampons are scarce and pricey.

All numbers in **North Sinai** (el-Arish) are prefixed ☎062; in **South Sinai** ☎064.

The Sinai: some history

Fifty million years ago the Arabian Plate began shearing away from the African landmass, tearing the Sinai Peninsula from the mainland while the Red Sea inundated the gap. Hot springs on the sea bed indicate that the tectonic forces which created Sinai are still active – the gulf is widening by three inches each year. In **prehistoric times** the climate was less arid and Sinai supported herds of gazelles which Stone Age people trapped and slaughtered in stone enclosures.

Bronze Age Semites from Mesopotamia were the first to exploit Sinai's lodes of copper ore and turquoise, foreshadowing the peninsula's colonisation by the III Dynasty pharaohs, who enslaved its Semitic population to work the mines, build roads and fortresses. According to Egyptian mythology, it was in Sinai that Isis sought the dismembered body of Osiris, and Hathor, "Our Lady of Sinai", was also associated with the region. **Pharaonic rule** lasted until the Hyksos invasion from the north, and was later reasserted by the XVIII Dynasty. Amongst the tribes subjugated by the Ramessid pharaohs and sent to work in Egypt were the Hebrews, or latterday **Israelites**.

THE EXODUS

Enshrined in the Old Testament and by centuries of tradition, the **Exodus of the Israelites** is reckoned by scholars to have taken place in the reign of Merneptah (1236–1223 BC). The event remains a conundrum as no archaeological evidence of the Israelites' journey through Sinai has ever been found – although recent excavations at Qantara (on the edge of the Suez Canal, see p.511) suggest that this may have been the town from which they left.

To identify their route and various crucial sites, scholars have compared Biblical descriptions with physical features and tried to reconcile myths with realities. The **Sea of Reeds**, north of Suez, or other sites along the isthmus are now deemed likelier crossing points than the miraculously parted **Red Sea**. From there, the Israelites are thought to have proceeded down the coast until **Wadi Feiran** and followed it inland to arrive at **Mount Sinai**; although a contrary theory has them trekking across northern Sinai and receiving the Ten Commandments at **Jebel Halal**. Either way, the subsequent forty years in the wilderness are only explicable in terms of a lengthy stay at "Kadesh Barnea", which some identify as **Ain Kadeis** or Ain Kedirat, southeast of El Quseima, where there are extensive ruins.

CHRISTIANITY AND ISLAM

Over the next millennium or so, Sinai was invaded by Assyrians, Hittites and Babylonians, recaptured by Egypt, and conquered in turn by the Persians and Greeks. While the Ptolemies built ports along the Mediterranean coast, Semitic tribes from Petra established themselves between Aqaba and Gaza, both ultimately succumbing to the **Romans**. Whether or not the **Holy Family** previously crossed Sinai to escape Herod's massacre, the region had begun to attract hermits even before Emperor Constantine legalised **Christianity**, which rooted itself in cathedrals and **monasteries** under Justinian's patronage.

In 639–40 the **Arabs** swept into Sinai, fired with the zeal of **Islam**. The new faith suited local tribes, which turned to plundering the desert monasteries while the Arabs sacked the cathedral cities. Northern Sinai eventually became a pawn in the **Crusades**, the area between Aqaba and Rafah belonging to the Frankish Kingdom until its collapse at Acre.

THE BEDOUIN

Most of Sinai's population are **Bedouin** who claim descent from the tribes of the Hejaz, and thus rate themselves amongst the purest Arab genealogies. Only the Jebeliya tribe is anomalous, tracing its origins to the Caucausus.

Traditionally, each tribe roamed its own territory in search of grazing and settled around local oases. The Mizayna claimed the land between Sharm el-Sheikh and Nuweiba; the Tarabeen a swathe from Nuweiba to El Arish; the Jebeliya the Saint Catherine's region, and so on*. Tribal and family honour were paramount, raids and camel-rustling a perpetual cause for blood feuds which might persist for generations. Agriculture or fishing was a hand-to-mouth activity, secondary to herding goats and camels – the latter being the measure of a tribe's wealth, with racing camels (*hageen*) esteemed above all. Though devout Muslims, the Bedouin retained pagan superstitions and practices from the "time of darkness", with their own common law (*'urf*) instead of regular Islamic jurisprudence.

Unsurprisingly, the Bedouin took advantage of discarded weaponry to resist outside authority, attempts to settle the nomads having little success until the 1970s, when Israel constructed water tanks, schools and clinics at various sites. By providing employment and exposing the Bedouin to Western comforts, the coastal resorts had an equally profound effect on traditional lifestyles. Nowadays, many earn their living through tourism, taxi driving or construction work, and stone huts with corrugated iron roofs and TV antennae are more common than black tents. But for Bedouin women, still confined to the domestic sphere, changes have been less fundamental. Where grievances are discernable by outsiders, they usually focus on administrators and entrepreneurs from mainland Egypt, whom many Bedouin regard as here on sufferance.

---

*The number of **tribes** in Sinai is uncertain, ranging from 14 to 27 depending on which of their subdivisions are counted. Other tribes include the Sawalha, Alekat, Walad Shaheen and Tiyahah. Collectively, they are known as the *Tawarah* ("Arabs of Tor"), after the ancient name of the peninsula, or simply as *al-Arab*.

After the Crusades, the victorious Mamlukes reopened Sinai's trade routes but the peninsula remained Egypt's Achilles heel, as the Ottoman Turks and Mohammed Ali demonstrated with their conquests of 1517 and 1831.

TWENTIETH-CENTURY SINAI

Sinai's strategic importance increased with the completion of the **Suez Canal**, and in 1892 Britain compelled Turkey to cede it as a buffer zone. Backed by Germany, the Turks retook it in 1914, laying roads and water pipelines along the northern coast and across the interior. Anglo-Egyptian forces only dislodged them – and went on to take Jerusalem – after a prolonged campaign.

During World War II Sinai witnessed little fighting, but the **creation of Israel** brought the territory right back into the frontline. In 1948 the Israelis repulsed Arab attacks from all sides and took the **Gaza Strip** and **el-Arish** before an armistice was signed, only withdrawing under British pressure. By closing the Gulf of Aqaba to Israeli shipping and nationalising the Suez Canal, however, Nasser brought together British and Israeli interests. It was Israel's advance into Sinai in October 1956 that was the agreed pretext for Anglo-French intervention; though militarily successful, the three states were compelled to quit by international opposition, UN peacekeeping forces establishing a buffer zone in Gaza and guaranteeing free passage through the Gulf of Aqaba.

But further **Arab-Israeli wars** were inevitable. When Egypt ordered the UN to leave and resumed its blockade in **1967**, Israel launched a pre-emptive strike and captured the entire peninsula, which it retained after the **Six Day War** and fortified with the Bar-Lev Line along the east bank of the Suez Canal. In the **October War of 1973**, Egypt broke through into Sinai but then suffered a devastating counterattack across the canal.

US-sponsored peace negotiations ultimately culminated in President Sadat's historic visit to Jerusalem, the **Camp David Accords** and a peace treaty signed in 1979, which led to Egypt's decade-long expulsion from the Arab League. Under its terms Israel evacuated all settlements founded during the occupation of Sinai and the territory reverted to Egypt; a phased transition completed in 1982, except for the disputed enclave of Taba, finally resolved in 1989. A Multinational Force of Observers (**MFO**) based at Na'ama Bay monitors Sinai's "banded" demilitarised zones from orange-flagged outposts around the peninsula.

ALONG THE GULF COASTS

Sinai rises and tapers as the peninsula runs towards its southern apex, red rock meeting golden sand and deep blue water along two gulf coasts. Even the **Gulf of Suez**, as E.M. Forster noted, looks enticing from offshore – "an exquisite corridor of tinted mountains and radiant water" – though it's nowadays transformed after dark into a vision of Hades by the flaming plumes of oil rigs.

For most travellers, however, Suez is merely an interlude before the **Gulf of Aqaba**, whose amazing coral reefs and tropical fish attract visitors to **Na'ama Bay** and other resorts. Their beach scene is the best Egypt can offer and should aquatic pursuits pall – if such a thing is possible – there are opportunities for making trips into the wild **interior** by jeep or camel. Even from the beach, the view of the mountains of Sinai and Saudi Arabia is magnificent. All things considered, it's not surprising that some people choose to spend their entire holiday here.

Approaches to the Gulf Coasts

Aside from those arriving from Israel or Jordan, most travellers approach the gulf coasts from **Cairo**, **Suez** or **Hurghada**, which generally entails following a zigzag route.

FROM CAIRO

Most people come from Cairo by **East Delta Company buses** from the **Sinai Terminal** (*Mahattat Seena*) in the Abbassiya district. To get there from Tahrir Square, catch a #32 minibus to the overpass just before the terminal, or a slower #54 or #56 bus going all the way (also boardable on Ramses Square). Taxis accept £E2–3 for the ride out, but try to overcharge for the journey back. Since bookings can only be made on the spot and telephone enquiries (☎824-753/824-999) are unrewarding, you'll have to check schedules and reserve seats the day before (earlier during Ramadan).

At the time of writing, five buses daily ran to **Sharm** (7–8hr; £E20), leaving at around 7.30am, 10am, 1pm, 11.30pm and midnight. **Nuweiba** can be reached (8hr; £E28) via the 7am bus to **Saint Catherine's Monastery**, which runs onto

---

SNORKELLING AND DIVING

The Red Sea offers some of the finest snorkelling and diving grounds in the world, accessible for a fraction of the cost of reaching the Seychelles or the Great Barrier Reef (unless you live nearby, of course). It's also a cheap place to learn open-water diving and gain a PADI or CMAS certificate, which entitles you to dive anywhere in the world.

If you're planning to do a lot of **snorkelling**, it's cheaper to buy your own gear in Alexandria, Cairo or Israel rather than rent it from dive shops along the Aqaba coast. At Dahab the rented masks are so leaky that you have to surface every couple of minutes to empty them of water. Coral reefs and spiny urchins can rip unprotected feet to shreds, so you should always wear plastic "jellybean" sandals or flippers. Wearing flippers, it's easier to walk *backwards* across reef flats if the water is too shallow to allow you to float above them. However cool the water may feel, the sun's rays (water can multiply the effects of ultraviolet) can still burn exposed flesh, so always wear a T-shirt and use waterproof sunscreen.

You must have PADI, CMAS or some other internationally recognised **certificate** to rent scuba **diving** equipment. Many people visit Na'ama Bay simply to acquire this on diving **courses**. A full course costs around $200 (dive shops quote prices in dollars, though most accept Egyptian currency). If you're certified but haven't logged a dive in the past three months, most dive shops insist on a trial dive, and they also offer introductory dives (US$40), too, for those who aren't sure about laying down the money for the full course.

Qualified divers can also take courses in night diving or wreck-salvage, organised at Hurghada (see *The Red Sea Coast and Eastern Desert* chapter).

Taba (9hr; £E30); and also by a direct overnight bus **through the Sinai interior** (7hr). Direct buses to **Dahab** (7hr; £E20) – leaving about 7.30am and noon – may also stop at Saint Catherine's. All services are billed as A/C, and halt at one or more resthouses along the Gulf of Suez; on-board snacks are grossly overpriced.

Rapid access to Sharm and great views of the peninsula might alternatively entice you onto **Air Sinai flights** (Tues, Thurs, Fri & Sat; $65 one-way).

FROM SUEZ

Although buses from Cairo usually bypass Suez, travellers coming from southern Egypt or northern Sinai can avail themselves of fairly reliable connections at Suez City. All transport from there uses the **Arba'in terminal**, where a "Tourists' Friends" kiosk is helpfully informative. Unless schedules have changed, the 9.30am **Saint Catherine's** bus runs onto **Nuweiba** (6hr; £E13) and **Taba** (7hr; £E15), while the 10.30am *service* to **Sharm** (5hr 30mins; £E10) carries on to **Na'ama Bay** and **Dahab** (£E13). In addition, there are direct buses to **Sharm** and **Nuweiba** at 2pm. The group rate for a **service taxi to Sharm** is £E90–100; other destinations are negotiable.

FROM HURGHADA

The third option is to travel directly from Hurghada to **Sharm** by **air** (Fri only; one-way US$60) or **ferry** (see p.570 for details), or charter a seven-seater **taxi** for the 750km drive (£E40–50 per person).

Between Suez and Sharm el-Sheikh

The 338km between Suez and Sharm el-Sheikh takes only a couple of hours by bus or *service* taxi, and there's little point in stopping unless you've got private transport. Such attractions as exist along (or off) the route are otherwise awkward to reach (or leave), so most travellers pass them by.

If you're not already booked on a through-service to Sinai, Suez is the place to catch a bus or *service* taxi – an easier, surer way than hoping to cadge a ride at the **Ahmed Hamdi Tunnel**, 17km north of Suez (£E10 by taxi). The tunnel – named after an Egyptian general killed in the October War – is the only road-crossing between Sinai and Egypt proper, so most traffic uses it.

South along the Gulf of Suez

Heading south by road, the **Gulf of Suez** is sensed before it appears as a glint on the horizon, beyond the sands that rim the west for much of the way.

Ain Musa
Roughly 40km south of the Ahmed Hamdi Tunnel, a turning towards the coast leads in 2km to **AIN MUSA**, the **"Springs of Moses"**. According to scholastic conjecture and local legend, it was here that the Israelites halted after crossing the Red Sea, and Moses threw a tree into the bitter spring of Marah, which miraculously became drinkable (Exodus 15).

Of the twelve springs mentioned in Exodus, seven remain, yielding enough brackish water to sustain a small oasis. Many of the palm trees, however, were decapitated during various Sinai conflicts; an Israeli battery stationed here shelled Suez and Port Tewfiq during the War of Attrition, until Egypt recaptured Ain Musa in 1973. The attraction of camping at the springs is limited by Ain Musa's lack of food and water, and transportation out: ask around the village before waiting for a bus on the highway.

Sudr and Hammam Faroun
Famed amongst cognoscenti for the variety of seashells washed up on its beach, **SUDR** is marred by a reeking oil refinery which doesn't seem to bother the middle-class Egyptians who frequent its **Tourist Village** (chalets from £E40).

The coast improves 55km to the south, where a blunted natural pyramid marks the site of **HAMMAM FAROUN** (Pharaoh's Bath). Arab folklore attributes the near-boiling **hot springs** around the seaward side of this 494-metre-high rock formation to the pharaoh's struggles to extricate himself from the waves. The unspoilt beach and primitive, laid-back ambience are disappearing as a Rheumatology Clinic materialises. Would-be campers are advised to bring food and be prepared to hitch out; there should be local traffic to el-Tor, if nowhere else.

A detour to the Turquoise Mines

Travellers with a sturdy car might consider detouring 30–40km inland to visit a pharaonic rock temple and turquoise mines at Sarabit el-Khadim. To get there, you turn off the highway several kilometres north of ABU ZENIMA, onto a road up Wadi Humor, which veers southeast after 21km; once past the manganese mines, take the second turning on the left (south) and the temple lies ahead.

Sarabit el-Khadim

Built on a summit – hence its name, "Heights of the Slave" – the **rock temple** at **SARABIT EL-KHADIM** has several courts full of stelae inscribed by Middle and New Kingdom officials. Although its sanctuary was dedicated to Hathor, "Mistress of Turquoise" (see p.281), Sopdu, god of the Eastern Desert, was also worshipped here. Hewn out during the XII Dynasty and seemingly abandoned during Ramses VII's reign, the temple was found by Niebuhr in 1792, but not excavated until the beginning of this century.

Neighbouring ravines and valleys were mined for turquoise and copper from the III Dynasty onwards, as numerous hierogylphic and Proto-Sinaitic **inscriptions** attest. The richest crop is in the **Wadi Mukattab** (Valley of Inscriptions) leading into Wadi Maraghah, where ancient mine-workings and stelae were damaged when the **turquoise mines** were revived and went bust in 1901. Though Bedouin still glean some by low-tech methods, the amount of turquoise that remains isn't worth the cost of industrial extraction.

On from Sarabit

If Sharm el-Sheikh is your destination, follow Wadi Maraghah eastwards into Wadi Sidri, and down to meet the Gulf highway at ABU RUDEIS. To reach Saint Catherine's Monastery or Dahab it's quicker to turn southeast inland, where a 12km spur connects the mines with **the road to Feiran Oasis and Saint Catherine's**, which leaves the Gulf highway 43km south of Abu Rudeis.

El-Tor and Ras Mohammed

Between Abu Zenima and el-Tor the "coast road" keeps veering inland, giving a wide berth to airstrips and oil terminals. The chewed-up, derrick and pipeline-strewn landscape is depressing, and **EL-TOR** does nothing to cheer you up. Seedy-looking and jerrybuilt, the administrative capital of southern Sinai offers no incentive to stay at its two hotels, but a fair chance of local buses or *service* taxis (£E3) to Sharm el-Sheikh, 108km away.

Ras Mohammed

Though it's not apparent from the road, there are reefs just off the coast right down to **RAS MOHAMMED**, a miniature peninsula at the southern tip of the Sinai. Designated a **nature reserve** in 1983, its rich ecology enjoys a measure of isolation thanks to a lack of public transport. Buses can drop you at the highway turn-off 25km west of Sharm (barely signposted), but there's still another 24km to cover; follow the road to the beach, and then southeast along the shoreline. Although visitors are welcome, campers need a special permit from the police in el-Tor. A Visitor's Centre should open shortly.

Ras Mohammed's underwater **Shark Observatory** gives a stunning view of marine life, Jaws and all, whilst diverse bird life flits around the **Mangrove Lagoon**. Children can safely bathe in its warm, sandy shallows, in contrast to the deeps beyond the reef barrier, where boats from Sharm bring **divers** to see barracuda, sharks, giant Napoleon fish and manta rays. Ras Mohammed's fish and coral are amongst the finest in the world, but under normal conditions the sea is too rough and the sights lurk too deep for good **snorkelling**. For novices, it can even be a frightening experience.

CORAL REEFS AND TROPICAL FISH

Created by the same tectonic stresses which formed the Dead Sea and East African Rift Valley, the **Red Sea basin** is two miles deep in places, yet effectively separated from the Indian Ocean by an underwater "sill" at Bab el-Mandab, roughly 100m below the surface. Circulation between the Red Sea and the Gulf of Aqaba is similarly limited by the 170-metre-deep Tiran Strait, although the gulf itself attains depths of 1830m. As neither is fed by rivers and their rate of evaporation far exceeds any rainfall, both are exceptionally warm and salty – providing an ideal environment for tropical fish and coral reefs.

It's the warmth of the Red Sea water that is responsible for the Sinai's particular brilliance of coral – a revelation if you have previously snorkelled in such places as Hawaii or the Carribean, whose reefs will ever after seem dull by comparison.

Coral reefs

The **coral reefs** which fringe the Sinai coastline from el-Tor to Taba have been created by generations of minuscule polyps extracting calcium from the seawater and depositing limestone exoskeletons on the remains of their ancestors. Fossilised reefs form the bedrock for living ones, which can grow 4–5cm a year, but are easily bruised or killed; if snapped off (which is strictly illegal), coral loses its colour within hours of being removed from the sea. Snorkellers and divers should avoid touching the reef for its sake and their own good (see below).

Reefs come in all shapes and sizes, some more encrusted with coral growths than others, but the idealised representation should give you an idea of where different species might be found. Some corals live a thousand feet down: the presence of sharks is usually a sign of a reef's good health.

Just below the shoreline, the warm water and eroded, sand- and rubble-covered bottom of the **lagoon** attracts starfish, sea slugs and stinging anemones. Clams and sea urchins hide in crevices, while small yellow anemone fish and schools of viridian and carmine damselfish flit about. Other species found here include azure and opal blennies, tentacled clown fish and multitudes of butterfly fish.

Beyond lies the **reef flat**, a barren, fossilised shelf curving up towards the **reef crest**, overgrown with organ pipe corals and anemones. Damselfish, angelfish, snappers and parrotfish are ubiquitous, while seaworms and eels emerge from deep **caves** below the crest. Mountain and staghorn corals encrust the upper **slope**, whose lower section merges into bare terraces or sandy shelves overgrown with **seagrass**, the habitat of sea horses and pipefish.

Close to the surface further out are **pillars** whose own richly developed coral formations attract damselfish, basslets, wrasses and grunts, to name but a few. The **forereef** tends to draw larger fish, octopus and squids, with stingrays and mantas (whose wingspans can reach 16ft) gliding along the seabed.

Tropical fish and other creatures

The Red Sea's flora and fauna are related to tropical Indo-Pacific species, with no observable migration from the Mediterranean, although blue-speckled parrotfish have travelled the other way. The following are the most basic notes for identification – and avoiding the odd dangerous species.

Wherever soft, stinging anemones cling to the reef you're likely to see yellow **anemone fish**, recognisable by their twin vertical stripes. Equally commonplace are **angelfish**, with their long dorsal fins diminishing to filaments. Crescent angelfish are blue at the front, with a yellow vertical stripe and black hindquarters, while Emperor

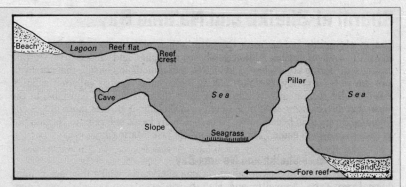

angelfish are horizontally pinstriped in blue and yellow, and the larger Arabian angelfish (up to 50cm long) is blue all over but for a yellow splotch. The same colour scheme in reverse appears on **butterfly fish** favouring sunny slopes and forereefs; around lagoons, pillars and crests you'll also see Racoon butterfly fish, striped in yellow and black, with a black and white eye patch.

Slopes and forereefs are the habitat of small **goatfish** with horizontal stripes of blue and yellow (or yellow and black in the case of Forsskal's goatfish). Diverse types of **parrotfish** and **snappers** frequent deeper water alongside crests and pillars. Parrotfish are easily recognisable by their beaky mouths and vibrant colours; snappers are similarly sized, with silvery scales striped and spotted in red, green or electric blue. Likewise bulky and diversely hued are **wrasses**, related to the bigger **Napoleon fish**, which can dwarf a person. Dugongs or **seacows** are equally large and harmless, unlike small, sharp-toothed and armoured **triggerfish**, **filefish** and **porcupine fish**, more commonly found in deeper water.

Dangers of the deep . . .
Considering all the **dangerous creatures** around, it's remarkable that most visitors experience nothing worse than the odd cut from sharp coral. Poisonous species include spiny **scorpion fish**, wildly coloured **turkeyfish** and **dragonfish**, and the oddly finned **lionfish**, resembling the baddies' subs in *Stingray*. By not touching anything remotely fitting their description you should avoid danger from that source.

The lethal **stonefish**, camouflaged as a gnarled rock, is harder to spot but fortunately rare. You're more likely to be at risk from stinging **purple anemones** and burning **fire coral**, or **black sea urchins** with needle-like spines, nestling in crevices. Dark caves sometimes harbour razor-toothed **moray eels**, which may bite if they feel threatened. **Stingrays** can deliver a painful dose of venom but purple **jellyfish** rarely cause irritation.

Although makos, hammerheads and other **sharks** frequent the deep waters around Ras Mohammed and the Tiran Strait, they're luckily seldom found near the coast. However, blood in the water can attract them from afar, so never enter the sea with an open wound, or when menstruating. Hammerheads are the only species prone to attack without provocation (which in shark terms can mean thrashing about, panic-stricken), though some divers consider **barracuda** more aggressive. Sighting either predator near the shore, climb out as quickly and calmly as possible and spread the word; if you're diving in deeper water, keep quiet and still and pray you'll be ignored.

Sharm el-Sheikh and Na'ama Bay

Sharm el-Sheikh and **Na'ama Bay** are the first of three sets of "twin" resorts along the Gulf of Aqaba. Although Sharm is bigger and closer to the diving grounds, its boring atmosphere and limited accommodation ensure that most visitors stay at Na'ama Bay, 7km north along the coast, which has superior facilities, and splendid reefs nearby. Na'ama is dearer than Dahab and Nuweiba, to the north, but also classier, with much better snorkelling; it attracts more divers and would-be divers than beach bums. Note that many locals still refer to Na'ama Bay by its former Israeli name, "Marina Sharm" (or just "Marina").

Access: Sharm el-Sheikh and Na'ama Bay

Buses from Cairo to Sharm call at Na'ama afterwards, whilst the ones coming down **from Taba**, **Nuweiba** and **Dahab** will even stop outside *Gafy Camp*, *Farouz Village*, the *Ghazala* and other hotels on request.

Landing at the **airport** northeast of town you have to rely on costly taxis. Arriving by **ferry from Hurghada** the port is only a few hundred metres from Sharm's bus terminal. From here, yellow open-sided *Tuf-Tuf* buses supposedly run every hour between mid-morning and 7pm, charging 50pt a ride.

For speedier **transport between Sharm and Na'ama** flag down cruising minibuses which charge £E1 a head for a full load, £E6 if there's only two of you, and perhaps £E10 for a quick return journey. Providing you select the right turn-off, hitching can also be good.

Sharm el-Sheikh

A hunk of sterile blocks on a plateau commanding docks and other installations, **SHARM EL-SHEIKH** was developed by the Israelis after their capture of it in the 1967 war. Their main purpose was to thwart Egypt's blockade of the Tiran Strait and to control overland communications between the Aqaba and Suez coasts. Tourism was an afterthought – though an important one, helping to finance the Israeli occupation and settlements, which Egypt inherited between 1979 and 82. Since then, Sharm's infrastructure seems to have expanded and deteriorated simultaneously, and for all its services there's nothing welcoming about the "Bay of the Sheikh".

Practicalities

Taking the road that curves uphill, you'll pass a flagposted **police** station, the **tourist police**, and a **youth hostel** (on the left at the top; ☎637). A bed in the A/C, segregated dormitories costs £E6 (£E7 for non-IYHF members), including breakfast. Providing you don't mind sharing with noisily gregarious Egyptian teenagers, the hostel offers better value than anywhere in Na'ama Bay, though guests are locked out between 9am and 2pm and after curfew (11pm; winter 10pm), and alcohol and card games are forbidden. Next door is the *Cliff Top* hotel, with A/C singles (£E42) and doubles (£E68); more basic bungalows (singles £E27, doubles £E50, triples £E70); several large tents with comfortable cots and electric lighting (£E14 per person); and space to pitch tents (negotiable). Room rates include half board, while hotel showers and toilets are available to those who opt to **camp**.

At the top of the hill, where buses from Cairo drop passengers, three **banks** changing travellers' cheques (Mon–Sat 8.30am–2pm & 6–9pm, Sun 10am–noon), a **post office** (Sat–Thurs 8am–3pm) and 24-hour **telephone** exchange (internal calls only) cluster around a square of sorts. There's also a couple of **supermarkets**, less well-stocked and no cheaper than the one in Na'ama Bay. Ask locals for directions to the **beach**, hidden behind bungalows and fences. At the bottom of the hill, past Sharm's **hospital**, a sliproad curves round into the **bus terminal** where tickets are sold from an inconspicuous hutch. Here you'll find *Sandy Palace*, the only **restaurant** (daily 9am–11pm) worth the name, near the cheaper *Fisherman's Café* and a row of **dive shops** including *South Sinai Travel*. The main road continues 1km farther south to Sharm el-Sheikh's port and the main police station, where tourists who've just arrived in Egypt need **to register**.

Ferries

The schedule of **ferries between Sharm and Hurghada** changes regularly, so check details and reserve tickets well in advance. At the time of writing, **sailings from Sharm** are on the *Mimi Misre* (Tues, Thurs, Fri & Sun) and *Golden Sun* (Mon, Wed & Fri); both leave at 8am and charge £E55. Tickets may be available through *South Sinai Travel*, or sold the evening before at the *Cliff Top Hotel* and Na'ama Bay's *Gafy Camp*. Although the advertised crossing time is five and a half hours, bad weather and mechanical breakdowns often prolong the journey.

Buses and flights

Daily **buses** between **Sharm and Cairo** are either sleek vehicles with A/C (departing Sharm around 5.30am, 11.30pm & midnight; £E20), or cronky ones without (7am, 10am, 1pm & 4.30pm; £E14). The ticket office is sometimes loath to reserve seats, especially on through-services from Nuweiba, which are often full when they arrive. It's worth turning up early, too, for the 8am bus to **Dahab and Saint Catherine's Monastery** (both £E9) or for the 9am and 5pm services to **Dahab and Nuweiba** (£E12); the jam-packed 9am bus runs on to **Taba** (£E5).

Rates for seven-seater **service taxis to Cairo** are highly negotiable – drivers usually start by quoting £E35–40 a head; Taba and Suez are also offered, though Egyptians would feel miffed at paying over £E90 for the whole cab-fare to Taba, or £E100 for Suez. Other destinations are even more subject to negotiation.

The airline office on Sharm's main square can tell you about *Air Sinai* **flights** to Cairo (US$70), Saint Catherine's (US$50) and Hurghada (US$60) from the airport north of Na'ama Bay.

Na'ama Bay

Despite its fine beach and upmarket facilities, **NA'AMA BAY** only rises above its Hebrew name ("pleasant") because of the amazing snorkelling and diving in its vicinity. If meeting other travellers and sunbathing are your priorities, there's a funkier, cheaper beach scene at Dahab, further up the coast. At Na'ama women sunbathers need to have a thick skin to ignore the gawping. However, walk around with a mask and flippers and you'll blend in perfectly – everyone in Na'ama respects underwater pursuits.

Hotels and diving shops are the main points of reference in Na'ama: *Tuf-Tufs* and buses from Cairo drop you on the parking lot outside the original *Marina Sharm Hotel*, and everything else is ranked parallel to the beach.

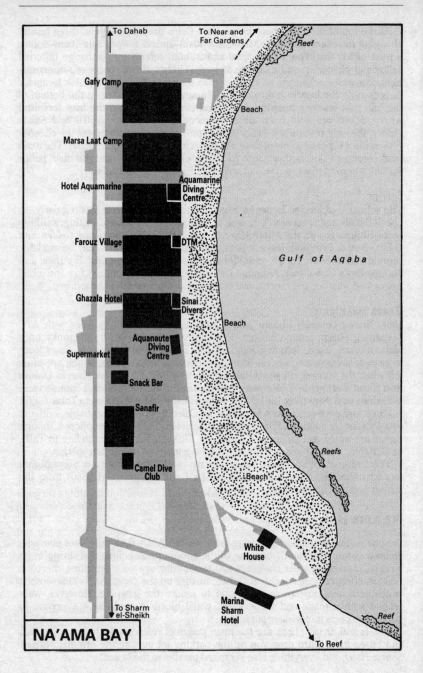

To Dahab

To Near and
Far Gardens

Reef

Gafy Camp

Beach

Marsa Laat Camp

Hotel Aquamarine

Aquamarine
Diving
Centre

Farouz Village

DTM

Gulf of Aqaba

Ghazala Hotel

Sinai
Divers

Beach

Aquanaute
Diving
Centre

Supermarket

Snack Bar

Reefs

Sanafir

Camel Dive
Club

Beach

White
House

To Sharm
el-Sheikh

Marina
Sharm
Hotel

Reef

To Reef

NA'AMA BAY

Accommodation

Expect to find the odd new hotel or tourist village that isn't marked on our map; several places are under construction at the time of writing.

Hotel Aquamarine. The cheapest option in Na'ama, recently renovated, with rooms from around £E40.

Sanafir Tourist Village (☎551-10). Superior to any other budget accommodation, this tastefully designed, spotlessly clean hotel charges £E85 for a double room with bath, and offers much cheaper **reed huts** with mattresses, lighting and fans (singles £E25, doubles £E35, triples £E40). Hot showers are always available and prices include an excellent buffet breakfast. Other good value meals and drinks are served around the sunken courtyard and Bedouin-style tent come lunchtime and evening – just beware of the gas that's sprayed to discourage mosquitoes. It's worth reserving huts or rooms in advance.

Marina Sharm Hotel. Geodesic fibreglass bungalows for US$25 single and US$38 double. Ordinary single and double rooms cost $35 and $45 respectively, or $55 and $65 for larger, ritzier quarters on the fifth floor; a $5 breakfast is obligatory.

Ghazala Hotel (☎649-602). Slick A/C hotel favoured by Germans. Singles (US$70), doubles (US$85) and triples (US$105). Non-residents can use the freshwater **swimming pool**, at least during the low season; in winter you have to look like a rich paying guest.

Farouz Village, run by the Hilton chain. A/C chalets at prices a little above the *Ghazala*.

CAMPSITES

Na'ama's **campsites** – positioned next door to each other – are the pits. Fresh water can usually be had at *Marsa Laat* but only between 7 and 8.30am and 6 and 7.30pm at *Gafy's*, which otherwise uses sea water; toilets and showers at both places are filthy. It's forbidden **to sleep on the beach** at Na'ama.

Gafy Camp. This has has a couple of two-person bungalows (£E35) and loads of ripped tents, the size of which determines whether you're charged £E3 or £E7 for a cot; to pitch your own tent costs £E3 per person. Sometimes the owner insists that guests pay for bed and breakfast (£E11), or even full board (£E20).

Marsa Laat Camp. Charges £E5 for a mattresses in a cramped tent with no light; £E7 for a cot in a larger tents with lighting; or £E3 per head for those with tents.

Snorkelling around Na'ama Bay

Snorkelling is one of the joys of Na'ama Bay, and you owe it to yourself to indulge. When trying out different sites, bear in mind that the sea is usually calmest in the morning, an important factor when you've got to walk or swim over serrated coral reefs. If you've never snorkelled before and find breathing through a tube unsettling, start with the baby reefs just off the beach near the *Sanafir* and *White House*, where the sea is only waist deep. By the time you've circled a reef and seen its profusion of rainbow-hued fish, snorkelling should feel like fun and you'll be ready to move onto bigger things. Unfortunately, all the other reefs involve some walking: drinking water, a hat and proper footwear are the minimum essentials, and it's wise to start early.

North of the bay

The best **reefs** – aptly known as coral gardens – run **north of Na'ama Bay**, and distinctions between them are somewhat arbitrary. Whenever you're considering a site, look for a safe descent from the rocks, and the shortest, smoothest reef flat, with dark water beyond its edge.

Beginners might prefer to swim there from the nearest shallow beach, or the pontoon pier one headland before the **Near Gardens**. You can reach them on foot (30–45min) by following the uphill path beyond *Gafy Camp* across arid buffs until the fence of the Marine Institute, and then down to the coast; it takes longer if you walk along the shore all the way. Plummeting to unseen depths beyond its crest, the reef has spawned offshore pillars (including a brain-shaped one harbouring a moray eel – keep your distance) and fantastic encrustations – the perfect habitat for angelfish, parrotfish and blue snappers. From here you can walk (30min) on to the equally amazing **Far Gardens**, up the coast.

South of the bay
South of Na'ama Bay there's yet another reef, less attractive for its coral than for its fish, plus the fact that you can walk there in fifteen minutes. The path starts beyond the *Marina Sharm Hotel*; follow it down into a wadi where you skirt the wire of a military outpost to reach the beach with caves and reefs at its far end. But don't swim here on an incoming tide, or windy days – the waves can easily bash you against the reef.

Diving centres, courses and excursions

Much of Na'ama's appeal lies in its excellent diving centres and extensive range of other activities, trips and equipment hire. Divers with "the bends" can be treated in Na'ama's **decompression chamber**; happily, it's a rare occurrence.

Diving centres and courses
Na'ama's five **diving centres** (daily 8am–6pm) run the cheapest open-water diving courses in the world, which partly accounts for the resort's popularity. At the time of writing all five outfits – *Camel Dive Club*, *Aquanaute Diving Centre*, *Sinai Divers*, *DTM* and *Aquamarine Diving Centre* – hire gear and offer training.

Regular **five-day diving courses** progress from theory to open-water training, and should gain you an internationally recognised PADI certificate (mailed from the USA). Prices are the same everywhere: currently US$200 for the course, plus US$25 for the certificate. Total novices or people who haven't dived for some time may be required to make an introductory dive (US$40) to show their capabilities. Although these rates include all the necessary gear, anyone can **hire equipment** from dive shops using their passport or driving licence as security. You'll economise by paying in Egyptian currency.

Diving excursions
Most centres run **excursions to Ras Mohammed and the Tiran Straits** (see p.525) for the equivalent of US$45, bookable in advance; note that Sinai-only visas aren't valid for Ras Mohammed. Priority is given to divers, and the majority of sites are too deep and turbulent for snorkellers anyway. However, *Camel Dive Club* does a special snorkelling trip to the shallower reefs of Ras Mohammed and/or the Tiran Straits (depending on the weather) for roughly $20 a head, and Fox (see below) can do likewise for a few dollars more. The Straits, like **Tiran and Sanafir Island**, offer exciting diving, with a good chance of seeing hammerheads and other sharks, manta rays and barracuda, or huge Napoleon fish the size of baby elephants. But the currents are strong, and the water chilling; bring high-calorie drinks and snacks to boost your energy.

Sinai Divers also runs snorkelling excursions to the less demanding reefs of **Ras Nasrani** and **Ras Umm Sidd** (dolphins and turtles); the US$35 charge excludes equipment rental.

Boat trips

The *Nautico Red Sea Diving Club* near the *Marina Sharm Hotel* also runs **trips in glass-bottomed boats** (£E10) for those who want to see marine life without getting wet. These are hourly rates unless specified otherwise, though you can pay for waterskiing, boating or pedallo-ing by the half-hour if desired.

Jeep and camel trips

The *Sanafir* can put you in touch with Fox, a cool dude of Bedou-Turkic extraction who sports wraparound shades and Bermuda shorts, and runs **jeep trips** (US$20–30 a head; minimum four persons). One itinerary takes you to **Ras Nasrani** for a preprandial snorkel, followed by tea with the Bedouin in **Wadi el-Att**, and sunset in the mountains. Another focuses on the coastal mangrove forest at **Nabeq**, further up the coast, with a dozen shipwrecks sunk as insurance fiddles; then you visit Sharm after a seafood lunch. The day trip to **Saint Catherine's** – which includes climbing Mount Sinai – is worth considering if you're short on time.

Adventurous, hardy types can also reach **Saint Catherine's monastery by camel**, paying $25 apiece per day for the guidance of Hussein Ahmed el-Bedoui, another well-known local character. It's an amazing trip through wild, spectacular scenery, but folks who haven't ridden camels before will be tortured by aching muscles halfway into their four-day (*inshallah*) journey. Try a three-to-four hour camel ride (which Fox can also arrange, though it's cheaper to do so in Dahab) and see how you feel afterwards before signing up for the big one.

These **longer trips** are only feasible during winter, when Fox runs jeep safaris to **Sarabit el-Khadim** (see p.525), the **Coloured Canyon** (see p.540), and other places in the mountainous interior. Overnight trips cost around US$35 a head; two days and two nights US$80 per person; this includes everything. Interested parties should contact Fox in Cairo (5 Sharia Ismail Barakat, Dokki) well in advance.

Other equipment hire

Farouz Village can supply **motorbikes**, **bicycles**, **fishing boat**s or **pedallo-kayak**, plus **horse-riding** lessons; whilst *DTM* rents out a **speedboat** and stuff for **waterskiing** (£E100) and **windsurfing** (£E50 for half a day).

Food, nightlife and other practicalities

Walk along Na'ama's "strip" and you'll pass most of the options for **eating and drinking**. Besides their own in-house restaurants, the *Ghazala* and *Farouz Village* both maintain places on the beach, serving *kofta*, kebab and pizzas. You can compare prices – which aren't cheap, however much they vary – for yourself, but it's worth mentioning a few features of the Na'ama culinary scene.

The cheapest juices, beer, grills, fish dishes and omelette-type meals are sold at *Snack Bar* next to the supermarket. A kiosk outside *Gafy Camp* undercuts them with pasta dishes, but the quality and standards of hygiene are much lower. For a nice ambience and not too expensive Stella Export, pizzas and salads, the *Sanafir*'s al fresco bar-restaurant is recommended. If you're into splurging, try the melon juice at the *Farouz* beach-bar, or a barbecue at the *White House* restaurant. In 1981 this was the setting for a mini-summit between Sadat and Begin, who humiliated his Egyptian counterpart by having the Israeli air force bomb an Iraqi nuclear reactor even as their meeting occurred.

Nightlife

Nightlife boils down to whatever's happening in the places above. From 8pm onwards, one of the beach-bars will probably feature an Egyptian band playing *Lulakky* and a medley of Western pop hits, while vastly amplified rock 'n' reggae booms from the kiosk near *Gafy Camp*, and a torch-singer croons somewhere amidst the *Farouz Village*. At the same time, there's a video – usually a major American film – shown in the *Ghazala*'s outdoor lounge.

Shops and services

Na'ama's **supermarket** (9am–2pm & 5–10pm) stocks yogurt, soft drinks, tampons, and anything you might need underwater or on the beach. Most tourists drink several litres of bottled **water** a day, so it's worth going for the cheapest supplier, which happens to be the *Hotel Ghazala*; for *Cleopatra Lights*, Egypt's most acceptable smoke, try the "bazaar" in *Farouz Village*.

It's in *Farouz Village*, too, that you'll find Na'ama's resident **doctor**. During banking hours you can **change money** at reception in the *Ghazala*, *Farouz Village* or *0*. The latter can place **international calls**.

Transport

Buses are the chief way of **moving on**. Because schedules change and Sinai buses are quite erratic anyway, the information given here (and posted outside *Marina Sharm Hotel*) should always be compared with what locals say.

Northbound services usually take on passengers outside the *Marina Sharm Hotel*, whereas buses going the other way may only stop on the high road near the *Ghazala* and *Farouz Village* turn-offs. Expect them five to ten minutes after, or fifteen to twenty minutes before, their scheduled departure times from Sharm el-Sheikh (detailed above). Particularly on Fridays, you might find it impossible to get a seat on the Taba bus, or the second morning bus to Cairo. Other services to the capital or Dahab and Nuweiba are likelier to have seats, and there's rarely any difficulty with the bus to Saint Catherine's.

Dahab

Jagged mountains ranged inland of Na'ama Bay accompany the road northwards to provide a magnificent backdrop for **DAHAB**'s tawny beaches, from which its Arabic name – "gold" – derives.

Don't be discouraged by Dahab **"town"**, 1km inland, where buses stop outside the *Bank of Egypt* if they're not going on to the depot nearer the **tourist village** on the coast. Fastidious tourists opt for the tourist village's A/C doubles with bathrooms (US$50), but most budget travellers forego the option of pitching a tent or renting a straw-roof hut (US$10) there in favour of staying at the **Bedouin village** 3km up the coast (£E3 a person). Most buses to Dahab carry on to there (50pt extra), or you can catch a *service* taxi from outside the bank (£E1). The road to the Bedouin village turns off near the microwave mast and curves around the coast; walking in the heat isn't recommended.

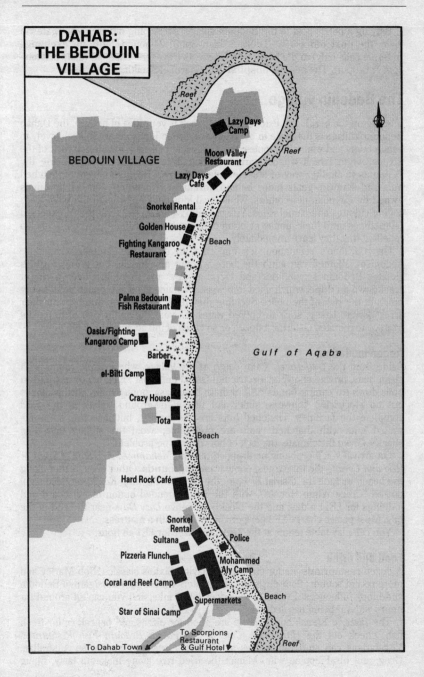

DAHAB: THE BEDOUIN VILLAGE

BEDOUIN VILLAGE

Reef

Lazy Days Camp

Moon Valley Restaurant

Reef

Lazy Days Cafe

Snorkel Rental

Golden House

Beach

Fighting Kangaroo Restaurant

Palma Bedouin Fish Restaurant

Oasis/Fighting Kangaroo Camp

Gulf of Aqaba

Barber

el-Bilti Camp

Crazy House

Tota

Beach

Hard Rock Café

Snorkel Rental

Sultana

Police

Pizzeria Flunch

Mohammed Aly Camp

Coral and Reef Camp

Supermarkets

Beach

Star of Sinai Camp

To Scorpions Restaurant & Gulf Hotel

To Dahab Town

Reef

Barring a police post in the Bedouin village, everything official congregates in town: the **post office** (Sat–Thurs 8.30am–3pm), 24-hour **telephone exchange** (internal calls only) and a **bank** which accepts travellers' cheques (daily 8.30am–2pm & 6–9pm). The nearest **hospital** is in Sharm el-Sheikh.

The Bedouin village

If lazing on the beach and listening to acid rock is your idea of heaven, the Dahab Bedouin Villlage is the place to be. Nowhere else in Egypt caters so exclusively to beach bums and wannabe-hippies; the music and laid-back **ambience** reek of the Sixties, when Israeli troops started coming here for R & R, introducing the Bedouins to another way of life. Nowadays, the *real* Bedouin village of thatched huts and scrawny goats hides behind dozens of restaurants and campgrounds owned by Egyptian newcomers, while local kids wander beneath the palm trees selling culottes and camel rides. Visitors either stay longer than they'd expected (sometimes until their money or brain cells are gone) or find the whole scene so repellent that they leave immediately.

Given Dahab's reputation, it's important to stress the limitations on pure hedonism. Women can sunbathe here without any hassle, but **going topless** violates Bedouin sensibilities and Egyptian law, and there has been a recent crackdown on **dope**, which used to be easily obtainable: if you consume, it's very much at the risk of the police deciding they need to make up numbers on their arrest forms. Lastly, stick to bottled water to avoid the slight risk of **hepatitis** from contaminated cisterns; a dozen or so cases of infection occur every year.

Accommodation

Aside from the *Gulf Hotel*, 200m south of the village, where triple rooms with clean beds, private showers, electric lights and fans cost £E14, **accommodation** boils down to "campgrounds". All of them have basic huts, usually with padlocks but no electricity; showers, sinks and hole-in-the-ground toilets in the yard complete the facilities. Thatched huts are the coolest, but insecure, so stone-walled huts with thatched roofs are preferable; avoid the stifling tin-roofed shacks. Given the climate, the lack of hot water is no problem.

On arrival you'll probably be dropped outside *Mohammed Aly*, *Star of Sinai* or *Reef and Coral* – the three most popular **campgrounds**. Other sites further along the beach include the dismal *El Bolti*; the *Oasis* or *Fighting Kangaroo* (also sign-posted "Crazy White House"), with the recommended option of full board and lodgings for £E11 a day; and the bleakly primitive *Lazy Days* near the end of the bay. Most places charge £E3 per person, or £E4 with a mattress.

You can play table tennis at the *Lazy Days Café* for £E1 an hour.

Food and drink

A dozen **restaurants** vie for custom by playing Sixties classics, Bob Marley and more recent sounds; floor cushions and posters reflect their amalgam of Bedouin and hippy influences. Everywhere serves soft drinks, and you can sit around for hours without being hassled to eat.

The *Pizzeria Flunch* and *Sultana* are good for pizzas and pancakes; for fresh fish, check out the *Hard Rock Café* or the *Palma Bedouin Fish Restaurant*. Vegetarians can stuff themselves at *Fighting Kangaroo*, run by an Australian, Greg, and his Filippina wife, Manai; the fried rice alone makes a tasty, filling meal. The *Scorpions Restaurant* south of the village does great chicken, chips and salad, screens diving videos and has video games. Food at the *Crazy House* is second rate, while kebabs at the *Sharkaw Restaurant* are downright dangerous. *Tota*, with its boat-like frontage, is the only place serving beer.

Most of these places are open until midnight, though the choice of food diminishes after 9pm. Three **supermarkets** (7.30am–midnight) stock bottled water, ices, pitta bread (sweet bread hawked by kids may cause diarrhoea) and candles.

Moving on

A couple of taxi drivers living in the village take full advantage of the fact that **moving on** means getting into town, where all the buses leave from. Although locals only pay 50pt for the ride, tourists in a hurry are ripe for overcharging, and it's wise to arrange early-morning departures the night before at *Mohammed Aly* or the *Star of Sinai* campgrounds. **Buses** to Sharm, calling at Na'ama, leave town around 8.30am, 2pm, 5pm and 8pm. The latter bus is the A/C *service* to Cairo; a non-A/C bus also departs at 8am. Of the two buses to Nuweiba (10.30am & 6.30pm), the evening one is the most crowded because it carries on to Taba. A bus to Saint Catherine's leaves Dahab around 9.30am.

Snorkelling and diving

Dahab's best **reefs** are at either end of the spit of land occupied by the **tourist village**; the ones north and south of the Bedouin settlement aren't so good (though there's easy snorkelling offshore of the *Golden House* campground), with a littered seabed between them.

The tourist village's **diving centre** rents better quality masks, fins and flippers than shops in the Bedouin Village – where leaky masks are a real problem – and also hires windsurfing boards ($6 per hour/$20 a day). As in Na'ama, it's cheaper to pay for **equipment** in £E than US$.

Courses and excurions

At the Bedouin Village, the *Fighting Kangaroo, Palm Beach Camp* or the *1001 Nights Café* can put you in touch with the guys running five-day PADI **diving courses** ($200), while the tourist village centre runs introductory dives ($40) and **scuba excursions** to Ras Mohammed (US$45, including equipment).

The *Crazy House* arranges overnight trips to the **Blue Hole**, 2km further north, so divers can admire nocturnal lobsters (£E25) and consume them (£E20) next morning. Greg at the *Fighting Kangaroo* offers a package of two dives at different sites – the Blue Hole, some small islands, or the underwater fissure known as the **Canyon** – for the equivalent of $45; a lobster feast is an optional extra.

Camel trekking

In its own way, **camel trekking** is as much fun as snorkelling, particularly once you get used to steering. Pull firmly and gradually on the nose rope to change direction; a camel should stop if you turn its head to face sideways. Couching the animal – entailing thrusting one's face close to its muzzle and growling "*kkhhurr, kkhhurr*" – is best left to the Bedouin boys who handle their camels with great aplomb. Bring water, food and a hat, plus something to protect your calves against chafing (see "Camels" in *Basics* for advice on posture) and the ferocious sun.

Trips

Enquire at the *Moon Valley Restaurant* or the *Star of Sinai* campground about day excursions **to Wadi Gnay**, a Bedouin hamlet with palms and a brackish spring, roughly three hours' ride into the wildly rugged interior. Foreigners have to give their passport details and obtain a permit (£E2) before leaving Dahab village; don't pay for the ride (£E25 per person) until you return.

Greg at the *Fighting Kangaroo* can also organise an overnight camel trek **to Ras Shaen** for £E35 a head. After several hours in the saddle, most tourists are painfully stiff the following day.

Nuweiba

Since Israel withdrew from Sinai tourists visiting **NUWEIBA** have diminished from a flood to a trickle and its once-thriving *moshav* (cooperative village) has gone to seed. It's possible that the resort's fortunes might revive now that a cross-Sinai bus service makes it readily accessible from Cairo but for the present, Nuweiba's reefs are as isolated as any you'll find. The tourist village, however, pretends that nothing has changed, overcharging accordingly, which is why many budget travellers prefer to sleep out near the Bedouin Village just up the coast. For others, Nuweiba is simply a stepping stone to Taba on the border with Israel, or the place to catch ferries to Aqaba in Jordan (see below).

Buses from points south call at Nuweiba "town", which is basically the **port**, before continuing 8km north to the **tourist village** – or vice versa coming from Taba. Nuweiba's Bedouin mostly live in two large villages named after local tribes: **Mizayna**, 4km south of the port, and **Tarabeen**, 2km beyond the resort village. *Service* taxis charge £E3–5 for the ride between Nuweiba town and the tourist village, whence you can walk to Tarabeen in about twenty minutes.

Accommodation

The **tourist village** proper offers A/C rooms and bungalows with private baths (singles £E44–84, doubles £E75–116; half board £E24, full board £E40), and a bar which excludes Bedouin lest they disturb the sedate clientele. Across the wire, another section of the sandy beach is dotted with thatched cabins (£E18 per head) and flapping tents; guests are charged £E18 a cot, or £E6 per head in one of the "older tents" (a fact that reception isn't keen to reveal).

Heading towards **Tarabeen**, clean doubles with hot showers (£E22) can be had at the low brownstone hotel beyond the former *moshav*, though many travellers prefer to doss on the beach (stashing their gear at the hotel restaurant) or rent a shack at the aptly named *Blue Bus* (negotiable rates).

The cafeteria opposite the campsite entrance sells overpriced beer, soft drinks and *kushari*. The fishermen's huts sell freshly caught fish with chips and salad, and the slightly dearer, nameless hotel restaurant nearer Tarabeen offers more varied fare. Richer tourists patronise *Macondo's* (2–4pm & 8pm–midnight), where a set meal of fish, rice, tahina, salad and melon costs around £E20.

The village around the old *moshav* contains three cheap and simple **restaurants** – *Sharkawi* (6.30am–1am) is the best – plus a couple of **supermarkets**. A **bakery** lurks within the huge corrugated-iron shed near the generator plant.

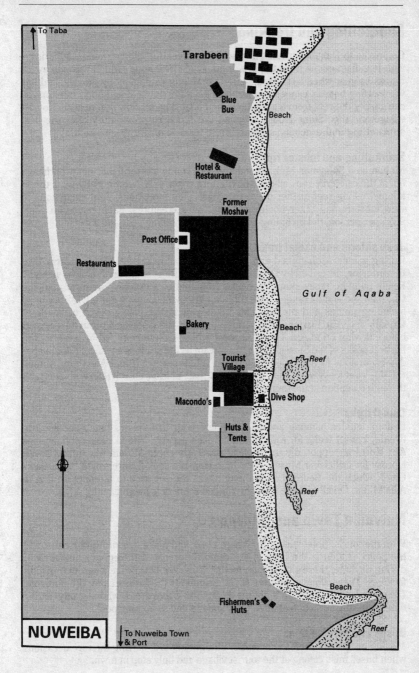

Tarabeen

To Taba

Blue Bus

Beach

Hotel & Restaurant

Former Moshav

Post Office

Restaurants

Gulf of Aqaba

Beach

Bakery

Reef

Tourist Village

Macondo's

Dive Shop

Huts & Tents

Reef

Beach

Fishermen's Huts

Reef

NUWEIBA

To Nuweiba Town & Port

Snorkelling and trekking

Compared to Dahab, Nuweiba is quiet and uneventful – some would say boring – with few distractions from the beach. Its single dive shop (which was still awaiting scuba gear when last heard) rents snorkelling equipment by the day, and has windsurfing boards, canoes and facilities for waterskiing at an hourly rate; or you can survey the reef from a glass-bottomed boat. The shallow reef near the tourist village and the "Stone House" beyond the southern promontory offer the best **snorkelling** in the vicinity; **surfing** is also feasible on Tarabeen beach.

Snorkelling and lobster rips

Mohammed Suleyman Mohammed, the cool young lobster fishermen who hangs out at the cafeteria, runs all-day **snorkelling trips to Nuweiba al-Dune**, a three-kilometre-long reef further down the coast; plus three-hour night excursions to view lobsters and other nocturnal underwater creatures. Each excursion costs £E25 per person, not including the rental of snorkelling gear and a wetsuit.

Jeep safaris and camel treks

During winter, Mohammed and two other operators organise **jeep safaris into the interior**, described by Doughty as a "labyrinthine solitude of rainless valleys". Really gung-ho types should consider Mohammed's two-day circuit around the Ghazlani and Gunna ranges, with three nights spent camping out (£E135 per head including guides and meals). This takes you to the palmy oases of **Wadi al Qusaib** and **Ain Furtaga**, with a hike through the fantastic **Coloured Canyon** before driving on to **Ain Umm Ahmed**, whose deep torrent fed by snow on the highest peaks of the Sinai shrinks to a stream as the seasons advance. For cheaper day excursions to the Coloured Canyon (£E35 per head) and Ain Umm Ahmed (£E45), contact *South Sinai Travel* or Emad el-Moazen's *Wilderness Company* through reception at the tourist hotel.

Camel treks

Bedouin guides hanging around the cafeteria or fishermen's huts may also run two-day **camel treks** for roughly US$30 each per day. The likeliest destination is **Ain Koudra**, supposedly the Biblical Hazeroth where Miriam was inflicted with leprosy for criticising Moses. Near its spring is a rock fissure called "Christian's Gate", which the Bedouin once thought was the entrance to a tunnel leading to Asia Minor. On all of these trips the rugged scenery is magnificent.

Nuweiba Town and transport

With the tourist hotel willing to change **cash** and make **international calls**, and the police station at the back of the campsite prepared to **register** new arrivals during daytime, there's no reason to visit Nuweiba Town except for its transport facilities. These alone guarantee some custom for the **hotels** along the port road (*Zaharaa* is the cheapest), if not the *El Sayedin Beach Hotel*, whose grotty setting diminishes the attraction of its A/C bungalows and swimming pool.

Buses and service taxis

Moving on from Nuweiba is normally straightforward, barring the rare occasions when buses miss calling at the tourist village and only stop in town.

Buses to Dahab (70min), Na'ama Bay and Sharm (3hr) are supposed to leave around 7am, 2pm and 4pm; and buses to Saint Catherine's (2hr) at 6.30am, 11am and 2pm. The last two carry on to Cairo via Suez. Another new A/C bus runs to the capital across the Wilderness of the Wanderings. There are also buses from the port area to Suez (5.30am, 6.30am & 7am). If you can't get aboard one of the buses to Taba (6.30am, 10am or noon, and 3.30pm), **service taxis** should do the run for £E40, perhaps slightly less. The fare to Dahab (£E40) and Sharm (£E55) is likewise negotiable and divided between however many passengers are travelling.

The ferry to Aqaba

Getting the ferry across to Aqaba in Jordan involves a little effort and uncertainty, but most travellers consider it worthwhile.

If you're coming directly from Cairo, the 11pm bus arrives in Nuweiba around 6am, while the morning service from Taba pulls in two hours later; both services stop near the **port**. Foreigners can usually walk straight in after showing their passports, unlike Egyptian migrant workers who have to queue for hours outside. **Customs** and the **ticket office** are located inside, as is a **bank** which opens at 9am. Although Westerners are usually whisked through proceedings, it's best to turn up at least ninety minutes before the boat is scheduled to depart.

Ferry services

Normally two **ferries** a day sail from Nuweiba, leaving between 10am and noon and 2 and 4pm. The boats are used by Egyptians bound for Jordan and the Gulf states, so are always crowded during major holidays like Ramadan (when workers travel home) and throughout the *hadj* season. To cope with the increased demand, a third evening service is sometimes laid on, but if an extra boat can't be found unlucky travellers may be stranded in town until the next day. The Jordanian vessel is a lot cleaner than the Egyptian ferries.

Because fares are based on oil prices reckoned in US$, the cost of **tickets** fluctuates (£E40–60 for a 2nd class single). Bloody-minded officials occasionally demand a recent exchange receipt covering this sum of money; some travellers are also conned into paying an "exit tax" which doesn't have any legal basis. If you're planning to return this way, it's cheaper to buy a single, and then your ticket back in Aqaba, rather than a return ticket from Nuweiba.

On boarding you'll be asked to hand over your passport and may be invited into the A/C first class lounge to sit out the journey (3–4hr) in comfort. Your passport will be returned at Aqaba customs, or, if you go searching for it, on the boat.

Visas

Jordanian **visas** (valid for 14 days or one month) are issued on board, or immediately after disembarkation. Things go quicker if you've already obtained one in Cairo, but British, Canadian, US, Australian and New Zealand citizens shouldn't have any trouble getting one on the spot. Charges vary according to nationality but it's cheaper to buy one here than in Cairo.

Travellers whose passports show **evidence of a visit to Israel** will not be allowed to land in Jordan, although a Taba entry stamp alone might be overlooked (but don't count on it). If you're lucky enough to have two passports, be sure to get a Nuweiba exit stamp in the one lacking any sign of Israel. Passing through Jordanian customs and immigration is a slow and tedious business.

Aqaba and Petra: some notes

Taxis and infrequent buses connect downtown **AQABA** with its port, 10km away. Aqaba's cheapest lodgings cluster around Municipality Square and the central post office: the *Jerusalem* and *Cliff Top* **hotels** are good ones to try.

Once you've tired of snorkelling (the best reefs are just south of the Marine Research Centre), Aqaba hasn't a lot to keep you. To move on, look for the bus terminal two blocks uphill of Municipality Square. From here you can catch a morning minibus or shared taxi (total fare 25JD) **to Petra** – the amazing rock-hewn city "half as old as time", as featured in *Indiana Jones and the Last Crusade*. The best budget places to stay around Petra are the *Student House* and *Musa Spring Hotel* in Wadi Musa. Minibuses and *JETT* buses from Petra run to the Jordanian capital, **Amman**.

Taba and the road to Israel

There are a few places of interest along the road to Taba. Roughly 20km north of Nuweiba, the new family-style resort at **BASATA** lets guests camp or rent huts on the beach for a few pounds (kitchen available), and it's possible to reserve rooms (£E25–35) at *Sally Land* from Cairo (☎743-689 between 5.30 and 10pm).

Eight kilometres before Taba you'll pass a motel named after **Pharaoh's Island**, just offshore, with a **Crusader fort** built to levy taxes on Arab merchants whilst ostensibly protecting pilgrims travelling between Jerusalem and Saint Catherine's. It's a nice little boat trip and there's a cafeteria on the island. Driving from Nuweiba to Taba takes about an hour.

Taba

TABA itself amounts to little more than a tourist complex, *Nelson's Village*, the deluxe *Sonesta Hotel* and 700m of palm-fronded beach. Yet it took ten years of bitter negotiations before international arbitration finally returned this disputed border enclave to Egypt on March 15, 1989. Hitherto, Israel had claimed that Taba lay outside the jurisdiction of the Camp David Accords, and then demanded US$60 million compensation for its investment in tourist facilities. For both sides the dispute was as much about saving face and exacting political capital. An apt symbol of relations between Egypt and Israel is the concrete platform erected for the handover ceremony, standing in the middle of nowhere.

The Israeli border – and on to Eilat

Because most transport and businesses shut down during the Israeli *shabbat*, it's unwise **to cross the border** on Fridays. Both checkpoints are open 24 hours, but officials are loath to do anything outside of 7am–9pm. The Egyptians levy a £E13 **exit tax** (also payable in US$), while the Israelis issue free one-month **visas** to British and most other EC nationals, US, Australian and New Zealand citizens. Say at the outset if you want them to stamp your entry card rather than your passport – an Israeli visa will certainly disqualify you from visiting other Arab countries, even if they don't notice your Taba exit stamp (for more about this, see the Aqaba stuff above and "Red Tape" in *Basics*). From the checkpoint you can catch a shared taxi (NIS 10) or #15 bus into Eilat.

Israel's number one holiday resort combines reefs and beaches with upfront hedonism and hustle. Thieving is rife and sleeping on the beaches can be risky, so it's advisable to find a proper bed in **EILAT** (almost impossible during Passover and other major Jewish holidays) – the Youth Hostel on the road into town and a cluster of places along HaNegev Street north of the main bus station are probably the cheapest options. The tourist office on Hatmarim Boulevard near the youth hostel is very helpful with local information.

THE INTERIOR

The **interior of Sinai** is a baking wilderness of jagged rocks, drifting sand and wind-scoured gravel pans, awesomely beautiful in its desolation. Yet life flourishes around its isolated springs and waterholes, or whenever rain falls, renewing the vegetation across vast tracts of semi-desert. Hinterland settlements bestride medieval pilgrimage routes which the Turks transformed from camel tracks into dirt roads, then the Egyptians and Israelis improved and fought over. Both sides also built and bombed the airstrips which the MFO now use to monitor the Sinai's demilitarised zones.

As a result, the only readily accessible part is **Saint Catherine's Monastery**, **Mount Sinai** and **Wadi Feiran Oasis**, although some other, smaller oases can be reached by jeep-safaris or camel treks from the Aqaba coast (as previously detailed). The **Plateau of el-Tih** (The Wanderings) via **Nekhl** and the thrice-embattled **Mitla Pass** can also be traversed, aboard the new cross-Sinai bus between Cairo and Nuweiba. However, because of the unexploded ordnance lying around, independent motoring is officially restricted outside the Saint Catherine's–Feiran Oasis area.

Saint Catherine's Monastery and Mt Sinai

Venerated by Christians, Jews and Muslims as the site of God's revelation of the Ten Commandments, **Mount Sinai** overlooks the valley where Moses is said to have heard the Lord speaking from a burning bush.

The bush is now enshrined in **Saint Catherine's Monastery**, nestling in a valley at the feet of the Mount, surrounded by high walls and lush gardens. As tourists have followed pilgrims in ever greater numbers the sacred mount has seen unseemly quarrels over sleeping space, and the monastery itself shows signs of strain. Yet for most travellers it remains a compelling visit, while other seldom visited peaks offer equally magnificent views if you're prepared to make the effort to reach them.

The Monastery of Saint Catherine

Open Mon–Thurs & Sat 9am–noon; closed Fri, Sun and public holidays; free.

The **Monastery of Saint Catherine** is a Greek Orthodox – rather than Coptic – foundation. Its origins date back to 337 AD, when the Byzantine **Empress Helena** ordered the construction of a chapel around the putative **Burning Bush**, already a focus for hermits and pilgrimage. During the sixth century, the site's

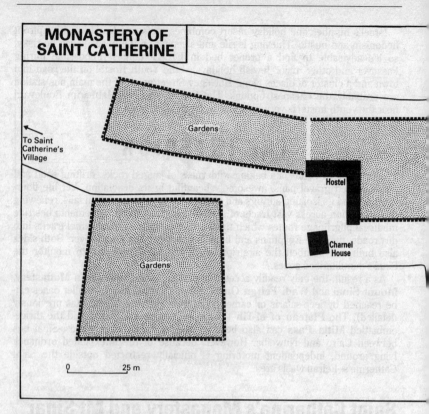

MONASTERY OF SAINT CATHERINE

Gardens

To Saint
Catherine's
Village

Hostel

Charnel
House

Gardens

0   25 m

vulnerability to raiders persuaded Emperor Justinian to finance a fortified enclosure and basilica, and to supply two hundred guards – half of them Greeks or Slavs – from whom the Jebeliya Bedouin claim descent.

Although the Prophet Mohammed is said to have guaranteed the monastery's protection after the Muslim conquest, the number of monks gradually dwindled until the "discovery" of Saint Catherine's relics (see below), which ensured a stream of pilgrims and bequests during the period of Crusader domination (1099–1270). Since then, it has had cycles of expansion and decline, on occasion being totally deserted. Today, Saint Catherine's accepts only monks of Greek origin (mostly from Mount Athos), who currently number seventeen.

Visiting the monastery

Modestly dressed visitors are currently admitted through a small gate in the northern wall near **Kléber's Tower** (named after the Napoleonic general who ordered its reconstruction) rather than the main portals facing west, one of which has a funnel for pouring boiling oil onto attackers. Built of granite, 10–15m high and 2–3m thick, the walls are essentially unchanged since Stephanos Ailisios designed them in the sixth century. Inside, however, restoration is proceeding apace and large sections of the monastery may be temporarily off-limits.

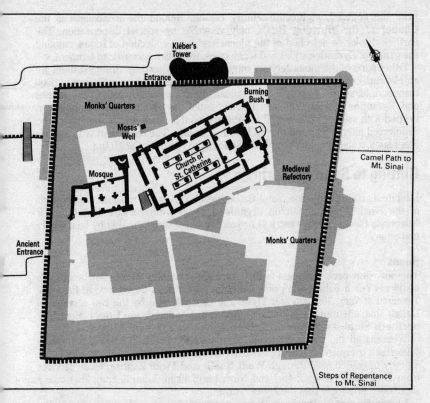

Kléber's
Tower

Entrance

Burning
Bush ■

Monks' Quarters

Moses'
Well

Church of
St. Catherine

Mosque

Medieval
Refectory

Camel Path to
Mt. Sinai

Ancient
Entrance

Monks' Quarters

Steps of Repentance
to Mt. Sinai

Emerging from the passage, a right turn takes you past **Moses' Well**, where the then-fugitive from Egypt met Zipporah, one of Jethro's seven daughters, whom he married at the age of forty. Walking the other way and around the corner, you'll see a thorny evergreen bush outgrowing an enclosure. This is the transplanted descendant of the **Burning Bush** whence God spoke to Moses: "Come now therefore, and I will send thee unto Pharaoh, that thou mayest bring forth my people the children of Israel out of Egypt" (Exodus 3:10). Sceptics may be swayed by the news that it's the only bush of its kind in the entire peninsula, and that all attempts to grow cuttings from it elsewhere have failed. The Bush was moved to its present site when Helena's chapel was built over its roots, behind the apse of the Church of Saint Catherine.

A granite basilica, **Saint Catherine's Church** was erected by Justinian between 542 and 551; the walls and pillars and the cedar-wood doors between the narthex and nave are all original. Its twelve pillars – representing the months of the year and hung with icons of the saints venerated during each one – have ornately carved capitals, loaded with symbolism. At the far end, a lavishly carved and gilded iconostasis rises towards a superb mosaic depicting Jesus flanked by Moses and Elijah, with Peter, John and James kneeling below – unfortunately roped-off and hard to see behind the ornate chandeliers and censers suspended from the coffered, eighteenth-century ceiling. Behind the iconostasis is the **Chapel of the Burning Bush**, only viewable by special dispensation. The narthex displays a selection of the monastery's vast collection of **icons**, running the gamut of Byzantine styles and techniques, from wax encaustic to tempera.

Other parts of the monastery are often closed to laypersons. Amongst them are an eleventh-century **mosque**, added to placate Muslim rulers; a **library** of 3000 manuscripts, surpassed only by the Vatican's; and a **refectory** with Gothic arches and Byzantine murals. You can usually enter the **charnel house**, however, heaped with monks' skeletons; the cemetery itself is small, so corpses have to be disinterred after a year and moved into the ossuary. The cadaver in vestments is Stephanos, a sixth-century guardian of one of the routes to the Mount.

Getting to Saint Catherine's

Despite its isolated location, Saint Catherine's is one of the most accessible parts of the Sinai. You can visit on **organised tours** from Na'ama Bay, Cairo or Hurghada (see respective entries) or you can make your own way by bus, *service* taxi or air.

Buses

The only drawback to **buses** is their variable schedules. When last heard, you could get reach Saint Catherine's **from Cairo** (8hr) on buses leaving the Sinai Terminal at 7am, 10.30am and 11pm, and probably also by the two services to Dahab that are routed via Saint Catherine's. Coming **from Upper Egypt or northern Sinai**, it's quicker to catch a bus from Suez (9.30am & 1pm).

Whereas all the above approach Saint Catherine's via **Wadi Feiran Oasis** (described overpage), the daily bus from Sharm (8am) and Dahab (9.30am) uses a newly upgraded road through **Wadi Nasib and Wadi Zaghra**, while services from Taba (10am & 1pm; 4hr) and Nuweiba (6.30am, 11am & 2pm; 2hr) take a more northerly route past the **Jebel Gunna**.

Leaving Saint Catherine's, buses normally collect passengers outside the *Cafeteria Catherine*. The Cairo service leaves around 1.30pm; buses to Nuweiba at 1.30pm and 2.30pm; and the Dahab and Sharm bus at about 1pm. It's best to arrive early and not place much trust in the later bus to Nuweiba.

Service taxis

For a group of travellers, another option is to engage a seven-seater **service taxi** at **Taba** (£E120) or **Suez** (£E80–90) and split the cost. Taxis usually run in the morning and afternoon if enough customers are interested, and hike their fares once the last bus has left. With hard bargaining, you could probably charter a private taxi for around £E130. Leaving St Catherine's, occasional *service* taxis may run to Dahab (£E7–8 a head) and other places depending on demand – prices double once the last bus has gone.

Flights

Travellers who can afford it might consider getting *Air Sinai* **flights** from Hurghada (Mon; US$60 one-way), Cairo (Mon & Sat; US$55) or Sharm el-Sheikh (2–3 weekly; US$40), simply for the amazing views of the peninsula. Flights from Cairo afford the longest look, passing over the Wilderness of the Wanderings as well as the southern mountains. Make reservations well beforehand.

Saint Catherine's village and accommodation

Buses often drop people outside the tourist village facing the monastery turn-off, 1km from **Saint Catherine's village**, before halting near the *Cafeteria Catherine* or the *Café al-Ekhlas*, whence sporadic minibuses run to the monastery gates. Arriving at the **airport**, 20km away, you'll be at the mercy of local taxis unless the holiday village sends its own bus (£E3).

Accommodation

Many travellers leave their packs in the monastery's storeroom (£E1.50) and ascend the camel path **to sleep out on Mount Sinai**. However, with night-time temperatures around 10°C during summertime and near-zero over winter (when frosts and snow aren't uncommon) a sleeping bag is essential. The nearest place you can pitch a tent – which is technically forbidden but seldom enforced – is Elijah's Hollow (see below). No one seems to use *Zeitouna Campsite* (stone huts or tent-sites £E5 per person), 5km along the road to Nuweiba.

Less alfresco **accommodation** includes the *El Salam Hotel* near the airport (singles £E40, doubles £E50); *Saint Catherine's Tourist Village* (singles US$50, doubles US$80 half-board); the adjacent *Hotel El Faroz*, with tiny huts (£E20 per bed) and dingy doubles with bathrooms (£E80); and the monastery's own *hostel*. At the latter, bunk beds (£E15; breakfast included) in cramped rooms with no access to showers can be reserved through the Greek Orthodox Patriarchate in Cairo (behind the Mosque of Beybars on Midan Zahir), or by asking at the monastery between 5 and 7pm (the gates are locked at 9.30pm).

Other facilities

The only tourist facilities in the Sinai interior are spread out along the two roads into Saint Catherine's village, which is essentially a cul-de-sac.

Past the *Hotel El Faroz* stands a tiny supermarket (Tues–Sun 8am–3pm & 5–9pm), a **petrol** station and the 24-hour *Cafeteria Catherine*, serving soup, beans, pasta, chicken and salad for £E10. The *Café al-Ekhlas* on the other road offers slightly less generous **meals**.

Nearby are the **post office** (Sat–Thurs 8am–2pm), **telephone exchange** (daily 8am–midnight; international calls) and well-stocked *Supermarket Katreen*, with a **hospital** and the **tourist police** opposite a **bank** (daily 10am–2pm & 6–9pm) which changes money and traveller's cheques. It's possible to register your passport at the **police** station on the hill above the shops.

Ascending Mount Sinai

Whilst some archaeologists question whether **Mount Sinai** was really the Biblical mountain where Moses received the Ten Commandments, it's hard not to agree with John Lloyd Stephens that "among all the stupendous works of Nature, not a place can be selected more fitting for the exhibition of Almighty power". A craggy, sheer-faced massif of grey and red granite "like a vengeful dagger that was dipped in blood many ages ago", its loftiest peak rises 2285m above sea level. Strictly speaking, it's only this that the Bedouin call *Jebel Musa* (Mount Moses), though the name is commonly applied to the whole massif. Some Biblical scholars reckon that Moses proclaimed the Commandments from Ras Safsaf, at the opposite end of the ridge, which overlooks a wide plain where the Israelites could have camped.

Walking to the summit

Neither of the two **routes to the summit** requires a guide.

The longer but easier ascent is via the switchback **camel path**, starting 50m behind the monastery. You can hire a camel for most of the ascent (US$10) but it's really worth the effort of walking (2hr 30min). Don't be misled by the peak with a conspicuous chapel, which is not Mount Sinai. Refreshment stalls along the way hike their prices the higher one gets, culminating in a guy on the top selling tea for £E2 a glass.

Beyond the cleft below the summit, the path is joined by the other route, known as the *Sikket Saiyidna Musa* (Path of our Lord Moses) or **Steps of Repentance**. Hewn by a penitent monk, the 3750 steps make a much steeper ascent from the monastery (90min), which is hell on one's leg muscles.

At present, the only building on the summit is a small **chapel** sited near the cave where God sheltered Moses: "I will put thee in a cleft of the rock, and will cover thee with my hand while I pass over" (Exodus 33:22). However, the Ministry of Tourism has recently revived President Sadat's idea of constructing an ecumenical centre atop the holy mount, for Christians, Jews and Muslims to pray together – a standing provocation to fundamentalist zealots of each faith, if it ever materialises. Meanwhile, the view over scores of arid peaks is breathtaking, particularly at sunset.

Many people ascend by the camel path and descend by the steps. Start your ascent around 5pm (earlier during winter) to avoid the worst of the heat and arrive in time to watch the spellbinding sunset. With a torch, you could also climb the camel path (but not the steps) by night.

Descending the steps you'll enter a depression containing a 500-year-old cypress tree, known as the Plain of Cypresses or **Elijah's Hollow**, where pilgrims pray and sing. Here Elijah heard God's voice (I Kings 19:9–18) and hid from Jezebel, being fed by ravens. One of the two chapels is dedicated to him, the other to his successor, Elisha.

Mount Catherine and Feiran Oasis

Nineteenth-century travellers were far less circumscribed than their present-day equivalents, who need to get permission from the village mayor and hire a Bedouin guide (£E30 a day, plus £E20 per camel) before embarking on any of the numerous Mount Sinai area trails described in Victorian editions of *Murray's Handbook*. Nowadays it's really only dedicated **hiking** or **camel trekking** buffs that bother to exploit the area's full potential.

As the shortest of these **wilderness routes** take five to six hours and the longer ones several days, you need to be fit and carry ample food and water; careless travellers can easily perish. A few trekkers go a stage further by living with Bedouin in their scattered camps.

Mount Catherine

Egypt's highest peak, **Mount Catherine** (*Jebel Katerina*; 2642m) lies roughly 6km south of Mount Sinai, and can be reached on foot in five to six hours. The path starts behind the village and runs up the Wadi el-Leja on Mount Sinai's western flank, past the deserted Convent of the Forty and a Bedouin hamlet. Shortly afterwards the trail forks; the lower path winding off up a rubble-strewn canyon, *Shagg Musa*, which it eventually quits to ascend Mount Catherine – an exhausting climb. On the summit are a chapel with water, a meteorological station and two rooms for pilgrims to stay overnight. The **panoramic view** encompasses most of the peninsula, from Hammam Faroun and the Wilderness of the Wanderings to the Arabian mountains beyond the Gulf of Aqaba.

According to tradition, it was on this peak that priests found the remains of **Saint Catherine** during the ninth or tenth century. Believers maintain that she was born in 294 AD in Alexandria of a noble family, converted to Christianity and subsequently lambasted Emperor Maxentius for idolatry; confounding fifty philosophers who tried to shake her faith. Following an attempt to break her on a spiked wheel (hence Catherine Wheels) which shattered at her touch, Maxentius had her beheaded; her remains being transported to the Sinai by angels. Others doubt that she ever existed and regard her cult as an invention of Western Catholicism, validated by "the land of her supposed sufferings" because of medieval France's demand for "holy oil" and other relics.

West to Wadi Feiran

It's thought that the ancient Israelites reached Mount Sinai by the same route that buses coming from the west use today, via Wadi Feiran and Wadi el-Sheikh. Travelling this road, you might glimpse the **Tomb of Nabi Salah** near the **Watiyyah Pass**, where Bedouin converge for an annual **moulid** (usually after the date harvest). Celebrants smear themselves with "lucky" tomb dust, sacrifice sheep, race camels, bury their dead and pray, before enacting a fantasia (*mesamerah*) and feasting on roast camel stuffed with sheep. Beyond the pass lies EL TAFRA, a small and dismal oasis village.

Roughly 60km from Saint Catherine's the road passes a huge walled garden marking the start of **WADI FEIRAN OASIS**. A twisting, granite-walled valley of palms and tamarisks, this was the earliest Christian stronghold in the Sinai, with its own bishop and convent, ruined during the seventh century but now rebuilt. More anciently, Wadi Feiran was supposedly the *Rephidim* of the Amalakites, who denied its wells to the thirsty Israelites, causing them to curse Moses until he smote the Rock of Horeb with his staff, and water gushed forth. Refreshed, they joined battle with the Amalakites next day, inspired by the sight of Moses standing on a hilltop, believed to have been the conical one that the Bedouin call **Jebel el-Tannuh**, with ruined chapels lining the track to its summit (1hr).

Other **hiking** possibilities in the area include **Jebel el-Banat** (1510m), further north, and the highly challenging ascent of **Jebel Serbal** (2070m), south of the oasis. This is approached via the broad and rugged Wadi Aleyat, with a few springs at its upper end. From here you can either follow a goat track up a steep, boulder-strewn ravine called **Abu Hamad** (5hr) or take the longer but less precipitous **Sikket er-Reshshah** (Path of the Sweaty) to the summit. From the main peak on the ridge there's a wonderful view of the oasis, countless mountains and wadis, with a narrow ledge jutting over a 1200m precipice. Although Feiran lacks any tourist accommodation, you could probably camp out somewhere in the palm groves with local consent.

En route to the coast, **motorists** might consider detouring north to the turquoise mines of Jebel Abu Alaqa and the rock-hewn temple at Sarabit el-Khadim (see p.525).

The Wilderness of the Wanderings

Separating the granite peaks of southern Sinai from the sandy wastes of the north is a huge table-land of gravel plains and fissured limestone, riven by wadis – the **Wilderness of the Wanderings** (*Badiet el-Tih*). Life exists in this desert thanks to sporadic rainfall between mid-October and mid-April; two or three downpours are enough to send yellow torrents surging down the **Wadi el-Arish**, rejuvenating clumps of *rhtum* (broom) and *ghraghada* (a prickly tribulus with fleshy leaves enjoyed by camels) and refilling the cisterns (*harabas*) which irrigate groves of palms and tamarisks. During Byzantine times, the cisterns sustained dozens of villages along the Sinai–Negev border; nowadays, the largest irrigated gardens are in Wadi Feiran and Wadi el-Arish.

Crossing the Wilderness via Nekhl and the Mitla Pass

On moonlit nights it's possible to glimpse the great Wilderness from the windows of the new direct night service bus between Cairo and Nuweiba (reserve seats the day before). For most of its 290km length the newly upgraded road follows the former *Darb el-Hadj* pilgrimage trail from Suez to Aqaba.

The route from Nuweiba

Travelling the route **from Nuweiba**, the road heads north to EL-THAMMED before cutting west across the Wadi el-Arish. **NEKHL**, at the heart of the peninsula, features another derelict castle built by Sultan al-Ghuri in 1516. South of one of the wadi's many tributaries lies **Ras el-Gindi** (also accessible by a minor road leaving the Suez coast at Sudr), a **ruined fortress** erected by Salah al-Din.

Moving west, the road climbs through the 480-metre-high **Mitla Pass**, one of three cleavages in the central plateau. When Ralph Bagnold attempted this route from Cairo by Model-T Ford in the early 1920s, it was choked with "yellow undulating cushions" of sand which buried the wire-mesh road laid by the British during World War I. The outcome of three Arab-Israeli conflicts was arguably determined at the Metla Pass in some of the bloodiest tank **battles** in history. During the war of 1956, an Israeli parachute battalion seized and held the road until the arrival of armoured columns coming up from el-Kuntila and el-Thammed, which subsequently dominated the interior. Having deployed their tanks in expectation of a similar strategy, the Egyptians were likewise wrongfooted during the 1967 War, when the Israelis advanced from Abu Ageila, captured the passes and then systematically annihilated their encircled foes, leaving the roadside littered with charred vehicles. In the October War of 1973, Egyptian forces failed to exploit their breakthrough along the Bar-Lev Line by taking the Mitla and Giddi passes; many blamed their subsequent defeat on the cautiousness of the Commander-in-Chief, General Ismail.

NORTHERN SINAI

While jagged mountains dominate the gulf coasts and interior of the peninsula, **northern Sinai** is awash with sand – pale dunes rising from coastal salt marshes and lagoons to meet gravel plains and wadis far inland. A succession of waterholes along the coastal strip between Egypt and Palestine has made this *Via*

MORE ON THE SINAI BEDOUIN

Nomadic Bedouin are keen observers of the Sinai's furtive **wildlife**. Hares and foxes can lead them to waterholes; desert sandgrouse, gazelles and the rare mountain ibex (*bedan*) make good hunting; and flocks must be guarded against the depredations of the jackal (*taaleb*), wolf (*dib*) and hyena (*dhaba*). The latter has a mythological counterpart, the *dhabia*, believed to have the power of mesmerising solitary travellers into entering its lair. Other creatures imbued with supernatural significance are the dreaded horned viper, known as *Abu Jenabiya* (Father of Going Sideways), and the fox, personifying wisdom and cunning. *Abu l'Husain* (Father of the Fortress) is a favourite character in children's tales.

Storytelling holds a special place in Bedouin culture, where poetic imagery and Koranic rhetoric sprang naturally from the lips of shepherds exposed to a rich oral heritage since childhood. When food is lacking for guests, hospitality can still be rendered in words: "Had I known that you would honour me by walking this way, I should have strewn the path between your house and mine with mint and rose petals!". Although professional reciters (*rawi*) of Arabic poetry are now rare, most Bedouin can reel off folktales, which usually begin with the phrase "*Kan ma kan . . .*" (There was, there was not).

Conversation is the expected reward for Bedouin **hospitality**, which traditionally stretched to three days, each named after a stage in the ritual: *salaam* (greeting), *ta'aam* (eating) and *kalaam* (speaking). Before the rising of the morning star on the fourth day, hosts helped their guests prepare for departure; those who lingered beyond the drying of the dew were as welcome "as the spotted snake". Honour can now be satisfied by three servings of tea or coffee (accepting further offers is rude), and it's no longer mandatory to slaughter an animal. The old Sinai custom that allowed a man to kill his neighbour's sheep in order to feed eminent guests caused so many disputes that the British abolished it.

Tribal honour and authority have always outweighed fealty to whichever government controlled the Sinai, and the Bedouin have a long tradition of **smuggling**. Hashish and guns were the favoured contraband under British administration, when Bedouin trackers were employed by the police to follow smugglers across the almost featureless gravel plains. Prior to Israel evacuating the Sinai in 1982, stolen cars and a tank were buried here for eventual resale in Egypt; the Israelis tried to find them by comparing photographs of sand dunes! Despite helicopter spotters and border patrols, some Bedouin still manage to slip across the frontier between Sinai and the Negev Desert, and thence into Jordan – or so locals privately boast.

Maris the favoured route for trade and invasions since late pharaonic times. However, few of the settlements have ever amounted to much, nor deserve a visit nowadays. Although Egyptians have begun flocking to the palmy beaches at **el-Arish**, most foreigners just zip through on direct buses between Cairo and Tel Aviv or Jerusalem, crossing over at **Rafah**; Khan Yunis and Gaza City, just across the border, are briefly covered after el-Arish.

Short of flying *Air Sinai* (Sun & Thurs; US$55 one-way) from Cairo to el-Arish, access to northern Sinai from mainland Egypt means crossing the Suez Canal. Daily buses from the Sinai Terminal in Abbassiya (7am, 8am & 1pm; £E12) and irregular *service* taxis from Koulali Square (£E11; mostly in the morning) travel **from Cairo** to el-Arish in five to six hours, using the car ferry north of Ismaliya. Coming **from Port Said or Suez**, it's easier to catch a *service* taxi to west Qantara, cross over by the free "people ferry", and then ride another *service* taxi or bus along the coast to el-Arish. With no north–south transport across the Sinai peninsula, it's only possible to **travel between the Mediterranean and Aqaba coasts** via Cairo or Suez. If the advertised bus service between Suez and el-Arish (4hr 30min) isn't running, as is often the case, you'll need to travel to Qantara and switch vehicles – luckily, a fairly swift process.

The road from Suez to El-Arish

Roughly 40km out of QANTARA (see p.511) towards el-Arish the road passes south (and out of sight) of **Pelusium**. This fortress-town (recorded in the Bible as the "Strength of Egypt") guarded Egypt's western border for many centuries. Legend has it that the army of Cambyses induced the garrision here to surrender without a fight by driving cats (the sacred animal of the goddess Bastet) before them. In Roman times, it was somewhere near here that Ptolemy XII ordered the murder of Pompey whilst competing for the throne against his sister, Cleopatra.

The coastal strip is suitably desolate, with salt marshes, windblown dunes and a long-abandoned railway line. Over the next 200km, a few dunes, palms and Bedouin barely enliven the swathes of sand and scrub that separate the ramshackle villages named after wells. Whereas nineteenth-century guidebooks compared the merits of vital watering holes like BIR EL-ABD ("brackish water and some telegraph-men's huts") and MAZAR ("it is better not to camp near the well on account of the camel ticks"), modern travellers can drive through without a qualm on the bus.

The provision of government schools, medical posts and water tanks in such villages has enticed many **Bedouin** to foresake nomadic lives, though others still roam the desert with their flocks, pursuing the grazing. From the road you can sometimes glimpse black-garbed women in veils or leather masks spangled with coins; girls in peacock-robes with hennaed tresses; aloof boys and men or a black tent pitched in the desert. Women are responsible for weaving the goats-hair *beit shaar* ("house of hair") and striking, packing, unloading and erecting them whenever the family moves on; in Bedouin divorces the husband gets the domestic animals while the woman keeps the tent. The colour of the cross-stitched embroidery on a woman's robe and hood indicates whether she's married (red) or not (blue).

El-Arish

Originally a Roman garrison town named *Rhinocolorum* ("Noses Cut Off"), after the fate of dissidents exiled there, **EL-ARISH** has experienced more than its fair share of invasions. Happily the latest one is peaceful and largely welcomed – Egyptian tourists attracted to the palm-shaded beaches and bracing rollers. But Westerners have been slow to follow, which is why the tourist poster advertising el-Arish superimposes their images on the beach – real *khawagas* are rarely seen outside of buses or the Egoth Oberoi.

Whether through cause or effect, el-Arish is more conservative than the Aqaba coast resorts, with restrictions on booze and dress and a relatively subdued night-life. However, for a group of travellers into renting a beach flat and providing their own entertainment, el-Arish could be the place.

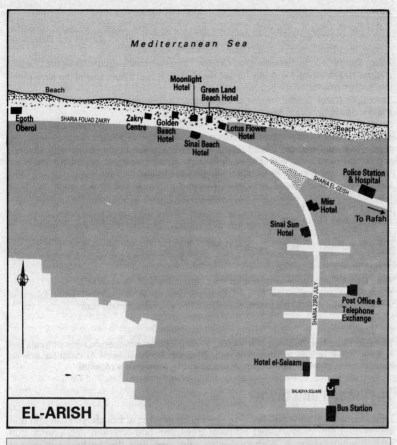

Mediterranean Sea

Beach

Moonlight Hotel

Green Land Beach Hotel

Egoth Oberoi

SHARIA FOUAD ZAKRY

Zakry Centre

Golden Beach Hotel

Sinai Beach Hotel

Lotus Flower Hotel

Beach

Police Station & Hospital

SHARIA EL-GEISH

Misr Hotel

To Rafah

Sinai Sun Hotel

SHARIA 23RD JULY

Post Office & Telephone Exchange

Hotel el-Salaam

BALADIYA SQUARE

Bus Station

EL-ARISH

The dialling code for calling Arish from outside is ☎068.

Arriving and finding somewhere to stay

From a visitor's standpoint there are really only two streets in town. Arriving from the west, you'll cruise along **Fouad Zakry** – parallel to the beach – until it swings inland and downhill to become **23rd July Street**. This eventually turns into a **souk** of wooden-shuttered stores that look like a set from a Wild West movie and terminaes in **Baladiya Square**, with its raucous mosque and fuming **bus station**. Minibuses (20pt) and *service* taxis (50–75pt) constantly shuttle between the souk and the beach, sparing the 2–3km walk and stopping at any point along the way.

Outside of July–September there shouldn't be any problem **finding somewhere to stay**. New places are springing up every year, mostly aimed at middle-class Egyptians. Only if you're in a group, or you don't feel happy without A/C and mod cons, is it worth booking in advance. Places listed on the following page are ranked in their order of appearance as you come in from the west.

HOTELS AND VILLAS

Hotel Egoth Oberoi (☎341-988; ☎778-033 direct from Cairo). Luxurious singles (US$100), doubles (US$135) and triples (US$160), half board included plus 15 percent tax. Deferential service, nightclub acts, a pool and tennis courts for guests only.

Zakry Centre, next to *American Fried Chicken*. Upmarket, family-sized villas on the beach.

Golden Beach Hotel. Single (£E10) and double (£E18) beach huts. One of the more primitive "tourist villages" on the beach.

Moonlight Hotel. Another warren of simple rooms nearby, priced per bed (£E10). Friendly and disorganised.

Sinai Beach Hotel (☎341-713). A swanky building on Fouad Zakry Street. Doubles (£E45) and triples (£E60) with private bathrooms and A/C. Breakfast £E4.

Maxim's Restaurant (☎342-850). Rents two-to-three-person beach chalets with kitchens and hot showers for £E55–60 (£E70 with balcony). Groups of six can get full bed and board for £E40 each per day. The owner speaks English and German.

Green Land Beach Hotel (☎340-601). Nearer the mosque just off the beach. Adequate double (£E18), triple (£E25) and quadruple (£E30) rooms, mostly with shared bathrooms. Breakfast £E3, lunch £E9.

Lotus Flower Hotel (☎342-270) Next door. Suites with bathroom and TV, sleeping up to six, for £E60; less out of season.

Sinai Sun Hotel (☎341-855). Singles (US$25), doubles (US$30), triples (US$44) and suites (US$75), with bathrooms, A/C, TV and breakfast. You can make reservations in Cairo (☎913-292) or Port Said (☎221-242).

Misr Hotel. Simple place with basic facilities farther downhill. Doubles £E12.

Hotel el-Salaam, around the corner Baladiya Square, above the *Aziz Restaurant*. Rooms of varying sizes for £E5–10 (£E12 with bathroom). Hot water and friendly staff.

CAMPING

El-Arish Camping, 7km west of town (£E1 by taxi). Spacious two-person tents with cots and lighting (£E6), or £E3 to pitch your own. It might also be possible to camp for free on beaches nearer town, but police permission (not always granted) is required.

The beach and town

Despite the huts and chalets lining several kilometres of **beach**, you can still find uncrowded stretches shaded by palm trees, the odd wrecked anti-aircraft gun adding a surreal touch. With cooler, rougher seas than the Aqaba coastline and no reefs, Arish's beach is better for bracing dips and idle sunbathing than snorkelling or diving (there's no dive shop, anyway). Foreigners often get invited to join family gatherings and for solo women travellers this can be a good way to avoid hassle from lecherous youths. Visitors are exhorted to stay off the beach after dark and dress modestly when in town; rules enforced by the police.

The Bedouin market and handicrafts museum

For a town of 35,000 inhabitants, el-Arish offers few sights or entertainments. On Wednesdays families ride into town for the **Bedouin market**, to sell embroidered dresses and camel saddles. If you're serious about buying, check out the tackier stuff in tourist shops on 23rd July Street to establish standards and prices before looking for something superior – and haggling like mad – at the Bedouin souk.

You might also try to take a look at the town's sporadically open **museum** of handicrafts and stuffed Sinai wildlife, out along the Rafah road (catch a bus or *service* taxi). Arish's only other "sight" is the multicoloured minaret halfway along 23rd July Street.

Nightlife and food

Smoking *sheeshas* over backgammon in a café on 23rd July Street is usually all that Arish can offer in the way of **nightlife** – and that's an exclusively male pursuit. Otherwise, the **outdoor restaurant** opposite the *Hotel Oberoi* and an unmarked **dance hall** on the beach nearer town occasionally host entertainers during high season. The cheapest places to eat are the *fuul* and *taamiya* joints around Baladiya Square or the simple **restaurants** along 23rd July Street. *Aziz* (below the *Hotel el-Salaam*) and *Sammar* (300m up the road) do good *kofta* and salad, or chicken and chips, at reasonable rates. Fish stuffed with lemon (£E20) can be had at *Maxim's* on the beach. Only the *Egoth Oberoi* sells alcohol.

Other practicalities

If needed, the **tourist police and information** kiosk can be found on Fouad Zakry, just before the beach; the main **police** station (☎120/1/2) and municipal **hospital** (☎340-010; ambulances ☎340-123) lie east along Sharia el-Geish, which forks off inland. *Pharmacy Fouad* (daily 9am–midnight) on 23rd July can recommend a doctor.

One block further north and across the road, a side street leads to the building housing Arish's **post office** (Sat–Thurs 9am–3pm) and 24-hour **telephone exchange** (international calls possible).

Transport

To be certain of a seat on direct buses **from el-Arish to Cairo** (7am, 10am, 3pm, 4pm & 5pm), you have to book the day before. A spur-of-the-moment alternative is to catch one of the regular buses to **Qantara** (hourly) or **Ismaliya** (every 90min; 4hr 30min), and then a *service* taxi from there. During the morning, there should also be direct **service taxis** from el-Arish to Cairo, where passengers are usually dropped at Koulali Square.

Twice-weekly **flights** to Cairo depart from the airport south of town along the Bir Lahfan road.

North to Rafah, Gaza and Israel

Travelling from **el-Arish to the border town of Rafah** and **crossing into Israel** is usually fairly easy. You should be aware, though, that the road north of Rafah to Tel Aviv runs through the Gaza Strip and violent confrontations between Israeli forces and Palestinian refugees often occur on Fridays, Palestinian or Muslim holidays – days to avoid travelling on. Keep in mind, too, that the entire Strip is currently under curfew (8pm–4am), so it's advisable to leave el-Arish before midday to avoid getting stuck in Gaza.

Rafah

Buses (every 30min–1hr) and *service* taxis make short work of the 41km from el-Arish to **RAFAH**. The Egyptian part of this divided town consists of a large chunk of Rafah refugee camp, separated by barbed wire from the larger camp and town proper on the Israeli side. Before returning the Sinai to Egypt as part of the Camp David peace treaty, Israel redrew the border, separating families and friends who shout messages to each other across the wire every morning.

Tourists are charged £E13 **exit tax** (also payable in US$) before leaving Egypt and **crossing the border** (open winter 9am–5pm; summer 10am–6pm). Although North Americans, Antipodeans and Europeans should get free **Israeli visas** on the spot, a few unfortunates experience heavy baggage searches and *Shin Bet* questioning.

Beyond the checkpoint you'll pass (on your left) the turning for Rafah's unexpectedly fine beach, while straight ahead lies a junction where taxis collect and dump passengers. From here you can get a ride into Rafah town (*Rafah Balad*) or Khan Yunis, and maybe even Gaza.

On to Gaza and Tel Aviv

If there's no direct service available at Rafah, simply change taxis in **KHAN YUNIS**. Try not to get stuck, however. The only place to stay in this shabby, ultra-conservative market town is a mega-costly hotel on nearby Katif Beach.

GAZA CITY has three **hotels**, of which the best budget choice is the *Hotel al-Waleed* on Omar al-Mukhtar Street, ten to fifteen minutes' walk towards the sea from Palestine Square. As well as being the heart of Gaza, this is the departure point for **service taxis** to Jerusalem, Beersheva and points east. Towns along the coastal road as far as Tel Aviv can be reached by taxis from Shujaiya Square, at the far end of Wahida Street. A taxi between the two depots costs US$1.

CHAPTER EIGHT

THE RED SEA COAST AND EASTERN DESERT

For 1250km, from Suez to the Sudanese border, turquoise waves lap rocky headlands and windswept beaches along a coastline separated from the Nile Valley by arid hills and mountains. Like Sinai, the region's infertility and sparse population belie its mineral wealth and strategic location, and there are further points in common in the wildlife, Bedouin nomads and long monastic tradition. But while Sinai is an international crossroads, with multiple attractions, the Red Sea Coast and the Eastern Desert are a cul-de-sac where tourism is largely confined to a single resort.

An *entrepôt* since ancient times, the **Red Sea Coast** was once a microcosm of half the world, as Muslim pilgrims from as far away as Central Asia sailed to Arabia from its ports. Though piracy and slaving ceased towards the end of the nineteenth century, smuggling still drew adventurers like Henri de Monfried long after the Suez Canal had sapped the vitality of the Red Sea ports. Decades later, the coastline assumed new significance with the discovery of oil and its vulnerability to Israeli commando raids, which led to large areas being mined – one reason why tourism didn't arrive until the 1980s.

Although Cairenes appreciate the beaches at **Ain Sukhna**, south of Suez, the real lure consists of fabulous **reefs** and **water sports** around **Hurghada**. Aside from diving buffs, few tourists visit **Port Safaga** or **el-Quesir**, and anywhere beyond them feels like the end of the world. However, connections between the three ports and the Nile Valley are actually quite effective.

Crossing the **Eastern Desert** by bus gives little idea of its spectacular highlands. Apparently devoid of life, the granite ranges and limestone wadis harbour ancient temples and quarries, gazelles and ibexes, and Bedouin. While you might not have the inclination, stamina or money for long excursions into the interior, thousands of Copts visit the **Red Sea monasteries**, and truck-loads of dervishes converge on **Wadi Humaysara** for the **Moulid of al-Shazli**. If totally off-the-beaten-track destinations are your thing, the Eastern Desert has more to offer than appears.

WARNING – MINEFIELDS

Large areas of Red Sea coastline and many wadis are still mined. Any area with barbed wire fencing (however rusty) is suspect. Don't wander off public beaches or into the desert without a guide.

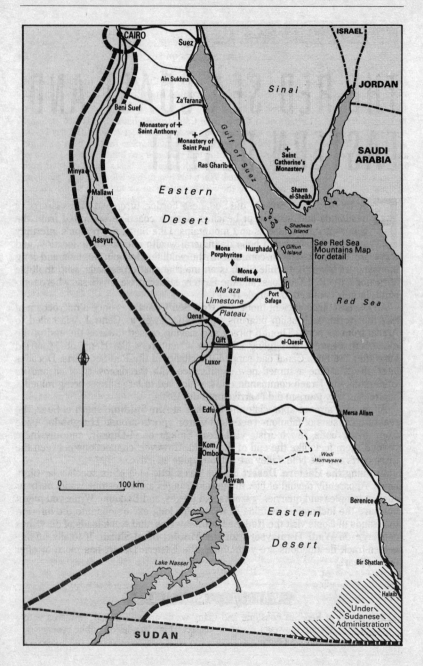

Approaches to Hurghada

Almost everyone heads straight for **Hurghada**, whose multiplicity of approaches makes it more accessible than its isolated location suggests. Vehicles go flat out along the coastal highway and desert roads, but a full tank of petrol is essential – there are few if any pumps en route. Getting to the Red Sea monasteries is covered separately, and some of the desert routes from the Nile are described in more detail later on.

● **From Cairo** Daily *EgyptAir/ZAS* **flights** from Cairo to Hurghada (1hr; US$65 one-way) need to be booked several days in advance during peak season (Oct & Nov). The day before should be sufficient for **buses** from Ahmed Helmi Terminal, near Ramses Station; to get there, cross the iron bridge, bear right past the taxi rank and you'll find it behind a row of fruit stalls – the ticket hutch is off to the left, though Hurghada buses actually depart from farther down the street, outside the terminal. When last heard, they left at 7.30am, 3pm, 9pm, 9.30pm, 10.30pm and 11pm daily, doing the 540km journey in six to twelve hours. Tickets range from £E8–12 for nominally A/C services to £E20 for a *Superjet*. Additional A/C 7am and 10pm buses stop at Hurghada and Port Safaga en route to el-Quesir. During the morning, there might also be **service taxis** from the neighbouring depot to Ahmed Helmi.

● **From Suez** The 410km from Suez can be covered in four to five hours by **service taxi** (£E10), or at a less perilous speed by **buses** (6–8hr) from the city's adjacent Arba'in terminal. Although buses are inconveniently scheduled (5am, 5.30am, 6am & 5pm, 5.30pm, 6pm), and few vehicles have A/C, seats (£E10–11) can usually be obtained at an hour's notice.

● **From Sinai** Suez can serve for connections if you can't afford direct transportation from Sinai. *Air Sinai* flies to Hurghada several times weekly from **Sharm** (US$50), and once a week from **Saint Catherine's** (US$70); early bookings are advised. The same goes for **ferries from Sharm**, which sail daily except Saturday, taking anywhere from five to fifteen hours depending on the weather and the state of the vessel (around £E55 one-way).

● **From the Nile Valley** Especially during winter, hordes of travellers seek a change from the Nile Valley. Daily **buses from Luxor** (6am & noon; £E9) may be standing-room only even before reaching **Qena** and taking the desert road towards Port Safaga and Hurghada (4–5hr). There's more chance of a seat on buses starting from Qena at 6.30am, 4pm, 5.30pm and 7pm, all of which run onto Suez, passing the turn-off for Saint Paul's Monastery (3–4hr; £E7). **Service taxis from Qena** (£E8) take hairpin bends at reckless speed, while *EgyptAir* has two to three weekly **flights from Luxor** (1hr; US$30). Most days, usually in the morning, a few **service taxis** may also cross the desert between Beni Suef and Za'farana, or Qift and Quesir; Edfu to Mersa Allam is less likely.

Between Suez and Hurghada

Without private transport or a firm intention to visit the Red Sea monasteries (see overpage), it's hardly worth stopping **between Suez and Hurghada**. Except for the first 30km, chewed up by tanks in the 1973 War, the road is excellent, with little traffic, and most of the blind corners are over by the time drivers get accustomed to speeding on the straights. Heading south past oil-related grot which recurs at intervals all along the coast, you'll see parched highlands rising inland. The **Jebel Ataqa** is the northernmost range in the Eastern Desert and an old Bedouin smuggling route by which hashish reached Cairo; Henri de Monfreid (author of *Hashish*) sent his cargo this way.

Ain Sukhna

Roughly 50km south of Suez, a series of beaches, coves and parked cars marks **AIN SUKHNA**, where middle-class Cairenes come to picnic at weekends. Ain Sukhna's name derives from the hot springs that originate in the Jebel Ataqa, but it's the sea that attracts people. Dark patches offshore indicate **coral reefs**, while rusty barbed wire fences delineate areas sown with land-mines (along the shore and beneath the cliffs); the **beaches** frequented by Egyptians should be okay.

Buses will drop you on request but getting a lift out again could be problematic, and with no shops around it's necessary to bring supplies if you're going to camp. The *Ein Sukhna* **hotel** charges £E40–55 for a double room or bungalow.

Za'farana

Charlie Pye-Smith reckoned **ZA'FARANA** "an ideal set for an Eastern spaghetti western", with dogs outnumbering its human population; a lighthouse, petrol pump and a couple of cafés. With nowhere to stay, it's only worth visiting in the hope of *service* taxis or hitchable traffic in the direction of Saint Anthony's or Saint Paul's Monastery (see below). Locals can point out a stretch of beach that's free of mines, Za'farana's sole amenity. The town's name means "saffron", after the spice boats that once docked here.

Ras Gharib and on to Hurghada

The next bus stop is at **RAS GHARIB**, 101km south: a drab and smelly township with a desalination plant, artesian wells and offshore oil rigs. Just south along the coast is the Mallaaha salt pan, where Ma'aza Bedouin once profited from breaking the British empire's salt monopoly.

From Ras Gharib to Hurghada is 145km of nothingness.

The Red Sea Monasteries

Secreted amidst the arid Red Sea Hills, Egypt's oldest **monasteries** – dedicated to **Saint Paul** and **Saint Anthony** – trace their origins back to the infancy of Christian monasticism, observing rituals that have scarcely changed over sixteen centuries. This tangible link with the primitive church gives them a special resonance for Coptic believers, but you don't have to be religious to appreciate their tranquil atmosphere and imposing setting – there's also scope for **bird-watching** and **hiking** in the vicinity.

Getting there – and staying

Though neither monastery is directly accessible by public transport, they can still be reached in several ways.

One option is to join pilgrim **tours** arranged **from Cairo** by the Coptic Patriarchate (22 Sharia Ramses, Abbassiya; ☎821-274), *YMCA* (27 Sharia al-Gumhorriya; ☎917-360) or *Egyptian Centre of International Cultural Cooperation* (11 Sharia Shagar al-Durr, Zamalek; ☎341-5419); Coptic churches in Minya, Assyut and Luxor may also run tours on a non-profitmaking basis.

An alternative is to travel from Hurghada, Suez or Za'farana. **Tours** from Hurghada are strictly commercial, with the best deal offered by *Misr Travel*, which does tours to both monasteries for £E85, including lunch. For those undeterred by bargaining, **hired taxis** are another option. A six- to eight-hour excursion should cost about £E120 from Suez, £E150–70 from Cairo or Hurghada; taxis from Za'farana might do a four- to five-hour jaunt for around £E60–70. An overnight stay for your driver adds at least £E20 to these rates.

The cheapest method combines **public transport, hitching and walking**. Outside of the hottest months, this shouldn't be dangerous providing you bring ample water and minimal luggage. Any bus from Cairo or Suez to Hurghada can drop you at the **turn-off for Saint Paul's Monastery**, 26km south of Za'farana, which is recognisable by its plastic-roofed shelter and "Hassan Alam Contracting" sign. Young Copts alight here, confident of hitching to the monastery, 13km uphill, for there's a fair amount of traffic along the well-paved road. If pilgrims visiting both sites don't offer you a lift, Saint Anthony's Monastery can be approached via **service taxis** running between Beni Suef and Za'farana. From the signposted turn-off 33km west of Za'farana, it's 15km uphill to the monastery, with reasonable hitching prospects. To drive from one to the other (82km) takes about ninety minutes; it's also possible to hike across the mountains (see below).

If you don't mind austerity, **staying** awhile might appeal. Both monasteries now have extramural guesthouses for visitors, though to stay at Saint Paul's you must obtain prior permission from the Patriarchate in Cairo. Contrary to assertions in other guidebooks, women can now stay at *both* monasteries. Neither of the monasteries has showers or cooking facilities and you'll need to bring food and bedding (drinking water is supplied). A donation of money or staples like tea, oil, rice or sugar is definitely appropriate. Respect conventions on dress and behaviour; smoking and drinking alcohol are forbidden.

> *Both Saint Anthony and Saint Paul monasteries are open 9am–5pm daily; they are closed to visitors during Lent and the pre-Christmas fast (Nov 25–Jan 7).*

The Monastery of Saint Anthony

West of Za'farana a wide valley cleaves the Galala Plateau and sets the road on course for the Nile, 168km away. Called **Wadi Arraba**, its name derives from the carts which once delivered provisions to the monastery, though legend attributes it to the pharaoh's chariots that pursued the Israelites towards the Red Sea. Turning off the road and south into the hills, it's possible to spot the monastery sited beneath a dramatic ridge of cliffs.

Lofty walls with an interior catwalk surround the **Monastery of Saint Anthony** (*Deir Amba Antonyus* or *Deir Qaddis Antwan*), whose lanes of two-storey dwellings, churches, mills and gardens basically amounts to a village. Despite importing produce from its own farm near Beni Suef, the community remains largely self-sufficient – and utterly dependent on its **spring**, where Arab legend has it that Miriam, sister of Moses, bathed during the Exodus.

An English-speaking monk like Father Zakariya or Brother Discours will give you a partial tour of the monastery, which varies with each visitor; don't expect to see everything. The oldest of the five **churches** – featuring thirteenth-century murals and graffiti – is dedicated to the monastery's namesake, who may be buried underneath it. During Lent (when the gates are locked and deliveries are winched over the walls), monks celebrate the liturgy in the twelve-domed Church of Saint Luke, dating from 1776. Other highlights include the **keep**, a soot-blackened **bakery** and a **library** of over 1700 manuscripts.

All of these buildings are recent compared to the monastery's foundation, shortly after Anthony's death in 356. A sojourn by Saint John the Short (whose body was later stolen by other monks) is all that's known of its early **history**, but an influx of refugees from Wadi Natrun, and then Melkite monks, occurred during the sixth and seventh centuries. Subsequently pillaged by Bedouin and razed by Nasr al-Dawla, the monastery was restored during the twelfth century by Coptic monks, from whose ranks several Ethiopian bishops were elected. After a murderous revolt by the monastery servants, it was reoccupied by Coptic, Syrian and Ethiopian monks. Today's brethren include many university graduates and ex-professionals – not unlike the kind of people drawn to monasticism in the fourth century AD.

Saint Anthony's Cave

Early morning or late afternoon is the best time to ascend to **Saint Anthony's Cave**, 2km from, and 276m above, the monastery (carry water). After a gentle start the path becomes extremely steep, with rickety handrails (1–2hr), but the stunning views from 680m above the Red Sea reward your effort. Technicolour wadis and massifs spill down into the azure gulf, with Sinai's mountains rising beyond. The *maghara* where Anthony spent his last 25 years contains medieval graffiti and modern *tilbas* – scraps of paper supplications inscribed "Remember, Lord, your servant", which pilgrims stick into cracks in the rock. **Bird life** – hoopoes, desert larks, ravens, blue rockthrushes and pied wagtails – is surprisingly abundant, and by sleeping out you might glimpse shy **gazelles** around dawn.

Hiking to Saint Paul's

Though not something to undertake lightly, fit, experienced walkers might consider **hiking over the mountains to Saint Paul's**. Brother Discours has a detailed, slightly confusing map of the region, and a German traveller recently accomplished the three-day hike – but its inherent risks can't be overstated. Running out of water and getting lost will almost certainly prove fatal.

The Monastery of Saint Paul

The **Monastery of Saint Paul** has always been overshadowed by Saint Anthony's. Its titular founder, Paul the Theban, was only sixteen when he fled Alexandria to escape Decius's persecutions, making him the earliest known hermit. But when visited by Anthony, Paul acknowledged his spiritual superiority by giving him a tunic of palm leaves, and was content to play second fiddle during his lifetime (228–348). *Deir Amba Bula* (or *Deir Mari Bolus*) was a form of posthumous homage by Paul's followers: its turreted walls are built around the cave where he lived for decades. The monastery's fortunes subsequently followed those of its more prestigious neighbour.

The monastery is smaller than Saint Anthony's and a little more primitive-looking, too. In its main **Church of Saint Paul**, the murals, too, are less fluid – though better preserved thanks to gung-ho restoration. A monk will show you round the chapels and identify their icons: notice the angel of the furnace with Shadrach, Meshach and Abednego, and the ostrich eggs hung from the ceiling – a symbol of the Resurrection. The southern sanctuary of the larger **Church of Saint Michael** contains a gilded icon of the head of John the Baptist on a dish. When Bedouin raided the monastery, its monks retreated into the **keep**, supplied with spring-water by a hidden canal.

SAINT ANTHONY

The life of **Saint Anthony** (251–356) coincided with a sea change in Christianity's position. When Anthony was orphaned at the age of eighteen, he placed his sister in a convent, sold his possessions and became a hermit. Christians at the time faced growing persecution – the "Era of Martyrs" from which the Coptic calendar is dated – but the transformation of Christianity into a state religion in 313 caused many believers to view the church as tainted by worldliness and foreign influences, and the hermit's life as a purer alternative. Admirers pursued Anthony ever deeper into the wilderness, camping out beneath Mount Qalah, where he dwelt in a cave until his death at the age of 105.

Icons depict the saint clothed in animal skins, barefoot and white-bearded, with an escort of lions. A century later, the Greek scholar Athanasius recounted his privations and visions in that prototypical work of Christian hagiography, the *Life of Anthony*, basis for the depictions of Anthony in the Wilderness throughout the next millennia of Coptic and Western art.

Hurghada (Ghardaka)

It's worth taking **HURGHADA**'s claims to be a seaside resort with a handful of salt. Unlike Sinai, where soft sand and gorgeous reefs are within easy reach and women left unhassled, Hurghada's public beaches are distant and uninviting, whilst the best marine life is far offshore.

Paying for boat excursions and superior private beaches is virtually unavoidable if you're to enjoy Hurghada's assets, and although conditions for windsurfing, scuba diving and deep-sea fishing are great, facilities aren't cheap, with real bargains mostly limited to accommodation.

Hurghada town is itself a treeless hodge-podge of utilitarian structures, as if someone had been "playing Lego with breeze blocks", as Charlie Pye-Smith put it. The bleakness of this new Governorate capital, however, is softened by a relaxed ambience and lively nightlife – a cosmopolitan veneer imparted by tourism. During wintertime peak season, tour groups fly in from abroad and templed-out backpackers flock here from the Nile Valley. Even over summer, it's popular enough to mean you should book bus seats early if you're hoping to move on to Sinai afterwards.

Orientation and getting around

Hurghada town proper is separated from the coast by "Ugly Mountain", an aptly named barren rock massif. Coming in from the north along Sharia Abdel Aziz Mustapha, crisp new flats and administrative buildings give way to hotels, shops and then mudbrick homes – delineating Hurghada's transformation from a small fishing village. Restaurants, bazaars, tourist agencies and most of the budget hotels cluster within a few blocks of the bus station.

West of here, a highway runs 2km south to Hurghada's **port** and on down the coast, past Moon Valley resort (4km), the *Sheraton Hotel* (6km) and a succession of **holiday villages** climaxing in the *Jasmine Village* (15km) and a new, as yet unnamed resort complex (20km). Heading out this way you'll pass the turn-off for the desert **airport**.

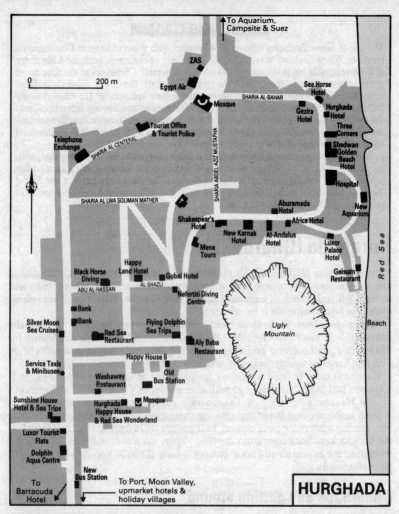

To Aquarium, Campsite & Suez

ZAS

Egypt Air

Mosque

SHARIA AL-BAHAR

Sea Horse Hotel

Gezira Hotel

Hurghada Hotel

Three Corners

Tourist Office & Tourist Police

Telephone Exchange

SHARIA AL-CENTRAL

SHARIA ABDEL AZIZ MUSTAPHA

Shedwan Golden Beach Hotel

Hospital

SHARIA AL LWA SOLIMAN MATHER

Aburamada Hotel

New Aquarium

Shakespear's Hotel

New Karnak Hotel

Al-Andalus Hotel

Africa Hotel

Luxor Palace Hotel

Red Sea

Mena Tours

Happy Land Hotel

Gobal Hotel

Geisum Restaurant

Black Horse Diving

ABU AL-HASSAN

AL-SHAZLI

Nefertiti Diving Centre

Ugly Mountain

Bank

Bank

Silver Moon Sea Cruises

Flying Dolphin Sea Trips

Beach

Red Sea Restaurant

Aly Baba Restaurant

Happy House II

Service Taxis & Minibuses

Weshaway Restaurant

Old Bus Station

Sunshine House Hotel & Sea Trips

Hurghada Happy House & Red Sea Wonderland

Mosque

Luxor Tourist Flats

Dolphin Aqua Centre

To Barracuda Hotel

New Bus Station

To Port, Moon Valley, upmarket hotels & holiday villages

0   200 m

HURGHADA

While walking is fine for **getting around** town, the port is best reached by local buses (25pt) or minibuses (50pt), both frequent. In the mornings minibuses convey workers as far south as *Jasmine Village*; later in the day they might run no further than the *Sheraton*. A taxi to the *Sheraton* costs £E4–5, £E10 to the airport; Hurghada **taxi** rates are the highest in Egypt. *Giftun Village* **rents cars** (£E15 daily plus 15pt per km) while **bicycles** can be hired from *Bebo* (opposite Nefertiti Diving Centre) and the *Andalus Hotel* for about £E3 a day; however, strong head-winds can make cycling along the coast a trial.

With the competition between dive shops and travel agencies, there's little point in enquiring at the main **tourist office** (daily 9am–2pm) about things to see or do. The **tourist police** (☎440-765), in the same building, are open 24 hours.

All telephone numbers in the Hurghada area are prefixed ☎62.

Accommodation

Except during December and January – when you might have to settle for whatever's going for a night or two – the pace of new construction ensures that hotels usually have **vacancies**. Prices quoted are for low season; upmarket hotels hike them ten to twenty percent – and may insist on half or full board – over winter.

Hurghada's fresh **water** has to be piped from the Nile Valley, so depending on your hotel's storage capacity it might be cut off for several hours a day. Profligate consumption means that others go short. A long-promised solar-powered desalination plant hasn't so far progressed beyond a weathered noticeboard.

Cheap hotels and tourist flats

Since Captain Mohammed Awad opened his *Hurghada Happy House* a decade ago, cheap hotels and tourist flats have proliferated. Most are small, with simple facilities and a homely atmosphere. It's often possible to negotiate reductions for long stays, or when business is slack.

Happy House I (☎440-540), **Happy House II**, **Happy Home**. These basic, clean and friendly lodgings near the bus station are operated by Capt. Mohammed and a relative, Raouf Ezzat. Most rooms have fans and three beds, rented individually (£E5). Shared kitchen and hot showers. Breakfast £E1.50.

Sunshine House (☎441-463). Emad Mohammed, the Captain's engaging nephew, runs this larger block of doubles (£E8) and triples (£E9) with fans and mosquito nets. Sleeping on the roof is free. Shared hot showers, a good kitchen and direct telephone link to Cairo. Newly built restaurant and diving centre. Guests get a £E5 reduction for Giftun Island trips and can make bookings here for the Sharm ferry.

Luxor Tourist Flats (☎441-373). Five small doubles and triples across the way. Negotiable rates (£E3–4 per head). Hot showers and kitchen.

Shakespear's Hotel. Large spartan rooms with balconies and two to four beds. Rates per head (£E4–5) vary according to how many share a room. Hot showers and kitchen. Rarely full.

New Karnak Hotel. Fairly basic, but welcoming. Doubles (£E15) and triples (£E22) only. Water supply more unreliable than usual.

Africa Hotel (☎440-629). Clean and airy with shared bathrooms. Singles (£E6), doubles (£E12) and triples (£E15). Breakfast included.

Luxor Palace Hotel (☎441-458). Singles (£E7.50), doubles (£E15) and triples (£E21) are spotless; all have fans; some have sea views; hearty breakfasts. Popular with tour groups.

Happy Land Hotel (☎441-373). Clean, agreeable singles (£E10), doubles (£E12) and triples (£E18) with fans. Shared hot showers. Like the *Gobal*, located amidst the tourist bazaar.

Gobal Hotel (☎440-623). Immaculate singles (£E12), doubles (£E18) and triples (£E24 including breakfast) with fans. Shared bathrooms with hot water. Inexpensive restaurant.

Mid-range hotels

Hurghada's mid-range hotels mostly cater to groups or middle-class Egyptians; they can usually guarantee private bathrooms, if not fancier amenities. The following places are all in town – rather than in the daggy port area.

Abu Ramada Hotel (☎440-617). Okay doubles (£E17), mostly with fans and some with private bathrooms (£E23). Extra beds £E6. Breakfast included. Popular with school parties.

Al-Andalus Hotel (☎440-639). Nice rooms with fans and mosquito nets. Singles £E13, doubles £E17 (£E25 with bathroom), triples £E30 (£E32). Bicycle rental £E3 daily.

Barracuda Hotel (☎440-625). Clean, simple rooms with fans and hot showers. Doubles £E23 (£E36 with half board), triples £E30 with breakfast. Kitchen facilities and rooftop restaurant. Private water supply. Can make reservations for Sharm ferry.

Hurghada Hotel (☎440-393). Roomy but stuffy cabins with bathrooms near a stony beach. Singles (£E10), doubles (£E27) and triples (£E36, including breakfast). Disco in the main building.

Upmarket hotels and holiday villages

South of Port Hurghada smart hotels and holiday villages, private beaches and marinas are multiplying rapidly. With ample water sports and well-stocked bars, their guests are cocooned from negative local reactions to Western-style beach-wear and behaviour, as hedonism (at a price) is permitted. Places below are in order of appearance, heading south. Upmarket hotels in the town itself are less worth the outlay.

SOUTH OF THE PORT: ON THE BEACH

Moon Valley Village (☎440-074). This tasteful enclave of well-fanned rooms overlooking a garden has outgrown its origins as a backpacker colony. Rates for singles (£E50), doubles (£E65) and triples (£E90) drop a bit over summer, and include breakfast. Restaurant. Private beach with small coral reef (diving courses). Accessible by taxi (£E3) or minibus (50pt).

Sheraton Hotel (☎440-785). Futuristic pile perched beside the sea. Rooms with all mod cons from £E100. Pool, sports facilities and private beach.

Hotel Samaka (☎440-227). Conglomerate of bungalows (A/C midday and evenings) focused around a diving centre. Singles (US$35), doubles (US$55) and triples (US$70) are fifteen percent dearer over winter. Reserve through *Zosser Tours* (☎258-0678) in Cairo.

Giftun Village (☎406-656). This German-run complex inspired the *Samaka*. Well-appointed chalets with fans, a private beach and Barakuda Club for windsurfing and diving. Singles (US$60), doubles (US$75) and triples (US$90) similarly dearer over winter. Car rental. Reserve through Cairo's *Victoria Hotel* (☎918-766).

Hor Palace. Less agreeable-looking version near the Marina whence boats sail for Giftun Island. Doubles with shared bathrooms for US$45 per person (half board).

Magawish Village (☎440-759). Formerly a *Club Med*, this still offers varied sports facilities and kids' activities, and 24-hour A/C. Singles (US$50), doubles (US$60) and triples (US$80) at half board. Diving courses and fishing. Bank and international calls facility. In season, reserve from Cairo (1 Sharia Talaat Harb; ☎392-4737).

IN TOWN

Gezira Hotel. On the northeast side of town, 200m from a beach of sorts. Spacious A/C rooms with private bath and telephone, around an elegant, verdant courtyard. Whether you have breakfast only or half board determines the price of singles (£E45–60), doubles (£E70–95) and triples (£E100–130). Bar, restaurant and nightly disco.

Shedwan Golden Beach (☎440-240). Flashy reception and dowdier A/C rooms. Freshwater pool, squash and tennis courts (£E5 per hour for non-residents). Diving centre beside a rather scummy lagoon. Half and full board rates for singles (£E120–140), doubles (£E150–170) and triples (£E190-230). Banking services and international calls.

Sea Horse Hotel (☎441-704). Comfortable rooms with private baths, A/C and balconies. Rates (for breakfast-only to full board) range between £E65 to £E90 for singles, £E70–120 for doubles and £E100–160 for triples. Twenty percent reduction over summer.

Camping

With rooms so cheap, saving money hardly justifies camping. For those with tents, the most accessible **sites** are behind the *Geisum Restaurant* and the *Hurghada Hotel*, charging £E3 and £E5 per person respectively. Facilities are minimal but may improve, unlike at the decaying *National Youth Camp*, 4km north of town, whose tent-like huts (£E7 a head) are often full.

Camping out elsewhere along the coast doesn't seem an attractive option given the risk of mines and the distances involved; permission from the Frontiers Office near *EgyptAir* (Sat–Thurs 10.30am–2pm & 7–9.30pm; bring two 20pt stamps) is also obligatory. But Giftun Island could be an idyllic spot if you brought water and food and arranged the boat rides with a tour operator (see below).

Beaches and reefs

Until the completion of a new beach beside Ugly Mountain, the scruffy windblown swathe that distances itself from the highway between the *Sheraton* and *Samaka* hotels remains the only public beach in Hurghada. Its prurient gawpers are another reason why most foreigners opt to pay for smoother sand and liberal standards on **private beaches**. Among these, **Shedwan Beach**, just north of the *Sheraton Hotel*, is soft and clean, with a small offshore reef; its £E5 entry charge includes soft drinks to that value, plus freshwater showers. For £E10 you can use the hotel's own beach (but not its pool). And if you can talk your way past the security, some of the **holiday villages** also have nice, residents-only beaches.

Reefs

Three small **reefs** (off Ugly Mountain, Coral and Shedwan beaches) offer a taste of the amazing feast of darting fish and rainbow-hued corals submerged further offshore. The marine life of the Red Sea Coast rivals that in the Gulf of Aqaba, since both hold countless species in common, but the Red Sea Coast favours island corals over coastal reefs, while sharks and dolphins prevail in its deeper, rougher waters. Nonetheless, much of the information about reefs and **snorkelling** in Sinai (see p.526 and p.523) is relevant to Hurghada – especially the cautionary advice. Familiarise yourself with the appearance of dangerous fire-corals, lionfish and other nasties, using the pictorial charts in Captain Mohammed's *Red Sea Wonderland* emporium or any of the other diving shops.

Giftun Island and other sea trips

Most hotels take bookings for **all-day excursions to Giftun Island**, run by local operators like Emad (*Sunshine Sea Trips*) or Adel Shazli (*Nefertiti Diving Centre*), who currently charge £E20 per person. Hotels usually add £E5 commission; this should include mask, snorkel and flipper rental – be sure that everything fits. You'll need to sign up and surrender your passport the night before; check that details are correctly noted, since the authorities will prevent wrongly documented passengers from boarding. Also, bring a hat, sunscreen lotion and lots of water. A fish, rice and salad lunch is eaten on board or on the silken sands of Giftun Island's beach. Sadly, the reefs clustered just offshore are suffering from their own popularity, as fleets of vessels drop anchor onto their delicate fronds. Other clumps in deeper waters are less at risk.

Overnight excursions to Giftun – with meals, music and campfires – are organised by Emad, *Silver Moon Sea Cruisers* and *Flying Dolphin Sea Trips* (£E50–75 per person), whilst Adel Shazli runs a three-day visit to the reefs around **Gobal Island**, farther up the gulf (£E45). Captain Mohammed (see "Cheap hotels"), who pioneered trips to the deeps, sometimes allows snorkellers to accompany his scuba-diving clients to northern reefs like **Abu Ramada**.

Captain Mohammed leaves the **House of Sharks**, 21km south of town, to Emad and Raouf (of *Happy House II*). These offshore reefs can be heavy going in rough weather, never mind the presence of tiger sharks and hammerheads, moray eeels and stonefish – but both men swear they have never had a serious accident and they won't go when seas are rough. The charge (£E15–17 per person) includes equipment rental.

Diving, windsurfing and water sports

Hurghada's expense, relative to the Sinai, hasn't stopped it from becoming a major **diving** centre. Germans, Dutch and Belgians fly in to pursue their hobby at holiday villages, whilst the less well-off compare deals at dive shops and agencies.

For those already **dive-certified**, the *Dolphin Aqua Centre* offers the cheapest outing – two dives around Giftun Island, with lunch, for £E90 (£E60 for one dive). The same outfit offers five-day PADI certificate **courses** for £E350 plus US$50; a similar course of nine dives cost US$200 at *Silver Moon Sea Cruisers*; £E420 at the *Moon Valley Hotel*; DM395 at the *Giftun Village*; and US$400 at *Flying Dolphin Sea Trips*. (A calculator or experience in international banking could be useful when doing the rounds.) **Novices** are charged around £E120 for two obligatory introductory dives. For really gung-ho types, *Flying Dolphin* runs **specialist courses** in night-diving and wreck salvage.

Windsurfing, fishing and boat trips

Powerful gusts also make Hurghada great for **windsurfing**. A couple of places in town can rent boards and wetsuits, but the widest range is definitely held by the *Barakuda Club* (daily 10–11am & 4–5pm) at *Giftun Village*. Board hire costs £E22 an hour, £E55 for a half day, or £E82 all day. The equivalent rates for wetsuits are £E3, £E7 and £E13; prices at the *Samaka* are identical.

Flying Dolphin, *Giftun Village* and others can arrange **deep-sea fishing** trips (1–5 days). Popular with groups of Japanese and German businessmen – and priced accordingly – they can be temporarily subsumed into international fishing tournaments (usually held in February and July).

And for those who can't face swimming amidst (or hunting) the Red Sea's flora and fauna, *Silver Moon* quotes £E15 for a ride in a **glass-bottomed boat** over the reefs near the *Sheraton*.

The Aquarium and Temple of the Arts

To see tropical fish without the bother or expense of a trip to the reefs, pay a visit to the new **Aquarium** on Sharia al-Bahr (daily 9am–10pm; £E4), which has effectively superseded the old aquarium 4km north of town, where half a dozen fish lurk in murky outdoor tanks beside the sea. Nearby the latter is a dismal **museum** (daily 8am–5pm) with stuffed and modelled examples of everything from sea cows to Napoleon fish, rendered in lurid colours. Both places are offically free, but a little *baksheesh* to the curators is in order.

Another, weirder tourist attraction that was underway during my visit was the "**Temple of the Arts**", a gallery of fake-pharaonic statuary out towards the Magawish. If you're in the area, it's bizarre enough to warrant a look.

Eating, nightlife and facilities

The centre of Hurghada is stuffed with stalls and cafés (especially along Abu Hassan al-Shazli), and budget-priced **restaurants** compete for custom. Purely because of its rooftop terrace and seniority, the *Red Sea Restaurant* is full most nights, though calamari, prawn and fish portions (£E5–6) are maybe a bit smaller than at *Happy Land Restaurant* on the highway. The native-style *Habbak* serves chicken, salads and veg dishes for around £E4; *Columbo Restaurant* over the road from *Shakespear's Hotel* offers regular customers a bargain three meals a day plus soft drinks for £E12; or for excellent pizzas try *Chez Pascal* (aka *Three Corners*). Fancier **hotel restaurants** provide opportunities to splurge.

The *Cha Cha Disco*, Hurghada's liveliest **nightspot**, is scheduled to move to the beach near the *Geisum Restaurant*; open until 3am, it has a minimum charge of £E9.50, so you might as well sink a few beers. Smaller, slicker discos at the nearby *Gezira* and *Hurghada* hotels don't levy any admission charge.

Practicalities

Also near the *Gezira* and *Hurghada* hotels, you'll find Hurghada's **hospital** and **first aid** (☎440-490) post.

The two **banks**, *Banque Misr* (Sun–Thurs 8.30am–9pm, Fri & Sat 9am–1.30pm & 5–9pm) and the *National Bank of Egypt* (daily 8.30am–2pm & 6–9pm), both take traveller's cheques and are firmly ensconced on the main street. The **post office** shack near the tourist police is poised to move next door to *Sunshine Sea Trips;* to phone Cairo it's usually quicker to use phones in hotels or the *Elad el Din Bazaar* than go through the nearby 24-hour **telephone exchange**.

Moving on

A number of **overland excursions** are organised by Hurghada agencies. The wild ravines and ancient glyph-hewn quarries of the **Red Sea Mountains** (see section following) can be visited courtesy of *Silver Moon*, and the same company also runs excursions to Luxor, Saint Catherine's and Cairo. *Misr Travel* offers the best value trips to Saint Anthony's and Saint Paul's Monastery (£E85 per person, including lunch).

Moving on by **regular transport**, you've the usual choice between **buses** and **service taxis** and the odd **flights**, plus a **ferry link across the Gulf of Suez** to Sharm el-Sheikh.

Buses or service taxis

Service taxis leave either from the square beside Hurghada's old mosque or from the minibus stand on the highway. You'll have to verify whether your bus is leaving from the old mosque depot or the new bus terminal towards the port.

Mornings are the best time to catch seven-seater **service taxis** to Luxor (4hr; £E6), Aswan (6hr; £E9), Suez (4hr; £E10) or Cairo (5–7hr; £E15), and for groups to engage a vehicle to take them all the way to Sharm el-Sheikh (£E30–40 each – one way to avoid spending 18 hours on buses and a tedious interlude at Suez).

Buses to Luxor (6am & 11am, £E6; 3pm, £E12) take around four to five hours, with no respite for passengers crammed into the aisles; which is even more the case for indeterminately prolonged journeys to Aswan (7am & 3pm; £E16). Of the services to Cairo via Suez, only the 5am is easily bookable the night before; the

7am (£E10), 3pm (£E18) and two 9pm-ish jobs (£E15) all arrive in town half full of passengers from Quesir, farther down the coast. There's also allegedly a 7am bus to Alexandria (£E16).

Flights

If you've got the money and book early during winter, **flights** are the best way of reaching Cairo, Luxor, Sharm el-Sheikh or Saint Catherine's.

See *EgyptAir* (daily 8am–8pm; ☎440-788) or *ZAS* (10am–9pm; ☎440-019) regarding daily flights to the capital; the former also handles planes to Luxor (Wed, Fri & Sun) and takes bookings for *Air Sinai*'s oversubscribed flights to Sharm (Fri) and Saint Catherine's Monastery (Mon).

To Sharm el-Sheikh by ferry

A popular travellers' route is to catch a boat from **Hurghada to Sharm el-Sheikh** across the Gulf of Suez. Depending on mechanical factors and the weather, the crossing can take anywhere from five to fifteen hours. Bring food and water for the journey.

Because of impending deregulation, it's hard to predict which boats and operators will be running in the future. The *Golden Sun* – featured on tourist posters – was undergoing repairs when last heard, whilst reponsibility for **bookings** had passed from *Les Voyages* to *Silver Moon Sea Cruisers* (daily 9am–2pm & 5–9pm), although Emad and some hotels also had a pipeline. It's equally hard to predict **schedules**, but there should be a boat most days. Make enquiries as soon as you arrive – don't wait until the night before departure, since boats carry only 25 persons. Bring your passport when you buy your ticket (currently £E55 one-way).

En route to Sharm you'll pass (port side) **Shadwan Island**, guarding the entrance to the Gulf of Suez: a barren chain of reddish hills furrowed by ravines. Its lighthouse was of keen interest to Henri de Montfried when he navigated his boat, the *Fat-el-Rahman*, through these waters in the early 1920s, with 400 *okes* (600 kilos) of hashish secreted in its hold.

The Red Sea Mountains

Inland of Hurghada the barren plains erupt into the **Red Sea Mountains**, which follow the coast southwards towards Ethiopia. This geologically primitive range of granite, porphyry and breccia contains Egypt's highest mountains outside Sinai, rearing up to 2187m (over 7000 feet) above sea level. During winter, peaks exceeding 1500m draw moisture from rising masses of air, while in summertime they precipitate brief, localised storms accompanied by violent lightning and flash floods. Hardy desert plants flourish in their wake, providing grazing for feral ruminants and the flocks of a few thousand nomads. Roaming their vast tribal lands, these Bedouin (see p.573 and p.575) are perfectly at home in the wilderness – unlike isolated groups of miners and soldiers, who feel almost as exiled as the slaves who quarried here in ancient times.

Exploring the mountains

Short of befriending some Bedouin and tagging along with them, the Red Sea Mountains are really only accessible via **day excursions from Hurghada**. Compare the rates and itineraries offered by *Silver Moon* and *Flying Dolphin Sea*

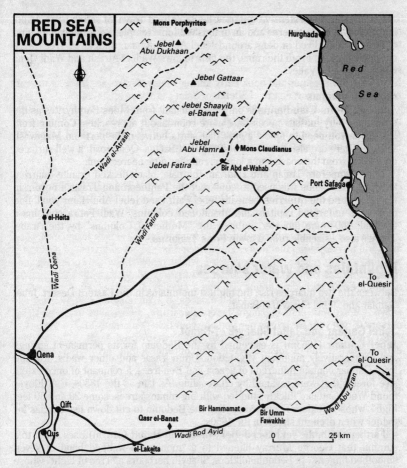

RED SEA MOUNTAINS

Mons Porphyrites

Hurghada

Jebel Abu Dukhaan ▲

Red

Jebel Gattaar ▲

Sea

Jebel Shaayib el-Banat ▲

Jebel Abu Hamr ▲ ♦ Mons Claudianus

Jebel Fatira ▲ Bir Abd el-Wahab

Port Safaga

Wadi el-Atrash

Wadi Fatira

el-Heita

Wadi Qena

To el-Quesir

To el-Quesir

Qena

Wadi Abu Ziran

Qift

Bir Hammamat

Bir Umm Fawakhir

Qus

Qasr el-Banat

Wadi Rod Ayid

el-Lakeita

0   25 km

Trips. The former charges groups of up to seven persons $35 (lunch included) for each of its three itineraries: to **Mons Claudianus**, **Wadi el-Shaayib** and **Safaga beach**; to **Mons Porphyrites** and **Wadi Umm Sidr**; or to **Wadi Naggaat** and a couple of **Roman forts**. Longer itineraries or overnight stays are negotiable, though you may not be able to find other tourists to share the cost.

Two Roman quarries

Twenty kilometres **north of Hurghada**, a *piste* quits the highway and climbs inland towards **Jebel Abu Dukhaan**, the 1161-metre-high "Mountain of Smoke". Anciently known as **Mons Porphyrites**, this was the Roman empire's main source of fine red porphyry, used for columns and ornamentation. Blocks were dragged 150km to the Nile, or by a shorter route to the coast, whence they were shipped to far-flung sites such as Baalbek or Constantinople.

Roundabout the extensive quarries lies a **ruined town** of rough-hewn buildings with two large cisterns and an unfinished Ionic temple. Rock hyraxes (a kind of large rodent) lived in dens around Jebel Abu Dukhaan until all its trees were cut down for fuel. From the ruins, the *piste* follows Wadi el-Atrash and Wadi Qena down to the Nile Valley.

Mons Claudianus

Although **Mons Claudianus** is only 50km distant from Mons Porphyrites as the crow flies, lofty massifs necessitate more roundabout approaches. Coming from Hurghada you need to follow a *piste* that starts between the port and Magawish Village. There are also two routes off the Port Safaga–Qena road: a well-surfaced one, 41km from the coast, and a longer, rougher *piste* nearer Qena.

Under emperors Trajan and Hadrian, the pale, black-flecked granite quarried at Mons Claudianus was used to construct the Pantheon and Trajan's Forum in Rome. Around the **quarries** beneath Jebel Fatira and Jebel Abu Hamr you'll find numerous unformed capitals and abandoned columns; Wadi Fatira contains a cracked, 200-tonne monster, dubbed the "Mother of Columns" by the Arabs. There's also a sizeable ruined town, **Fons Trajanus**.

Mountains and water sources

Between the two quarries rise the highest mountains in the Eastern Desert: Jebel Gattaar and Jebel Shaayib el-Banat.

Jebel Gattaar and Jebel Shaayib el-Banat

Jebel Gattaar (1963m) is esteemed by the Bedouin for its permanent springs and comparatively abundant vegetation. Umm Yasar and other wadis draining from Gattaar contain hundreds of acacia and Ben-trees, a remnant of once extensive forests that were ravaged by charcoaling. As late as the 1880s, E.A. Floyer found Wadi Gattaar "thickly studded with big mimosa-trees, some 20 and 30 feet high", whose reckless felling compelled the Bedouin to cut down live acacias for fodder when drought struck in the 1950s.

Farther south, the yet loftier **Jebel Shaayib el-Banat** (2187m) rises sheer to a summit that George Murray likened to a "monstrous webbed hand of seven smoothed fingers". In Bedouin folklore, Shaayib harbours a "Tree of Light" whose leaves can cure blindness; the world's only other one is believed to be in Lebanon.

Wadi Naggaat and the Ma'aza Limestone Plateau

Early Christian hermits made their home in **Wadi Naggaat**, between Abu Dukhaan and Jebel Shaayib. *Naggaat* means "dripping place", a Bedouin term for a particular type of water source which falls from cliffs to irrigate maidenhair ferns, reeds and mosses, and fills pools where ibexes and people drink.

But with only four *naggaat* in the Eastern Desert and not enough rope to plumb the 50-metre-deep well of Bir Gattaar, the Bedouin must also use surface springs and gravel seeps. These are far more common in the granite Red Sea Mountains than on the **Ma'aza Limestone Plateau** that separates the range from the Nile Valley; one reason why Bedouin dislike this "Place of Strayings". Its mysterious **Bir Sheitan** (Pool of Satan) is popularly believed to be replenished by Nile water via an underground passage but is actually dependent on rainfall; the shade from the overhanging rocks prevents evaporation. It is shunned by the mountain Bedouin on account of being allegedly frequented by cannibal "near-men" and "murderous" Mutayar tribesmen, who come up from the Valley to hunt ibex and collect wormwood.

THE MA'AZA BEDOUIN, GAZELLES AND IBEXES

From Saint Anthony's Monastery to the Qift–Quesir road, 90,000 square kilometres of highland form the stamping ground of the **Ma'aza** (Goat) tribe of **Bedouin**, who migrated here from Arabia in the 1700s. As their name suggests, goats form the basis of their livelihood, although gathering plants and hunting are also important. Herbalists buy wormwood, henbane, argel and Ben-tree seeds from the nomads, while hunters from the Gulf Emirates used to hire them as guides until the Ma'aza grew disgusted with their wanton slaughter of Barbary sheep (now extinct), ibexes and gazelles.

The Ma'aza themselves only hunt with dogs, rocks and knives, sprinting after their quarry. Whereas **gazelles** are regarded as everyday food, ibex meat is prized because it supposedly enables them to run up mountains without tiring. The sound of rutting **ibexes** locking horns in September attracts the foul botfly, which squirts its larvae into their mouths and nostrils. Smashing dead branches with rocks makes the same noise – something to remember should you camp out in these mountains as botfly can also live as parasites in humans.

South of Hurghada

Down the coast from Hurghada, **Port Safaga** (58km) more or less marks the ebb tide of tourism, with scarcely a trickle of foreigners going on south to **el-Quesir** (a further 85km). Up to this point, connections with Cairo and the Nile Valley are assured, with roads cutting across the Eastern Desert, on old camel routes. Ask around Hurghada's bus station and taxi ranks before 9am or late in the afternoon regarding transport.

Farther south, all communications become tenuous and bureaucratic obstacles loom as you head **towards the border with Sudan**. Even equipped with a Sudanese visa obtained in Cairo, the chances of entering the Sudan this way are virtually nil. For the intrepid who fancy taking the route whatever, the odd *service* taxi might run to Mersa Allam or perhaps even Berenice (but see below).

Port Safaga and the road to Qena

The tourist component of **PORT SAFAGA** consists of a German-managed *CMAS* **diving centre** and the pricey *Safaga* hotel. Only experienced divers (or those willing to pay a lot for extensive courses) will be able to handle the rough sea beds here, where bizarre flora and fauna lurk fathoms down.

Amongst the big fish prevalent in these waters are **hammerhead sharks**, reputedly the most aggressive shark species. Research suggests that sharks track their victims with two forms of biological sensor. At long range and when closing on its kill, the hammerhead senses vibrations in the water, but in the final seconds it tunes into electromagnetic fields "bounced" off its target. Because the sharks aren't genetically "programmed" to interpret signals reflected by oxygen-tanks or the steel bars of diving cages, they frenziedly bite them instead of the divers – or that's one theory, anyway.

The road to Qena and off to the quarries

Safaga is primarily a commercial **port** for shipping out phosphates (an extraction plant fumes just inland) and importing US grain sent as food aid, which is trucked across the Eastern Desert to the Nile Valley. The imminent reopening of a long-abandoned freight railway will end a windfall for the Ma'aza Bedouin, who feed their flocks on grain spilt **along the desert road to Qena** (161km). Indeed, elders may spend their final years here: the pickings are good and they get to meet everybody.

Besides trucks, there are several **service taxis** and **buses** daily in each direction. Those with four-wheel drive vehicles might also consider the two routes leading off **towards Mons Claudianus** (see previous section). The turn-off west of Safaga gets there in 25km via Bir Abd el-Wahab, whereas the rougher *piste* outside Qena follows its euphonymous wadi to el-Heita before forking right up Wadi el-Atrash towards Jebel Abu Dukhaan (roughly 150km).

El-Quesir and the route to Qift

EL-QUESIR, 85km south of Safaga, is likewise into phosphates extraction, but has fewer inhabitants and more of a sense of history about it. A small **fort** built by Sultan Selim overlooks the town, which was the largest Muslim port on the Red Sea until the tenth century. In pharaonic times, it was from here that boats sailed to the "Land of Punt" (thought to be Yemen or Somalia), as depicted in reliefs within Hatshepsut's temple at Deir el-Bahri. The Romans later knew it as *Leukos Limen* (White Harbour).

Flaubert saw the port's last flickers of exoticism in the 1840s. Crude pearl-fishers' *pirogues* resembling dug-out tree-trunks shared the harbour with graceful Arab *dhows* whose outsize sterns and high prows mimicked calligraphic flourishes. Not only Arab and African pilgrims changed boats here; Flaubert encountered fur-capped Tartars from Bukhara and even a French Consul ("garrulous, insipid, deadly, knows everything and everybody"). Nowadays, Quesir's **Friday market** draws Ma'aza and Ababda Bedouin. On the edge of town are a few cheap chalets where it's possible **to stay**.

The desert road to Qift

The modern road from **el-Quesir to Qift** (216km) follows the earliest known route across the Eastern Desert, partially explored by the V Dynasty but not fully established until Ramses IV's time (1164–57 BC), when wells were dug at intervals. In those days, the main attraction was hard, dark breccia – used for statues and sarcophagi – found in the **Wadi Hammamat**, roughly midway between Quesir and Qift.

When Flaubert travelled this way by camel, it was necessary to drink from an earthy source "reached by sliding under a rock", in the vicinity of a maimed animal "uttering its death-rattle", while other parties "breasted ahead" over sand dunes in a haze of dust, "as though they were wading through clouds". Nowadays the hardships and romance have gone, and vehicles rarely stop at the great well of **Bir Hammamat**, dug by 8000 men for Ramses IV; nor at **Bir Umm Fawakhir** (92km from Quesir), which is marked with hieroglyphs – and where plans are afoot to reopen ancient mines specified on an Egyptian survey map of c.1400 BC.

Roughly 100km further on from Bir Umm Fawakhir, you might glimpse the sizeable ruins of **Qasr el-Banat** (Fortress of the Maidens), scratched with

Greek, Coptic and Sinaitic characters, and formerly reputed to be haunted. Nowadays, the only way-station as such is **el-Lakeita**, a tiny oasis-village whose cistern bears a faint inscription from the reign of Tiberius Claudius.

To Mersa Allam and the Moulid of al-Shazli

The Qift–Quesir road marks the boundary between **Ma'aza** tribal land and **Ababda** territory. Though traditional rivals, the Ma'aza and Ababda may graze and water their flocks on each other's preserves should their own land be drought-stricken. Tribal politics are conditioned by the harsh environment and long memories; the names of wells and landmarks are often historically specific. For example, Bir Umm Howeitat, near the Umm Rus goldmine inland of Mersa Umbarak, is named after the Saudi Bedouin who harried the Ma'aza in their original homeland and later in Sinai.

The fishing village of **MERSA ALLAM**, 132km from Quesir, is the furthest south along the coastal road that you can go without military permission. Travellers into off-the-beaten-track destinations and totally "authentic experiences" might care to use the Mersa Allam–Edfu road (230km) to visit the (usually) October-held **Moulid of Abul Hassan al-Shazli**.

The Moulid of Abul Hassan al-Shazli
Outside Egypt, **Abul Hassan al-Shazli** (who died in 1258) is known as al-Shadhili, hence the name of his Sufi order, the *Shadhiliyya*. He is buried high in the mountains, 100km southeast of a turn-off where pilgrim trucks circle three times around the tomb of another Sufi sheikh, Salim, to avoid incurring his jealousy. According to believers, the Prophet Mohammed himself buried al-Shazli in **Wadi Humaysara**.

The wadi is unmarked on survey maps: **Jebel Abu Hammamid** seems the closest designated spot. It is here that, during the **moulid**, tents are pitched for morning *zikrs* and snack-stalls are erected for the Sufis that converge here from all over Egypt. Pilgrims make little heaps of stones and take home *baraka*-imbued dust. To discover when the *moulid* is due (usually, but not invariably, in October), ask locals in Hurghada or Edfu. Arranging a ride will require much palaver, but you shouldn't have any problem identifying the pilgrim trucks, festooned with banners and loudspeakers.

The far south: Berenice to the Sudanese border

In times past, foreigners occasionally continued 145km south to **BERENICE**, named after the wife of Ptolemy II, on whose instigation a trading port was established here in 275 BC. Abandoned during the fifth century AD, the site was excavated by Belzoni in 1818; a Temple of Semiramis (whose sanctuaries depict Tiberius worshipping Min) are the highlight of the **ruins**, which cover two square kilometres, five minutes' walk from the modern town.

Inland of here lie the ancient **Emerald Mines of Wadi Sakait**, worked from pharaonic to Roman times and under the khalifs; Mohammed Ali had them reopened, but few gems remained to be found by then, and the mines were soon abandoned. Nearby is a small Ptolemaic rock temple with Greek inscriptions, dedicated to Isis and Serapis. The offshore island of Topazos gave its name to topaz, once abundant there.

Nowadays **the far south** is exploited for different purposes. Following the Iranian Revolution, the Ras Banas air base was earmarked for use as a staging-post for the US Rapid Deployment Force (later reconstituted as Central Command). Egyptian forces participated in joint **wargames** where paratroops were dropped to defend "oil wells" and "hostile" tanks were bombed by sorties of B-52s. Intended to counter the Iranian "threat" to Saudi Arabia, these operations waned after Iran was embroiled in war by Iraq, and the US "forward base" withdrew to Diego Garcia. However, when Iraq invaded Kuwait in August 1990 – catching Western Intelligence by surprise – the only units immediately available for airlift into Saudi Arabia were Egyptian special forces (perhaps only five hundred men initially).

Judging by events in the Middle East at time of writing, the coastline down to **BIR SHATLAN** (where Sudanese administration takes over before the "state" border at **HALAIB**) will be **off-limits** for the forseeable future. It's also probable that only Sudanese and Egyptians living in the Red Sea provinces will be allowed to cross **the border**.

PART THREE

THE

CONTEXTS

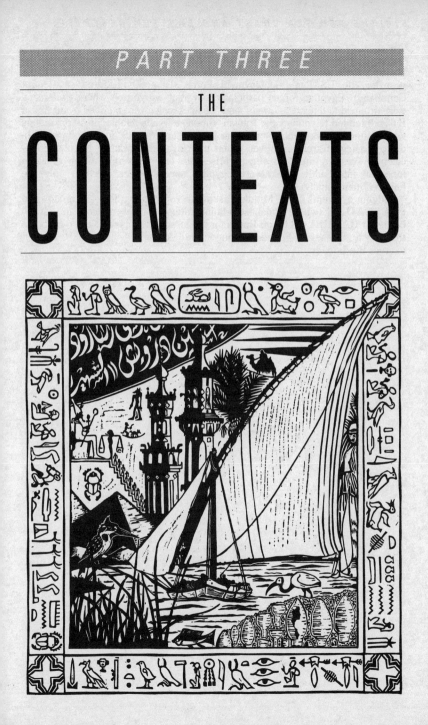

THE HISTORICAL FRAMEWORK

The present borders of Egypt are almost identical to those in pharaonic times, territories such as Sinai and Nubia being essentially marginal to the heartland of the Nile Valley and its Delta, where Egyptian civilisation emerged some five thousand years ago. The historical continuity is staggering, the pharaonic era alone lasting for thirty centuries, before being appropriated by Greek and Roman emperors.

Egypt's significance in the ancient world was paramount, and the country has never been far from the frontline of world history. Although neither Christianity nor Islam was born in Egypt, both are stamped with its influence. In modern times, when the Arab world sought to rid itself of European masters, Egypt was at the forefront of the anti-colonial struggle, while its peace treaty with Israel altered the geopolitics of the Middle East.

UNCERTAINTIES . . .

Any attempt to precis this vast span of history inevitably runs the risk of obscuring social dynamics and ordinary people amid a roll call of dynasties and great men (plus a few notable women). Whilst the continuity of so many aspects of Egyptian life supports this conservative view, dramatic watersheds and subtle fluxes are also a feature of Egyptian history. Nor are the facts graven on stone. Egyptology is riddled with uncertainties, not least in its chronology of dynasties and kings.

Whilst opting for consistency – we have taken our system of **dates** from that set out by T.G.H. James – it's only fair to mention the margins of error. These are up to a hundred years in the period around 3000 BC; seventy-five years around 2000 BC; and between ten and fifteen years around 1000 BC. From 500 BC onwards, dates are fairly precise until the Ptolemaic era, when the chronology gets hazy, only firming up again in Roman times.

THE BEGINNINGS

Stone tools from the gravel beds of Upper Egypt attest to the presence of **hunter-gathering hominids** in the area over 250,000 years ago, when the Sahara was a savannah that supported zebras, elephants and other game. Drastic climatic changes late in the **Palaeolithic** era (c.25,000 BC) caused widespread **desertification**, which compelled the nomadic tribes to settle around the **Nile and the oases**. While most still lived by hunting and fishing, a primitive pastoral and agricultural life emerged even before cereal cultivation, sheep and goat herding filtered through from the Near East (c.7000 BC).

During the **Neolithic** era, Middle Egypt and the Delta had **settled communities** that cultivated wheat and flax, herded flocks and wove linen. Although some reverted to a nomadic lifestyle after the rains of the Neolithic subpluvials checked the process of desertification, others remained to develop into agricultural societies.

PRE-DYNASTIC EGYPT

Nothwithstanding the Delta's exposure to Levantine and Aegean influences, the impetus for development came from southern Egypt, where archaeologists have identified three main cultures. The earliest is known as the **Badarian**, after the village of el-Badari where Brunton carried out excavations in the 1920s. The Badarians were farmers, hunters and miners; they made fine pottery, carved bone and ivory, and traded for turquoise and wood.

The **Naqada I** period, from about 4000 BC onwards, was characterised by larger settlements and a distinctive style of pottery: burnished red clay ware with black rims and white zoomorphic decorations. Clay and ivory figurines show Naqada menfolk sporting beards and penis-shields, raising a possible ethnic connection with their Libyan neighbours. The granite mace-heads found in graves could have been used for war, or simply for ritual purposes.

Graves from the **Naqada II** period contain copper tools and glazed beads that signify advances in technology, and extraneous materials such as lapis lazuli, indicating trade with Asia. The graves themselves evolved from simple pits into painted tombs lined with mats and wood, or, later still, brick. The development of extensive irrigation systems (c.3300 BC) boosted productivity and promoted links between communities.

THE TWO LANDS

By this time, the communities of Upper and Lower Egypt existed in two loose **confederations**. As power coalesced around Naqada in the south and Behdet in the Delta, each confederation became identified with a chief deity and a symbol of statehood: Seth and the White Crown with **Upper Egypt**, Horus and the Red Crown with the **Delta**.

Later, each acquired a new capital (Hierakonpolis and Buto, respectively) and strove for domination over the entire region. The eventual triumph of the southern kingdom resulted in the **unification of the Two Lands** (c.3100 BC) under the quasi-mythical ruler **Menes** (aka Narmer), and the start of Egypt's Dynastic period.

THE ARCHAIC PERIOD (c.3100–2686 BC)

The **Early Dynastic** or **Archaic Period** was the formative epoch of Egyptian civilisation. Its beginnings are a mix of history and myth, relating to the foundation – supposedly by Menes – of the city of **Memphis**. Located at the junction between Upper and Lower Egypt, this was the first imperial city on earth.

From this base, Djer and Den, the third and fifth kings of the **I Dynasty**, attempted to bring Sinai under Egyptian control. Writing, painting and architecture became increasingly sophisticated, whilst royal tombs at Saqqara and Abydos developed into complex *mastabas*.

Equally indicative of future trends was the dissolution of the unified kingdom as centralised authority waned towards the end of the dynasty. Although this was restored by **Raneb** (or Hotepsekhemwy), founder of a new line of rulers, regional disputes persisted throughout the **II Dynasty** (c.2890–2686 BC).

These disputes probably also inspired the **contendings of Seth and Horus**, a major theme in Egyptian mythology. The *Stela of Peribsen* shows a temple facade surmounted by the figure of Seth, rather than Horus, the traditional symbol of kings. However, the rivalry between the two regions and their respective deities appears to have been resolved under **Khasekhem**, the last king of the dynasty – paving the way for an era of assurance.

THE OLD KINGDOM (c.2686–2181 BC)

During the **Old Kingdom** – which began with the **III Dynasty** – advances in technology and developments in culture raised Egypt to an unprecedented level of civilisation.

The main figure of the III Dynasty was **King Zoser** (or Djoser), whose architect, **Imhotep**, built the first **Step Pyramid** at Saqqara in the twenty-seventh century BC. The pyramid's conception and construction were a landmark and later generations deified Imhotep as the ultimate sage. On the economic and political front, the III Dynasty also sent expeditions into Sinai, to seek turquoise and copper and subjugate the local Bedouin.

Pyramid-building and expansionism were likewise pursued during the **IV Dynasty** (c.2613–2494 BC). It's first king, **Snofru** (aka Sneferu), raised two pyramids at Dashur, and made incursions into Nubia and Libya. His successors, **Cheops** (Khufu), **Chephren** (Khafre) and **Mycerinus** (Menkaure), erected the **Pyramids of Giza**, expanded trade relations with the Near East, and developed mining activities in Nubia, where a copper-smelting factory was established at the Second Cataract. Though Snofru's line expired with the death of **Shepseskaf**, his widow Queen **Khentkawes** is believed to have married a high priest to produce an heir.

A debt to the priesthood of **Heliopolis** may explain the increased **worship of Re** during the **V Dynasty** (c.2494–2345 BC), whose rulers styled themselves "son of Re" and built elaborate sun-temples at Abu Ghurab. Their pyramids at Abu Sir and Saqqara were smaller than those of the previous dynasty but more finely worked. It was **Unas**, the last pharaoh of the dynasty, who introduced religious texts into his pyramid – descriptions of the underworld and afterlife that subsequently inspired the *Book of the Dead*. Meanwhile, the tombs of nobles grew larger and farther away from the royal pyramids, suggesting that their independence was increasing.

This trend continued during the **VI Dynasty** (c.2345–2181 BC) when nobles were buried in their own **nomes** (provinces). Whilst punitive expeditions carried the pharaoh's banner deep into Nubia, Libya and Palestine, domestic power ebbed to the *nomarchs*, reaching the point of no return under **Pepi II** (aka Neferkare), whose death heralded the **end of the Old Kingdom**.

FIRST INTERMEDIATE PERIOD (c.2181–2050BC)

After Pepi's death, decades of provincial rivalry and chaos ensued, with petty dynasties claiming the mantle of the Old Kingdom. The Greek historian Manetho records seventy rulers during the brief **VII Dynasty** (c.2181–2173), whilst an unknown number of kings vainly asserted their claims from Memphis during the **VIII Dynasty** (c.2173–2160).

When rains failed over the Ethiopian highlands, famine struck Egypt, exacerbating civil disorders. Weak principalities sought powerful allies such as **Heracleopolis**, the dominant city of the Twentieth Nome, whose ruler, **Achthoes**, gained control of Middle Egypt, assumed the throne-name Meryibre, and founded the **IX Dynasty** (c.2160–2130).

Whereas most of the north came under the control of the IX and **X Dynasty** (c.2130–2040) kings of Heracleopolis, Upper Egypt was contested by the rulers of Edfu and Thebes. After vanquishing his rival, the Theban ruler Inyotef Sehertowy tried to extend his power beyond Upper Egypt, founding the **XI Dynasty** (c.2133–1991 BC). The struggle between north and south was only finally resolved by **Nebhepetre Mentuhotpe II**, who reunited the whole country under one authority, establishing the Middle Kingdom.

THE MIDDLE KINGDOM (c.2050–1786 BC)

During Mentuhotpe's fifty-year reign the mines and trade routes were reopened; incursions into Libya, Nubia and Sinai resumed; and arts and crafts flourished again. His successors, Mentuhotpe III and IV, were most notable for their expeditions to the Land of Punt. Inscriptions from Wadi Hammamat name the vizier in charge of the second expedition as **Amenemhat** (or Ammenemes), who subsequently founded the **XII Dynasty** (c.1991 BC).

Amenemhat returned the capital to Memphis and safeguarded the Nile Delta from raiders by constructing the Walls of the Prince, a fortified *cordon sanitaire*. Northern Nubia was annexed, and trade extended farther into Palestine and Syria.

Under Amenemhat's son, **Senusert I** (aka Sesostris I), the administrative capital was transferred to the **Fayoum**, where massive waterworks were undertaken. Amenemhat II curbed the power of the *nomarchs*, whilst Senusert III may have abolished the office completely. These kings also built **the last pyramids**, at Lahun, Lisht and Hawara. But as Egypt's population and state expenditure grew, the stability of the kingdom was eroded by bad harvests and popular unrest, causing another breakdown in centralised authority.

SECOND INTERMEDIATE PERIOD (c.1788–1567BC)

Under the enfeebled XIII and XIV dynasties, Asiatic nomads gained control of the Delta and gradually extended their power southwards. Known to the Egyptians as the **Hyksos** ("princes from foreign lands"), they established a new Delta capital, **Avaris**, where the recent discovery of Minoan frescoes points to Aegean ties. The Hyksos maintained links with countries as far afield as Persia, Palestine and the Sudan. Though Egyptian chronicles describe their rule as anarchic, evidence such as the *Rhind Mathematical Papyrus* suggests that the Hyksos fostered native culture, took Egyptian names and ruled as pharaohs.

From 1650 BC onwards, Hyksos rule was challenged by the **XVII Dynasty** of Theban kings, who claimed all of Egypt. The balance of power shifted back and forth, with Nubia allied to whichever state recognised its independence. Eventually, the Theban ruler Wadikheperre Kamose besieged Avaris, and his successor **Ahmosis** finally expelled the Hyksos from Egypt in 1567 BC, ushering in a new era.

THE NEW KINGDOM (1567–1085 BC)

The **XVIII Dynasty** founded by Ahmosis inaugurated the **New Kingdom**, a period of stability, wealth and expansion, whose rulers include some of the most famous names in Egyptian history. During this era **Nubia** was brought under Egyptian control, yielding gold, ivory, ebony, gems and, most importantly, slaves. The professional armies of the pharaohs also invaded the Near East, Syria and Palestine, establishing colonies governed by Egyptian viceroys or local satraps. One result was an influx of immigrants into Egypt, bringing new customs, ideas and technology.

The effects are evident at **Thebes**, capital of the New Kingdom, where a spate of temples and tombs symbolise the pre-eminence of the god **Amun** and the power of the pharaohs. While **Tuthmosis I** (c.1525–1512 BC) built the first tomb in the Valley of the Kings, his daughter **Hatshepsut** raised the great mortuary temple of Deir el-Bahri, ruling as pharaoh (c.1503–1482 BC) despite her stepson's claim on the throne. Having belatedly assumed power, **Tuthmosis III** embarked on imperial conquests, extending Egyptian power beyond the Fourth Cataract in Nubia, and across the Euphrates to the boundaries of the Hittite empire. His successor **Amenophis II** (c.1459–1425 BC) penetrated deeper into Nubia, while **Tuthmosis IV** (c. 1425–1417 BC) further strengthened the empire by marrying a princess of Mitanni, a state bordering the Hittites.

The zenith of Egyptian power coincided with the reign of **Amenophis III** (c.1417–1379 BC). With the empire secure and prosperity at home, the king devoted himself to the arts and the construction of great edifices such as Luxor Temple. During the same period, a hitherto minor aspect of the sun-god was increasingly venerated in royal circles – the **cult of Aten** that the pharaoh's son would subsequently enshrine above all others.

THE AMARNA REVOLUTION

By changing his name from Amenophis IV to **Akhenaten** and founding a new capital at Tell el-Amarna, the young king underlined his commitment to a new **monotheistic religion** which challenged the existing priesthood and bureaucracy. Since the story of Akhenaten and **Nefertiti** is related in detail on p.253, suffice it to say that the **Amarna revolution** barely outlasted his reign (c.1379–1362 BC) and that of his mysterious successor, **Smenkhkare**, who died the following year.

The boy-king **Tutankhamun** (1361–1352 BC) was easily persuaded to abjure Aten's cult and return the capital to Thebes, heralding a **Theban counter-revolution** that continued

under **Ay** and **Horemheb**. Though Horemheb (c.1348–1320 BC) effectively restored the *status quo ante*, his lack of royal blood and, more importantly, an heir, brought the XVIII Dynasty to a close.

THE XIX DYNASTY

The **XIX Dynasty** began with the reign of Horemheb's vizier, **Ramses I** (c.1320–1318 BC), whose family was to produce several warrior kings who would recapture territories lost under Akhenaten. **Seti I** (c.1318–1304 BC) reasserted pharaonic authority in Nubia, Palestine and the Near East, and began a magnificent temple at Abydos. His son **Ramses II** (c.1304–1237 BC) completed the temple and the reconquest of Asia Minor; commemorating his dubious victory at Qadesh with numerous reliefs, but later concluding a treaty with the Hittites. At home, Ramses usurped temples and statues built by others, and raised his own monumental edifices – notably the Ramesseum at Thebes and the sun-temples at Abu Simbel.

His son **Merneptah** (c.1236–1217 BC) faced invasions by the "Sea Peoples" from the north and Libyans from the west, but eventually defeated the latter at Pi-yer in the western Delta. He is also thought to be the pharaoh of the **Exodus**, although the only non-Biblical reference to the Israelites describes an Egyptian victory against these "nomads". The XIX Dynasty expired with **Seti II** (c.1210 BC), to be followed by a decade without a ruling dynasty.

THE XX DYNASTY

The **XX Dynasty**, begun by Sethnakhte (c.1200), was the last of the New Kingdom. His successor **Ramses III** (c.1198–1166 BC) repulsed three great invasions by the Libyans and Sea Peoples, and built the vast temple-cum-pleasure palace of **Medinet Habu**. But strikes by workmen at the royal necropolis and an assassination attempt within the king's harem presaged problems to come. Under the eight kings who followed (all called Ramses), Egypt lost the remains of its Asiatic empire, and thieves plundered the necropolis. **Ramses XI** (c.1114–1085 BC) withdrew to his residence in the Delta, delegating control of Upper Egypt to **Herihor**, high priest of Amun, and Lower Egypt to vizier **Smendes**.

THE LATE PERIOD
(c. 1085 – 322 BC)

This division was consolidated under the **XXI Dynasty** (c.1085–945 BC), the successors of Herihor and Smendes ruling their respective halves of Egypt from **Thebes** and **Tanis**. However, each was vulnerable to foreign invaders and internal fragmentation. The Tanite kings were ousted by land-hungry Libyans, who founded their own **XXII Dynasty** (c.945–715 BC). Upper Egypt remained stable for longer, but likewise eventually succumbed to invasions from the south.

THE NUBIAN KINGS

The Nubian ruler Piankhi advanced as far north as Memphis, while his brother **Shabaka** went on to conquer the Delta and reunite the Two Lands. His rule launched the **XXV Dynasty** of **Nubian kings** (c.747–656 BC), which was marked by a revival of artistic and cultural life, and renewed devotion to Amun (as evinced by reliefs at Karnak and Luxor).

By the reign of Tanutamun, however, Egypt was menaced by the **Assyrians**, who occupied Memphis in 667 BC and then raided Thebes, whereupon Tanutamun withdrew to Nubia.

THE SAÏTE DYNASTY

The vacuum was filled by **Psammetichus I**, son of a Delta prince who found favour with the Assyrians. After they withdrew and became embroiled with the Persian empire, he declared himself pharaoh and eventually reunited the Two Lands. The **XXVI Dynasty**, with its capital at **Saïs** in the Delta, was the last great age of pharaonic civilisation. Whilst harking back to the glories of the Old Kingdom in art and architecture, it adopted new technologies and permitted colonies of Greek merchants at Naucratis, and Jewish mercenaries at Elephantine. **Necho II** (610–595 BC) defeated Josiah, King of Judah, at Megiddo, but was routed by the Babylonians. He is also credited with starting to build a canal to link the Nile with the Red Sea. Though **Psammetichus II** (595–589 BC) enjoyed several victories, his successor **Apries** was overthrown following defeat in Cyrenacia, the throne passing to **Amasis** "the Drunkard", who relied on Greek allies to stave off the Perisian empire.

PERSIAN RULE

The **Persian invasion** of 525 BC began an era of rule by foreigners that essentially lasted until Nasser eventually overthrew Egypt's monarchy in 1952.

Mindful of the Assyrians' mistake, the Persian emperors **Cambyses** and **Darius I** kept a tight grip on Egypt. Besides completing Necho's canal and founding a new city near Memphis, called **Babylon-in-Egypt** (today's "Old Cairo"), they built and restored temples to enhance their legitimacy. But **rebellions** against Xerxes and Artaxerxes testified to Egyptian hatred of this foreign **XXVII Dynasty**.

Ousted by Amyrtaeus, sole ruler of the XXVIII Dynasty, the Persians constantly assailed the native rulers that followed. Though **Nectanebo I** (380–343) of the **XXX Dynasty** managed to repulse them with Greek help, his successor's campaign in Phoenicia failed. Finally, bereft of allies, **Nectanebo II** (360–343 BC) was crushingly defeated by Artaxerxes III, and fled to Nubia. Egypt remained under Persian control until 332 BC, when their entire empire succumbed to **Alexander the Great**.

THE PTOLEMIES
(332 – 30 BC)

Alexander's stay in Egypt was brief, though long enough for him to adopt local customs. He offered sacrifices to the gods of Memphis and visited Amun's temple at Siwa; reorganised the country's administration, installing himself as pharaoh; and founded the coastal city of Alexandria. Upon his death in 323 BC, Alexander's generals divided the empire, Ptolemy becoming ruler of Egypt and establishing the **Ptolemaic Dynasty**.

Under **Ptolemy I** (305–282 BC), **Greek** became the official language and Hellenistic ideas had a profound effect on Egyptian art, religion and technology. Although Greek deities were also introduced, the Ptolemies cultivated the Egyptian gods and ruled much like Egyptian pharaohs, erecting great cult temples such as Edfu and Kom Ombo. They also opened new ports, established the Library of Alexandria and had Hebrew scriptures translated into Greek by Jewish rabbis. The first synagogue in Egypt was founded at Leontopolis in the Delta.

It was dynastic disputes that led to the loss of Ptolemaic control. **Roman intervention** in Egypt grew until, under Ptolemy XII Auletes (80–51 BC), Egypt was almost totally dependent on Rome. **Julius Caesar** attacked Egypt in 54 BC, taking Alexandria by force.

The most famous queen of Egypt, **Cleopatra VII** (51–30 BC) was also the last of the Ptolemies. Under the protection of Julius Caesar – whom she bore a son, Caesarion – Cleopatra managed to prolong her family's rule. After Caesar's death, she formed a similar alliance with **Mark Antony** to preserve Egyptian independence. Their joint fleets, however, suffered disaster against the **Emperor Octavian** at the Battle of Actium, and both committed suicide rather than face captivity. Egypt subsequently was reduced to the status of a province of the Roman Empire (30 BC).

ROMAN RULE AND THE RISE OF CHRISTIANITY

The **Roman emperors**, like the Ptolemies, adopted many of the Egyptian cults, building such monuments as Trajan's kiosk at Philae, and temples at Dendara and Esna. Their main interest in the new colony, however, lay in its potential as grain supplier to Rome. With this end constantly in mind, trade routes were ensured by Roman garrisons at Alexandria, Babylon (Old Cairo) and Syene (Aswan). In terms of culture, language and administration, **Hellenistic influence** barely diminished and Alexandria continued to thrive as an important centre of Greek and Hebrew learning.

Although the **Holy Family's flight to Egypt** from Palestine cannot be proven, Egypt's Jewish colonies would have been a natural place of refuge, and several sites remain associated with the episode. According to Coptic tradition, however, **Christianity** was brought to Egypt by **Saint Mark**, who arrived in the time of Nero. Mark converted many to the new underground faith, founding the Patriarchate of Alexandria in 61 AD.

Politically, the most significant ruler was **Trajan** (98–117 AD), who reopened Necho's Red Sea Canal. Trade flourished with the export of glass, linen, papyrus and precious stones. But the *fellaheen* were growing increasingly discontented with heavy taxation and forced recruitment into the Roman army.

THE COPTS

First-century Egypt was fertile ground for the spread of Christianity. The religion of the old gods had lost its credibility over the millennia of political manipulations and disasters, while the population – Egyptians and Jews alike – was becoming increasingly anti-Roman and nationalistic in its outlook. The core of Christianity, too, had a resonance in ancient traditions, with its emphasis on resurrection, divine judgement and the cult of the great mother.

Inevitably, as Egypt's Christians – who became known as **Copts** – grew in political confidence, there was conflict with the Roman authorities. In 202 AD, **persecutions** began, reaching their height under **Diocletian** (284–305), when thousands of Coptic Christians were massacred. Copts date their calendar from the massacres in 284.

The legalisation of Christianity and its adoption as the imperial religion by **Constantine** in 313 did little to help the Copts. The Roman leaders, from their new capital at **Byzantium**, embraced an orthodox faith which differed fundamentally from their Egyptian co-religionists – and persecutions continued. An attempt to reconcile differences at the **Council of Nicaea** (325) failed and the split had become irrevocable by the time it was formalised at the **Council of Chalcedon** (451 AD), following which the Copts established their own patriarchate at Alexandria.

The same period also saw the emergence of **monasticism**, which took root in the Egyptian deserts. The monasteries of Saint Catherine in the Sinai, those of Wadi Natrun and Sohag, and Saint Anthony's and Saint Paul's in the Red Sea Hills, all originated in these years.

THE COMING OF ISLAM

Apart from a brief invasion in 616, Egypt remained under **Byzantine rule** until the **advance of Islam** in the seventh century. Led by the Prophet Mohammed's successor, Abu Bakr, the Muslim armies defeated the Byzantine army in 636 AD. General **Amr Ibn al-As** then advanced towards Babylon-in-Egypt, which surrendered after a brief siege, to be followed by Heliopolis (640) and finally the imperial capital of Alexandria (642).

Amr built his capital, Fustat, north of the fortress town of Babylon-in-Egypt, in what is today Old Cairo. However, Egypt was but a province in the vast Islamic empire that was governed from Damascus and Baghdad. As in Roman times, Egypt's primary role was as a bread basket.

Arabisation and Islamicisation was a gradual and uneven process, with intermittent periods of religious toleration and discrimination. Much depended on the character of the Khalifs, and their own power struggles, whose impact was felt throughout the Islamic empire. In 750, the empire's ruling **Ummayad** dynasty was defeated by the armies of Abu al-Abbas (a descendant of Abu Bakr) and an **Abbasid** khalifate came to power in Baghdad, administering Egypt, along with its other territories, for the next two centuries.

THE TULUNIDS (868– 905 AD) AND IKHSHIDIDS (935–969)

In 868, **Ahmed Ibn Tulun**, sent to administer Egypt on behalf of Khalif al-Mu'tazz, declared the territory independent. He and his successors, the **Tulunids**, ruled for 37 years, during which time economic stability and order were restored. Like previous rulers, Ibn Tulun built a new capital city, **al-Qitai**, whose vast mosque still remains. The dynasty did not long outlive him, however. His spendthrift son, Khomaruya, was assassinated, as were his heirs, and by 905 Abbassid rule was reimposed.

Egypt remained under the direct control of Baghdad until 935, when Mohammed Ibn Tughj was appointed governor and granted the title *Ikhshid* (ruler or king) by the khalif. Like the Tulunids, the **Ikhshidid dynasty** functioned virtually independent of the khalifate. Severe taxation, though, led to popular discontent and the death in 965 of Tughj's second son, Ali, combined with famine, drought and political instability, opened the way for an invasion of the **Shi'a Fatimids** from Tunisia.

THE FATIMID ERA (969–1171)

The early **Fatimid khalifs** ruled half the Muslim world, with Egypt forming the central portion of an empire that included North Africa, Sicily, Syria and western Arabia. **Gohar**, commander of the khalifal forces, built the city of **al-Qahira** (the Triumphant) as a new capital in 969, its walls containing opulent palaces and

the prestigious mosque-university of al-Azhar. **Khalif al-Muizz** installed himself in the city and from there ruled the empire. Trade with India, Africa and Europe expanded, the burdensome tax system was abolished, and a vast multiracial army that included Europeans, Berbers, Sudanese and Turks, was formed.

Whilst al-Muizz and his successor al-Aziz (975–996) were efficient and tolerant rulers, under whom Egypt's economy prospered and the arts flourished, the third khalif – **al-Hakim** (996–1021) – was a mad and capricious despot. His laws outraged the population, whilst his support of Byzantine against Latin Christians, and destruction of the Church of the Holy Sepulchre in Jerusalem, later provided a pretext for the First Crusade. His mysterious disappearance (see p.97) was taken by his followers – he championed Shia against Sunni Islam – as proof of messianic stature.

By the long reign of al-Hakim's grandson, **al-Mostansir** (1035–94), decay had set in. The empire was largely controlled by army commanders, administration was chaotic and famine added to the troubles. A series of governors imposed control over the army and restored peace and prosperity to Egypt for a further hundred years, but the loss of Syria to the Seljuk Turks, and new forces in Europe, left the empire increasingly vulnerable.

The **First Crusade** (1097–99), and those that followed, were motivated as much by the desire to acquire estates as to restore Christian dominance to the Holy Land. Egypt, however, was not attacked until 1167, by which time the Crusader kingdom held the former Fatimid coastal area of Palestine. Outraged at the fraternisation between Franks and Fatimids, the Seljuk Sultan, Nur al-Din, sent an expedition to Cairo to repel them. The sultan's deputy, Shirkoh, occupied Upper Egypt, while his nephew, Salah al-Din al-Ayyubi – known to Europe as Saladin – took possession of Alexandria.

THE AYYUBIDS (1171–1249)

On the death of the last Fatimid khalif in 1171, **Salah al-Din** became ruler of Egypt. To this day he remains a hero in the Arab World, a ruler renowned for his personal modesty, generosity, culture and political acumen. Having no pretensions to religious leadership, Salah al-Din chose for himself the secular title of *al-sultan* (the power) rather than that of *khalif*, giving his family's name – the Ayyub – to the dynasty which succeeded him. Of his 24-year reign, he spent only eight years in Cairo, the rest being spent in **liberating the former Crusader territory**. By 1183, Syria had been won back and in 1187 Jerusalem was recaptured.

In Cairo, Salah al-Din built a fortress – today's Citadel – and expanded the Fatimid walls to enclose the city. In order to propagate Sunni orthodoxy, he also introduced the Seljuk institution of the *madrassa* or teaching mosque, thus turning Cairo into a great centre of learning. Hospitals were endowed, too, and the pharaonic canal at Fayoum was reopened.

Following his peaceful death in Damascus in 1193, Salah al-Din's eastern territories fragmented into principalities, though Egypt remained united under the Ayyubids. His nephew, **al-Kamil** (1218–38), repulsed the Fifth Crusade. The last of the dynasty, **Ayyub** (1240–49), built up a formidable army of Turkish-speaking Qipchak slaves from the Black Sea region, and he himself married a slave girl, **Shagar al-Durr** (Tree of Pearls).

It was Shagar al-Durr who took power following Ayyub's death, ruling openly as *sultana* until the Abbasid khalifs insisted that she take a husband, quoting the Prophet's words: "Woe to the nations ruled by women." Jealous of her power and warned by astrologers that he would die at a woman's hands, her husband, Aybak, planned to take a second wife, whereupon she had him murdered. She herself was assassinated soon afterwards, but her henchman, **Beybars the Crossbowman**, clawed his way to power, inaugurating the Mamluke era.

THE MAMLUKES (1250–1517)

Beybars was a commander among the foreign troops – the Mamlukes – on whom the latter-day Ayyubids depended. Following his accession, **Mamluke amirs** retained control of Egypt for the next three centuries, each sultan intriguing his way up the ranks to assume the throne by coup d'état or assassination.

BAHRI MAMLUKES (1250–1382)

The **Bahri (River) Mamlukes**, named after their garrison by the Nile and predominantly Turkic, formed the first of these military dynasties. The dynasty was founded by **Qalaoun**, who poisoned Beybars's heirs to inherit the throne. He sponsored numerous buildings in Cairo, and established relations as far afield as Ceylon and East Africa, concluding treaties with the Hapsburg Emperor Rudolph and other European princes. His son, **Khalil**, forced the remaining Crusaders from their stronghold in Acre in 1291.

Qalaoun's son **Mohammed al-Nasir** (1294–1340) was another great builder and power-broker. He concluded treaties with the Mongols, after defeating them in Syria, and strengthened political and trade ties with Europe. After his death a series of weak relatives were barely able to hold the throne in the face of conflicts between rival Mamluke factions.

BURGI MAMLUKES (1382–1517)

In 1382, the sultanate was seized by **Barquq**, one of the Circassian **Burgi (Tower) Mamlukes** from the garrison below the Citadel. To finance his campaigns against the **Mongols**, who by 1387 were on the borders of Syria, he had to impose punitive taxes that beggared the economy.

Hardships were exacerbated by famine and plague during the reign of his son, **Farag** (1399–1405), and it was only under Sultan **Barsbey** (1422–37) that Egypt regained some of its power. Barsbey established friendly relations with the new power in the north, the Ottoman Turks, and expanded trade in the Indian Ocean. But although the next hundred years saw relative peace and security, the Egyptian economy remained ropy.

The country experienced a brief revival under the rule of **Qaitbey** (1468–1495), though his lavish building programme imposed a huge burden. The forty-sixth, and penultimate sultan, **Qansuh al-Ghuri** (1501–16), suffered the loss of customary revenues after Vasco da Gama discovered the Cape of Good Hope, dealing a crippling blow to Egypt's spice trade monopoly. Worse was to come, as the **Ottoman Turks** consolidated their northern empire, defeating the Shi'ite Persians and then attacking Mamluke territory in northern Syria. In 1516, al-Ghuri was killed in battle and his successor, Tumanbey, was executed in Cairo by the Ottomans in 1517.

OTTOMAN EGYPT (1517–1798)

Even after the Turkish conquest, the Mamlukes remained powerful figures, running the administration of what was now a province of the vast Ottoman Empire. Government was provided by a series of **pashas**, career officials trained in Istanbul. As long as taxes were received, the Ottomans interfered little with Egyptian affairs and Cairo retained its importance as a religious, if not cultural or commercial, centre.

The Mamluke army continued to grow with the import of Caucasian slaves and by the end of the sixteenth century had become powerful enough to depose a pasha, although the Ottomans still held overall control. The growing power of the highest rank of the military corps – **the Beys** – posed a challenge to that of the pashas. Their arbitrary taxes, profligate ways and internal rivalry dominated events.

Meanwhile, economic decline, accelerated by changes in European shipping routes, and an outbreak of plague in 1819, left the country in a sorry shape. The French traveller Volney, visiting around 1784, described a depopulated country, whose capital was crumbling and surrounded by mounds of rubbish.

FRENCH OCCUPATION

At the end of the eighteenth century, Egypt became a pawn in the struggle for power between France and Britain. **Napoleon** saw Egypt as a means to disrupt British commerce and eventually overthrow their rule in India. In 1798, his fleet landed at Alexandria, where he issued a proclamation that began with the Islamic *bismillah* ("In the name of God . . ."), stated his aim of liberating Egypt from the "riff-raff of slaves", and concluded that he respected Allah, his Prophet and the Koran more than the Mamlukes did.

Although Napoleon routed the Mamlukes at Imbaba and occupied Cairo, he left his fleet exposed at Abu Qir Bay, where it was attacked and destroyed by the British under Nelson. With his grand vision in tatters, and facing a declaration of war from the Ottoman sultan, Napoleon returned secretly to France. General Kléber, whom he left in charge, had a victory over the Ottomans, but was then assassinated. When his successor, General Menou, took charge, declared his conversion to Islam, and

proclaimed Egypt a French **protectorate**, the British invaded from Abu Qir and occupied Alexandria. Combined Ottoman-British forces then took Damietta and Cairo, and the French were forced to surrender. Under the Capitulation Agreement, the archaeological treasures gathered by Napoleon's savants were surrendered to Britain – which is why the Rosetta Stone ended up in the British Museum rather than the Louvre.

MOHAMMED ALI AND HIS HEIRS

After the expulsion of the French a power struggle ensued, which was won by **Mohammed Ali**, an officer in the Albanian Corps of the Ottoman forces. Widely regarded as the founder of modern Egypt, his dynasty was to change Egypt more radically than any ruler since Salah al-Din.

The Ottomans confirmed Mohammed Ali as pasha in 1805, whereupon he proceeded to decapitate – literally and figuratively – what remained of the Mamluke power structure. The first time was on the occasion of his accession, where he tricked the beys into a coup attempt; six years later, he dispensed with the rest of the Corps, inviting 470 of them to a feast at the Citadel and slaughtering the lot.

Whilst nominally a vassal of the Ottoman sultan, Mohammed Ali's control was absolute. He confiscated private land for his own use and set about modernising Egypt with European expertise, building railroads, factories and canals. Meanwhile, his son Ibrahim led a murderous campaign to subjugate northern **Sudan**, of which the only positive result was the introduction of a special kind of **cotton** – henceforth Egypt's major cash crop.

When Mohammed Ali died insane in 1849, his power greatly reduced after disastrous adventurism in Greece and Syria, he was succeeded by **Abbas** (1848–54), who closed the country's factories and schools and opened Egypt to free trade, thus delaying the country's industrial development for the next century.

Abbas's successor, **Said Pasha** (1854–63), granted a concession to a French engineer, **Ferdinand de Lesseps**, to build the **Suez Canal**. The project was completed in 1869, by which time **Khedive Ismail** (1863–79) was in power. An ambitious and enlightened ruler, Ismail transformed Cairo, spending lavishly on modernisation. However, exorbitant interest rates had to be paid on loans from European lenders. Egyptian indebtedness spiralled and, to stave off bankruptcy, Ismail sold his Suez Canal shares to the British government in 1875.

He was deposed and succeeded by his son **Tewfiq** (1879–92), whose own financial control was limited by the French and British, to the disgust of patriotic Egyptians. A group of army officers forced him to make power-sharing concessions and to appoint their leader, **Ahmed Orabi**, as Minister of War. France and Britain responded by sending in the gunboats, shelling Alexandria and landing an army at Ismailiya, which subsequently routed Orabi's forces at Tell el-Kebir and restored Tewfiq as a puppet ruler under British control.

BRITISH OCCUPATION ... AND NATIONALISM

Britain's stated intention was to set Egyptian affairs in order and then withdraw, but its interests dictated a more active and permanent involvement. From 1883 to 1907, Egypt was controlled by the British Consul-general, Sir Evelyn Baring, later **Lord Cromer**, who coined the term "Veiled Protectorate" to describe the relationship.

The emergence of the Mahdi in the Sudan accelerated the trend towards direct British involvement in military and civil affairs. The Sudan was nominally an Egyptian khedival possession – a status quo which the British, ostensibly, moved to protect. However, Britain was clearly pursuing its own interests, and dominating Egyptian government, to the extent of replacing its key officials with British colonial personnel. Egyptian resentment at this usurpation of authority found expression both under Tewfiq's son, **Abbas II**, who came to power in 1892, and in a nationalist movement led by a young lawyer, **Mustafa Kamil**. To ameliorate the situation, the British made a series of reforms and allowed Orabi to return from exile in Ceylon.

Economically, however, Egypt was effectively a colony, with Britain supplying all the country's manufactured goods, and in turn encouraging Egyptian dependence on cotton exports. In order to grow cotton, the *fellaheen* had to take out loans; when prices fell, many were forced to sell up to large landowners.

TOWARDS INDEPENDENCE

Politically, things came to a head when Turkey entered **World War I** on the side of Germany, in November 1916. Egypt was still nominally a province of the Ottoman Empire, so to protect its interests – the Suez Canal and free passage to the East – Britain declared Egypt a protectorate. By 1917, **Fouad**, the sixth son of Ismail, was khedive of Egypt, Sir Reginald Wingate its High Commissioner.

The **nationalist movement** flourished under wartime conditions. In 1918, its leader, **Sa'ad Zaghloul**, presented the High Commissioner with a demand for autonomy, which was rejected. The request to send a delegation (*Wafd*) to London led to Zaghloul's arrest and deportation to Malta, a decision rescinded after nationwide anti-British riots. In 1922 Britain abolished the protectorate and recognised Egypt as an independent state, but kept control of the legal system, communications, defence and the Suez Canal. In March 1922, Fouad assumed the title of king.

The years between independence and World War II saw a struggle for power between the king, the British and the nationalist **Wafd Party**. Backed by the masses, the latter won landslide elections but King Fouad retained power and the backing of the British. His son, **King Farouk**, succeeded him to the throne in 1935 and a year later signed a twenty-year **Anglo-Egyptian treaty** which ended British occupation but empowered British forces to remain in the Suez Canal Zone. In 1937, Egypt joined the League of Nations; but the outbreak of World War II halted Egypt's move to complete independence.

WORLD WAR II

During **World War II**, Egypt served a vital strategic asset as a British base in the Middle East. The Wafd leadership went along with support for the Allies – on the tacit understanding that full independence would be granted after the war – keeping internal tensions controlled. Cairo itself, however, became an extraordinary centre of international power-broking, with its British political-military command and exiled Balkan royals and governments.

Rommel's Afrika Korps came within sixty-five kilometres of Alexandria, but was repulsed by the **Eighth Army** under General **Montgomery** at the **Battle of el-Alamein** in

October 1942. Thereafter the tide of war turned in the Western Desert Campaign and the Allies continued to advance across North Africa, through Libya and Tunisia.

POSTWAR MANOEUVRINGS

On **conclusion of the war**, the Wafd demanded the evacuation of British troops and unification with Sudan — in opposition to British plans for the latter's self-government. Popular resentment was expressed in anti-British riots and strikes, supported by the **Muslim Brotherhood**, which led to clashes with British troops. In January 1947, British troops were evacuated from Alexandria and the Canal Zone.

Following the declaration of the state of **Israel** in May 1948, Egypt joined Iraq, Syria and Jordan in a military invasion. The defeat of the Arab forces was followed by a UN-organised treaty in February 1949 which left the coastal **Gaza Strip** of Palestine under Egyptian administration. Many of the Egyptian officers who fought in this war were left disgusted by the incompetence and corruption of their superiors; it was from their ranks that many of the leading lights of the 1952 revolution were to emerge.

THE 1952 REVOLUTION

For the present, the country experimented with democracy, holding its first **elections** in ten years. The Wafd won a majority and formed a government with Nahas Pasha as prime minister. A course for crisis was set, as the **Suez Canal** — which the British still controlled — loomed increasingly large. In 1952, Nahas was dismissed by King Farouk after abrogating the 1936 Treaty with Britain, and the army was sent out onto the streets to quell anti-British protests.

Reaction was swift. On July 23, 1952, a group of conspiratorial **Free Officers** seized power and forced the **abdication of King Farouk**. General Naguib, the official leader of the group, was made commander of the armed forces and became prime minister, but real power lay in the hands of the nine officers of the **Revolutionary Command Council** (RCC), foremost amongst whom was Colonel **Gamal Abd al-Nasser**.

Under RCC direction, the Constitution was revoked, political parties dissolved, the monar-chy abolished and Egypt declared a **republic** (July 26, 1953). Meanwhile, a struggle for power was taking place behind the scenes, as Naguib attempted to step beyond his figure-head status and moderate the revolutionary impulses of the RCC. After his implication in an attempt on Nasser's life at Alexandria in 1954, Naguib was placed under house arrest. Nasser became acting head of state and in June 1956 was confirmed as president.

THE NASSER ERA

President Nasser dominated Egypt and the Arab World until his death in 1970, his ideology of Arab nationalism and socialism making him supremely popular with the masses (if not always their governments) from Iraq to Morocco. Under his leadership, Egypt was at the forefront of **anti-colonialism**, lending support to liberation struggles in Algeria, Black Africa and other regions. Nasser also helped to set up the **Non-Aligned Movement**, with India and Indonesia, in 1955.

DIPLOMACY AND WAR

Nasser's most urgent priority, from the start, was to assert Egyptian control over the **Suez Canal**. In 1954 he reached agreement for the withdrawal of British troops from the Canal Zone, though the canal's management and profits were to remain in foreign hands. At the same time he was seeking credits from the World Bank to finance construction of the Aswan High Dam, and for weapons to rearm Egyptian forces, depleted from the 1948 war.

When the Soviet Union offered to supply the latter, the United States vetoed loans for the dam. Committed to the Aswan plan, Nasser had little alternative but to **nationalise the Suez Canal**, in order to secure revenue. This he did in July 1956.

His action was regarded by the West, and especially by Britain, as a threat to vital interests, and an unholy alliance was formed to combat the "Arab Hitler". Britain and France concluded a secret agreement with Israel, whose **invasion of Sinai** in October 1956 was to provide the pretext for their own military intervention. Following massive bombardment of the zone, and British paratroop landings in Port Said, the United States stepped in to impose a solution, threatening to destabilise the British economy unless their forces were withdrawn. The American motivation was to keep Britain and France from control of the Middle East, and the Arabs from moving en masse into the Soviet camp. In the event, the canal was reopened under full Egyptian control and Nasser emerged from the **Suez Crisis** as a champion of Arab nationalism.

On a wave of **pan-Arabist** sentiment, Egypt and Syria united to form the **United Arab Republic** (UAR) in 1958: an unworkable arrangement which foundered within three years. Nasser also intervened in the **Yemen civil war**, supporting the revolutionary faction, to the extent of authorising the use of poison gas against royalist forces. On a broader political front, he moved closer to the Soviet Union, accepting technical and military assistance on a massive scale, to help build the Aswan Dam and to counter an increasingly well-armed, US-supplied Israel. Most significantly, meeting in Cairo in 1964, the **Arab League** set aside funds for the formation of the **Palestine Liberation Organisation**.

War was again on the horizon. When Israel threatened to invade Syria in 1967, Nasser sent Egyptian forces into Sinai; ordered UN monitors to withdraw; and blockaded the Tiran Straits, cutting shipping to the Israeli port of Eilat. Israel responded with a preemptive strike, destroying the Egyptian air force on the ground and seizing the entire Sinai. This **Six Day War** resulted in permanent Israeli occupation of Sinai and Gaza Strip, the West Bank and the Golan Heights. It was a shattering defeat for the Arabs, and Nasser in particular, who proferred his resignation to the public, only resuming the presidency after vast demonstrations of support on the streets.

The Six Day War had no official resolution, merely subsiding into a **War of Attrition**, which was to drag on for the next two years. From their positions in Sinai, Israeli forces bombarded Egypt's Canal Cities and even Cairo and Middle Egypt suffered bombing raids. Egypt, meanwhile, was rearming with Soviet assistance and struggling to deal with millions of refugees from the Canal Zone and the newly occupied Gaza Strip.

PROGRESS AND REPRESSION

Amid the political drama of Suez and the wars with Israel, it is easy to overlook the **social achievements** of the Nasser era. One of the first acts of the RCC was to break up the old feudal estates, transferring **land** to the *fella-heen*. As a result of the **Aswan Dam**, the amount of land under cultivation increased by fifteen percent – exceeding Egypt's population growth for the first time. The Dam's electricity also powered a huge new **industrial base**, which was established virtually from scratch.

Similarly radical progress was made in the fields of **education and health care**. The number of pupils in school doubled, and included both sexes for the first time. As a result of a huge programme of local health centres, and the doubling of the number of doctors, average life expectancy rose from 43 to 52 years.

The downside of Nasser's socialism was a heavily bureaucratic, often Soviet-modelled, system. Political life was stifled by the merging of all parties into the **Arab Socialist Union** (*ASU*). Opponents of the regime were not tolerated: censorship, torture, show trials and political internment were widespread.

Nevertheless, **Nasser's death** – from a heart attack – in September 1970 was a profound shock to the whole Arab World. His funeral procession in Cairo was the largest the country has ever seen.

EGYPT UNDER SADAT

Nasser's successor was his vice-president, **Anwar Sadat**, whom the ASU hierarchy confirmed as president in October 1970. His role was to reform an Egypt demoralised by defeat in the 1967 war, economic stagnation and austerity. His first significant act was to announce a **"corrective revolution"**, reversing the policy of centralised economic control, and expelling over a thousand Soviet advisors.

Again, however, social and economic affairs were overshadowed by military developments. In concert with Syria and Jordan, Egypt launched a new campaign against Israel. On October 6, 1973, Egyptian forces crossed the Suez Canal, storming the "invincible" Bar-Lev Line to enter Israeli-occupied Sinai. This **October War** (aka Ramadan/Yom Kippur War) ultimately turned against the Arabs, but enhanced their bargaining position and dealt a blow to Israeli self-confidence. In addition, Egypt regained a strip of territory to the east of the Suez Canal.

THE OPEN DOOR POLICY

After the war, extensive changes took place in Egypt. An amnesty was granted to political prisoners, press censorship was lifted and some political parties, including the Muslim Brotherhood, were allowed. Equally important was Sadat's economic policy of *infitah* or **"open door"**, designed to encourage private and foreign investment and to reduce the role of the state in the economy.

Helped by Gulf Arab investments – a reward for the October War – and stimulated by the reconstruction of the Canal Cities, the economy boomed. However, the benefits were distributed totally unevenly. Whilst the number of millionaires rose from 500 to 17,000 between 1975 and 1981, and an affluent middle class developed, the condition of the urban poor and peasants worsened. Some five million families subsisted on less than US$30 a month, and one and a half million Egyptians migrated to work in the Gulf states.

In 1977, when the IMF insisted on the removal of subsidies on basic foodstuffs, there were nationwide **food riots**. Sadat saw the crunch coming and needed a dramatic injection of Western capital.

CAMP DAVID AND AFTERWARDS

In 1977 Sadat went to Jerusalem, the first (and to date only) Arab leader to visit Israel. This drastic step, accompanied by a total realignment of Egyptian foreign policy towards the United States, has been explained in two ways. One theory holds that it was solely motivated by the desire for US investment; the other, by Israel's acquisition of nuclear weapons, which rendered impossible a military solution in the region.

Under the resulting, US-sponsored **Camp David Agreement** of 1978, Egypt recognised Israel's right to exist and Israel agreed to withdraw from the Sinai. This independent peace treaty, which failed to resolve the Palestinian issue, outraged Arab opinion. Meeting in Baghdad, the Arab League Council decided to withdraw their ambassadors to Egypt, sever economic and political links, and transfer the League's headquarters from Cairo to Tunis.

At home, Sadat encouraged the rise of Islamic political forces to counter leftist influences. But as the Muslim Brotherhood grew stronger and protested against the economic

slump and Camp David, Sadat clamped down, with wholesale arrests of critics. In this charged atmosphere, **Sadat's assassination** by Muslim militants in October 1981 was not altogether surprising, although Western intelligence, as ever, was caught on the hop.

THE 1980S AND 1990S: PRESIDENT MUBARAK

Sadat's policies have for the most part been continued, with rather more caution, by his successor, **President Hosni Mubarak**, who took office in 1981 and remains in power at the time of writing, a decade on.

THE ECONOMY

The country's **economy** was left in dire straits at the end of the Sadat era, and the root problems seem intractable. Egypt's **population** increases by a million every nine months – 1991 estimates put the total at around sixty million – and the country imports sixty percent of its foodstuffs. To pay for this, a huge **national debt** has arisen, in excess of US$50 billion, and without **US aid** (Egypt is the second largest recipient, after Israel), the economy would collapse.

Egyptian **domestic revenues**, such as they are, depend on a narrow base, which is highly vulnerable to the political climate: tolls on shipping through the Suez Canal, remittances from Egyptians working abroad, crude oil production, and tourism. All of these were badly hit by the **Gulf War** in 1990–91, which led to over a million refugees returning from Kuwait and Iraq and wiped out the tourist industry for the best part of a year. Further cause for gloom is provided by the increased use of synthetic fibres, which threatens to undermine Egypt's important cotton exports.

In terms of **domestic politics**, Mubarak has encouraged a freer system, allowing both the Wafd Party and some Islamic groups to participate in elections. Opposition, however, is still restricted, with left-wing students (still influenced by Nasserist ideals) and Muslim fundamentalists the targets of perennial clampdowns.

Despite this, things occasionally erupt, as when Central Security conscripts rioted in 1986 over the threat of extended service and arrears in wages, or the workers' occupation of the Helwan iron and steel mill in 1989.

FOREIGN AFFAIRS AND THE FUTURE . . .

Mubarak's **foreign policy** involves a delicate balancing of priorities. He has maintained a "cold peace" with Israel, whom he openly criticised over their invasion of Lebanon in 1982, the bombing of Tunis in 1985, and the attempted suppression of the Palestinian intifada in the Occupied Territories. Simultaneously, he has moved to restore ties with the Arab states, which in 1990 readmitted Egypt to the Arab League, whose headquarters have now returned to Cairo.

Ties with the **US**, however, remain paramount, which explains Egypt's support for action against Iraq during the Gulf War. In return for supplying a small military force, and providing political "legitimacy", they were rewarded with the writing-off of US$7 billion debts, and further military as well as economic aid.

For **the future**, Egypt's stability is affected to some extent by progress towards a lasting peace settlement in the Middle East, and particularly a just resolution of the Palestinian problem. However, it is the problems of poverty and overpopulation, and the scarcity of water and fertile land that will really determine the issue.

ISLAM

It's difficult to get any grasp of Egypt without first knowing something of Islam. What follows is a very basic background: some theory, some history and an idea of Egypt's place in the modern Islamic world.

BEGINNINGS: PRACTICE AND BELIEF

Islam was a new religion born of the wreckage of the Graeco-Roman world around the south of the Mediterranean. Its founder, a merchant named **Mohammed** from the wealthy city of Mecca (now in Saudi Arabia), was chosen as God's Prophet: in about 609 AD, he began to hear divine messages which he transcribed directly into the **Koran**, Islam's Bible. This was the same God worshipped by Jews and Christians – Jesus is one of the minor prophets in Islam – but Muslims claim He had been misunderstood by both earlier religions.

The distinctive feature of this new faith was directness – a reaction to the increasing complexity of established religions and an obvious attraction. In Islam there is no intermediary between man and God in the form of an institutionalised priesthood or complicated liturgy; and worship, in the form of prayer, is a direct and personal communication with God. Believers face five essential requirements, the so-called **"Pillars of Faith"**: prayer five times daily; the pilgrimage (*hadj*) to Mecca; the Ramadan fast; a religious levy; and, most fundamental of all, the acceptance that "There is no God but God and Mohammed is His Prophet".

THE PILLARS OF FAITH

The Pillars of Faith are still central to Muslim life, articulating and informing daily existence. Ritual **prayers** are the most visible. Bearing in mind that the Islamic day begins at sunset, the five daily times are sunset, after dark, dawn, noon and afternoon. Prayers can be performed anywhere, but preferably in a mosque. In the past, and even today in some places, a *muezzin* would climb his minaret each time and summon the faithful.

Nowadays, the call is likely to be pre-recorded; even so, this most distinctive of Islamic sounds has a beauty all its own, especially when neighbouring *muezzins* are audible simultaneously. Their message is simplicity itself: "God is most great (*Allahu Akbar*). I testify that there is no God but Allah. I testify that Mohammed is His Prophet. Come to prayer, come to security. God is great." Another phrase is added in the morning: "Prayer is better than sleep."

Prayers are preceded by ritual washing and are spoken with the feet bare. Facing Mecca (the direction indicated in a mosque by the *mihrab*), the worshipper recites the *Fathah*, the first chapter of the Koran: "Praise be to God, Lord of the worlds, the Compassionate, the Merciful, King of the Day of Judgement. Only thee do we worship and thine aid do we seek. Guide us on the straight path, the path of those on whom thou hast bestowed thy grace, not the path of those who incur thine anger nor of those who go astray." The same words are then repeated twice in the prostrate position, with some interjections of *Allahu Akbar*. It is a highly ritualised procedure, the prostrate position symbolic of the worshipper's role as servant (Islam literally means "submission"), and the sight of thousands of people going through the same motions simultaneously in a mosque is a powerful one. On Islam's holy day, Friday, all believers are expected to attend prayers in their local grand mosque. Here the whole community comes together in worship led by an *imam*, who may also deliver the *khutba*, or sermon.

Ramadan is the name of the ninth month in the lunar Islamic calendar, the month in which the Koran was revealed to Mohammed. For the whole of the month, believers must obey a rigorous fast (the custom was originally modelled on Jewish and Christian practice), forsaking all forms of consumption between sunrise and sundown; this includes food, drink, cigarettes and any form of sexual contact. Only a few categories of people are exempted: travellers, children, pregnant women and warriors engaged in a *jihad*, or holy war. Given the climates in which many Muslims live, the fast is a formidable undertaking, but in practice it becomes a time of intense celebration.

The pilgrimage, or **hadj**, to Mecca is an annual event, with millions flocking to Mohammed's birthplace from all over the world. Here they go through several days of rituals, the central one being a sevenfold circumambulation of the Ka'ba, before kissing a black stone set in its wall. Islam requires that all believers go on a *hadj* as often as is practically possible, but for the poor it may well be a once-in-a-lifetime occasion, and is sometimes replaced by a series of visits to lesser, local shrines – in Egypt, for instance, to the mosques of Saiyida Zeinab or el-Hussein.

Based on these central articles, the new Islamic faith proved to be inspirational. Mohammed's own Arab nation was soon converted, and the Arabs then proceeded to carry their religion far and wide in an extraordinarily rapid territorial expansion.

DEVELOPMENT IN EGYPT

Islam's **arrival in Egypt**, in 640 AD, coincided with widespread native resentment of Byzantine rule and its particular version of Christianity. By promising to respect Egyptian Christians and Jews as "people of the Book", the Muslim leader **Amr** got acquiescence, if not immediate support, from the population, in the wake of the Arab conquest. For many Egyptians who had found Christianity a more valid religion than the old pagan, polytheistic theology, Islam must have seemed a logical simplification, capturing the essence of human relationships with an all-powerful god.

Early on, the spread of Islam was accompanied by a somewhat bizarre conflict of interest. The Arabs wished to spread the faith, yet their administration depended on finance raised by a poll tax levied on non-Muslims. A balance was maintained for a while, but towards the end of the ninth century, rulers began to use the tax as a punitive measure, alongside a series of repressive acts directed against the Christian and Jewish faiths. Khalif al-Hakim, in particular, embarked on a programme of destroying churches and synagogues. However, it was not until the eleventh century that Cairo attained a **Muslim majority**, and not until the thirteenth century for Egypt as a whole.

The original Arab dynasties of Egypt subscribed to **Sunni Islam** – the more "orthodox" branch of the religion, dominant then, as now, in most parts of the Arab world. However, the Fatimid dynasty, which took control of

Egypt in 969, signalled a shift to **Shi'ite** Islam, which was to continue (among the rulers, at least) until late in the twelfth century. Under the Ayyubid dynasty that followed, Egypt reverted, permanently, as it turned out, to Sunni adherence, with orthodoxy propagated through the new institution of the *madrassa* – a theological college attached to a mosque.

Orthodoxy, by its very nature, has to be an urban-based tradition. Learned men – lawyers, Koranic scholars and others – could only congregate in the cities where, gathered together and known collectively as the *ulema*, they regulated the faith. In Sunni Islam, the *ulema* divide into four schools (*madhahib*): *Hanbali*, *Maliki*, *Hanafi* and *Shafi'i* – the last two of which predominate in Egypt. The *ulema* of Cairo's great **mosque of al-Azhar** is regarded as the ultimate theological authority by most Sunnis outside of the Gulf Arab states.

SHEIKHS AND SUFIS

Alongside this formal religious establishment, Egypt also developed a **popular religious culture**, manifested in the veneration of sheikhs and the formation of Sufi brotherhoods – both of which remain important today.

Sheikhs are basically local holy men: people who developed reputations for sanctity and learning. There is no set process for their sanctification in Islam – only acclamation – so the names change with the locality. Similar to sheikhs are individuals revered simply as *saiyid* (lord) or *saiyida* (lady), often due to their direct decent from the Prophet's line. Important Egyptian examples include Saiyid el-Hussein, Mohammed's grandson and the son of Ali, and the Prophet's granddaughters, Saiyida Zeinab and Saiyida Nafisa.

Although the Koran explicitly prohibits monasticism and isolation from the community, Islam soon developed religious orders dedicated to asceticism and a mystical experience of God. Collectively known as the **Sufis**, these groups generally coalesced around a charismatic teacher, from whom they derived their name. The largest of these brotherhoods (*tariqas*) in Egypt are the **Rifai**, the **Ahmediya** and the **Shadhiliyya** – who can be seen at *moulids* ("saint's day" festivals) parading with their distinctive banners.

TOWARD CRISIS

With all its different forms, Islam permeates almost every aspect of Egyptian society. Unlike Christianity, at least Protestant Christianity, which has accepted the separation of church and state, Islam sees no such distinction. Civil law was provided by the *sharia*, the religious law contained in the Koran, and intellectual life by the *madrassas* and al-Azhar.

The religious basis of Arab study and intellectual life did not prevent its **scholars and scientists** from producing work that was hundreds of years ahead of contemporary "Dark Age" Europe. The medical treatises of Ibn Sina (known in Europe as Avicenna) and the piped water and sewage systems of Fustat are just two Egyptian examples. Arab work in developing and transmitting Graeco-Roman culture was also vital to the whole development of the European Renaissance.

By this time, however, the Islamic world was beginning to move away from the West. The **crusades** had been one enduring influence towards division. Another was the Islamic authorities themselves, who were increasingly suspicious (like the Western church) of any challenge and actively discouraging of innovation. At first it did not matter in political terms that Islamic culture became static. But by the end of the eighteenth century, Europe was ready to take advantage. Napoleon's expedition to Egypt in 1798 marked the beginning of a century in which virtually every Islamic country came under the control of a **European power**.

Islam cannot, of course, be held solely responsible for the Muslim world's material decline. But because it influences every part of its believers' lives, and because East–West rivalry had always been viewed in primarily religious terms, the nineteenth and twentieth centuries saw something of a **crisis in religious confidence**. Why had Islam's former power now passed to infidel foreigners?

REACTIONS: FUNDAMENTALISM

Reactions and answers veered between two extremes. There were those who felt that Islam should try to incorporate some of the West's secularism and materialism; on the other side, there were movements holding that Islam should turn its back on the West, purify itself of all corrupt additions and thus rediscover its former power.

The earliest exponent of the latter view was the **Muslim Brotherhood** (*Ikhwan el-Muslimeen*), founded in Ismailiya by **Hassan el-Banna** in 1928. The Brotherhood preached a moral renewal of Islam, established a network of schools and training centres, and set up clandestine paramilitary groups. It was as much against the corrupt feudal and khedival institutions as western imperialism.

Within fifteen years, the Brotherhood had spread throughout Egypt and spawned offshoots throughout the Middle East. Its terrorist activities prompted a violent state response, with its banning by King Farouk, whose royal bodyguards are believed to have assassinated el-Banna in 1949.

After Egyptian independence, and the revolution of 1952, the legitimised Brotherhood rapidly became disillusioned with Nasser's secular nationalism. In 1954 two Brothers attempted to assassinate him during a public meeting in Alexandria. Mass arrests followed and the Brotherhood went underground again, not surfacing in public until the Sadat era, when the government regarded it as a useful counterweight to the left.

By this time the Brotherhood itself had moderated its strategy, if not its ideals, and its tacit co-operation with the state led to the emergence of more radical groups. These are commonly lumped under the heading of **Islamic Jihad**, although the groups themselves are legion, with a mass of small autonomous cells. One such group, *al-Taqfir w'al-Higrah* (Repentance and Holy Flight), gained notoriety for attacking boutiques and nightclubs in Cairo during the bread riots of 1977. Another faction, established within Egypt's military academy, planned a coup d'état but was nipped in the bud. Most famous – and effective – was the group known simply as *al-Jihad*, which assassinated Sadat and then attempted to launch a revolution in Assyut. Their alleged spiritual leader, **Sheikh Omar Abd al-Rahman**, has been on trial at various points in the last decade.

More overt and quasi legal are the *Gamaat Islamiya* (Islamic Societies), which dominate student unions and professional associations in Middle Egypt and other regions.

MONUMENTAL CHRONOLOGY

*The chronology below is designed for general reference of monuments and dynasties or rulers. For simplicity, only the **major figures of each dynasty** or era are listed; likewise the monuments and artefacts.*

*The following **abbreviations** are used: EAM (Egyptian Antiquities Museum in Cairo); IAM (Islamic Arts Museum in Cairo) and BM (British Museum in London).*

c.250,000 BC	**Hunter-gathering hominids** roam the savannahs.	Stone tools have been discovered in gravel beds of Upper Egypt and Nubia.
c.25,000 BC	**Late Paleolithic** era. Onset of desertification.	Ostrich eggs and flints have been found beneath dunes of Great Sand Sea.

PRE-DYNASTIC EGYPT

c.5000 BC	**Badarian culture**.	Pottery, jewellery and ivory excavated at village of el-Badari in Upper Egypt.
c.4000 BC	**Naqada I culture.**	Burnished pottery and granite mace heads have been found near Qus in Upper Egypt.

ARCHAIC PERIOD (c.3100–2686 BC)

c.3100 BC	**Unification of the Two Lands** (Upper and Lower Egypt) by **Menes**.	Foundation of Memphis; Palette of Narmer (EAM); Stela of Peribsen (BM).

OLD KINGDOM (c.2686–2181 BC)

2686–2613 BC	**III Dynasty** *Zoser; Sekhemkhet; Huni.*	Step Pyramid and Unfinished Pyramid built at Saqqara; Collapsed Pyramid at Maidum (?).
2613–2494 BC	**IV Dynasty** *Snofru; Cheops; Chephren; Mycerinus.*	Bent Pyramid at Dahshur; Great Pyramids of Giza.
2494–2345 BC	**V Dynasty** *Userkaf; Sahure; Neferefre; Nyuserre; Unas.*	Sun Temples and Pyramids at Abu Sir; several further pyramids at Saqqara.
2345–2181 BC	**VI Dynasty** *Teti; Pepi I; Pepi II.*	More pyramids at Saqqara.

FIRST INTERMEDIATE PERIOD (c.2181–2050 BC)

2181–2160 BC	**VII and VIII Dynasties**. Period of anarchy and fragmentation of power.	
2160–2130 BC	**IX Dynasty** *Achthoes.*	Capital at Heracleopolis, near Beni Suef.
2130–2040 BC	**X Dynasty**	
2133–1991 BC	**XI Dynasty** *Inyotef Sehertowy; Nebhepetre Mentuhotpe II.*	Ruined mortuary temple at Deir el-Bahri; Mentuhotpe's statue (EAM).

MIDDLE KINGDOM (c.2050–1786 BC)

1991–1786 BC	**XII Dynasty** *Amenemhat I; Senusert I and II; Amenemhat III.*	Pyramids at Lahun, Lisht and Hawara; rock tombs at Beni Hassan and Aswan; site of Medinet Ma'adi.

SECOND INTERMEDIATE PERIOD (c1786–1567 BC)

1786–1603 BC	**XIII and XIV Dynasties**	
1674–1567 BC	**XV (Hyksos) Dynasty** *Khyam; Apophis I and II.*	Capital at Avaris in the Delta (with Minoan frescoes); *Rhind Mathematical Papyrus* (BM).
1684–1567 BC	**XVI and XVII Dynasty**. Expulsion of the Hyksos by Ahmosis.	Tombs at Qarat Hilwah.

NEW KINGDOM (c.1567–1085 BC)

1567–1320 BC	**XVIII Dynasty**. Two Lands reunited; period of imperial expansion. *Ahmosis; Amenophis I; Tuthmosis I and II; Hatshepsut; Tuthmosis III; Amenophis II and III; Akhenaten; Smenkhkare; Tutankhamun; Ay; Horemheb.*	Temple of Deir el-Bahri; site of Tell el-Amarna; royal tombs in the Valleys of the Kings and Queens at Thebes; Luxor and Karnak temples; Tutankhamun's gold (EAM).
1320–1200 BC	**XIX Dynasty** *Ramses I; Seti I; Ramses II; Merneptah; Seti II.*	Serapeum at Saqqara; temples at Abydos and Abu Simbel; Ramesseum and royal tombs at Thebes.
1200–1085 BC	**XX Dynasty** *Sethnakhte; Ramses III (and eight other minor and hopeless Ramses).*	Temple of Medinet Habu and further royal tombs at Thebes.

LATE PERIOD (1085–322 BC)

1085–945 BC	**XXI Dynasty**. Authority divided between Tanis and Thebes. *Smendes; Herihor; Psusennes I and II.*	Capital at Tanis; Treasure of Tanis (EAM); *Book of the Dead* (BM).
945–715 BC	**XXII Dynasty** *Sheshonq.*	Ruins at Tanis; Sheshonq's relief at Karnak.
818–715 BC	**XXIII and XXIV Dynasties**	
747–656 BC	**XXV (Nubian) Dynasty** *Piankhi; Shabaka; Taharqa; Tanutamun.*	Reliefs at Luxor; Kiosk of Taharqa at Karnak; statue of Amenirdis (EAM).
664–525 BC	**XXVI (Saïte) Dynasty** *Psammetichus I; Necho II; Psammetichus II; Apries; Amasis.*	Ruins of Naucratis; stelae at Ismailiya.
525–404 BC	**XXVII (Persian) Dynasty**. Persian invasion. *Cambyses; Darius I; Xerxes; Artaxerxes I.*	Temple of Hibis at Kharga Oasis; completion of Nile–Red Sea canal; foundation of Babylon-in-Egypt (Cairo).

404–380 BC	**XXVIII and XXIX Dynasties**. *Amyrtaeus.*	Temple of el-Ghweeta.
380–343 BC	**XXX Dynasty** *Nectanebo I and II.*	Additions to Philae and Karnak; ruined temple of Amun at Siwa Oasis.

PTOLEMAIC ERA (332–30 BC)

332–30 BC	**Fourteen Ptolemies** ruled Egypt, the line expiring with with **Cleopatra VII** (51–30 BC). Influx of Hellenistic and Judaistic influence; extensive trade with Mediterranean world; foundation of **Alexandria**.	Construction (or modification) of temples of Edfu, Esna, Kom Ombo, Dendara and Philae; catacombs in Alexandria; Sanctuary of Amun at Siwa Oasis; ruins of Karanis and Qasr Qaroun in the Fayoum.

ROMAN AND BYZANTINE PERIOD (30 BC–640 AD)

30 BC	Octavian (Augustus) annexes Egypt to the **Roman Empire**.	Tomb of Kitnes and Temple of Dush in Kharga Oasis.
45 **AD**	Saint Mark brings **Christianity** to Egypt.	Muzawaka Tombs in Dhakla Oasis.
249–305	**Persecution of Coptic Christians** under Decius and Diocletian.	"Pompey's Pillar" at Alexandria.
313	Edict of Milan **legalises Christianity**.	Foundation of monasteries of Wadi Natrun, St Anthony, St Paul and St Catherine.
395	Partition of Roman Empire into East and West; Egypt falls under Eastern, **Byzantine**, sphere.	Necropolis of el-Bagawat at Kharga Oasis.
451	Council of Chalcedon leads to **expulsion of Copts from Orthodox Church**.	Numerous objects in Coptic Museum (Cairo).

ARAB DYNASTIES (640–1517)

640–642	**Arab conquest** of Egypt; **introduction of Islam**.	Mosque of Amr and ruins of Fustat in Cairo.
661–750	Egypt forms part of **Umayyad Khalifate**, ruled from the dynasty's capital at Damascus.	Ceramics and pottery (IAM).
750–935	**Abbasids** depose Umayyads and form new dynasty, ruling from Baghdad. In 870 Egypt's governor, **Ibn Tulun**, declares independence, founding a dynasty which rules until 905.	Mosque of Ibn Tulun in Cairo.
935–969	**Ikhshidid dynasty** takes power in Egypt.	
969–1171	**Shi'ite Fatimid dynasty** conquers Egypt and seizes the Islamic Khalifate, which it rules from Cairo.	Mosques of al-Azhar, al-Hakim and al-Aqmar, Mausoleum of Imam al-Shafi'i, and various fortified gates, in Cairo.
1171–1249	**Salah al-Din** founds **Ayyubid dynasty** and liberates land conquered by the Crusaders. Egypt returns to **Sunni Islam**. Intrigues of **Shagar al-Durr** open the way to **Mamluke** takeover.	Madrassa-Mausoleum of al-Silah Ayyub in Cairo; ruins of Shali in Siwa Oasis. Mausoleum of Shagar al-Durr in Cairo.

MAMLUKE DYNASTIES (1250–1517)

1250–1382	**Bahri Mamlukes**. *Qalaoun; Khalil; Mohammed al-Nasir.*	In Cairo: Qalaoun's Maristan-Mausoleum-Madrassa, Mosques of al-Nasir, House of Uthman Katkhuda, and Qasr Bashtak.
1382–1517	**Burgi Mamlukes** *Barquq; Farag; Barsbey; Qaitbey; Qansuh al-Ghuri.*	In Cairo: Barquq's Mausoleum, Madrassa and Khanqah of Barsbey, Mosque of Qaitbey, and the Ghuriya. Also, Fort Qaitbey in Alexandria.

OTTOMAN PERIOD (1517–1798)

1517	**Selim the Grim conquers Egypt**. For the next three centuries the country is ruled as an Ottoman province from Constantinople (Istanbul).	In Cairo: Mosques of Suleyman al-Silahdar and Suleyman Pasha; Sabil-Kuttab of Abd al-Rahman Katkhuda. Terbana Mosque in Alexandria.
1798–1802	French occupation of Egypt. Capitulation Agreement of 1802 leaves British in effective control of the country.	Treasures shipped off to Louvre/British Museum. Graffiti left on numerous temples.

PASHAS, KHEDIVES AND KINGS (1805–1952)

1805	**Mohammed Ali** seizes power.	Mohammed Ali Mosque in Cairo; Ras el-Tin Palace and Mahmudiya Canal in Alexandria.
		Belzoni, Mariette and others pioneer digs at pharaonic sites in the Nile Valley and Delta.
1848–54	Reign of **Abbas I**.	
1854–63	Reign of **Said Pasha**.	Suez Canal begun.
1863–79	Reign of **Khedive Ismail**.	Completion of Suez Canal; Central Cairo boulevards constructed.
1879–92	Reign of **Khedive Tewfiq**. British crush the **Orabi Revolt** (1882–83).	Howard Carter discovers Tutankhamun's tomb at Thebes (1922), at the tail end of a period of intensive excavations throughout Egypt.
1935–1952	Reign of **King Farouk**; during World War II Egypt stays under British control	Construction of Midan Tahrir in Cairo.
1952–53	Farouk overthrown by Free Officers. **Egypt declared a Republic**.	

MODERN EGYPT (1952–)

1956	**Nasser** becomes President; **Suez Crisis**.	Major industrialisation programme, and construction of schools, hospitals and public housing. Massive damage to Canal Cities during Six Day War.
1967	**Six Day War**.	
1970	**Nasser dies** and is succeeded as president by **Sadat**.	High Dam at Aswan completed (1970).
1973	**October War**.	
		Mohandiseen district of Cairo built, along with hundreds of new hotels, shops, etc.
1977–78	Food Riots. Sadat's trip to Jerusalem leads to **Camp David** agreeement.	
1981	**Assassination of Sadat**. Presidency assumed by **Hosni Mubarak**.	First line of Cairo metro completed.

MUSIC

As with other cultural spheres, Egypt's musical traditions date back to pharaonic times, though the primary influences are Arab and Islamic. Given Egypt's status in the Arab World, it is no surprise that Cairo is the centre of the Arab recording industry – a dominance partly acquired by the collapse of its rivals in the Lebanon, Libya and Kuwait. Egypt's sixty-million population makes it the most important market for Arab music, and the amazingly high proportion of youth (over thirty million Egyptians are under 25) has ensured a big demand for contemporary sounds.

The different types of folk or popular music you come across varies greatly with the region and environment: Cairo, the Nile Valley, the Delta and the desert all have their own characteristic sounds, rhythms and instruments. Often their songs reflect the rituals of everyday life: weddings, *moulids*, harvest festivals, old stories of village life or triumphs. What follows is the briefest of introductions to the various major forms.

RELIGIOUS MUSIC

During Ramadan and other major festivals you'll encounter **religious music** – renditions of **Koranic verses**, or praises to Allah, teased out in any numer of ways.

Performers may be *munshids* – professional reciters who move from one festival to another – or simply the *muezzin* or *imam* of the local mosque. In everyday religious life, *muezzins* all have their individual styles of phrasing, which are sometimes jealously guarded. In a celebrated court case in the 1980s an Egyptian judge ruled that no copyright existed on any expression of the Koran, since God himself created it.

Recitals at *moulids* are often more participation than performance, with dozens of Sufi devotees chanting and swaying to the accompaniment of a drum. These recitals, known as *zikrs*, can last for days.

CLASSICAL ARAB MUSIC

Antecedents of **Classical Arabic music** can be traced back to the **Bedouin** reciters and singers of the Arabian peninsula, but also to the more refined **court music** of the great khalifal cities of Baghdad and Damascus, and Ottoman Constantinople.

During this century, the form has been characterised by oriental scales, passionate rhetoric, bravura soloists, massed orchestras and male choirs. The most famous exponent of recent decades has been **Umm Kalthoum** (aka Oum Khalsoum), who until her death in 1975 was the most popular singer in the Arab World. Her career coincided with the advent of long-distance broadcasting and she was essentially the first Arab music star. In Egypt, she was a national institution, known as "The Mother of Egypt" and accorded a weekly concert on radio (and, later, TV). Although she is still widely played today, the genre itself has become ossified and its admirers tend to be amongst the older generation.

REGIONAL/ETHNIC MUSIC

SAIYIDI

The music of Upper Egypt – known like its people as *Saiyidi* – has a characteristic rhythm which horses are trained to dance to. It is based upon two instruments: the *nahrasan*, a two-sided drum hung over the chest and beaten with sticks; and the *mismar saiyidi*, a kind of wooden trumpet. Performances often involve monologues, ripe with puns and wit. One of the famous names of the genre, **Omar**

Gharzawi, is known for his rebuttals of the stereotyped image of stupid, hot-headed Saiyidis. Another contemporary monologuist, **Shoukoukou**, has a special instrument (a joke clapping doll, sold at festivals) named after him. On a more official standing is *Rais* ("Boss") **Met'al al-I'nawi**, often chosen by the government to represent Egypt at foreign music festivals.

FELLAHI

The northern counterpart to Saiyidi music, found in the Delta, is known as **fellahi** (peasant) music. It is generally softer, with a fondness for the *matsoum* (one and a half) rhythm, and use of instruments like the *rababa*, a two-stringed viol, and the *mismar*, a kind of oboe.

SAWAHEELI

Found along the Mediterranean coast and Canal Zone, **Sawaheeli** music is characterised by the use of a guitar-like stringed instrument, the *sinseemeya*. Another form, specific to Alexandria, also features the accordion, the result of the city's Greek and Turkish influences.

BEDOUIN

There are two kinds of **Bedouin** music: one found in the Western Desert, towards Libya, the other in the Eastern Desert and Sinai. Both have songs recounting old intrigues, activities and stories to a strong rhythmic accompaniment. This has been a major influence on *al-Jeel* music (see below).

NUBIAN

Performed in their own language, in the southern reaches of the Nile Valley, **Nubian** music has more African than Arab roots. It relies a lot on hand-clapping and the *duf*, a kind of tambourine. More urbanised versions — found in Aswan or Khartoum — have opted for brass sections and female choruses.

URBAN MUSIC

In Cairo and other cities, rural traditions have mixed with the more elite Classical styles, and adapted to reflect urban preoccupations and the faster pace of life. Over the last couple of decades, this **urban music** has come to reject the melodrama, ornate melodies and scales of classical Arab music, while its lyrics express the concerns of the more freewheeling post-Nasser years. By the mid-1980s, two main types of music had developed: **Shaabi** and **al-Jeel**.

SHAABI

Shaabi ("people") music was born in the working-class quarters of Cairo, where millions of second- and third-generation rural migrants live. It blends the traditional form of the *mawal* (plaintive vocal improvisations) with a driving beat. Its lyrics are often raunchy or satirical, politically and socially provocative. You will never hear this music on the media. It is not so much banned as beneath the contempt of the middle classes and "respectable society", who see its rudeness and social criticism as coming from another Egypt. It is to be heard, however, at weddings and parties throughout working-class Cairo and at some of the nightclubs along Pyramids Road.

The original Shaabi singer was **Ahmed Adaweer**, who, from 1971 on, introduced the idea of street-language and subsequently broke every rule in the book. He was basically a punk, and the youth of the backstreets loved him. Later exponents introduced elements of rap and disco into the Shaabi sound, rather in the manner of Algerian *Raï* music.

AL-JEEL

Al-Jeel means "the generation" and is the latest post-Shaabi sound. It takes disco elements a step further, using drum tracks and synthesised backing, and mixes these with Nubian and Bedouin rhythms. The latter came in large part through the influence of Libyan musicians, who had fled to Cairo in the late 1970s after Gaddafi's "cultural revolution", where he clamped down on Western musical influences.

Al-Jeel lyrics, in contrast to Shaabi, are usually about love or the country and rarely stray into sensitive areas. Singers and musicians, too, are less crucial than the arrangers and producers who put the songs and cassettes together. Nevertheless, performances remain a focus for discontented youth, echoing the West's 1960s idea that "rock music" was in some undefined way radical or even revolutionary.

EGYPTIAN MUSIC: A CASSETTOGRAPHY

Cassettes are the medium for almost all recorded Egyptian music. Introduced in the early 1970s, they have proved robust, cheap and very easy to copy – piracy is such a problem that it has its own special police division in Cairo. Outlets are street corner kiosks, small shops and market stalls, most of which tend to specialise in either Shaabi or al-Jeel, or the old oriental musics, traditional and modern. There are no charts as such, though you will soon know when a song is the city's "number one"; if it's big, producers can expect to sell up to a million copies.

The following is a highly **selective list of artists and cassettes** to start you off in Cairo cassette browsing. In Britain or North America, you can find a limited range of records, too – mostly Umm Kalthoum and the like, though with a few more contemporary releases by the new "World Music" labels. By far the most compelling of these is David Lodge's brilliant **Yalla: Hitlist Egypt** collection (Mango/Island, 1990), which devotes a side each to Shaabi and al-Jeel.

RELIGIOUS MUSIC
Sheikh Mohammed el-Hosni *Doa Khetm el-Koran il-Karim*. Highly emotional.

CLASSICAL ARABIC MUSIC
Umm Kalthoum *al-Atalaal* and *Enta Omri*. Two of her greatest live recordings – among dozens of releases.

SAYAIDI MUSIC
Ahmed Ismail and Sohar Magdy. Anything by this duo is worth acquiring.

NUBIAN MUSIC
Khedr *Ya Sahabba*. Sung in an obscure Nubian dialect – and popular mainly among Nubians.

BEDOUIN MUSIC
You won't find cassettes in Cairo but may strike lucky in the Sinai or Mersa Matrouh.

SHAABI MUSIC
Ahmed Adaweer *al-Tareek*. The father of it all at his best.

Magdy Shabeeni *Hasanahan*. Big on social comment and aggressive rhythms.

Hassan el-Asmar *Mish Hasheebak*. Classic Shaabi lyrics of hard urban life.

AL-JEEL MUSIC
Ehab Tawfek *Maraheel*. Promising New Wave newcomer.
Mohammed Foad *Shamf*.

BOOKS

Publishers are detailed below in the form of British Publisher/American Publisher, where both exist. Where books are published in one country only, UK or US follows the publisher's name.

Abbreviations: o/p (out of print); U.P. (University Press); AUC (American University in Cairo Press). AUC books are most easily available in Cairo.

GENERAL/TRAVEL

Robert Curzon *Visits to Monasteries in the Levant* (Random Century, UK/US). Famed account, by a man later made Viceroy of Egypt, of youthful adventurings in Egypt, Palestine and Greece in the 1830s. Several chapters deal with Egyptian monasteries, where Curzon got the monks drunk and stole their antiquarian manuscripts.

E.W. Lane *Manners and Customs of the Modern Egyptians* (East-West Publications/State Mutual Bank). Facsimile editions of this encyclopaedic study of life in Mohammed Ali's Cairo, first published in 1836. Highly browsable.

Karl Baedeker *Egypt: Handbook for Travellers*; ***Murray's Handbook for Travellers in Egypt***. These were the classic Egypt guides – used by generations of tourists from the 1870s until World War II. Each features splendid engravings and site plans, extensive essays on Egyptology and religion, and embarrassingly colonial attitudes. Of the numerous Baedeker editions, the **1929 revision** – which includes the discovery of Tutankhamun's tomb – is the one to hunt for in secondhand bookshops (it sells for £100/

US$160; a facsimile edition, published in the 1980s is out of print but can often be found for £20/US$30 or so). The **Murray's** is of greatest interest for its coverage of Sinai, featuring walker's routes covered nowhere else, before or since. It sells for around £30/US$50.

Gerard de Nerval *Journey to the Orient* (Michael Haag/Hippocrene). Stoned on hash, de Nerval thrilled to Mohammed Ali's Egypt; splendour and squalor, eroticism and cruelty – the Orientalist fantasy that still colours perceptions today. A whacky read.

Gustav Flaubert *Flaubert in Egypt* (Michael Haag/Hippocrene). A romp through the brothels, baths and sites by the future author of *Madame Bovary*, who cared little for monuments but delighted in Egyptian foibles and vices. Skilfully edited by Francis Steegmuller.

Amelia Edwards *A Thousand Miles up the Nile* (Random Century, UK/US). Verbose, patronising classic from the mid-nineteenth century. All books on Egypt have their Amelia quotes – this one included.

Henri de Monfreid *Hashish* (Penguin, UK/US). A latterday swashbuckler who followed a spell in Djibouti jail by smuggling hash on the Red Sea during the 1920s. The latter half relates his dealings with the Suez underworld.

Bimbashi McPherson *The Man Who Loved Egypt* (Ariel, UK). Edited letters of a paternalist British administrator, interesting for the light they cast on Cairo in the early twentieth century (when he headed the secret police).

E.M. Forster *Alexandria: A History and a Guide* (Michael Haag/Hippocrene). A foreword by Lawrence Durrell and stylishly erudite notations by Michael Haag enhance Forster's 1922 guidebook. Forster's companion piece was *Pharos and Pharillon* (o/p), a diverse colllection of essays on Alexandrian life.

Jan Morris *Destinations* (Oxford U.P, UK). This collection of essays includes an interesting if overblown piece on Cairo.

Charlie Pye-Smith *The Other Nile* (Penguin, UK/US). Witty and insightful account of a tour in the early 1980s, interwoven with recollections of trips into Sudan and Ethiopia, before coups and famine made them inaccessible.

Stanley Stewart *Old Serpent Nile: A Journey to the Source* (John Murray, UK). Stewart managed to travel from the Nile Delta to the

Mountains of the Moon in Uganda in the late 1980s and relates his adventures in spare, taut prose. The most up-to-date Egypt travelogue.

Christopher Pick *Egypt: A Traveller's Anthology* (John Murray, UK). Mixed bag of observers from the last two centuries, including Disraeli, Mark Twain, Vita Sackville-West, Flaubert, E.M. Forster and Freya Stark.

Deborah Manley *The Nile: A Traveller's Anthology* (Cassell, UK). A better anthology to go for: nicely illustrated and with selections gathered from some very obscure sources.

CAIRO

Desmond Stewart *Great Cairo, Mother of the World* (AUC). Entertaining and erudite history of the city, from pharaonic times through to the Nasser era. Readily available in Cairo.

James Aldridge *Cairo* (o/p). Covers much the same ground as Stewart, but is slightly more up-to-date, bringing the story to the mid-1960s. Equally readable.

Richard Parker *Islamic Monuments of Cairo: A Practical Guide* (AUC). Excellent and detailed handbook to the monuments and history of seventh- to nineteenth-century Cairo.

Trevor Mostyn *Egypt's Belle Epoque: Cairo 1869–1952* (Quartet, UK). Expat highlife and diplomatic intrigue, from the time of Ismail to the revolution which overthrew King Farouk.

Artemis Cooper *Cairo in the War* (Hamish Hamilton, UK). Excellent account, with a more detailed focus on the period 1939–45.

THE DESERT

R.A. Bagnold *Libyan Sands: Travels in a Dead World* (Michael Haag/Hippocrene). One of a band of motorised explorers of the Libyan Desert during the 1920s and 30s, Bagnold later wrote the seminal work on dune-formation, *The Physics of Blown Sand and Desert Dunes* – a book continuously in print since 1939 and used by NASA to interpret satellite photos of Mars. *Libyan Sands*, despite the restrained prose, is compelling boy's own stuff, and the sheer range of journeys – to all the oases, 'Uweinat, the Great Sand Sea and the Forty Days Road – make it an enduring bible for desert buffs.

Ahmed Fakhry *The Oases of Egypt* (AUC; currently o/p). Fakhry's unfinished trilogy is still the last word on the Western Desert Oases.

Volume I, covering Siwa, is fascinating; volume II, on Bahariya and Farafra, is heavier going; while Fakhry's death in 1973 aborted the volume on Dakhla and Kharga. Until the AUC reprints them with updated material (as is promised), the first two remain rare, sought-after works: the AUC Library and Siwa's *Cafeteria Shali* have reading copies of Volume I.

Burton Bernstein *Sinai: The Great and Terrible Wilderness* (Weidenfeld, UK). Mixture of travel writing and history, describing Sinai on the eve of its handover to Egypt in 1979. Dated but still the best book on the region.

Michael Asher *In Search of the Forty Day Road; Impossible Journey* (Penguin, UK/US). Asher's camel journeys, in the Sudanese desert and from Mauretania to the Nile, respectively, evoke all the hardships and magic of the desert.

ANCIENT HISTORY

GENERAL WORKS

T.G.H. James *An Introduction to Ancient Egypt; Ancient Egypt: The Land and its Legacy; Egyptian Painting; Egyptian Sculpture* (all published by the British Museum, London). James was the keeper of the Egyptian Antiquities department of the British Museum until the mid-1980s, and an acknowledged expert. Beginners could find no better companion than James's *Introduction. The Land and its Legacy* is a coffee-table book, good for pre-visit reading; the *Painting* and *Sculpture* volumes are accessibly written and lavishly illustrated.

George Hart *A Dictionary of Egyptian Gods and Goddesses* (Routledge, UK/US). Indispensible guide to the deities and myths of ancient Egypt, profusely illustrated with line drawings. Hart's *Egyptian Myths* (British Museum Publications, UK) is equally informative, covering similar ground.

Geoffrey T. Martin *The Hidden Tombs of Memphis* (Thames and Hudson, UK/US). A detailed account of recent discoveries at Memphis, most notably the Tomb of Maya, a contemporary of Tutankhamun.

John Taylor *Egypt and Nubia* (British Museum Publications, UK). Covers the history of Nubia from 4000 BC to the dawning of the Christian era, focusing on ancient Nubian art and relations with Egypt.

Richard Parkinson *Voices from Ancient Egypt: An Anthology of Middle Kingdom Writings* (British Museum Publications, UK). All kinds of literature, from spells and curses to state propaganda. The material for once brings to life people rather than monuments.

Peter France *The Rape of Egypt* (Barrie & Jenkins, UK). Interesting background on the characters and personalities of the early archaeologists, and a no-holds-barred indictment of imperialist looting.

Martin Bernal *Black Athena* (Free Association Press/Rutgers U.P.; 2 vols.). These dense, provocative works assert the "Africanness" of ancient Egyptian civilisation and its contribution to Greek and Roman culture. The first two volumes (1987 and 1991; two more are to follow) show a formidable breadth of enquiry, though Egyptologists and Classicists nit-pick holes everywhere.

PYRAMIDOLOGY

I.E.S. Edwards *The Pyramids of Egypt* (Pelican/Penguin) Richly illustrated, closely argued survey of all the major pyramids, recently updated to take account of new discoveries and theories though Mendelssohn (see below) is conspicuously absent.

Kurt Mendelssohn *The Riddle of the Pyramids* (Thames and Hudson, UK/US). An attempt to resolve the enigma of the Maidum and Dahshur pyramids, which postulates a "pyramid production line" and caused a stir in the world of Egyptology during the 1980s.

Tom Valentine *The Great Pyramid: Man's Monument to Man* (o/p). A 1970s cocktail of whacky Pyramid-theories replete with abstruse calculations and dubious assertions.

THE AMARNA PERIOD/TUTANKHAMUN

Cyril Aldred *Akhenaten, King of Egypt* (Thames and Hudson, UK/US). Conventional account of the Amarna period by one of Britain's leading postwar Egyptologists.

Julia Samson *Nefertiti and Cleopatra* (Rubicon Press/Intl. Spec. BK). Fascinating account of Egypt's most famous queens, by the Petrie Museum's expert on Amarna civilisation. She concludes that Smenkhkare, Akhenaten's mysterious successor, was actually Nefertiti; her coverage of Cleopatra is less controversial.

Christiane Desroches-Noblecourt *Tutankhamen: Life and Death of a Pharaoh* (Penguin, UK). Briliantly illustrated, detailed study of all aspects of the boy-pharaoh and his times.

Thomas Hoving *Tutankhamun: the Untold Story* (Hamish Hamilton/Simon & Schuster). Lifts the lid on archaeological backbiting and the tomb thefts by Carter and Carnarvon.

Philipp Vandenberg *The Curse of the Pharaohs* (o/p); *Nefertiti* (Hodder, UK). Sensationalism decked out as Egyptology. Thought (and chuckle) provoking, providing you suspend critical faculties.

PTOLEMAIC, ROMAN AND COPTIC EGYPT

Alan Bowman *Egypt After the Pharaohs* (British Museum Publications/University of California Press). Scholarly, nicely illustrated study of an often overlooked period.

Lucy Hughes-Hallet *Cleopatra: Histories, Dreams and Distortions* (Bloomsbury/Harper Collins). Fascinating deconstructive analysis of Cleopatra in history and myth down through the ages.

Barbara Watterson *Coptic Egypt* (Scottish Academic Press, UK). Covers Coptic history and culture from ancient times to the present.

Otto Meinardus, *Monks and Monasteries of the Egyptian Desert* (AUC). A history and guide to Egypt's Coptic monasteries.

MEDIEVAL AND MODERN HISTORY

THE CRUSADES

Amin Maalouf *The Crusades through Arab Eyes* (Al-Saqi Books, UK). Lebanese writer and journalist, Maalouf has used the writings of contemporary Arab chroniclers of the Crusades to retrace two centuries of Middle Eastern history. His conclusion is that present-day relations between the Arab World and the West are still marked by the battle that ended seven centuries ago.

Steven Runciman *A History of the Crusades* (Penguin UK/US, 3 vols). Highly readable narrative, laced with anecdote and scandal. Runciman's hero is Salah al-Din, rather than Richard the Lionheart, who is depicted (like most of the other traditional Western good guys) in all his murderous ferocity.

COLONIAL OCCUPATIONS

Peter Mansfield *The British in Egypt* (Weidenfeld, UK). Interesting account of how Egypt passed from being the "veiled protectorate" to an outright imperial possession. Mansfield is also author of *The Arabs* (Penguin, UK/US), a clear, perceptive and wide-ranging introduction to the Arab World from the arrival of Islam to the 1970s.

Anthony Sattin *Lifting the Veil: British Society in Egypt 1768–1956* (J.M. Dent, UK). A fascinating slice of social history, charting the rise and fall of British tourists and expatriates in Egypt. Classic photographs, too.

Barrie Pitt *The Crucible of War* (Cape/Paragon House). Blow-by-blow account of the Battle of el-Alamein.

Corelli Barnett *The Desert Generals* (Kimber/ Indiana U.P.). Barnett concludes that Montgomery was a less assured general than his predecessors, let alone Rommel.

POST-INDEPENDENCE

Robert St John *The Boss* (o/p). Racy, anecdotal biography of Nasser, written a decade before his death. Interesting, albeit dated since its publication in 1960.

A.J. Barker *Arab-Israeli Wars* (Ian Allan, UK). An illustrated account of the 1948, 1956, 1967 and 1973 wars, by a military historian. Photographs (and sympathies) come largely from the Israeli side.

Mohammed Heikal *Cutting the Lion's Tail; The Road to Ramadan; The Autumn of Fury* (all o/p, though most libraries will turn up one or another). These three books cover, respectively, the Suez Crisis, the 1973 War, and Sadat's rise and fall. As a confidante of Nasser's since the Revolution, one-time editor of *Al-Ahram* and Minister of Information, Heikal provides a genuinely inside view.

David Hirst and Irene Beeson *Sadat* (o/p). Revealing political biography of the man whom Kissinger described as "the greatest since Bismarck". Published in 1970, the book stops short of his assassination.

Anwar Sadat *In Search of Identity* (Harper Collins, US). An anodyne, ghosted autobiography which reveals less about the character of Egypt's assassinated president than either Heikal or Hirst and Beeson.

Raymond William Barker *Sadat and After* (Taurus & Co., UK). Heavyweight but fascinating critique of Egyptian society from six different perspectives, including those of the Muslim Brotherhood, Nasserists, Marxists and Osman Ahmed Osman, each presented sympathetically. A *tour de horizon* of contemporary Egyptian political thought.

ANTHROPOLOGY AND SOCIOLOGY

R. Critchfield *Shahhat: An Egyptian* (AUC). A wonderful book, based on several years' resident research with the Nile Valley *fellaheen*, across the river from Luxor. Moving, amusing and shocking, by turn.

Nayra Atiya (ed.) *Khul-Khaal: Five Egyptian Women* (Virago/Syracuse U.P.; also AUC). Equally gripping, this should be read alongside *Shahhat*. It presents the lives and views of five women from different backgrounds.

Nawal El Saadawi *The Hidden Face of Eve* (Zed Books/Beacon). Egypt's best-known woman writer, Saadawi has been in conflict with the Egyptian authorities most of her life. This is her major polemic, covering a wide range of topics – sexual aggression, female circumcision, prostitution, divorce and sexual relationships.

Huda Shaarawi *Harem Years: Memoirs of an Egyptian Feminist 1879—1924* (Virago/ Feminist Press). A unique document from the last generation of upper-class Egyptian women, who spent their childhood and married life in the segregated world of the harem.

Rana Kabbani *Egypt's Myths of Orient* (Pandora Press, UK). An easier read than Edward Said's heavyweight *Orientalism* (Penguin, UK/US), this book unravels the erotic fantasies and myths which Western travellers, painters and poets built up about the east. Starting with the Crusades and on through the Victorians, Kabbani shows how the East was portrayed as sexually voracious and thus intellectually and morally inferior.

Joseph Hobbs *Bedouin Life in the Egyptian Wilderness* (Texas U.P., US). Fascinating, albeit academic account of the Khushmaan clan of Ma'aza Bedouin living in the Jebel Galala of the Eastern Desert.

Lila Abu Lughod *Veiled Sentiments: Honour and Poetry in a Bedouin Society* (California U.P., US). Anthropological study devoted to the Awlad Ali tribe of the Western Desert.

Nemat Guenena *The "Jihad". An "Islamic Alternative" in Egypt* (Cairo Papers Vol. 9, Summer 1986). As the quotation marks imply, a cautiously academic investigation into the beliefs and social profile of Egypt's leading radical fundamentalist group.

ISLAM

A.J. Arberry (trans.) *The Koran* (Oxford U.P., UK) The Oxford translation is the best English-language version of Islam's holy book, whose revelations and prose style form the basis of the Muslim faith and Arab literature. Arberry's scholarship is also evident in *Sufism: An Account of the Mystics of Islam* (Mandala, UK) and *The Koran Interpreted* (Macmillan, US).

H.A.R. Gibb *Islam* (Oxford U.P.; published in the US by Princeton U.P. as *Studies on the Civilization of Islam*). Concise exposition of the historical development and nature of Islam.

Titus Burckhardt *Art of Islam: Language and Meaning* (o/p). Superbly illustrated, intellectually penetrating overview of Islamic art and architecture.

EGYPTIAN FICTION

André Chedid *The Sixth Day* (Serpent's Tail/Consort Book Sales); *From Sleep Unbound* (Serpent's Tail/Ohio U.P.). French-based author, whose metaphor-laden plots and clinical prose are not exactly beach reading.

Gamal al-Ghitani *Incidents in Zafraani Alley* (Egyptian Book Organisation – only available in Egypt); *Zayni Barakat* (Penguin, UK/US). *Incidents* is a highly accessible, darkly humorous read, which could be interpreted as a satire on state paranoia and credulous fundamentalism. *Zayni Barakat* is a more convoluted, elliptical drama set in the last years of Mamluke rule – an allegorical comment on Nasser's Egypt.

Nabil Naoum Gorgy *The Slave's Dream and Other Stories* (Quartet, UK). The amorality of man and nature is the main theme of this collection of tales, apparently influenced by Borges and Bowles.

Gamil Attiyah Ibrahim *Down to the Sea* (Quartet, UK). A stumbling translation mars what is by all accounts – in the original – a fascinating exploration of life in Cairo's Cities of the Dead.

Yusuf Idris *The Cheapest Nights; Rings of Burnished Brass* (Heinemann/Three Continents Press). Two superb collections by Egypt's finest writer of short stories, who died in 1991. Uncompromisingly direct, yet ironic.

Naguib Mahfouz *Miramar; Midaq Alley; The Thief and the Dogs; Respected Sir; The Search; Wedding Song; The Beggar; The Beginning and the End; Autumn Quail* (variously published by Quartet in the UK, and Doubleday or Three Continents Press in the US; most are available in Egypt as AUC editions, except *The Children of Gebelawi*, which is banned). Awarded the Nobel Literature Prize in 1989, Mahfouz is the Grand Old Man of Egyptian letters. His novels have a rather nineteenth-century feel, reminiscent in plot and characterisation of Balzac or Victor Hugo; most are set in Cairo or Alexandria. Favoured themes include the discrepancy between ideology and human problems, hypocrisy and injustice, and taking personal responsibility.

Alifa Rifaat *Distant View of a Minaret* (Heinemann, UK/US). A well-known writer in her fifties expresses her revolt against male domination and suggests solutions within the orthodox Koranic framework.

Nawal El Saadawi *Woman at Point Zero* (Zed Books/Humanities Press); *The Fall of the Imam* (Methuen/Humanities Press); *God Dies by the Nile* (Zed Books/Humanities Press); and others. Saadawi's novels are informed by her work as a doctor and psychiatrist in Cairo, and by her feminist and socialist beliefs; they range through subjects virtually taboo in Egypt. *Point Zero*, her best, is a powerful and moving story of a woman condemned to death for killing a pimp. You will find very few of her books on sale in Egypt, though *The Fall of the Imam* is the only one officially banned.

ANTHOLOGIES

Margot Badran and Miriam Cooke (eds.) *Opening the Gates: a Century of Arab Feminist Writing* (Virago Press/Indiana U.P.). Mix of fiction and polemic, including a fair number of Egyptian contributors.

W.M. Hutchins (ed./trans.) *Egyptian Tales and Short Stories of the 1970s & 80s* (AUC). Includes stories by Nawal el Saadawi, Amira Nowaira, Gamal al-Ghitani and Fouad Higazy.

Marylin Booth (ed./trans.) *My Grandmother's Cactus: Stories by Egyptian Women* (Quartet, UK/US). Short stories by the latest generation of women writers, including Radwa Ashour, Salwa Bakr, Etidal Osman, Neamet el-Biheiri, Ibtihal Salem and Sahar Tawfiq.

Inea Bushnaq *Arab Folktales* (Penguin/Pantheon). Great collection of folk stories from across the Arab world, including many from Egypt, with interesting thematic pieces putting them in context. Highly recommended.

POETRY

C.P. Cavafy *Collected Poems* (Chatto and Windus/Princeton U.P.). Elegiac evocations of the Alexandrian myth by the city's most famous poet. An excerpt from *The City* appears under "Alexandria" in this book.

FOREIGN NOVELISTS

Noel Barber *A Woman of Cairo* (Coronet, UK). Ill-starred love and destiny amongst the Brits and Westernised Egyptians of King Farouk's Cairo, interwoven with historical events and characters. From that perspective, a good insight on those times.

Gillian Bradshaw *The Beacon at Alexandria* (o/p). A woman learns medicine in secret, disguises herself as a man and practices it in sectarian strife-ridden Alexandria, and later in barbarian-haunted Thrace.

Moyra Caldecott *Daughter of Amun* (Arrow, UK). Romanticised account of the rise and fall of Queen Hatshepsut.

Agatha Christie *Death on the Nile* (Fontana). Egypt's most famous murder: a classic piece of skulduggery, solved by Hercules Poirot, on a Nile cruise boat. Christie wrote the book in Aswan, staying at the Old Cataract Hotel.

Lawrence Durrell *The Alexandria Quartet*. (Faber/NAL-Dutton). Endless sexual and metaphysical ramblings, occasional relieved by a dollop of Alex atmosphere, from one of the century's most overrated writers.

Ken Follet *The Key to Rebecca* (Fontana/NAL-Dutton). Fast-paced thriller based on the true story of a German spy, Eppler, who operated in Cairo during 1942. Follet exercises artistic licence when describing the outcome, but the belly dancer Sonia, and Sadat's involvement, are largely faithful to history.

Anton Gill *City of the Horizon* (Bloomsbury, UK). The first volume of Gill's trilogy pits the scribe Huy against conspirators as Tutankhamun is enthroned and Horemheb amasses power. To be continued in the forthcoming *City of Dreams* and *City of the Dead*.

Robert Irwin *The Arabian Nightmare* (Dedalus/Penguin). Brilliant, paranoid fantasy set in the Cairo of Sultan Qaitbey, where a Christian spy contracts the affliction of the title. As his madness deepens, reality and illusion spiral inwards like an opium-drugged walk through a *medina* of the mind.

Olivia Manning *The Levant Trilogy* (Penguin, UK/US). The second half of this six-volume blockbuster of love 'n' war finds the Pringles in Egypt, where Harriet mopes and Guy's as crass as ever, until . . . you'll know the lump-in-the-throat finale from the TV series starring Emma Thompson and Kenneth Branagh.

Michael Pearce *The Mamur Zapt and the Men Behind* (Collins/Doubleday). Nefarious deeds and political conspiracy in British-ruled Egypt, from the stews of Cairo to the cotton-fields of the Delta. A cracking yarn.

EGYPT SOCIETIES

Journal of Egyptian Archaeology and *Egyptian Archaeology*. Published by the Egyptian Exploration Society, the *Journal* is the world's leading forum for all matters Egyptological: all the new theories and discoveries get printed here first. *Egyptian Archaeology* magazine, illustrated and with a popular slant, is also published by the Society. Membership opf the society costs £20 per annum; for details contact: The Secretary, Egyptian Exploration Society, 3 Doughty Mews, London WC1N 2PG (☎071/242 1880).

LANGUAGE

Egyptians are well used to tourists who speak only their own language, but an attempt to tackle at least a few words in Arabic is invariably greeted with great delight and encouragement, and as often as not the exclamation "You speak Arabic better than I do!". Whatever else you do, at least make an effort to learn the Arabic numerals and polite greetings.

Although most educated and urban Egyptians will have been taught some English and are only too happy to practise it on you, a little Arabic is a big help in the more remote areas. French may also come in handy in some cities such as Alexandria, where Greek is also spoken by older folk; German, too, is increasingly understood in tourist-related spheres.

EGYPTIAN ARABIC

Although Arabic is the common and official language of 23 countries, the spoken dialect of each can vary considerably. Egyptian Arabic, however, because of the country's vast film, television and music industry, is the most widely understood in the Arab world.

PRONUNCIATION

Transliteration from Arabic script into English presents some pronunciation problems, since some letters have no equivalents. The phonetic guide below should help: everything is pronounced.

ai	as in eye	ey/ay	as in day
aa	as in bad but lengthened	ee	as in feet
'a	as when asked to say ah by the doctor	kh	as in Scottish loch
a'	a glottal stop as in bottle	gh	like the French "r" (back of the throat)

Note that **double consonants** should always be pronounced separately.

BASICS

Yes	aiwa (or) na'am	Come in, please	itfaddal (m) / itfaddali (f)
No	la	(to m/f)	
Thank you	shokran	Excuse me	'an iznak (m) / 'an iznik (f)
You're welcome	'afwan	Sorry	aasif (m) / asfa (f)
Please (to m/f)	min fadlak (m) / fadlik (f)	God willing	n sha' Allah

GREETINGS AND FAREWELLS

Welcome/hello	ahlan w-sahlan	Good evening (evening of	masa' il-kheer
(response)	ahlan bik (m) / biki (f) / bikum (pl)	goodness)	
		(response – evening of light)	masa' in-nur
Hello (formal)	assalaamu aleikum	How are you (m/f) ?	izzayak (m) / izzayik (f)
(response)	wa-aleikum assalaam	I (m/f) am fine, thanks be to	qwayyis (m) / qwayyisa
Greetings	sa'eeda	God	(f) il-hamdu lilla
Nice to meet you	fursa sa'eeda	Good night	tisbah (m) / tisbahi (f)
Good morning (morning of goodness)	sabah il-kheer		'ala kheer
(response – morning of light)	sabah in-nur	And to you (m/f)	wenta (m) / wenti (f) bi-kheer
		Goodbye	ma'a salaama

QUESTIONS AND DIRECTIONS

What is your (m/f) name?	*ismak (m) / ismik (f) ey?*	. . . the airport?	*. . . il-mataar?*
My name is . . .	*ismi . . .*	. . . the toilet?	*. . . il-twalet?*
Do you (m/f) speak Arabic?	*titkallim (m) / titkallimi (f) 'Arabi?*	. . . a restaurant?	*. . . mat'am?*
English?	*ingleezi?*	Left/right/straight ahead	*shimaal/yimeen/alatool*
French?	*fransawi?*	Near/far	*areeb/ba'eed*
I speak English	*ana batkallim ingleezi*	Here/there	*hinna/hinnak*
I don't speak Arabic	*ana ma-batkallimsh 'arabi*	When does the bus leave?	*il-autobees yissafir imta?*
I understand (a little)	*ana fahem (shwaiya)*	When does the train leave?	*il-atr yissafir imta?*
I don't understand	*ana mish fahem*	. . . arrive?	*. . . yoosal?*
What's that in English?	*ya'ani ey bil-ingleezi?*	What time (is it)?	*issa'a kam?*
Where is Hotel . . . ?	*feyn funduk il . . . ?*	First/last/next	*il-awil/il-akhir/et-tani*
. . . the bus station?	*. . . mahattat il-autobees?*		
. . . the train station?	*. . . mahattat il-atr?*		

REQUESTS AND SHOPPING

Do you (m/f) have . . . ?	*fi 'andak (m) / 'andik (f) . . . ?*	(but)	*(wa-laakin)*
. . . cigarette(s)	*. . . sigara/sagayir*	bigger/smaller	*akbar/asghar*
. . . matches	*. . . kibreet*	How much (is it)?	*bi-kam (da)?*
. . . newspaper	*. . . gurnal*	It's too expensive	*da ghaali awi*
I (m/f) want something . . .	*ayyiz (m) / ayyza (f) haga . . .*	big	*kebir awi*
. . . else	*. . . tanya*	small	*sughayyar awi*
. . . better than this	*. . . ahsan min da*	That's fine	*maashi*
. . . cheaper	*. . arkhas min da*	There is/is there?	*fi/fi?*
. . . like this	*. . . zay da*	I (m/f) don't want . . .	*mish ayyiz (m)/ ayyza (f) . . .*

ACCOMMODATION

Do you (m/f) have a room?	*fi 'andak (m) / 'andik (f) ouda?*	. . . hot water?	*. . . mayya sukhna?*
I (m/f) would like to see the rooms	*ayyiz/ayyza ashuf il-owad*	. . . a shower?	*. . . doush?*
		. . . a balcony?	*. . . balcona?*
Can I see the rooms?	*mumkin ashuf il-owad?*	. . . air conditioning?	*. . . takyeef hawa?*
Is there . . . ?	*fi . . . ?*	. . . a telephone?	*. . . telifoon?*
		How much is the bill?	*kam il-hisab?*

REACTIONS AND SMALL TALK

I (m/f) don't understand	*ana mish fahem (m) / fahma (f)*	Let's go	*yalla*
I (m/f) don't know	*ana mish 'arif (m) / 'arfa (f)*	Go away	*imshi*
I (m/f) am tired/unwell	*ana ta'aban (m) / ta'abana (f)*	Never mind	*maalesh*
I (m/f) am hungry	*ana gawa'an (m) / gawa'ana (f)*	It doesn't matter	*mush muhim*
I (m/f) am thirsty	*ana 'atshaan (m) / 'atshaana (f)*	There's no problem	*ma feesh mushkila*
I (m/f) am (not) married	*ana (mish) mitgawwiz (m) / mitgawwiza (f)*	It's not possible	*mish mumkin*

CALENDAR

day	*youm*	tomorrow	*bukkra*	Tuesday	*youm it-talaata*
night	*leyla*	yesterday	*imbaarih*	Wednesday	*youm il-arb'a*
week	*usbu'a*	later	*bahdeen*	Thursday	*youm il-khamees*
month	*shahr*	Saturday	*youm is-sabt*	Friday	*youm il-gum'a*
year	*sana*	Sunday	*youm il-ahad*		
today	*innaharda*	Monday	*youm il-itnayn*		

MONEY

Where's the bank?	*feyn il-bank?*	Egyptian pound	*giney*
I (m/f) want to change . . .	*ayyiz/ayyza aghayyar . . .*	half pound	*nuss giney*
. . . money	*. . . floos*	quarter pound	*rub'o giney*
. . . British pounds	*. . . ginay sterlini*	Piaster	*irsh/saagh*
. . . US dollars	*. . . dolar amrikani*	2 piastres	*irshayn*
. . . travellers' cheques	*. . . shikaat siyahiyya*	5 piastres	*khamsa irsh/saagh*

NUMBERS

0	*sifr*	10	*'ashara*	20	*'ashreen*	100	*miyya*
1	*wahid*	11	*hidarsha*	21	*wahid wa-*	150	*miyya wa-*
2	*itnayn*	12	*itnarsha*		*'ashreen*		*khamseen*
3	*talaata*	13	*talatarsha*	30	*talaateen*	200	*mitayn*
4	*arb'a*	14	*arb'atarsha*	40	*arb'aeen*	300	*talaata miyya*
5	*khamsa*	15	*khamastarsha*	50	*khamseen*	500	*khamsa miyya*
6	*sitta*	16	*sittarsha*	60	*sitteen*	1000	*alf*
7	*sab'a*	17	*sab'atarsha*	70	*sab'aeen*	2000	*alfayn*
8	*tamanya*	18	*tamantarsha*	80	*tamaneen*	3000	*talaat alaaf*
9	*tes'a*	19	*tis'atarsha*	90	*tis'een*	4000	*arb'at alaaf*

ARABIC NUMERALS

1	١	10	١٠	19	١٩	80	٨٠
2	٢	11	١١	20	٢٠	90	٩٠
3	٣	12	١٢	21	٢١	100	١٠٠
4	٤	13	١٣	22	٢٢	200	٢٠٠
5	٥	14	١٤	30	٣٠	300	٣٠٠
6	٦	15	١٥	40	٤٠	400	٤٠٠
7	٧	16	١٦	50	٥٠	1000	١٠٠٠
8	٨	17	١٧	60	٦٠		
9	٩	18	١٨	70	٧٠		

GLOSSARY OF EGYPTIAN TERMS

This is just a basic glossary of Egyptian terms in everyday use. For Islamic and architectural terms, see the special glossary on p.84; for pharaonic symbols and architectural terms, see p.238 and p.274.

Common alternative spellings are given in brackets.

ABU Literally "father": a term of repsect often used for a saint.

AIN (AYN, EIN) Spring.

AMIR (EMIR) Commander, prince.

BAB Gate

BAHR River, sea, canal.

BARAKA Blessing.

BEIT (BAYT) House.

BEY (BAY) Lord or noble; an Ottoman title.

BIR (BEER) Well.

BIRKA (BIRQA, BIRKET) Lake.

BURG Tower.

CADI (QADI) Judge.

CALECHE Horse-drawn carriage.

CORNICHE Seafront or riverfront promenade.

DARB Path or route.

DEIR Monastery or convent.

FELUCCA Nile sailing boat.

GALABIYYA Loose flowing robe worn by men.

GEZIRA Island.

GHIRD (GHARD) Sand dune.

HADJ (HAJ) Pilgrimage to Mecca.

HAGG/HAGGA One who has visited Mecca.

HAIKAL Sanctuary of a Coptic church.

HAMMAM Turkish bath.

HANTOUR Horse-drawn carriage.

JEBEL (GEBEL, GABAL, etc) Hill or mountain.

KHALIG Gulf or canal.

KHEDIVE Viceroy.

KOM Mound of rubble and earth covering an ancient settlement.

KUBRI Bridge.

MADRASSA School, theological college.

MASR (MISR) Popular name for Egypt, and Cairo.

MASTABA Oblong tomb chamber, or mudbrick bench.

MIDAN (MAYDAN) Square.

MIHRAB Niche indicating the direction of Mecca, to which all Muslims pray.

MIT Village.

MOULID Anniversary celebration of a Muslim or Christian holy person or saint.

MUEZZIN Prayer caller.

PASHA (PACHA) Ruler – a lord or prince.

QALA Fortress, citadel.

QARAT Peak, ridge.

QASR Palace, fortress, mansion.

QUBBA Dome, and by extension any domed tomb.

RAS Cape, headland, peak.

SHARIA Street (literally "way"). Also laws based on Koranic precepts, which Muslim fundamentalists wish to see applied in Egypt.

WADI Valley or watercourse (usually dry).

WAHAH Oasis.

INDEX

Abu Simbel Temple 383
Abu Sir Pyramids 188
Abu Sir 478
Abu Zenima 524
Abydos Temple 271
Accommodation 31
Agami 477
Aghurmi 442
Ahmed Hamdi Tunnel 524
Ain Dalla 420
Ain es-Siliyin 405
Ain Musa 524
Ain Sukhna 559
Akhenaten 253
Akhmim 269
al-Maraqi 443
al-Qasr (Bahariya) 415
al-Qasr (Dakhla) 425
Alexandria 449–475
  Abu Qir 470
  Accommodation 455
  Anfushi Tombs 465
  Beaches 468
  Catacombs of Kom es-Shoqafa 467
  Fine Arts Museum 461
  Food and nightlife 471
  Fort Qaitbey 465
  Getting about 454
  Graeco-Roman Museum 462
  History 449
  Listings 473
  Mahmudiya Canal 468
  Montazah Palace 469
  Moving on 474
  Orientation and arrival 452
  Pompey's Pillar 467
  Roman Theatre 461
Amarna art and religion 254
American Express 17
Aqaba, Jordan 542
Armant 343
Asasif Tombs 322
Ashmunein 252
Assyut 262
Aswan 356–373
  Accommodation 361
  Agha Khan's Mausoleum 366
  Eating and drinking 368

Elephantine Island 363
  Entertainments 368
  Excursions 370
  Felucca journeys 372
  First Cataract 371
  History 357
  Kitchener's Island 365
  Monastery of Saint Simeon 366
  Moving on 372
  Sehel Island 371
  Tombs of the Nobles 366
  West Bank 365
Aswan Dams 374

Bahariya Oasis 413
Baksheesh 23
Balaat 426
Baltim 499
Banks 16
Baris 433
Basata 542
Bashendi 426
Bawiti 414
Bedouin: Eastern Desert 573; *Sinai* 521, 551
Behna 496
Beni Hassan tombs 247
Beni Marr 265
Beni Suef 241
Berenice 575
Bilbeis 496
Bir el-Abd 552
Bir Hammamat 574
Bir Shatlan 576
Bir Umm Fawakhir 574
Books 603
Bubastis 495
Bulaq 433
Bureaucracy 11–12
Burg el-Arab 478
Buses 27

Cairo
  ☞ See **Cairo chapter index** on p.50
Camels 30
Campsites 32
Canal Zone 500–516
Car rental 28
Cartouches 238
Christianity in Egypt 125, 584
Chronology of monuments 596
Cleopatra Bath 443
Colonial history 588
Colossi of Memnon 316
Coloured Canyon 540

Consulates, Egyptian (overseas) 12
Consulates, Foreign (in Egypt) 25
Copts 12, 584
Coptic festivals 42, 247, 266, 268, 343, 411,
　497–8
Coral reefs 526
Costs 14
Currency 15
Customs 13

Dahab 534
Dakhla Oasis 421
Damanhur 491
Damietta (Dumyat) 498
Darow Camel Market 355
Dashur 190
Dasuq 493
Deir Aba Hur 246
Deir Abu Maqar 398
Deir Abu Mina 478
Deir al-Abyad 268
Deir al-Adhra 246
Deir al-Ahmar 268
Deir al-Azab 411
Deir al-Suryani 396
Deir Anba Baramus 397
Deir Anba Bishoi 396
Deir Anba Samwil 411
Deir el-Bahri Temple 329
Deir el-Malak 411
Deir el-Medina Temple 338
Deir el-Muharaaq 266
Deir Manayus w al-Shuhada 346
Deir Mari Girgis 411
Dendara Temple 280
Dimeh es-Siba 407
Dirunka (Convent of the Virgin) 266
Disabled access 43
Diving 523
Doctors 18
Drink 36–37
Driving in Egypt 29; *desert driving* 392
Dush Temple 433

Eastern Desert 557–576
Edfu Temple 346
Eilat, Israel 543
el-Alamein 479
el-Arish 552
el-Bagawat Necropolis 430
el-Ballas 285
el-Balyana 271
el-Ghweeta Temple 432
el-Hayiz 418

el-Kab 350
el-Kharga 427
el-Lakeita 575
el-Madamud 285
el-Mahalla el-Kubra 494
el-Mansura 497
el-Quesir 574
el-Qusiya 266
el-Till 257
el-Tor 525
Esna Temple 344
Farafra Oasis 418
Fatnis Island 443
Fayoum 399
Fayoum City 400
Felucca journeys 30, 372–373
Ferries from Europe 5
Festivals 40
　see also Coptic and Islamic Festivals
Fish, Tropical 526
Flights from Australasia 11
Flights from Europe 3
Flights from the USA and Canada 8
Flights, Internal 30
Food 33–35
Forty Days Road 355, 432
Fuwa 493

Gamasa 499
Garagos 285
Gaza City, Gaza Strip 556
Giftun Island 567
Giza Pyramids 169
Gods and goddesses
　Amun 301
　Bastet 495
　Geb 149
　Hapy 345
　Hathor 281
　Heliopolitan Cosmogony 149
　Hermopolitan Cosmogony 251
　Horus 350
　Isis 377
　Khnum 345
　Khonsu 301
　Mut 301
　Nut 149
　Osiris 277
　Ptah 178
　Re 149
　Sekhmet 309
　Shu 149
　Sobek 404
　Sokar 178

Theban Triad 301
Thoth 251
Great Sand Sea 445
Guides 23

Halaib 576
Hammam Faroun 524
Hannoville 478
Harraniyya 177
Hatshepsut 329
Health 18
Heracleopolis 241
Hermopolis 252
Hibis Temple 429
History 579–592
Hitching 28
Holiday companies, UK-based 6
Holiday companies, US-based 11
Hospitals 18
Hotels 31
Hurghada 563
Inoculations 18
Insurance 21
Islam 593
Islamic dynastic history 585
Islamic holidays and festivals 40, 205, 280, 296, 346, 403, 440, 473, 489, 575
Ismailiya 506
Israel, overland routes to Egypt 7, 542, 555

Jebel 'Uweinat 446
Jebel Dakhrour 443
Jebel el-Banat 549
Jebel Gattaar 572
Jebel Serbal 549
Jebel Shaayib el-Banat 572
Jews of Egypt 128
Jordan, ferry routes to Egypt 541

Kafr el-Sheikh 493
Kalabsha Temple 381
Karnak Temple 299
Kerdassa 177
Khan Yunis, Gaza Strip 556
Kharga Oasis 427
Kom Ombo Temple 351
Kom Oshim 407

Lahun Pyramid 409
Lake Manzala 499
Lake Qaroun 405
Lake Zeitun 444
Language 609
Lisht Pyramids 411

Luxor 286–299
Accommodation 287
Activities 295
Eating and drinking 296
Excursions 298
Festivals 296
History 286
Luxor Museum 294
Luxor Temple 292
Maidum Pyramid 410
Mallawi 245
Maps 22
Mazar 552
Media 39
Medinet Habu Temple 340
Medinet Ma'adi 408
Mediterranean Coast 449–487
Mersa Allam 575
Mersa Matrouh 482
Middle Egypt 241–269
Minya 242
Mit Damsis 497
Mitla Pass 550
Monasteries (see also under *Deir* prefixes)
General information 43
Burnt Monastery 266
Dirunka 266
Red Monastery 268
Saint Anthony 561
Saint Catherine 543
Saint Damyanah 498
Saint Menas 478
Saint Paul 562
Saint Simeon 366
White Monastery 268
Mons Claudianus 572
Mons Porphyrites 571
Monuments, visits/permits 43
Mosques, visiting 43
Moulids see *Coptic* and *Islamic Festivals*
Mount Catherine 548
Mount Sinai 547
Mubarak, Hosni 591
Mummification 318
Music 600
Mut 422

Na'ama Bay 529
Nabeq 533
Nadura Temple 429
Nag Hammadi 278
Nag Lohlah 343
Naqada 285
Nasser, Gamal Abd al- 589

Naucratis 492
Nefertiti 253
Nekhl 550
Nile cruises 30
Nile Delta 488–499
Nile Valley 236–389
Nubians 356
Nuweiba 538

Ottoman history 587
Oxyrhynchus 241

Pelusium 552
Pharaoh's Island 542
Pharaonic history 580
Pharaonic symbols 238
Pharmacies 18
Philae 376
Police 24
Port Fouad 515
Port Safaga 573
Port Said 511
Postal services 38
Pre-Dynastic history 579
Ptolemaic history 583
Public holidays 42
Pyramids 168
  Abu Sir 188
  Giza 169
  Hawara 409
  Lahun 409
  Lisht 411
  Maidun 410
  Saqqara, North 178
  Saqqara, South 190
  Zawiyat al-Ayran 177
Qantara 511
Qara Oasis 444
Qasr al-Farafra 418
Qasr es-Sagha 407
Qasr Qaroun 408
Qattara Depression 445
Qena 279
Qift 285
Qurna 316
Qus 285

Rafah 555
Ramadan 40
Ramesseum Temple 336
Ras el-Bahr 499
Ras el-Gindi 550
Ras Gharib 560
Ras Mohammed 525
Ras Nasrani 533

Red Sea Coast 557–576
Red Sea Mountains 570
Registration 14
Resthouses 32
Riziq 343
Roman history 583
Rosetta (Rashid) 490

Sadat, Anwar 590
Saïs 493
Sammanud 494
Saqqara, North 178
Saqqara, South 190
Sarabit el-Khadim 525
Service taxis 28
Shadwan Island 570
Sharm el-Sheikh 528
Sidi Abd el-Rahman 481
Sidi Barrani 487
Silsilah 351
Sinai 517–556
Siwa Oasis 434
Siwa Town 437
Snorkelling 523
Sohag 266
Sollum 487
Studying in Egypt 44
Sudan, ferry connection 388
Sudr 524
Suez 502

Taba 542
Tanis 496
Tanta 492
Tarabeen 538
Tehna al-Gabel 247
Telephones 38
Television 39
Tell el-Amarna 252
Tell el-Kebir 497
Tell el-Maskhuta 497
Temple Architecture 274
Teneida 426
Theban Necropolis 310–343
Thomas Cook 9, 17
Tombs of the Nobles (Aswan) 366
Tombs of the Nobles (Thebes) 332
Tourist offices 21–22
Trains, domestic 26
Trains, from Europe 5
Travel agencies 22
Travel permits 14
Tuna al-Gabel 251
Tutankhamun 255, 321 (tomb)

Underworld 319
Upper Egypt 269–389

Valley of the Kings 317–328
Valley of the Queens 339
Visas 11–12

Wadi el-Arish 550
Wadi el-Att 533
Wadi Feiran Oasis 549
Wadi Humaysara 575
Wadi Naggaat 572
Wadi Natrun 394
Wadi Sakait 575

Water 19
Watiyyah Pass 549
Western Desert Oases 390–448
White Desert 417
Wilderness of the Wanderings 550
Women travellers 25
Working in Egypt 44

Youth hostels 32

Za'farana 560
Zagazig 494
Zawiyat al-Ayran Pyramids 177
Zerzura 447

HELP US UPDATE

We've gone to a lot of effort to ensure that this first edition of *Egypt: The Rough Guide* is accurate and up-to-date. However, Egyptian information isn't always the most reliable commodity: telephone numbers and bus schedules are in a constant state of flux; areas of sites close and reopen after excavations; and, of course, restaurants, hotels and other tourist facilities raise prices or lower standards as they see fit.

If you find we've got something wrong or left something out, we'd like to know: any suggestions, comments or corrections would be much appreciated, but if you can remember the address, the price, the time, the phone number, so much the better.

We'll credit all contributions, and send a copy of the next edition (or any other Rough Guide if you prefer) for the best letters. Send them along to:
Dan Richardson, The Rough Guides, 149 Kennington Lane, London SE11 4EZ.

MEDITERRANEAN WILDLIFE

THE ROUGH GUIDE

MEDITERRANEAN WILDLIFE: THE ROUGH GUIDE is an essential companion for anyone interested in the fauna and flora of the Mediterranean region, featuring detailed country-by-country wildlife site guides to France, Greece, Italy, Morocco, Portugal, Spain, Tunisia, Turkey and Yugoslavia, with practical details on how to get to the sites and where to stay nearby. Introductory sections provide a keynote guide to the plant and animal species, while background articles analyse the environmental issues facing the Mediterranean in the 1990s.

Written and researched by Pete Raine, with a team of international wildlife contributors. Illustrated throughout with line drawings by Tessa Lovat-Smith.

Published by Harrap Columbus, price £7.99